MW00774510

thomson.com
changing the way the world learns

Understanding American Government

FOURTH EDITION

SUSAN WELCH
THE PENNSYLVANIA STATE UNIVERSITY

JOHN GRUHL
MICHAEL STEINMAN
JOHN COMER
UNIVERSITY OF NEBRASKA—LINCOLN

JAN P. VERMEER
NEBRASKA WESLEYAN UNIVERSITY

West / Wadsworth

I(T)P® **an International Thomson Publishing Company**

Belmont, CA • Albany, NY • Bonn • Boston • Cincinnati • Detroit • Johannesburg
London • Los Angeles • Madrid • Melbourne • Mexico City • Minneapolis / St. Paul
New York • Paris • Singapore • Tokyo • Toronto • Washington

■ Production Credits

Editor: Clark Baxter
Developmental Editor: Sharon Adams-Poore
Marketing Manager: Jay Hu
Production Editors: Peter Krall, Emily Autumn
Designer: Roz Stendahl, Dapper Design
Copy Editor: Sheryl Rose
Indexer: Schroeder Editorial Services
Illustrator: Randy Miyake
Cover Image: Tony Stone Worldwide
Compositor: Carlisle Communications
Printer: West Publishing Company

Printed in the United States of America
2 3 4 5 6 7 8 9 10

■ Photo Credits

1 (top) Joseph Kossuth Dixon, Courtesy Library of Congress; **1** (bottom) Schapiro, Liaison International; **2** AP/Wide World Photos; **4** Tomas Muscionico/Contact Press; **5** Brown Brothers; **6** Sebastiao Slagado; **22** Courtesy of Winterthur Museum; **24** Dennis Brack Ltd./Black Star; **27** The Metropolitan Museum of Art, Bequest of Charles Allen Munn, 1924 (24-90-35); **28** Historical Society of Pennsylvania; **39** The Granger Collection; **44** Roland Freeman/Magnum Photos, Inc.; **48** Sygma; **51** The Bettmann Archives; **56** U.S. Dept. of Agriculture; **58** AP/Wide World Photos; **61** Bettmann; **68** © 1988, J. B. Diederich, Contact Press Images, Inc.; **71** (top) Woodfin Camp & Associates; **71** (bottom) Brown Brothers; **72** Robb Kendrik Photography; **80** Black Star; **83** From the Collections of the St. Louis Mercantile Library Association; **104** Washington D.C. Fencer's Club, © Neal Slavin Studio, Inc., **107** © 1986 Ken Heinen; **111** Donna Binder/Impact Visuals; **115** Gotham Book Mart, New York, N.Y.; **116** Michael Salas; **117** The Bettmann Archives; **119** Courtesy of Christian Coalition; **121** © 1989 Shelly Katz/Gamma Liaison; **122** Lynn Johnson; **129** Pierre Gleizes/Greenpeace; **131** AP/Wide World Photos; **138** Andy Levin; **140** P. F. Bentley/Time Magazine; **144** The Granger Collection; **145** (left) The Granger Collection; **145** (right) The Granger Collection; **138** Courtesy of

—Continued following index

For more information, contact Wadsworth Publishing Company, 10 Davis Drive, Belmont, CA 94002, or electronically at http://www.thomson.com/wadsworth.html

International Thomson Publishing Europe
Berkshire House 168-173
High Holborn
London, WC1V 7AA, England

Thomas Nelson Australia
102 Dodds Street
South Melbourne 3205
Victoria, Australia

Nelson Canada
1120 Birchmount Road
Scarborough, Ontario
Canada M1K 5G4

International Thomson Publishing GmbH
Königswinterer Strasse 418
53227 Bonn, Germany

International Thomson Editores
Campos Eliseos 385, Piso 7
Col. Polanco
11560 México D.F. México

International Thomson Publishing Asia
221 Henderson Road
#05-10 Henderson Building
Singapore 0315

International Thomson Publishing Japan
Hirakawacho Kyowa Building, 3F
2-2-1 Hirakawacho
Chiyoda-ku, Tokyo 102, Japan

International Thomson Publishing Southern Africa
Building 18, Constantia Park
240 Old Pretoria Road
Halfway House, 1685 South Africa

Library of Congress Cataloging-in-Publication Data

Understanding American government / Susan Welch ... [et al.]—4th ed.
p. cm.
Includes bibliographical references and index.
ISBN: 0-314-20153-X (pbk. : alk. paper)
1. United States—Politics and government. I. Welch, Susan.
JK271.U53 1997
320.973—dc20 96–36719

BRIEF CONTENTS

PART ONE

The American System 1

CHAPTER 1 AMERICAN DEMOCRACY 2

CHAPTER 2 THE CONSTITUTION 22

CHAPTER 3 FEDERALISM AND THE GROWTH OF GOVERNMENT 48

PART TWO

Links Between People and Government 71

CHAPTER 4 PUBLIC OPINION 72

CHAPTER 5 INTEREST GROUPS 104

CHAPTER 6 POLITICAL PARTIES 138

CHAPTER 7 ELECTIONS 166

CHAPTER 8 THE MEDIA 212

CHAPTER 9 MONEY AND POLITICS 252

PART THREE

Institutions 279

CHAPTER 10 CONGRESS 280

CHAPTER 11 THE PRESIDENCY 324

CHAPTER 12 THE BUREAUCRACY 360

CHAPTER 13 THE JUDICIARY 392

PART FOUR

Civil Liberties and Rights 423

CHAPTER 14 CIVIL LIBERTIES 424

CHAPTER 15 CIVIL RIGHTS 464

PART FIVE

Public Policies 515

CHAPTER 16 THE BUDGET 516

CONTENTS

Preface xiv

PART ONE

The American System 1

CHAPTER 1
AMERICAN DEMOCRACY 2

YOU ARE THERE: Is Politics Necessary? 3

American Diversity 5

Ethnic and Economic Diversity 5

NEW POPULISM 8

Diversity and the Public Interest 9

NEW POPULISM: Controlling Immigration 11

Characteristics of Democracy 12

Value of the Individual 12

Political Equality 13

Majority Rule 14

Minority Rights 14

Direct and Indirect Democracy 14

Classical Democracy 14

Contemporary Theories of American Democracy 15

Pluralism 15

Elitism 16

Current Views 16

Conclusion: Is Government Responsive? 17

EPILOGUE: Politics, Representation, and Democratic Government 18

Key Terms 19

Further Reading 19

Notes 20

CHAPTER 2
THE CONSTITUTION 22

YOU ARE THERE: The Case of the Confidential Tapes 23

The Articles of Confederation 25

National Government Problems 25

State Government Problems 26

The Constitution 26

The Constitutional Convention 26

AMERICAN DIVERSITY: Founding Mothers 27

Features of the Constitution 31

Motives of the Founders 34

Ratification of the Constitution 36

Changing the Constitution 38

Conclusion: Is The Constitution Responsive? 40

SYMBOLIC SOLUTIONS FOR COMPLEX PROBLEMS: Making English the Official National Language 41

EPILOGUE: The President Complies 44

Key Terms 45

Further Reading 45

Notes 46

CHAPTER 3
FEDERALISM AND THE GROWTH OF GOVERNMENT 48

YOU ARE THERE: Can Uncle Sam Help Baby-Sit? 49

Federal and Other Systems 51

Federal Systems 51

Unitary Systems 51

Confederal Systems 52

The Political Bases of Federalism 52

The Constitutional Bases of Federalism 53

Major Features of the System 53

Interpretations of Federalism 54

Federalism and the Growth of Government 55

Early Nationalist Period 56

Pre-Civil War Period 57

The Civil War to the New Deal 57

The New Deal 58

From the New Deal to the Great Society 59

NEW POPULISM: A New Western Saga: Cowboys versus the Government? 60

New Federalism 60

Contemporary Federalism 63

Federal-State Relations 63

Interstate Relations 65

SYMBOLIC SOLUTIONS FOR COMPLEX PROBLEMS: Should the Federal Government Turn Welfare Over to the States? 66
State-Local Relations 67
Conclusion: Is Federalism Responsive? 68
EPILOGUE: Ros-Lehtinen Supports the Bill 69
Key Terms 69
Further Reading 70
Notes 70

PART TWO

Links Between People and Government 71

CHAPTER 4
PUBLIC OPINION 72

YOU ARE THERE: The President Considers the Nation's Rising Concern over Crime 73
Nature of Public Opinion 74
Formation of Public Opinion 75
Agents of Political Socialization 76
Impact of Political Socialization 80
Measuring Public Opinion 80
Early Polling Efforts 80
Emergence of Scientific Polling 81
Polls and Politics 82
NEW POPULISM: Teledemocracy: If Politicians Can't Do the Job, Can We? 84
How Informed Is Public Opinion? 87
Public Opinion 88
Ideology 88
Social Welfare and the Proper Role of Government 89
Social Issues 90
Race 91
Political Tolerance 93
Trust in Government 94
AMERICAN DIVERSITY: We Are Not Just Liberals and Conservatives 95
Conclusion: Is Government Responsive to Public Opinion? 98
EPILOGUE: The President Follows the Polls 99
Key Terms 100
Further Reading 100
Notes 100

CHAPTER 5
INTEREST GROUPS 104

YOU ARE THERE: Do You Leave Congress to Lead a Civil Rights Organization? 105
Group Formation 106
Why Groups Form 107
Why People Join 108
Who Joins? 108
Have Americans Stopped Joining? 109
Types of Interest Groups 109
Private Interest Groups 109
NEW POPULISM: The Angriest White Males 111
Public Interest Groups 116
Tactics of Interest Groups 123
Direct Lobbying Techniques 123
Indirect Lobbying Techniques 125
Protest and Civil Disobedience 128
Success of Interest Groups 129
Resources 129
Competition and Goals 131
Conclusion: Do Interest Groups Help Make Government Responsive? 132
EPILOGUE: Mfume Joins the NAACP 133
Key Terms 134
Further Reading 134
Notes 134

CHAPTER 6
POLITICAL PARTIES 138

YOU ARE THERE: Should the Republicans Offer the Voters a "Contract"? 139
What Are Political Parties? 141
Development and Change in the Party System 142
Preparty Politics: The Founders' Views of Political Parties 143
First Party System: Development of Parties 144
Second Party System: Rise of the Democrats 144
Third Party System: Rise of the Republicans 144
Fourth Party System: Republican Dominance 145
Fifth Party System: Democratic Dominance 145
Has the Fifth Party System Realigned? 146
The Parties Today 149

Characteristics of the Party System 149
Two Parties 149
Fragmentation 150
Moderation 150
Minor Parties in American Politics 151
NEW POPULISM: Do We Need a Third Party? 152
Party in the Electorate 153
Party Identification 153
Characteristics of Democrats and Republicans 153
Party in Government 153
Party Organization 155
National Party Organization 156
State and Local Party Organizations 158
Big-City Party Organizations 158
The Nominating Process 158
Caucuses 158
Conventions 158
Primaries 158
Conclusion: Do Political Parties Make Government More Responsive? 160
EPILOGUE: The Republicans Adopt a Contract 161
Key Terms 162
Further Reading 163
Notes 163

CHAPTER 7
ELECTIONS 166

YOU ARE THERE: To Resign or Not? 167
The American Electorate 169
Early Limits on Voting Rights 169
Blacks and the Right to Vote 169
AMERICAN DIVERSITY: Blacks and Hispanics in Office 170
Women and the Right to Vote 173
Other Expansions of the Electorate 173
Voter Turnout 174
Political Activism in the Nineteenth Century 174
Progressive Reforms 174
AMERICAN DIVERSITY: Women in Office 175
Recent Turnout 176
Who Does Not Vote? 177
Why Turnout is Low 177
SYMBOLIC SOLUTIONS FOR COMPLEX PROBLEMS? Same Day Voter Registration 182
Other Campaign Participation 184
Presidential Nominating Campaigns 185
Who Runs for President and Why? 185
AMERICAN DIVERSITY: Can an African American Be Elected President? 186
How a Candidate Wins the Nomination 187
Presidential Caucuses and Conventions 189
Presidential Primaries 189
Reforming the Nomination Process 190
The National Conventions 191
Independent and Third-Party Nominees 193
General Election Campaigns 193
Campaign Organization 194
Images and Issues 194
The Electoral College 195
Campaign Strategies 197
The Media Campaign 198
Campaign Funding 201
Voting 201
Party Loyalties 201
Candidate Evaluations 203
Issues 203
NEW POPULISM: The Angry White Male 204
Parties, Candidates, and Issues 205
Conclusion: Do Elections Make Government Responsive? 206
EPILOGUE: Bob Dole Resigns from the Senate 207
Key Terms 207
Further Reading 208
Notes 208

CHAPTER 8
THE MEDIA 212

YOU ARE THERE: Should You Pull Him Out of "the Closet"? 213
The Media State 215
Roles of the Media 215
Concentration of the Media 216
Atomization of the Media 217
NEW POPULISM: Talk Radio 218
Relationship Between the Media and Politicians 220
Symbiotic Relationship 221
Adversarial Relationship 224

Relationship between the Media and Recent Administrations 225
Relationship between the Media and Congress 229
Bias of the Media 230
Political Bias 231
Commercial Bias 234
Impact of the Media on Politics 239
Impact on the Public Agenda 239
Impact on Public Opinion 240
Impact on Political Parties and Elections 240
Conclusion: Are the Media Responsive? 243
EPILOGUE: Signorile Reveals Official's Homosexuality 245
Key Terms 246
Further Reading 246
Notes 246

CHAPTER 9
MONEY AND POLITICS 252

YOU ARE THERE: Quid Pro Quo? Or No? 253
The Development of Laws to Regulate Money and Politics 255
Money in Nineteenth-Century American Politics 255
Early Reforms 256
The Role of Money in Election Campaigns 256
Campaign Finance Laws 257
Loopholes in the Reforms 258
How the System Works 259
The Impact of Campaign Money 262
Does the Campaign Finance System Deter Good Candidates? 263
Does Money Win Elections? 263
Does Money Buy Favorable Policies? 264
Reforming the Campaign Money System 268
SYMBOLIC SOLUTIONS FOR COMPLEX PROBLEMS? Public Funding for Congressional Campaigns 270
Conflicts of Interest 271
Conclusion: Does the Influence of Money Make Government Less Responsive? 272
EPILOGUE: DeConcini Intervenes 274
Key Terms 276
Further Reading 276
Notes 277

PART THREE
Institutions 279

CHAPTER 10
CONGRESS 280

YOU ARE THERE: Should You Risk Your Career? 281
Members and Constituencies 284
Members 284
Constituencies 285
SYMBOLIC SOLUTIONS FOR COMPLEX PROBLEMS? Term Limits 286
Congressional Campaigns and Elections 288
The Advantages of Incumbency 288
AMERICAN DIVERSITY: Women in Congress 289
Unsafe at Any Margin? 292
Challengers 294
Campaigns 295
NEW POPULISM: The 1994 Congressional Elections 296
Voting for Congress 298
The Representative on the Job 298
Informal Norms 298
Working Privately and "Going Public" 299
Voting by Members 300
How Congress Is Organized 302
How Congressional Organization Evolved 302
Leaders 304
Committees 304
Staff 309
AMERICAN DIVERSITY: Black Power in Congress 310
What Congress Does 311
Lawmaking 311
Overseeing the Federal Bureaucracy 314
Budget Making 315
Conclusion: Is Congress Responsive? 317
EPILOGUE: Margolies-Mezvinsky Supports the President and Loses Her Job 319
Key Terms 320
Further Reading 320
Notes 321

CHAPTER 11
THE PRESIDENCY 324

YOU ARE THERE: Retreat Again? 325

Presidential Job Description 327

Qualifications 327

Tenure 327

Succession 327

Rewards 328

Growth of the Modern Presidency 328

The Presidency Before the New Deal 328

Development of the Personal Presidency 330

Presidential Power 332

Persuading the Washingtonians 333

Persuading the Public 335

Presidential Popularity 338

Limits of Presidential Power 338

Roles of the President 339

Growth of Presidential Staff 339

Administrative Leadership 341

SYMBOLIC SOLUTIONS FOR COMPLEX PROBLEMS? The Line-item Veto 342

Domestic Policy Leadership 345

Foreign Policy Leadership 346

Military Leadership 350

Symbolic Leadership 353

Party Leadership 354

Conclusion: Is The Presidency Responsive? 355

EPILOGUE: The President Stands Firm 356

Key Terms 357

Further Reading 357

Notes 357

CHAPTER 12
THE BUREAUCRACY 360

YOU ARE THERE: Attacking AIDS 361

Bureaucracy 363

Nature of Bureaucracy 363

Public and Private Bureaucracies 363

SYMBOLIC SOLUTIONS FOR COMPLEX PROBLEMS? Slashing the Bureaucracy 366

Federal Bureaucracy 367

Growth of the Bureaucracy 367

Why the Bureaucracy Has Grown 368

Types of Bureaucracy 368

NEW POPULISM: Are Bureaucrats the Enemy? 371

Bureaucratic Functions 373

Making Policy 373

AMERICAN DIVERSITY: Women and Minorities in the Civil Service 374

Administering Policy 378

Other Functions 378

Expectations About the Federal Bureaucracy 378

Responsiveness 379

Neutral Competence 379

AMERICAN DIVERSITY: Presidential Administrative Appointments 383

Controlling the Bureaucracy 383

President 383

Congress 384

Courts 385

Interest Groups and Individuals 385

Conclusion: Is the Bureaucracy Responsive? 387

EPILOGUE: The Surgeon General Chooses Neutral Competence 388

Key Terms 389

Further Reading 389

Notes 389

CHAPTER 13
THE JUDICIARY 392

YOU ARE THERE: Friend or Foe? 393

Development of the Courts' Role in Government 394

Founding to the Civil War 395

Civil War to the Depression 397

Depression to the Present 398

Courts 399

Structure of the Courts 399

Jurisdiction of the Courts 400

Judges 400

Selection of Judges 400

AMERICAN DIVERSITY: Do Women Judges Make a Difference? 402

Tenure of Judges 407

Qualifications of Judges 407

Independence of Judges 408

Access to the Courts 408
Wealth Discrimination in Access 408
Interest Group Help in Access 409
Restrictions on Access 409
Proceeding Through the Courts 411
Deciding Cases 411
Interpreting Statutes 411
Interpreting the Constitution 411
Restraint and Activism 413
Following Precedents 414
Making Law 415
The Power of the Courts 415
Use of Judicial Review 415
Use of Political Checks Against the Courts 418
Conclusion: Are the Courts Responsive? 419
EPILOGUE: Exclusion of Japanese Is Upheld 420
Key Terms 421
Further Reading 421
Notes 421

PART FOUR

Civil Liberties and Rights 423

CHAPTER 14

CIVIL LIBERTIES 424

YOU ARE THERE: Does Religious Liberty Include Animal Sacrifice? 425
The Constitution and the Bill of Rights 426
Individual Rights in the Constitution 426
The Bill of Rights 427
Freedom of Expression 428
Freedom of Speech 428
Freedom of the Press 433
Libel and Obscenity 435
AMERICAN DIVERSITY: Can They Be "As Nasty as They Wanna Be"? 439
Freedom of Religion 440
Rights of Criminal Defendants 446
Search and Seizure 446
Self-Incrimination 447
Counsel 448
Jury Trial 448
Cruel and Unusual Punishment 449
SYMBOLIC SOLUTIONS FOR COMPLEX PROBLEMS? Capital Punishment 450
Rights in Theory and in Practice 452
Right to Privacy 452
Birth Control 452
Abortion 453
Homosexuality 456
Right to Die 457
Conclusion: Are the Courts Responsive in Interpreting Civil Liberties? 458
EPILOGUE: The First Amendment Protects Animal Sacrifice 458
Key Terms 459
Further Reading 459
Notes 459

CHAPTER 15

CIVIL RIGHTS 464

YOU ARE THERE: Compromise or Continue to Fight? 465
Race Discrimination 467
Discrimination Against African Americans 467
AMERICAN DIVERSITY: Black Masters 469
Overcoming Discrimination Against African Americans 471
Continuing Discrimination Against African Americans 479
Discrimination Against Hispanics 485
Discrimination Against Native Americans 488
Sex Discrimination 490
Discrimination Against Women 490
Discrimination Against Men 498
Affirmative Action 498
NEW POPULISM: Opposition to Affirmative Action 501
Are Civil Rights Enough? 504
Conclusion: Is Government Responsive in Granting Civil Rights? 507
EPILOGUE: Hamer Continues to Fight 508
Key Terms 509
Further Reading 509
Notes 509

PART FIVE

Public Policies 515

CHAPTER 16

THE BUDGET 516

YOU ARE THERE: Support the Budget Compromise? 517

Fundamentals of Budgeting 519

Evolution of Budgeting Processes 519

Purposes of Budgeting 522

Limits on Budgeting 523

Operation of the Current Budgeting Process 524

Issues in Budgeting 526

Where Does the Money Go? 526

The Deficit and its Causes 529

Dealing with the Deficit 533

SYMBOLIC SOLUTIONS FOR COMPLEX PROBLEMS?
Balancing the Budget by Constitutional Amendment 534

Budgeting as Politics 539

Conclusion: Is Government Responsive in Its Budgeting? 540

EPILOGUE: Kasich Goes Along 541

Key Terms 542

Further Reading 542

Notes 542

Appendix A: The Declaration of Independence 543

Appendix B: Constitution of the United States 545

Appendix C: Federalist Paper #10 557

Appendix D: Federalist Paper #51 561

Glossary 565

Index 573

Presidents, Elections and Congresses 1789–1993 588–591

PREFACE

The fourth edition of our text, *Understanding American Government*, tries, as did the previous editions, to interest students in learning about the exciting, important, and controversial issues in American public life. We believe an introductory course succeeds if most students develop an understanding of major ideas, an interest in learning more about American government, and an ability to begin to understand and evaluate the news they hear about American political issues. Although a firm grounding in the essential "nuts and bolts" of American government is crucial, other approaches are helpful in motivating students' interest in government.

We offer the essential "nuts and bolts" of American government, but we also want the student to understand why (and sometimes how) these important features have evolved, their impact on government and individuals, and why they are controversial (if they are) and worth learning. For example, we prefer students to leave the course remembering why campaign finance laws were created and why they have the impact they do than to memorize specific dollar limitations on giving for different types of candidates from different types of organizations. The latter will change or will soon be forgotten, but understanding the "whys" will help the student understand the campaign finance issue long after the course is over.

We have also tried to interest students by describing and discussing the impact of various features of government. For example, students who do not understand why learning about voter registration laws is important may "see the light" when they understand the link between such laws and low voter turnout. Therefore, a particular emphasis throughout the book is on the *impact* of government: how individual features of government affect its responsiveness to different groups (in Lasswell's terms, "Who gets what and why?"). We realize that nothing in American politics is simple; rarely does one feature of government produce, by itself, a clear outcome. Nevertheless, we think that students will be more willing to learn about government if they see some relationships between how government operates and the impact it has on them as citizens of America.

This shorter edition of *American Government* retains the emphases and personality of the longer edition. But this condensed edition is aimed at several different audiences. The book can be used as a core text by instructors who wish to assign readings in addition to the main text. This shorter version is also appropriate for instructors who find that their students are not able to cover in one quarter or semester all the policy chapters in the standard version. The book is perfect for the instructor who feels guilty about requiring students to purchase a large text and then does not assign some of the chapters.

This book, however, is not a typical "essentials" book, covering only the basics with little attention to examples, explanation, and interpretation. It is, of course, examples and interpretation that bring concepts to life. We have tried to make sure that "less length" is not synonymous with "less interesting."

We are delighted to have the opportunity to write another edition and to improve the text further in ways suggested by our students and readers. We have been extremely pleased by the reaction of instructors and students to our previous editions. We were especially gratified—twice—to have won the American Government Textbook Award from the Women's Caucus for Political Science of the American Political Science Association.

Changes in the Fourth Edition

This edition contains a wealth of new material. Over the past several years, voter anger with government and politicians has grown. Along with that is increasing public support for new laws that limit the power of government or elected officials, such as term limits, the balanced budget amendment, and limits on taxing power. In two new features found in many chapters, we focus on helping students understand and evaluate the anger and the policies sometimes suggested by those who claim to be "fed up" with government and politics.

One of these features, *The New Populism*, examines the roots and manifestations of discontent with government, comparing today's unrest with the populist movement of the late nineteenth century. For example, in Chapter 3 we examine the discontent of many westerners with federal government control of western lands; in Chapter 7 we focus on the "angry white male"; and in Chapter 8 we explore "talk" radio as a manifestation of new populism.

A second feature, *Symbolic Solutions for Complex Problems?*, analyzes policy suggestions to see if they would likely help solve the problems they are directed toward or whether they are merely symbolic solutions—ideas that sound good but would have little impact. Symbolic Solutions boxes focus on popular ideas such as term limits (Chapter 10), public financing of campaigns (Chapter 9), the line item veto (Chapter 11), slashing the bureaucracy (Chapter 12), and turning welfare over to the states (Chapter 3).

We have also added a brand new chapter on The Budget (16), which shows how the budgetary process fits into the broader political process and how current budgetary controversies reflect long-standing political debates between the parties and factions within the parties. This chapter should enable students to understand the arguments over the budget that dominate politics now.

We have also incorporated the results of the 1996 presidential and congressional elections. See especially the "You Are There" in Chapter 7, focussing on Robert Dole's decision to resign from the Senate to invigorate his run for president.

In addition to these new features, we have extensively revised the entire text. In Chapter 1, we explore the suggestion that Americans, though vastly proud of the American system in general, do not like the manifestations of democracy they see in their political institutions, particularly Congress—disagreement, lobbying, negotiation, and delay. We return to that paradox in later chapters as we discuss the seemingly growing anger toward and impatience with government.

In Chapters 6, 7, and 10, we have integrated much material about the Republican victories in the 1994 elections and the Republican efforts to bring about greater changes as a result. In many chapters we have integrated new information about the Clinton administration. The impact of new technology on politics receives more consideration in this edition, especially in Chapters 4 and 8. The discussion of affirmative action in Chapter 15 has been expanded and revised.

Special Features

Student interest and analytic abilities grow when confronted with a clash of views about important issues. Today there is much discussion about how to stimulate the critical thinking abilities of students. Beginning with the first edition, our text has provided features especially designed to do this by involving students in the controversies—and excitement—of American politics.

YOU ARE THERE. Each chapter opens with a scenario called "You Are There." In a page or two the student reads about a real-life political dilemma faced by a public official or a private citizen involved in a controversial issue. Students are asked to put themselves in that individual's shoes, to weigh the pros and cons, and to decide what should be done. The instructor may want to poll the entire class and use the "You Are There" as a basis for class discussion. In the "Epilogue" at the end of the chapter, we reveal the actual decision and discuss it in light of the ideas presented in the chapter.

One-half of the *You Are There* features in this edition are new. They feature such timely topics as the development of the Republicans' "Contract with America" (Chapter 6), the dilemma of a Democratic Representative pondering the Clinton budget bill (Chapter 10), and the Henry Foster nomination for Surgeon General (Chapter 11).

AMERICAN DIVERSITY. In many chapters, American Diversity boxes illustrate the impact of the social diversity of the American population on political life. The boxes help students understand how diversity of backgrounds and attitudes shape views of politics and positions on issues.

THE NEW POPULISM. This new feature, described above, analyzes why voters are angry, and some of the manifestations of that anger. These boxes help explain the complexity and diversity of public opinion.

SYMBOLIC SOLUTIONS FOR COMPLEX PROBLEMS? Another new feature, already described, helps students evaluate whether commonly discussed solutions to complex public problems might work, or whether some might be only symbolic or might actually make the problems worse.

BOXES. In each chapter several boxes highlighting interesting aspects of American politics draw the students into the material. Many illustrate how government and politics really work in a particular situation—how a corporation lobbies for government benefits, how a seemingly powerless group is able to organize for political action, how interest groups solicit money by mail, and how political polls are done—while others highlight features of government that may be of particular interest to students, such as a box on Ideology in the Electorate which divides voters in a new way and allows students to categorize themselves.

Several other features help students organize their study:

OUTLINE. Each chapter begins with an outline of its contents.

KEY TERMS. Key terms are boldfaced within the text and listed at the end of each chapter.

FURTHER READING. A brief, annotated list of further readings contains works that might be useful to a student doing research or looking for further reading.

GLOSSARY. A glossary at the end of the book defines terms that may be unfamiliar to students.

The Organization and Contents of the Book

While the basic organization of American government books is fairly standard, our text has a unique chapter on money and politics and the new and unusual chapter on the budget. Other features include a civil rights chapter that integrates a thorough treatment of constitutional issues concerning minorities and women, a discussion of the civil rights and women's rights movements, and contemporary research on the political status of these groups. We include in this chapter the special legal problems of Hispanics and Indians.

The organization of the book is straightforward. After material on democracy, the Constitution, and federalism, the book covers linkages, including money and politics, then institutions, and finally policy. Civil liberties and rights are treated after the chapter on the judiciary. But the book is flexible enough that instructors can modify the order of the chapters. Some instructors will prefer to cover institutions before process. Others may prefer to discuss civil liberties and rights when discussing the Constitution. Still others may wish to integrate the budgetary policy chapter into their coverage of Congress and the Presidency.

Supplementary Materials

The supplementary materials complement the book.

INSTRUCTOR'S MANUAL. Written by Jeff Walz, the instructor's manual provides lectures, lecture suggestions, and in-class exercises for each chapter. Suggestions for out-of-class papers and projects are also provided. A student questionnaire is included to allow instructors to collect student data that can be used in class throughout the semester as a comparison with national poll data presented in the book.

INSTRUCTIONAL MATERIALS ON DISKETTES. The lectures and other material in the instructor's manual are provided on computer diskettes. So is the student questionnaire, which will spare instructors the trouble of having it retyped or re-entered on computer disks.

STUDENT STUDY GUIDE. An excellent Student Guide, written by Susan Rigdon, provides students with exercises emphasizing the major points of each chapter. Chapter objectives and key terms are reviewed. Practice multiple choice questions are provided. Unlike many such guides, this one also helps the students learn to write essays, thus emphasizing the improvement of analytic skills. Essay writing tips are given, then illustrated for each chapter.

VIDEODISC. Developed to support concepts in the book, our disk combines use of video clips, charts, and graphs. It is approximately 50 minutes long and is comprised of 4- to 6-minute segments that can be used to enhance lectures.

VIDEOTAPES. Qualified adopters are entitled to choose from West's Political Science Video Library. A list of tapes is available upon request. In addition, the *Government by Consent* video collection and the *Equal Justice Under the Law* series are available.

TRANSPARENCY ACETATES. Fifty full-color acetates of important maps and graphs from the text are offered to adopters.

ACKNOWLEDGMENTS

We would like to thank the many people who have aided and sustained us during the lengthy course of this project. Our current and former University of Nebraska and Penn State colleagues have been most tolerant and helpful. We thank them all. In particular, we appreciate the assistance of John Hibbing, Philip Dyer, Robert Miewald, Beth Theiss-Morse, Louis Picard, John Peters, David Rapkin, Peter Maslowski, David Forsythe, W. Randy Newell, and Steven Daniels who provided us with data, bibliographic information, and other insights that we have used here. We are especially grateful to Philip Dyer, Alan Booth, Louis Picard, Robert Miewald, and John Hibbing who read one or more chapters and saved us from a variety of errors.

We are also grateful to the many other readers of our draft manuscript. Without their assistance the book would have been less accurate, complete, and lively.

Reviewers include:

Alan Abramowitz, State University of New York at Stony Brook.
Larry Adams, Baruch College-City University of New York
Danny M. Adkison, Oklahoma State University
James Alt, Harvard University
Margery Marzahn Ambrosius, Kansas State University
Kevin Bailey, North Harris Community College
Kennette M. Benedict, Northwestern University
Timothy Bledsoe, Wayne State University
Jon Bond, Texas A&M University
Paul R. Brace, New York University
Joseph V. Brogan, La Salle University
James R. Brown, Jr., Central Washington University
Chalmers Brumbaugh, Elon College
Richard G. Buckner, Jr., Santa Fe Community College
Ronald Busch, Cleveland State University
Carl D. Cavalli, Memphis State University
Richard A. Champagne, University of Wisconsin, Madison
Michael Connelly, Southwestern Oklahoma State University
Gary Copeland, University of Oklahoma
George H. Cox, Jr., Georgia Southern College
Paige Cubbison, Miami-Dade University
Landon Curry, Southwest Texas State University
Jack DeSario, Case Western Reserve University
Robert E. DiClerico, West Virginia University
Ernest A. Dover, Jr., Midwestern State University
Georgia Duerst-Lahti, Beloit College
Ann H. Elder, Illinois State University
Ghassan E. El-Eid, Butler University
C. Lawrence Evans, College of William and Mary
Murray Fischel, Kent State University
Bobbe Fitzhugh, Eastern Wyoming College
Marianne Fraser, University of Utah
Jarvis Gamble, Owens Community College
David Garrison, Collin County Community College
Phillip L. Gianos, California State University—Fullerton
Doris A. Graber, University of Illinois—Chicago
Ruth M. Grubel, University of Wisconsin—Whitewater
Stefan D. Haag, Austin Community College
Larry M. Hall, Belmont University
Edward Harpham, University of Texas—Dallas
Peter O. Haslund, Santa Barbara City College
Richard P. Heil, Fort Hays State University
Peggy Heilig, University of Illinois at Urbana
Craig Hendricks, Long Beach City College
Marjorie Hershey, Indiana University
Samuel B. Hoff, Delaware State College
Robert D. Holsworth, Virginia Commonwealth University
Jesse C. Horton, San Antonio College
Gerald Houseman, Indiana University
Jerald Johnson, University of Vermont
Loch Johnson, University of Georgia
Evan M. Jones, St. Cloud State University
Henry C. Kenski, University of Arizona
Matt Kerbel, Villanova University
Marshall R. King, Maryville College
Orma Lindford, Kansas State University
Peter J. Longo, University of Nebraska—Kearney
Roger C. Lowery, University of North Carolina—Wilmington
H. R. Mahood, Memphis State University
Jarol B. Manheim, The George Washington University
A. Nick Minton, University of Massachusetts—Lowell
Matthew Moen, University of Maine
Michael Nelson, Vanderbilt University
Bruce Nesmith, Coe College
Walter Noelke, Angelo State University

Thomas Payette, Henry Ford Community College
Theodore B. Pedeliski, University of North Dakota
Jerry Perkins, Texas Tech University
Toni Phillips, University of Arkansas
C. Herman Pritchett, University of California—Santa Barbara
Charles Prysby, University of North Carolina—Greensboro
Sandra L. Quinn-Musgrove, Our Lady of the Lake University
Donald R. Ranish, Antelope Valley Community College
Linda Richter, Kansas State University
Jerry Sandvick, North Hennepin Community College
James Richard Sauder, University of New Mexico
Eleanor A. Schwab, South Dakota State University
Earl Sheridan, University of North Carolina—Wilmington
Edward Sidlow, Northwestern University
Cynthia Slaughter, Angelo State University
John Squibb, Lincolnland Community College
M. H. Tajalli-Tehrani, Southwest Texas State University
Kristine A. Thompson, Moorehead State University
R. Mark Tiller, Austin Community College
Gordon J. Tolle, South Dakota State University
Susan Tolleson-Rinehart, Texas Tech University
Bernadyne Weatherford, Rowan College of New Jersey
Richard Unruh, Fresno Pacific College
Jay Van Bruggen, Clarion University of Pennsylvania
Kenny Whitby, University of South Carolina
Clifford J. Wirth, University of New Hampshire
Ann Wynia, North Hennepin Community College
Mary D. Young, Southwestern Michigan College

We are also grateful to those instructors who have used the book and relayed their comments and suggestions to us. Our students at the University of Nebraska have also provided invaluable reactions to the previous editions.

Others too have been of great assistance to us. Susan Rigdon, Margery Ambrosius, and Harry Basehart helped revise previous editions of this book, and devoted more time to it than they ever bargained for. Eric Tiritilli, Jeff Walz, Staci Beavers, and Michael Moore helped produce the ancillary materials for the book.

Several people at West Publishing also deserve our thanks. Clark Baxter has been a continual source of encouragement and optimism from the beginning of the first edition through the last decision on this edition. We are greatly in debt to David Farr, who designed and produced the first two editions of the book, and to Peter Krall, who produced this edition.

Finally, the contribution of our spouses—Kathy Vermeer, Nancy Comer, Linda Steinman, and Alan Booth—can hardly be summarized in a sentence or two. But we are very appreciative that they were supportive all the time and patient most of the time.

ABOUT THE AUTHORS

SUSAN WELCH received her A.B. and Ph.D. degrees from the University of Illinois at Urbana-Champaign. She is currently Dean of the College of the Liberal Arts and Professor of Political Science at The Pennsylvania State University. Her teaching and research areas include legislatures, state and urban politics, and women and minorities in politics. She has edited the *American Politics Quarterly.*

JOHN GRUHL, a Professor of Political Science, received his A.B. from DePauw University in Greencastle, Indiana and his Ph.D. from the University of California at Santa Barbara. Since joining the University of Nebraska faculty in 1976, he has taught and done research in the areas of judicial process, criminal justice, and civil rights and liberties. He won University of Nebraska campus wide distinguished teaching awards in 1979 and 1986 for excellence in undergraduate teaching, and became a charter member of the University's Academy of Distinguished Teachers in 1995.

MICHAEL STEINMAN graduated from George Washington University with a B.A. in 1964. His M.A. and Ph.D. degrees are from the University of Chicago. An Associate Dean of the College of Arts and Sciences and Professor of Political Science at the University of Nebraska-Lincoln, he teaches courses in public administration and does research in policing and domestic violence. In 1984 he won a campus wide distinguished teaching award for his development and implementation of a Keller Plan Introduction to American Government course.

JOHN COMER is a Professor of Political Science at the University of Nebraska. He received his A.B. in political science from Miami University of Ohio in 1965, and his Ph.D. from the Ohio State University in 1971. His teaching and research focus on interest groups, public opinion, voting behavior, and political parties.

JAN P. VERMEER is Professor of Political Science at Nebraska Wesleyan University. He received his B.A. from the University of California, Santa Barbara, and his A.M. and Ph.D. from Princeton University. He has won two campus-wide teaching awards, most recently in 1996. His research has centered on media and politics and on congressional elections.

PART ONE

The American System

Italian immigrants arrive at Ellis Island, New York, in 1910. (right) Elementary students in Brentwood, California, reflect the multicultural present and America's future. (below)

1 American Democracy

You Are There

Is Politics Necessary?

It is November, 1992. You are a 21 -year-old first-time voter and must make a choice from among George Bush, Bill Clinton, and Ross Perot. You consider yourself an independent and are skeptical about what the candidates are saying. You are not sure if they are talking about the things most Americans care about.

Like many Americans, you do not really trust government and politicians. You have heard about the Vietnam War and the Watergate and Iran-contra scandals. You do not know much about them, but do know that they involved many government officials who were not always honest with the public. You also know that the taxpayers are footing the bill for the recent collapse of many banks and savings and loans, and that many members of the House of Representatives overdrew their checking accounts in the House bank, some more than 100 times, without any consequences. President Bush criticized them but he had already broken his promise not to raise taxes. You wonder whether these politicians are working for most Americans or for the "special interests."

Then too, you know that times are not good. The economy is stagnant and the cities are crumbling. Many people are out of work and you worry about getting a good job after you graduate. Like most other Americans, you feel that the country is headed in the wrong direction. And what are the politicians doing about it? Not much, at least that you can see. The president blames Congress while Congress blames the president. Republicans blame Democrats while Democrats blame Republicans. Maybe, you think, politics is just mudslinging rather than solving problems.

The two major party candidates seem to promise more of the same. Republican candidate and incumbent George Bush has been a politician most of his life. People joked that he had "the longest resume in Washington" even before he became president. As president, he does not appear to have much vision or interest in tackling our domestic problems. Although Democratic candidate and Arkansas governor Bill Clinton is an "outsider" to Washington politics, he has wanted to be president for a long time and is a "career politician" who shades the truth to avoid offending voters. You still do not know how he avoided the draft during the Vietnam War and whether he has cheated on his wife, though you are not sure these things are all that important anyway. His admission that he tried marijuana without inhaling seems to justify his nickname, "Slick Willie."

There is a third candidate, Ross Perot, a multibillionaire Texas businessman. In an appearance on the "Larry King Live" television show, Perot declared that he would run for president if volunteers could get his name on the ballot in all 50 states. Minutes later, phone lines were jammed as thousands called to volunteer their help.

Perot's message resonates with you and other Americans fed up with government as usual. He promises quick fixes to America's problems, fixes that could be devised by smart people sitting around a table. Running as a sort of national "Rotor-Rooter candidate,"[1] Perot drills home the idea that Americans must come to grips with the reality of the budget deficit and the sinking economy. He argues that he can fix these problems along with the entire laborious political process. He claims he will "have the House and Senate dancing like Ginger Rogers and Fred Astaire." Appealing to a public fed up with politicians and stalemate, Perot's ratings soared. His informal down-to-

CONTINUED

OUTLINE

American Diversity
- Ethnic and Economic Diversity
- Diversity and the Public Interest

Characteristics of Democracy
- Value of the Individual
- Political Equality
- Majority Rule
- Minority Rights
- Direct and Indirect Democracy

Classical Democracy

Contemporary Theories of American Democracy
- Pluralism
- Elitism
- Current Views

Conclusion: Is Government Responsive?

earth style on talk shows is a striking contrast to the other candidates and their handlers.

One of Perot's favorite lines is "It's that simple." But you wonder if it *is* that simple. Many of Perot's positions are undefined. Most are one-liners. The media, reflecting as well as stimulating public concern, are looking for more information about Perot to determine how he would fix national problems. And, after some digging, the media found some information that was not flattering. For example, Perot has a penchant for hiring investigators to look into the backgrounds and lifestyles of his employees. At times in his career, he simply quit whatever he was doing when the going got rough. He left the Navy early because he did not get along with his commander and left the board of directors of General Motors when it did not support his view of what GM policies should be.

Moreover, Perot's behavior seems unpredictable. He hired Hamilton Jordan, Jimmy Carter's White House chief of staff, and Ed Rollins, Ronald Reagan's 1984 presidential campaign manager, to run his campaign. But Perot then seemed unhappy about "selling out" to professional politicians. Jordan and Rollins urged him to have a full-fledged campaign with extensive advertising in the media, many public appearances, and position papers. However, growing uncertain about whether he wanted to spend the millions it would take to do all this and becoming fed up with what he thought were personal attacks against him, he soon fired Jordan and Rollins. Later, he withdrew from the race on the day of Bill Clinton's acceptance speech at the Democratic Convention. But he even hedged doing this. After weeks of hesitating, he said he would take a poll to see if he should reenter the race. After polling his own volunteers, he reentered the race on October 1, 1992.

Ross Perot is caught in a flood of media attention.

These moves make you wonder if Perot has the temperament to be president. He is used to being the boss in his businesses. In fact, bumper stickers proclaim "Ross for Boss." He tells his employees what to do and can fire them if they do not obey or if they do not move fast enough to please him. But politicians in our government of shared powers and checks and balances cannot order each other around. They have to persuade each other to work together. The president has to persuade members of Congress to pass the laws and the budgets he wants. Then he has to persuade bureaucratic agencies to implement the laws the way he wants them implemented. We get impatient when politicians take what seems like an infinite amount of time to do something. But in a diverse society, there are always competing interests that want politicians to do contradictory things.

You do not know whether Perot has the temperament to persuade rather than order. During the campaign, he showed a short temper dealing with the press, snapping at reporters who asked reasonable questions. Perhaps more significantly, Perot did not have the ability, or willingness, to persuade others when he served on GM's board. Although economists concede that he knew what he was talking about regarding GM's problems, he could not bring about changes in GM because he did not forge alliances with other board members or key executives. He quit after his complaints got nowhere. Would he behave this way as president?

Perot says he knows what we need. A vote for him may be a vote to give politics a backseat. But can he really get government to work? Is his lack of political experience going to benefit the nation? Can we really take politics out of governing, and would we be better off if we did?

How do you vote?

Inconsistencies dominate American politics. Americans cherish the symbols of democracy, but deplore its realities.[2] We visit Washington to marvel at the Washington Monument, the Jefferson and Lincoln Memorials, the Capitol, and the White House. We show these symbols of our democracy to our children, hoping they will revere them. We cherish the Declaration of Independence and the Constitution.

But at the same time that we prize these symbols of democracy, we condemn the reality of democracy. We define debates over issues as quarrels or "bickering"; we call compromises "selling out"; we label conflict as mere self-interest; we tag interest groups and political parties as "special interests." We have no tolerance for the slow pace of government's dealing with the nation's problems. In other words, we love the concept of democracy, but hate the rough and tumble, the give and take, and the conflict that is democracy in action.[3]

Why do we act as if we dislike democracy in action? Has government failed? Are the laws it enacts not what the people want? Is it the fault of the media, emphasizing mostly the negative side of government? Are average citizens actually shut out of the process? Or is the problem really the fault of citizens, and not government at all?

We can begin to answer these questions by exploring why American government is characterized by conflict and compromise. One major reason is, of course, that Americans do not agree on either the nature of the problems that confront us, or their solutions. If we all agreed, there would be no need for debate, bargaining, compromise, or delays. Another major reason is that we have chosen a representative democracy as our form of government. Most Americans, even those highly dissatisfied with the way government actually works, do not want a king, a dictator, or an emperor to make decisions for us.

In this chapter we will look at some of the differences among Americans, and we will examine democracy as a form of government. In later chapters we will explore some specifics about our political processes and institutions that have led Americans to distrust and dislike the workings of our political system. And at the end of each chapter, we will ask how well the U.S. political system responds to the needs and concerns of the citizens.

➤American Diversity

"Here is not merely a nation but a teeming Nation of nations."[4] Poet Walt Whitman's statement tells us a lot about our country and its politics. America is a diverse nation, peopled by individuals from all over the world. We are a conglomeration of different religions, races, ethnic groups, cultural traditions, and socioeconomic groups.

■ Ethnic and Economic Diversity

Diversity exists because all of us are immigrants or descendants of immigrants. Even those we call native Americans crossed a land bridge from Asia about 50,000 years ago. The next major wave of immigration occurred in the early 1600s with people from Britain, Holland, France, and Spain. These first European colonists came for a variety of reasons, some to find a place to practice their religion, others to escape political tyranny, and still others to make their fortunes. British culture and the English language soon became dominant. Although all immigrants have had to adapt to this culture, succeeding generations have helped modify it into a unique, American culture.

The immigration of Africans began in 1619 and continued through the early 1800s. Unlike other immigrant groups, most blacks did not come freely. They were brought in chains as slaves. This fact has had a profound impact on American culture and politics.

A fourth major wave of immigration occurred in the mid-1800s. It included millions of people from Ireland fleeing the potato famine and Germans escaping political turmoil. Most immigrants since then also came for economic, religious, and political reasons. Starting in the late 1800s and continuing until World War I, another influx included many Chinese and Japanese laborers and millions of Italians, Poles, and Jews.

Beginning in the 1970s, the latest major wave has included Vietnamese, Cambodians, Russian Jews, and

These 1910 immigrants from Bohemia and Bulgaria illustrate the European character of most early twentieth century immigration. Meals served at Ellis Island around this time featured beef stew, boiled potatoes, rye bread with herring for Jews, and crackers and milk for women and children.

Russian emigrants wait at Moscow Airport for their flight to America.

Latin Americans. Most are Asians and Mexicans. The entry of 6 million legal and at least 2 million illegal immigrants in the 1980s accounted for over one-third of the nation's growth in that decade. By 1995, immigration rose to an estimated 1,100,000 newcomers annually, more than 800,000 of whom enter the country legally.[5] Immigration has fueled the growth of Sunbelt states like California, Texas, and Florida and has ensured that industrial states such as New York and Illinois would not lose population.[6]

The Statue of Liberty welcomes newcomers by proclaiming, "Give me your tired, your poor, your huddled masses yearning to breathe free. . . ." Nevertheless, "old Americans," worried about threats to what they regard as the American "character," do not always share this sentiment. Native Americans resisted the first European immigrants and with good reason. The "Know-Nothings" won popularity in the 1840s by spreading fear of a Catholic takeover. Patriotic fervor during World War I produced hostility toward Americans of German birth or descent. For example, in 1918, Iowa's governor required all groups of two or more people to speak only English, even when using the telephone.[7] From 1924 to 1965, federal law limited immigration from most areas outside western Europe. As indicated in the New Populism box, the debate continues about whether today's immigrants are an asset or a problem for our society.

Although each generation of immigrants has faced resentment from preceding generations, each has contributed to the building of America. Early European immigrants settled the eastern seaboard and pushed west to open the frontier. African immigrants helped build the South's economy with their slave labor. Germans helped develop the Midwest into an agricultural heartland, while Irish, Italian, Polish, and Russian newcomers provided labor for America's industrial revolution and turned many cities into huge metropolises. Chinese immigrants helped build the transcontinental railroad linking East and West, and Japanese and Hispanics helped California become our top food producer. All immigrant groups have gone on from their initial roles to play a fuller part in American life.

There is evidence that America is a melting pot for millions. Among white ethnic groups, so much intermarriage has occurred that many people cannot identify their ancestry. In the 1990 census, 100 million Americans could name no specific ancestry or reported multiple ancestries.[8] This blending continues. For example, although more than 90% of Italian-Americans age 65 and over have two parents of Italian ancestry, only 18% of Italian-American children under 5 have. Jews, who as recently as 35 years ago were restricted by quotas from enrolling at universities and joining private clubs and were discriminated against in hiring by many universities, banks, and corporations, are now blending into the melting pot partly through intermarriage and partly through the reduction of discrimination. Today, the efficiency of the melting pot means that for many Americans of white, European ancestry, the most common "ethnic experience" is eating ethnic foods.[9]

However, for many others whose skin color or language mark them as different, integration into America's melting pot has been much slower. For example, comprising 12% of the population, blacks were Americans long before the ancestors of most whites. Yet they have experienced the most consistent and severe discrimination.

Hispanics (including several diverse groups of Spanish origin, primarily Mexican-Americans, Cuban-Americans, and Puerto Ricans) comprise about 9% of the population. Like blacks, Hispanics tend to be less educated and have lower incomes than other white Americans. Although they also face discrimination, Hispanics are growing in number and integrating into the larger society faster than blacks.

Asian-Americans, the fastest growing minority, are about 3% of the population. They have achieved considerable economic success despite harsh discrimination in the past and more subtle forms today. For example, although Asian-Americans are represented far beyond their population share at most top universities, many suspect that some universities have set informal admissions quotas to limit their numbers.

Despite the discrimination still faced by many Americans whose ancestry is not European, racial boundaries are beginning to erode. For example, one government study showed that 6% of people considering themselves black, one-third who considered themselves Asian, and 70% of those who considered themselves American Indian were thought to be white by survey researchers. A study of infant deaths showed that many infants were classified by a different race at death than on their birth certificates. A quarter of those who identified themselves as American Indian to the Census did not claim American Indian ancestry. Interracial marriages and interracial children are becoming increasingly common. More than half the births to an American Indian parent and one-third of the births to an Asian-American parent had one parent of a different race. One-fourth of the children born to a Hispanic parent had a non-Hispanic other parent.[10]

Despite the important fact that white America has resisted the assimilation of blacks much more than of Asians or Hispanics, even these racial barriers are beginning to erode slightly. The number of black-white marriages has tripled and the number of births of babies with one black and one white parent has quintupled in the past twenty years.

All of these examples indicate that once seemingly clear notions of "race" as either black or white are becoming confused as we become an increasingly multiracial society. In the 1990 Census, 75 multiracial categories were named, along with 600 American Indian tribes and 70 categories of Hispanics. One survey showed that one-third of African Americans believe that blacks are not a single race, and almost half of both black and white respondents believed that government should not collect information on race at all.[11]

Ethnic and racial diversity is not the only cleavage in society, though it has been the most controversial one in the past decade (and many times before in American history). Religious differences certainly exist,

New Populism

Americans are fed up. Majorities think the country is in "deep and serious trouble," believe the American dream will be difficult to achieve for their children, are suspicious of the press, schools, and religious and business leaders, think society is too tolerant of people who misbehave, and are angry at leaders who "say one thing and do another." Reflecting this concern, one journalist noted "a tidal wave of discontent," and an author titled his recent book *Why Americans Hate Politics.*[1]

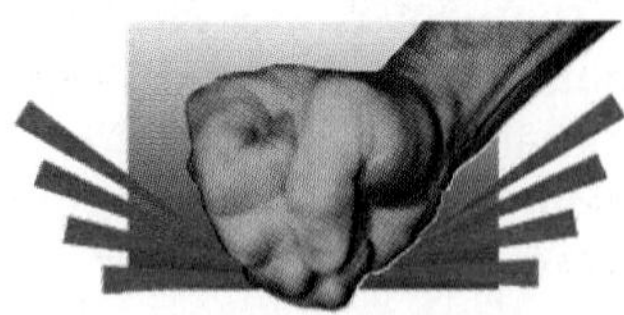

In short, many Americans are frustrated and angry, especially with government, believing the country is going in the wrong direction and our leaders do not see or care. An expanding economy and falling unemployment have not convinced most Americans that the country is on the right path. Frustrated with George Bush, the Republican president, voters threw him out in 1992. Not satisfied with that change, and equally frustrated with a Congress controlled by Democrats, voters threw many of them out in 1994, giving Republicans control of both houses of Congress for the first time since the Eisenhower Administration. Indeed, many Americans are so angry at Congress and the president, they would like to make laws themselves through national referenda.[2]

None of this is new in American history. We have a long tradition of distrust and anger directed at government and other powerful institutions. After all, in 1776, we revolted against the British government because many Americans thought it was remote and unrepresentative of our interests. Andrew Jackson became president in 1828 by running as a frontiersman opposed to the power of the eastern elites.

What we call the *populist movement* began in the late 1800s in the rural Midwest, when many Americans, especially farmers and small business owners, believed the national government to be the pawn of big interests (then called "trusts") such as big business, the railroads, and banks. Novels such as Frank Norris's *The Octopus* and L. Frank Baum's *The Wizard of Oz* dramatized the struggle of good, hard-working people against these powerful interests. In the view of populists, these interests worked against the common people. In general **populism** describes movements that celebrate "the people" in contrast with the greed and immorality of the powerful. Populist movements frequently give people a way to vent their frustrations when they feel powerless in the face of big business, big money, and big government. That frustration often arises when the ideals of democracy (everyone counts equally) conflict with the reality of society (some people have much more power than others). Because populism is characterized by resentment toward elites and often by faith in a popular leader, it is different from simply an affirmation or the democratic right of all to participate.[3]

The populist movement of the late 1800s, led by the great orator and Democratic leader William Jennings Bryan, combined religious conservatism with economic radicalism. Although Bryan was narrowly defeated for president all three times he ran (in 1896, 1900, and 1908), he made a mark on American history with his mobilization of the common people against the business elites of the time and in favor of moral traditionalism (such as outlawing the sale of liquor and fighting the teaching of evolution in the schools). Populist calls for regulation of big business presaged some of the regulations passed in this century and their concerns with moral issues are reflected in our current debates over prayer in the schools, abortion, and other such issues.

CONTINUED 

and sometimes spill over into politics. For example, many Catholics and fundamentalist Protestants are against abortion, while many mainline Protestants are pro-choice.

Economic diversity also divides our nation. Though we think of ourselves as a land of opportunity, most people who are born poor stay poor. Opportunities knock harder and more often for those who are born into the upper and middle classes. And, although our society is not as class conscious as many others, our personal economic situations play an important part in shaping our views toward politics and our role in it. In 1992, for example, most poor Americans did not vote and most who did voted for Bill Clinton. Most well-off Americans did vote, and voted for George Bush.

Regional and residential differences can also be important, especially when they are intertwined with economic interests. Midwestern farmers, who produce the food we eat, have quite different views on farm bills than big-city dwellers who are interested in buying food at a cheap price. Suburban dwellers in affluent communities and residents of decaying urban areas usually have quite different notions of whether the government should help local schools.

Despite a sometimes overwhelming diversity, most Americans share some common goals and values.

Populists also distrusted the institutions of government and representative democracy, such as legislatures and political parties, believing that these were controlled by powerful interests working against the common people. Early in this century, some of these beliefs underpinned successful efforts in many states to allow citizens to make laws themselves through initiatives (proposals put on the ballot by groups of individuals) or referenda (proposals put on the ballot by a vote of the legislature) and to remove officials in recall elections.

In the last decade, the label "populist" has again become fashionable.[4] Most politicians call themselves populists, trying to portray themselves as representatives of the average citizen. One recent author wrote about contemporary populism by using Jesse Jackson (champion of the liberal Democrats) and Pat Robertson (champion of the conservative Christian Republicans) as examples.[5] Ross Perot is often cited as a new populist, and both Bill Clinton and Newt Gingrich are sometimes called populists too.

Today, the moral and religious emphasis of populism is more likely to be found among Republicans, while the economic emphasis is found among Democrats. Thus Republican populists are most likely to emphasize returning to the traditional moral and cultural values of this society, while Democratic populists are more likely to emphasize improving the standard of living for the average person and curbing big business.

Because populism has been an important part of American history and has recently reemerged as a major theme, and because populist ideals underlie discussions over many contemporary issues, throughout the book we will discuss the ideas of New Populism as they pertain to specific problems. As we will see in these boxes, the term *populism* means many things to many people, but underlying each use is a resentment that government and others (such as business or media elites) who hold great power in society are not acting in a way to promote the best interests of "ordinary" people.

1. See E. J. Dionne, Jr., *Why Americans Hate Politics* (New York: Simon and Schuster, 1991).
2. The poll results are from "Opinion Outlook," *National Journal,* February 4, 1995, p. 324; and Kevin Phillips, "The Voters Are Already Tapping Their Feet," *Washington Post National Weekly Edition,* November 21–27, 1994, p. 24.
3. See Allen D. Hertzke, *Echoes of Discontent: Jesse Jackson, Pat Robertson, and the Resurgence of Populism* (Washington, D.C.: CQ Press, 1993).
4. See the following for comprehensive recent studies of the populist tradition: Michael Kazin, *The Populist Persuasion* (New York: Basic Books, 1995) and Christopher Lasch, *The Revolt of the Elites and the Betrayal of Democracy* (New York: W. W. Norton, 1995).
5. Hertzke, *Echoes of Discontent.*

Indeed, these goals and values are often what attracts new immigrants. We idealize our nation's Founders and the reasons they fought a revolution. Most Americans support our form of government[12] and believe that America is a land of opportunity for those willing to work hard.

Shared values reduce the strains produced by our differences. They also allow us to compete intensely on some issues but cooperate on others. For example, Protestant fundamentalists and Catholic leaders disagree strongly about aid to parochial schools but agree on opposing abortion. Rich and poor differ over the role government should play in reducing unemployment but largely agree about protecting the environment. Jews and blacks sometimes disagree over the use of quotas, but both tend to favor more public spending for social programs. Majorities of Americans of all ancestries who have been in the United States for a generation want to tighten immigration laws but disagree how to do it. Thus, although most Americans share some basic beliefs, our "nation of nations" is cross-cut with cleavages.

Diversity and the Public Interest

Diversity produces different perceptions of the world. As a result, people tend to define society's problems differently and have conflicting views about what government should do about them. This means that, although government officials typically justify their actions in terms of the "public interest," that interest is usually impossible to define to everyone's satisfaction. Thus, whether a policy will further the public interest is almost always a matter for political debate. People disagree about what government should do and whether government is responsive because they have different views of their own interests and those of society.

The existence of disagreement leads to **politics,** the competition to shape government's impact on society's problems and goals. Government can coerce us to do things because it is supposed to represent the public interest.[13] Politics, though, entails not only conflict but cooperation. It brings people together when they realize that cooperation is the only way to address problems. For some issues, they discover that their shared values are more important than their differences.

FIGURE 1
Mexican Immigrants

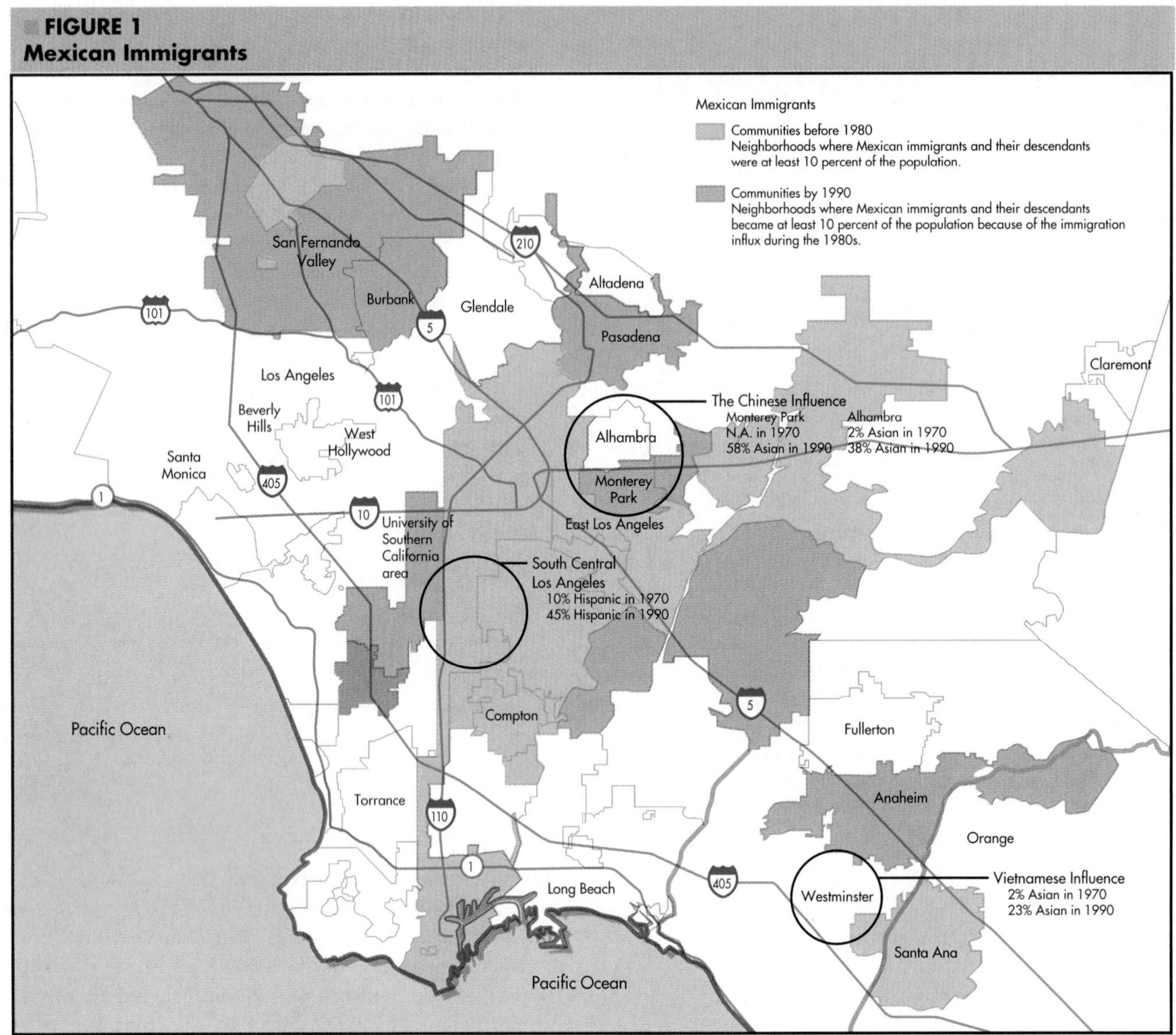

The huge influx of immigrants in the 1980s, especially from Mexico, changed the face of the Los Angeles area.
Source: Based on Gallup Polls via *The New York Times,* Sunday, September 18, 1994, pp. E4–5.

Although the conflict in politics gives us reason to be skeptical about individuals' and groups' claims that they seek the public interest, cooperation in politics gives us reason to accept the possibility that the public interest can be achieved. Thus, the Greek philosopher Aristotle wrote 2,000 years ago that politics is the most noble thing in which people can engage, partly because it helps them to know themselves and partly because it forces them to relate to others. Individuals have their own needs, but they have to consider other citizens' needs too.

The conflict and cooperation in politics are channeled through government. We call our form of government a "democracy." And although we all like the idea of a democracy, most of us forget how messy the process of reaching compromises on contentious issues can be. It is easy to see when others should bend a little (or a lot) to resolve a conflict, but it is hard for us to give in on points we feel strongly about ourselves. Because we all want to be true to our principles but still reach a consensus with others, politics in a democracy is going to be stormy and controversial.

New Populism

Controlling Immigration

Immigration, and the seeming inability of government to control it, is one of the issues about which many Americans are angry. Substantial majorities, believing that immigrants cost taxpayers money because of their use of welfare, public schools, and hospitals, would like to see immigration limited. This anger is particularly strong in states where immigrants are concentrated; about 72 percent of America's immigrants live in California, Florida, Illinois, New Jersey, New York, and Texas. There the pressure on public services is most acute and the resentment against immigrants most pronounced (and conversely, some states are barely touched by immigration; for example, in 1992 when California had over 330,000 new immigrants, Wyoming had 281).[1]

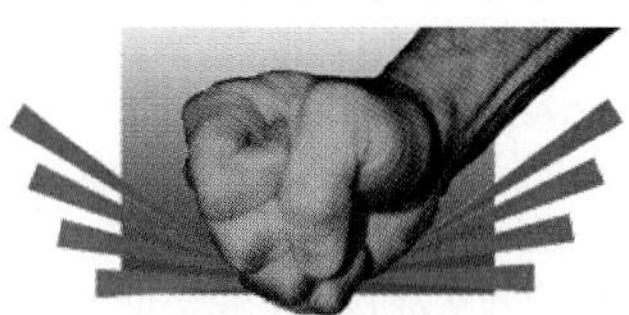

Dislike of immigrants and a variety of other kinds of minorities is part of the populist tradition, though the targets of hostility have varied over time. Around the turn of the century, populists opposed immigration because a large proportion of immigrants were Catholics or Jews coming from southern and eastern Europe, a mix that seemed threatening to the dominant Anglo-Saxon, Protestant group. In the 1930s, Father Charles Coughlin appealed to a mass following by arguing that a Jewish conspiracy ran the government. In 1968 Governor George Wallace (D-Ala.) won a substantial following among white working-class voters in his race for president by running on the race issue. (Governor Wallace had stood "in the schoolhouse door" to try to prevent blacks from attending the University of Alabama.)

Today, the dramatic influx of new residents has triggered resentment similar to earlier anti-immigration feelings. In the last twenty years, America has experienced the second largest wave of immigration in its history (the largest since the 1910s and 1920s). Most of today's immigrants are Asians or Latin Americans, and relatively few are from Europe. In 1992, for example, about 15% of the nearly 1,000,000 legal immigrants were from Europe, over one-third from Asia (the largest groups being Vietnamese, Filipino, Chinese, and Indian), nearly 40% from Mexico and Central America, and the remainder from the rest of the world.[2] Illegal immigrants presumably come largely from Mexico and Central America.

The size of this immigration flood (over 7 million arrived during the 1980s) triggered a number of negative responses. One that most Americans believe is that immigrants take jobs away from other residents. California, Florida, New Jersey, and Texas do have jobless rates well above the national average, which exacerbates concern over the impact of immigrants on unemployment. However, the evidence that immigrants deprive other residents of jobs is not clear. Immigrants, particularly illegal ones, do take some low-paying, unskilled jobs, especially in restaurants, food processing plants, and other traditional low-wage industries. They also take very low paying seasonal farm work jobs, which most other Americans do not want. Most legal immigrants, many of whom are well educated and skilled, do not deprive other residents of jobs. In fact, they increase total employment and generate more economic activity and benefits.[3]

In states with large immigrant populations, taxpayers are concerned that they have to carry the cost of the services immigrants use, believing that immigrants do not pay taxes. That concern is not new; it has often taken some time before new immigrants can successfully shoulder their portion of the tax burden. But immigrants do pay taxes. Everyone pays sales taxes, for instance. However, many illegals, who make up about 13% of all immigrants, do not pay income tax or contribute to Social Security through payroll deductions. They are often hired on a cash basis and avoid these taxes (as do some citizens and legal aliens). Newcomers increase demand for state and local public services, particularly health care and education. In New York City, for example, some schools are so crowded, largely because of immigration, that one out of 11 students lacks a desk or a chair, and some classes are held in hallways, on staircases, and even in closets. Such conditions force the schools to seek more tax revenues from an already unhappy public.[4] Although federal funds help to pay for many of these services, this assistance is shrinking as the federal government cuts funding to the states.

Part of the concern about immigration reflects noneconomic issues. Some native-born Americans fear non-English languages, different cultural traditions and religious practices, and nonwhite skin colors. In 1991, Republican presidential candidate Patrick Buchanan complained that immigration is about to "submerge" our "predominantly Caucasian Western society" and warned about a "dilution" of our European heritage.[5] A newspaper criticized immigrants who "bring with them their non-Christian Third World cultures, poverty-mindedness and a tendency toward crime."[6]

This does not mean that everyone who opposes immigration is racist. Some people just do not like change, or are afraid of so much change at a time when our economy is performing sluggishly and when the country faces so many problems related to poverty and crime.

What does the public want done about immigration? Most (about 60%) would like to see tighter controls on legal

CONTINUED 

immigration and more effort to curb illegal immigration. Federal legislation in 1986 and 1990 did try to make it more difficult to enter the country illegally by imposing significant penalties for employers who hire illegal workers. However, our long, thinly patrolled borders make it extremely difficult to keep people out. Employer penalties have proven less than completely effective because illegals can buy forged Social Security cards and other papers, and because some employers are willing to risk penalties in order to hire cheap labor (obviously, illegal workers cannot complain to the government about less than minimum wages or safety standards). Although the public wants greater controls over illegals, and 65% say they are willing to spend federal tax money to patrol the Mexican border more thoroughly, only half favor a national identity card, which could help control illegal immigration.[7]

Citizens in some states are taking action on their own. For example, in 1994 60% of the voters in California (which has about 40% of the nation's illegal immigrants) voted for Proposition 187, the "Save Our State" initiative. Challenged in the courts as unconstitutional, it seeks to deny most state and local services, including public education and nonemergency health care, to illegal immigrants and their children.[8] Citizens are making efforts to put similar propositions on the ballots in other states, and a number of states have filed lawsuits arguing that Washington is responsible for higher state and local spending necessitated by the failure of its immigration policies. A number of proposals in Congress call for eliminating or reducing welfare and other services for illegal, and sometimes even legal, immigrants. Even liberals such as Senator Ted Kennedy of Massachusetts and former member of Congress Barbara Jordan have argued for more aggressive efforts to control immigration.

Populism has always been a "people's movement" with a focus on resentment of political, social, or economic elites. But historically populism has always included a resentment and dislike of those of "the people" who were different and weaker, including immigrants, Catholics and Jews, blacks and Asians. Today, one focus of this resentment is immigrants. Yet, in the case of immigration, it is easier to resent and dislike than it is to make dramatic changes in the status quo. In fact, despite the rhetoric so prevalent in discussions of immigration, Americans have very mixed feelings about what to do about it. Almost all Americans want to reduce illegal immigration, and a solid majority wants to reduce legal immigration too. But only about half believe we should stop providing government health and education benefits to immigrants (even legal ones) and their children. About half also believe we should deny American citizenship to children born here to immigrants who have not become U.S. citizens themselves.

Despite the anger over immigration, it appears likely that anti-immigrant legislation is more likely to pass in states where the most immigrants live. National opinion patterns are divided, suggesting that stringent new legislation might be difficult to pass nationally. On the other hand, there seems clear support for limiting immigration, even if there are no clear views on how to treat new residents once they are here. Deep down, most people realize that immigrants who risk all they have to come to the United States, willing to work hard to make a better life for themselves, embody just those qualities on which the American dream has always been built.

---

1. *Statistical Abstract of the United States, 1994.* Table 10.
2. *Statistical Abstract of the United States, 1994.* Table 8.
3. "Illegal Aliens Depress Wages for Some in US," *New York Times,* March 20, 1988, p. 16; Thomas Muller and Thomas Espenshade, *The Fourth Wave: California's Newest Immigrants* (Washington, D.C.: Urban Institute Press, 1985), pp. 101–22; Philip Martin, "Labor Intensive Agriculture," *Scientific American* 249 (October 1983), p. 57; Leon Bouvier and Robert Gardner, "Immigration to the U.S.: The Unfinished Story," *Population Bulletin* 41 (November 1986): pp. 28–31; Peter Passell, "So Much for Assumptions about Immigration and Jobs," *New York Times,* April 15, 1990, p. 4E; K. F. McCarthy and R. B. Valdez. *Current and Future Effects of Mexican Immigration in California* (Santa Monica, Calif.: The Rand Corporation, 1986).
4. "Students Without Desks," *New York Times,* February 6, 1995, p. E16.
5. George F. Will, "Buchanan Takes Aim," *Washington Post National Weekly Edition,* December 16–22, 1991, p. 28.
6. This quote from the *Christian American* is reported in Dick Kirschten, "Building Blocs," *National Journal,* September 26, 1992, p. 2173.
7. Information in this paragraph is from Dick Kirschten, "Immigration: Second Thoughts," *National Journal,* January 21, 1995, pp. 150–151.
8. Survey data are reported in Bruce Nelan, "Not Quite So Welcome Anymore," *Time* (Special Issue on the New Face of America; Fall, 1993), pp. 10–13.

Characteristics of Democracy

Democracy was invented by ancient Greek city-states (the term *democracy,* meaning authority of the people, is a Greek term). The principles that shape our democracy are also rooted in the Judeo-Christian tradition and in British history.

Value of the Individual

Democracy emphasizes the value of the individual.[14] This principle has roots in the Judeo-Christian belief that every individual is equal and has worth before God. It also shaped the works of the British philosophers Thomas Hobbes and John Locke. Briefly, they wrote that individuals give some of their rights to government so it can protect them from each other. Individuals then use their remaining liberties to pursue their individually defined visions of the good life. These ideas are part of social contract theory, which we discuss in Chapter 2.

Influenced by these ideas, early Americans emphasized liberty over other goals of government. This is reflected in the Declaration of Independence and the Constitution and Bill of Rights. James Madison, for example, justified the Constitution by writing that government's job is to protect the "diversity" of interests and abilities that exists among individuals. Liberty is also reflected in our long tradition of rights, deriving from Britain's. Usually these are rights against the government—for example, government shall not deny freedom of assembly, and government shall not engage in unreasonable searches and seizures. Essentially, this means the overall right to be left alone by the government. Such individualistic values have molded popular expectations. Immigrants often came and still come to America to be their own bosses: to farm their own farms, manufacture or sell their own products, and worship their own way. Although the opportunities for many individuals to get ahead in America are limited by prejudice and poverty, living in a society with an explicit commitment to individual worth can be exciting and liberating.

Political Equality

Although the Judeo-Christian belief that all people are equal in the eyes of God reflects one type of equality, it led logically to other types, such as political equality. The ancient Greek emphasis on the opportunity and responsibility of all citizens to participate in ruling their city-states also contributed to our notion of political equality. Thus, the Declaration of Independence proclaimed that "all men are created equal." This did not mean that all people are born with equal virtues or abilities. It meant that all (at the time excluding male slaves and all women) are born with equal standing before government and entitled to equal rights.

Inevitably, some people use their virtues or abilities to amass more wealth and power than others and have more influence over government. The ancient Greeks feared that democracy could not tolerate extremes of wealth and poverty. They thought a wealthy minority, out of smugness, and an impoverished minority, out of desperation, would try to act independently of the rest of the people and consequently disregard the public interest. Early Americans worried less about this. They thought they could create a government that would protect individual diversity and still survive (as we will discuss more fully in Chapter 2).

Americans have always considered themselves relatively equal politically and socially if not economically. Alexis de Tocqueville, a perceptive Frenchman who traveled through the United States in the 1830s, observed that Americans felt more equal than Europeans did. De Tocqueville attributed this feeling to the absence of a hereditary monarchy and aristocracy in this country. There was no tradition in America of

"We can't come to an agreement about how to fix your car, Mr. Simons. Sometimes that's the way things happen in a democracy."

Source: Drawing by Handelsman; © 1987 The New Yorker Magazine, Inc.

looking up to kings and queens and aristocrats as one's "betters."

A belief in political equality leads to **popular sovereignty,** or rule by the people. Abraham Lincoln expressed this concept when he spoke of "government of the people, by the people and for the people." If individuals are equal, no one person or small group has the right to rule others. Instead, the people collectively rule themselves. Of course, not all the people can be a president, a member of Congress, or a judge. But these officials are not the rulers; they are the representatives of the people, who together have authority as the rulers.

Majority Rule

Commitments to the principles of individual worth and political equality lead to majority rule. That is, when there are disagreements over policies, majorities rather than minorities decide. If individuals are equal, then policies should be determined according to the desires of the greater number. Otherwise, some individuals would be bestowed with more authority than others.

Majority rule helps provide the support necessary to control the governed. Those in the minority go along because they accept this principle and expect to be in the majority on other issues. At a minimum, the minority expects those in the majority to respect their basic rights. If these expectations are not fulfilled, the minority is less likely to accept majority rule and tolerate majority decisions. Thus, majority rule necessarily entails minority rights.

Minority Rights

Although majority rule is important, it sometimes conflicts with minority rights. Majorities make decisions *for* "the people" but in doing so do not *become* "the people." "The people" includes members of the majority *and* members of the minority. As a result, majorities that harm minority rights diminish everyone's rights. Sadly, as James Madison and other writers of the Constitution feared, majorities in the United States have sometimes forgotten this and denied minorities their rights. For example, the government put Americans of Japanese descent into special camps during World War II. At other times, blacks were slaves; religious minorities could not practice their beliefs; those with unpopular opinions lost basic rights; and women could not vote.

Thus, democratic principles sometimes contradict each other. These principles are goals more than depictions of reality. Americans have struggled for two centuries to reconcile practice with democratic aims and to perfect a system of government that was revolutionary for its time and remains the envy of many around the world.

Direct and Indirect Democracy

Our description of democracy must include one additional refinement. Democracies may be either direct or indirect. A **direct democracy** permits citizens to vote on most issues. The best example of a direct democracy is the town meeting, which has been the traditional government of many New England towns for more than 350 years. Although town meetings today are often attended by relatively small numbers of citizens, they still offer one of the few opportunities people have to rule themselves directly. Citizens attending them make their own laws (e.g., whether to put parking meters on the main street) and elect officers to enforce them (such as the police chief and city clerk).

Our national government is an **indirect democracy,** or a **republic.** Citizens have an indirect impact on government because they select policymakers to make decisions for them. Thus, members of Congress, not rank-and-file citizens, vote bills into law.

Classical Democracy

Democratic principles come alive when individuals participate in government. The ancient Greek philosopher Aristotle concluded that there were three types of government in the city-states of his day: democracies, societies ruled by the many; monarchies, societies ruled by one person—kings, queens, or emperors; and aristocracies, societies ruled by a few elites. Aristotle's definition of democracy emphasized the importance of citizen participation in government through debating, voting, and holding office. We call this vision **classical democracy.**

In a classical democracy, citizens are committed to learning about and participating in government. They are well informed, discuss public affairs regularly, tell public officials what they think, and vote. Some political theorists think that, compared to individuals who do not take their roles as democratic citizens seriously, those who do are more likely to see the complexities in issues and, while disagreeing with each other, still share common goals and work together to accomplish them.[15]

Political scientists initially accepted the classical democratic view as a fairly accurate picture of American politics. However, by the 1940s and using information from surveys and voter turnout records, they discovered that many fewer citizens take advantage of their democratic rights than classical democratic theory predicts. For example, voting is a routine political activity. It is the easiest way to participate in politics and the least costly in terms of time and energy. Yet only one-half of Americans vote in presidential elections and only one-third have voted in recent congressional elections. Even fewer vote in purely local elections. Instead of being motivated to participate in politics as in a classical democracy, most citizens are little involved. In fact, one-fifth of the electorate does nothing at all political, not even discussing politics.[16]

Only about one-tenth of the population takes full advantage of opportunities to participate. These activists, the "gladiators" of politics, give money to candidates, make phone calls, distribute leaflets, write letters to legislators, attend meetings or join neighbors to work for a common end (such as neighborhood preservation).

Why does the reality of political participation fall short of classical democratic expectations? One recent analysis argues that many Americans do not participate because they are turned off by, among other things, long political campaigns in which sound bites and negative campaigning replace meaningful dialogue about issues.[17] Another and more enduring explanation is that political participation is class-based: People who participate tend to have more money and education. The American working class and lower class, unlike their counterparts in many European countries, lack strong trade unions and political parties to represent them. American trade unions involve mostly the middle and better-off classes. American political parties appeal more to middle-class than working-class interests too. Thus, the poor do not have strong organizations to promote their political participation.

The poor also tend to belong to fewer organizations of any kind (civic groups, labor unions, or issue-oriented groups) than the middle or upper classes. As a result, they have fewer opportunities to be drawn into political action through such associations.

In addition, political participation requires both time and money. Many poor adults are single heads of families with little spare time for political activity or resources for transportation and babysitters.

Race and ethnicity explain political participation too, but not as well. Blacks and Hispanics participate less than others, but this is due primarily to their average lower education and income levels. At each education and income level, blacks and Hispanics participate at about the same rates.

Age also explains participation in politics. Young people participate much less than their elders. The middle-aged—the highest participators—are more apt to be established in a career and family life and have more time and money to devote to political activities. They are also less apt to be infirm than older people.

Thus, American government is not a classical democracy. Only a small minority of citizens fully participates in politics. Majorities cannot rule when most people do not take advantage of their rights by voting or trying to influence government or each other.[18] Furthermore, those who do participate are not representative of the whole population in class and other social characteristics. This can have an important impact on the kind of public policy we have. Elected officials chosen by people with more money and education are unlikely to have the same perspectives as those chosen by people with less money and education.

➤Contemporary Theories of American Democracy

Revelations of low levels of participation prompted political scientists to find other ways to explain the workings of American democracy.

Pluralism

In the 1950s, many political scientists thought they knew how American democracy operated. In a theory called **pluralism,** they sought to reconcile democratic principles with the evidence that most people do not participate actively in politics.

Pluralists maintain that government is responsive to groups of citizens working together to promote their common interests.[19] Individuals join others with like beliefs to influence government.

The pluralist view maintains that enough people belong to enough interest groups that government ultimately hears everyone. This produces, according to pluralist theory, a kind of balance in which no group loses so often that it stops competing. As a result, no group or small number of groups can dominate government. This encourages people to continue to "play the game" by finding ways to compromise with each other. It also leads government to avoid major policy changes to maintain the balance and the popular support that comes with it.

Pluralist theory is attractive because it says democracy can "work" without everyone participating in politics. Actual participation is by group leaders and paid staff who represent rank-and-file members to government. There is some validity to this theory. Thousands of interest groups in Washington employ experts to represent them in congressional corridors, bureaucratic agencies, and courtrooms.

Elitism

Problems with pluralist theory, especially its failure to acknowledge the limited power of citizens with average or below-average incomes, led some political scientists to search for another explanation of how American democracy works. A second school of thought gained considerable support in the 1960s. This theory, called **elitism,** stated that American democracy was much less democratic than pluralists believed.

Elite theory maintains that the holders of a few top jobs in key parts of the society rule. They are the leaders of major corporations (such as IBM, Exxon, General Motors, and AT&T), major universities (such as Harvard, Chicago, and Stanford), major foundations (Ford, Rockefeller, and Johnson) and major media outlets (the *New York Times, Washington Post,* CBS, NBC, and ABC). Elite jobs are also found in important parts of government, such as the Defense Department. One political scientist identified 7,314 key jobs in major organizations such as these.[20]

Shared backgrounds help tie many elite members together. This was a major conclusion of one of the most famous elite theorists, the sociologist C. Wright Mills.[21] He noted that many elite members had gone to the same prep schools and universities and belonged to the same church denominations. Having like backgrounds and heading key organizations, they developed similar views about how government should work.

Elite theory does not limit elite membership to those with elite backgrounds, however. One does not have to attend a prep school like Choate, graduate from Princeton, and be an Episcopalian. Anyone committed to elite views who rises to the top of a major organization can belong. Elite theory includes important labor leaders among the chosen few even if their backgrounds do not include silver spoons.

Elite theory is believable. A 1990 survey reported that 77% of a large sample believed that government is run by "a few big interests."[22] It is often hard to know what is *really* going on in Washington, and easy to be frustrated when the process yields outcomes we do not like. Elite theory offers a plausible explanation: "They" have met in posh, smoke-filled rooms to cut a deal. Anyone who knows anything about tax law has probably had such thoughts. This belief about elite domination of government makes populist appeals even more attractive.

Although elite theorists acknowledge that elite members compete with each other, they see intraelite competition as jockeying for more benefits rather than as a major threat to elite cohesion or to the status quo. Overall, most elite members agree that serving the public interest—and their own interests at the same time—requires protecting the status quo.

Elite theory is useful because it reminds us that tremendous inequalities of resources exist, enabling some parts of society to influence government more than others.

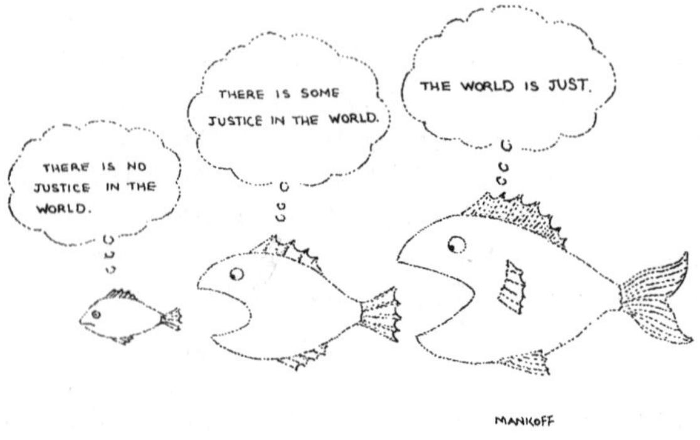

Source: Drawing by Mankoff; © 1981 The New Yorker Magazine, Inc.

Current Views

Political scientists have had spirited debates about whether pluralism or elitism is the best explanation of American politics. Gradually, most have come to see that neither explains everything. As Chapter 5 shows, many people and issues fall through the cracks of interest group representation. The poor are especially unlikely to be organized and to have many resources to fight political battles. Besides, elites do not decide everything and sometimes lose important battles. For example, environmentalists have won big victories over major oil and utility companies.

Sometimes policy reveals a mix of influences. For example, President Bush's energy program of drilling for more oil, fighting to preserve access to Persian Gulf oil, and promoting nuclear power reflected elite views in the energy business. But it is also likely that most Americans preferred this approach over changing their lifestyles to decrease U.S. energy consumption and dependence on foreign resources. Thus, both elite and pluralist theory can be used to explain Bush's energy program.

Current perspectives on how government works stress the "veto" many interest groups have in issues affecting them. Some political scientists have labeled this **hyperpluralism,** suggesting a pluralist system run wild. With so many interests, it is difficult to find common ground to work out solutions to problems. The close ties of many interests to congressional committees and subcommittees considering legislation allow them to stop policy ideas they dislike. And modern technology heightens their impact. A witness to congressional hearings on tax reform reported that lobbyists used cellular phones to produce floods of protest by phone or fax the instant anyone "even *thought*" about something they opposed.[23] So many powerful groups have clout that attempts to alter the status quo or change national priorities are extremely difficult. Presidents Carter, Reagan, and Clinton found this out when they tried to produce major changes in energy, budget, and health care policy, respectively. The Clinton White House tried to work with more than 1,100 interest groups on health care reform, to no avail.[24] Efforts to bring about major changes in national domestic priorities are extremely difficult.

The difficulties created by interest group vetoes often contribute to gridlock and what one observer calls the "blame game."[25] Gridlock occurs when policies are not enacted or administered effectively because the president and Congress cannot agree on what to do. Politicians representing different interests often blame each other for this inaction, or play the "blame game," when they see that gridlock is likely to keep them from getting what they want. For example, although they agreed privately that cuts were needed, Democrats in Congress accused Republicans of hurting the elderly by supporting Social Security cuts to lower the budget deficit; and congressional Republicans blame President Clinton for budget deficits, though his are smaller than his Republican predecessors. The blame game encourages elected officials to distrust each other and furthers public cynicism about government's responsiveness and effectiveness.

Given the presence of many strong groups and their veto opportunities, passing a law means fashioning compromises out of competing group views.[26] In addition to being slow, it often leads to vaguely worded laws giving actual policymaking authority to bureaucrats who work less visibly with interest group help. In effect, agencies and interest groups, not Congress, often legislate. Thus, chemical industry lobbyists help write regulations on hazardous waste, and military contractors help the Pentagon write weapons contracts.

The growth of bureaucratic policymaking makes our democracy more indirect than the writers of the Constitution intended. Most citizens cannot monitor and influence the actions of a president, 535 members of Congress organized into over 300 committees and subcommittees, *and* bureaucratic agencies. The leaders of major interest groups can, and this gives them considerable power. The possibility that these leaders may be relatively independent of their rank-and-file memberships makes them even more important.

These views challenge both pluralism and elitism by concluding that government responds to many but not all groups. This suggests a hybrid explanation of American government stressing the clout of more powerful groups, whose leaders may belong to a larger, more diversified elite.

➤Conclusion: Is Government Responsive?

In America, these days, few people seem pleased with their government. Does that mean that government is not responsive to them? This is a difficult question to answer. Let us look, for example, at the health care debate that occupied the political landscape during much of 1994. President Clinton proposed a major reform of the health care system and the public overwhelmingly appeared to agree that a dramatic overhaul was necessary and important. By the time the debate in Congress was over and interest groups had lobbied both the public and the Congress, public opinion had shifted to a very divided and not very enthusiastic stance toward health care reform. Congress killed Clinton's bill. Is this an example of elite power or pluralist democracy? Is this an example of a responsive government or an unresponsive one? Clearly the lack of public support for the health care bill by the end of the debate was reflected in congressional action, and in that sense government was responsive. On the other hand, special interests with a financial stake in the existing system were responsible for the change in public opinion, and that suggests an elitist interpretation of events and a government not very responsive to the "real" desires of the public. Whichever interpretation we choose, however, it is clear that the entire process contributed to public frustration with government. The president and Congress attacked an important issue with great fanfare, spent months debating the issue, and ended up doing nothing. The fact that the lack of passage of a bill was congruent with public opinion is lost in the larger focus on government as ineffective.

Democracy assumes that majorities control government. Indirect democracy assumes that people control their representatives. Most people, of course, do not try to control government directly or the organizations and leaders who say they represent them. Nonetheless, in contemporary American government, the number of organized interests and their effectiveness in making their views known have both multiplied, so that government officials are besieged by a cacophony of views. And this has happened in an era when the workings of government are increasingly in public view. The result has been a feeling by most people that government is out of their control and unrepresentative of their interests.

We have argued that much of this is a necessary component of a democratic system in a large and diverse nation. Nonetheless, to say we must live with debate, compromise, and slowness in our system does not mean we cannot improve and speed the workings of government. In the next twelve chapters, we will examine carefully the major institutions and processes of our democracy to see if we can shed light on how they contribute to public dissatisfaction and how they might be improved.

EPILOGUE

Politics, Representation, and Democratic Government

Like 44% of the other young voters who went to the polls, you decided to vote for Bill Clinton. Ross Perot received 19% of the total popular vote, higher than any third-party candidate in this century except Teddy Roosevelt in 1912. Perot did especially well among independents, garnering about 30% of their vote. His vote among younger voters was about 23%, only slightly higher than among the public as a whole.

The lack of fit between the personal characteristics needed to be a successful business leader and those needed to be a successful politician illustrates why Perot was attractive to millions of disillusioned Americans. This lack of fit also illustrates why he was not an especially good presidential candidate. Millions of Americans were looking for a decisive, independent leader to break the policy deadlock in Washington. Perot was decisive in business and had, at many points, moved quickly to end commitments that were not working to his advantage. But one needs patience to be successful in politics. As a business owner, a person may be able to achieve quick results by telling employees what to do and accepting their resignations if they do not want to do it. In politics, one can be successful only to the extent that one can negotiate. There are many competing interests at stake in most political decisions. Majority coalitions built by persuasion, patience, and correct perceptions of other interests are the keys to political success.

Building coalitions by reconciling diverse interests is what politics is. At its worst, the political process can lead to gridlock when no leader, party, or other force is able to bring diverse interests together. At its best, this process can bring people and interests together and produce decisions that benefit most if not all. Politics occurs because people almost always disagree. In democratic systems, a variety of institutions have evolved over the centuries that seek to ensure the representation of different interests in society when political decisions are made. Political parties, interest groups, and elections are examples of such institutions. Their often cumbersome nature reflects the difficulty of reconciling diverse interests in a complex society and the structures of our own government, designed to make sure most interests are heard.

Like many other frustrated citizens, Perot expressed disdain for much of the political process, including parties and interest groups. Like most Americans, he finds the democratic process, with its compromises and delays, messy and unpalatable. Perhaps not surprisingly, the party he created to sustain his candidacy, United We Stand America, has been plagued by internal dissension and has lost much of its strength. Some former state and local party officers charge that Perot, in the words of one, wants a party of "automatons who are out there as window dressing."[27] By 1995, Perot's popularity had fallen so low that no one in a national survey volunteered his name as someone to support for president in 1996.[28] Even more striking, only 12% of voters now admit voting for Perot in 1992, when he received 19% of the vote.[29]

Nevertheless, the conditions that fueled Perot's candidacy in 1992 have not changed. In 1996, Steve Forbes, a rich businessman who had never held elected office, entered the race for the Republican presidential nomination and won two primaries, including a key early contest in Arizona. The fact that he had never held office was actually an asset. Just before the primary season started, almost one-quarter of the electorate said they would be more likely to vote for a candidate who had never held political office than for one with experience in office.[30] Forbes built his campaign on a proposal for a flat income tax to replace the involved system now in use, which attracted the support of many who look for simple solutions to complex problems. Thus, many Americans continue to demand tax cuts, but oppose spending cuts that affect them (half of our households receive some sort of federal financial payment).[31] They want democracy but no arguments or compromises.

POOR SUSAN, SHE MARRIED A MEMBER OF A RIGHT-WING PARAMILITARY GROUP.

So the political ground remains fertile for candidates who use the rhetoric that made Perot a national figure. Quick fixes look good to those who are poorly informed about government and who resent the debating, compromises, and slowness of democracy. But quick fixes and free lunches have much in common. There is no such thing as either. Politics is necessary to govern a democratic society. Ignoring politics and the institutions we have to represent ourselves, such as political parties and interest groups, will not eliminate politics. Rather, it would eliminate the most effective ways yet developed for the public to influence government's decisions.

Key Terms

populism
politics
popular sovereignty
direct democracy
indirect democracy
republic
classical democracy
pluralism
elitism
hyperpluralism

Further Reading

John E. Chubb and Paul E. Peterson, *Can the Government Govern?* (Washington, D.C.: Brookings Institution, 1989). *A collection of case studies showing how the public interest often suffers when elected officials and bureaucrats avoid hard policy choices by playing the blame game with each other and "special interests."*

Marilyn P. Davis, *Mexican Voices/American Dreams: An Oral History of Mexican Immigration to the United States* (New York: Owl/Holt, 1990). *The author describes the Mexican immigrant experience in the words of the immigrants themselves.*

William Greider, *Who Will Tell the People: The Betrayal of American Democracy* (New York: Simon & Schuster, 1992). *A populist perspective that views Washington politics as a "grand bazaar" where wealthy interest groups exchange favors with public officials who want to maintain their power.*

Alan D. Hertzke, *Echoes of Discontent: Jesse Jackson, Pat Robertson, and the Resurgence of Populism* (Washington, D.C.: CQ Press, 1993), *Hertzke examines two contemporary examples of populism, while providing a good historical context for this important phenomenon in American politics.*

John R. Hibbing and Elizabeth Theiss-Morse, *Congress as Public Enemy: Public Attitudes toward American Political Institutions* (Cambridge: Cambridge University Press, 1995). *The authors argue that the public is fed up with Congress because Congress is where the internal workings of democracy—the debates, appeals to self, partisan, and group interest, compromises, and inefficiencies—are most obvious.*

Harold Lasswell, *Politics: Who Gets What, When, How* (New York: New World Publishing, 1958). *A classic treatment of some very practical political problems.*

Michael Pertschuk, *Giant Killers* (New York: W. W. Norton, 1986). *A public interest lobbyist describes several major congressional battles in the 1980s showing that the side with money and status does not always win.*

Hedrick Smith, *The Power Game: How Washington Works* (New York: Random House, 1988). *A Pulitzer Prize winning journalist's account of the colorful personalities and complex alliances that shape national policymaking. Loaded with good anecdotes.*

➤Notes

1. A label given to Perot by analyst Kevin Phillips. See Howard Fineman, "Running Scared," *Newsweek*, November 2, 1992, p. 47.

2. See John Hibbing and Elizabeth Theiss-Morse, *Congress as Public Enemy: Public Attitudes toward American Political Institutions* (Cambridge: Cambridge University Press, 1995); Hibbing and Theiss-Morse, "Civics Is Not Enough; Teaching Barbarics in K-12," *PS* Vol. XXIX (March 1996), pp. 57–62). Gabriel A. Almond and Sidney Verba, *The Civic Culture* (Boston: Little, Brown, 1965), p. 64.

3. Hibbing and Theiss-Morse, *Congress as Public Enemy: Public Attitudes toward American Political Institutions* (Cambridge: Cambridge University Press, 1995).

4. Walt Whitman, *Leaves of Grass and Selected Prose*, Lawrence Buell, ed. (New York: Random House, 1981), p. 449.

5. Tom Morganthau, "What Color Is Black?" *Newsweek*, February 13, 1995, p. 65.

6. The data in this paragraph are from Barbara Vobejda, "The Land of the Immigrant and the Home of Diversity," *Washington Post National Weekly Edition*, March 18-24, 1991, p. 34; and Dick Kirschten, "Second Thoughts," *National Journal*, December 21, 1995, p. 151.

7. Robert Reinhold, "Resentment Against New Immigrants," *New York Times*, October 26, 1986, p. 6E.

8. Bureau of the Census, *General Social and Economy Characteristics: U.S. Summary* (Washington, D.C.: U.S. Government Printing Office, 1990), Part 1, Table 12.

9. Richard D. Alba, "The Twilight of Ethnicity Among Americans of European Ancestry: The Case of Italians," in Richard Alba, ed., *Ethnicity and Race in the U.S.A.: Toward the Twenty-First Century* (London: Routledge & Kegan Paul, 1985), pp. 134–58. Discussed in David Brinkerhoff and Lynn White, *Sociology*, 2d ed. (St. Paul, Minn.: West Publishing, 1988), p. 259.

10. Antonio McDaniel, "The Dynamic Racial Composition of the United States," *Daedalus* (Winter 1995), pp. 179–198; Lawrence Wright, "One Drop of Blood," *New Yorker* (July 25, 1994), pp. 46–55.

11. Reported in Morganthau, "What Color Is Black?" p. 64. Data on black-white intermarriage is found in Susan Kalish, "Interracial Baby Boomlet in Progress?" *Population Today* 20 (December 1992), pp. 1–2.

12. Ronald Inglehart, "The Renaissance of Political Culture," *American Political Science Review* 82 (December 1988), p. 1213.

13. H. H. Gerth and C. Wright Mills, trans. and eds., *From Max Weber: Essays in Sociology* (New York: Oxford University Press, 1958), p. 78.

14. Louis Hartz, *The Liberal Tradition in America* (New York: Harcourt, Brace, 1955).

15. For a discussion of this see Mark Warren, "Democratic Theory and Self-Transformation," *American Political Science Review* 86 (March, 1992), pp. 8–23.

16. This discussion draws on Sidney Verba and Norman Nie, *Participation in America* (New York: Harper & Row, 1972); and Stephen Earl Bennett and Linda L. M. Bennett, "Political Participation," in Samuel Long, ed., *Annual Review of Political Science* (Norwood, N.J.: Ablex Publishing Group, 1986).

17. E. J. Dionne, Jr., *Why Americans Hate Politics* (New York: Simon & Schuster, 1991).

19. Robert A. Dahl, *A Preface to Democratic Theory* (Chicago: University of Chicago Press, 1956), p. 142.

19. See Arthur F. Bentley, *The Process of Government* (Chicago: University of Chicago Press, 1908); and David Truman, *The Governmental Process* (New York: A. A. Knopf, 1951).

20. Thomas R. Dye, *Who's Running America? The Bush Era* (Englewood Cliffs, N.J.: Prentice-Hall, 1990), p. 12.

21. C. Wright Mills, *The Power Elite* (New York: Oxford University Press, 1956).

22. Cited in Allen D. Hertzke, *Echoes of Discontent: Jesse Jackson, Pat Robertson, and the Resurgence of Populism* (Washington, DC: CQ Press, 1993), p. 235.

23. Reported in Robert Wright, "Hyper Democracy," *Time*, January 23, 1995, p. 18.

24. David S. Broder, "Can We Govern?" *Washington Post National Weekly Edition*, January 31–February 6, 1994, p. 23.

25. Hedrick Smith, *The Power Game: How Washington Works* (New York: Random House, 1988), chapter 17.

26. For example, see Theodore J. Lowi, *The End of Liberalism*, 2d ed. (New York: W. W. Norton, 1979).

27. Dan Balz, "Turf War Among the Grass Roots," *Washington Post National Weekly Edition*, May 2–8, 1994, p. 12.

28. "Opinion Outlook," *National Journal*, January 21, 1995, p. 194.

29. Calvin Trillin, "Statistically Scary," *Time Magazine*, May 13, 1996, p. 37.

30. Nancy Gibbs, "Knock 'Em Flat," *Time*, January 29, 1996, p. 27.

31. Michael Wines, "Taxpayers Are Angry. They're Expensive, Too," *New York Times*, November 20, 1994, p. E5.

2 The Constitution

You Are There

The Case of the Confidential Tapes

In June 1972, a security guard for the Watergate building in Washington, D.C., noticed that tape had been placed across the latch of a door to keep it from locking. The guard peeled off the tape. When he made his rounds later, he noticed that more tape had been placed across the latch. He called the police.

The police encountered five burglars in the headquarters of the Democratic National Committee. Wearing surgical gloves and carrying tear gas guns, photographic equipment, and electronic gear, they had been installing wiretaps on the Democratic party's phones.

No one expected this break-in to lead to the White House. The *Washington Post* assigned two young reporters who usually covered local matters to the story. But the unlikely pair of Bob Woodward, a Yale graduate, and Carl Bernstein, a college dropout, were ambitious, and they uncovered a series of bizarre connections. The burglars had links with President Richard Nixon's Committee to Reelect the President (CREEP).

The administration dismissed the break-in as the work of overzealous underlings. Even the press called it a "caper." Indeed, it was hard to imagine that high officials in the administration could be responsible. In public opinion polls, Nixon enjoyed an enormous lead, almost 20%, over the various Democrats vying for their party's nomination to challenge him in the fall election. Risky tactics seemed unnecessary.

But Woodward and Bernstein discovered that White House staff members had engaged in other criminal and unethical actions to sabotage the Democrats' campaign. They had forged letters accusing some of the Democrats' candidates of homosexual acts. Later they had obtained and publicized psychiatric records, causing the Democrats' vice presidential nominee to resign.

Nixon won reelection handily, but the revelations forced his two top aides to resign and prompted the Senate to establish a special committee to investigate what was being called the **Watergate scandal.** When investigators happened to ask the president's appointment secretary if there was a taping device in the Oval Office, he said, "I was hoping you fellows wouldn't ask me about that." Then he revealed what only a handful of aides had known—that Nixon had secretly tape-recorded conversations in nine locations in the White House, the Executive Office Building across the street, and Camp David in Maryland. Nixon had intended to create a comprehensive record of his presidency to demonstrate his greatness.[1]

The tapes could confirm or refute charges of White House complicity in the break-in and cover-up, but Nixon refused to release them. Special Prosecutor Archibald Cox filed suit to force Nixon to do so, and federal trial court Judge John Sirica ordered him to do so. After the federal appeals court affirmed the trial court's decision, Nixon demanded his attorney general fire Cox. The attorney general and deputy attorney general both refused and resigned in protest. Then the third-ranking official in the Justice Department, Robert Bork, fired the special prosecutor. (Bork later would be nominated to the Supreme Court by President Reagan.)

The public furor over this "Saturday Night Massacre" was so intense that Nixon finally did release some tapes. But one crucial tape contained a mysterious 18-minute gap that a presidential aide speculated was caused by "some sinister force."

◄ *Soon after their deaths, the Founders became venerated by the people. Here George Washington is pictured ascending to heaven.*

CONTINUED 

The Articles of Confederation
- National Government Problems
- State Government Problems

The Constitution
- The Constitutional Convention
- Features of the Constitution
- Motives of the Founders
- Ratification of the Constitution
- Changing the Constitution

Conclusion: Is the Constitution Responsive?

OUTLINE

To mollify critics Nixon appointed a new special prosecutor, Leon Jaworski. After his investigation, Jaworski presented evidence to a grand jury that indicted seven of the president's aides for the cover-up, specifically for obstruction of justice, and even named the president as an "unindicted coconspirator."

The House Judiciary Committee considered impeaching the president, and Jaworski subpoenaed more tapes. Nixon issued edited transcripts of the conversations but not the tapes themselves. As a compromise he proposed that one person listen to the tapes—a senator who was 72 years old and hard of hearing. Frustrated, Jaworski went to court, where Judge Sirica ordered Nixon to release the tapes. When Nixon refused, Jaworski appealed directly to the Supreme Court.

You are Chief Justice Warren Burger, appointed to the Court by President Nixon in 1969 partly because of your calls for more law and order. Three of your brethren also were appointed by Nixon. In the case of *United States v. Nixon,* you are faced with a question that could lead to a grave constitutional showdown with the president. Special Prosecutor Jaworski claims he needs the tapes because they contain evidence pertaining to the upcoming trial of the president's aides indicted for the cover-up. Without all relevant evidence, which possibly could vindicate the aides, the trial court might not convict them.

Washington Post reporters Carl Bernstein (left) and Bob Woodward uncovered the Watergate scandal.

President Nixon claims he has **executive privilege**—authority to withhold information from the courts and Congress. Although the Constitution does not mention such a privilege, Nixon claims the privilege is inherent in the powers of the presidency. Without it presidents could not guarantee confidentiality in conversations with other officials or even foreign leaders. This could make it difficult for them to govern.

There are few precedents to guide you. Many past presidents exercised executive privilege when pressed for information by Congress. In these instances, Congress ordinarily acquiesced rather than sue for the information, so the courts did not rule on the existence of the privilege. Once, in 1953, the Eisenhower administration invoked the privilege, and the Supreme Court upheld the claim. However, this case involved national security.[2]

In addition to considering the merits of the opposing sides, you also need to consider the extent of the Court's power. The Court lacks strong means to enforce its rulings. It has to rely on its authority as the highest interpreter of the law in the country. Therefore, if the Court orders Nixon to relinquish the tapes and Nixon refuses, there would be little the Court could do. The refusal would show future officials they could disregard your orders with impunity.

In this high-stakes contest, do you and your brethren on the Court order Nixon to turn over the tapes, or do you accept his claim of executive privilege?

Early settlers came to America for many reasons. Some came to escape religious persecution, others to establish their own religious orthodoxy. Some came to get rich, others to avoid debtors' prison. Some came to enrich their families or companies in the Old World, others to flee the closed society of that world. Some came as free persons, others as indentured servants or slaves. Few came to practice self-government. Yet the desire for self-government was evident from the beginning.[3] The settlers who arrived in Jamestown in 1607 established the first representative assembly in America. The pilgrims who reached Plymouth in 1620 drew up the Mayflower Compact in which they vowed to "solemnly & mutually in the presence of God, and one of another, covenant and combine our selves together into a civill body politick." They pledged to establish laws for "the generall good of the colonie" and in return promised "all due submission and obedience."[4]

During the next century and a half, the colonies adopted constitutions and elected representative assemblies. Of course, the colonies lived under British rule; they had to accept the appointment of royal governors and the presence of British troops. But a vast ocean separated the two continents. At such a distance, Britain could not wield the control it might at closer reach. Consequently, it granted the colonies a measure of autonomy, with which they practiced a degree of self-government.

These early efforts toward self-government led to conflict with the mother government. In 1774 the colonies established the Continental Congress to coordinate their action. Within months the conflict reached flashpoint, and the Congress urged the colonies to form their own governments. In 1776 the Congress adopted the Declaration of Independence.

After six years of war, the Americans accepted the British surrender. At the time it seemed they had met their biggest test. Yet they would find fomenting a revolution easier than fashioning a government and drafting a declaration of independence easier than crafting a constitution.

THE ARTICLES OF CONFEDERATION

Even before the war ended, the Continental Congress passed a constitution, and in 1781 the states ratified it. This first constitution, the **Articles of Confederation,** formed a "league of friendship" among the states. As a confederation, it allowed each state to retain its "sovereignty" and "independence." That is, it made the states supreme over the national government.

Under the Articles, however, Americans would face problems with both their national and state governments.

National Government Problems

The Articles established a Congress, with one house in which each state had one vote. But the Articles strictly limited the powers that Congress could exercise, and they provided no executive or judicial branch.

The Articles reflected the colonial experience under the British government. The leaders feared a powerful central government with a powerful executive like a king. They thought such a government would be too strong and too distant to guarantee individual liberty. Additionally, the Articles reflected a lack of national identity among the people. Most did not view themselves as Americans yet. As Edmund Randolph remarked, "I am not really an American, I am a Virginian."[5] Consequently, the leaders established a very decentralized government that left most authority to the states.

The Articles satisfied many people. Most people were small farmers and, although many of them sank into debt during the depression that followed the war, they felt they could influence the state governments to help them. They realized they could not influence a distant central government as readily.

But the Articles frustrated bankers, merchants, manufacturers, and others in the upper classes. They envisioned a great commercial empire rather than the agricultural society the country had. More than local trade, they wanted national and even international trade. For this they needed uniform laws, stable money, sound credit, and enforceable debt collection. They needed a strong central government that could protect them against debtors and against state governments sympathetic to debtors. The Articles provided neither the foreign security nor the domestic climate necessary to nourish these requisites of a commercial empire.

After the war the army disbanded, leaving the country vulnerable to hostile forces surrounding it. Britain maintained outposts with troops in the Northwest Territory (now the Midwest), in violation of the peace treaty, and an army in Canada. Spain, which had occupied Florida and California for a long time and had claimed the Mississippi River Valley as a result of a treaty before the war, posed a threat. Barbary pirates from northern Africa seized American ships and sailors.

Congress could not raise an army, because it could not draft individuals directly, or finance an army, because it could not tax individuals directly. Instead, it had to ask the states for soldiers and money. The states, however, were not always sympathetic to the problems of the distant government. And although Congress could make treaties with foreign countries, the states made, or broke, treaties independently of Congress. Without the ability to establish a credible army or negotiate a binding treaty, the government could not get the British troops out of the country. Neither could it get the British government to ease restrictions on shipping or the Spanish government to permit navigation on the Mississippi River.

In addition to an inability to confront foreign threats, the Articles demonstrated an inability to cope with domestic crises. The country bore a heavy war debt that brought the government close to bankruptcy.

Since Congress could not tax individuals directly, it could not shore up the shaky government.

The states competed with each other for commercial advantage. As independent governments, they imposed tariffs on goods from other states. The tariffs slowed the growth of businesses.

In short, the government under the Articles seemed too decentralized to ensure either peace or prosperity. The Articles, one leader concluded, gave Congress the privilege of asking for everything, while reserving to each state the prerogative of granting nothing.[6] A similar situation exists today in the United Nations, which must rely on member countries to furnish troops for its peacekeeping forces and dues for its operating expenses.

State Government Problems

There were other conflicts closer to home. State constitutions adopted during the Revolution made the state legislatures more representative than the colonial legislatures had been. And most state legislatures began to hold elections every year. The result was heightened interest among candidates and turnover among legislators. In the eyes of national leaders, there was much pandering to voters and horsetrading by politicians as various factions vied for control. The process seemed up for grabs. According to the Vermont Council of Censors, laws were "altered—realtered—made better—made worse; and kept in such a fluctuating position that persons in civil commission scarce know what is law."[7] In short, state governments were experiencing more democracy than any other governments in the world at the time. National leaders, stunned by the changes in the few years since the Revolution, considered this development an "excess of democracy."

Moreover, state constitutions made the legislative branch the most powerful. Some state legislatures began to dominate the other branches, and national leaders called them "tyrannical."

The national leaders, most of whom were wealthy and many of whom were creditors, pointed to the laws passed in some states that relieved debtors of some of their obligations. The farmers who were in debt pressed the legislatures for relief that would slow or shrink the payments owed to their creditors. Some legislatures granted such relief.

While these laws worried the leaders, **Shays's Rebellion** in western Massachusetts in 1786 and 1787 scared them. Boston merchants who had loaned Massachusetts money during the war insisted on being repaid in full so they could trade with foreign merchants. The state levied steep taxes that many farmers could not pay during the hard times. The law authorized foreclosure—sale of the farmers' property for the taxes—and jail for the debtors. The law essentially transfered wealth from the farmers to the merchants. The farmers protested the legislature's refusal to grant any relief from the law. Bands of farmers blocked entrances to courthouses where judges were scheduled to hear cases calling for foreclosure and jail. Led by Daniel Shays, some marched to the Springfield arsenal to seize weapons. Although they were defeated by the militia, their sympathizers were victorious in the next election and the legislature did provide some relief from the law.

Both the revolt and the legislature's change in policy frightened the wealthy. To them it raised the specter of "mob rule." Nathaniel Gorham, the president of the Continental Congress and a prominent merchant, wrote Prince Henry of Prussia, announcing "the failure of our free institutions" and asking if the prince would agree to become king of America. (The prince declined.)[8] Just months after the uprising, the Congress approved a convention for "the sole and express purpose of revising the Articles of Confederation."

To a significant extent, then, the debate at the time reflected a conflict between two competing visions of the future American political economy—agricultural or commercial.[9] Most farmers considered the government under the Articles responsive to their concerns, but most leaders, who envisioned a commercial empire, considered the goverment too weak to give rise to such an empire. The combination of national problems and state problems prompted leaders to push for a new government.

The Constitution

The Constitutional Convention

The Setting

The **Constitutional Convention** convened in Philadelphia, then the country's largest city, in 1787. That year the Industrial Revolution was continuing to sweep Europe and beginning to reach this continent. The first American cotton mill opened in Massachusetts and the first American steamboat plied the Delaware River.[10]

State legislatures chose 74 delegates to the convention; 55 attended. They met at the Pennsylvania State

American Diversity

Founding Mothers

Charles Francis Adams, a grandson of President John Adams and Abigail Adams, declared in 1840, "The heroism of the females of the Revolution has gone from memory with the generation that witnessed it, and nothing, absolutely nothing remains upon the ear of the young of the present day."[1] That statement is still true today; in the volumes written about the revolutionary and Constitution-making eras, much is said of the "founding fathers" and very little about the "founding mothers." Although no women were at the Constitutional Convention, in many other ways women contributed significantly to the political ferment of the time. The political role of women during the Constitution-making era was probably greater than it would be again for a century.

Before the Revolutionary War, women were active in encouraging opposition to the British. Groups of women, some called the "daughters of liberty," led boycotts of British goods as part of the protest campaign against taxation without representation. A few women were political pamphleteers, helping to increase public sentiment for independence. One of those pamphlet writers, Mercy Otis Warren, of Massachusetts, was thought to be the first person to urge the Massachusetts delegates to the Continental Congress to vote for separation from England.[2] Throughout the period before and after the Revolution, Warren shared her political ideas in personal correspondence with leading statesmen of the time, such as John Adams and Thomas Jefferson. Later she wrote a three-volume history of the American Revolution.

Many women were part of the American army during the battles for independence. Most filled traditional women's roles as cooks, sewers, and nurses, but some disguised themselves as men (this was before a military bureaucracy mandated preenlistment physical exams) and fought in battle. One such woman, wounded in action in 1776, is the only Revolutionary War veteran buried at West Point. Still other women fought to defend their homes using hatchets, farm implements, and pots of boiling lye in addition to muskets.

Following independence, some women continued an active political role. Mercy Warren, for example, campaigned against the proposed Constitution because she felt it was not democratic enough.

Independence did not bring any improvement in the political rights of women. In fact, after the Constitution was adopted, some rights that women had held before were gradually lost, such as the right of some women to vote. It was to be another century before the rights of women became a full-fledged part of our national political agenda.

1. Quoted in Linda Grant DePauw and Conover Hunt, *Remember the Ladies* (New York: Viking Press, 1976), p. 9.
2. Alice Felt Tyler, *Freedom's Ferment* (New York: Harper & Row, 1962).

This English political cartoon satirizes a gathering of leading women in North Carolina who drew up a resolution to boycott taxed English goods and tea.

House—now Independence Hall—in the same room where some of them had signed the Declaration of Independence 11 years before.

Delegates came from every state except Rhode Island. That state was controlled by farmers and debtors who feared that the convention would weaken states' powers to relieve debtors of their debts.

The delegates were distinguished by their education, experience, and enlightenment. Benjamin Franklin, of Pennsylvania, was the best-known American in the world. He had been a printer, scientist, and diplomat. At 81 he was the oldest delegate. George Washington, of Virginia, was the most respected American in the country. As the commander of the revolutionary army, he was a national hero. He was chosen to preside over the convention. The presence of men like Franklin and Washington gave the convention legitimacy.

The delegates quickly determined that the Articles were hopeless. Rather than revise them, as instructed by Congress, the delegates decided to start over and draft a new constitution.[11] But what would they substitute for the Articles?

The Predicament

The delegates came to the convention because they suffered under a government that was too weak. Yet previously Americans had fought a revolution because they chafed under a government that was too strong. "The nation lived in a nearly constant alternation of fears that it would cease being a nation altogether or become too much of one."[12] People feared both anarchy and tyranny.

This predicament was made clear by the diversity of opinions among the leaders. At one extreme was Patrick Henry, of Virginia, who had been a firebrand of the Revolution. He felt the country would become too strong, perhaps even become a monarchy, in reaction to the current problems with the Articles. Although chosen as a delegate to the convention, he said he "smelt a rat" and did not attend. At the other extreme was Alexander Hamilton, of New York, who had been an aide to General Washington during the war and had seen the government's inability to supply and pay its own troops. Since then he had called for a stronger national government. He wanted one that could veto the laws of the state governments. And he wanted one person to serve as chief executive for life and others to serve as senators for life. He did attend the convention but, finding little agreement with his proposals, participated infrequently.

In between were those like James Madison, of Virginia, who was a nationalist but less extreme than Hamilton. Small and frail, timid and self-conscious as a speaker, he was nonetheless intelligent, savvy, and audacious. He had been instrumental behind the scenes in convening the convention and securing George Washington's attendance. (He publicized that Washington would attend without asking Washington first. Washington, who was in retirement, did not plan to attend but reluctantly agreed to because of the expectation that he would.)[13] Drawing upon his study of governments in history to learn why many had

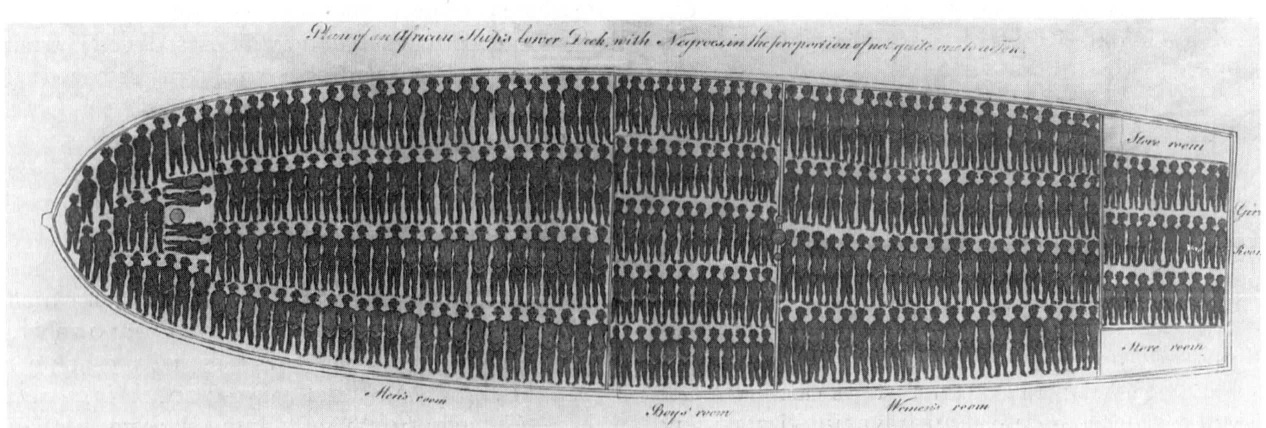

This plan of a slave ship shows the overcrowding that led to inhumane conditions, rampant diseases, and high rates of mortality.

failed, Madison had secretly drafted a plan for a new government that was a total departure from the Articles. Madison's ideas set the agenda for the convention. In the end, his views, more than anyone else's, would prevail, and he would be called the Father of the Constitution.[14]

Consensus

Despite disagreements, the delegates did see eye to eye on the most fundamental issues. They agreed that the government should be a republic—an indirect democracy—in which people could vote for at least some of the officials who would represent them. This was the only form of government they seriously considered. They also agreed that the national government should be supreme over the state governments. At the same time, they thought the government should be limited, with checks to prevent it from exercising too much power.

They agreed that the national government should have three separate branches—legislative, executive, and judicial—to exercise separate powers. They thought both the legislative and executive branches should be strong.

Conflict

Although there was considerable agreement over the fundamental principles and elemental structure of the new government, the delegates quarreled about the specific provisions concerning representation, slavery, and trade.

REPRESENTATION There was sharp conflict between delegates from large states and small states. Large states sought a strong central government that they could control; small states feared a government that would control them.

When the convention began, Edmund Randolph introduced the Virginia Plan drafted by Madison. According to this plan, the central government would be strong. The legislature would have more power than under the Articles, and a national executive and national judiciary also would have considerable power. The legislature would be divided into two houses, with representation based on population in each.

But delegates from the small states calculated that the three largest states—Pennsylvania, Virginia, and Massachusetts—would have a majority of the representatives and could control the legislature. These delegates countered with the New Jersey Plan, introduced by William Paterson. According to this plan, the central government would be relatively strong, although not as strong as under the Virginia Plan. But the primary difference was that the legislature would be one house, with representation by states, which would have one vote each. This was exactly the same as the structure of Congress under the Articles, also designed to prevent the large states from controlling the legislature.

The convention deadlocked. George Washington wrote that he almost despaired of reaching agreement. To ease tensions Benjamin Franklin suggested that the delegates begin each day with a prayer, but they could not agree on this either; Alexander Hamilton insisted they did not need "foreign aid."

Faced with the possibility that the convention would disband without a constitution, the delegates compromised. Delegates from Connecticut and other states proposed a plan in which the legislature would have two houses. In one, representation would be based on population, and members would be elected by voters. In the other, representation would be by states, and members would be selected by state legislatures. Presumably the large states would dominate the former, the small states the latter. The delegates narrowly approved this **Great Compromise,** or Connecticut Compromise. Delegates from the large states still objected, but those from the small states made it clear that such a compromise was necessary for their agreement and, in turn, their states' ratification. The large states, though, did extract a concession that all taxing and spending bills must originate in the house in which representation was based on population. This provision would allow the large states to take the initiative on these important measures.

The compromise was "great" in that it not only resolved this critical issue but paved the way for resolution of other issues.

SLAVERY In addition to conflict between large states and small states over representation, there was conflict between northern states and southern states over slavery, trade, and taxation.

With representation in one house based on population, the delegates had to decide how to apportion the seats. They agreed that Indians would not count as part of the population but differed about slaves. Delegates from the South, where slaves were one-third of the population, wanted slaves to count fully in order to boost their number of representatives. They argued that their use of slaves produced wealth that benefited the entire nation. Delegates from the North, where most states had outlawed slavery or at least the slave trade after the Revolution, did not want slaves to count at all. Gouverneur Morris, of Pennsylvania, said the southerners' position "... comes to this: that the inhabitant of Georgia and South Carolina who goes to the coast of Africa, and in defiance of the most sacred laws of humanity tears away his fellow creatures from their dearest connections and damns them to the most cruel bondages, shall have more votes in a government instituted for the protection of the rights of mankind than the citizen of Pennsylvania or New Jersey who views with a laudable horror so nefarious a practice."[15] Others pointed out that slaves were not considered persons when it came to rights such as voting. Nevertheless, southerners asserted that they would not support a constitution if slaves were not counted at least partially. In the **Three-fifths Compromise,** the delegates agreed that three-fifths of the slaves would be counted in apportioning the seats.

As a result the votes of southern whites would be worth more than those of northerners in electing members to the House of Representatives and presidents (because the Electoral College would be based on membership in Congress). Between 1788 and 1860, nine of the 15 presidents, including all five who served two terms, were slaveowners.[16]

Although northerners had to accept this compromise in order for southerners to support the Constitution, northerners apparently did not contest two other provisions addressing slavery. Southerners pushed through one provision forbidding Congress to ban the importation of slaves before 1808 and another requiring free states to return any escaped slaves to their owners in slave states. In these provisions southerners won most of what they wanted; even the provision permitting Congress to ban the slave trade in 1808 was hardly a limitation because by then planters would have enough slaves to fulfill their needs by natural population increases rather than importation. In return, northerners, representing most shippers, got authority for Congress to regulate commerce by a simple majority rather than a two-thirds majority. Thus, northerners conceded two provisions reinforcing slavery in order to benefit shippers.[17]

Yet the framers were embarrassed by the hypocrisy of claiming to have been enslaved by the British while allowing enslavement of blacks. The framers' embarrassment is reflected in their language. The three provisions reinforcing slavery never mention "slavery" or "slaves"; one gingerly refers to "free persons" and "other persons."

The unwillingness to tackle the slavery issue more directly has been called the "Greatest Compromise" by one political scientist.[18] But an attempt to abolish slavery would have led the five southern states to refuse to ratify the Constitution.

TRADE AND TAXATION Slavery also underlay a compromise on trade and taxation. With a manufacturing economy, northerners sought protection for their businesses. In particular, they wanted a tax on manufactured goods imported from England. Without a tax, these goods would be cheaper than northern goods; but with a tax, northern goods would be more competitive—and prices for southern consumers more expensive. With an agricultural economy, southerners sought free trade for their plantations. They wanted a guarantee that there would be no tax on agricultural products exported to England. Such a tax would make their products less competitive abroad and, they worried, amount to an indirect tax on slavery—the labor responsible for the products. The delegates compromised by allowing Congress to tax imported goods but not exported ones. Tariffs on imported goods would become a point of controversy between the North and South in the years leading up to the Civil War.

With all issues resolved, a committee was appointed to write the final draft. Gouverneur Morris was the member of the committee most responsible for the polished style of the document. He was also largely responsible for the stirring preamble. In earlier drafts the preamble had not referred to "the people" but had listed the states. Morris's change signaled a shift in emphasis from the states to the people directly.

After 17 weeks of debate, the Constitution was ready. On September 17, 1787, 39 of the original 55 delegates signed it. Some delegates had left when they saw the direction the convention was taking, and three others refused to sign, feeling that the Constitution gave too much authority to the national government. Most of the rest were not entirely happy with the result—even Madison, who was most responsible for the content of the document, was despondent that his plan for a national legislature was compromised by having one house with representation by states—but they thought it was the best they could do. Benjamin Franklin had some qualms, but he

The Founders and the People

Democracy is "the worst of all political evils."
—Elbridge Gerry

"[T]he people have ever been and ever will be unfit to retain the exercise of power in their own hands."
—William Livingston

"[T]he people [should] have as little to do as may be about the government."
—Roger Sherman

"Notwithstanding the oppression and injustice experienced among us from democracy, the genius of the people is in favor of it, and the genius of the people must be consulted."
—George Mason

"It seems indispensable that the mass of citizens should not be without a voice in making the laws which they are to obey, in choosing the magistrates who are to administer them."
—James Madison

In part these statements reflect the Founders' support for republicanism and opposition to democracy, as they defined the terms. But in a more general sense, these statements reflect the Founders' ambivalence about "the people." Rationally they believed in popular sovereignty, but emotionally they feared it. Perhaps no statement illustrates this ambivalence more than the one by New England clergyman Jeremy Belknap: "Let it stand as a principle that government originates from the people; but let the people be taught . . . that they are not able to govern themselves."

Source: Richard Hofstadter, *The American Political Tradition and the Men Who Made It* (New York: Vintage, 1948), pp. 3–17.

was more optimistic. Referring to the sun painted on the back of George Washington's chair, he remarked that throughout the proceedings he had wondered whether it was a rising or setting sun. "But now . . . I have the happiness to know that it is a rising and not a setting sun."

Features of the Constitution

William Gladstone, a British prime minister in the nineteenth century, said the American Constitution was "the most wonderful work ever struck off at a given time by the brain and purpose of man."[19] To see why it was unique, it is necessary to examine its major features.

A Written Constitution

The Founders established the idea of a written constitution, first in the Articles of Confederation and then more prominently in the Constitution itself. Other Western countries had constitutions that served as their supreme law, but these constitutions were not written or, if written, not as a single document. For example, the British constitution, which consisted of various customs, declarations, acts of Parliament, and precedents of courts, was partly unwritten and partly written. To Americans this was no constitution at all. They felt that a constitution should be a fundamental law above all other laws—not a mixture of customs and laws.

This belief is reflected in Americans' use of social contract theory. A **social contract,** not a literal contract like a business contract, is an implied agreement between the people and their government. The people give up part of their liberty to the government, which in exchange protects the remainder of their liberty. The Mayflower Compact was a very general form of social contract, whereas the written Constitution, stipulating the powers and limits of government, was a more specific form of social contract.

A Republic

As explained in Chapter 1, the Founders distinguished between a **republic** and a **democracy.** They created a republic. Also called an "indirect democracy," this form of government is one in which people vote for representatives who make decisions for them.

The Founders opposed a "direct democracy" in which the will of the people becomes law. Some city-states of ancient Greece and medieval Europe had direct democracies but could not sustain them. The Founders thought a large country would have even less ability to do so because people could not be brought together in one place in order to act. The Founders also believed human nature was such that people could not withstand the passions of the moment and would be swayed by a demagogue to take unwise action. Eventually, democracy would collapse into tyranny. "Remember," John Adams wrote, "democracy never lasts long. It soon wastes, exhausts, and murders itself. There never was a democracy yet that did not commit suicide."[20]

The Founders favored a republic because they firmly believed the people should have some voice in government for it to be based on the consent of the governed. So the Founders provided that the people could elect representatives to the House and that the state legislators, themselves elected by the people, could select senators and members of the Electoral College, who would choose the president. In this way the people would have a voice but one filtered through their presumably wiser representatives.

The Founders considered a democracy radical and a republic only slightly less radical. Because they believed the country could not maintain a democracy, they worried that it might not be able to maintain a republic either. When the Constitutional Convention closed, Benjamin Franklin was approached by a woman who asked, "Well, Doctor, what have we got, a republic or a monarchy?" Franklin responded, "A republic, madam, if you can keep it."

Fragmentation of Power

Other countries assumed that government must have a concentration of power to be strong enough to govern. However, when the Founders made our national government more powerful than it had been under the Articles, they feared they also had made it more capable of oppression, and therefore they fragmented its power.

The Founders believed people were selfish, coveting more and more property, and that leaders lusted after more and more power. They assumed such human nature was unchangeable. Madison speculated, "If men were angels, no government would be necessary." But, alas, Madison said, men are not angels. Therefore, "In framing a government which is to be administered by men over men, the great difficulty lies in this: you must first enable the government to control the governed; and in the next place oblige it to control itself."[21] The Founders decided the way to oblige government to control itself was to structure it to prevent any one leader, group of leaders, or factions of people from exercising power over more than a small part of it. Thus, the Founders fragmented government's power. This is reflected in three concepts they built into the structure of government—federalism, separation of powers, and checks and balances.

FEDERALISM The first division of power was between the national government and the state governments. This division of power is called **federalism.** Foreign governments had been "unitary"; that is, the central government wielded all authority. At the other extreme, the U.S. government under the Articles had been "confederal," which meant that although there was some division of power, the state governments wielded almost all authority. The Founders wanted a strong national government, but they also wanted, or at least realized they would have to accept, reasonably strong state governments as well. They invented a federal system as a compromise between the unitary and confederal systems.

SEPARATION OF POWERS The second division of power was within the national government. The power to make, administer, and judge the laws was split into three branches—legislative, executive, and judicial (see Figure 1). In the legislative branch, the power was split further into two houses. This **separation of powers** contrasts with the British parliamentary system in which its legislature, Parliament, is supreme. Both executive and judicial officials are drawn from it and responsible to it. Madison expressed the American view of such an arrangement when he said that "the accumulation of all powers, legislative, executive, and judiciary, in the same hands

FIGURE 1
Separation of Powers

Branch:	**Legislative Congress**		**Executive Presidency**	**Judicial Federal Courts**
	House	Senate	President	Judges
Officials chosen by:	People	People, (originally, state legislatures)	Electoral College, whose members are chosen by the people (originally, by state legislatures)	President, with advice and consent of Senate
For term of:	2 years	6 years	4 years	Life ("good behavior")
To represent primarily:	Common people Large states	Wealthy people Small states	All people	Constitution

Separation of powers, as envisioned by the Founders, means not only that government functions are to be performed by different branches, but also that officials of these branches are to be chosen by different people, for different terms, and to represent different constituencies.

. . . may justly be pronounced the very definition of tyranny."[22]

To reinforce the separation of powers, officials of the three branches were chosen by different means. Representatives were elected by the people (at that time mostly white men who owned property), senators were selected by the state legislatures, and the president was selected by the Electoral College, whose members were selected by the states. Only federal judges were chosen by officials in the other branches. They were nominated by the president and confirmed by the Senate. Once appointed, however, they were allowed to serve for "good behavior"—essentially life—so they had much independence. (Since the Constitution was written, the Seventeenth Amendment has provided for election of senators by the people, and the state legislatures have provided for election of members of the Electoral College by the people.)

Officials of the branches were also chosen at different times. Representatives were given a two-year term, senators a six-year term (with one-third of them up for reelection every two years), and the president a four-year term. These staggered terms would make it less likely that temporary passions in society would bring about a massive switch of officials or policies.

The Senate was designed to act as a conservative brake on the House, due to senators' selection by state legislatures and their longer terms. After returning from France, Thomas Jefferson met with George Washington over breakfast. Jefferson protested the establishment of a legislature with two houses. Washington supposedly asked, "Why did you pour that coffee into your saucer?" "To cool it," Jefferson replied. Similarly, Washington explained, "We pour legislation into the senatorial saucer to cool it."[23]

CHECKS AND BALANCES To guarantee separation of powers, the Founders built in overlapping powers called **checks and balances** (see Figure 2). Madison suggested that "the great security against a gradual concentration of the several powers in the same department consists in giving those who administer each department the necessary constitutional means and personal motives to resist encroachments by the others. . . . *Ambition must be made to counteract ambition.*"[24] To that end, each branch was given some authority over the others. If one branch abused its power, the others could use their checks to thwart it.

Thus, rather than a simple system of separation of powers, ours is a complex, even contradictory, system of both separation of powers and checks and balances. The principle of separation of powers gives each branch its own sphere of authority, but the system of checks and balances allows each branch to intrude into

FIGURE 2
Checks and Balances

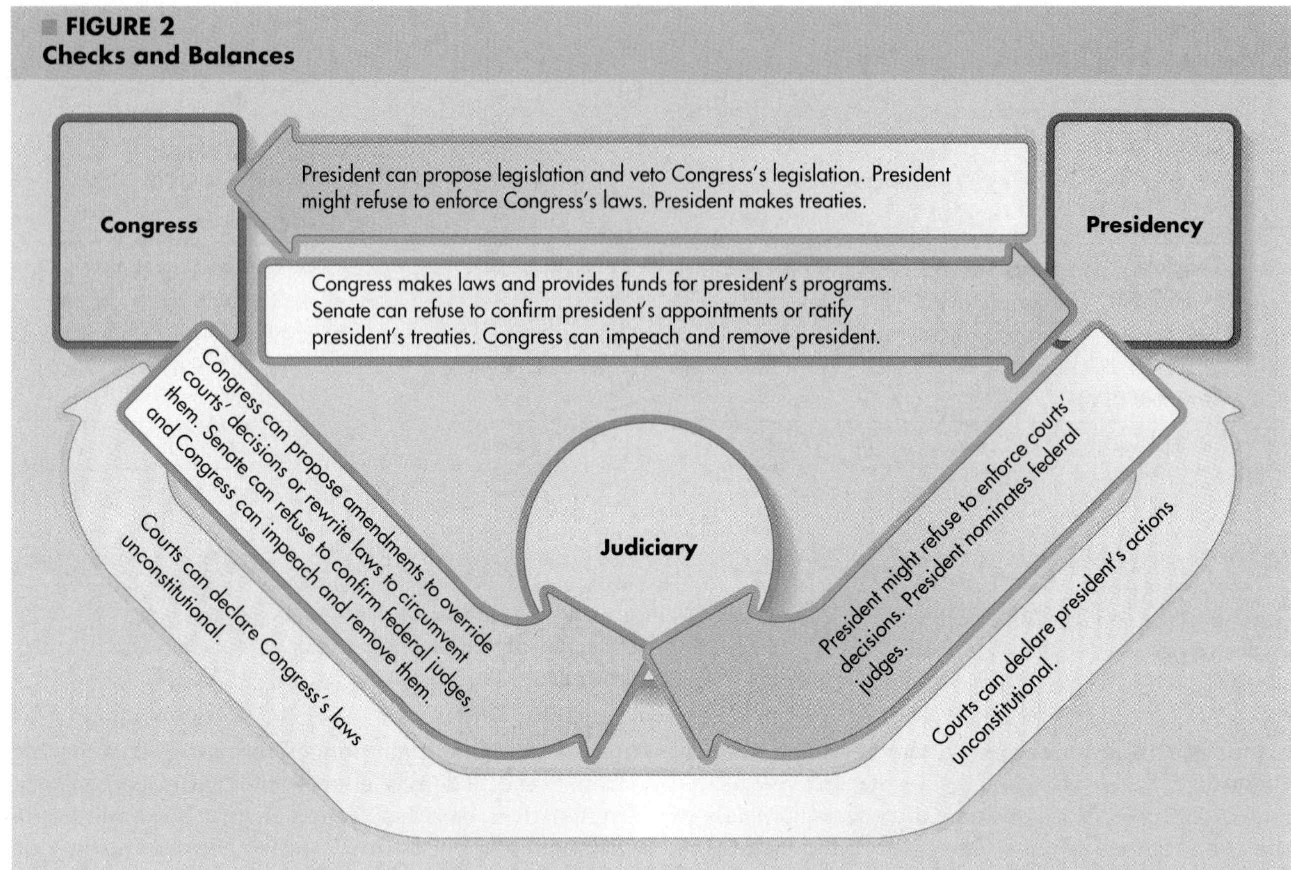

Most of the major checks and balances between the three branches are explicit in the Constitution, though some are not. For example, the courts' power to declare congressional laws or presidential actions unconstitutional—their power of "judicial review"—is not mentioned. And the president's power to refuse to enforce congressional laws or judicial decisions is not mentioned or even implied. In fact, it contradicts the Constitution, but sometimes it is asserted by the president nonetheless.

the other branches' spheres. For example, because of separation of powers, Congress makes the laws, but due to checks and balances, the president can veto them and the courts can rule them unconstitutional. In these ways all three branches are involved in legislating. One political scientist calls ours "a government of separated institutions sharing powers."[25]

With federalism, separation of powers, and checks and balances, the Founders expected conflict. They invited the parts of government to struggle against each other in order to limit each other's ability to dominate all. At the same time, the Founders hoped for "balanced government." The national and state governments would represent different interests, and the branches within the national government would represent different interests. The House would represent the "common" people and the large states, the Senate the wealthy people and the small states, the president all the people, and the Supreme Court the Constitution. The parts of government would have to compromise to get anything accomplished. Although each part would struggle for more power, it could not accumulate enough to dominate the others. Eventually its leaders would have to compromise and adopt policies in the interest of all of the parts and their constituencies. Paradoxically, then, the Founders expected narrow conflict to produce broader harmony.

Motives of the Founders

To understand the Constitution better, it is useful to consider the motives of the Founders. Were they selfless patriots, sharing their wisdom and experience? Or were they selfish property owners, protecting their interests? To answer these questions it is necessary to look at the philosophical ideas, political experience, and economic interests that influenced these men.

Philosophical Ideas

The Founders were exceptionally well educated intellectuals who incorporated philosophical ideas into the Constitution. At a time when the average person did not dream of going to college, a majority of the Founders graduated from college. As learned men, they shared a common library of writers and philosophers.

The framers of the Constitution reflected the ideals of the Enlightenment, a pattern of thought emphasizing the use of reason, rather than tradition or religion, to solve problems; they studied past governments to determine why they had failed in the hope they could apply these lessons to the present.

From all accounts they engaged in a level of debate at the convention that was rare in politics, citing philosophers ranging from the ancient Greeks to the modern British and French. Even when they did not mention them explicitly, their comments seemed to reflect the writings of particular philosophers.

The views of John Locke, a seventeenth-century English philosopher, underlay many of the ideas of the Founders. In fact, his views permeate the Declaration of Independence and Constitution more than those of any other single person.

Locke, like some previous philosophers, believed people had **natural rights.** These rights were inherent; they existed from the moment people were born. And they were inalienable; they were given by God so they could not be taken away. One of the most important was the right to property. When people worked the land, clearing it and planting it, they mixed their labor with it. This act, according to Locke, made the land their property. Some people, due to more work or luck, would accumulate more property than others. Thus, the right to property would result in inequality of wealth. Yet he thought it would lead to greater productivity for society. This view of property appealed to Americans who saw an abundance of land in the new country.

Locke wrote that people came together to form government through a social contract that established a **limited government,** strong enough to protect their rights but not too strong to threaten these rights. This government should not act without the consent of the governed. To make its decisions, this government should follow majority rule. (Locke never resolved the conflict between majority rule and natural rights—that is, between majority rule and minority rights for those who disagree with the majority.)

The views of Charles de Montesquieu, an eighteenth-century French philosopher, also influenced the debate at the convention and the provisions of the Constitution itself. Others had suggested separation of powers before, but Montesquieu refined the concept and added that of checks and balances. The Founders, referring to him as "the celebrated Montesquieu," cited him more than any other thinker.[26] (Presumably they cited him more than Locke because by this time Locke's views had so permeated American society that the Founders considered them just "common sense.")[27]

The principles of the system of mechanics formulated by Isaac Newton, an eighteenth-century British mathematician, also pervaded the provisions of the Constitution. As Newton viewed nature as a machine, so the Founders saw the constitutional structure as a machine, with different parts having different functions and balancing each other. Newton's principle of action and reaction is manifested in the Founders' system of checks and balances. The natural environment and the constitutional structure both were viewed as self-regulating systems.[28]

Political Experience

Although the Founders were intellectuals, they were also practical politicians. According to one interpretation, they were "first and foremost superb democratic politicians" and the convention was "a nationalist reform caucus which had to operate with great delicacy and skill in a political cosmos full of enemies."[29]

The Founders brought extensive political experience to the convention: 8 had signed the Declaration of Independence; 39 had served in Congress; 7 had been governors; many had held other state offices; some had helped write their state constitutions. The framers drew upon this experience. For example, while they cited Montesquieu in discussing separation of powers, they also referred to the experience of colonial and state governments that already had some separation of powers.

As practical politicians, "no matter what their private dreams might be, they had to take home an acceptable package and defend it—and their own political futures—against predictable attack."[30] So they compromised the difficult issues and ducked the stickiest ones. Ultimately, they pieced together a Constitution that allowed each delegate to go home and announce that his state won something.

"Religious freedom is my immediate goal, but my long-range plan is to go into real estate."

Economic Interests

Historian Charles Beard sparked a lively debate when he published *An Economic Interpretation of the Constitution* in 1913.[31] Beard argued that those with money and investments in manufacturing and shipping dominated the Constitutional Convention and state ratification conventions and that they produced a document that would increase their wealth. (At least 40 of the 55 delegates to the Constitutional Convention held bonds from the government, based on loans they had made to the government to finance the Revolutionary War, and of course expected to be repaid. These loans, ranging from a few dollars to more than $100,000, could be repaid easier by a strong national government than a weak one.)[32] Later scholars questioned Beard's conclusions, pointing out that support for the Constitution was not based strictly on wealth; Elbridge Gerry, one of the richest men in the country, opposed the Constitution, whereas Hamilton and Madison, both of more modest means, supported it.[33]

Although some of Beard's specific points do not hold up, his underlying position that the Founders represented an elite that sought to protect its property from the masses seems more valid. The delegates to the Constitutional Convention were an elite. They included prosperous planters, manufacturers, shippers, and lawyers. About one-third were slaveowners. Most came from families of prominence and married into other families of prominence. Not all were wealthy, but most were at least well-to-do. Only one, a delegate from Georgia, was a yeoman farmer like most men in the country. In short, "this was a convention of the well-bred, the well-fed, the well-read, and the well-wed."[34]

The Founders supported the right to property. The promise of land and perhaps riches enticed most immigrants to come to America.[35] A desire for freedom from arbitrary taxes and trade restrictions spurred some colonists to fight in the Revolution.[36] And the inability of the government under the Articles to provide a healthy economy prompted the Founders to convene the Constitutional Convention. They probably agreed with Madison that "the first object of government" is to protect property.[37]

The Founders' emphasis on property was not as elitist as it might seem, however. Land was plentiful and, with westward expansion, even more would be available. Already most men were middle-class farmers who owned some property. Many who owned no property could foresee the day when they would, so most Americans wanted to protect property.

The Founders diverged from the farmers in their desire to protect other property in addition to land, such as wealth and credit. Of the 55 delegates, 40 were owners of government bonds that had depreciated under the Articles, and 24 were moneylenders.[38] So the delegates included provisions to protect commerce, including imports and exports, contracts, and debts, and provisions to regulate currency, bankruptcy, and taxes.

Political scientists and historians disagree about which of these three influences on the Founders—philosophical, political, or economic—was most important. Actually the influences are difficult to separate because they reinforce each other; the framers' ideas point to the same sort of constitution that their political experience and economic interests do.[39]

Ratification of the Constitution

The Constitution specified that ratification would occur through conventions in the states and that the document would take effect with approval of conven-

Constitutional Provisions Protecting Property

"The Times, Places and Manner of holding Elections for Senators and Representatives, shall be prescribed in each State by the Legislature thereof."	Allows state to set property qualifications to vote.
"The Congress shall have Power . . . To coin Money."	Centralizes currency.
"No State shall . . . emit bills of credit."	Prevents states from printing paper money.
"Congress shall have Power . . . To establish uniform Laws on the subject of Bankruptcies."	Allows Congress to prevent states from relieving debtors of obligation to pay.
"No State shall . . . pass any . . . Law impairing the Obligation of Contracts."	Prevents states from relieving debtors of obligation to pay.
"The United States shall guarantee to every State [protection] against domestic Violence."	Protects states from debtor uprisings.
"Congress shall have Power . . . To provide for calling forth the Militia to execute the Laws of the Union, suppress insurrections."	Protects creditors from debtor uprisings.

tions in 9 of the 13 states. The framers purposely did not provide for approval by the state legislatures because they feared that some legislatures would reject it because it reduced their power. Too, the framers wanted the broader base of support for the new government that ratification conventions would provide.

Technically the procedures for ratification were illegal. According to the Articles of Confederation, which were still in effect, any changes had to be approved by all 13 states. However, the framers suspected that they would not find support in all states.

Indeed, ratification was uncertain. Many people opposed the Constitution, and there was a lively campaign against it in newspapers, pamphlets, and mass meetings. And although the procedures required ratification by only nine states, the framers realized they needed support from all of the largest states and much of the public to lend legitimacy to the new government.

Knowing opponents would charge them with setting up a national government to dominate the state governments, those who supported the Constitution ingeniously adopted the name **Federalists** to emphasize a real division of power between the national and state governments. They dubbed their opponents **Antifederalists** to imply that they did not want a division of power between the governments.

The Antifederalists faulted the Constitution for lacking a bill of rights. The Constitution did contain some protection for individual rights, such as the provision that the writ of habeas corpus, which protects against arbitrary arrest and detention, cannot be suspended except during rebellion or invasion, and the provision that a criminal defendant has a right to a jury trial. But the framers made no effort to include most of the rights people believed they had, because most states already had a bill of rights in their own constitutions. They also thought that by fragmenting power no branch could become strong enough to deny individual rights. Yet critics demanded provisions protecting various rights of criminal defendants and freedom of the press. In response, the Federalists promised to propose amendments guaranteeing these rights as soon as the government began.

The Antifederalists criticized the Constitution for other reasons. Localists at heart, they were wary of entrusting power to officials far away; they correctly claimed that republics historically worked only in small geographical areas where the population was more homogeneous and the officials were closer to the people. They worried that the central government, to function effectively, would accumulate too much power and the presidency would become a monarchy or Congress an aristocracy. One delegate to the Massachusetts convention blasted the Federalists:

> These lawyers, and men of learning and moneyed men, that talk so finely, and gloss over matters so smoothly, to make us poor illiterate people swallow down the pill, expect to get into Congress themselves; they expect to . . . get all the power and all the money

into their own hands, and then they will swallow up all us little folks . . . just as the whale swallowed up Jonah![40]

But the Antifederalists had no alternative plan. They were divided; some wanted to amend the Articles, while others wanted to reject both the Articles and the Constitution in favor of some yet undetermined form of government. Their lack of unity on an alternative was instrumental in their inability to win support.[41]

Ratification was quick in some states, a bitter struggle in others. Within three months after the Constitutional Convention, Delaware became the first state to ratify, and six months later New Hampshire became the necessary ninth. Virginia and New York followed but they ratified only by narrow margins. Indeed, New York ratified only by three votes after New York City threatened to secede from the state if the state did not ratify. So the Constitution took effect and the new government began in 1788, with George Washington becoming president. Within one year, North Carolina and Rhode Island, both of which initially rejected the Constitution, became the last states to approve it.

Changing the Constitution

The framers expected their document to last; Madison wrote, "We have framed a constitution that will probably be still around when there are 196 million people."[42] Yet because the framers realized it would need some changes, they drafted a Constitution that can be changed either formally by constitutional amendment or informally by judicial interpretation or political practice. In doing so, they left a legacy for later governments. "The example of changing a Constitution, by assembling the wise men of the state, instead of assembling armies," Jefferson noted, "will be worth as much to the world as the former examples we had given them."[43]

By Constitutional Amendment

That the Articles of Confederation could be amended only by a unanimous vote of the states posed an almost insurmountable barrier to any amendment at all. The framers of the Constitution made sure this experience would not repeat itself. On the other hand, they did not make amendment easy; although the procedures do not require unanimity, they do require widespread agreement.

PROCEDURES The procedures for amendment entail action by both the national government and the state governments. Amendments can be proposed in either of two ways—by a two-thirds vote of both houses of Congress or by a national convention called by Congress at the request of two-thirds of the state legislatures. Congress then specifies which way amendments must be ratified—either by three-fourths of the state legislatures or by ratifying conventions in three-fourths of the states. Among these avenues, the usual route has been proposal by Congress and ratification by state legislatures (see Figure 3).

AMENDMENTS In the first Congress under the Constitution, the Federalists fulfilled their promise to support a bill of rights. Madison drafted the amendments, Congress proposed them, and the states ratified 10 of them in 1791. This **Bill of Rights** includes freedom of expression—speech, press, assembly, and religion (First Amendment). It includes numerous rights for those accused of crimes—protection against

FIGURE 3
Avenues for Constitutional Amendment

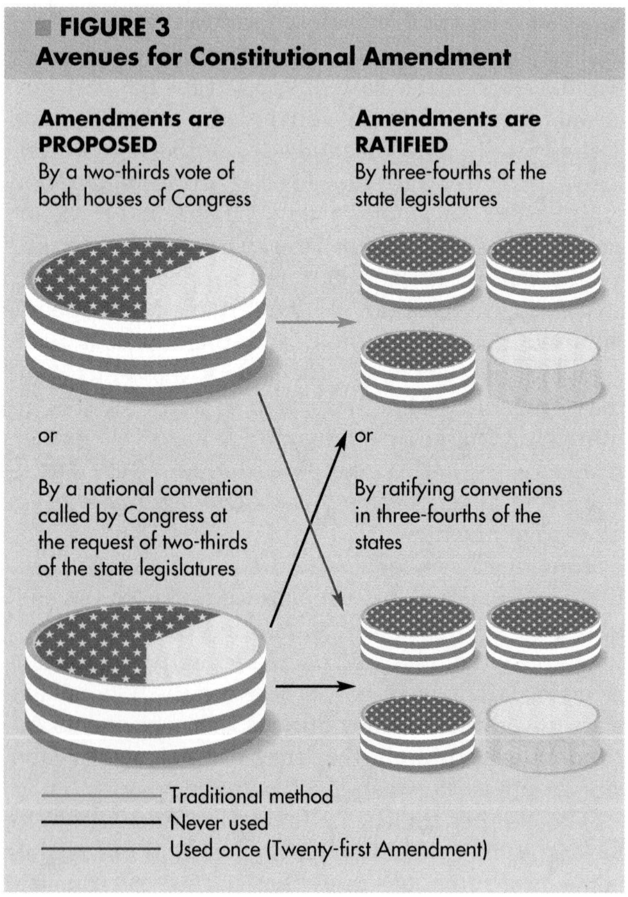

The Federalist Papers

Out of the great debate over ratification came a series of essays considered the premier example of American political philosophy. Titled the **Federalist Papers,** these essays were written by Alexander Hamilton (*left*), James Madison (*center*), and John Jay. At the urging of Hamilton,[1] the authors wrote 85 essays that appeared in New York newspapers during the ratification debates there. The authors tried to convince delegates to the convention to vote for ratification.

In the fashion of the time, the papers were published anonymously—by "Publius" (Latin for "Public Man"). They were so unified in approach that few of the authors' contemporaries could discern their pens at work. Given the arguments and compromises at the Constitutional Convention, one political scientist speculated that the framers who read the essays "must have discovered with some surprise what a coherent and well-thought-out document they had prepared."[2]

Despite the unity of the papers, political scientists have identified the authors of individual ones. Hamilton wrote most of those describing the defects of the Articles, Madison most of those explaining the structure of the new government, including the famous #10 and #51 (reprinted at the back of this book). Before he became sick, Jay, who was secretary of foreign affairs, wrote a few concerning foreign policy.

Actually there is little evidence that the essays swayed any of the delegates. Yet they have endured because readers see them as an original source of political thinking and as one of the best guides to the intentions of the Framers.

1. Although Hamilton worried that the Constitution would not establish a strong enough government, he thought it was preferable to the Articles, which he despised.
2. John P. Roche, ed., *Origins of American Political Thought* (New York: Harper & Row, 1967), p. 163.

unreasonable searches and seizures (Fourth), protection against compulsory self-incrimination (Fifth), guarantee of due process of law (Fifth), the right to counsel and a jury trial in criminal cases (Sixth), and protection against excessive bail and fines, and cruel and unusual punishment (Eighth). It also includes a jury trial in civil cases (Seventh).

In addition to these major rights, the Bill of Rights includes two amendments that grew out of the colonial experience with Great Britain—the right to bear arms for a militia (Second) and the right not to have soldiers quartered in homes during peacetime (Third). The Bill of Rights also includes two general amendments—a statement that the listing of these rights does not mean these are the only ones people have (Ninth) and a statement that the powers not given to the national government are reserved to the states (Tenth).

Among the other 17 amendments to the Constitution, the strongest theme is the expansion of citizenship rights:

- Abolition of slavery (Thirteenth, 1865)
- Equal protection, due process of law (Fourteenth, 1868)
- Right to vote for black men (Fifteenth, 1870)
- Direct election of senators (Seventeenth, 1913)
- Right to vote for women (Nineteenth, 1920)
- Right to vote in presidential elections for District of Columbia residents (Twenty-third, 1960)
- Abolition of poll tax in federal elections (Twenty-fourth, 1964)
- Right to vote for persons eighteen and older (Twenty-sixth, 1971)

Another theme is the increase of federal power. Many amendments, notably those regarding voting, take authority away from the states and authorize Congress to enforce these rights by "appropriate legislation."

Most amendments proposed by Congress were ratified by the states, although some were not. Recently, two proposed amendments were not ratified. One would have provided equal rights for women (this amendment will be discussed in Chapter 15), and the other would have given congressional representation to the District of Columbia, as though it were a state.

These and other recent amendments have had time limits for ratification—usually seven years—set by Congress. But an amendment preventing members of Congress from giving themselves a midterm pay raise, written by Madison and passed by Congress in 1789, had no time limit. Once Michigan ratified it in 1992, it reached the three-fourths mark and became the Twenty-seventh Amendment.

Although the Constitution expressly provides for change by amendment, its ambiguity about some subjects and silence about others virtually guarantee change by interpretation and practice as well.

By Judicial Interpretation

If there is disagreement about what the Constitution means, who is to interpret it? Although the Constitution does not say, the judicial branch has taken on this role. To decide disputes brought to them, the courts must determine what the relevant provisions of the Constitution mean. By saying the provisions mean one thing rather than another, the courts can, in effect, change the Constitution. Woodrow Wilson called the Supreme Court "a constitutional convention in continuous session." The Court has acted as a safety valve, diffusing pressure for new amendments by interpreting the Constitution in such a way as to bring about the same results as new amendments.

By Political Practice

Political practice has accounted for some very important changes. These include the rise of political parties and the demise of the Electoral College as an independent body. They also include the development of the cabinet to advise the president and the development of the committee system to operate the two houses of Congress.

The Founders would be surprised to learn that only 17 amendments, aside from the Bill of Rights, have been adopted in about 200 years. In part this is due to their wisdom, but in part it is due to changes in judicial interpretation and political practice, which have combined to create a "living Constitution."

Conclusion: Is the Constitution Responsive?

Soon after ratification, the Constitution became accepted by the people. It took on the aura of a secular Bible. People embraced it, consulted it for guidance, cited it for support, and debated the meaning of its provisions.

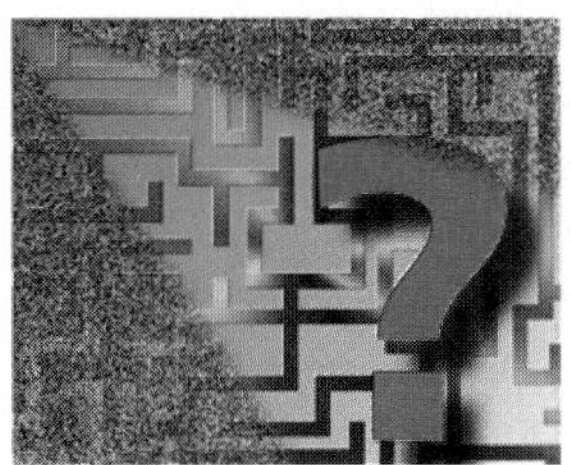

Symbolic Solutions for Complex Problems?

Making English the Official National Language

In some chapters we have a box examining what we consider largely a symbolic solution for what is actually a complex problem. The proposal is symbolic in that it appears to address the problem, but because of the complexity of the problem, the solution is not likely to solve the problem or, possibly, even ameliorate it.

The symbolic solution tends to be a simple solution—we could title these boxes "Simple Solutions for Complex Problems?"—and a simple solution is not likely to solve a complex problem. (There might, of course, be exceptions, as there are to other generalizations.)

People tell pollsters they favor many of these ideas. But we want students to recognize that these ideas, so appealing at first glance, are more symbolic than substantive. We want students to recognize that politicians, political parties, and interest groups might urge adoption of these ideas because they are trying to rally people to their side for other reasons. They might see these ideas as ways to gain support in an election campaign or in a policy fight. At a time when national problems seem intractable, it is tempting for politicians to claim they can solve them, even if they cannot. And it is tempting for politicians to claim they can solve them quickly, as most of these proposals imply, even when they cannot. Or proponents might see these as ways to advance some hidden agenda. (For example, before the 1994 elections Republicans called for term limits for members of Congress at least in part because they saw term limits as a way to oust entrenched Democrats from Congress.)

Our belief is that citizens should demand real solutions for real problems and that they should not allow themselves to be manipulated or appeased by proposals that merely pretend to address the problems. Symbolic actions can be useful, especially as protests in the early stages of controversies, but they must give way to substantive efforts if problems are to be resolved.

We do need to emphasize, however, that reasonable people can disagree and some readers might want to adopt these proposals even if they are largely symbolic. Other readers might want them for other reasons. We will elaborate in individual boxes.

In this chapter we focus on the proposal for a constitutional amendment making English the official national language. Two-thirds of the public supports this proposal, according to a recent survey.[1] This proposal is a reaction to the influx of immigrants in recent decades. Some native-born Americans are sincerely worried about the tide of immigrants, as Chapter 1 explained, while other native-born Americans are simply annoyed by the inability of many immigrants to speak English.

Of course, the U.S. has had waves of immigrants before. However, most waves have not been as large and have not included as diverse a group of people as now. In the past, most immigrants were Europeans. Now, many are Latin Americans, many are Asians, and some are Middle Easterners as well. Los Angeles offers election ballots in Spanish, Chinese, Japanese, Vietnamese, Korean, and Tagalog. Its county courts provide interpreters for about 80 languages. (Even so, confusion occurs. A police officer testified that he had read a suspect his Miranda rights in the Tai-shan dialect of Chinese, but the judge discovered that the man understood only the Cantonese dialect, so he had to disregard the confession.)[2]

Groups like *U.S.English* and *English First* have sounded the alarm: "If this continues, the next American president could well be elected by people who can't read or speak English!" Seventeen states have passed laws making English their official language, and some members of Congress have proposed a constitutional amendment for the entire country.

It is not clear what effect the amendment would have. Election ballots and other forms now printed in various languages probably would be printed only in English, and bilingual education programs in public schools probably would be scaled back. The amendment would not restrict private, religious, or ceremonial use of foreign languages.

But no doubt there would be different interpretations of the amendment by different branches of the government in different parts of the country. When California made English its official language in the 1980s, one city council fired librarians for buying foreign language books and subscribing to foreign language magazines. In some cities teachers forbade students from speaking foreign languages among themselves, and hospitals forbade employees from speaking any language but English. One official reprimanded a worker who spoke Spanish to a co-worker in the hallway, and another fired workers who spoke Filipino to patients who spoke that language.[3]

Despite uncertainty about the interpretation of an amendment, might one nonetheless prompt people who do not speak English to learn the language?

The underlying assumption is that immigrants are taking longer to learn English than in the past and that some are refusing to learn it at all. It is true that some immigrant communities are so large that people can survive without learning English. Some Mexican immigrants in parts of the Southwest and some Cuban immigrants in parts of Florida speak Spanish alone. Contrary to some perceptions, however, most immigrants feel pressure to learn English. It helps them land jobs and function in the broader society.[4] Their children, who grow up and attend schools in this society, learn English and put more pressure on them.

A survey of Hispanics in 40 cities found that more than 90% thought U.S. citizens and residents should learn English.[5] A survey of Hispanics in South Florida found that 98% thought it was important for their children to read and write "perfect English."[6] And their children apparently agree. More than four-fifths of immigrant children in south Florida and more than two-thirds of those in San Diego prefer English to their familial language.[7]

Another study of immigrants underscored the value they put on succeeding in school. These families are more likely to have rules about doing homework and maintaining grades (including rules limiting television) than they are to have requirements about performing household chores or part-time jobs.[8] Their efforts to succeed in school as a way to make it in society reflect similar efforts by past immigrants.

It should not be surprising, then, that current immigrants are mastering English. Of 17.3 million Spanish speakers in the United States, less than 10% do not speak English.[9] Cuban-Americans are learning it as fast or faster than any previous group in history.[10] Mexican-Americans are learning it as they stay longer in the U.S. Although most of those who come for work and plan to return to Mexico do not speak English or do not speak it well, most of those who plan to remain in the U.S. learn to speak more English and almost all of their children learn to speak fluent English.[11] Thus, the process takes time, but it does work.

Consequently, a constitutional amendment making English the official national language would be little more than a symbolic solution. Immigrants already are learning English.

Some advocates of an amendment acknowledge that it would be a symbol—a symbol of national unity at a time when there is more diversity than ever before. To this extent, the debate is not just about prodding immigrants to learn English; it is also about persuading them to assimilate—to shed their foreign ways and adopt our "American ways." Yet it is hard to see what an amendment would accomplish beyond what learning English and adapting to society already are accomplishing. And if the fear is of too much immigration, changing immigration laws is a much more direct solution.

In fact, an amendment might be counterproductive. It could encourage more xenophobia—fear of foreigners—and more intolerance of diversity. It could result in more discrimination against even legal immigrants. Abolition of bilingual ballots might disfranchise some, and abolition of bilingual forms might make it difficult for some to receive government services for which they are eligible. An amendment also would restrict freedom of speech. A federal court struck down Arizona's law as a violation of the First Amendment.

1. Margot Hornblower, "Putting Tongues in Check," *Time*, October 9, 1995, p. 49.
2. Otto Friedrich, "The Changing Face of America," *Time*, July 8, 1985, p. 29.
3. Eloise Salholz, "Say It in English," *Newsweek*, February 20, 1989, p. 23; Margaret Carlson, "Only English Spoken Here," *Time*, December 5, 1988, p. 29; Elaine Elinson, "On the Job, English Only Rules Are on the Rise," *Civil Liberties* (Fall, 1990), p. 5.
4. Learning English without a Spanish accent helps even more. Alberto Dávila, Alok D. Bohara, and Rogelio Saenz, "Accent Penalties and the Earnings of Mexican Americans," Social Science Quarterly, 74 (December, 1993), pp. 902–16.
5. Lynne Duke, "English Spoken Here," *Washington Post National Weekly Edition*, December 21–27, 1992, p. 37.
6. Salholz, "Say It in English," p. 23.
7. Joel Kotkin, "Can the Melting Pot Be Reheated?" *Washington Post National Weekly Edition*, July 11–17, 1994, p. 23.
8. Nathan Caplan, Marcella H. Choy, and John K. Whitmore, *Children of the Boat People: A Study of Educational Success* (Ann Arbor: University of Michigan Press, 1992).
9. 1990 Census of the Population, Social and Economic Characteristics, Part I, Table 13; less than 5% of Asian-language speakers and less than 2% of other language speakers do not speak English.
10. Thomas Boswell and James Curtis, *The Cuban American Experience* (Totowa, N.J.: Rowman & Allanheld, 1983), p. 191.
11. Kevin F. McCarthy and R. Burciaga Valdez, *Current and Future Effects of Mexican Immigration in California—Executive Summary* (Santa Monica: Rand Corporation, 1985), p. 27.

The Constitution has proven to be so popular that many countries have copied parts of it. Almost all of the 170-plus nations in the world today have a constitution written as a single document. Many have provisions similar to those in our Constitution. The Kenyan constitution speaks of "freedom of expression," the Costa Rican gives the "right to petition," and the German says that "all persons shall be equal before the law." And officials and groups in, of all unlikely places, South Africa and Russia, considered provisions in our Constitution when they changed theirs.[44]

But the brevity of our Constitution remains unique; with just 89 sentences, it is far shorter than those of other nations. Because it is short, it is necessarily general; because it is general, it is necessarily ambiguous; because it is ambiguous, it is necessarily open to interpretation. This provides succeeding generations the opportunity to adapt the Constitution to changing times. The longer, more detailed, and less flexible constitutions of other nations become outdated and periodically need complete revision.

In 1987 our Constitution celebrated its bicentennial as the oldest written constitution in the world. During the same 200 years, France, for example, had 10 distinct constitutional orders, including five republics, two empires, one monarchy, one plebiscitary dictatorship, and one puppet dictatorship during World War II.

Although our Constitution, and the institutions it established, have been responsive enough to survive, are they responsive enough to allow us to solve our problems? Can a constitution written by a small circle of men whose fastest mode of travel was horseback continue to serve masses of diverse people, some of whom have traveled by spaceship?

Intended to construct a government responsive to the masses of people to a limited extent, the Constitution set up a republic, which allowed the people to elect some representatives who would make their laws. This gave the people more say in government than people in other countries enjoyed at the time.

But the Constitution was intended to construct a government unresponsive to the masses of people to a large extent. It was expected to filter the public's passions and purify their selfish desires. Consequently, the Founders limited participation in government, allowing people to vote only for members of the House of Representatives—not for members of the Senate or the president.

Moreover, the Founders fragmented the power of government. Federalism, separation of powers, and checks and balances combine to make it difficult for any one group to capture all of government. Instead, one faction might control one branch, another faction another branch, and so on, with the result a standoff. Then the factions must compromise to accomplish anything.

Since the time of the founding, changes in the Constitution, whether by amendment, interpretation, or practice, have expanded opportunities for participation in government. But the changes have done little to modify the fragmentation of power, which remains the primary legacy of the Founders.

This structure has prevented many abuses of power, though it has not always worked. During the Vietnam War, for example, one branch—the presidency—exercised vast power while the others acquiesced. This structure also has provided the opportunity for one branch to pick up the slack when the others became sluggish. The overlapping of powers ensured by checks and balances allows every branch to act on virtually every issue it chooses to. In the 1950s President Eisenhower and Congress were reluctant to push for civil rights for blacks, but the Supreme Court did so by declaring segregation unconstitutional in a series of cases.

But the system's very advantage has become its primary disadvantage. In their efforts to fragment power so that no branch could accumulate too much, the Founders divided power to the point where the branches sometimes cannot wield enough. In their efforts to build a government that requires a national majority to act, they built one that allows a small minority to block action. This problem has become increasingly acute as society has become increasingly complex. Like a mechanical device that operates only when all of its parts function in harmony, the system moves only when there is consensus or compromise. Consensus is rare in a large heterogeneous society; compromise is common, but it requires a long time as well as the realization by competing interests that they cannot achieve much of what they want without compromise. Even then, compromise often results in only a partial solution.

At best the system moves inefficiently and incrementally. At worst it moves hardly at all; the Constitution has established a government that is slow to respond to change. Characterized by one political scientist as a "negative, do-nothing system,"[45] the government is most likely to respond to the status quo and the groups that want to maintain it.

This sluggishness periodically stimulates populist movements anxious to make the system more responsive to their desires. Currently such populist sentiments abound in the country.

Yet some political scientists believe many people actually prefer a constitutional structure that is inefficient and incremental. Because the people are suspicious of government, they may be reluctant to let one party dominate it and use it to advance that party's policies. In surveys many people say they think it is good for one party to control the presidency and the other to control Congress. In presidential and congressional elections, typically half or more of the voters split their ticket between the two major parties. As a result, between 1968 and 1996 opposing parties controlled the executive and legislative branches for all but six years.

During the election of 1992, rising voices complained of "gridlock," and voters elected a Democratic president and a Democratic Congress. But the Democratic Congress itself was split between northerners and southerners and between members who most wanted to solve social problems they thought had been neglected and those who most wanted to reduce the deficit. Therefore, Clinton did not have a working majority. Then in the congressional elections in 1994, voters elected Republican majorities in both houses of Congress. Thus, voters who complained of gridlock just two years before cast their ballots in a way to produce more gridlock. In the elections of 1996, voters reelected Clinton and retained Republican majorities in both houses of Congress, thus dividing control of the government again.

EPILOGUE

The President Complies

Chief Justice Warren Burger announced the unanimous decision in the case of *United States v. Nixon:* The president must turn over the tapes.[46] The Court acknowledged the existence of executive privilege in general but rejected it in this situation because another court needed the information for an upcoming trial and because the information did not relate to national security.

The Court emphasized that courts would determine the legitimacy of claims of executive privilege, not presidents, as Nixon wanted. Because of separation of powers, Nixon argued, neither the judicial nor legislative branch should involve itself in this executive decision. However, this president, who as a high school student in Whittier, California, had won a prize from the Kiwanis Club for the best oration on the Constitution, ignored the system of checks and balances, which limits separation of powers. In this case, checks and balances authorized the courts to conduct criminal trials of the president's aides and Congress to conduct impeachment proceedings against the president. To do so, the courts and Congress needed the information on the tapes.

Within days of the Court's decision, the House Judiciary Committee passed three articles of impeachment. These charged Nixon with obstruction of justice, by covering up a crime; defiance of the committee's subpoenas for the tapes; and abuse of power. Nevertheless, some Republicans maintained there was no "smoking gun"—that is, no clear evidence of crimes. They said the impeachment effort was strictly political.

Regardless, Nixon's support in Congress dwindled, and he found himself caught between a rock and a hard spot: Releasing the tapes would furnish more evidence for impeachment, but not releasing them would spur impeachment. He reportedly considered disregarding the decision but, after 12 days of weighing his options, complied with the order.

Releasing the tapes did reveal a smoking gun. Although the tapes did not show that Nixon participated in planning the break-in, they did show that he participated in covering it up. When the burglars blackmailed the administration, Nixon approved paying them hush money. He ordered the head of his reelection committee to "stonewall it" and "cover up." He and an aide formulated a plan to have the

Richard Nixon, after submitting his resignation as president, prepares to leave Washington.

CIA thwart the FBI in its investigation of the scandal. When his top aides were subpoenaed to appear before the grand jury, he encouraged them to lie.

In addition to this evidence of crimes, the tapes revealed much vulgarity and profanity in Nixon's conversations. Such language undercut the public's positive image of Nixon.

The tapes, printed as a book that became an instant best-seller, repelled the public. When it became clear that public opinion would force the House to impeach him and the Senate to remove him, Nixon decided to resign. On August 9, 1974, he became the first American president to do so. Vice President Gerald Ford became the new president.

Although the smoking gun had been found, some people still thought the crimes relatively minor and the punishment excessively harsh. But Nixon was not driven from office solely or even primarily because of the break-in. Rather, he lost the public's trust because of the cover-up. He had campaigned for president on a "law and order" platform and had sworn an oath of office "to take care that the laws be faithfully executed." During the cover-up, he had repeatedly proclaimed that he was innocent of any wrongdoing. As the evidence came to light, the hypocrisy and lying became too much for the public to stomach. Ultimately, Nixon could not lead the public he had misled for so long.

Despite depression and cynicism about the scandal, many people saw that the system had worked as it was supposed to. The Founders had divided power to make it difficult for any one branch to amass too much power. In the face of the president's efforts to exercise vast power, the courts, with their orders to turn over the tapes, and Congress, with its Senate Watergate Committee hearings and House Judiciary Committee impeachment proceedings, checked the president's abuse of power. In addition, the media, with its extensive publicity, first prompted and then reinforced the actions of the courts and Congress.

However, although the system worked, it worked slowly. More than two years elapsed between the break-in and the resignation. For more than half the length of a presidential term, the president and many of his aides were so preoccupied with Watergate they could not devote sufficient attention to other problems facing the country.

When the affair was over, 21 of the president's men were convicted and sentenced to prison for their Watergate crimes. Except for one, a burglar who was most uncooperative and who served 52 months, the men served from 4 to 12 months. Nixon, who could have and probably would have been prosecuted after leaving office, received a pardon in advance from President Ford.

Nine years after the resignation, the security guard who discovered the break-in was convicted for shoplifting in Augusta, Georgia. Unemployed, he had stolen a pair of shoes for his son. Unlike the president's men, he received the maximum sentence—12 months for the $12 shoes.

Yet the story is not over. Congress passed a law mandating that other, unreleased tapes and documents be turned over to the National Archives, which was to make public any that related to Watergate or had "general historic significance." However, the Archives, prodded by Nixon's team of lawyers, has delayed releasing all but a handful of tapes.[47] In one of these, Nixon is heard remarking to his chief of staff, "I always wondered about that taping equipment, but I'm damn glad we have it, aren't you?"[48]

Key Terms

Watergate scandal
executive privilege
Articles of Confederation
Shays's Rebellion
Constitutional Convention
Great Compromise
Three-fifths Compromise
social contract
republic
democracy
federalism
separation of powers
checks and balances
natural rights
limited government
Federalists
Antifederalists
Federalist Papers
Bill of Rights

Further Reading

Leonard W. Levy, ed., *Essays on the Making of the Constitution* (New York: Oxford University Press, 1969). *Essays that address the question, Was the Constitution an undemocratic document framed and ratified by an undemocratic minority for an undemocratic society?*

Clinton Rossiter, 1787: *The Grand Convention* (New York: Macmillan, 1966). *A lively account of the Constitutional Convention and the ratification campaign.*

Theodore H. White, *Breach of Faith* (New York: Atheneum, 1975). *A chronicle of the Watergate scandal as a Greek tragedy in which actors on both sides behaved in such ways as to fulfill their destinies.*

Bob Woodward and Carl Bernstein, *All the President's Men* (New York: Simon and Schuster, 1974). *Riveting account of journalistic sleuthing by the two reporters who broke the Watergate story.*

➤Notes

1. Nixon thought he might be considered an American Disraeli. (Benjamin Disraeli, a British prime minister in the nineteenth century, was a Tory who had progressive ideas.) Nixon praised Robert Blake's biography of Disraeli, and one cabinet secretary remarked, in 1971, "The similarities are great, Mr. President, but what a pity that Blake could not quote Disraeli's conversation." Nixon did not destroy the tapes, even after they became a liability, apparently for this reason. Sidney Blumenthal, "The Longest Campaign," *The New Yorker*, August 8, 1994, p. 37.

2. *United States v. Reynolds*, 345 U.S. 1 (1953).

3. The Indians, of course, had their own governments, and the Spanish might have established St. Augustine, Florida, or Santa Fe, New Mexico, before the English established Jamestown. These Spanish settlements were extensions of Spanish colonization of Mexico and were governed by Spanish officials in Mexico City.

4. This is not to suggest that the Pilgrims believed in democracy. Apparently they were motivated to draft the compact by threats from some on the Mayflower that when the ship landed they would "use their owne libertie; for none had power to command them." Thus, the compact was designed to bind them to the laws of the colony. Richard Shenkman, *I Love Paul Revere, Whether He Rode or Not* (New York: Harper Collins, 1991), pp. 141–42.

5. David Hawke, *A Transaction of Free Men* (New York: Scribner's, 1964), p. 209.

6. Louis Fisher, *President and Congress* (New York: Free Press, 1972), p. 14.

7. Gordon S. Wood, "The Origins of the Constitution," *This Constitution: A Bicentennial Chronicle* (Summer 1987), pp. 10–11.

8. Eric Black, *Our Constitution* (Boulder, Colo.: Westview Press, 1988), p. 6. Shays, eventually pardoned by Massachusetts, settled in New York and became a staunch Federalist (Black, p. 8).

9. For development of this idea, see Kenneth M. Dolbeare and Linda J. Medcalf, "The Political Economy of the Constitution," *This Constitution: A Bicentennial Chronicle* (Spring 1987), pp. 4–10.

10. Black, *Our Constitution*, p. 59.

11. The Constitution, however, would reflect numerous aspects of the Articles. See Donald S. Lutz, "The Articles of Confederation as the Background to the Federal Republic," *Publius* 20 (Winter 1990), pp. 55–70.

12. Robert McCloskey, *The American Supreme Court* (Chicago: University of Chicago Press, 1960), p. 29.

13. Fred Barbash, "James Madison: A Man for the '80s," *Washington Post National Weekly Edition*, March 30, 1987, p. 23.

14. According to a poll in 1987, the bicentennial of the Constitution, only 1% of the public identified Madison as the one who played the biggest role in creating the Constitution. Most—31%—said Thomas Jefferson, who was a diplomat in France during the convention. Black, *Our Constitution*, p. 15.

15. Paul Finkelman, "Slavery at the Philadelphia Convention," *This Constitution: A Bicentennial Chronicle* (1987), pp. 25–30.

16. Finkelman, "Slavery at the Philadelphia Convention," p. 29.

17. Finkelman, "Slavery at the Philadelphia Convention.

18. Theodore J. Lowi, *American Government* (Hinsdale, Ill.: Dryden Press, 1976), p. 97.

19. C. Herman Pritchett, *Constitutional Law of the Federal System* (Englewood Cliffs, N.J.: Prentice-Hall, 1984), p. xi.

20. Richard Hofstadter, *The American Political Tradition and the Men Who Made It* (New York: Random House, 1948), p. 13.

21. *Federalist Paper #51.*

22. *Federalist Paper #47.*

23. Max Farrand, *The Framing of the Constitution of the United States* (New Haven: Yale University Press, 1913).

24. *Federalist Paper #51.*

25. Richard E. Neustadt, *Presidential Power and the Modern Presidents* (New York: Macmillan, 1990), p. 29.

26. Donald S. Lutz, "The Relative Influence of European Writers on Later Eighteenth-Century American Political Thought," *American Political Science Review* 78 (March 1984), pp. 139–97.

27. Alpheus T. Mason and Richard H. Leach, *In Quest of Freedom: American Political Thought and Practice*, 2nd ed. (Englewood Cliffs, N.J.: Prentice-Hall, 1973), p. 51.

28. For development of this idea, see Martin Landau, "A Self-Correcting System: The Constitution of the United States," *This Constitution: A Bicentennial Chronicle* (Summer 1986), pp. 4–10.

29. John P. Roche, "The Founding Fathers: A Reform Caucus in Action," *American Political Science Review* 56 (March 1962), pp. 799–816.

30. Ibid.

31. Charles Beard, *An Economic Interpretation of the Constitution* (New York: Macmillan, 1913).

32. Although Beard admired the Founders, especially those who championed a strong national government, he came under sharp attack for portraying them as anything other than disinterested national patriots. An Ohio newspaper proclaimed, "Scavengers, hyena-like, desecrate the graves of the dead patriots we revere." Ellen Nore, "Charles A. Beard's Economic Interpretation of the Origins of the Constitution," *This Constitution* (Winter 1987), p. 39.

33. R. E. Brown, *Charles Beard and the Constitution* (Princeton: Princeton University Press, 1956); Forrest MacDonald, *We the People* (Chicago: University of Chicago Press, 1976).

34. James MacGregor Burns, *The Vineyard of Liberty* (New York: Alfred A. Knopf, 1982), p. 33.

35. Bernard Bailyn, *Voyagers to the West* (New York: Alfred Knopf, 1986), p. 20.

36. The Boston Tea Party, contrary to myth, was not prompted by higher taxes on British tea. Parliament lowered the taxes to give the British East India Company, facing bankruptcy, an advantage in the colonial market. This threatened American shippers who smuggled tea from Holland and controlled about three-fourths of the market. The shippers resented Parliament's attempt to manipulate the economy from thousands of miles away. Shenkman, *I Love Paul Revere, Whether He Rode or Not*, p. 155.

37. *Federalist Paper #10.*

38. Black, *Our Constitution*, p. 21.

39. Calvin C. Jillson and Cecil L. Eubanks, "The Political Structure of Constitution Making," *American Journal of Political Science* 29 (August 1984), pp. 435–58.

40. Jonathan Elliot, *The Debates in the Several State Conventions on the Adoption of the Federal Constitution as Recommended by the General Convention at Philadelphia, in 1787*, 2nd ed., 5 vols. (Philadelphia, 1896), vol. II, p. 102; as quoted in Cecilia M. Kenyon, "Men of Little Faith," in John P. Roche, ed., *Origins of American Political Thought* (New York: Harper & Row, 1967), pp. 197–98.

41. For Antifederalist thinking, see W. B. Allen and Gordon Lloyd, eds., *The Essential Antifederalist* (Lanham, Md.: University Press of America, 1985).

42. "A Fundamental Contentment," *This Constitution: A Bicentennial Chronicle* (Fall 1984), p. 44.

43. Charles Warren, *The Making of the Constitution* (Boston: Little, Brown, 1928), p. xiv.

44. "South Africa Looks at U.S. Constitution," *Lincoln Sunday Journal-Star (New York Times),* October 7, 1990; David Remnick, " 'We, the People,' from the Russian," *Washington Post National Weekly Edition,* September 10–16, 1990, p. 11.

45. Harold J. Spaeth, *Supreme Court Policy Making* (San Francisco: W. H. Freeman, 1979), p. 13.

46. 418 U.S. 683 (1974).

47. Seymour M. Hersh, "Nixon's Last Cover-up: The Tapes He Wants the Archives to Suppress," *The New Yorker,* Dec. 14, 1992, pp. 76–95.

48. "Tapes Confirm Nixon Approved Hush Money," *Lincoln Journal* (AP), June 5, 1991.

3 Federalism and the Growth of Government

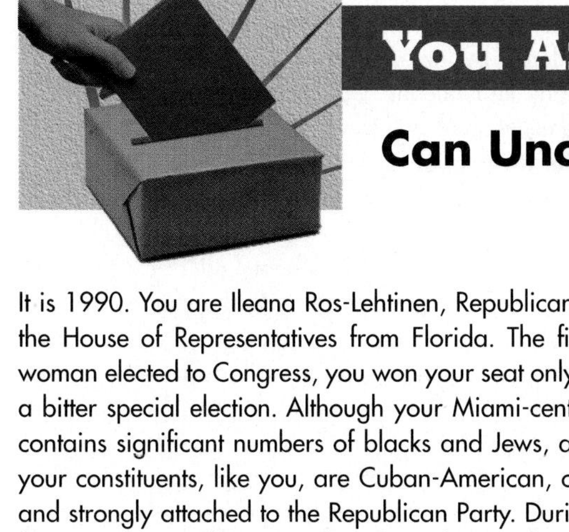

You Are There

Can Uncle Sam Help Baby-Sit?

It is 1990. You are Ileana Ros-Lehtinen, Republican member of the House of Representatives from Florida. The first Hispanic woman elected to Congress, you won your seat only last year in a bitter special election. Although your Miami-centered district contains significant numbers of blacks and Jews, a majority of your constituents, like you, are Cuban-American, conservative, and strongly attached to the Republican Party. During your first few months in office, you have voted strongly conservative, winning a perfect score from some conservative interest groups who rate voting patterns of members of Congress.[1]

You are facing a choice concerning a package of legislation relating to children. The bill would give $2.5 billion to the states to increase existing grant programs for child care, begin funding state programs for before-and-after-school day care for "latchkey" children, help poor and lower-middle-income families pay for child care, and require states to set quality, health, and safety standards for child-care providers.

Support for the bill is broad. More than 100 organized groups have endorsed the legislation. Over 60% of the public, including those who are not parents as well as those who are, believe the federal government should do something to make child care more available and affordable.[2] Both parties are seeking to show the public that they are concerned about children.

There is much to be concerned about. One out of five children is poor. Nineteen percent of all white children, 30% of all Hispanic children, and 54% of all black children live in homes with only one parent.[3] The census projects that only 39% of all newborns will live with both parents until they are 18. Growing numbers of children, many of them children of cocaine addicts, live with neither parent. And every night, 100,000 children are among the nation's homeless.[4]

To make matters worse, teenage pregnancy, higher than in any other industrial nation in the world, is increasing, bringing a new cycle of poverty-stricken and often one-parent families. Children born into such homes are themselves likely to be poor, suffer ill health, bear children early, drop out of school, and end up on welfare or in prison.

Contributing to these woes, the Reagan administration cut back many programs designed to help children, including programs to provide nutrition and health care for low-income pregnant women and their babies, vaccinations, Head Start, school breakfasts and lunches, and food stamps. But now, people are becoming concerned. As Jesse Jackson argued, "We can either fund Head Start and child care and day care on the front side of life, or welfare and jail care on the back side of life."[5] Conservatives and business people, normally against federal involvement in family life, have also decided that the problem of America's children can no longer be ignored. They realize that our society will not be able to function in the future, let alone be competitive in the international economic arena, with a generation of ill-fed, ill-educated, ill-trained young people outside the mainstream of society. A recent report by a group of major corporate executives called for drastic increases for funding early childhood programs.

◄ *State and federal officials worked together to rescue victims and track down perpetrators of the 1995 bombing of the federal building in Oklahom City.*

CONTINUED 

OUTLINE

Federal and Other Systems
- Federal Systems
- Unitary Systems
- Confederal Systems

The Political Bases of Federalism

The Constitutional Bases of Federalism
- Major Features of the System
- Interpretations of Federalism

Federalism and the Growth of Government
- Early Nationalist Period
- Pre–Civil War Period
- The Civil War to the New Deal
- The New Deal
- From the New Deal to the Great Society
- New Federalism

Contemporary Federalism
- Federal-State Relations
- Interstate Relations
- State-Local Relations

Conclusion: Is Federalism Responsive?

Among the many needs of America's children and their families is quality day care. Over half of the women with children under 3 and almost three-quarters of women with children from 3 to 17 work in the paid labor force. And the number of working women increases each year as economic pressures force families to work harder to stay afloat. But many parents cannot afford day care and do not have trustworthy friends and relatives to baby-sit. Some go on welfare so they can stay home with their children, others leave their children in dirty or dangerous environments, and others worry constantly about tenuous day-care arrangements. And even families that can afford day care cannot always find quality arrangements.

The child-care bill tries to increase the supply of day-care centers, strengthen their health and safety standards, and help families pay for them. President Bush dislikes this bill and has threatened to veto it. The bill is also opposed by conservatives in the Republican party, one of whom thundered that it would "Sovietize the American family by warehousing babies."[6] The alternative offered by two conservative legislators, and supported by many Republicans, would authorize less money for grant programs, require no standards for the quality of child care, and offer nothing for latchkey children.

How should you vote? On the one hand, you are in favor of the goals of the bill. You are a former teacher and know the problems faced by parents who cannot find adequate child care. On the other hand, you are concerned about the contents of the bill. It is costly. It sets up federal standards that you oppose. You believe such involvement will increase the size of the federal bureaucracy and cause problems for day-care providers. You are not much in favor of the federal government getting more involved in family life and encroaching on areas left to the states, and you would like to support your fellow Republicans. What do you decide?

Most Americans claim to believe that state governments are more responsive to them than the federal government (Table 1), but over the past 60 years they have asked the federal government to get involved in almost every policy issue imaginable. Many Americans decry the growth of big government, and yet few realize that over the past 25 years, the size of state governments has doubled while the federal government has grown hardly at all. Most Americans want small government, but they also want a government powerful enough to keep the peace abroad and responsive to their needs at home.

TABLE 1 The Public Trusts the States More

	STATE	FEDERAL
Which government do you trust to:		
do a better job running things	70%	27%
establish rules about who can receive welfare	70	25
set rules for workplace safety	55	42
set Medicare and Medicaid regulations	52	43
set environmental rules for clean air and clean water	51	47
protect civil rights	35	61

Source: Washington Post–ABC Poll, reported in Richard Morin, "Power to the States," *Washington Post National Weekly Edition*, March 27–April 2, 1995, p. 37.

These issues of the size and scope of the federal government relative to the states are not new. They are the same issues that the Founders debated at the Constitutional Convention in 1787. The issue of whether the states or the national government should have the final say in political decisions was the central conflict in the Civil War (1861-1865), which ultimately determined that the national government, not the states, was supreme.

Because of this outcome, and because of the tasks we ask government to do, we live in a nation with a strong central government. Yet we vigorously disagree about just how strong that government should be. Critics accuse the national government and its programs of being too large, too expensive, and too intrusive on the rights of the states and the people. Yet when members of Congress suggest cutting programs severely or transferring responsibilities back to the states, the public outcry is vociferous. And even though our system of powers at both the national and state levels contributes to the messiness of democracy that the public dislikes, there is little support for streamlining or centralizing powers at the national level.

These contradictions are perhaps endemic to a federal system. In this chapter we will examine the nature of American federalism and how it has changed as government has grown.

Federalism is the only domestic issue in the United States over which several million Americans fought and 500,000 died. This photograph shows the remains of Richmond, Virginia, after a Civil War battle.

FEDERAL AND OTHER SYSTEMS

Federal Systems

The term **federalism** describes a system in which power is constitutionally divided between a central government and subnational or local governments (in the United States the subnational governments are the states). Both levels of government receive their grants of power from a higher authority—the will of the people as expressed in a constitution, for example. Each level can deal directly with individuals to tax, regulate, or provide benefits.

Power granted to each level is not necessarily exclusive. In fact, in the United States only one power is left solely to the states, and that is the power to determine whether they shall exist. States cannot be abolished or altered without their own consent.

Nearly 90% of all nations are unitary systems, but several large nations are federal systems—for example, Germany, Canada, India, and Brazil. Federal systems vary greatly in their basic economic and political characteristics; they are similar only in the fact that each has a written constitution allocating some powers to the national and some to the subnational governments.

Unitary Systems

In contrast to the federal system, in a **unitary system** the national government creates subnational governments and gives them what power it wishes. Thus, the national government is supreme. In Britain, for example, the national government can give or take away any power of the subnational governments or can even abolish them, as it did with some counties several years ago. And, in unitary Sweden, the national parliament abolished 90% of its local governments from 1952 to 1975.

In the United States, the 50 states are each unitary with respect to their local governments; cities, counties, and school districts can be altered or even eliminated by state governments.

The distinction between unitary and federal is not at all related to the distinction between democracy and authoritarianism. Some unitary systems are among the most democratic in the world (Britain and Sweden); others are authoritarian (Egypt and Ghana). Nor are only federal systems decentralized. All modern governments have to decentralize power because a central government, even in a unitary system, cannot run every local service or deal with every local problem.

Confederal Systems

The third arrangement between central and subnational governments is confederal. In a **confederal system** the central government has only those powers given to it by the subnational governments; it cannot act directly on citizens. Two examples of confederal systems are the United States under the Articles of Confederation and the United Nations. The lack of central authority in such systems makes them basically unworkable in modern nations.

The Political Bases of Federalism

Why do some nations choose a federal form of government while others do not? The Founders of the United States chose federalism as one means of limiting governmental power. Another reason for choosing federalism was that it could help deal with national diversity. Federal systems are often, though not always, ethnically, linguistically, religiously, or racially diverse. We in the United States are not as diverse as peoples in India, for example, but we are a nation of many ethnic groups, races, religions, and political traditions.

Our states also reflect this diversity. Despite our national media networks, franchises and chains bringing the same products to all parts of the country, and transportation systems that carry us across the nation in only a few hours, there are still significant differences among us, and not just in whether we prefer Texas chili or New England clam chowder. In different states and regions, we have developed somewhat different political styles and attitudes. Most governors of Pennsylvania, for example, could never be elected in Idaho, and vice versa. Ways of looking at politics, partisan preferences, ideology, appropriate ways of organizing for political action, and other political features vary greatly across our nation.

Distinctive ways of looking at, and participating in, politics are called **political cultures.**[7] In the United States, three cultures predominate, each having a regional and, to some extent, ethnic base (see Figure 1).

One is the *moralistic* political culture, found in states of the upper Midwest and New England that are populated by Scandinavians or descendants of the Yankee Puritans who arrived from England. In this culture, politics is seen as a way of improving life, and people have a strong sense that they should participate. Politics is relatively free of corruption.

A second type is the *individualistic* political culture, most typical in the large band of industrial states of the Midwest and East populated by immigrant groups from Eastern and Southern Europe and from Ireland. In these states, the ultimate objective of politics is not so much to create a better public life but rather to get things for yourself and your group. The traditional machine politics of many large cities are good examples of the individualistic political culture.

In a *traditionalistic* culture, still present in some of the South, politics is left to a small elite. Politics is not seen as a way to further the public good but as a way to maintain the status quo. Louisiana politics offers an example: There it has been said that "a politician's first obligation is to entertain, his second not to get caught stealing, and his third to govern."[8]

In some areas, immigration patterns of this century have blurred cultural patterns; the West, for example, is populated by a mix of people from all three cultures.

Although these cultural patterns are regional, there are cultural differences within regions. The political corruption and shady political dealing tolerated by Illinoisians would never be accepted by Minnesotans. Nevada and Utah share a common border but very different political cultures.

In addition to cultural and ethnic differences, states are diverse in their economic well-being. For example, despite the growth in the southern economy since the 1950s, residents of most southern states still lag behind the rest of the United States in income and education.

Thus, state boundaries mean something beyond identifying the government to which state taxes are

FIGURE 1
Political Cultures Vary Among States

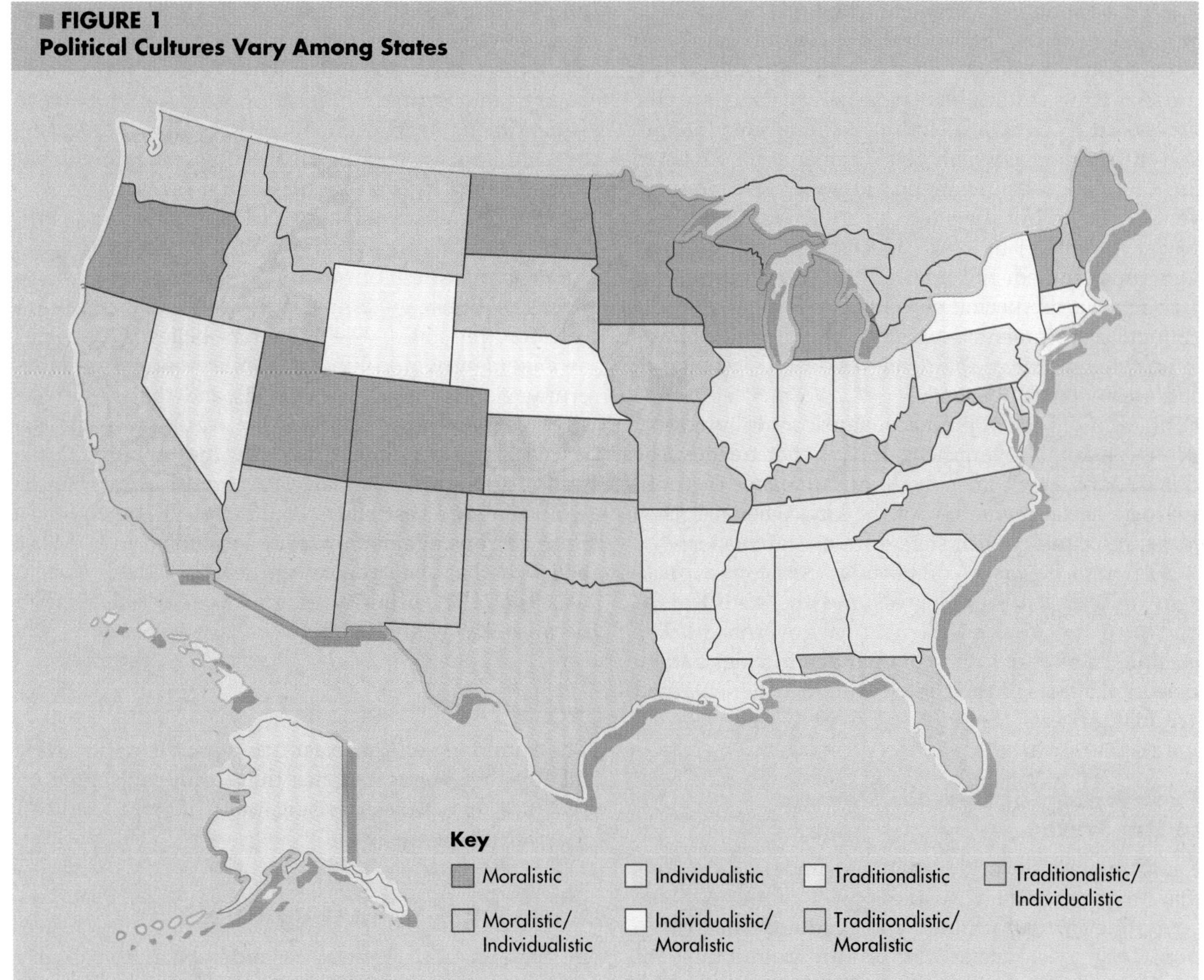

Source: Daniel Elazar, *American Federalism: A View from the States,* 3rd ed. (New York: Harper & Row, 1984), p. 135.

paid. In policy areas as diverse as economic development, welfare, and regulation of personal morality (such as gambling and prostitution), states vary widely. Federalism, even with a strong national government, does provide some autonomy for states to adopt and maintain policies consistent with their own political cultures.

The Constitutional Bases of Federalism

Major Features of the System

As we saw in Chapter 2, the Founders were unsure how to solve the problem of national versus state powers. All wanted limited government. Although they saw federalism as one way to limit government power by dividing it, there was little debate over the concept of federalism, and the main outlines emerged only as the Founders dealt with other issues. The major features of nation-state relationships outlined by the Constitution include a strong national government, prohibition of certain powers to the states, and some limitations on national powers.

Strong National Government

Although the Founders did not all agree on how strong the national government should be, all did agree that they wanted a national government stronger than that of the Articles of Confederation. They wanted a national government able to tax without the permission of the states, and one able to carry out foreign and domestic policies without the states' consent. Thus, the Constitution grants many specific powers to Congress, including taxation and regulation of commerce, which gives tremendous power to the national government and allows it to be independent of the will of the state governments. Congress's power to make all laws **"necessary and proper,"** sometimes called the **implied powers clause,** for carrying out its specific powers also strengthened the national government. This grant of power soon was interpreted to mean that Congress could legislate in almost any area it wished.

In addition, the **supremacy clause** contributed to a strong national government. It says that treaties, the Constitution, and "laws made in pursuance thereof" are to be the supreme law of the land whenever they come into conflict with state laws or state actions.

Although it was a compromise decision, a president independent of Congress and the state legislatures also strengthened the national government. The president's power to be commander in chief and to execute the laws of the United States further enlarged national powers.

Prohibition of Certain Powers to the States

The Constitution forbids states to undertake actions that might conflict with the power of the national government; they cannot enter into treaties, keep troops or navies, make war, print or coin money, or levy import or export taxes on goods. These prohibitions reaffirmed that the national government was to be supreme in making foreign policy and regulating interstate commerce. Under the Articles, the national government was limited in both these areas. The new Constitution also forbade states to infringe on certain rights of individuals. For example, a state could not pass a law making an action a crime and then punish citizens who committed the "crime" before it was made illegal (called an *ex post facto* law).

Some Limitations on National Powers

The Constitution prohibits the creation of new states within existing states, the combination of two states, or the change of existing state boundaries without the approval of the legislatures of the affected states.

The Tenth Amendment granted to the states and to the people those powers not granted by the Constitution to the national government. At the time, this was considered a significant limit on national powers. Since then, the broad construction of Congress's "necessary and proper" powers has made the Tenth Amendment inconsequential. Recently there have been attempts to breathe life into this amendment, but thus far they have had only limited success.[9]

These three features—a strong national government, prohibition of certain powers to the states, and some limitations on national powers—ensured a strong national government as well as a significant role for the states. The Founders believed that this arrangement would limit the ability of any one government to tyrannize its citizens and that the diversity of interests in the system would prevent the formation of a national majority that could trample minority rights. Similarly, a central government would ensure that states could protect the rights of their citizens against arbitrary local majorities. Many believed that the primary virtue of a federal system was that the authority of government was limited because it was divided between two levels.

Interpretations of Federalism

The Founders left the exact details of the nation-state relationship vague because they could not agree on specifics. It is not surprising that different views of federalism emerged.[10]

Nation-Centered Federalism

In *The Federalist Papers,* Alexander Hamilton clearly articulated the view that national power was to be supreme. This nation-centered view of federalism rests on the assumption that the Constitution is a document ratified by the people. The states have many powers, but the national government has the ultimate responsibility for preserving the nation and the viability of the states as well. Nation-centered federalism was the view held by northerners in justifying a war to prevent the southern states from seceding in 1861.

State-Centered Federalism

Another view, later used by southerners to justify their defiance of the central government before the Civil War, held that the Constitution is a product of state action. In this view, the states created the union. State-centered federalists argue that the grant of powers to Congress is limited to those items specifically mentioned in Article I. Madison said, "The powers delegated . . . to the federal government are few and defined. Those which are to remain in the state governments are numerous and indefinite."[11] In this view, any attempt by Congress to go beyond these explicitly listed powers violates state authority.

Dual Federalism

Dual federalism is the idea that the Constitution created a system in which nation and state each have separate grants of power, with each supreme in its own sphere. In this view, the two levels of government are essentially equal. Their differences derive from their different jurisdictions, not from any inequality.

Cooperative Federalism

The term **cooperative federalism** refers to the continuing cooperation among federal, state, and local officials in carrying out the business of government. The term encompasses the relationship of federal and state officials when distributing payments to farmers, providing welfare services, planning highways, organizing centers for the elderly, and carrying out all the functions that the national and state governments jointly fund and organize. It also refers to informal cooperation in locating criminals, tracking down mysterious diseases, and many other activities. A person speaking of cooperative federalism is not evaluating the legalistic relationship of national and state governments but rather referring to day-to-day joint activities.

Federalism and the Growth of Government

In 200 years, our national government has grown from a few hundred people with relatively limited impact on the residents of 13 small states to a government employing millions, affecting the daily lives of most of the population of more than 260 million people. This transformation is closely related to the changing way in which Americans understand the federal system.

Over the years, the dominant interpretations of federalism have shifted among the nation-centered, state-centered, and dual views. Changing interpretations have reflected court opinions, pressing economic needs, the philosophies of those in the executive and legislative branches, and changing public demands. The most

Federalism and the "Mischiefs of Faction"

Probably the most influential work of American political theory was written by James Madison in *Federalist Paper* #10 (reprinted in the appendix to this book). This work helps explain the attraction of a federalist system for Madison and many of the other Founders.

In *Federalist* #10, Madison asserted that it is inevitable that factions—groups of citizens seeking some goal contrary to the rights of other citizens or to the well-being of the whole country—will threaten the stability of nations. To cure the "**mischiefs of faction**" Madison said government had either to remove the causes of faction or to control its effects.

Madison believed the government could never remove the causes of faction because this would require changing selfish human nature, which he thought impossible. It also would require taking away freedom by outlawing opinions and strictly regulating behavior. People would inevitably have different ideas and beliefs, and government, he thought, should not try to prevent this.

Because one could not remove the causes of faction without too greatly inhibiting freedom, Madison recommended that a properly constructed government should control its effects. If a faction were less than a majority, Madison believed it could be controlled through majority rule, the majority defeating the minority faction. However, if the faction were a majority, then a greater problem arose, but one for which Madison had an answer.

To control a majority faction, one had only to limit the ability of a majority to carry out its wishes. Madison believed this was impossible in a small democracy, where there is little check on a majority determined to do something. But in a large federalist system, there are many checks on a majority faction—more interests competing with each other and large distances to separate those who might scheme to deprive others of liberty. As Madison noted, "The influence of factious leaders may kindle a flame within their particular States, but will be unable to spread a general conflagration through the other States." Having many states and having them spread over a large territory were, in Madison's view, major checks against majority tyranny.

In a spirit of optimism amidst the turmoil of the Civil War, Congress in 1862 established federal support for the land grant colleges, a striking example of intergovernmental cooperation in the nineteenth century. Today many of these institutions are among our finest universities. Here, students plow on the campus of The Pennsylvania State University, one of the first land grant colleges.

general trend has been away from state-centered and toward nation-centered federalism, but there have been significant shorter-term trends in the opposite direction. Moreover, the term *cooperative federalism* has come into use, since World War II, to describe everyday relations between national and state officials.

Early Nationalist Period

Very soon after the Constitution was ratified, the federal courts became the arbiters of the Constitution. (Note that we are using "federal" to mean "national," a confusing but common usage. "Federal government" normally means "national government.") John Marshall, chief justice of the United States from 1801 to 1835, was a firm nationalist, and the decisions of his court emphasized the need for a strong national government. The Marshall-led Supreme Court not only held that decisions of the state courts could be overturned by the federal courts, it also, in the case of *McCulloch v. Maryland,* gave approval to the broad interpretation of Congress's implied powers in the Constitution.

McCulloch v. Maryland

The broad interpretation of the clause giving Congress the right to make all laws "necessary and proper" to carry out the powers that the Constitution gives it grew out of a case involving the establishment of a national bank. Because the Constitution does not explicitly grant Congress the authority to charter banks, many people thought Congress may have been infringing on rights the Constitution left to the states. Ironically, it was John Calhoun, later to become the leading states' rights advocate, who introduced a bill to charter a Bank of the United States (B.U.S.).

Once established, the bank was immediately unpopular because it competed with smaller banks operating under state laws and because some of its branches engaged in reckless and even fraudulent practices. When the government of Maryland levied a tax on the notes—what we would now call currency—issued by the Baltimore branch of the bank, the constitutionality of the B.U.S. was called into question and a case was brought to the Supreme Court.

In ***McCulloch v. Maryland,*** John Marshall wrote one of his most influential decisions.[12] Pronouncing the tax unconstitutional, Marshall wrote that "the power to tax involves the power to destroy." The states should not have the power to destroy the bank, he stated, because the bank was "necessary and proper" to carry out Congress's powers to collect taxes, borrow money, regulate commerce, and raise an army. Marshall argued that if the goal of the legislation is legitimate and constitutional, "all means which are appropriate, which are plainly adapted to that end, which are not prohibited, but consistent with the letter and spirit of the Constitution, are constitutional."

Thus, Marshall interpreted "necessary" quite loosely. The bank was probably not necessary, but it was "useful." This interpretation of the implied powers clause allowed Congress to wield much more authority than the Constitution gave it explicitly.

Although there was some negative reaction—"a deadly blow has been struck at the sovereignty of the states," cried one Baltimore newspaper—the Court maintained its strongly nationalistic position as long as Marshall was chief justice.

Early Growth of Government

At the same time the courts were interpreting national powers broadly, the national government was exercising its powers on a rather small scale. The federal government had only 1,000 employees in the administration of George Washington, and this number had increased to 33,000 during the presidency of James Buchanan 70 years later. It raised relatively little revenue. But state governments were also small and had limited functions. There were only a few federal-state cooperative activities. For example, the federal government gave land to the states to support education and participated in joint federal-state-private ventures, such as canal-building projects initiated by the states.

Thus, the early nationalist period was characterized by the growth of nation-centered federalism in legal doctrine, by small-scale state and national government, and by a few intergovernmental cooperative activities responding to the needs of an expanding nation.

Pre-Civil War Period

In 1836, the Court began to interpret the Tenth Amendment as a strict limitation on federal powers, holding that powers to provide for public health, safety, and order were *exclusively* powers of the state government, not of the national government. This dual federalism interpretation eroded some of the nation-centered federal interpretations of the Marshall Court while continuing to uphold the rights of the federal courts to interpret the Constitution.

At the same time, champions of the state-centered view of federalism were gaining ascendance in the South. Southern leaders feared that the federal government, dominated by the increasingly populous North, would regulate or even abolish slavery. John Calhoun, one of the leading proponents for the state-centered view, even went so far as to say that a state could nullify laws of Congress (the doctrine of nullification). According to Calhoun, a state could withdraw from the Union if it wished. When the South did secede from the Union in 1861, it called itself the Confederate States of America, emphasizing the supremacy of the states embedded in a confederal system. After the Civil War, the vision of state-centered federalism largely lost its credibility.

The Civil War to the New Deal

After the Civil War, vast urbanization and industrialization took place throughout the United States. Living and working conditions for many city dwellers were appalling. Adults as well as children who moved into the cities often took jobs in sweatshops—factories where they worked long hours in unsafe conditions for low pay.

Spurred by revelations of these unsafe and degrading conditions, states and sometimes Congress tried to regulate working conditions, working hours, and pay through such means as child labor and industrial safety laws. Beginning in the 1880s, a conservative Supreme Court used the dual federalism doctrine to rule unconstitutional many of these attempts. It often decided that Congress and the states had overstepped their powers. From 1874 to 1937, the Supreme Court found 50 federal and 400 state laws unconstitutional.[13] Before the Civil War, in contrast, the Court overturned only 2 congressional and 60 state laws.

At the same time that the Court was limiting both state and national action in regulating business and industry, both levels of government were slowly expanding. The revenues of both grew—the United States through an income tax finally ratified in 1913, the states and localities through gasoline and cigarette taxes, higher property taxes, and some state income taxes. Federal support for state programs also grew through land and case grants given by the federal government to the states.[14] By the late 1920s, however, most governmental functions still rested primarily in state and local hands. The states were clearly the dominant partner in providing most services, from health and sanitation to police and fire protection. The federal government provided few direct services to individuals, nor did it regulate their behavior. The Great Depression signaled a dramatic shift in this arrangement.

President Roosevelt's confidence, along with the hopes people had in his New Deal programs, led to public support for the expansion of the role of the federal government.

The New Deal

To grasp the scope of the changes that have taken place in our federal structure between 1930 and today, consider the report of a sociologist who studied community life in Muncie, Indiana.[15] In 1924 the federal government in Muncie was symbolized by little more than the post office and the American flag. Today, two-thirds of the households in Muncie depend in part on federal funds—federal employment, Social Security, welfare payments, food stamps, veterans benefits, student scholarships and loans, Medicare and Medicaid, and many other smaller programs.

In large part, the Great Depression brought about these changes. During the stock market crash of 1929, wealthy people became poor overnight. In the depths of the Depression one-fourth of the work force was unemployed, and banks failed daily.

Unlike today, there was no systematic national program of relief for the unemployed then—no unemployment compensation, no food stamps, no welfare, nothing to help put food on the table and pay the rent. Millions were hungry, homeless, and hopeless. States and localities, which had the responsibility for providing relief to the poor, were overwhelmed; they did not have the funds or organizational resources to cope with the millions needing help. And private charities did not have enough resources to even begin to assume the burden.

The magnitude of the economic crisis led to the election of a Democrat, Franklin Delano Roosevelt, in 1932. He formulated, and Congress passed, a program called the **New Deal.** Its purpose was to stimulate economic recovery and aid the victims of the depression who were unemployed, hungry, and often in ill health. New Deal legislation regulated many activities of business and labor, set up a welfare system for the first time, and began a large scale federal-state cooperation in funding and administering programs through federal **grants-in-aid.** These grants-in-aid provided federal money to states (and occasionally to local governments) to set up programs to help people—for example, the aged poor or the unemployed.

These measures had strong political support, although they were opposed by many business and conservative groups and initially by the Supreme Court, which was still following the dual federalism doctrine. But after the reelection of Roosevelt in 1936, the Court became more favorable toward New Deal legislation, and later resignations of two conservative judges ensured that the Court would be sympathetic to the New Deal (see Chapter 13 for more on the Court and the New Deal.)

The Court decisions approving New Deal legislation were, in a sense, a return to the nation-centered federalism of John Marshall's day. But although the Supreme Court ratified much of the New Deal, it also approved more sweeping *state* regulations of business and labor than had the more conservative pre-New Deal Court. Thus, the change in court philosophy did not enlarge the federal role at the expense of the powers of the state. *It enlarged the powers of both state and federal government.* In doing so, it responded to preferences on the part of taxpayers for a more active government to cope with the tragedy of the Depression. The limited government desired by the Founders became less limited as both state and national government grew.

Changes in patterns of taxing and spending soon reflected the green light given to federal involvement with the states and localities. As Figure 2 indicates, the federal share of spending for domestic needs (omitting spending for the military) nearly tripled from 17% in 1929, before the New Deal, to 47% in 1939, a decade later. The state share stayed constant while the local share dropped dramatically. Local governments did not spend less, but the state and federal governments spent more. Likewise state spending increased, but not as much as federal spending. The federal government raised more revenue and in turn gave much of it to the states and localities in the form of grants-in-aid to carry out programs such as unemployment compensation, free school lunches, emergency welfare relief, farm surpluses to the needy, and other programs.

FIGURE 2
The New Deal Increased Federal and State Spending More Than Local

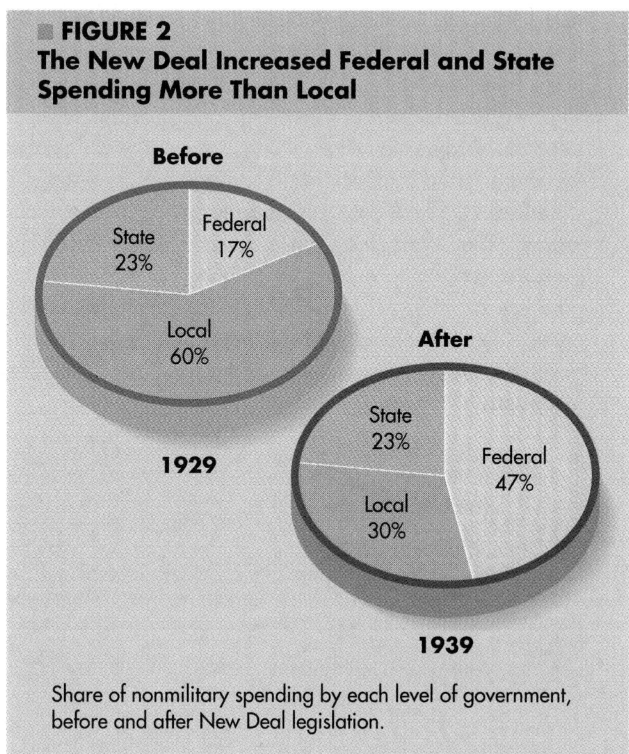

Share of nonmilitary spending by each level of government, before and after New Deal legislation.

Source: "Significant Features of Fiscal Federalism," *Advisory Commission on Intergovernmental Relations* (Washington, D.C.: U.S. Government Printing Office, 1979), p. 7.

The New Deal brought a dramatic change in the relationship of the national government to its citizens. Before this, when the national government directly touched the lives of citizens, it usually was to give or sell them something, such as land for settlers or subsidies for businesses helping develop the frontier.[16] With New Deal programs the federal government directly affected the lives of its citizens through its regulations (of banks and working conditions, for example) and its redistributive policies designed to protect the poor (such as Social Security and Aid to Dependent Children).

From the New Deal to the Great Society

During the years that followed the initiation of the New Deal, federal aid to states increased steadily but not dramatically. But federal support to the states carried conditions. For example, local administrators of Aid to Dependent Children programs had to be hired through a merit system, not because of political or personal connections. Construction funds for highways could be spent only on highways whose designs met professional standards. Thus, federal "strings" accompanied federal money.

By the 1950s, some public officials became uneasy about the growing size of the federal goverment and its involvement in so many state and local programs. Yet under President Eisenhower, a Republican concerned about the growth of federal involvement, many new federal grants-in-aid to the states were added, ranging from the massively expensive interstate highway program to collegiate programs in science, engineering, and languages. Federal grants-in-aid spending nearly tripled during his administration (1952-1960).

The 1960s witnessed an explosion in federal programs. Mostly a consequence of President Lyndon Johnson's Great Society, new programs of federal aid mushroomed both in number and in cost. Federal support for state and local activities extended to almost every area imaginable, including former state and local preserves such as local law enforcement, urban mass transit, and public education.

A new feature of the Great Society era was an increasing number of grants going directly to localities. Because they believed the state legislatures were unresponsive to their interests, urban and other local governments now demanded, and got, direct federal support that bypassed states.

New Populism

A New Western Saga: Cowboys versus the Government?

Midwestern and prairie farmers battled big railroads, big business, and big government in the first populist movement of the late nineteenth century. Today, some populist themes are echoed in the battle by western farmers and ranchers against big government.

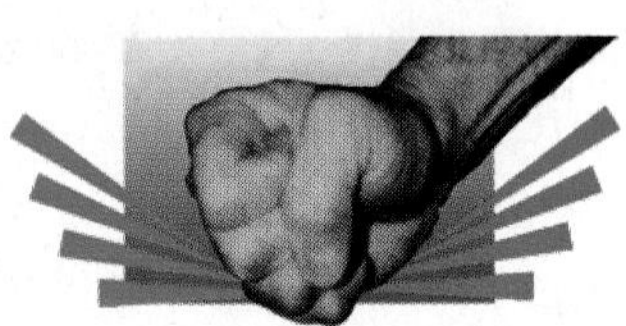

Several key issues have recently inflamed simmering controversies. Many westerners are angry that the federal government controls huge amounts of land in most western states. In most nonwestern states, the government owns less than 5 percent of land; in several western states (Alaska, Idaho, Oregon, Utah), the government owns over 50 percent.[1] In Nevada, it owns 87 percent. The federal government owns this land in part to protect natural resources considered valuable for the entire country (lumber, minerals, and places of great scenic beauty such as the Grand Tetons and the Grand Canyon). As the landowner, the federal government, through the Bureau of Land Management (BLM) and the Forest Service, places restrictions on how the land can be used. It limits the number of cattle that can graze the land, how much timber can be cut from forested lands, and, in some areas, what kind of vehicles can drive on the land. It places other restrictions on land use in order to protect endangered species. Although the government tries to balance the interests of farmers and ranchers with environmental concerns, any regulation creates angry protests. As one irate state legislator noted, "The federal government has a stranglehold on the rural West."[2]

The antagonism of many westerners to the federal regulations is growing. They have enlisted the machinery of local governments; at least 35 (and perhaps as many as 300) counties in the West have said that federally owned lands in the county fall under their jurisdiction.[3] Individually, some westerners are also defying the federal government. Although the BLM has canceled some ranchers' grazing permits, it cannot always keep them from grazing their herds anyway. As one BLM official notes, "We can't protect the resource because we are afraid our employees will be shot."[4] Another claims that "Folks are taking the law into their own hands. We're going to have anarchy and chaos in eastern Nevada."[5]

At the same time, of course, the federal government provides farmers and ranchers with grazing rights, water rights, and mining subsidies far below market costs. When the Clinton administration tried to increase the price to farmers and ranchers for these goods, that too raised a storm of protest.[6] Thus, some farmers and ranchers who want to be free of federal regulations are nonetheless willing to accept federal handouts.

Land is not the only issue igniting controversy. Gun restrictions and even the income tax are sparking opposition. In some western states, protesters have turned to violence. Pipe bombs have been found, cars have been bombed, and shots have been fired. Most, however, are trying to fight the federal government by organizing groups to push local land control, to elect representatives sympathetic with western interests, and to use the courts to fight the federal government.

What is at stake is a perception that a way of life is slipping away. Environmentalists, tourists, and recreational vehicle drivers want to see wildlife, not cattle herds. But ranchers do not want reduced grazing rights and increased regulations; they think of themselves as independent people who live where there are few rules and a strong sense of freedom. "What they really want is to build walls against the future," said a member of a conservative think tank.[7]

These developments are hardly new to American history. The West may have been "won" by hardy pioneers seeking to escape the confines of the cities, but government financed much of its exploration and settlement. Thus, the conflict between the wish for freedom from government and the desire for aid from it has strong roots in western history.

1. *Statistical Abstract of the United States, 1994* (Washington, D.C.: U.S. Government Printing Office, 1994), Table 354.
2. Christopher John Farley, "The West Is Wild Again," *Time* (March 20, 1995), p. 46.
3. Erik Larson, "Unrest in the West," *Time* (October 23, 1995), p. 54.
4. Tom Kenworthy, "Dueling with the Forest Service," *Washington Post National Weekly Edition,* February 27–March 5, 1995, p. 31.
5. Ibid.
6. Farley, "The West Is Wild Again," p. 46.
7. Larson, "Unrest in the West," p. 55.

The vast increase in programs and the multiplying requirements and conditions of the grants made federal aid ever more complex. State and local officials felt hamstrung by the increasingly burdensome regulations.

New Federalism

The continuing expansion of the federal government during the 1950s and its explosive growth in the 1960s led to a reaction in the 1970s. Alarmed at the

New Deal Legislation Passed During Roosevelt's First Term

March 9, 1933	Emergency Banking Act
March 31, 1933	Civilian Conservation Corps created
May 12, 1933	Agricultural Adjustment Act
May 12, 1933	Federal Emergency Relief Act
May 18, 1933	Tennessee Valley Authority created
June 5, 1933	Nation taken off gold standard
June 13, 1933	Home Owners Loan Corporation created
June 16, 1933	Federal Deposit Insurance Corporation created
June 16, 1933	Farm Credit Administration created
June 16, 1933	National Industrial Recovery Act
January 30, 1934	Dollar devalued
June 6, 1934	Securities and Exchange Commission authorized
June 12, 1934	Reciprocal Tariff Act
June 19, 1934	Federal Communications Commission created
June 27, 1934	Railroad Retirement Act
June 28, 1934	Federal Housing Administration authorized
April 8, 1935	Works Progress Administration created
July 5, 1935	National Labor Relations Act
August 14, 1935	Social Security Act
August 26, 1935	Federal Power Commission created
August 30, 1935	National Bituminous Coal Conservation Act
February 19, 1936	Soil Conservation and Domestic Allotment Act

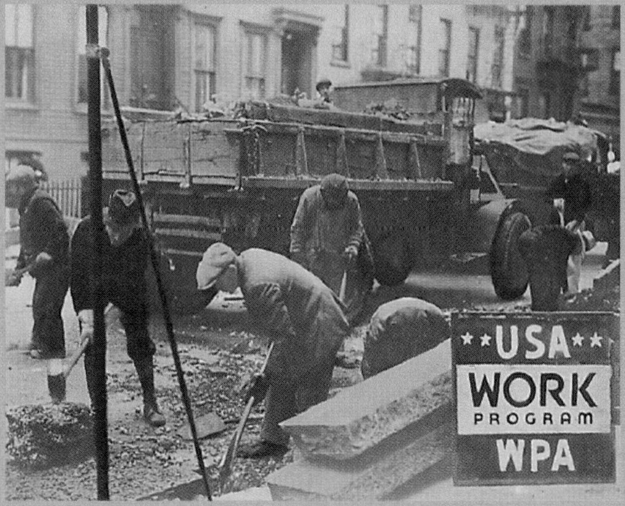

Franklin Roosevelt took office on March 4, 1933. He immediately sent to Congress a group of legislative proposals, many of which Congress passed within 100 days. Roosevelt's program, known as the New Deal, enlarged the role of the federal government. Shown in the photo are civilians employed in the Works Progress Administration (WPA), a New Deal agency that built the schools, roads, airports, and post offices in many towns in the late 1930s. Though the term "boondoggle" was coined in reference to some WPA projects, the agency was successful in putting millions to work and improving the nation's public buildings, roads, and bridges.

Source: List compiled by Lee Epstein and Thomas Walker, *Constitutional Law for a Changing America: Institutional Powers and Constraints* (Washington, DC: CQ Press, 1992), p. 283.

growth of the national government, elected officials of both parties called for reevaluation of the scope of federal activity. Republican leaders were especially vocal in their belief that the national government was becoming too large and that many federal activities could be better handled by the states.

Both President Nixon (1968–1974) and President Reagan (1980–1988) advocated a **new federalism.** Their definitions were quite different.

President Nixon proposed two important innovations: **general revenue sharing** and **block grants.** General revenue sharing gave states and cities money to spend as they saw fit, subject to only a few conditions (for example, the money could not be used to support activities that discriminated on the basis of race, age, or sex). This program was in place from 1972 through

Are States Really Closer to the People?

Much of today's rhetoric suggests that many federal government programs, such as health care, welfare, education, and environmental protection, for example, should be turned over to the states because the states are "closer to the people." But what does that mean?

Those who argue that states are closer to the people point to the relative smallness of states. The United States has 257 million residents. Although 7 states have over 10 million people, and California has over 30 million, most (32) states have fewer than 5 million residents. Thus, it should be possible for individuals to have more say in state government than national. Moreover, states are, on the whole, more homogeneous in their cultures than the nation, and these state cultures lead to different policy preferences: Residents of traditionalistic states, on average, have different views of desirable government action than residents of individualistic or moralistic states. Thus, leaving policymaking to the states means that public policy can be more sensitive to the preferences of state communities. Being closer to the people may also mean that state governments can respond more quickly to changes in the public mood; state legislators are closer to the grassroots than national legislators. Finally, smaller government should be more efficient.

However, reality is not always as simple as a slogan. Except in a few very small states, where town meetings still prevail, it is difficult for individuals to have much say in their state government as well as their national government. States are not small entities, even if they are a lot smaller than the federal government. In fact, states have more employees than the federal government and are growing faster (see figure). Moreover, most people know a lot more about what is going on in Washington than they do about what is going on in Lincoln, Springfield, Sacramento, or Harrisburg, to name a few state capitals, and in that sense have more tools to make the federal government responsive than they do the state government. (How many talk shows or CNN clones focus on what is going on in the statehouse?) There is also evidence that being "closer to the people" also means being more susceptible to the pressures of big money, and the relative homogeneity of state populations may make it easier to steamroller the rights of small groups. Finally, there is no evidence that state governments are less corrupt or more efficient than the federal government.[1] Indeed, federal pressure has been a major influence on professionalizing of state bureaucracies.

Number of Employees in the Federal and State Governments, 1975–1993

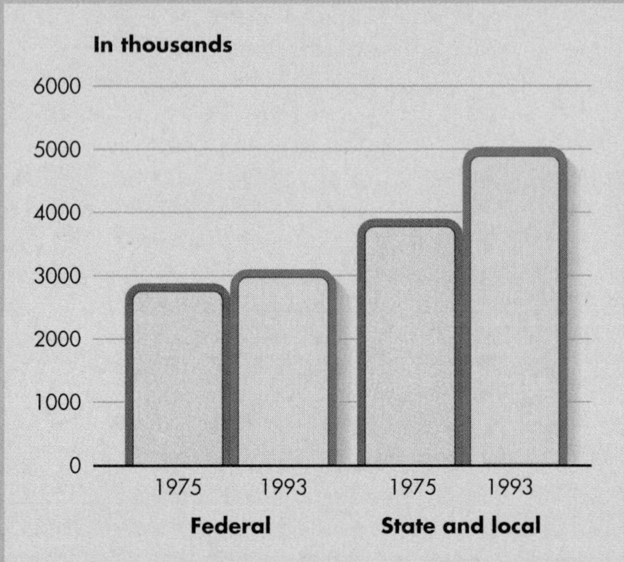

Source: *Statistical Abstract of the United States, 1995,* Tables 540 and 508.

These problems with state governments do not mean that turning some federal programs back to the states is necessarily a bad idea. The problems do suggest, though, that we need to look beyond slogans to the reality of politics, national and state.

1. See for recent discussions, Richard Cohen, "States Aren't Saints Either," *Washington Post National Weekly Edition,* April 3–9, 1995, p. 28; R. W. Apple, "You Say You Want a Devolution," *New York Times,* January 29, 1995, Section 4, p. 1.

1987. Block grants gave states and localities some leeway on spending federal funds for designated purposes, such as community development. Because the limitations that accompany them are less rigid than those on grants-in-aid, states welcomed them. But block grants still enable Congress and the president to set priorities for spending by designating the purposes for which the funds can be used. In 1996 Congress turned welfare over to the states by making it a block grant, giving states some discretion in running its aid programs.

Although Jimmy Carter began to decrease federal spending on grants to states and localities, it was Ronald Reagan who made curbing the growth of the federal government a main theme of his administration. Using a dual federalist rhetoric, Reagan articulated a vision of a smaller federal government and more powerful states.[17] He suggested that he would propose radical changes in the relationships between the federal government and the states. But in fact he did little of that. Though he persuaded Congress to drop a few grants, consolidate other grants, and eliminate general revenue sharing, Reagan's major impact on nation-state relationships was through his budget priorities. By massively increasing military spending and running huge deficits requiring ever larger interest payments, the amount of money available for domestic spending shrank. Money spent on federal grants-in-aid declined substantially relative to overall spending during the 1980s.

Thus, whereas the centerpiece of Nixon's "new federalism" was to provide *more* unrestricted or minimally restricted federal funds to states and localities, Reagan's "new federalism" was directed toward dramatically *reducing* federal support to the states. States and localities were told to support new programs with their own resources.

Despite Republican control of the White House throughout most of the 1970s and 1980s, the federal government continued to grow. State activity also increased. Many states modernized and expanded their tax systems and were then able to take advantage of the economic boom in the 1980s. With these resources, the states enacted hundreds of new programs in many areas, especially education, child care and child protection, and economic development. Moreover, as the federal government has backed away from increased regulations, state regulation increased in areas as diverse as the insurance industry, environmental protection, and consumer affairs.

Today, however, cuts in federal aid to states mean cuts in state support for services such as education, housing, and Medicaid. In 1996, many states found it difficult to budget for various programs, because the federal budget deadlock made it impossible to predict how much grant money and other federal funds they could count on. This demonstrates how much states depend on federal money to deal with their needs.

The new Republican majority in Congress took an additional step in 1995 to return power to the states. They passed legislation allowing states once again to set speed limits on interstate and other federal highways. States were quick to respond, with western states, especially, raising the speed limit to 70 or 75 miles per hour.

Contemporary Federalism

Today's federalism is a mixture of cooperation and conflict. One expert calls it "competitive federalism," because states and the federal government are competing for leadership of the nation's domestic policy.[18] In this section, we will review some of the major features of today's federalism, and then return to some of the areas of conflict and contention that are the subject of current debate.

Federal-State Relations

Cooperation

Much federal-state activity is cooperative. Given the large number of governments in the United States (Table 2), it is essential that they cooperate. And they do. States and the federal government work together in a myriad of activities in almost every area of policy.

TABLE 2 Number of Government Units in the United States

Part of the reason that intergovernmental relations in the United States are so complex is that there are so many governments. Though the number of school districts has decreased dramatically in the last forty years, and the number of townships has declined slowly, the number of "special districts"—created for a single purpose, such as parks, airports, or flood control management—continues to grow.

	STATES	COUNTIES	MUNICIPALITIES	TOWNSHIPS AND TOWNS	SCHOOL DISTRICTS	SPECIAL DISTRICTS
1942	48	3,050	16,220	18,919	108,579	8,299
1992	50	3,043	19,296	16,666	14,556	33,131

Source: *Statistical Abstract of the United States*, 1993 (Washington, D.C.: U.S. Government Printing Office, 1993), Table 466.

One example of informal but intensive cooperation is the National Disease Control Center, which helps state and local governments with health emergencies. National and state police and other crime-fighting agencies share data on crimes and criminals. Another area of cooperation is joint regulatory activity. The federal government and the states jointly regulate some businesses and industry. The federal government sets standards, and each state decides whether to enforce the standard itself or let the federal government do it. Joint activity is found in several areas, including occupational safety and environmental regulation.

Another important area of federal-state cooperation is federal grants to states. The federal government gives funds to states to cope with problems that do not stop at state borders. Federal grant-in-aid programs represent a compromise between those who want a nationally administered program and those who want to keep a program at the state or local level. Unemployment compensation, administered by the states under federal regulation and funding, is a good example. Moreover, despite some examples of inefficiency, major federal programs have succeeded in helping state and local governments meet real needs and, along the way, they have increased the professionalism of state and local bureaucrats.

Federal programs often serve the interests of state and local officials, who would rather have programs paid for by federal taxes than state and local taxes. And the system greatly benefits many different kinds of interest groups that demand national action when they are spurned by the states. Groups of all ideological stripes pragmatically seek federal aid. For example, both conservatives and liberals supported a federal grant program helping states collect child support money from nonpaying divorced or unmarried fathers.

States and Localities as Lobbyists

A crucial part of the relationship of the states to the federal government concerns lobbying. The importance of federal money to states and localities and the need for coordination between federal and state bureaucracies have stimulated the organization of

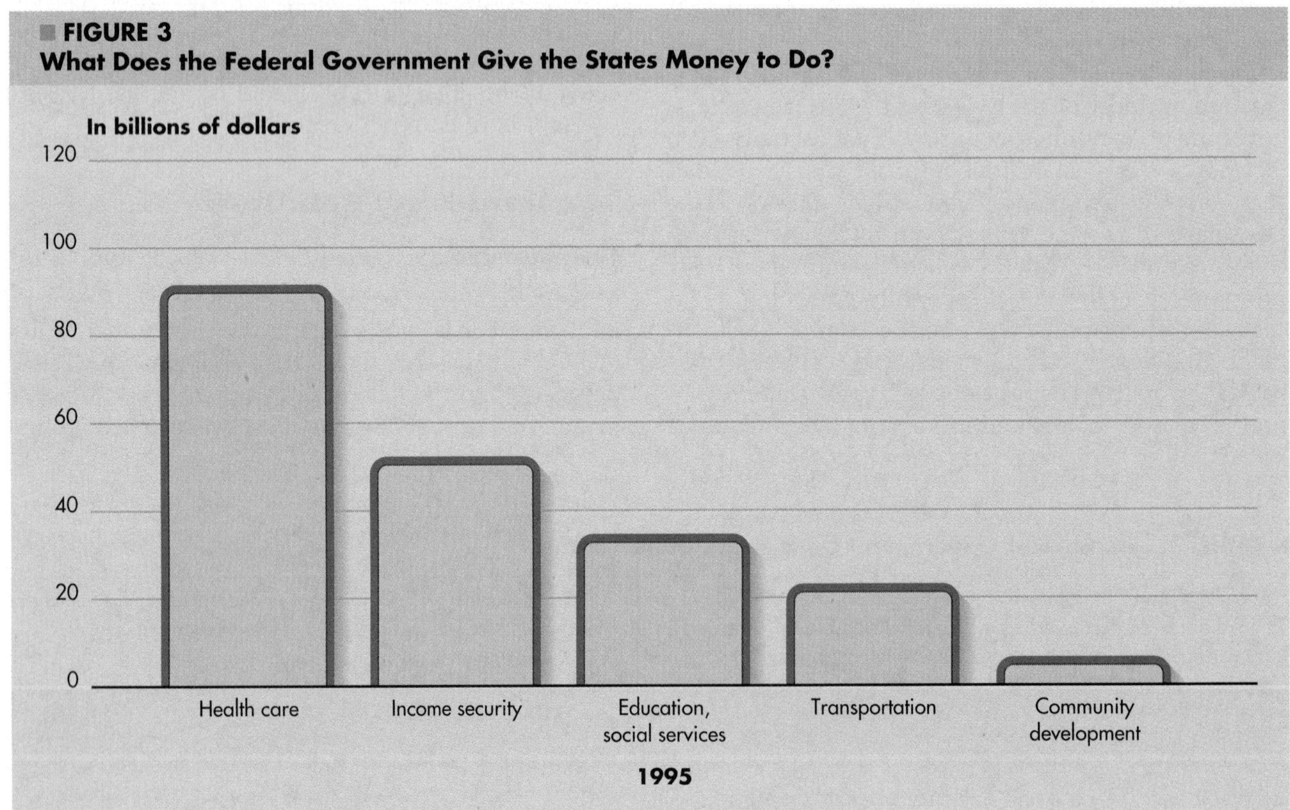

Most of the $228 billion the federal government gave to the states went for programs in these areas.
Source: *Statistical Abstract of the United States,* Washington, D.C.: U.S. Government Printing office, 1995, Table 479.

groups of state and local officials, such as the National Conference of State Legislatures, the National League of Cities, and the American Public Welfare Association. These groups lobby for favorable legislation for states and localities and work with federal agencies to ensure that new regulations are implemented in a way acceptable to the states. Most of these organizations have multimillion-dollar budgets and employ a sizable staff of lobbyists and researchers. Many individual states and cities have their own Washington lobbyists, and these lobbyists appear to have some positive effect on increasing federal aid.[19]

Conflict

Current federal-state relations are also characterized by conflict. One of the sharpest clashes concerns the so-called **unfunded mandates.** These are federal laws requiring states to do something, usually to regulate. Often the federal government transfers money to the states to cover part of the cost of the activity, but not always. For example, the federal government requires the states to deduct child support from the wages of parents who fall behind on payments. The state is also to deduct payments automatically from paychecks of fathers of children whose mothers are on welfare.[20] States that fail to carry out these mandates risk losing the federal contributions to their welfare funds.

Environmental regulations are, overall, the most expensive federal mandates. Meeting federal standards for clean air and water is projected to cost billions. Other recent federal regulations include a mandate that states and localities provide for the education of illegal immigrants and one that requires, among other things, public buildings, sidewalks, and transportation to be accessible to the handicapped.

The burdens of these and other mandates led to a plank in the Republicans' 1994 "Contract with America" calling for legislation to reduce such mandates. Some conservatives would like to abolish unfunded mandates completely. Others believe that unfunded mandates are sometimes beneficial, but that their costs should be made more public at the time legislation is passed. Still others believe the attack on unfunded mandates is really an attack on all regulatory action by the federal government. This group believes that expecting states to enact significant regulations in some areas is impracticable.

Another area of conflict is more basic. Some favor a radical shift in federal-state responsibilities, with a return to some form of dual federalism. States would handle many more programs than they do now, and the federal government would shrink in size, scope, and cost.

Proponents of this view do not all have the same assumptions. Some believe that government has a role to play in solving societal problems, and the states are capable of handling that role. Others believe that government has no role, and that turning programs over to the states will kill them.

Even though most people agree there are some areas that the federal government should leave to the states, the problem is there is little consensus on what those areas are. For example, some argue that the federal government should leave health care to the states but centralize welfare programs at the federal level. Others believe exactly the opposite.

Interstate Relations

Constitutional Requirements

The Constitution established rules governing states' relationships with each other. One important provision is the **full faith and credit clause,** which requires states to recognize contracts. If you marry in Ohio, Pennsylvania must recognize your marriage. The Constitution also provides that if a fugitive from justice flees from one state to another, he or she is supposed to be extradited, that is, sent back to the state with jurisdiction.

Voluntary Cooperation

Most state-to-state interaction is informal and voluntary, with state officials consulting with officials in other states about common problems and states borrowing ideas from one another. Sometimes states enter into formal agreements, called interstate compacts, to deal with a common problem—operating a port or allocating water from a river basin, for example.

Interstate Competition

Changing economic patterns and an overall loss of economic competitiveness by the United States in the world market have stimulated vigorous competition among the states to attract new businesses and jobs. They advertise the advantages of their states to prospective new businesses: low taxes, good climate, a skilled workforce, low wages, and little government regulation. This growing competition prompts states to give tax advantages and other financial incentives to businesses willing to relocate there.

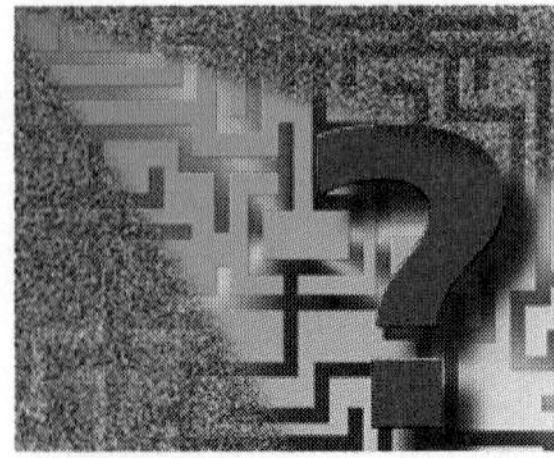

Symbolic Solutions for Complex Problems?

Should the Federal Government Turn Welfare Over to the States?

Americans are angry at government, and one of the favorite specific objects of public wrath is the welfare program. A particular object of hostility is Aid to Families with Dependent Children, the program that supports a total of almost 14 million people: poor children, their mothers, and sometimes their fathers.[1] Although most Americans believe government should do more to help the poor, most also believe we spend too much for welfare.[2]

The AFDC program has been a joint federal and state program. Most funding is provided by the federal government, which also writes the rules under which welfare is administered. States have some discretion in how they operate the program but are very much limited by the federal rules. Many state leaders believe they could run the programs better than does the federal government.

Recent legislation gives the responsibility for the AFDC program back to the states. Given the political climate, it is not surprising that many members of Congress, along with state officials, believe that welfare could be given to the states to administer.

Welfare reform, long demanded by politicians of both parties, was a plank in the Republicans' "Contract with America," and was incorporated in the Republicans' welfare reform bill introduced early in the 1995 congressional session. One of its key provisions was to consolidate federal support for AFDC and many other antipoverty programs (such as food stamps and food aid to women, infants, and children) into block grants to be paid to the states. The states, in turn, could decide how much money they wanted to spend, declare eligibility standards for those who receive the money, and set priorities among different programs. Different states, then, could have different standards and programs. The federal government could withdraw from these programs.

But is turning welfare over to the states a real solution or only symbolic? The answer to that question, in turn, depends on the definition of the problem the proposal is designed to solve.

Some believe that the problem with welfare is that it is too expensive. Turning the program over to the states would not, in itself, reduce the costs of welfare. Congress could cut the welfare budget whether or not the program is turned over to the states. In fact, many governors are reluctant to support a block grant approach to welfare unless Congress declared that states would get a fixed level of funding for each recipient. They are fearful that, if block grants are adopted, the federal government will shrink the amount of funds it puts into this program, leaving states holding the bag.

Others believe that the problem with welfare is that it is not responsive to local needs and conditions. States, in theory, could respond more quickly and efficiently to evolving needs. Some states might discover they did not need one particular program, but would need more support for another program. Being smaller, states should be able to run programs with less red tape. Many governors believe that if they had the money, they would know what to do with the welfare system. On the other hand, larger states have the same diversity of interests as the nation as a whole—huge urban areas and small rural communities, rich and poor, black and white. It is likely that the same controversies would emerge in the states as in Congress.

Still others believe that the problem with the welfare program is that it is too complex, with too many regulations and too many overlapping programs for the poor. At first blush, the block grant solution seems a real solution to complexity. States could get federal funds without conditions. Said one state representative, "Send us the unfettered authority. We'll do it. That's our job."[3] If that happened, the federal government would leave it to individual states to decide who is eligible for aid. Yet some of those most committed to the idea of letting the states run the welfare system also favor limiting access to welfare by, for example, noncitizens and teenagers who have babies. If the federal government attaches strings to its aid, prohibiting states from denying aid to these or other groups, we might soon see a system little different from today's, with the states having to follow hundreds of federal regulations. Many Republicans, as well as Democrats, are reluctant, however, to turn the administration of the program entirely over to the states.

Indeed a system of block grants might even increase complexity in the system. Individuals might be eligible for welfare assistance in one state and not another (under the existing system, there is a uniform standard of eligibility, though monthly payments vary greatly from one state to another). States differ in their capacity to raise money, too, and the poorest states have less capacity and more demand. The current system tries to remedy this by giving larger amounts of assistance to poorer states.

Still others say that the problem with welfare is that it encourages immorality by offering cash benefits for having

Source: Oliphant © 1995 Universal Press Syndicate.

babies whether or not a person is able to care for and support children. There is little evidence that individuals do have children just because of welfare, but even if it were true, turning the system over to the states without other changes in the system is not likely to change the incentive structures. Incentives for having babies, for holding jobs, for living in a two-parent household could be changed whether or not the system is run by the federal government or by the states. The problem is that there is no agreement on just how the incentives *should* be changed.

The solution of turning welfare over to the states seems to be mostly symbolic if it is targeted to the problems of cost, incentives, or simplicity. It might be a partial real solution to the problems of allowing different communities and regions to deal with welfare in different ways. It seems unlikely, though, that such a solution will really get at the basic dilemmas at the heart of the system: We want to be generous to the children, but not so generous that it encourages their parents to stay on welfare. And we would like to help the adults on welfare make something of themselves so they can hold jobs, but we do not want to spend money on job training, health benefits, and child care that would enable more of them to have a reasonable chance of doing this. Balancing these disparate objectives is difficult whether the program is run by the federal government or the states.

1. *Statistical Abstract of the United States, 1994* (Washington, DC: U.S. Government Printing Office, 1994), Table 577.
2. Richard Morin, "What the Public Really Wants," *Washington Post National Weekly Edition,* January 9–15, 1995, p. 37; Jeffrey L. Katz with Alissa Rubin and Peter MacPherson, "Major Aspects of Welfare Bill Approved by Subcommittee," *CQ* (February 18, 1995), p. 525.
3. Rochelle L. Stanfield, "The New Federalism," *National Journal* (January 28, 1995), p. 229.

Critics believe that these offers serve mostly to erode a state's tax base and have little impact on most business relocation decisions. Evidence indicates that low taxes are not the primary reason for business relocation.[21] Nevertheless, without some special break for business, states now feel at a competitive disadvantage in recruiting them. Business interests pressure states to adopt legislation more favorable to business.

State-Local Relations

Another important feature of contemporary federalism is the relationship of states to their localities—counties, cities, and special districts. These relationships are defined by state constitutions; they are not dealt with in the federal constitution. States differ in the autonomy they grant to their localities. In some states, **home rule** charters give local governments

A little-known example of federal-state-local cooperation is firefighting in wilderness areas. In 1988, more than 15,000 firefighters converged to fight summer fires in Yellowstone and surrounding areas. Led by members of the U.S. Forest Service and other federal agencies, the firefighters were sent by state and local governments of every state.

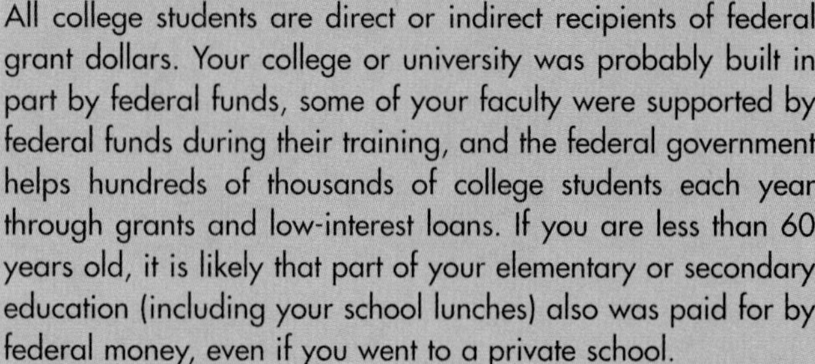

Who, Me? Students as Recipients of Federal Aid

All college students are direct or indirect recipients of federal grant dollars. Your college or university was probably built in part by federal funds, some of your faculty were supported by federal funds during their training, and the federal government helps hundreds of thousands of college students each year through grants and low-interest loans. If you are less than 60 years old, it is likely that part of your elementary or secondary education (including your school lunches) also was paid for by federal money, even if you went to a private school.

If you live in a city with a municipal bus or subway system, your bus fare is lowered by as much as half because it is partially supported by federal dollars. Even if you do not ride a bus or subway, the federal government has paid for part of your transportation—whatever it is—by contributing to the funding of many streets and roads. If you drive to another city during your school holidays, you drive over highways for which Uncle Sam has paid up to 90% of the cost. If you fly, you fly into airports that are partially paid for by the federal government.

If you or your parents have been unemployed, your unemployment compensation is paid in part by the federal government through a grant program. If one of your parents died while you were a youngster, you probably received Social Security benefits, and if you have lived in poverty, you may have received AFDC (Aid to Families with Dependent Children).

If you feel that you have been affected by none of these grants, here is a final example. If you have a flush toilet, it is probably connected to a sewer paid for by, you guessed it, Uncle Sam, who has spent hundreds of millions in grants to local communities for sewer construction.

considerable autonomy in such matters as setting tax rates, regulating land use, and choosing their form of local government. In many states, cities of different sizes have different degrees of autonomy. Although localities are creatures of their states, whereas states exist independently of the national government, some of the same problems that affect national-state relations also affect state-local relations. City and county officials often wish for more authority and fewer mandates from the state.

➤ Conclusion: Is Federalism Responsive?

Across the United States, our beliefs in democracy, freedom, and equality bind us together. In many ways we are becoming more alike, as rapid transportation, television and other forms of instant communication, fast-food franchises, hotel chains, and other nationwide businesses bring about an increasing similarity in what we think about, our tastes in culture and food, and even political activities. But to say that Alabama is more like New York than it used to be is certainly not to say they are alike. Our federal system helps us accommodate this diversity by allowing both state and federal governments a role in making policy.

Our Founders probably did not foresee a federal system like the one we have now; the federal government has surpassed the states in power and scope of action. Yet one of the paradoxes of our system is that as the national government has gained extraordinary power, so have the states and localities. All levels of government are stronger than in the eighteenth century. Federal power *and* state power have grown hand in hand.

It is probably foolish to pretend to know how the Founders might deal with our complex federal system. However, many of them were quite astute politicians who would undoubtedly recognize that our system evolved because various groups over time

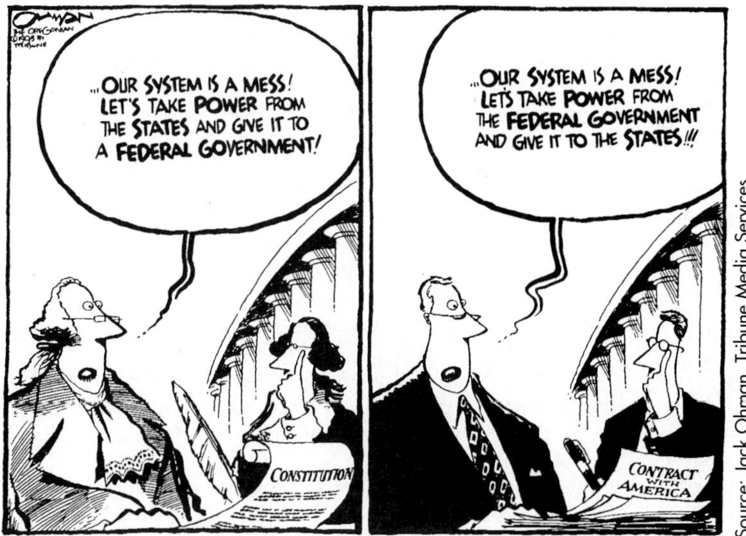

Source: Jack Ohman. Tribune Media Services

demanded national action. Yet we continue to believe in local control and grassroots government. Our system is a logical outcome of our contradictory impulses for national solutions and local control.

Is such a complex system responsive? It is very responsive in that groups and individuals making a demand that is rejected at one level of government can go to another level. The federal system creates multiple points of access, each with power to satisfy political demands. Yet the system is less responsive in that the same multiple levels and points of access also block demands. Civil rights groups, for example, were able to win voting rights for blacks in most states before the 1960s. But they were still blocked in several states until the national government acted. Thus federalism creates opportunities for influence, but it also creates possibilities for roadblocks to achieving national political action. This, of course, is what Madison foresaw.

Does this complex federal system contribute toward the anger many Americans feel toward their government? Although hard evidence is not available, it certainly seems that the multiple points of access, and the ability to stop action at many levels, contributes to Americans' sense that their government is out of the control of the people.

EPILOGUE

Ros-Lehtinen Supports the Bill

Representative Ros-Lehtinen was one of only 47 Republicans who supported the child-care bill (119 voted no). But most Democrats supported it, so it passed 265-145. Later in 1990, the Senate and House agreed on a version of the bill, which was signed by President Bush. The bill became the first significant child-care legislation in 19 years.

Those who might otherwise resist the expansion of federal power into the area of child care and family life voted for this bill because they believe that America's children need help. It is probably not coincidental that, though a large majority of Republicans voted against the bill, a large majority of Republican *women* voted for it.

Although the funds spent in this bill are not large by federal budget standards, the decision to fund the program in a time of budgetary scarcity illustrates why and how federal programs have grown over the years. Conservatives as well as liberals often see the federal government as the appropriate agent to carry out what they believe are worthy policies. Resistance to a bigger federal government takes second place to a desired policy objective. In this light, big government is bad only when it wants to do something you do not want it to do.

➤Key Terms

federalism
unitary system
confederal system
political culture
"necessary and proper"
implied powers clause
supremacy clause
dual federalism
cooperative federalism
"mischiefs of faction"
McCulloch v. Maryland
New Deal
grants-in-aid
new federalism
general revenue sharing
block grants
unfunded mandates
full faith and credit clause
home rule

➤Further Reading

Daniel Elazar, *American Federalism: A View from the States*, 3rd ed. (New York: Harper & Row, 1984). *Explores the development of intergovernmental relations and examines American political cultures.*

Paul Peterson, Barry Rabe, and Kenneth Wong, *When Federalism Works* (Washington, D.C.: Brookings Institute, 1986). *Challenges prevailing wisdom to argue that most federal grant programs work.*

Jeffrey Pressman and Aaron Wildavsky, *Implementation* (Berkeley, Calif.: University of California Press, 1973). *The difficulties of translating federal laws into working programs when dealing with a multiplicity of state and local governments.*

Alice Rivlin, *Reviving the American Dream: The Economy, the States, and the Federal Government* (Washington, D.C.: Brookings Institute, 1992). *An analysis of the fiscal relations between the federal government and the states by Clinton's budget director.*

David Walker, *The Rebirth of Federalism* (Chatham, N.J.: Chatham House, 1995). *A recent look at contemporary trends.*

John Steinbeck, *The Grapes of Wrath* (New York: Viking, 1939). *A novel portraying the conditions facing the country that set the stage for the New Deal.*

➤Notes

1. Grant Ujifusa and Michael Barone, "Almanac of American Politics 1990," Washington, D.C.: *National Journal*, 1991, pp. 288-90.

2. *Congressional Quarterly Weekly Report*, July 2, 1988, p. 1834.

3. Spencer Rich, "More Kids Live in One-Parent Household," *Washington Post National Weekly Edition*, March 20-26, 1989, pp. 2934-39.

4. See Julie Kosterlitz, "Not Just Kid Stuff," *National Journal*, November 19, 1988, pp. 2934-29; Calvin Tomkins, "A Sense of Urgency," *New Yorker*, March 27, 1989, pp. 48-74; Ellen Goodman, "Tough Look at Spending on Children," *Lincoln Star*, March 21, 1989, p. 8.

5. "The Emerging Child Care Issue," *Time*, May 16, 1988, p. 42.

6. Antifeminist Phyllis Schlafly, quoted in "The Emerging Child Care Issue."

7. Daniel Elazar, *American Federalism: A View from the States*, 3rd ed. (New York: Harper & Row, 1984).

8. Paul Taylor, "End of the Louisiana Hayride," *Washington Post National Weekly Edition*, March 18, 1985, p. 13.

9. A 1976 Supreme Court decision used the Tenth Amendment as a reason to forbid the federal government to extend minimum wage and hour laws to state and local government employees. See *National League of Cities v. Usery*, 426 U.S. 833 (1976). This decision was partially overruled in 1985. See *Garcia v. San Antonio Metropolitan Transit Authority*, 83 L.Ed. 2d 1016 (1985).

10. The following discussion is drawn from Richard Leach, *American Federalism* (New York: W. W. Norton, 1970), chapter 1. See also Christopher Hamilton and Donald Wells, *Federalism, Power and Political Economy: A New Theory of Federalism's Impact on American Life* (Englewood Cliffs, N.J.: Prentice Hall, 1990).

11. James Madison, Alexander Hamilton, and John Jay, *The Federalist Papers*, # 45. Several editions.

12. *McCulloch v. Maryland*, 4 Wheat. 316 (1819).

13. Alfred Kelly and Winfred Harbeson, *The American Constitution: Its Origins and Development* (New York: W. W. Norton, 1976).

14. Daniel Elazar, *The American Partnership* (Chicago: University of Chicago Press, 1962).

15. Perhaps because he is a sociologist (!), Theodore Caplan did not fully appreciate the extent of federal involvement in Muncie, even in 1924—the support of veterans, schools, roads, and hospitals by federal land grants. Nevertheless, his major point is valid: The federal presence there was nothing compared to now. Caplan is quoted in Daniel Walker, *Toward a Functioning Federalism* (Cambridge, Mass.: Winthrop, 1981), pp. 3-4.

16. Theodore Lowi, *The Personal President* (Ithaca, N.Y.: Cornell University Press, 1985).

17. Paul Peterson, Barry Rabe, and Kenneth Wong, *When Federalism Works* (Washington, D.C.: Brookings Institute, 1986). See also John Schwartz, *America's Hidden Success*, 2nd ed. (New York: W. W. Norton, 1988); David Walker, *The Rebirth of Federalism: Slouching toward Washington* (Chatham, N.J.: Chatham House, 1995).

18. Alice Rivlin, *Reviving the American Dream: The Economy, the States and the Federal Government* (Washington, D.C.: Brookings Institute, 1992).

19. Neil Berch, "Why Do Some States Play the Federal Aid Game Better than Others?" *American Politics Quarterly* 20 (July, 1992) pp. 366-377.

20. See Mary Ann Glendon, *Abortion and Divorce in Western Law* (Cambridge, Mass.: Harvard University Press, 1987), pp. 87-88; see also Susan Welch, Sue Thomas, and Margery Ambrosius, "Family Policy," in Virginia Gray and Herbert Jacob, *State Politics and Policy*, 5th ed. (Boston: Little, Brown, 1995).

21. Enid F. Beaumont and Harold Hovey, "State, Local and Federal Development Policies: New Federalism Patterns, Chaos, or What?" *Public Administration Review* 45 (March/April 1985), pp. 327-32; Barry Rubin and C. Kurt Zorn, "Sensible State and Local Development," *Public Administration Review* 45 (March/April 1985), pp. 333-39.

PART TWO

Links Between People and Government

Journalists fill the Los Angeles Coliseum for the 1984 Olympics. Teddy Roosevelt called the presidency a "bully pulpit" from which he could speak, through the press, to the people to persuade them to support his programs.

4 Public Opinion

You Are There

The President Considers the Nation's Rising Concern over Crime

It is January 1994 and you are President Clinton, about to speak to the nation in your annual State of the Union address. The speech will identify the issues you want Congress to consider in the coming year, and help mobilize the public behind your program. You need something to demonstrate to the American people that you are not out of step with moderate middle America but a "new kind of Democrat" who is sympathetic to the needs and wants of average citizens. A tough anticrime bill might be such a policy.

Republicans have called you another "tax and spend Democrat." In your first year in office you pushed through an economic plan that boosted taxes on the wealthy but also increased gas taxes that will affect the middle class. You supported the North American Free Trade Agreement (NAFTA). In the long run it should help the economy, but in the short run it might prompt some U.S. corporations to relocate their factories in Mexico, costing some blue collar workers their jobs. You have been criticized on noneconomic issues, too. Some believe your positions on abortion, gays in the military, and other social issues are too liberal.

You are looking for a policy that will counter the perception that you are always on the liberal side of issues. You realized early in your career that it is beneficial to be "tough on crime." After losing your first election for governor of Arkansas to an opponent who ran on a law-and-order platform, you came out in favor of capital punishment, setting execution dates for 26 prisoners.[1] Even in the midst of the hectic presidential campaign, you rushed back to Arkansas to deny clemency to a condemned murderer who was so brain-damaged that he seemed unaware what was going on. You said, "I can be nicked on a lot, but no one can say I'm soft on crime."[2]

Americans are increasingly concerned with crime. Public opinion polls show that one in five Americans, more than on any other issue including the economy, report crime is the main problem facing the nation, a rise of 15% since June. Even though the crime rate has declined recently, it is higher than a decade ago, and public concern is triggered by news stories of violent crime, such as the murder of a twelve-year-old in California and the shooting of passengers on a New York City railway train.

A crime bill is now working its way through Congress. One provision is dubbed "three strikes and you're out." It has an appealing sound and means life imprisonment for anyone convicted of three serious crimes. Taking a tough position on crime is likely to gain approval with the public and outflank the Republicans who would otherwise use the issue against you and your party in the next election. Moreover, you genuinely believe that repeat violent offenders have to be put away permanently so they will be unable to commit other crimes.

On the other hand, you recognize that "three strikes and you're out" is an oversimplified response to a difficult issue. First, most crime is caused by lack of jobs, family breakdown, and drugs. Putting criminals behind bars will not affect these conditions. Second, longer sentences will only stress the nation's prison system, which is so overcrowded that many convicts already serve less time than they should. Mandatory sentences

CONTINUED 

OUTLINE

Nature of Public Opinion

Formation of Public Opinion

Agents of Political Socialization

Impact of Political Socialization

Measuring Public Opinion

Early Polling Efforts

Emergence of Scientific Polling

Polls and Politics

How Informed is Public Opinion?

Public Opinion

Ideology

Social Welfare and the Proper Role of Government

Social Issues

Race

Political Tolerance

Trust in Government

Conclusion: Is Government Responsive to Public Opinion?

that fail to consider the specifics of each case often result in jail terms when a less severe penalty would save the taxpayers money and open prison space for more violent criminals. Imprisonment for minor crimes like drug possession often leads to more violent crimes once a person is released.

Moreover, even the most violent criminals usually do not continue their violent behavior as they get older. Thus, the "three strikes" law would require the government to pay hundreds of thousands of dollars to confine inmates well beyond the years when they are likely to commit crimes. Finally, crime is largely a matter handled by state and local governments. Most criminals have violated state laws and are punished by the states. It is unlikely that a federal "three strikes" law will have a significant impact on crime.

Weighing these factors, do you support "three strikes and you're out," and win favor with the public as well as undermine the Republicans on the issue? Or do you try to educate the public by informing them of the costs and limitations of building more prisons and putting more and more people behind bars? Or perhaps you do nothing, and hope that when the media turn their attention to another issue, the concern with crime will diminish.[3]

Our feelings about public opinion are contradictory. On the one hand, in a democracy we want leaders to be responsive to public opinion. Yet often we complain that our elected officials do not lead but simply follow the latest trends in public opinion polls. And these public opinion polls are contradictory, too. Many Americans are angry with government. They do not trust it; they think it is too big and spends too much money. At the same time, they like the services government provides them, and very few Americans are willing to cut spending so drastically as to eliminate their favorite service or program.

In this chapter we will explore public opinion to better understand these contradictions. We will describe how public opinion is formed and measured and discuss the pattern of public opinion on some important issues. For example, are Americans really as angry and mistrustful as the media portray? Finally, we will assess the extent to which government is responsive to public opinion. Because political science is primarily interested in opinions that affect government, the focus of this chapter is public opinion about political issues, personalities, institutions, and events.

➤Nature of Public Opinion

We can define **public opinion** as the collection of individual opinions toward issues or objects of general interest, that is, those that concern a significant number of people. Public opinion can be described in terms of direction, intensity, and stability. Direction refers to whether public opinion is positive or negative. Generally it is mixed: Some individuals have a positive opinion, others negative. Intensity refers to the strength of opinion. Intense opinions are more likely to be the basis for behavior. Gun enthusiasts strongly opposed to gun control are likely to act on their opinions and vote against members of Congress who support gun registration.

Most public issues are not of interest to most people. Individuals may feel intensely about one or two issues that directly affect them, but not everyone, or even a majority, is intense about the same issues. The relative absence of severe economic and social divisions in the United States explains the lack of intense opinions. With the possible exception of the racial and states' rights issues that almost destroyed the nation in the 1860s, there has been nothing like the long-standing, divisive class and religious conflicts of many European nations.

Opinions also differ in stability. An opinion is more likely to change when an individual lacks intensity or information about an issue. The opinions of citizens toward the country are more stable than their opinions of presidential candidates. For example, polls following the party nominating conventions in 1992 showed Bill Clinton's margins over George Bush seesawing back and forth from day to day (Figure 1). At this stage of the campaign, many voters were undecided. Some opposed Bush but did not know enough about Clinton to support him firmly. They would see something on television or read something in the press favorable to Clinton and report a preference for him, and then see something unfavorable and shift to Bush.[4]

FIGURE 1
The Presidential "Poller Coaster"

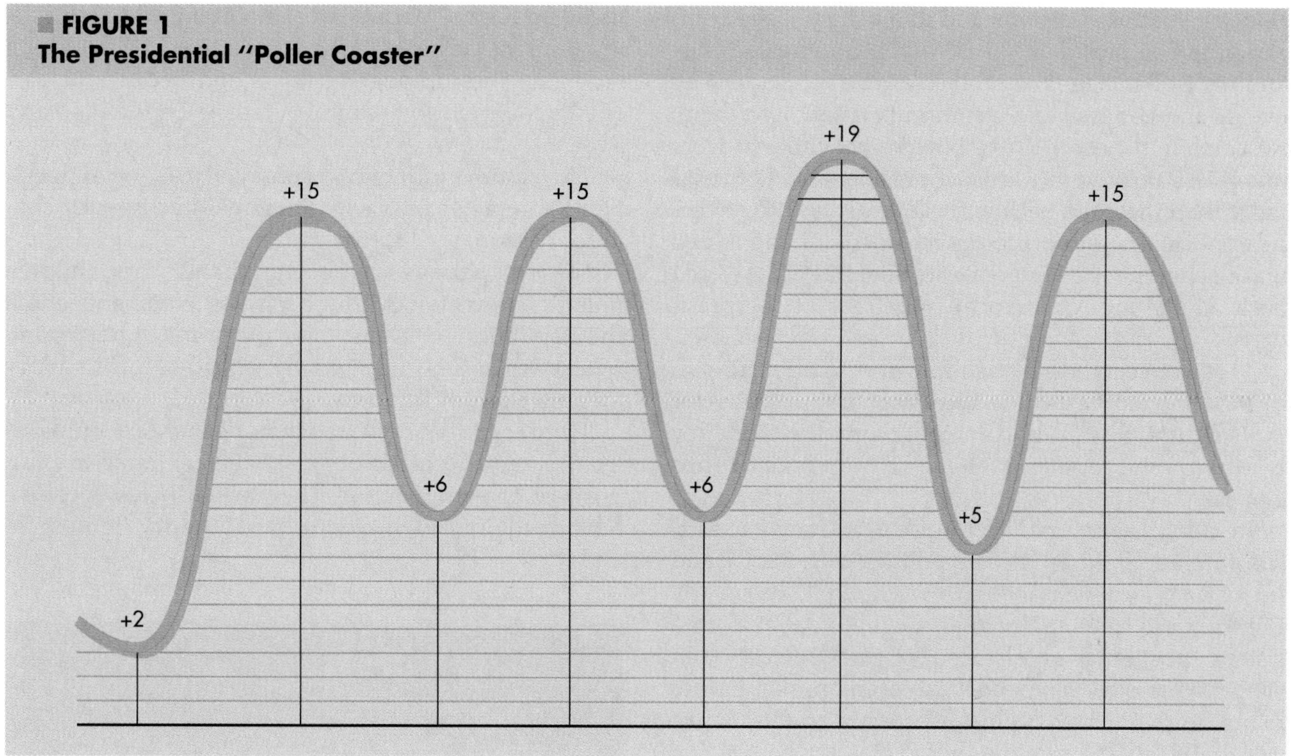

Clinton's margins over Bush rose and fell dramatically early in the 1992 campaign. *Source: USA Today,* October 3, 1992. Polls taken August 20–September 2, 1992. The term "poller coaster" was coined by Richard Morin, "The Ups and Downs of Political Poll-Taking," *Washington Post National Weekly Edition,* October 5, 1992, p. 37.

➤FORMATION OF PUBLIC OPINION

People have opinions about issues and objects because they learn them in a process called **political socialization.**

As with other types of learning, individuals learn about politics by being exposed to new information from parents, peers, schools, the media, political leaders, and the community. These sources are referred to as **agents of political socialization.** Individuals also can learn about politics through direct personal experience.

Political learning begins at an early age and continues through life. Reasoning capacity as well as the demands placed upon an individual influence what is learned.[5] Very young children are unable to distinguish the political from the nonpolitical world. In fact, young children have difficulty separating political figures from cartoon characters. Some confuse the political with the religious. Twenty-five percent of a sample of five- and six-year-olds reported that the president takes his orders directly from God.[6] By first grade, however, children begin to see government as distinct and unique.[7]

The inability to understand abstract concepts or complex institutions means the child's conception of government is limited. Most identify government with the president.[8] Children can recognize the president—they see him on television—and understand that he is a leader of the nation much as the parent is a leader of the family. In general, experiences with parents and other adult figures provide children with a basis for understanding remote authority figures such as the president.[9] Positive feelings toward parents are also responsible for positive feelings toward the president. Children describe the president as good and helpful[10] and view him as more powerful than he really is.[11]

With age, children develop greater capacity to learn, and greater demands are placed upon them. They are introduced to political ideas and institutions by parents, teachers, and peers. Their conception of government broadens to include Congress and such things as voting, freedom, and democracy. The idealization of the president gives way to a more complex and realistic image. The process can be accelerated by events and parental and community reaction to them. Research in the early 1970s showed that children were much less positive toward the president and government than they had been in the 1960s. The 1970s were a period when support for government among adults was declining. The Watergate scandal in 1973 lowered both adults' and children's evaluations of the president.[12]

These effects did not last, however. Although children socialized in the late 1960s and early 1970s were more cynical toward government than others, as they matured their opinions changed and became less cynical.[13]

In adolescence, political understanding expands still further. Children discuss politics with family and friends. Political activity, however limited, begins. By their middle teens, individuals begin to develop consistent positions on issues.[14] Some fifteen- and sixteen-year-olds have political opinions similar to many adults'. They begin to recognize faults in the system but still believe the United States is better than other countries. They rate the country low in limiting violence and fostering political morality, but they rate it high in providing educational opportunities, a good standard of living, and science and technology.[15] For most, the positive feelings toward American government learned earlier are reinforced.

In adulthood, opinions toward specific policies and personalities develop, and political activity becomes more serious. Most Americans have not developed a critical perspective, and few are asked or pushed to criticism by the schools, press, political parties, or political institutions. Although disillusionment with government in general increases, it is basically passive and directed toward political leaders rather than institutions.[16] In the absence of a major upheaval, depression or war, for most, the positive feelings developed toward government early in life are likely to remain and perhaps even cushion the impact of such events if they occur.[17]

Agents of Political Socialization

Family

Children are not born little Republicans and Democrats. Most learn these allegiances from the family. Individuals are influenced by the family throughout life. Families are particularly important in shaping the opinions of children, however, because of the strong emotional ties among members and because of parents' near exclusive control of their children's early lives.

The family influences opinions in several ways. First, parents share their opinions directly with children, who may adopt them.

Second, parents say or do things that children imitate. They may overhear parents' comments about the Republican or Democratic party, for example, and repeat what they hear. Many initially learn a party identification in this way.

Third, children may transfer or generalize opinions from parents to other objects. When children are less positive toward parents, they are also less positive toward the president and other authority figures.[18]

This boy, at a white supremacist rally, likely was socialized in these views by his parents.

Fourth, the family shapes the personality of the child. This may affect the child's political opinions. For example, the family contributes to self-image. Individuals who are self-confident are more likely to participate in politics than others.

Fifth, the family places children in a network of social and economic relationships that influences how they view the world and how the world views them. White children who live in a middle-class suburb will likely view themselves and the world around them differently than black children who live in a large city ghetto.

The influence of the family is strongest when children clearly perceive what the parents' opinion is and that the matter is important to the parents. In the case of party identification, cues are frequent and unambiguous. In one study, 72% of a sample of high school seniors could identify their parents' party identification, whereas no more than 36% could identify their parents' opinion on any other issue.[19]

Today, however, the family has less opportunity to influence the child. Parents no longer have exclusive control during a child's preschool years, and the number of households with both parents working or with a single parent who works means that children have fewer daily contact hours with parents. Consequently, other agents of socialization are becoming more influential. For example, we turn more often to the schools to deal with problems the family dealt with in the past.

School

A child of our acquaintance who came to the United States at the age of five could not speak English and did not know the name of his new country. After a few months of kindergarten, he knew that George Washington and Abraham Lincoln were good presidents, he was able to recount stories of the Pilgrims, he could draw the flag, and he felt strongly that the United States was the best country in the world. This child illustrates strikingly the importance of the school in political socialization and how values and symbols of government are explicitly taught in American schools, as they are in schools in all nations.[20]

Schools promote patriotic rituals, such as beginning each day with the Pledge of Allegiance, and include patriotic songs and programs in many activities. In the lower grades, children celebrate national holidays such as Presidents' Day and Thanksgiving and learn the history and symbols associated with them. Such exercises foster awe and respect for government.

In the upper grades, mock conventions, elections, Girls' and Boys' State, and student government introduce students to the operation of government. School clubs often operate with democratic procedures and reinforce the concepts of voting and majority rule. The state of Illinois even let the state's elementary school children vote to select the official state animal, fish, and tree, conveying the message that voting is the way we decide things.

Curricula and textbooks also foster commitment to government; civics or government courses are offered in most schools and in many places are required of all students. Textbooks, particularly those used in elementary grades, emphasize compliance with authority and the need to be "good" citizens and appear to foster these traits. They are less successful in teaching political participation skills and support for democratic values. Even textbooks in advanced grades often present idealized versions of the way government works and exaggerated views of the responsiveness of government to citizen participation.

Nor does the curriculum make much difference. Civics instruction has only a modest impact on knowledge of and interest in politics, sense of political efficacy (feelings that one can influence government), levels of tolerance, and political trust.[21] Nor do teachers, generally speaking, have much impact, though there is evidence that they have more impact if they are believable.[22] Consequently, only a minority of a sample of 17-year-olds could list four or more ways to influence politics. Sixty percent of a sample of high school seniors favored allowing the police and other groups to censor books and movies.[23]

The failure of the schools to develop participation skills and commitment to democratic values often is attributed to the "hidden curriculum."[24] Schools are run by teachers and administrators with little input from students. In such an environment, it is not surprising that students fail to develop participation skills and democratic values.

Education—the skills that it provides and experiences it represents—does make a difference, however. People who have more years of formal education are generally more interested in and knowledgeable about politics.[25] They are also more likely to participate in politics and to be politically tolerant. But educated Americans are no more likely than others to appreciate that democratic politics and government involves disagreements, arguments, bargaining, and compromise—in other words, to understand the reality of politics in a democratic society.

The major impact of schooling is that it helps create "good" citizens. Citizens are taught to accept political authority and the institutions of government and to channel political activity in legitimate and supportive ways. Thus, the schools provide a valuable function for the state.

Studies have shown the liberalizing influence of a college education. Many go to college to get a job that pays a high salary. Some attend to expand their knowledge and understanding of the world. Others enroll because their parents want them to or simply because everyone else does. Probably no one goes to become more liberal in his or her opinions. But becoming more liberal is often the result.[26]

College students are more liberal than the population as a whole, and the longer they are in college the more liberal they become. Seniors are more liberal than freshmen, and graduates are more liberal than undergraduates.

Why does college lead to liberal opinions? One explanation is that a college education leads to greater self-confidence. As a result, college graduates are less likely to feel threatened by changes in society and more likely to accept them. Support for change is a component of liberalism.

Another explanation is that college leads to a broadened perspective on the world. Individuals begin to look beyond their immediate environment and see themselves as part of a larger world community. This leads to an increased tolerance of different opinions and an awareness of the conditions that are faced by the less fortunate and by those in other parts of the world; all are components of liberalism.

Still another explanation is that liberal college professors indoctrinate students. A Carnegie Commission survey showed that 64% of the social science faculty in the nation's colleges identified themselves as liberal and only 20% regarded themselves as conservative. Faculty in other disciplines are much less likely to be liberal, however. For example, 30% of the business and 55% of the natural science faculty identified themselves as liberal. Although the potential for influence exists, and college professors, no doubt, affect some students, their impact is probably not great. The broadened outlook that leads to greater tolerance of ideas is likely to make students more resistant to indoctrination.

Evidence also suggests that students' attitudes vary over time. During the height of the Vietnam War, 1968–1971, students were more likely to identify themselves as liberal in outlook than were students before and after. (Liberal attitudes are discussed more fully later in the chapter.) In recent years, college students have moved to the center. For example, 24% of college freshmen identified themselves as liberal in 1990 compared to 38% in 1970. Over the same time period, however, there was only a 2% shift to conservatism. Thus, the big change was from liberal identification to middle of the road. At the same time, college faculty changed very little. Thus, students are not simply a reflection of their college classroom teachers. At large universities, where the largest percentage of students attend college, the environment is sufficiently diverse to reinforce all points of view.

Although students are more conservative than they were in the late 1960s, they remain predominantly liberal. They are much more likely to be pro-choice on the abortion issue, for example, than the general public. A comparison of college and noncollege youth also revealed substantial differences. Eighteen percent of college youth agreed that money is very important, compared to 40% of the noncollege youth. Thirty-six percent of the college students responded that abortion is morally wrong; 64% of the noncollege youth took that position.

Still another explanation for the liberalizing influence of college is that it attracts those who are more liberal in the first place. Some evidence suggests that this may be true for some issues. Whereas 68% of 1990 college freshmen thought the courts treat criminals too leniently, 83% of the public thought so. Fifty-six percent of college freshmen favored busing to achieve racial balance in the schools, whereas only 33% of the adult population favored it.

The most distinctive characteristic of college freshmen in 1994 was their lack of interest in politics. Only 16% said that they frequently discuss politics and only 32% considered it important to keep up with political affairs. These figures, which have been declining since the late 1960s, represent an all-time low.[27]

Although some liberals attend college and have their opinions reinforced, and others are influenced by college faculty, liberal opinions most likely result from increased political awareness and a broadened world perspective.

Peers

In many instances, peers simply reinforce the opinions of the family or school. When there is a conflict between peer and parental socialization, peers sometimes win but only on issues of special relevance to youth. For example, peer influence is more important than family influence on the issue of whether 18-year-olds should be allowed to vote, but parental influence appears to be more significant with respect to partisanship and vote choice.[28] Peers have the most influence when the peer group is attractive to the individual and when the individual spends more time with the group. The influence of peer groups on young teenagers and young adults may be increasing as many, particularly in the nation's inner cities, have joined gangs to satisfy needs traditionally provided for in the family.

Opinions on Abortion

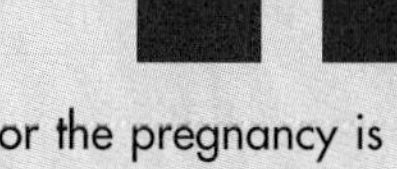

Issues that involve moral questions have the greatest potential to be divisive. Slavery was a moral issue that almost destroyed the nation. In the first decades of this century, prohibition—banning the sale of alcoholic beverages—was a divisive moral issue. In 1992, whether gays should be permitted to serve in the military emerged as another divisive moral issue.

Abortion is the most contentious such issue. In the 1970s, abortion emerged as a moral issue. There are two dimensions to public opinion on this issue. One involves the health and safety of the mother or child. The vast majority of Americans endorse legal abortion when the mother's health may be endangered, the child is likely to have a serious defect, or the pregnancy is the result of rape or incest. This pattern of opinion has been reasonably stable over the past decade.

The other dimension relates to the personal preferences of the mother. Americans are divided on whether a legal abortion is acceptable when the family has a low income and does not want any more children or when the mother is unmarried and does not want to marry the father.

Although the accompanying tables do not reveal intensity, the patterns in boxes a, b, and c show agreement, or consensus, whereas boxes d, e, and f reveal disagreement, or conflict.

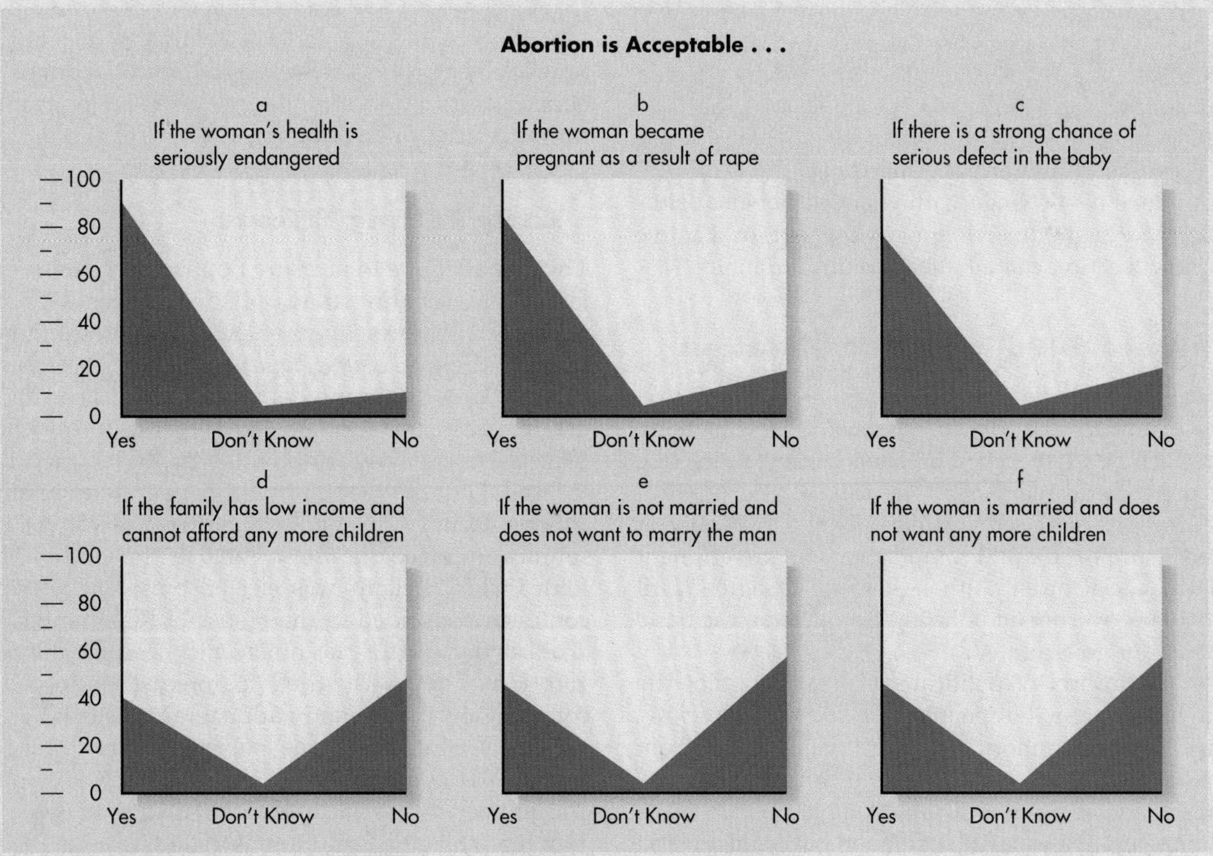

Abortion is Acceptable . . .

a
If the woman's health is seriously endangered

b
If the woman became pregnant as a result of rape

c
If there is a strong chance of serious defect in the baby

d
If the family has low income and cannot afford any more children

e
If the woman is not married and does not want to marry the man

f
If the woman is married and does not want any more children

100
80
60
40
20
0
Yes
Don't Know
No

Source: Surveys by the National Opinion Research Center, General Social Surveys, 1993.

Mass Media

The primary effect of the media on children is to increase their level of information about politics. For adults the media primarily influence what people think about, that is, the issues, events, and personalities they pay attention to,[29] but the media also influence opinions about issues and individuals. Research shows that changes in public opinion tend to follow sentiments expressed by television news commentators.[30] We will examine the impact of the media in more detail in Chapter 8.

Adult Socialization

Not all political socialization occurs in childhood. It is a lifelong process; opinions change as we have new experiences.

Citizens' encounters with government have the potential to change their opinions about politics. Many Americans who were particularly hard hit by the Great Depression, for example, became active in the political process for the first time. Most of these new voters voted Democratic in 1932, and many have voted Democratic ever since. The war in Vietnam was another event that influenced masses of people. Some took to the streets to protest the war; others rejected their country and traveled to Canada to avoid the draft. Watergate was yet another event that affected the opinions of millions of Americans.

Opinions also change with changed personal situations. Marriage, divorce, unemployment, or a move to a new location can all affect political opinions.[31]

Impact of Political Socialization

Each new generation of Americans is socialized to a large extent by the preceding generations. In many ways each new generation will look and act much like the one that came before. In this sense, political socialization is biased against change. Typically it leads to support for and compliance with government and the social order. Although many disagree with particular government policies, few question the basic structure of government.

Yet the impact of political socialization is not the same for all groups of people. The socialization experiences of poor minority children are different from those of rich white ones. Children from low-income families are more cynical about government; black children feel less able to influence government and are less inclined to trust it.[32]

Measuring Public Opinion

Public opinion typically is measured by asking individuals to answer questions in a survey. If done properly, this is the most accurate way to measure public opinion. Before the use of polls, other techniques were employed: Elected officials relied on opinions of people who wrote or talked to them; journalists tried to gauge public opinion by talking selectively to individuals; letters written to newspaper editors or newspaper editorials were thought to reflect public opinion.

These techniques can lead to distortions. Letters to public officials and newspapers are more likely to come from people with extreme opinions[33] or from those with writing skills, that is, people with more education. Nor will opinions culled from a few conversations match the pattern of opinion for the nation as a whole. Editorial opinion is even less likely to provide an accurate picture of public opinion because most newspaper publishers tend to be conservative, which often is reflected in their editorials. In most presidential elections in this century, newspapers have favored the Republican candidate by about three to one.[34]

Polling to measure public opinion is an obvious improvement, but the result of a poll cannot be equated with public opinion. A poll is an instrument for measuring public opinion.

Early Polling Efforts

The first attempts to measure popular sentiments on a large scale were the **straw polls** (or unscientific polls) developed by newspapers in the nineteenth century.[35] In 1824, the *Harrisburg Pennsylvanian,* in perhaps the first poll assessing candidate preferences, sent reporters to check on support for the four presidential contenders that year. In July, the paper reported that Jackson was the popular choice over John Quincy Adams, Henry Clay, and William H. Crawford. Jackson also received the most votes in the election, but John Quincy Adams was elected president after the contest was decided in the House of Representatives. Toward the end of the nineteenth century, the *New York Herald* regularly tried to forecast election outcomes in local, state, and national races. During presidential election years, the paper collected estimates from reporters and political leaders across the country and predicted the Electoral College vote by state.

Straw polls are still employed today. Some newspapers have interviewers who ask adults at shopping

Words Do Make a Difference

A major problem for public opinion pollsters is designing questions that accurately measure what the public believes about issues. "It's not the case that a few words don't make a lot of difference in a poll question." What? Get the picture? Poorly worded questions, such as those with double negatives, can confuse the public and lead pollsters to draw the wrong conclusions.

This was illustrated recently in a poll sponsored by the American Jewish Committee to find out the proportion of Americans who doubt that the Holocaust (the mass murder of millions of Jews by the Nazis in World War II) happened. The survey asked the following question: "As you know, the term Holocaust usually refers to the killing of millions of Jews in Nazi death camps during World War II. Does it seem possible or does it seem impossible to you that the Nazi extermination of the Jews never happened?" The results: 22% said it was possible that the Holocaust never happened: another 12% were not sure. The conclusion: About one-third of the country either doubted the truth of the Holocaust or was uncertain.

Since no reputable historian or anyone with the slightest knowledge of world affairs denies that the Holocaust happened, this "finding" was shocking. Commentators reflected on how the public could be so ignorant of one of the major events, not just of twentieth century history, but of all recorded history. On further investigation, however, it seems that the question wording influenced the responses.

Another version of the question asked "Does it seem possible to you that the Nazi extermination of Jews never happened, or do you feel certain that it happened?" This time only 1% said it was possible the Holocaust never happened. Eight percent were unsure, and 90% said they were certain the Holocaust happened.

Why the difference? A study of 13 polls with estimates of Holocaust doubters from 1% to 46% found that studies with high estimates used double-negative wording. For example, to express that the Holocaust happened, one had to respond "impossible" that it "never happened." Such wording often results in a response that is exactly the opposite of what is intended.

What do Americans really know about the Holocaust? Nine of 10 have heard of the Holocaust; however, only two-thirds are able to correctly explain the Holocaust. In 1992, knowledge of the Holocaust increased with publicity surrounding the opening of the Holocaust Museum in Washington and the release of the Academy Award–winning movie *Schindler's List.*

Source: Richard Morin, "From Confusing Questions, Confusing Answers," *Washington Post National Weekly Edition,* July 18–24, 1994, p. 37.

centers and other locations their voting preferences. Some have readers return coupons printed in the papers. Television and radio stations often ask questions and provide two telephone numbers for listeners to call—one for yes, one for no. The votes are electronically recorded.

The major problem with straw polls is that there is no way to ensure that the sample of individuals giving opinions is representative of the larger population. Generally speaking, they are not.

The famed *Literary Digest* poll is a good example. This magazine conducted polls of presidential preferences between 1916 and 1936. As many as 18 million ballots were mailed out to persons drawn from telephone directories and automobile registration lists. Although the purpose was less to measure public opinion than to boost subscriptions, the *Digest* did have a pretty good record. It predicted the winners in 1924, 1928, and 1932. However, in 1936, the magazine predicted Alfred Landon would win, but Franklin Delano Roosevelt won by a landslide. The erroneous prediction ended the magazine's polling, and in 1938 the *Digest* went out of business.

A bias in the *Digest*'s polling procedure that the editors failed to consider led to erroneous results. At the time, owners of telephones and automobiles were disproportionately middle- and high-income individuals who could afford a telephone or car in the depths of the Depression; these people were much more likely to vote for Landon (a Republican) than were lower-income people.[36] Since the survey was drawn from telephone directories and auto registrations, lower income people were disproportionately excluded from the poll.

Emergence of Scientific Polling

Scientific polling began after World War I, inspired by the new field of business known as marketing research. After the war, demand for consumer goods rose, and American business, no longer engaged in the production of war materials, turned to satisfying consumer demand. Businesses used marketing research to identify what consumers wanted and, perhaps more important, how products would be packaged so consumers would buy them. For example, the American Tobacco Company changed from a green to a white package during World War II because it found that a white package was more attractive to women smokers.[37]

Also important to the development of scientific polling was the application of mathematical principles of probability. To check the rates of defects in manufactured products, random or spot inspections of a few items, called a sample, were made. From these, projections of defects among the entire group of items could be made. From this use of sampling, it was a small step to conclude that sampling a small number of individuals could provide information about a larger population.

In the early 1930s, George Gallup and several others, using probability-based sampling techniques, began polling opinions on a wide scale. In 1936, Gallup predicted that the *Literary Digest* would be wrong and that Roosevelt would be reelected with 55.7% of the vote. Roosevelt received 62.5%.

Increasingly, polls were used by government. In 1940, Roosevelt became the first president to use polls on a regular basis, employing a social scientist to measure trends in public opinion about the war in Europe. Most major American universities have a unit that does survey research, and there are hundreds of commercial marketing research firms, private pollsters, and newspaper polls.

Polls and Politics

For politicians, polls have become what the oracle of Delphi was to the ancient Greeks and Merlin was to King Arthur: a divine source of wisdom. In the recent budget debate with President Clinton, Republicans used polls that told them that promising to "put the government on a diet" would be popular. Polls directed Clinton to counter by accusing the Republicans of trying to cut Medicare. When the media wanted to make sense out of the debate, they conducted still more polls.[38]

John Kennedy commissioned 16 polls during his three years as president. Richard Nixon conducted 233 over six years in the White House. Bill Clinton spent $4.5 million on polls in his first two and a half years in office, enough to buy 150 polls.[39] In addition, members of Congress, state officeholders, political parties, political candidates, and media poll. The number of polls is staggering.

Pollsters can conduct a poll at a moment's notice and have the results within a few hours. But can polls be taken at face value?

On clearly defined issues that the public has thought about carefully and on which they hold strong views, such as how they will vote in tomorrow's election, a well-designed poll can accurately reflect the winner. For example, the average results in six major polls in 1992 showed 44% for Clinton, 37% for Bush, and 15% for Perot. The actual vote was 43% for Clinton, 38% for Bush, and 19% for Perot.[40] The polls correctly gauged Clinton's and Bush's support but underrepresented Perot's vote. Some Perot voters may have been excluded from pollsters' estimates of likely voters if they did not vote in recent elections. Some may have been unwilling to acknowledge their support for Perot because of the stigma attached to voting for third party candidates. Others may have shifted to Perot at the last minute owing to his election eve media blitz and were missed by the polls.[41]

On issues that the public has not thought much about and where choices are less clearly defined, polls rarely provide a meaningful guide to what the public thinks. Poll results on the appeal of Steve Forbes jumped up and down when he was seeking the Republican nomination in early 1996, when voters did not know much about him.

Even when issues are well defined and opinions are fairly stable, it is increasingly difficult to obtain a sample that provides a representative picture of public opinion. Many respondents refuse to be interviewed,[42] some because they do not want to be bothered, others because they fear they will be asked to buy something or contribute money. Nonrespondents, those who refuse or cannot be reached, number from one-half to two-thirds of those called, and these people are more likely to be better educated, more affluent, and live in suburbs rather than cities and rural areas.[43] The result is a distorted and biased picture.

Another problem for pollsters is the tendency of some respondents to express an opinion when they do not have one. No one wants to appear ignorant. Some respondents volunteer an answer even though they know little or nothing about a subject. The problem is getting worse as pollsters increasingly probe topics on which the public has no opinion and on which there is little reason to believe it should. For example, pollsters have asked whether the public thought President Reagan's colon cancer was serious and whether the bloody glove originally fit O.J. Simpson.[44]

Although polls can be biased because of these problems, some pollsters and politicians consciously distort poll results. Today, many pollsters come from political consulting backgrounds and poll exclusively for members of one political party. Rather than provide accurate information about public opinion, their

SLOP Surveys Are Sloppy Surveys

SLOP is an acronym for self-selected listener opinion polls. SLOP surveys are telephone call-in polls used increasingly by radio and television stations and even by newspapers. Why attach such a negative label to call-in polls? The answer is simple: The results are meaningless because those who call in do not reflect the views of the general public.

An example was CBS's survey to gauge public reaction to President Bush's 1992 State of the Union address. The program allowed viewers to dial and then respond to a series of recorded questions by pushing buttons on their telephone. The views of more than 300,000 respondents were recorded. In an effort to measure representativeness, CBS, at the same time, conducted a survey of 1,241 adults. A comparison of the two polls revealed that the results differed by 10% or more on seven of the nine questions. One question asked whether respondents were better off or worse off than four years ago. In the call-in poll, 54% said they were worse off, compared to 32% in the scientific survey. Viewers who felt they were worse off called in greater proportions than viewers who felt they were better off. In other words, viewers who are more angered or concerned may be more likely to use their telephones to express their opinions.

Another problem with call-in polls is that people can call in more than once. *Parade* magazine conducted a call-in poll on abortion and received more than 300,000 responses. It later acknowledged that 21 percent of the callers may have voiced their opinion more than once. Obviously, if the views of some people are counted two or more times, the results will not be representative of the general public.

Despite these problems, SLOP surveys are likely to continue. As one pollster put it, ". . . it's a good show. And who's going to give up a good show just for the truth?"

Sources: Richard Morin, "Another Contribution to SLOPpy Journalism," *Washington Post National Weekly Edition,* February 10, 1992, p. 38. Richard Morin, "Numbers from Nowhere: The Hoax of the Call-in 'Polls,' " *Washington Post,* February 9, 1992, p. B3.

Harry Truman exults in incorrect headlines, based on poll results and early returns, the morning after the 1948 election.

goal is to present their client in the most favorable light.[45]

An example of misuse is the "push poll." A pollster asks whether the person called is for John Jones, Mary Smith, or undecided in the upcoming congressional election. If the answer is Smith or undecided, the person is asked: "If your were told that Smith's hobby is driving a high-powered sports car at dangerous speeds through residential neighborhoods and seeing how many children and pets she can run over, would that make a difference in your vote?" You are asked your preference again. The idea is to see if certain "information" can "push" voters away from the opposition candidate or a neutral opinion toward support for the candidate favored by those doing the poll.[46] Learning the weaknesses of the opposition has always been a part of politics, but push polls seek to manipulate, rarely focus on a candidate's issue positions, and often distort a candidate's record and the facts.

An even more vicious tactic is to pump thousands of calls into a district or state under the guise of conducting a poll but with the intent of spreading false information about a candidate.[47] Steve Forbes accused the Dole campaign of spreading false information under the guise of a poll when both were campaigning for the Republican presidential nomination in Iowa. Both the push poll and the phony poll are corruptions of the political process as well as violations of polling ethics.

In spite of problems and abuses, polls still provide a valuable service to the nation. If direct democracy of the New England town meeting type is the ideal, the use of public opinion polls is about as close as the modern state is likely to get to it. Polls help interpret the meaning of elections. When voters cast their ballots for one candidate over another, all anyone knows for sure is that a majority preferred one candidate. Polls can help reveal what elections mean in terms of policy preferences, and thus help make the government more responsive to voters. For example,

New Populism

Teledemocracy: If Politicians Can't Do the Job, Can We?

Many Americans believe that politicians are out of touch with the realities of today's world. Working and middle-class people with jobs feel they are working harder but falling further behind. Men with high school educations are, on average, less well off than their parents' generation. White men resent affirmative action and the opportunities it offers, but women and minorities know that despite affirmative action they still have not attained equality in the workplace. Families need two incomes, and maybe more, to stay even with increasing demands. The poor are falling further behind. "Being middle class used to mean you were comfortable. Today being middle class means you're scared."[1]

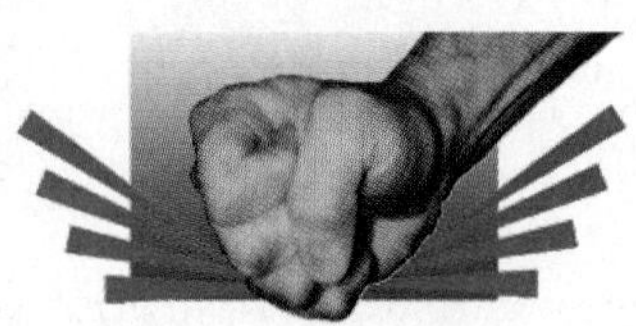

These feelings have several political manifestations. In 1992, they stimulated Ross Perot to run for president and enabled Bill Clinton to win. In 1994, they helped the Republicans take over Congress. They lend support to calls for term limits. And they have encouraged consideration of "teledemocracy," which is a name for many different versions of electronic town meetings. Teledemocracy is a new populist idea because it assumes that we would be better off if we bypassed our political leaders and made government decisions ourselves. Indeed, as one commentator argues, "nostalgia is growing for a high-tech update of Athenian democracy or of . . . townspeople gathered around a cast-iron stove in rural Vermont."[2]

Town meetings have indeed been a tradition of many New England towns for 350 years. They are an exercise in direct democracy: Citizens in a local community come together to discuss public issues and make local laws.

During the 1992 presidential election campaign, Ross Perot talked about the possibility of an electronic town meeting in which everyone in the nation could be part of a discussion and preference vote on some policy. His idea was to link Americans electronically. During the campaign, he had a satellite broadcast that linked rallies in six different states. Participants could hear one another cheer as Perot spoke to them from Florida. President Clinton employed a similar format when he participated in a televised question-and-answer session with citizens in four cities. Citizens in television studios in Atlanta, Miami, and Seattle could interact directly with the president in a Detroit studio.

"Teledemocracy" would go a long way toward transforming our representative democracy into a direct democracy. The president, or perhaps the leadership of Congress or the political parties, would identify a problem such as the deficit or health care reform. Then the president, the Cabinet secretaries, members of Congress, policy experts, or even ordinary citizens would lay out the arguments, pro and con, and ask Americans to register their preferences by pushing a button. Although their preferences would not be binding, elected politicians would probably feel tremendous pressure to follow them as though they were.

If the technology existed to do it—which it does not yet—would teledemocracy be a good idea? Perot—and

President Reagan interpreted his election and reelection to mean voters wanted less government. However, polls suggested that voters simply lacked confidence in his opponent, President Carter in 1980 and Walter Mondale in 1984. There was little evidence that voters wanted less government. Similarly, the Republicans claimed their victory in the 1994 congressional elections was an indication that voters supported the party's "Contract with America," but polls showed that most Americans had never heard of it (see You Are There, Chapter 6).

Polls, however, also have a down side. Their standing in the polls may discourage otherwise viable candidates from entering a race, leaving the field to others with less of a chance of winning or who lack the skills necessary to govern effectively. George Bush's standing in the polls in January 1991, at the start of the Gulf War, made him appear a sure winner in the 1992 presidential election. Several prominent Democrats chose not to seek the presidency in 1992, leaving the field to others and limiting voters' choice.

Others have suggested that polling has changed the nature of political campaigns. Prior to polling, the purpose of campaigns was to reveal the candidates' views on the issues and their solutions to the pressing problems of the day. Instead, polls focus attention on the electorate and what they think. Polls find out what the voters want, and the candidates develop images to suit the market.

Newt Gingrich too—envisions it as a cure for government gridlock and the influence of special interests. The idea that citizens might bypass the machinery of representative democracy and directly influence government decisions has a gut-level appeal, especially if government is not responding quickly to problems facing the country. Teledemocracy appeals to those Americans who are displeased by the processes of modern democracy, including lobbying and compromise. However, most issues that cause gridlock do so because they are difficult and complex and have no easy solutions. There are not just two options, for example, to solving our health care problems. Dozens or more decisions need to be made, each involving complex options. How could these be explained in a short television program? Legislative bills are often hundreds of pages long with many complex provisions.

The Founders' fear of a tyrannical majority moved by passion led them to create a representative democracy with checks and balances to ensure that decisions would be filtered and made deliberately rather than hastily. Checks and balances guard against popular whims and demagoguery while protecting minority rights. A long process of writing, rewriting, and amending legislation contributes, in many cases, to better legislation that takes into account the complex interests of society. Bills passed without taking account of minority viewpoints or complex issues can be very bad bills. As one political scientist notes, "Look at history. The reality of human experience is that emotional responses have turned to utter tragedy time and time again." It was Hitler, after all, who pioneered the electronic referendum, using radio broadcasts to drum up votes to support his rise to power.

Proponents like Perot and Gingrich believe that teledemocracy would increase participation. It could stimulate interest and get people to think about alternatives and trade-offs involved in choosing one policy rather than another.

Yet rates of participation were low in an early experiment with electronic democracy at the local level. It is likely that the same interested, educated people who participate in politics now would be the major participants in teledemocracy. And of course, not everyone has a computer to participate in teledemocracy. There is now about one computer for every ten adults,[3] a figure likely to grow substantially. Still, the poor are clearly at a disadvantage in this sort of voting system.

This vision of an electronic national referendum is perhaps extreme. However, in other respects, direct democracy is already here. Citizens are wired to Washington through public opinion polls, talk radio, faxes, phones, and e-mail. From C-SPAN's studios just off Capitol Hill, lawmakers chat with callers live—including those who have been monitoring lawmakers' activities via the C-SPAN cameras. More messages pass through the Beltway barrier than ever before, and politicians pay attention to them.

Judging from what we already have, more direct democracy is unlikely to moderate middle-class anger. It may make it worse. Intensely held opinions unfiltered by the political process lead to dubious laws that do not address real issues. For example, "three strikes and you're out" was created by talk radio and won support in the White House and Congress through telephone polls, talk shows, and faxes. It is unlikely to affect crime, but is likely to further frustrate citizens with government when they find that in spite of "three strikes" laws crime is still a major problem.

1. "Why Are We So Angry," *U.S. News and World Report* (November 7, 1994), p. 31.
2. Kevin Phillips, "Virtual Washington," *Time,* Spring 1995, p. 60.
3. Ibid., p. 65.

The ease of polling also means that judgment and leadership have given way to the sentiments expressed in public opinion polls. Politicians rarely make a decision without one. Rather than educate the public regarding the merits of particular policies, politicians seem to follow the polls blindly.

For example, when Rodney King, a black man who was stopped for speeding, was beaten by four white police officers in Los Angeles in 1992, the incident created a furor, and when the officers' first trial resulted in a verdict of not guilty, it led to a riot. President Bush was in a quandary about what to do. His aides were divided. Some said he should give speeches emphasizing the need for racial harmony, and some said he should propose programs providing urban renewal for big cities. But others said he should do neither. So he tried to follow the polls. At first, he defended the police and called their chief "an American hero." After the first trial he declared, "The system has worked." But in a couple of days, he said he was "stunned" and felt "a deep sense of personal frustration and anguish" from the verdict. As the public changed their responses in the polls, he changed his messages to the public. Ultimately, analysis of the polls showed no clear mandate, so Bush did not do anything except approve some emergency aid to cope with the destruction from the riots.[48]

Focus Groups: Measuring or Manipulating Public Opinion?

Ever wonder where the ideas for political ads come from? Many come from people like you, meeting in focus groups. A focus group is a dozen or so ordinary people who are brought together to share their opinions on everything from grocery products to television sitcoms. They are also used by political candidates to examine voters' attitudes. Focus group leaders ask questions such as, "If George Bush came to your house for dinner, what would you talk about?" or "If the candidate were a color, what would he be?" Sessions are taped and consultants spend hours poring over every word and gesture in an effort to find out what is on voters' minds.

Unlike in public opinion polls, the samples are not drawn scientifically, nor is a great deal of time spent ensuring that questions used to measure opinions are fair and unbiased. The only requirement is that participants feel comfortable enough with each other to share their thoughts. It is considered risky to mix people of different social characteristics, for example, blue- with white-collar workers, blacks with whites, even men with women. According to Bill Clinton's pollster, "The key to a focus group is homogeneity. The more homogeneity, the more revealing."

A 1985 episode from Macomb County, Michigan, a region of predominantly white suburbs with many "Reagan Democrats," illustrates the point. After years of winning elections, the Democrats hired a pollster to conduct focus groups to find out why, in the 1980s, they began losing. He found white, middle-class Democrats turning away from the party because of race. These Democratic defectors saw hiring preferences for blacks as a threat to their own livelihoods and the black-majority city of Detroit as a "sinkhole" for their tax dollars. Each group listened to a quotation from Robert Kennedy exhorting whites to honor their "special obligation" to blacks. Virtually every participant reacted angrily. One said, "I can't go along with that." Another remarked, "No wonder they killed him."

The findings are somewhat unexpected because public opinion polls reflect a different picture. The hostility toward affirmative action and spending for minorities would not have been revealed in a mixed group, nor is it likely that the depth of feeling would have been reflected in a public opinion poll. Yes–no–I don't know answers in public opinion polls reveal the substance but not the texture of public opinion. Feelings censored from public comments often rise to the surface in focus groups. These feelings are likely to come into play when people vote.

The 1992 presidential campaigns used more focus groups than ever. Every ad was tested with a focus group. The Clinton campaign began holding focus groups in New Hampshire even before the candidate announced. Personal responsibility and welfare reform, centrist themes from Clinton's earlier days, bombed when tested in focus groups. With high unemployment and depressed real estate values, New Hampshire residents did not want to hear about personal responsibility. And instead of viewing welfare recipients as freeloaders, they recognized them as people who lost their jobs to the recession and could no longer make it—people very much like themselves. In response to this information, Clinton abandoned his message and developed a new one, tailored to New Hampshire.

Between New Hampshire and the convention, the Clinton campaign convened focus groups at every major crisis. When Paul Tsongas challenged him, focus groups directed the campaign to contrast Tsongas's theme of sacrifice with Clinton's "people first" message. When Jerry Brown rose in the polls, focus groups revealed that the campaign should confront him on the issues rather than on his image as "Governor Moonbeam." Focus groups were behind the idea to profile Clinton's humble beginnings at the Democratic National Convention. His Georgetown, Yale, and Oxford education had given many voters the impression that he was a Bush-style blue-blood.

On the Republican side, focus groups pushed the campaign to capitalize on voters' image of Clinton as a "slick politician." Focus groups revealed Barbara Bush as one of Bush's positives, so she was profiled during the Republican National Convention.

Focus group participants invariably come away with a sense of empowerment, a feeling that someone is genuinely interested in their opinions. Most forget what they suspected at the beginning, that they are being used for the $50 fee. To be sure, politicians are interested in their opinions, but not to make the system more responsive to them. Rather, politicians use their opinions to produce a potent message that will influence their vote. As a former Perot pollster put it, "They're the guinea pigs allowing us to exploit the electorate."

Source: Elizabeth Kolbert, "Test-Marketing a President," *The New York Times Magazine,* August 30, 1992, p. 18.

As the number of polls, both good and bad ones, continues to increase, their importance for the public as well as those who want the information they provide may decline. A leading pollster makes the point that the sheer number of polls may lead everyone to take them less seriously. If polls show public opinion to bounce around, preventing an accurate reading on some issues, it may call into question results where polls can provide a more reliable measure of what the public thinks. And if all politicians are driven by poll results, no one will gain political advantage from information provided by them.[49]

➤How Informed Is Public Opinion?

Many Americans are uninformed or misinformed concerning government and politics. Only one-fourth can name their two senators,[50] and only one-third can name their U.S. representative.[51] More than one-third do not know the party of their representative,[52] and 40% do not know which party controls Congress.[53]

Many Americans are unable to identify prominent political personalities. (See Table 1.) Six years after he was elected vice president, 23% could not identify George Bush. More people can identify the judge on the television show "The People's Court" than can identify the Chief Justice of the United States.[54] In spite of increases in education, levels of knowledge regarding politics have not changed much since the 1940s.[55]

Only a small percentage of Americans can identify a single piece of legislation passed by Congress.[56] Nearly 60% are ignorant of a plan passed by the House of Representatives in 1995 to balance the federal budget.[57]

Misperception regarding government policies is widespread. While polls show Americans in favor of reducing the size of the federal government, seven out of ten are unaware that the number of federal employees has decreased in recent years.[58] Seven out of ten feel that the country spends too much on foreign aid, and two out of three say the country should cut spending on foreign aid. However, one-half estimate foreign aid to be about 15 times greater than it is. Asked what an appropriate spending level would be, the average answer is 8 times more than the country actually spends. Thus, 70% think the country spends too much on foreign aid but many would support an amount substantially higher.[59]

TABLE 1 Political Ignorance of the Public

	PERCENTAGE UNABLE TO IDENTIFY
Who is in Washington:	
Vice president	40
Speaker of the House	46
Their Senate representatives	54
Majority leader in Senate	66
Their House representative	67
What goes on in Washington:	
That the number of federal employees decresed in past three years	72
That the government spends more on Medicare than on foreign aid	73
That the House passed a plan to balance the budget	75
That the Senate passed a plan to balance the budget	78

Source: Richard Morin, "Tuned Out, Turned Off," Washington Post National Weekly Edition February 5–11, 1996), pp. 6–8.

Another example of Americans not knowing what they think they know is the 24% who agreed and 19% who disagreed that the Public Affairs Act of 1975 should be repealed. The problem is that they offered an opinion on something that does not exist.[60] The question was a ploy to see how many would volunteer an answer when they have no opinion.

Most Americans do not think much about politics. Their major concerns are family and work. Lack of concern for government means that politicians can sometimes ignore what the public wants and what it needs. That is, politicians can be less responsive to the public.

Although the public may not pay much attention to politics and is uninformed on many things, some political scientists argue that average citizens know what they like and dislike and can make sound political judgments on this basis.[61] Most do take a more active interest in politics when they see their personal situation directly affected. Eighty percent know that Congress passed a law requiring employers to provide family leave following the birth of a child or a family emergency. Family leave touches people directly.

Americans may know what they like and dislike, but lack of knowledge and information about government and politics compromises their ability to make sound judgments. Polls show that less politically knowledgeable Americans find it difficult to sort through the claims and counterclaims of politicians to determine which policies are in their best interest. Some support candidates and policies that work against their self-interest.[62]

Adding to the problem are public officials who fail to educate the public on issues. Politicians often do not like to discuss issues, especially controversial ones. When they do, public awareness increases. After President Reagan made an issue of American support for the Nicaraguan contras, for example, awareness of the issue and the side the United States was supporting jumped from 25% to 59%.[63]

PUBLIC OPINION

Public opinion polls cover virtually every aspect of American life. Polls have reported the number of California drivers with paraphernalia hanging from their rearview mirrors and Iowans with ornaments on their lawns. Political polls examine opinions about political issues and political candidates, whether the American people are liberal or conservative, and whether this influences their positions on issues and preferences for political candidates. Although it is important to know how Americans stand on current issues and how they feel about political candidates, it is also important to know what they think about government: its founding principles, political institutions, and political leaders. This is especially true in a time when the media are filled with discussions of voter anger at government.

We begin by discussing ideology, what it is, what the labels liberal and conservative mean, and whether Americans identify themselves as liberal or conservative. We then look at how ideology relates to opinions on specific issues such as social welfare, social issues, and race. We also explore how ideology is related to political tolerance, whether Americans are willing to extend rights and liberties to individuals who do not share their opinions. Finally, we look at trust in government: Do Americans trust their government to do the right thing, and are liberals more trusting than conservatives?

Ideology

The term **ideology** refers to a highly organized and coherent set of opinions. In the extreme, one who is ideological takes a position on all issues consistent with his or her ideology. *Liberalism* and *conservatism* are terms used to describe the current major ideologies in American politics. Liberals are sometimes identified by the label "left," and conservatives by the label "right."

A **liberal** is someone who believes in a national government active in domestic policies, providing help to individuals and communities in areas such as health, education, and welfare. In the New Deal era of Roosevelt, liberalism was seen as a way to use government authority to expand opportunities and improve the quality of life for all. With this as their platform, the Democrats came to power in the 1930s and dominated American politics through the 1960s. Since the 1960s, liberalism has been identified with some less popular policies, particularly the civil rights policies of the Democrats. These policies threatened the white-dominated social order in the South and white ethnic communities in the North. Blacks increased their support of the Democratic Party, and many whites, especially in the South, increased their support of the Republican Party. The term was also linked to the anti-Vietnam protests and to Supreme Court decisions that expanded the rights of persons accused of crimes, legalized abortion, and barred mandatory prayers in public schools.

A **conservative** is someone who believes that the domestic role of government should be minimized and that individuals are responsible for their own well-being. However, conservatives often support increases in military spending and recently, the label has also been attached to those, often affiliated with fundamentalist religions, who favor government action banning abortions and approving mandatory school prayers.

To what extent are Americans ideological? Do the ideological labels liberal and conservative describe the opinions of the American people? One way to find out whether a person is liberal or conservative is to ask. The greatest percentage of Americans opt for the middle, identifying themselves as moderate or centrist. Comparing the percentage of liberals to conservatives reveals conservatives to be slightly more numerous. These distributions have changed very little in the past 15 years.

Self-identifications are helpful, but one cannot be sure that individuals actually know what the label means or that they support the positions identified with the label. To determine whether the labels distinguish Americans in terms of issue positions, we need to look at specific issues.

On a number of issues liberals and conservatives take different positions. However, on most issues a majority of liberals and conservatives take the same position. On social welfare issues, for example, most liberals and conservatives endorse increased spending for health care, education, the environment, and to combat drugs. Majorities of liberals and conservatives have similar feelings on issues of race and are supportive of civil liberties for all Americans whether or not they share their views. Both tend to agree on the failings of the government. All of this means that most Americans are not very ideological. While many call themselves liberals and conservatives, these groups do not represent cohesive blocs of citizens with opposing issue positions seeking to control the government to enact their position into law.

Why aren't Americans more ideological? First, we are not very interested in politics. Much of what we find important in life falls outside of politics. We are concerned about our families and jobs, which for most are not directly and immediately affected by government. Lack of interest leads to lack of intensity. Even where majorities of liberals and conservatives disagree—as, for example, on abortion, prayer in school, and busing—feelings of most are not very intense, perhaps because most are not touched by these issues.

Second, political candidates and parties do not usually mobilize their followings with ideological or issue appeals. Both candidates and parties try to be all things to all people, for reasons we will discuss more fully in Chapter 6, and often blunt the ideological or issue content of their message in order to attract support from both the right and the left.

Nonetheless, our political leaders of both parties are more ideological than the rank and file. Obviously political leaders are more interested in politics, and this contributes to the intensity of their feelings. And while a few years ago scholars talked of "the end of ideology," today they remark on its increase in American political debates.

Social Welfare and the Proper Role of Government

Government programs to help individuals deal with economic hardship started during the Great Depression in the 1930s. These included programs to provide aid for the elderly (Social Security), unemployed, and poor (Aid to Dependent Children). Most Americans supported government assistance of this kind in the 1930s and support it today.

Still, Americans have mixed feelings about social welfare spending (see Figure 2). Support is high for Social Security and for helping the poor. About half feel that the nation is spending too little to assist the poor and poor children, and slightly fewer think we spend too little on Social Security.[64] Nearly 85% favored provisions of the Clinton health care plan that would have subsidized medical costs for the low-income and unemployed.

On the other hand, support for "welfare," especially Aid to Dependent Children, is much lower. Polls show most (60% to 80%) support reforms that would require persons on welfare to work and get off welfare after two years. Over 50% feel, however, that it is unfair for the government to cut off payments after two years if there is no other source of income. Most Americans (75%) believe the answer to welfare is job training and are willing to pay more in the short term to provide it. Americans appear to favor helping the poor, but they do not like "welfare," which for decades has been the target of both government officials and the media. They believe that requiring work and training for jobs is the key to welfare reform.

Americans approve increased spending for education, health care, the environment, drug rehabilitation, and crime and law enforcement. For example, two-thirds favor increased spending for improving and protecting the nation's health. Although less than a majority, sizable numbers favor increases in spending for the nation's highways and bridges, mass transportation, and parks and recreation. Only small minorities, less than 10%, oppose additional funding in these areas.

In spite of these sentiments, Americans think their taxes are too high. Seventy-six percent favor a middle-class tax cut. Forty-one percent prefer fewer services to reduce taxes, while only 20% say the government should provide more services and increase taxes.

Consistent with Republican goals to devolve functions of government from the national to state levels, 75% want the states to take over many of the responsibilities performed by the national government.[65] Only 12% say that the national government does the best job of spending tax dollars in an efficient and constructive manner. Thirty-two percent say that state governments do the best job.

The preference for state over national government is linked to lack of confidence in the national government.

Complaints include that the government wastes money, spends too much on the wrong things, takes too long to solve problems, and offers ineffective solutions to problems. It is possible (indeed likely) that the greater visibility of the national government compared to state governments in turn leads to this relative lack of confidence. If our state legislatures were covered by television to the extent that Congress is, it is probable the evaluations by the public would be quite different.

Americans have not, however, given up on the national government. They want it managed better and want to see better performance from government employees. Few want to see the government made smaller by cutting spending and programs.

Social Issues

Beginning in the 1960s, so-called social issues have been important sources of political debate. These issues generally relate to family, school, and church. More specifically, they include opinions on abortion, prayer in public schools, restrictions on pornography, tolerance of homosexuals, crime, and the role of women in society.

Social issues have led to a clash of values between those seeking to preserve traditional moral standards and those seeking to establish new ones. Many Americans feel that government policy has encouraged the decline in moral standards and increased permissiveness. Spurred by a rising crime rate in the 1960s and 1970s, Americans felt increasingly that the courts were not being severe enough with criminals. Forty-eight percent responded that the courts were not harsh enough with criminals in 1965; 86% felt this way in 1993.[66] Increasing numbers of Americans, 59% in 1993, were also willing to endorse the death penalty for murder.[67]

The position of liberals and conservatives on social issues is opposite of what it is on social welfare. On social welfare issues, liberals are likely to support government action, but on social issues they are more likely to reject government involvement. Liberals generally prefer to leave questions of religious belief and sexual morality to individuals to decide for themselves, while conservatives are more willing to call upon government to enforce particular standards of behavior.

Conservatives, for example, are more likely to favor a ban on abortion and to require prayer in public schools (see Figure 3). They are more willing to support capital punishment. Conservatives are considerably more likely than liberals to respond that homosexual relations are always wrong and somewhat more likely to subscribe to the traditional roles for women. For example, conservatives are more likely to feel that women should take care of the home and leave running the country to men.

Liberals and conservatives do not differ on all social issues, however. They are similar in their attitudes

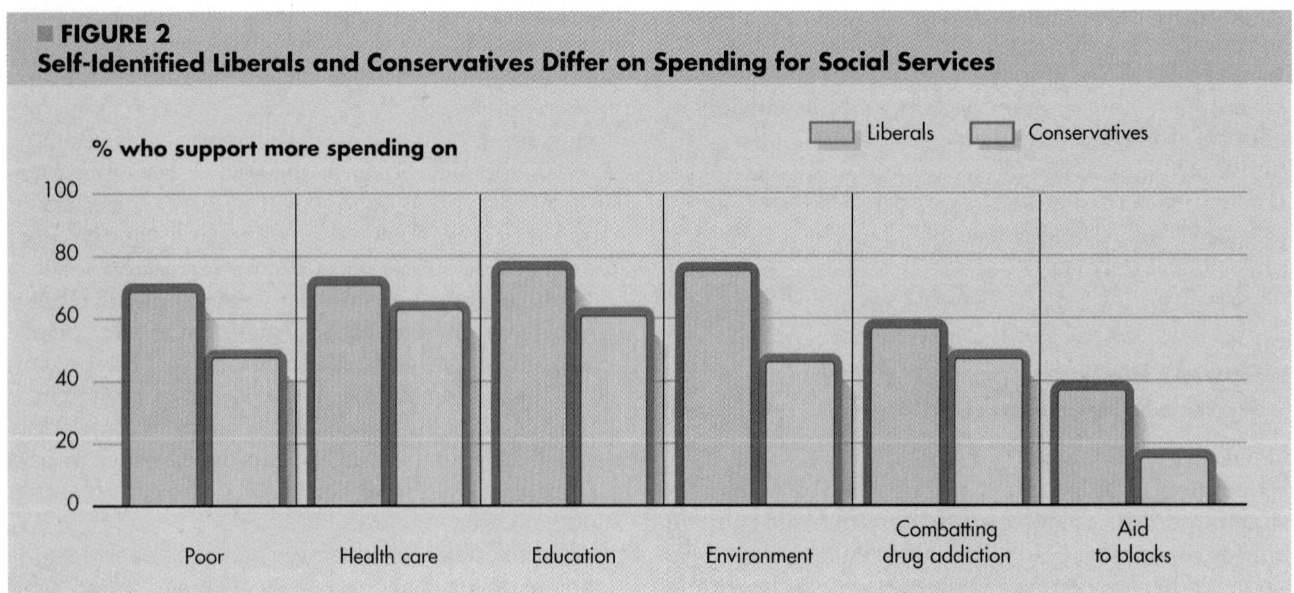

Source: 1993 General Social survey.

FIGURE 3
Self-Identified Liberals and Conservatives Differ on Social Issues

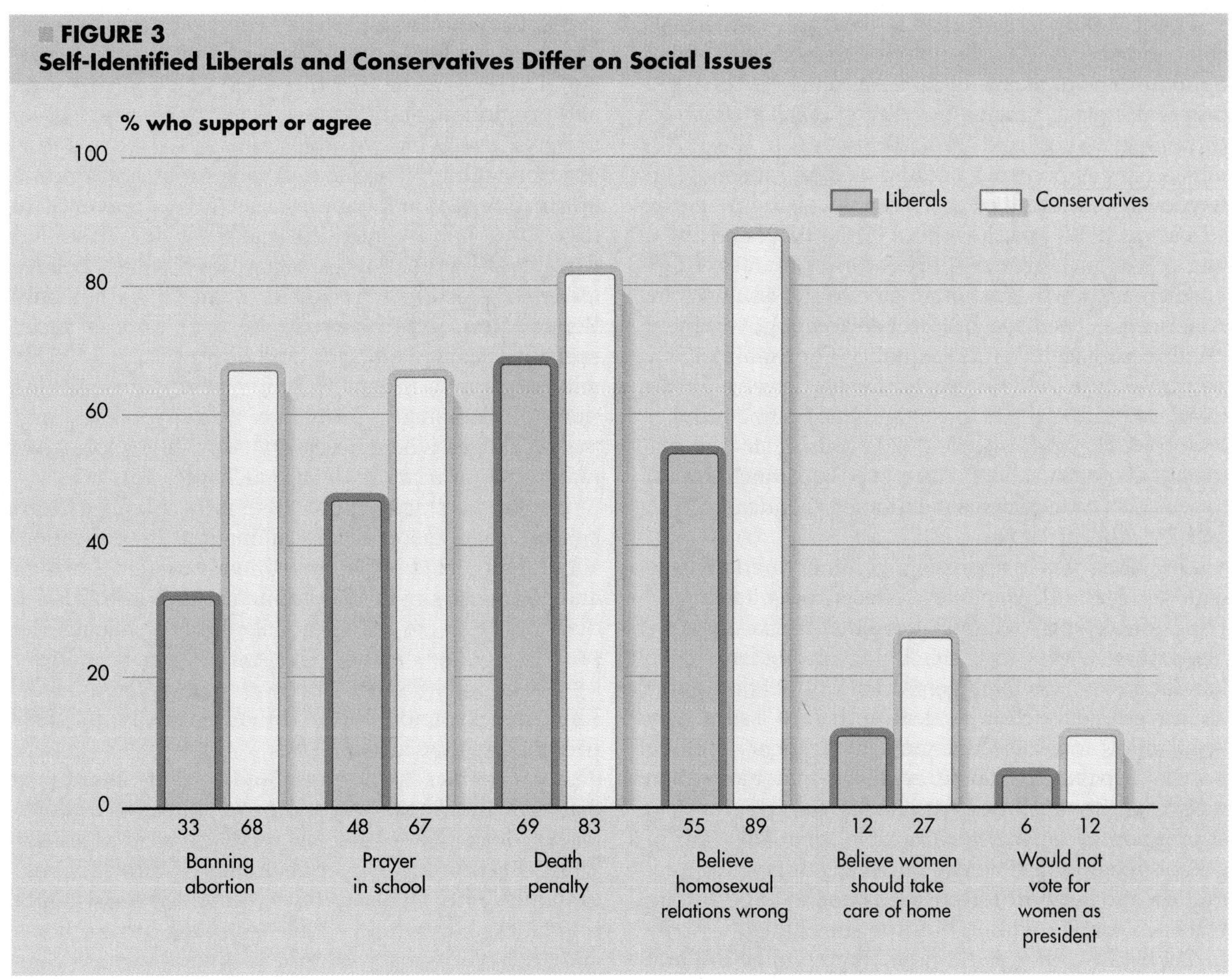

Source: 1993 General Social Survey.

about whether they would vote for a woman president; a high percentage of both liberals and conservatives say they would. Nor is there much difference between them in their strong support for the death penalty.

Race

Public opinion has influenced as well as responded to the progress of the black struggle for equality. Although the historical record extends to colonial times, the polling record begins in the 1940s. It shows white America increasingly opposed to discrimination and segregation, at least in principle.[68] In fact, the change might be characterized as revolutionary. For example, whereas only one-third accepted the idea of black and white children going to the same schools in 1942, in the 1980s more than 90% approved. The percentage believing that whites do not have a right to keep blacks out of their neighborhood has nearly doubled since 1963, and a 1989 survey found that only one-third of white Americans live in all-white neighborhoods, and two-thirds claim they have a fairly close friend who is black (80% of blacks claim they have a fairly close white friend).[69] Thirty-eight percent were against laws forbidding intermarriage in 1963; 79% were opposed in 1990.[70]

Only 37% expressed a willingness to vote for a black candidate for president in 1958; in 1986, 86% expressed such willingness. These findings suggest that white America is becoming much more tolerant of racial diversity. Although the North continues to be more supportive of black rights than the South, whites in both regions show increased acceptance of blacks.

Public opinion can change because individuals change or because older individuals with one set of opinions are replaced by a new generation with a different set. Changes in whites' racial opinions through 1960 occurred for both reasons. In the 1970s, most changes occurred because of replacement. Difference in socialization between those born in the 1920s and 1930s and those born in the 1950s and 1960s has led to much greater support for racial integration.

There is, however, another side to the issue. White America has been much slower to accept government initiatives to achieve racial equality. For example, 38% approved the federal government's ensuring fair treatment for blacks in jobs in 1964; the same number endorsed the idea in the 1970s. Busing to achieve racial balance in schools has never had much appeal to whites. Thirteen percent endorsed the idea in 1972, and 25% did in 1986.

Unwillingness to endorse government initiatives to end segregation sometimes reflects racist feelings.[71] For example, most whites believe that blacks are more likely than whites to prefer living on welfare, to be lazy, and to be less intelligent.[72] Lack of white support for government action to deal with race issues may also reflect an objection to government's telling people what to do. Some evidence that more than racism is involved is that blacks too are far less supportive of busing, for example, than they are of school integration. The gap between support for integration and support for busing is not as large among blacks as among whites, but it is substantial.[73]

There are other indications that whites are not necessarily motivated by racism when they will not support government initiatives to end segregation. Since 1966, 90% or more of whites have indicated a willingness to send their children to a school where a few blacks attend, and 80% have been willing to send their children to a school where half of the students are black, a substantial increase since 1958, when only 50% were willing. Most white Americans have no objection to a black living next door or to a family member bringing a black guest to dinner (see Figure 4). Although a small minority still find it difficult to accept blacks and be close to them, by most measures a majority of white Americans do not have this problem. Even where whites would be a minority—a school or neighborhood with mostly blacks—half report it would not bother them.[74]

A third reason that white Americans are reluctant to accept government intervention is that most have closed their eyes to the racial prejudice that still exists. Less than one-fourth of whites see the discrimination in education and housing. Only a small majority of whites recognize the discrimination in hiring and promotion, and they overwhelmingly reject racial preferences (even without quotas) to redress this discrimination.[75] Three out of four Americans oppose affirmative action programs that give preference to minorities and women to make up for past and current discrimination. A majority of whites believe affirmative action hurts white men.[76] It is not only Republicans and conservatives who oppose racial preferences, but Democrats and liberals as well.[77] This may explain President Clinton's pledge to examine the government's affirmative action policies and make changes where necessary (we will explore affirmative action in more detail in Chapter 15).

Blacks see things quite differently. About a third believe that there is discrimination in education, about half believe discrimination exists in housing and getting an unskilled job, and about two-thirds see discrimination in getting a skilled job or managerial position and equal pay.[78] The average black American sees discrimination in three or four of these areas. Thus, blacks and whites differ markedly in their perceptions that racism exists.

What do blacks believe should be done about race discrimination? Although the polling record for blacks does not extend as far back as it does for whites, blacks have overwhelmingly endorsed integration. Nearly all blacks have responded consistently that blacks and whites should go to the same schools and that blacks have a right to live anywhere they want to. Intermarriage is approved by three of four blacks.

Like whites, blacks have become somewhat less supportive of government initiatives. In 1964, 92% thought the national government should ensure blacks fair treatment in jobs; in 1974, 82% did. Support for government assistance in school integration has varied considerably, although in 1986 about the same proportion approved it as in 1964 (more than 80%). Some blacks fear that government initiatives will only antagonize whites. Others believe government aid hurts blacks by making them too dependent. Still others believe government is ineffective in bringing about an end to discrimination.

Self-identified liberals and conservatives also differ on race issues. Liberals are somewhat more likely to oppose laws that ban racial intermarriage, to disagree that whites have a right to keep blacks out of their neighborhood, and to accept sending their children to

FIGURE 4
Whites Have Grown More Accepting of Neighborhood Integration

Residential segregation is the lynchpin of racial separation in America. Such segregation influences the quality and nature of schools, employment opportunities, and the amenities of daily life. In the past twenty years, American cities have become somewhat less segregated, stimulated in part by whites changing attitudes about residential segregation.

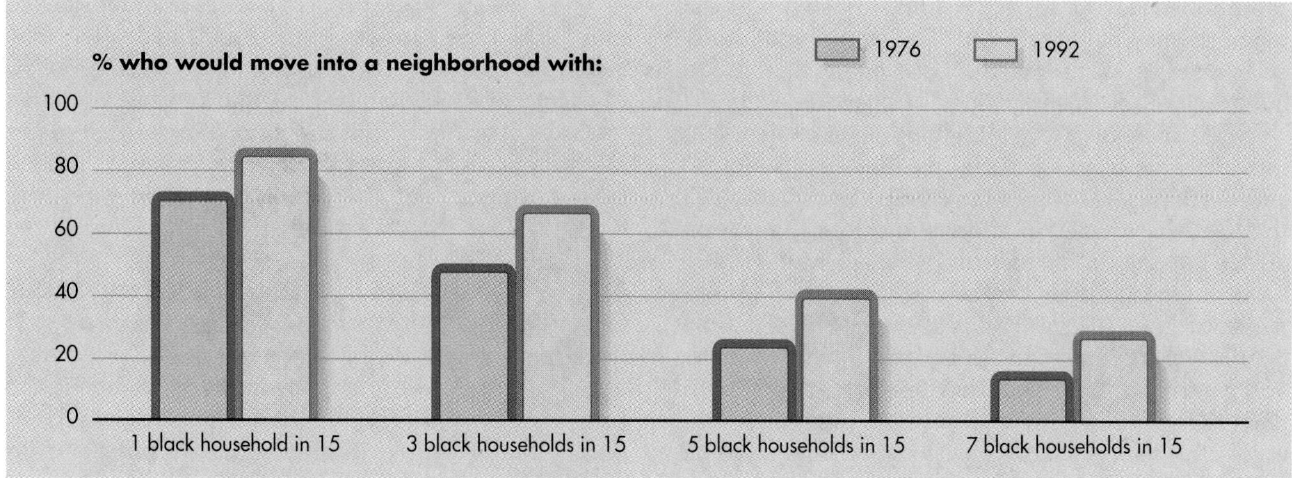

Source: Douglas Massey and Nance Denton, *American Apartheid* (Cambridge: Harvard University Press, 1993).

a school where most are a different race. They are also more likely to endorse busing and say they would vote for a black candidate for president. However, these differences are fairly small (except for attitudes toward busing they range from 5 to 9 percentage points), and majorities of both liberals and conservatives favor the proequality stance in all instances except busing.

Political Tolerance

Political tolerance is the willingness of individuals to extend procedural rights and liberties to people with whom they disagree. Tolerance is important because it embodies many elements essential to democratic government, such as freedom of speech and assembly.

J. William Fulbright, former senator from Arkansas, once said, "Americans believe in the right to free speech until someone tries to exercise it." In other words, people are tolerant in the abstract but not when called upon to support speakers they disagree with. More than 85% of Americans claim to believe in free speech for all,[79] yet a 1954 nationwide survey found that only 37% of the respondents would allow a person opposed to churches and religion to speak in their communities.[80] Even fewer would permit an admitted communist to speak. More highly educated people were more tolerant than those with less education, and political elites were more tolerant than the general public.

The finding that elites were more tolerant than the general public was reassuring. After all, many elites are in a position to deprive people of rights, and elites help shape public opinion. Later studies reveal, however, that elites are more tolerant than the general public largely because they are better educated. There is no "elite" distinction apart from education.[81] Elites, however, do influence the opinions of the general public on civil liberties. When elites agree among themselves, the general public is more likely to reflect this consensus.[82]

More recent studies suggest that Americans have become substantially more tolerant of communists, socialists, and atheists.[83] However, overall levels of tolerance may not have increased that much.

In the 1950s, people perceived communists and socialists as a major threat. As the perception of the threat diminished, so did people's fears. Research on tolerance, therefore, has first asked people which groups they dislike and then assessed their tolerance toward those groups.[84] Two-thirds or more thought that members of their least-liked group should be banned from being president and from teaching in the public schools. Many responded that the group should be outlawed, indicating a high degree of intolerance. On the other hand, in the 1970s, the public was more willing to allow their least-liked group to speak and teach than they were to allow communists to do so in 1954.[85] This suggests that tolerance may have increased. Thus, although intolerance remains, it seems that the public has grown more tolerant since the 1950s.

While increased levels of political tolerance since the 1950s are a reason to be positive, job insecurity and declining real wages have helped promote negative feelings toward minorities and immigrants and others outside the mainstream. A majority of whites, for example, agree that equal rights for racial minorities have gone too far. Eighty-two percent agree that people coming to live in the U.S. should be restricted and controlled more than they are now.[86] Such sentiments are not likely to lead to a loss of civil liberties unless political elites direct citizens' fears in an attempt to gain political advantage.

In general, liberals tend to be more tolerant than conservatives, at least toward communists, atheists, racists, and those who would support a military government. For example, in 1990, 74% of those who identified themselves as liberals in a national survey indicated a willingness to allow a communist to speak in their community; 66% of the conservatives took this position.[87]

Trust in Government

An important dimension of public opinion is the trust or support citizens have for their government, its institutions, its officials, and fellow citizens. With high levels of trust, citizens might do everything government demands. They would pay their taxes and, if called upon to do so, defend the government. They might also gullibly accept anything officials tell them. At low levels of trust, citizens would be more skeptical; they might even disobey the law. At the lowest levels, they might try to overthrow the government or commit violent acts against it, as with the Oklahoma City bombing. Thus, democratic government "depends on a fine balance between trust and distrust."[88]

Public trust of government has declined significantly in the last 30 years. In the early sixties, Americans were supportive of the government. A comparison of five nations—the United States, Britain, West Germany, Italy, and Mexico—found Americans to be the most positive about the responsiveness and performance of government; 95% of the Americans sampled pointed to the government when asked what aspects of the nation they were proud of.[89] The picture that emerged was one of trust and confidence.

The pattern, however, changed sometime in the mid-1960s. Trust in government declined after 1964 and continued to decline through 1980 (see Figure 5). The pattern was characteristic not only of opinions toward government but of opinions toward all major institutions in society, including the medical profession, business, and the press. Government responsiveness also was rated less positively during the 1960s and 1970s.

Why have levels of trust and confidence declined? One answer is the performance of government itself. In the mid to late 1960s, the nation was divided over a number of issues, including what to do about the war in Vietnam and the civil rights demands of blacks. Many people wanted the government to do everything possible to win the war in Vietnam, whereas others wanted an immediate withdrawal of U.S. forces; the Johnson and Nixon policies of limited and prolonged war were unresponsive to both sides.

The civil rights struggle also divided the nation. Some wanted government to do more to speed the progress of blacks and other minorities, whereas others

FIGURE 5
Trust in Government Declined During the 1960s and 1970s

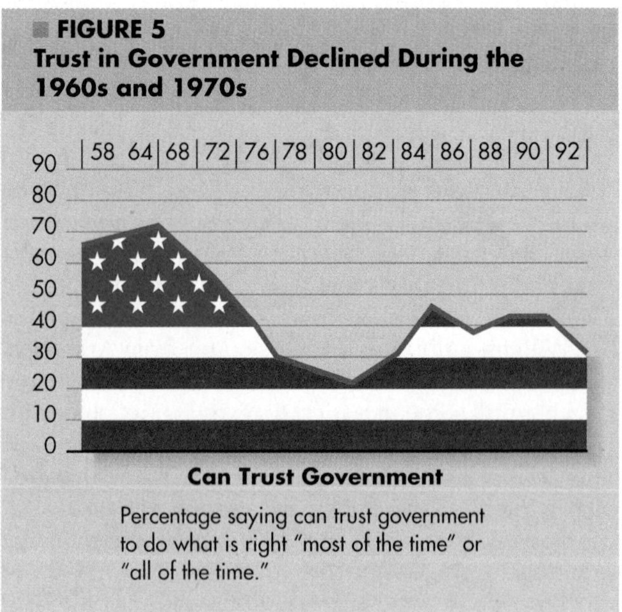

Percentage saying can trust government to do what is right "most of the time" or "all of the time."

Source: National Election Studies, the Center for Political Studies.

American Diversity

We Are Not Just Liberals and Conservatives

While liberalism and conservatism continue to be meaningful in American politics, social, economic, and technological changes are creating divisions that cut across traditional ideological lines. One analysis suggests that four cultural, two economic, and one foreign policy dimension define seven political groupings that are identified by the following labels: liberal activist, conservative activist, populist traditionalist, steward, dowager, ethnic conservative, and agnostic.

Liberal and conservative activists reflect the traditional ideological groupings. They represent about 35 percent of the population and the foundations of the Democratic and Republican parties. *Liberal activists* (20% of voters) believe prevention rather than punishment is the answer to crime. They are more concerned with rising prices than they are with the deficit or high taxes. They see the job of government as helping families achieve the American dream. They want to keep abortion legal and think more can be done to promote the rights of women and minorities. They oppose increases in military spending. They are predominantly young, educated, single, working women; 65% voted for Bill Clinton in 1992. However, they do not like Clinton's move to the right on some issues and would prefer him and the Democrats in Congress to challenge the conservative policies of the Republican majority in Congress. They believe that Americans can be united around liberal issue positions.

Conservative activists (15% of voters) are the mirror opposite. They see the cure for crime in punishment, not prevention. They want taxes lowered and the deficit brought under control. They believe that individuals need to take responsibility for themselves and not expect government to solve their problems. They oppose abortion and think the cause of women's, gay, and civil rights has gone too far. Conservative activists favor increases in military spending. Two-thirds are high-income, college-educated, married men. Seventy-three percent voted for Bush in 1992.

Among *populist traditionalists* (15% of voters), who are predominantly blue-collar males under 45, job security and providing for their family are the big concerns. Many are union members but feel the union is powerless to deal with the problems they face. They do not trust government and are divided on whether the government should help families get ahead. Taxes are considered too high, which they see as robbing them of the prosperity they work hard to achieve. The debate among conservative and liberal activists on issues like abortion is irrelevant to them, although they feel abortion should be illegal. They do not oppose efforts of minorities to get ahead but feel the civil rights movement has gone too far. They believe American jobs should be protected by trade barriers limiting foreign-made goods. This group, which at one time would have been a mainstay of the Democratic party, gave Clinton 31% of its vote and Bush 42%. Populist traditionalists feel left out by the changes taking place in society and would prefer to return to the past where they feel more at home and more secure.

Stewards (15% of voters) have little use for government, except perhaps at the local level. They prefer the tax money they send to Washington be transferred to local government where they feel it can be spent more effectively. They are worried about crime and advocate harsher penalties and capital punishment. They also believe too many people are dependent on government. They want abortion to remain legal and are concerned with the growing strength of the religious right. Stewards are well-off financially; many are retired. They are upbeat about their and the nation's future. In spite of this, 22% turned their back on the traditional parties and voted for independent candidate Ross Perot in 1992, more than any other group; 36% voted for Bush, 33% for Clinton.

Dowagers (7% of voters) are elderly and female. They have worked all their lives in low- and middle-level positions and support themselves on Social Security and small pensions. Some are Democrats, some Republicans, but they are generally liberal when it comes to government helping people get ahead. They believe in protecting workers and assisting families that have fallen on hard times, as many of them did during the Depression. They value hard work and think something needs to be done about people who are on welfare and never get off. Forty percent voted for Clinton, 37% for Bush.

Ethnic conservatives (16% of voters) are composed of African Americans, Hispanics, and white ethnics. Most are low-income, blue-collar workers. They are concerned about crime, which is widespread in their communities and neighborhoods, but stress the need for prevention rather than punishment. Although many grew up in Democratic homes and believe the government should bolster programs for the needy, they are suspicious of liberals. They are antiabortion and religion plays an important part in their lives. Clinton garnered 43% of their vote, while Bush received 35%.

WHICH VOTER GROUP ARE YOU IN?

To find out which voter group you belong to, take this quiz. For each question, circle your position every time it appears on the horizontal line (also, be sure to circle "either answer" wherever it appears). Then add up the number of circles in each vertical column, and write the total at the bottom. The group with the highest number is yours. If you have the same score in more than one group, you share the cultural views of each group.

	A	B	C	D	E	F	G
On the issue of abortion, are you. . .	pro-life	pro-choice	undecided	pro-choice	pro-life	pro-life	pro-choice
Which radical agenda worries you more. . .	gay and feminist	religious right	religious right	religious right	gay and feminist	gay and feminist	religious right
Do you think the civil rights movement has gone. . .	too far	too far	not far enough	not far enough	too far	not far enough	too far
On business, are you more likely to side with. . .	labor	manage-ment	neither	labor	manage-ment	labor	either answer
On foreign aid, do you think that the U.S. should. . .	increase spending	decrease spending	decrease spending	decrease spending	increase spending	either answer	decrease spending
Concerning military defense spending, do you think the U.S. should. . .	increase spending	decrease spending	decrease spending	decrease spending	increase spending	either answer	decrease spending
On the issue of gun control, are you more likely to. . .	resist restrictions	favor gun control	favor gun control	favor gun control	resist restrictions	favor gun control	either answer
Concerning crime, should the government focus more on. . .	punish-ment	punish-ment	punish-ment	prevention	punish-ment	prevention	prevention
Should the government help families achieve the American dream or make people get ahead on their own?	help	no help	no help	help	no help	help	no help
Do you think that the women's movement has gone. . .	too far	too far	too far	not far enough	too far	either answer	too far
Add up the total number of circles in each column	______	______	______	______	______	______	______

A. ***Populist Traditionalists***–Union Democrats traditionally, but cast as isolationist vote for Perot in '92. Celebrity example: Rosanne's husband, Dan

B. ***Stewards***–Moderate Republicans turned off by the religious right in '92, came home in '94, 1996? Celebrity example: Thurston Howell

C. ***Dowagers***–Not very well informed. Clinton voters still voting for FDR. Celebrity example: Golden Girls

D. ***Liberal Activists***–Control nominating process of the Democrats. May alienate swing voters with liberal views on social issues. Celebrity example: Murphy Brown

E. ***Conservative Activitists***–Control the Republican nomination. Also can alienate swing voters with conservative social views. Celebrity example: Alex P. Keaton

F. ***Ethnic Conservatives***–Traditional Democrats who may defect from the party over issues related to social values and crime. Celebrity example: Louise Jefferson and Edith Bunker

G. ***Agnostics***–Strongly supported Clinton in 1992. Distinctly turned off by purely partisan bickering on the issues. Celebrity example: Frasier

American Diversity

Agnostics (12% of voters) are in their 40s and 50s and part of the protest generation of the 1960s. They favor crime prevention to punishment. They support increases in government assistance to the needy and decreases in defense spending. Not particularly religious, they see society threatened by the religious right. They favor gun control. They are the most tolerant of cultural diversity. Forty-seven percent voted for Clinton, 31% for Bush.

Although the categories oversimplify, they give some idea of the ideological diversity that exists today and why it is difficult for political institutions to win favor with more than a minority of Americans. Winning the support of one group is likely to drive the others away. Many Americans remain middle of the road, but this may be changing. With Americans no longer aligned from liberal to conservative but along several distinct dimensions, the middle may be getting smaller and smaller.

Using the accompanying questions, you find out which grouping you are in.[1]

1. "The New America," *U.S. News and World Report* (July 10, 1996), pp. 18–23.

thought government was moving too fast. Once more, government chose a middle course responsive to neither side.[90]

Following on the heels of these seemingly intractable problems, the early 1970s brought news of Watergate and corruption in government, and after 1973 the nation experienced economic problems, inflation, high interest rates, and unemployment. The government was little more successful in dealing with these than it was with the problems of the 1960s. Levels of trust again declined.

Between 1980 and 1984, levels of trust and confidence in government increased modestly. People seemed to respond to what appeared to be an improved economy and a few foreign policy successes. Reagan's personal popularity seemed to inspire confidence on the part of the American people.

Reagan's involvement in the Iran-contra scandal, a sense that his administration lacked compassion, and popular dissatisfaction with domestic and foreign policy diminished his appeal, however, and no doubt contributed to a decline in trust between 1984 and 1986.[91] In the 1990s, trust has continued to fall and in 1994 it was at a record low.[92] Congress and the president (both Bush and Clinton) have been deadlocked over crucial issues, from health care reform to budget deficits.

This brief overview suggests that policy failure is responsible for declining trust. Citizens have become increasingly oriented to government in terms of the services (jobs and high standard of living) they expect government to provide. When performance falls short of expectations, trust in government also falls.[93] One study documents the link between confidence in government and the state of the economy. Between 1966 and 1980, every percentage increase in unemployment lowered confidence in government by almost 3%.[94]

However, others theorize that declining trust can be traced not to policy but to process.[95] This view holds that declining trust is highly correlated with the increasing visibility of government. As Americans see more of their federal government on a day-to-day basis, through C-SPAN and newscasts, they like it less and trust it less. Talk radio and television interpret what are normal parts of the democratic process—lobbying, bargaining, negotiating, and compromise —as cynical acts done only for the self-interest of an individual, interest group, or political party. Of course, there is plenty of self-interest in politics, as in any other form of human endeavor, but compromise and negotiation are a necessary part of a democratic process. Since most Americans seem neither to understand nor like that part of the process, the more exposure the process gets, the less the public likes it.

Probably both policy and process have contributed to declining trust of government. Moreover, the two reinforce each other. Policy deadlock contributes to negative reactions to process, but even when the process yields significant policies, the public visibility of the mechanics of the policy process, with its negotiations and deals, still contributes to cynicism and mistrust.

Levels of trust among liberals and conservatives are frequently influenced by the party that occupies the White House. During Republican administrations, liberals tend to be less trusting; when Democrats hold office, liberals are more trusting.[96] Extremists are distrustful regardless of who occupies the White House. Americans who join militias and talk about government as an alien force are clearly examples of those having high levels of distrust. These Americans no longer believe that government sometimes makes mistakes or is simply too big to be effective; they have come to believe that it is directed by a force out of control of ordinary Americans (foreigners, communists, Jews, "the New World Order," and others are favorite suspects).

Those holding these extreme beliefs are a small fraction of the population. Most Americans generally believe that government is good, if sometimes misguided. However, if trust continues to decline, more Americans may be open to the arguments of those who believe that government is the enemy.

The pattern of low trust of government by the public is not unique to the United States.[97] In America a recent poll showed 8 out of 10 thought the country was going in the wrong direction. Seventy percent responded this way in Canada, and 44% in Japan. Large numbers do not trust their government to do what is right. Moreover, many see a bleak future ahead. Forty percent of Americans respond that future generations of Americans will be worse off than people today. In Canada, more than 50% respond this way. To a large extent, this reflects the economic uncertainty that global competition and technological change are producing, particularly among the less skilled and educated, and the inability of governments to do much about it. Countries have less power than ever in controlling their economies. Companies can move operations and individuals can transfer capital across national boundaries at will. While this creates economic opportunity, it also creates anxiety. Individuals are unclear what they need or should do to protect themselves and their families.

At the same time, however, Americans as well as citizens in other industrialized countries report that they are contented with the lives they lead. Citizens' negative response to government and their concern for the future may result from what they read and see in the news and the political rhetoric of politicians as much as it does from their personal situation.[98] Thus, the declining levels of trust might be due to the expanding scope of the media in developed countries.

➤Conclusion: Is Government Responsive to Public Opinion?

Our interest in public opinion stems in part from the belief that in a democracy government should be responsive to the wishes of the people. But is it? Political scientists have had only limited success answering this question because of the difficulty in measuring influence.

The most direct way to assess whether public policy is responsive to public opinion is to compare changes in policy with changes in opinion. The largest study of this type examined several hundred public opinion surveys done between 1935 and 1979. From these surveys, the researchers culled hundreds of questions, each of which dealt with a particular policy and had been asked more than one time. On more than 300 of these questions, public opinion had changed. The authors of the study compared changes in these 300 opinions with changes, if any, in public policy. They found congruence between opinion and policy changes in more than two-thirds of the opinions. Congruence was most likely when the opinion change was large and stable and when the opinion moved in a liberal direction.

The authors acknowledged that in about one-half of the cases, the policy change may have caused the opinion change, but in the other half the opinion change probably caused the policy change or they both affected each other. Although in many instances policy was not congruent with public opinion, on important issues, when changes in public opinion were clear-cut, policy usually became consistent with opinion.[99]

Although policy usually changes with changes in opinions, sometimes it does not. One reason is that reelection does not rest with the entire public but with the voting public, and those who vote often differ in their policy preferences from those who do not.[100] To the extent that elected public officials are responsive to voters, and voters differ from nonvoters, public policy will not reflect public opinion.

Then too, elected public officials must not only pay attention to the direction of public opinion but also to its intensity. It may be advantageous for an elected official to vote in support of a minority opinion that is intensely held. A minority with intense feelings is more likely to vote against a candidate who does not support its position than is a group with weak preferences. When elected officials are confronted with an intense minority—for example, the gun lobby—public policy may not reflect public opinion.

Moreover, public opinion is not the only influence on public policy, nor is it necessarily the most important. Interest groups, political parties, other institutions of government, and public officials' own preferences also influence policy, and they may or may not agree with public opinion. Where the preferences of the various influences do not agree, policy generally will reflect a compromise among them.

Finally, there is nothing sacred about public opinion. Even when a majority of the public favors a course of action, one should not assume that this is the most desirable course; the public can be wrong. This possibility led the Founders to establish a government that was partially insulated from the influence of public opinion. In other words, we do not have complete and immediate correspondence between opinion and policy because the Founders did not want instant government responsiveness. They built a federal system with separation of powers and many checks and balances to ensure that the majority could not steamroll the minority. Thus one should not expect public policy to reflect public opinion perfectly. The fact that policy usually comes to reflect large and stable majorities does indicate, however, that government is eventually responsive on important issues. Indeed, some observers think politicians pay too much attention to public opinion, to the point that leaders are fearful of leading or of offending the competing groups pulling in opposite directions. The result is more gridlock.

EPILOGUE

The President Follows the Polls

Driven by growing public sentiment that crime was the number one problem facing the nation, in his State of the Union address the president called on Congress to pass a "strong, smart, tough crime bill," including "three strikes and you're out." He was rewarded with his longest standing ovation (22 seconds) of the speech. He also called for 100,000 more police officers, a ban on semiautomatic weapons, boot camps for young offenders, and drug treatment for prison inmates. Although he argued for tougher penalties for those who commit violent crimes, he also called for more job training and national service that could provide jobs and strengthen families and thus help in the fight against crime.

This support at least temporarily pulled the rug out from under Republicans who have traditionally been the hard-liners on crime. Months later, when asked which party they thought could best handle the crime problem, the public gave the Democrats a slight edge, 39–32%, reversing a traditional Republican advantage and an indication that this aspect of Clinton's "new Democrat" politics are paying off.[101]

"My third felony was a smart move. Folks on the outside are still waiting for health care."

Source: Drawing by Handelsman. © 1994. The New Yorker Magazine, Inc.

Key Terms

public opinion
political socialization
agents of political socialization
straw polls
ideology
liberal
conservative
political tolerance

Further Reading

Herbert Asher, *Polling and the Public: What Every Citizen Should Know* (Washington, D.C.: CQ Press, 1988). *An introduction to polling methodology and the influence of polls on American politics as well as advice to citizens on how to evaluate polls.*

P. Brace and B. Hinckley, *Follow the Leader: Opinion Polls and the Modern President* (New York: Basic Books, 1992). *A survey of how recent presidents have allowed the results of public opinion polls to influence their position on issues.*

B. I. Page and R. Y. Shapiro, *The Rational Public: Fifty Years of Trends in American's Policy Preferences* (Chicago: University of Chicago Press, 1992). *An examination of the influence of public opinion on public policy using public opinion polling information generated over the past fifty years.*

T. E. Mann and G. R. Orren, eds., *Media Polls and American Politics* (Washington, D.C.: Brookings, 1992). *Several essays focusing on the influence of media-conducted polls on American political institutions and elections.*

Celinda Lake, *Public Opinion Polling: A Handbook for Public Interest and Citizen Advocacy Groups* (Washington, D.C.: Island Press, 1987). *A step-by-step treatment for lay audiences on how to conduct a public opinion poll.*

Notes

1. Michael Kramer, "Frying Them Isn't the Answer," *Time* (March 14, 1994), p. 34.

2. Ibid.

3. Material is drawn from: Richard Morin, "Public Enemy No. 1: Crime," *Washington Post National Weekly Edition* (January 24–30, 1994), p. 37; Richard Lacayo, "Lock 'Em Up," *Time* (February 7, 1994), pp. 51–59; Michael Kramer, "Tough, But Smart?" *Time* (February 7, 1994), p. 29.

4. Richard Morin, "The Ups and Downs of Political Poll-Taking," *Washington Post National Weekly Edition* (October 5, 1992), p. 37.

5. T. E. Cook, "The Bear Market in Political Socialization and the Costs of Misunderstood Psychological Theories," *American Political Science Review* 79 (December 1985), pp. 1079–93.

6. S. W. Moore et al., "The Civic Awareness of Five-and Six-Year- Olds," *Western Political Quarterly* 29 (August 1976), p. 418.

7. R. W. Connell, *The Child's Construction of Politics* (Carlton, Victoria: Melbourne University Press, 1971).

8. F. I. Greenstein, *Children and Politics* (New Haven, Conn.: Yale University Press, 1965), p. 122; see also F. I. Greenstein, "The Benevolent Leader Revisited: Children's Images of Political Leaders in Three Democracies," *American Political Science Review* 69 (December 1975), pp. 1317–98; R. D. Hess and J. V. Torney, *The Development of Attitudes in Children* (Chicago: Aldine, 1967).

9. Hess and Torney, *Development of Attitudes in Children;* Connell, *Child's Construction of Politics.*

10. Greenstein, *Children and Politics;* Greenstein, "The Benevolent Leader"; and Hess and Torney, *Development of Attitudes in Children.*

11. Connell, *Child's Construction of Politics.*

12. F. C. Arterton, "The Impact of Watergate on Children's Attitudes toward the President," *Political Science Quarterly* 89 (June 1974), pp. 269–88; also F. Haratwig and C. Tidmarch, "Children and Political Reality: Changing Images of the President," paper presented at the 1974 Annual Meeting of the Southern Political Science Association; J. Dennis and C. Webster, "Children's Images of the President and Government in 1962 and 1974," *American Politics Quarterly* 4 (October 1975), pp. 386–405; R. P. Hawkins, S. Pingree, and D. Roberts, "Watergate and Political Socialization," *American Politics Quarterly* 4 (October 1975), pp. 406–36.

13. M. A. Delli Carpini, *Stability and Change in American Politics: The Coming of Age of the Generation of the 1960s* (New York: New York University Press, 1986), pp. 86–89.

14. R. Merelman, *Political Socialization and Educational Climates* (New York: Holt, Rinehart and Winston, 1971), p. 54.

15. R. Sigel and M. Hoskin, *The Political Involvement of Adolescents* (New Brunswick, N.J.: Rutgers University Press, 1981).

16. J. Citrin, "Comment: The Political Relevance of Trust in Government," *American Political Science Review* 68 (September 1974), pp. 973–1001; J. Citrin and D. P. Green, "Presidential Leadership and the Resurgence of Trust in Government," *British Journal of Political Science* 16 (1986), pp. 431–53.

17. It is plausible to assume that the content of early political socialization influences what is learned later, but the assumption has not been adequately tested. Thus, we might expect the positive opinions toward government and politics developed early in childhood to condition the impact of traumatic events later in life. D. Easton and J. Dennis, *Children and the Political System: Origins of Regime Legitimacy* (New York: McGraw-Hill, 1969); R. Weissberg, *Political Learning, Political Choice and Democratic Citizenship* (Englewood Cliffs, N.J.: Prentice-Hall, 1974). See also D. D. Searing, J. J. Schwartz, and A. E. Line, "The Structuring Principle: Political Socialization and Belief System," *American Political Science Review* 67 (June 1973), pp. 414–32.

18. D. Jaros, H. Hirsch, and F. Fleron, Jr., "The Malevolent Leader: Political Socialization in an American Subculture," *American Political Science Review* 62 (June 1968), pp. 564–75.

19. K. Tedin, "The Influence of Parents on the Political Attitudes of Adolescents," *American Political Science Review* 68 (December 1974), pp. 1579–92.

20. On the impact of the public schools and teachers on political socialization, particularly in the area of loyalty and patriotism, see Hess and Torney, *Development of Attitudes in Children.*

21. K. Langton and M. K. Jennings, "Political Socialization and the High School Civics Curriculum," *American Political Science Review* 62 (September 1968), pp. 852–77.

22. D. Goldenson, "An Alternative View about the Role of the Secondary School in Political Socialization: A Field Experimental Study of the Development of Civil Liberties Attitudes," *Theory and Research in Social Education* 6 (March 1978), pp. 44–72.

23. The study of 17-year-olds is reported by E. Shantz, "Sideline Citizens," in Byron Massiales, ed., *Political Youth, Traditional Schools*

(Englewood Cliffs, N.J.: Prentice-Hall, 1972), pp. 69–70; the study of high school seniors is reported by H. H. Remmers and R. D. Franklin, "Sweet Land of Liberty," in H. H. Remmers, ed., *Anti-Democratic Attitudes in American Schools* (Evanston, Ill.: Northwestern University Press, 1963), p. 62.

24. R. Merelman, "Democratic Politics and the Culture of American Education," *American Political Science Review* 74 (June 1980), pp. 319–32.

25. G. Almond and S. Verba, *Civic Culture* (Boston: Little, Brown, 1965); John R. Hibbing and Elizabeth Theiss-Morse, "Civics Is Not Enough: Teaching Barbarics in K-12," forthcoming, *P.S.*

26. Material for this section is drawn from E. C. Ladd and S. M. Lipset, *The Divided Academy* (New York: McGraw-Hill, 1975); C. Kesler, "The Movement of Student Opinion," *The National Review* (November 23) 1979, p. 29; E. L. Boyer, *College: The Undergraduate Experience in America* (New York: Harper & Row, 1986); "Fact File: Attitudes and Characteristics of This Year's Freshman," *The Chronicle of Higher Education* (January 11, 1989) pp. A33–A34; General Social Survey, National Opinion Research Center, 1984, p. 87.

27. Rene Sanchez, "Don't Know Much About Politics," *Washington Post National Weekly Edition,* January 16, 1995, p. 37.

28. M. K. Jennings and R. G. Niemi, *The Political Character of Adolescence* (Princeton, N.J.: Princeton University Press, 1974), p. 243.

29. M. McCombs and D. Shaw, "The Agenda Setting Function of the Media," *Public Opinion Quarterly* 36 (Summer 1972), pp. 176–87.

30. B. I. Page, R. Shapiro, and G. R. Dempsey, "What Moves Public Opinion?" *American Political Science Review* 81 (March 1987), pp. 23–44.

31. H. Weissberg, "Marital Differences in Voting," *Public Opinion Quarterly* 51 (1987), pp. 335–43.

32. P. R. Abramson, *Political Attitudes in America* (San Francisco: Freeman, 1983), pp. 150, 213; see also Paul R. Abramson, *The Political Socialization of Black Americans* (New York: Free Press, 1977).

33. P. E. Converse, A. R. Clausen, and W. Miller, "Electoral Myth and Reality," *American Political Science Review* 59 (1965), pp. 321–26.

34. J. P. Robinson, "The Press as Kingmaker: What Surveys Show from the Last Five Campaigns," *Journalism Quarterly* 49 (Summer 1974), p. 592.

35. For a review of the history of polling, see Hennessy, *Public Opinion,* 4th ed., (Monterey, CA: Brooks/Cole Publishing Co., 1983), pp. 42–44, 46–50. See also C. Roll and A. Cantril, *Polls: Their Use and Misuse in Politics* (New York: Basic Books, 1972), pp. 3–16.

36. P. Squire, "The 1936 Literary Digest Poll," *Public Opinion Quarterly* 52 (1988), pp. 125–33; see also Don Cahalan, "The Digest Poll Rides Again," *Public Opinion Quarterly* 53 (1989), pp. 107–13.

37. Hennessy, *Public Opinion,* p. 46.

38. "Consulting the Oracle," *U.S. News and World Report* (December 4, 1995), pp. 52–55.

39. Ibid.

40. "Polls Came Close to Nailing Election," *Lincoln Journal* (November 11, 1992).

41. Many questioned the polls because some pollsters, Gallup in particular, showed Bush overcoming a substantial Clinton lead and closing to within two percentage points a week before the election. Some argued that this was not a real surge but resulted from a change by Gallup in reporting Bush's support among likely rather than registered voters the week before the election. R. Morin, "Surveying the Ups and Downs of Election '92," *Washington Post National Weekly Edition* (November 9, 1992), p. 37.

42. "All Things Considered," National Public Radio, October 30, 1992.

43. "Consulting the Oracle," p. 53.

44. Ibid.

45. R. Morin, "Surveying the Surveyors," *Washington Post National Weekly Edition* (March 2, 1992), p. 37.

46. David Broder, "Push Polls Plunge Politics to a New Low," *Lincoln Star* (October 9, 1994), p. 5E.

47. Ibid.

48. Ann Devroy, "George Bush's Identity Crisis," *Washington Post National Weekly Edition* (August 24–30, 1992), pp. 6–7.

49. Richard Morin, "When the Method Becomes the Message," *Washington Post National Weekly Edition,* December 19–25, 1994, p. 33.

50. Richard Morin, "Tuned Out, Turned Off," *Washington Post National Weekly Edition* (February 5–11, 1996), pp. 6–8.

51. Ibid.

52. Ibid.

53. Richard Morin, "They Know Only What They Don't Like," *Washington Post National Weekly Edition,* October 3–9, 1994, p. 37.

54. 1986 National Election Study, Center for Political Studies, University of Michigan; "Wapner Top Judge in Recognition Poll," *Lincoln Star,* June 23, 1989, p. 1 (*Washington Post* syndication).

55. Michael X. Dellli Carpini and Scott Keeter, "U.S. Public Knowledge of Politics," *Public Opinion Quarterly* (Winter, 1991), pp. 583–612.

56. Morin, "They Know What They Don't Like."

57. Morin, "Tuned Out, Turned Off."

58. Ibid.

59. Richard Morin, "Foreign Aid: Mired in Misunderstanding," *Washington Post National Weekly Edition,* March 20–26, 1995, p. 37.

60. Richard Morin, "What Informed Public Opinion?" *Washington Post National Weekly Edition,* April 10–16, 1995, p. 36.

61. V. O. Key, *The Responsible Electorate* (Cambridge, Mass.: Harvard University Press, 1966); N. Nie, S. Verba, and J. R. Petrocik, *The Changing American Voter* (Cambridge, Mass.: Harvard University Press, 1976), chapter 18.

62. Morin, "Tuned Out, Turned Off."

63. B. Sussman, "When Politicians Talk about Issues People Listen," *Washington Post National Weekly Edition,* August 18, 1986, p. 37.

64. Data in this section are summarized in *The Public Perspective* 6, no. 2 (February/March, 1995), pp. 39–46.

65. Data here are from Peter Hart Research Associates Survey for the Council for Excellence in Government, March 16–18, 1995.

66. Gallup Survey, December 16, 1993.

67. Ibid.

68. This section draws heavily on H. Schuman, C. Steeh, and L. Bobo, *Racial Attitudes in America* (Cambridge, Mass.: Harvard University Press, 1985); data summaries are drawn from the General Social Surveys of the National Opinion Research Center, University of Chicago, and National Elections Studies of CPS, University of Michigan; see also L. Sigelman and S. Welch, *Black Americans' Views of Racial Inequality* (Cambridge, Mass.: Cambridge University Press, 1991).

69. *Washington Post National Weekly Edition,* October 30, 1989, p. 37.

70. "Whites Retain Negative Views of Minorities, a Survey Finds," *New York Times,* January 10, 1991, p. C19; M. Jackman,

"General and Applied Tolerance: Does Education Increase Commitment to Racial Inequality?" *American Journal of Political Science* 22 (1978), pp. 302–24; M. Jackman, "Education and Policy Commitment to Racial Equality," *American Journal of Political Science* 25 (1981), pp. 256–69; D. Kinder and D. Sears, "Prejudice and Politics," *Journal of Personality and Social Psychology* 40 (1981), pp. 414–31.

71. "Whites Retain Negative Views."

72. H. Schuman and L. Bobo, "Survey-Based Experiments on White Attitudes toward Residential Integration," *American Journal of Sociology* 94 (1988), pp. 272–94; W. R. Merriman and E. Carmines, "The Limits of Liberal Tolerance: The Case of Racial Politics," *Polity* 20 (1988), pp. 519–26; see also Schuman, Steeh, and Bobo, *Racial Attitudes*.

73. L. Sigelman and S. Welch, "A Dream Deferred: Black Attitudes toward Race and Inequality," unpublished manuscript, 1989. Almost all blacks support school integration, only 50% to 60% support busing.

74. 1990 General Social Survey.

75. ABC/*Washington Post* Poll, 1981.

76. Richard Morin, "No Place for Calm and Quiet Opinions," *Washington Post National Weekly Edition* (April 24–30, 1994), p. 34.

77. Martin Gilens and Paul Sniderman, "Affirmative Action and the Politics of Realignment." Paper presented at the Midwest Political Science Association Meeting, Chicago, Ill., 1995; Paul Sniderman and Thomas Piazza, *The Scar of Race* (Cambridge, Mass: Harvard University Press, 1993).

78. ABC/*Washington Post* Poll, 1981 and 1986.

79. J. Sullivan, G. Marcus, S. Feldman, and J. Pierson, "Sources of Political Tolerance: A Multivariate Analysis," *American Political Science Review* 75 (March 1981), pp. 92–106.

80. S. Stouffer, *Communism, Conformity, and Civil Liberties* (New York: John Wiley and Sons, 1954).

81. R. W. Jackman, "Political Elites, Mass Publics, and Support for Democratic Principles," *Journal of Politics* 34 (August 1972), p. 753.

82. H. McClosky and J. Zaller, *The American Ethos: Public Attitudes toward Capitalism and Democracy* (Cambridge, Mass.: Harvard University Press, 1986).

83. C. Z. Nunn, H. H. Crockett, Jr., and J. A. Williams, *Tolerance for Nonconformity* (San Francisco: Jossey-Bass, 1976).

84. J. Sullivan, J. Pierson, and G. Marcus, "An Alternative Conceptualization of Tolerance: Illusory Increases 1950s–1970s," *American Political Science Review* 73 (September 1979), pp. 781–94. For a critique of this study, see P. M. Sniderman, P. E. Tetlock, J. M. Glaser, D. P. Gress, and M. Hout, "Principled Tolerance and the American Mass Public," *British Journal of Political Science* 19 (January 1989), pp. 25–46.

85. P. Abramson, "Comments on Sullivan, Pierson, and Marcus," *American Political Science Review* 74 (June 1980): pp. 780–81.

86. "Polls Find Americans Angry, Anxious, Less Altruistic," *Lincoln Journal* (September 21, 1994), p. 9.

87. 1990 General Social Survey.

88. Judith Shklar, quoted in Paul Taylor, "In Watergate's Wake: The Good, the Bad, and the Ugly," *Washington Post National Weekly Edition*, June 22, 1992, p. 25.

89. Almond and Verba, *Civic Culture*, pp. 64–68.

90. A. Miller, "Political Issues and Trust in Government, 1964–1970," *American Political Science Review* 68 (September 1974), pp. 951–72.

91. S. M. Lipset and W. Schneider, *The Confidence Gap* (New York: Free Press, 1983), pp. 63–64.

92. "Clinton's High Victory Rate Conceals Disappointments," *Congressional Quarterly Weekly Report* (December 31, 1994), pp. 3619–3623.

93. A. Miller and S. Borrelli, "Confidence in Government During the 1980s," *American Politics Quarterly* 19 (April 1991), pp. 147–73.

94. T. J. Lowi, *The Personal President* (Ithaca, N.Y.: Cornell University Press, 1985), pp. 64–68.

95. J. Hibbing and E. Theiss-Morse, *Congress as Public Enemy: Public Attitudes Toward Political Institutions* (Cambridge: Cambridge University Press, 1995).

96. 1990 General Social Survey.

97. Richard Morin, "I'm OK; My Government's Not," *Washington Post National Weekly Edition* (July 26–August 1, 1993), p. 37.

98. Ibid.

99. Benjamin Page and Robert Shapiro, "Effects of Public Opinion on Policy," *American Political Science Review* 77 (March 1983), pp. 175–90.

100. Sidney Verba and Norman H. Nie, *Participation in America: Political Democracy and Social Equality* (New York: Harper & Row, 1972), chapter 15.

101. Dan Balz, "Taking a Positive View," *Washington Post National Weekly Edition* (March 7–13, 1994), p. 13.

5 Interest Groups

You Are There

Do You Leave Congress to Lead a Civil Rights Organization?

You are Kweisi Mfume, member of the House of Representatives from a predominantly black district in Baltimore. You were elected in 1986 and have won reelection with more than 80% of the vote ever since. It is now 1995 and you have to decide whether to leave Congress and lead the country's oldest and largest civil rights organization. Your path to Congress has been an unusual one.

When you were twelve, your father left your family to fend for itself in the inner city slums. At sixteen, your mother died in your arms. You dropped out of high school and held a number of dead-end jobs. At nineteen, the one person you thought was trying to help blacks, Martin Luther King, Jr., was shot down. When some inner city blacks rioted because of it, so did you. You hung out on street corners, smoked, drank, and fathered five sons out of wedlock before your twenty-second birthday.

You were not called to serve in Vietnam. Several of your friends were killed there. Having been spared, you wondered why. At this point, you started to turn your life around. You changed your name from Frizzell Gray to Kweisi Mfume, which means "conquering son of kings" in Swahili. You finished high school, graduated from college with honors and got a master's degree in international relations from Johns Hopkins. As a popular talk-radio show host, you developed a following and were elected to the Baltimore City Council, where you promoted the interests of inner city residents. Later, you ran and won a seat in Congress.

In Congress, you quietly developed an expertise in banking issues. Your focus is on helping minority-owned businesses get started. You sponsored the Minority Business Development Act. With bipartisan support, you proposed an urban spending program to attack problems in the nation's cities, including proposals to reform welfare, establish a national service, and provide for environmental cleanup.

In 1992 you were elected leader of the Congressional Black Caucus, an organization of the black members in Congress. Under your leadership, the caucus, with 38 members—the largest number of blacks to serve in Congress at one time—became an effective bargaining agent for black interests. Although you were willing to work with President Clinton following his election in 1992, you made it clear that black members should not be taken for granted. You complained that he appointed too few blacks to administrative positions. You refused meetings with him that simply provided photo opportunities rather than substantive discussions. You withheld support when you felt the president's efforts to balance the budget fell too hard on the poor and minorities. Because the president needs black support to win legislative approval of his policies, you, as leader of the caucus, have some leverage.

Although the Republicans won control of the House in 1994, the potential for black influence on the White House and in Congress remains high, and you have an extraordinary opportunity to shape and direct that influence.

However, you have been asked to leave Congress and take over the leadership of the National Association for the

Interest groups represent almost every group's interest, and fence with other groups over public issues. This organization fences more literally.

CONTINUED

OUTLINE

Group Formation
- Why Groups Form
- Why People Join
- Who Joins?
- Have Americans Stopped Joining?

Types of Interest Groups
- Private Interest Groups
- Public Interest Groups

Tactics of Interest Groups
- Direct Lobbying Techniques
- Indirect Lobbying Techniques
- Protest and Civil Disobedience

Success of Interest Groups
- Resources
- Competition and Goals

Conclusion: Do Interest Groups Help Make Government Responsive?

Advancement of Colored People (NAACP), the oldest and largest civil rights organization in the nation. From its inception, the NAACP fought segregation and in the 1950s won major victories when the Supreme Court invalidated separate schools for blacks and whites. In the 1960s, it joined with other civil rights groups in organizing nonviolent marches, sit-ins, and other mass-action protests. As part of the civil rights movement, the organization can claim considerable credit for the civil rights laws passed in the 1960s.

But the NAACP of the 1990s is not what it was in the 1960s. The organization has been weakened by internal strife. It has lost members and has fallen into debt. The former president was fired for mismanagement. Some feel the organization has moved away from its commitment to integration and to work with mainstream groups toward more extremist approaches to combat discrimination. Several prominent black leaders have suggested that the organization has outlived its usefulness.

Staying in Congress has its advantages. The residents of the 7th District will likely continue to reelect you until you retire. You will be guaranteed a forum to speak out on the issues of greatest importance to African Americans and an opportunity to shape legislation affecting these issues. Your influence will be somewhat less now that the Republicans control Congress, but this may change in the next election. Joining the NAACP is riskier. The organization may not be able to recover—it needs more members and more money. Or the organization may survive but not be able to generate the support and resources to make it an effective agent for promoting African Americans' concerns. On the other hand, the right person might be able to restore the organization and push its agenda to the center of the policy debate in the United States.

Do you stay in Congress where your reelection is assured and your role as an insider in policymaking can continue? Or do you leave Congress and take over leadership of the weakened NAACP, where you might or might not succeed?[1]

In the United States everything from fruits to nuts is organized. From apple growers to filbert producers, every interest has an organization to represent it. These organizations touch every aspect of our lives; members of the American College of Obstetrics and Gynecology bring us into the world, and members of the National Funeral Directors Association usher us out.

Organizations that try to achieve at least some of their goals with government assistance are called **interest groups.** Fruit and nut growers want government subsidies and protection from imported products; doctors and funeral directors want to be free of government controls. The efforts of interest groups to influence government are called **lobbying.** Lobbying may involve direct contact between a lobbyist, or consultant or lawyer, as they prefer to be called, and a government official; or it may involve indirect action, such as attempts to sway public opinion, which will in turn influence officials.

People organize and lobby because these are ways for them to enhance their influence. As one Washington lobbyist put it, "Democracy is not a spectator sport. If you want to have a hand in shaping the nation, you must get into it with more than your one vote on the Tuesday after the first Monday in November."[2] Or as another put it, somewhat more forcefully, "The modern government is huge, pervasive, intrusive into everybody's life. If you just let things take their course and don't get involved in the game, you get trampled on."[3]

The Founders feared the harmful effects of interest groups. Madison was intent on "curing the mischiefs of faction" through separation of powers, checks and balances, and federalism. Today, many people bemoan the "mischiefs of faction" or "special interests" because they seem to block government actions favoring the larger interests of society.[4] Sometimes it seems that everyone is represented in Washington but the people.

Do interest groups undermine the people's interests? Or do they make government more responsive by giving people greater representation in the political process? These are the difficult questions we explore in this chapter.

➤Group Formation

Throughout most of its history, America has been a nation of joiners. As early as the 1830s, the Frenchman Alexis de Tocqueville, who traveled in America, noted the tendency of Americans to join groups: "In no country in the world has the principle of association been more successfully used or applied to a greater multitude of objects than in America."[5] Even now Americans are more likely than citizens in other countries to belong to groups.[6]

The United States is especially fertile for the growth of groups. Compared to most other countries, it is racially, religiously, and ethnically diverse. These differences give rise to different interests and views on public issues and often lead to the formation of groups that express those views.[7]

Groups can organize because of the freedom to speak, assemble, and petition government, guaranteed in the First Amendment to the Constitution. Without such freedom, only groups favored by the government—or groups whose members are willing to be punished for their actions—could exist.

The federal structure also encourages the proliferation of groups. It is not enough to have a national organization. Because state and local governments have significant power, groups also must be organized at those levels to protect their interests.

Why Groups Form

The formation of groups occurs in waves.[8] In some periods formation is rapid and extensive, whereas at other times there is very little activity.

Social and economic stress often account for these surges.[9] The stress of the Revolutionary War period activated groups for and against independence. The slavery controversy in the decades before the Civil War energized groups on both sides of the issue. After the war, rapid industrialization led to the formation of trade unions and business associations. Economic problems in agricultural areas spurred the development of farm groups.

In 1773 a group of colonists organized to protest British taxes on tea by throwing tea into Boston Harbor. In 1989 groups organized to protest a congressional pay increase by sending teabags to their representatives in Washington.

The greatest surge in group formation occurred between 1900 and 1920. Stimulated by the shocks of industrialization, urbanization, immigration, and the government's response to them, groups such as the United States Chamber of Commerce, American Medical Association, American Farm Bureau Federation, National Association for the Advancement of Colored People (NAACP), Socialist and Communist parties, and countless others formed.[10]

The 1960s and 1970s witnessed an interest group explosion, directed primarily toward Washington. As the national government expanded in power and influence in the post–World War II period, it increasingly became the center of interest group efforts to satisfy demands for favorable public policy. Spurred by the success of civil rights and war protest movements in the 1960s, other groups representing racial minorities, women, consumers, the poor, the elderly, and the environment organized. Business lobbying surged in the late 1970s as a response to the success of consumer and environmental groups in prompting government to increase the regulation of occupational safety and environmental standards.[11]

Technological changes also accelerate group formation. A national network of railroads and the telegraph contributed to the surge in the early 1900s. Computer-generated direct mail appeals, to solicit funds and mobilize members to action, as well as WATS lines (wide-area telephone service), increased the ability of groups to form and mobilize in the 1960s and 1970s. The number of groups increased by 60% between 1960 and 1980, and the number sending representatives to Washington doubled.[12] The spread of personal computers and the growing system of computer networks known as the Internet in the 1990s facilitates communication between persons with an endless variety of narrow interests. PCs and the Internet are particularly useful for persons who wish to organize citizens but who lack financial resources for more sophisticated approaches.[13] For example, members and sympathizers of militia groups are able to use the Internet to keep each other informed about group activities.

Group organizers also play a role in group formation.[14] These entrepreneurs often come from estab-

For Right to Undress, Nudists Flex Right to Redress

For those of you who get the urge to go skinny-dipping in the public pool or tan in the nude at the neighborhood park, the 17,000-member Naturalist Society, the nation's most politically active organization of nudists, is out to help.

While the National Park Service allows nude beaches in remote areas, conflicts occur at more accessible beaches. Members argue that they "are tired of always moving farther down the beach." To protect their right to clothing-optional recreation, as members call it, the organization retained a Washington lobbyist to make its case to Congress.

The first task of their newly hired lobbyist is to make the issue less attention grabbing. The strategy is to become just another pestering group in Washington. When the smirks fade from the faces of official Washington, the group believes it will be taken more seriously.

Politically, nudists are divided into conservative and liberal camps. Conservatives tend to join the Florida-based Sunbathing Association, which claims 36,000 members. They prefer to be left alone and gravitate toward private clubs. Liberals are more likely to join the Naturalist Society and use public beaches.

Besides beach access, nudists are addressing other issues as well, including child custody and jobs. Many have lost children and jobs because of their penchant for nude recreation.

Source: "The Right to Undress," *Common Cause Magazine* (January/February 1991), pp. 6–7.

lished groups. They gain experience and then strike out on their own. Many civil rights activists of the 1950s and early 1960s founded organizations in the late 1960s. Some used their skills to organize groups against the war in Vietnam and later to organize groups for women's rights and environmental causes.[15] Thus the formation of one group often opens the door to the formation of others.

The government is also important to group formation. Government attempts to deal with perceived problems often generate organized opposition groups, such as the increase in business lobbying in response to environmental lobbying. In addition, government provides direct financial assistance to some groups, particularly nonprofit organizations. Groups as diverse as the American Council of Education, the National Governors Association, and the National Council of Senior Citizens obtain a large percentage of their budgets through federal grants and contracts.[16]

Why People Join

Most people join groups voluntarily because of the benefits groups provide.[17] Some are attracted to groups for political or ideological reasons. Members of Common Cause join because they support the group's goals of campaign finance reform and ethics in government. The benefits are the psychological satisfaction of being identified with the cause and the prospect that the group will succeed. Some groups offer monetary benefits to members such as discounted prices for goods and services. The large nonfarm membership of the Farm Bureau often is attributed to the cut-rate insurance policies offered through the organization.[18] The American Association of Retired Persons (AARP) provides health, home, and auto insurance; a motor club; a travel service; investment counseling; discount drugs and medicines; and a magazine. These services attract members and generate millions of dollars for the organization. Two-thirds of AARP's revenue comes from business activities that provide discount services to members. Groups also provide social benefits. Some people join groups to make friends.

Because most groups seek to expand their membership and people join for different reasons, most groups provide a mix of benefits. The National Rifle Association (NRA) lobbies against gun regulation and control. Some people join for this reason. Others join to secure other NRA services: *The American Rifleman* (a monthly magazine), a hunter's information service, low-cost firearm insurance, membership in local gun clubs, and shooting competitions.[19] Still others join because they enjoy associating with fellow gun enthusiasts.

Some people join groups because they are coerced. For example, in some states lawyers must join the state bar association to practice law.

Who Joins?

Not all people are equally likely to join groups.[20] Those with higher incomes and education are more likely to belong. They can afford membership dues, have the leisure necessary to take part, and have the social and intellectual skills that facilitate group participation. They also appear more attractive to many groups and therefore are more apt to be recruited.

Whites more often belong to groups than blacks, but mostly because of their higher average income and education.[21]

Have Americans Stopped Joining?

A new and to some a disturbing trend is that membership in organizations where members interact face to face is declining.[22] For example, church membership and church-related activities have declined over the past 20 years. Membership in labor unions, once the most common organizational affiliation among American workers, has been declining for nearly four decades. Membership in the PTA is down over the past generation. In general, membership in and volunteering for civic and fraternal organizations are down. The impulse to join with others in common pursuits has lessened to such a degree that it has influenced recreational activity. Although more Americans than ever bowl, league bowling is down by more than 40%. If the decline represented just a loss of revenue from the pizza and beer consumed by leagues, only bowling proprietors would care. However, the decline also means the loss of close personal friendships that foster discussion of public issues and trust among citizens, which are important to the success of democratic government.[23]

Although important politically, mass-membership organizations like the National Organization for Women and the American Association of Retired Persons (AARP) do not link members socially. Members do not know each other. They pay dues and are on a mailing list. Their ties are to common symbols, leaders, and ideals, but not to one another. In terms of connecting citizens to one another, AARP and the bowling league are not the same thing.[24]

Types of Interest Groups

Interest groups come in all shapes and sizes. Some have large memberships, such as the American Federation of Labor-Congress of Industrial Organizations (AFL-CIO) with 13 million members. Others have small memberships, such as the Mushroom Growers Association with 14 members.

Two types of groups do not have any members.[25] Corporations do not have members but act as interest groups when they lobby government. Some Washington-based groups also do not have members. They lobby on behalf of specific interests and are funded by the government, private foundations, other groups, or fees from consulting. The Children's Defense Fund (CDF) is one such group. Founded in 1973, its staff of 90, funded entirely from private funds, lobbies on behalf of a broad range of issues involving children.[26]

Some groups have members, but their sole purpose is financial support. Supporters are "checkbook" members, and the group is simply the staff. Supporters' main links to the organization are occasional checks they send to it. They may receive a newsletter and requests to write their senator or representative, but they do not interact with other members nor participate in decision making. Some public interest groups, such as Congress Watch, Ralph Nader's organization, have this organizational structure. Many **political action committees (PACs)** do also. They raise money through direct mail and channel it to political candidates. How to spend the money, some of which goes to staff, is determined solely by the staff.

Some interest groups are formally organized, with appointed or elected leaders, regular meetings, and dues-paying members. Some are large corporations whose leaders are the corporate officers hired by boards of directors. Others have no leaders and few prescribed rules.

Thus, interest groups can be distinguished according to their membership and organizational structure. They also can be distinguished by their goals.

Private Interest Groups

Private interest groups pursue chiefly economic interests that benefit their members.

Business

Business organizations are the largest and most powerful interest groups (see Figure 1). Some have argued that the major cleavage in American politics is between business groups on the one hand and government and not-for-profit institutions on the other.[27] E. E. Schattschneider notes that "the struggle for power is largely a confrontation of two major power systems, government and business."[28]

However, throughout the 1980s and 1990s, government often supported the interests of business regardless of which party controlled the White House or Congress.[29] Republicans traditionally favor business, and Democrats recently have supported business more than in the past, due to contributions to Democrats by business and the election of more moderate

FIGURE 1
Business Interests Dominate the Contemporary Interest Group System

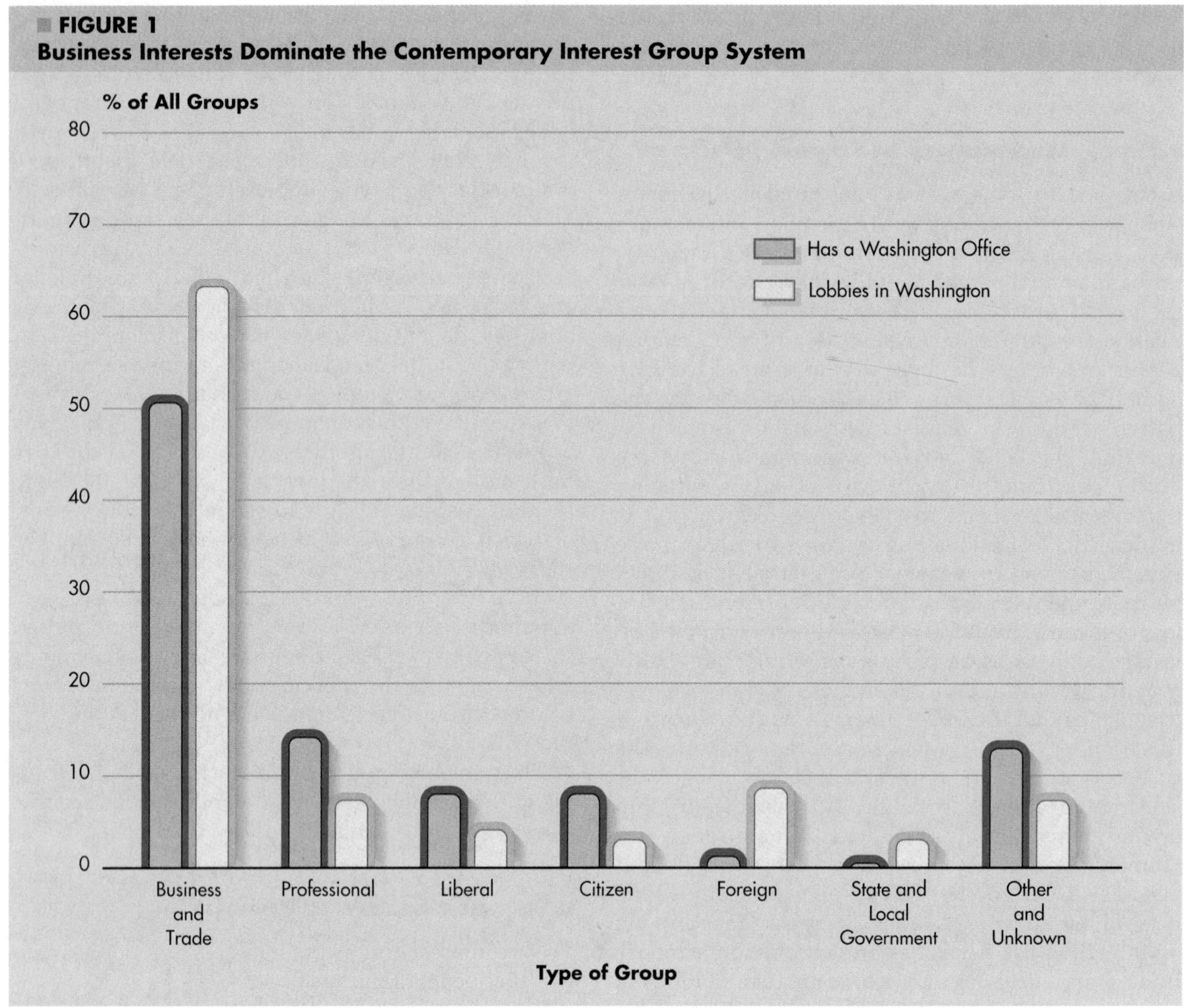

Note: Groups with a Washington office number 2,810, and 6,601 groups lobby there. "Liberal" groups are those representing women, minorities, the poor, labor, and the elderly. "Citizen" includes public interest groups such as Common Cause.
Source: K. L. Schlozman and J. T. Tierney, *Organized Interests and American Democracy* (New York: Harper & Row, 1986), p. 67.

and conservative Democrats. Under Clinton, business won major international trade agreements. It was able to secure "most favored nation" trade privileges for China in spite of human rights violations by that country. Despite courting by the Clinton administration, business lobbies defeated the administration's economic stimulus package and health care reform proposal, which would have required employers to provide employee health insurance. They also stymied labor's goal of prohibiting permanent replacement of striking workers.

With Republican control of Congress in 1994, business can expect even more success.[30] Environmental regulations and product liability laws are likely to change in favor of business.

Business is not monolithic, however. The Chamber of Commerce, one of the most important business groups, represents a great range of different businesses. The National Association of Manufacturers and the Business Roundtable represent big business.

Other organizations represent small business: the National Federation of Independent Business and the

New Populism

The Angriest White Males

Although most interest groups seek to achieve their goals through lawful and democratic processes, a few of the angriest are going far beyond changing government by "throwing the rascals out" through the voting process. They are working to overthrow the government itself. A group of separatists calling themselves the Freemen declared their independence from the United States, labeling the government a "de facto corporate prostitute." They reject government authority, refuse to pay taxes, and question the validity of U.S. currency. Holed up in a ranch in Montana surrounded by the FBI, 20 well-armed Freemen refused to negotiate the standoff for several months. The bombing of the federal building in Oklahoma City was apparently the work of a few anti-government terrorists who sought revenge against the national government and federal agents for the raid on the Branch Davidian religious sect in Waco, Texas. So-called militia groups have sprung up across the country who also despise the federal government.

These individuals and groups live in a world of paranoia, hate and fear. They believe that government has betrayed the people and subverted the Constitution. They believe that government has sold out to a mysterious "New World Order," a one-world government. They believe that "the nation is already under siege by troops hovering in black helicopters who have embedded interstate road signs with directional codes that only they can read."[1] Some groups also believe that Jews, blacks, or immigrants are trying to take over the government. And some even believe that bar codes in grocery stores are secret codes ordered by a foreign government, that bar codes on dollars allow government agents to drive by houses and determine how much money the occupants have, and that the government has installed electronic devices in car ignitions to stall autos on the day the "New World Order" takes over.[2]

Historians point out that the paranoid strain in American politics runs deep; only a few years ago, many people believed that it was the Communists who were about to take over America. With the demise of Communism, coupled with our own economic and social troubles, many people look closer to home to find an enemy.

Militias collect weapons, cache food, train in the woods, and await an invasion from a United Nations force. Although their rage is, theoretically, against the forces of the "New World Order," in practice it is directed at federal agents and policies. Members have a particular hatred for gun control laws, believing that such laws are part of a plot by foreign agents to disarm America and take over. They are especially angry at the Bureau of Alcohol, Tobacco, and Firearms for the 1993 raid on the Branch Davidians which ended in a mass suicide of the Davidians, and more generally because this agency enforces gun control.

A small number of Americans are deeply suspicious of the government.

Of course, not all members of militia are males, and not all believe in all these conspiracy theories. Nor did most start out by believing any of these theories, but rather by being angry at government for being unresponsive to their concerns, whether they want to own assault weapons, think they should be able to graze their cattle on public lands, or believe that government has gone too far in protecting the rights of minorities.

Experts estimate that active members of the militia total less than 100,000 nationwide, but the concerns that fuel their hatred and fear resonate with many more Americans. In fact, a recent poll showed that four of ten Americans believe that the government threatens their freedom.[3]

---

1. "Inside the World of the Paranoid," *New York Times* (April 30, 1995), Section 4, p. 1.
2. Jill Smolowe, "Enemies of the State," *Time* (May 8, 1995), pp. 60–69.
3. Steven Thomma, "Poll Shows 4 of 10 Distrust Government," *Centre Daily Times* (April 29, 1995), p. 1. Another common set of conspiracy theories is found among urban blacks, some of whom believe that AIDs and drug traffic are white plots to destroy the black community.

National Small Business Association. These groups often, but not always, ally with big business.

In addition to these general groups, hundreds of trade associations represent single industries, such as builders, used-car salespeople, and restaurant owners. Many corporations also lobby in Washington.

Labor

Although there are more than 100 labor unions in the United States, the AFL-CIO is probably the most important politically. It is a confederation of 88 trade and industrial unions with 13 million members. It has a staff of 500 and includes some of the most skillful lobbyists in Washington. Through its Committee on Political Education (COPE), it provides substantial sums of money as well as a pool of campaign workers to candidates for public office, typically Democratic candidates. In recent years labor has lobbied hard to eliminate the right of employers to hire replacement workers for striking employees; to defeat the North American Free Trade Agreement between the U.S., Mexico, and Canada, which may mean a loss of American jobs; and to adopt national health care reform.

The political influence of labor unions has waned since the 1960s. One reason is that membership has declined. Only 16% of the nonagricultural work force belongs to unions (see Figure 2). Declining membership reflects changes in the economy. In the 1970s and 1980s, millions from the "baby boom" generation entered the job market but could not find jobs. Slowdowns in manufacturing, such as steel and auto production, added to unemployment. The oversupply of workers, along with a fear of inflation and presidents hostile to unions, created pressures to keep wages low. Labor's bargaining position with business weakened, and there was little reason for union workers to look to unions for help or for nonunion workers to join. Additionally, global competition robbed labor of its most powerful weapon—the strike. Fearful that they will be replaced or that their employers will suffer in the competitive marketplace, employees are unwilling to strike. In recent testimony, the AFL-CIO signaled its willingness to curb the right to strike if Congress would restrict the right of business to use replacement workers during a strike.[31]

Some businesses also frustrated union efforts to organize workers by opting for a "progressive management" approach to keep workers satisfied. Others threatened to fire pro-union employees or predicted dire consequences from unionization; both tactics are illegal. Such tactics increased in the 1980s in part because Reagan, and to a lesser extent Bush, appointed only probusiness people to the National Labor Relations Board (NLRB), the agency that hears cases involving threats and intimidation against employees who support unionization.[32] Previous presidents had appointed representatives of both business and labor to the board.

Until recently unions have also been unwilling to appeal to nonmanufacturing sectors of the economy. With the exception of teachers and government employees, unions have shown little interest in organizing younger workers, women, and those in clerical and service occupations. In general, union organizing activity has decreased in recent years.[33] Labor's political influence has also declined because its membership is located primarily in the Northeast and Midwest, which are declining in population and losing representation in Congress. In the South and Southwest, where population is increasing, opposition to unions is strong and only a small percentage of the work force is unionized.

Energized by the Republican takeover of Congress in 1994 and the election of new leadership, the AFL-CIO sent out 1,000 organizers into selected communities during the summer of 1996 to campaign for labor's friends and against its enemies. The union also funneled millions to Democratic candidates in an effort to turn back Republican successes in 1994. A new and confrontational generation of union leaders feel that the old contract between workers, employers, and the government is broken. They hope to restore labor's position as a key player in American politics. The goal is to organize workers in industries and regions of the country where unions are weak or nonexistent. Changing economic circumstances for workers hold out the prospect of success. Besides, labor has little to lose.[34]

Agriculture

Agricultural interests are represented by a variety of general and specialized groups. The American Farm Bureau Federation, the largest of the general agriculture interest groups, began when the federal government established the agricultural extension service with agents in rural locations to help farmers. To encourage cooperation with agents, the govern-

FIGURE 2
Union Membership Has Decreased

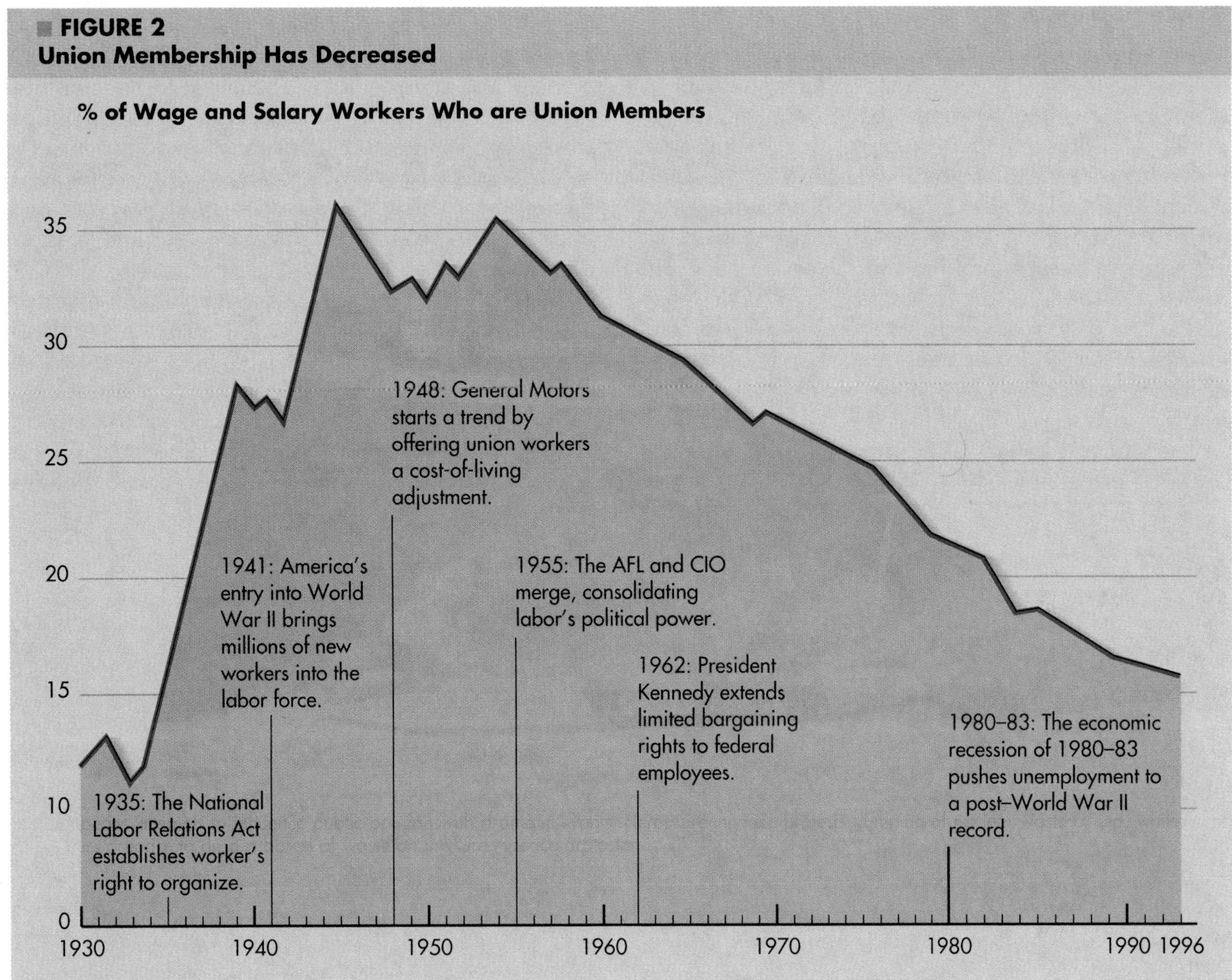

Sources: Christoph Blumrich, *Newsweek*, September 5, 1983, p. 51; *Statistical Abstract of the United States*. 1990; *Lincoln Journal*, March 1993.

ment offered grants to states that organized county farm bureaus. By 1919 a national organization was formed.

Despite its roots, the Farm Bureau today is staunchly opposed to government intervention in the economy, including subsidies to farmers. This reflects the conservative ideology of the large and wealthy farm interests that dominate the organization. Despite opposition to government subsidies, many members benefit from them.

The National Farmers' Union, which is considerably smaller than the Farm Bureau, represents small farming interests. It strongly supports government subsidies to farmers.

The American Agriculture Movement (AAM) began as a protest movement by farmers who were badly hurt by falling prices in the mid-1970s.[35] Dissatisfied with the position of both the Farm Bureau and the Farmers' Union, AAM called for a national farmer's strike until the government adopted a policy that included guaranteed income levels for farmers. Today AAM has a small, permanent lobbying staff in Washington and speaks out primarily on issues that benefit small farmers and ranchers.[36]

Along with the general interest groups, hundreds of commodity organizations promote specific products and operate much like business trade associations. Examples include cattle, cotton, milk, tobacco, and wool producers. Large agribusiness firms such as Cargill also have powerful lobbies in Washington.

Professionals

Most professions—occupations that require considerable specialized instruction or training, such as medicine, law, and teaching—have organizations to protect and promote their interests. Doctors have the powerful American Medical Association (AMA)[37] which has worked first to keep government out of medicine and then to shape Medicare and other government health programs in ways that benefit doctors. Although still influential, the AMA is no longer unchallenged; consumer and public interest groups, insurance companies, and national chains of hospitals and clinics are now highly involved in health-care issues.

The American Bar Association (ABA) represents the legal profession. The ABA supports the economic interests of lawyers and has promoted structural and procedural reforms of the courts.[38] The ABA also advises the president and Senate on the qualifications of those being considered for federal judgeships. The National Bar Association represents the nation's black lawyers. It deals with professional matters of particular interest to black lawyers and, like the ABA, passes judgment on the qualifications of federal judges.

The National Education Association has a membership of 1.7 million teachers.[39] Perhaps its greatest national lobbying successes have been the establishment of the cabinet-level Department of Education in 1979 and defeating Reagan's attempts to dismantle it.

Even political scientists have a professional association, with 12,000 members. The American Political

Corporate Lobbies: Big Winners in the Government Sweepstakes

When one thinks of special interests seeking special favors from the government, the image of disgruntled farmers or abortion activists marching on Washington comes to mind. President Reagan used the label to identify labor unions, teachers, and women's groups when he charged that Walter Mondale, the Democratic party nominee for president in 1984, was the candidate of special interests. However, if the term refers to groups that are the most powerful and successful in winning "goodies" from the federal government, it applies to America's biggest and wealthiest corporations.

Corporations lobby Congress and government agencies for a variety of benefits including subsidies and tax breaks. In 1994, business received $50 billion in direct subsidies and another $50 billion in tax breaks. One of the leading beneficiaries of government largess is agribusiness, which receives nearly $30 billion in subsidies. Large, profitable ranchers are allowed to graze their livestock on federal lands at a fraction of what it would cost on private property. One hundred million dollars is doled out by the government to companies to advertise their products abroad. Sunkist Growers, Inc., received $18 million to promote citrus products. The American Soybean Growers got $10 million, Gallo wines $5 million, and McDonalds $.5 million to push Chicken McNuggets.

Mining companies are permitted to extract minerals from public lands for nothing. The "biggest prize" went to a Toronto-based company that has mined $9 billion worth of gold from public lands since 1987. The founder of the company collected $32 million in salary in 1992.

Pharmaceutical companies are also big winners. U.S. taxpayers paid out $32 million dollars over 15 years to develop Taxol, an anticancer drug. Bristol-Myers Squibb was given exclusive rights to market the drug in 1991, at which time it charged $986 for a three-week supply. Estimates are that the company recouped eight times its production costs. Taxpayers paid once to develop the drug and again to use it.

These benefits are often justified on the grounds that they promote competitiveness with companies that enjoy unfair marketing advantages. For example, the $100 million provided firms to advertise their products overseas is supposed to help American firms overcome the advantages enjoyed by foreign companies that are subsidized by their governments. However, most of the firms are reaping huge profits, and subsidies and tax breaks are only a small part of the overall net worth of corporate America.

Programs like food stamps ($25 billion in 1994) and Aid to Families with Dependent Children ($15 billion in 1994) are often criticized as "giveaways" that should be cut in periods of tight budgets and deficits. Few call for elimination of corporate "giveaways." One reason is that corporations lobby effectively to keep them.

Source: James P. Donahue, "The Corporate Welfare Kings," *Washington Post National Weekly Edition* (March 21–27, 1993), p. 24.

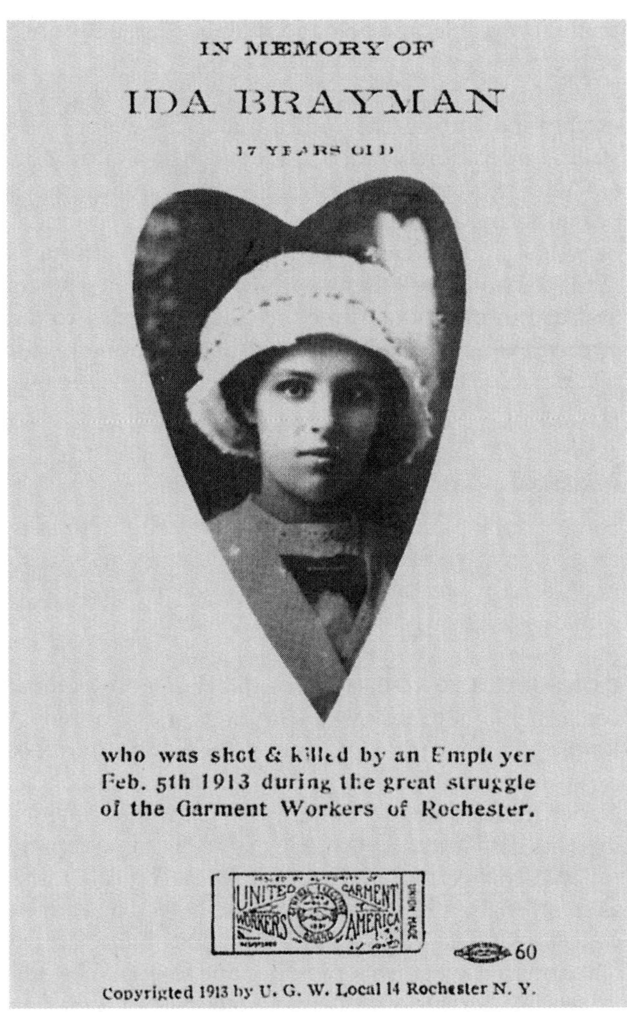

This postcard commemorates the death of a 17-year-old woman striking for recognition of her union, an eight-hour day, and extra pay for overtime and holidays.

Science Association and other social science organizations also support an umbrella organization whose staff seeks to educate Congress and bureaucrats about the value of social science research.

Elderly

While the population of the nation as a whole has tripled since 1900, the number of elderly has increased eightfold. Today, persons over 65 are over 12% of the population. Several groups, sometimes called the "gray lobby," represent their interests.

Founded in 1958 to provide insurance to the elderly, the American Association of Retired Persons (AARP), with 33 million members, is the nation's largest and one of its most powerful interest groups. Recruited by direct mail and word of mouth, AARP attracts 8,000 new members a day. For $8, anyone over 50 can join and use the numerous benefits provided by the organization[40] (see Table 1).

With 1800 employees and 18 lobbyists, AARP has become a potent political force. AARP's lobbying efforts are directed primarily at preserving and expanding government benefits to the elderly, which total about $14 billion each month.[41] The Reagan administration quickly dropped the idea of cutting cost-of-living increases in Social Security to reduce the nation's deficit when AARP and others protested. Reagan's budget director lamented, "These are people who have plenty of time on their hands, who are well organized, who vote regularly, and they are a massive political force."[42] Although programs for the elderly represent one-third of the budget, politicians are reluctant to touch them. Those who have suggested doing so have earned themselves the AARP label "granny-basher." Mindful of their political influence, Clinton got AARP to support his effort to reform health care by including long-term nursing home care.

Influence is exercised primarily by a flood of correspondence to members of Congress from AARP members. There is no congressional district where the AARP is not 50,000 strong.[43]

To counterbalance the power of the gray lobby, a number of groups such as Americans for Generational Equity and the Children's Defense Fund have formed, but they are small by comparison.

Foreign Governments

Foreign interests also lobby in Washington. Mexico has a 16-member Washington office that geared up to support NAFTA. In addition to spending $1 million to

TABLE 1 AARP Is a Big Business

ACTIVITY	AARP'S 1994 REVENUE IN MILLIONS OF DOLLARS
Health insurance	$120.0
Visa/MasterCard	8.7
Auto/home insurance	35.0
Car rental	4.5
Mutual funds	7.6
Pharmacy	4.3
Motor club	1.9

polish the country's image, it distributed more than 100,000 pieces of mail, including state-by-state analyses of NAFTA's impact, to members of Congress. Most countries recruit lobbyists from the ranks of former members of Congress and the bureaucracy. Since 1974, 47% of former employees of the U.S. Office of Trade Assistance have worked for foreign governments, the most prominent for Japan. Though it happens frequently, most people consider it unethical for former government employees to leave government and take jobs with interest groups, corporations, or foreign governments and use their knowledge and skills to lobby government. Many officials of OTA helped draw up the rules for U.S. trade, then left and helped foreign governments beat the rules. As one writer put it, "No wonder we are losing the trade war."[44] The Clinton administration attempted to close the revolving door by requiring top political appointees to refrain from lobbying their agencies for five years after leaving government and from representing foreign governments forever.[45] However, two of his senior advisors left to take jobs with major lobbying firms. Both said they would not lobby government, but they were hired because of their contacts in the Clinton administration.

Public Interest Groups

Public interest groups, of which there are more than 2,500 with 40 million members,[46] lobby for benefits that cannot be limited or restricted to their members. The National Taxpayers Union lobbies for reduced taxes not only for themselves but for everyone who pays taxes. Amnesty International lobbies for the rights of political prisoners around the world even though none of its members are prisoners. Although nearly all groups think of themselves as pursuing the public interest, the label applies only to those working for other than personal or corporate interests. "Public interest" does not mean that a majority of the public necessarily favors the goals of these groups.

Public interest groups are not new, but their numbers and size increased dramatically during the late 1960s and early 1970s. Several factors account for this surge. Americans were becoming increasingly distrustful of government, which appeared to favor special interests over more general interests. The need for a balance between the two led many to join public interest groups. Many middle-class Americans also had the financial means to support public interest groups. The new technology mentioned earlier also made it possible to reach and mobilize large numbers of them.[47]

While many of the public interest groups that were established during the 1960s and 1970s were "shoestring" operations staffed by idealistic social reformers with few professional skills, the public interest organizations of today have larger budgets and memberships and a cadre of professionals—attorneys, management consultants, direct-mail fund-raisers, and communications directors—handling day-to-day operations and seeking to influence government with a variety of strategies and tactics.[48]

Multiple-Issue Groups

Some public interest groups are multiple-issue groups, involved with a broad range of issues. Others have a narrower focus and are often referred to as single-issue groups.

CONSUMER GROUPS One of the more famous consumer organizations is the network founded by Ralph Nader. Author of *Unsafe at Any Speed,* a book exposing safety defects in Corvair automobiles, Nader testified before Congress, which was considering the 1965 Auto Safety Act. Nader became famous practically overnight when the press revealed that General Motors had hired a private detective to try to collect evidence that could discredit him. Greatly embarrassed when this ploy became known, GM had to pay Nader an out-of-court settlement for harassment. No "dirt" was ever found—Nader then and now lives a Spartan life and is apparently totally devoted to his work.

AARP members review publications targeted for senior citizens.

With the settlement and funds from book royalties and lecture tours, Nader founded a wide variety of public interest organizations, the most famous of which is called Public Citizen. Nader's staff members, called "Nader's Raiders" to characterize their zeal, are willing to accept low wages and work long hours. Their reward is the chance to influence government to pass and enforce laws protecting consumers and workers and reducing government waste.

Nader's organizations research and publicize problems and lobby in Congress. Current causes include problems in the nuclear industry, costs of health care, consumer protection, and congressional campaign finances.

Although consumer groups achieved many of their objectives in the 1960s and 1970s, since then they have had less success. Their main target, business, reasserted its political dominance.

WOMEN'S GROUPS Groups advocating women's equality have mushroomed in the past two decades and range from large, mass-based organizations with a broad agenda, such as the National Organization for Women (NOW), to much smaller groups with very specific interests such as electing women to public office.

NOW is the largest women's group with 150,000 members in all 50 states.[49] With a national board made up of regional representatives and national salaried officers, NOW is well organized. It has field representatives and organizers, researchers, lobbyists, and specialists in various policy areas such as reproductive freedom and economic rights.

NOW is funded largely from membership dues but has actively solicited funds by mail. It also receives income from subscriptions and selling such things as T-shirts and posters. Private foundations interested in promoting women's rights also provide significant funding.

Although NOW began as a protest movement, today its focus is on lobbying at the national, state, and local levels. It provides leadership training and

The first wave of women's organizations campaigned for women's right to vote. Here, some of 20,000 marchers parade for women's rights in New York City in 1917.

education for local and state groups and works with a shifting coalition of other women's rights groups.

In recent years the women's movement has divided between groups pushing an ideological agenda, like NOW, which continues to see abortion as a major concern, and more pragmatic groups such as the National Women's Political Caucus, which sees its task as electing women to public office regardless of their stands on the issues.

EMILY—short for "Early Money Is Like Yeast" (it makes the dough rise) is an organization that recruits, trains, and endorses pro-choice Democratic women candidates and then works to fund and elect them to public office. The organization holds seminars for candidates, campaign managers and press secretaries. It helped elect five women to the Senate and 34 to the House. In 1994, it contributed over $8 million to Democratic candidates, the largest contributor to the party. In 1996 it spent $10 million to get out the vote.[50]

RELIGIOUS GROUPS Religious groups often lobby on political issues. The National Council of Churches, representing liberal Protestant denominations, has spoken out on civil rights, human rights, and other social issues. Catholic groups have been active in both antiabortion and antinuclear movements. Jewish groups have been involved in lobbying for liberal issues, such as the rights of workers and minorities.

Jewish groups have been particularly active in lobbying for Israel. Since its beginning in 1951, the pro-Israel lobby has lost on only three key decisions, all involving the sale of U.S. arms to Egypt and Saudi Arabia. The success of Jewish groups in lobbying for Israel reflects their commitment, organization, and political skill, and an opposition Arab lobby that is weak by comparison.[51]

Identified by a "born again" experience, a desire to win converts to Jesus Christ, and a literal interpretation of the Bible, members of the Christian right, sometimes called fundamentalists, spurred by what they saw as a decline in traditional values, became active in politics in the 1970s.[52] The National Association of Evangelicals, representing conservative Protestant denominations, gained in visibility and prestige as the membership in conservative churches increased while membership in mainline churches declined.[53]

Opposed to abortion, divorce, homosexuality, and women's rights, conservative Christians were the major force behind the effort of television evangelist Pat Robertson to win the Republican presidential nomination in 1988. Local churches worked to secure names on endorsing petitions and funds. Although he did not win the nomination, Robertson did win a number of delegates to the Republican National Convention.

Following his loss of the nomination, Robertson converted a mailing list of two million names into the Christian Coalition under the leadership of Ralph Reed. Unlike the religious right groups of the 1980s, which were primarily concerned with spreading their message through television and radio, the Coalition runs training seminars at which participants are taught how to win control of the Republican party from the ground up. Operating quietly in the early 1990s, Reed cautioned his followers never to mention the Christian Coalition among Republicans. By 1992, the organization had gained dominance or leverage in twenty state parties.[54]

The Coalition has 1.2 million members, half of which pay $15 annual dues. Each state has a chapter and nineteen states have full-time field staffs who raise their own salary. The Coalition has emerged as a political powerhouse that includes schools, newspapers, magazines, radio and television stations, and thousands of politically mobilized churches. The organization is seen by religious right leaders as a counterweight to a "liberal establishment," which Robertson believes is controlled by "secular humanists who are exerting every effort to debase and eliminate Bible-based Christianity from our society."[55]

The network involved itself heavily in political campaigns in 1992 and 1994. The Coalition raised money, registered voters, ran phone banks, and graded legislators.[56] In the 1994 congressional elections, the group distributed 33 million voter guides, many through churches on the Sunday before the election, which compared Republicans and Democrats on several "key" issues.[57] Opponents of the Coalition charged the guides were biased against Democrats, claiming, for example, that support of the Clinton health care plan was identified in the guide as support for "Federal Government Control of Health Care." Sixty percent or more of the candidates supported by the Coalition won. Prior to the election in 1996, the Coalition distributed 45 million voter guides.[58]

Now the most powerful organization in the Republican party, the Coalition hopes to broaden its appeal. If, however, it moves any distance to the left, it may lose the enthusiasm and support of its supporters on the right. Already some supporters have become agitated by efforts to merge family and social issues with the traditional economic concerns of the Repub-

'94 Christian Coalition

VOTER  GUIDE

WASHINGTON
Congressional
District 5

Tom Foley (D)	ISSUES	George Nethercutt (R)
Opposes	Term Limits for Congress	Supports
Opposes	Balanced Budget Amendment	Supports
Supports	Taxpayer Funding of Abortion	Opposes
Opposes	Parental Choice in Education (Vouchers)	Supports
No Response*	Voluntary Prayer in Public Schools	Supports
No Response*	Homosexuals in the Military	Opposes
Supports	Banning Ownership of Legal Firearms	Opposes
No Response*	Capital Punishment for Murder	Supports
Supports	Federal Government Control of Health Care	Opposes
Supports	Raising Federal Income Taxes	Opposes

*Each candidate was sent a 1994 Federal Issues Survey by certified mail or facsimile machine. When possible, positions of candidates on issues were verified or determined using voting records and/or public statements.

Paid for and authorized by the Christian Coalition; Post Office Box 1990; Chesapeake, Virginia 23327-1990. The Christian Coalition is a pro-family citizen action organization. This voter guide is provided for educational purposes only and is not to be construed as an endorsement of any candidate or political party.

★ Vote on November 8 ★

Voter guides were distributed to churches on the Sunday before the election in 1994.

lican party. On the other hand, unwillingness to compromise on issues such as abortion, feminism, and church-state relations runs the risk of dividing the party.[59]

The Interfaith Alliance began in 1994 to counter the message and political activity of the Christian Coalition and other conservative religious groups. Comprised of mainstream and minority religious and secular groups, it has 42 chapters in 17 states, representing 20,000 individuals, and hundreds of churches, faith, and civic organizations. The group holds rallies and public forums dealing with family values, poverty, and discrimination. It opposes prayer in schools but takes no position on abortion. Like the Coalition, it produces voter guides and campaign literature. The organization elected members to local school boards and was active in a number of presidential primaries in 1996.[60]

GAYS AND LESBIANS Gay rights organizations have a shorter history than most other major political groups. The first groups formed after World War II in an era when, on the rare occasions when gays came to public attention, they were labeled as deviates. For example, in 1954, after a raid of a bar where gay men congregated, a Miami newspaper headline noted, "Perverts Seized in Bar Raids." Early gay and lesbian groups focused largely on sharing information about how to survive and how to fight police repression.[61]

In the middle 1960s, a few gays followed the example of the civil rights movements and organized small public demonstrations. Other gays argued that such public demonstrations undermined the safety and well-being of the homosexual subculture, which by then existed underground in many large cities. Nonetheless, during the '60s the gay rights movement became more radical and visible. Like Vietnam War protesters, women's rights advocates, and civil rights activists, many gays embarked upon active protests to challenge the status quo. News of a violent confrontation between gays and the police after a 1969 police raid of a gay bar in New York City helped fuel this new "gay liberation" movement. Street protests became common in large cities. Gays began forming clubs on campuses. By 1972, the issue of civil rights for gays began to be discussed in presidential campaigns, and in 1973 the American Psychiatric Association removed homosexuality from its lists of mental disorders.

Although some states decriminalized homosexual acts, many barriers remained. In some states, homosexual acts remained criminal. Gays and lesbians could be dismissed from the military if discovered. Being gay often meant losing a job, being evicted, or losing custody of a child, if divorced.

The AIDS epidemic, which began in 1981, opened a new chapter in the fight for rights of gays and lesbians. The media attention on AIDS and its impact on the gay community led to new discussions about discrimination against gays. It also revealed that many entertainers and other celebrities were gay.

Today, some gays and lesbians mostly want freedom from discrimination in jobs and other areas of life. Others want recognition of same-sex marriages. Not surprisingly, the goals of gay rights groups also differ. Some work reasonably comfortably within the mainstream; for example, the Human Rights Campaign Fund is a political action group that raised more than $4 million for candidates in the 1992 election. Others focus on specific issues, such as the Gay Men's Health Crisis, which seeks to support those with AIDS. Groups like Act Up or Queer Nation are oriented toward dramatic political action. Though most gays and lesbians vote Democratic, the Log Cabin Federation is a group of gay Republicans.

Evidence accumulates that lobbying by gay and lesbian groups is paying off. In a recent poll, 70% agreed that gays should have equal rights in hiring and firing; 78% favored increasing efforts for AIDS research, prevention, and care; and 57% supported a bill to ban workplace discrimination against gays.[62] However, the public is less supportive of lifestyle changes such as legalizing gay marriages.

ENVIRONMENTAL GROUPS Environmental groups are another example of multiple issue groups. Earth Day 1970 marked the beginning of the environmental movement in the United States. Spurred by an oil spill in California, what was to be a "teach-in" on college campuses mushroomed into a day of national environmental awareness with an estimated 20 million Americans taking part. A minority movement in the 1970s, the environmental lobby today is large and active and its values are supported by most Americans.[63]

Some environmental groups, such as the National Audubon Society, Sierra Club, and the Natural Resources Defense Council, have permanent offices in Washington with highly skilled professionals who carry out a full range of lobbying activities. All experienced substantial growth in membership and finances during the 1980s, when the Reagan administration threatened to undo the environmental gains of the 1970s.[64]

The so-called "Greens" are environmental groups that shun conventional lobbying approaches and are more confrontational. Groups like Greenpeace, Earth First!, and the Sea Shepherds seek a "green cultural revolution." Local citizen groups have also organized in support of local environmental concerns such as the location of toxic or nuclear waste dumps. Citizens, skeptical of government and corporate claims that such facilities are safe, want them located elsewhere.[65]

OTHER MULTIPLE-ISSUE INTEREST GROUPS Common Cause, a multiple-issue group established in 1970 by John Gardner, attracted nearly 100,000 members in the first six months of its existence. Much of the group's lobbying program has been directed toward improving the accountability of government. The group successfully lobbied for campaign finance reform, which placed stricter rules on reporting campaign expenditures and contributions and provided public financing for presidential elections. The organization also supports further finance reform, including public funding of congressional elections.

A new organization, The Fair Government Foundation, founded after the 1994 elections by Republican Senator Paul Coverdell of Georgia, sees itself as a counterweight to Common Cause. Although small by comparison—it has a budget of $300,000 and two full-time staff—it opposes public funding of elections and views any limits on spending as a violation of the First Amendment.[66]

Other multiple-issue interest groups include the American Civil Liberties Union, concerned with protecting the constitutional rights of citizens; the League of Women Voters, concerned with government reform and expanding women's roles and participation; and the Children's Defense Fund, concerned with protecting the nation's children.

Single-Issue Groups

Single-issue groups pursue public interest goals but are distinguished by their intense concern for a single issue and their reluctance to compromise. Members of the National Rifle Association (NRA) passionately oppose most forms of government control of firearms. For years, in spite of a majority of Americans who support gun control, the NRA has successfully lobbied Congress to prevent significant gun control. The group has members in every congressional district and is well organized to mobilize them. It spent a great deal of money in a losing battle to defeat the Brady Act, which requires a five-day waiting period in order to purchase a gun. It also failed to prevent a ban on sales of assault weapons. The House did vote to repeal the ban in 1996.

While the NRA remains a major political force, antigun sentiment is growing as more and more Americans respond to increasing gun violence that touches cities, suburbs, and small towns. The result is an increase in the political influence of antigun groups such as Handgun Control and politicians more willing to take on the NRA. The image of the NRA has been damaged by its unwillingness to accept reasonable gun control measures. To restore its image, the

Pressure on Congress and state legislatures from the National Rifle Association has meant that even guns like these are readily available in most states.

group has shifted emphasis from guns to criminal justice. Its Crime Strike division has made a point of calling for tougher sentences, more prisons, and a crackdown on drug crimes. Its image was tarnished even more, however, when a fund-raising letter at the time of the bombing of the federal building in Oklahoma City referred to federal law enforcement officers as "jackbooted government thugs, wearing black, armed to the teeth, who break down a door, open fire with an automatic weapon and kill or maim law-abiding citizens." The jackboot reference, which is associated with Nazi stormtroopers, led former president George Bush (a longtime NRA member and supporter) to resign his membership. The organization lost more than 300,000 members in 1995.

The abortion controversy has generated a number of single-issue groups. The National Right to Life Committee seeks a constitutional amendment banning all abortions. The committee works to elect candidates who favor such an amendment and defeat those who do not. After the 1989 and 1992 Supreme Court decisions allowing more state regulation of abortion, pro-life groups turned their attention to state legislators. They pushed for laws requiring informed consent, waiting periods, and parental consent for minors. In 1996, the organization activated its 8 million members and contributed heavily on behalf of Republican candidates.

Operation Rescue is a confrontational antiabortion group that attempts to prevent women seeking abortions access to abortion clinics. Many "rescuers" have been arrested and jailed because of their activities. The group graduated its first class of abortion protesters from its military-style boot camp in Florida. The 22 men and women, ranging in age from 16 to 67, learned a number of skills to assist them in their fight against abortion. From a private detective, they learned how to obtain information about people, for example, that license plates can be used to obtain home addresses. The purpose is to identify people who perform abortions: to pray or picket in front of their homes, confront them in the supermarket, and identify them as "murderers" to their neighbors and children.

A lawyer lectured on how to file lawsuits against local officials, police, abortion doctors, and activists in an effort to bog them down in paperwork. Students were instructed in how to infiltrate abortion clinics. One scenario has a man and woman stage an argument in the waiting area, one pleading with the other not to go through with the abortion. In another, a student uses a borrowed urine sample from a pregnant woman and goes through all the steps of obtaining an abortion up to reclining on the operating table. The purpose is to disrupt clinic operations. Students also learn the art of phone taps and long-distance surveillance. Graduates are expected to return home and teach others what they have learned. These tactics, including the murder of two doctors by deranged right-to-lifers, have limited access to abortion because many physicians do not wish to be harassed and simply refuse to perform abortions.[67] The application of federal racketeering laws to those who disrupt clinic activities may limit these tactics in the future.

Anti-abortion activists picked up considerable support in Congress following the 1994 elections, but abortion issues were set aside in favor of issues identified in the "Contract with America" (see You Are There, Chapter 6).

Abortion did not become much of an issue in the 1996 Republican presidential nomination, but Republican activists did divide over whether the party's platform would contain a pro-life plank. The party appeared, however, to avoid a major public conflict by permitting pro choice Republicans to register their opinion in an appendix to the platform. With Clinton's veto of a ban on late-term abortions, the issue may become important in the general election.

Members of the national Abortion Rights Action League and Planned Parenthood are fervently committed to protecting women's right to abortion. Planned Parenthood is the oldest, largest, best-financed, and most powerful single advocate of reproductive freedom for women, including birth control and abortion.

Since 1988, the organization has mounted a major effort to win policymakers to the pro-choice point of view. Using the theme that Americans want abortion to be safe and legal, ads were placed in national newspapers. Testimony was provided by physicians who treated botched abortions in the days when abortion was illegal, by clergy involved in counseling, and by women who underwent illegal abortion because they had no choice. Three months before the 1989 Supreme Court decision allowing state regulation of abortion (for more on this see Chapter 14), 300,000 pro-choice activists staged a march in Washington. Calling the event the "March for Women's Lives," the goal was to recast the issue in terms of freedom and choice rather than abortion. The march slogan, "Who Decides, You or Them?" became the rallying cry in several state elections in 1989. The three-day event received substantial publicity and demonstrated to members of Congress that the movement could mobilize a large number of supporters.[68]

Single-issue groups have increased in number since the mid-1960s. Some view this with alarm, because when groups clash over a highly emotional issue and are unwilling to compromise, government cannot resolve the issue.[69] The issue commands excessive time and energy of policy makers at the expense of broader issues that may be more important.

On the other hand, single-issue groups have always been part of politics.[70] These groups may even be beneficial because they represent interests that may not be well represented in Congress. Fears about single-issue groups may result from the groups' own exaggerated claims of influence, their heavy media

The right-to-life movement is considered a single-issue group.

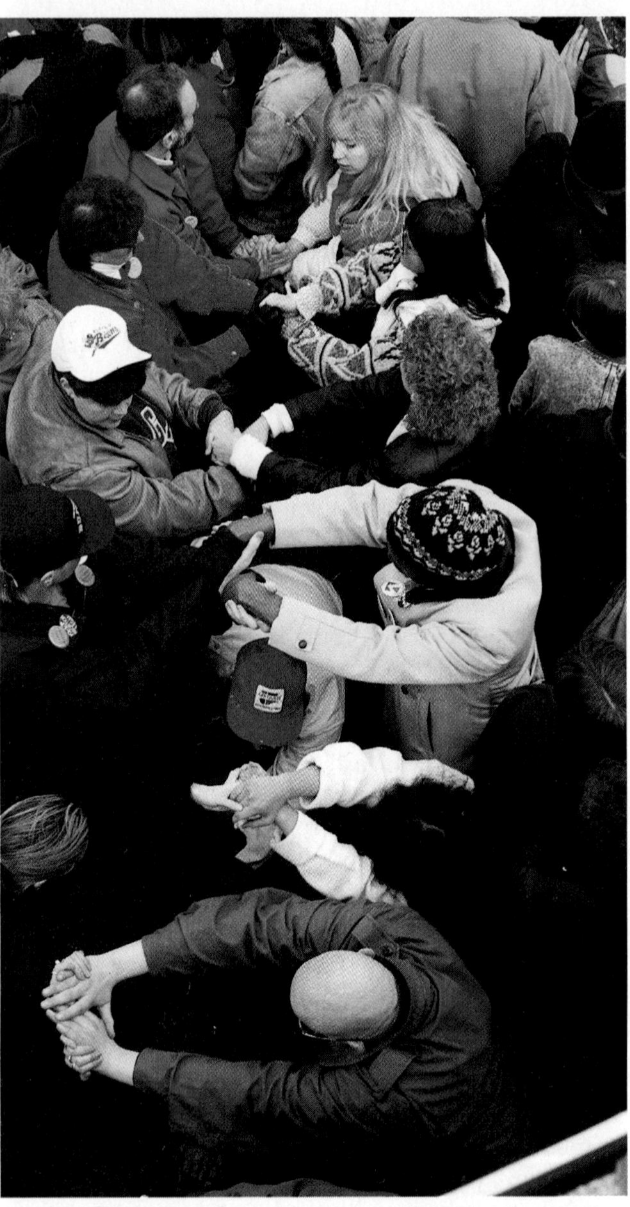

Pro-choice advocates form a human corridor to protect patients and workers entering a clinic in Buffalo.

coverage, and in the case of some anti-abortion groups, their resort to violence.

Tactics of Interest Groups

Interest groups engage in a variety of tactics to secure their goals. Some try to influence policymakers directly, whereas others seek to mold public opinion and influence policymakers indirectly. Sometimes interest groups form broad coalitions or engage in protest activity, both of which involve direct and indirect techniques.

Direct Lobbying Techniques

Direct lobbying techniques involve personal encounters between lobbyists and public officials. Some lobbyists are volunteers; others are permanent, salaried employees of the groups they represent; and others are contract lobbyists, "hired guns" who represent any individual or group willing to pay for the service. Contract lobbyists include the numerous Washington lawyers affiliated with the city's most prestigious law firms. Many have worked for government, so they can boast of contacts in government and access to policymakers to plead their clients' cases. Most firms recruit from the ranks of both Republicans and Democrats to assure access regardless of which party controls government.

Making Personal Contacts

Making personal contacts, in an office or in a more informal setting, is the most effective lobbying technique. Compared to other forms of lobbying, direct personal contact is relatively inexpensive, and it minimizes problems of misinterpretation by allowing questions to be answered on the spot.

Lobbyists know that contacting every legislator is unnecessary, whereas contacting key legislators, those who sit on the committees having jurisdiction over matters of interest to the lobbyists, and staff serving those committees, is critical.[71] Conventional wisdom also suggests that only those legislators who support a group's position or who are known to be undecided should be contacted directly.[72] Putting undue pressure on known opponents may jeopardize prospects for working together in the future on other issues.

To a large extent lobbying is building relationships based on friendship. As Leon Panetta, when he was chair of the House Budget Committee, put it, "The most effective lobbyists here are the ones you don't think of as lobbyists." Referring to one prominent Washington lobbyist, Panetta said, "I don't think of him as a lobbyist. He's almost a constituent, or a friend." Barbara Boxer, then a Democratic representative from California, referring to the same gentleman, described him as "a lovely, wonderful guy. In the whole time I've known him, he's never asked me to vote for anything." At a gathering she joked that he was almost "a member of the family."[73]

Providing Expertise

Some lobbying groups do research and present their findings to public officials. One of the major strengths of Ralph Nader's organization, and the public interest movement in general, is the ability to provide public officials, particularly Congress, with accurate and reliable information.

Lobbyists often have a great deal of knowledge and expertise that is useful in drafting legislation. A legislator may ask a lobbyist to draft a bill or both may work together in drafting legislation. Sometimes interest groups themselves draft legislation and ask a sympathetic legislator to introduce it. General Electric drafted a tax reform measure that saved it millions in taxes. There is nothing illegal about this.

Testifying at Hearings

Testifying at congressional hearings is designed to establish a group's credentials as a "player" in the policy area as well as to convince its own constituents that it is doing its job. A member of a prominent Washington law firm with responsibility at his firm for prepping witnesses to testify identified the Boy Scout motto, "Be Prepared," as the most important principle to follow in getting ready for a hearing. Beyond that, he offers a few other tips: Keep it short. Time is at a premium in Washington. No one has an hour to listen to you. Don't read your statement. Good salespeople don't have prepared statements. They know the product and can talk to you about it. Don't be arrogant. Some witnesses are short with members because they believe committee members don't understand their business. Too bad. Most members of Congress don't care about your business; they are going to make a decision based on what they hear. Don't guess. If you don't know the answer to a question, say so and promise to supply the answer

The Ten Commandments of Lobbying

I Thou shalt speak only the truth, and speak it clearly and succinctly; on two pages and in 15-second sound bites.

II Thou shalt translate the rustle of thy grassroots into letters, phone calls, and personal visits.

III Thou shalt not underestimate thy opponent, for he surely packeth a rabbit punch.

IV Help thy friends with reelection; but in victory, dwelleth not on the power of thy PAC.

V Thou shalt know thy issue and believe in it, but be ready to compromise; half a loaf will feed some of thy people.

VI Runneth not out of patience. If thou can not harvest this year, the next session may be bountiful.

VII Love thy neighbor; thou wilst need him for a coalition.

VIII Study arithmetic, that thou may count noses. If thou can count 51, rejoice. Thou shalt win in the Senate.

IX Honor the hard-working staff, for they prepare the position papers for the members.

X Be humble in victory, for thy bill may yet be vetoed.

Source: Ernest Wittenberg and Elisabeth Wittenberg, *How to Win in Washington* (Cambridge, Mass.: Blackwell, 1989), p. 16.

later. Don't be hokey, but illustrate whenever possible. It is easier to focus on a wrecked fender in a hearing room than to visualize a set of statistics.[74]

Another advantage of testifying is that it provides free publicity. Staging sometimes occurs. A lobbyist might request a sympathetic legislator to ask certain questions that the lobbyist is prepared to answer or to indicate in advance what questions will be asked. Sometimes celebrities are invited to testify. In a not unprecedented but certainly rare move, Mrs. Clinton, the principal player in developing the president's health care reform, testified before several congressional committees. This White House effort prompted a former Reagan aid to quip, they "do PR the way (former chair of the Joint Chiefs) Colin Powell does war: maximum use of force."[75]

Giving Money

Lobbyists try to ensure access to legislators, and giving money is one way to guarantee this. Justin Dart, a longtime financial backer of Ronald Reagan, once said that having a dialogue with a politician is fine, "but with a little money they hear you better."[76] One Democrat commented in a similar vein, "Who do members of Congress see? They'll certainly see the one who gives the money. It's hard to say no to someone who gives you $5,000."[77]

The primary way groups channel money to legislators is through campaign contributions. Groups, including businesses and unions, may set up political action committees (PACS) to give money to campaigns of political candidates.

The number of PACs has grown dramatically since the mid-1970s as has the amount of money they have contributed. (We discuss PACs more fully in Chapter 9).

Lobbying the Bureaucracy

For lobbyists, the battle is not over when a bill is passed. Lobbyists also must influence bureaucrats who implement policy. For example, regulations outlawing sex discrimination in educational institutions were drafted largely in the Department of Education with only broad guidelines from Congress. Both women's rights groups and interests opposing them lobbied for years to influence the regulations.

In influencing bureaucrats, interest groups use most of the tactics already described. They also try to influence who gets appointed to bureaucratic positions. Someone opposed by the major agricultural interest groups is not likely to be appointed secretary of agriculture. Nor is someone unsympathetic to labor apt to be appointed head of the Labor Department. The auto industry vetoed a number of Clinton's nominees to head the National Highway Traffic Safety Administration. While consumer groups want someone interested in promoting automobile safety, the industry is looking for someone more sympathetic to their interests and concerns. Of course, groups do not always succeed in their opposition. President Reagan appointed as heads of several agencies persons strongly opposed by interest groups sympathetic to the agency's activities. He appointed a secretary of the interior opposed to many governmental efforts to protect public land and an Environmental Protection Agency head who opposed most government efforts to protect the environment.

The influence of groups in the appointment process is especially crucial in the case of appointments to regulatory agencies such as the Food and Drug Administration. By influencing appointments to an agency, the regulated industry can improve its prospects of favorable treatment.

Lobbying the Courts

Like bureaucrats, judges also make policy. Some interest groups try to achieve their goals by getting involved in cases and persuading courts to rule in their favor. Although most groups do not initiate litigation, some use it as their primary tactic. Litigation has been employed extensively by civil liberties organizations, particularly the American Civil Liberties Union (ACLU), civil rights organizations such as the NAACP, environmental groups such as the Sierra Club, and public interest groups such as Common Cause. Litigation often is used by groups that lack influence in Congress and the bureaucracy.

Groups can file civil suits, represent defendants in criminal cases, or file friend of the court briefs, which are written arguments asking the court to decide a case a particular way.[78]

Some groups use the courts to make their opponents negotiate with them. Environmental groups frequently challenge developers who threaten the environment in order to force them to bear the costs of defending themselves and to delay the project. The next time, developers may be more willing to make concessions to avoid lengthy and costly litigation.

Groups try to influence the courts indirectly by lobbying the Senate to support or oppose judicial nominees.

Indirect Lobbying Techniques

Traditionally, lobbyists employed tactics of direct persuasion almost exclusively—providing information, advice, and occasionally pressure. More recently, interest groups are going public, that is, mobilizing their activists and molding and activating public opinion. A recent study of 175 lobbying groups found that most were doing more of all kinds of lobbying activity, but the largest increases were in going public.[79] Talking with the media increased the most, and mobilizing the grass roots to send letters and telegrams and make telephone calls was second.

Mobilizing the Grass Roots

The constituency of an interest group—the group's members or those whom the group serves—can help communicate the group's position to public officials. The National Rifle Association is effective in mobilizing its members. The NRA can generate thousands of letters within a few days. As one senator remarked, "I'd rather be a deer in hunting season than run afoul of the NRA crowd."[80]

Conservative Christian minister Jerry Falwell activated his "gospel grapevine" to flood the White House and Congress in opposition to the president's plan to lift the ban on homosexuals in the military. Warning of a new radical homosexual rights agenda, he urged viewers of his "Old Time Gospel Hour" to call and register their opinions.

Grassroots lobbying was the hallmark of the effort to derail or modify health care reform. Industries affected by the proposed change lined up their own supporters. Cigarette companies rallied tobacco growers to oppose increases in cigarette taxes. The Pharmaceutical Manufacturers Association had the presidents of 26 drug companies write letters to 600,000 workers asking them to write Congress warning of dangers in price controls. Insurance agents provided their clients with a booklet called "A Citizen's Guide to Health Care Reform" and urged them to contact their representatives. The AMA sent 660,000 physicians and 48,000 medical students a questionnaire marked "For Patients" with 10 questions on Clinton's health care proposal. The chief lobbyist for the National Federation of Independent Business, which also opposed the Clinton plan, says "You use the people back home to sensitize members of Congress and staff. I get listened to on the Hill because they know I have 600,000 small businessmen behind me back home. The grass roots gives me standing."[81]

Appeals to write or phone policymakers often exaggerate the severity of the problem and the strength of the opposition. Only the threat of imminent failure or a monstrous adversary with superior resources is sufficient to move most members. Because of the difficulty in mobilizing members and the cost in time and money, grassroots efforts are typically a last resort. Besides, as one lobbyist put it, members of Congress "hate it when you call in the dogs."[82]

To be successful, mass letter writing and phone calls must look sincere and spontaneous. Groups often send members sample letters to help them know what to write, but letters that appear unique are most effective. Campaigns producing thousands of postcards generally are not effective unless representatives do not hear from the other side.

Sometimes grassroots lobbying involves more than phoning or writing letters. A lobbyist for the nation's hospitals opposed to the Clinton plan for health care reform encouraged hospital administrators across the nation to get acquainted with their representative, work with the member to organize town meetings to discuss issues, and guide the member on a tour of the local hospital to point out how many people are employed and what the hospital means to the local community. "If done well, the member summoned to

Washington's "Super Lobbyist"

There are thousands of lobbyists or, as they prefer to be called, political consultants, in Washington, but the label "super lobbyist" applies to only a small number. Thomas H. Boggs, of the Washington law firm of Patton, Boggs, and Blow, is one. The firm has more than eighty lawyers, but it is referred to as "Boggs's firm." Boggs, son of the late Democratic Majority Leader Hale Boggs and former Democratic Representative Lindy Boggs of Louisiana, is reputed to be one of the capital's most powerful lobbyists.

Like most successful lobbyists, Boggs is intelligent and personable. He is also cunning and calculating. His approach is soft-sell rather than hard-line pressure. He understands the political process, especially in the House of Representatives, and has a keen sense of what motivates politicians. A few years ago he was able to win over liberal Representative Charles Rangel, a Harlem Democrat, to retain import duties on steel because some of the imported steel would come from apartheid South Africa. He convinced the late Representative William Ketchum, a conservative Republican, to retain the import duties because the company Boggs represented was located in Ketchum's district and would be hurt by competition with a foreign steel maker. Boggs points with pride to his ability to build coalitions comprising both liberals and conservatives and notes this ability as one reason he is successful.

While Boggs is a Democrat, most on his client list—one of the longest in Washington with nearly 500 names—are corporations. Being a Democrat, however, is not a handicap. It means he has access to Democratic members of Congress who are most likely to oppose business. Republicans typically vote with business. As one corporate lobbyist put it, "Republicans usually vote with you anyway. So Tommy knows he has most of them, and every time he gets a Democrat, particularly a liberal, that's icing on the cake."

As do most lobbying firms in Washington, Patton, Boggs, and Blow employ both Republicans and Democrats. The bipartisan approach and the mix of clients who are occasionally on opposite ends of issues smacks of conflict of interest. This leaves Boggs and his firm open to the charge that they are driven chiefly by money rather than moral purpose. As a lobbyist for Ralph Nader's organization put it, "Some attorneys and lobbyists have a reputation of trying to persuade their clients to do the right thing. Nobody ever says that about Tommy Boggs." Boggs is uncomfortable when conversations turn to what he hopes to contribute to society or about his political philosophy. He simply responds, "I enjoy playing the game."

And Boggs knows how to play the game. During a policy strategy session at the Carter White House, Boggs suddenly walked in. The ploy enabled him to brag about his access to the White House and added credibility to his claim that he could advise his business clients on what the "opposition" was up to. While Boggs has had some notable successes over the years—for example, he gets much of the credit for the Chrysler bailout—he does not win all the time. However, he convinces people that he can make things happen. Even if the belief in his power and influence is exaggerated, it does not matter to Boggs, as long as his clients and would-be clients hold this belief.

Boggs's chief asset is his ability to raise money for congressional candidates. He contributes himself, generally the $25,000 maximum allowed by law. More important, he gets his clients to contribute. Boggs also calls upon a network of Washington lobbyists to contribute. "I hit these guys," he says, "and I know they'll come back and hit me up."

While very important to his success, fund-raising is only part of Boggs's job. He can be seen prowling the corridors of Congress, talking with members, and picking up whatever political information he can. Like any well-connected lobbyist, he attends as many as ten receptions per week, two or more some evenings. The schedule is hectic and no one claims Boggs does not work hard for his clients.

Sources: A. R. Hunt, "The Washington Power Brokers," ed. P. Woll, *Behind the Scenes of American Government*, 6th ed. (Little, Brown and Company: Boston, Mass., 1987); *National Journal* (September 14, 1985).

the Oval Office can turn to the president and say 'I can't go with you on this, Mr. President, because I promised the people in my district.' "[83]

Molding Public Opinion

Groups use public relations techniques to shape public opinion through the media. Ads in newspapers, magazines, and on television supply the public with information, foster a positive image of the group, or promote a public policy. By themselves ads have little impact in moving policymakers to action or shifting public opinion dramatically in the short run. They are most effective in combination with other tactics.

Groups also may stage events such as rallies or pickets to attract media coverage to their cause. For example, those opposed to racial segregation in South Africa won considerable attention picketing and protesting outside the South African embassy in Washington, D.C. They were especially effective because they enlisted members of Congress, community leaders, and other celebrities in their protests. Arrests of members of Congress and other celebrities for trespassing kept the issue in the limelight for months.

Those arguing in favor of tort reform (limiting damages courts will award to those injured in auto accidents, air disasters, unsuccessful surgeries or other mishaps) focus on the few outrageous huge settlements for seemingly innocuous injuries. Those arguing against such changes focus on the poor widows left penniless after being permanently incapacitated by the rapacious behavior of a wealthy corporation.[84]

A tactic increasingly used by interest groups to influence public opinion is rating members of Congress. Groups may choose a number of votes crucial to their concerns such as abortion, conservation, or consumer affairs. Or they may select many votes reflecting a liberal or conservative outlook. They then publicize the votes to their members with the ultimate objective of trying to defeat candidates who vote against their positions. The impact of these ratings is probably minimal unless they are used in a concerted effort to target certain members for defeat.

Caps Off to the Beer Lobby

Do you like to have a beer now and then? If so, perhaps membership in the Beer Drinkers of America is for you. But then again maybe it is not. While an organization for beer drinkers may seem slightly odd, an organization for beer producers and sellers seems quite likely.

A "fact sheet" put out by the organization says that the group has a membership of 700,000 beer drinkers. Their mission is to mobilize members to fight things such as taxes on beer, restrictions on advertising, and deposit laws, ostensibly on behalf of beer drinkers.

How did the group get started? One version is that a few fellow beer drinkers decided to oppose a proposed tax on beer on the ballot in New Mexico back in 1987. (We can visualize a couple of mad-as-hell couch potatoes sitting in a mobile home in the desert flinging empties at the TV and clamoring they weren't going to take it any more.) A more plausible version is that the group was the brainchild of a lobbyist trying to help a client beat back the beer tax. The lobbyist and a friend persuaded one beer company to put up some seed money and many beer retailers to spread the word. In less than a year, 4,000 signed on. Today, money comes from two beer companies and from beer wholesalers who pressure their employees to join. Of the 700,000, only 150,000, most of whom are employed by the beer industry, actually pay dues; the rest support the group by signing petitions and writing letters.

Unfortunately for all the real beer drinkers in the country, the organization is a tool of the industry. Why all the deception? The industry hopes to use the group to scare members of Congress. Members might vote against the industry but they don't want to go back to their districts having voted against "Joe Six Pack." Increasingly groups try to couch their real intent behind a name that they know will conjure positive images on the part of the public and maybe policymakers.

Source: Sean Holton, "Beer Biz Leaves 1 Drinker Foaming," *Orlando Sentinel* (September 12, 1993), pp. 1A, 7A.

Coalition Building

Coalitions, networks of groups with similar concerns, help individual groups press their demands. Coalitions can be large and focused on many issues or small and very specific. For example, 7-Eleven stores, Kingsford charcoal, amusement parks, and lawn and garden centers joined the Daylight Saving Time Coalition to lobby Congress to extend daylight saving time. All wanted additional daylight hours to snack, grill, play, or till the soil, which would mean more money in their pockets.

Coalitions have formed around health care reform. The AFL-CIO, American Airlines, Chrysler Corp, the American College of Physicians and the League of Women Voters support health care reform, and the American Conservative Union, United Seniors Union, Citizens for a Sound Economy, and National Taxpayers have joined a coalition of Citizens Against Health Rationing. Similarly, more than 2,700 companies and trade associations were members of USA*NAFTA, a coalition supporting the trade agreement.[85]

Coalitions demonstrate broad support for an issue and also take advantage of the different strengths of groups. One group may be adept at grassroots lobbying, another at public relations. One may have lots of money, another lots of members.

The growth of coalitions in recent years reflects a number of changes in the policy process.[86] Issues have become increasingly complex. Legislation often affects a variety of interests, which makes it easier to form coalitions among groups representing the interests. In addition, changes in technology make it easier for groups to communicate with each other and with constituents. And the number of interest groups is larger than it used to be, especially the number of public interest groups. Many such groups have limited resources, and coalitions help them stretch their lobbying efforts. Some "black hat" business groups, with image problems, seek to associate themselves with "white hat" organizations ranging from labor unions to consumer groups.[87] The decentralization of Congress and the weakness of political parties also have led to coalition building to win needed majorities at the various stages of the policy process.

Coalitions vary in their duration—some are short-term, whereas others are permanent. Coalitions involved with the health care issue are likely to remain only until the issue is resolved. Coalitions supporting and opposing NAFTA ceased to exist when Congress approved the measure.

On the other hand, the Leadership Conference on Civil Rights is a permanent coalition of 185 civil rights, ethnic, religious and other groups (Elks, Actors Equity, YMCA, and the National Funeral Directors and Morticians Association). Unlike short-term coalitions, permanent ones need to be sensitive to how today's actions will affect future cooperation. Some issues may be avoided even though a majority of coalition members want to deal with them. When a coalition is unified, however, it can be formidable.

In elections, coordination among PACs in channeling money to political candidates is widespread. Business PACs, for example, take their lead from the Business-Industry Political Action Committee (BIPAC). Information is shared on candidates' issue positions, likelihood of winning, and need for funding.

Protest and Civil Disobedience

Groups that lack access or hold unpopular positions can protest. They can target policymakers directly or indirectly through public opinion. In recent years, issues as diverse as abortion, American support for the contras in Nicaragua, busing to promote school integration, nuclear weapons, and the poor farm economy in the Midwest have generated protest marches and rallies.

Peaceful but illegal protest activity, where those involved allow themselves to be arrested and punished, is called civil disobedience. Greenpeace is an environmental and peace group that practices civil disobedience. It started in 1971 when a group of environmentalists and peace activists sent two boats to Amchitka Island in the Aleutians to protest a U.S. underground nuclear weapon test. The boats were named *Greenpeace,* linking the environment and peace. Although the boats failed to reach the island, the publicity generated by the affair led Washington to cancel the test.

Throughout the 1970s and 1980s, Greenpeace staged a number of such protests. To protest dumping of toxic wastes and sewage in the ocean, 13 Greenpeace activists lowered themselves from a New York bridge and hung there for eight hours, preventing any sewage barges from carrying wastes out to sea. All were arrested. To protect endangered whales, members placed themselves in the path of a harpoon, narrowly missing being struck. Others parachuted over coal-powered power plants to protest acid rain. Their goal was to generate publicity and dramatic photographs that would activate the general population.

Protest can generate awareness of an issue, but to be successful, it must influence mass or elite opinion. Often it is the first step in a long struggle that takes years to resolve. Sometimes the first result is hostility toward the group using it. Antiwar protest by college students in the 1960s and 1970s angered not only government officials, who targeted the leaders for harassment, but also many citizens. In the early years of the women's movement, the media labeled many female protestors "bra burners" even though it is not clear if any woman ever burned a bra.

Greenpeace attempts to influence public opinion with dramatic events. Here, Greenpeace protests dumping of nuclear waste at sea, while dumpers prepare to drop a barrel of waste on the Greenpeace protestors.

Extended protests are difficult because they demand more skill by the leaders and sacrifices from the participants. Continued participation, essential to success, robs participants of a normal life. It can mean jail, physical harm, or even death and requires discipline to refrain from violence, even when violence is used against them.

The civil rights movement provides the best example of the successful use of extended protest and civil disobedience in twentieth-century America. By peacefully demonstrating against legalized segregation in the South, black and some white protesters drew the nation's attention to the discrepancy between the American values of equality and democracy and the southern laws that separated blacks from whites in every aspect of life. Protesters used tactics such as sit-ins, marches, and boycotts. Confrontations with authorities often won protesters national attention and public support, which eventually led to change.

All tactics can be effective, but some lend themselves better to some groups than others. For example, business groups with great financial resources can pay for skillful lobbyists and donate to political candidates. Labor unions have many members and can help candidates canvass and get out the vote. Public interest groups rely on activating public opinion and, where members are intensely committed to a cause, protest.

Success of Interest Groups

Although no interest group gets everything it wants from government, some are more successful than others. Politics is not a game of chance, where only luck determines winners and losers. Knowing what to do and how to do it—strategy and tactics—are important, as are resources, competition, and goals.

Resources

Although large size does not guarantee success, large groups have advantages. They can get the attention of public officials by claiming to speak for more people or by threatening to mobilize members against them.

The geographical distribution of members of a group is also important. Because organized labor is concentrated in the Northeast, its influence is less strong elsewhere. The Chamber of Commerce, on the other hand, has members and influence throughout the country.

Other things being equal, a group with well-educated members has an advantage because highly educated people are more likely than others to communicate with public officials and contribute to lobbying efforts.

Group cohesion and intensity are also advantages. Public officials are unlikely to respond to a group if it cannot agree on what it wants or if it does not appear to feel very strongly about its position. For example, in recent years the NAACP has suffered from deep splits within its leadership over tactics and allies. Such splits diminish the clout of a group.

A large **market share,** the number of members in a group compared to its potential membership, is another advantage. For years the American Medical Association enrolled a large percentage (70% or more) of the nation's doctors as members. As its membership (as a percentage of the total number of doctors) has declined, so too has its influence.

The more money a group has, the more successful it probably will be. Not only does money buy skilled lobbyists and access to elected officials, it is also necessary for indirect lobbying efforts.

Knowledge is a major resource too. If leaders of a group are experts in a policy area, they are more apt to get the attention of public officials. Knowledge of how things get done in Washington is also helpful,

Organizing Protest: The Montgomery Bus Boycott

The 1955 Montgomery, Alabama, bus boycott was the first successful civil rights protest, and it brought its 26-year-old leader, Dr. Martin Luther King, Jr., to national prominence. Montgomery, like most southern cities, required blacks to sit in the back of public buses while whites sat in the front. The dividing line between the two was a "no man's land" where blacks could sit if there were no whites. If whites needed the seats, blacks had to give them up and move to the back.

One afternoon, Rosa Parks, a seamstress at a local department store and a leader in the local chapter of the National Association for the Advancement of Colored People (NAACP), boarded the bus to go home. The bus was filled and when a white man boarded, the driver called on the four blacks behind the whites to move to the back. Three got up and moved, but Mrs. Parks, tired from a long day and of the injustice of always having to move for white people, said she did not have to move because she was in "no man's land." Under a law that gave him the authority to enforce segregation, the bus driver arrested her.

That evening a group of black women professors at the black state college in Montgomery, led by Jo Ann Robinson, drafted a letter of protest. They called on blacks to stay off the buses on Monday to protest the arrest. They worked through the night making 35,000 copies of their letter to distribute to Montgomery's black residents. Fearful for their jobs and concerned that the state would cut funds to the black college if it became known they had used state facilities to produce the letter, they worked quickly and quietly.

The following day black leaders met and agreed to the boycott. More leaflets were drafted calling on blacks to stay off the buses on Monday. On Sunday, black ministers encouraged their members to support the boycott, and on Monday 90% of the blacks walked to work, rode in black-owned taxis, or shared rides in private cars.

The boycott inspired confidence and pride in the black community and signaled a subtle change in the opinions of blacks toward race relations. This was obvious when, as nervous white police looked on, hundreds of blacks jammed the courthouse to see that Rosa Parks was safely released after her formal conviction. And it was obvious later that evening at a mass rally when Martin Luther King cried out, "There comes a time when people get tired of being trampled over by the iron feet of oppression. There comes a time when people get tired of being pushed out of the glittering sunlight of life's July, and left standing amidst the piercing chill of an Alpine November." After noting that the glory of American democracy is the right to protest, King appealed to the strong religious faith of the crowd, "If we are wrong, God Almighty is wrong. . . . If we are wrong, Jesus of Nazareth was merely a utopian dreamer. . . . If we are wrong, justice is a lie." These words and this speech established King as a charismatic leader for the civil rights movement.

Each day of the boycott was a trial for blacks and their leaders. Thousands had to find a way to get to work and leaders struggled to keep a massive carpool going. However, each evening's rally built up morale for the next day's boycott. Later which is why many groups employ former members of Congress and the executive branch as lobbyists.

Finally, public image is important. A negative public image often troubles new, change-oriented groups, such as the animal rights movement. Many of the country's traditional interest groups, big business and organized labor, also suffer from a poor image, being viewed as too powerful and self-serving.

Few groups are blessed with all resources, but the more resources a group has, the better its chances of getting what it wants from government.

Competition and Goals

Success also depends on group competition and goals.

Many groups are successful because they face weak opponents. Supporters of gun control have public opinion on their side, but their main opposition, the National Council to Control Handguns, has a membership of only 400,000 and a budget of $7.5 million, a fraction of the NRA's. Used-car dealers successfully lobbied against "the lemon law," which would have required them to tell customers of any defects in cars. Few lobbyists represented the other side. These mismatches between groups occur most often on highly technical issues where one side has more expertise or the public has less interest.

When a group competes with other groups of nearly equal resources, the outcome is often a compromise or a stalemate. The Clean Air Act was not rewritten for years because the auto industry, which wanted a weaker law, and the environmental lobby, which wanted a tougher one, were about equal in strength. The increased clout of the environmental forces finally led to a strengthening of the law in 1990.

the rallies became prayer services, as the black community prayed for strength to keep on walking, for courage to remain nonviolent, and for guidance to those who oppressed them.

The city bus line was losing money. City leaders urged more whites to ride the bus to make up lost revenue, but few did. Recognizing the boycott could not go on forever, black leaders agreed to end it if the rules regarding the seating of blacks in "no man's land" were relaxed. Thinking they were on the verge of breaking the boycott, the city leaders refused. Police began to harass carpoolers and issue bogus tickets for trumped-up violations. Then the city leaders issued an ultimatum: Settle or face arrest. A white grand jury indicted more than 100 boycott leaders for the alleged crime of organizing the protest. In the spirit of nonviolence, the black leaders, including King, surrendered.

The decision to arrest the leaders proved to be the turning point of the boycott. The editor of the local white paper said it was "the dumbest act that has ever been done in Montgomery."[1] With the mass arrests, the boycott finally received national attention. Reporters from all over the world streamed into Montgomery to cover the story. The publicity brought public and financial support. The arrests caused the boycott to become a national event and its leader, Martin Luther King, a national figure. A year later, the U.S. Supreme Court declared Alabama local and state laws requiring segregation in buses unconstitutional, and when the city complied with the Court's order, the boycott ended.

Rosa Parks became a hero of the civil rights movement. She has been honored many times since then, and millions saw her appearance at the 1988 Democratic National Convention.

Rosa Parks being fingerprinted after her arrest.

1. Taylor Branch, *Parting the Waters, America in the King Years* (New York: Simon and Schuster, 1988), p. 83.

Sources: Taylor Branch, *Parting the Waters,* chapters 4 and 5; and Juan Williams; *Eyes on the Prize* (New York: Viking Press, 1987).

Groups that work to preserve the status quo are generally more successful than groups promoting change; it is usually easier to prevent government action than to bring it about. Separation of powers among the Congress, executive branch, and the courts; checks and balances within each branch; and division of authority between the states and national government provide interest groups with numerous points in the political process to exercise influence. Groups wishing to change policy have to persuade officials throughout the political process to go along; groups opposed to change only have to persuade officials at one point in the process. Groups promoting change must win over the House, Senate, White House, bureaucracy, and courts; groups against change need convince only one of them.

Groups are more likely to be successful in securing very narrow and specific benefits than they are in promoting broad policy changes. For example, corporations are concerned with broad policy issues, but they are more likely to be successful in obtaining exemptions from major policy initiatives than they are in winning or losing on the policy itself. The tax code is riddled with exemptions for corporations; the beneficiaries are rarely identified by name. The 1986 changes in the tax code contained an exemption for Phillips Petroleum, identified in the bill as a "corporation incorporated on June 13, 1917, which has its principle place of business in Bartlesville, Oklahoma."[88] Phillips was not concerned about the basic tax changes because it was not affected by them. Such exemptions are unlikely to receive media attention and become controversial. In this way, politicians are able to satisfy a major interest group without risking a hostile public reaction.

➤Conclusion: Do Interest Groups Help Make Government Responsive?

Interest groups provide representation that helps make government more responsive. Although elected officials are representatives, they cannot adequately represent all interests in our diverse society. Interest groups pick up some of the slack by representing the views and opinions of their members and constituents and communicating these to political decision makers. This does not mean that all members agree with everything group leaders say or do, or that group leaders are accountable to their members. Group leaders often develop perspectives somewhat different from those of their members. In most instances, however, groups do represent and speak for at least some of the interests of their members. In voluntary organizations particularly, leaders are likely to reflect the interests of their members. If they do not, members can simply exercise their option to leave. Even "checkbook" members can withhold their support if they disagree with group leaders.

Interest groups do not represent, however, all interests or all interests equally. In 1960, E. E. Schattschneider described the pressure system as small in terms of members and biased toward business and the wealthy. At that time no more than 1,500 groups were included, and more than 50% represented either corporations or trade and business associations.[89] Few groups represented consumers, taxpayers, the environment, women, and minorities.

The pressure system has changed since Schattschneider wrote, but its bias remains. The number of interest groups exploded in the 1960s and 1970s, with many of the new groups representing consumers, environmentalists, minorities, and other nonbusiness interests, but these were more than offset by an increase in the number of corporations in the pressure system.

Business interests still dominate, as we saw earlier. Indeed, business had a greater presence in Washington in the 1980s than it did in the 1960s. Nearly two-thirds of the groups in Washington in the 1980s represented either corporations or trade associations. Groups representing minorities, women, the poor, and elderly are less than 10% of all groups with an office in Washington and only 5% of all groups that lobby.

This bias in the pressure system is a big advantage for business and wealthy interests, and it may be increasing. Over the past three decades, business groups have gained in numbers and influence relative to other groups. Labor unions and the Democratic party, strong supporters of legislation to improve the welfare of the working class, often in opposition to business and wealthy interests, have declined or shifted their focus. As one political analyst put it, "The nature of representative government in the U.S. has changed, so that more and more of the weight of influence in Washington comes from interest groups, not voters."[90] And interest groups are predominantly looking out for the interests of business. The declining level of prosperity of the middle and working classes is one reflection of this change.

Interest group strength is relevant to the debate between those who think our system reflects pluralism and those who think it is run by elites. People who argue that we have a pluralist system emphasize group competition and the ability of individuals to organize themselves to influence government. Those who think we have an elitist government point to the inequality of group competition. On some issues, such as those involving economic benefits for workers, there is competition among groups. On other issues, such as tax policy, there is little.

James Madison foresaw the inevitable development of interest groups and wanted to create a government that would hold them in check. That is, he wanted government to prevent one or more of them from doing harm to others or to the nation as a whole. Madison thought a system of checks and balances and competition among groups would accomplish this. Just as he thought, competing groups can slow the political process. In recent years, we have called this gridlock. But when there is no competition, the nation suffers. Similarly, it suffers when so many interests are involved in politics that it is difficult for government to take action. Government's capacity to do its job is limited by both the bias in the pressure system and the large number of interest groups. Moreover, the built-in checks and balances that Madison thought would preserve the system threaten it by allowing groups to block needed action.

How can we preserve the constitutional rights of interest groups to form and petition government and still keep government responsive to the needs of unorganized or poorly organized interests that lack the resources to press their demands? Recognizing and correcting imbalances in group strength is not simple or easy. Groups currently enjoying an advantage will fight to keep it.

Source: Reprinted by permission: Tribune Media Services

EPILOGUE

Mfume Joins the NAACP

Kweisi Mfume took over the leadership of the NAACP believing he could accomplish more there than in Congress. Explaining his decision, he said, "There is too much hate, too much violence, too much disrespect, and too little government intervention in problems of the day. There is a despair and helplessness in the eyes of too many young people. I watch people be born and die in a world not changing fast enough. It's difficult to bring about the kind of change I want as an individual member of Congress. I could stay and do a little or leave and do a lot."[91]

While his first priority will be eliminating the organization's debt and rebuilding its budget, two areas where he hopes to make a mark are economic development and youth membership. Inner cities desperately need more jobs and more minority-owned and -operated businesses. And the NAACP needs to overcome its image as an organization dominated by an older generation out of step with the younger generation. Mfume hopes to place greater emphasis on the NAACP's national scholarship competition.

To accomplish these goals, Mfume will draw on his talents for building coalitions, which helped him in Congress. He will seek help from Republicans as well as Democrats and whites as well as blacks.

Beyond his immediate goal of rescuing the organization from its recent troubles, he hopes to reignite the racial optimism of the 1960s. He says that "Americans of all colors share a common destiny."[92] His ability to sell this idea may determine whether the NAACP has a future and whether racial equality becomes a reality.

➤Key Terms

interest groups
lobbying
political action committees (PACs)
private interest groups
public interest groups
single-issue groups
coalitions
market share

➤Further Reading

Jeffrey M. Berry, *The Interest Group Society*, 2nd ed. (Boston: Little, Brown, 1989). *A general survey of interest groups in American politics. It covers political action committees, lobbyists and lobbying, the internal dynamics of groups, and the problems that interest groups present to society.*

Jeffrey Birnbaum, *The Lobbyists: How Influence Peddlers Get Their Way in Washington* (New York: Times Books, 1993). *A study of lobbyists' activities surrounding major issues considered by Congress in the 1989–1990 session.*

Mark Green, *The Other Government* (New York: W. W. Norton, 1975). *An examination of the role of Washington lawyers in representing clients before the government.*

Michael Pertschuk, *Giant Killers* (New York: W. W. Norton, 1986). *How low-budget lobbies can sometimes defeat the big guys by superior organization, tactics, and luck.*

E. E. Schattschneider, *The Semi-Sovereign People* (New York: Henry Holt & Company, 1975). *A classical statement on how interest group politics benefit business and corporate interests by limiting the involvement of citizens in the political process.*

Ernest Wittenberg and Elisabeth Wittenberg, *How to Win in Washington: Very Practical Advice about Lobbying, the Grassroots and the Media* (Cambridge, Mass.: Basil Blackwell, 1989). *A "how to" book for average citizens.*

➤Notes

1. Michael Barone and Grant Ujifusa, *The Almanac of American Politics 1994* (Washington, D.C.: National Journal, 1993); "A Child of the Movement," *U.S. News and World Report* (December 25, 1995–January 1, 1996), p. 62; "The Last Best Hope," *Newsweek* (February 12, 1996), p. 71.
2. Ernest Wittenberg and Elisabeth Wittenberg, *How to Win in Washington* (Cambridge, Mass.: Blackwell, 1989), p. 24.
3. Jeffrey Birnbaum, *The Lobbyists* (New York: Times Books, 1992), p. 32.
4. M. A. Peterson and J. L. Walker, "Interest Group Responses to Partisan Change: The Impact of the Reagan Administration upon the National Interest Group System," in A. J. Cigler and B. A. Loomis, eds., *Interest Group Politics*, 2nd ed. (Washington, D.C.: CQ Press, 1987), p. 162.
5. A. de Tocqueville, *Democracy in America* (New York: Knopf, 1945), p. 191.
6. G. Almond and S. Verba, *Civil Culture* (Boston: Little, Brown, 1965), pp. 266–306.
7. D. Truman, *The Governmental Process* (New York: Knopf, 1964), pp. 25–26.
8. Ibid., p. 59.
9. Ibid., pp. 26–33.
10. J. Q. Wilson, *Political Organization* (New York: Basic Books, 1973), p. 198.
11. G. K. Wilson, *Interest Groups in America* (Oxford: Oxford University Press, 1981), chapter 5; see also G. K. Wilson, "American Business and Politics," in Cigler and Loomis, *Interest Group Politics*, pp. 221–35.
12. K. L. Schlozman and J. T. Tierney, "More of the Same: Washington Pressure Group Activity in a Decade of Change," *Journal of Politics* 45 (May 1983); pp. 335–56.
13. Christopher H. Foreman, Jr., "Grassroots Victim Organizations: Mobilizing for Personal and Public Health," in Allan J. Cigler and Burdett A. Loomis, *Interest Group Politics*, 4th ed. (Washington, D.C.: CQ Press, 1994), pp. 33–53.
14. R. H. Salisbury, "An Exchange Theory of Interest Groups," *Midwest Journal of Political Science* 13 (February 1969): 1–32.
15. J. M. Berry, *The Interest Group Society* (Boston: Little Brown, 1984), pp. 26–28.
16. J. L. Walker, "The Origins and Maintenance of Interest Groups in America," *American Political Science Review* 77 (June 1983), pp. 398–400; see also *National Journal* (August 1981), p. 1376.
17. Wilson, *Political Organization*, chapter 3.
18. C. Brown, "Explanations of Interest Group Membership Over Time," *American Politics Quarterly* 17 (January 1989), pp. 32–53.
19. C. Brown, "Explanations of Interest Group Membership." The National Rifle Association. Annual Meeting of Midwest P.S. Association, 1987.
20. National Opinion Research Center, General Social Surveys, 1987.
21. N. Babchuk and R. Thompson, "The Voluntary Associations of Negroes," *American Sociological Review* 27 (October 1962), pp. 662–65; see also P. Klobus-Edwards, J. Edwards, and D. Klemmach, "Differences in Social Participation of Blacks and Whites," *Social Forces* 56 (1978), pp. 1035–52.
22. Robert D. Putnam, "Bowling Alone: America's Declining Social Capital," *Journal of Democracy* (January, 1995), pp. 65–78, see also Robert J. Samuelson, "Join the Club," *Washington Post National Weekly Edition* (April 15–21, 1996), p. 5.
23. Ibid.
24. Ibid.
25. M. T. Hayes, "The New Group Universe" in Cigler and Loomis, *Interest Group Politics*, pp. 133–45.
26. C. Tomkins, "A Sense of Urgency," *New Yorker*, March 27, 1989, pp. 48–74.
27. Walker, "The Origins and Maintenance of Interest Groups in America."
28. E. E. Schattschneider, *Semi-Sovereign People* (New York: Holt, Rinehart, and Winston, 1960), p. 118.
29. David Broder and Michael Weisskopf, "Finding New Friends on the Hill," *Washington Post National Weekly Edition* (October 3–9, 1994), p. 11.
30. Peter Behr, "The Corporate Winning Streak," *Washington Post National Weekly Edition* (January 30–February 5, 1995), p. 24.
31. F. Swoboda, "Striking Out as a Weapon Against Management," *Washington Post National Weekly Edition* (July 13, 1992), p. 20.
32. P. E. Johnson, "Organized Labor in an Era of Blue Collar Decline," in A. J. Cigler and B. A. Loomis, eds., *Interest Group Politics*, 3rd ed. (Washington, D.C.: CQ Press, 1991), pp. 33–62.

33. Ibid., p. 47.

34. Frank Swoboda, "Leadership Labor in the Vineyards," *Washington Post National Weekly Edition* (November 6–12, 1995), p. 20; Jeffrey Birnbaum and Eric Pooley, "New Party Bosses," *Time* (April 8, 1996), pp. 28–32.

35. A. J. Cigler and J. M. Hansen, "Group Formation Through Protest: The American Agriculture Movement," in A. J. Cigler and B. A. Loomis, eds., *Interest Group Politics* (Washington, D.C.: CQ Press, 1983), chapter 4.

36. A. J. Cigler, "Organizational Maintenance and Political Activity on the Cheap: The American Agriculture Movement," in Cigler and Loomis, *Interest Group Politics,* pp. 81–108.

37. On the AMA, see L. H. Zeigler and G. W. Peak, *Interest Groups in American Society,* 2nd ed. (Englewood Cliffs, N.J.: Prentice-Hall, 1972), pp. 225–58.

38. For a discussion of the ABA, see M. Green, "The ABA: The Rhetoric Has Changed But the Morality Lingers On," *Washington Monthly* (January 1974): 21–27.

39. The education lobby is treated in R. Stanfield, "The Education Lobby Reborn," *National Journal,* August 9, 1983, pp. 1452–56.

40. J. Tierney, "Old Money, New Power," *New York Times Magazine,* October 23, 1988, p. 69.

41. "Grays on the Go," *Time,* February 22, 1988, p. 69.

42. "Gray Power," *Time,* January 4, 1988, p. 36.

43. "Our Footloose Correspondents," *New Yorker,* August 8, 1988, p. 70.

44. "Grapevine," *Time* (November 28, 1988, p. 24; see also D. Kaul, "Perot Raises Worthwhile Point Regarding Foreign Lobbyists," *Lincoln Journal-Star* (October 25, 1992), p. 5B.

45. *Congressional Quarterly Weekly Report* (December 12, 1992), p. 3792.

46. A. S. McFarland, *Common Cause* (Chatham, N.J.: Chatham House, 1984); see also A. S. McFarland, *Public Interest Lobbies: Decision Making on Energy* (Washington, D.C.: American Enterprise Institute, 1976).

47. R. G. Shaiko, "More Bang for the Buck: The New Era of Full Service Public Interest Groups," in Cigler and Loomis, *Interest Group Politics,* p. 109.

48. Ibid., p. 120.

49. For a discussion of the evolution of NOW and its success in lobbying Congress, see A. N. Costain and W. D. Costain, "The Women's Lobby: Impact of a Movement on Congress," in Cigler and Loomis, *Interest Group Politics.*

50. Birnbaum and Pooley, "New Party Bosses."

51. E. M. Uslaner, "A Tower of Babel on Foreign Policy," in Cigler and Loomis, *Interest Group Politics,* p. 309.

52. K. Wald, *Religion and Politics* (New York: St. Martin's Press, 1985), pp. 182–212.

53. James L. Guth, John C. Green, Lyman A. Jellstedt, and Corwin E. Wmidt, "Onward Christian Soldiers: Religious Activist Groups in American Politics," in Cigler and Loomis, *Interest Group Politics,* p. 57.

54. Sidney Blumental, "Christian Soldiers," *New Yorker* (July 18, 1994), p. 36.

55. Ibid., p. 37.

56. David Von Drehle and Thomas B. Edsall, "The Religious Right Returns," *The Washington Post National Weekly Edition* (August 29–September 4, 1994), p. 6.

57. "Prodding Voters to the Right," *Time* (November 21, 1994), p. 62.

58. Ibid.

59. "Religious Right Returns," p. 6.

60. Charles Levendosky, "Alternative Religious Voice Finally Being Raised," *Lincoln Journal-Star* (March 3, 1996), p. 7b.

61. The source for most of the next paragraphs is Eric Marcus, *Making History: The Struggle for Gay and Lesbian Equal Rights 1945–1990* (New York: Harper-Collins, 1992). Also see Jeffrey Schmalz, "Gay Politics Goes Mainstream," *New York Times Magazine* (October 11, 1992), pp. 18ff.

62. Gabriel Rotello, "94 Was a Good Year for Gay Rights," *Lincoln Journal-Star* (January 7, 1995), p. 10.

63. C. J. Bosso, "Adaption and Change in the Environmental Movement" in Cigler and Loomis, *Interest Group Politics,* pp. 155–56.

64. Ibid., p. 162.

65. Ibid., p. 169.

66. Tim Curran, "Common Cause Gets Rival," *Roll Call* (February 6, 1995), p. 41.

67. Sarah Tippit-Melbourne and Nancy Traver, "Camp for Crusaders," *Time* (April 19, 1993), p. 40.

68. A. Rubin, "Interest Groups and Abortion Politics in the Post-Webster Era," in Cigler and Loomis, *Interest Group Politics,* pp. 249–251; *Congressional Quarterly Weekly Report* (March 27, 1993), pp. 755–57.

69. D. Broder, "Let 100 Single-Issue Groups Bloom," *Washington Post,* January 7, 1979, pp. C1–C2; see also D. Broder, *The Party's Over: The Failure of Politics in America* (New York: Harper & Row, 1972).

70. Wilson, *Interest Groups,* chapter 4.

71. P. M. Evans, "Lobbying the Committee: Interest Groups and the House Public Works and Transportation Committee, in the Post-Webster Era," in Cigler and Loomis, *Interest Group Politics,* pp. 257–76.

72. Berry, *Interest Group Society,* p. 188.

73. Jeffrey Birnbaum, *The Lobbyists* (New York: Times Books, 1992), p. 40.

74. Ernest Wittenberg and Elisabeth Wittenberg, *How to Win in Washington* (Cambridge, Massachusetts: Blackwell, 1989), p. 24.

75. David Broder and Spencer Rich, "The Health Care Battle Begins," *Washington Post National Weekly Edition* (September 27–October 3, 1993), p. 6.

76. E. Drew, *Politics and Money: The New Road to Corruption* (New York: Macmillan, 1983), p. 78.

77. Ibid.

78. For an article dealing with the success of interest group litigation at the district court level see L. Epstein and C. K. Rowland, "Debunking the Myth of Interest Group Invincibility in the Courts," *American Political Science Review* 85 (March 1991): 205–20.

79. S. Kernell, *Going Public* (Washington, D.C.: CQ Press, 1986), p. 34.

80. R. Harris, "If You Love Your Grass," *New Yorker,* April 20, 1968, p. 57.

81. Michael Weisskopf, "Letting No Grass Roots Grow Under Their Feet," *The Washington Post National Weekly Edition* (October 18–24, 1993), pp. 20–21.

82. Evans, "Lobbying the Committee," p. 269.

83. Sandra Boodman, "Health Care's Power Player," *Washington Post National Weekly Edition* (February 14–20, 1994), pp. 6–7.

84. Birnbaum, *The Lobbyists,* p. 40.

85. Dan Balz and David Broder, "Take Two Lobbyists and Call Me in the Morning," *The Washington Post National Weekly Edition* (October 18–24, 1993), pp. 10–11.

86. Much of the information in this section is taken from B. A. Loomis, "Coalitions of Interests: Building Bridges in the Balkanized State," in Cigler and Loomis, *Interest Group Politics,* 2nd ed., pp. 258–74.

87. Birnbaum, *The Lobbyists,* p. 83.

88. Dan Clawson, Alan Neustadtl, and Denise Scott, *Money Talks* (New York: Basic Books, 1992), p. 91.

89. Schattschneider, *Semi-Sovereign People,* chapter 2.

90. Kevin Phillips, "Fat City," *Time* (September 26, 1995), p. 51.

91. "A Child of the Movement."

92. "The Last Best Hope."

6 Political Parties

You Are There

Should the Republicans Offer the Voters a "Contract"?

You are Newt Gingrich, a Republican member of the House of Representatives from Georgia. Although it is early 1994, you sense that your party has a good chance to gain many congressional seats in the November elections, and an outside chance to become the majority party. Voter anger, coupled with the redistricting that changed many district lines in 1992, led a record number of House incumbents (48) to retire. Four other incumbents were defeated in primary elections, leaving 52 seats open. This offers a large opportunity for Republicans to take control of the House. If they do, you will likely become the Speaker of the House, the most powerful office in the House of Representatives.

You have been a key member of the Republican congressional party almost from your first day in Washington. You were one of the first to discover the potential of C-SPAN to get your messages to the public. Your political action committee, GOPAC, raises money from conservative business leaders and uses it to recruit and train Republican candidates who believe in your conservative message.[1] You even provide a list of words tested in focus groups that Republican candidates should use in the campaign: Democrats are to be associated with decay, sickness, stagnation, corruption and waste, and Republicans with change, truth, morality, courage, and family, for example. In the last election, 21 of 47 newly elected Republicans were GOPAC recruits.

Now you are focusing on the strategies and tactics that will ensure a successful 1994 congressional campaign. At a meeting with fellow Republican members of the House, Richard Armey (Texas), Bill Paxon (New York), Tom DeLay (Texas), and others, you discuss the possibility of offering voters a specific platform of actions that your party would take if elected.[2]

Such a possibility is unheard of in off-year (non–presidential election) congressional elections. During presidential election years, parties offer platforms of promises. Though often vague, these platforms distinguish the two major parties, and the winning presidential candidate usually will try to follow through on at least some of the more specific ideas. But congressional elections are generally much less focused on national party goals. These elections tend to be highly individual, with incumbents having great advantages, and both incumbents and challengers tend to focus on local and state issues.

In recent campaigns, candidates have waged highly negative campaigns, both responding to and fueling voter anger at politics and politicians. And during this election year, voters are even more angry than in 1992, when they spurned George

CONTINUED 

The Republican party has tried to pull blue-collar workers away from their traditional home in the Democratic party. Former President Ronald Reagan was especially effective in luring these voters.

What Are Political Parties?

Development and Change in the Party System

- Preparty Politics: The Founders' Views of Political Parties
- First Party System: Development of Parties
- Second Party System: Rise of the Democrats
- Third Party System: Rise of the Republicans
- Fourth Party System: Republican Dominance
- Fifth Party System: Democratic Dominance
- Has the Fifth Party System Realigned?

The Parties Today

Characteristics of the Party System

- Two Parties
- Fragmentation
- Moderation
- Minor Parties in American Politics

Party in the Electorate

- Party Identification
- Characteristics of Democrats and Republicans

Party in Government

Party Organization

- National Party Organization
- State and Local Party Organizations
- Big-City Party Organizations

The Nominating Process

- Caucuses
- Conventions
- Primaries

Conclusion: Do Political Parties Make Government More Responsive?

Newt Gingrich looms large at Republican gathering.

Bush's bid for a second term. Fueled by radio and television talk show hosts, Americans said they were fed up with politics as usual: with politicians attuned more to special interest groups than voters, members of Congress who had been in Washington so long they had forgotten the people back home, and elected officials who were unwilling to balance the federal budget. Americans were dubious about their economic futures, terrified of crime, and furious at the breakdown in morality. They blamed government for these problems, or at least for not doing something about them. They especially blamed Democrats, who had controlled Congress for forty years. Most of all, the public seemed to believe that government was no longer accountable to the people.

You think, however, that playing on the voters' negative feelings may not be quite enough to win the majority that you want. Negativism will win some votes, but you believe that the voters want something more positive. Providing a "platform" for this midyear election might be unique enough to draw voters' attention and give a focus to the campaign rhetoric of Republican candidates throughout the nation.

However, there are potential drawbacks to this idea. Exactly what should be part of such a platform? Like the Democrats, your party has significant divisions among its members, especially over issues of morality such as abortion rights and school prayer, and over budget issues too. Political parties in the U.S. are not tightly disciplined organizations characterized by shared values on all major issues. Drawing up a platform that everyone could agree on would not be an easy task, and a public fight among members over the terms of such a platform would negate any benefits of having one at all.

Moreover, if such a platform could be constructed, there would be a danger that Republicans would be labeled a failure if they could not carry out that platform. Being specific about what the party wanted to do might make it easier for Democrats and other skeptics to point to all the platform promises that were not accomplished. And the more specific the platform, the easier it would be to spot and criticize these failures.

There is also the prospect that you will misread public opinion and the whole thing will backfire. Support for abstract positions such as reducing the size of government have more appeal than specific government programs targeted for elimination.

What do you decide? Do you go ahead with a Republican platform, risking party division and possible failure to deliver on your promises? Or do you follow a more traditional approach, focusing almost entirely on what is wrong with the Clinton presidency and the Democratic Congress?

George Washington warned against the "baneful" effects of parties and described them as the people's worst enemies. More recently, a respected political scientist, E. E. Schattschneider, argued that "political parties created democracy and that democracy was impossible without them."[3] The public echoes these contradictory views. Many believe that parties create conflict where none exists, yet most identify with one of our two major parties.[4]

These same feelings exist among candidates for office. They often avoid political parties by establishing their own personal campaign organizations and raising their own funds. If elected, they often do not follow the party line. At the same time, candidates for national and state offices are nominated in the name of political parties, they rely on parties for assistance, and they have little chance of winning unless they are Democrats or Republicans.

In this chapter, we examine American political parties to see why they are important and why many observers believe that if they become less important and effective, our system of government may not work as well as it does.

➤What Are Political Parties?

Political parties are a major link between people and government. They provide a way for the public to have some say about who serves in government and what policies are chosen. Political parties generally are defined as organizations that seek to control government by recruiting, nominating, and electing their members to public office. They consist of three interrelated components: the **party in the electorate,** those who identify with the party; the **party in government,** those who are appointed or elected to office as members of a political party; and the formal **party organization,** the party "professionals" who run the party at the national, state, and local levels (see Figure 1).[5]

In linking the public and government policymakers, parties serve several purposes. They help select public officials by recruiting and screening candidates and then providing campaign resources. They help empower citizens by activating and interesting them in politics. Individually, citizens have little power, but collectively, through parties, they can influence government.

Many voters feel an attachment to a political party, an affiliation they acquire early in life and which aids them in deciding among competing candidates. Some voters simply vote their party identification, regardless of candidates or issues. But parties also help many people vote on the basis of issues. Parties are associated, however dimly, in the voters' minds with issues. In the recent past, the Democratic party has favored an expanded role for the national government in maintaining the economic well-being of Americans, whereas the Republican party has supported a more limited role. Most voters understand this difference. Knowing a candidate belongs to a particular party is a clue to the candidate's general stand on the issues, and voters therefore do not need to study each candidate's position in great detail.

The party in government plays an important role in organizing and operating government; it formulates policy options and ultimately decides which to support or oppose. When political parties represent individuals from widely different backgrounds and interests, parties aid society by aggregating and mediating conflicts and contributing to political and social stability.

However, parties are seen by the public as a part of the "mess in Washington." Many believe that parties contribute to the lack of government action and that partisan debates are mostly meaningless squabbles. Thus the public tends to believe that parties create differences where none existed, rather than being

FIGURE 1
The Three Components of Political Parties

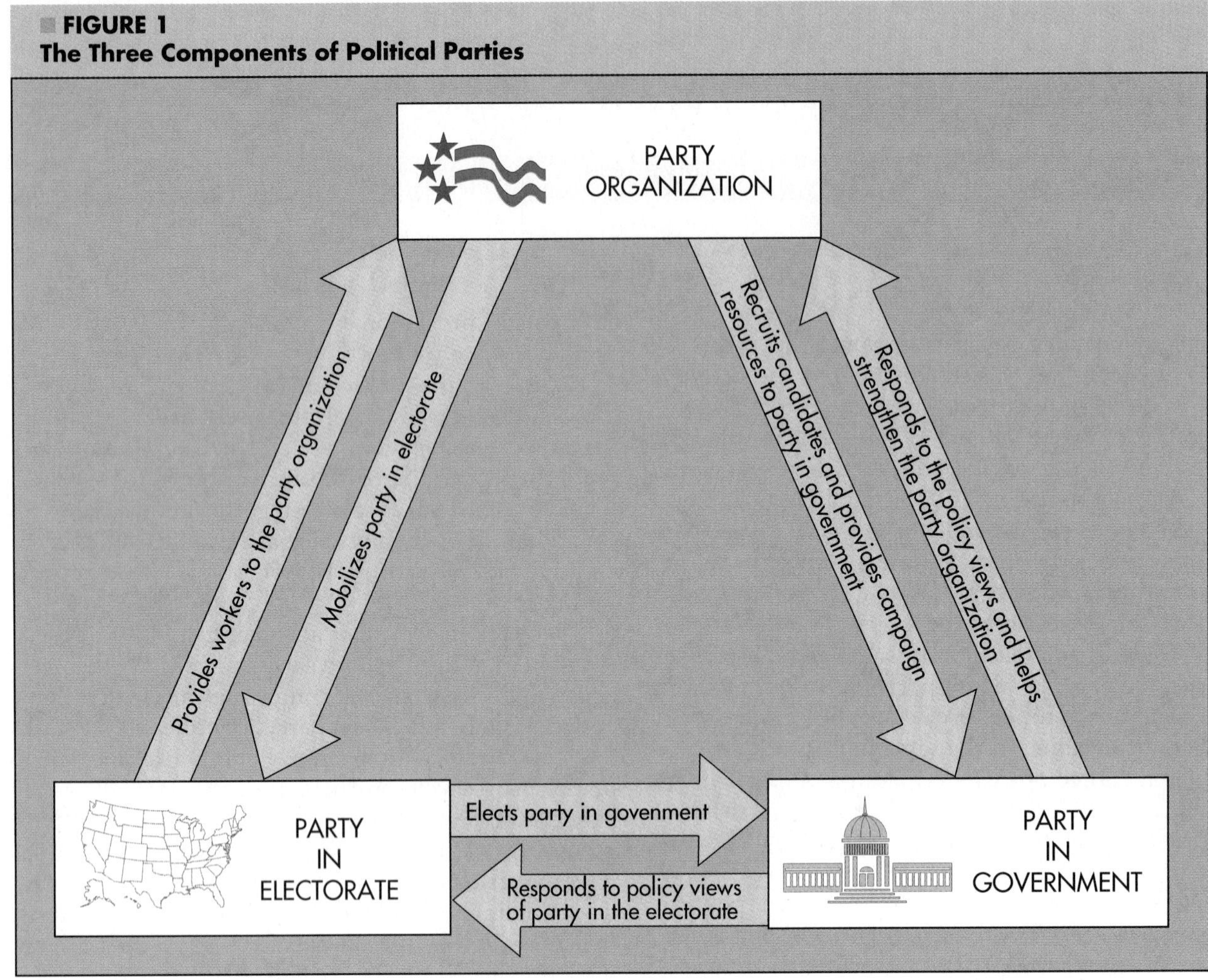

institutions that reflect and represent Americans' real differences in views on how to solve the nation's problems.

➤Development and Change in the Party System

Most Americans think of the Democratic and Republican parties as more or less permanent fixtures, and indeed they have been around a long time. The Democratic party evolved from the Jacksonian Democrats in 1832, and the Republican party was founded in 1854. Nevertheless, the current party system is only one of five distinct party systems that have existed in American history (see Figure 2).

In tracing the development of these systems, we need to keep two things in mind. First, parties developed after the nation's founding, they grew to be very powerful in the late nineteenth century, and they have declined in influence since then.

Second, there have been periods of stability in the party system when one party has dominated American politics and won most elections. There have also been periods of transition and instability when neither party has dominated, and control of government has been divided between the parties or has shifted back and forth. In transition periods, issues emerge that are difficult to resolve, and voters establish new party loyalties based on them. The transition from one stable party system to another is called a **realignment.**

FIGURE 2
The Five American Party Systems

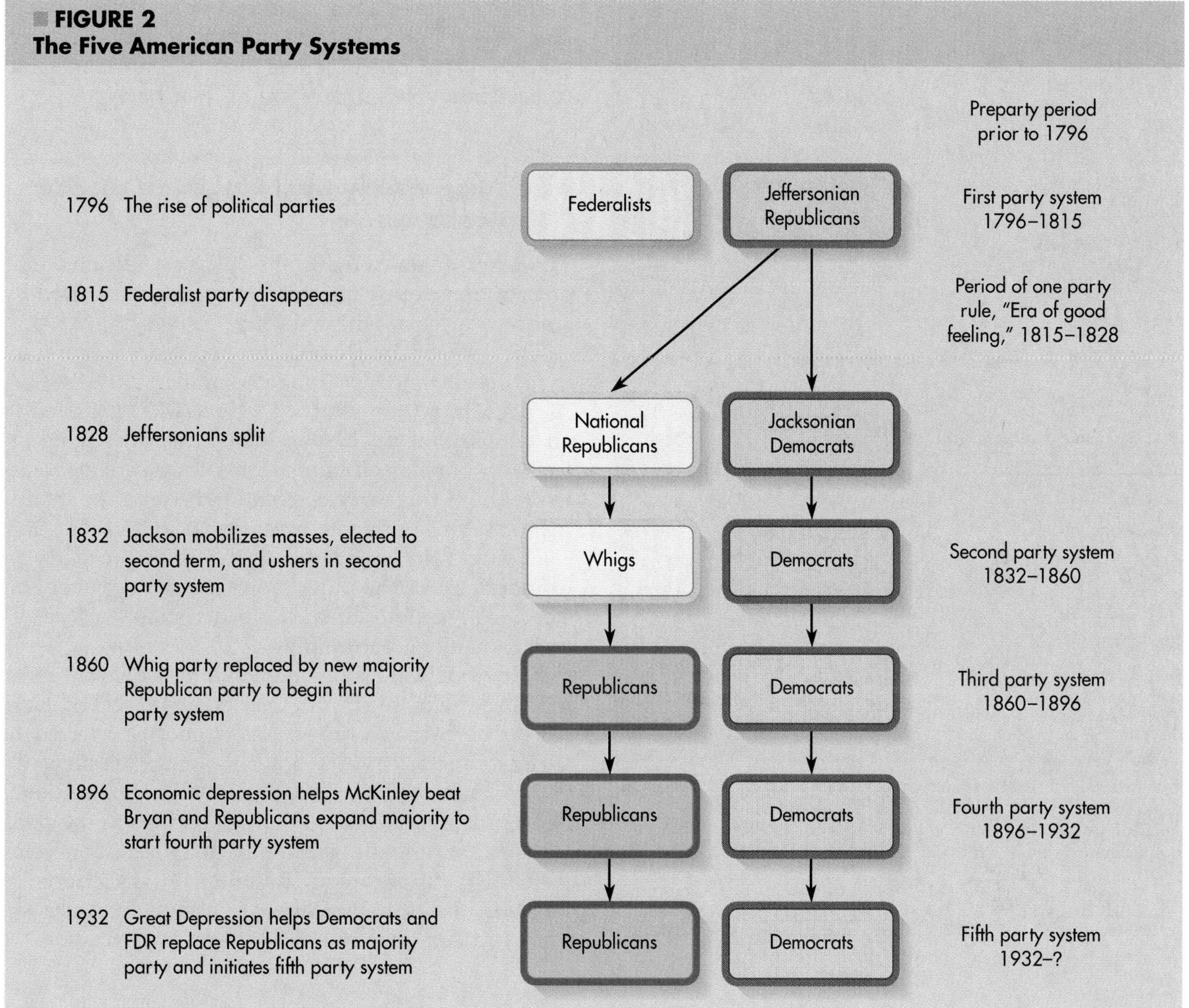

Preparty Politics: The Founders' Views of Political Parties

Most of the Founders viewed political parties as dangerous to stable government. This antiparty feeling was rooted in three basic beliefs. First, the Founders thought parties created and exploited conflicts that undermined consensus on public policy. Second, they thought parties were instruments by which a small and narrow interest could impose its will on society. And third, they believed parties stifled independent thought and behavior.[6]

Madison feared political parties as much as interest groups because he felt both pursued selfish interests at the expense of the common good. He referred to both as "factions" in *Federalist #10.* John Adams dreaded what he considered the greatest political evil, the formation of rival political parties.

Therefore, it is not surprising that the Constitution does not mention political parties. Nevertheless, it created a system in which parties, or something like them, were inevitable. When the Founders established popular elections as the mechanism for selecting political leaders, an agency for organizing and mobilizing supporters of political candidates was needed. Indeed, despite their antiparty feelings, several of the Founders were active in the first parties.

The factions that developed into the first political parties were already vying with each other in Washington's administration. Thomas Jefferson (*second from left*) and Alexander Hamilton (*fourth from left*) are pictured here with Washington (*right*).

Thomas Jefferson and James Madison, for example, were the founders of the first political party.

First Party System: Development of Parties

With Washington's unanimous election to the presidency in 1788, it appeared the nation could be governed by consensus. But differences of opinion soon arose. Alexander Hamilton, Washington's secretary of the treasury, supported a strong national government. His following, the Federalists, were opposed by Thomas Jefferson, secretary of state, who feared a strong central government. The conflict led Jefferson to challenge Federalist John Adams for the presidency in 1796. Jefferson lost, but he then recruited able leaders in each state, founded newspapers, established political clubs, and in 1800 ran again and won. Jefferson's victory demonstrated the utility of political parties.

By Jefferson's second term, more than 90% of members of Congress were either Federalists or Jeffersonians (later called Jeffersonian Republicans) and consistently voted in support of their party.[7]

Second Party System: Rise of the Democrats

The Jeffersonian Republicans split into factions. One of these developed into the Democratic party, led by Andrew Jackson, who won the presidency in 1828.

The Jacksonian Democrats emphasized the common person and encouraged popular participation. As a result of their efforts, the vote was expanded to all white adult males. Presidential electors were selected in popular elections rather than by state legislatures, and the party convention became the instrument used to nominate presidential and other party candidates. No longer did members of the party in Congress select the party's presidential nominee. Instead, conventions opened up decisions to local as well as national party elites.

Many political leaders deplored Jackson's efforts to mobilize the masses. John Quincy Adams called Jackson a "barbarian." An Adams supporter referred to Jackson's victory as "the howl of raving Democracy."[8]

Jackson's popular appeal and the organizational effort of his party brought large numbers to the polls for the first time. By 1828, more than a million votes were cast for president. Building on the efforts of Jefferson, Jackson introduced a uniquely American idea, a mass-population-based party organization.

Third Party System: Rise of the Republicans

The conflict over slavery brought a new party alignment. Abolitionists and proslavery factions split the Whig party, which had been the primary opposition to the Democrats. By 1860, the Whigs disappeared and a new party, the Republicans (not related to the Jeffersonian or National Republicans), emerged. The Republicans (also known as the GOP—Grand Old Party), reflecting abolitionist sentiment, nominated Abraham Lincoln for president. Northern Democrats who opposed slavery joined Republicans to form a new majority party.

After the Civil War, the Republicans usually won the presidency and controlled Congress. After 1876,

In 1828, opponents of Andrew Jackson called him a jackass. Political cartoonists and journalists began to use the donkey to symbolize Jackson and the Democratic Party. In the 1870s, Thomas Nast popularized the donkey as a symbol of the party in his cartoons and originated the elephant as a symbol of the Republican Party. His 1874 cartoon showed the Democratic donkey dressed as a lion frightening the other animals of the jungle, including the Republican elephant.

however, elections were close and the parties evenly matched in Congress.

Parties were strong during this period. They controlled nominations for office and mobilized voters through extensive local organizations. Big-city political machines provided employment and other help for many new immigrants in exchange for their allegiance. Corruption—vote buying and political payoffs—linked poor immigrants, big business, and party leaders in strong party machines.

Fourth Party System: Republican Dominance

The election of 1896 ushered in another party alignment. Democrat William Jennings Bryan appealed to southerners and farmers of the plains. He played to their hostility toward the Northeast, with its large corporations and growing ethnic working class. His was a religious appeal too, pitting fundamentalists against Catholics. But his appeal was too narrow and the Democrats were soundly defeated.

During this period a third party, the Progressives, became popular. The Progressives championed political reform, especially of big-city machines. Although the Progressives did not win the presidency, their ideas eventually were enacted into law. These included voter registration and the secret ballot, which reduced election fraud; the direct primary, which allowed rank-and-file voters to nominate their party's candidates and reduce control by party bosses; and civil service reform, which reduced political patronage. These reforms, intended to check corruption, all weakened political parties. They gave parties, and their bosses, less control over elections and jobs.

Fifth Party System: Democratic Dominance

In the 1920s, the Republicans began to lose support in the cities. The party ignored the plight of poor immigrants and in Congress pushed through quotas limiting immigration from southern and eastern Europe. After the Depression hit in 1929, these immigrants, along with many women voting for the first time, joined traditional Democrats in the South to elect Franklin Roosevelt in 1932. This election reflected another party alignment.

The **New Deal coalition,** composed of city dwellers, blue-collar workers, Catholic and Jewish immigrants, blacks, and southerners, elected Roosevelt to an unprecedented four terms. The coalition was an odd alliance of northern liberals and southern conservatives. It stuck together in the 1930s and 1940s because of Roosevelt's personality and skill and because northerners did not seriously challenge southern racial policies.

But the coalition came unglued after Roosevelt's death. The Republicans, by nominating a popular war hero, General Dwight D. Eisenhower, won the presidency in 1952 and 1956. Although the Democrats regained the White House in 1960, the civil rights movement and the Vietnam War divided them sharply, and they lost again in 1968 and 1972.[9] They won in 1976 by nominating a southerner—Jimmy Carter—and because the Republicans suffered from the Watergate scandal. Even though the Democrats dominated Congress until 1994, they had much less success in winning the presidency. Democrats have won the White House only twice since 1964, suggesting that the fifth party system may have ended.

Has the Fifth Party System Realigned?

The fifth party system has changed, but has a major realignment occurred? Many of the signs that preceded major realignments of the party system have been present for some time. **Ticket splitting,** voting for a member of one party for one office but a member of another party for a different one, is at a high level (see Figure 3). In the 1980s, ticket splitting was two to three times that in the 1950s.[10] This is most evident at the national level. The Republicans have occupied the White House and the Democrats have controlled Congress most of the time since 1968.

Another sign of change is the increased number of citizens who do not choose to identify with a political party. Many voters who became eligible to vote for the first time during the 1980s and 1990s have not been attracted to either party, and some older voters lack firm attachments to their party.

Realigning periods also are characterized by compelling issues that fracture the unity of the major parties.[11] In the years before 1860, slavery was such an

FIGURE 3
Declining Partisan Loyalties

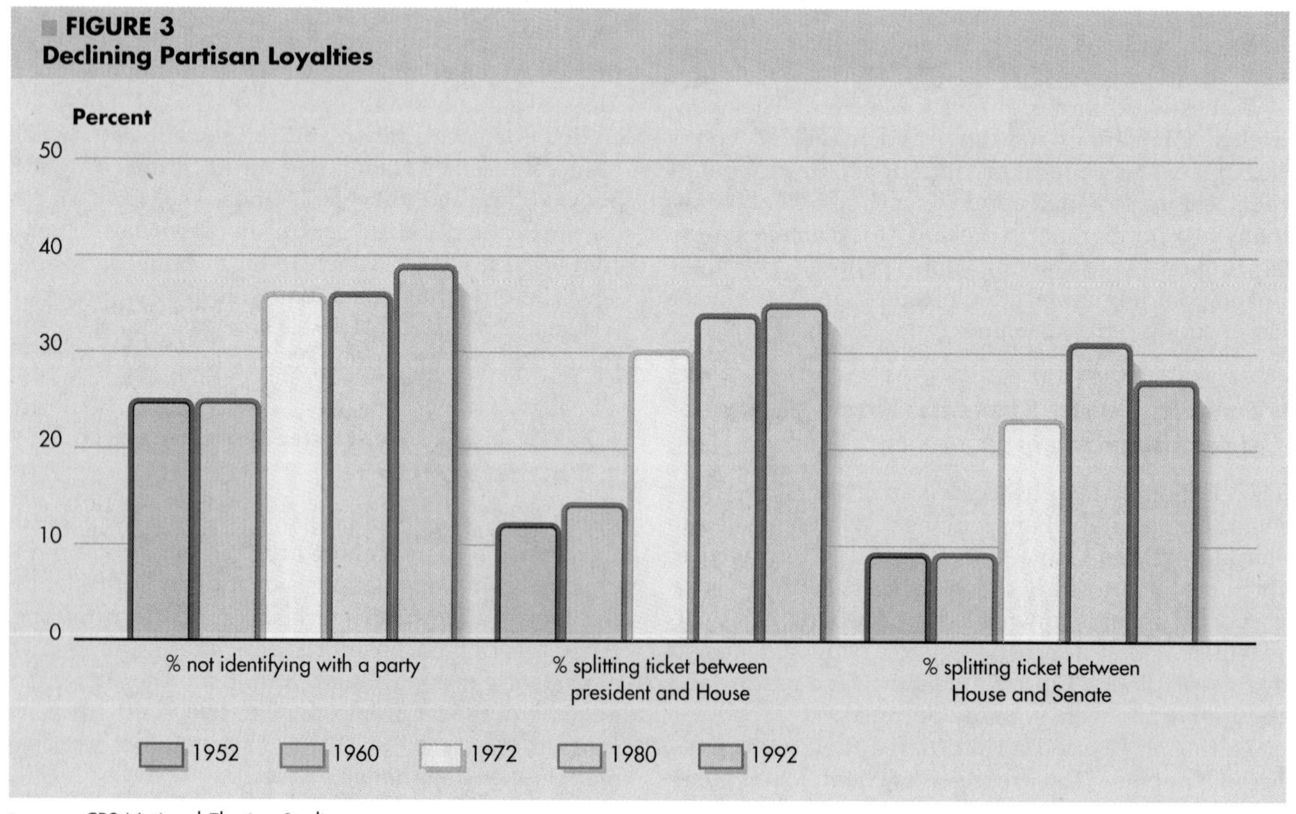

Source: CPS National Election Studies.

issue. It divided the Democrats and destroyed the Whigs. In 1932, economic issues led many Republicans away from their party to the Democrats. As memories of the Depression and influence of Depression-era economic issues fade, the potential exists for new issues to mobilize and realign voters.

While a major realignment has not occurred, the fifth party system has changed since the 1960s. Blue-collar ethnics and Catholics have found the Democrats much less attractive.[12] As New Deal policies succeeded, blue-collar workers became much less concerned with economic security and turned their attention to other issues. Many were upset with the party's promotion of civil rights. Divisions in the party over the Vietnam War pushed many who were in favor of the war, particularly union members, to the Republicans. Some objected to the Democratic party's positions on social issues such as opposition to capital punishment, prayer in schools, and support for abortion and the rights of criminal defendants.

However, in the 1980s, economic concerns returned. Today blue-collar workers find their standard of living eroding, and feel left behind and left out.[13] This has not moved them back to their Democratic roots, however. They feel resentful at what they believe to be the Democrats' favoritism toward minorities and policies that seem to free citizens of personal responsibility for their actions (for example, crime policies that some see as "coddling criminals"). The big-city machines that once mobilized workers to vote Democratic are gone, and the labor unions, which did the same, are dramatically weakened.

Other changes drove some voters to the Democratic party. Northern white Protestants and white-collar workers are somewhat less Republican than they used to be. Many of them are employed by government and more sympathetic to government's role in solving societal problems. The Democrats are also appealing increasingly to better-educated voters, who support Democratic initiatives such as health care reform, commitment to the environment, and abortion rights.[14]

In general, then, there has been some evidence of slight realignment focused on issues of government size and scope, with parties becoming slightly more homogeneous.[15] Although only a modest realignment has occurred nationally, a regional one, confined to the South, has certainly occurred. Long a bastion of Democratic party strength, the South began to drift away in the 1950s and showed major signs of change in 1964. For the first time in a century, the Republicans carried Alabama, Georgia, Louisiana, Mississippi, and South Carolina in the presidential election. Upset with the civil rights policies of the national Democratic party, many white southerners voted for Barry Goldwater, the Republican nominee.

Since 1968 Republicans have carried the South in all presidential elections, except for Jimmy Carter's election in 1976. Although the Georgian carried the region, a majority of white southerners voted for Ford. Carter won the region on the strength of the black vote. Clinton carried his home state, Arkansas, and that of his running mate, Tennessee. He also picked up Louisiana, but, like Carter, lost the majority of white Southerners.

White southerners increasingly vote for Republicans in congressional races too. In 1994 they cast the majority of their votes for Republicans. The shift has led a few Democratic members of Congress to change their party in an effort to take advantage of the changing loyalties of white southerners. Five Democratic House members and two Democratic senators shifted to the GOP following the 1994 elections. For the first time since Reconstruction, a majority of governors, U.S. house members, and senators from the eleven southern states are Republican.[16]

The change in party identification among white southerners is the main reason that polls have shown a decline in Democratic loyalties nationwide. The shift of white southerners to the Republican party makes the South not only more Republican, but it makes the Republicans more conservative. The change also gives the party system a somewhat more ideological look. The southern Democrats who changed tend to be conservatives and are more ideologically compatible with policies of the Republican party.

The race issue, which spurred this realignment, continues to play a role. Where white southerners in the 1950s and 1960s claimed "betrayal" by the national Democratic party for its policies urging equality for blacks, they now say they object to its policies accepting affirmative action for minorities. The polarization between the races has sharpened the realignment. Defection of white southerners from the Democratic party has left a Republican party that is largely white and a Democratic party that is largely black. Whites who are asked their party affiliation sometimes retort, "I'm white, aren't I?" meaning "I'm Republican."[17] Racial segregation of parties ensures white political supremacy and black political irrelevance. There is little incentive for white politicians to pay attention to the needs of blacks.

There also has been some **dealignment.**[18] More individuals have opted for independence as parties become less and less relevant. Increasing numbers say that there is nothing that they like or dislike about parties, suggesting that citizens are indifferent toward them. Similarly, the number who have something positive to say about one party and something negative to say about the other has declined, again suggesting that parties are not as important to citizens as they were in the 1950s and 1960s.[19] Candidates and issues have become more important.

The Electorate of the 1990s

We have discussed the divisions within each of the two major parties. One survey organization has tried to describe these divisions more specifically by focusing on what different subgroups of the voting population really want. Though these sketches are necessarily to some extent superficial and time-bound, they do capture some of the complexity of the voting public.

Largely Republican

Enterprisers: 12% of registered voters, 74% Republican. Antigovernment, antiwelfare, probusiness. Largely male, white, middle-aged, affluent and college-educated. Key issue: Opposed to health care reform. Heroes: Ronald Reagan, Colin Powell, and Rush Limbaugh. Villains: Bill and Hillary Clinton, Ted Kennedy, and gay rights activists.

Moralists: 20% of registered voters, 65% Republican. Antigovernment, antiwelfare, and anti–big business. Religious and socially intolerant. White, middle-aged, average income and education. Key issues: Support for prayer in school and harsher sentences for criminals. Heroes: Ronald Reagan and Colin Powell. Villains: Gay rights activists.

Libertarians: 4% of registered voters, 54% Republican. Antigovernment, anti–social welfare, and probusiness. Tolerant but not religious. Male, white, highly educated and affluent. Key issues: Cutting taxes and welfare. Hero: Colin Powell. Villains: Ted Kennedy, Louis Farrakhan, Jerry Falwell.

Largely Independent

New Economy Independents: 19% of registered voters, 52% independent (27% Democratic). Strong environmentalists, but oppose government regulation. Pro–social welfare, but not sympathetic to blacks. Female, young and middle-aged, white-collar professionals and service workers, average income; 40% are working women. Key issues: Support for health care reform, stricter gun control, government spending for job training, and gay rights. No heroes. Villain: Jerry Falwell.

Bystanders: None of the registered voters, but 8% of the population, 52% independent. Environmentalist. Young, female, less education and income. Key issues: none. Heroes: none. Villains: Tobacco companies.

Embittered: 7% of registered voters, 39% independent, 36% Democrat; 25% African-American. Antigovernment, antipolitician, and antibusiness. Religious and socially intolerant. Believe discrimination is barrier to black progress. Low skill, low income. Support school prayer and oppose government-funded abortions. Hero: John Kennedy. Villains: Insurance companies, MTV, Rush Limbaugh.

Largely Democrat

Seculars: 10% of registered voters, 46% Democrat (31% independent who lean Democrat). Somewhat progovernment. Anticorporations. Strong commitment to environment. Tolerant. White, relatively young, highly educated and affluent. Favor government funding for abortion, gun control, and gay rights. Oppose school prayer. Hero: Hillary Clinton. Villains: Rush Limbaugh, Jerry Falwell, Oliver North, Louis Farrakhan, tobacco companies.

New Democrats: 8% registered voters, 62% Democrat, but most voted for Bush in 1988. Progovernment, proenvironment, more probusiness than other Democratic groups. Religious but not intolerant. Female, average income and education, high proportion of minorities, employed in social service and educational occupations. Key issues: Support for health care reform and job training. Heroes: Hillary Clinton and Colin Powell. Villain: Rush Limbaugh.

New Dealers: 8% registered voters, 82% Democrat. Faith in government, but distrust politicians and big business. Conservative on race and social welfare programs. Strongly religious, moderately tolerant. Oldest group: one-third over 65. Labor unions, low income, no college. Oppose government-funded abortions and support prayer in schools, health care reform, and use of military force. Heroes: Franklin Roosevelt, John Kennedy, Jimmy Carter, Al Gore. Villain: Jerry Falwell.

Partisan Poor: 8% registered voters, 89% Democrat. Progovernment, anti–big business; 41% nonwhite, blue collar, very poor. Favor government spending to help poor, job training, health care reform, and school prayer. Heroes: John Kennedy, Jimmy Carter, Bill and Hillary Clinton. Villain: Rush Limbaugh.

Source: *The New Political Landscape.* Times Mirror Center for the People and the Press, October 1994.

The tendency toward dealignment may increase the length of time it takes for a realignment, or postpone a realignment altogether. That is, some people who might have switched parties do not care enough about them to switch. Some observers see a "rolling realignment" that has been moving the country to the right and toward the Republicans in fits and starts since the early 1970s.

THE PARTIES TODAY

Generally each party is more ideologically homogenous than it used to be, with most Republicans considering themselves conservative. In fact, the Republican party represents an uneasy coalition of traditional conservatives, motivated primarily by a desire to minimize government intervention in the economy, and new conservatives, motivated primarily by a desire to institutionalize their religious and moral values. Called the religious right, the new conservatives want to increase government intervention in such areas as abortion, prayers in school, and pornography. In many states, the religious right controls the Republican party. Since the 1992 Republican National Convention, the right has avoided open confrontations with moderate Republicans, and national party leaders have stressed issues such as lower taxes and smaller government, on which both agree. With white born-again Christians 17% of the electorate, party success in 1996 and beyond may depend on keeping more divisive issues such as abortion in the background.

Class differences are also apparent among conservatives. Many traditional conservatives are upper-middle and upper class, while many new conservatives are lower-middle class. The two factions were united in their hate for communism and their support for Reagan. But now the disintegration of the Soviet Union and the Communist bloc and the retirement of Reagan leave them with less in common.[20]

In spite of these differences, Republicans won control of Congress in 1994 for the first time in 40 years. They increased their strength in the states, controlling 26 state legislatures and electing 30 state governors. Some herald this as a long-awaited Republican realignment.

The Democrats, reeling from their defeat in 1994, are also divided. Some want to return to their liberal roots by appealing to working men and women and denouncing Republican support for big business and wealthy taxpayers. Others want the party to appeal to moderates who want lower taxes, less government, and more local control. A Clinton advisor says, "We can't define ourselves as the party of government."[21] The party is unlikely, however, to win back control of Congress unless it can appeal to both its liberal base and the moderate middle. The key is to offer solutions to or, at least, assistance in dealing with problems and real concerns of voters, namely stagnant incomes, job security, and family care. Even if the party runs on these issues, it may lose to a Republican party that has raised more money, registered more voters, and recruited good candidates to challenge Democratic incumbents.

PAC contributions shifted sharply in favor of Republicans following the 1994 election. When the Democrats controlled Congress, nearly all PACs contributed more to Democrats than Republicans. Now PACs give more to Republicans. Although the passage of the "motor voter" bill, which allows citizens to register to vote when they renew their driver's license, was expected to help Democrats, it has primarily helped Republicans. In the South, Democrats have been unable to recruit candidates to run under the party's label.

Polls continue to show a slight advantage for the Democrats in the number of voters who identify with the party, but this support is strong only among older voters and minorities. Older voters have been shaped by the New Deal. A Democratic pollster quipped that "there are a lot of Democrats, the bad news is they will be dead by the next election."[22] Although African Americans vote overwhelmingly Democratic in presidential elections, large numbers have supported Republicans in state-wide races.

The Democrats' strategy to win back Congress in 1996 is to convince voters that the Republican majority is out of step with mainstream Americans. Failure to do so may mean permanent minority status for the nation's oldest political party. At the presidential level, President Clinton hopes to defeat Robert Dole by coopting traditional Republican positions that are popular, such as balancing the budget, and attacking Republican positions that are unpopular, such as rolling back environmental regulations.[23]

CHARACTERISTICS OF THE PARTY SYSTEM

The American party system is characterized by some intriguing and even unique qualities.

Two Parties

First, the American party system is a **two-party system.** Only two parties win seats in Congress, and only two parties compete effectively for the presidency. The development and perpetuation of two parties is rare among the nations of the world.

In Western Europe, for example, **multiparty systems** are the rule. Italy has 9 national parties and several regional parties; France and Germany have 4. Great Britain, although a predominantly two-party system, now has at least 3 significant minor parties. Multiparty systems also are found in Canada, which has 3 parties, and Israel, which has more than 20.

Why do we have a two-party system? The most common explanation is the nature of our election system.[24] Public officials are elected from **single-member districts** under a **winner-take-all** arrangement. This means only one individual is elected from a district or state—the individual who receives the most votes. This contrasts with **proportional representation** election schemes, where seats in the national legislature go to political parties roughly according to the proportion of the popular vote the parties' candidates receive.

In single-member district, winner-take-all systems, only the major parties have much chance of winning legislative seats. Without much hope of developing a base to build on, minor parties tend to die off or merge with one of the major parties. However, this explanation might not account for the difference. It may be the party system that influences the election system rather than the reverse. Where only two parties exist, it is to their advantage to maintain an election system that undermines the development and growth of minor parties. For example, legislatures, controlled by the two parties, have tried to make it as difficult as possible for third parties to get on the ballot (though the courts have struck down much of this restrictive legislation). Where several parties exist, it is to their advantage to establish an election system that benefits many parties.[25]

Fragmentation

The federal system, with its fragmentation of power between state and national levels, leads to fragmentation within parties. State and local parties have their own resources and power bases separate from those of the national parties.

Power also is fragmented at each level. At the national level, power is shared among the president and members of Congress. No one controls the party. Presidents often have a difficult time winning support for their policies among their party members in Congress.

As parties have weakened, this problem has become more apparent. In 1992 House Republicans supported President Bush 71% of the time, Senate Republicans 73%. In 1993 House Democrats supported President Clinton 77% of the time, Senate Democrats 87%. Even on major issues, congressional Democrats broke with Clinton. For the North American Free Trade Agreement (NAFTA), two of the top three majority leaders in the House actually led the opposition and two of the top three majority leaders in the Senate joined the opposition. Three Democratic committee chairs and 17 subcommittee chairs in both the House and Senate joined with Republicans in defeating a Democratic-sponsored crime bill. To their dismay, these leaders later learned that the party's failure to pass legislation dealing with crime and other issues contributed to voters' disgust with the party and the Republican takeover in the 1994 elections.

These defections illustrate members' independence from their party. To be reelected, they need to satisfy only a plurality of the voters in their district or state, not the president. When Clinton considered a gas tax increase to reduce the deficit, Democratic Senator Herbert Kohl (Wis.) told him the increase would be no more than 4.3 cents per gallon. Clinton had to accept this figure because the bill's outcome was in doubt and the senator's vote was crucial. Kohl, a multimillionaire, paid for his initial election campaign and could pay for a reelection bid, so he felt no obligation to his party. Such independence makes it difficult to forge a unified party.

Moderation

American political parties are moderate; there are no extremely liberal or extremely conservative major parties. One reason for this is that the people themselves are moderate (see Figure 4). To attract the most voters, the parties try to appear moderate.

Because parties try to attract many voters, both have liberals as well as conservatives, though the Democratic party has more liberals and fewer conservatives than the Republican party. This combination prompts parties to moderate their appeals and nominate moderate candidates. When liberal or conservative candidates do get nominated, they usually move toward the middle on some issues or at least portray themselves as moderate. Reagan, when running for

FIGURE 4
Parties Aim Their Campaigns to the Middle, Where the Voters Are

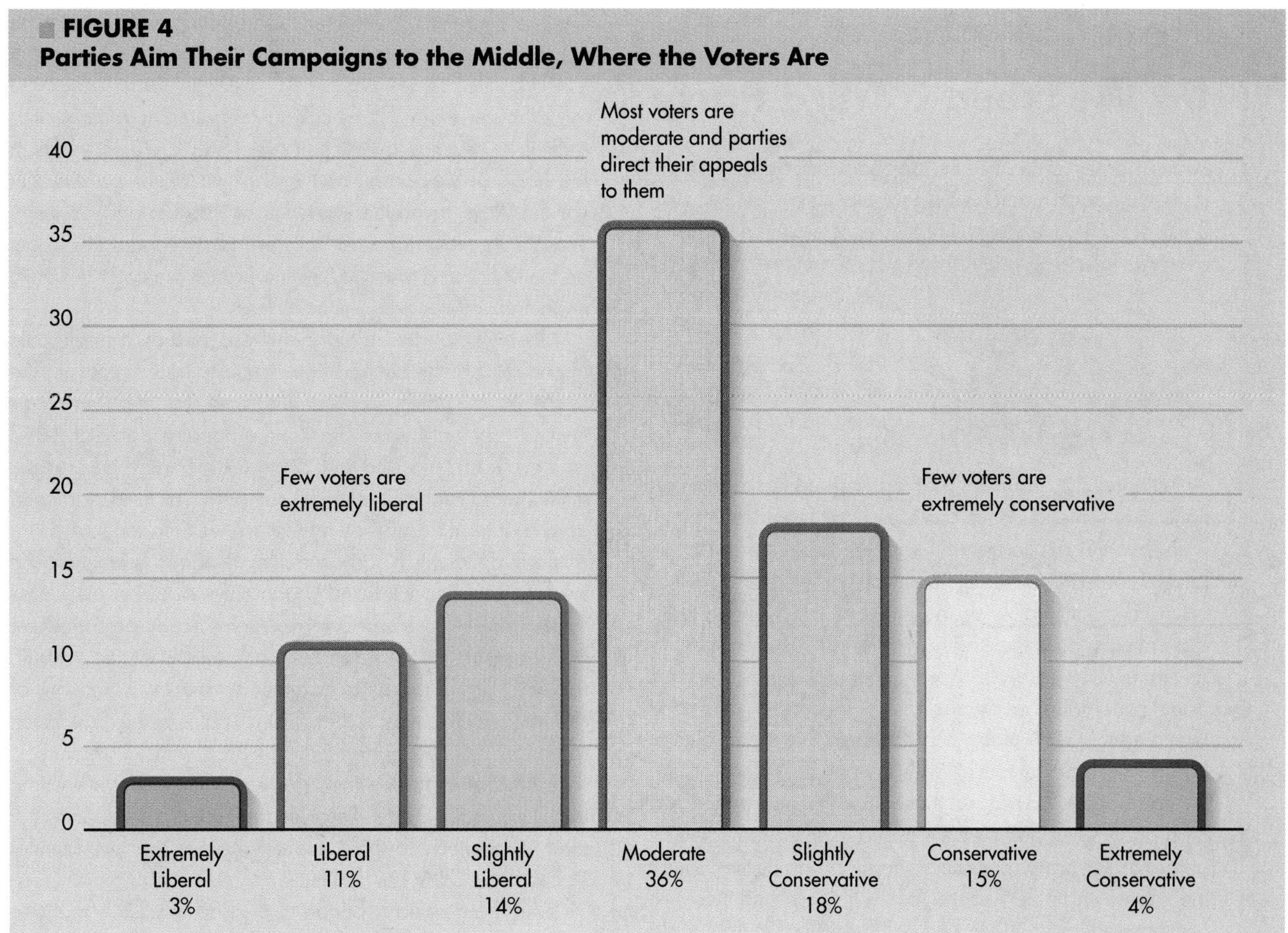

Source: Data from 1990 General Social Survey, National Opinion Research Center. The labels (such as "liberal") were self-descriptions.

reelection, embraced a conciliatory stance toward the Soviet Union in contrast to his earlier "evil empire" posture. Bill Clinton became a "new kind" of Democrat. The implication is that, unlike those in the past who catered to minorities and special interests, he would deal with the problems of middle America.

Minor Parties in American Politics

Sometimes called "third parties," minor parties are as varied as the causes they represent. Some are one-issue parties, like the American Know-Nothing party (1856), which ran on a platform opposing immigrants and Catholics, and the Prohibition party (1869 to the present), which campaigns to ban the sale of liquor.

Other parties advocate radical change in the American political system. Economic protest parties, such as the Populist party of 1892, sometimes appear when economic conditions are especially bad and disappear when times improve. Since the 1920s, the Communist party has espoused the adoption of a Communist system.

Some parties are simply candidates who failed to receive their party's nomination and decided to go it alone. In 1968, Alabama Governor George Wallace split from the Democratic party to run for president as the candidate of the conservative American Independent Party. Failing to get the Republican nomination, John Anderson launched a third-party campaign in 1980. Though both Wallace and Anderson had significant public support, neither won a large number of votes nor had much influence on the election outcome.

Ross Perot's third-party candidacy in 1992 had no association with either party. He simply decided to run (see Chapter 7). Although he polled 19% of the

New Populism

Do We Need a Third Party?

Populist anger at politicians, big government, and existing institutions occasionally leads to a movement to start a new political party, one that will better represent the needs of the average voter. The populist tag was sometimes attached to the attempts to form a third party by Ross Perot and his movement in 1992 and George Wallace and his supporters in 1968.

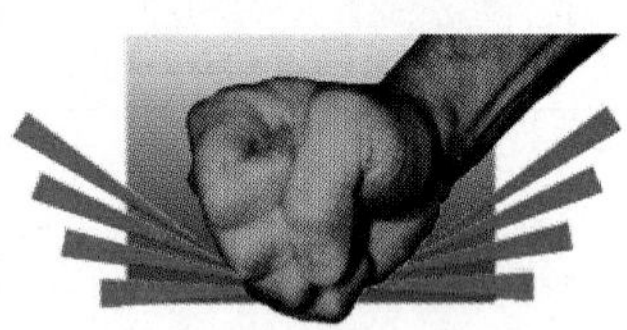

The populist argument that existing leaders and institutions have somehow been corrupted and separated from the wishes of the public fits well with the desire of third-party leaders to oust the existing political parties and their leaders. And in an era when the public seems to have lost its close allegiance to the existing parties, and is alienated from government in general, it would seem fairly easy for third-party candidates to be successful. Indeed, a recent poll indicated that 82% of the public believe that the parties are "pretty much out of touch" with the people.[1]

Other polls also suggest there is substantial support for a third party. Over half of those polled in 1994 indicated that a third major party is needed.[2] Support was highest among men, those under 30, independents, liberals, and those who are more educated. Over half of those polled in 1995, after Republicans took over control of Congress, still wanted a third party. Even 48% of Republicans did.[3]

Despite such sentiments, third parties have rarely had much success. Think of all the attention that Perot's candidacy received in 1992—but he garnered less than 20% of the vote. He certainly did his best to mobilize the disgruntled, angry voters into his camp. Yet he was unsuccessful in making the kind of impact he wanted. He did not even win one state.

Many voters might consider a third party an antidote to the "business as usual" politics in Washington. Yet when faced with the choice of voting against a candidate of their own party, or voting for a relatively unknown quantity with no ties to the party structure, many voters spurn the third party and choose the tried and true. Though their anger remains, it is often expressed with a vote for the nonincumbent of the major party. Thus, angry voters threw out George Bush in 1992 rather than electing Ross Perot, and the same angry voters threw out the Democratic Congress in 1994.

Although many issues calling for solutions remain, it is difficult to establish a new party. Not only are most voters in the habit of supporting one of the two major parties, but various laws favor the existence of the two-party system. These laws make it harder for third-party candidates to get on the ballot and give the existing parties the edge in public financing of presidential elections.

Most third parties in history have started on a small scale in one region. The 1948 Dixiecrat party had its roots in the South as a protest against the move by the Democrats toward more rights for blacks; the Populist party of 1892 was rooted in the Midwest. With the pervasiveness of the mass media today, it is easier for potential third parties to gain a national audience if they are well funded.

Forming a third party requires dynamic and energetic leaders with financial and organizational resources. Jesse Jackson and Ross Perot are two such forceful personalities. Both had substantial resources; Jackson's were his strength and visibility in the black community and in its network of churches. Perot was a billionaire, able to buy as much television time as he wanted. But even with his resources, Jackson did not form a third party, but chose to work within the Democratic party. Perot organized a third party, but after his failure to gain more votes in the presidential election, his party has sputtered.

Even if a new party began to develop, it is likely that one or both of the existing parties, seeing the appeal of the new party, would adopt some of its ideas to avoid further defections to the new party. The Prohibition party died when prohibition became law, and the Socialist party faded when Roosevelt's New Deal included new social legislation.

Thus, while the new wave of populism in the country is certainly stimulating discussions of a new third-party movement for 1996, if recent history is any guide, the 1996 election will be decided by the two major parties and not an upstart. Populists will throw incumbents out, but only within the two-party system.

---

1. Joel Kotkin, "Catching the Third Wave," *Washington Post National Weekly Edition* (February 6–12, 1995): 24.
2. Times Mirror Center for People and the Press, as reprinted in the *New York Times* (September 21, 1994): A21.
3. Laurence I. Barrett, "Party of Spoilers," *Time* (March 13, 1995): 91.

vote, his candidacy did not influence the election's outcome.

Minor parties face many obstacles in trying to establish themselves. Because a sizable portion of the electorate is firmly attached to the existing parties, minor party candidates find it difficult to attract voter support and money and to develop lasting state and local organizations. Even voters who favor the ideas or candidates of a minor party often will not vote for them because in a close race between the major party candidates, a vote for a minor party is seen as a "wasted" vote. And most third-party movements die after their candidate's defeat. Perot was able to overcome some of these problems by drawing on his personal fortune. His "United We Stand America" movement from his campaign in 1992 became the Reform party in 1996 and served as the organizational base for his run for the presidency in 1996.

Party in the Electorate

The party in the electorate—those individuals who identify with a political party—are a party's grassroots supporters. **Party identification** is a psychological link between individuals and a party; no formal or organization membership is necessary. In contrast, European parties do have members; members pay dues and sign a pledge that they accept the basic principles of the party. The percentage of voters who are members ranges from 1 or 2% in some countries to over 40% in others.

Party Identification

A majority of Americans identify with a political party (see Table 1). In 1992, 36% said they were Democrats, 25% Republicans, and 38% independent.

In Chapter 4, we discussed how political socialization leads to party identification early in childhood. Political scientists used to think that changes in party identification after childhood were rare except for those that occurred during major party realignments. But in fact people change their party identification more often. This can happen because they change jobs or residence, or because they develop policy views that conflict with their original party. As we have seen, for example, the national Democratic party's increased support for civil rights and other liberal policies caused many white southerners to leave the party.

TABLE 1 Party Identification, 1960–1992

AFFILIATION	1960	1972	1980	1992
Strong Democrat	21	15	18	18
Weak Democrat	25	25	23	18
Independent Democrat*	8	11	11	14
Independent	8	13	13	12
Independent Republican*	7	11	10	12
Weak Republican	13	13	14	14
Strong Republican	14	10	9	11
Apolitical, do not know	4	2	2	0

*Independents who lean toward the Democrats or Republicans.

Source: University of Michigan Survey Research Center CPS/NES.

Characteristics of Democrats and Republicans

Although people from all walks of life are found in each party, individuals with certain characteristics are more likely to be found in one than the other (see Table 2). Blacks and Hispanics are more likely than non-Hispanic whites to be Democrats. Jews and Catholics are more likely than Protestants to be Democrats.

High-income professionals and those in business are most apt to be Republicans; low-income blue-collar workers are most likely to be Democrats. Skilled blue-collar workers and white-collar workers are more evenly divided between the parties. Women are more likely than men to be Democrats.

Party in Government

Nationally, the party in government is the party's elected members of Congress and, for the party that occupies the White House, the president. The party in government links the party in the electorate to their government. The job of the party in government is to enact policies that party voters favor. This seems like a simple idea, but political scientists have waged great debates over how close the link between the party in government and the party in the electorate should be.

TABLE 2 Characteristics of Republicans, Democrats, and Independents

	REPUBLICAN	DEMOCRAT	INDEPENDENT
Total	25%	36%	38%
Age 18–29	26	28	46
30–49	27	37	36
50 and over	28	44	28
Less than high school education	19	50	31
High school graduate	24	40	36
Some college education	28	34	37
College graduate	35	31	34
Men	30	31	39
Women	23	42	36
White	31	30	39
Black	4	70	26
Hispanic	29	21	50
Asian	50	25	25
Protestant	33	35	32
Catholic	21	43	35
Jewish	5	68	27
Professional and business	30	33	37
Other white collar	27	36	37
Blue collar	25	37	38
Under $15,000	19	46	36
$15,000–$24,999	22	44	34
$25,000 and over	32	33	35
Conservative	49	21	32
Middle of the road	26	36	39
Liberal	9	57	35

Source: CPS/NES 1992.

Proponents of a **responsible party government** believe parties should take clear and contrasting positions on issues and enforce them on their members. "Responsible" party government would be responsible in that

- voters would have a choice between parties advocating different programs;
- a party would make sure that its members in office vote for these programs;
- therefore, if a party had a majority, it would enact its program into law.

Under these conditions, voting for one party rather than another would have definite policy consequences. It would increase the prospects for popular control of government because a voter would know what a vote for one party means for public policy. Great Britain is an example of responsible party government. Political parties there are heavily involved in developing, articulating, and implementing public policy. If a party member defects too often from important policy positions, party leaders can deny him or her the right to stand for reelection as the party's candidate.

The American system is not a responsible party government. Political parties do not always offer clear and contrasting positions. When they do, party leaders are limited in authority to ensure that members support the "party," that is, the position of the president or party's leaders in Congress.

Although the American system is not a responsible party government, it has some elements of party responsibility. The party links presidents with the members of their party in Congress. Members of the president's party in Congress support his policies more often than members of the opposition. Parties also have important organizational and leadership functions in Congress.

Party influence is also visible in congressional voting[26] and increased dramatically during the 1980s. This reflects the realignment of the South. In the days before blacks were allowed to vote and before the Republicans offered real challenges in most Southern districts, the vast majority of Southern members of Congress were conservative Democrats, Democrats who voted like Republicans. As white conservatives have moved into the Republican party, districts with conservative white majorities are much more likely to elect Republicans rather than conservative Democrats. Districts with large numbers of black voters are more likely than before to elect blacks or moderate or liberal white Democrats. Thus voting patterns of representatives from the South are divided along party lines. The movement of parties and voters in the South was reflected in the nation as a whole in 1994, with Republican voters moving to the right and Democratic voters moving to the left. Eighty percent of self-identified conservatives voted Republican and 82% of self-identified liberals voted Democratic.[27] As a result, Democratic members of Congress from the North as well as the South are more likely to act and vote differently from Republicans.

FIGURE 5
Party Unity Is on the Rise in Congress

The average percentage of times that Democrats and Republicans in Congress voted with their party on votes where a majority of Democrats opposed a majority of Republicans.

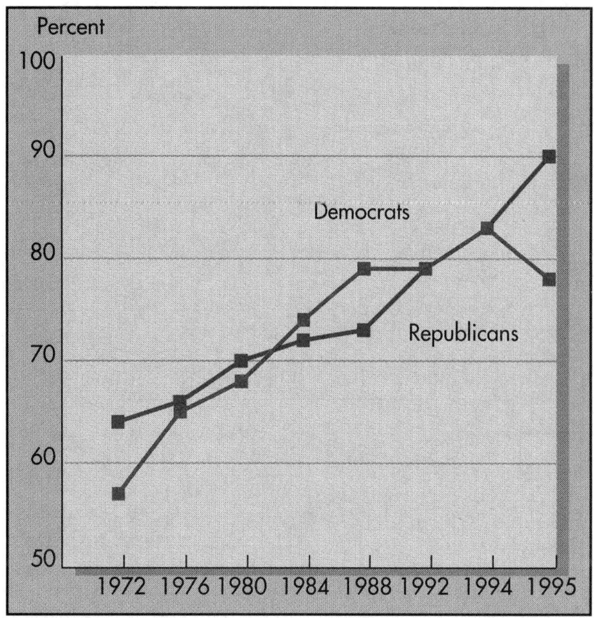

Source: Party unity voting studies in *Congressional Quarterly Almanac* for the respective years, Washington, D.C.: Congressional Quarterly.

Winning control of both houses of Congress in 1994 for the first time in 40 years pushed the level of party unity even higher. A number of conservative Republicans, committed to a very conservative agenda, were elected in 1994. Eager to retain control of Congress, moderate incumbent Republicans supported the program to show voters that the party can enact legislation and govern effectively.[28] Moderate Democrats, on the other hand, found themselves unable to support the GOP's agenda. Division between the parties reached record highs. Sixty-nine percent of the votes in the Senate and 73% of the votes in the House saw a majority of Republicans opposing a majority of Democrats. On these votes, Senate Republicans voted with their party on average 89% of the time, House Republicans 91%. Senate Democrats voted with their party 81%, House Democrats 80%. (See Figure 5.) Democrats concerned with their loss of Congress were somewhat more likely to defect from their party in support of the conservative GOP agenda than Republicans were to defect from theirs. Party voting rivaled European-style parliaments, which are often used as examples of responsible party government.[29]

With President Clinton exercising his veto over Republican-passed legislation and Republican fears that the voters will hold them responsible for failing to deal with the nation's problems, party unity in Congress may decline in 1996 as both compromise in an effort to win public approval.

Much higher levels of party voting would require major changes in the operation of government. Party leaders would have to be given more power to maintain party discipline in Congress. A greater tie between the president and Congress also would be required. This could be accomplished on a continuing basis only through a constitutional change providing for a parliamentary system similar to Britain's, in which Congress would elect the president. Such a change is unlikely.

➤Party Organization

The party organization is the third component of the political party. The major levels of party organization—national, state, and local—coincide with political units responsible for administering elections. Within the local parties there are further subdivisions. The smallest unit

Source: Tony Auth, Universal Press Syndicate, Reprinted with permission.

is usually the precinct-level organization. Several precincts comprise a ward or district; several wards comprise the city or county organization.

Although party organization seems hierarchical (organized from the top down), it is not. Party organization is a layered structure with each layer linked to, but independent of, the others. Higher levels cannot dictate to or impose penalties on lower levels to ensure compliance.

Party organization is only loosely connected with the party in government. This contrasts with the British system, in which the party leaders in Parliament try to maintain a tight grip on the party organization.

National Party Organization

The head of the party organization is the national chair. Although selected by the party's presidential nominee, the national chair is not a major political figure.

Responsibilities of the national party chair include managing the national headquarters, overseeing the national party apparatus, planning the national convention, and coordinating the presidential campaign efforts of the national organization with those of the nominee's personal organization. Fund-raising and promotion of the party also fall on the chair. The new chair of the Republican party built a television studio and launched GOP-TV, the Republican National Committee network that carries his weekly talk show; started a slick magazine; and founded the National Policy Forum, a quasi–think tank intended to develop Republican positions on issues. He also reduced the party's $4 million debt.[30]

Members of the **national committee** are selected by state party committees or conventions, and membership usually is awarded on the basis of service to the party. Duties of the committee are few but important: It chooses the site of the national convention and the formula for determining the number of delegates each state sends to it.

Both parties also have two national campaign committees that are growing in influence. In the 1980s both parties raised more money than ever from a variety of sources. Money came from PACs and large and small contributors. Both party organizations opened permanent headquarters and expanded their staffs.[31]

The national party organizations have become increasingly active in recruiting candidates to run for office. The Republicans' programs to help their candidates are better developed, but the Democrats' are catching up. Since 1984, the Republican organization has provided every female Senate primary candidate a $1,500 campaign contribution (once a similar amount has been raised by the candidate). Specific candidates have been encouraged to run. In an effort to convince a Nebraskan to run for the Senate, the Republican national organization invited her to Washington to tour the capital, dine with senators, and see what life in the Senate is like (she ran and lost). Occasionally, the organizations have discouraged individuals from running, especially where another candidate appeared to have a better chance of winning.

Training in managing a campaign is also available from the national party organizations. Both parties hold how-to seminars and help candidates design campaign strategies; they help research issues and write speeches; and they conduct polls and work with state and local party organizations to get out the vote.

National party organizations are heavily involved in campaign financing. They contribute directly to candidates and raise funds for them through direct mail and by encouraging PACs to contribute. They also assist candidates in raising their own funds.

While the national parties are not as powerful as they were a century ago, they are active. They play the role of intermediary between candidates and voters and between candidates and other political actors, such as campaign consultants and PAC leaders, who possess the skills and resources needed to communicate with the electorate.

The growing capacity of parties to offer candidates such help may be partly responsible for the increased party voting in Congress in recent years. National party organizations, however, are growing in power at the expense of state and local ones.[32] The national party's greater fund-raising capacity coupled with generous PAC donations means that members of Congress are less dependent on state and local parties than ever.

A Day in the Life of a Machine Politician

George Washington Plunkitt was a ward leader in the infamous Tammany Hall machine, the Democratic party organization that governed New York City for seven decades in the late nineteenth and early twentieth centuries. Although Plunkitt was on the city payroll, he did not have a free ride. The demands of his job were exhausting. Yet by providing needed services to his constituents he had many opportunities to build support for the party. Now government provides many of these services, thus making parties less vital. Entries from Plunkitt's diary illustrate the pervasive role of the party:

2:00 A.M. Aroused from sleep by a bartender who asked me to go to the police station and bail out a saloon keeper who had been arrested for violating the excise law. Furnished bail and returned to bed at three o'clock.

6:00 A.M. Awakened by fire engines. Hastened to the scene of the fire . . . found several tenants who had been burned out, took them to a hotel, supplied them with clothes, fed them, and arranged temporary quarters for them.

8:30 A.M. Went to the police court to secure the discharge of six "drunks," my constituents, by a timely word to the judge. Paid the fines of two.

9:00 A.M. Appeared in the municipal district court to direct one of my district captains to act as counsel for a widow about to be dispossessed. . . . Paid the rent of a poor family and gave them a dollar for food.

11:00 A.M. At home again. "Fixed" the troubles of four men waiting for me: one discharged by the Metropolitan Railway for neglect of duty; another wanted a job on the road; the third on the subway; and the fourth was looking for work with a gas company.

3:00 P.M. Attended the funeral of an Italian. Hurried back for the funeral of a Hebrew constituent. Went conspicuously to the front both in the Catholic church and the synagogue.

George Washington Plunkitt holds forth in his unofficial office, a bootblack stand at the New York County Court House.

7:00 P.M. Went to district headquarters to preside over a meeting of election district captains, submitted lists of all the voters in their districts and told who were in need, who were in trouble, who might be won over [to Tammany] and how.

8:00 P.M. Went to a church fair. Took chances on everything, bought ice cream for the young girls and the children, kissed the little ones, flattered their mothers, and took the fathers out for something down at the corner.

9:00 P.M. At the clubhouse again. Spent $10 for a church excursion. Bought tickets for a baseball game. Listened to the complaints of a dozen pushcart peddlers who said they were being persecuted by the police. Promised to go to police headquarters in the morning and see about it.

10:30 P.M. Attended a Hebrew wedding reception and dance. Had previously sent a handsome wedding present to the bride.

12:00 P.M. In bed.

Source: Alistair Cooke, *Alistair Cooke's America* (New York: Alfred A. Knopf, 1973), pp. 290–91; adapted from William L. Riordon, *Plunkitt of Tammany Hall* (New York: E. P. Dutton, 1963), pp. 91–93.

State and Local Party Organizations

Each state and local party has a chair and committee to direct the activities of their party activists. In some communities, parties may be so weak and unimportant that there is little party organization. Because of this, someone who wants to become active in the party organization only has to show up at party meetings and be willing to work.

Big-City Party Organizations

Unlike most local party organizations today, the **political machine,** which flourished in some of the nation's largest cities in the late nineteenth and early twentieth centuries, was strong and powerful. At the head of the machine was a boss, who often served as mayor and directed operations in such a way as to maintain control over the city and the organization.

The machine relied on the votes of the poor and working class, many of whom had only recently immigrated from Europe. Most accounts of machine politics are negative, dwelling on graft and corruption. However, the machine provided a number of valuable services. In a period when there were no welfare agencies, the machine provided jobs, food, and fuel for the thousands of immigrants who had no place else to turn. In return, party leaders expected individuals to vote for machine candidates.

Business also benefited from machines. The machine provided (for a fee) permits for business expansion, licenses, new roads, utilities, and police and fire protection.

The key to the machine's success was **patronage,** that is, giving jobs to party loyalists when the party controlled local government. An army of city employees, whose jobs depended on the political success of the machine, would dutifully bring family and friends to the polls on election day. One of the last of the big-city bosses, Mayor Richard Daley, head of the Chicago machine during the 1960s and 1970s, controlled 35,000 public jobs and, indirectly through public contracts, 10,000 private ones.[33]

Reformers disturbed by corruption and by lower-class control of city politics eventually passed laws making it difficult for machines to operate. Merit examinations for city jobs, nonpartisan elections, secret ballots, and voter registration undercut the means that machines had to secure voter loyalty. Political machines were dealt another blow when the federal government assumed responsibility for welfare needs in the 1930s; individuals no longer had to rely on the machine. And with a more educated population and greater employment opportunities, patronage jobs were no longer as desirable.

The Nominating Process

The major function of political parties is to nominate and elect candidates to office. Often many candidates of one party want to run for the same office. Parties have devised three ways—caucuses, conventions, and primaries—to choose among these contenders.

Caucuses

A **caucus** is a meeting. In the early eighteenth century, party candidates were nominated by a small number of party leaders and officeholders in a caucus. It was criticized by many because so few people actually participated.

Conventions

By 1830, the increased number of voters in elections and the desire of parties to win their continued support led to new procedures to involve more voters in nominations. Caucuses of local residents selected delegates to attend county, state, and national conventions. These conventions then nominated candidates for public office.

Party conventions usually were controlled by party leaders who decided what happened and who was nominated. The leaders often made decisions behind the scenes in "smoke-filled rooms."

Primaries

In the early 1900s Progressive reformers argued that nominating conventions ignored the rank-and-file voter. Because they believed that party leaders in their "smoke-filled rooms" were corrupt and not to be trusted, reformers established the **direct primary** to increase citizen participation and check the influence of party bosses in nominations. The primary allows the voters in an election to choose the party's candidates. Today all states use primary elections, sometimes in conjunction with caucuses and conventions, to nominate candidates.

Primaries vary from state to state according to who is eligible to vote in them. A **closed primary** limits participation to those who are registered with a party or declare a preference for a party. Thus only Democrats can vote in the Democratic party's primary. An **open primary** imposes no such limits; regardless of party registration, one may vote in either party's primary.

Party leaders and others favoring strong parties oppose open primaries. They argue that only voters who are party supporters should be permitted to vote in the party's primary. They fear that independents and opposition partisans will vote for candidates who are less sympathetic to the party's position on issues or who are less likely to win.

A minority of states use runoff primaries, which pit the two highest vote-getters in the primary against each other for the party's nomination. Over the years, the inability of the Republican party to compete effectively for office in the South meant that the winner of the

Why Not Return to the "Smoke-Filled Rooms"?

In addition to attracting a small and unrepresentative group of voters to the ballot box, primaries have other flaws. In some ways, the primary process is less responsive to voters than party conventions, where candidates were once selected by a small group of party leaders meeting in smoke-filled hotel rooms.

Primaries do not necessarily provide voters with much choice. Many primaries are uncontested. Often the presence of an incumbent deters challengers, or at least strong challengers. In either case, incumbents are generally renominated.

Primaries also may make the general election less competitive. The minority party (that is, the party less likely to win the general election) often has no strong candidate who can mount an effective campaign in the general election. In preprimary days, party leaders generally made sure there were strong candidates running in the general election regardless of election prospects.

Another problem with primaries is that the electorate may nominate a candidate known by his or her party peers to be incompetent, difficult to work with, or lacking in character and integrity. Although the convention system does not guarantee that such candidates will be avoided, party leaders are more likely to know the real strengths and weaknesses of potential candidates than are voters, who must rely on the media for information. Indeed, voters have so little information about primary candidates that success often turns on name recognition.

Primaries hurt the most, however, by freeing candidates from supporting the party's program. It is nearly impossible for party leaders to withhold nominations from candidates who are party members in name only or who often vote with the other party. Thus, the party bonds are weakened and members can feel free to vote and act however they want.

This might seem desirable. But when candidates vote completely independent of their party, it is more difficult for voters to cast an informed vote. When parties offer a clear choice, voters know what they are voting for and can reward or punish the parties for what they do or plan to do in office. Thus, party voting can make government more responsive to the voters.

Some commentators have advocated returning to convention nominations. If we did so, the abuses that we associate with the smoke-filled rooms of a century ago are less likely to occur today because of the greater likelihood of exposure by the media and hostile voter reaction. In states and localities where the parties are competitive, it is likely that conventions would produce strong candidates. This would give voters a real choice in the general election. However, in locales dominated by one party, the convention system would not necessarily produce stronger candidates than a primary. At the presidential level, smoke-filled rooms produced the likes of Franklin Roosevelt and John Kennedy. Perhaps the greatest argument for smoke-filled rooms is Harry Truman. Although a product of machine politics, Truman was honest and incorruptible. Tapped to be FDR's vice president in 1944 by party bosses who knew Roosevelt would not live out his term, Truman became an excellent president.

Why haven't we returned to the convention system? Primaries are widely accepted. They *seem* more democratic because more people are involved than in conventions, where only party activists participate. But the sheer number of people involved is only one aspect of democracy and probably not the most important. Democracy also implies that those making the nominations are representative of the public; primary electorates are not. Moreover, a democratic process must offer some choice, and primaries adversely affect competition.

Although it is unlikely that we will abolish primaries and return to conventions, in recent years party leaders have asserted more control in some states through preprimary endorsements. Parties endorse candidates for nomination. The endorsed candidates are listed first on the primary ballot or are simply publicized as the "official" party candidate. Although on occasion the preferred candidate is defeated, the voters usually go along with the party's choice. Such arrangements promote party strength and ultimately responsiveness to voters.

Democratic party's primary was virtually assured of winning the general election. Due to the large number of Democratic candidates, sometimes the winner of the primary did not have a majority of the vote. In those cases, some southern states used a runoff election between the two highest vote-getters in the primary.

Although primaries have increased citizen participation in nominations, turnout in primaries is quite low and unrepresentative. Turnout reached record lows in the 1992 presidential primaries, when average turnout in Democratic primaries was 12% and in Republican primaries 8%. While Montana and New Hampshire had record high turnouts, 11 states recorded new lows.[34] Voters in primaries are unrepresentative of the public at large. Primary voters tend to have higher incomes and education and to be older, more interested in politics, and more partisan.[35]

The primary also hurts the party organization and undermines the party in government. Candidates can bypass party leaders and appeal directly to voters. Candidates who oppose the party's issue positions can run and win the party's nomination, especially in elections in which voters do not know much about the candidates.

Conclusion: Do Political Parties Make Government More Responsive?

Although the Founders had little use for political parties, parties did develop, and during the nineteenth century they were the major link between the public and government. Following the Progressive reforms of the early twentieth century, the importance of parties began to decline.

Compared to a century ago or even a few decades ago, each of the components of political parties has

Divided We Stand?

Since 1981, we have had **divided government.** For all but two years, one party controlled the White House and the other the Congress. The Founders made divided government possible by dividing authority between the executive and legislative branches and providing that members of each would be elected in different ways and for different terms. This contrasts with parliamentary systems, in which voters vote for members of the legislative branch and they in turn choose the executive leader of the nation.

In the first half of the twentieth century, divided government did not occur very often. From 1900 to 1950, only 4 of 26 presidential and midterm elections resulted in divided government. However, from 1952 to 1994, 14 of 22 elections did.[1] Even with Reagan's overwhelming victory in 1980, the Republicans failed to win control of the House of Representatives. While the party captured the Senate, their dominance lasted only until 1986, when the Democrats regained majority control. President Bush faced both a House and Senate controlled by the Democrats, and now President Clinton faces a Republican Congress.

Some believe that divided government is partially responsible for our failure to solve many of our important problems. The term *gridlock* has often been used to suggest this policy stalemate. The continuing attempt to reduce the federal deficit is a striking example. While nearly everyone agreed that the deficit is a significant problem, it continues to grow. The parties disagree over which programs to cut to reduce spending and which taxes to raise, if any, to increase revenue. The president presents a program and Congress does not accept it. Or Congress comes up with their own plan and the president vetoes it. The result is a lot of squabbling and little action. Divided government produces "conflict, delay, inadequate and ineffective policies or no policies at all."[2]

Gridlock, however, is also the result of responsiveness to the public. Gridlock can be a reflection of democracy. Perhaps gridlock accurately reflects the public's view. Most people do not want to cut programs—at least their programs—or increase taxes. Since we must do one or the other to reduce the deficit, inaction reflects public sentiment.

Moreover, united government will probably not eliminate gridlock. From 1946 to 1990, as many major laws passed during periods of divided government as in periods of united government. Adoption of policies that address major problems are usually the result of strong presidential leadership, significant events, and changes in public opinion rather than united government.[3]

1. M. Fiorina, *Divided Government* (New York: Macmillan, 1992), p. 7.
2. J. L. Sundquist, "Needed: A Political Theory for the New Era of Coalition Government in the United States." *Political Science Quarterly 103 (1988)*, p. 629.
3. D. R. Mayhew, "Divided Party Control: Does It Make a Difference?" *PS: Political Science and Politics*, December 1991, pp. 637–40.

declined. Political parties no longer control or have much influence over who can run for party office. In spite of name recognition, endorsements, and a cache of money to throw at the 1996 nomination, the Republican party could not prevent Steve Forbes, a multimillionaire magazine publisher, and Pat Buchanan, a television personality—neither of whom had ever been elected to anything—and a host of others from entering the race and challenging the establishment candidate, Robert Dole. These candidates were taken seriously. They got airtime, coverage by national newspapers and magazines, and into presidential debates. They attacked Dole, undermining his chance of winning the presidency, and there was nothing much he or the party could do about it. Today, anyone can claim to belong to a party and run for the party's nomination for president or any other office. In the past, the party organization could discourage candidates with little chance of winning an election, withhold its support, or threaten sanctions if necessary.

Today, political parties compete with interest groups, pollsters, campaign consultants, and the media, which provide the resources parties provided in the past. Party workers are less important today as candidates appeal directly to voters through television. Money flows directly from interest groups to candidates. Campaign messages are tailored by focus groups and public opinion polls to appeal to mass audiences. Voters less committed to political parties are more easily swayed by such appeals. Less beholden to political parties than candidates in the past, elected officials are less likely to vote with the party.

Parties have tried to adapt to the current political environment. They are involved in recruiting, funding, and developing campaign strategies for party candidates. State and national party organizations are raising money and engaged in party-building activities. Party voting in Congress is very high. Despite these trends, politics remains fragmented.

Split-ticket voting and the divided government it produces make it unclear how one's vote will affect what government does. It is hard for voters to reward or punish officeholders for what they do. If each officeholder stands alone, there are no unifying and simplifying forces allowing voters to throw the incumbents out. Elections become less meaningful because voters have little idea what they are voting for. And because elections are the chief means by which most voters can influence government, government may become less responsive to the average voter. At the same time, voters look at Congress and state legislatures and see parties as instruments of delay and deadlock, not realizing that it is often lack of party discipline, and not the reverse, that causes the deadlock. Citizens have a greater prospect of influencing the direction of government if they elect party loyalists to office. This factor is what led E. E. Schattschneider to reflect on the inevitability and necessity of parties in our American democracy.

EPILOGUE

The Republicans Adopt a Contract

Newt Gingrich and his fellow Republican leaders did introduce a "Contract with America" as a Republican "platform" for the 1994 election. The "Contract" was a 10-point platform, based on results of focus groups, consultation with business groups and other interests, and questionnaires sent to Republican candidates. The "Contract" promised that bills reflecting its provisions would be brought to a vote in the first 100 days of the new Congress. Republican leaders announced the "Contract" in September and published it as an ad in *TV Guide* in late October, only two weeks before the election.

The "Contract" proposed:

1. An amendment requiring a balanced federal budget by 2002, a constitutional amendment mandating a balanced budget amendment, and a line-item presidential veto.

2. An anticrime bill requiring mandatory prison sentences for crimes committed with a gun, limiting appeals in death penalty cases, giving police more leeway in seizing evidence, and building new prisons.

3. Welfare reform, involving prohibitions on mothers under 18 getting welfare, time limits for those receiving welfare, and cuts in overall welfare spending.

4. A family reinforcement act, including stricter enforcement of child support laws, stronger child pornography laws, and tax breaks for adoption and care of the elderly.

5. A middle-class tax cut.

6. A bill forbidding U.S. troops to serve under United Nations command and increasing spending on the military.

7. A bill raising the Social Security earnings limit (currently, Social Security recipients pay income tax—at the same rate as other Americans—on most of their Social Security earnings if they have a total income over a set amount).

8. A tax cut on capital gains (capital gains are profits from sale of property and other capital such as stocks and bonds), and a bill making government regulation of business more difficult.

9. A legal reform bill requiring losers in lawsuits to pay their opponent's legal fees and limiting juries from ordering corporations and doctors to pay a set amount to individuals harmed by defective products or medical malpractice.

10. A constitutional amendment setting term limits of six years in the House of Representatives and twelve years in the Senate.

The "Contract" avoided abortion and other moral issues on which the party was divided. It also avoided reform in campaign finance, also a subject over which Republicans differ.

Did the "Contract" win votes for the Republicans? Voters did defeat some incumbent Democrats and elect many new Republicans, but polls showed that most Americans never heard of the contract, or did not know what it said.[36] Nonetheless, it may have influenced some voters, especially more informed ones.

In other ways, the "Contract" was useful for the Republicans. It not only gave them a positive program to run on in the last weeks of the campaign, but it gave them a set of priorities for the new Congress.

The "Contract" also energized the Democrats, once they recovered from their colleagues' defeats, because it gave them a target to aim at. They said the "Contract" was economically unrealistic in calling for a balanced budget and at the same time income tax cuts (including those based on Social Security earnings), capital gains tax cuts, and increased military spending. They also said that the "Contract" benefited the rich more than others. The Democrats' message apparently got across. Near the close of the first 100 days, a majority of Americans told pollsters that the primary danger in Congress was that the Republicans would go too far in helping the rich and cutting needed services for ordinary people.[37]

The Republicans did have more trouble implementing the "Contract" than they expected in the postelection euphoria. Although they only promised to bring the provisions to a vote, citizens who supported the "Contract" likely expected them to get the provisions adopted. In the first 100 days, the Republicans passed, and President Clinton signed, some measures. Yet Republicans in the House failed to pass the term limits amendment, and the Republican majority in the Senate failed to pass the balanced budget amendment—the two most visible planks in the platform. The Republicans also came up short on some other measures. Those in the House, led by Gingrich, passed most provisions, but those in the Senate, who tend to be more moderate, weakened or blocked numerous provisions. And, of course, the Democrats voted against most provisions.

Regardless of whether the provisions of the "Contract" eventually are passed or defeated, and regardless of whether the Republicans eventually are helped or hurt, the "Contract" was a healthy step toward more responsible party government. Attentive voters saw that one party made explicit promises before an election and made real efforts to deliver them after the election. Voters can evaluate the party's effectiveness, and, to the extent adopted, the effectiveness of the "Contract." This provides, according to one political scientist, "democratic accountability at its best."[38]

➤Key Terms

party in the electorate
party in government
party organization
realignment
New Deal coalition
ticket splitting
dealignment
two-party system
multiparty systems
single-member districts
winner-take-all
proportional representation
party identification
responsible party government
national committee
political machine
patronage
caucus
direct primary
closed primary
open primary
divided government

➤Further Reading

David S. Broder, *The Party's Over: The Failure of Politics in America* (New York: Harper & Row, 1972). *Argues that the only way America will be able to meet the difficult challenges of the future is for the political parties to assert themselves and exercise more influence in American politics.*

Paul Herrnson, *Party Campaigning in the 1980s* (Cambridge, Mass.: Harvard University Press, 1988). *Documents the revival of the national parties in the 1980s.*

Edwin O'Connor, *The Last Hurrah* (New York: Bantam Books, 1957). *A warm, intimate novel set in Boston in the 1950s that contrasts the old-style party election campaigns with new media-oriented ones.*

William L. Riordon, *Plunkitt of Tammany Hall* (New York: Dutton, 1963). *A series of witty talks by a ward boss of New York City's Democratic party machine. A slice of Americana, this book discusses "honest graft" and other aspects of "practical politics" and in the process demonstrates why political machines flourished.*

Mike Royko, *Boss: Richard J. Daley of Chicago* (New York: New American Library, 1971). *An intriguing account of how the Chicago political machine operated under the late mayor Richard J. Daley.*

James L. Sundquist, *Dynamics of the Party System* (Washington, D.C.: Brookings Institution, 1973). *Analyzes the concept of realignment based on a review of the major party realignments in American history.*

➤Notes

1. Thomas B. Rosenstiel, "Gingrich Created Army," *Lincoln Star* (December 20, 1994): p. 1ff.
2. Dan Balz, "10 Hard Acts to Follow Up," *Washington Post National Weekly Edition* (November 28–December 4, 1994): 6.
3. E. E. Schattschneider, *Party Government* (New York: Holt, Rinehart and Winston, 1960), p. 1.
4. Jack Dennis, "Trends in Public Support for the American Party System," in *Parties and Elections in an Anti-Party Age*, ed. Jeff Fishel (Bloomington, Ind.: Indiana University Press, 1978).
5. Frank Sorauf, *Political Parties in the American System*, 4th ed. (Boston: Little, Brown, 1980).
6. Richard Hofstadter, *The Idea of Party System: The Rise of Legitimate Opposition in the United States, 1780–1840* (Berkeley: University of California Press, 1969).
7. Theodore J. Lowi, *The Personal President: Power Invested, Promise Unfulfilled* (Ithaca, N.Y.: Cornell University Press, 1985).
8. James MacGregor Burns, *The Vineyard of Liberty* (New York: Knopf, 1982).
9. Kevin Phillips, *The Emerging Republican Majority* (New York: Doubleday, 1969).
10. Everett Carll Ladd, *Where Have All the Voters Gone?* (New York: W. W. Norton, 1982), p. 78; 1984 and 1988 data are from the 1984 and 1988 CPS National Election Study.
11. James L. Sundquist, *Dynamics of the Party System: Alignment and Realignment of Political Parties in the United States* (Washington, D.C.: Brookings Institution, 1973).
12. J. R. Petrocik and F. T. Steeper, "The Political Landscape in 1988," *Public Opinion Magazine* (September/October 1987), pp. 41–44; H. Norpoth, "Party Realignment in the 1980s," *Public Opinion Quarterly* 51 (Fall 1987), pp. 376–90.
13. Thomas Edsall, "The Democrats' Class and Gender Gap," *Washington Post National Weekly Edition* (June 6 1994): p. 12.
14. Thomas Edsall, "The Fissure Running through the Democratic Party," *Washington Post National Weekly Edition* (June 6–12, 1994): p. 11.
15. Ibid.
16. Katharine Q. Seelye, "Democrats Across U.S. Continue to Flee Party," *Lincoln Journal-Star* (October 7, 1995), p. 1A.
17. John Petrocik, "Realignment," *Journal of Politics* 49 (May 1987), pp. 347–75; George Rabinowitz, Paul-Henri Gurian, and Stuart MacDonald, "The Structure of Presidential Elections and the Process of Realignment," *American Journal of Political Science* 28 (November 1984), pp. 611–35; D. Broder, "The GOP Plays Dixie," *Washington Post National Weekly Edition,* September 12–18, 1988, p. 4; T. B. Edsall, "A Serious Case of White Flight," *Washington Post National Weekly Edition,* September 10–16, 1990, p. 13.
18. Walter Dean Burnham, *Critical Elections and the Mainstream of American Politics* (New York: W. W. Norton, 1970); Helmut Norpoth and Jerrold Rusk, "Partisan Dealignment in the American Electorate," *American Political Science Review* 76 (September 1982), pp. 522–37; David W. Rhode, "The Fall Elections: Realignment and Dealignment," *The Chronicle of Higher Education* (December 14, 1994), pp. B1–B2.
19. Martin P. Wallenberg, *The Rise of Candidate-Centered Politics* (Cambridge: Harvard University Press, 1991).
20. D. Sarasohn, "Wall Falls on Reagan Coalition," *Lincoln Sunday Journal Star,* February 18, 1990, p. 1C; John C. Green, "The Christian Right and the 1994 Election" 28 (March 1995), pp. 5–8.
21. Steven Roberts, "Near Death Experience," *U.S. News and World Report*, November 6, 1996, p. 28.
22. Ibid.
23. Ann Devroy, "More to the Right, Mr. President—Now Grab the GOP Agenda," *Washington Post National Weekly Edition*, October 16–22, 1995, p. 13.
24. Maurice Duverger, *Political Parties* (New York: John Wiley & Sons, 1963). See also Edward R. Tune, "The Relationship between Seats and Votes in Two-Party Systems," *American Political Science Review* 67 (1973), pp. 540–54.
25. See also Lowi, *Personal President*. He makes the point that two parties survived in the United States despite the use of multimember districts in elections for Congress in the nineteenth century.
26. William R. Shaffer, *Party and Ideology in the United States Congress* (Lanham, Md.: University Press of America, 1980).
27. David Broder, "Polarization Growing Force for Political Parties," *Lincoln Journal-Star,* January 22, 1995, p. 4B.
28. Dan Carney, "As Hostitilies Rage on the Hill, Partisan-Vote Rate Soars," *Congressional Quarterly Weekly Report*, January 27, 1996, pp. 199-200.
29. Ibid.
30. Lloyd Grove, "A Good Ol' Boy Going in for the Kill," *Washington Post National Weekly Edition,* August 22–28, 1994, pp. 13–14, 32.
31. Frank J. Sorauf, *Money in American Elections* (Glenview, Ill.: Scott, Foresman, 1988), pp. 121–53; Paul Herrnson, *Party Campaigning in the 1980s* (Cambridge, Mass.: Harvard University Press, 1988).

32. Xandra Kayden, "The Nationalization of the Party System," in Michael Malbin, ed., *Parties, Interest Groups, and Campaign Finance Laws* (Washington, D.C.: American Enterprise Institute, 1980).

33. Milton L. Rakove, *Don't Make No Waves, Don't Back No Losers* (Bloomington, Ind.: Indiana University Press, 1975).

34. "Turnout for Primaries Declines to Record Low," *Lincoln Journal-Star,* June 26, 1992.

35. Austin Ranney, *Participation in American Presidential Nominations, 1976* (Washington, D.C.: American Enterprise Institute, 1977). See also Austin Ranney, "Parties in State Politics," in Herbert Jacob and Kenneth Vines, eds., *Politics in the American States,* 3rd ed. (Boston: Little, Brown, 1980), pp. 61–99.

36. Richard Morin, "Myths and Messages in the Election Tea Leaves," *Washington Post National Weekly Edition,* November 21–27, 1994, p. 37.

37. Kevin Phillips, "GOP's Big-Bang Revolution Turns into a Wet Firecracker," *Lincoln Journal (Los Angeles Times),* April 4, 1995, p. 3.

38. Thomas Mann, quoted in John F. Starks, "100 Days of Attitude," *Time* (April 10, 1995), p. 32.

7 Elections

You Are There

To Resign or Not?

You are Bob Dole, the majority leader of the U.S. Senate, and it is May 1996. After a spirited primary season, during which other contenders for the Republican presidential nomination focused their attacks on you, you have won commitments from enough delegates to guarantee you the party's nomination. But you have made little headway in narrowing President Clinton's lead in the polls, and you are getting very frustrated.

You caught the presidential bug when you ran for vice president with Gerald Ford in 1976. You ran, unsuccessfully, for the Republican presidential nomination in 1980 and 1988, losing to Ronald Reagan and to George Bush. But this time you have the presidential nomination sewn up, disposing of Phil Gramm, Pat Buchanan, Lamar Alexander, and Steve Forbes, not to mention several other minor candidates.

You have served in Congress for thirty-five years, the last twenty-eight in the Senate. You have been the Republican leader since 1985, serving as majority leader twice, once in the 99th Congress under President Reagan and again in the 104th Congress with President Clinton in the White House. You find the position challenging and satisfying. "I did not become majority leader to lose" legislative battles, you said, and you have worked hard to build consensus behind the scenes.[1] Indeed, one of your strengths of your presidential candidacy has been your success as a legislative leader. It has allowed you to claim that you are a "doer not a talker," as opposed to Clinton who is, in your eyes, a talker not a doer.[2] Although you would be the first to run for the presidency from the position of Senate majority leader, you were confident that you could launch a successful campaign from that post. You planned to use your Senate position to demonstrate that you could get things done. That would make it easier to criticize Clinton for being ineffective, a view you think most people hold. For instance, you planned to induce the Senate to pass a health insurance reform measure that would allow people changing jobs to take their health coverage with them, rather than lose it (called "portability"). If you could swing that, the contrast between you and the president, who proposed a far reaching and ultimately unsuccessful health reform plan, would be clear to all.

It has not worked out that way. You have not been able to spend your time on the campaign trail meeting voters because you have had to be on the Senate floor so much. You have not been able to take clear positions on political issues, because you have had to work for compromises behind the scenes. You have not been able to get the Senate to adopt legislation that Clinton might veto, making the president take controversial positions, because Democrats have used Senate rules to thwart you at every step. In the public mind, you are being tied to the increasingly unpopular Speaker of the House, Newt Gingrich,

CONTINUED 

OUTLINE

The American Electorate
- Early Limits on Voting Rights
- Blacks and the Right to Vote
- Women and the Right to Vote
- Other Expansions of the Electorate

Voter Turnout
- Political Activism in the Nineteenth Century
- Progressive Reforms
- Recent Turnout
- Who Does Not Vote?
- Why Turnout Is Low

Other Campaign Participation

Presidential Nominating Campaigns
- Who Runs for President and Why?
- How a Candidate Wins the Nomination
- Presidential Caucuses and Conventions
- Presidential Primaries
- Reforming the Nomination Process
- The National Conventions
- Independent and Third-Party Nominees

General Election Campaign
- Campaign Organization
- Images and Issues
- The Electoral College
- Campaign Strategies
- The Media Campaign
- Campaign Funding

Voting
- Party Loyalties
- Candidate Evaluations
- Issues
- Parties, Candidates, and Issues

Conclusion: Do Elections Make Government Responsive?

because the Speaker and the majority leader make many joint appearances to comment on legislation in progress. Your experience in the Senate itself is turning into a liability; you are being seen as an insider in Washington at a time when all insiders are suspect.

Meanwhile, you trail Clinton in every pre-election poll, sometimes by as much as 25%. You are convinced that part of the gap results from your primary opponents' attacks on you, while Clinton, with no opposition for the Democratic nomination, enjoyed more positive news coverage. But you expected your ratings to go up as the divisiveness of the nominating season passed, but they have not. You know that the normal convention "bounce" in the polls should help, but probably not enough. Clinton's margin looks daunting and perhaps insurmountable.

It is all very frustrating, because few people see Clinton as a great president. The Whitewater investigations have cast doubt on Clinton's character. Moreover, Clinton has not come across as a strong, decisive leader. In March, only about two of every five voters thought Clinton had done well enough in his first term to merit a second.[3] The Republican victories in 1994's congressional elections were widely seen as the voters' rejection of Clinton's presidency. And yet you have not been able to take advantage of Clinton's weaknesses. You need to do something to jump-start your campaign.

You have considered giving up your position as majority leader. That would free up a great deal of time, allowing you to campaign more often and to take clear positions without having to compromise later; the new majority leader would have to fashion the compromises. And it would allow you to remain in the institution you love, "the club," as one reporter put it, in which you have "held nearly a lifetime's membership."[4]

But you have also considered another idea: resigning from the Senate altogether. It certainly would be a drastic change, and it might have a dramatic effect on the race. But you are a cautious man and you find this idea a disturbing one. Your wife, Elizabeth Dole, expressed her doubts. Your home state, Kansas, would lose two strong advocates, because Nancy Kassebaum, your colleague from Kansas, has already announced that she will not seek reelection in November. More importantly, you would be turning your back on the institution you have loved and served for over a quarter of a century. If anything, you are Bob Dole, Senator. Of course, if you lost the race for president, you would not be able to return to the Senate in January.

Would resigning really make a difference in the race? It may not change anything. One Democrat pointed out the obvious: "If they think he can leave the Senate and wipe out a 35-year history, they're wrong."[5] Or it might make your chances worse. The biggest risk is that voters would see your resignation from the Senate as just another political maneuver by just another politician. Depending on how the media report the decision, you could be seen as taking a desperate gamble to change the odds in a losing campaign, instead of as a courageous statesman willing to risk his Senate seat for the greater good of his party and nation. You might also jeopardize your image of authenticity, in contrast to Clinton's changeable ways.

On the other hand, if you stay in the Senate, you would probably lose the election anyway. Unless Clinton stumbles over the summer, you would still be trailing in the polls on Labor Day, and few candidates behind at that point have ever won.[6]

What do you do? Do you resign as majority leader but remain in the Senate, or do you resign from the Senate to campaign for president? Or do you continue as majority leader and hope that Clinton stumbles and the polls improve?

Americans have fought and died in wars to preserve the rights of citizens to choose their leaders through democratic elections. Some have even died here at home, trying to exercise these rights. Still, most Americans take these important rights for granted; about half do not bother to vote, and even fewer participate in politics in other ways.

Moreover, the process by which we choose our leaders, especially the president, has been sharply criticized in recent years. Critics charge that election campaigns are meaningless and offer little information to the voters, that candidates pander to the most ill-informed and mean-spirited citizens, and that public relations and campaign spending, not positions on issues or strength of character, determine the winners.

In this chapter, we analyze why voting is important to a democracy and why, despite its importance, so few do it. We then examine political campaigns and elections to see how they affect the kinds of leaders and policies we have. We will see that the lack of participation by many reinforces the government's responsiveness to those who do participate, especially those who are well organized.

➤The American Electorate

During the more than two centuries since the Constitution was written, two important developments have altered the right to vote, termed **suffrage.** First, suffrage gradually has been extended to include almost all citizens aged 18 or over. Second, deciding who may vote now lies largely in the hands of the federal government. The electorate has been widened mostly through constitutional amendments, congressional acts, and Supreme Court decisions.

Early Limits on Voting Rights

Although the Declaration of Independence stated that "all men are created equal," at the time of the Constitution and shortly thereafter, the central political right of voting was denied to most Americans. States decided who would be granted suffrage. In some only an estimated 10% of the white males could vote, whereas in others 80% could.[7]

Controversial property qualifications for voting existed in many states. Some argued that only those with an economic stake in society should have a say in political life. But critics of the property requirement repeated a story of Tom Paine's:

> You require that a man shall have $60 worth of property, or he shall not vote. Very well . . . here is a man who today owns a jackass, and the jackass is worth $60. Today the man is a voter and he goes to the polls and deposits his vote. Tomorrow the jackass dies. The next day the man comes to vote without his jackass and he cannot vote at all. Now tell me, which was the voter, the man or the jackass?[8]

Because the Constitution gave states the power to regulate suffrage, the elimination of property requirements was a gradual process. By the 1820s, most were gone, although some lingered to mid-century.

In some states, religious tests also were applied. A voter had to be a member of the "established" church or could not be a member of certain religions (such as Roman Catholic or Jewish). However, religious tests disappeared even more quickly than property qualifications.

By the time of the Civil War, state action had expanded the rights of white men. However, neither slaves, Indians, nor southern free blacks could vote, although northern blacks could in a few states.[9] Women's voting rights were confined to local elections in a few states.[10]

Blacks and the Right to Vote

The Civil War began the long, slow, and often violent process of expanding the rights of blacks to full citizenship. Between 1865 and 1870, three amendments were passed to give political rights to former slaves and other blacks. One, the Fifteenth Amendment, prohibited the denial of voting rights on the basis of race and thus gave the right to vote to black men.

For a short time after the ratification of this amendment, blacks voted and even were elected to office in the South, where 90% of blacks lived. They could exercise these rights in part because of a northern military presence and because the national government monitored southern politics closely during the period known as **Reconstruction**. Although blacks did not dominate politics or even receive a proportional share of offices, white southerners saw blacks' political activities as a threat to their own dominance. They began to prevent blacks from voting through intimidation that ranged from mob violence and lynchings to economic sanctions against blacks who attempted to vote.

In 1876, a compromise ended Reconstruction. Southern Democrats agreed to support Republican Rutherford B. Hayes for president in the disputed 1876 election in return for northern military withdrawal and a hands-off policy toward activities there.

During Reconstruction, blacks were elected to the United States Congress for the first time. Shown here are those elected to the Forty-first Congress in 1868.

American Diversity

Blacks and Hispanics in Office

Before the Voting Rights Act, few African Americans held major public office. Only a handful were members of Congress and few were state legislators, mayors of major cities, or other important political officers. Following the Voting Rights Act, southern blacks began to have the political clout to elect members of their own race to office for the first time. Progress, slow to be sure, has occurred; in 1968, there were only 23 black legislators in southern legislatures, but by 1993, there were nearly 250, including 42 in Mississippi. Virginia, the heart of the Confederacy, elected the nation's first black governor, Douglas Wilder. And 16 black members of Congress represent southern constituencies.

The number of northern black officeholders also has increased, reflecting heightened black political activity there too. Richard Hatcher, who became mayor of Gary, Indiana, in 1968, was the first black mayor of a major U.S. city. By 1993 there were 38 black mayors in northern and southern cities of 50,000 or more. This includes not only cities where blacks are a majority, such as New Orleans, Detroit, Baltimore, and Birmingham, but also cities where blacks are a minority, such as Seattle and Denver.

Nationally, the number of black officeholders has increased from an estimated 1,200 in 1969 to over 8,000 in 1993. Although this is far from proportional representation, it is a dramatic increase.

Hispanics too have improved their representation in political office. From a total of little more than 3,000 Hispanic public officials in 1985, their numbers have grown to nearly 5,200.

In sum, though progress seems slow, blacks and Hispanics, like other ethnic groups, are beginning to achieve political clout through elections.

Sources: *Statistical Abstract of the U.S.* 1994 (Washington Government Printing Office, 1994), Tables 443 and 444. Joint Center for Political Studies. *National Roster of Black Elected Officials* (Washington, D.C., 1993).

By the end of the nineteenth century, blacks were effectively disenfranchised in all of the South. The last black southern member of Congress served to 1901. Another would not be elected until 1972.

The loss of black voting rights was legitimized in southern constitutions and laws. **Literacy tests** were often required, supposedly to make sure voters could read and write and thus evaluate political information. A **grandfather clause** exempted illiterate people whose grandfathers had the right to vote before 1867, that is, before blacks could legally vote in the South. Most blacks were illiterate, having been denied education. The **poll tax** also discouraged voting by poor blacks. The tax, though only a couple of dollars, was often a sizable proportion of their monthly income. And the **white primary** kept blacks from participating in the selection of the nominees for the general election. Because the Democrats always won the general election, the real contests were in the Democratic primaries.

Less formal means also were used to exclude blacks from voting. Registrars often closed their offices when blacks tried to register, or whites threatened blacks with the loss of jobs or housing if they tried to vote. Polling places were sometimes located far from black neighborhoods or were moved at the last minute without notifying potential voters. If these means failed, whites threatened or practiced violence. In one election in Mobile, whites wheeled a cannon to a polling place and aimed it at about 1,000 blacks lined up to vote.

The treatment of blacks by the southern establishment was summarized on the floor of the Senate by South Carolina Senator Benjamin ("Pitchfork Ben") Tillman, who served from 1895 to 1918. As he put it, "We took the government away. We stuffed ballot boxes. We shot them. We are not ashamed of it."

Over time, the Supreme Court and Congress outlawed the "legal" barriers to black voting in the South. The Court invalidated the grandfather clause in 1915 and the white primary in 1944. Through the Twenty-fourth Amendment, Congress abolished the poll tax for federal elections in 1964, and the Court invalidated the tax for state elections in 1966.[11] But threats of physical violence and economic reprisals still kept most southern blacks from voting. Although many blacks in the urban areas of the rim South (North Carolina, Florida, Texas, Tennessee) could and did vote, those in the rural South and most in the Deep South could not; in 1960, black registration ranged from 5% to 40% in southern states.[12]

The Voting Rights Act

Today black voting rates approach those of whites. In the deep South, much of this dramatic change was brought about by the passage of the **Voting Rights Act** (VRA) in 1965, which made it illegal to interfere with anyone's right to vote. The passage of this act was one of the major successes of the civil rights movement, discussed in more detail in Chapter 15. The act suspended the use of literacy tests and, most important, it sent federal voter registrars into counties where less than 50% of the voting age population (black and white) was registered. The premise of this requirement was that if so few had registered, there must be serious barriers to registration.[13] Those who sought to deter blacks from voting through intimidation now had to face the force of the federal government.

Though black registration had been increasing in the rim states of the South (Virginia, North Carolina, Texas, for example), due to voter registration and education projects, the impact of the VRA in the Deep South was dramatic.[14] Within a year after federal registrars were sent, hundreds of thousands of southern blacks were registered, radically changing the nature of southern politics. In the most extreme case, Mississippi registration of blacks zoomed from 7% to 41%. In Alabama the black electorate doubled in four years.

Political effects were profound. Not only have dozens of blacks been elected, but white politicians must now court black voters to get elected. Even Strom Thurmond, the staunch South Carolina segregationist who ran for president on an anti–civil rights platform in 1948 and who held the longest filibuster—24 hours, 18 minutes—against the 1957 civil rights bill in the Senate, has attracted black support after he voted to extend the Voting Rights Act.[15]

The Voting Rights Act was renewed and expanded in 1970, 1975, and 1982. It now covers more states and other minorities, such as Hispanics, Asians, Native Americans, and Eskimos, and thus serves as a basic protection for minority voting rights. For example, states must provide bilingual ballots in counties in which 5% or more of the population does not speak English.

Blacks line up to vote in Peachtree, Alabama, after enactment of the Voting Rights Act of 1965.

Racial Gerrymandering

This North Carolina district (12), shown in purple on the maps, was drawn to create a black majority district. It consists of parts of 10 counties along the I-85 interstate and includes the predominantly black sections of Durham, Greensboro, Winston-Salem, and Charlotte. As one reporter noted, "In most electoral contests, candidates try to focus on finding out what the voters want. But in the 12th, the candidates face a challenge just *finding out who the voters are.*"[1]

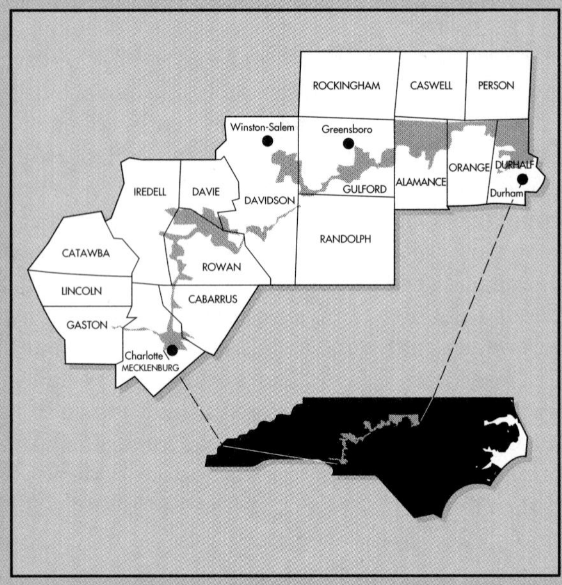

The practice of drawing strangely shaped districts to fulfill political objectives, called "gerrymandering," is hardly new in American politics. The name originated in 1812 when the Massachusetts legislature carved out a district that historian John Fiske said had a "dragonlike contour." When painter Gilbert Stuart saw the misshapen district, he drew in a head, wings, and claws and exclaimed, "That will do for a salamander!" Editor Benjamin Russell replied, "Better say Gerrymander," after Elbridge Gerry, then governor of Massachusetts.[2] Since then gerrymandering has been widely used by politicians to benefit their own political parties.

The Supreme Court has ruled that racial gerrymandering, the drawing of district lines to concentrate racial minorities, is constitutionally suspect, and a variety of other cases on this issue are pending in state and federal courts.

Supporters of racial gerrymandering, under the Voting Rights Act amendments of 1982, believe it is the best way to increase minority representation. It allows members of a minority racial group to elect members of their own race. But others argue that low numbers of racial and ethnic minorities in Congress cannot appropriately be changed by the use of deliberate gerrymanders. Some also object to the creation of minority-dominant districts because they see the dangers of thereby creating other districts with fewer minorities. These other districts will be more white than before, with representatives who are less sensitive to the interests of minorities.

One possible reform that meets the objectives of both groups is cumulative voting. Under a system of **cumulative voting,** members of Congress would not be elected from single-member districts, but from at-large districts in which several members of Congress would be elected at the same time. Voters would each have a number of votes equal to the number of seats in the district. They could apportion their votes among the candidates in any way that they preferred.

If, for example, the district included six seats in the House of Representatives, each voter would have six votes. The voter could give all six to one candidate, give one to each of six different candidates, or use any other method to distribute the six votes.

Members of any group, including racial, ethnic, religious, political, or economic groups, could target their votes on the candidates most likely to represent the group's interests. In the case of minority voters, the preferred candidates might be members of the minority group but could also be sympathetic members of some other group.

This election procedure could produce greater racial and ethnic diversity in representative bodies such as Congress without creating new districts on the basis of race or ethnicity. Cumulative voting has less potential for creating barriers between groups, since there would be no group basis for the creation of districts. This procedure is not totally new to the United States; it was used for many years in Illinois to elect members of their state's House of Representatives. Still, acceptance of cumulative voting for congressional districts seems remote.

1. Charles Mahtesian, "Blacks' Political Hopes Boosted by Newly Redrawn Districts," *Congressional Quarterly Weekly Report* (April 25, 1992), p. 1087.
2. *Guide to Congress,* 2nd ed. (Washington, D.C.: Congressional Quarterly, Inc., 1976), p. 563; *Congressional Quarterly, The Race to Capitol Hill,* (February 29, 1992), pp. 103–105.

Other sources: Kenneth J. Cooper, "Wrong Turns on the Map?" *Washington Post National Weekly Edition,* January 31–February 6, 1994, p. 14; Bruce E. Cain, "Voting Rights and Democratic Theory Toward a Color-Blind Society?" *The Brookings Review,* Winter 1992, pp. 46–50; Carol M. Swain, "The Voting Rights Act: Some Unintended Consequences," *The Brookings Review,* Winter 1992, p. 51; George R. Will, "Districting by Pigmentation," *Newsweek,* July 12, 1993, p. 72; Lani Guinier, *The Tyranny of the Majority: Fundamental Fairness in Representative Democracy,* reviewed in David J. Garrow, "Lani Guinier in Her Own Words," *Washington Post National Weekly Edition,* April 4–10, 1994, p. 35; Douglas Amy, *Real Choices/New Voices: The Case for Proportional Representation Elections in the United States* (New York: Columbia University Press, 1993).

The 1982 renewal and its subsequent judicial interpretation expanded the nature of the Voting Rights Act. In addition to protecting minorities' voting rights, the act now requires states with large minority populations to draw boundaries specifically to increase the probabilities that minorities will win seats. After the 1990 Census, eleven new congressional districts were created for blacks and six for Hispanics. All but one were actually won by blacks and Hispanics in the 1992 election. Partly as a result of this redistricting, blacks were elected to Congress for the first time since Reconstruction in Alabama, Florida, North Carolina, South Carolina, and Virginia. Hispanics were elected for the first time ever in Illinois and New Jersey. In all, 39 blacks and 19 Hispanics were elected to Congress, a dramatic increase from the 25 blacks and 10 Hispanics serving before the 1992 election.[16] Whether these gains will be maintained is likely to depend on the outcome of court challenges to these gerrymanders.

Women and the Right to Vote

When property ownership defined the right to vote, women property owners could vote in some places. When property requirements were removed, suffrage came to be seen as a male right only. Women's right to vote was reintroduced in the 1820s in Tennessee school board elections.[17] From that time on, women had the vote in some places, usually only at the local level or for particular kinds of elections.

The national movement for women's suffrage did not gain momentum until after the Civil War. Before and during that war, many women helped lead the campaign to abolish slavery and establish full political rights for blacks. When black men got the vote after the Civil War, some women saw the paradox in their working to enfranchise these men when they themselves lacked the right to vote. Led by Susan B. Anthony, Elizabeth Cady Stanton, and others, they lobbied Congress and the state legislatures for voting rights for women.

The first suffrage bill was introduced in Congress in 1868 and reintroduced each year thereafter until 1893. Most members were strong in their condemnation of women as potential voters. One senator claimed that if women could hold political views different from their husbands it would make "every home a hell on earth."

When Wyoming applied to join the union in 1889, it already had granted women the right to vote. Congress initially tried to bar Wyoming for that reason but then relented when the Wyoming territorial legislature declared, "We will remain out of the Union 100 years rather than come in without the women." Still, by 1910 women had complete suffrage rights in only four states.

Powerful interests opposed suffrage for women. Liquor interests feared that women voters would press for prohibition because many women had been active in the temperance (antiliquor) movement. Other businesses feared that suffrage would lead to reforms to improve working conditions for women and children. Southern whites feared that it would lead to voting by black women and then by black men. Political bosses feared that women would favor political reform. The Catholic church opposed it as contrary to the proper role of women. According to some people, suffrage was a revolt against nature. Pregnant women might lose their babies, nursing mothers their milk, and women might grow beards or be raped at the polls (then frequently located in saloons or barber shops).[18] Others argued less hysterically that women should be protected from the unsavory practices of politics and should confine themselves to their traditional duties.

About 1910, however, the women's suffrage movement was reenergized, in part by ideas and tactics borrowed from the British women's suffrage movement. A new generation of leaders, including Alice Paul and Carrie Chapman Catt, began to lobby more vigorously, reach out to the working class, and engage in protest marches and picketing, new features of American politics. In 1917, when the National Women's party organized around-the-clock picketing of the White House, their arrest and forced feeding during jail hunger strikes embarrassed the administration and won the movement some support. These incidents, plus contributions by women to the war effort during World War I, led to adoption of the Nineteenth Amendment guaranteeing women the vote in 1920. Although only 37% of eligible women voted in the 1920 presidential election, as the habit of voting spread, women's rates of voting equaled those of men.

Other Expansions of the Electorate

Federal constitutional and legislative changes extended the franchise to young adults. Before 1971, many states required a voting age of 19 or more. The service of 18-year-olds in the Vietnam War brought protests that if these men were old enough to die for their

Women's contributions to the war effort during World War I helped lead to the ratification of the women's suffrage amendment in 1920. Here Broadway chorus women train as Home Guards during the war.

country, they were old enough to vote. Yielding to these arguments and to the general recognition that young people were better educated than in the past, Congress adopted and the states ratified the Twenty-sixth Amendment giving 18-year-olds the right to vote.

Only convicted felons, the mentally incapable, noncitizens, and those not meeting minimal residence requirements are unable to vote now. Voting has come to be an essential right of citizenship rather than a privilege just for those qualified by birth or property. Paradoxically, however, as the *right* to vote has expanded, the proportion of eligible citizens *actually* voting has contracted.

➤Voter Turnout

Political Activism in the Nineteenth Century

In 1896, an estimated 750,000 people—5% of all voters—took train excursions to visit presidential candidate William McKinley at his Ohio home during the campaign.[19] This amazing figure is but one indication of the high level of intense political interest and activity in the late nineteenth century.

In those days, politics was an active, not a spectator, sport. People voted at high rates, as much as 80% in the 1840 presidential election,[20] and they were very partisan. They thought independents were corrupt and ready to sell their votes to the highest bidder. Elaborate and well-organized parties printed and distributed the ballots. Voters, after being coached by party leaders, simply dropped their party's ballot into the box. Split-ticket voting and secrecy in making one's choice were impossible.

Progressive Reforms

The **Progressive reforms** of the early twentieth century brought radical changes to election politics. Progressive reformers, largely professional and upper middle class, sought to eliminate corruption from politics and voting. But they also meant to eliminate the influence of the lower classes, many of them recent immigrants. These two goals went hand in

American Diversity

Women in Office

Even before women were given the right to vote nationally, they held political office. Women officeholders in colonial America were rare but not unknown. In 1715, for example, the Pennsylvania Assembly appointed a woman as tax collector.[1]

Elizabeth Cady Stanton, probably the first woman candidate for Congress, received 24 votes when she ran in 1866.[2] It was not until 1916 that the first woman member of Congress, Jeannette Rankin (R-Mont.), was actually elected. In 1872, Victoria Claflin Woodhull ran for president on the Equal Rights party ticket teamed with abolitionist Frederick Douglass for vice president.

More than 17,500 women now hold elective office, but many of these offices are minor. Inroads by women into major national offices have been slow. Geraldine Ferraro's 1984 vice presidential candidacy was historic but not victorious. In recent years, women have only gradually increased their membership in Congress. But in the 1992 elections, women candidates won striking increases in national legislative office. Women nearly doubled their numbers in the House of Representatives, from 27 to 48 seats, and tripled their numbers in the Senate, from two to six. A seventh woman won the unexpired senatorial term of Lloyd Bentsen when he became the Secretary of the Treasury in 1993.

Real progress has been made in state and local governments. Women hold 20% of all statewide elective offices, although only one woman, Christine Whitman (R-N.J.), is a governor. In 1965, only 5% of the state legislators were women; today 21% are. In ten states, after the 1992 elections, women held more than 27% of state legislative seats.[3]

More than 20% of the city council seats in medium and large cities are now occupied by women, a proportion that is steadily growing. Seventeen percent of the mayors of cities of 30,000 and more are women.

Does it make a difference in terms of policy to have women officeholders rather than men? Studies of the behavior of women members of Congress and other legislative bodies indicate that they are, on the whole, more liberal than men.[4] Women tend to give issues relating to women, children, and the family higher priority than male legislators do.[5] Women are also less likely to be involved in corrupt activities.

More and more women are getting graduate and professional education and working outside the home. These changes, coupled with increased public support for women taking an active role in politics, suggest that the trend toward more women in public office will continue.

Barbara Boxer and Dianne Feinstein celebrate their 1992 election as U.S. senators from California. This is the first time any state has elected two women senators. Boxer received 57% of the women's vote but only 44% of the men's.

1. Joseph J. Kelley, *Pennsylvania: The Colonial Years* (Garden City, N.Y.: Doubleday, 1980), p. 143.
2. Elisabeth Griffin, *In Her Own Right* (New York: Oxford University Press, 1983).
3. Data are from Center for the American Woman and Politics, National Information Bank on Women in Public Office, Rutgers University. Fact Sheets 1991 and 1993.
4. Susan Welch, "Are Women More Liberal Than Men in the U.S. Congress?" *Legislative Studies Quarterly* 10 (February 1985), pp. 125–34.
5. Sue Thomas and Susan Welch, "The Impact of Gender on the Priorities and Activities of State Legislators," *Western Political Quarterly,* 1991.

hand, because the lower classes were seen as the cause of corruption in politics.

The Progressive movement was responsible for several reforms: primary elections, voter registration laws, secret ballots, nonpartisan ballots (without party labels), and the denial of voting rights for aliens, which removed a major constituency of the urban party machines. The movement also introduced the merit system for public employment to reduce favoritism and payoffs in hiring.

The reforms, adopted by some states at the beginning of the century, and by others much later, were largely effective in cleaning up politics. But the reformers also achieved, to a very large extent, their goal of eliminating the lower classes from politics. Taking away most of the reason for the existence of

Some Account of some of the Bloody Deeds of

GEN. JACKSON.

Jacob Webb. *David Morrow.* *John Harris.* *Henry Lewis.* *David Hunt.* *Edward Lindsey.*

Eight photos, each marked with a blue band along the top, illustrate American campaign tactics throughout the years. In this photo from the 1828 campaign, Andrew Jackson's opponents accused him of executing soldiers he commanded (as symbolized by the coffins). Jackson won anyway.

the political parties—choosing candidates and printing and distributing ballots—caused the party organization to decline, which in turn produced a decline in political interest and activity on the part of the electorate. Without strong parties to mobilize voters, only the most interested and motivated participated. The new restrictions on voting meant that voters had to invest more time, energy, and thought in voting. They had to think about the election months in advance and travel to city hall to register.

As a consequence, politics began to be a spectator activity. Voter turnout declined sharply after the turn of the century.

Turnout figures from the nineteenth century are not entirely reliable and not exactly comparable with today's. In the days before voter registration, many aliens could vote and some people voted twice. In some instances, more people voted in a state election than lived there! Nevertheless, it is generally agreed that turnout was very high in the nineteenth century and that it has diminished substantially; it dropped from more than 77% from 1840 to 1896 to 54% in the 1920–1932 era, when the Progressive reforms were largely in place. During the New Deal era, when the Democratic party mobilized new groups of voters, turnout rose again, but it has never achieved anything close to the levels of the nineteenth century.

Recent Turnout

Between 1964 and 1988, turnout in presidential elections slowly declined, from 62% to 50%. In 1992, turnout increased slightly, to 54%, but in 1996, it continued to decline, dipping to 49%. That is, of all citizens who could have registered and voted, less than half voted. This means that only one-fourth of potential voters voted for the winner of the presidential election.

The turnout for off-year congressional elections is even lower. It has not exceeded 45% since World War II, and in 1994 it was 39%. Turnout in primary elections is also low. In 1986 it was an astoundingly low 10%.

Although nations count their turnouts differently, it is clear that Americans vote in much lower proportions than citizens of other Western democracies (Figure 1). Only Switzerland, which relatively recently gave women the right to vote, approximates our low turnout levels.

Within the United States, turnout varies greatly among the states. In the 1992 presidential election, for example, 72% of Maine's citizens voted, but only 42% of Hawaii's did. Turnout tends to be higher in the northern plains and mountain states and lower in the South.[21]

These differences suggest that not only are there certain kinds of people who are unwilling to vote, but there are also certain kinds of laws and political traditions that depress voting turnout.

Who Does Not Vote?

Before we can explain why some people do not vote, we need to see who the nonvoters are. The most important thing to remember is that voting is related to education, income, and occupation, that is, to socioeconomic class. For example, if you are a college graduate, the chances are about 80% that you will vote; if you have less than a high school education, the chances are only about half that.[22] Differences between higher- and lower-income people are also quite large. Two out of three nonvoters have below average incomes.[23] This class gap in turnout is widening. Although voting among all groups of Americans has declined in the past 30 years, the proportion of college-educated persons who participated fell by less than 10% while that of high school-educated persons dropped by nearly 20%.

Though many people take it for granted that those in the working class vote at lower rates than those in the middle and upper classes, in the United States these differences are far wider than in other nations[24] and far wider than in nineteenth-century America. So there appears to be something unique about the contemporary American political system that inhibits voting participation of all citizens, but particularly those whose income and educational level are below the average.

Why Turnout Is Low

There are a number of possible reasons more Americans, especially low-income and young Americans, do not vote.

Satisfaction Among Voters

One reason sometimes given for low rates of voter turnout is that nonvoters are satisfied; failing to vote is a passive form of consent to what government is doing.[25] This argument falls flat on two counts. First, voter turnout has decreased in an era when public trust in government has decreased, not increased. Levels of trust and voting turnout both started declining after 1964. And second, voter turnout is lower precisely among those groups of citizens who have least reason to be content, not those who have most

In 1840, the Whigs plastered slogans on huge balls that party members rolled across the country. From this gimmick came the phrase "keep the ball rolling."

FIGURE 1
Turnout in the United States is Lower Than in Most Other Democracies

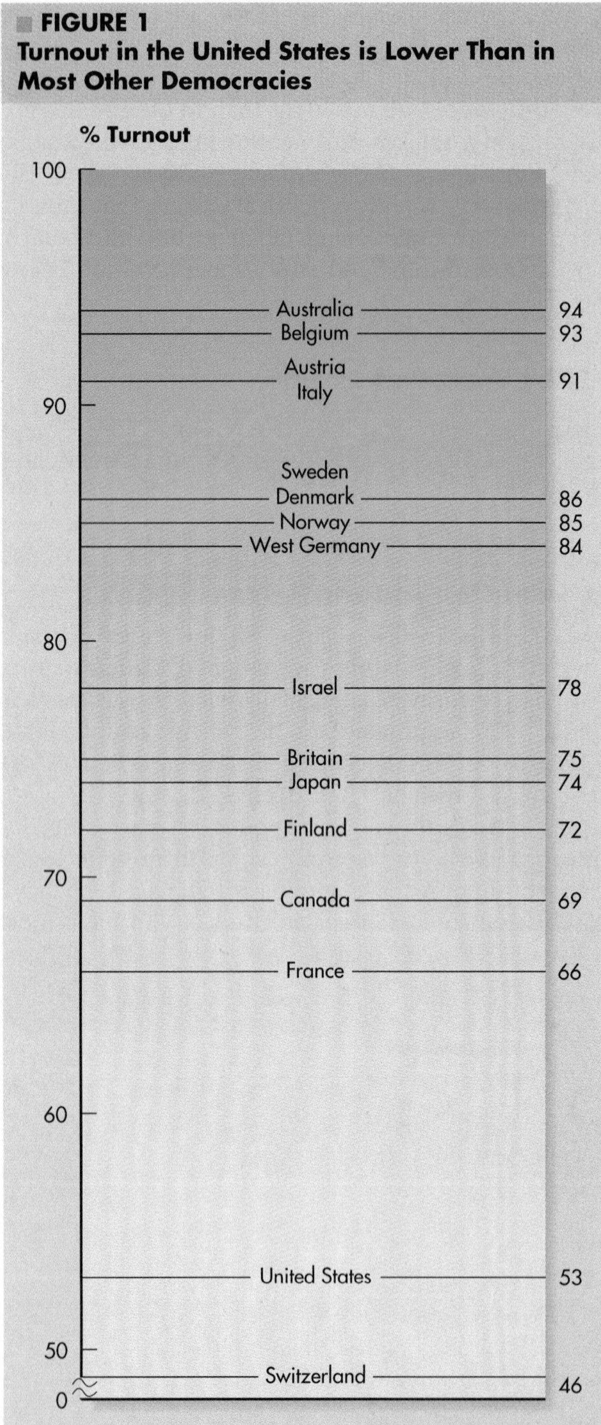

Sources: Data are from national elections between 1986 and 1989. Richard Flickinger and Donley Studlar, "The Disappearing Voter?" *West European Politics* 15 (April 1992), pp. 1–16.

reason to be so. If staying at home on election day was an indication of satisfaction, one would expect turnout to be lower among the well-off, not among the working class and the poor.

Voters Are "Turned Off" by Political Campaigns

About one-third of a group of nonvoters in the 1990 election, when asked why they did not vote, gave reasons suggesting they were disgusted with politics.[26] In explaining the low turnout in the 1988 campaign, one analyst commented, "The media consultants, media and politicians gave this nation an awful election, and the public responded with appropriately awful turnouts."[27] The analyst was condemning the lack of real issues in the campaign, the negative advertising, and the constant attention paid by television to the polls telling people how they were going to vote (in 1988, there were 140 campaign polls, according to one count).[28] These analyses surely contain some grains of truth, but how many? After all, people who are most likely to pay attention to the media, watch the ads, hear about the polls, and follow the campaigns are the most likely to vote, not the least. It is possible that the increasingly media-oriented campaigns have decreased overall turnout during the past generation (and we will have more to say about these campaigns later in the chapter). In fact, turnout is inversely related to media spending; the more the candidates spend, the lower the turnout. Moreover, voters who watch negative political ads are less likely to vote or to feel their vote counts.[29] The increase in negative advertising, then, helps explain declining turnout. However, negative advertising and other media attention cannot explain the class bias in nonvoting.

In addition to the *quality* of the campaigns, some people think turnout has declined because our elections are so frequent, campaigns last so long, and so many offices are contested that the public becomes bored, confused, or cynical.[30] At the presidential level, the sheer quantity of coverage, much of it focused repetitively on "who's winning," may simply bore people. Moreover, the continual public opinion polling and the widely publicized results may lead some to believe they don't need to vote.

At the local level voters elect so many officeholders, all the way down to weed and mosquito control commissioners, that many have no idea for whom or what they are voting. This proliferation of elective of-

Young People Vote Less

Ratification of the Twenty-sixth Amendment to the U.S. Constitution in 1971 gave 18–20 year olds the right to vote. Political observers expected that the campus activism of the Vietnam and civil rights era would be reflected in high voting turnouts among young people.

But in 1972, their first presidential election, less than half of young voters turned out, and even that small turnout has declined precipitously since. As the figure indicates, only 38% of 18–20 year olds voted in 1992, compared with over 60% of their elders.

Why the low vote? One might expect that young people are more alienated from politics than their elders, but this does not seem to be true. Young voters are more trusting and less cynical. Others attribute low voting turnout to the high degree of mobility of young adults; they change their residences frequently, and perhaps do not have time or do not take time to figure out how and where to register. Many young people are preoccupied with major life changes, going to college, leaving home, starting their first full-time job, getting married, starting a family. Then too, young people do not have the habit of voting.

In an attempt to encourage young adults to vote in 1992, MTV featured a number of conversations with the political candidates, as well as ads urging young people to vote: "Choose or Lose." Madonna, for example, warned the audience that if they did not vote, they were "going to get a spankie."

Source: Census Bureau, Richard L. Berke, "Is the Vote, Too, Wasted on Youth?" *New York Times* (June 30, 1991), p. 2.

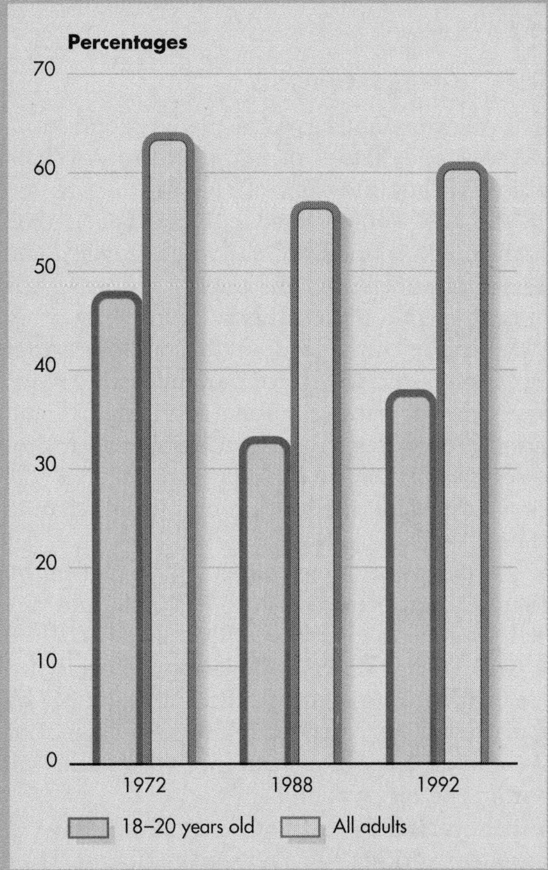

Current Population Reports, "Voting and Registration in the Election (various editions)," U.S. Census, series P20.

fices, thought by some to promote democracy and popular control, may promote only voter confusion and alienation. The problem is compounded because elections for different offices are held at different times. For example, most states have decided to hold elections for governor in nonpresidential election years. This decision probably reduces presidential election turnout by 7% and may reduce by one-third the number of those who vote for governor in those states.[31]

Primary elections are another problem. One estimate is that holding primary campaigns diminishes the general election turnout by 5%.[32]

By contrast, in Britain the time between calling an election (by the current government) and the actual election is only a month. In March, 1992, Prime Minister John Major called an election; in April it was held. All campaigning was done during that time. There are no primaries. Moreover, as in most other parliamentary democracies, British citizens vote only for their representative in parliament and (at one other time) for the local representative. Voters are not faced with choices for a myriad of offices they barely recognize.

Barriers to Registration

Having to register first has kept many people from voting. About one-quarter of nonvoters surveyed in 1990 indicated they did not vote because it was too difficult. As one commentator put it, "The United States is the only major democracy where government assumes no responsibility for helping citizens cope with voter registration procedures."[33] In many other nations, voter registrars go door to door to register voters, or voters are registered automatically when they pay taxes or receive public services. Difficult registration procedures have a special impact on low-income Americans, who were 17% less likely to vote in states with difficult registration procedures than in other states.[34]

Some states make it more convenient to register by having registration periods lasting up to election day (most states require registration at least 25 days before the election), registration in precincts or neighborhoods instead of one county office, registration by mail, registration offices open in the evenings and Saturday, and a policy of not purging voters who fail to vote from the registration lists.

In other jurisdictions, voter registrars try to hinder groups working to increase registration. They may refuse to allow volunteers to register voters outside the registration office or let only selected volunteers handle registration (for example, allowing members of the League of Women Voters or the Christian Right as volunteers but not the NAACP or organizations targeted toward registering lower-income groups).[35] One estimate is that voting turnout would be 9% higher if all states' procedures were similar to those of states that try to facilitate voter registration.[36]

To try to increase registration, Congress recently passed a law to make registration easier; it allows people to register at public offices such as welfare offices and drivers' license bureaus (for this reason it is called the **"motor voter"** law.)[37] Evidence shows the greatest expansion of voter registration in American history; after eight months of the law, five million new voters registered. A related proposal suggests that registration be automatically updated when voters file change of address cards with the post office when they move. One estimate is that the mobility of our society reduces voting by as much as 9% because voters have to reregister after they move.[38]

Some states have also tried to make voting itself easier. For instance, when Oregon conducted a special election to fill the U.S. Senate vacancy left by the resignation of Bob Packwood, voters could mail in their ballots at their convenience, as long as the ballots arrived by the deadline. Turnout was substantially higher.

Failures of Parties to Mobilize Voters

Traditionally political parties mobilized voters to turn out. As parties have declined in importance, they have become less effective in this role. The lack of effectiveness on the part of political parties in mobilizing millions of nonvoters, most of them working class or poor, is another reason for low voter turnout. Because of their low income, most of these nonvoters are Democrats. If mobilized, they would probably vote for Democrats, although in some elections the

Voter turnout was higher in the days when campaigns were more fun and involved more people. Songs were often written about the candidates, and, here, a book about teddy bears reflects Theodore (Teddy) Roosevelt's popularity.

preferences of nonvoters have simply reflected the preferences of voters.[39]

Republicans are most fearful of this potential electorate. One conservative analyst wrote that a national registration plan, by tapping the voting power of the poor, "has the potential for altering the American party system."[40]

Even some Democrats are wary. The party has embraced social and economic reforms that attracted many middle-class and some business groups. The goals of these groups sometimes conflict with those of the poor, and the party's leaders do not want to threaten these constituencies. Moreover, in recent years the party has muted its appeals to the working

Gay Power

In recent years, homosexuals have become more politically active. Spurred by the crisis of AIDS among the gay community and the initially slow response of the federal government to the disease, gays have begun to organize to exercise political clout.

How much clout can gays have? Even the number of gays in the U.S. is a politically sensitive question. Many gay activists argue that 10% of the population is gay. Various recent surveys of sexual activity indicate the number may be considerably lower, perhaps as low as 1%. Sexual orientation is not a question asked in standard national surveys, and if it were, it might not elicit truthful answers, so that it is difficult to know the accuracy of the estimates. Whatever the numbers, homosexuals have been "coming out of the closet" in significant numbers in recent years.

Gay issues are now being openly considered in political campaigns. "Gay rights" includes a number of different things. Most discussed have been ending the ban on homosexuals in the military and giving homosexuals equal rights to jobs and housing. Some gay activists want legal recognition of same-sex marriages and a general acknowledgement of homosexuality as an acceptable lifestyle. The public overwhelmingly supports nondiscrimination in jobs and in the military but is not supportive of homosexual lifestyles and same-sex marriages.

Barney Frank (D-Mass.), one of three openly gay members of Congress, at a fund-raiser.

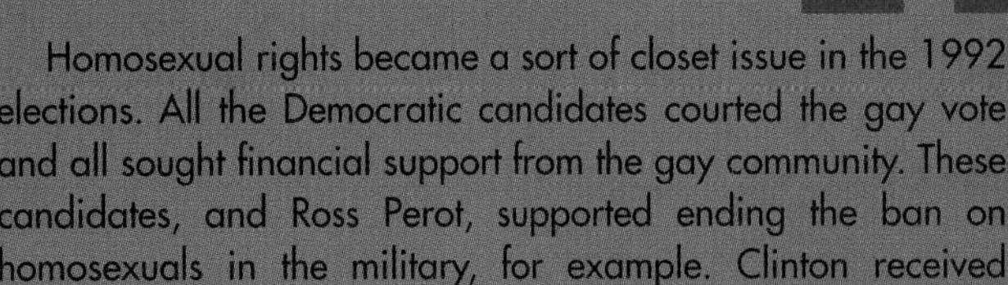

Homosexual rights became a sort of closet issue in the 1992 elections. All the Democratic candidates courted the gay vote and all sought financial support from the gay community. These candidates, and Ross Perot, supported ending the ban on homosexuals in the military, for example. Clinton received strong support from the gay community; in some areas gays are a significant political force. In California, for example, perhaps as many as 10% of all voters are gay.

Most Republicans are less supportive of homosexual rights. Such rights are anathema to many fundamentalist Christians, who consider homosexuality a sin and refuse to think that it could be an acceptable lifestyle. These fundamentalists, and other conservatives, are an important part of the Republican constituency and are strongly opposed to extension of rights to gays. At the 1992 Republican convention, some speakers overtly attacked gays and gay rights. However, as one conservative political analyst remarked, "The gay-bashing turned people off."

President Bush, who had at least a dozen aides and officials who were gay, personally did not engage in direct gay-bashing. He and other top Republicans used more subtle attacks on gays and gay lifestyles, for example by calling for a return to "family values," a term that can mean almost anything but was intended to be a code word for traditional family values.

In 1994, a number of openly gay candidates were elected, including three members of Congress and state legislators in Arizona, California, Missouri, and Washington. These successes are coming at a time when the gay community is being weakened through the AIDS epidemic, which has already caused about 150,000 deaths, two-thirds gay men. But AIDS has been important in encouraging gays to come out of the closet, and possibly has been important in encouraging broader tolerance of gays. Twice as many people now say they know someone who is a homosexual than did so a decade ago. Even though there is no consensus on homosexual issues, it seems clear that gays are gaining legitimacy in the political process.

Sources: Jeffrey Schmalz, "Gay Politics Goes Mainstream," *New York Times Magazine* (October 11, 1992), p. 18ff. Much of this box is drawn from the Schmalz article; Bill McAllister and Michael Weisskopf, "Breaking Through the 'Lavender Ceiling,' " *Washington Post National Weekly Edition* (November 14–20, 1994), p. 14.

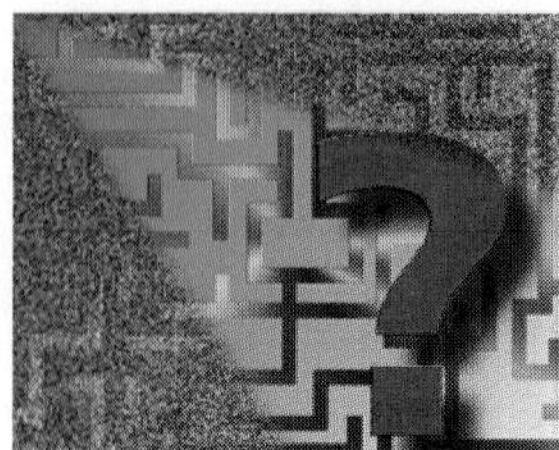

Symbolic Solutions for Complex Problems?

Same Day Voter Registration

Voting turnout in the U.S. is second from lowest among the nations of the industrialized world. This is a source of great concern to many who prize our democratic traditions and value citizen participation. As we have explained, there are a number of explanations for this low turnout, and a number of proposed remedies for it.

One popular proposal is to allow voters to register when they go to the polling place on election day. This would reduce the costs of voting by reducing the time spent in finding and going to the registration office and the foresight necessary to remember to do so weeks or months in advance of the election. Moreover, by allowing same-day registration, states would put less premium on permanence of residence. Since Americans are a mobile population, this would increase the number of citizens eligible to vote.

But is same-day voter registration just a symbolic solution, making us feel as if we are increasing citizen participation but really not? Or is same-day registration a real solution that might allow us to increase voter turnout? And if it is such a solution, are its benefits greater than the drawbacks of such a registration system?

As we have seen, states that make registration difficult (closing registration long before the election, not allowing absentee registration, not having regular office hours at the registrar's office, and so forth) have voter turnout about 9% less than states that make registration easier.[1] Since same-day registration is another way of making registration easier, we would expect it to improve turnout.

Three states (Maine, Minnesota, and Wisconsin) adopted same-day registration beginning in the 1970s, and that allows us to compare turnout between them and the other states. Since those three states have adopted same-day registration, their turnout in presidential elections has increased over 3%. The turnout rates in the other states, on average, have decreased almost 2% during that same time.[2] In other words, with everything else staying the same, same-day registration appears to improve voting turnout by about 5%. Other indicators of turnout change also suggest that same-day registration does lead to increased turnout.

Does the increase in turnout outweigh possible negative effects of this change? Opponents of the reform believe that it might lead to increased voter fraud; it might be easier for voters to vote multiple times, for example, if they do not have to register before the election. However, the existing system does not protect very well against voter fraud for someone determined to vote more than once, either. With the expansion of sophisticated computer tools, we might expect that the means to combat voter fraud are increasingly at hand, same-day voting or not.

Ultimately, though, we have to decide whether the expansion of the electorate by 5%, or, in another estimate, 8 million voters, is worth the additional risks that slightly more multiple voting might take place. And, whether or not we adopt same-day voting, we need to consider other means of increasing voter turnout too.

1. Steven Rosenstone and Ray Wolfinger, "The Effect of Registration Laws on Voter Turnout," *American Political Science Review* 72 (March, 1978), pp. 22–45; G. Mitchell and C. Wlezien, "Voter Registration Laws and Turnout, 1972–1982," paper presented at the annual meeting of the Midwest Political Science Association, 1989.
2. Mark J. Fenster, "The Impact of Allowing Day of Registration Voting on Turnout in U.S. Elections from 1960 to 1992," *American Politics Quarterly* 22 (January, 1994), pp. 74–87.

class. This further reduces the incentives of working-class people to vote, and in turn decreases the incentive of Democrats to appeal to working class voters.[41] However, increasing voter turnout has now become a partisan issue with most Democrats backing attempts to increase turnout (such as the motor voter plan), and most Republicans opposing them.

Voting as a Rational Calculation of Costs and Benefits

Nonvoting also may be the result of a rational calculation of the costs and benefits of voting. Economist Anthony Downs argues that people vote when they believe the perceived benefits of voting are greater than the costs.[42] If a voter sees a difference between the parties or candidates, and favors one party's position over the other, that voter has a reason to vote and can expect some benefit from doing so. For that reason, people who are highly partisan vote more than those less attached to a party, and people with a strong sense of political efficacy, the belief they can influence government, vote more than others.

Voters who see no difference between the candidates or parties, however, may believe that voting is not worth the effort it takes and that it is more rational to abstain. And in fact, 40% of nonvoters in 1990 gave only the excuse that they were "too busy," suggesting a large degree of apathy.[43] For some voters, however, the act of voting itself is worthwhile,

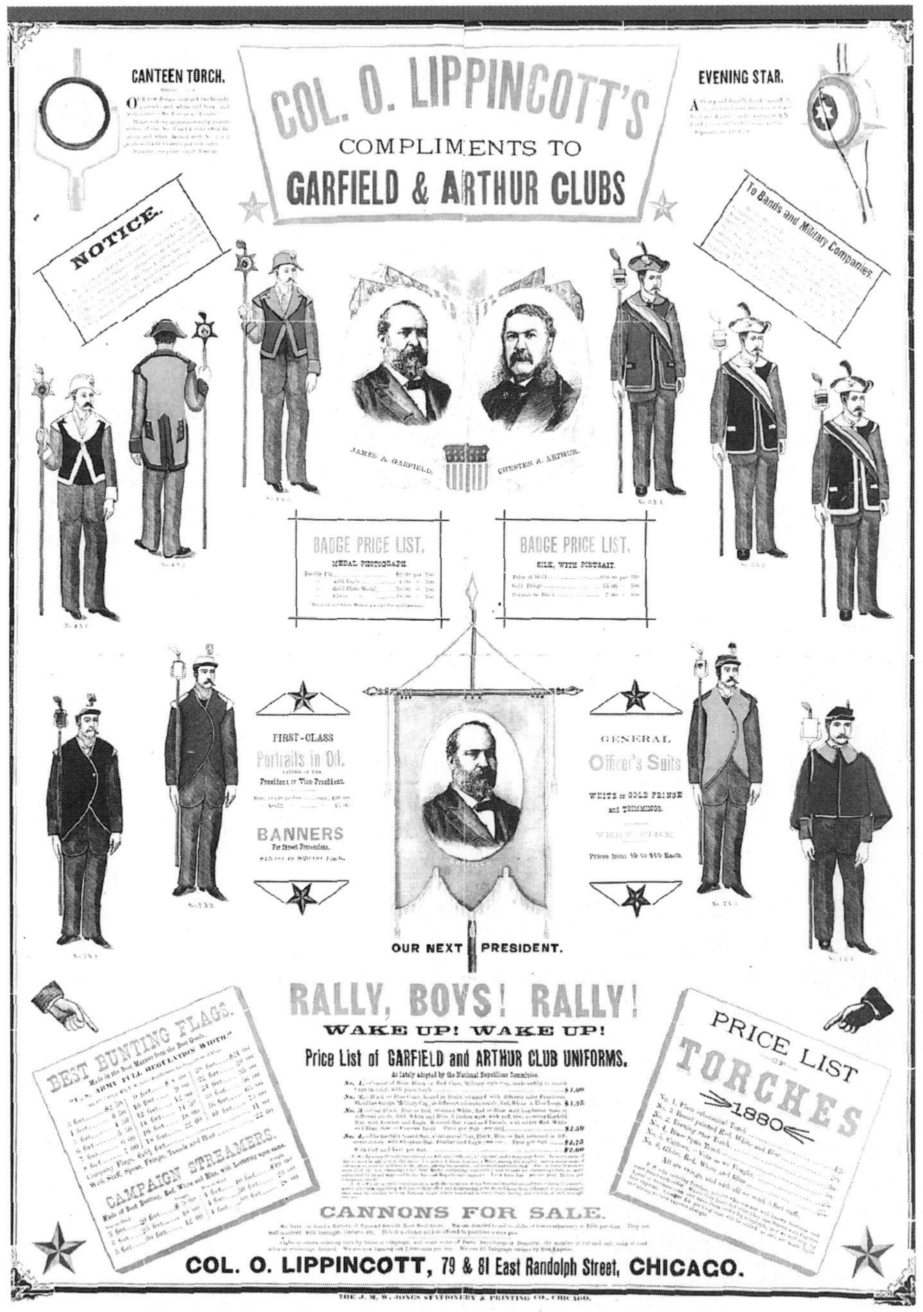

Today, most citizens take part in political activities as "couch potatoes" watching television. During the third party era, most eligible voters (largely white males) participated actively. Torchlight parades and rallies were frequent, and businesses sprang up to supply the necessary torches, banners, flags, and uniforms.

Collection of the New York Historical Society

even if they do not see a difference between the candidates. They vote out of a sense of civic duty, a belief that their responsibilities as citizens include voting. Most voters feel gratified that they have done their duties as citizens. In fact, more voters give this as an explanation for voting than any other reason, including the opportunity to influence policy.[44]

Downs assumes that the costs of voting are minimal, but, in reality, for many people the time, expense, and possible embarrassment of trying to register are greater than the perceived benefits of voting. This is especially true for lower-income people who perceive that neither party is attentive to their interests. Moreover, it is possible that the frequency, length, and media orientation of campaigns lower the perceived benefits of voting for people of all incomes by trivializing the election and emphasizing the negative.

➤Other Campaign Participation

We have seen that only about half of all Americans vote in presidential elections, and even fewer vote in off-year congressional races. Still fewer participate actively in political campaigns. For example, in a recent year, about one-quarter of the population said that they worked for a party or candidate. About an equal proportion claimed that they contributed money to a party or candidate. Smaller proportions attended political meetings or actually belonged to a political club.

Unlike voting, rates of participation in campaigns have not declined over the past 20 years. This suggests that people are not less political than they used to be, but that something about elections themselves has decreased voter turnout. Indeed, more people give money to candidates and parties than they used to, probably because, unlike 20 years ago, candidates and parties now use mass mailing techniques to solicit funds from supporters.[45] Campaigners do a better job of mobilizing donors than they do voters.

Just as there is a strong class basis to voting, there is also a strong class basis to participation in campaign activities. Those with more education and income are more likely to participate. A recent study found that those with only eight grades of education or less participated, on average, in only one of 12 types of political participation aside from voting, whereas those with college education participated in 3 or 4. Those with some college education actually had increased their participation over the past 20 years, whereas those with less than a high school education had decreased theirs. Thus the class bias in

Wendell Willkie, Republican presidential candidate in 1940, rides into Elwood, Indiana. In the days before television, motorcades allowed many people to see the candidates and allowed the candidates to generate enthusiasm among the voters.

participation, as in voting alone, has increased over time.[46]

Gender, race, age, and regional differences in participation also appear. Even taking education into account, men usually participate slightly more than women, whites somewhat more than blacks, older people more than younger people, and southerners more than northerners. But these differences change over time. Young people participated more than their elders, and blacks more than whites, during the late 1960s and early 1970s.[47] These were times of heightened interest in politics generally, and the anti–Vietnam War and civil rights movements drew many young and black people into political activity.

Presidential Nominating Campaigns

Many Americans believe in the Horatio Alger myth, that with hard work anyone can achieve great success. This myth has its parallel in politics, where it is sometimes said that any child can grow up to be president. In fact, only a few run for that office and even fewer are elected.

Soliciting votes by giving speeches and making appearances was once considered beneath the dignity of the presidential office. William Jennings Bryan was the first presidential candidate to break this tradition. In 1896 he traveled more than 18,000 miles and made more than 600 speeches in an effort to win voters. Although Bryan lost the election to William McKinley, his approach to campaigning became the standard. This photo illustrates how the term "stump speech" to refer to candidates' boilerplate campaign speeches may have developed.

Who Runs for President and Why?

In deciding whether to run for president, individuals consider such things as the costs and risks of running and the probabilities of winning.[48] Most people have little chance of being president: They are unknown to the public, they do not have the financial resources or contacts to raise the money needed for a national campaign, they have jobs they could not leave to run a serious campaign, and their friends would probably ridicule them for even thinking of such a thing.

But a few people are in a different position. Take, for instance, a hypothetical U.S. senator from Texas or a governor of California. By their vote-gathering ability in a large state, they have demonstrated some possibility that they could win. Their decision to run might hinge on such considerations as whether they think they could raise the money necessary to run a campaign, whether they are willing to sacrifice a good part of their private life and their privacy for a few years, and whether they would lose the office they currently hold if they run and lose.

These calculations are real. Most candidates for president are, in fact, governors or senators.[49] In 1996, however, Bob Dole originally planned to use his position as majority leader of the Senate to demonstrate he could get things done. Democrats in the Senate, though in the minority, foiled this plan by making it difficult for Dole to maneuver. He decided to resign both his leadership position and his Senate seat to run as "just a man" for the presidency. Vice presidents also frequently run for president, but in this century only George Bush has won.

Why do candidates run? An obvious reason is to gain the power and prestige of the presidency. But they may have other goals as well, such as to gain support for a particular policy or set of ideas. Ronald Reagan, for example, clearly wanted to be president in part to spread his conservative ideology. Jesse Jackson wants to be president in part to help those at the bottom of the social ladder. Candidates with no real hope of winning a major party nomination also often have policy goals. Eugene McCarthy ran in 1968 to challenge Lyndon Johnson's Vietnam policy.

Sometimes candidates run to gain name recognition and publicity for the next election. Most successful candidates in recent years have run before. George Bush lost the nomination in 1980 before being elected

American Diversity

Can an African American Be Elected President?

The Jesse Jackson campaigns of 1984 and 1988 and that of Douglas Wilder in 1992 raise the question of whether a black person can be elected president. Or, more generally, will the American presidency continue to be held only by white, non-Jewish males?

These questions sound familiar. In 1960, some doubted that a Catholic could ever be elected president. At that time, only 71% of all voters said they would vote for a Catholic for president.[1] The only previous major-party Catholic candidate, Alfred Smith, had been soundly defeated by Herbert Hoover in 1928. But then John F. Kennedy was elected. Since then, two Catholics, Geraldine Ferraro and Sargent Shriver, have run as vice presidential nominees without much attention paid to their religion.

But race has been a more pronounced cleavage in American society than religion. Racism persists, and race influences all kinds of political debates, from welfare reform to the all-volunteer military. The party realignment that has occurred in the South is shaped by racial as well as class issues.[2] A majority of white southerners, resentful of the Democratic party's support of the civil rights struggle, has turned to the Republican party.

Race was important in the 1988 campaign. It surfaced when the Republicans succeeded in tying Willie Horton to Dukakis. It also came up when Jesse Jackson's prominence in the Democratic party was highlighted and made to seem somehow illegitimate and frightening. A campaign letter from the California Republican party asked, "Why is it so urgent you decide now? . . . Here are two [reasons]." Below were two photos, one of Bush and Reagan, the other of Jackson and Dukakis. "If [Dukakis] is elected to the White House," it continued, "Jesse Jackson is sure to be swept into power on his coattails."[3]

This is not to say that all of those who voted against Jackson in the primaries or against the Democrats in the general election are racists. Many argue that it might very well be possible for a black to be elected president, but not Jesse Jackson. In foreign as well as domestic policy, Jackson has been identified with the most liberal wing of the Democratic party. And his public career has largely been in the civil rights movement rather than in government.

Declining Numbers Oppose Blacks, Women, and Jews for President

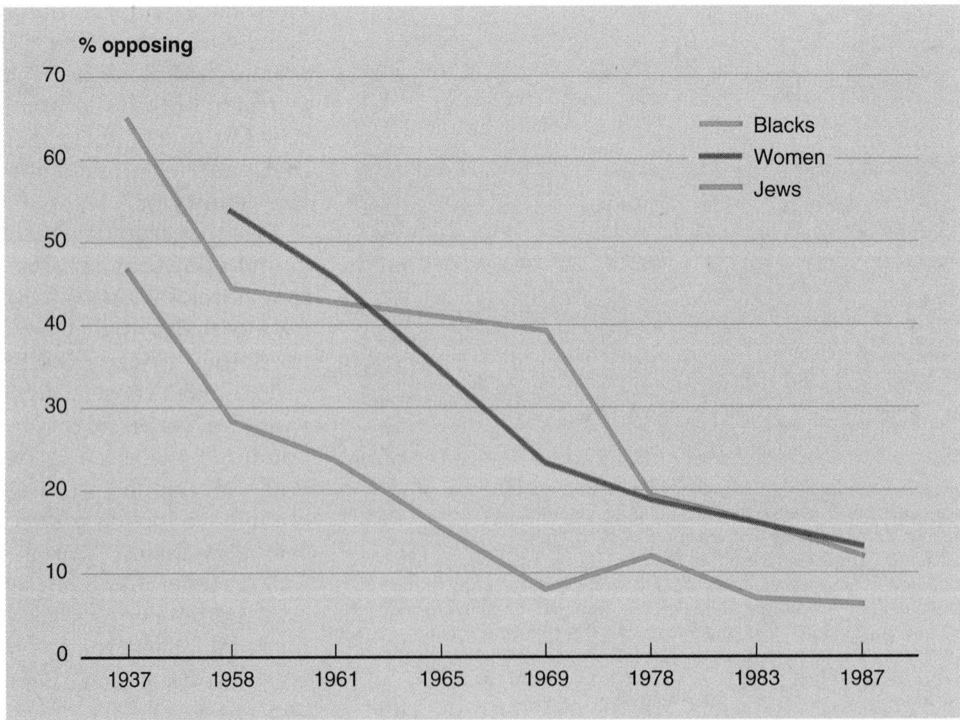

Source: Gallup Polls. The question asked was, "If your party nominated a generally well-qualified man for president and he happened to be a black [Jew], would you vote for him?" or, "If your party nominated a woman for president, would you vote for her if she were qualified for the job?" No questions were asked about blacks until 1958. The 1961 data for blacks are from 1963. Gallup has not asked these questions since 1987.

During the 1980s, Jackson became a symbol of the hopes of African Americans that a black might one day be president. However, in 1992, Douglas Wilder, the first black ever elected governor of a U.S. state, announced his candidacy. He began campaigning but did not make it even to the New Hampshire primary. He dropped out when his public opinion polls back home in Virginia plummeted. Realizing his candidacy was a long shot, he decided that protecting his political base in Virginia was more important than running what was likely to be an expensive and futile race.

Undoubtedly there will come a time when a black man or woman will be president, just as will white women, Jews, and others who are not white, Christian males. Colin Powell, formerly chairman of the Joint Chiefs of Staff (the nation's highest military post) was widely considered a potential 1996 candidate, for example. As the figure shows, 12% to 13% of the public say they would not vote for a black or a woman who was their party's nominee, and a slightly lower proportion say they would not vote for a Jew. Although 12% to 13% is a sizable bloc of voters, more people today say they would vote for a black, Jew, or woman than said they would vote for a Catholic in 1960. John Kennedy's victory suggests that 12% to 13% is not an insurmountable barrier.

1. Barry Sussman, "A Black or Woman Does Better Today Than a Catholic in '60," *Washington Post National Weekly Edition,* November 21, 1983, p. 42.
2. Earl Black and Merle Black, *Politics and Society in the South* (Cambridge, Mass.: Harvard University Press, 1973).
3. "Though This Be Meanness, Yet There is a Method in It," *Washington Post National Weekly Edition,* October 10–16, 1988, p. 26.

in 1988; Ronald Reagan lost in 1976 before his victory in 1980; Richard Nixon lost in 1960 before winning in 1968.

Sometimes candidates run for the presidency to be considered for the vice presidency, probably viewing it as an eventual stepping-stone to the presidency. But only occasionally, such as when Reagan chose Bush in 1980 or Kennedy chose Johnson in 1960, do presidential candidates choose one of their defeated opponents to run as a vice presidential candidate. In 1988, 1992, and 1996 nominees passed over their defeated rivals in choosing vice presidential running mates.

How a Candidate Wins the Nomination

Presidential candidates try to win a majority of delegates at their party's national nominating convention in the summer preceding the November election. Delegates to those conventions are elected in state caucuses, conventions, and primaries. Candidates must campaign in state after state to win the support of those who attend caucuses and conventions and of primary voters.

Normally, candidates formally announce their candidacies in the year preceding the presidential election year. Then their aim is to persist and survive the long primary and caucus season that begins in February of election year and continues until only one candidate is left. Candidates use a number of methods to try to maximize their chances of survival. They carefully choose the primaries they will enter and to which they will devote their resources. Candidates must enter enough primaries so they are seen as national, not regional, candidates, but they cannot possibly devote time and resources to every primary or caucus. Especially important are the early events—the Iowa caucus and the New Hampshire primary—and the larger state primaries in the middle of the season.

Candidates also try to survive by establishing themselves as *the* candidate for a particular policy or constituency. In 1996, Pat Buchanan hoped to win the loyalties of the most conservative members of the Republican Party, but he was unsuccessful in enlisting enough of these voters to offset his unpopularity with other Republicans.

To compete successfully, candidates also need considerable media coverage. They must convince reporters that they are serious candidates with a real chance of winning. Journalists and candidates establish expectations for how well each candidate should do based on the results of polls, the quality of a candidate's campaign organization, the amount of money and time spent in the campaign, and the political complexion of the state. If a candidate performs below expectations, even though garnering the most votes, it may be interpreted by the press as a weakness and hurt the campaign. On the other hand, a strong showing when expectations are low can mean a boost to a candidate's campaign.

Consequently, candidates try to lower media expectations. It is not enough to win a primary; you have to win by at least as much as the media claims you should, or you will be seen as a loser. In the Republican race in 1988, Pat Robertson's organizers tried to counter media predictions for the Iowa caucuses by urging supporters to tell pollsters that they were not going to attend the caucuses. Because pollsters do not count people who do not plan to vote,

The train "whistlestop" campaign was a staple of many presidential races. Here President Harry Truman gives a speech from the back of a train in 1948.

this tactic could result in an artificially low prediction—and then a surprisingly high vote.[50]

Sometimes even losers are portrayed as winners if they do better than expected. For example, in 1968 in the New Hampshire primary, antiwar candidate Senator Eugene McCarthy won 40% of the vote against President Johnson, who had become increasingly unpopular because of the Vietnam War. Although McCarthy did not win, he did much better than expected, and the press interpreted the vote as a repudiation of Johnson's leadership.

In sum, then, the primary season is a game among the media, the candidates, and the voters, with the candidates trying to raise voter enthusiasm and lower media expectations simultaneously.

The common wisdom about presidential primaries is that the key ingredient is "momentum." That is, a candidate needs to win early, or at least do better than expected, to gain momentum, then keep winning to maintain momentum. Jimmy Carter's 1976 victory in the Iowa caucuses, which attracted tremendous media attention, which in turn led to further primary wins, is an illustration. It is important for candidates to convince their supporters that they remain viable. Without that, fund-raising, which is crucial to the continuing success of a campaign, becomes impossible.

Early in the primary season, candidates try to find the position, slogan, or idea that will appeal to the most voters. To take advantage of what appeared to be America's distrust of Washington, D.C., Jimmy Carter tried to create an image of an honest person who would never tell a lie. In 1984, Ronald Reagan presented himself as the candidate embodying traditional America. As one of his staff aides wrote in a campaign memo, "Paint RR as the personification of all that is right with, or heroized by, America."[51]

Candidates must avoid making a big mistake or, worse yet, being caught covering up a mistake or untruth. Edmund Muskie's front-running candidacy ground to a halt in 1972 when he cried at a public appearance while denouncing a newspaper attack on his wife. Gary Hart's 1988 candidacy collapsed when the media discovered that his marriage did not prevent him from having affairs with a series of other women. He compounded the damage by lying. The Muskie incident was taken by the media and public to indicate that he could not handle the stress of a campaign or, by inference, the presidency. The Hart incident raised questions about his character and honesty.

Incumbent presidents seeking renomination do not have the same problems as their challengers. No

In the 1950s, at the dawn of the television age, Democratic party leaders instruct their delegates on how to behave on camera.

incumbent who sought renomination has been denied it in this century.

In addition to these general strategies, candidates must deal specifically with the particular demands of caucuses, conventions, and primaries.

Presidential Caucuses and Conventions

Some states employ caucuses and conventions to select delegates to attend presidential nominating conventions. In 1996, one or both parties in 18 states selected delegates in caucuses.

The Iowa caucuses, except for their timing and newsworthiness, are similar to those in other states. Normally the campaign in Iowa starts months before the caucuses are actually held. In 1988, presidential candidates spent a total of 999 days campaigning in Iowa. Campaigning is, in large part, personal. Democrat Bruce Babbitt reported that one caucus attender, a tropical fish hobbyist, said he would deliver his vote to Babbitt if he could tell him the "pH and sediment density of the Congo River at its mouth." Babbitt assigned a staffer to look into the question.[52]

In early February, the caucuses are held in private homes, schools, and churches, and all who consider themselves party members can attend. They debate and vote on the candidates. The candidates receiving the most votes win delegates to later county and state conventions. The number of delegates is proportional to the vote that the candidate received at the caucuses (assuming the candidate got at least 15%).

Iowa, as the first state to hold its caucuses, normally gets the most attention. In 1996 several Republican candidates, including Bob Dole, Steve Forbes, and Pat Buchanan, worked hard to win some of the handful of convention delegates at stake. The candidates hoped a strong showing would impress the nation's political pros and would establish them as serious contenders. That would attract further media attention and the financial donations important to continuing the campaign.

Presidential Primaries

Delegates to presidential nominating conventions are also selected in direct primaries, sometimes called **presidential preference primaries.** In these elections, governed by state laws and national party rules, voters indicate a preference for a presidential candidate, delegates committed to a candidate, or both. Some states have preference primaries, but delegates are actually selected in conventions. These primaries are often called "beauty contests" because they are meaningless in terms of winning delegates. Like other primaries, presidential primaries can be open or closed.

Until 1968, presidential preference primaries usually played an insignificant role in presidential nominations. Only a handful of states employed primaries to select delegates. The conventional wisdom was that primary victories could not guarantee nomination but a loss would spell sure defeat.

The insignificance of most primaries was illustrated in 1968 by Vice President Hubert Humphrey's ability to win the party's nomination without winning a single primary. In some states, when Lyndon Johnson decided not to seek reelection, it was too late for Humphrey to get on the primary ballot. In other states, he entered but did not win. Humphrey was able to win the nomination anyway because a majority of the delegates to the convention in 1968 were selected through party caucuses and conventions, where party leaders supportive of Humphrey had considerable influence.

Humphrey's nomination severely divided the Democratic party. Many constituencies within the party, particularly those opposed to the Vietnam War, were hostile to Humphrey and believed that the nomination was controlled by party elites out of step with the preferences of rank-and-file Democrats.

Delegate Selection Reform

The response of the Democratic party to these complaints was to change delegate selection procedures in order to make delegates more representative of Democratic voters. One change established quotas for blacks, women, and young people to reflect the groups' percentages in each state's population. These reforms significantly increased minority and female representation in the 1972 convention, and, quite unexpectedly, made the primary the preferred method of nomination. Criteria of openness and representativeness could be more easily satisfied through primary selection. In recent years, more than 70% of the Democratic delegates were chosen in primaries.

The Democrats have replaced quotas for minorities with guidelines urging minority involvement in party affairs. However, the quota that half the delegates must be women remains.

The Democratic party reforms diminished the participation of party and elected officials. Critics felt that this weakened the party and increased the probability of nominating a candidate who could not work with party leaders. Since 1984, 15% to 20% of the delegates have been "superdelegates" appointed from among members of Congress and other party and public officials. The change was to help ensure that the party's nominee would be someone who could work with other elected officials within the party.

The Republican party has not felt as much pressure to reform its delegate selection procedures. Republicans have tried to eliminate discrimination and increase participation in the selection process.

In 1988, a new feature of the primary season emerged. So-called **Super Tuesday** was a day when most southern states held primaries simultaneously. Southern politicians thought this arrangement would force the parties to nominate candidates more to the liking of southern voters. Though Super Tuesday captured the attention of the candidates and the media, it has not had much impact on the final outcome for either Democrats or Republicans. Those who thought the Super Tuesday arrangement would give a boost to the most conservative Democratic candidate neglected to consider the impact of the black vote, which in some southern states is a large portion of the entire Democratic vote.

Reforming the Nomination Process

Each election year political observers discuss changing the presidential nomination process. They correctly complain that primaries tend to weaken political parties and have very low, unrepresentative turnouts. Moreover, the current system gives disproportionate influence to two small states, Iowa and New Hampshire, that come first in the process. Voters in most other states do not get to see most candidates; they have already been weeded out by the time the April, May, and June primaries occur. Moreover, some charge that the current system is influenced too much by the media, which exaggerates the victories of the winners and makes the losers seem weaker than they actually are.

Until recently, we could defend the primary system by pointing out two advantages of giving small states that select their delegates early a disproportionate influence in the process. For one thing, only in these first small states did candidates come in contact with voters on a personal basis. Moreover, when small states came first, the candidates could test their popularity without spending millions of dollars. Those who were successful could then attract funds for the larger, more expensive races. This system gave little-known candidates a better chance than most alternative arrangements would have.

But by 1996, large states such as California, New York, Texas, Florida, and Illinois moved their primaries earlier into the primary season in order to increase their influence on the nominating process. Now candidates can no longer bank on doing well in the first small state primary elections and then having some momentum to help in raising large sums of money. The demands for fund-raising have grown, because candidates must have money in hand long before the first primary in order to book and run the massive television campaigns needed to reach primary voters in these large states. As a result, little-known candidates have a tougher battle now than in previous election years.

Some observers are glad that we no longer have the "smoke-filled rooms" where party bosses chose nominees. Nevertheless, the primary system has weakened political parties, and the small primary electorate is unrepresentative of the general public. Indeed, these voters might be less representative of the public than the party bosses who met in smoke-filled rooms. And they probably know less about the nominees than did the party bosses. But the days when party leaders could anoint the nominees are probably gone forever.

The National Conventions

Once selected, delegates attend their party's national nominating convention in the summer before the November election. Changes in party rules have reduced the convention's role from an arena where powerful party leaders came together and determined the party's nominee to a body that ratifies a choice based on the outcome of the primaries and caucuses.

In the "old" days, often many ballots were necessary before a winner emerged. In 1924, it took the Democrats 103 ballots to nominate John W. Davis. Now nominees are selected on the first ballot. In most election years, some experts predict a close nomination race, which would force the decision to be made at the convention. But in fact, the recent national party conventions served the purposes they have served for nearly 40 years—to endorse the nominee and his choice for vice president, to construct a party platform, to whip up enthusiasm for the ticket among party loyalists, and to present the party favorably to the national viewing audience. Thus, even without the nomination job, national conventions give meaning to the notion of a national party.

Before 1972, delegates were predominantly white and male. After 1972, the percentage of delegates who were black, women, and under 30 increased substantially. In 1996, 53% of the Democratic and 36% of the Republican delegates were women; 17% of the Democratic and 3% of the Republican delegates were black. The latter figures are fairly close to the percentage of blacks among each party's supporters.

Convention delegates are still unrepresentative in terms of education and income. Compared to the population, delegates to national party conventions are well educated and well-off financially. To spend a week at a convention requires more money and free time than the average American has.

Delegates also tend to be more ideologically extreme than each party's rank and file. Democratic delegates are generally more liberal and Republican delegates more conservative than their party's supporters (see Figure 2).

The Activities of the Convention

National party conventions are full of color and excitement. They are a montage of balloons, placards, and demonstrations. Candidates and their lieutenants scurry in search of uncommitted delegates. Behind-the-scenes negotiators try to work out differences

FIGURE 2
National Convention Delegates Are More Ideologically Extreme Than Rank and File Members

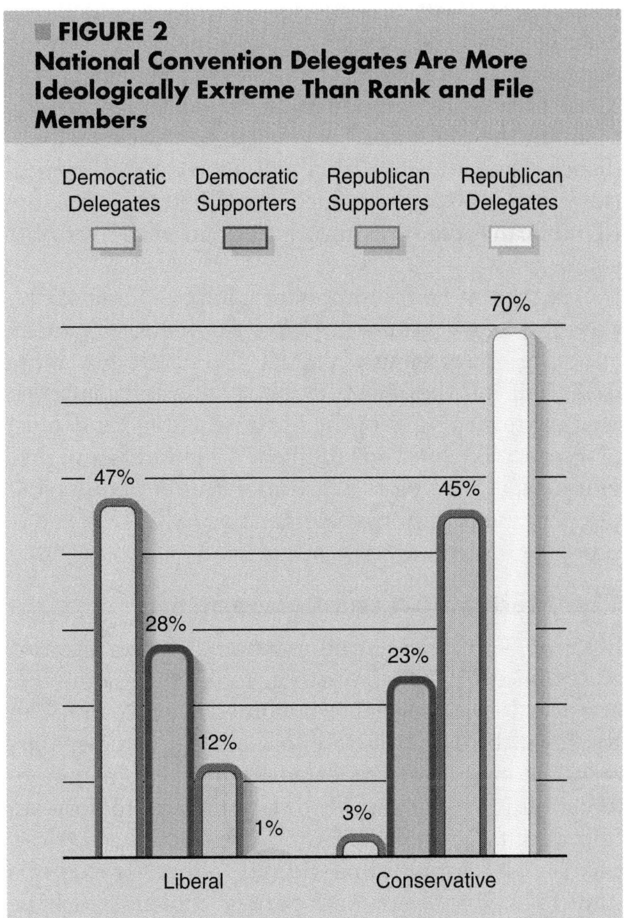

Sources: Data are from delegate and public surveys reported in *New York Times*, July 13, 1992, p. B6, and August 7, 1992, p. A18; *Washington Post National Weekly Edition*, August 16, 1992, p. A19.

among factions of the party. Journalists are everywhere covering everything from the trivial to the momentous. The keynote address reviews the party's glorious past and speaks to a promising future. Each candidate is placed in nomination by a party notable who reviews the candidate's background and experience. The roll call of the states ratifies the party's choice, and on the last night delegates cheer the acceptance speeches of the presidential and vice presidential nominees. Those who contested the nomination often join the nominees on the platform at the end in a display of party unity.

Aside from these very visible aspects, each convention has three important committees. The credentials committee reviews any challenges that may arise to the right of specific delegates to participate. The rules committee formulates convention and party rules, such as those governing delegate selection. The platform committee drafts the party's platform. The contents of the platform can generate conflict. For example, months before the 1996 GOP convention convened, moderate Republicans suggested the party reconsider its commitment to an absolute pro-life plank in the platform. That suggestion was met with disbelief and hostility from anti-abortion members of the party, who threatened to fight to keep the Republicans' platform firmly committed to a pro-life stance.

Apart from being important symbols of the direction the party wants to take, do platforms mean anything? Surprisingly, amidst the platitudes, more than half of the most recent platforms contained pledges regarding proposed future actions, and most of those pledges were fulfilled.[53] Platforms do provide observant voters with information about what the party will do if elected.

The Media and the Convention

Before 1932, nominees did not attend the convention. Acceptance of the nomination took place sometime afterward in a special ceremony. In 1932, Franklin Roosevelt broke with tradition and delivered his acceptance speech to the convention and to a nationwide radio audience; he did not want to lose an opportunity to deliver his message to the American people. The Republicans did not follow his example until 1944. Since then, both parties' conventions have closed with the acceptance speeches of the presidential and vice presidential nominees.

With the beginning of radio coverage in 1924 and television coverage in 1940, the conventions have become media events. The parties try to put on a show they hope will attract voters to their candidates. Polls usually show the party's candidate doing better during and after the party's convention, called the "convention bounce," though the effect does not last long.[54]

Major addresses, such as the acceptance speech, are planned for peak viewing hours. Potentially disruptive credentials and platform proceedings often are scheduled for the early morning hours. Conventions have become tightly organized and highly orchestrated affairs where little is left to chance. The stakes are too high.

Control, however, has its limits. If there are deep cleavages in the party, it may be impossible to prevent them from surfacing at the convention during prime time. The 1968 Democratic Convention was filled with conflict—conflict inside the convention between the supporters of Hubert Humphrey and opponents of the Johnson policies on the Vietnam War and conflict outside the convention on the streets of Chicago between antiwar demonstrators and the Chicago police. Television covered both events, associating the division in the convention with the turmoil outside, and dimmed Humphrey's chances of winning the election.

Selecting a Vice Presidential Nominee

Selection of a vice presidential candidate normally is done by the party's presidential nominee, then merely ratified at the convention, although in 1956, Democratic nominee Adlai Stevenson broke with tradition and left the decision to the convention.

Presidential candidates usually select a vice presidential nominee who can "balance" the ticket in terms of region (Kennedy from Massachusetts chose Johnson of Texas in 1960), ideology (the more liberal Dukakis picked the more conservative Bentsen), Washington experience (in 1980, Washington outsider Reagan chose Washington insider Bush), and other characteristics. Gender traditionally has not been part of a ticket balancing effort, but Walter Mondale's historic choice of Geraldine Ferraro in 1984 suggests that presidential nominees must now consider gender.

Bush's selection of Indiana Senator Dan Quayle, however, did not illustrate any of the usual strategic considerations except that Quayle was from a different part of the country than Bush. Quayle was youthful and charming but had little experience and was considered a lightweight. During the campaign,

As a vice presidential candidate, Geraldine Ferraro drew large crowds and especially ignited the enthusiasm of many women.

Bush's advisers would not let Quayle appear on network news shows or get close to metropolitan areas with major media markets.

Most observers believe Clinton's choice of Senator Albert Gore, Jr., was more astute. Although Gore did not "balance" the ticket in traditional terms or come from a pivotal state with a lot of electoral college votes (Tennessee), he in fact did balance some of Clinton's weaknesses. Gore was a war veteran, while Clinton avoided service in Vietnam, and Gore's credentials as a family man had never been challenged. Gore had foreign policy expertise while Clinton did not. Perhaps more important, Gore's own moderate political philosophy strengthened Clinton's image as a moderate; Gore's youth strengthened Clinton's credibility as a candidate for change; and Gore's reputation as an environmentalist played well to younger voters.

In 1996 Bob Dole surprised most observers and picked former New York representative Jack Kemp, a past Reagan cabinet member and Buffalo Bills quarterback, as his vice presidential running mate. Although Kemp and Dole disagreed on a number of issues, especially whether cutting taxes or cutting the federal deficit is more important, Kemp gave the Republican ticket an image of vigor and energy. Because Kemp was firmly identified with the Reagan tax cuts, his nomination made Dole's goal of completing the Reagan revolution more credible. Moreover, Dole's choice of Kemp gave conservative Republicans another reason to support the ticket enthusiastically.

Do vice presidential choices affect the election outcome? In most cases probably not. As a cynical observer commented, "Pick anyone . . . if Quayle can't sink a ticket, nobody can."[55]

Independent and Third-Party Nominees

Independent and third-party candidates also run. Although most of these candidates are invisible to all but avid political devotees, recent years have seen stronger independent candidates emerge, such as George Wallace in 1968, John Anderson in 1980, and Ross Perot in 1992. Ross Perot's Reform Party was again on the ballot in many states in 1996, and consumer advocate Ralph Nader conducted an independent candidacy for president, too. Such candidacies have become more viable because voters identify less strongly with parties and express more dissatisfaction with politics as usual. A strong independent candidate who draws more support from one major party candidate than the other could influence the outcome of the election. Many people predicted that Perot would have this effect in 1992, but he siphoned voters almost equally from Bush and Clinton. In 1996, Perot had little effect on the election outcome.

It is not easy for independent candidates to get on the ballot. State laws control access to the ballot, and Democratic and Republican legislators and governors make those laws. Thus the candidates of the Democratic and Republican parties are automatically placed on the ballot in all 50 states, but independent candidates must demonstrate significant support to get on the ballot through petitions signed by voters.

General Election Campaigns

We take it for granted that the election campaign determines who wins. But consider this: Only once since 1952 has the candidate who was ahead in the polls in July, before the national conventions, lost. That year was 1988. Dukakis led in the preconvention period by 6 to 10 points.[56] This suggests that although campaigns can make a difference, a lot of other factors determine who is elected.

Campaign Organization

Staffing the campaign organization is crucial, not only to get talented people but also to get those with considerable national campaign experience and a variety of perspectives. In 1988, most of the Bush team were old hands in national campaigns, having had significant roles in Reagan's. Dukakis's staff members were much less experienced and, perhaps even more damaging, did not always appreciate that campaigns are run differently in California, Texas, or Illinois than in Massachusetts, Dukakis's home state. In 1992 the situation was different. Bush's team lacked the confidence and experience of Clinton's.

The candidate's own personal organization is only one part of the overall campaign organization. The national party organization and state parties also have some responsibilities, especially in registering potential party voters, getting them to the polls, and trying to make sure that the presidential candidate's local appearances will help the party's congressional and state candidates.

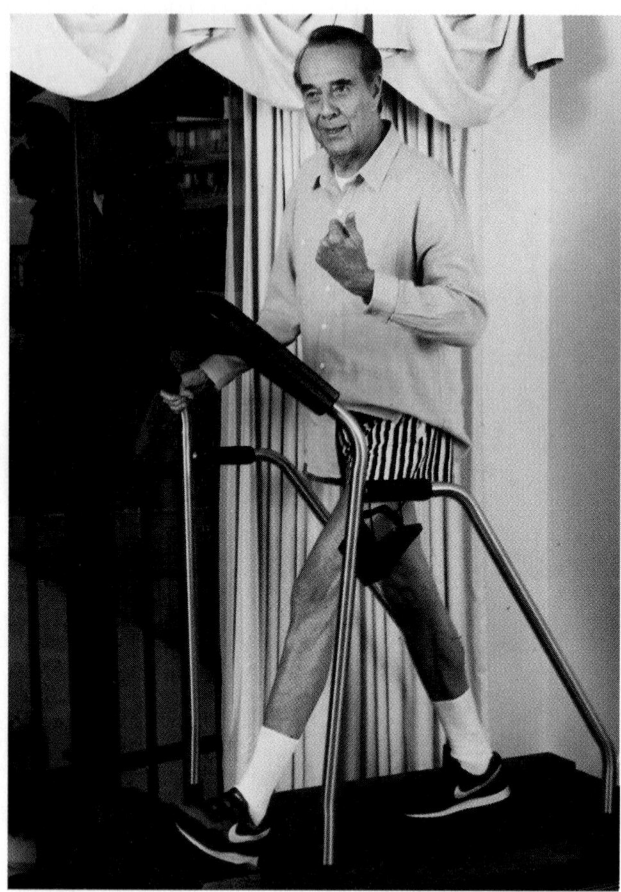

The 72-year-old Senator Robert Dole, the Republican presidential nominee, tries to demonstrate his vigor despite his age by having his picture taken while exercising on a treadmill.

Images and Issues

Largely through the media, candidates try to create a favorable image and portray the opponent in an unfavorable way. The Bush campaign was remarkably successful at creating a negative image for Dukakis in 1988 but much less so for Clinton in 1992. Dukakis seemed not to grasp the damage the Bush campaign was doing to him. The Clinton team answered every attack Bush made, but at the same time they stayed focused on their own campaign message. In 1996, Bob Dole tried to present himself as experienced but not too old to be president.

Issues also can be the basis for an appeal to voters. As they did in 1992, Democrats traditionally have used the "pocketbook" issues, arguing that economic times are better when Democrats are in the White House. In 1984, however, Reagan was successful in focusing on economic issues and taking credit for a strong economic recovery.

Issue appeals are usually general, and often candidates do not offer a clear-cut choice even on the most important controversies of the time. For example, the 1968 presidential election offered voters little choice on Vietnam policy, because the positions of candidates Nixon and Humphrey appeared very similar.[57] Voters who wanted to end the war by withdrawing and others who wanted to escalate the war had no real choice of candidates.

Ideally, the major campaign themes and strategies have been put into place by the end of the summer, but these themes and strategies are revised and updated on a daily, sometimes hourly, basis as the campaign progresses. Decisions are made not just by the candidate and the campaign manager but by a staff of key advisers who include media experts and pollsters. Sophisticated polling techniques are used to produce almost daily reports on shifts in public opinion across the nation and in particular regions. Thus, media ads can be added and deleted as polls reflect their impact. Campaign trips are modified or scratched as the candidate's organization sees new opportunities. And media events can be planned to complement the paid advertising the candidate runs.

The Electoral College

All planning for the campaign has to take into account the peculiar American institution of the **Electoral College.** In the United States voters do not elect the president directly, although this may surprise those who thought they voted for Clinton or Bush. In fact they voted for Clinton's or Bush's electors, who formed part of the Electoral College.

Electors are party notables who gather in each state capitol in December after the presidential election to cast their votes for president and vice president. Each state has as many electors as its total representation in Congress (House plus Senate) (see Figure 3). The smallest states (and the District of Columbia) have 3, whereas the largest state—California—has 54.

With the exception of Maine and Nebraska, which divide their Electoral College votes according to who wins in each congressional district, all of each state's electoral votes go to the candidate winning the most votes in that state, no matter how slim the margin. If

FIGURE 3
Clinton Wins Electoral Votes in the Industrial Heartland, Northeast, and Pacific Coast

The numbers inside the states indicate the electoral votes, out of a total of 538.

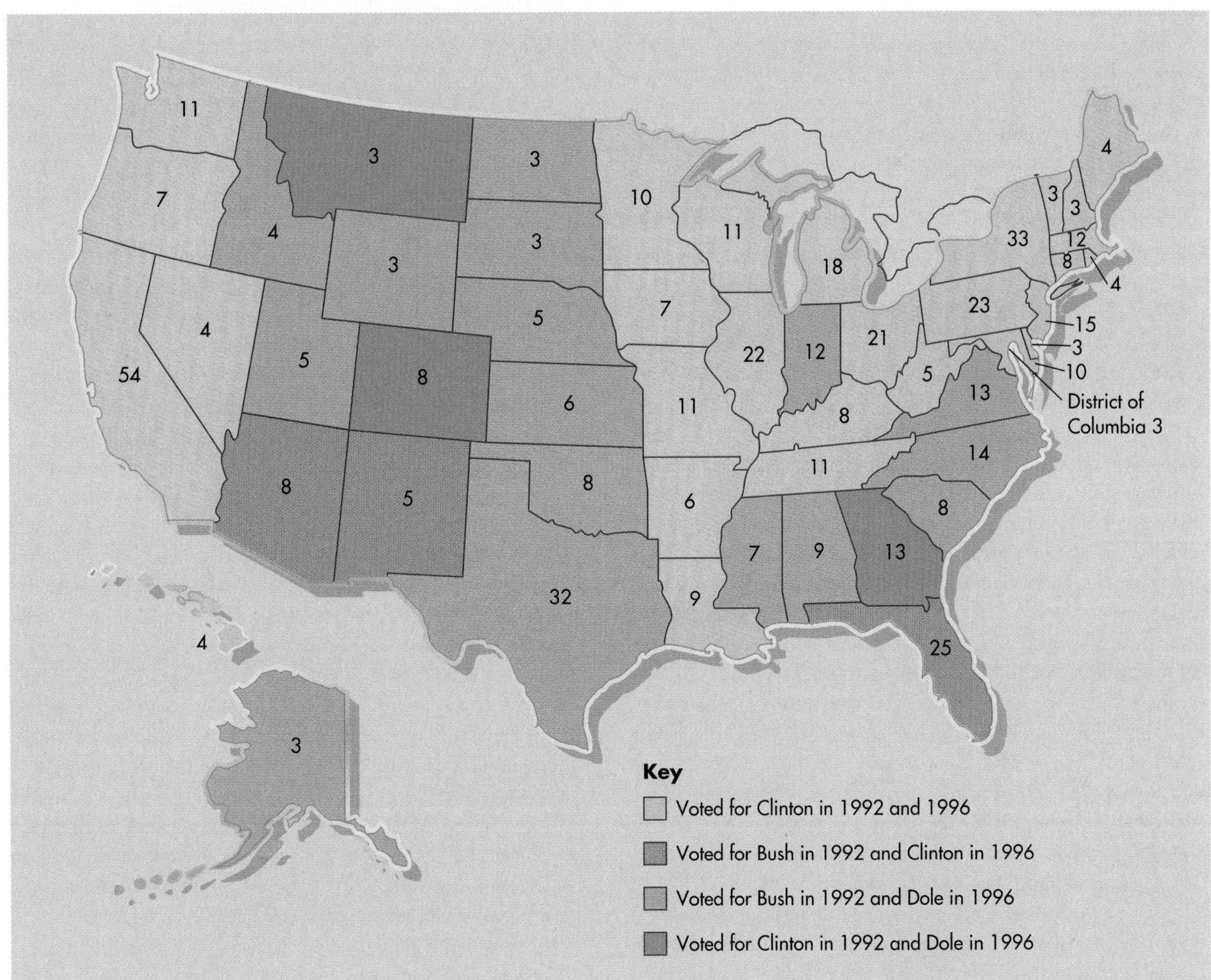

Source: Richard Scammon and Alice McGilliuray, *American Votes 19* (Washington, D.C.: Congressional Quarterly, 1991), pp. 9–13; *Congressional Quarterly Weekly Reports,* November 7, 1992, p. 3549; and Rhodes Cook, "1996 Presidential Election," Nov. 9, 1996, p. 3190.

one candidate wins a majority of the electors voting across the United States, that candidate wins. If no candidate wins a majority, the election is decided in the House of Representatives, where each state has one vote and a majority is necessary to win. This has not happened since 1824, when John Quincy Adams was chosen. If voting in the Electoral College for the vice president does not yield a majority, the Senate chooses the vice president; again each state has one vote.

The Role of the Electoral College

Critics frequently suggest that the Electoral College, a complex and sometimes puzzling institution, should be reformed or abolished. One reform would keep the overall system but eliminate electors as individuals; electoral votes would automatically be cast according to a state's popular vote.

Abolishing the Electoral College in favor of a direct popular election is another reform idea that has some support. Votes would be counted nationwide; state totals would not matter. This proposal has been offered as a constitutional amendment in Congress several times but has never won approval. Even if passed in Congress, it probably would fail to obtain ratification by the necessary three-fourths of the state legislatures because large states would oppose it.

One reason that some argue for abolishing the Electoral College is that there are some undemocratic aspects to it, just as the Founders intended. The Electoral College makes it possible for the candidate with the most popular votes to lose the election. This has occurred three times: John Quincy Adams (1824), Rutherford B. Hayes (1876), and Benjamin Harrison (1888).

Critics of the Electoral College argue that these historical anomalies should not happen; in a democratic system, the person with the most votes should win. Further, the Electoral College often converts candidates with a plurality but not a majority of the popular vote into majority winners in the Electoral College. This may give a greater legitimacy to the winners. In 1960 John F. Kennedy won only 49.7% of the popular vote but a substantial 56% of the Electoral College vote. Significant margins of popular votes can be turned into the appearance of consensus too. For example, in 1984 President Reagan won 59% of the popular vote, but because he won in 49 states, he won 97% of the Electoral College vote.

Another undemocratic feature of the current system is the **faithless elector,** an elector who decides to cast a vote for a personal choice, not for that of his or her state's voters. Occasionally electors do stray from their pledge—in 1988 a West Virginia elector voted for Lloyd Bentsen for president and later said she wished she had voted for Kitty Dukakis. Even though the intent of the Founders was to allow electors to cast their votes any way they desired, many people believe that in our more democratic era electors should be bound by the wishes of the voters. However, no faithless elector has ever made a difference in the outcome of an election.

Some people favor abolishing the College because direct election is a more understandable system. However, we still need to formulate rules to deal with situations where no candidate gets a majority and that makes the popular vote alternative more complicated than at first glance.

The major reason we retain the Electoral College system, though, is that in the current system, voters in large states receive more attention from candidates. A 1-vote margin in Pennsylvania yields the candidate 29 electoral votes, a 1-vote margin in North Dakota only 3 electoral votes. So it is more important to get that extra vote in Pennsylvania than in North Dakota. Rational candidates and parties will direct their resources and perhaps tailor their policy views accordingly.

Although political scientists have debated the actual extent of the large state bias in the current system, most believe it does exist and is significant.[1] Urbanites, especially central city residents, have more clout in the Electoral College system than they would have under a direct election system. Minority groups benefit too, because they are disproportionately located in urban areas. (However, one should not overstate this clout. The more liberal candidates, presumably those favored by the more urban interests, have lost most presidential elections since 1968.)

Supporters of the system argue that this urban bias is fair when viewed in the context of our other political institutions. The Senate, for example, overrepresents the interests of smaller, rural states because each state, regardless of population, has two votes. Many of the institutions of Congress, too, work in a way that gives an advantage to more conservative interests, often identified with rural America. The complex committee system and diffused power structure make dramatic changes in the status quo difficult.

Defenders of the Electoral College argue that to abolish it would remove a balance that exists in American politics: the conservative, rural bias of Congress on the one hand and the liberal, urban bias of the Electoral College on the other.

1. Lawrence Longley and James Dana, Jr., "New Empirical Estimates of the Biases of the Electoral College for the 1980s," *Western Political Quarterly* 37 (March 1984), pp. 157–75.

The Founders assumed that the Electoral College would have considerable power, with each elector exercising independent judgment and choosing from among a large number of candidates. They did not foresee the development of political parties. As state parties developed, the electors became part of the party process, pledged to party candidates. Thus, electors usually rubber stamp the choice of voters in each state rather than exercise their own judgment.

Because of the winner-take-all feature of the Electoral College, the system gives an advantage to large states and their urban populations. The 11 largest states have a majority (270) of the 538 votes. Candidates concentrate their efforts on these states.

The Electoral College is based on states, so it encourages campaigns designed to win "states." In this sense, it reinforces the federal system.

Campaign Strategies

Developing a strategy is an important element of a presidential campaign. But every strategy is surrounded by uncertainty, and even political pros cannot always predict the impact of a particular strategy.

Candidates seek to do three things: mobilize those who are already loyal to them and their party, persuade independent voters that they are the best candidate, and try to convert the opposition. Most candidates emphasize mobilizing their own voters. Democrats have to work harder at this than Republicans because Democratic voters often do not vote and are more likely to vote for the other party than are Republicans.

Both parties must try to persuade independent voters because independents are the swing voters; their votes determine the outcome. In 1964, when Johnson trounced Republican Goldwater, 80% of Republicans voted for Goldwater. And in 1988, when Dukakis was soundly beaten by Bush, 75% of Democrats voted for Dukakis. It was the independent voters who determined the outcomes.

The crucial strategic question is where to allocate resources of time and money: where to campaign, where to buy media time and how much to buy, and where to spend money helping local organizations. Candidates must always remember that they have to win a majority of the Electoral College vote. The most populous states, with the largest number of electoral votes, are vital. Prime targets are those large states that could go to either party, such as Illinois, Texas, California, and New York.

Candidates also have to expand their existing bases of support. Most of the western states have been solidly Republican in their presidential loyalties. Republicans have been able to build on their solid western base and their strength in the South. They only have to carry a few of the large industrial states to win.

The Clinton family became more prominent in Clinton's 1992 campaign after his campaign team discovered the public knew little about them.

Democrats have a strategic problem given the western Republican bloc. Between the end of Reconstruction and 1948, the South was solidly Democratic, but there have been no solidly Democratic states in presidential elections since then (although Washington, D.C., has been solidly Democratic). Since 1976, the Democrats have consistently lost the South. During the 1980s some strategists believed the Democrats should try to win back the South by choosing more conservative candidates. Others argued for a strategy to win without the South, aiming for the industrial states of the East and Midwest along with California and a few other states of the West. This was largely Clinton's strategy in 1992 and 1996, though he did win his home state and Gore's (Arkansas and Tennessee) and picked up Louisiana too. The non-southern strategy was used successfully by the Republicans between the 1870s and the 1920s, when they were able to capture the White House regularly without ever winning a southern state.

The Media Campaign

The media campaign consists of paid advertising, personal appearances on talk shows, debates, and coverage on news broadcasts and in print media. Candidates have the most control over paid advertising and the least over news coverage; but even there, campaigns spend hundreds of hours devising strategies to show their candidates to best advantage.

Campaigns are expensive because they rely so heavily on the media to get the candidate's message to the voters. As one observer argued, "Today's presidential campaign is essentially a mass media campaign. It is not that the mass media entirely determine what happens. . . . But it is no exaggeration to say that, for the large majority of voters, the campaign has little reality apart from the media version."[58]

Impact of the Media

The media, through news coverage, personal appearances by candidates, and paid advertisements, help shape voters' opinions and choices in three ways. They inform, they help set the campaign agenda, and they help persuade voters.[59] In Chapter 8, we will discuss these effects.

Use of the Media

MEDIA EVENTS Candidates try to use the media to their advantage by staging media events that allow them to be photographed doing and saying noncontroversial things in front of enthusiastic crowds and patriotic symbols. As Bush campaign strategist Roger Ailes proclaimed 20 years ago, "This is the beginning of a whole new concept. This is the way they'll be elected forevermore. The next guys will have to be performers."[60]

Candidates and their advisers try to design settings that will encourage television reporters to focus their stories on the candidate and put his or her policies in the best light.[61] In 1988, George Bush almost literally wrapped himself in the flag, frequently "pledging allegiance," until negative media reaction led his advisers to decide that they were overdoing it.

Candidates spend most of their time going from media market to media market, hoping to get both national and local coverage.[62] Some candidates are much better than others at using the media. Bob Dole was plagued by media coverage that emphasized his lagging standing in the polls.

ADVERTISING Paid advertisements allow candidates to focus on points most favorable to their case or to portray their opponents in the most negative light. Most political ads are quite short, 30 or 60 seconds in length. Television ads were first used in the 1952 campaign. One, linking the Democratic Truman administration to the unpopular Korean War, showed two soldiers in combat talking about the futility of war. Then one of the soldiers is hit and dies. The other one deliberately exposes himself to the enemy and is also killed. The announcer's voice says, "Vote Republican."[63] Today's ads are perhaps less melodramatic but still appeal to viewers' emotions. One classic set of ads that had a strong emotional response was the 1984 Reagan ads, depicting his policies as putting the country on the road to greatness again ("It's morning in America").[64]

Some ads are issue oriented. In 1988, for example, one Dukakis ad focused on the Democrat's plans for helping families pay for college education for their children.

Negative ads have come increasingly to dominate media advertising. Sometimes these ads have more impact on public opinion than do positive ads. Candidates believe their media consultants who tell them, "People won't pay any attention [to positive ads]. Better to knock your opponent's head off."[65] And they see it reflected in the polls, where negative ads can sometimes have a dramatic short-term effect on a candidate's standing.

Although the 1988 campaign probably set a modern record for negative campaigning, the phenomenon is as American as apple pie. When Thomas Jefferson faced John Adams in 1796, a Federalist editorial called Jefferson "mean spirited, low-lived . . . the son of a half-breed Indian squaw" and prophesized that if he were elected, "Murder, robbery, rape, adultery and incest will be openly taught and practiced."[66] When Andrew Jackson ran for president in 1832, his mother was called a prostitute, his father a mulatto (someone of mixed races, black and white), his wife a profligate woman, and himself a bigamist.[67]

Negative Campaigning in 1988 and 1992

Almost all observers agree that negative campaigning was a successful strategy in the 1988 presidential election. Over 60% of the public thought that Bush's campaign was dirty, but he won handily anyway. (Forty percent thought Dukakis's campaign was dirty.)[1] Bush successfully painted a picture of Dukakis as "not a patriot, no believer in law and order, no manly man, no lover of family . . . one of those loose lovers of 'them' and 'their' ways."[2] He did this in part by hitting Dukakis hard for vetoing a bill which would have made the Pledge of Allegiance mandatory in Massachusetts schools each day. Though Dukakis did this because he felt the bill was unconstitutional, Bush's campaign used the veto to challenge Dukakis's patriotism. And the Bush campaign linked Dukakis to Willie Horton, a convict who was furloughed from the Massachusetts prison system while Dukakis was governor. Horton, while on furlough, raped a woman and terrorized her and her fiance. Though 40 other states and the federal government had furlough programs, the Bush campaign used the Horton incident to portray Dukakis as soft on crime. The impact of this is illustrated by the fact that three years later, focus groups of voters remembered little about the 1988 election except the Horton ads.[3]

Election analysts feared that the success of negative advertising in 1988 would set the stage for even more in 1992. But, much to the surprise of many, negative campaigning did not work so well in 1992. By October, the Bush campaign, failing to find its own focus, was reduced simply to portraying Clinton as a taxer and spender, a liar and a coward, and even a possible Soviet sympathizer. In a truly desperate moment, Bush claimed, "My dog Millie knows more about foreign affairs than these two bozos!" (the bozos were Clinton and Gore). And, during the last week of the campaign, reporters at the *Washington Post* and other news organizations received messages from high-ranking Republican officials passing on rumors that Clinton was having an affair which was being covered up by the Secret Service. These calls urged the press to report the rumors.[4]

Why was this negative strategy less successful in 1992 than in 1988? One possibility is that Clinton was a better candidate than Dukakis. Indeed, recalling the fate of the Dukakis campaign, Clinton's team was ready to respond to any negative the Bush campaign could offer. For example, when the Clinton campaign caught wind of upcoming Bush television ads, they prepared counterattacks to launch immediately. And often they did get wind of one (both campaigns sometimes did this by intercepting satellite transmissions as ads were beamed to local stations or by getting a friendly television employee to play the ad). When the Bush campaign aired its "Night of the Living Dead" ad, which depicted Arkansas as a barren state populated by a lonely buzzard, Clinton's response was broadcast only 24 hours later.[5] During the Republican convention, James Carville, Clinton's campaign manager, ordered his staff to be ready to answer any line of the keynote address within an hour.

But the major difference between 1988 and 1992 may be that the voters were less receptive to negative campaigning because they were more concerned about real issues. A poor economy tends to focus voters' concerns. In 1992, the economy was sour and so were the voters. At several times in the campaign, voters indicated they were fed up with personal attacks. Early in the primary season, polls showed that voters were tired of hearing about Clinton's alleged womanizing. During the second presidential debate, the one with audience participation, both the moderator and a participant from the audience indicated they were annoyed with personal attacks and wanted to hear about the issues.

Edward Rollins, the Republican consultant who ran Ronald Reagan's 1984 campaign, summed up the 1992 campaign by noting, "It is not that negative campaigning does not work, it is that the voters this year did not want it. And George Bush talked about the draft about 200 times and his economic agenda about three times."[6] The lesson of the campaign may be, then, not that dirty campaigns do not work at all, but rather that there are some circumstances under which they will not work.

1. Richard Morin, "Relieved Rather than Elated," *Washington Post National Weekly Edition*, November 7–13, 1988, p. 42.
2. Gus Tyler, "After the Brawl Was Over," *New Leader*, November 28, 1988, p. 7.
3. Deborah Tannen, "Lies, Damned Lies, and Political Ads," *Washington Post National Weekly Edition*, September 21–27, 1992.
4. Ann Devroy, "The Low Road that Went Nowhere," *Washington Post National Weekly Edition* (November 9–15, 1992), p. 7.
5. Howard Kurtz, "In Advertising Give and Take, Clinton Camp Took and Responded," *Washington Post*, November 6, 1992, p. A10.
6. Devroy, "The Low Road . . .", p. 7.

Families all across the country gathered in front of their TV to watch the first televised presidential debates in 1960, featuring Senator John F. Kennedy (D-Mass.) and Vice President Richard Nixon (R).

A British observer of American elections in 1888 described them as a "tempest of invective and calumny . . . imagine all the accusations brought against all the candidates for the 670 seats in the English Parliament concentrated on one man, and read . . . daily for three months." [68]

In the old days, newspapers were the main medium of negative campaigning, but now television is. Some people blame the media, the campaign advisers and consultants, and the candidates themselves for negative advertising. But really the finger should be pointed at the public itself. When issues, rather than negative advertising, boost candidates in the polls, negative advertising diminishes. And if voters punished candidates who used negative advertising, it would disappear even more quickly. Of course, many voters respond to negative advertising by not voting, as we have seen.

But why does negative advertising sometimes work when most people say they do not like it? People may say they like to hear about issues, but their actions belie their words. Politics is just not that important to most people, and indeed many are woefully ignorant about specific issues. If one out of seven Americans cannot find the United States on a world map, how interested are they going to be in a discussion of foreign policy?[69] As it turns out, candidates can use negative advertising to let voters know how they and their opponents differ on issues.[70] Negative ads tend to present issues vividly, so candidates find them useful to reach voters who are not particularly attuned to listening to debates on specifics.

There are checks on negative campaigns.[71] One check is the press, which could point out errors of fact. A second is the voter, who might become outraged. The third is the candidate under attack, who in most cases will hit back.[72] In 1992, the press evaluated candidates' ads critically, Clinton countered negative ads aggressively, and voters made their displeasure with attack ads known. In 1996, each candidate made a campaign issue out of his opponent's negative ads and responded in kind with more negative ads.

TELEVISED DEBATES Candidates also use televised debates as part of their media campaigns. In

1960 Kennedy challenged Nixon to debate during their presidential campaign. Nixon did not want to debate because as vice president he was already known and ahead in the polls. He remembered his first election to the House of Representatives when he challenged the incumbent to debate and, on the basis of his performance, won the election. Afterward he said the incumbent was a "damn fool" to debate. Nevertheless, Nixon did agree to debate, and when the two contenders squared off, presidential debates were televised to millions of homes across the country for the first time.

Nixon dutifully answered reporters' questions and rebutted Kennedy's assertions. But Kennedy came to project an image. He sought to demonstrate his vigor, to compensate for his youth and inexperience. He also sought to contrast his attractive appearance and personality with Nixon's. So he quickly answered reporters' specific questions and then directly addressed viewers about his general goals.

Kennedy's strategy worked. He appealed to people and convinced them that his youth and inexperience would not pose problems. While Kennedy remained calm, Nixon became very nervous. He smiled at inappropriate moments, his eyes darted back and forth, and beads of sweat rolled down his face.

According to public opinion polls, people who saw the debates thought that Kennedy performed better in three of the four. (The only debate in which they thought Nixon performed better was the one in which the candidates were not in the same studio side by side. They were in separate cities, and with this arrangement Nixon was less nervous.) Yet people who heard the debates on radio did not think Kennedy performed as well. They were not influenced by the visual contrast between the candidates. Clearly, television made the difference.

There were no more presidential debates for 16 years. The candidates who were ahead did not want to risk their lead. But every presidential election since 1976 has featured debates between the candidates, including 1984 when Reagan enjoyed a large lead in the polls over Mondale. Now candidates find it hard to refuse to debate. In 1992 Bush agreed to debate Clinton after the Clinton campaign started sending a person dressed as a chicken to Bush rallies to pressure Bush to debate.

Because candidates have different strengths, each campaign wants the other to agree to a format that builds on their candidate's strengths. The "debate about debates" is a typical campaign issue that frequently overshadows other, more important issues. It has become as predictable a part of campaigns as the debates themselves.

Campaign Funding

Success in raising money is one of the keys to a successful political campaign. Although some of the money for presidential campaigns comes from public funds, much is raised privately. In Chapter 9 we will discuss campaign funding and its impact on politics.

Voting

For 40 years political scientists have argued about how voters make their choices. Are parties most important? Issues? Personalities? Political scientist Stanley Kelley has argued that voters go through a simple process in deciding how to vote. They add up the things they like about each candidate and party and they vote for the candidate with the highest number of "likes." If there is a tie, they vote on the basis of their party identification, if they have one. If they do not, they abstain. On the basis of this simple idea, Kelley explains more than 85% of the variation in voting choice.[73]

In making these calculations, then, voters consider three things:

- The party of the candidate, which has a great effect on how the voter views everything else about him or her.
- The candidate's personality, style, and appearance.
- The issue stands of the candidates and parties.

Despite considerable disagreement as to exactly how each of these is weighted in the voter's mind, political scientists can offer some general conclusions.

Party Loyalties

One's party loyalty, called party identification, is probably the most important factor influencing a person's vote: Democrats tend to vote for Democrats and Republicans for Republicans. This is most true for lower-level contests such as state legislative elections, but it is also true for presidential races because party preference influences how a voter perceives a candidate's personality and issue stance. For some people, party identification is their only source of

Source: The New Yorker Magazine, Inc.

"We'll probably vote for the least qualified candidate. We have no judgment skills."

information about candidates, and they vote on the basis of it alone.

However, since the turn of the century, and even since the 1950s, party has become less important to voters. There are more independents and more people who vote contrary to their partisan loyalties. Party loyalties seem to be in flux, and parties themselves have been weakened by competition from the media and interest groups. Nevertheless, if you are guessing how a person will vote, the best single bit of information to have is the person's party identification.[74]

How do people get to be Republicans and Democrats? Socioeconomic class is a very important predictor of the vote: the lower the income, the more likely to vote Democrat. But this general rule is cross-cut with distinctive ethnic and religious patterns (we use ethnic here to refer to differences of national origin and race).

For example, Jews are much more likely to vote Democratic than other whites of similar income. On the whole, they have a higher-than-average income, yet in 1992 about three-fourths of Jewish voters voted Democratic. As a group, they were exceeded in their Democratic allegiance only by blacks.[75]

Catholics used to be predominantly Democratic. They still are, but not consistently. Although 60% supported Democratic congressional candidates, and they favored Clinton over Bush by 44% to 36%, only half voted for Dukakis and a majority voted for Reagan in 1980 and 1984.

Blacks are probably the most distinctive group politically. About 90% consistently vote Democratic, and this loyalty has increased over the past 25 years.

Hispanics who, like blacks, also have lower-than-average incomes, are not as universally Democratic as blacks and have voted Republican in significant numbers in recent elections. Although almost three-quarters voted Democratic in congressional elections, just about 60% voted for Dukakis in 1988 and Clinton in 1992.

Hispanics vote Republican more than they previously did for several reasons. One is that many Hispanics are moving into the middle class. Another is that Republicans have made a great effort to lure Hispanic voters. Moreover, a growing number are Cuban Americans, largely located in Florida, whose most intense political opinion is anticommunism. Cuban Americans are much more likely to be Republican than either Mexican Americans or Puerto Ricans.

White Protestants generally give a majority of their vote to the Republicans and have done so for decades. However, as for other groups, income differences are important in determining the vote of Protestants.

Ethnicity and religion are important in determining the vote because they are shorthand terms for many other factors influencing political behavior—class, historical treatment within the society, and basic culture and values. Jews are predominantly Democratic, for example, because as a persecuted minority throughout much of their history, they have learned to identify with the underdog, even when their own economic circumstances move them into the middle or upper class. Catholics were sometimes discriminated against too; this discrimination plus their working-class status propelled them to the party of Roosevelt. As Catholics have moved into the middle class and as tolerance toward Catholics has grown, Catholics, like Protestants, have tended to vote their income. Moreover, evangelical Protestants (such as Southern Baptist and Assembly of God) are much more likely to vote for Republicans than are mainline Protestants (such as Episcopalians or Presbyterians).

Candidate Evaluations

Candidates' personalities and styles have had more impact as party influence has declined and as television has become voters' major source of information about elections. Reagan's popularity in 1984 is an example of the influence of a candidate and his personality. The perceived competence and integrity of candidates are other facets of candidate evaluation. Voters are less likely to support candidates who do not seem capable of handling the job, regardless of their issue positions. Jimmy Carter suffered in 1980 because of voter evaluations of his competence and leadership.

Issues

Issues are a third factor influencing the vote. Although Americans are probably more likely to vote on issues now than they were in the 1950s, issues only influence some voters some of the time. In 1984 and 1988, for example, voters' issue positions overall were closer to the positions of Mondale and Dukakis than to Reagan or Bush. And, in the 1996 election, 18% of those voters who considered themselves liberal voted for Bob Dole and 21% of those who considered themselves conservative voted for Bill Clinton.

Still, although other factors also influence voters, many do cast issue votes. To cast an issue vote, voters have to be informed about issues and have opinions. In recent elections, more than 80% of the public could take a position on issues such as government spending, military spending, women's rights, and relations with the Soviet Union.[76] Knowledge about these issues may have been vague, but individuals were able to understand the issues enough to define their own general positions.

Also, for voters to cast issue votes, candidates must have detectable policy differences. A substantial minority of voters are able to detect some differences among presidential candidates. In recent elections the percentages able to identify correctly general differences between the major party candidates varied between 36 and 62%.[77]

In the 1972 through 1988 elections, more than 70% of those who could correctly identify the positions of the candidates as well as their own position on an important issue cast a vote consistent with their own position.[78] We call this issue voting. Issues with the highest proportion of issue voting were those that typically divided Republicans and Democrats, such as government spending, military spending, and government aid to the unemployed and minorities. However, because only one-third to two-thirds of the electorate was able to define both their own and the candidates' positions on each issue, the proportion of the total electorate that can be said to cast an "issue vote" is usually less than 40%, and for some issues it is much less.[79]

Some scholars have suggested that issue voting is really more of an evaluation of the current incumbents. If voters like the way incumbents, or the incumbent's party, have handled the job in general or in certain areas—the economy or foreign policy, for example—they will vote accordingly, even without much knowledge about the specifics of the issues.

New Populism

The Angry White Male

If 1992 was the year of the woman in politics, 1994 was the year of the "angry white male." Feeling "left behind and left out," white men turned in large numbers to the Republicans in that off-year election.[1] Sixty-two percent of white male voters voted for Republican House candidates, compared to only 55% of women, the largest gender gap ever reported.[2]

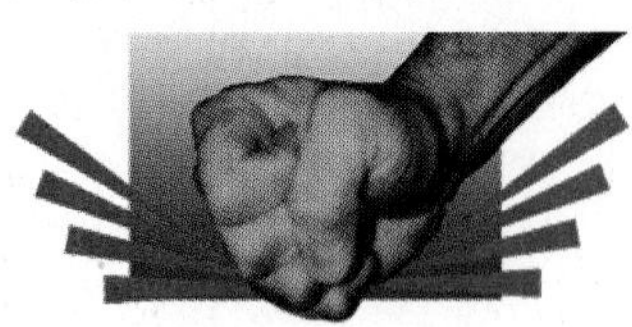

The term "angry white male" is not very precise. Obviously, not all white males are angry. Moreover, middle and upper class white males have traditionally voted Republican, so no special explanations are needed for their 1994 vote. But consider the lower and working class white males, who traditionally have been loyal to the Democratic party . Why did they move toward the Republicans in 1994? What will they do in 1996?

Some analysts believe that the issues of the 1994 campaign, such as taxes, spending, crime, and gun control, were issues of particular importance to men and to Republicans. Others argue that the shift of white men to the Republican party was based on much broader issues of social and economic change. During the 1980s, the economic status of those with only high school educations declined. Although the economy has been strong in recent years, many people have faced layoffs as American corporations "downsize" and jobs go elsewhere or nowhere. Indeed, during the 1980s, the median hourly wage for men fell 10%.[3] More families needed two earners to make it, putting more women in the workforce and giving them an increasing amount of power within families.

Even though these economic declines for working class men occurred mostly under Republican administrations, many white males blame the Democrats. They identify the Democrats with cultural changes which, they feel, have pushed them aside. Although white men receive higher wages than any other group and control most businesses, educational institutions, legislative bodies, and other centers of power in America, working class white men do not share

Source: Powell, LA Times Syndicate, Inc. Reprinted from The Washington Post National Weekly Edition, Feb. 26-Mar. 3, 1996, p. 33.

in this power.[4] They see their high-paying, skilled, blue-collar jobs move overseas or disappear altogether. But they believe that others are moving ahead. They see gains made by women and minorities in getting better jobs and access to higher education.

As one survey of white working class Detroiters found, "These white Democratic defectors express a profound distaste for blacks, a sentiment that pervades almost everything they think about government and politics. . . . Blacks constitute the explanation for [the whites'] vulnerability and for almost everything that has gone wrong in their lives."[5]

Angry white males are also angry with women, especially with women's increasing economic and political power. In 1994, white males who voted Republican were twice as likely as other white men to think it unimportant that women be elected to office, for example.[6]

Working class white males believe that public policies, especially affirmative action, are working to move women and minorities ahead, but not them. They overestimate how effective these policies are. (See Chapter 15.) They are angry with the Democrats since the Democratic party has most strongly supported civil rights laws since the 1960s.

Angry white males, then, seem caught between two forces. Predominantly working class, their economic fortunes are not rosy. The rich are getting richer, but the working class is not. Because they are white males, no government policies seem to be directed toward helping them. Indeed, many minorities and women view them as oppressors or at the least, beneficiaries of the existing system, not people who also need help. The resentment generated by these forces, then, propelled many "angry white males" to pull the Republican lever in the 1994 election.

During the Republican primaries in 1996, Patrick Buchanan tapped into these discontents. He coupled Republican opposition to affirmative action and changes in the traditional family structure with an attack on the North American Free Trade Agreement and the General Agreement on Tariffs and Trade which, he said, have cost Americans their jobs. Although he did not win the nomination, he remains convinced that many Democrats and independents, especially working class males, can be brought into the Republican fold with these positions.[7] But Buchanan's economic stance conflicts with the party's traditional stands on business and trade. It is unlikely that Republicans will change their views in order to attract more "angry white males."

And so these voters find themselves pulled in contrary directions. Should they direct their anger at Democrats for their support of affirmative action and civil rights? Or should they turn on Republicans whose economic policies encourage increasing economic divisions between rich and poor? Politicians from George Wallace in 1968 through H. Ross Perot in 1992 and Patrick Buchanan in 1996 have combined economic and cultural issues to appeal to exactly these voters.

1. Thomas B. Edsall, "The Democrats' Gender and Class Gap," *Washington Post National Weekly Edition* (June 6, 1994), p. 12.
2. Richard Morin and Barbara Vobejda, "It Was the Year of the Angry (White) Man," *Washington Post National Weekly Edition* (November 11–20, 1994), p. 37; "Portrait of the Electorate: Who Voted for Whom in the House," *New York Times* (November 13, 1994), p. 24.
3. Thomas Edsall, "The U.S. Male, Caught in a Cultural Shift," *Washington Post National Weekly Edition* (May 8–14, 1995), p. 25.
4. Ibid.
5. Herbert Hill, "Black Workers, Organized Labor, and Title VII of the 1964 Civil Rights Act," in Herbert Hill and James Jones, eds., *Race in America* (Madison: University of Wisconsin Press, 1993), p. 329.
6. Richard Morin, "And How Did the Voters Judge the Media?" *Washington Post National Weekly Edition* (December 5–11, 1994), p. 37.
7. Thomas B. Edsall, "Tapping into the Politics of Rage," *Washington Post National Weekly Edition* (February 19–25, 1996), p. 14.

Voting on the basis of past performance is called **retrospective voting.** There is good evidence that many people do this, especially according to economic conditions.[80] Voters support incumbents if national income is growing in the months preceding the election. Since World War II, the incumbent party has won a presidential election only once when the growth rate was less than 3% (Eisenhower in 1956) and lost only once when it was more than 3% (Ford in 1976). Unemployment and inflation seem to have less consistent effects on voting, and economic conditions two or three years before the election have little impact on voting.[81] An economic recovery helped Reagan get reelected in 1984 and helped put Bush in the White House in 1988. Clinton's criticism of Bush's handling of the economy helped him in 1992, and the strong economy of 1996 virtually guaranteed his reelection.

Parties, Candidates, and Issues

All three factors—parties, candidates, and issues—clearly matter. Party loyalties are especially important because they help shape our views about issues and candidates. However, if issues and candidates did not matter, the Democrats would have won every presidential election since the New Deal. Republican victories suggest that they often have had more attractive candidates (as in 1952, 1956, 1980, and 1984) or issue positions (in 1972 and in some respects in 1980).

However, the Democrats' partisan advantage shrank throughout the 1980s. Though there are still more Democrats than Republicans, the margin is modest and the number of independents is growing.

Party loyalties have been even more important in congressional voting. The Democrats controlled the House continuously between 1954 and 1994, and controlled the Senate most of those years. However, the Democratic lock on the House was broken in the 1994 election, which found the Republicans winning control in a sweeping victory. Clearly, issues overcame traditional partisan habits in that election. Exactly which issues mattered, however, was less than clear.

Conclusion: Do Elections Make Government Responsive?

Although election campaigns are far less successful in mobilizing voters and ensuring a high turnout today than they were in the past century, in a democracy, we expect elections to allow us to control government. Through them we can "throw the rascals out" and bring in new faces with better ideas, or so we think. But other than to change the party that controls government, do elections make a difference?

In the popular press, we hear a lot about "mandates." A president with a **mandate** is one who is clearly directed by the voters to take some particular course of action—reduce taxes or begin arms control talks, for example. George Bush had a substantial majority in his 1988 victory. But did he have a mandate? If so, what for? The campaign hardly talked about the budget deficit even though the election-day polls showed that this was the issue of concern to the largest group of voters. They, in turn, gave an overwhelming majority of *their* votes to Dukakis. On other issues, such as protecting the environment, Bush portrayed himself as a liberal. On many issues, ranging from abortion to day care to defense policy, the two candidates clearly differed. But did Bush's victory mean that he was to limit abortions, leave it to the states to fund day care, or continue the Reagan defense policy? Did he have a mandate on any of these issues?

Like most things in politics, the answer is not simple. Sometimes elections have an effect on policy, but often their effects are not clear-cut. In 1992, some voters chose a candidate on the basis of the economy, others the budget deficit issue, others on health care, and so on. Only one issue (the economy) was the primary concern of even a quarter of the voters.

In the surprising 1994 election, specific policy issues appeared to have little impact. Instead, voters appeared to be expressing their negative views about government generally. Though Republicans presented a "Contract with America," it is not clear which, if any, of the points of that contract, including a balanced budget amendment, term limits, cutting back welfare, spending cuts, and increasing military spending, have majority support.

Typically, even presidents are given a very vague mandate. Reagan's huge election victory in 1984 did not mean that the public agreed more with him than with Mondale on the issues, but mainly that they liked him and approved of the upturn in the economy. Still, over time a rough agreement develops between public attitudes and policies.[82]

It is primarily political parties that translate the mix of various issues into government action because voters' issue positions influence their party loyalties and their evaluations of candidates. A vote for the candidate of one's own party is usually a reflection of agreement on at least some important issues.[83] Once in office, the party in government helps sort out the issues for which there is a broad public mandate from those for which there is not.

Elections that appear to be mandates can become "mandates for disaster." More than one observer has pointed out that every twentieth-century president who has won election by 60% or more of the popular vote soon encountered serious political trouble. After his landslide in 1920, Warren Harding had his Teapot Dome scandal involving government corruption. Emboldened by his 1936 triumph, Franklin Roosevelt tried to pack the Supreme Court and was resoundingly defeated on that issue. Lyndon Johnson won by a landslide in 1964 and was soon mired in Vietnam. Richard Nixon smashed George McGovern in 1972 but then had to resign because of Watergate. Ronald Reagan's resounding victory in 1984 (a shade less than 60%) was followed by the blunders of the Iran-contra affair. Of these presidents, only Roosevelt was able to recover fully from his political misfortune. Reagan regained his personal popularity but seemed to have little influence on policy after Iran-contra. One recent observer has argued that these disasters come because "the euphoria induced by overwhelming support at the polls evidently loosens the president's grip on reality."[84]

Elections can point out new directions for government and allow citizens to make it responsive to their needs, but the fact that many individuals do not vote means that the new directions may not reflect either the needs or wishes of the public. If election turnout falls too far, the legitimacy of elections may be threatened. People may come to believe that election results do not reflect the wishes of the majority. For this reason, it was a healthy thing for our democratic system that election turnout increased in 1992, halting a slow and steady decline. If elections promote government responsiveness to those who participate in them, higher turnouts help increase responsiveness.

EPILOGUE

Bob Dole Resigns from the Senate

On Tuesday, June 11, 1996, Bob Dole gave up his Senate seat to devote his full attention to his campaign for president. Meeting the press, his colleagues, and his supporters in a room in the Hart Senate Office Building in May, Dole announced his intentions in a speech many hailed as one of his best ever. "I will seek the presidency with nothing to fall back on but the judgment of the people and nowhere to go but the White House or home," he said. "I will then stand before you without office or authority, a private citizen, a Kansan, an American, just a man."[85]

Reporters called the move a "big gamble,"[86] as it was, but the potential reward, winning the presidency, was worth the risk. Dole's campaign, according to one campaign staffer, got "a huge psychological lift. . . . Everyone who has been upset now has a reason to get optimistic."[87]

Nevertheless, Dole did not benefit much from his resignation. During the summer, he continued to trail President Clinton by between ten and twenty points in all the public opinion polls, despite being freed from his Senate duties so he could campaign full-time. But he could not find a message that attracted support. He proposed to cut income taxes fifteen percent and cut federal spending enough to balance the budget by 2002, but the electorate was not impressed.

Faced with a sagging campaign, Dole looked forward to a large convention "bounce" in the polls, enough to bring him within striking distance of Clinton. Dole's selection of former congressman and professional football player Jack Kemp as his running mate, Elizabeth Dole's impressive "Oprah"-like performance during the convention, and the generally positive tone of the Republican convention did indeed help Dole make up a lot of ground. Unfortunately, President Clinton benefitted from a similar "bounce" after the Democratic convention, leaving Dole as far behind as before on Labor Day.

Although some polls showed Dole edging closer to Clinton by the end of September, the president retained a significant edge. Two presidential debates, with Reform Party candidate H. Ross Perot excluded over his vigorous objections, gave Dole a chance to demonstrate how he compared to Clinton, but Clinton easily retained his lead.

At the end, the president won reelection rather handily. Dole even lost Florida and Arizona, states that had been considered safely Republican the year before. As the results came in, Dole retired from public life, no longer having his Senate seat to return to. He had bet all he had on the campaign, and he lost.

➤Key Terms

suffrage
Reconstruction
literacy tests
grandfather clause
Progressive reforms
motor voter law
presidential preference primaries
Super Tuesday
poll tax
white primary
Voting Rights Act
cumulative voting
Electoral College
faithless elector
retrospective voting
mandate

➤Further Reading

Lucius Barker, *Our Time Has Come: A Delegate's Diary of Jesse Jackson's 1984 Presidential Campaign* (Urbana, Ill.: University of Illinois Press, 1988); Adolph Reed, *The Jesse Jackson Phenomenon* (New Haven: Yale University Press, 1986). *Barker provides a unique account of Jackson's 1984 campaign from his viewpoint as a political scientist and Jackson delegate. Reed's account of Jackson is relatively unsympathetic.*

Taylor Branch, *Parting the Waters: America in the King Years* (New York: Simon & Schuster, 1988). *An excellent, readable account that illustrates the impact of political protest in changing America's race laws and to a considerable extent its attitudes about race.*

Robert Darcy, Susan Welch, and Janet Clark, *Women, Elections, and Representation* (Lincoln, Neb.: University of Nebraska Press, 1994). *An examination of the potential barriers faced by women candidates.*

Kathleen Hall Jamieson, *Packaging the Presidency* (New York: Oxford University Press, 1984). *The history and impact of presidential campaign advertising. Jamieson's followup,* Dirty Politics *(New York: Oxford University Press, 1992) argues that the media encourage negative and dishonest campaigning by their focus on the horse race.*

Allan Lichtman and Ken De Cell, *The Thirteen Keys to the Presidency* (Madison Books, 1990). *Focusing on 13 factors—"Keys"—that help explain presidential election outcomes, these authors correctly predict every election since 1860.*

Frances Fox Piven and Richard Cloward, *Why Americans Don't Vote* (New York: Pantheon, 1988). *The authors attribute nonvoting to restrictive registration laws and the disinterest of parties in mobilizing the working class.*

Theodore H. White, *The Making of the President*, 4 vols. (New York: Atheneum Publishers, 1961, 1965, 1969, 1973). *Journalistic accounts of presidential elections from 1960 to 1972. White was the first journalist to travel with the candidates and give an inside view of campaign strategy.*

➤Notes

1. Quoted in Alan Ehrenhalt, *Politics in America: The 100th Congress* (Washington, D.C.: CQ Press, 1987), p. 550.
2. Quoted in Jerelyn Eddings, "Reinventing Bob Dole," *U.S. News & World Report*, May 27, 1996, p. 28.
3. Steven V. Roberts, "The End of the Beginning," *U.S. News & World Report*, March 1, 1996, p. 30.
4. Sidney Blumenthal, "Comment: Our Next Prime Minister," *The New Yorker*, May 20, 1996, p. 5.
5. Eddings, "Reinventing Bob Dole," p. 32.
6. Robert Shogan, "Need for Dole Policy Agenda Is Taking on Greater Urgency," *The New York Times*, June 12, 1996, p. A13.
7. William Flanigan and Nancy H. Zingale, *Political Behavior of the American Electorate* (Boston: Allyn and Bacon, 1972), p. 13. See also Chilton Williamson, *American Suffrage from Property to Democracy* (Princeton, N.J.: Princeton University Press, 1960).
8. James MacGregor Burns, *Vineyard of Liberty* (New York, Alfred A. Knopf, 1982), p. 363.
9. August Meier and Elliot Rudwick, *From Plantation to Ghetto* (New York: Hill and Wang, 1966), p. 69.
10. Robert Darcy, Susan Welch, and Janet Clark, *Women, Elections, and Representation* (New York: Longman, 1987).
11. Grandfather clause: *Guinn v. United States,* 238 U.S. 347, (1915); white primary: *Smith v. Allwright*, 321 U.S. 649, (1944).
12. Data on black and white voter registration in the southern states are from the *Statistical Abstract of the United States* (Washington, D.C.: U.S. Bureau of the Census, various years).
13. All of Alabama, Mississippi, South Carolina, and Louisiana, substantial parts of North Carolina, and scattered counties in five northern states were included in the area covered by registrars. Any changes in election procedures had to be approved by the Department of Justice or the U.S. District Court for the District of Columbia. States or counties had to show a clear record of not discriminating for ten years before they could escape this supervision.
14. Richard Limpme, "Mass Mobilization or Government Intervention? The Growth of Black Registration in the South," *Journal of Politics* 57 (May, 1995), pp. 425–42.
15. Weston Kosova and Thomas Rosenstiel, "Strom Thurmond: Home on the Hill—Or Over It?" *Newsweek*, May 6, 1996, pp. 36–38.
16. Bob Benenson, "Arduous Ritual of Redistricting Ensures More Racial Diversity," *Congressional Quarterly Weekly Report* (October 24, 1992), p. 3385. For a very thorough review of the legal and behavioral impact of the Voting Rights Act, see Joseph P. Viteritti, "Unapportioned Justice: Local Elections Social Science and the Evolution of the Voting Rights Act," *Cornell Journal of Law and Public Policy* (Fall, 1994), pp. 210–270.
17. Darcy, Welch, and Clark, *Women, Elections and Representation.*
18. The discussion in this paragraph is drawn largely from Lois Banner, *Women in Modern America* (New York: Harcourt Brace Jovanovich, 1974), pp. 88–90; Glenn Firebaugh and Kevin Chen, "Vote Turnout of Nineteenth Amendment Women," *American Journal of Sociology* 100 (January 1995), pp. 972–996.
19. Richard Jensen, "American Election Campaigns: A Theoretical and Historical Typology," paper delivered at the 1968 Midwest Political Science Association Meeting, quoted in Walter Dean Burnham, *Critical Elections and the Mainsprings of American Politics* (New York: W. W. Norton, 1970), p. 73.
20. Frances Fox Piven and Richard A. Cloward, *Why Americans Don't Vote* (New York: Pantheon, 1988), p. 30.
21. Daniel Elazar, *American Federalism: A View from the States* (New York: Thomas Y. Crowell, 1972).
22. Piven and Cloward, *Why Americans Don't Vote,* p. 162. See also G. Bingham Powell, Jr., "American Voter Turnout in Comparative Perspective," *American Political Science Review* 80 (March 1986), pp. 17–44.
23. Piven and Cloward, *Why Americans Don't Vote,* pp. 17–18. Data are from 1980.
24. Powell, "American Voter Turnout," p. 30; Piven and Cloward, *Why Americans Don't Vote,* p. 119.
25. George Will, "In Defense of Nonvoting," *Newsweek,* October 10, 1983, p. 96.
26. Richard Morin, "The Dog Ate My Forms, and, Well, I Couldn't Find a Pen," *Washington Post National Weekly Edition,* November 5–11, 1990, p. 38.
27. Curtis Gans, quoted in Jack Germond and Jules Witcover, "Listen to the Voters—and Nonvoters," *Minneapolis Star Tribune,* November 26, 1988. This effect was foreshadowed by Michael J.

Robinson, "American Political Legitimacy in an Era of Electronic Journalism," in *Television as a Social Force,* ed. Douglass Cater and Richard Adler (New York: Praeger), 1975.

28. Ibid.

29. Priscilla Southwell, "Voter Turnout in the 1986 Congressional Elections," *American Politics Quarterly* 19 (January 1991), pp. 96–108; Stephen Ansolabehere, Shanto Iyengar, Adam Simon, and Nicholas Valentino, "Does Attack Advertising Demobilize the Electorate?" *American Political Science Review* 88 (December, 1994), pp. 829–838.

30. Curtis B. Gans, "The Empty Ballot Box," *Public Opinion* 1 (September/October 1978), pp. 54–57. See also Austin Ranney, *Channels of Power* (New York: Basic Books, 1983); and Richard Boyd, "The Effect of Election Calendars on Voter Turnout," paper presented at the Annual Meeting of the Midwest Political Science Association, April 1987, Chicago, Illinois.

31. Boyd, "The Effect of Election Calendars."

32. Ibid.

33. Piven and Cloward, *Why Americans Don't Vote,* p. 17.

34. Benjamin Ginsberg, *The Consequences of Consent: Elections, Citizen Control and Popular Acquiescence* (Reading, Mass.: Addison-Wesley, 1982), p. 37.

35. See Piven and Cloward, *Why Americans Don't Vote,* pp. 196–97 for illustrations of these kinds of informal barriers.

36. Raymond Wolfinger and Steven Rosenstone, *Who Votes?* (New Haven: Yale University Press, 1980), table 6.1.

37. James A. Barnes, "In Person: Marsha Nye Adler," *National Journal,* February 18, 1989, p. 420.

38. Peverill Squire, Raymond Wolfinger, and David Glass, "Residential Mobility and Voter Turnout," *American Political Science Review* 81 (March 1987), pp. 45–66. See also Samuel C. Patterson and Gregory A. Caldeira, "Mailing in the Vote: Correlates and Consequences of Absentee Voting," *American Journal of Political Science* 29 (November 1985), pp. 766–88.

39. For review of this literature, see John Petrocik, "Voter Turnout and Electoral Preference," in Kay Schlozman, ed., *Elections in America* (Boston: Allen & Unwin, 1987).

40. Kevin Phillips and Paul Blackman, *Electoral Reform and Voter Participation* (Stanford, Calif.: American Enterprise System, 1975).

41. Kim Quaile Hill, Jan Leighley, and Angela Hinton-Anderson, "Lower-Class Mobilization and Policy Linkage in the U.S. States," *American Journal of Political Science* 39 (February, 1995), pp. 75–86.

42. Anthony Downs, *An Economic Theory of Democracy* (New York: Harper & Row, 1957).

43. Morin, "The Dog Ate My Forms."

44. Kay Lehman Schlozmand, Sidney Verba, and Henry Brady, "Participation's Not a Paradox: The View from American Activists," *British Journal of Political Science* 25 (January, 1995), pp. 1–36.

45. Norman H. Nie, Sidney Verba, Henry Brady, Kay Lehman Schlozman, and Jane Junn, "Participation in America: Continuity and Change," paper presented at the Annual Meeting of the Midwest Political Science Association, Chicago, Illinois, April 1988. The standard work on American political participation is Sidney Verba and Norman Nie, *Participation in America* (New York: Harper & Row, 1972).

46. Ibid.

47. Paul Allen Beck and M. Kent Jennings, "Political Periods and Political Participation," *American Political Science Review* 73 (1979), pp. 737–50; Nie et al., "Participation in America."

48. The following discussion draws heavily from John Aldrich, *Before the Convention* (Chicago: University of Chicago Press, 1980).

49. Ibid. See also David Rohde, "Risk Bearing and Progressive Ambition: The Case of Members of the United States House of Representatives," *American Journal of Political Science* 23 (February 1979), pp. 1–26.

50. "Political Grapevine," *Time,* February 8, 1988, p. 30.

51. "The Fall Campaign," *Newsweek,* Election Extra (November/December 1984), p. 88.

52. Bruce Babbitt, "Bruce Babbitt's View from the Wayside," *Washington Post National Weekly Edition,* February 24–March 6, 1988, p. 24. The 999 days figure is from the *Congressional Quarterly Weekly Report,* February 1, 1992, p. 257.

53. Gerald Pomper and Susan Lederman, *Elections in America* (New York: Longman, 1980), chapter 7.

54. Michael J. Robinson, "Where's the Beef?," in Austin Ranney, ed., *The American Election of 1984* (Durham, N.C.: Duke University Press, 1985).

55. "Conventional Wisdom Watch," *Newsweek,* November 21, 1988, p. 18.

56. See *Congressional Quarterly,* July 23, 1988, p. 2015; Thomas Holbrook, "Campaigns, National Conventions and U.S. Presidential Elections," *American Journal of Political Science* 38 (November, 1994), pp. 973–98.

57. Benjamin Page and Richard Brody, "Policy Voting and the Electoral Process," *American Political Review* 66 (1972), pp. 979–95.

58. Thomas F. Patterson, *Mass Media Elections* (New York: Praeger, 1980), p. 3.

59. The discussion of the functions of the media relies heavily on the excellent summary found in Stephen Ansolabehere, Roy Behr, and Shanto Iyengar, "Mass Media and Elections," *American Politics Quarterly* 19 (January 1991), pp. 109–39.

60. *Congressional Quarterly Weekly Reports,* July 30, 1971, p. 1622, quoted in Ansolabehere, Behr, and Iyengar, "Mass Media and Elections," p. 109.

61. Martin Schram, *The Great American Video Game: Presidential Politics in the Television Age* (New York: William Morrow, 1987).

62. Patterson, *Mass Media Elections,* p. 4.

63. Robert McNeil, *The Influence of Television on American Politics* (New York: Harper & Row, 1968), p. 182.

64. Elisabeth Bumiller, "Selling Soup, Wine and Reagan," *Washington Post National Weekly Edition,* November 5, 1984, pp. 6–8.

65. Paul Taylor, "Pigsty Politics," *Washington Post National Weekly Edition,* February 13–19, 1989, p. 6.

66. Eileen Shields West, "Give 'em Hell These Days Is a Figure of Speech," *Smithsonian* (October 1988), pp. 149–51. The editorial was from the *Connecticut Courant.*

67. Charles Paul Freund, "But Then, Truth Has Never Been Important," *Washington Post National Weekly Edition,* November 7–13, 1988, p. 29.

68. Quoted in Freund, "But Then, Truth Has Never Been Important," p. 29.

69. Freund, "But Then, Truth Has Never Been Important," p. 29.

70. Richard Harwood, "The Press and the Making of a President," *Washington Post National Weekly Edition,* January 22–28, 1996, p. 28.

71. In her book, *Packaging the Presidency* (New York: Oxford University Press, 1984), Kathleen Jamieson also argued that there are checks on misleading advertising, but later ("Is the Truth Now Irrelevant in Presidential Campaigns?" see note 73) she argued that these checks did not work well in 1988. See Jamieson, *Dirty Politics: Deception, Distraction and Democracy* (New York: Oxford University Press, 1992).

72. Kathleen Hall Jamieson, "Is the Truth Now Irrelevant in Presidential Campaigns?" *Washington Post National Weekly Edition,* November 7–13, 1988, p. 28.

73. Stanley Kelley, Jr., *Interpreting Elections* (Princeton, N.J.: Princeton University Press, 1983); Stanley Kelley, Jr., and Thad W. Mirer, "The Simple Act of Voting," *American Political Science Review* 68 (June 1974), pp. 572–591.

74. J. Merrill Shanks and Warren E. Miller, "Partisanship, Policy and Performance: The Reagan Legacy in the 1988 Election," *British Journal of Political Science* 21 (April 1991), pp. 129–97; Eugene DeClerq, Thomas Hurley, and Norman Luttbeg, "Voting in American Presidential Elections," *American Political Quarterly* 3 (July 1975), updated and reported in David B. Hill and Norman Luttbeg, *Trends in American Electoral Behavior,* 2nd ed. (Itasca, Ill.: F. E. Peacock, 1983), p. 50.

75. Lee Sigelman, "If You Prick Us, Do We Not Bleed? If You Tickle Us, Do We Not Laugh? Jews and Pocketbook Voting," paper prepared for presentation at the 1990 American Political Science Meeting; Susan Welch and Lee Sigelman, "The Politics of Hispanic Americans," *Social Science Quarterly* (1991); *New York Times,* November 5, 1992, p. B9.

76. Paul Abramson, John H. Aldrich, and David Rohde, *Change and Continuity in the 1988 Elections* (Washington, D.C.: CQ Press, 1990), p. 172.

77. Ibid., p. 165.

78. Ibid.

79. Ibid., p. 170.

80. Morris Fiorina, *Retrospective Voting in American National Elections* (New Haven: Yale University Press, 1981).

81. Edward Tufte, *Political Control of the Economy* (Princeton, N.J.: Princeton University Press, 1978); Douglas Hibbs, "The Mass Public and Macroeconomic Performance," *American Journal of Political Science* 23 (November 1979), pp. 705–731; John Hibbing and John Alford, "The Electoral Impact of Economic Conditions: Who Is Held Responsible?" *American Journal of Political Science* 25 (1981), pp. 423–39.

82. Benjamin I. Page and Robert Shapiro, "Effects of Public Opinion on Policy," *American Political Science Review 77* (March 1983), pp. 175–90.

83. Abramson, Aldrich, and Rohde, *Change and Continuity.* See also Benjamin Page and Calvin C. Jones, "Reciprocal Effects of Party Preferences, Party Loyalties and the Vote," in Richard Niemi and Herbert Weisberg, *Controversies in Voting Behavior,* 2nd ed. (Washington, D.C.: CQ Press, 1984).

84. Arthur Schlesinger, Jr., *Wall Street Journal,* December 5, 1986.

85. Quoted in Richard Stengel, "The Hard Way," *Time,* May 27, 1996, p. 25.

86. Jerelyn Eddings, "Reinventing Bob Dole," *U.S. News and World Report,* May 27, 1996, p. 28.

87. Quoted in Eddings, "Reinventing Bob Dole," p. 29.

8 The Media

You Are There

Should You Pull Him Out of "the Closet"?

You are Michelangelo Signorile, a homosexual activist and a writer for *OutWeek,* a homosexual magazine. It is 1991 and you have to decide whether to publicize the fact that a high-ranking official in the Department of Defense is gay. You think that publication would be newsworthy given the department's stance against homosexuality in the military services. But you also are concerned about the ethical issues involved in publicizing this aspect of the person's private life.

Your own background in the media and in the movement led you to hold these conflicting views. After college you worked for a public relations firm with clients in the entertainment business. When your clients sought publicity for their latest projects, you fed tidbits of information about them to the writers of gossip columns in newspapers. In this way, you planted their names in these columns. When the AIDS epidemic spread in the 1980s, you joined ACT UP (AIDS Coalition To Unleash Power), a group that used protest to gain publicity for its demands that the government invest more resources in the fight against the epidemic.

You know from your public relations work that gossip columnists prattle on about anything in a celebrity's private life except a celebrity's homosexuality. That is taboo. Columnists talk about a straight actor's affairs but not a gay actor's relationships. Sometimes they even pretend that a gay actor is straight by writing that he or she is "dating" someone of the opposite sex. The result, you feel, is to send a message that homosexuality is "so utterly grotesque that it should never be discussed."[1]

This message, you believe, reflects an unconscious conspiracy to keep homosexuals locked in "the closet"—that is, to keep them from revealing their sexual identity, sometimes even to their closest friends and relatives. You think this conspiracy is perpetuated by the government, the media, and the entertainment industry—even including some powerful homosexuals in these institutions who go along out of fear that their power, prestige, and income would plummet if the truth were revealed.

In recent years some gays have tried to reveal the homosexuality of other gays, but the mainstream media normally have not reported the revelations. In 1990 activists held a press conference on the steps of the Capitol and identified three members of the Senate and five members of the House of Representatives as gay. Activists also altered a billboard of an incumbent senator running for reelection—"Closeted Gay. Living a Lie. Voting to Oppress"—and demonstrated outside the homes of some members. But most media did not report these efforts.[2] (In 1989 the media did address the homosexuality of a representative who had a long relationship with a male prostitute who operated out of the member's apartment. The journalists considered this situation scandalous and covered it.)

You were sympathetic with these efforts, and, still disgusted by the gossip columnists' practice of hiding the homosexuality of entertainers, you criticized their practice and implied that two columnists themselves were homosexuals. Your exposé prompted another writer to compare you with Senator Joseph McCarthy

CONTINUED 

Journalists accompany American troops as they land in Haiti in 1994.

OUTLINE

The Media State

Roles of the Media

Concentration of the Media

Atomization of the Media

Relationship between the Media and Politicians

Symbiotic Relationship

Adversarial Relationship

Relationship between the Media and Recent Administrations

Relationship between the Media and Congress

Bias of the Media

Political Bias

Commercial Bias

Impact of the Media on Politics

Impact on the Public Agenda

Impact on Public Opinion

Impact on Political Parties and Elections

Conclusion: Are the Media Responsive?

(R.-Wis.), who shrilly and often falsely accused government employees of being communists in the 1950s.

Other journalists see no sinister motives behind the silence on homosexuality. They deny the existence of any conspiracy to keep homosexuals locked in "the closet." They say they do not publicize a person's homosexuality because of the likely consequences of the public's prejudices.

Now you have information that an assistant secretary of defense in the Bush administration is gay. You have no doubt about the accuracy of the information. Should you report it in *OutWeek*?

The official has a high position and considerable visibility. During the recent Persian Gulf War, he was the primary spokesman for the department.

Since the war the department's policy of discharging gay and lesbian military personnel has come under heavy fire. In the past decade the Pentagon has discharged perhaps 13,000 soldiers, sailors, airmen and women, and marines for homosexuality.[3] This policy rankles you and others in the gay and lesbian community. But you do not know whether the assistant secretary has any influence over the policy or whether he might be working on the inside to overturn it. Do these factors matter?

Although the policy does not apply to civilian officials, such as the assistant secretary, does the situation—being a gay spokesman for a department that discharges gay and lesbian personnel—reflect hypocrisy? If so, is the hypocrisy sufficient for you to reveal his homosexuality?

Or should a concern for privacy override your distaste of hypocrisy? There is no legal right to privacy for one's sexuality, but should there be an ethical right? Many gays think there should be. One called privacy "the central protection" for gays. Forsaking it would cause anguish for people and would ignore the complexities of their lives. Perhaps there are good reasons to allow some to remain in "the closet."[4]

Or do the media routinely disregard privacy to such an extent that it is irrelevant to consider? Reporters already cover out-of-wedlock births, abortions, affairs, and divorces of public figures. Is it pointless to try drawing the line at homosexuality?

Or are the media generally so invasive of people's private lives that their current practices should not serve as a guide for covering homosexuality? Reporting of people's "scandalous" conduct used to focus on their malfeasance or incompetence in public office. Now it has extended to their private behavior, including instances that occurred before they became public officials. Sometimes it has extended to their aides, who were not elected and do not hold public office. In the past decade officials or candidates have been exposed for having a "shotgun" wedding, having affairs while married, smoking marijuana while in college, attending parties where others used cocaine, telling racist or sexist jokes, and a variety of other things.[5] Should people be defined publicly according to the way they lead their private lives or solely according to the way they perform their jobs? If some aspects of their private lives are relevant, is their sexual identity as heterosexual or homosexual relevant?

In this debate, it is not clear whether privacy helps or hurts the lives of gays. Keeping homosexuality secret certainly props up the walls of "the closet." This practice might make life more difficult for gay teenagers, who see few gay adults and who feel isolated. But challenging this practice might complicate the already difficult lives of gay adults still in "the closet."

So what do you do with the information?

Michelangelo Signorile

A "medium" transmits something. The mass media—which include newspapers, magazines, books, radio, television, movies, and records—transmit communications to masses of people.

Although the media do not constitute a branch of government or even an organization established to influence government, such as a political party or interest group, they have an impact on government. In addition to providing entertainment, the media provide political information, sometimes directly through the news, other times indirectly in a program or story addressing a public problem such as crime or drugs. Either way, people obtain most of their information about government and politics from the media.

➤The Media State

The media have developed and flourished to an extent the Founders could not have envisioned. As one political scientist noted, the media have become "pervasive . . . and atmospheric, an element of the air we breathe."[6] Without exaggeration, another observer concluded, "Ancient Sparta was a military state. John Calvin's Geneva was a religious state. Mid-nineteenth century England was Europe's first industrial state, and the contemporary United States is the world's first media state."[7]

Americans spend more time being exposed to the media than doing anything else. In a year, according to one calculation, the average full-time worker puts in 1,824 hours on the job, 2,737 hours in bed, and 3,256 hours exposed to the media (in a day, almost 9 hours exposed to the media).[8] Seventy-seven percent of adults read newspapers; the average person does so for three-and-a-half hours a week. The average person also reads two magazines for one-and-a-half hours a week.[9] Eighty-eight percent of American homes have a radio, and 98% have a television.[10] The average adult watches television three hours a day and the average child four. By the time the average child graduates from high school, he or she has spent more time in front of the tube than in class.[11] By the time the average American dies, he or she has spent one-and-a-half years just watching television commercials.[12]

Roles of the Media

American newspapers, which originated in colonial times, were the only regular media in the country for almost two centuries. Although newspapers gained readers, political magazines appeared in the nineteenth century, and newsweeklies began in the 1920s, there were no "mass media" until the advent of the broadcast media. Radio, which became popular in the 1920s, and television, which became popular in the 1950s, reached people who could not or would not read.

People bought television sets to watch entertainment programs, but they also began to watch newscasts. At first the newscasts, lasting only 15 minutes and consisting solely of an anchor and a few correspondents talking, were not compelling. In 1963 the networks expanded the time to 30 minutes and altered the format to emphasize visual interest. That year, for the first time, people said they got more political information from television than from any other source.

As television grew in popularity, newspapers waned. People did not need them for the headlines anymore. Although newspapers began to provide in-depth analysis of news, which television did not, they struggled for readers and advertisers, and some folded.

These trends continued. In the 1970s and 1980s, the number of adults in the country increased 34% and the number of households increased 41%, but the circulation of daily newspapers remained stagnant.[13] The number of young adults (from 18 through 29) who are regular readers of daily newspapers declined the most—50% in the last two decades. Now only one-third are regular readers.[14]

Consequently, television has become the most important of the media for politics. According to surveys, people pay more attention to it and put more faith in it than in other media. This makes positive coverage on television essential for politicians.

Nevertheless, television has not fully eclipsed newspapers. Most people who say they get the bulk of their political information from television admit they do not watch the news daily, whereas more people who get the bulk of their political information from newspapers read the news sections daily. Because newspapers require more effort or provide more depth, they leave a longer-lasting impression; people remember what they read in newspapers better than what they watch on television.[15]

Moreover, national newspapers such as the *New York Times* and *Washington Post,* which blanket the country with in-depth international and national news, influence opinion leaders who, in turn, influence other persons.

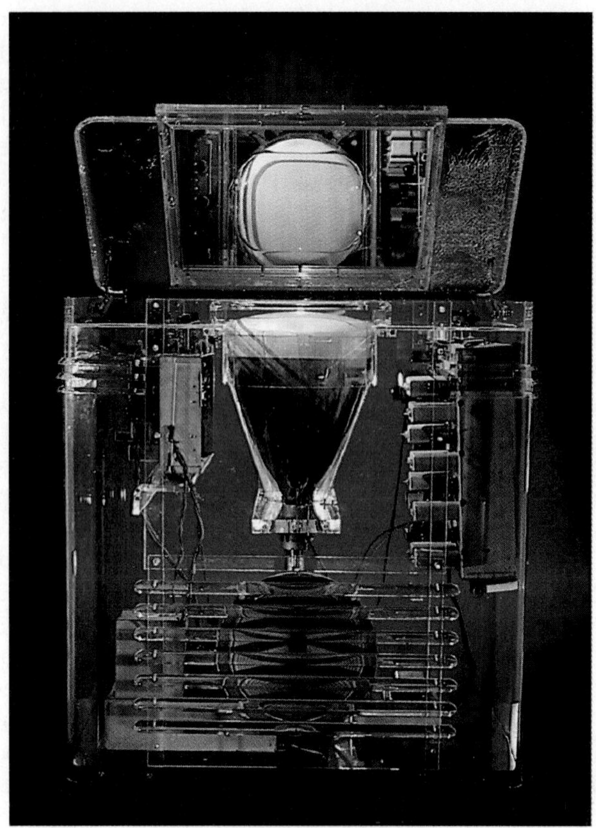

This television made its debut in the Hall of Television at the New York World's Fair in 1939. President Franklin Roosevelt opened the fair by appearing on the tiny screen (top).

Coverage of the Persian Gulf War in 1991 reflected the contemporary roles of broadcast and print journalism. Although the networks had little film footage of the war itself, they provided immediacy and drama. When the Scud missile attacks threatened, reporters on the scene announced, "There go the sirens. We'll probably have an attack here in five minutes." Reporters in Israel, where poison gas attacks were feared, broadcast while putting on gas masks or scurrying to sealed rooms. The live reports, beamed via satellite, often were unedited and rough yet compelling, almost hypnotic, for many viewers. But they were also fragmentary and sometimes contradictory. Newspapers presented more complete and accurate accounts the next day.

Concentration of the Media

In the late nineteenth century, journalism started to become big business, and news organizations began to focus less on crusading for their causes and more on maximizing their profits.[16] Although for decades most media remained local media, owned by local individuals or companies, in the middle twentieth century economic pressures forced many organizations to join large chains or conglomerates. These chains and conglomerates came to dominate the business and to constitute a national media.[17]

Although media in this country, compared with those in other Western democracies, remain relatively decentralized—in the United States there are approximately 1,700 daily newspapers, 10,800 radio stations, and 1,600 television stations[18]—these numbers are misleading. Chains own papers that have over 70% of the circulation in the country.[19] Further, in most cities with more than one paper, economic pressures have caused competing papers to merge. As a result, by 1991 only 12 cities had separately owned, fully competitive papers, compared with 35 a decade earlier.[20]

Media conglomerates own newspapers, magazines, radio stations, and television stations. The result is that just 10 corporations control the following:

- 58 newspapers, including the *New York Times, Washington Post, Los Angeles Times,* and *The Wall Street Journal;*
- 59 magazines, including *Time* and *Newsweek;*
- 41 book publishers;
- 3 major radio and television networks;
- 62 radio stations;
- 34 television stations;
- 201 cable television systems; and
- 20 record companies.[21]

Similarly, a small number of businesses garner a disproportionate amount of revenue. Six magazine companies, among 11,000 in the country, account for half the magazine revenue, and 6 book publishers, among 2,500 in the country, account for more than half the book revenue.[22] Fifty radio stations (of 10,800) generate half the radio profits.[23]

These trends are likely to continue because the media business is big business. The media industry is the nation's ninth largest, just below aerospace and just above electronics equipment.[24] And the industry is growing. Conglomerates are combining computer operations, cable systems, and telephone systems with their publishing and broadcasting businesses. These huge corporations are competing with each other to control the flow of information and delivery of entertainment throughout the country and even the world. For example, in 1995 Disney, the world's largest telecommunications corporation, bought ABC; and Time Warner, the world's second largest telecommunications corporation, merged with Turner Broadcasting, which owns CNN. Microsoft, the computer software giant, linked with NBC to launch a 24-hour news service on cable and on the Internet.

Equally important as the growth of chains and conglomerates is the dominance of a few sources of news. One wire service—AP—supplies the international and national news for most newspapers. Three magazines—*Newsweek, Time,* and *U.S. News and World Report*—control the market of news magazines. Four radio networks—ABC, CBS, NBC, and Mutual—furnish the news for most radio listeners, and four television networks—ABC, CBS, NBC, and CNN—furnish the news for most television viewers. Consequently, the media present quite homogeneous international and national news.

Atomization of the Media

Despite the growing concentration of the media during the twentieth century, a quite different trend—the atomization of the media—also has been developing in recent years. Where concentration of the media led to a national media, atomization of the media is fragmenting the influence of this national media. The major newspapers and broadcast networks are beginning to lose their dominance, while other media, some not even considered news organizations, are starting to play a significant role in politics.

Viewership of network news declined through the 1980s. In 1991 it reached its lowest mark since 1961.[25] The networks offer newsmagazine shows, such as CBS's "60 Minutes," to boost ratings. Yet the networks struggle to retain viewers.

During the same years, viewership of local news increased to a level half again as large as that of network news.[26] Technological innovations enable local stations to present more compelling newscasts than before. Many stations offer combined local and national newscasts by joining a consortium of other stations, spread across the country but linked by satellite, to share coverage of events of national interest.

Expansion of cable television threatens the networks further. Now reaching 60% of American households, cable offers many competing channels and promises more specialized programs. Although much of cable's menu duplicates the networks' (and reflects Bruce Springsteen's complaint, "57 Channels, and Nothin' On"), its offerings will become increasingly focused—"narrowcasting" that will appeal to small segments of the audience, rather than the networks' broadcasting that is designed to appeal to the general audience.

Already CNN, a 24-hour news station on two channels, attracts a large audience, and C-SPAN, which covers Congress at length and with little editing on two channels, has a significant audience. Even MTV, the music channel, offers some coverage of politics in formats to attract young viewers.

Other national cable networks cater to blacks and to Hispanics. A cable system in Los Angeles and New York City caters to Jews. A cable channel in California broadcasts in Chinese, one in Hawaii broadcasts in Japanese, while one in Connecticut and Massachusetts broadcasts in Portuguese. Stations in New York City also program in Greek, Hindi, and Korean.

These developments reflect a more diverse country than the one that existed when television was born, and they pose a serious challenge to the networks. "Forty years ago," observed the media critic for *Rolling Stone,* "television news consisted of middle-aged white men reading . . . news into a camera. Today, network news consists of middle-aged white men reading . . . news into a camera."[27]

The popularity of radio and television talk shows also threatens the dominance of major newspapers and broadcast networks. Many radio stations have some talk shows, and about 10% of the stations have an all-talk format, the fastest growing format in the business.[28] According to one 1993 survey, 17% percent of the public say they listen to these shows regularly; 25% more say they listen sometimes. (Eleven percent have tried to call in; 6% have gotten on the air.)[29] According to another 1993 survey, 44% of the public said these shows are their primary source of political information.[30] With millions of people listening, talk radio is a force in politics. It attracts a middle-class audience that serves as a national jury on governmental controversies.

The atomization of the media was especially apparent during the 1992 presidential campaign. *The Star,* a supermarket tabloid, published allegations by Gennifer Flowers, a former nightclub singer, that she had had a 12-year affair with Bill Clinton while he was governor of Arkansas. The major media hesitated repeating the *Star*'s story—they had nothing but scorn for the tabloids which, they insisted, did not practice true journalism—but within days the networks and most newspapers gave in, under the pretense of de-

New Populism
Talk Radio

Perhaps no phenomenon more clearly reflects new populism than the rise and popularity of talk radio. Both the hosts and the callers to these shows demonstrate righteous anger toward the government and public officials and an intense desire to change their practices and policies.

Hosts

A survey of 112 hosts in the 100 largest media markets in the country found that a majority of hosts describe themselves as moderates, with a minority of equal numbers of liberals and conservatives. A majority also call themselves independents, with a minority of partisans, slightly more of whom lean toward the Democrats than toward the Republicans. In these ways the hosts are roughly representative of the American public.[1]

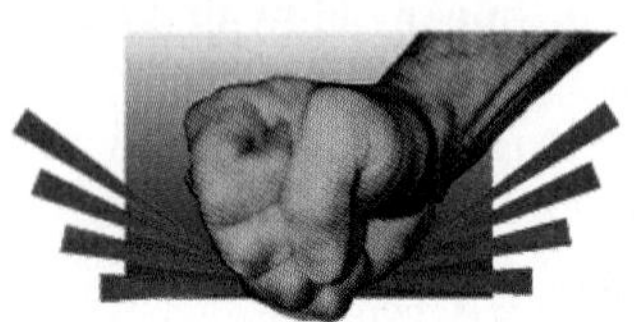

The hosts, however, are more educated and less religious than the public. (Thirty percent of the hosts say they have no religious affiliation, whereas only 10% of the population says this.) The hosts also are more libertarian than the public. They are more likely to oppose restrictions on abortion and on homosexuals teaching in public schools or serving in the military, and they are more likely to oppose banning books from school libraries and reinstating prayers in school classes.

Significantly, the hosts are far more critical of the government and its representatives than the public is. Although more voted for Clinton than for Bush or Perot in 1992, they expressed more criticism of Clinton and of Congress (before the elections of 1994) than the public did.

Thus, the hosts do not fit neatly into the usual liberal and conservative categories. They reflect some attitudes of each.

But these conclusions from the survey are somewhat misleading, because the survey treats all hosts equally. Conservative hosts have a much larger audience, and therefore a considerably greater influence, than liberal hosts.[2] Rush Limbaugh, for example, has the most popular show, with 4.5 million listeners tuning in to 600 stations across the country. (And this does not include his talk television show.)[3]

Callers

The callers are more likely to be conservatives than liberals and more likely to be Republicans than Democrats. In fact, conservatives and Republicans are more than twice as likely to get on the air. (And men are almost twice as likely to get on the air as women.)[4]

Almost all the hosts acknowledge that their callers are not typical of the people in their city. The hosts say that their callers are more critical of Congress, the Democratic party, and President Clinton (and far more critical of Hillary Clinton).[5] They are also more opposed to abortion and more hostile to homosexuals. But, most important, the hosts report that their callers reflect an angrier tone than do most people.

Impact

With these attitudes, the hosts and callers have had a considerable impact on politics in recent years. When Congress voted itself a substantial pay raise in 1988, several hosts decided to coordinate an attack. They sent faxes to other stations, and the hosts urged listeners to phone or fax their representatives and to send tea bags to them. The deluge caused Congress to postpone and scale back the raise.

When *USA Today* reported congressional check kiting in 1992, talk shows turned to the issue. Most people ignored the newspapers' explanation that members who overdrew their checking accounts at the House of Representatives "bank" essentially had borrowed money from each other rather than taken any from the taxpayers. Cued by talk show hosts, people considered these overdrafts from the House "bank" equivalent to overdrafts from their own checking accounts. The vitriol prompted the retirement of some members and the reelection defeat of others.

When it came out that President Clinton's first choice for attorney general—Zoe Baird, a $500,000 a year corporate lawyer—and her husband had hired illegal aliens to provide day care for their children, listeners contacted their senators. As calls mounted, it became clear that she could not be confirmed and her nomination was withdrawn.

For all three incidents, citizens' anger was fueled by talk shows reflecting middle-class indignation that officials were making too much money, getting too many benefits, and not playing by the rules other people had to play by. Although the major media initially had not considered these incidents important and had not covered them prominently, listeners of the talk shows had a different opinion.

Listeners' outrage has also influenced more substantive policies. When a girl was murdered by a career criminal in California, the host of a talk show drafted the outline of the "three strikes and you're out" sentencing policy (which mandates life in prison for persons convicted of three felonies).[6] After the idea caught on in California, it spread to the rest of the country through other talk shows. Although many criminal justice experts said the policy would provide minimal benefit and would cause some harm and considerable expense for society, the torrent of opinion prompted President Clinton and Congress to adopt the policy for the federal courts.

Talk radio might have had an impact on politics in other ways as well. In particular, it might have contributed to Republican victories in the congressional elections in 1994. Voters nationwide favored Republicans by just 2%, but voters who were talk-radio listeners favored Republicans by 28%.[7] Although people who tune in talk radio are disproportionately Republicans (26% of Republicans compared with 14% of independents and 12% of Democrats listen regularly, and 50% of Republicans compared with 41% of independents and 35% of Democrats listen sometimes),[8] the size of this difference suggests that the dynamics of talk radio might have persuaded some listeners to support Republicans or at least galvanized some listeners who already leaned toward Republicans to vote. It is possible that enough listeners did so in close races that they enabled the Republicans to win and wrest control of Congress from the Democrats.

Source: *Washington Post National Weekly Edition*, July 19–23, 1993, p. 37.

The anger over the airwaves might have a broader impact on society also. "When I started out in 1979," a host in Washington, D.C. recalls, "I believed that talk radio could become a unifying force, a way to help bridge our differences through the sharing of ideas and knowledge." But in recent years, she laments, "talk radio has become one more force to separate rather than unite us."[9] Stations encourage hosts to have strong views and make sharp attacks, rather than to promote full discussion of complex issues, because the former is entertaining—and boosts the ratings for the show—even if it heightens the hostility in society.

Some hosts have followed this approach to the extreme. A Colorado Springs host urged listeners to take their guns to Washington to protest proposals to ban assault weapons. (Not long after, a deranged Colorado Springs man did take his gun to Washington and shot at the White House.) A Phoenix host, in a show about Jim Brady, the press secretary for President Reagan who was wounded when the President was shot, criticized Brady's wife, who has campaigned for gun control. "You know," the host said, "she ought to be put down. A humane shot at a veterinarian's would be an easy way to do it. Because of all her barking and complaining, she really needs to be put down."[10] G. Gordon Liddy, one of the Watergate burglars and now a popular host, advised listeners to shoot for the head of federal agents because they wear bulletproof vests.

1. Nationwide sample from May and June, 1993. "The Vocal Minority in American Politics," Times Mirror Center for the People and the Press, Washington, D.C., July, 1993.
2. Richard Corliss, "Look Who's Talking," *Time,* January 23, 1995, p. 22.
3. David Remnick, "Radio Free Limbaugh," *Washington Post National Weekly Edition,* February 28–March 6, 1994, p. 23.
4. "The Vocal Minority in American Politics," pp. 9–10.
5. This survey was conducted before the Whitewater investigation and the proposals for health care reform led to more criticism of Hillary Clinton.
6. Robert Wright, "Hyper Democracy," *Time,* January 23, 1995, p. 16.
7. "Victory by the Numbers," *Time,* November 21, 1994, p. 64.
8. "The Vocal Minority in American Politics," pp. 7–8.
9. Diane Rehm, "Can We Talk about Talk Radio?" *Washington Post National Weekly Edition,* September 19–25, 1994, p. 23.
10. Timothy Egan, "Talk Radio or Hate Radio? Critics Assail Some Hosts," *New York Times* (January 1, 1995), p. 11.

bating the propriety of reporting personal matters. The Clintons felt obligated to appear on "60 Minutes" to refute the allegations (while sidestepping the question of whether he had ever committed adultery). Whereupon Flowers appeared on "A Current Affair," a syndicated television show, rated Clinton as a lover on a scale from 1 to 10, and sang "Stand By Your Man." Thus, Flowers did not need to take her story to the major media; she got the tabloid media to tell it and pay her for it (an estimated $150,000 by the *Star* alone).[31] The continuing coverage precipitated a drop in Clinton's standing during the presidential primaries.

Then Ross Perot announced his candidacy for president on CNN's "Larry King Live," a talk show, rather than through a press conference with the networks. Other candidates followed on various talk shows. Clinton fielded questions on the "Phil Donahue Show" and on MTV, and played the saxophone on the "Arsenio Hall Show." President Bush,

Ross Perot jokes during preparation for the Larry King show.

who initially called these appearances "weird," eventually courted sports fans on ESPN and country music fans on the Nashville Network.

Candidates saw these shows as ways to communicate with the voters without having their messages "filtered"—that is, condensed, simplified, distorted, or challenged—by the press. Clinton even bought television time for half-hour shows, "electronic town meetings," in which he took questions from voters in several cities.

Because of the expanding role of fringe media, mainstream journalists glimpse a shrinking role for themselves. They no longer monopolize the market of political information; they no longer control the gates through which such information must pass.

In fact, according to one journalism professor, many citizens see no purpose in having journalists intervene in politics. "Max in Seattle feels as well represented by Julie's question from Houston as he would be by Sam Donaldson's inquiry from New York." (Actually, Max might prefer Julie's to Sam Donaldson's. Many citizens are annoyed by the "cult of toughness" among journalists that leads them to challenge public figures with "a level of shamelessness and aggression that ordinary people cannot manage.")[32]

Although the new use of media may be more democratic, in appealing to a broader segment of the population and allowing participation by a portion of the population, it also is less analytical. Most citizens are not versed in issues or knowledgeable about candidates and officials to the extent that professional journalists are. Many citizens are not able to separate the blarney from the gospel truth when candidates and officials open their mouths.

This problem is aggravated by the fact that some fringe media are less than scrupulous about the accuracy of the information they disseminate. In their quest for an audience, some fringe media pay for stories, possibly encouraging people to lie for the money; many fringe media sensationalize stories, possibly distorting the truth. Of course, the mainstream media also are commercial enterprises subject to the pressures of the marketplace (as will be addressed later in the chapter). However, these established media at the same time are subject to the pressures of tradition. Reporters at major newspapers and broadcast networks often speak of their responsibility to follow certain journalistic norms, while members of the fringe media sometimes reflect the views of a radio talk show host who asserts, "The news isn't sacred to me. It's entertainment . . . designed to revel in the agony of others."[33]

With such views, concern for the accuracy of information is not foremost. For example, when Vince Foster, deputy counsel for President Clinton, apparently committed suicide in a park, a right-wing group sent a fax to news organizations linking the suicide to the Whitewater land deal. The group passed the rumor that Foster died at an administration "safe house" and later was moved to the Washington park. Talk show host Rush Limbaugh reported the rumor. Other talk show hosts repeated it, while some added the rumor that Foster was murdered. A few financial speculators spread the rumors as a way to manipulate the stock market, and the next day newspaper business sections repeated the rumors in articles about their effect on the stock market. Thus, the rumors, through announcement and repetition by the media, came to seem true to many people—yet they remained just rumors.[34]

➤Relationship Between the Media and Politicians

"Politicians live—and sometimes die—by the press. The press lives by politicians," according to a former presidential aide. "This relationship is at the center of our national life."[35]

Politicians and journalists need each other. Politicians need journalists in order to reach the public and to receive feedback from the public. They scan the major newspapers in the morning and the network newscasts in the evening. President Lyndon Johnson watched three network newscasts on three televisions simultaneously. Journalists need politicians in order to cover government. They seek a steady stream of fresh information to fill their news columns and newscasts. Just two days after the election of Bill Clinton, a chorus of reporters complained of a "news blackout" by the incoming administration.[36] A week later the chorus forced the president-elect to call a press conference to pacify the press corps, though he had no news yet and hardly any voice after the long campaign.[37]

The close relationship between the media and politicians is both a **symbiotic relationship,** meaning they use each other for their mutual advantage, and an **adversarial relationship,** meaning they fight each other.

Symbiotic Relationship

President Lyndon Johnson told individual reporters, "You help me and I'll help make you a big man in your profession." He gave exclusive interviews, told outrageous tales, and invited reporters to bunk overnight at his Texas ranch.[38] In return he expected favorable coverage.

Reporters get information from politicians in various ways. Some reporters are assigned to monitor **beats.** Washington beats include the White House, Congress, Supreme Court, State Department, Defense Department, and some other departments and agencies. Other reporters are assigned to cover specialized subjects, such as economics, environmental problems, and energy issues, which are addressed by several branches, departments, or agencies.

The government has press secretaries and public information officers who provide reporters with ideas and information for stories. The number of these officials is significant; in one recent year the Defense Department employed almost 1,500 people just to handle press relations.[39]

The government supplies reporters with a variety of news sources, including copies of speeches, summaries of committee meetings, news releases, and news briefings about current events. Officials also grant interviews, hold press conferences, and stage "media events." The vast majority of reporters rely on these sources rather than engage in more difficult and time-consuming investigative reporting.

Interviews show the symbiotic nature of the relationship between reporters and politicians. During the early months of the Reagan presidency, *Washington Post* writer William Greider had a series of 18 off-the-record meetings with budget director David Stockman. Greider recounted:

> Stockman and I were participating in a fairly routine transaction of Washington, a form of submerged communication which takes place regularly between selected members of the press and the highest officials of government. Our mutual motivation, despite our different interests, was crassly self-serving. It did not need to be spelled out between us. I would use him and he would use me. . . . I had established a valuable peephole on the inner policy debates of the new administration. And the young budget director had established a valuable connection with an important newspaper. I would get a jump on the unfolding strategies and decisions. He would be able to prod and influence the focus of our coverage, to communicate his views and positions under the cover of our "off the record" arrangement, to make known harsh assessments that a public official would not dare to voice in the more formal setting of a press conference, speech, or "on the record" interview.[40]

Interviews can result in **leaks**—disclosures of information some officials want to keep secret. Other officials in the administration, Congress, or bureaucracy use leaks for many reasons. Officials in the administration might leak information about a proposed policy to test the water for it, without committing themselves or their offices to it, in case intense opposition surfaces. Or they might leak to warn their president or fellow officials about the foolishness of a pending policy. Or, engaged in infighting with other officials, they might leak to make the competitors or their policies look bad. Or officials who feel slighted might leak to call attention to their ideas or to force public debates rather than closed-door decisions on issues.

Most presidents get enraged by leaks. Reagan said he was "up to my keister" in leaks, and Nixon established a "plumbers" unit to plug leaks by wiretapping aides and reporters to hear where leaks were coming from. However, despite accusations that leaks are from low-level employees in the opposite party, most are from high-ranking officials in the same party. "The ship of state," one experienced reporter noted, "is the only kind of ship that leaks mainly from the top."[41]

During the Vietnam War, President Lyndon Johnson himself ordered an aide to leak the charge that steel companies were "profiteering" from the war. After an executive complained, Johnson assured him that the statement was inappropriate and that "if I find out some damn fool aide did it, I'll fire the sonuvabitch!"[42]

In the presidential campaign of 1988, there was much speculation about whom George Bush would choose to be his running mate. Bush's campaign manager, James Baker, leaked the fact that Senator

The pervasiveness of the media has increased tremendously. Andrew Jackson was the first president to have his photograph taken. Modern presidents must expect to have their photograph taken almost anywhere at almost any time.

Dan Quayle was one of the finalists. Baker saw this as a way to discourage Bush from choosing Quayle; he thought once the press published this fact, there would be so much opposition that Bush would have to select someone else. (Baker's ploy failed because the press did not take the idea seriously enough to criticize it.)[43]

After President Bush nominated Clarence Thomas to the Supreme Court, a Republican leaked the fact that Thomas had experimented with marijuana in college. The purpose was to innoculate Thomas from the greater controversy that might arise if the press discovered and revealed this fact closer to the vote on confirmation.[44] Then a Democrat, presumably, leaked the FBI report on Anita Hill's charges that Thomas sexually harassed her. The report had been secret and Hill had refused to go public before. Once the information came to light, Hill felt forced to go public, and the Senate nearly denied confirmation.

When reporters get information before other reporters, they can **scoop** them. In 1980 NBC correspondent Chris Wallace scooped his colleagues in reporting that Reagan would choose Bush as his running mate. Although Wallace was first by just seconds, this helped him win a promotion to NBC White House correspondent.[45] Usually, however, reporters are reluctant to be out front if their information is controversial. Reporters who are willing to be out front often find their editors reluctant. "There is an institutional reluctance to take on some of these stories," an investigative reporter for a national newspaper said. The editors "don't want to get too far ahead of the curve." Most journalists are more comfortable following the pack than scooping it.[46]

The interdependence between reporters and politicians can result in less news for the public. Reporters who want to continue to receive information and rub shoulders with powerful politicians may feel obligated to treat their sources favorably or at least not as skeptically as they treat others. When the Watergate burglary occurred, most newspapers dismissed it as an inconsequential "caper." With their close ties to high officials, reporters in the Washington press corps did not dig to unearth the story behind the burglary. Instead, two young reporters—Bob Woodward and Carl Bernstein—who covered local news for the *Washington Post* got the story. As one of the *Post's* editors noted, they were not part of "the Establishment"; they did not mind embarrassing administration officials.

Before the Iran-contra affair came to light, some reporters relied on Lt. Col. Oliver North for information. Although many reporters suspected that North was involved in supplying the contras with arms despite congressional restrictions on such aid, North had been a valuable source and, as one reporter remarked, "his romantic derring-do and colorful antics made him more fun to talk to than other bureaucrats."[47] Reporters did not investigate North's involvement until the story broke in an obscure Lebanese magazine. If they had been willing to sacrifice their access to him, they could have publicized the affair far sooner.

Press conferences also show the symbiotic nature of the media-politician relationship. Theodore Roosevelt, the first president who cultivated close ties to correspondents, started the **presidential press conference.**[48] He held irregular and informal sessions while being shaved. Later presidents, uncomfortable with the "cross-examination," offered few sessions and demanded questions in advance.[49] But Franklin Roosevelt realized that the press conference could help him reach the public. Newspaper publishers detested him and criticized him in editorials, but by holding frequent sessions and permitting questions on the spot he provided a steady stream of news, which editors felt obligated to publish. This news publicized his policies and his efforts to implement them.

John Kennedy saw that the press conference could help him reach the public more directly, by allowing the networks to televise it live.[50] Then editors could not filter his remarks.

Televising a press conference seems inherently contradictory. If a president wants to answer reporters, he can do so in private. If he wants to communicate with the public, he can do so in a formal speech, without risking an embarrassing question. So why would a president opt for a televised press conference? He might perform better in the less formal setting of a press conference. Or, like the youthful Kennedy, he might feel a need to demonstrate his competence to the watchful public.[51] With his intellect and wit, Kennedy expected to excel at these, and he did.

As a result, presidents and their aides transformed the conference into a carefully orchestrated media show. Now an administration schedules a conference when it wants to convey a particular message. It might even limit questions to that topic. Aides identify potential questions, and the president rehearses appropriate answers. (Former press secretaries admit that they predicted at least 90% of the questions asked and often the exact reporters who asked them.)[52] Aides prepare a seating chart, and during the conference the president calls on the reporters he wants. Although he cannot ignore those from the major media, he can call disproportionately on those he knows will lob soft questions. Consequently, the conference usually helps the president.

Beaming the conference to the nation results in less news than having a casual exchange around the president's desk, which used to reveal his thinking on programs and decisions. Appearing in millions of homes, the president cannot be as open, cannot commit himself to a policy prematurely, and cannot allow himself to make a gaffe in front of the huge audience.

Televising the conference does not even provide much accountability, because one is scheduled when the administration wants and nearly every aspect is scripted or predicted in advance. For the most part, the conference offers an illusion of accountability.

The transformation of the conference frustrates reporters and prompts them to act as prosecutors. As one press secretary observed, they play a game of "I gotcha."[53] After Clinton's first conference, one reporter criticized him because "he didn't say a single thing he didn't mean to."[54] The reporter considered the conference a game in which the press tries to best the president, and this time the press lost because it could not trick him into saying something imprudent.

Still, reporters value the conference and criticize presidents who hold sessions infrequently. Editors consider the president's remarks news, so the conference helps reporters do their job. It also gives them a chance to bask in the limelight.

Media events also show the symbiotic nature of the media-politician relationship. These events, staged for television, usually pair a photo opportunity and a speech to convey a particular impression of a politician's position on an issue.

The "photo op" frames the politician against a backdrop of things that symbolize clear values—for example, children or flags. Photo ops for economic issues often use factories, whether bustling to represent a success or abandoned to represent a failure. The backdrop is designed to be visually interesting to attract the cameras. The strategy is the same as that for advertisements of merchandise: Combine the product (the politician) with the symbols in hope that the potential buyers (voters) will link the two.[55] In the 1992 campaign, President Bush peered into the Grand Canyon to demonstrate his credentials as an environmentalist, despite his limited record; Governor Clinton appeared at a bowling alley to demonstrate his credentials as an average "Joe," despite his Yale and Oxford education.

When the United States sent troops to distribute food in Somalia in 1992, Pentagon public affairs officials notified news organizations of the landing beach and time. They intended to create a photo op to gain worldwide publicity for this humanitarian mission and national publicity for the military. They hoped to show off the marines' amphibious landing capabilities and demonstrate the military's need for its large budget even with the economy in the dumps and the former Soviet Union falling apart.[56] Officials did not foresee the ridiculous spectacle of troops hitting the beach and sneaking toward the town in camouflage fatigues—while photographers swarmed all around and spotlights lit up the night sky.

The speech in a media event is not a classical oration or even a cogent address with a beginning, middle, and end. It is an informal talk that emphasizes a few key words or phrases or sentences—almost slogans, because television editors allot time only for a short **sound bite.** And the amount of time is less and less. In 1968 the average sound bite of a presidential contender on the evening news was 42.3 seconds, but in 1988 it was just 9.8 seconds and in 1992 7.3 seconds.[57]

Speech writers plan accordingly. "A lot of writers figure out how they are going to get the part they want onto television," a former presidential aide explained. "They think of a news lead and write around it. And if the television lights don't go on as the speaker is approaching that news lead, he skips a few paragraphs and waits until they are lit to read the key part."[58] This does not result in coherent speeches, but the people watching on television will not know and the few watching in person do not matter because they are just props. More significantly, this does not result in adequate explanations for people in either group.

It is tempting to use media events to convey desirable but inaccurate impressions. When polls showed that the public thought Reagan slighted education because he cut federal money for student loans and schools, he traveled across the country to meet with teachers and students in a series of media events. Then, according to an aide, "The polls absolutely flip-flopped. He went from a negative rating to a positive rating [on education] overnight."[59] Yet he did not change his policies at all. Bush unveiled his anticrime package at a police academy, but later it was noticed that his budget proposed cutting funds for this academy.[60]

Perhaps more than any other source of news, media events illustrate the reliance of politicians on television, and of television on politicians. The head of CBS News said, "I'd like just once to have the courage to go on the air and say that such and such a candidate went to six cities today to stage six media events, none of which had anything to do with governing America."[61] Yet television fosters these events, and despite occasional swipes by correspondents, networks continue to show them.

Sound bite journalism leads to sound bite politics.

Adversarial Relationship

Although the relationship between the media and politicians is symbiotic in some ways, it is adversarial in others. Since George Washington's administration, when conflicts developed between Federalists and Jeffersonians, the media have attacked politicians and politicians have attacked the media. In John Adams's administration, Federalists passed the Sedition Act of 1798, which prohibited much criticism of the government. Federalists used the act to imprison Jeffersonian editors. Not long after, President Andrew Jackson proposed a law to allow the government to shut down "incendiary" newspapers. Even recently a former press secretary commented, "There are very few politicians who do not cherish privately the notion that there should be some regulation of the news."[62]

The conflict stems from a fundamental difference in perspectives. Politicians want the media to help them accomplish their goals, so they hope the media will pass along their messages to the public exactly as they deliver them. But journalists see themselves as servants not of the government but of the public. They question officials until the public knows enough about a matter to hold the officials accountable. According to correspondent Sam Donaldson, "My job is not to say here's the church social with the apple pie, isn't it beautiful?"[63] But some go beyond skepticism to cynicism. In the eyes of Clinton aide George Stephanopoulos, they walk in the door "assuming that something is wrong and asking, 'What are you hiding?' "[64]

In contemporary society, information is power. The media and the government, especially the president, with the huge bureaucracy at his disposal, are the two primary sources of information. To the extent that the administration controls the flow of information, it can achieve its policy goals. To the extent that the media disseminate contradictory information, they can ensure that the administration's policy goals will be subject to public debate.

Inevitably politicians fall short of their goals, and many blame the media for their failures. They confuse the message and the messenger, like Czar Peter the Great, who, when notified that the Russian army had lost a battle in 1700, promptly ordered the messenger strangled.

When President Kennedy became upset by the *New York Times* coverage of Vietnam, he asked the paper to transfer the correspondent out of Vietnam. (The paper refused.) When President Nixon became angry with major newspapers and networks, he had Vice President Agnew lash out at them. He also ordered the Department of Justice to investigate some media companies for possible antitrust violations and the Internal Revenue Service to audit a newspaper and a reporter for possible income tax violations.

The wariness between the media and politicians has increased since the Vietnam War and Watergate scandal fueled cynicism about government's performance and officials' truthfulness. Today the media are less trusting of politicians and less trusted by them.[65]

The conflict between the media and politicians also stems from the nature of the modern media. Now there are so many media with so much space to fill that they have a voracious appetite for news. As they cover the same small circle of top officials, reporters are exposed to the same messages and the same policies day after day. They get bored, forgetting that the public has not paid as much attention and absorbed as much information, and they search for new stories and new angles on old stories. As a result, they often magnify the trivial and distort the important. This is due more to the needs of the media than any desire to conspire against officials.[66]

The rise of the fringe media exacerbates this conflict. This development means more media are seeking news and also more media are deviating from journalistic norms. Once the fringe media publicize an incident, the mainstream media tend to follow, even if the accuracy of the news is in question, because they fear losing their audience. Sometimes the mainstream media follow under the guise of addressing the political ramifications of the incident or the journalistic ethics involved in publicizing it. In this way, charges in the fringe media wind up in the mainstream media as well. Hence an increase in stories about personal shortcomings—sex, drugs, or alcohol—in politicians' lives and questions about their "character."[67]

However, it would be incorrect to think that the relationship between the media and politicians usually is adversarial. In fact, it normally is symbiotic. Although journalists like to think of themselves and try to portray themselves as adversaries who stand up to politicians, most rely upon politicians most of the time.[68]

Thus, despite the impression created by media coverage of Watergate, few journalists engage in investigative reporting. An examination of 224 incidents of criminal or unethical behavior by Reagan administration appointees found that only 13% were uncovered by reporters. Most were discovered through investigations by executive agencies or congressional committees, which then released the information to the press. Only incidents reflecting personal peccadillos of government officials, such as sexual offenses, were exposed first by reporters.[69] Even the $2 billion scandal involving influence peddling at the Department of Housing and Urban Development (HUD) went unnoticed by nearly all reporters until the department's inspector general and a congressional committee probed the payoffs. Yet HUD had been considered "a feeding trough" by Washington insiders for several years.[70]

Relationship between the Media and Recent Administrations

Franklin Roosevelt created the model that most contemporary presidents follow when interacting with the media. Newspaper publishers had no use for Roosevelt and his policies. In fact, a former correspondent recalls, "The publishers didn't just disagree with the New Deal. They hated it. And the reporters, who liked it, had to write as though they hated it, too."[71] Roosevelt saw he was not going to get favorable coverage, but he still wanted to reach the public. He used press conferences to provide a steady stream of news. This tactic enabled him to circumvent the publishers but gain access to their readers. He also used radio—a series of **fireside chats**—to advocate his policies and reassure his listeners in the throes of the Depression. He had a fine voice but, more important, a superb ability to speak informally—he commented about his family, even his dog, in a way to appeal to average people. (He drew so many listeners that he was granted as much air time as he wanted, but he was shrewd enough to realize that too much would result in overexposure.) This tactic enabled him to avoid the filters of reporters and editors and take his case directly to the people.

Reagan Administration

In his younger years, Reagan idolized FDR and developed an imitation of him that included an appropriate accent and even a cigarette holder.[72] As president, Reagan duplicated Roosevelt's success in using the media. Before Reagan lost some effectiveness during his second term, the media dubbed him the Great Communicator for his uncanny ability to communicate his broad themes.

The Reagan administration approached its relationship with the media as "political jujitsu."[73] A jujitsu fighter tries to use the adversary's force to his or her own advantage through a clever maneuver. The administration knew the media would cover the president extensively to fill their news columns and newscasts. Aide Michael Deaver explained the strategy: "The media, while they won't admit it, are not in the news business; they're in entertainment. We tried to create the most entertaining, visually attractive scene to fill that box, so that the networks would have to use it."[74]

Deaver spared no effort or expense to satisfy the demands of television and enhance the image of the president at the same time. Deaver sent advance agents days or weeks ahead of the president to prepare the "stage" for media events—the specific location, backdrops, lighting, and sound equipment. A trip to Korea was designed to show "the commander in chief on the front line against communism." The advance man went to the demilitarized zone separating North and South Korea and negotiated with the army and the Secret Service for the most photogenic setting possible. He demanded that the president be able to use the most exposed bunker, which meant that the army had to erect telephone poles and string 30,000 yards of camouflage netting from them to hide Reagan from North Korean sharpshooters. The advance man also demanded that the army build camera platforms on a hill that remained exposed but offered the most dramatic angle to film Reagan surrounded by sandbags. Although the Secret Service wanted sandbags up to Reagan's neck, the

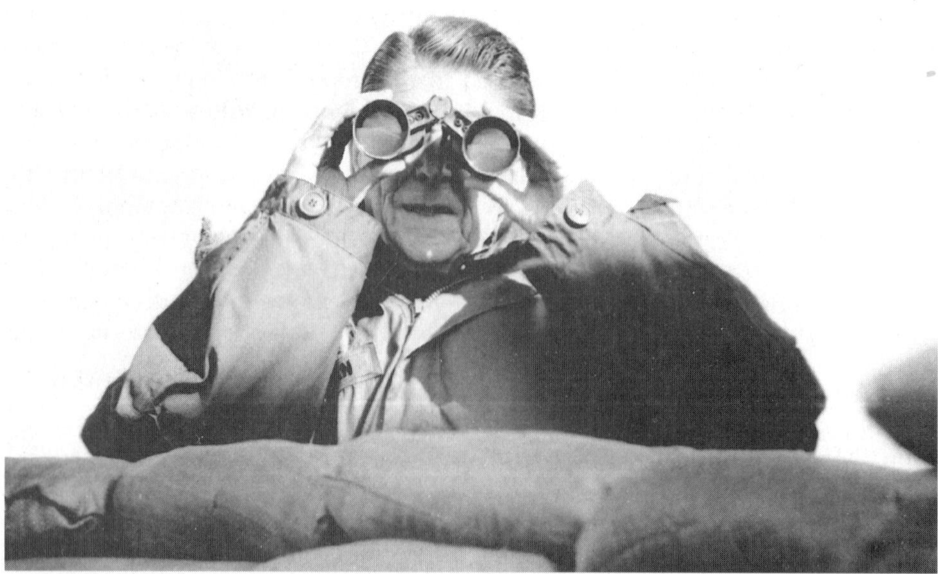

President Reagan, staged to reflect "American strength and resolve" in Korea.

advance man insisted that they be no more than four inches above his navel so viewers would get a clear picture of the president wearing his flak jacket and demonstrating "American strength and resolve."[75]

It did not seem to matter if there was little connection between what the president was doing and what actually was happening. When U.S. planes shot down two Libyan jets, Reagan was helicoptered to the deck of an aircraft carrier—off the coast of California, not Libya—for a triumphant photo op.[76]

To set the agenda, and to prevent the media from setting it, the administration tried to control the president's appearances and restrict his comments. Aides especially worried that off-the-cuff comments would reveal Reagan's limited command of the facts and details behind his policies or would result in a blooper, such as the time he said that trees cause most air pollution. To keep such comments from damaging his image or at least overshadowing his message of the day, aides provided few opportunities for reporters to ask questions. When reporters asked questions inside a building, aides frequently demanded that the television lights be shut off so any answers could not be televised; outside they often ordered the helicopter's engines revved up so the questions would be drowned out. Aides scheduled few press conferences. Although conferences normally benefit presidents, they are subject to less control than media events and were considered too risky.

Paradoxically, Reagan was highly visible but not very accessible. By alternately using and avoiding the media, his administration succeeded in managing the news more than any other administration.

Bush Administration

Bush rejected some of Reagan's efforts to manipulate the media and, anyway, he lacked most of Reagan's appeal on television. So his administration deemphasized television appearances in favor of frequent press conferences and get-togethers with reporters. Occasionally he telephoned reporters to talk or jog with him. In these settings his grasp of issues came across. He tried to impress reporters and, like Roosevelt, charm them, in hope that he would receive favorable coverage. Journalists did consider Bush more accessible and open than Reagan.

For the invasion of Panama in 1989 and war with Iraq in 1991, however, the Bush administration insisted on strict control and censorship rather than accessibility and openness. When the United States invaded Panama to force General Manuel Noriega from office, reporters were delayed arriving in Panama and then delayed transmitting their dispatches back to the United States. They were prevented from seeing most battles out of fear that they would witness civilian casualties.[77] Despite later indications of many civilian casualties, we may never learn fully what happened in this operation.[78]

Because there were few negative news stories, the Pentagon and Bush administration were satisfied with the results and used a similar system when the United States fought Iraq. About 100 reporters at a time, of 800 on the scene, were escorted to locations where American troops were living or fighting. Reporters were permitted to interview soldiers only when supervised by their officers. Reporters who ventured off on their own were arrested, detained, and threatened with the loss of their credentials (as one who had the temerity to interview Saudi Arabian shopkeepers discovered).[79]

Before dispatches could be sent back to the United States, they had to be cleared by military censors. Though the stated purpose was to prevent release of information that could jeopardize the safety of U.S. troops, sometimes the apparent purpose was to prevent release of information that could put the U.S. military in a bad light. One censor blocked a story that said pilots were watching pornographic movies before bombing missions, while another changed a story that said pilots were "giddy" after a mission. (Instead, the censor described them as "proud.")[80] Yet, according to reporters, censorship was not as much of a problem as lack of access and information.

The Pentagon was most sensitive about casualties, whether American or Iraqi. Officials' concern went far beyond the possibility that television might show a dead soldier before his or her kin could be notified. They worried that pictures of dead or wounded Americans would cause the public to turn against the war. Likewise, they worried that information about injured Iraqi civilians or destroyed homes would weaken support for the war.

As a result of the administration's management of the news, television showed film of one precise bombing attack after another. Commentators lauded the "smart" bombs that were so accurate it was like having them "delivered by Federal Express." Yet after the war one official said only 7% of the bombs were "smart" bombs, and another said only 25% of the other bombs hit their targets. This means that at least 61,000 tons of bombs landed where they were not supposed to.[81]

Polls showed that most Americans approved the military's control of the news, and a majority even thought the military should have more control of the news. Only 19% thought the military was "hiding bad news from the public."[82]

Clinton Administration

Clinton emulates Roosevelt and Reagan in their use of the media. Like Reagan he tries to focus on an issue and highlight a message of the day or week to influence public opinion on that issue. Like Roosevelt, he tries to leapfrog reporters to reach citizens directly. He holds frequent press conferences and periodic question-and-answer sessions with citizens. On television, these sessions are analogous to Roosevelt's fireside chats on radio.

The administration, which considers network television too broad and too unfocused to reach the many groups that contemporary presidents must reach, uses "narrowcasting" to reach groups who have more specific concerns than the national media usually address. For example, when a commission proposed eliminating numerous military bases, press conferences and question-and-answer sessions were held with regional and local media in the three states taking the hardest hits. In Florida additional questions arose about a policy to convert defense plants to domestic factories and about policies concerning Haiti and Cuba.[83] These questions were more specific than ones typically asked by national reporters.

The give-and-take of question-and-answer sessions could be tricky for a president; questions from citizens are less predictable than those from reporters. But Clinton is knowledgeable about issues and comfortable when improvising. He also is articulate. As one television critic observed, "We now have a president capable of speaking in complete sentences, each one with a subject, a verb and its various clauses arranged in grammatical order. Not only that, but each sentence . . . progresses logically to the next."[84]

Unlike Roosevelt and Reagan, however, Clinton is not enthralling. He lacks discipline and, as a result, talks too long and gives too many details for most listeners. He strays from his message of the day or week and thus blurs this message. Consequently, he does not effectively communicate his proposals and programs, and many people do not really know what he stands for.

Clinton also has been hampered by a staff that has been inexperienced and incompetent in handling the White House press corps. Too often reporters' calls have gone unanswered or their interview requests have not been granted. Too often reporters' questions have received misleading or false replies. Later the staff would have to acknowledge that certain replies were "misstatements" or were "rendered inoperative," leaving the reporters more cynical than ever.

The youthfulness of the staff has contributed to these problems. At the beginning of the administration, 63 of the 450 members of the White House staff

Source: Oliphant copyright 1993 Universal Press Syndicate.

were younger than 24. (A generation gap between the young staffers and the middle-aged reporters also has created tensions. "As a father of a kid in college," one reporter admitted, "I find it somewhat off-putting to talk to male White House aides wearing earrings. It's like coming home and finding your kids got into the liquor cabinet.")[85]

Various slights, whether intended or imagined, have aggravated these problems. Upon taking office Clinton insulted the major media by giving his first interview not to a national reporter, but to the political correspondent from MTV. Other actions were considered direct challenges to the press. The administration closed a White House passageway between the staff offices and the press room. Reporters had hung out in the hallway to buttonhole aides but had clogged the hallway. The administration also revamped the White House travel office, which makes plane and hotel arrangements for reporters covering the president on trips. After the administration discovered mismanagement in the office, it scaled back the VIP treatment lavished on reporters. Then reporters complained that they received cold food instead of hot food and cheap domestic champagne instead of the usual expensive imported champagne.

As a result of the administration's bumbling and dissembling and the press corps' overreacting, Clinton has received sharply negative coverage. He had no "honeymoon" from criticism, as new presidents normally have. During his first four months, according to a study of network news, 64% of all references to him were negative, compared with 41% for President Bush at the same point. Some of this coverage was due to Clinton's own missteps, but some was not. According to an analysis of three issues—national service, educational reform, and PAC reform—Clinton received much less favorable coverage than his predecessor, although he did more and fulfilled his campaign promises more fully than Bush did in the same areas.[86]

Most damaging has been the overall charge that Clinton has reneged on his commitments. Although Clinton has kept many promises—like most presidents, he has kept more than he has broken—the media have focused on the ones he has not kept and the ones he has not been able to keep.[87] The media, showing little recognition that bargaining and ultimately compromising are necessary for any president, have characterized Clinton as a "waffler" and a "compromiser." (Serious observers do ask whether Clinton has had to give in as quickly as he has in some disputes, but journalists have gone far beyond questions about tactics.) Thus, the media have reinforced the naive belief of some citizens that politicians need not and should not bargain and compromise. This impression leads to disillusionment with virtually all politicians.

Are reporters as unsophisticated as their coverage suggests? Or are they as alienated from their government and its officials as other citizens now, and as inclined to exaggerate?

Some reporters observed that their colleagues felt "they had blown it" in covering the Reagan and Bush administrations and were determined not to be conned by this administration. Thus, they have looked for manipulation or hypocrisy behind every act.[88] Some political scientists speculated that the media have compensated for favoring Clinton over Bush in the election by being harsher on Clinton in office—perhaps, subconsciously, as a way to prove their critics wrong.[89] Some political scientists speculated that the media have accelerated their normal tendency to oversimplify and overdramatize, to declare "winners" and "losers."[90] In the first weeks of the administration, mistakes led some media to herald "the beginning of the end" and compare Clinton to Carter.

Relationship between the Media and Congress

Members of Congress also use the media but have much less impact. Since 1970 nearly all have hired his or her own full-time press secretary who churns out press releases, distributes television tapes, and arranges interviews with reporters.[91] The Senate and House of Representatives have established recording studios for members, allowed television cameras into committee rooms, and supported the creation of C-SPAN. Yet members still have trouble attracting the eye of the media. One president can be the subject of the media's focus, whereas 535 members of Congress cannot. Only a handful of powerful (or, occasionally, colorful) members receive much notice from the national media. Other members get attention from their home state or district media, but those from large urban areas with numerous representatives get little publicity or scrutiny even there.[92]

Since the congressional elections of 1994, Speaker of the House Newt Gingrich (R.-Ga.) has gotten extraordinary coverage, even for a leader of Congress,

For the congressional elections of 1994, Republicans campaigned against Democrats by linking them to President Clinton and by linking him to former President Carter. Both presidents, they charged, were failures. *Time* magazine reinforced the Republicans' theme by running this series of computer-generated images showing Clinton becoming Carter.

because he was the point man for the Republican takeover of Congress and has been the leader of the Republican agenda in Congress. Other powerful Republicans in Congress also have received increased coverage because of their controversial agenda to reduce and eliminate governmental programs.

➤Bias of the Media

Every night Walter Cronkite, former anchor for CBS Evening News, signed off, "And that's the way it is." His statement implied that the network reported the news exactly the way it happened, that the network held a huge mirror to the world and reflected an image of the world to the viewers—without any distortion. Yet the media do not hold a mirror. They hold a searchlight that seeks and illuminates some things instead of others.[93]

From all the events that occur in the world every day, the media can report only a handful as the news of the day. Even the fat *New York Times,* whose motto is "All the News That's Fit to Print," cannot include all the news. The media must decide what events are newsworthy. When the Wright brothers invited reporters to Kitty Hawk, North Carolina, to observe the first plane flight in 1903, none considered it newsworthy enough to cover. After the historic flight, only seven American newspapers reported it, and only two reported it on the front page.[94]

After the media decide what events to report, they must decide where to report them—on the front page or top of the newscast, or in a less prominent position. Then they must decide how to report them. Except for magazines, most media attempt to be "objective"; that is, they try to present facts rather than their opinions. Where the facts are in dispute, they try to present the positions of both sides. They are reluctant to evaluate these positions, although sometimes they do explain or interpret them.

In making these decisions, it would be natural for journalists' attitudes to affect their coverage. As one

acknowledged, a reporter writes "from what he hears and sees and how he filters it through the lens of his own experience. No reporter is a robot."[95]

Political Bias

Historically, the press was politically biased. The party papers, which were established by political parties, parroted the party line. Even the independent papers, which succeeded them, advocated one side or the other. Publishers', editors', and reporters' attitudes seeped—sometimes flooded—into their prose. But papers gradually abandoned their ardor for editorializing and adopted the practice of objectivity to retain as many of their readers as possible.

Yet the public thinks the press is still biased. According to one survey, 41% think the press is "out to get" the groups they identify with: Executives believe the press is out to get businesses, and laborers believe it is out to get unions. Liberals believe it is biased against liberals, and conservatives believe it is biased against conservatives.[96]

Indeed, the public seems more critical today, when most media at least attempt to be objective, than in the past, when they did not even pretend they were. Then, citizens could subscribe to whichever local paper reflected their own biases (without ever recognizing that the paper reflected any biases). Now, as local newspapers have been eclipsed by national broadcast networks, and as independently owned media have been eclipsed by chains and conglomerates, the public has fewer choices and is more sensitive to perceptions of bias.

Bias for Established Institutions and Values

The media generally do reflect a bias for established institutions and values. This should not come as a surprise. Because the media are major businesses owned by large corporations, and because they need to retain their readers and viewers to make a profit, they consciously or unconsciously mirror the mainstream.

The media have a long history of bias against other ideologies, such as communism or even democratic socialism. The failures of noncapitalist economic systems are played up, the successes played down. In foreign policy matters, the U.S. government line usually is adopted. During the cold war, this meant harsh attacks on the Soviet Union and leftist Latin American countries.[97]

During the Persian Gulf War, this meant embracing the administration's goals and questioning little of its propaganda.[98] Although this was partly due to the administration's manipulation of the news, it was also partly due to the media's own bias. Even when journalists obtained contradictory information, news organizations hesitated reporting it until later.[99] The result was "a frenzy of jingoism" during the fighting.[100]

Correlated with the media's support for established institutions and values is their reliance upon government officials for their news. A study of front-page stories from the *New York Times* and *Washington Post* over two decades found that 74% were based on statements by U.S. government officials.[101] This is striking considering that these papers have far more staffers and resources to do investigative journalism than other papers. Such heavy reliance upon government officials means that the stories are likely to bear their strong imprint. Similarly, a study of ABC's "Nightline," which features news and interviews, found that 80% of the Americans interviewed on the program were from the government or corporate establishment (and 90% of these were white males). The watchdog group Fairness & Accuracy In Reporting (FAIR) found that representatives from peace, environmental, consumer, or labor groups were "hardly visible."[102]

Reporters turn to officials for news because it is easy and because, ironically, they want to avoid charges of bias. Reporters believe their peers, superiors, and the public all consider officials newsworthy. Ignoring them or downplaying them could be interpreted as showing bias against them.[103]

Bias for Particular Candidates and Policies

Most debate about media bias revolves around charges that the media exhibit a preference for particular candidates and policies over others. Conservative groups, in particular, claim that the media are biased toward liberal candidates and policies, and they have gone so far as to mount an effort to buy CBS in order to change its newscasts.

In studying media bias, social scientists have examined the characteristics and behavior of journalists. They have found that journalists are not very representative of the public. They are disproportionately college-educated white males from the upper middle class. Further, they are disproportionately urban and secular, rather than rural and religious. They are disproportionately Democrats or independents leaning to the Democrats, rather than Republicans or independents leaning to the Republicans. Likewise, they identify themselves disproportionately as liberals rather than conservatives.[104]

But journalists do differ among themselves. Those who work for the prominent, influential organizations— large newspapers, wire services, news magazines, and radio and television networks—are more likely to be Democrats and liberals than those who work for nonprominent organizations—small newspapers and radio and television stations.[105]

Journalists in prominent organizations are more likely than the public to support the liberal position on issues. Large majorities support homosexuals' right to teach in public schools and affirmative action. They are also suspicious of big business, believing it is the sector of society that exerts the most influence but should exert much less.[106] At the same time, they support capitalism. Large majorities think businesses should be owned privately rather than publicly; businesses should be regulated less than they are; and businesses are fair to their workers. According to one study, 73% do not think that our institutions "need overhaul."[107] Thus, although these journalists are likely to be liberals, they are hardly extreme liberals or radicals.

These findings might seem to support the charge that the media are biased against conservatives, but this assumes that journalists' attitudes necessarily color what they report. Several factors mitigate the effect of journalists' attitudes. For one thing, journalists do not seem to have intense opinions. Most did not become journalists because of a commitment to political ideology but because of the opportunity to rub elbows with powerful people and be close to exciting events. "Each day brings new stories, new dramas in which journalists participate vicariously."[108] As a result, most "care more about the politics of an issue than about the issue itself,"[109] which makes them less likely to voice their views about the issue.

In addition, media organizations pressure journalists to muffle their views, partly out of a conviction that it is more professional to do so and partly out of a desire to avoid the headaches that could arise otherwise—debates among their staffers; complaints from their local radio and television affiliates; complaints from their audience; perhaps even complaints from the White House, Congress, or the Federal

Communications Commission (FCC), which licenses them.

Sometimes media executives or editors pressure reporters because they have contrary views. Reporters learn not to explore certain subjects, not to ask certain questions. Reporters who pursue the stories regardless might find their copy edited, with the most critical portions deleted. The *New York Times*, despite its liberal reputation, altered reporters' stories on foreign affairs to hew more closely to administrations' conservative policies.[110] CBS toned down correspondents' stories about Reagan's economic policies.[111] Reporters who pursue the stories might find themselves transfered to another beat. One who covered El Salvador for the *New York Times* wrote a series of reports about the government's massacre of nearly a thousand peasants. The reports contradicted Reagan's assertions that the nation was making great strides in human rights. Under pressure, the *Times* pulled the reporter off this beat.[112] Ultimately, reporters who pursue the stories could find themselves fired.[113]

For all of these reasons the media do not exhibit nearly as much **political bias** as would be expected from their journalists' attitudes. Although they do show a bias for established institutions and values, they do not show much bias for particular candidates in elections.

To measure bias, researchers use a technique called "content analysis." They scrutinize newspaper and television stories to determine whether there was an unequal amount of coverage, unequal use of favorable or unfavorable statements, or unequal use of a positive or negative tone. They consider insinuating verbs ("he conceded" rather than "he said") and pejorative adjectives ("her weak response" rather than "her response"), and for television stories they evaluate the announcer's nonverbal communication—voice inflection, eye movement, and body language.

Studies of coverage of several presidential campaigns found relatively little bias. The media typically gave the two major candidates equal attention and rarely made a favorable or unfavorable statement about them or used a positive or negative tone discussing them.[114] The studies did find some bias against incumbents, front-runners, and emerging challengers.[115] For these candidates, the media apparently took their watchdog role seriously.

Overall, then, there is less bias than the public believes or the candidates feel. When candidates complain, they usually are objecting to bad news, and they probably are trying to manipulate the media. The strategy is to put reporters on the defensive so they will be tougher on the candidates' opponents in the future.

Yet the way in which the media cover campaigns can have different implications for different candidates. The media report the facts, and all the details that contribute to the facts: that one candidate is leading while the other is trailing, that one campaign is surging while the other is slipping. This coverage has positive implications for the former—swaying undecided voters, galvanizing campaign workers, and attracting financial contributions—and negative implications for the latter. Such coverage does not benefit one party over the other party in election after election, but it can benefit one party's candidate over the other party's candidate in a particular election. It helped the Democrat Carter in 1976 and the Republican Bush in 1988; it hurt the Republican Ford in 1976 and the Democrat Carter in 1980.[116] Some people, especially supporters of the losers, consider such reporting biased. Journalists, however, consider it a reflection of reality.

There were numerous accusations of bias—for Clinton and against Bush—during the 1992 election, but the media's continuing coverage of the success of Clinton's campaign and the failure of Bush's campaign accounts for most (though not all) of the tilt.[117] During the primaries, Clinton faced much negative news, but during the general election he received more positive coverage.[118] As he climbed in the polls, his characterization by the press changed from "Slick Willie" to a dogged survivor. Meanwhile, Bush presided over a slow economy and ran a hesitant campaign, and he fell in the polls. He was portrayed as an incumbent in trouble, like "a baseball team that was favored to win the pennant but stumbled early and never regained its stride."[119]

The same reporting continues for politicians in office. The press focuses on the extent to which Clinton is "winning"—persuading fellow Democrats or the Republicans to adopt his policies, and getting the public to support him and his policies—or "losing." As Clinton the candidate benefited from these reporting conventions, Clinton the president has suffered from them.

There are two exceptions to the generalization that overt political bias in elections is minimal. First, the media usually give short shrift to third-party candidates. However, the media did pay much attention to Ross Perot's presidential bid in 1992. They took him seriously because he said he would spend $100 million on his campaign and because polls showed he could compete with Bush and Clinton.

Second, newspapers traditionally print editorials and columns that express opinions. In editorials before elections, papers often endorse candidates. Most owners are Republican, and this is one time many seek to influence the content of their papers. Since the first survey in 1932, more papers have endorsed the Republican presidential candidate, except in the election between Democratic President Lyndon Johnson and Republican Senator Barry Goldwater in 1964 and in the election between Clinton and Bush in 1992.[120]

The relative lack of bias in coverage of elections does not necessarily mean there is a lack of bias in coverage of other events. Because elections are highly visible and candidates are very sensitive about the coverage, the media might take more care to be neutral here than elsewhere. Researchers have not examined coverage of other events as much. Some think that journalists' liberal attitudes do surface. A study of coverage of nuclear energy found an evolution from slightly pro- to strongly antinuclear power during the 1970s,[121] while one of school busing found a tilt for busing during the same decade,[122] and one of abortion found a tilt toward choice in the late 1980s.[123] Yet an analysis of news about the Iranian hostage seizure and the Soviet invasion of Afghanistan, both in 1980, revealed a slight conservative bias.[124]

FIGURE 1
Bad News about Presidential Candidates Increases

In presidential campaigns in the 1960s and '70s, candidates received primarily positive coverage. In the 1980s and '90s, however, they have faced more negative coverage, according to an analysis of articles in *Newsweek* and *Time*.

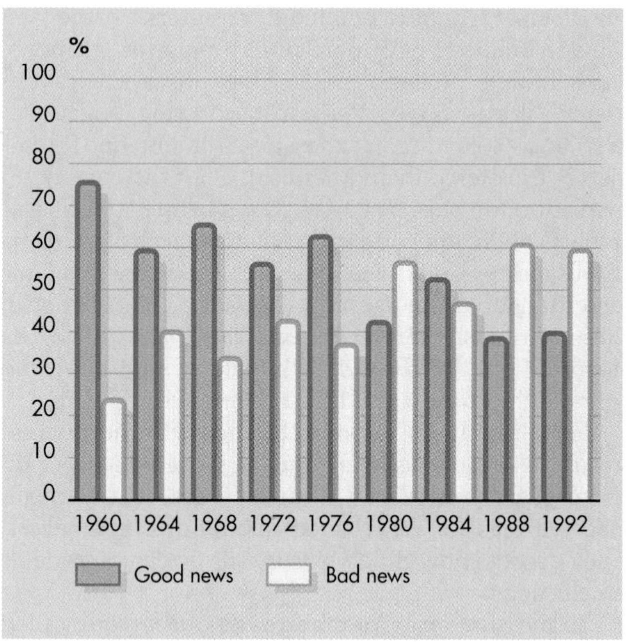

Note: Analysis is based on paragraphs that can be categorized one way or the other. It does not include statements about "the horse race."

Source: Thomas E. Patterson, *Out of Order* (New York: Vintage, 1994), p. 20.

Bias Against All Candidates and Officials

Some critics charge that there is a general bias against all candidates and officials—a negative undercurrent in reporting about government, regardless of who or what is covered. President Nixon's first vice president, Spiro Agnew, called journalists "nattering nabobs of negativism." Critics think this bias increased after the Watergate scandal made reporters more cynical.

There seems to be considerable validity to this charge.[125] Analyses of newspapers, magazines, and television networks show that the overwhelming majority of the stories about government are neutral.[126] However, the rest of the stories are more often negative than positive.[127] Moreover, the number of stories that are negative is increasing. (See Figure 1.)

As a result, the media often convey the impression that neither the candidates are worthy of the office they seek nor the officials of the office they hold. They ultimately convey the impression that the political process itself is contemptible.[128]

Despite a tendency toward negativism, the tone appears to vary depending on the medium and the institution covered. Television is more critical than newspapers and magazines,[129] and Congress is more criticized than the president.[130] For example, after reporting that the Supreme Court gave Congress 30 days to revamp an independent regulatory commission, NBC anchor David Brinkley remarked, "It is widely believed in Washington that it would take Congress 30 days to make instant coffee."[131] The tone also appears to vary from the national media to the local media. The national media, whose reporters are better educated and more experienced in national affairs, are far more critical.

Commercial Bias

Except for public radio and television networks and stations, American media are private businesses run for a profit. They must attract readers and listeners and viewers. With an audience, they can sell advertising. The larger the audience, the higher the price they can charge for advertising. A change of 1% in the ratings of a television news program in New York City, for example, can mean a difference of $5 million in advertising for a station in a year.[132] The opportunity to make a profit is so enormous that CBS's "60 Minutes," the most watched program during some recent years, made more money in its first decade on the air than the entire Chrysler Corporation in the same decade.[133]

The need to attract an audience shapes the media's presentation of the news and leads to a **commercial bias.** Sometimes this means that the media deliberately print or broadcast what advertisers want. At the request of the gas company sponsoring the drama "Judgment at Nuremberg," one network bleeped the words "gas ovens" from descriptions of the Nazis' war crimes.[134] Other times the media censor themselves. When the auto industry was pressuring Congress to repeal seat belt and air bag regulations in the 1970s, the *New York Times* publisher urged the editors to present the industry position because it "would affect the advertising."[135] In articles on health numerous magazines avoided references to the dangers of smoking for fear of losing advertising from tobacco companies. *Ms.* magazine, generally attentive to women's health, even avoided references to the increased dangers of smoking during pregnancy (at a time when it still accepted advertising).[136]

Usually, though, commercial bias means that the media must print or broadcast what the public wants, and this means that the media must entertain the public. This creates a "conflict between being an honest reporter and being a member of show business," network correspondent Roger Mudd confessed, "and that conflict is with me every day."[137]

The dilemma is most marked for television. Many people who watch television news are not interested in politics; a majority, in fact, say it covers too much politics.[138] Some watch the news because they were watching another program before the news and left the television on, others because they were going to watch another program after the news and turned the television on early. Networks feel pressure "to hook them and keep them."[139]

Therefore, networks try to make the everyday world of news seem as exciting as the make-believe world they depict in their other programs. One network instructed its staff: "Every news story should, without any sacrifice of probity or responsibility, display the attributes of fiction, of drama. It should have structure and conflict, problem and denouement, rising action and falling action, a beginning, a middle and an end."[140] As one executive says, television news is "info-tainment."[141]

Source: BIZARRO cartoon by Dan Piraro, reprinted by permission of Chronicle Features, San Francisco, California.

Although television anchors and newscasters help determine the content of their newscasts, they are not hired strictly for their journalistic experience and ability but partly for their appearance and personality. They become show business stars. To enhance their appeal, networks and stations shape their image, ordering them to change their hairstyle and even, with tinted contact lenses, their eye color. They set up clothes calendars so newscasters will rotate their outfits regularly.

Although appearance is important for both men and women newscasters, it is especially crucial for women. While viewers accept men aging on the screen, they do not seem to accept women aging. As one woman anchor commented, "The guys have got white hair, and the girls look like cheerleaders."[142] Indeed, according to one calculation, although a third of local anchors are women, only 3% are past 40; of the men 50% are past 40 and 16% are past 50.[143]

The commercial bias of the media has a number of consequences. One is emphasis on human interest stories. In 1980 UPI and CBS carried seven times more stories about President Jimmy Carter's beer-drinking brother, Billy, than about the Strategic Arms Limitation Talks (SALT) between the United States and the Soviet Union.[144] By 1990, the networks had mentioned President Bush's dog, Millie, in more stories than they mentioned three cabinet secretaries.[145]

In 1988 a pair of whales got trapped under ice in the Arctic. Their plight and rescue efforts, which took three weeks, new technology, and cooperation with the Soviet Union, received daily coverage. Yet efforts to restrict whaling, which results in the slaughter of many whales, receive less attention because they involve more complex policies and less human interest.

The emphasis on human interest also means an emphasis upon crime and sex.[146] During the 1976 presidential campaign, Carter gave an interview to *Playboy* magazine and, in a short portion of the long interview, admitted that he had "looked on a lot of women with lust. I've committed adultery in my heart many times." The media seized upon this quotation and ignored the rest of the interview. During the 1992 presidential primaries, Clinton gave his first major speech on the economy. The same day Senator Bob Kerrey (Neb.), one of his Democratic rivals, was overheard, by a boom mike, telling a lesbian joke to an official next to him. The media focused on Kerry's joke rather than Clinton's speech.

In contrast, during the 1988 presidential campaign, Democratic candidate Michael Dukakis proposed that college graduates repay their college loans by having a percentage of their job salary withheld, so those with a lower salary would pay a lower amount. A television reporter complained that the proposal was "complicated" and "boring."[147]

The emphasis on human interest leads to another consequence of commercial bias—a **game orientation** in political reporting.[148] The underlying assumption is that politics is a game and politicians, whether candidates campaigning for election or officials performing in office, are the players. The corollary to the assumption is that the players are self-centered and self-interested. They are seeking victory for themselves and defeat for their opponents and are not concerned about the consequences of their proposals or the government's policies. Thus, through this game filter, politicians' strategies and tactics are highlighted, and new developments are presented according to how they help some players and hinder others. The substance and impact of the proposals and policies are slighted.

The game orientation appeals to journalists because it generates human interest. It offers new story lines as new information comes to light, much like a board game with "chance" cards injects unexpected scenarios and alters the players' moves and the game's outcomes. This orientation also appeals to journalists because it is easy and relatively free from charges of partisan or ideological bias. (Stories highlight which contestants are winning, not which ones should win or what consequences might result.) Analyzing policy lacks all of these advantages for journalists.

The game orientation attracts an audience, but it creates more public cynicism. The assumption that politics is a game and the corollary that the players are concerned solely with their own interests leads to the conclusion that their strategies and tactics are based mostly on manipulation and deception. Journalists, casting their wary eyes on politicians, look for manipulation and deception and interpret even sincere action in those ways.

For elections, the game orientation results in what is called "horse-race coverage," with "front-runners," "dark horses," and "also-rans." This coverage accounts for much of the total coverage of campaigns.[149] For example, in 1988 one-third of all network television stories about the presidential primaries referred to candidates' poll standings.[150] This is remarkable so early in the campaign, when most citizens know little about most candidates. It is likely that many viewers knew where the candidates were running in the race but not where they stood on the issues.

Horse-race coverage is not new and is not confined to television. An examination of presidential election coverage by metropolitan newspapers from 1888 through 1988 shows that the race was a staple of journalism long before the advent of broadcast media.[151] Yet other research suggests that the proportion of coverage focusing on the race has been increasing in recent decades. (See Figure 2.)

The emphasis upon human interest stories and horse-race aspects of an election led one observer to summarize the 1976 presidential campaign as follows:

> I saw President Ford bump his head leaving an airplane.... I saw Carter playing softball in Plains, Georgia. I saw Carter kissing [daughter] Amy, I saw Carter hugging [mother] Lillian. I saw Carter, in dungarees, walking hand in hand through the peanut farm with [wife] Rosalyn. I saw Carter going to church, coming out of church.... I saw Ford misstate the problems of Eastern Europe—and a week of people commenting about his misstatement. I saw Ford bump his head again. I saw Ford in Ohio say

FIGURE 2
Game Orientation in Presidential Campaigns Increases

In presidential campaigns in the 1960s, policy and leadership issues received approximately equal coverage with the strategies and tactics and the successes and failures that reflect the game orientation. In the 1970s, '80s, and '90s, however, policy and leadership issues have received a much smaller proportion of the coverage, according to an analysis of articles on the front page of the *New York Times.*

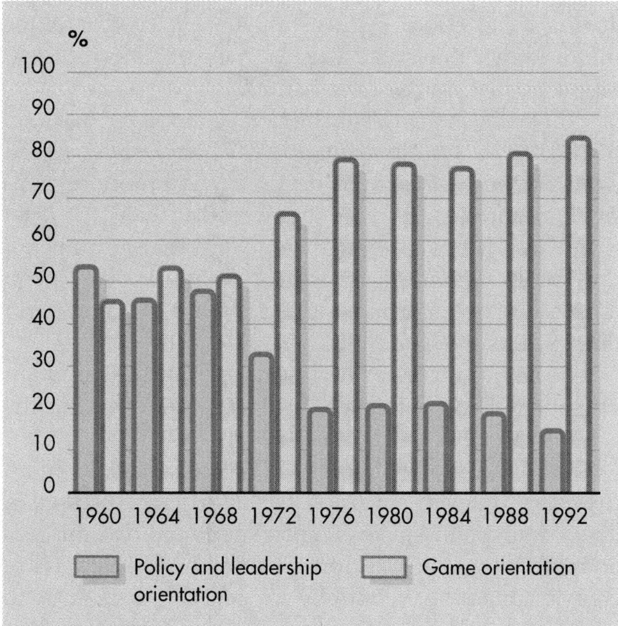

Note: Analysis is based on articles that can be categorized one way or the other. It does not include other orientations, which received about 15% of the coverage.

Source: Thomas E. Patterson, *Out of Order* (New York: Vintage, 1994), p. 74.

> how glad he was to be back in Iowa. I saw marching bands and hecklers, and I learned about the size of crowds and the significance of the size of crowds. . . .
>
> But in all the hours of high anxiety that I spent watching the network news, never did I hear what the candidates had to say about the campaign issues. That was not news.[152]

Even after elections, the game orientation continues. During Reagan's first term, social programs were cut, income taxes were cut significantly, and military spending was increased sharply, but the main theme of media coverage was whether Reagan was "winning" or "losing" his battles with Congress and the bureaucracy. Similarly, during Clinton's first term, the main theme was whether Clinton was "triumphing" or "failing" in his efforts to prod Congress to adopt his policies.

The emphasis on human interest leads to another consequence of commercial bias—an emphasis on controversy rather than agreement. Stories about conflict provide drama. Reporters, one admits, are "fight promoters" rather than consensus builders.[153] (Newt Gingrich observed that if Thomas Edison invented electric light today, the media would report it by saying that "the candlemaking industry was threatened."[154]) Reporters frame disputes as struggles between opposite camps. They depict attack and counterattack, using dueling sound bites from politicians and interjecting metaphors from wars. They talk about politicians who are "targets," who are "under fire," who receive "shots across their bow." They talk about politicians who engage in "search-and-destroy missions" and who "hold back no ammunition." Occasionally they refer to a "cease-fire," but eventually they return to a "war of attrition" with "do-or-die" battles. Ultimately they lament the politicians who "crashed in flames."[155]

With little awareness of a middle ground and with little attention to any nuance, the emphasis on conflict polarizes disputes and at the same time simplifies them. In the 1992 presidential campaign, Vice President Quayle included one sentence about the TV character Murphy Brown in a half-hour speech about poverty, work, and contemporary lifestyles: "It doesn't help matters when prime-time TV has Murphy Brown [who decided to become a single mother] mocking the importance of fathers, by bearing a child alone and calling it just another 'lifestyle choice.' " This sentence became the biggest story in the news for a week. People heard the reactions of representatives of the network and of producers and writers of the show, and they heard the reactions of representatives of civil rights, feminist, pro-choice, and pro-life groups. But people heard little about the main point of the speech—that the breakdown of the family had important consequences for American society.

In the 1993 and 1994 debates over health care reform, the media focused more on the conflicts among the Clinton administration, members of Congress, and coalitions of interest groups than on the substantive provisions of the various proposals.[156] Few people, despite their interest in health care reform, learned enough to make a reasoned judgment about the proposals.

The commercial bias of the media leads to certain consequences for television specifically. One is emphasis on events, or those parts of events, that have visual interest. The networks have people whose job is to evaluate all film for visual appeal. Producers seek the events that promise the most action; camera operators shoot the parts of the events with the most action; and editors select the portions of the film with the most action.[157] Television thus focuses on disasters, crimes, and protests far more than they actually occur, and when it covers other events, it focuses on the most exciting aspects of them. It distorts reality in order to hold the viewers' attention. In the summer of 1988, fires raged through Yellowstone National Park. Television showed a wall of flame night after night and called the park "a moonscape." As one lifeless scene followed another on the screen, NBC's Tom Brokaw intoned, "This is what's left of Yellowstone tonight." The effect, according to a journalism study, was to create the impression that our first national park was completely burned. Yet three-fourths of the park, including its famed geysers and waterfalls, was nearly unscathed. Further, fire plays a natural and necessary role in the ecosystem of the park.[158]

The emphasis on visual interest often results in coverage of the interesting surface of events over the underlying substance—the protest but not the cause. When Iranians seized the American embassy and employees in 1980, the demonstrators discovered television's appetite for visual interest and teased it almost every night for more than a year. As the cameras arrived, they erupted with wild chants and threats, hung Jimmy Carter effigies, and shredded American flags. Yet the reasons for the seizure, rooted in Iranian problems, American policies, and superpower conflicts, were only briefly mentioned.[159]

Another consequence of commercial bias for television is that it covers the news very briefly. In a half-hour newscast, there are only 21 minutes without commercials. In that time, the networks broadcast only about one-third as many words as the *New York Times* prints on its front page alone. Although television conveys visual impressions as well, the contrast in the amount of information these media transmit is striking.

The stories are short—about one minute each—because the time is short and because the networks think viewers' attention spans are short. Indeed, a survey found that a majority of 18- to 34-year-olds who have remote controls typically watch more than one show at once.[160] Thus, networks do not allow leaders or experts to explain their thoughts about particular events or policies. Instead, networks take sound bites to illustrate what was said. Their correspondents usually do not have enough time to explain the events or policies or to provide background information about them.

A network correspondent was asked what went through his mind when he signed off each night. "Good night, dear viewer," he said. "I only hope you read the *New York Times* in the morning."[161]

The networks have tried to expand to a full hour newscast, but local affiliates have resisted because the networks would sell commercials for the extra time and the affiliates would lose revenue they generate during this period. Regardless, there is no guarantee that a longer newscast would be a better newscast. It might be just more of the same.

When the chairman of the board of one network, in conversation with Reagan aide Michael Deaver, asked what the networks could do to provide more responsible reporting, Deaver answered, "Easy, . . . just eliminate ratings for news. You claim that news is not the same as entertainment. So why do you need ratings?" The chairman sighed, "Well, that's our big money-maker, the news."[162]

The same is true for individual stations. One financial analyst estimated that 40–50% of their profits come from news programs.[163]

Overall, commercial bias of the media results in no coverage, delayed coverage, or superficial coverage of many important stories. When members of Congress bounced checks at the House bank, one recalled, there was a "massive scramble to get the list of who bounced checks. . . . It was ya-hoo! . . . Reporters were lusting after it." But few were paying any attention to the "$400 billion worth of hot checks being written by the federal government."[164] The media considered the deficit too difficult to explain to readers and viewers. Not until Perot made it a campaign issue did most media begin to address it.

Even scandals, which might be expected to interest citizens, get limited coverage if they are complicated. When a career civil servant presented evidence of the HUD scandal in the 1980s, a *Washington Post* reporter said it was not worth looking into and a Washington television investigator said it was not "sexy" enough.[165] Although financial publications and business pages of newspapers reported the looming savings and loan scandal of the 1980s, political reporters and editors ignored it for years. They did not understand the substance and were not interested in it. A banking reporter later said, "You would relay this to your editors, but because it involved banking regulations, their eyes would glaze over."[166] The crisis was too complicated and too dull until it could be personalized and sensationalized. Finally, Charles Keating—

the chair of a failed S&L and a highflier with three private jets, one with gold-plated bathroom fixtures—was linked to the scandal. Then "looted Rembrandts and party girls on yachts" were discovered, and both the media and the public took notice.[167] Yet by this time, officials estimated, the industry needed a $500 billion bailout from the taxpayers to prevent even more insolvent S&Ls from collapsing (and taking depositors' savings with them).

In sum, the commercial bias of the media, especially television, limits the quality of the news presented. This, more than any political bias, makes it difficult for citizens, particularly those who rely on television, to become well informed.

Impact of the Media on Politics

It is difficult to measure the impact of the media on politics. Different media provide different coverage and reach different though overlapping audiences. Other factors also influence people's knowledge, attitudes, and behavior toward politics. Thus, it is exceedingly difficult to isolate the impact of particular media on particular groups of people. But there is considerable agreement that the media have a substantial impact on the public agenda, public opinion, political parties, and elections.

Impact on the Public Agenda

The most important impact of the media is **setting the agenda**—influencing the process by which problems are considered important and alternative policies are proposed and debated.[168] The media publicize an issue, and people exposed to the media talk about the issue with their fellow citizens. Eventually enough consider it important and expect officials to try to resolve it.[169]

The media's impact is most noticeable for dramatic events that occur suddenly, such as the dismantling of the Berlin Wall. The impact is less noticeable for issues that evolve gradually. Watergate required months of coverage before making it on the public agenda, and AIDS required the death of actor Rock Hudson before making it.[170]

Even for issues that evolve gradually, however, cumulative coverage by the media can have an impact. In 1989 and 1990 people told pollsters that drug use was the "most important problem" facing the country. Although by this time drug use had remained flat, or even had declined slightly, the media lavished attention on it so people assumed it had increased sharply. Once the media's attention was focused on other problems, drug use, which had been cited by a majority of respondents, now was cited by less than a tenth of them. Similarly, in 1993 and 1994 people told pollsters that crime was the "most important problem." Yet the crime rate had been relatively steady (up a bit for some crimes, down a bit for other crimes). Only the amount of media coverage had changed significantly.[171] Between 1992 and 1993 the amount of time devoted to crime on network newscasts had increased 100%.[172]

The impact usually is greatest for stories that appear on the front page of the newspaper or top of the newscast rather than those buried in the back or at the end.[173] Many people who do not follow the news fully check the beginning of the newspaper or newscast for the "important" stories. Without being aware of it, they are accepting the media's role in identifying these stories as the important ones.

And the media's impact usually is greatest on people who are most interested in politics, because they are most likely to follow the news and discuss it with others.[174] Yet the impact varies according to the personal experiences of the audience. For instance, people with recent unemployment in their family will be more sensitive to news about unemployment than other people.

In shaping the agenda, the most prominent print organizations normally are the most powerful. The *New York Times* is preeminent for international politics, the *Washington Post* for domestic politics, and the specialized *Wall Street Journal* for economic matters. The AP wire service is influential, and *Newsweek* and *Time* magazines are also. Other media take their cues from these organizations. Even the television networks get most of their stories from these print media.[175]

However, in recent years radio and television call-in shows set the agenda for some issues. In the 1992 presidential campaign, tabloid newspapers and non-news television programs set the agenda for Clinton's sexual affairs.

For years the major media "controlled the gates through which news passed. If they didn't report it, by and large the rest of us didn't hear about it."[176] But now the mainstream media have no monopoly; the fringe media also can open the gates for some issues.

The media's power to influence the agenda has important implications. The media play a key role in deciding which problems government addresses and which it ignores. They also play a key role in increasing or decreasing politicians' ability to govern and to get reelected. By publicizing some issues, the media create a golden opportunity for politicians with the authority and ability to resolve these issues. At the same time, the media create a pitfall for those who lack the power to resolve these issues. Thus, the Iranian seizure of the American embassy and hostages became the prominent issue in the country in 1980. Every night CBS's Walter Cronkite signed off, "And that's the way it is, the ______ day of American hostages in captivity," as if anyone needed reminding. President Carter's lack of success in persuading Iranian officials to release the hostages or in directing an American invasion to rescue them cost him dearly in his reelection bid that year.

Yet the role of the media in shaping the agenda should not be overstated. Individuals' knowledge and experience lead them to consider some things unimportant even when the media do cover them. And, of course, individuals' interests prompt the media to cover some things in the first place.[177]

Moreover, politicians play an important role in shaping the agenda. For much legislation, such as bills to improve safety in automobiles, workplaces, and coal mines, Congress initiates action and then the media publicize it.[178] For presidential elections, candidates usually establish the agenda of policy issues. By emphasizing issues they think will resonate with the public and reflect favorably on themselves, candidates pressure the media to cover these rather than other issues that might not rebound to their credit. On the other hand, the media usually establish the agenda of nonpolicy issues, involving the candidates' personality and behavior.[179] The media are able to set the agenda for nonpolicy issues because these are more likely to catch the public's fancy.

Impact on Public Opinion

Social scientists long thought that the media influenced the things people thought about but not the opinions they held about these things. Some contemporary research, however, demonstrates that the media do have a substantial impact on public opinion as well as on the public agenda. A comparison of the networks' newscasts with the public's policy preferences in a wide variety of foreign and domestic issues for 15 years during the 1970s and 1980s shows that the media influence opinion about issues.[180] Other research shows that the media influence opinion about particular presidents.[181] They affect opinion indirectly—by providing the news and transmitting the views of various opinion leaders—as well as directly—through editorials and commentaries intended to sway opinion.

There is much speculation that the media have contributed to the public's cynicism toward government in recent decades. The media have undermined the public's perception of the integrity of government and officials not just by reporting real shortcomings of programs and administrators, but by engaging in several practices already addressed in this chapter. The negative bias in coverage of all candidates and officials directly undermines them, while the game orientation in coverage of them more subtly undermines them. The emphasis on conflict leads to a focus on politicians' most extreme statements, which alienates the public and, at the same time, polarizes it. The practice of objectivity—reporting what he said versus what she said without evaluating the truth of either—passes along some false statements and some misleading ones and confuses the public.[182] Many people complain, "You can't believe any of them."

Some researchers have concluded that the result of these practices is to foster **media malaise** among the public.[183] This is a feeling of cynicism and distrust, perhaps even despair, toward government and officials. Indeed, according to a 1995 survey, the public is even more cynical than journalists themselves. Seventy-seven percent of the public gave government officials a low rating for honesty and ethics, while only 40% of the journalists did so.[184] Apparently journalists view their practices as ways to expand their audience, but the public, while deploring these practices, sees them as reflections of reality. So cynical coverage by the press leads to even more cynical attitudes in the citizenry.

The cynical attitudes have important implications for politics. They probably reduce satisfaction with candidates and officials and reduce turnout in elections. At the same time, they probably increase votes for "outsiders" who present themselves as "nonpoliticians."

Impact on Political Parties and Elections

In addition to their overall impact on the public agenda and public opinion, the media have had a major impact on political parties and elections in various other ways.

Political Parties

The media have contributed to the decline of political parties on the national level. In the young republic, political parties created and controlled most newspapers. Naturally, the papers echoed the parties' views and the journalists bowed to the parties' leaders. (The editor of one Democratic Party paper made sure a pail of fresh milk was left on the White House doorstep for President Andrew Jackson every morning, even if the editor had to deliver it himself.[185]) People received much of their political information, however biased, from these papers.

After independent newspapers arose, the party papers disappeared. People began to get much of their political information from the independent newspapers. Eventually people came to get it from independent radio and television networks and stations as well. Thus, people are no longer dependent upon parties for their political information.

In other ways as well, the media, especially television, have contributed to the decline of parties. In place of selection by party bosses, television allows candidates to appeal directly to the people. If candidates succeed in the primaries, parties have little choice but to nominate them. In place of campaign management by party bosses, television requires new expertise, so candidates assemble their own campaign organization. Television advertising requires substantial amounts of money, so party funds are inadequate and candidates approach other donors. Television also gives voters information so they can make up their own minds about how to vote, rather than rely on the party organization to tell them. Thus, the media have supplanted parties as the principal link between people and their leaders.

Types of Candidates

Television has encouraged new types of candidates for national offices. No longer need candidates be experienced politicians who worked their way up over many years. Celebrities from other fields with name recognition can move into prominent positions even without political experience. It is not coincidental that in recent years the House has had an actor (Fred Grandy, R-Ia.—"Gopher" on "Love Boat"), a professional baseball pitcher (Jim Bunning, R-Ky.), a professional football quarterback (Jack Kemp, R-N.Y.), and a professional basketball player (Tom McMillen, D-Md.) and the Senate has had a professional basketball player (Bill Bradley, D-N.J.) and two astronauts (John Glenn, D-Oh., and Harrison Schmitt, R-N.M.).[186] Nor is it coincidental that the Senate has had a television commentator (Jesse Helms, R-N.C.) and a businessman who appeared in his company's commercials (Rudy Boschwitz, R-Minn.). Alternatively, unknowns with talent can achieve rapid name recognition and move into prominent positions. Jimmy Carter, who had served one term as governor of Georgia, was relatively unknown elsewhere in the country when he ran for the Democratic nomination for president in 1976. But through effective use of television, he won enough primaries so the party had to nominate him, even though the leaders were uncomfortable with him.

Washington, Jefferson, and Lincoln in the Media Age

How would three of America's greatest presidents have fared in the media age? George Washington cut an impressive figure, but he had a speech impediment.

Thomas Jefferson was tall—six feet, two inches, when the average American man was about five feet, five inches—but he was shy, even awkward, with people. And apparently he never made a political speech.

Abraham Lincoln was also tall, but he was gangly. According to contemporaries, he was homely in different ways at different times. One newspaper called him "the ugliest man in the Union."[1] He had a "ploughed" face and a "doughnut" complexion, protruding ears, and "spider" legs.[2] He also had a high-pitched voice.

A modern observer speculated how television would cover the Gettysburg Address, which, though brief, would not be brief enough: The cameras would focus on the network correspondent describing the scene and recalling the battle, while in the background Lincoln would be speaking. Finally, the cameras would focus on Lincoln concluding, "government of the people, by the people, for the people, shall not perish from the earth."[3]

Are there contemporary Washingtons, Jeffersons, and Lincolns who might make effective leaders but who would not qualify because they are ineffective on television?

1. Thomas E. Patterson, *Out of Order* (New York: Vintage, 1994), p. 9.
2. Marcus Cunliffe, "What Did Abraham Lincoln Look Like?" *Washington Post National Weekly Edition*, February 27, 1984, p. 35.
3. Thomas Griffith, "Always Articulate on Sunday," *Time*, June 6, 1983, p. 55.

At the same time that television has allowed newcomers to run, it also has imposed new requirements on candidates for national offices. They must demonstrate an appealing appearance and performance on camera; they must be telegenic. President Franklin Roosevelt's body, crippled from polio and often on crutches or in a wheelchair, would not be impressive on television. President Harry Truman's style—"Give 'em hell"—would not be impressive on television either. Although effective in whistlestop speeches, it would be too "hot," too intense, to come into people's homes every day. A "cool," low-key style is more effective.

President Reagan was the quintessential politician for the television age. He was tall and trim with a handsome face and a smooth, reassuring voice. As a former actor he could project his personality and convictions and deliver his lines and jokes better than any other politician. It is not an exaggeration to conclude, as one political scientist did, "Without a chance to display his infectious smile, his grandfatherly demeanor, and his 'nice guy' qualities to millions of Americans, Ronald Reagan, burdened by his image as a superannuated, intellectually lightweight movie actor with right-wing friends and ultraconservative leanings, might never have reached the presidency."[187]

Television has not created the public desire for politicians with an appealing personality. "When candidates shook hands firmly, kissed babies, and handed out cigars, the thrust was not on issues."[188] Yet television has exacerbated this emphasis on the right image.

Campaigns

The media affect nomination and election campaigns through their news and commentary and candidates' advertisements. They help set the campaign agenda and help shape public opinion, as already explained. They also inform and persuade.

The media provide information about the candidates and the issues, and they also interpret this information.[189] The public learns about the candidates and the issues,[190] but in the process the public is influenced in making its choices.

Information about the candidates can have a major impact especially at the nomination stage. In presidential elections, a party without an incumbent president running for reelection might field a dozen candidates. The media cannot cover all adequately, so they narrow the field by considering some "serious" and giving them more coverage. Once the primaries begin, they label some "winners" and others "losers," and they give the "winners" more coverage. In the Democratic race in 1976, Carter finished second to "uncommitted" in the Iowa caucuses. This was enough to give him 23 times more coverage in *Time* and *Newsweek*, and 5 times more coverage on network television, than any of his rivals. Finishing first by just 4% in the New Hampshire primary landed him on the covers of *Time* and *Newsweek* and brought him 25 times more coverage on network television than the runner-up.[191] In the Democratic race in 1992, even before a single primary, the press proclaimed Clinton the front-runner and several magazines put his picture on their cover, although half of the public did not know who he was.[192]

By making these judgments, the media strongly influence the election process at this stage.[193] Because few people have formed opinions about the candidates this early, they are open to impressions from the media. Therefore, when the media declare some candidates winners, they help create a bandwagon effect.[194] When they declare others losers, they make it hard for these candidates to attract contributors and volunteers and eventually supporters in the next primaries.

The media also can persuade voters directly. This can be seen in several ways.

Televised debates do not sway most viewers because people tend to engage in **selective perception,** which is a tendency to screen out information that contradicts their beliefs. Consequently, most people conclude that their candidate performed better.[195] However, the debates do sway some viewers, usually those who have moderate education and some interest in politics but who are not decided or, if decided, not strongly committed to one candidate. In 1960 the debates might have caused enough voters to cast their ballots for Kennedy that he won the election.[196]

Media commentary about the debates also sways some viewers. In 1976 Ford erroneously said there was "no Soviet domination of Eastern Europe." People surveyed within 12 hours after the debate said they thought Ford won. But the media zeroed in on this slip, and people surveyed later said they thought Carter won (see Table 1). In the first debate in 1984, Reagan appeared tired and confused. By a modest margin, people polled immediately after the debate said Mondale won. But the media focused on Re-

TABLE 1 Media Commentary Influenced Perceptions of 1976 Debates

CANDIDATE VIEWERS FELT WON DEBATE	VIEWERS INTERVIEWED WITHIN 12 HOURS AFTER DEBATE	VIEWERS INTERVIEWED FROM 12 HOURS TO 48 HOURS AFTER DEBATE
Ford	53%	29%
Carter	35	58
Undecided	12	13

According to a study of people in Erie, Pennsylvania, and Los Angeles, media commentary on Ford's gaffe caused many to change their minds about which candidate won the debate. A majority of those interviewed before the commentary sunk in thought Ford won, whereas a majority of those interviewed later thought Carter won.

Source: Thomas E. Patterson. *The Mass Media Election* (New York: Praeger, 1980), p. 123.

agan's age and abilities and, by increasingly large margins, people polled in the days after the debate said Mondale won. Perhaps viewers did not catch Ford's statement or, due to selective perception, notice Reagan's doddering, but the media called attention to them, which prompted many viewers to reconsider and reverse their verdict.

Newspaper endorsements of candidates also sway some readers, especially those with a ninth- through twelth-grade education. People with less education are less likely to read editorials, while those with more education have more sources of information and more defined ideologies to guide their decisions.[197] Even if endorsements sway only a small percentage of voters, they could determine the outcome of tight races.[198] Endorsements are thought to have little effect on well-publicized races, although one study of the 1964 presidential election concluded that endorsements of President Johnson by monopoly newspapers in 223 counties across the North added about 5% to the vote he would have received in these counties otherwise.[199] Endorsements probably have more effect on relatively unpublicized races, such as for state legislator or local tax assessor, because voters have little other information to guide them.

Conclusion: Are the Media Responsive?

The media have to be responsive to the people to make a profit. They present the news they think the people want. Because they believe the majority desire entertainment, or at least diversion, rather than education, they structure the news toward this end. According to a number of studies, they correctly assess their consumers.[200] For the majority who want entertainment, network television provides it. For the minority who want education, the better newspapers and magazines provide it. Public radio, with its hour-and-a-half nightly newscast, and public television, with its hour nightly newscast, also provide quality coverage. The media offer something for everyone.

When officials or citizens get upset with the media, they pointedly ask, "Who elected you?" Journalists reply that the people—their readers or listeners or viewers—"elected them" by paying attention to their news columns or newscasts. At the same time, however, the people criticize the media. Almost three-fourths tell pollsters that the media get in the way of society's efforts to solve its problems. Only one-fourth say that the media help to solve the problems.[201]

To say the media are responsive, however, is not to say they perform well. Giving the people what they want most is not necessarily serving the country best. As one reporter lamented, "People seem to 'know' everything now—hearing the same news bulletins repeated around the clock—but they seem to understand precious little of what's really going on."[202] The media personalize and dramatize the news. The result is to simplify the news. Superficial coverage of complex events leaves the public unable to understand these events and, ultimately, unable to force the government to be responsive.

The media reflect a crisis *du jour* mentality in which everything is important for a day or a week or occasionally a month. But almost no political development is important for long. So the media lurch from a supposed crisis to a real crisis, and back again. In the Clinton years, for example, the media have flitted from the caning of a teenager in Singapore to the making of nuclear weapons in North Korea; from a civil war in the former Yugoslavia to the appropriate commemoration for the fiftieth anniversary of the end of World War II with Japan; from the president's haircut in an airplane, which cost $200, to his first budget bill, which reduced the deficit; from the Clintons' possible corruption in the Whitewater land deal to the effort by a friend of the Clintons to get a White House job in the "Travelgate scandal"; from the secrecy of the health care task force to the substance of health care reform; from the denial of a presidential appointment for Zoe Baird because she hired illegal aliens to the denial of a presidential appointment for Kimba Wood because—well, somebody must remember; it was considered important. The headlines and the stories clamoring for attention go by in such a blur that after a while they all become a jumble for many people. They leave no sense of what's actually a crisis, what's just a problem, what's merely an irritant, and what's truly a triviality.[203]

Thus, most news coverage is episodic—an event is presented as a single, idiosyncratic occurrence—rather than thematic—the event is presented as an example or reflection of a larger pattern. For instance, a story might focus on one hungry person or group of persons rather than on malnutrition as a national problem. Episodic coverage is more common because it is more entertaining—dramatic, with human interest—than thematic coverage. But episodic coverage makes it hard for people to see the connection between problems in society and the actions of government and its officials. Then people do not hold their leaders accountable for addressing or resolving the problems.[204]

Moreover, by bombarding the public with instances of conflict, without much coverage of constructive compromises that sometimes flow from such disagreement, and by portraying interest groups and lobbying as evil rather than as ways the public is represented, the media contribute to the public's distaste for democratic processes.

The media's shortcomings are aggravated by a declining interest in politics and a decreasing number of people who read newspapers and, to a lesser extent, watch newscasts. Although the public is better educated now than in the 1960s, it is less likely to follow the news and less able to answer questions about the government.[205] People under 35 especially reflect these trends. To keep these vanishing readers, many newspapers have revamped their formats. While some have improved their quality, more have emulated *USA Today* and reduced their substance to hold the attention spans of younger readers weaned on television. (One radio station advertises, "You can get the facts without straining your brain."[206]) This has disturbing implications. Citizens who are not aware of the news or who do not understand it cannot fulfill their role in a democracy.

Thus, the problem is a circular one. Politicians try to use the media to manipulate the public, but they must follow the conventions of the media, which are determined by the demands of the public. Therefore, the public is an accomplice in its own exploitation.[207]

These trends come at a time when the media, despite their shortcomings, provide more news than ever and—with journalists better educated and better able to address complex topics—more effective news

than ever. Because the media are somewhat responsive and effective, they have become powerful enough to serve as a check on government in many situations. This was evident during the major crises of recent decades. During the war in Vietnam, the media stood up to two presidents when Congress and the courts were relatively passive. During the Watergate scandal, the media led Congress and the courts in standing up to a president. The media serve as a check on the government in countless other situations. As a former government official noted, "Think how much chicanery dies on the drawing board when someone says, 'We'd better not do that; what if the press finds out?' "[208]

EPILOGUE

Signorile Reveals Official's Homosexuality

Michelangelo Signorile decided to publish information revealing that the assistant secretary of defense, Pete Williams, was homosexual.[209] Initially the mainstream media refused to report the story. Most reporters on the Pentagon beat did not ask questions about the revelation or write articles about it. Most editors spiked the articles that reporters did write. Eventually one reporter asked Williams directly. He refused to answer: "As a government spokesman, I stand here and I talk about government policy. I am not paid to discuss my personal opinions about that policy or talk about my personal life, and I don't intend to."[210] In subsequent weeks some mainstream newspapers and magazines decided to cover the story and name the official after all.

The brouhaha put the military's policy of discharging homosexuals on the agenda for the 1992 election. Candidate Bill Clinton criticized the hypocrisy of the situation and promised to change the policy. After Clinton's election, Williams, a political appointee of the Bush administration, left government for the private sector.

"Outing," as the practice of identifying gays and lesbians who remain in "the closet" came to be called, spread. While some activists engaged in outing through their writing, others sent faxes across the country, nailed posters to telephone poles, and confronted persons in public. Supermarket tabloids, always alert for sensational stories, engaged in outing of actors. Unlike the gay activists, these papers were motivated by the desire to boost circulation and increase profits.

Many homosexuals felt threatened by the spread of outing. Signorile remembers, "I was called every name in the book and fended off angry people everywhere I went."[211] Many heterosexuals who felt that the media already were too intrusive into private lives also criticized the practice. One political scientist called it "a despicable new movement."[212]

Signorile acknowledges the media might be too intrusive, but he says if the media cover the private lives of heterosexuals they legitimately can cover the private lives of homosexuals. "Journalists," he adds, "are not in the business of providing comfort or making people feel better. They're in the business of telling the truth, whatever it is, whenever it is pertinent to a story."[213]

But when is a person's homosexuality "pertinent to a story"? Signorile would limit outing to public figures—famous persons who make lots of money from the public or wield considerable power over the public—and to situations that reflect hypocrisy, such as persons in government or the media who act contrary to the interests of homosexuals. Signorile admits these criteria are fuzzy and decisions need to be made on a case-by-case basis.

And he admits he is uneasy about some of what has happened. "I can't say I felt great about all this. It wasn't the outing I had a problem with, but the fact that I was using it as a bludgeoning and blackmailing tool. That wasn't what I originally had in mind. But as has been true in every revolution, there is always a person or group who kicks things off by doing something brutal. . . . We were under siege at the time, and I was operating with a siege mentality."[214]

His goal in outing is "to give courage to millions of gay people who stay in the closet out of fear and shame."[215] He especially wants to show gay teenagers, who are left "feeling alone, like freaks" and who experience more depression and suicide than straight teenagers, that there are gay adults who have made it—as Eddie Murphy and Oprah Winfrey show black kids.[216]

With these words, Signorile indicates that he might be more an activist than a journalist. But in these times, when anyone with a fax machine or an Internet account can be a "journalist," the ethics of reporting have become more blurred.

➤Key Terms

symbiotic relationship
adversarial relationship
beats
leaks
scoop
presidential press conference
media events
sound bite
fireside chats
political bias
commercial bias
game orientation
setting the agenda
media malaise
selective perception

➤Further Reading

The print media themselves are the primary sources for further reading. A good metropolitan newspaper or a weekly newsmagazine is essential. For political junkies, the *Washington Post National Weekly Edition,* a compilation of the newspaper's best articles and cartoons about politics during the week, is wonderful.

Timothy Crouse, *The Boys on the Bus* (New York: Random House, 1972). *An irreverent account of press coverage of elections by a writer who reported on the reporters rather than on the candidates along the presidential campaign trail in 1972.*

Mark Hertsgaard, *On Bended Knee* (New York: Farrar, Straus & Giroux, 1988). *An indictment of media coverage of the Reagan presidency. The author's thesis is that Reagan turned news hounds into lap dogs.*

Kathleen Hall Jamieson and David S. Birdsell, *Presidential Debates* (New York: Oxford University Press, 1988). *A history of presidential debates and a set of proposals for their reform.*

John R. MacArthur, *Second Front: Censorship and Propaganda in the Gulf War* (Hill and Wang, 1992). *A searing critique of media coverage of the war.*

Joe McGinniss, *The Selling of the President 1968* (New York: Simon & Schuster, 1969). *An account of the often-comical efforts by Richard Nixon's advisers to transform him into a media candidate.*

Nan Robertson, *The Girls in the Balcony: Women, Men, and the* New York Times (Random House, 1992). A history of piggery at the country's most famous newspaper.

Tom Rosenstiel, *Strange Bedfellows: How Television and the Presidential Candidates Changed American Politics, 1992* (New York: Hyperion, 1993). A critical examination of media coverage of the 1992 campaign.

➤Notes

1. Michelangelo Signorile, *Queer in America: Sex, the Media, and the Closets of Power* (New York: Random House, 1993), p. 78.
2. Larry J. Sabato, *Feeding Frenzy: How Attack Journalism Has Transformed American Politics* (New York: Free Press, 1991), pp. 192–93.
3. Signorile, *Queer in America,* p. 138.
4. Ibid., p. 148.
5. Sabato, *Feeding Frenzy,* pp. 1, 8–22.
6. James David Barber, *The Pulse of Politics* (New York: W. W. Norton, 1980), p. 9.
7. Kevin Phillips, "A Matter of Privilege," *Harpers,* January 1977, pp. 95–97.
8. Richard Harwood, "So Many Media, So Little Time," *Washington Post National Weekly Edition,* September 7–13, 1992, p. 28.
9. Thomas R. Dye and L. Hannon Zeigler, *American Politics in the Media Age* (Monterey, Calif.: Brooks/Cole Publishing, 1983), pp. 123–24.
10. Edwin Diamond, *The Tin Kazoo* (Cambridge, Mass.: MIT Press, 1975), p. 13.
11. Doris A. Graber, *Mass Media and American Politics* (Washington, D.C.: Congressional Quarterly, 1980), p. 2.
12. William Lutz, *Doublespeak* (New York: Harper & Row, 1989), pp. 73–74.
13. Richard Harwood, "Nobody Reads Anymore," *Washington Post National Weekly Edition,* December 26, 1988–January 1, 1989, p. 29.
14. Sabato, *Feeding Frenzy,* p. 50.
15. Thomas E. Patterson, *The Mass Media Election* (New York: Praeger, 1980), pp. 58–60, 62–63.
16. Timothy E. Cook, *Making Laws and Making News: Media Strategies in the U.S. House of Representatives* (Washington, D.C.: Brookings Institution, 1989), p. 19.
17. J. Fred MacDonald, *One Nation Under Television: The Rise and Decline of Network TV* (New York: Pantheon, 1991); Robert S. Lichter, Stanley Rothman, and Linda S. Lichter, *The Media Elite* (Bethesda, MD, 1986), pp. 5–7.
18. Otto Friedrich, "Edging the Government Out of TV," *Time,* August 17, 1987, p. 58; Edmund L. Andrews, "A New Tune for Radio: Hard Times," *New York Times,* March 1992.
19. Benjamin M. Compaine, *Who Owns the Media?* (White Plains, N.Y.: Knowledge Industry Publications, 1979) pp. 11, 76–77.
20. Alex S. Jones, "At Many Papers, Competition Is at Best an Illusion," *New York Times,* September 22, 1991.
21. Michael Parenti, *Inventing Reality* (New York: St. Martin's, 1986), p. 27.
22. Paul Farhi, "You Can't Tell a Book by Its Cover," *Washington Post National Weekly Edition,* December 5–11, 1988, p. 21.

23. Andrews, "A New Tune for Radio."

24. Harwood, "So Many Media, So Little Time."

25. Elizabeth Kolbert, "For Talk Shows, Less News is Good News," *New York Times,* June 28, 1992, p. E-2.

26. Carol Matlack, "Target Television," *National Journal,* February 1, 1992, p. 263.

27. Judith Miller, "But Can You Dance to It?" *New York Times Magazine,* October 11, 1992, p. 33.

28. Howard Fineman, "The Power of Talk," *Time,* February 8, 1993, p. 25.

29. "The Vocal Minority in American Politics," Times Mirror Center for the People and the Press, Washington, D.C., July, 1993.

30. Richard Corliss, "Look Who's Talking," *Time,* January 23, 1995, p. 23.

31. William A. Henry III, "Handling the Clinton Affair," *Time,* February 10, 1992, p. 28.

32. Richard Harwood, "The Growing Irrelevance of Journalists," *Washington Post National Weekly Edition,* November 2–8, 1992, p. 29.

33. Corliss, "Look Who's Talking," p. 25.

34. Tom Rosenstiel, *The Beat Goes On: President Clinton's First Year with the Media* (New York: Twentieth Century Fund, 1994), p. 35.

35. Dom Bonafede, "Press Paying More Heed to Substance in Covering 1984 Presidential Election," *National Journal,* October 13, 1984, p. 1923.

36. "All Things Considered," National Public Radio, November 5, 1992.

37. "Comment: Take Five," *New Yorker,* November 23, 1992, p. 4.

38. Thomas M. DeFrank, "Playing the Media Game," *Newsweek,* April 17, 1989, p. 21.

39. Charles Peters, *How Washington Really Works* (Redding, Mass.: Addison-Wesley Publishing, 1980), p. 18.

40. William Greider, "Reporters and Their Sources," *Washington Monthly* (October 1982), pp. 13–15.

41. Daniel Schorr, "A Fact of Political Life," *Washington Post National Weekly Edition,* October 28–November 3, 1991, p. 32.

42. Howard Kurtz, "How Sources and Reporters Play the Game of Leaks," *Washington Post National Weekly Edition,* March 15–21, 1993, p. 25.

43. Elizabeth Drew, "Letter from Washington," *New Yorker,* September 12, 1988, p. 92.

44. Ann Devroy, "The Republicans, It Turns Out, Are a Veritable Fount of Leaks," *Washington Post National Weekly Edition,* November 18–24, 1991, p. 23.

45. William A. Henry III, "Scrounging for Good Air," *Time,* September 3, 1984, p. 7.

46. Christopher Georges, "Confessions of an Investigative Reporter," *Washington Monthly,* March, 1992, p. 41; Timothy Crouse, *The Boys on the Bus* (New York: Random House, 1972).

47. Jonathan Alter, "When Sources Get Immunity," *Newsweek,* January 19, 1987, p. 54.

48. Samuel Kernell, *Going Public: New Strategies of Presidential Leadership* (Washington, D.C.: Congressional Quarterly, 1986), p. 59.

49. Woodrow Wilson also tried to cultivate correspondents and host frequent sessions, but he did not have the knack for this activity and he scaled back the sessions. Kernell, *Going Public,* pp. 60–61. He did perceive that "[s]ome men of brilliant ability were in the group, but I soon discovered that the interest of the majority was in the personal and the trivial rather than in principles and policies." James Bennet, "The Flack Pack," *Washington Monthly,* November 1991, p. 27.

50. Dwight Eisenhower actually was the first president who let the networks televise his press conferences, but he did not do so to reach the public. When he wanted to reach the public, he made a formal speech. The networks found his conferences so untelegenic that they stopped covering the entire session each time. Kernell, *Going Public,* p. 68.

51. Kernell, *Going Public,* p. 104.

52. Bennet, "The Flack Pack," p. 19.

53. Dom Bonafede, " 'Mr. President,' " *National Journal,* October 29, 1988, p. 2756.

54. Garry Wills, ". . . But Don't Treat It as a Game," *Lincoln Journal* (Universal Press Syndicate), March 26, 1993.

55. Charles Hagen, "The Photo Op: Making Icons or Playing Politics?" *New York Times,* February 9, 1992, p. H28.

56. "Media Lights' Glare Inhibits Maneuvers," *Lincoln Journal* (AP), December 9, 1992; Jonathan Alter, "Did the Press Push Us into Somalia?" *Newsweek,* December 21, 1992, p. 33.

57. Kiku Adatto, cited in Howard Kurtz, "Networks Adapt to Changed Campaign Role," *Washington Post,* June 21, 1992, p. A19.

58. Lance Morrow, "Time Essay," *Time,* August 18, 1980, p. 78.

59. Steven R. Weisman, "The President and the Press," *New York Times Magazine,* October 14, 1984, p. 71.

60. Ronald H. Brown, "Republican Baloney About Crime," *Washington Post National Weekly Edition,* April 30–May 6, 1990, p. 29.

61. David Halberstam, "How Television Failed the American Voter," *Parade,* January 11, 1981, p. 8.

62. George E. Reedy, *The Twilight of the Presidency* (New York: New American Library, 1970), p. 112.

63. Thomas Griffith, "Winging It on Television," *Time,* March 14, 1983, p. 71.

64. "Talking about the Media Circus," *New York Times Magazine,* June 26, 1994, p. 63.

65. Sabato, *Feeding Frenzy.*

66. Sabato, *Feeding Frenzy,* p. 53.

67. See Sabato, *Feeding Frenzy,* for additional reasons for this increase.

68. W. Lance Bennett, *News: The Politics of Illusion,* 2nd ed. (New York: Longman, 1988).

69. John David Rausch, Jr., "The Pathology of Politics: Government, Press, and Scandal," *Extensions* (University of Oklahoma), Fall 1990, pp. 11–12.

70. Michael Riley, "Where Were the Media on HUD?" *Time,* July 24, 1989, p. 48.

71. William Rivers, "The Correspondents after 25 Years," *Columbia Journalism Review* 1 (Spring 1962), p. 5.

72. James David Barber, *Presidential Character* (Englewood Cliffs, N.J.: Prentice Hall, 1992), p. 238.

73. Hedrick Smith, *The Power Game* (New York: Random House, 1988), p. 403.

74. Timothy J. Russert, "For '92, the Networks Have to Do Better," *New York Times,* March 4, 1990.

75. Smith, *Power Game,* p. 420.

76. Adam Hochschild, "All the President's Patsies," *Mother Jones,* July/August 1988, p. 52.

77. When Reagan ordered the invasion of Grenada in 1983, the administration excluded reporters. For two days the only news that reached the public came from the administration, and it was uniformly positive about both the need for and the success of the invasion. However, in response to criticism from the media, the Pentagon established a pool system for future wars. Representative

groups of reporters would be allowed to cover the action and share their information with other media. The military could transport and protect a few pools more easily than a huge number of individual reporters. But what the Pentagon did not admit was that the military, while appearing to cooperate, could control reporters' access to battles, individuals, and other sources of information more easily as well.

78. Patrick J. Sloyan, "The War the Administration Isn't Going to Let You See," *Washington Post National Weekly Edition,* January 21–27, 1991, p. 23; Vicki Kemper and Deborah Baldwin, "War Stories," *Common Cause,* March/April 1991, p. 18; Stanley W. Cloud, "How Reporters Missed the War," *Time,* January 8, 1990, p. 61.

79. Howard Kurtz, "The Press Pool's Chilling Effect on Covering the War," *Washington Post National Weekly Edition,* February 18–24, 1991, p. 12.

80. Howard Kurtz, "Keeping It All Pretty Quiet on the Mideastern Front," *Washington Post National Weekly Edition,* February 4–10, 1991, pp. 34–35.

81. Calculated from David Sarasohn, "Not So Smart," *Lincoln Journal* (Newhouse News Service), April 2, 1991.

82. Richard Morin, "The New War Cry: Stop the Press," *Washington Post National Weekly Edition,* February 11–17, 1991, p. 38.

83. Sidney Blumenthal, "The Syndicated Presidency," *New Yorker,* April 5, 1993, p. 45.

84. Robert P. Laurence, "Mr. President Proves He Has a Way with Words," *San Diego Union-Tribune,* March 24, 1993.

85. Rosenstiel, *The Beat Goes On,* pp. 8–9.

86. William Glaberson, "The Capitol Press vs. the President: Fair Coverage or Unreined Adversity?" *New York Times,* June 17, 1993, p. A11; Christopher Georges, "Bad News Bearers," *Washington Monthly,* July/August, 1993, pp. 28–34.

87. Thomas E. Patterson, *Out of Order* (New York: Vintage, 1994), pp. 14, 244.

88. Howard Kurtz, "Rolling with the Punches from the Press Corps," *Washington Post National Weekly Edition,* January 24–30, 1994, p. 10; James Fallows, "The Media's Rush to Judgment," *Washington Monthly,* January/February, 1994, pp. 10–11.

89. Mark P. Petracca, "Letters," *Washington Monthly,* September, 1993, p. 2; Larry J. Sabato, cited in Howard Kurtz, "Is It Splitsville for Clinton and the Media?" *Washington Post National Weekly Edition,* February 8–14, 1993, p. 14.

90. Larry J. Sabato, cited in Glaberson, "The Capitol Press vs. the President."

91. Stephen Hess, *Live from Capitol Hill!* (Washington, D.C.: Brookings Institution, 1991), p. 62; Cook, *Making Laws & Making News,* p. 2.

92. Hess, *Live from Capitol Hill!,* p. 102.

93. Edward Jay Epstein, *News from Nowhere* (New York: Random House, 1973), p. 13.

94. Graber, *Mass Media and American Politics,* p. 62.

95. Milton Coleman, "When the Candidate Is Black Like Me," *Washington Post National Weekly Edition,* April 23, 1984, p. 9.

96. Roper Organization, "A Big Concern about the Media: Intruding on Grieving Families," *Washington Post National Weekly Edition,* June 6, 1984.

97. Parenti, *Inventing Reality,* chapters 7–11; Charles E. Lindblom, *Politics and Markets* (New York: Basic Books, 1977); MacDonald, *One Nation Under Television.*

98. John R. MacArthur, *Second Front: Censorship and Propaganda in the Gulf War* (New York: Hill and Wang, 1992); James Bennet, "How They Missed That Story," *Washington Monthly,* December 1990, pp. 8–16. For a more detailed analysis, see Barbara Allen, Paula O'Loughlin, Amy Jasperson, John L. Sullivan, *"The Media and the Gulf War: Framing, Priming, and the Spiral of Silence,"* Polity 27, (Winter, 1994), pp. 255–84.

99. E.g., a videotape of Iraqis being killed reached two networks, but they refused to show it. Barber, *Presidential Character,* pp. 481–82.

100. Christopher Dickey, "Not Their Finest Hour," *Newsweek,* June 8, 1992, p. 66.

101. Leon V. Sigal, *Reporters and Officials* (Lexington, Mass.: D. C. Heath, 1973), pp. 120–21.

102. Lucy Howard, "Slanted 'Line'?" *Newsweek,* February 13, 1989, p. 6. See also Stephen Hess, *Live from Capitol Hill!,* p. 50. This tendency is less typical of local news.

103. Cook, *Making Laws & Making News,* p. 8.

104. Lichter et al., *The Media Elite,* pp. 21–25. See also Hess, *Live from Capitol Hill!,* Appendix A, pp. 110–30.

105. John Johnstone, Edward Slawski, and William Bowman, *The Newspeople* (Urbana, Ill.: University of Illinois Press, 1976), pp. 225–26.

106. Stanley Rothman and S. Robert Lichter, "Media and Business Elites: Two Classes in Conflict?" *The Public Interest* 69 (1982), pp. 111–25.

107. S. Robert Lichter and Stanley Rothman, "Media and Business Elites," *Public Opinion* (October/November, 1981), p. 44.

108. Stephen Hess, *The Washington Reporters* (Washington, D.C.: Brookings Institution, 1981), p. 89; Lichter et al., *The Media Elite,* pp. 127–28.

109. James Fallows, "The Stoning of Donald Regan," *Washington Monthly* (June 1984), p. 57. Most individual reporters also probably care more about their career than ideology, but this could lead to bias. In 1976 one media analyst ran into an old friend, an NBC correspondent. When the analyst asked how she was doing, she answered, "Not so great. My candidate lost." That is, the candidate she had covered during the presidential primaries lost his bid for the nomination. Because reporters often follow "their" presidential candidate into office, she lost her chance to become NBC's White House correspondent. Graeme Browning, "Too Close for Comfort?" *National Journal,* October 3, 1992, p. 2243.

110. Parenti, *Inventing Reality,* pp. 38, 56–57.

111. Mark Hertsgaard, "How Ronald Reagan Turned News Hounds into Lap Dogs," *Washington Post National Weekly Edition,* August 29–September 4, 1988, p. 25.

112. Joel Millman, "How the Press Distorts the News from Central America," *Progressive* (October 1984), p. 20.

113. Epstein, *News from Nowhere,* pp. 206–207. This, however is less of a problem than it used to be. Hess, *Washington Reporters.*

114. C. Richard Hofstetter, *Bias in the News* (Columbus, Ohio: Ohio State University Press, 1976); Doris Graber, *Mass Media and Politics* (Washington, D.C.: Congressional Quarterly Press, 1980), pp. 167–68; Michael J. Robinson, "Just How Liberal Is the News?" *Public Opinion* (February/March 1983), pp. 55–60; Maura Clancy and Michael J. Robinson, "General Election Coverage: Part I," *Public Opinion* 7 (December/January 1985), pp. 49–54, 59; Michael J. Robinson, "The Media Campaign, '84; Part II" *Public Opinion* 8 (February/March 1985), pp. 43–48.

115. Clancy and Robinson, "General Election Coverage"; Robinson, "The Media Campaign '84"; Michael J. Robinson, "Where's the Beef? Media and Media Elites in 1984," in Austin Ranney, ed., *The American Elections of 1984* (Durham, N.C.: Duke University

Press, 1985), p. 184; Michael J. Robinson, "News Media Myths and Realities: What Network News Did and Didn't Do in the 1984 General Campaign," in Kay Lehman Schlozman, ed., *Elections in America* (Boston: Allen & Unwin, 1987), pp. 143–70.

116. Patterson, *Out of Order,* p. 131.

117. Ibid., pp. 100–07.

118. Research by Robert Lichter and Richard Noyes, cited in Richard Harwood, "The Press and the Making of a President," *Washington Post National Weekly Edition,* January 22–28, 1996, p. 28.

119. Patterson, *Out of Order,* p. 106.

120. "Clinton Gains More Support from Big Papers," *Lincoln Journal-Star* (New York Times), October 25, 1992.

121. Stanley Rothman and S. Robert Lichter, "The Nuclear Energy Debate," *Public Opinion* 5 (August/September 1982), pp. 47–48; Stanley Rothman and S. Robert Lichter, "Elite Ideology and Risk Perception in Nuclear Energy Policy," *American Political Science Review* 81 (June 1987), pp. 383–404.

122. Lichter et al., *The Media Elite,* chapter 7.

123. Sabato, *Feeding Frenzy,* p. 87, and sources cited therein.

124. Robinson, "Just How Liberal Is the News?" p. 59.

125. James Fallows, *Breaking the News: How the Media Undermine American Democracy* (New York: Pantheon, 1996.)

126. Hofstetter, *Bias in the News;* Hess, *Live from Capitol Hill!,* pp. 12–13.

127. Robinson, "Just How Liberal Is the News?" p. 58; Arthur H. Miller, Edie N. Goldenberg, and Lutz Erbring, "Type-Set Politics," *American Political Science Review* 73 (1979), p. 69; Patterson, *Out of Order,* p. 6; Charles M. Tidmarch and John J. Pitney, Jr., "Covering Congress," *Polity* 17 (Spring 1985), pp. 463–83.

128. Patterson, *Out of Order,* pp. 25, 245.

129. Michael Baruch Grossman and Martha Joynt Kumar, *Portraying the President* (Baltimore: Johns Hopkins University Press, 1981).

130. Michael J. Robinson and Margaret A. Sheehan, *Over the Wire and on TV* (New York: Russell Sage Foundation and Basic Books, 1983).

131. Michael J. Robinson, "Three Faces of Congressional Media," in Doris A. Graber, ed., *Media Power in Politics* (Washington, D.C.: Congressional Quarterly, 1984), pp. 215–16.

132. "Anchorwoman Verdict Raises Mixed Opinions," *New York Times,* August 9, 1983.

133. Theodore H. White, *America in Search of Itself* (New York: Harper & Row, 1982), p. 186.

134. George F. Will, "Prisoners of TV," *Newsweek,* January 10, 1977, p. 76.

135. Parenti, *Inventing Reality,* p. 48.

136. David Owen, "The Cigarette Companies: How They Get Away with Murder, Part II," *Washington Monthly* (March 1985), pp. 48–54.

137. Martin A. Linsky, ed., *Television and the Presidential Elections* (Lexington, Mass.: D. C. Heath, 1983).

138. Barry Sussman, "News on TV: Mixed Reviews," *Washington Post National Weekly Edition,* September 3, 1984, p. 37.

139. Bill Carter, "Networks Fight Public's Shrinking Attention Span," *Lincoln Sunday Journal-Star* (New York Times), September 30, 1990.

140. Epstein, *News from Nowhere,* p. 4.

141. William A. Henry III, "Requiem for TV's Gender Gap," *Time,* August 22, 1983, p. 57.

142. Tom Jory, "TV Anchorwoman's Suit Exposes Subtle Bias in Hiring," *Lincoln Journal,* July 31, 1983, p. 1A.

143. Marlene Sanders and Marcia Rock, *Waiting for Prime Time: The Women of Television News* (Urbana, Ill., University of Illinois Press, 1988), pp. 147–48, cited in Hess, *Live from Capitol Hill!,* p. 120. Some of this pressure comes from women viewers. Barbara Walters receives more letters about her hair—"Why did you cut your hair?"—than about the stories she broadcasts. "Hair Anxiety Hounds Newswomen," *Lincoln Journal-Star,* December 12, 1995.

144. Robinson, "Just How Liberal Is the News?" p. 60.

145. "Tidbits and Outrages," *Washington Monthly* (February 1990), p. 44.

146. This, of course, is not a recent development. When independent newspapers competed for readers in the nineteenth century, they began to engage in "yellow journalism"—sensationalizing news, especially of crimes.

147. Patterson, *Out of Order,* p. 161.

148. Ibid., pp. 53–59 and generally.

149. For 1976 presidential campaign: Thomas E. Patterson, *The Mass Media Election* (New York: Praeger, 1980), p. 24. For 1984 presidential campaign: Henry E. Brady and Richard Johnson, "What's the Primary Message: Horse Race or Issue Journalism?," in Gary R. Orren and Nelson W. Polsby, ed., *Media and Momentum* (Chatham, N.J.: Chatham House, 1987), pp. 127–86. For 1988 presidential campaign: Stephen Ansolabehere, Roy Behr, and Shanto Iyengar, "Mass Media and Elections: An Overview," *American Politics Quarterly* 19 (January 1991), p. 119. For 1992 presidential campaign and in general: Patterson, *Out of Order.* For 1992 congressional campaigns: Charles M. Tidmarch, Lisa J. Hyman, and Jill E. Sorkin, "Press Issue Agendas in the 1982 Congressional and Gubernatorial Election Campaigns," *Journal of Politics* 46 (November 1984), p. 1231.

150. S. Robert Lichter, Daniel Amundson, and Richard Noyes, "The Video Campaign: Network Coverage of the 1988 Primaries" (Washington, D.C.: American Enterprise Institute for Public Policy Research, 1988), p. 65.

151. Lee Sigelman and David Bullock, "Candidates, Issues, Horse Races, and Hoopla: Presidential Campaign Coverage, 1888–1988." *American Politics Quarterly* 19 (January 1991), pp. 5–32. And so was emphasis upon human interest. In 1846 the *New York Tribune* described the culinary habits of Representative William "Sausage" Sawyer (D.-Oh.), who ate a sausage on the floor of the House every afternoon: "What little grease is left on his hands he wipes on his almost bald head which saves any outlay for Pomatum. His mouth sometimes serves as a finger glass, his shirtsleeves and pantaloons being called into requisition as a napkin. He uses a jackknife for a toothpick, and then he goes on the floor again to abuse the Whigs as the British party." Cook, *Making Law & Making News,* pp. 18–19.

152. Parenti, *Inventing Reality,* p. 15, quoting Malcolm MacDougall, "The Barkers of Snake Oil Politics," *Politics Today* (January/February 1980), p. 35.

153. David S. Broder, "Can We Govern?" *Washington Post National Weekly Edition,* January 31–February 6, 1994, p. 23.

154. "Newtspeak: The Gospel According to Gingrich," *Time,* December 25, 1995–January 1, 1996, p. 78.

155. Kathleen Hall Jamieson, *Dirty Politics: Deception, Distraction, Democracy* (New York: Oxford University Press, 1992), pp. 184–85.

156. William Glaberson, "The New Press Criticism: News as the Enemy of Hope," *New York Times,* October 9, 1994, p. E1; Tom Hamburger, Ted Marmor, and Jon Meacham, "What the Death of Health Reform Teaches Us about the Press," *Washington Monthly,* November, 1994, pp. 35–41.

157. Epstein, *News from Nowhere,* pp. 179, 195.

158. T. R. Reid, "Media Wrong about Yellowstone," *Lincoln Journal* (Washington Post), July 24, 1989.

159. David L. Altheide, "Format and Symbol in Television Coverage of Terrorism in the United States and Great Britain," *International Studies Quarterly* 31 (1987), pp. 161–76.

160. John Horn, "Campaign Coverage Avoids Issues," *Lincoln Sunday Journal-Star,* September 25, 1988.

161. John Eisendrath, "An Eyewitness Account of Local TV News," *Washington Monthly* (September 1986), p. 21.

162. Michael Deaver, "Sound-Bite Campaigning: TV Made Us Do It," *Washington Post National Weekly Edition,* November 7–13, 1988, p. 34.

163. Hess, *Live from Capitol Hill!,* p. 34.

164. Stanley W. Cloud and Nancy Traver, "Mr. Smith Leaves Washington," *Time,* June 8, 1992, p. 65.

165. "Letters," *Washington Monthly,* May, 1992, p. 2.

166. Howard Kurtz, "Asleep at the Switch," *Washington Post National Weekly Edition,* December 21–27, 1992, p. 6.

167. Larry Martz, "For the Media, a Pyrrhic Victory," *Newsweek,* June 22, 1992, p. 32. See also Hobart Rowen, "Uncle Sam's Underwriter," *Washington Post National Weekly Edition,* May 15–21, 1989, p. 5.

168. Donald L. Shaw and Maxwell E. McCombs, *The Emergence of American Political Issues: The Agenda-Setting Function of the Press* (St. Paul, Minn.: West, 1977). For a review of agenda-setting research, see Everett M. Rogers and James W. Dearing, "Agenda-Setting Research: Where Has It Been, Where Is It Going?" *Communication Yearbook* 11 (Newberry Park, Calif.: Sage, 1988), pp. 555–94.

169. Lutz Erbring, Edie N. Goldenberg, and Arthur H. Miller, "Front-Page News and Real-World Clues: A New Look at Agenda-Setting by the Media," *American Journal of Political Science* 24 (February 1980), pp. 16–49.

170. Michael Bruce MacKuen and Steven Lane Coombs, *More Than News* (Beverly Hills: Sage, 1981), p. 140; Rogers and Dearing, "Agenda-Setting Research," pp. 572–76; G. E. Lang and K. Lang, *The Battle for Public Opinion* (New York: Columbia University Press, 1983), pp. 58–59.

171. Richard Morin, "Public Enemy No. 1: Crime," *Washington Post National Weekly Edition,* January 24–30, 1994, p. 37.

172. Molly Ivins, "Hard Questions, Easy Answers," *Lincoln Journal* (Creators Syndicate), July 7, 1994.

173. Shanto Iyengar and Donald R. Kinder, *News That Matters* (Chicago: University of Chicago Press, 1987), pp. 42–45.

174. Erbring et al., "Front-Page News," p. 38; MacKuen and Coombs, *More Than News,* pp. 128–37.

175. Lichter et al., *The Media Elite,* p. 11.

176. Carl Sessions Stepp, "Establishment Media Have Lost Control of Campaign News Flow," *Lincoln Journal* (Hartford Courant), November 4, 1992.

177. Rogers and Dearing, "Agenda-Setting Research," p. 569; MacKuen and Coombs, *More Than News,* p. 101; Erbring et al., "Front-Page News," p. 38.

178. Rogers and Dearing, "Agenda-Setting Research," p. 577, citing Jack L. Walker, "Setting the Agenda in the U.S. Senate," *British Journal of Political Science* 7 (October 1977), pp. 423–45. See also Cook, *Making Laws & Making News,* pp. 116, 130–31.

179. Robinson and Sheehan, *Over the Wire;* Robinson, "The Media Campaign, '84," pp. 45–47.

180. Benjamin I. Page, Robert Y. Shapiro, and Glenn R. Dempsey, "What Moves Public Opinion?" *American Political Science Review* 81 (March 1987), pp. 23–43. Critical news and commentaries about presidents seem to lower their popularity. Darrell M. West, "Television and Presidential Popularity in America," *British Journal of Political Science* 21 (April 1991), pp. 199–214. Even television's "framing" of events, as isolated incidents or parts of patterns, affects viewers' opinions about these events. Shanto Iyengar, *Is Anyone Responsible? How Television Frames Political Issues* (Chicago: University of Chicago Press, 1991).

181. Iyengar, *Is Anyone Responsible?* Chs. 6, 8.

182. Kathleen Hall Jamieson, quoted in Howard Kurtz, "Tuning Out the News," *Washington Post National Weekly Edition,* May 29–June 4, 1995, p. 6; William Raspberry, "Blow-by-Blow Coverage," *Washington Post National Weekly Edition,* November 6–12, 1995, p. 29.

183. Michael J. Robinson, "Public Affairs Television and the Growth of Political Malaise," *American Political Science Review* 70 (1976), pp. 409–32; Miller, Goldenberg, and Erbring, "Type-Set Politics."

184. "Study: Public More Cynical Than Media," *Champaign-Urbana News Gazette (New York Times),* May 22, 1995.

185. Thomas Griffith, "Leave Off the Label," *Time,* September 19, 1984, p. 63.

186. After one term, however, Schmitt was defeated by an opponent whose slogan was, "What on Earth has he ever done?"

187. Doris A. Graber, "Kind Pictures and Harsh Words: How Television Presents the Candidates," in Kay Lehman Schlozman, ed., *Elections in America* (Boston: Allen & Unwin, 1987), p. 141.

188. Ibid., p. 116.

189. The discussion of the functions of the media relies heavily on the excellent summary found in Stephen Ansolabehere, Roy Behr, and Shanto Iyengar, "Mass Media and Elections," *American Politics Quarterly* 19 (January 1991), pp. 109–39.

190. Bruce Buchanan, *Electing a President: The Markle Commission Report on Campaign '88* (Austin, Tex.: University of Texas Press, 1990); Montague Kean, *30-Second Politics* (New York: Praeger, 1989). Marion Just, Lori Wallach, and Ann Crigler, "Thirty Seconds or Thirty Minutes: Political Learning in an Election," paper presented at the Midwest Political Science Association Meeting, April 1987, Chicago, Illinois.

191. David Paletz and Robert Entrum, *Media—Power—Politics* (New York: Macmillan, 1981), pp. 35ff.

192. Patterson, *Out of Order,* p. 44.

193. Ansolabehere et al., "Mass Media and Elections," pp. 128–29; Christine F. Ridout, "The Role of Media Coverage of Iowa and New Hampshire in the 1988 Democratic Nomination," *American Politics Quarterly* 19 (January 1991), pp. 45–46, 53–54; Marc Howard Ross, "Television News and Candidate Fortunes in Presidential Nomination Campaigns," *American Politics Quarterly* 20 (January, 1992), pp. 69–98.

194. Henry Brady, "Chances, Utilities, and Voting in Presidential Primaries," paper delivered at the Annual Meeting of the Public Choice Society, Phoenix, Arizona, cited in Ansolabehere, Behr, and Iyengar, "Mass Media and Elections;" Bartels, *Presidential Primaries* and the Dynamics of Public Choice (Princeton: Princeton University Press) 1988.

195. Lee Sigelman and Carol K. Sigelman, "Judgments of the Carter-Reagan Debate," *Public Opinion Quarterly* 48 (1984), pp. 624–28.

196. Theodore H. White, *The Making of the President 1960* (New York: Atheneum House, 1961), p. 333.

197. MacKuen and Coombs, *More Than News,* p. 222.

198. For a review, see MacKuen and Coombs, *More Than News,* pp. 147–61.

199. Robert S. Erickson, "The Influence of Newspaper Endorsements in Presidential Elections," *American Journal of Political Science* 20 (May 1976), pp. 207–33.

200. Graber, *Mass Media,* p. 244; Doris Graber, *Processing News: How People Tame the Information Tide* (New York: Longman, 1984). A 1993 survey concluded that almost half of Americans over 16 have such limited reading and math skills that they are unfit for most jobs. One task the survey included was to paraphrase a newspaper story. Many people could scan the story but not paraphrase it when they finished it. Paul Gray, "Adding Up the Under-Skilled," *Time,* September 20, 1993, p. 75.

201. "The New Political Landscape," *Times Mirror Center for the People & the Press,* October 1994, p. 4.

202. Greider, "Reporters and Their Sources," p. 19.

203. Idea for this paragraph from James Fallows, "Did You Have a Good Week?" *Atlantic Monthly,* December 1994, pp. 32, 34.

204. Iyengar, *Is Anyone Responsible?*

205. Stephen Earl Bennett, "Trends in Americans' Political Information," *American Politics Quarterly* 17 (October 1989), pp. 422–35; Richard Zoglin, "The Tuned-Out Generation," *Time,* July 9, 1990, p. 64.

206. Howard Kurtz, "No More 'Extra, Extra' for Major Newspapers," *Washington Post National Weekly Edition,* November 6–12, 1995, p. 34.

207. Walter Goodman, "What's Bad for Politics is Great for Television," *New York Times,"* November 27, 1994, p. H-33.

208. Peters, *How Washington Really Works,* p. 32.

209. Signorile wrote the article for *Outweek,* but before publication that magazine folded and the article was included in *The Advocate,* another homosexual magazine.

210. Signorile, *Queer in America,* p. 145.

211. Ibid., p. 92.

212. Sabato, *Feeding Frenzy,* p. 192.

213. Signorile, *Queer in America,* p. 149.

214. Ibid., pp. 303–04.

215. Ibid., p. ix.

216. Ibid., p. 81.

9 Money and Politics

You Are There

Quid Pro Quo? Or No?

You are U.S. Senator Dennis DeConcini.[1] A moderate Democrat, you have represented Arizona since 1976. It is now 1987, and you are facing a decision whether to pressure federal savings and loan regulators to go easy on Lincoln Savings and Loan, owned by Charles Keating, your constituent, acquaintance, and campaign donor.

You have known Keating for over a decade. He is a millionaire real estate developer who has, over the years, made generous campaign donations to local, Arizona, and national officeholders. He and his associates gave over $100,000 to campaign funds of Phoenix city council members around 1980, after which they made zoning decisions in his favor. Although Keating is a Republican, he joined your campaign finance committee and raised more than $33,000 for your 1982 campaign. He raised another $48,000 for you between 1985 and 1987 in preparation for your 1988 campaign. You returned the favors. You tried to get President Reagan to appoint Keating ambassador to the Bahamas. Your efforts were rebuffed, probably because Keating earlier had been in trouble with the Securities and Exchange Commission over an alleged bank fraud. And you have called on the president's chief of staff many times to lobby on behalf of a Keating associate for a spot on the Federal Home Loan Bank Board. Now Keating wants you to help him in his fight with the Federal Home Loan Bank Board and its regulators. The board wants to limit the investment activities of Keating's Lincoln Savings and Loan, owned by Keating's Arizona corporation.

Considering this problem, you think about the savings and loan industry. Before 1980, it was a boring business, investing only in houses. It operated according to the 3-6-3 principle: Offer 3% on savings, loan at 6% for home mortgages, and hit the golf course at 3 P.M.[2] But in the 1970s, inflation cut heavily into the industry's profits; other financial institutions offered much higher interest rates on savings, while charging far more on loans. To help the industry, and at the urging of both Presidents Carter and Reagan, Congress stepped in to deregulate. Deregulation allowed savings and loan institutions to pay higher interest, and in order to raise funds to pay that higher interest, Congress allowed them to invest in anything—from junk bonds to real estate. Then, it allowed S&L depositors to have an unlimited number of accounts, each insured up to $100,000. These moves were expected to make S&Ls more attractive to investors and more lucrative for owners. As President Reagan said in signing some S&L deregulation, "I think we've hit the jackpot."[3]

After the deregulation legislation, the Reagan administration was lax in enforcement of the new laws. The S&L regulatory agency, the Federal Home Loan Bank Board, lost half its veteran staff due to budget cuts and poor morale. Those who remained were told by their boss to let S&Ls pretend to be solvent even when they were not, in the hope that they would become stronger eventually.[4]

But two years after deregulation, a new chair of the board feared that insolvent S&Ls were undermining the stability of the whole banking system. The board voted to tighten investment

Ted Welch makes another call to try to raise $20 million for Lamar Alexander's (R-Tenn) presidential bid.

CONTINUED

OUTLINE

The Development of Laws to Regulate Money and Politics

Money in Nineteenth-Century American Politics

Early Reforms

The Role of Money in Election Campaigns

Campaign Finance Laws

Loopholes in the Reforms

How the System Works

The Impact of Campaign Money

Does the Campaign Finance System Deter Good Candidates?

Does Money Win Elections?

Does Money Buy Favorable Policies?

Reforming the Campaign Money System

Conflicts of Interest

Conclusion: Does the Influence of Money Make Government Less Responsive?

regulations, especially concerning real estate, declaring that only a small proportion of any S&L's investments could be in real estate (most were supposed to be invested in low-risk outlets). This new regulation threatened the stability of S&Ls like Keating's, which had gone overboard in high-risk real estate investments. The board began investigating Keating's S&L, demanding documents and evidence concerning the value of real estate and other investments it had made. By 1987, Keating was complaining that the regulators were harassing his Lincoln S&L.

Keating asks you, along with several other senators, to help him get the regulators off his back. You have mixed feelings about this, though you are basically sympathetic. Helping constituents is part of your job. Keating is not just an average constituent, he is a big fund-raiser and donor to your campaigns. As far as you know, he is an honest businessman. In fact, a managing partner of the prestigious national accounting firm of Arthur Young & Company has written a letter to a fellow senator, John McCain (R-Ariz.), vouching for the Lincoln S&L and charging that it is being harassed by regulators. A respected economist, Alan Greenspan (later to become chair of the Federal Reserve Board), has written a letter to several senators also attesting to the S&L's financial health.

On the other hand, there are some warning signals. Your banking aide, an Arizonan whose family is in the S&L business, warns you that Keating takes too many risks. She recommends avoiding him. Others are suspicious too. Senator Jake Garn (R-Utah), for example, has said he will have nothing to do with Keating. Moreover, you are mindful of Senate ethics rules requiring senators not only to refrain from wrongdoing but from conduct giving "the appearance of wrongdoing."[5] While doing favors for constituents is a key element of your job, putting pressure on regulators on behalf of a large campaign contributor could certainly give "the appearance of wrongdoing."

What do you do? Do you help your constituent and campaign donor by trying to get federal regulators to go easy on the Lincoln S&L? That is, do you follow the practice of quid pro quo (tit for tat)? Or do you let the regulatory process work, perhaps closing down the S&L and the parent company in Arizona and angering a rich donor and fund-raiser?

Former Speaker of the House of Representatives Tip O'Neill once said, "There are four parts to any campaign. The candidate, the issues . . . , the campaign organization, and the money. Without money you can forget the other three."[6] Thus, conventional wisdom holds that "money is the mother's milk of politics." But we are not sure if that milk is pure or tainted. On one hand, without money, candidates or people with new political ideas could never become known in our massive and complex society. Television spreads names and ideas almost instantaneously, so having money to buy television time means your ideas will be heard. In that sense, money contributes to open political debate.

On the other hand, money can be a corrupting influence on politics. At the least, it can buy access to those making decisions. At the worst, it can buy decisions. Money allows some points of view to be trumpeted while others are forced to whisper. Some candidates or groups can afford to spend hundreds of thousands of dollars for each prime time minute of national television or for prestigious Washington law firms to lobby; others can afford only mimeographs and letters. Money increases inequities in political life.

Money, then, leads to a dilemma in politics. In our largely capitalist society, we expect substantial differences in wealth and income. In most cases, we see nothing wrong when those with great income buy goods and services that others cannot afford. But in politics, many people feel uneasy when those with great wealth are able to buy political favors. We feel so uneasy that we have outlawed certain kinds of buying of political favors, such as politicians paying voters for their votes or interest groups paying politicians and bureaucrats for their support.

But we are uneasy about other ways of limiting the influence of money. Many people feel that individuals or groups should be allowed to contribute as much money to candidates as they want, and that candidates should be permitted to buy as much media time as they want and can afford. This view holds that contributing money and buying media time are forms of constitutionally guaranteed freedom of speech. The opposite view says that this distorts the democratic process.

In this chapter, we first focus on the development of laws that regulate how money can influence politics, then we turn to the role and impact of money in elections, and finally we briefly examine conflict of interest on the part of decision makers in Congress and the executive branch.

➤The Development of Laws to Regulate Money and Politics

Concern about the illegitimate influence of money on politics is as old as the Republic. In his campaign for the Virginia House of Burgesses in 1757, George Washington was accused of vote buying. He had given out 28 gallons of rum, 50 gallons of rum punch, 34 gallons of wine, 46 gallons of beer, and 2 gallons of cider.[7] Because there were only 391 voters in his district, he had provided more than a quart and a half of beverages per voter![8]

Obviously, George Washington survived these charges, and his constituents probably survived the effects of the rum and cider. But most discussions of the impact of money on politics were more sober. In his well-known analysis of controlling factions, James Madison, in *Federalist #10,* recognized that "the most common and durable source of factions has been the various and unequal distribution of property." Madison went on to say that although ideally no one should be allowed to make decisions affecting his or her own self-interest, almost any subject of legislation—taxes, tariffs, debts—involves self-interest. For those making laws, "every shilling with which they overburden the inferior number is a shilling saved to their own pockets."[9]

Madison hoped that the design of the new nation, with the power of the government divided among the branches of government and between the nation and the states, would mean that no one interest or faction would overwhelm the others. The interest of one person or group would check the interest of another.

This view of counterbalancing interests is an optimistic one and has not always worked. Over the decades, Americans have found it necessary to make additional rules to restrict the ways that those with money can try to influence policymakers.

This Puck cartoon mocks President U.S. Grant's involvement in various corrupt activities. Grant (dressed in the flag suit) is shown supporting various political bosses and profiteers.

Money in Nineteenth-Century American Politics

The influence of money on politics has shaped several epochs of American history. For example, from the earliest westward expansion of the nation, charges of graft and corruption surrounded the government's sale and giveaway of land. Indeed, the West was developed by giving land to speculators and railroads, sometimes after bribes. When Congress was debating whether to give federal land to the railroads, the lobbyists "camped in brigades around the Capitol building."[10]

The impact of money on political life was probably at its peak in the late nineteenth century. The United States grew from a small agrarian society to a large industrialized one. Oil exploration and refining, the growth of the steel industry, the expansion of the railroad companies, and other large corporations produced many millionaires. This was the era of "robber barons," when the owners of giant corporations (called "trusts") openly bought political favors.

At the turn of the century, rich New Yorkers, wearing vine leaves on their heads, enjoy their wealth.

Business contributions to campaigns and to politicians were routine. One railroad president justified bribery of political officials by noting, "If you have to pay money to have the right thing done, it is only just and fair to do so."[11] Mark Hanna, a Republican fund-raiser in the presidential election of 1896, assessed banks at a fixed percentage of their capital and also collected substantial sums from most insurance companies and large corporations.[12] However, Cornelius Vanderbilt, one of the wealthiest men of his time, refused to contribute to election campaigns, believing it was cheaper to buy legislators after they were elected!

Early Reforms

Around the turn of the century, the Progressive reformers and their allies in the press, called the **Muckrakers,** began to attack this overt corruption. They wanted to break the financial link between business and politicians. In 1907 a law prohibited corporations and banks from making contributions to political campaigns, and a few years later Congress mandated public reporting of campaign expenditures and set limits on campaign donations. Prohibitions against corporate giving to political campaigns were broadened over time to forbid utilities and labor unions from giving as well.

The **Teapot Dome scandal** of 1921 stimulated further attempts to limit the influence of money on electoral politics. The secretary of the interior in the Harding administration accepted almost $400,000 from two corporations and then allowed them to lease oil reserves in California and Wyoming (one reserve was called the "Teapot Dome"). This led to the Federal Corrupt Practices Act (1925), which required the reporting of campaign contributions and expenditures.

Because none of these laws was enforced, each had only a momentary effect. Nevertheless, the reforms did seem to make open graft and bribery less acceptable and less common. Instead of outright bribes, political interests now sought to influence politicians through campaign contributions.

Labor unions, for example, set up **political action committees (PACs)** funded from dues. These committees raised "voluntary" money from members to support candidates for elections. Then many businesses did the same.

The Role of Money in Election Campaigns

In 1971 changed conditions caused new laws to be passed.

"Honest Graft"

The influence of money on local politics reached a high point in the late nineteenth century. Urban machines used money to cement a complex network of businesses, voters, and political party organizations. Business payoffs to government and party officials for licenses and contracts, and party payoffs to voters for their support, were the norm. Graft was tolerated and even expected.

As we saw in Chapter 6, George Washington Plunkitt was a famous leader of the New York City Democratic machine, Tammany Hall. Plunkitt, born in 1842, began life as a butcher's helper and ended up a millionaire through deals made in his role as a party leader and public official. He held a number of state and local public offices; at one point, he held four at the same time. He drew a salary for three of them simultaneously.

Plunkitt's view of graft illustrates the casual attitude about the influence of money on politics common among many of his time:

> There's all the difference in the world between [honest graft and dishonest graft]. There's an honest graft, and I'm an example of how it works. I might sum up the whole thing by sayin': "I seen my opportunities and I took 'em."
>
> Just let me explain. . . . My party's in power in the city, and it's goin' to undertake a lot of public improvements. Well, I'm tipped off, say, that they're going to lay out a new park at a certain place. I see my opportunity and take it. I go to that place and I buy up all the land I can in the neighborhood. Then the board of this or that makes its plan public, and there is a rush to get my land, which nobody cared particular for before. Ain't it perfectly honest to charge a good price and make a profit on my investment and foresight? Of course, it is. Well, that's honest graft.
>
> Tammany was beat in 1901 because the people were deceived into believin' that it worked dishonest graft. . . . [They supposed] Tammany men were robbin' the city treasury or levyin' blackmail on disorderly houses, or workin' in with the gamblers and lawbreakers. . . . Why should the Tammany leaders go into such dirty business when there is so much honest graft lyin' around?
>
> . . . I don't own a dishonest dollar. If my worst enemy was given the job of writin' my epitaph . . . he couldn't do more than write: George W. Plunkitt. He Seen His Opportunities, and He Took 'Em.

Source: William L. Riordon, *Plunkitt of Tammany Hall* (New York: E. P. Dutton, 1963).

Campaign Finance Laws

Prompted by the increasing use and cost of television in campaigns, in 1971 Congress passed a law regulating spending on advertising. The law limited donations that candidates could make to their own campaigns and required candidates to disclose the names and addresses of donors of more than $100.

In the course of the Watergate investigations, it became clear that corporations were not abiding by these restrictions. Several corporations secretly funded President Nixon's reelection campaign. For example, an ITT Corporation subsidiary gave the Republican National Committee $400,000[13]—and then Nixon's Justice Department negotiated a settlement favorable to ITT in a pending legal dispute. Altogether, 21 individuals and 14 corporations were indicted for illegal campaign contributions, mostly but not entirely to Nixon's reelection campaign.

In response to these scandals, Congress again attempted to regulate campaign financing by passing the **Federal Election Campaign Act** in 1974. The following are key provisions of that law, the basics of which, along with individual state laws, regulate campaign finance today:

- Public financing of presidential campaigns. Each candidate is given tax dollars for his or her campaign, as we will see in more detail later.
- Limits on contributions by individuals and committees to presidential and congressional campaigns.
- Limits on overall expenditures by candidates' organizations in presidential campaigns.
- Limits on overall expenditures by national party committees.
- Limits on expenditures by PACs.
- Limits on contributions by individuals to PACs and to candidates.
- Prohibitions on cash contributions of more than $100.
- Establishment of a bipartisan Federal Election Commission to enforce the law.

Limits on spending by candidates' organizations in congressional races and limits on so-called **independent spending,** spending by groups not under the control of candidates, were also part of the 1974 act. These limits were ruled unconstitutional and no longer obtain.

Because of the importance of money in campaigns, both elected officials and those who want something from the officials have looked for ways to get around the campaign finance laws.[14]

Loopholes in the Reforms

The objectives of the 1974 law were to make the campaign finance system more open, to limit spending, and to force candidates to be less reliant on a few big donors. The law has not worked as it was intended, however. In 1976, the Supreme Court knocked a hole in it when it ruled that some portions of the act were unconstitutional.[15] In a case brought by an alliance of civil libertarians and conservatives, the Court struck down several spending limits for campaigns that were not publicly funded, that is, congressional campaigns. The Court argued that spending restrictions violated individuals' rights of free speech because spending in a campaign enables candidates to get their message out. Thus, spending is a form of expression protected by the Constitution.

In addition to the holes knocked into the law by the Supreme Court, it became clear that there were other loopholes in the law. (*Loophole* is a common term for aspects of a law that intentionally or unintentionally limit its effectiveness or restrict its coverage.) One important loophole was created by a little-noticed portion of the law reaffirming the right of unions and corporations to establish PACs using voluntary contributions. Now that there were limitations on the amount of money individuals could give to campaigns, PACs became the vehicle by which individuals could channel more money to their favorite candidates. Individuals could give a limited amount directly to candidates, and then $5,000 to each of several PACs, which in turn could give it to candidates.[16]

PACs quickly sprang up. Business and trade PACs multiplied especially quickly, from around 100 in 1974 to more than 4,700 today. Labor had dominated the PAC game before 1974; now, with fewer than 400 PACs, it finds itself completely outnumbered.

Several other loopholes also have been exploited by candidates, parties, and PACs. Individuals and PACs can avoid most rules and limitations by independent spending. In 1985, the Supreme Court ruled that PACs can spend unlimited amounts working on behalf of issues or candidates, publicly funded or not, as long as they do not give funds directly to parties or candidates.[17]

The Court assumed this spending would be meaningfully independent. However, "independent spending" often is done by organized groups with indirect links to the candidate. Today, interest groups and political parties themselves also can spend as much as they want as long as they are not actually campaigning for a candidate. Instead, they can engage in "issues advocacy" even if it only helps candidates of one party. The AFL-CIO, for instance, spent as much as $35 million in an advertising campaign in 1996 urging support for many of President Clinton's priorities. But instead of running the ads all across the nation, the union has targeted its television ads at congressional districts with Republican incumbents.[18] Because contributions to groups engaged in "issues advocacy" are not limited by law, large donors can provide a great deal of indirect support to candidates for office without violating laws limiting campaign contributions.

In addition to the "independent spending" loophole, there is also the **soft money** loophole. Donors who want to give more than their legal federal maximum can give to national party committees, which channel to state parties, which spend under less stringent state regulations. Soft money need not be reported to the federal government nor, sometimes, to the states.

Soft money is used for such things as voter registration drives, direct mailings, polling, and advertisements for nonfederal party candidates. Soft money, including union dues and corporate funds, also can be used at the federal level by national party committees for capital improvements such as new buildings and computers. Both parties have building funds to which corporations and labor unions contribute freely. And private donors and corporations pay for large proportions of the costs of each party's national convention.

The soft money loophole allows people with money to spend as much as they want on their favorite presidential candidate or party. For 1996, the Democrats received $80 million in soft money from special interests, the Republicans $74 million. Sometimes the parties resort to questionable tactics to raise money. In late 1995, Republican National Committee chairman Haley Barbour sent letters to lobbyists offering incentives for contributing to the party. A contributor could be photographed with the GOP presidential candidates or have drinks in a private skybox at the Republican convention, depending on the size of the contribution. Dinner with President Clinton and Vice President Gore was the carrot the Democratic National Committee dangled in front of potential donors. One hundred thousand dollars would qualify.[19] As one observer commented, "Soft money is where rich people can play again."[20]

Yet another loophole is sometimes called "back pocket PACS." Members of Congress organize their own PACS and register them only at the state level. Since many states have lax campaign finance laws, this allows these state-registered PACs to receive contributions that are illegal under federal law, for example, from corporations and labor unions. Charles Keating's corporation gave $200,000 to a back pocket PAC run by John Glenn (D-Ohio).[21]

A final problem with the campaign finance laws is that inflation has changed the real value of the contribution and spending limits. The amount each candidate can spend does increase with inflation, but no other part of the system is indexed to inflation. The maximum $1,000 contribution is now worth only $340 in 1974 dollars. Thus the contribution limits are unrealistically low.

How the System Works

Presidential Elections

Presidential candidates who accept public financing, as most do, may not spend more than $33 million to get the nomination. (The money comes from a voluntary checkoff of $3 on individuals' tax returns; the spending limit increases each year to take inflation into account.) Candidates who do not accept public funding, such as Ross Perot in 1992, can spend as much as they can raise. Once candidates receive their parties' nomination, public funding pays them each about $55 million for the general election campaign (also adjusted each election for inflation), and they can accept several million more from their party's national committee. At this point, fund-raising is officially over for the candidates.

However, money plays a bigger role in practice than in theory. Presidential campaigns cost far more than the amount publicly funded.[22] The discrepancy is due to the independent spending and soft money loopholes. (President Clinton came under attack in 1996 for accepting large contributions that came, indirectly, from an Indonesian businessman.) The increasing number of private individuals and corporations donating huge amounts indicates that we have come full circle back to the conditions that led to the campaign finance reforms. As one observer indicated, "The fat cats have returned."[23]

Congressional Elections

Candidates for Congress rely on three sources of funding: PAC contributions, individual donations, and donations from their political parties. PAC contributions make up about a third of the funds for House seats and a quarter for Senate seats (Figure 1). Over time, PAC funds have grown in importance to candidates.

PACS There are vast differences in the funding activity of PACs. Although there are 4,700 PACs, about one-third do not contribute to any candidates, while about 400 give over $100,000 each. Less than 10% of the PACs give three-fourths of the dollars. Thus, the number of key PACs is relatively small. Some of the biggest spenders include well-known groups such as the National Rifle Association, the Teamsters, and the American Medical Association. But they also include less well-known groups such as the Association of Trial Lawyers, the American Federal-State-County-and-Municipal Employees, and the American Institute of CPAs.[24]

PACs differ in the targets of their donations, but some patterns are clear. PACs show a distinct preference for Republicans in presidential races and for incumbents, whether Republicans or Democrats, in congressional races. For the latter, PACs usually want to give to candidates they believe will win so they will have access to policymakers.

If they guess wrong, they often give to the winners *after* the election. After the surprise Republican victories in the 1994 congressional elections, PACs raced to help winning Republicans pay their campaign debts (Figure 2). As one noted, "We gave to Democrats because they were in control, and we're likely to do the same for Republicans. The balance of power has shifted, and those who affect our company and our customers are in another party."[25] After the election, health care lobbyists paid $1,000 each to attend a breakfast for Republican Senate winner Fred Thompson (Tenn.) although many had contributed to Thompson's opponent before the election. Perhaps they were mindful of the warning by Newt Gingrich (R-Ga.) that if the Republicans took power, those not on board would "suffer the two coldest years in Washington."

Although the majority of PACs are business related and ideologically sympathetic to the Republicans, before 1994 they gave predominantly to the Democrats because they were the majority party. Now that the Republicans control both houses of Congress, we are likely to see an even more lopsided split of PAC money, because ideological sentiment and the practical politics of supporting incumbents both point toward the Republicans.[26]

FIGURE 1
Congressional Campaign Spending Rises Faster Than PAC Contributions

Congressional campaign spending rose sharply in 1992 after slow growth in the 1980s.

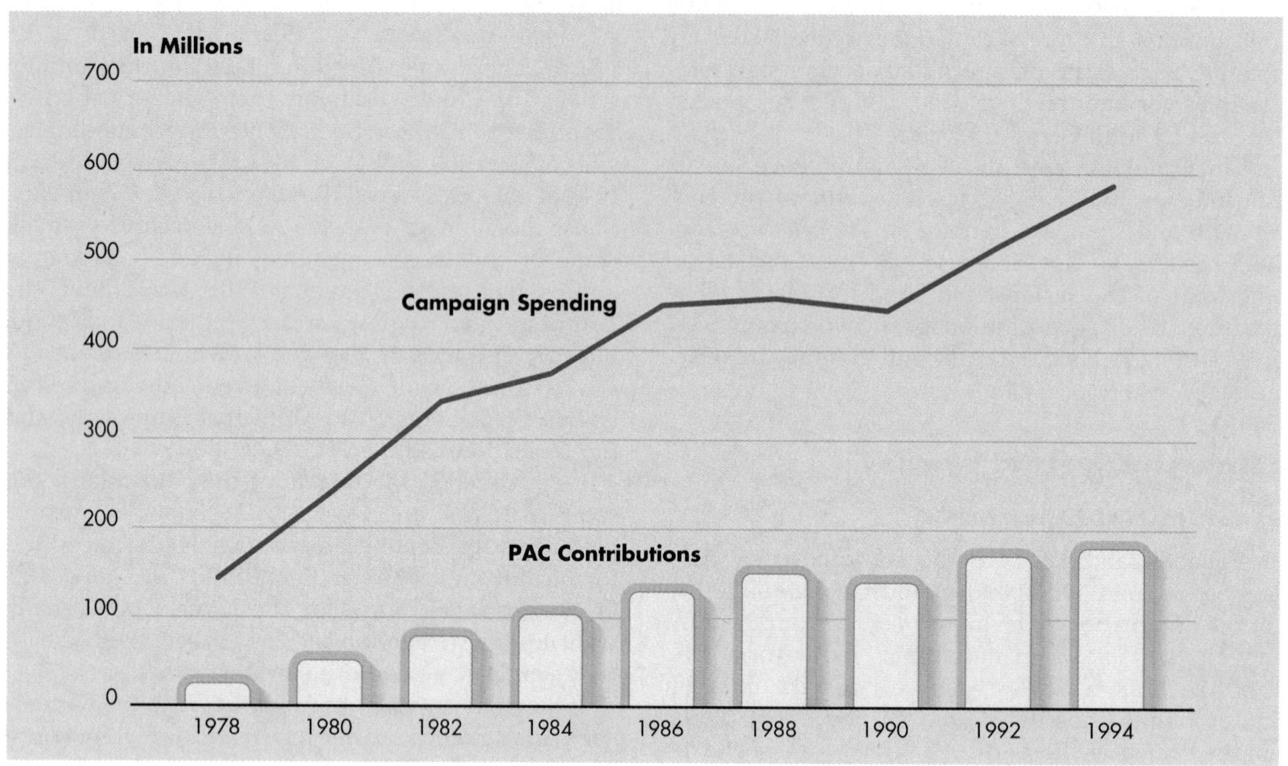

Source: *National Journal,* February 10, 1990, p. 353.

What other criteria guide PAC donations?[27] Most PACs give money to members in districts where the PACs have a substantial interest, such as a union PAC with a large number of members or a corporate PAC with a large factory.

PACs also target contributions to members of key congressional committees. For example, PACs organized by defense contractors give to members who serve on the Armed Services Committees, which have a big role in deciding what weapons to purchase. Unions and shipping companies involved in the maritime industry give to those on the House Merchant Marine and Fisheries Committee and its Senate counterpart, Commerce, Science, and Transportation.[28] Members of congressional committees that specialize in tax law (Ways and Means, and Finance) and business regulations (Commerce) receive generous contributions from business PACs.

Women's PACs, including EMILY's List, one of 1992's biggest spending PACs, focus most of their money on nonincumbents. Their goal is to get more women elected, which means supporting nonincumbents with strong chances of winning.

SPECIAL INTERESTS AS VICTIMS? PAC contributions to congressional campaigns are products of mutual need. PACs need access to and votes of members of Congress, and members of Congress need (or think they need) large sums of money to win elections. Thus, PAC donations are useful to members and to PACs. The question is whether they are useful to the public.

Although PACs try to buy access and sometimes votes, members of Congress are not simply victims of greedy PACs. Indeed, as one recent observer remarked, "There may be no question that the money flowing into campaign coffers is a crime. But there is a question whether the crime is bribery of public officials or extortion of private interests."[29]

Members themselves are increasingly aggressive in soliciting PACs for donations. They fear defeat in the next election and think that raising a lot of money can protect them. Senators, for example, must raise more than $18,000 *each week* during all six years of their term to fund an average-cost winning reelection campaign. A senator from a high-cost state needs to raise $60,000 a week. On the other hand, many incumbents raise millions even when they face little-known opponents. Phil Gramm (R-Tex.) continued to solicit funds from lobbyists even after he had raised more than $6 million and his opponent had only $20,000.

Thirty years ago most fund-raising by members of Congress was done in their home districts. Members did not want their constituents to think they were influenced by Washington lobbyists. Today, half of the PAC funds are raised in Washington.[30] Members of Congress continually hold fund-raisers to which dozens of lobbyists for PACs are invited. Well-known lobbyists get hundreds of invitations to these fund-raisers every year.[31] Indeed, the number of these

PAC Man

Leadership PACs, organized and run by members of Congress, offer a convenient way to avoid some of the campaign finance limits for congressional candidates.

Some of the largest of these PACs are run by candidates for congressional offices such as majority leader, party whip, and committee chair. The founders of these PACS provide funds to lesser known candidates in tacit exchange for support in leadership races. Other personal PACs do not give much money to fellow candidates, but instead use the money to promote the leader's own candidacy and ideologies, using the money for campaign materials and sometimes for travel and luxury items on the campaign trail.

Candidates from both parties have such personal PACs. By far the largest are Campaign America and GOPAC. Campaign America, run by Robert Dole (R-Kan.), raised over $6 million in the 1994 election cycle, but spent only a small fraction of this on candidates. GOPAC, run by Newt Gingrich (R-Ga.), raised nearly $4 million but spent only $59 on candidates (as of July, 1994). The largest Democratic leadership PAC, run by Richard Gephardt (D-Mo.), raised about $1 million and spent $200,000 on other Democratic candidates.[1]

All of these leadership PACs have been under attack for being inconsistent with the spirit of the rules governing political action committees, but GOPAC was the subject of major controversy. Because it kept its donor list secret, GOPAC was sued by the Federal Election Commission and was the subject of ethics complaints in two states and in Congress. The *New York Times* labeled it a "stealth PAC."[2] Of the nearly $4 million GOPAC raised, it reported the donors for less than $500,000.[3]

Speaker Gingrich argued that GOPAC was not a political action committee at all, but was an educational institution, and he noted that only 10% of its funds went to federal candidates (so only this part was subject to federal regulation). However, fund-raising letters from GOPAC offered donors a chance to have input on the Republican legislative agenda, and noted that GOPAC helped elect 41 new GOP freshmen in the 1992 elections.

GOPAC activity focuses on providing candidates with training seminars and instructional materials, many featuring Speaker Gingrich. GOPAC was also used to promote Gingrich's college course, "Renewing American Civilization," which is available by video and satellite across the nation. Indeed, corporate donors to GOPAC have been invited to help shape the content of the course and have had their products promoted in the course. Course presentations noted that, for example, McDonald's is "the most successful worldwide seller of food in the history of the human race," and Milliken (carpets) "offers its customers a choice of over 1,000 colors and patterns." (The owner of the latter company had given over $250,000 to GOPAC.)[4]

Because Speaker Gingrich had led the attacks on former Majority Leader Jim Wright (D-Tex.) for his questionable ethics practices, Democrats reveled in the opportunity to attack Gingrich for his bad judgment (and possibly illegal actions). After continued Democratic attacks on his apparent conflicts of interest and violation of ethics laws, in May, 1995, Speaker Gingrich announced that he was disbanding GOPAC and disclosing the names of donors to it.

1. Eliza Newlin Carney, "PAC Men," *National Journal* (October 1, 1994), pp. 2272–2273.
2. Ibid., p. 2272.
3. Jonathan D. Salant, "Ethics Spotlight Puts Heat on Speaker Gingrich," *CQ* (March 4, 1995), p. 639.
4. Serge F. Kovaleski and R. H. Melton, "And Now a Word from Our Sponsor," *Washington Post National Weekly Edition* (March 27–April 2, 1995), p. 12.

FIGURE 2
PACs Give Postelection Donations to Winners

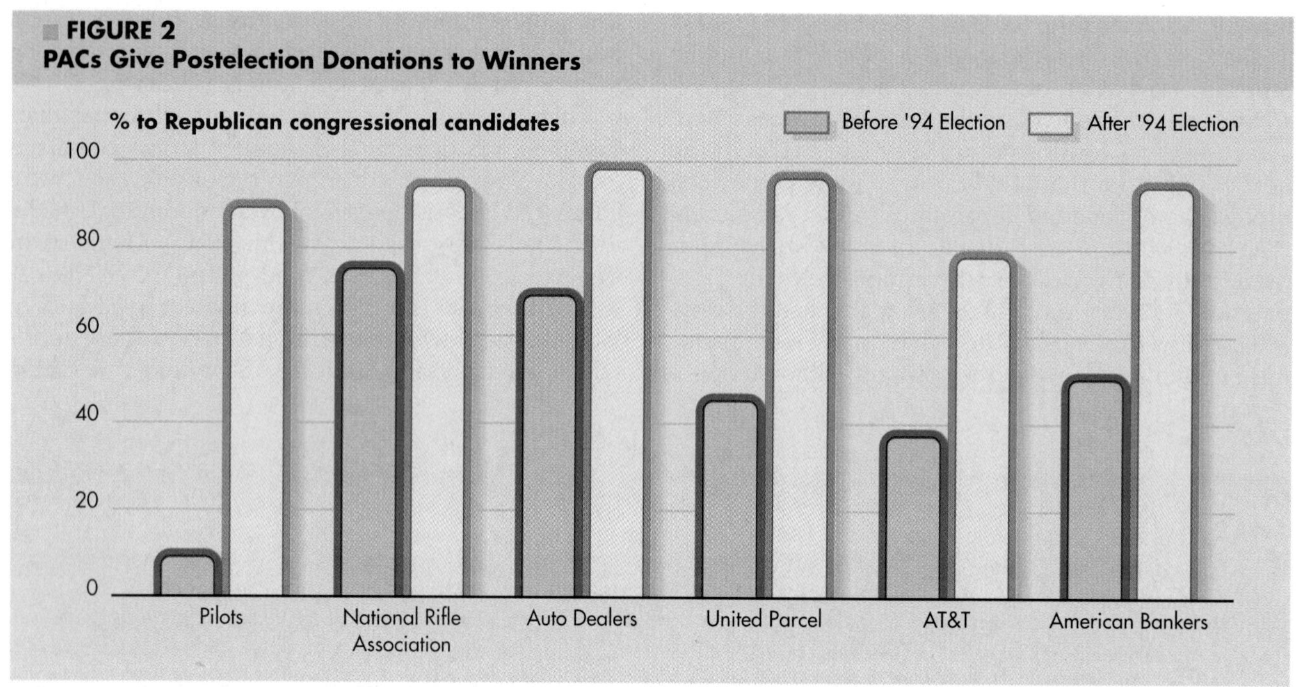

Source: Jonathan Salant and David Cloud, "To the '94 Election Victors Go the Fund-Raising Spoils," *Congressional Quarterly*, April 15, 1995, p. 1056.

events in Washington is so large that a private company sells a monthly newsletter listing all of them. One Washington insider says of being asked by incumbents to give money, "Unless you give your max [the maximum the law allows], unless you lay out your $5,000 at a fundraiser, you don't have access. . . . you don't get in the door. They don't ever return your phone calls."[32]

Some members keep lists on their desks of which PACs have given to them, an implicit indication that those groups will have access. Others play one PAC off against another. They might tell a representative of a bank PAC that they received contributions from savings and loan PACs and that the bank PAC should contribute or possibly miss out.[33]

NON-PAC SOURCES OF FUNDS Donations from individuals are a second important source of congressional campaign funds. Large donations come from business executives, lawyers, and entertainers.

Party organizations, such as the Democratic Congressional Campaign Committee and its Republican counterpart, and the Republican Senate Campaign Committee and its Democratic counterpart, are the third source of funds. These party groups together gave almost $100 million in the 1994 campaign.

There is no question that the nature of raising money for campaigns has changed. Whatever the problems with the current system, however, we should be careful not to contrast it with an idealized version of the past. After all, almost 100 years ago Mark Twain observed: "It could probably be shown by facts and figures that there is no distinctly native American criminal class except Congress." Big interests always have had influence and access in Washington. The ways in which they exercise that influence are different now. In some ways, this influence is more open because the campaign finance reforms have made public the organizations working for special interests and the money they spend doing it. Thirty years ago we would not have known how much each member of Congress received from each lobbying group; today we do.

The Impact of Campaign Money

We have discussed several aspects of money in elections: how much there is, who contributes it, and how they do so. Now we turn to the question of what difference campaign money makes. An obvious question is whether money influences the outcomes of elections. But we also will focus on two other kinds of potential effects of money and the way it is raised: the recruitment of good candidates and the policy decisions of elected leaders.

Does the Campaign Finance System Deter Good Candidates?

When John Glenn, an unsuccessful Democratic candidate in 1984, was asked whether running for president had been worth it despite his defeat, Glenn replied: "My family was humiliated. I got myself whipped. I gained 16 pounds. And I'm more than $2.5 million in debt. Except for that, it was wonderful."[34]

Other presidential candidates have lamented the difficulties and humiliations of having to raise money; Richard Cheney, Jack Kemp, and Dan Quayle, all potential 1996 presidential candidates, bowed out early in 1995 indicating that the magnitude of necessary fund–raising was one reason. Texas Senator Phil Gramm, however, may be the exception who enjoys fund–raising. "I don't have any trouble asking people for support. I believe in what I am doing."[35]

The necessity of raising a lot of money deters congressional candidates too. As one leading congressional scholar noted, "Raising money is, by consensus, the most unpleasant part of a campaign. Many candidates find it demeaning to ask people for money and are uncomfortable with the implications of accepting it."[36] Senator Brock Adams (D-Wash.), who had served in the House until 1976 and then ran a decade later for the Senate, was shocked at the changes in fund-raising. "I never imagined how much of my personal time would be spent on fund raising. . . . I do not think a candidate for the U.S. Senate should have to sit in a motel room in Goldendale, Washington, at 6 in the morning and spend three hours on the phone talking to political action committees."[37] And, once elected, many new members of Congress are surprised and chagrined to find that they must begin raising funds for their next campaign almost before they are sworn into office.

Does Money Win Elections?

Money probably helps win some elections, but other factors also determine the outcomes. The evidence is mixed as to the impact of money on winning presidential primaries. Some candidates are never considered serious because they do not have sufficient money to mount a large campaign. In that sense, money is crucial. But money alone cannot win. Sometimes the biggest spenders get nowhere. Beyond some point, money might not matter as much. In 1984 and 1988, spending by the major Democratic and Republican presidential primary candidates in each state bore little relationship to whether they won that state.[38]

By the time presidential candidates are nominated, they already have spent a great deal. The name recognition achieved during the primaries and at the national conventions carries into the general election campaign. Presidential candidates receive extensive free media coverage in news stories. The amount that they spend after the convention is less likely to be as crucial. This is just as well for the health of the two-party system, because if money determined elections, the Republicans would have won every presidential election since World War II. However, of the presidential elections lost by the Democrats during that time, probably only the election of 1968 between Richard Nixon and Hubert Humphrey was close enough that it might have turned out differently had the Democrats been able to spend more.[39] When elections are close, as in 1968, the Republicans definitely have the advantage by having more money.[40]

In congressional races, incumbents usually start with a huge advantage. Their name is recognized by many of their constituents. Challengers must buy advertising to achieve similar recognition. Thus, the ability of the challenger to raise money is crucial. As Figure 3 shows, challengers to incumbents have a

Luckovich, *Atlanta Constitution*, reprinted in *Newsweek*, December 25, 1995–Jan 1. 1996, p. 62.

very low probability of winning unless they raise $500,000 or more. One study found that every $10,000 spent by a House challenger increases his or her vote total by more than 2%. The amount of money incumbents spend seems unrelated to whether they win or not. As challengers spend more, so do incumbents.[41]

Recent elections offer contrasting lessons about the impact of money on elections. In 1994 the biggest two spenders in Senate races, Michael Huffington (R-Cal.) and Oliver North (R-Va.), both lost as did four of the top six House spenders.[42]

But in 1992, supposedly an anti-incumbent year, 26 of 27 Senate incumbents outspent their challengers, and 23 were reelected. In 1994, another anti-incumbent year, over 90% of House incumbents, most with a substantial funding advantage, were reelected. Nonetheless, 34 Democratic incumbents were beaten, partially due to the much better funding of Republican challengers than most challengers in the past.

The fact that most challengers cannot raise the amounts of money that incumbents have readily available is probably an important reason most incumbents are reelected. In 1990, for example, only 35 House incumbents faced opponents who raised as much as half the amount the incumbent did.[43]

Candidates need more money than ever. In the past, the parties often ran coordinated campaigns for their entire slate of candidates, and many voters cast a straight party ticket. But candidates must now appeal directly to the voters themselves. Television makes that possible, but only for candidates with money. Other ways of reaching voters also cost large sums. The decline of parties means candidates must raise large amounts of money to run their campaigns.

Does Money Buy Favorable Policies?

Everyone agrees that money buys access. Both anecdotal and systematic evidence suggests that money also buys votes, although only under some conditions.

There is now a significant amount of research on the impact of PACs on legislators' behavior in committees and in voting. There appears to be a link between campaign contributions and favorable action in committees, where voting patterns are less visible to the public, than roll-call votes in the whole chamber. In committees, legislators with PAC support are more active in speaking, negotiating, and offering

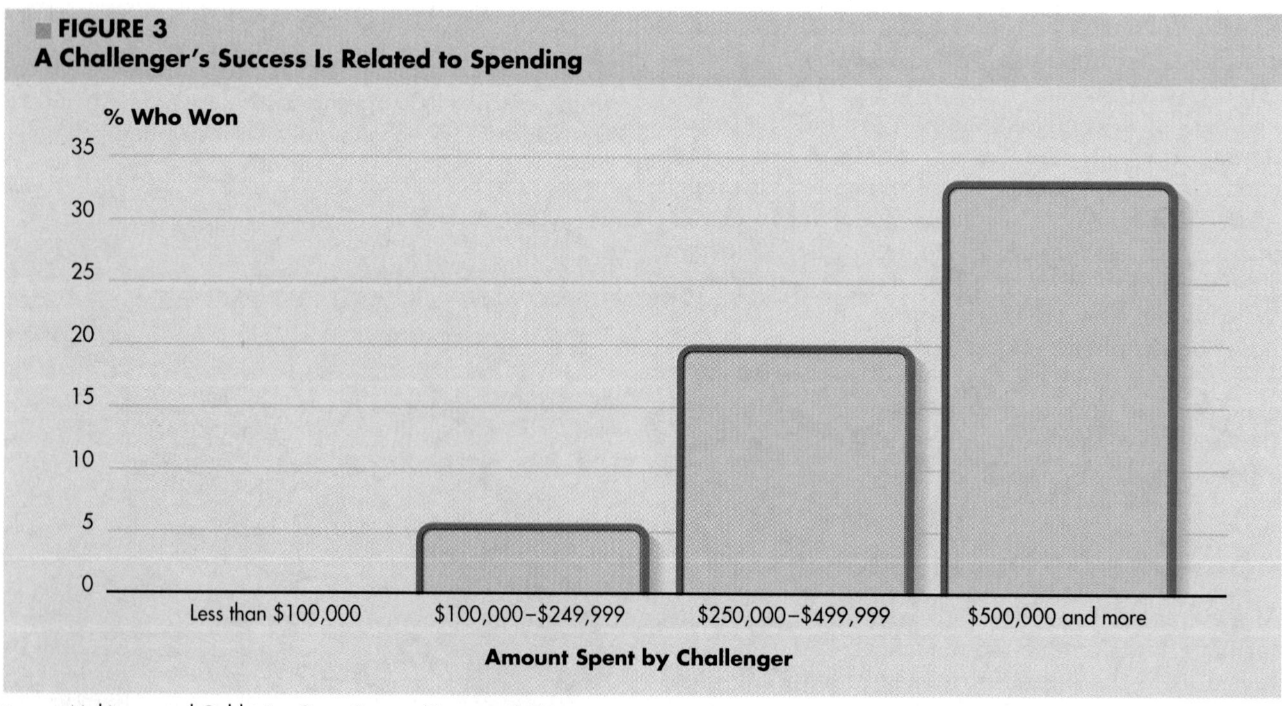

Source: Makinson and Goldstein, *Open Secrets.* (See note 24.)

amendments on behalf of positions favored by the PACs.[44]

The research on voting is not completely consistent but suggests that PACs may influence voting, especially on votes that are less visible.[45] Most issues are not of great importance to the public and are not widely publicized. "The plain truth is that most issues before Congress do not involve great moral principles, and the lobbyists understand that a little persuasion will often do the trick."[46] Or more bluntly, "You can't buy a Congressman for $5,000. But you can buy his vote. It's done on a regular basis."[47]

A recent survey of members found that about one-fifth admit that political contributions have affected their votes on occasion, and another one-third are not sure.[48] Analysis of voting has revealed that contributions from the AFL-CIO affected voting on the minimum wage legislation, and contributions from the trucking interests led senators to vote against deregulation of trucking. Those senators facing reelection that year were most susceptible.[49] Donations also affected voting in such disparate areas as minimum wage legislation, business regulation, and gun control.[50]

One classic example concerns used-car legislation. Auto dealers spent $675,000 in the 1980 congressional elections. This investment seemed to pay off when in 1982 Congress voted against a rule requiring dealers to inform prospective buyers of any known defects in used cars. The senators who opposed the measure

How Congressional Candidates Spend Their Money

Common wisdom suggests that much of the explanation for expensive political campaigns is the high cost of television advertising. A closer look suggests that this common wisdom is somewhat wide of the mark.

The 1988 campaign budgets of two rank-and-file House members, Florida Republican Michael Bilirakis and Virginia Democrat Frederick Boucher, reveal something about how campaign money is used. Most campaign spending goes toward two things: campaign organization and advertising. Campaign organization includes obvious costs such as office space, supplies, phone, and postage, and for incumbents, salaries for key campaign personnel. Challengers, who have fewer funds, often must rely on volunteers to staff their campaign.

Campaign Spending by Three House Candidates

	Bilirakis (Incumbent, unopposed)	Boucher (Incumbent, opposed)	Brown (Challenger)
Organization	61%	28%	65%
Advertising	8	44	21
Fund–raising	14	5	0
Travel	9	3	5
Consulting	8	20	9
Total spending	$190,000	$600,000	$158,000
% of vote	100%	63%	37%

Source: Sam Miller, "Always Run Scared," *National Journal*, June 16, 1990, pp. 1456–57.

But for many candidates, especially incumbents, organizational expenses can include items that have very little to do with wooing voters. Indeed, a study of congressional campaign spending revealed that half of all campaign spending is unrelated to contacting voters. With little accountability in how money is spent, some candidates run up tens of thousands of dollars worth of food bills, donate hundreds of thousands of dollars to educational institutions, spend days at lavish resorts, and buy decorations for their offices.

Representative Bilirakis's organizational expenses included sending flowers to constituents, treating them to meals at restaurants and clubs, and giving money to local party clubs and charity groups.

Overall, House candidates spend only 23% on television advertising, while Senate candidates, who need to reach larger audiences, spend around 30%. Advertising expenses among these three candidates range widely from 8% by Representative Bilirakis who was unopposed, to 44% by Representative Boucher. Boucher did have an opponent, John Brown, but like most congressional challengers, Brown was underfunded. Boucher had almost four times as much to spend as Brown. Boucher spent almost half of his $600,000 campaign budget on advertising. (Most advertising costs are for television time, though, depending on the locale, candidates might also buy radio and newspaper ads.) Boucher won easily, perhaps discouraging future opponents. In 1990 he had no opposition.

Sources: Charles Babcock, "The Big Spenders on the Hill," *Washington Post National Weekly Edition* (September 14–20, 1992), p. 34. Drawn from Sara Fritz and Dwight Morris, *Handbook of Campaign Spending*.

received twice as much money from the auto dealers' PAC as those who voted for it; the representatives who opposed the measure received five times as much money as those who voted for it.[51] The relationship between PAC money and votes still existed even when taking into account the party and ideology of the members. For conservatives, who might have voted against requiring auto dealers to list defects anyway, PAC contributions made only a marginal difference in their voting; but for liberals, PAC money substantially raised the probability that they would vote with the used-car dealers.[52] " 'Of course it was money,' one House member said. . . . 'Why else would they vote for used-car dealers?' "[53]

House Democratic leaders were rebuffed by some Democratic members who said they could not vote against a capital gains tax cut (which would benefit the wealthy) because it would anger their business contributors. "I get elected by voters. I get financed by contributors. Voters don't care about this, contributors do."[54]

The relationship between PAC contributions and voting should not be exaggerated, however.[55] Even on these low visibility votes, a member's party and ideology are important. The constituency interests of members are also key factors. For example, members with many union workers in their districts are going to vote for those interests regardless of how much or little they get in PAC contributions.[56] Members without these constituents, though, may be more swayed by PAC contributions.

Money not only can help buy votes and access, it can buy congressional influence with federal regulators. This type of influence is well illustrated by the relationship of Charles Keating and Senator DeConcini outlined earlier in this chapter. While this was an extreme case of favor giving, as long as members feel dependent on big donors for campaign funds, these "favors" are likely to remain common.

Although research on the impact of PAC contributions on the behavior of members of Congress is plentiful, we know less about how contributions affect the decisions of presidential candidates. Large donations to presidential campaigns probably are less successful in gaining influence than they are in other campaigns. Presidential candidates tend to have widely publicized views, and presidents' actions are subject to intense scrutiny and publicity. Once in office presidents need donors less than donors need them, thus making the leverage of a campaign

"I appreciate your offer, but I'm afraid I'm already bought and paid for."

Mailing for Dollars

The Environmental Defense Fund once sent out a mass fund-raising mailing promising new members a copy of the book *50 Simple Things You Can Do to Save the Earth.* The book's number-one suggestion: Stop junk mail. Ironically, environmental groups, like others, fill mailboxes with junk mail, which destroys millions of trees a year and eventually amounts to 3% of the volume in our landfills. Yet they persist with the mailings because they bring in new members and new funds.

PACs and political parties soliciting funds send out hundreds of millions of letters annually. For example, the National Rifle Association sends 12 million letters monthly, and the American Association of Retired People sends 50 million a year just prospecting for new members.[1]

Because most people look forward to mail more than other daily activities such as television, eating, and hobbies,[2] mail solicitations provide an interesting diversion in their day. Many read the letters, are convinced by the arguments, and write checks.

Getting a good response from mail solicitations appears to be both an art and a science. Here are some of the tricks of the trade used by successful PACs.

The *mailing list* is one key to success. Letters are not sent out randomly. Rather, you are likely to receive such mailings if you have already contributed to a candidate or cause or even if you buy goods from mail-order catalogs. One estimate is that Americans in professional occupations spend eight months of their lives simply opening and sorting political and business junk mail. Mailing lists of potential contributors are shared among like-minded groups.

The *envelope* should be personalized, with real stamps, not metered ones. Often the words URGENT or REPLY REQUIRED stimulate a better response. One PAC sent out a mailing with the words FEDERAL TAX REDUCTION INFORMATION ENCLOSED prominently displayed on the envelope. The letter dealt with the activities of a PAC working to reduce taxes.

The *letter* often is written on expensive-looking paper. The text is written in short paragraphs to capture the reader's attention. A letter from the Independent Action PAC (IAPAC) had about 14 paragraphs per page, many of them just a sentence long. The prose usually is written at the sixth- to eighth-grade level—short, simple language. On the other hand, the letter is often fairly long. Four pages is typical, but many are longer.

The *opening paragraph* is usually an attention grabber such as, "I need your advice," or "This is the most urgent letter I have ever written."[3]

The *language* is usually emotional, overblown, and very negative. One 1995 Democratic fund-raising letter called Newt Gingrich a terrorist. (The authors later apologized.) The National Rifle Association's labeling of government agents as "jackbooted thugs" caused former President Bush to resign his membership. One National Conservative PAC letter from Jesse Helms warned, "Your tax dollars are being used to pay for grade school courses that teach our children that cannibalism, wife swapping, and the murder of infants and the elderly are acceptable." Campaigning against PACs, IAPAC warned that "money doesn't just talk, it leads many elected officials around on a leash."

Mailers use a personal approach, and their letters are sprinkled with "you"s. A mailing from the National Taxpayers Union offered instructions as to how "you can save America from Washington." Well-heeled PACs sometimes use computers to intersperse your name throughout the letter.

Enclosures are common. Solicitors often promise you something for your membership or send along a small gift, such as a signed picture, sticker, or pin. "While trying to appeal to you with flattery for your intelligence and compassion, direct mail packages are designed on the assumption you are a self-indulgent idiot," commented one observer.

A *donor card* is crucial. Cards, which allow you to check a box for the amount of your contribution, are enclosed to make it easy for you to give. They can be pretty emotional, too. For example, one conservative PAC offered recipients two choices on the donor card. If they contributed to the PAC, they could stick a stars and stripes flag on the card. If they refused to contribute, they should stick on the white flag of surrender!

Calvin and Hobbes **by Bill Watterson**

Source: Bill Watterson, Universal Press Syndicate, 1995.

1. Jill Smolowe, "Read This!!!!!!!!" *Time,* November 26, 1990, p. 63.
2. Larry Sabato, "Mailing for Dollars," *Psychology Today* 18 (October 1984), pp. 38–43. This box draws heavily on the Sabato article.
3. Sabato, "Mailing for Dollars." The remainder of the quotations are from this article, unless otherwise noted.

donation uncertain. Contributors sometimes find, as did one contributor to the campaign of Teddy Roosevelt, "We bought the son of a bitch but he did not stay bought."[57]

Still, analyses of large donors to, and fund-raisers for, the Bush campaign reveal that many were given special favors or benefits from the government. The Department of Labor reduced a proposed fine by nearly 90% against a large sugar farmer who gave $200,000 to the campaign.[58] The president proposed incentives for using corn-based ethanol in auto fuels, a proposal that would cost consumers at the pump but yield Archer-Daniels-Midland, which gave the Republican campaign more than $1 million, a profit of $30 to $75 million.

Although it is impossible to prove a cause-and-effect relationship in these cases, clearly large donors who expect favorable treatment have plenty of precedents to lead them to that conclusion. Thus, the leader of a watchdog group said, "The point is, we're not just electing politicians. It's a package deal. We're also electing their patrons and their priorites."[59]

The influence of big money in presidential campaigns probably makes both parties more conservative. The biggest contributors to the Republicans in recent elections have been among the most conservative people within the party. The big contributors to the Democrats are, on the whole, less liberal than the mainstream of the party.

Large contributions to presidential campaigns often lead to appointments to public office. This "spoils system" has been with us since at least the time of Andrew Jackson, so it cannot be blamed on modern PACs, "independent spending," and soft money. Many times these appointments are to minor offices without much significant policy impact—for example, ambassadorships to small nations.

➤Reforming the Campaign Money System

Many believe the current system of raising funds is undesirable. The concentration of congressional fund-raising efforts on Washington lobbyists increasingly gives the appearance, and perhaps the reality, of simply buying elections and then votes. The conservative *Wall Street Journal* colorfully described the system in Washington as "the mutants' saloon in 'Star Wars'—a place where politicians, PACs, lawyers, and lobbyists for unions, business, or you-name-it shake each other down full time for political money and political support."[60]

We have seen repeatedly that public confidence and trust in government have diminished greatly over time. Some reasons for this decline have nothing to do with money. But public trust was certainly affected by the illegal contributions in the Watergate scandal, and it is likely that revelations about big money lobbying since then have not improved the public's view of the honesty of public officials.

There is some evidence that the public is reacting against the growth of big money in campaign finance. Though many issues were involved in the defeat of Democratic incumbents in 1994, most members of the House who were defeated in 1990 and 1992 had some conflict-of-interest allegations leveled against them.

Several proposals to reform the system have been offered, most focusing on congressional campaign spending.[61] One major proposal, a combination of public financing and limits on spending, is discussed in this chapter's Symbolic Solutions box. Another idea comes from Speaker Newt Gingrich, who favors strengthening the parties. "Since we cannot effectively stifle . . . special-interest voices," Gingrich said, "let us submerge them in appeals from the parties."[62] Strong parties could insulate legislators from pressures contributors might exert on them. Other ideas include allowing parties to give more to candidates; raising the amounts individuals can contribute (inflation has eroded the value of the limits set in the early

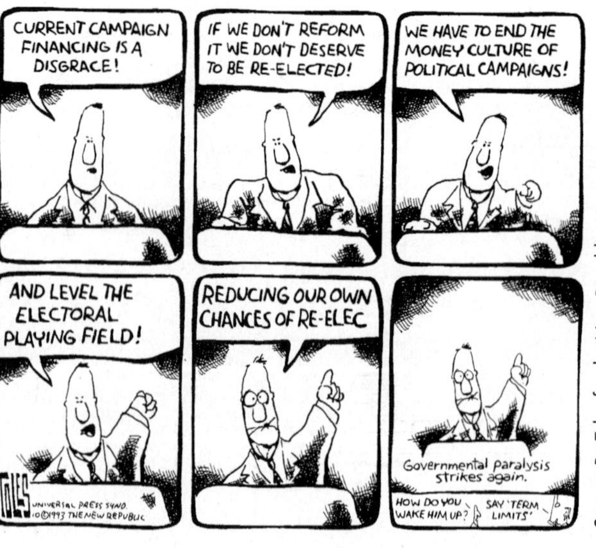

Source: By Toles for the New Republic Magazine, Inc.

1970s) and limiting further the amount PACs can give; forcing PACs to disclose more about their operations; or giving tax credits for campaign contributions only to congressional candidates in one's own state (or to presidential candidates).

Some proposals would allow candidates free media time and prohibit purchase of additional time, as is common in other nations. Candidates would be given time and be required to use it in slots of at least 5 or 10 minutes. No 30-second slash-and-burn commercials

Doctors' Orders

Big money does not always win key congressional votes. One example was the 1982 battle between the American Medical Association (AMA) and a variety of groups including Ralph Nader's Congress Watch, a public interest group.[1] The AMA was fighting to get Congress to overturn a ruling of the Federal Trade Commission (FTC), a federal regulatory agency. The FTC had ruled that doctors could not engage in price fixing, that is, deciding as a group what minimum fees to charge and punishing doctors who charge less. The FTC also had ruled that doctors could advertise their services. In other words, the FTC was applying to doctors the same rules that the Supreme Court had applied to lawyers and that the FTC itself applies to other businesses; automakers, for example, cannot agree to fix the price of cars, nor can they punish other car manufacturers who advertise. If automakers tried to fix prices, they would be in violation of antitrust laws that forbid such collusion.

The AMA wanted to be free to do its own regulating; it wanted Congress to pass a special law exempting doctors from antitrust regulations and from the clutches of the FTC. Given the antigovernment sentiment of the time, the AMA seemed close to achieving a victory. The exemption passed the House and cleared a key Senate committee.

The AMA was thought to be one of the strongest lobbying forces in Washington. It had fought against government regulation of medicine for more than 30 years. Its legitimacy was reinforced by the idea that it was an association of friendly, helpful, lifesaving doctors.

For the anti-AMA forces to win on this issue, they had to challenge the legitimacy of the AMA. To do that, they turned the wealth and power of the AMA against it. The FTC itself unleashed a blitz of public relations pointing out that the AMA was trying to set prices and regulate the economics of medicine. Congress Watch noted that when the FTC permitted advertising of eyeglasses and contact lenses, prices went down and consumers saved $100 million. But most important, Congress Watch showed that the AMA was trying to buy Congress.

Indeed, the AMA had contributed more money to congressional candidates than any other organization except the National Association of Realtors. It gave $1,700,000 in campaign contributions to the House and Senate cosponsors of the antitrust exemption bill and another $280,000 to members of committees that would hold hearings on the bill. Forty-four members of Congress received $10,000 or more from the AMA.

In a series of press releases, Congress Watch pointed out exactly which members were taking campaign money from the AMA. These names often were picked up by the members' home media, which editorialized against them. A New York representative was narrowly defeated in the primary election after his links with the AMA were exposed. This defeat led the *New York Times* to say: "Opportunistic congressmen who flack for special interests may wind up paying for their jobs."[2] Copies of the editorial were distributed to congressional offices by the anti-AMA lobby.

Gradually, the AMA lost its reputation as a group of selfless individuals interested in the public's health and began to be tagged as a greedy group interested in its own economic health. This perception was furthered by a Congress Watch news release pointing out that the average doctor earned more than $86,000 the year before.

Meanwhile, Congress Watch accompanied its publicity campaign with one-on-one lobbying of members of Congress. Soon, members who originally cosponsored the AMA bill decided to back off and the Senate voted overwhelmingly against it.

This outcome illustrates a key point about the influence of campaign money. It is more influential when the issue is not well publicized. When AMA foes were able to spotlight the money generously flowing from the AMA to those willing to do its bidding in Congress, the AMA's money began to be seen as a liability rather than an asset. When Congress Watch and other groups were able to focus the debate on the public interest versus the special interest, and to show members that their home constituents were watching, members opted for the public interest.

1. This example is drawn from Michael Pertschuk (former chair of the Federal Trade Commission and now involved in public interest lobbying), *Giant Killers* (New York: Norton, 1986), chapter 4.
2. Ibid., p. 108.

Symbolic Solutions for Complex Problems?

Public Funding for Congressional Campaigns

Although the 1974 campaign finance legislation provides public funding for presidential elections, it does not do so for congressional ones. Should we provide some public funding for congressional candidates? That idea has been discussed since at least 1907, when Republican President Teddy Roosevelt argued that one way to reduce graft in Congress was to provide public funding so members would not need to raise huge sums of money. That reasoning still motivates supporters of public funding. Would public funding reduce the mutual backscratching of special interest groups and members of Congress and allow the public to have a bigger voice? Or is public funding just a symbolic solution to a very complex issue?

Public funding is a symbolic solution in that it would send a message to voters that the impact of big money and special interests is being reduced. But would such a change really reduce the influence of special interests? And would there be other effects too?

Supporters of public funding believe it would reduce the reliance of members of Congress on special interests that provide them funding. Clearly no system would completely eliminate the influence of money on the behavior of all public officials. But providing a substantial part of the cost of campaigns through tax money, and setting limits on how much more members could spend, would take away some of the anxiety that members feel about raising money. As one observer noted, "A kind of fever takes over. Members hear that someone else is raising $500,000, and they think they have to raise $500,000, and soon everyone thinks he has to raise $500,000."[1] This anxiety preoccupies members of Congress with fund-raising and leads them to consider the impact of their decisions on their ability to raise funds. This is clearly an unhealthy situation.

Others, however, believe such a change would really be an "incumbent protection act," because challengers to congressional incumbents must spend a lot of money to be as well known as incumbents. A ceiling on campaign spending, which would likely come with public financing, might hurt challengers more than incumbents, who are already widely known.

Although that argument is plausible, the facts suggest that incumbents are already very well protected by the current laws. As we will see in the next chapter, most incumbents who run are reelected. In fact, in 1986 through 1992 nearly 96% of all House incumbents were reelected. Even in the anti-Democratic incumbent election of 1994 nearly 90% of all incumbents were reelected. It is hard to see how a change in the law could make incumbents safer than they already are.

---

would be allowed. Presidential candidates in 1992 made good use of free media time, not because of legislative mandates but because of offers by talk show hosts and others who wanted to interview them. Interest in congressional candidates is considerably less, however.

Opponents point out the practical difficulties of this reform in a federal system in which each congressional candidate must appeal to his or her own constituency. Unlike Western European nations, where citizens vote primarily for the national party, not for their local candidate, politics in the United States is decentralized. But this roadblock to reform may not be insuperable for, as Senator Robert Dole (R-Kan.) said, "If they can figure out the tax code, they can figure this out."[63]

However, our political leaders have no stake in serious reform. Ideologically, Democrats are more sympathetic to limiting the influence of big money, but practically, Democratic incumbents are heavily dependent upon their PAC "fixes." When a Republican president was in office, Democratic members could vote their ideological inclinations, resting assured that the president would veto any serious bills. When Clinton took office and voiced support for reform, Democratic members found innumerable ways to avoid passing a serious bill. Now that Republicans control Congress, Democrats rue their failure. Business interests, ideologically more in tune with Republicans, have begun to finance them heavily, as the new incumbents and majority party. Democrats are finding their sources of funding drying up.

Republicans traditionally have opposed ceilings on spending and public funding because of their anti–big government stance, their ability to raise more money than Democrats, and their fear that incumbents will benefit. Although Republicans are now the majority of incumbents, it is unlikely that this will outweigh their other objections to public funding.

One concern of either limits on candidate spending or limits on PACs' giving is that it would increase "independent" spending. Given the Supreme Court's current view of independent spending, that will be difficult to regulate. Many people believe it is better to have PACs contributing openly than to have independent spending accountable to no one.

One of the few clear lessons of campaign financing reform is that we cannot always foresee the impact it will have. No one imagined in 1974 that PACs and Washington lobbyists would come to dominate fund-raising and influence officials as they do today. As a director of a successful conservative PAC once said, "Whatever changes they make in the law, we'll turn them to our advantage."[2]

In sum, while it seems clear that public financing of congressional elections and caps on spending would send a symbolic message that campaign finance is being cleaned up, the problem is a complex one and there is little agreement what the other consequences would be.

1. Elizabeth Drew, *Politics and Money* (New York: Collier Books, 1983), p. 51.
2. Larry Sabato, *PAC Power* (New York: W. W. Norton, 1984), p. 172.

This Puck cartoon, "Jack and the Wall Street Giants," shows a brave but tiny Theodore Roosevelt challenging the large corporations of his time. Removing their influence in elections was but one way Roosevelt fought the trusts.

Walter Lippman, a former journalist, once said that Americans govern themselves "by fits and starts of unsuspecting complacency and violent suspicion." We think nothing is wrong, and then we think everything is wrong. So it is with our views of campaign money. For several years after the 1974 reforms, we thought the influence of money was in check. More recently many think it is out of control and the nation is in terrible jeopardy. Whether we are overreacting or not, the issue of campaign finance reform is again alive.

➤Conflicts of Interest

In addition to money's influence on political campaigns, it also leads to **conflicts of interest.** This term refers to officials making decisions that directly affect their personal livelihoods or interests. The campaign contribution system we have just described is certainly a huge conflict of interest. Presidents and members of Congress make decisions about policies affecting those who give them campaign money. But conflicts of interest are not confined to decisions involving campaign money. As Madison noted, almost every decision involves potential conflicts of interest. Decisions by presidents, bureaucrats, and members of Congress can affect their personal financial interests (including stocks, bonds, or other investments).

Despite periodic attempts to limit conflicts of interest, violations of ethics codes still occur in Congress and in the executive branch. In 1981, six House members and one senator were convicted in an FBI undercover operation known as Abscam. Five were even videotaped accepting cash. Incidents of blatant bribery such as this are rare, but conflicts of interests

This secretly filmed picture shows the acceptance of money in the Abscam episode. As one of the implicated members said: "I'm gonna tell you something real simple and short. In this business, money talks and b _ _ _s _ _ _ walks."

are more common. They are harder to deal with, however, because the issues are less clear-cut.

In trying to understand congressional behavior, it is difficult to untangle the effects of personal financial interests, constituency interests, and party loyalties. For example, people on the Agriculture Committee with agribusiness interests, as most have, often represent districts with large agricultural interests. If those members vote in favor of agricultural interests, they are voting both for their own interests and for their constituents' interests. And they are likely to think that they are advancing the national interest at the same time. It appears that the impact of these personal interests on voting is fairly small once constituency interests are taken into account.[64]

In the executive branch, decision makers operate under much less direct public and media scrutiny. Yet they too may be acting on matters that affect their personal economic position. Since the Carter administration, all high-level administrative officials have been required to file public financial disclosure statements to allow the public to see when they are making decisions that benefit their own financial interests. But the rules do not require officials to step aside on matters that would affect them financially. (The law is more strict for the judicial branch. Judges are forbidden to participate in cases in which they have any financial interest.)

It is also a conflict of interest to use one's government position to line up a job following a public service career. The Ethics in Government Act of 1978 tried to regulate this, but the law is not enforced very stringently. Because many companies that regularly deal with government think experience in government, especially in the agency that regulates the company's activities, is an asset, many officials take well-paying jobs in the industry they came to know while in government. Critics call this the "revolving door," referring to the movement of people from government service to the private sector and, sometimes, back again.

Using a government job to line up lucrative private employment also can involve **influence peddling**, using one's access to powerful people to make money. Former high government officials can and do use their access to former colleagues to win jobs representing clients in business and labor. A well-publicized case of influence peddling was that of Michael Deaver, the deputy chief of staff and one of President Reagan's closest advisers during his first term. Deaver left government, immediately set up a public relations and lobbying firm, and began soliciting clients largely on the basis of his close relationship with the president.[65]

Conflicts of interest can never be completely eradicated from government, but presidents can make their expectations clear. Presidents Bush and Clinton have shown more concern about ethical issues than their predecessors, though conflicts of interest have been regularly reported. Ironically, when such conflicts are made public instead of being ignored, public perceptions of lower ethical standards in government than elsewhere in society may be reinforced. There is little reason to think, however, that people in government are less ethical than those in business, labor, or other parts of the private sector.

Conclusion: Does the Influence of Money Make Government Less Responsive?

The influence of money in American politics is a perennial source of concern to those who want to live up to the democratic ideals of popular sovereignty and political equality. Our democratic values tell us that government should represent all, the poor as well as the rich, and that everyone should have an equal chance to influence government. We know that in the real world things do not work this way. We tolerate much inequality in access because that seems to be the way the world works in the private as well as in

What About Whitewater?

Since 1992, the topic of Whitewater keeps popping into the news. It is an alleged scandal that involves President Clinton, his wife Hillary Rodham Clinton, an obscure savings and loan in Arkansas, and a suicide in Washington, D.C. Although the story of Whitewater has persisted, most people long ago have forgotten, if they ever knew, what the supposed "scandal" is all about. Yet surfers on the Internet, as well as listeners on conservative talk radio, read and hear about nefarious plots allegedly connected to Whitewater.

The facts are less exciting than the lurid rumors. The facts appear to be that in the late 1970s, Bill and Hillary Clinton entered into a venture, called the Whitewater Development Company, whose purpose was to sell vacation lots in the Ozarks. The Clintons were a 50% partner in this deal, along with James McDougal, a political supporter of then-Governor Clinton. With an investment of $230,000, the Clintons lost somewhere between $45,000 and $68,000 in this venture, eventually selling their shares to McDougal.

Later, McDougal (but not the Clintons) purchased a savings and loan company, the Madison Guaranty, which, after a time, federal regulators declared to be insolvent. Meanwhile, Hillary Clinton, as a lawyer representing Madison Guaranty, petitioned the new state securities commissioner (who herself had formerly worked for a law firm that represented Madison), to permit the savings and loan to borrow money and remain in operation. But the appeal failed, and the savings and loan was taken over by the federal government in 1989, as part of the nationwide program to get the savings and loan industry back to financial solvency.

All of this happened long before Bill Clinton was in the White House, and thus has nothing to do with use or misuse of presidential power. Investigations by special prosecutors and Congress have revealed a kind of cronyism that often affects politics in small towns and small states and can lead to conflicts of interest. There have been charges that funds were siphoned from Madison to Clinton's gubernatorial campaign, but these have not been proven.

The plot thickened, however, when Vincent Foster, a former law partner of Hillary Clinton (he handled the Clintons' sale of their Whitewater holdings) and later a lawyer on the White House staff, committed suicide in a Washington park in 1993.

Immediately rumors spread that Foster had been murdered or had committed suicide because of Whitewater. The motive for a political killing is obscure at best. Foster was beset by many political problems and despaired of his perceived lack of success in his Washington role. However, White House counsel Bernard Nussbaum did remove Foster's Whitewater files before the police reached Foster's office, thus adding fuel to the flame. Clinton later fired Nussbaum.

In 1994 Attorney General Janet Reno appointed an independent counsel to investigate the entire Whitewater affair. Hillary Clinton was called to testify before a federal grand jury hearing evidence about Whitewater. Republicans in Congress launched an investigation of their own, complete with televised hearings. Several of Clinton's associates were tried and convicted in 1996 on charges related to the failure of Madison Guaranty. President Clinton himself testified by videotape for the defense in two of these trials.

Although several findings concluded that the Clintons violated no laws in the Whitewater matter, many congressional Republicans are convinced that the Clintons have been less than forthcoming and may in fact be hiding crucial evidence. While new revelations might throw entirely new light on the Clintons, for now it seems that sloppy financial record keeping, cronyism, and a lack of candor about their complicated deals are their major failings. Most of the public seem bored with the continuing story, or nonstory, which seems to have taken on a life of its own on the fringes of the news media.

the public sphere, and also because everyone is not equally interested in influencing government.

Nevertheless, our reaction to the influence of money seems to be cyclical. We tolerate it; then when stories of inside deals, influence peddling, and buying access and even votes become too frequent, we act to do something about it. We then slip back into apathy until the next cycle comes along.[66]

In recent history, the low point of the use of money to buy access was probably during the Watergate scandals associated with the 1972 election. We then reacted strongly to those scandals by passing new laws and in general cleaning up our campaign finance system. But as the years went by, people found ways to get around the laws. Now it appears we are in another era of growing concern over ethical standards in government.

We should not think of our times as the low point in government morality. In political campaigns, big money is certainly less influential than it was in the late nineteenth century or even during the early 1970s. Campaign funding regulations have cleaned up some of the unethical practices of the Watergate era. Although there are large loopholes in these regulations, they are an improvement over what came before. Disclosure laws have opened for public scrutiny the sources of campaign funds for candidates for federal offices. It is the disclosure laws that make us at least somewhat aware of the sources of private money seeking to influence the political system.

Some commentators believe the standards of public officials decreased during the 1980s. But their behavior reflected the ethical standards of the larger society. Making money in any way possible seems to have been the hallmark of the 1980s, the age of "pin-striped outlaws." Not only was the Reagan White House filled with people who resigned after embarrassing revelations of conflicts of interest or illegal activities, but also many leaders of the business world seemed intent on making their fast buck, regardless of the ethics or legality of their actions. Numerous Wall Street bankers bought and sold illegal insider tips, savings and loan officers looted their institutions, military contractors cheated government, and other executives made millions in shady deals that were barely legal. One businessman lamented, "We are all embarrassed by events that make the *Wall Street Journal* read more like the *Police Gazette*."[67]

We should not exaggerate the amount of money involved in politics. Corporations spend much more to attract consumers than politicians spend to attract voters. For example, Procter and Gamble spent nearly $2.7 billion on advertising in 1994, more than four times the cost of all congressional campaigns combined that year.[68] It is not the amount of money in politics as much as its possible effects that concerns us.

Those effects are hard to pin down. We have seen that it is difficult to measure the influence of money on political outcomes. Money sometimes influences votes and policies. Campaign contributions have some impact on voting in Congress. But sometimes money appears to have little or perhaps no impact at all. We do not know, for instance, whether presidential candidates are influenced by huge campaign donations or whether bureaucrats use promises of future jobs as trade-offs for current favors. We think that good candidates are hindered or deterred from running by a shortage of money or even just by the knowledge that they need to raise big money, but it is difficult to know exactly how many. Even though money is very tangible, its influence sometimes is quite intangible.

To the extent that money has an impact, it probably limits the responsiveness of government to the average citizen. It causes some policymakers to be more responsive to the big interests. This does not mean, though, that those with the most money always win. Organization and a sense of the public interest can sometimes defeat even big money.

In designing laws to regulate the use of money in political life, we need to realize that no system can protect us against all unethical or dishonest candidates and officials. Perhaps the best that reformers can reasonably hope for is a system in which politicians of average honesty will feel some obligation to put the public interest ahead of their private interest, so that they can better resist the temptation of money. Our current laws, especially our congressional campaign finance laws, do not always do that. As a result, we lose trust in officials and faith in government. We become increasingly angry and alienated. Perhaps, then, even a largely symbolic effort by our legislators to limit the influence of money on the political process is important, because it sends the signal that they are aware of our concerns. That is one step in retaining our trust in government.

EPILOGUE

DeConcini Intervenes

DeConcini decided to help Keating. Though he insists he did not arrange a meeting with the Federal Home Loan Bank Board chair, Edward Gray, DeConcini attended such a meeting and took the lead in presenting Lincoln S&L's case. Participants included four other U.S. senators, Alan Cranston (D-Cal.), John McCain (R-Ariz.), Donald Riegle (D-Mich.), and John Glenn (D-Ohio), all of whom had received substantial campaign contributions from Keating, ranging from Riegle's $78,000 to Cranston's nearly $1 million. Gray indicated he did not know the specifics of the Lincoln S&L case and offered to arrange a meeting between the five senators and the regulators. When that meeting was held, DeConcini asked the regulators to lay off the Lincoln S&L until a lawsuit to determine the legality of the board's actions was settled.

In 1993 Charles Keating, Jr. was sentenced to over 12 years in prison for defrauding the Lincoln Savings and Loan Association and its investors. He was also ordered to pay $122 million in restitution.

DeConcini cited the accountant's estimate of the good financial health of the S&L, asking, "You believe they'd prostitute themselves for a client?"[69] The regulators responded by noting that the Lincoln S&L case could involve criminal charges. At that point, the meeting adjourned and DeConcini stopped inquiring for a while. The next year, however, DeConcini made repeated calls to Gray's successor and to another board member inquiring whether the Lincoln S&L could be sold. The day after his last phone call, Keating's Arizona company declared bankruptcy; the following day, federal regulators took over the Lincoln S&L.

After the actions of the senators, called the Keating 5, came to light, they were the subject of a 14-month investigation by the Senate Ethics Committee. Hearings, broadcast over C-SPAN, enraged many. The senators defended their actions, noting that serving constituents is a routine part of their job. They claimed that if they were guilty, so were most other members of Congress. The investigating attorney argued that at least three of the group, including DeConcini, went far beyond the bounds of ethical behavior. He argued that even though there was no actual exchange of money for favors, the arrangement gave the appearance of such an exchange and brought discredit to the Senate and the government.

After the hearings, the committee found that Cranston, who was actively soliciting money from Keating even while he was intervening with the federal regulators, broke ethics rules linking "fund raising and official activities." The committee found that DeConcini and Riegle did not break rules but engaged in conduct that "gave the appearance of being improper." The committee noted that it "could not condone" their behavior. McCain and Glenn received the lightest sanction, merely being chastised for their "poor judgment."[70]

The collapse of Keating's S&L is estimated to be the largest in history. It will cost the taxpayers $2.5 billion to pay off the depositors whose accounts were insured. It was only a small but illustrative part of the shenanigans that led to the collapse of thousands of S&Ls all over the country (a drama that also spawned the Whitewater case). As one analyst indicated, "It's as though Jimmy Carter poured gasoline on the S&L house, a Democratically controlled Congress put a match to it, and the Reagan-Bush regime placed snipers on rooftops to shoot at firefighters."[71]

The pressure of the Keating 5 and other members of Congress delayed investigations of the failing S&Ls, postponing recognition of the magnitude of the savings and loan problem and thus escalating by many times the costs of bailing out depositors. Under pressure from constituents and donors, members also dragged their feet on legislation to begin the reorganization of the entire S&L industry. One estimate is that if action had been taken in 1986, the whole S&L bailout would have amounted to about $20 billion. Now estimates run at least to $500 billion, or about the cost of the Vietnam War. On average, each household in America will pay $5,000 for the bailout. As one commentator remarked, "Never has so much money gone to such key legislators who worked so hard for measures that cost taxpayers so dearly."[72]

Greed, criminality, and negligence led to this economic disaster. But of course, it was not just the greed of public officials that caused the S&L mess. Private enterprise contributed more than its share. In addition to the thousands of greedy and in some cases criminal S&L operators, real estate appraisers participated in the debacle by vastly inflating the estimates of the value of real estate that many S&Ls bought (thus making it look as if the S&Ls had more assets than they did). And, though DeConcini did not believe that the accountant who vouched for Lincoln S&L's financial health would prostitute himself for his clients, many did. That accountant took a job the next year with Keating's firm at a salary of $900,000. Economists, lawyers, and others were also willing to sell their good judgment. (Alan Greenspan, the economist who also testified to Lincoln S&L's financial strength, was paid by Keating's law firm to write the letter.)[73]

Has the Keating 5 scandal led to higher ethical standards in Congress and perhaps new campaign finance laws? Keating was quite open in acknowledging he was trying to buy influence with his campaign contributions. Asked if his financial support influenced several political figures to take up his cause, he replied, "I want to say in the most forceful way I can, I certainly hope so."[74] But even with this open acknowledgment of influence buying, no significant action has been taken to regulate campaign finance. The Democrats had their chance to limit campaign spending and blew it. The Republicans do not want to limit spending. Thus, real reform seems unlikely in the near future.

The pressures against cleaning up conflicts of interest are strong. There always are members who want to make more money and interest groups that are happy to help them do so in exchange for access or more tangible favors. As one journalist noted, "The mutual affinity of the wealthy and the politically powerful offers a seduction that not all members of Congress are able to resist."[75] For this reason, it is not surprising that most Americans believe that members lie, put the needs of special interests above the needs of the average citizen, and profit improperly from their positions.[76]

Nevertheless, Congress is probably cleaner today than in the past. In earlier decades, these activities would not excite the least discussion. In the nineteenth century, Daniel Webster received a cash retainer from the Second Bank of the United States while chairing the Senate Finance Committee. At the height of the debate over the bank's rechartering, he complained to its president that his retainer was too low![77]

➤Key Terms

Muckrakers
Teapot Dome scandal
Federal Election Campaign Act
independent spending
soft money
political action committees (PACs)
conflicts of interest
influence peddling

➤Further Reading

John M. Barry, *The Ambition and the Power* (New York: Viking, 1989). *The fall of Speaker Jim Wright set in the context of his successes as speaker and the enemies they created.*

Brooks Jackson, *Honest Graft: Big Money and the American Political Process* (New York: Knopf, 1988). *Jackson followed Tony Coehlo, then the chair of the Democratic Congressional Campaign Committee, around the country observing him raising money for Democratic candidates. Jackson believes that the success of Democrats in raising PAC money has blunted the threat of a PAC-financed Republican takeover of Congress but only at the cost of having Democrats more dependent on special-interest money.*

Larry Sabato, *PAC Power: Inside the World of Political Action Committees* (New York: W. W. Norton, 1984). *A fairly positive assessment of PACs.*

Frank Sorauf, *Inside Campaign Finance: Myths and Realities* (New Haven, Conn.: Yale University Press, 1992). *An overview that challenges conventional wisdom.*

➤Notes

1. Material on DeConcini and Keating is drawn from John R. Cranford, "Keating and the Five Senators: Putting the Puzzle Together," *Congressional Quarterly Weekly Report* (January 26, 1991), p. 221; Jim Calle and Bill Roberts, "Who Was Asleep When Keating Went Astray?" *Palm Beach Post* (January 8, 1990), p. 18; "Bonfire of the S&Ls," *Newsweek,* May 21, 1990, pp. 20–30.

2. "Bonfire," p. 27.

3. Ibid.

4. Ibid.

5. Phil Kuntz, "Senators Ponder How to Treat Appearance of Wrongdoing," *Congressional Quarterly Weekly Report* (January 26, 1991), p. 229.

6. Jimmy Breslin, *How the Good Guys Finally Won: Notes from an Impeachment Summer* (New York: Ballantine Books, 1974), p. 14.

7. Congressional Quarterly, *Dollar Politics,* 3rd ed. (Washington, D.C.: CQ Press, 1982), p. 3.

8. Ibid.

9. James Madison, *The Federalist Papers, #10.*

10. Haynes Johnson, "Turning Government Jobs into Gold," *Washington Post National Weekly Edition,* May 12, 1986, pp. 6–7.

11. Quoted in Richard Hofstadter, *The American Political Tradition* (New York: Vintage Books, 1958), p. 165.

12. Congressional Quarterly, *Dollar Politics,* p. 3.

13. Elizabeth Drew, *Politics and Money* (New York: Collier, 1983), p. 9.

14. Ibid.

15. *Buckley v. Valeo,* 424 U.S. 1 (1976).

16. See Marick Masters and Gerald Keim, "Determinants of PAC Participation among Large Corporations," *Journal of Politics* 47 (November 1985), pp. 1158–73; J. David Gopoian, "What Makes PACs Tick?" *American Journal of Political Science* 28 (May 1984), pp. 259–81; Larry Sabato, *PAC Power* (New York: W. W. Norton, 1984), chapter 3; Theodore Eismeier and Philip H. Pollock, "Political Action Committees," in Michael Malbin, ed., *Money and Politics in the United States* (Chatham, N.J.: Chatham House, 1984); John Peters, "Political Action Committees and the 1984 Congressional Elections," paper prepared for delivery to the Research Committee on Political Finance and Political Corruption at the World Congress, International Political Science Association, Paris, France, 1985.

17. *Federal-Election Commission v. National Conservative PAC,* 470 U.S. 480 (1985).

18. Ruth Marcus, "Taking Issue with Advocacy," *Washington Post National Weekly Edition,* April 15–21, 1996, p. 13.

19. Jeffrey H. Birnbaum, "The Appetizers Better Be Good . . . ," *Time Magazine,* December 11, 1995, p. 47.

20. Drew, *Politics and Money,* p. 105.

21. Peter Overby, "Back Pocket PACs," *Common Cause,* July/August, 1990, p. 26.

22. "Big Money's Election Year Comeback," *New York Times,* August 7, 1988, p. 5.

23. Carol Matlock, "Lobbying Focus," *National Journal,* November 5, 1988, p. 2868.

24. Larry Makinson and Joshua Goldstein, *Open Secrets: The Encyclopedia of Congressional Money and Politics* (Washington, D.C.: Congressional Quarterly Inc., 1994).

25. Michael Weisskopf, "To the Victors Belong the PAC Checks," *Washington Post National Weekly Edition* (January 2–5, 1995), p. 13. The remainder of the paragraph is also drawn from that source.

26. Jennifer Babson and Kelly St. John, "Momentum Helps GOP Collect Record Amounts from PACs," *Congressional Quarterly Weekly Report,* December 3, 1994, pp. 3456–3459.

27. See Kevin Grier and Michael Mangy, "Comparing Interest Group PAC Contributions to House and Senate Incumbents," *Journal of Politics* 55 (August, 1993): 615–643.

28. J. David Gopoian, "Change and Continuity in Defense PAC Behavior," *American Politics Quarterly* 13 (July 1985), pp. 297–322; Richard Morin and Charles Babcock, "Off Year, Schmoff Year," *Washington Post National Weekly Edition,* May 14–20, 1990, p. 15.

29. Gary Wasserman, "The Uses of Influence," *Washington Post National Weekly Edition,* January 11–17, 1993, p. 35.

30. Makinson and Goldstein, *Open Secrets,* p. 23.

31. Drew, *Politics and Money,* p. 68; Thomas B. Edsall, "More Than Enough Is Not Enough," *Washington Post National Weekly Edition,* February 9, 1987, p. 13. See also Edward Handler and John Mulkern, *Business in Politics* (Lexington, Mass.: D.C. Heath, 1982), pp. 1–34.

32. Johnson, "Turning Government Jobs into Gold," p. 7; Sabato, *PAC Power,* p. 84.

33. Amy Dockser, "Nice PAC You've Got There . . . A Pity if Anything Should Happen to It," *Washington Monthly* (January 1984), p. 21.

34. Meg Greenfield, "The Political Debt Bomb," *Newsweek,* April 6, 1987, p. 76.

35. John Harwood, "Cash Machine: Candidate Gramm Rarely Skips a Chance to Raise More Money," *Wall Street Journal,* February 17, 1995, p. 7, quoted in Nelson W. Polsby and Aaron Wildavsky, *Presidential Elections: Strategies and Structures in American Politics,* ninth edition (Chatham, N.J.: Chatham House Publishers, 1996) pp. 109–110n.

36. Gary Jacobson, *Money in Congressional Elections* (New Haven: Yale University Press, 1980), p. 61.

37. David Broder, "The High Road to Lower Finance?" *Washington Post National Weekly Edition,* June 29, 1987, p. 4; Diane Granat, "Parties' Schools for Politicians or Grooming Troops for Election," *Congressional Quarterly Weekly Report,* May 5, 1984, p. 1036.

38. Gary Orren, "The Nomination Process," in Michael Nelson, ed., *The Elections of 1984* (Washington, D.C.: CQ Press, 1986), chapter 2. See also Michael J. Robinson and Austin Ranney, eds., *The Mass Media in Campaign 1984* (Washington, D.C.: American Enterprise Institute, 1985); Michael Robinson, Clyde Wilcox, and Paul Marshall, "The Presidency: Not for Sale," *Public Opinion* (March/April 1989), pp. 49–52.

39. Nelson Polsby and Aaron Wildavsky, *Presidential Elections* (New York: Charles Scribner's Sons, 1984), p. 56.

40. David Nice, "Campaign Spending and Presidential Election Results," *Polity* 19 (Spring 1987), pp. 464–76, shows that presidential campaign spending is more productive for Republicans than Democrats.

41. Gary Jacobson, *Money in Congressional Elections*; Jacobson, "Public Funds for Congressional Campaigns: Who Would Benefit?" in Herbert E. Alexander, ed., *Political Finance* (Beverly Hills, Calif.: Sage Publications, 1979); Jacobson, "Parties and PACs in Congressional Elections," in Lawrence C. Dodd and Bruce I. Oppenheimer, eds., *Congress Reconsidered,* 3rd ed. (Washington, D.C.: CQ Press, 1985); Jacobson, *The Politics of Congressional Elections,* 2nd ed. (Boston: Little, Brown, 1987), chapter 4; Jacobson, "The Effects of Campaign Spending in House Elections," *American Journal of Political Science* 34 (May 1990), pp. 334–62; Christopher Kenny and Michael McBurnett, "A Dynamic Model of the Effect of Campaign Spending on Congressional Vote Choice," *American Journal of Political*

Science 36 (November 1992), pp. 923–37; Donald Green and Jonathan Krasno, "Salvation for the Spendthrift Incumbent," *American Journal of Political Science* 32 (November 1988), pp. 884–907.

42. "Campaign Spending in '93–'94: The Senate, The House," *Washington Post National Weekly Edition* (January 30–February 5, 1995), pp. 14–15.

43. Charles Babcock, "Money Isn't Everything," *Washington Post National Weekly Edition,* November 12–18, 1990, p. 15.

44. Jean Reith Schroedel, "Campaign Contributions and Legislative Outcomes," *Western Political Quarterly* 39 (September 1986), pp. 371–89; Richard L. Hall and Frank Wayman, "Buying Time: Moneyed Interests and the Mobilization of Bias in Congressional Committees," *American Political Science Review* 84 (September 1990), pp. 797–820.

45. Woodrow Jones and K. Robert Keiser, "Issue Visibility and the Effects of PAC Money," *Social Science Quarterly* 68 (March 1987), pp. 170–76; Janet Grenzke, "PACs and the Congressional Supermarket," *American Journal of Political Science* 33 (February 1989), pp. 1–24, found little effect of PAC money on a series of votes that were not obscure. Laura Langbein, "Money and Access," *Journal of Politics* 48 (November 1986), pp. 1052–64, shows that those who received more PAC money spend more time with interest group representatives.

46. Drew, *Politics and Money,* p. 79.

47. "Running with the PACs," *Time,* October 25, 1982, p. 20. The quotation is from Representative Thomas Downey (D-N.Y.).

48. "Congress Study Links Funds and Votes," *New York Times,* December 30, 1987, p. 7.

49. John Frendreis and Richard Waterman, "PAC Contributions and Legislative Behavior: Senate Voting on Trucking Deregulation," *Social Science Quarterly* 66 (June 1985), pp. 401–12. See also W. P. Welch, "Campaign Contributions and Legislative Voting," *Western Political Quarterly* 25 (December 1982), pp. 478–95; Jonathan Silberman and Garey Durden, "Determining Legislative Preferences on the Minimum Wage," *Journal of Political Economy* 84 (April 1976), pp. 317–29.

50. Laura Langbein, "PACs, Lobbies and Political Conflict: The Case of Gun Control," *Public Choice* 75 (1993), pp. 254–271; Laura Langbein and Mark Lotwis, "The Political Efficacy of Lobbying and Money: Gun Control in the House, 1986," *Legislative Studies Quarterly* 15 (1990), pp. 413–40; Jean Schroedel, "Campaign Contributions and Legislative Outcomes," *Western Political Quarterly* 39 (1986), pp. 371–389.

51. Adam Clymer, " '84 PACs Gave More to Senate Winners," *New York Times,* January 6, 1985, p. 13.

52. Kirk Brown, "Campaign Contributions and Congressional Voting," paper prepared for the annual meeting of the American Political Science Association, 1983, cited in Malbin, *Money and Politics,* p. 134.

53. Drew, *Politics and Money,* p. 79.

54. Tom Kenworthy, "The Color of Money," *Washington Post National Weekly Edition,* November 6–12, 1989, p. 13.

55. See Grenzke, "PACs and the Congressional Supermarket"; also see Frank Sorauf, *Money in American Elections* (Glenview, III.: Scott, Foresman, 1988).

56. Grenzke, "Political Action Committees and the Congressional Supermarket," *American Political Science Review* 84 (1990) pp. 417–438; John Wright, "Contributions, Lobbying and Committee Voting in the US House of Representatives," Henry Chappel, Jr., "Campaign Contributions and Voting on the Cargo Preference Bill," *Public Choice* 36 (1981), pp. 301–12.

57. Jasper Shannon, *Money and Politics* (New York: Random House, 1959).

58. "Study: Bush Donors Get Government Favors," *Lincoln Journal,* May 28, 1992. A *Los Angeles Times* news release.

59. Charles Lewis of the Center for Public Integrity, quoted in "Book Details Candidates' Extensive Financial Alignments," *Lincoln Journal* (Tribune Media Services), January 12, 1996, p. 5A.

60. "Cleaning Up Reform," *Wall Street Journal,* November 10, 1983, p. 26; Kenworthy, "The Color of Money."

61. Good discussions of proposed reforms are found in Malbin, *Money and Politics,* ch. 8; Drew, *Politics and Money,* ch. 20; and Sabato, *PAC Power,* ch. 6.

62. David S. Broder, "Gingrich the Heretic," *Washington Post National Weekly Edition,* November 20–26, 1995, p. 4.

63. Drew, *Politics and Money,* p. 151.

64. John Peters and Susan Welch, "Private Interests and Public Interests," *Journal of Politics* 45 (May 1983), pp. 378–96.

65. "Having It All, Then Throwing It Away," *Time,* May 25, 1987, p. 22.

66. Elizabeth Drew, "Letter from Washington," *New Yorker,* May 1, 1989, pp. 99–108; see also Don Bolz, "Tales of Power and Money," *Washington Post National Weekly Edition,* May 1–7, 1989, pp. 11–12.

67. "Having It All," p. 22.

68. "100 Leading National Advertisers: U.S. Ad Spending Totals," *Advertising Age,* September 27, 1995, p. 2.

69. "Bonfire of the S&Ls," p. 28.

70. Helen Dewar, "Much Ado About What?" *Washington Post National Weekly Edition,* March 11–17, 1991, p. 14.

71. Donald Kaul, "S&L Mess Response Baffling," *Sunday Journal-Star,* November 11, 1990, p. 3A, Tribune Media Services syndicate.

72. "Bonfire of the S&Ls," p. 28.

73. Ibid.

74. Jack Germond and Jules Witcover, "Looking for a Smoking Gun on Campaign Funds?" *National Journal,* December 2, 1989, p. 2956.

75. Drew, "Letter from Washington," p. 108.

76. Richard Morin, "They're All Crooks—Whatever Their Names Are," *Washington Post National Weekly Edition,* May 29–June 4, 1989, p. 39.

77. James Glassman, "Ethics, Schmethics—Congress Has Never Been Cleaner," *Washington Post National Weekly Edition,* June 5–11, 1989, p. 23.

PART THREE

Institutions

Bill Clinton, near his childhood home of Hope, Ark. (right).

Newt Gingrich at 7 (below).

10 Congress

You Are There

Should You Risk Your Career?

It is August 1993 and the House of Representatives is considering Bill Clinton's first budget bill. The bill, which includes a plan to substantially reduce the deficit, has been portrayed as a "make or break" moment in Clinton's presidential term. Failure to get the bill passed will further reduce his persuasive power and stature, perhaps (the hyperbolic media pronounced) ruin his presidency, because he is already seen as weak. On the other hand, the media and the interested public will see passage of the bill as a huge victory, the first step in bringing the nation's deficit under control.

You are Marjorie Margolies-Mezvinsky, a freshman Democratic member of Congress from suburban Philadelphia. You are faced with a representative's worst nightmare: On an important, well-publicized vote, you must either stand with the president of your party against the wishes of the majority of your district's voters, or vote with your district but contribute in large part to your president's defeat.

You are not a typical member of Congress. A graduate of Columbia University, you are a television newswoman married to a former Iowa congressional representative. You have eleven children, including biological children, stepchildren, adopted children from Korea and Vietnam, and refugee foster children. After covering the Clarence Thomas-Anita Hill hearings as a journalist, you decided to run for Congress yourself. Your opponent, a former state representative and county commissioner, was well known for his constituency work (called a "zen master of constituency service" by the local paper), but you attacked him for feeding at the public trough and for waffling ("pro-choice, that's me; multiple choice, that's Jon Fox").[1] You supported abortion rights, improved health care programs, and a middle-class tax cut.

You are finishing your first term in office and, like most other members, are greatly concerned about your reelection chances. Your district had been continuously represented by Republicans since 1916 (!) before you were elected. But in 1992, the voters of the district gave you a razor-thin majority (you won by only 1300 votes out of 254,000 cast) and a plurality to Bill Clinton, largely because of economic concerns and partly because of an anti-incumbent mood. Since coming to Congress, you have positioned yourself well. You are one of only five freshmen appointed to the powerful Energy and Commerce Committee. A position on that committee has given you access to important interests who have already contributed to your reelection campaign.

Clinton's budget bill calls for a combination of tax increases and spending cuts. It pleases no one entirely, but it is the first significant move toward reducing the deficit since the 1960s. But the bill is in jeopardy for two reasons. First, the Republicans, the minority party in the House, are united in opposition. Many Republicans had supported similar budget measures when they were proposed by George Bush. But now that it is Clinton's budget bill, they sensed an opportunity to deal a major blow to his presidency by defeating this key economic package. The Republicans have traditionally positioned themselves as fiscally conservative (even though it was a Republican president, Ronald Reagan, who ran the largest deficits in U.S. history), and they

CONTINUED

As the Republicans take control of Congress, a staff member for a departing Democrat packs to leave.

OUTLINE

Members and Constituencies
- Members
- Constituencies

Congressional Campaigns and Elections
- The Advantages of Incumbency
- Unsafe at Any Margin?
- Challengers
- Campaigns
- Voting for Congress

The Representative on the Job
- Informal Norms
- Working Privately and "Going Public"
- Voting by Members

How Congress Is Organized
- How Congressional Organization Evolved
- Leaders
- Committees
- Staff

What Congress Does
- Lawmaking
- Overseeing the Federal Bureaucracy
- Budget Making

Conclusion: Is Congress Responsive?

do not wish to relinquish this advantage to the Democrats. But many conservative Democrats are defecting because they oppose the various tax increases, including a proposed tax on fuel as an energy-saving measure.

You initially voted against the bill because you have told your constituents you will not support the bill. You had mixed emotions when it passed by six votes. The bill has come back to the House after House and Senate representatives reached agreement in a conference committee (when the Senate and House versions of a particular bill are not identical, a committee is set up to negotiate a common version of the bill, which is then sent to each house for ratification). Now the House must ratify the results of that negotiation. You have already prepared a statement explaining your "no" vote on the budget bill. You think it does not go far enough to reduce the deficit. In particular, you believe that it does not pare enough away from entitlements, those programs like Medicare, welfare, and Social Security. As part of your justification for the no vote, you indicate you believe that the president should call a "summit" meeting to discuss entitlement spending.

But now the president has spoken to you at length, pleading for your support. He, and anyone who follows the news, knows the vote is extremely close. He needs every vote, including yours. Given the unanimous opposition of the Republicans, most Democrats must stand firm or the bill will be defeated. You know that a defeat on this bill could have serious repercussions for his entire presidency.

But you do not really favor the bill. It does not go as far as you want on spending cuts, and there are too many tax increases in the bill. Moreover, you think your constituents are not in favor of it either. You want to be reelected, and you fear that because you have told your constituents you will not support the bill, your constituents will think you have sold out. To vote for the bill could mean committing political suicide in your Republican district; even under the best of circumstances you will have an uphill race. To waffle on this key issue could move your reelection chances from marginal to hopeless. What do you do?

Representative Margolies-Mezvinsky with her aides moments before she must vote.

Many Americans are angry at government, and they are most angry at Congress. Americans profess a love for democracy in the abstract, but paradoxically it is the very visibility of democratic processes that makes Congress the least loved branch of government.[2]

The public has the highest level of support for the Supreme Court, the institution that is the least democratic (Figure 1). The Court, however, is most isolated from the public. Little of the disagreement, negotiation, and compromise that take place on the Court becomes public. The public gives the president the next highest level of support. The president is certainly the most visible symbol of national government, but within the executive office, disagreement, negotiation, and compromise are somewhat concealed.

The public is least supportive of Congress, where the processes of democracy are exposed for all to see. C-SPAN and news broadcasts bring debate, disagreement, and compromise alive. The media also bring to every American who cares to listen the arguments of lobbyists and special interest groups, each trying to pull Congress in a particular direction. The public sees Congress as too powerful, impeding the president from carrying out his duties. Too often, for the

FIGURE 1
Public Perceives Congress as Most Powerful National Institution, and Likes It the Least

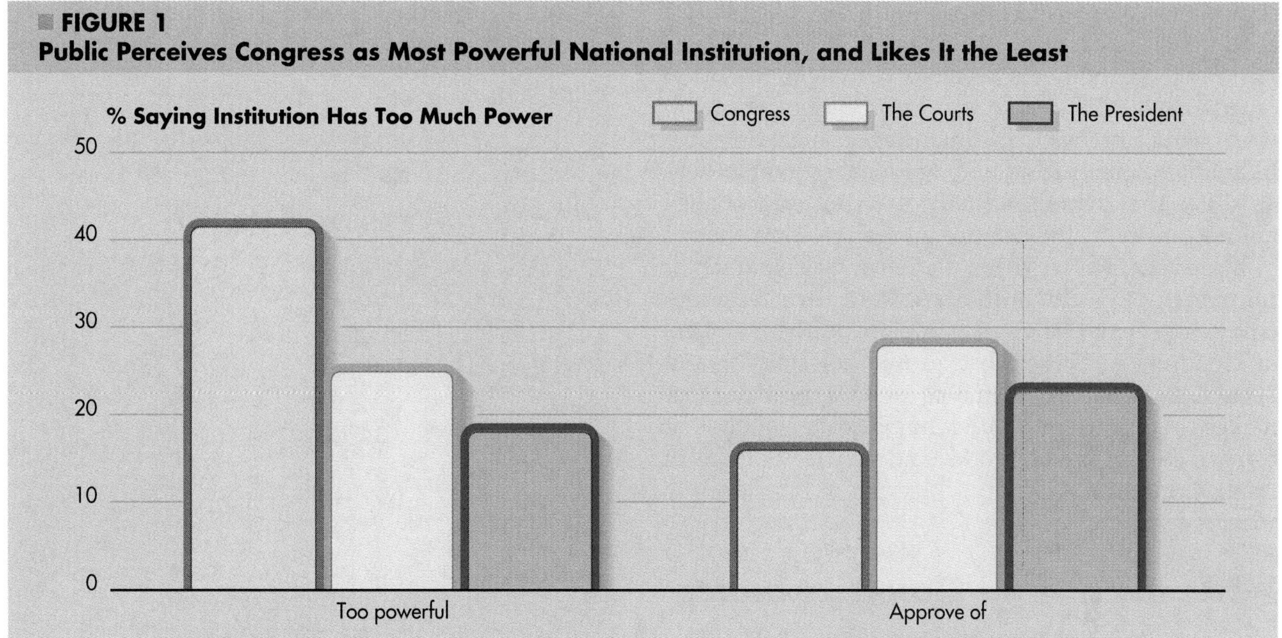

Source: John Hibbing and Elizabeth Theiss-Morse, *Congress as Public Enemy* (Cambridge, Cambridge University Press, 1995). Data are from 1993.

public's taste, the debate is rancorous rather than calm, and focused on how prospective legislation will affect private interests rather than the public interest. None of this is surprising, of course, in a complex society where people and groups do have quite different interests and views of the world. But, as two political scientists recently commented, "The people want democracy without the mess and Congress is a tangible reminder that democracy is messy."[3]

That being said, however, public attitudes about Congress are themselves complex. One famous political scientist once observed that Americans hate their Congress, but love their own member of Congress.[4] This is true, but attitudes are not that simple. Two-thirds of the public approve of their own representative, compared to about one-fourth who approve of the members of Congress as a whole and about the same percentage who approve of congressional leaders.

The public thinks that most members of Congress care more about power than about the best interests of the nation, care more about special interests than the people, and quickly lose touch with the people back home after being elected. Although almost half think that most members of Congress are doing the best job they can, only 30% believe that members have high personal moral codes and even fewer believe that members care deeply about the problems of ordinary citizens. In other words, the public thinks members of Congress are a rather crass and self-interested group.

Despite all this, nearly 90 percent approve of Congress as an abstract institution, separate from the people in it.[5] The idea of a Congress as enshrined in the Constitution is important and esteemed. It is the people *in* Congress and the way Congress works that the public dislikes.

In addition to the public's dislike for Congress' messy processes, Congress seems to be blamed for the nation's problems, and for taxes and government wastefulness. Conflicts of interest also mar its reputation. Members themselves greatly contribute to the poor image of Congress by belittling the institution and promising voters a change when they campaign for office. They denigrate Congress to get themselves elected.[6]

And if that were not bad enough, the public tends to believe there is one "public interest," and if Congress is not passing legislation to pursue that interest, there must be something wrong. Only a minority of the public, it seems, has a sophisticated understanding that there are many different interests in American society, and that Congress is the focus of controversy over which version of the public interest is adopted.

Individual members seem to be judged by other criteria than the whole Congress.[7] Members who work hard for their constituencies, doing favors for individual constituents and winning economic benefits for the district, usually are reelected. Policy failures of the institution do not seem to hurt them.

In this chapter, we try to understand this paradoxical pattern of citizen attitudes toward their representatives and their Congress by looking at the members of Congress and their backgrounds, elections, and behaviors. What do members of Congress do that makes them so popular back home? Then we look at Congress itself, how it works, and why it is a focus of public criticism.

Members and Constituencies

Alexis de Tocqueville was not impressed with the status of members of Congress, noting that they were "almost all obscure individuals, village lawyers, men in trades, or even persons belonging to the lower class." De Tocqueville would still find lawyers and men (and women) in trades, but in the modern Congress he would find few belonging to the lower class.

Members

The Constitution places few formal restrictions on membership in Congress. One must be 25 years old to serve in the House, and 30 in the Senate. One has to be a citizen for 7 years to be elected to the House, and 9 to the Senate. Members must reside in the states from which they were elected, but House members need not reside in their own districts.

Social Characteristics

Despite these rather loose requirements, Congress is not very representative of society. The process of recruiting, nominating, and selecting ensures that only certain types of individuals serve in Congress. Members tend to be very high in education, income, and occupational status compared to the rest of the population (see Table 1). Nearly all have college degrees, and a majority have graduate or professional degrees. Members are also quite well-off financially. Over one-fourth of the senators and one-ninth of the representatives are estimated to be millionaires. Although blue-collar workers constitute nearly one-third of the working population, there are no blue- collar workers in Congress. More than half the members of the House have served in their state legislature.[8]

TABLE 1 Members of Congress Are Not Representative of the Public in Race, Sex and Class

	POPULATION (%)	HOUSE (%)	SENATE (%)
Lawyer[a]	.6	40	54
Blue-collar[a]	30	0	0
Race & ethnicity[*b]			
Black	12	9	1
Hispanic	8	4	0
Asian	2	1	2
American Indian	1	0	1
Women[b]	51	12	9
Catholic[a]	23	26	20
Jewish[a]	4	5	9
Millionaires[a]	**	12	28
Mean age[a]	33	51	58

[a]Data are for 1993–94. [b]Data are for 1997–98.

* Does not include nonvoting Hispanic members from Puerto Rico, Guam, Samoa, and the Virgin Islands or the black nonvoting members from the District of Columbia.

**.05% (one-twentieth percent)

Source: *Congressional Quarterly Weekly Report,* November 12, 1994, pp. 7-12; Glenn R. Simpson, "Representative Moneybags," *Washington Post National Weekly Edition,* May 2-8, 1994, p. 25; *Congressional Quarterly Weekly Report,* supplement to No. 45, November 9, 1996.

By far the most common occupation of both senators and representatives is the law. Over the past decade, about 40% of the members of the House and 60% of the Senate were lawyers. Law and politics are closely linked. Many people enter law specifically because they see it as a stepping-stone to a political career. Lawyers can take time out from a legal practice to pursue a political career whereas most salaried or wage-earning individuals cannot. The personal contacts developed in politics also can be invaluable in obtaining legal clients, and many former members of Congress enter law firms at salaries far higher than they commanded before serving in Congress.

Congress always has been predominantly white, Anglo (that is, not Hispanic), and male. It is only slightly less so today, as Table 1 shows. White, non-Hispanic males, who make up less than 40% of the total population, represent about 80% of the House and 90% of the Senate. Thus, Congress is not very representative in its demographic characteristics.

Opinions and Party Identification

Members of Congress seek to represent their **constituencies**. Those in districts filled with farmers must represent farmers, whether or not they know anything about farming. Representatives of districts with large universities must be aware of the reactions of university constituents even if they personally think academics have pointed heads. This conception of representation is different and more complex than simply sharing demographic characteristics.

One way members represent their constituents is through shared opinions. The liberalism of districts is reflected in members' votes. Members are more likely to share specific opinions of constituents when the issue is important to constituents and when the opinions are strongly held.[9] However, there is evidence that members are more responsive to the opinions of independent voters than to their own partisans.[10] This is probably because members believe they can count on the support of their own partisans but need to appeal to voters not strongly committed to either party.

Political party loyalties are another route to representation. The party composition of Congress corresponds rather well with the party identification of the public. Just as Democrats have been more numerous than Republicans in the public, Democrats have held majorities in both houses of Congress most of the years since World War II (see endpapers). The Republican victory in 1994 corresponded with the increase in Republican partisans during the 1980s, though there are still more Democrats than Republicans in the population.

Constituencies

Senators' constituencies include all the residents of their respective states; each state elects two senators. The number of each state's representatives is based on its population. Members of the House are elected from districts within states, although six states have only one representative.

Initially, the House of Representatives had 59 members, but as the nation grew and more states joined the Union, the size of the House increased too. Since 1910, it has had 435 members except in the 1950s, when seats were temporarily added for Alaska and Hawaii. Each 10 years, in a process called **reapportionment,** the 435 seats are distributed among the states based on population changes.

Within a constant 435-seat House, states with fast-growing populations gain seats, while those with slow-growing or declining populations lose seats. Since World War II, population movement in the United States has been toward the South, West, and Southwest and away from the Midwest and Northeast. This has been reflected in the allocation of house seats. Since 1950, California has gained 22 seats and New York has lost 12, for example. In the latest reapportionment after the 1990 census, no Frost Belt state gained and only one Sunbelt state— Louisiana—lost.[11]

States that gain or lose seats and other states with population shifts within the state must redraw their district boundaries, a process called **redistricting.** This is always a hot political issue. The precise boundaries of a district can influence the election prospects of candidates and parties. In fact, districts often are formed with weird shapes to benefit the party in control of the state legislature. The term **gerrymander** is used to describe a district that is designed to maximize the political advantage of a party or a racial group.

Majority parties in state legislatures continue to secure political advantage by drawing districts of bizarre shapes, although the Supreme Court requires all congressional districts to be approximately equal in population. Before 1960, states were often reluctant to redistrict their state legislative and congressional boundaries to conform to population changes within the state. Such redistricting would endanger incumbents and threaten rural areas whose populations were declining. After decades without reapportioning, some legislative districts in urban areas were as much as 19 times the population of rural districts.

When state legislatures, frequently dominated by rural representatives, still refused to reapportion themselves, the Supreme Court in *Baker v. Carr* (1962) issued the first in a series of rulings forcing states to reapportion their legislative districts.[12] In 1964 the Court required congressional districts to be approximately equal in population, thus mandating the principle of "one person, one vote."[13] As a result, most states had to redraw district lines, some more than once, during the 1960s. These decisions fueled heated controversy, including a proposed constitutional amendment to overturn them. But after a while the principle of "one person, one vote" came to be widely accepted.

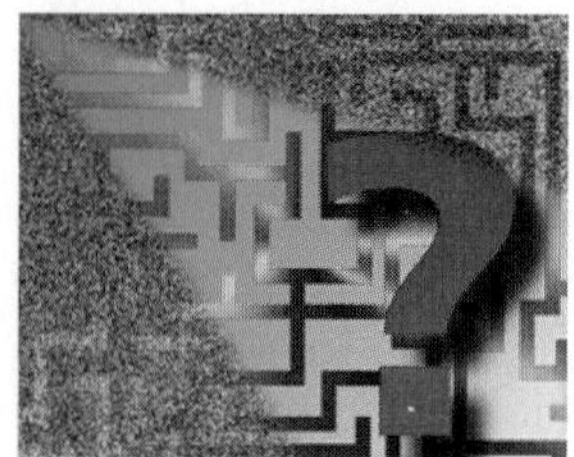

Symbolic Solutions for Complex Problems?

Term Limits

"Throw the rascals out!" is the battle cry of the decade. Fed up with politicians and politics, voters are calling for limits to the years that legislators can serve. Members of Congress and state legislators are the focus of voter anger, symbolizing everything that voters do not like about politics.

Over 70% of the public say they favor term limits.[1] Consequently, in 23 of 24 states that allow citizens to vote directly on bills, voters have adopted term limits for their members of Congress and state legislators (Mississippi is the exception; its citizens will vote on limits in 1996). In most states, the limits are twelve years; for Congress, that means a limit of two Senate and six House terms.

The Republican "Contract with America" pledged that Congress would vote on a constitutional amendment to set term limits within the first 100 days of the 1995 congressional session. It did so, rejecting them by a narrow vote.

Despite public support for limits, in 1995, in a 5-4 vote, the Supreme Court held term limits for members of Congress unconstitutional. The majority argued that permitting individual states to have diverse qualifications for Congress would "result in a patchwork of state qualifications, undermining the uniformity and national character that the Framers envisioned and sought to ensure."[2] The Court indicated that state laws added to the qualifications spelled out in the Constitution (age and citizenship), therefore, in effect, "amending" the Constitution. Only a constitutional amendment can amend the Constitution, so the state action was not legitimate. The Court ruling does not affect limits placed on terms of state legislators or other state and local officials, but does mean that for limits to be placed on members of Congress, a constitutional amendment to that effect must be passed. Thus supporters of term limits continue to push for such an amendment.

Are term limits merely a symbolic solution, perhaps assuaging the feelings of those who think government is out of control without changing the behavior of legislators at all? Or are term limits a good solution to a real problem of entrenched legislators forgetting about their constituencies and building personal empires? Or will term limits actually be a negative factor, exacerbating problems that already exist with government?

Term limits were part of our original governing document, the Articles of Confederation, but were not adopted by the Framers of the Constitution. Why do many people now favor term limits?

Some supporters cling to the mid-nineteenth-century image of "citizen lawmakers," who set aside their personal business for a few years to attend to the public's business, and then return home. Most supporters believe that by not having to worry about continuing to be elected, legislators can be free to consider the "public interest," not the "special interests," and will have no desire to build personal empires. Others also see term limits as a way to weaken the power of government by having a more rapid turnover of members of legislatures. Members without experience, this argument holds, could not learn the ropes fast enough to be able to wield power effectively. Still others saw term limits as a way to break the sixty-year-old stranglehold of the Democrats on Congress, a rationale that was undercut by the Republican victories in 1994.

Opponents, including many Republicans, argue that term limits are a very bad, and very radical, idea. Term limits are antidemocratic in that they restrict the ability of voters to elect whomever they please to Congress. If Congressman Smith is not doing a good job, his constituents can elect someone else. Term limits allow Congresswoman Jones to tell Congressman Smith's constituents they cannot elect Smith. Even though the results of democracy are not always ideal, as one commentator remarked, "democracy is like blowing one's nose—you should do it yourself, even if you do it badly."[3]

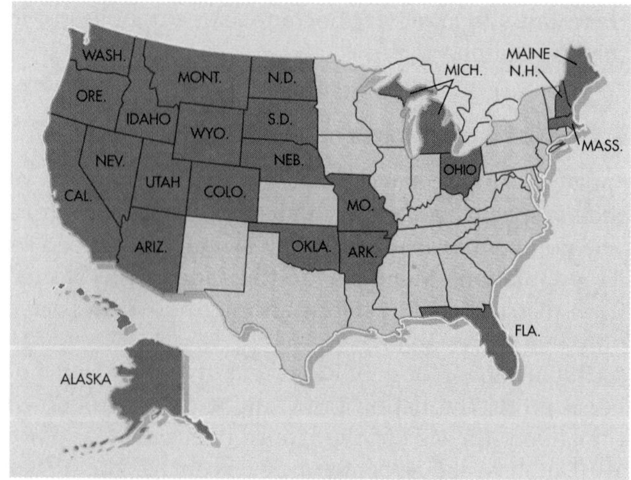

Blue areas show states that have passed term limits.

Opponents also point out that the world is a much more complex place than in the early nineteenth century when many legislators were "citizen legislators." Today, most people want their heart surgery done by "career cardiac surgeons," not by people who sell real estate or teach school for a career and take two years off to try being surgeons. They want their legal problems handled by "career lawyers," their teeth pulled by "career dentists," and their bridges designed by "career engineers." Likewise, opponents of term limits argue, it is appropriate to have laws drafted by "career legislators," or at least legislative bodies with a significant membership of experienced legislators.

Term limits also attack a problem that does not exist. They are a response to the very high-reelection rates of the late 1980s, when the reelection rate of House incumbents was over 90%. However, the elections of 1992 and 1994 show that when voters want change, they can effect change by voting incumbents out. The existing system allows plenty of turnover. In 1995, 45% of the members of the House were first elected in 1992 or 1994 and in the Senate 25% were first elected in these two elections. In other words, there is already considerable turnover in legislatures without term limits.

Term limits also break the tie between citizens and their representatives. If representatives are not responsible to their voters, to whom are they responsible? Opponents of term limits fear that these limits will strengthen the power of lobbyists, bureaucrats, and committee staffs. These unelected officials will have the knowledge about policies and procedures that legislators elected for only a few years cannot possibly have. It is sometimes said that it takes members four years to learn when they are being snookered by lobbyists or bureaucrats; it takes six years to begin to accomplish something.[4] Term limits of six or eight years would ensure a legislature full of individuals with less knowledge than the professional bureaucrats have. As one long-term Republican congressman noted about term limits: "Career politician is an epithet. But pass term limits, and professionals . . . will run this government. Only they will not be elected: they will be the faceless, nameless, try-to-get-them-on-the-phone, unaccountable permanent bureaucracy."[5] It is unlikely that this is the outcome favored by those who prefer term limits.

Term limits have actually gone into effect in Michigan, where voters limited the members of the lower house in the state legislature to six years and their upper house to eight. As predicted by opponents of term limits, observers believe that lobbyists have more influence than before.[6] Moreover, some newly elected members, knowing they can only serve six years, have already started looking for their next jobs—by currying favor with lobbyists.

1. David Broder, "Dumbing Down Democracy," *Lincoln Journal*, April 5, 1995, p. 18.
2. Quoted in Kenneth J. Cooper and Helen Dewar, "No Limits on the Term Limits Crusade," *Washington Post National Weekly Edition*, May 29–June 4, 1995, p. 14. The majority of the Court included John Paul Stevens, Anthony Kennedy, David Souter, Ruth Ginsburg, and Stephen Breyer.
3. Garry Wills, "Term Limits Attack Corrupt Electorate," *Lincoln Journal*, March 16, 1992, p. 6.
4. James J. Kilpatrick, "Cincinnatus' Time Is Past: Term Limits Are a Bad Idea," *Lincoln Journal*, September 3, 1992, p. 16.
5. Broder, "Dumbing Down Democracy."
6. Arlene Levinson, "Michigan First among 20 States Dealing with Term Limits," *Centre Daily Times*, April 23, 1995, p. 9A.

Because of the important role state legislatures play in the redistricting process in most states, both parties saw the 1990 state legislative elections as crucial. In the early 1980s, Democratic-controlled state legislatures were able to help Democratic candidates in states like California by drawing lines that concentrated Republican strength in a few areas and created districts with small Democratic majorities.[14] After the 1990 state legislative elections, which gave Republicans more clout, many states drew boundaries favoring Republicans, a factor in the Republicans' victories in 1994.

Another important aspect of redistricting is representation of women and minorities. Inroads into the House by women have been slow because of the large proportion of incumbents and their nearly perfect record of getting reelected. In 1992, however, there were many more open seats than usual, partly due to redistricting, and women were able to win about one-third of open seats.

Different factors influence the impact of redistricting on minority representation. An increase in the proportion of blacks or Hispanics serving in Congress will most likely depend on whether any more majority black or Hispanic districts are created. As we saw in Chapter 7, in 1992, 11 new districts were created with black majorities and 6 with Hispanic majorities; all but 1 were won by blacks and Hispanics. However, much of this redistricting was quite controversial because of the extensive use of gerrymandering to create them. Recent Supreme Court decisions have suggested that using race as a primary basis for creating districts is unconstitutional.[15]

The racial redistricting issue also affects the partisan composition of Congress. In some southern states, several Democratic districts were weakened in order to create one or two new majority black districts; Democratic black voters were redistricted from newly solid Democratic districts, leaving these districts with fewer Democrats and thereby creating Republican majorities.[16] The exact impact of this change is still being debated, but clearly the overall effect was to substantially weaken Democratic electoral strength in several states.[17]

This outcome was part of a deliberate strategy of the Republican party in several southern states. They often worked in concert with civil rights groups to encourage this type of redistricting, believing that it could result in new conservative Republican districts. Partly as a result, Republicans won 18 congressional seats for the first time in 1994. It will be ironic if conservatives on the Supreme Court stifle this development.

Congressional Campaigns and Elections

To understand Congress, one must understand the process by which its members are elected.[18] Because reelection is an important objective for almost all members of Congress and *the* most important objective for many, members work at being reelected throughout their terms. Most are successful, though senators are not as secure as members of the House. In recent years, as few as 55% and as many as 97% of senators have won reelection, while the success of House incumbents varied only from 88% to 98%.

The Advantages of Incumbency

Before they even take the oath of office, newly elected representatives are given an introduction to the advantages of incumbency. At meetings arranged by the Democratic and Republican leadership and by the House Administrative Committee, new members learn about free mailing privileges, computers and software to help them target letters to specialized groups of constituents, facilities to make videotapes and audiotapes to send to hometown media, and other "perks" designed to keep members in touch with their constituencies and not coincidently to help win reelection.

Incumbents win because, for a number of reasons, they are better known than nonincumbents and voters evaluate them more positively. Almost all voters can recognize the name of their representatives; they have seen them on television or received mail from them, and they can give a general rating of their performances (see Figure 2).[19] Although most voters can correctly identify their representatives as liberal or conservative, only a small minority know how their representatives voted on any issue.[20] Therefore, representatives have the advantage of name recognition without the disadvantage of having voters know how they really voted.

Representatives' high level of public recognition is not so surprising given that members of Congress spend most of their time and energy looking for and using opportunities to make themselves known to their constituents. Members visit their home districts or states an average of 35 times a year—at taxpayers' expense.[21]

FIGURE 2
Senate and House Incumbents Are Well Known to Voters

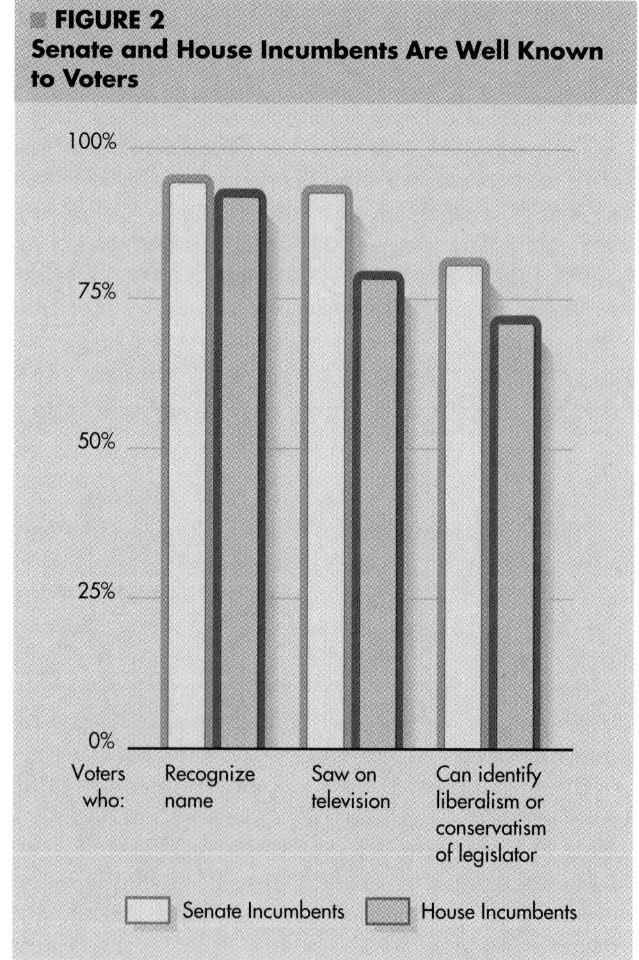

Source: John Alford and John Hibbing. "The Disparate Electoral Security of House and Senate Incumbents," paper presented at the American Political Science Meetings, September 1989, Atlanta, GA.

American Diversity

Women in Congress

Women make up more than 50% of the nation's population but only 9% of the Congress. The first woman in Congress was Representative Jeannette Rankin (R-Mont.), who was elected in 1916 even before women got the right to vote nationally. It was not until 1932 that the first woman served in the Senate. Hattie Caraway (D-Ark.) won the seat after the death of her husband, the former occupant. The first woman elected to the Senate without occupying the Senate seat of a deceased spouse was Margaret Chase Smith, a Republican from Maine who spent a distinguished career in the Senate from 1949 to 1973.

Many called 1992 "The Year of the Woman." Despite gains then and again in 1994 when both the Senate and the House added one woman member, women make up only 8% of the Senate and 11% of the House. These paltry proportions are a large increase from the 1980s when the percentage of women in the House remained around 5% indefinitely. Twenty-three states have at least 1 woman in their delegation.

The women in Congress are racially heterogeneous. One-quarter of the women members of the House and 1 of the 8 women Senators are black, Hispanic, or Asian.

In 1992 the proportion of women increased as much as it did in the House because women targeted the extraordinarily large numbers of open seats available. Indeed, of the 65 open seats in the 1992 election, 22 were won by women. However, 6 of these new incumbents were swept out of office in the 1994 Republican landslide.

Although gains were small in 1994, we may expect a growing proportion of women in Congress because more women are being elected to state legislatures and other offices that traditionally have been stepping-stones to Congress. Women fare about as well as men when they run for congressional seats.[1]

Women's problems are not over when they are elected, however. Women feel out of the congressional mainstream in many ways. These include small inconveniences, such as the lack of a women's restroom within 100 yards of the House floor and none at all in the Senate chamber. Only in recent years has the lavish congressional gym been open to women; before that the "ladies' health facility consisted of 10 hair dryers and a ping-pong table." More substantively, the leadership of both houses is all male. Said one woman who has tried for a seat on the prestigious Appropriations Committee three times, "Each time I've been nicely told that the women's slot is already filled on that committee." And in 1993, Nancy Johnson (R-Conn.), one of the Republicans' leading health-care experts, was told by her subcommittee chair at a public hearing that she must have learned about a particular health issue through "pillow-talk" with her physician husband. The chair later apologized, but the incident was not forgotten.[2]

But women do seem to be making a substantive difference. The Congressional Caucus for Women's issues reported that in 1993-94, Congress passed a record 66 bills of special importance to women. That nearly equals the number of such bills passed in the entire previous decade.[3]

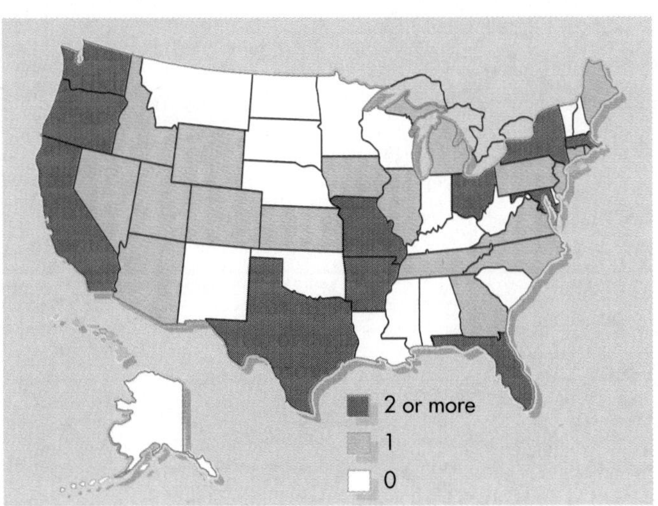

Source: Data from *Congressional Quarterly*, November 12, 1994, p. 10.

Number of Women Representatives by State.

1. For a recent analysis of Senate voting, see Philip Paolino, "Group-Salient Issues and Group Representation: Support for Women Candidates in the 1992 Senate Elections," *American Journal of Political Science* 39 (May, 1995), pp. 294-313; Barbara Burrell, "Did We Get More than One 'Year of the Woman'?" paper presented at the 1995 Annual Meeting of the Midwest Political Science Association, Chicago, Illinois.
2. Kevin Merida, "A Woman's Place on the Hill," *Washington Post National Weekly Edition* (April 11-17, 1994), p. 15.
3. Leslie Laurence, "Congress Makes Up for Neglect," *Lincoln Journal* (December 5, 1994), p. 8.

Sometimes members take unusual steps in an attempt to become better known. One member stood on the Capitol steps "dressed in an exterminator's outfit with plastic cockroaches glued to his shoulders." He then jumped up and down, shouting "squash one for the Gipper." This was to endear himself to owners and workers of an insecticide manufacturer in his district.[22]

Franking

Members gain name recognition by free mail privileges called **franking.** In just 6 months during 1989, Senator Alfonse D'Amato (R-N.Y.) sent out nearly 17 million pieces of mail at a cost of $2.65 million. With the exception of 1991, Congressional mailings have increased in volume every election year and fallen in the off-year.

Some restrictions are designed to make franking less blatantly political. For example, mass mailings cannot be sent out close to an election. Regardless, one political consultant estimates that the frank is worth at least $350,000 in campaign funds.[23]

Franking privileges become even more useful when combined with sophisticated word processing systems to target very specific constituency groups with "personalized" letters. Members can maintain incredibly specialized lists, not just of Republicans and Democrats but of those living near federal prisons, small-business owners, veterans, teachers, and government employees, for example. No group is too specialized or ostensibly apolitical to be targeted. Senator Charles Grassley (R-Iowa) even sent a letter to a thousand Iowans with abbreviated intestinal tracts in honor of Ostomy Awareness Month.[24]

This system can help keep representatives in touch with their constituents. But the frank and the computer together have turned most congressional offices into full-time public relations firms. Their value in reelection is reflected in the fact that members send out much more mail in their reelection year than in other years (see Figure 3).[25]

Media Attention

In addition to "old-fashioned" mail, members use increasingly sophisticated production equipment and technology to make television and radio shows to send home. For example, one evening, on any of three local television news shows, residents of Boise, Idaho, might have seen their congressional representative, Larry Craig (R-Idaho), state in an interview that he

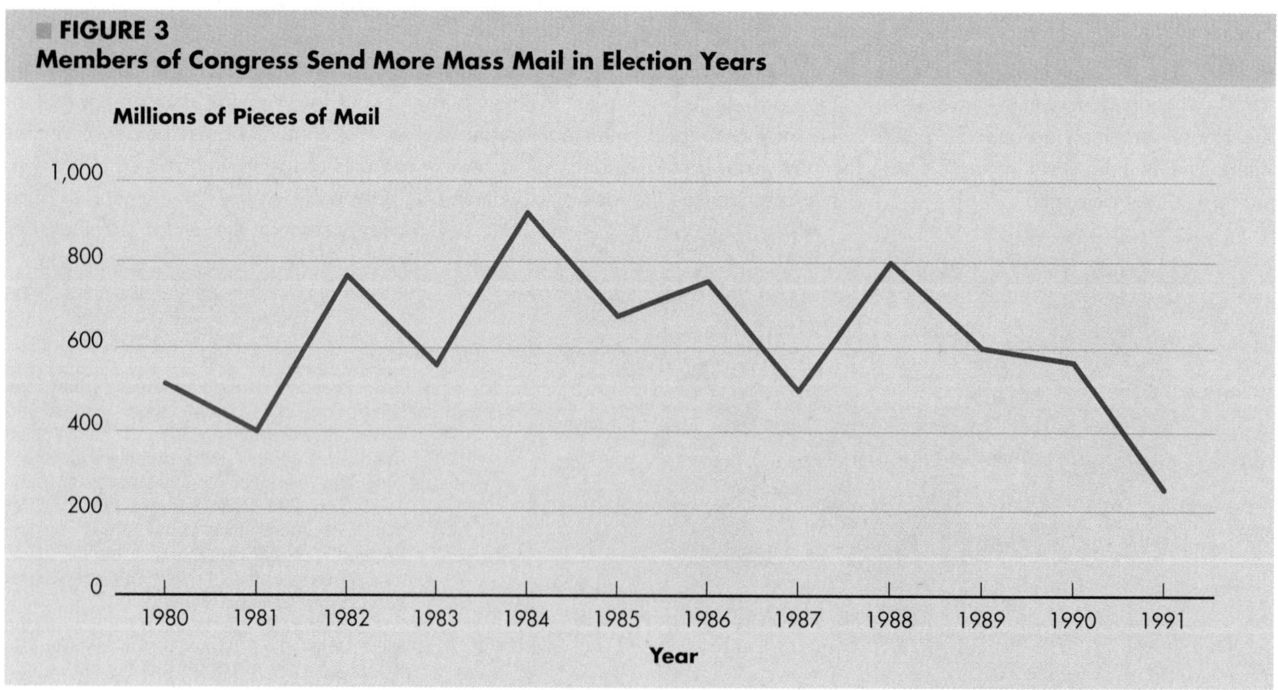

Source: *Vital Statistics of Congress*, 1993–1994 (Washington, D.C.: CQ Press, 1994), p. 163.

Earmarking: How to Pack the Pork

Earmarking is the practice of designating spending for specific projects, outside of any regular formulas or granting processes. Powerful members of Congress use their influence to attach their pet projects, intended to bring funds and jobs to voters in their districts, as footnotes to appropriations legislation. Earmarking has long been one method to serve up pork to the homefolks. (Another method is to quietly pressure bureaucrats to include a particular cut of pork in their recommended projects.)

As the pressures of the deficit have left less funding for general public works projects and have decreased bureaucratic discretion over these funds, the practice of earmarking has increased. For example, before 1987, few roads and bridges were earmarked in federal highway legislation. In 1987, the transportation act included 152 "demonstration projects." These, in theory, test something new but in reality are the priorities of influential members of Congress. By 1991, highway legislation included 452 demonstration projects, costing taxpayers more than $6 billion.[1]

Sometimes, the recipient state is not even consulted. In 1991, Senator Robert Dole (R-Kansas) added two home state projects, costing $104 million, to the federal transportation bill. The Kansas secretary of transportation said neither of these projects had been included in the first stage of the state's highway modernization plan. He was "not certain we'd make the same decision at the same time that Sen. Dole would about how and where to spend the money."[2]

There are some signs that the pressures of the deficit and of public disillusionment with such practices may be decreasing the amount of pork served up by Congress. In 1993, Congress killed a Texas project called the superconducting supercollider (SSC) that would have been the world's largest scientific experiment. Although the project had already cost $2 billion and had originally been estimated to cost $4.4 billion, the 1993 estimate had risen to $11 billion. In a lopsided vote in the House, representatives stripped funding for the SSC from the $22.2 billion appropriations bill. The Senate agreed to cancel the SSC, over the objections of many, including Senator Phil Gramm in whose home state of Texas the SSC was being constructed.

There are other signs that earmarking may be on the decline. A review by the House Science, Space and Technology Committee noted that four major appropriations bills in 1993 included only half as many earmarked projects as in 1991. This committee has been holding public hearings on earmarking to bring this practice into public view. "Earmarks" are like mushrooms—they grow best in the dark," noted the former chair of the committee.[3]

1. "Slicing the Pork Isn't Easy," *Governing*, January 1994, pp. 62–63.
2. "Dole Shows He's King of the Road," *The Wichita Eagle*, December 14, 1991, pp. 1A, 7A.
3. "A Little Less from the Pork Barrel," *Washington Post National Weekly Edition*, November 8–14, 1993, p. 37.

was strongly opposed to a pay increase for Congress and would not take it if it were passed. The viewers were not told that the "interviewer" was one of Craig's congressional staffers and that the camera crew was that of the Republican Congressional Campaign Committee, which also paid for the broadcast.[26]

Members also like to tape themselves at committee meetings asking questions or being referred to as "Mr. (or Madam) Chairman" (because many members are chairs of at least a subcommittee). The tape then is edited to a 30-second sound bite to be sent to local television stations. Often stations run these productions as news and do not tell their viewers that they are essentially campaign features prepared by the members. But television is not alone in portraying members' self-publicity as "hard news." Congressional staffers write press releases about accomplishments of the member and fax them to local newspapers, which often print them as written. Local media, whether print or television, are often short of national news with a local flavor and eagerly take whatever members give them.

Constituency Service

Members of Congress make themselves known in more routine ways. One is by providing **constituency service:** answering questions and doing personal favors for constituents who write or call for help.

This function, also called **casework,** is crucial for members and their staffs, who function as red-tape cutters for everyone from elderly citizens having difficulties with Social Security to small-town mayors trying to get federal grants for new sewer systems. Members provide information to students working on term papers and citizens puzzled about which federal agency to ask for assistance. Members can provide gifts of calendars, United States flags that were flown over the Capitol, and brochures and publications of the federal government.

Requests for service often come by mail. More than half the congressional office staffs work on the flood of mail that pours in. Some offices get 5,000 to 10,000 requests per year for assistance.[27] In addition to handling casework in Washington offices, most senators and representatives have one or more state or home district offices to deal personally with constituents and their casework. More than 35% of senators' staffs and 40% of all representatives' staffs are located in their home state or district.[28]

Citizens turn to their congressional representatives because they see them as allies in their struggles with bureaucracy.[29] Members of Congress, who are in large part responsible for the establishment of the huge Washington bureaucracy, are able to score with voters by helping them cope with the bureaucracy they have created.[30] Individual members may have limited power in trying to get important legislation passed, but in dealing with a constituent's problems, their power is much greater because of their clout with bureaucrats. A phone call or letter to a federal agency will bring attention to the constituent's problem.

Of course, not all casework is directed toward winning reelection. Some members say they enjoy their casework more than their policy roles, perhaps because the results of casework are often more immediate and tangible. Certainly, casework allows members to build nonpartisan and seemingly nonpolitical ties with their constituents, an advantage in this antipolitical era.

Pork Barrel

Another way members gain the attention of constituents is to obtain funds for special projects, new programs, buildings, or other public works in their districts or states. Such benefits, often called **pork barrel** projects, comprise about a seventh of the budget not devoted to entitlements and interest. They are sometimes defined as "federal spending with a zip code attached."[31] In the final days of one session of Congress, for example, a few of the last-minute pork barrel projects approved included a $3.6 million irrigation project for Maine's potato growers and a $400,000 fuel dock for a Hawaiian hotel.[32] These projects are desired by constituents because they provide jobs and business in the local district.

Because members consider pork barrel projects crucial to reelection chances, there is little support in Congress for eliminating projects known to be unwise or wasteful. Liberals and conservatives, Democrats and Republicans, protect these kinds of projects. Senator Alfonse D'Amato (R-N.Y.) is called "Senator Pothole" for his ability to win highway and transportation projects for New York. One conservative Kentucky Republican argued for a freeway in his district in 1995: "This project is not pork, [it is] a vital infrastructure necessity."[33] David Stockman, former President Reagan's director of the Office of Management and Budget, observed, "There's no such thing as a fiscal conservative when it comes to his district."[34]

Fund-Raising

Another advantage of incumbency is the opportunity to raise funds from the hundreds of PACs that populate Washington. Eager to gain access to members of Congress, PACs make fund-raising much easier for incumbents than challengers, as we pointed out in Chapter 9.

Unsafe at Any Margin?

Most members are reelected even if they have done relatively little constituency work or have obtained little federal money for their districts (see Figure 4).[35] Indeed, one Republican member remarked, "Let's face it, you have to be a bozo to lose this job."[36] Still, incumbents believe the best way to ensure victory is to be so good at constituency work, so successful in bringing pieces of pork to their districts, and so well known to the voters that no serious rival will want to run. Incumbents hope potential rivals will bide their time and wait for a better year or run for some other office.[37]

Given their advantages, you may wonder why incumbents worry about losing. But worry they do. One political scientist proclaimed that members feel "unsafe at any margin."[38] No matter how big their last victory, they worry that their next campaign will bring defeat. And despite the high reelection rate of incumbents, some are defeated. This fear prompts them to spend even more of their energies preparing for the next campaign.

But this fear is fairly remote, even in recent anti-incumbent elections. In 1994, only 9% of House incumbents lost (all of them Democrats). In 1992, only 7% did. Senators are somewhat more vulnerable. Fifteen percent lost in 1992 and 10% in 1994. Nonetheless, the electoral benefit of incumbency still exists for

■ **FIGURE 4**
House Incumbents Have Had Secure Jobs in Recent Years

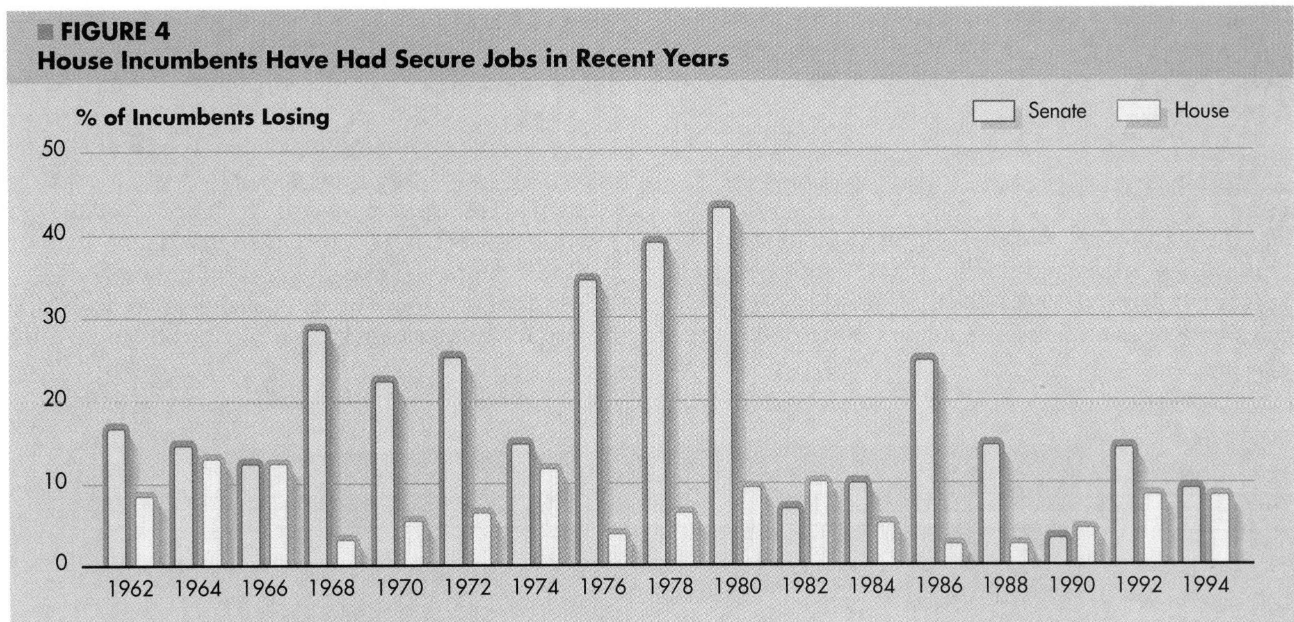

Notice that in the 1980s more House incumbents lost in the reapportionment year of 1982. In the 1970s more lost in the Watergate year, 1974, when many Republican defenders of President Nixon were defeated. In the 1960s reapportionment did not start until after 1962, so the elections of 1964 and 1966 reflected reapportionment.

Source: *Congressional Quarterly Weekly Report*, November 19, 1988, p. 18, and November 10, 1990, p. 3801; "Women, Minorities Join Senate," *CQ Almanac*, 1992, pp. 8A–14A; "Wave of Diversity Spared Many Incumbents," *CQ Almanac*, 1992, pp. 15A–21A, 24A.

Source: SIGNE, *Philadelphia Daily News*, Philadelphia, USA
CARTOONISTS & WRITERS SYNDICATE

the great majority of candidates who choose to run for reelection.[39] Turnover in Congress comes primarily from those who decide not to run, sometimes from fear of losing.

Challengers

Another reason for the uneasiness of incumbents is that as their media and public relations sophistication has grown, so has that of challengers. Still, without the advantages of the free frank and other opportunities to become well known to constituents, challengers have a difficult time. The best advice to someone who wants to be a member of Congress is to find an open seat.

To beat an incumbent, challengers need money. The more they spend, the more likely they are to win. In recent House campaigns, a challenger needed to spend at least $250,000 to have even a one in four chance of winning—and the cost continues to rise.[40]

Spending is important for challengers because they must make themselves known in a positive way, and

Source: © 1995 Mark Alan Stamaty. Excerpted from "WASHINGTOON" with permission.

they must suggest that something is wrong with the incumbent. Usually challengers will charge incumbents with ignoring the district, being absent from committee hearings or floor votes, being too liberal or too conservative, or voting incorrectly on a key issue. Sometimes, of course, the incumbent has been involved in a scandal, which offers a ready target for the challenger.[41]

Sometimes challengers will try unusual tactics to make themselves known. Tom Harkin (D-Iowa) worked in a series of blue-collar jobs when running for the House to show people in his district that he understood their problems. Meanwhile he got a lot of free publicity.

Senate challengers have a slightly better chance than House challengers. One reason is that there are stronger candidates to challenge incumbent senators because Senate seats are a bigger prize and because in a statewide constituency there are more potential challengers. Senate challengers are better known than House challengers.[42] They are often former governors or members of the House with a statewide reputation. For example, in 1988, about 80% of voters recognized the name of the person running against their incumbent senator; less than 60% recognized the challenger to their House incumbent.[43] Senate challengers can attract more money because they are better known.

Another reason Senate challengers have greater success is that most incumbents have constituencies (i.e., states) much larger than House districts. The greater population means that senators cannot have personal contact with as high a proportion of their constituents. Also they cannot satisfy as high a proportion since their constituencies are much more heterogeneous than House district constituencies.[44] Evidence indicates that senators from the largest states have about a six- or seven-point electoral disadvantage compared to senators from the smallest states. Senators from the smallest states do about as well as House members from their states.[45]

Campaigns

In the nineteenth century, political campaigns were organized largely by political parties, and the candidates had relatively little to do. Today, however, congressional campaigns are candidate-centered. Most candidates hire workers, raise money, and organize their own campaigns. They may recruit campaign workers from local political parties; interest groups they belong to; unions; church, civic, or other voluntary organizations; or simply groups of friends and acquaintances.[46]

Political parties do have a significant role, however. National and local parties also recruit potential candidates. Presidents make personal appeals to fellow party members who they think can run strong races, and national campaign committees also recruit aggressively. Said one Democratic congressional campaign chair, "I'm not looking for liberals or conservatives. That's not my bag. I'm looking for winners."[47] Parties also provide campaign money and assistance to candidates for polling, mailing, issue research, and getting out the vote.[48]

The Media Campaign

To wage a serious campaign, the challenger or a contender for an open seat must wage a media campaign. Candidates hire media consultants and specialists in polling, advertising, and fund-raising.

Media campaigning has attracted a new type of congressional candidate and hence a new type of congressional incumbent. The old-style politician who might have been effective in small groups but who cannot appear poised and articulate on television has given way to one who can project an attractive television image. Candidates are elected on the basis of their media skills, which may not be the same skills as those of a good lawmaker.

Moreover, fears grew that candidates were becoming less closely linked to parties than before and once elected, not as indebted to their party nor as obligated to reflect party views.[49] Political parties, however, recognized this problem. Since the early 1980s, national parties have increasingly provided useful services to congressional candidates—helping them manage their campaigns, develop issues, advertise, raise money, and conduct opinion polls. National parties also give substantial sums of money to congressional candidates.[50]

Campaign Money

The old adage says, "Half the money spent on campaigns is wasted. The trouble is, we don't know which half." This bromide helps explain why congressional campaigns are expensive. There is a kind of "campaign arms race" as each candidate tries to do what the other candidate does and a little more, escalating costs year by year.

New Populism

The 1994 Congressional Elections

"Revenge of the Right," proclaimed one headline. "The GOP Earthquake," declared another. "G.O.P. Celebrates Its Sweep to Power," announced a third. These reports of the 1994 election results suggested their importance and the surprise of many. Overnight, forty years of Democratic control of the House were ended, and almost overnight, President Clinton's legislative agenda lay in ruins. The Republicans, led by Newt Gingrich (R-Ga.), offered a new agenda.

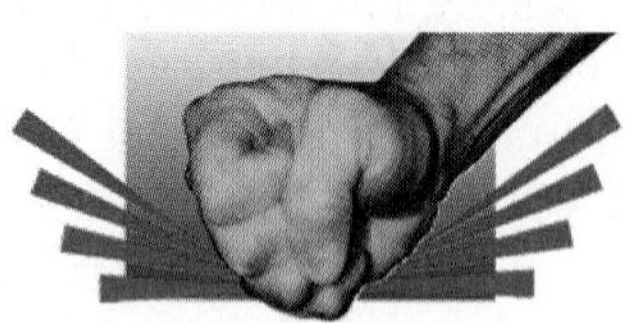

Today, the Republicans control both the House and Senate for the first time since 1954, and some have labeled this a "new populist" revolt. Though Republicanism and populism are certainly not the same, the Republican victory suggested a populist movement to throw out the old elites and try something new. On the other hand, the Republicans, as the party of the better off, represent many of those interests that the original populists fought against: big business and big banks. In that sense, it is ironic that the new populist label has been attached to some of their causes.

The Background

The 1994 election took place in the midst of an economic upturn and in a time when the nation was at peace. Normally these factors lead to high reelection rates for incumbents. But 1994 was different. Voters were angry in 1994, even more angry than in 1992, when they spurned George Bush's bid for a second term. The level of trust in government had plummeted to an all-time low. In 1964, 76 percent of a national sample said they trusted "the government in Washington to do what's right" most or all of the time. By 1992, only 29% said the same.[1]

Fueled by radio and television talk show hosts, Americans said they were fed up with politics as usual: with politicians attuned more to special interest groups than voters, and members of Congress who had been in Washington so long they had forgotten the people back home. Americans were dubious about their economic futures, terrified of crime, and furious at the breakdown in morality. They blamed government for these problems, or at least for not doing something about them, and for not being responsive to the people. They especially blamed Democrats, who had controlled Congress for forty years.

The Democrats, it seems, had grown complacent in power. Democratic congressional leaders quarreled with their president, did not seem inclined to support his key legislative initiative, health care, and grew increasingly dependent on campaign money from large interest groups. Republicans, for their part, had been out of power in Congress so long they seemed to perceive their major goal as obstructionism and had honed attacks on the institution to a fine point.

Voter anger, coupled with redistricting that changed many district lines in 1992, led near record numbers of House and Senate incumbents to retire (48 and 9, respectively). Many were in the South, where the president and Democratic party were very unpopular.

To characterize the 1994 campaign as highly negative is to understate its vitriolic nature. In addition to the usual partisan charges, candidates were commonly portrayed as liars and sometimes even as criminals. Indeed, being an incumbent itself was depicted as nearly a criminal act, as illustrated by a successful Republican Senate candidate from Tennessee who defeated the incumbent: "Bill Frist supports term limits to stop career politicians, and the death penalty to stop career criminals."[2]

Almost every nonincumbent, and even some incumbents, ran against government in general and Congress in particular, a common strategy in recent elections. For example, Fred Thompson (R- Tenn.) argued in his ad that "Congress is more the problem than the solution; they're out of touch and we're out of patience."[3]

The Campaign Results

Even though the election produced dramatic results, it was hardly a landslide. Republicans gained 52% of the contested House votes, a 2% increase over 1992.[4] Only 39% of the electorate voted, slightly more than in the 1990 off-year election.[5]

Although the election was not a landslide, Republican candidates got enough votes in enough districts for the party to win a majority in Congress. Before the 1994 election, the Democrats held a comfortable 60% margin in the House.[6] The Republicans gained 74 seats in the election to gain a slimmer, but clear, majority of 53%. The magnitude of the Democratic disaster can be illustrated by the fact that

Thomas Foley (D-Wash.), Speaker of the House, lost his seat. This marked only the first time since 1862 (and only the third time in history) that the sitting Speaker was defeated.

The table below shows some of the most important features of the House election results. First, although more Democratic than Republican incumbents won reelection, and although only 9% of all incumbents were defeated, all (35) were Democrats. About half these Democrats were first elected in 1992. *No* Republican incumbent was defeated. Further, Republicans won three-fourths of open seats, those where no incumbent was running. Republicans captured the House, then, because their incumbents who chose to run for election all won, and because they captured a very large majority of seats where no incumbent was running.

Composition of the 1995–96 House of Representatives*

104th Congress (1995–6)	Republicans	Democrats
Incumbents reelected	157	190
Total freshman	74	13
—who defeated incumbents	35	0
—who won open seats	39	13
Total members*	231	203

*One seat is held by an independent.

The Democrats lost seven Senate seats, a seemingly small number, but enough to give Republicans control of the Senate (53-47). Republicans have only controlled the Senate ten years in the past 62, so this new Republican majority is newsworthy too. Not one new Democratic senator was elected in 1994, a situation that has never occurred before.[7]

Election polls showed that voters had no single reason for their votes. Four of ten voters, for example, listed crime as the issue most affecting their voting; yet about half voted for Republicans and half for Democrats. Republicans claimed the majority of the votes from Republicans, independents, Perot voters, conservatives, males, whites, and those with at least some college education.[8] Democrats claimed a majority of votes from women, those with a high school education or less, blacks, Hispanics, moderates, liberals, and Democrats.

Not surprisingly, those who believed the country is "going in the right direction" voted heavily for the Democrats (76%), and those who believed the country is "off on the wrong track" gave 67% of their votes to the Republicans. About an equal number said their vote was in support of Clinton and against Clinton, while, surprisingly, a plurality of voters (38%) said their vote had nothing to do with Clinton.

Exit (postelection) polls did not find a large turn to the right in this election. Most showed about one-third of the voters claimed to be conservative, about half moderates, and the rest liberals.[9] There was only a slight move toward the Republicans, with about half the public identifying with Republicans, half with Democrats. Moreover, postelection polls showed that most Americans never heard of the Republicans' "Contract with America," or were unfamiliar with what it said.[10]

The election provides further evidence that Congress, far from being removed from the people, may be too close to the people. While it is certainly true that today's legislators are not "citizen legislators," it is also true that they are responsive to every nuance of public opinion. By being responsive to the tremendous variety of conflicting views, they cannot get much accomplished. One commentator noted that the effect of being in touch with everyone is "to turn a somewhat slow and contemplative system into something more like a 500-channel democracy, with the clicker grasped tightly in the hands of the electorate."[11] In 1992, the voters clicked off Republican George Bush; in 1994, they clicked off the Democratic Congress. Although it is possible that a Republican majority can cool the anger and win the trust of the voters, it seems more likely that voters will continue to have itchy clicker fingers.

1. "The Anger: Ever Deeper," *New York Times Magazine* (October 16, 1994), p. 37. For an analysis of the election, see Everett Carll Ladd, "The 1994 Congressional Elections," *Political Science Quarterly* 110 (1995), pp. 1-23.
2. Robin Toner, "Image of Capitol Maligned by Outsiders, and Insiders," *New York Times* (October 16, 1994), p. 1.
3. Toner, "Image of Capitol Maligned by Outsiders, and Insiders."
4. Richard Morin, "Myths and Messages in the Election Tea Leaves," *Washington Post National Weekly Edition* (November 21-27, 1994), p. 37.
5. Richard L. Berke, "Victories Were Captured by G.O.P. Candidates, Not the Party's Platform," *New York Times* (November 10, 1994), p. B1.
6. These electoral data are drawn from *Congressional Quarterly Weekly Report* (November 12, 1994), pp. 9ff.
7. Popular election of senators began in 1914, and no freshman class has ever been all Republican.
8. Mitofsky International survey data drawn from "How Groups Divided in the Vote for the U.S. House," *New York Times* (November 10, 1994), p. B4. The following two paragraphs are drawn from these data.
9. Morin, "Myths and Messages in the Election Tea Leaves."
10. Ibid.
11. Michael Wines, "Washington Really Is in Touch: We're the Problem," *New York Times* (October 16, 1994): Section 4, p. 2.

In 1992, winners of open seats in the House spent $620,000 on average. Successful campaigns against incumbents cost more. Million-dollar campaigns are no longer unusual. Because they are statewide, Senate races are much more expensive than House races. In 1992, winning Senate candidates spent more than $3.5 million, on average.

Voting for Congress

Just as for presidential elections, party loyalties, candidate evaluations, and issues are important factors in congressional elections.[51]

Party loyalties are even more important for congressional than for presidential elections because congressional elections are less visible, so more people base their vote on traditional party loyalties. Incumbency is also more important than in presidential races. The result is that increasingly, since about 1960, voters have split their tickets in voting for presidential and congressional candidates. This is both because voters favor congressional incumbents and because many Democrats desert their party when casting a vote for president but not for lesser offices. For example, one out of five Reagan voters in 1984 voted for a Democratic member of the House, leaving Reagan with only a 41% Republican House despite his commanding personal victory.

Until this television ad ran, former Senator Walter Huddleston (D-Ky.) was substantially ahead of his opponent. The ad pointed out that Huddleston had a poor attendance record (hence sending out bloodhounds to find him). When the local media focused on this ad, it helped bring victory to his challenger, Mitch McConnell. A result of Senator McConnell's victory in 1984 is that Senate attendance on roll-call votes has been at all-time highs.

Normally, the party of a winning presidential candidate gains seats during a presidential election year and loses a number of seats in the midterm election. This maintains a sort of equilibrium in party control of Congress.[52] Though in most recent elections these losses have been modest, in 1994, the Democrats lost nine Senate seats and nearly 50 House seats, surrendering control of both houses to the Republicans.

The Representative on the Job

Informal Norms

In addition to the formal requirements of the representative's job—which are few—there are **informal norms** learned from colleagues, staff, and the press. Like the subtle socialization of young people, new members of Congress learn the ways of their elders.[53] These norms help keep the institution running smoothly by attempting to diminish friction and competition among members. As in other American institutions, the norms of Congress have changed.

Thirty years ago, the most important norm was **institutional loyalty,** the expectation that members would respect their fellow members and the Congress itself, especially their own house. Personal criticism of one's colleagues was to be avoided, and mutual respect was fostered by such conventions as referring to colleagues by title, such as "The distinguished senator from New York," rather than by name. This norm has seriously eroded in the last two decades.

Reciprocity, also called "logrolling," is reflected in the statement, "you support my bill and I'll support yours." This is another norm that is increasingly threatened. Sam Ervin, the late Democratic senator from tobacco-growing North Carolina, is reported to have told an audience from North Dakota, "I got to know Milt Young [then a senator from North Dakota] very well. And I told Milt, 'Milt, I would just like you to tell me how to vote about wheat and sugar beets and things like that, if you just help me out on tobacco.' "[54]

Tied to the norm of reciprocity is the norm of **specialization.** Members cannot be knowledgeable in all areas, so they specialize in some area related to their committee work. The Senate traditionally has been more individualistic than the House and less willing to give priority to specialists. Many senators see themselves as potential presidential candidates who need to be well versed on a variety of issues. The Senate is also much smaller so there are fewer members to cover all the issues.

Specialization and reciprocity increase the influence of individual members but also facilitate the smooth running of the institution. By specializing, a member can become an expert. Reciprocity helps members' work be accepted by their colleagues.

Norms have changed as decentralization and a "go your own way" sentiment have become typical. Open meetings and media scrutiny have made it more difficult for members to "go along" on bills unpopular in their constituency. The increased fears of members for their electoral security reaffirm this basic caution and individualism.

Members have also become more willing to challenge the work of their colleagues, making it difficult for anyone to control Congress and direct its energies to the solution of public problems. On the other hand, the decline of these norms means that the institution is more democratic, because new members can have influence without being under the thumb of more senior members.

Working Privately and "Going Public"

A member's routine traditionally involved bargaining with other members, lobbyists, and representatives of the administration. Working privately, one-on-one in small groups, or in committees, members and staff discussed and debated issues, exchanged information, and planned strategies. Twenty years ago most issues were probably resolved this way. Even though many issues still are resolved through these private channels, much has changed in the way Congress operates.

Today members believe it is as important to "go public" as it is to engage in private negotiation.[55] **Going public** means to carry an issue debate to the public through the media. Congress goes public by televising floor debates and important hearings, and leaders and individual members go public by using the media to further their goals.

C-SPAN

From time to time, television networks broadcast important hearings, such as those for the Watergate scandal and for the Iran-contra affair. But more regular exposure comes daily on C-SPAN. In 1979, after considerable controversy and anxiety, the House began routinely to televise its proceedings. Fearful of being overshadowed by the House, and mindful of Ronald Reagan's advice on how to deal with televised coverage ("Learn your lines, don't bump into furniture, and, in kissing, keep your mouth closed"), in 1986 the Senate followed suit.[56] This coverage is available to more than 60 million people on cable television through C-SPAN. Estimates are that more than one-third of C-SPAN subscribers watch their legislators at least one hour a month.[57] Even more see them in session when network news programs use footage of members making speeches.[58]

Other Use of the Media

During the 1980s, other use of the media by congressional leadership increased tremendously. Newt Gingrich's (R-Ga.) rise to power has been attributed in part to his strategic use of television. He understands the potential of television and other technology. He uses language that appeals to the public (as one reporter noted, he's "absolutist, aggressive, hyperbolic, informed, topical, unpredictable, and studied in his use of supercharged symbolic language").[59] His stated goal is to shape the entire nation through the news media.

Even before becoming a party leader he illustrated strategic use of the media. He regularly stood on the House floor denouncing Democrats; because the camera is stationary, on TV it looked as if he was speaking to an interested audience of members. In reality he was talking to an empty chamber. The former Speaker of the House, Tip O'Neill, once ordered the House cameras to pan the chamber to expose Gingrich's make-believe performance, although the ensuing debate between Gingrich and O'Neill gave Gingrich even more publicity.

As leader, he continues to make use of the media to set the agenda for public debate. His issues become "the" issues, and he has often put Bill Clinton on the defensive. As one observer noted, "Bill Clinton is the Jello, Newt is the mold."[60]

The Democratic House leadership decided to use the media in reaction to former President Reagan's success in going public. In 1981 and 1982, Reagan was able to push many of his programs through Congress by bypassing members and appealing to the public. By influencing these constituents, the president was able to move Congress. In response, the congressional leadership of both parties now goes public too. Leaders regularly call producers of television talk shows to

Republican leaders in the style of the classic portrait of Washington crossing the Delaware. (*Clockwise, from upper left*: Newt Gingrich, Robert Dole, Richard Armey, and Phil Gramm.)

suggest guests. They meet with the press and often have prepared statements. Before important congressional votes on key issues, the leadership plans letters to the editors of important newspapers and floor speeches designed for maximum television coverage.

The more media-oriented among the rank-and-file members are also experts in providing short and interesting comments for the nightly network news, writing articles for major newspapers, appearing on talk shows and as commentators on news programs.

Voting by Members

We have seen that members of Congress represent their constituents through service and by obtaining special benefits for the district or state. A third major kind of representation is policy representation. In the eyes of most people, members are sent to Washington to make laws. By casting hundreds of votes each year, members try to represent the interests of their constituencies as they see them and in the process win support for reelection. Increasingly, constituencies are becoming more active in communicating with their legislators. Members are flooded with faxes, poll results, and mailgrams, often stimulated as a result of radio or television talk shows. These individuals, however, do not represent the entire constituency. Talk show callers and listeners, for example, are more likely than other voters to be conservative, Republican, and male.[61]

Constituency opinion is often uninformed, divided, or apathetic. Because most votes in Congress are on subjects the electorate knows little about, members cannot, and often do not want to, rely on a simple polling of constituents to tell them how to vote. The opinions of constituents do matter, but other influences are also important: the party, the president, the members' ideology, staffers, and other members' recommendations. Members look to these sources for cues as to how to vote.

Party

Forty to 60% of the ballots in Congress are party votes; that is, a majority of one party opposes a majority of the other. In these votes, party members support their party between 70% and 90% of the time. Party support increased during the 1980s and is now at near record highs.

There are several reasons for the continuing importance of the party. All members of Congress are elected on a partisan ballot, and Congress organizes itself on a partisan basis. Members tend to have policy views similar to others in their party, at least more similar than to those in the opposite party. Many members receive campaign support from the party, and party leaders try hard to influence party members to vote the "right" way. Party votes reflect different constituency needs, too, because Democratic and Republican constituencies are different.

Members have several constituencies, including not only their entire district but also constituencies within the district, such as voters of their party, major socioeconomic groups, and their own personal supporters.[62] Sometimes these constituencies may be in conflict. The representatives' personal constituency may be more liberal or conservative than the district as a whole. When members vote in conflict with what seems to be the sentiments of the majority of voters in the district, it may be that they are responding to their own supporters or partisans. Of course, in those rare instances where most of the representative's constituents feel strongly about an issue, the member cannot buck an overwhelming majority and expect to win reelection.

When neither the member or the member's constituents have strong feelings on an issue, it is certainly in the member's interest to go along with party leaders, who have some "perks" to dispense or pressure to exert. Although their efforts are usually low-key, party leaders sometimes turn on the heat. In a successful vote to override a Reagan veto, Democratic Senate leaders adopted a "baby-sitting" strategy to make sure that wavering Democrats did not get near anyone who might persuade them to uphold the president's veto. These Democrats were accompanied at all times by two other Democrats with the "right" views. For their part, Republicans called on Reagan to make personal appeals to wavering Republicans.

Ideology

The member's own ideology usually reflects both the party and constituency, but it can be an independent influence.[63]

On the whole, Democrats vote for more liberal measures than do Republicans. However, this has not been true of southern Democrats, who often deserted the Democratic leadership and voted with Republicans because they shared the more conservative Republican outlook. Thus, the Democrats, even when a majority in Congress, often did not have a "working majority," as President Clinton learned early in his first term.

The tendency of southern Democrats to behave like Republicans has diminished and probably will dwindle further. With the growing strength of southern Republicanism, southern conservatives run as Republicans and have a good chance of winning. A number of southern conservative Democrats have switched parties in recent years. Also, many southern districts are increasingly urban and contain voters who are more liberal than those of 30 years ago. African Americans, for instance, are now an important factor in many southern districts. The remaining Democrats in the South feel freer to vote in accordance with their own ideological preferences.

The President

The president is also a factor in congressional voting, partly due to his role as party leader.[64] The president appeals to fellow partisans to support a program and tries to persuade those in the other party to go along as well. Presidents can win support by granting or withholding favors, such as support for a member's proposed policy or pet project in his or her district.

Interest Groups

Interest group lobbyists are most effective when their interests overlap constituency interests or when the issue is technical or little publicized.

Staffers

Staff can be a very important influence on a member's vote. Staff members are likely to have done the research and briefed the member on an issue. They probably have the greatest influence on technical issues or those the member does not care much about.

Other Members

Members also are influenced by other members of their party or their state's delegation. Members also may turn to colleagues whose judgment or expertise they respect or whose ideology or background they share. In fact, on most routine bills, cues from trusted fellow members are the most important influence on members' votes.

How Congress Is Organized

An institution of 535 members without a centralized leadership that must make decisions about thousands of proposed public policies each year is not an institution that can work quickly or efficiently. Each year in the past 10, from 2,000 to 10,000 bills have been introduced in Congress, and 250 to 2,000 have been passed.

Although many of these bills are trivial, such as those proclaiming "National Prom Graduation Kick-off Day" or naming local courthouses, others deal with crucial issues. In addition to these bills, Congress must oversee the performance of the federal bureaucracy in implementing bills previously passed.

How Congressional Organization Evolved

Like all organizations, legislatures need some structure to be able to accomplish their purposes. Congress has a leadership system and a committee system, both organized along party lines. The Constitution calls for the members of the House of Representatives to select a **Speaker of the House** to act as its presiding officer and for the vice president of the United States to serve as president (or presiding officer) of the Senate. But the Constitution does not say anything about the powers of these officials, nor does it require any further internal organization.

The first House, meeting in New York in 1789, had slow and cumbersome procedures, but soon permanent committees were created, each with continuing responsibilities in one area, such as taxes or trade.[65] As parties developed, the selection of the Speaker became a partisan matter, and the Speaker became as much a party leader as a legislative one. As Speaker, Henry Clay (Ky.) used his powers to appoint committee members and chairs to maintain party loyalty and discipline. In the nation's early years, the House was the dominant branch, but its influence declined when it, like the rest of government, could not cope with the divisiveness of the slavery issue. By 1856 it took 133 ballots to elect a Speaker. In many instances there were physical fights on the House floor and duels outside.[66]

The Senate, a smaller body than the House, was less tangled in procedures and more informal and effective in its operation. Its influence rose as visitors packed the Senate gallery to hear the great debates over slavery waged by Daniel Webster (Mass.), John C. Calhoun (S.C.), and Henry Clay (who had moved from the House). During this era, senators were elected by state legislatures, not directly by the people. Thus they had strong local party ties and often used their influence to get presidential appointments for home state party members. But the Senate too became ineffective as the nation moved toward civil war. Senators carried arms to protect themselves as the eloquent debates over slavery turned to violence.

After the Civil War, strong party leadership re-emerged in the House, and it again became an effective legislative body. Speaker Thomas Reed (Me.) assumed the authority to name members and chairs of committees and to chair the Rules Committee, which decided which bills were to come to the floor for debate. A major consequence of the Speaker's extensive powers was increased party discipline. Members who voted against their party might be punished by a loss of committee assignments or chairships.

At the same time, both the House and the Senate became more professional. The emergence of national problems and an aggressive Congress made a congressional career more prestigious. Prior to the Civil War, membership turnover was high; members of the House served an average of only one term, senators only four years. After the war, the strengthening of parties and the growth of the one-party South made reelection easier.

This desire for permanent careers in the House produced an interest in reform. Members wanted a chance at desirable committee seats and did not want to be controlled by the Speaker. Resistance against the dictatorial practices of Reed and his successor Joseph Cannon (Ill.) grew. Cannon, more conservative than many of his fellow Republicans, used his powers to block legislation he disliked, to punish those who opposed him, and even to refuse to recognize members who wished to speak. In 1910 there was a revolt against "Cannonism," a synonym for the arbitrary use of the Speaker's powers.

The membership voted to strip the Speaker of his authority to appoint committees and their chairs and to remove the Speaker from the Rules Committee. The revolt weakened party influence because it meant party discipline could no longer be maintained by the Speaker punishing members through loss of committee assignments. And it gave committees and their chairs a great deal of independence from leadership influence.

The Senate also was undergoing a major reform. As part of the Progressive movement, pressure began to build for the direct popular election of senators. The election of senators by state legislatures had made many senators pawns of special interests—the big corporations (called "trusts") and

Oratory was important in the pre–Civil War Senate. Shown speaking is Henry Clay and standing ready to attack is John C. Calhoun (second from right). Daniel Webster is listening at left with a cupped ear.

railroads. In a day when millionaires were not as common as now, the Senate was referred to as the "Millionaires Club."

Not surprisingly, the Senate first refused to consider a constitutional amendment providing for its direct election, although in some states popular balloting on senatorial candidates took place anyway. Finally, under the threat of a call for a constitutional convention, which many members of Congress feared might consider other changes in the Constitution, a direct election amendment was passed in the House and Senate in 1912 and ratified by the states a year later.

These reforms of the early twentieth century dispersed power in both the House and Senate and weakened leadership. House members no longer feared the kind of retribution levied by Speaker Cannon on members who deviated from party positions. In the Senate, popular elections made senators responsive to diverse constituencies rather than to party leaders.

Leaders

Members of each party in each house meet to choose their leaders. The Speaker of the House is chosen by the majority party members and presides over the House. Typically someone who has served in the House a long time, the Speaker is usually a skilled parliamentarian and an ideological moderate. The institutional task of the Speaker is to see that legislation moves through the House. His (all speakers have been men so far) partisan task is to secure the passage of measures preferred by his party.

Trying to win partisan support is often difficult. The Speaker has some rewards and punishments to mete out for loyalty and disloyalty, but they are mild compared to the power wielded by Reed and Cannon. The Speaker, however, does have influence on which committees members will be assigned to, on which committees will be given jurisdiction over complex bills, on what bills will come to the House floor, and on how campaign funds are allocated. He also has the sole power to decide who will be recognized to speak on the floor of the House and whether motions are relevant. He has the authority to appoint members to the Rules Committee and to certain special committees, and he controls some material benefits, such as the assignment of extra office space. The current Speaker, Newt Gingrich (R-Ga.), has exercised more authority than his predecessors, in large part because of his strong support among Republican members. Gingrich managed to bypass seniority for committee chairs and then secured pledges from those chairs to support the GOP agenda. But, as has been true of previous Speakers, his main weapon is persuasion.

The party leadership in the House also includes a **majority leader,** a **minority leader,** and majority and minority **whips.** The majority leader is second in command to the Speaker, and the minority leader is, as the name suggests, the leader of the minority party. Whips originated in the British House of Commons, where they were named after the "whipper in," the rider who keeps the hounds together in a fox hunt. This aptly describes the whips' role in Congress. Party whips try to maintain contact with party members, see which way they are leaning on votes, and attempt to gain their support. Both parties have several assistant whips who keep tabs on their assigned state delegations.

The party apparatus in the House also includes committees to assign party members to standing committees, discuss policy issues, and allocate funds to party members running for reelection.

The party organization in the Senate is similar to that of the House except that there is no leader comparable to the Speaker of the House. The vice president is formally the presiding officer but in reality attends infrequently and has relatively little power. He is allowed to cast the tie-breaking vote in the rare instances in which the Senate is split evenly. Vice President Gore had such an opportunity in 1993. The Senate has an elected president pro tempore, a mostly honorific post with few duties except to preside over the Senate when the vice president is absent. Because presiding over the Senate on a day-to-day basis is considered boring, junior members usually do it.

The real leader in the Senate is the majority leader, a position now held by Trent Lott (R-Miss.). The minority party leader is normally in line to assume the majority leadership post when his or her party gains a majority of the Senate.

Committees

Standing Committees

Most of the work of Congress is done in committees. Observers of American politics take this for granted; yet the power of legislative committees is rather rare among western democracies. In Britain, for example, committees cannot offer amendments that change the substance of a bill.

Senate majority leader Lyndon Johnson, persuading. LBJ "used physical persuasion in addition to intellectual and moral appeals. He was hard on other people's coat lapels. If one were shorter than Lyndon he was inclined to move up close and lean over the subject of his persuasive efforts." Here that subject is Senator Theodore Green (D-R.I.). "If a Senator were taller than [Johnson], he would come at him from below, somewhat like a badger." Senator Edmund Muskie (D-Me.), who was taller, "emerged from a meeting with Johnson with the observation that he had not known until this meeting why people had the hair in their nostrils trimmed." Quotes are from Eugene McCarthy, *Up 'Til Now* (New York: Harcourt Brace, 1987).

Soon after its establishment, Congress set up four permanent committees; over the years the number slowly grew. Today there are 19 **standing committees** in the House and 17 in the Senate. Each deals with a different subject matter, such as finance or education or agriculture. Each has a number of subcommittees, totaling 84 in the House and 69 in the Senate. Nearly all legislation introduced in Congress is referred to a standing committee and then to a subcommittee. Subcommittees hold public hearings to give interested parties a chance to speak for or against a bill. They also hold **markup** sessions to provide an opportunity for the committee to rewrite the bill. Following markup, the bill is sent to the full committee, which also may hold hearings. If approved there, it goes to the full House or Senate.

Standing committees vary in size from 10 members to 61. Trying to accommodate members' desires for committee seats that allow them to help constituents has led to ever larger committees. Party ratios—that is, the number of Democrats relative to Republicans on each committee—are determined by the majority party. The ratios are generally set in rough proportion to party membership in the particular house, but the majority party gives itself a disproportionate number of seats on several key committees in order to ensure control. Conflict between the parties flared in 1995, when Republicans offered a seat on an influential committee to a Democrat if he would switch parties. He did, and the extra Republican seat further imbalanced the partisan makeup of the committee.

Committee Membership

New members and those members seeking committee changes express their preferences to their party's selection committee. As a general rule, preferences will be granted, although there is a self-selection process whereby junior members usually do not ask for the most prestigious posts.

Seats on some committees are sought after; others are shunned. The committees dealing with budgets and appropriations are always popular because having money to allocate gives members power and the ability to help their districts. Most members want committees that allow them to tell constituents that they are working on problems of the district. For example, members from agricultural districts strive to get on the agriculture committees.

The practice of filling committees with representatives whose districts have an especially strong economic interest in the subject matter makes committees rather parochial in their outlook and fills them with members who have financial interests in the businesses they make policies for.[67] Most members who sit on the banking committees own bank stock, the agriculture committees agribusiness stock, and the armed services committees stock in military contractors.[68]

In the media age, another criterion has become important for choosing a committee: media coverage. The work of some committees is more likely to be covered by television. In a five-year period, the Senate Foreign Relations Committee had 522 network television cameras covering it, whereas the Indian Affairs Committee had 0.[69] Getting on the right committee is important to those who want to become nationally known. When a journalist once asked Senator Joseph Biden (D-Del.) why he was so newsworthy, Biden replied, "It's the committees, of course." Biden had served on the three most publicized committees.

Committee Chairs

The chair is the leader and most influential member of a committee. Chairs have the authority to call meetings, set agendas, and control the committee staff and funds. In addition, chairs are usually very knowledgeable about matters that come before their committee, and this too is a source of influence. Some chairs have used their power to rule their committee with an "iron hand."

Usually, the member of the majority party with the longest service on a committee becomes its chair—the so-called **seniority rule.** Before the early 1900s, powerful Speakers of the House often would use their authority to reward friends and allies by appointing them as committee chairs. To protect themselves, committee members adopted seniority as the basis for selecting chairs. Chairs might be completely out of touch with most of the party, senile, alcoholic, or personally disliked by every member of the committee, but if they had served the longest and their party had a majority in the House, they were chairs regardless.

Many members believed the custom of seniority led to chairs who were out of step with the rest of the party and dictatorial in their committees. In response to those complaints, in the early 1970s both parties agreed that the seniority rule no longer had to be followed. A Committee on Committees in the Republican party and a Steering and Policy Committee in the Democratic party now recommend chairs. Then the members of the party vote on these recommendations.

In 1975, in a striking break with precedent, the Democratic membership stripped three senior Democrats of their chairs. They did so again in 1985 and 1994. The Republicans also violated the seniority principle in their choice of chairs in 1995.[70] In the House, Speaker Gingrich elevated less senior members who were more conservative over other Republicans on the committees, and announced a 6-year limit on chairs. Still, the seniority principle applies most of the time.

Why does Congress usually follow the seniority rule? It assumes that members with long service on the committee will have expertise in its subject matter, and that is usually true. It also eliminates potentially damaging intraparty fights over who will be chairs of important committees. Some people believe the seniority system is also the best protection for women and minorities as they gain seniority in the institution, although in this white male-dominated institution this is more a side effect than a reason for the system's persistence.

Choosing chairs by means other than strict seniority has ended the days of the autocratic chair. And the reform has brought about an interesting change in the behavior of senior members. Before 1975, committee chairs were much lower in support for their party in roll-call votes than other party members.[71] Since 1975, committee chairs have been much more likely to vote with their party than other members. The same pattern holds true of those who are second, third, and fourth in seniority on each committee. Thus, removing seniority as a sole criterion for choosing committee chairs has meant that senior party members are much less likely to deviate from their party's position. In that sense, the reforms have strengthened party influence in Congress.

Subcommittees

Each committee is divided into subcommittees with jurisdiction over part of the committee's subject. The House International Relations committee, for example has five subcommittees—one for Africa, one for Asia and the Pacific, and one for the Western Hemisphere, as well as one on trade and one on human rights.

Committee chairs traditionally dominated not only their committee but its subcommittees as well. Chairs chose the chairs of the subcommittees and controlled the subcommittees' jurisdiction, budget, and staff. Chairs thus could manipulate the subcommittees' action on proposed legislation as they saw fit. In the 1950s, southern chairs bottled up important civil rights legislation for years.

In another rejection of domineering committee chairs, House Democrats made a number of rules changes in 1973 and 1974, sometimes called the **subcommittee bill of rights.** These measures reduced the control of the whole committee, especially its chair, over the subcommittees. Similar changes took place in the Senate. These reforms allow more members, especially newer members, to share in important decisions. In this way they make Congress more democratic.

But by diffusing power, they also make it less efficient. Each subcommittee can operate semi-

The Power of Speaker Gingrich

No Speaker of the House since the days of Thomas Reed and Joseph Cannon has wielded as much power as Newt Gingrich. Within months of taking office, he transformed the speakership into a position from which he could not only rival President Clinton for national attention, but also lead the Republican majority in an effort to change the direction of the federal government. Why has he been able to galvanize the majority as no one else had in many years?

On the surface, the answer seems simple: Republicans in the 104th Congress recognize that they owe their majority status to Gingrich and his efforts. But why do they think so? Because over the past 10 years, Gingrich has personally recruited, trained, and financed an army of new Republicans who are remarkably loyal to him and his agenda.

About half of the Republicans in Congress are recruits from his so-called "farm team." Gingrich's political action committee, GOPAC, is considered by some to be a more important party organ than the Republican National Committee. One of GOPAC's strategies is to recruit and train candidates who are enthusiastic about Gingrich's vision for America, a combination of cultural conservatism and economic freedom. Training sessions on campaign tactics are held across the country, and campaign manuals and tapes detail campaign "do's" and "don'ts." Word lists coach candidates on how to talk like Newt. Candidates can call in and talk to Gingrich himself.

The plan started when Gingrich was first elected to the House, where he joined like-minded Republicans to plan a strategy to make the Republicans the party of the future. Initially the movement relied on C-SPAN to get the message out. Even though the House chamber was empty, Gingrich could reach millions of cable watchers. Later, GOPAC was established to raise money for Republican candidates from conservative business leaders.

The organization decided to make the House bank scandal a major issue and blame it on the Democrats. They also decided to endorse term limits as a way to appeal to angry voters.

The most famous GOPAC document is "Language, a Key Mechanism of Control," in which Gingrich provides a list of words tested in focus groups to use in discussing the opposition. Democrats were to be associated with decay, sick, pathetic, stagnation, corrupt, waste, and traitors. Republicans were to be identified with share, change, truth, moral, courage, family, peace, and duty.

Gingrich prepared audio tapes that prospective candidates listened to as they drove across their states. A former House member and now U.S. Senator from Pennsylvania, Rick Santorum, said, "I listened to those tapes all the time driving around in the car. They taught tactics you should use, basic philosophy, how to discuss the issues. I was a *disciple*."[1] Republican state legislators, potential House members of the future, were all sent tapes. As one House member said, "It is a network prepared to listen to what they perceive to be marching orders."[2]

With each election, more of these "farm team" members won seats in the House. By 1992, 21 of the 47 Republicans elected to the House were GOPAC recruits. By 1994, GOPAC had 33 more new members in the House. Moreover, Gingrich realized his dream, a Republican House majority.

The new Republican majority quickly adopted new rules for the House that had the effect of strengthening the Speaker, including introducing "term limits" for committee chairs. And they have stood behind him—some would say pushed him—during budget negotiations with the White House. Gingrich's relationship with his Republican colleagues is his strongest base. "There is a personal loyalty to him that is without precedent in recent history," said a former Republican representative. "I don't think anyone ever felt they owed their seat to [recent Democratic Speakers] Jim Wright, Tom Foley, or Tip O'Neill."[3]

---

1. Quoted in Connie Bruck, "The Politics of Perfection," *The New Yorker*, October 9, 1995, p.63 (emphasis in original).
2. Bruck, "Politics of Perfection," p. 63.
3. Quoted in Roger H. Davidson and Walter J. Oleszek, *Congress and Its Members*, 5th ed. (Washingon, D.C.: CQ Press, 1996), p. 169.

Source: Thomas B. Rosenstiel, "Gingrich created army," *Lincoln Star*, December 20, 1994, pp. 1 & 5.

independently of the parent committee. The multiplicity of subcommittees also contributes to government gridlock. Complex legislation might be sent to several subcommittees, each with its own interests and jurisdiction. In response, rules changes under the new Republican majority in Congress cut the number of subcommittees significantly, streamlining the legislative process and leaving fewer chairs with independent authority.

With so many committees and subcommittees, the average member is spread pretty thin. The typical senator sits on 11 committees and subcommittees; the average representative about 7. These multiple assignments mean that members have impossible schedules, and committees cannot obtain quorums because members have other committee hearings to attend. This leaves it to the committee chair, a few colleagues, and staff to do the work and make many of the decisions.

Other Committees

There are a few other types of congressional committees. Select or special committees, such as the Senate Watergate Committee, are typically investigative committees organized on a temporary basis to investigate and make recommendations. Joint committees include members from both houses. Another committee is the Conference Committee, which we will discuss later.

Evaluating Committee Government

The division of labor provided by committees and subcommittees enables Congress to consider a vast number of bills each year. If every member had to review every measure in detail it would be impossible to deal with the current workload. Instead, most bills are killed in committee, leaving many fewer for each member to evaluate before a floor vote. Committees also help members develop specializations. Members who remain on the same committee for some time gain expertise and are less dependent on professional staff and executive agencies for information.

But committee government also has disadvantages. In addition to the inefficiencies mentioned already, committees and especially subcommittees are often unrepresentative of Congress as a whole. As a result, they tend to be more responsive to narrow interests and constituencies and less responsive to national objectives.

Over time, members of congressional subcommittees develop close relationships with the interest groups and executive branch agencies affected by their work. These three sets of participants share a concern with a specific policy area. Over the years, the people in these three groups get to know each other, probably come to like and respect one another, and seek to accommodate each other's interests. Personal relationships foster favorable treatment of special interest groups.

The freedom and authority of individual members mean that Congress as a whole often cannot get things done because power is fragmented. Most members of the majority party in the Senate and about half of those in the House chair committees or subcommittees. These centers of power are somewhat independent from party leaders. Thus, Congress often has difficulty mounting a coherent alternative to the president.

On the other hand, the fragmentation of power means it is relatively easy for Congress to block presidential initiatives. In this sense, Congress remains a conservative institution, protecting the status quo. Whether one thinks this is a good idea or not depends on the particular nature of the changes being proposed. Congress has frustrated both conservative and liberal presidents.

Crumbling Committees?

Over the past decade there have been changes in the way Congress deals with important issues. Committee chairs and committees do not always have the power they used to. There is evidence of greater centralization, though not as much as at the turn of the century. Power is gravitating to all members of a few "power" committees, such as the Appropriations, Ways and Means, and Energy and Commerce committees in the House and the Finance Committee in the Senate. The power of these committees lies in their ability to control spending and raise revenue (as we will see later). As one observer commented, even the most senior member of Public Works finds it difficult to accomplish what the most junior member of Appropriations can do in winning home district pork barrel projects. The former chair of the Senate Appropriations Committee, Robert Byrd (D-W.Va.), was called the "Prince of Pork" for his success in bringing federal money to West Virginia.[72]

Power has also gravitated to party leaders. The formal leader of the House, the Speaker, has gained power, and party unity is on the upswing. Leaders, including some committee chairs, are also more powerful because more and more negotiations over important bills are taking place directly among the leaders of Congress and administration officials. For example, the Senate version of the Clean Air Act was drafted in a series of meetings between the Senate majority leader, other key senators, and Bush administration officials. The bill written in committee was largely ignored. Other issues, such as an anticrime bill, campaign finance legislation, and a congressional ethics package have been developed outside formal committee structures.

These new arrangements have some advantages. They overcome the paralysis that sometimes results from the divided partisan control of Congress and the presidency. Direct negotiations between the White House and congressional leaders can sometimes break long-standing deadlocks.

On the other hand, these new arrangements bypass mechanisms for accountability to the public and to most rank-and-file members. Bills are written without formal hearings and the opportunities to point out potential pitfalls and problems of the legislation. Rank-and-file members often are faced with voting on a huge package of legislation about which they know only what they read in the newspaper.

Moreover, without powerful committees, if the majority leaders are not strong, bargaining over legislation can become a complete free-for-all, with dozens of legislators striking individual deals for their favorite program. Without strong committees or leaders, individual members of Congress, often with no expertise or interest beyond a special interest, can hold a piece of legislation hostage in exchange for a tax loophole or bit of pork.

Thus, many people believe that Congress is still ripe for reform. The Republicans did make several changes when they took over in 1995, including abolishing three House committees and several subcommittees, eliminating proxy committee voters, and planning for a substantial reduction in staff. Despite this modest streamlining, the basic functioning of the Congress is unchanged. However, its burst of legislative energy early in 1995 suggests that when Congress fails to get things done, committee structure is only part of the reason. A cohesive House majority with strong leadership can pass legislation even with a complex committee structure. Conversely, if the public is divided and there is little strong leadership or incentive for members to carry out a legislative agenda, congressional structure only reinforces other impediments to action. As one member remarked, "How is a committee overhaul going to make me more courageous to do things I don't want to do now?"[73]

Staff

The term "Congress" encompasses not only our 535 elected representatives but also their staff of nearly 30,000 people.

Congress hires far more staff members than any other legislative body. Even with recent cuts, it is still by far the largest. The Canadian legislature, which is second in staff size, has only about 3,300 people.[74]

Types of Staff

Congressional staff members include those working in members' Washington and district offices, defined as "personal" staff, those working for congressional committees, those working for the special support agencies of Congress (the Congressional Research Service, Office of Technology Assessment, Congressional Budget Office, and the General Accounting Office), and auxiliary staff such as police.

House members have about 16 personal staff members, and the average senator has more than 40. Senators from states with larger populations have a larger staff than senators from smaller states. Leaders have many more staff than rank-and-file members. By far the largest proportion of members' personal staffs works on constituency service, both in the district offices and in Washington. Other staff members will be assigned to legislative duties, and one or more will do media work.

One of the main reasons for the tremendous growth and size of staff is the increasing demand for constituency service. As more citizens turn to Congress for help with the bureaucracy, Congress hires more staff to take care of them. Another main reason is that Congress has attempted to develop its own expertise and sources of information so it will not have to rely on the executive branch. Thus its committees have staff members who research and draft legislation as well as develop support for it.

Staff in the support agencies of Congress carry out various research functions, again enabling Congress to be independent of the executive branch. The General Accounting Office checks on the efficiency and effectiveness of executive agencies. The Congressional Research Service conducts studies of public issues and does specific research at the request of members. The Office of Technology Assessment provides long-range analyses of the effects of new and existing technology, and the Congressional Budget Office provides the expertise and support for Congress' budgeting job.

Impact of Staff

Some scholars have argued that although increased congressional staff may be necessary, it has created more problems than it has solved.[75] Large staffs create more paperwork and have a tendency to produce ever more research, committee work, and hearings. Information is collected that is impossible for members to digest. Large staffs have made members into

American Diversity

Black Power in Congress

Special interest caucuses are groups of members united by some personal interest or characteristic. There are more than 60 House caucuses, representing partisan, ideological, policy, or regional interests. One of these, the Black Caucus, was organized in 1969 by black members of Congress determined to gain some clout. This organization, which includes all African American members of Congress, has grown to 40 members and meets regularly, usually weekly. It also has more than 80 white associate members. Before 1994, the caucus, like other caucuses, had its own small staff. However, the Republican majority eliminated staff support for special interest caucuses, so now the caucus relies on its members to provide support from their staffs.

Paradoxically, at a time when the caucus is at its all-time high in its number of members, it is perhaps the weakest it has been in two decades. The reason is that all but two of its members are Democrats, and now they are the minority party in both houses. When the Democrats controlled the House, many black members had positions of power, chairing, in 1994, 26% of all House committees and many subcommittees too. Now with their party out of power, they chair no committees or subcommittees. Moreover, the caucus has little influence with the Republican majority because of its small Republican membership and the Democratic predispositions of the black constituents of Republican members of Congress.

As we have discussed, the success of blacks in getting several southern states to redistrict to form majority black districts helped weaken Democratic congressional representation in the South and contributed to the Republican majority. One analyst notes that "A lot of people say redistricting was a means to an end of getting more power for black people by getting more blacks in Congress; if redistricting was a means to an end, it turned out to be a dead end."[1] Others, such as Jesse Jackson, urge a continuation of the majority-minority redistricting strategy, arguing that the Democrats did poorly in 1994 partly because of low black turnout, which can be mobilized.

To be influential in these new circumstances, Black Caucus members will have to negotiate and find new allies. Yet they must also continue speaking for their constituency. In today's climate, this is a difficult task. For example, their proposed alternatives to both the Republican and the Clinton budget cuts are getting little publicity, and have even less chance of being seriously considered.

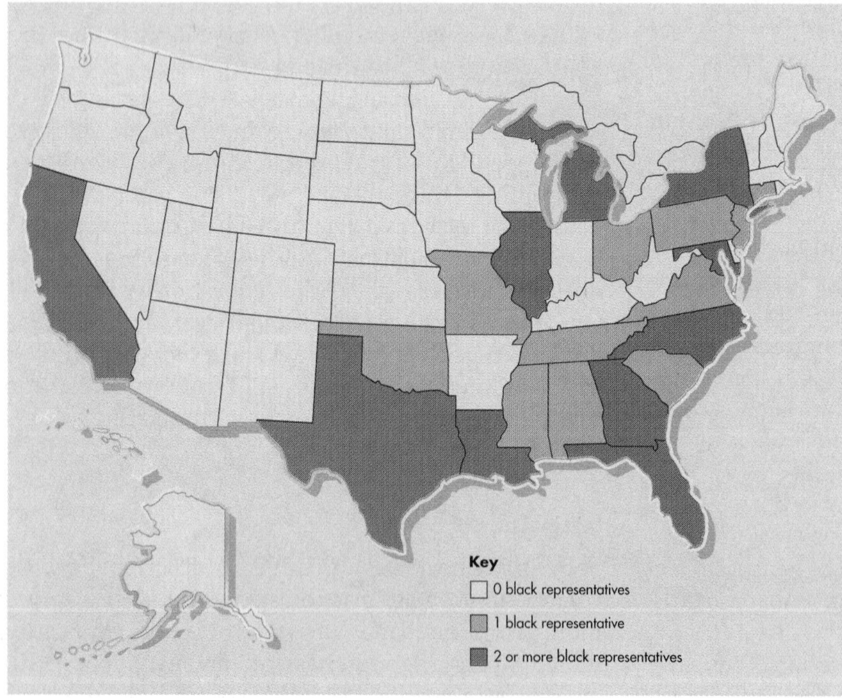

Number of African American members of Congress, by state.

1. Juan Williams, "How Black Liberal Strategy Failed Its Followers," *Washington Post National Weekly Edition,* November 28–December 3, 1994, p. 25; Steven Holmes "Did Racial Redistricting Undermine Democrats?" *New York Times,* November 13, 1994, p. 32.

executives who need to manage their offices rather than legislators with time to think about policy. Congressional staffs have reduced the amount of discussion members have with one another over policy issues. As former Senator David Boren (D-Okla.) complained, "Very often, I will call on a senator on an issue, and he won't know anything about it. He'll ask me to get someone on my staff to call someone on his staff. It shuts off personal contact between senators."[76] This means the compromises and adjustments necessary to make policy are sometimes made by technicians rather than elected representatives.

➤What Congress Does

The Founders intended Congress to be the dominant branch of government. The powers and role of Congress are spelled out in Article I of the Constitution, before attention is given to the president. Almost half the Constitution is devoted to a discussion of Congress. The importance of Congress also is reflected in the major, explicit constitutional powers the Founders gave it: to lay and collect taxes, coin money, declare war and raise and support a military, and regulate commerce with foreign governments and among the states. These and other powers specifically mentioned in the Constitution are called the enumerated powers of Congress.

Congress also has implied powers; that is, it can make all the laws "necessary and proper" to carry out its enumerated powers. Although the Founders did not necessarily foresee it, this tremendous grant of power covers almost every conceivable area of human activity.

Lawmaking

High school civics students learn the formal steps by which a bill becomes a law (see Figure 5). Although these procedures are important, at every step there are compromises, trade-offs, and understandings. In other words, there is politics.

A bill becomes a law if its supporters can get it through an obstacle course. Approval must be obtained at each obstacle or the bill fails. Those opposing a bill have an advantage because it is easier to defeat a bill than pass it. The need to win a majority at each stage of the process also means that individuals with varying interests must be satisfied. The end result is almost always a compromise.

Introduction

Bills may be introduced in either the House or the Senate, except for tax measures (which according to the Constitution must be introduced initially in the House) and appropriations bills (which by tradition are introduced in the House). This reflects the Founders' perceptions that on tax issues Congress should be especially responsive to the people and that the House would be more responsive than the Senate.

Only members of Congress are permitted to introduce bills. Interest groups or the president must find a congressional sponsor for a proposed bill. About half the legislation passed is initiated by the president.[77]

Referral and Committee Action

After a bill's introduction, it is referred to a standing committee by the Speaker of the House or the presiding officer in the Senate. The content of the bill largely determines where it will go, although the Speaker has some discretion, particularly over complex bills that cover more than one subject area.

Once the bill reaches a committee, it is assigned to a subcommittee. Bills receiving subcommittee approval go to full committee and if approved go to the whole House. Bills that get out of committee usually become law. Most bills, however, die in committee or subcommittee. Indeed, one of the main functions of committees is to screen bills with little chance of passage. (If a committee kills a bill, there are procedures that members can use to try to get the bill to the floor, but these are used infrequently.)

The committee and subcommittee markup stage is legally open yet barely visible to the public. Consequently, lobbyists attend hearings. For critical meetings, lobbyists will hire messengers to stand in line for them, sometimes all night, and then pack the hearing room. Members who depend on particular groups for financial or other support often face intense and direct pressure to vote a particular way in committee, and are sometimes mobbed by lobbyists when they leave the hearing room.

Scheduling and the Rules Committee

Once a bill is approved by committee, it is placed on one of five "calendars," each of which contains a particular type of bill (for example, all bills considered to be noncontroversial are placed on one calendar). Bills from each calendar are generally considered in the

FIGURE 5
How a Bill Becomes a Law

These formal steps do not include the informal negotiations, discussions, and compromises that take place throughout the process. Neither do they include the efforts interest groups make to influence the decisions or the information legislators receive from their constituents.

	HOUSE	SENATE	PRESIDENT
Bill Introduction ↓	Given a number Referred to committee	Given a number Referred to committee	
In Committee ↓	Referred to subcommittee Hearings held Markup Recommend passage or kill the bill Rules committee action (setting terms of debate)	Referred to subcommittee Hearings held Markup Recommend passage or kill the bill	
On the Floor ↓	Debate and amendment, if allowed under rule Vote on passage	Debate and amendment Vote on passage	
In Conference ↓	Conference Committee reconciles different versions Conference report adapted	Conference report adapted	
To President	Veto override (if necessary)	Veto override (if necessary)	Signs or vetoes

order that they are reported from committee. In the House, the **Rules Committee** sets the terms of the debate over the bill by issuing a rule on it. The rule either limits or does not limit debate and determines whether amendments will be permitted. A rule forbidding amendments means that members have to vote Yes or No on the bill; there is no chance to change it. If the committee refuses to issue a rule, the bill dies.

The Rules Committee is not as independent or powerful as it once was. In earlier years the committee was controlled by a coalition of conservative Democrats and Republicans who used the committee to block liberal legislative proposals. It now functions as an arm of the majority leadership.[78] Members are nominated by the Speaker, and the leadership uses the committee to fashion rules to control and expedite floor action.

Debate in the House

Debate on a bill is controlled by the bill managers, the senior committee supporters of the bill. The opposition too has its managers who schedule opposition speeches. "Debates" are hardly a series of fiery speeches of point and counterpoint. They are often boring, given to sparse audiences, some of whom are reading, conversing, or walking around. After the agreed-upon time for debate is over, the bill is reported for final action.

The Senate

Because the Senate is a smaller body, it can operate with fewer rules and formal procedures. It does not have a rules committee. A lot of work is accomplished through the use of unanimous consent agreements, which allow the Senate to dispense with standard rules and limit debate and amendments. As the Senate's workload has increased and its sense of collegiality decreased, unanimous consent agreements are both more desirable and more difficult to gain from opponents of a bill. A few senators can delay or kill important bills. (Table 2 summarizes House and Senate differences.) As one observer remarked, "The Senate has the same procedural rules as you would find on Monkey Island in the San Francisco Zoo."[79]

Without unanimous consent, there is no rule limiting debate and no restrictions on adding amendments. Opponents can add all sorts of irrelevant amendments to pending legislation. One senator held up an antibusing bill for eight months with 604 amendments.

The other major mechanism for delay in the Senate is the **filibuster.** This is a continuous speech made by

TABLE 2 Important Differences Between the House and Senate

HOUSE	SENATE
Constitutional Differences	**Constitutional Differences**
Must initiate revenue bills Initiates impeachment and passes impeachment bills Apportioned by population	Must give approval to many major presidential appointments Tries impeached officials Approves treaties Two senators from each state
Differences in Operation	**Differences in Operation**
More centralized, more formal: Speaker's assignment of bills to committee hard to challenge Rules Committee fairly powerful in controlling time and rules of debate (works with majority leaders) Nongermane amendments forbidden Majority party controls scheduling More impersonal Power less evenly distributed Members are highly specialized Emphasizes tax and revenue policy	Less centralized, less formal: Assignment of bills to committee appealable No rules committee; limits on debate come through unanimous consent or cloture of filibuster Nongermane amendments permitted Schedule and rules negotiated between majority and minority leaders More personal Power more evenly distributed Members are generalists Emphasizes foreign policy
Changes in the Institution	**Changes in the Institution**
Power is becoming centralized in the hands of key committees and the leadership House procedures are becoming more efficient with less debate and fewer amendments	Senate workload increasing and informality breaking down Members are becoming more specialized; debate and deliberation are less frequent

Sources: Louis A. Froman, *The Congressional Process: Strategies, Rules, and Procedures* (Boston: Little, Brown, 1967); Norman Ornstein, "The House and Senate in a New Congress" in Thomas Mann and Norman Ornstein, eds., *The New Congress* (Washington, D.C.: American Enterprise Institute, 1981), pp. 363–84.

one or more members to prevent the Senate from taking action. Before 1917, only unanimous consent could prevent an individual from talking. Today a **cloture** vote of three-fifths of the members can limit debate to only 20 more hours.

Like nongermane amendments, filibusters are used by both liberals and conservatives. The filibuster developed in the 1820s when the Senate was divided between slave and free states. Unlimited debate maintained the deadlock.[80] For over a century the filibuster was used primarily to defeat race and civil rights legislation; the 1964 Civil Rights Act was passed only after a cloture vote. Recently, filibusters have occurred on many different types of legislation.

During Clinton's first year in office, Republicans used the filibuster quite frequently. Not only did they use it to work against his economic proposals, but they also used it as a political tactic to embarrass the president. Even though the Democrats had a significant majority, their majority was not large enough to shut off the filibuster (unless some Republicans joined them). After that Republicans captured the Senate in 1994, Democrats resorted to the filibuster.

Filibusters protect the rights of congressional minorities and help ensure that controversial issues will get full consideration. On the other hand, they deny the majority the right to legislate, and contribute mightily to gridlock.[81] In the last decade they have been used far more frequently than in the past. In 1991–1992 alone they were used 35 times, compared with only 16 times during the entire nineteenth century. By in effect requiring 60 votes to pass controversial legislation, they make it difficult for a majority to legislate.

Conference Committee

Under the Constitution, the House and Senate must pass an identical bill before it becomes law. Thus the House and Senate versions of the bill must be reconciled. Sometimes the house that passed the bill last will simply send the bill to the other house for minor modifications. But if the differences between the two versions are not minor, a **Conference Committee** is set up to try to resolve them. The presiding officers of each house, in consultation with the chairs of the standing committees that considered the bill, choose the members of the committee. Both parties are represented.

To win approval, majorities of members from each house must agree to the Conference Committee version. Sometimes the bill is rewritten fairly substantially, and occasionally a bill is killed.

Once the Conference Committee reaches an agreement, the bill goes back to each house for ratification. It cannot be amended at that point so Congress must either "take it or leave it." This means the Conference Committee can be very influential.

Presidential Action and Congressional Response

The president may sign the bill, in which case it becomes law. The president may veto it, in which case it returns to Congress with the president's objections. The president also may do nothing, which means the bill becomes law after 10 days unless Congress adjourns.

Presidents infrequently veto legislation, but when they do, they usually are not overridden by Congress. A two-thirds vote in each house is required to override a presidential veto. Congress voted to override only 9 of former President Reagan's 78 vetoes, and only 1 of President Bush's 46.

Overseeing the Federal Bureaucracy

As part of the checks and balances principle, it is Congress's responsibility to make sure the bureaucracy is carrying out the intent of Congress in administering federal programs. This congressional **oversight** has become more important as Congress continues to delegate authority to the executive branch. For a variety of reasons, Congress is not especially well equipped, motivated, or organized to carry out its oversight function. Nevertheless, it does have several tools for this purpose.

One tool is the General Accounting Office, created in 1921, which functions as Congress's watchdog in oversight and is mostly concerned with making sure that money is used properly.

Another tool is the **legislative veto.** Used since 1933, it allows one or both houses of Congress, or on occasion a congressional committee, to block executive action. Congress adds the veto provision to some legislation. In the 1970s, it did much more than in the past in order to restrict agency activities. For example, all Federal Trade Commission rulings were subject to a legislative veto.

In 1983, the Supreme Court declared the legislative veto unconstitutional as a violation of the separation of powers principle. Legislation, the Court ruled, must be passed by both houses and signed by the president. Congress cannot take over executive functions. Even so, since that decision, more than 100 bills have passed with provisions for a legislative veto.[82] Though presumably they could not be enforced, legislative vetoes continue to be honored by federal agencies unwilling to risk congressional wrath by doing something Congress has vetoed.

Yet another method of oversight is committee hearings, although they are not very effective. Members can quiz representatives from agencies on the operation of their agencies, but often they go into great detail about some particular problem of minor importance and neglect broader policy questions. Poor attendance and the pressure of other business mean that members' attentions are usually not focused on congressional hearings. Nevertheless, officials in agencies view hearings as a possible source of embarrassment for their agency and spend a great deal of time preparing for them.

Political considerations also influence oversight. For example, a year before the Iran-contra scandal hit the front pages in 1986, two congressional committees began investigations of Colonel Oliver North's fundraising efforts for the Nicaraguan contras. The investigations were dropped in order not to challenge a popular president.

Congress's control over the budget is the major way it exercises oversight. Congress can cut or add to agencies' budgets and thereby punish or reward them for their performance.

Informal oversight is a common tool.[83] This can include requiring reports on topics of interest to members or committees. In a recent year the executive branch prepared 5000 reports for Congress.[84] Moreover the chair and staff of the committee or subcommittee relevant to the agency's mission are consulted regularly by the agency. But one can question whether much actual oversight gets done informally. Members of congressional committees and subcommittees with authority over an agency's budget get benefits for their constituents from that agency. By responding to congressional wishes, agencies get a favorable budget. There are few electoral or other incentives for members to become involved in the drudgery of more thorough oversight.[85]

Budget Making

An increasingly large part of the job of Congress is to produce a budget. The Constitution gives Congress the authority to control the federal purse by collecting taxes and spending money.

The topic of making budgets sounds dull and can be tedious. However, without money to implement laws, laws themselves would mean very little. It is one thing to pass legislation that provides funding for day care, improves Medicare benefits, combats drug addiction, regulates health and safety standards for workers, and provides financial aid to students. But without money in the budget to fund these programs, the programs are empty rhetoric. And in fact, sometimes laws are passed to give the impression that government is really doing something about a problem when in reality it is not doing much. Much of the "War on Drugs" fits this category. In other cases, those who support legislation do see that it is reasonably well funded initially, but later it may lose support and suffer funding cuts. During the Reagan administration, for example, many regulatory programs established during the 1970s, such as the Consumer Product Safety Commission and the Environmental Protection Agency, lost substantial parts of their funding and were forced to cut back their activities. Thus budgets are crucial in determining what government actually does.

There are two major features of congressional spending patterns. First, the process is usually incremental; that is, budgets of one year are usually slightly more than budgets of the past year. Normally, Congress does not radically reallocate money from one year to the next; members assume agencies should get about what they received the previous year. This simplifies the work of all concerned. Agencies do not have to defend, or members scrutinize, all aspects of the budget.[86]

A second feature is that Congress tends to spend slightly more on federal agencies in election years.[87] This tendency increases in times of unemployment and moderates in times of inflation. Members are also more likely to vote for increasing federal payments to individuals (such as veterans' benefits or Social Security) in the years they are up for reelection.[88]

These general tendencies cannot account for every year's budgeting. Reagan's domestic budget cuts and increased military spending in 1981 were clearly an exception to incrementalism. But his failure to win further cuts and increases in succeeding years testifies to the persistence of incrementalism.

Budget legislation goes through a similar but more complicated process as other bills.[89] To grasp the complexity, we have to understand the distinction between budget authorizations and budget appropriations. **Authorizations** provide agencies and departments with the legal authority to operate. Although authorizations also might specify funding

Overseeing the Pentagon

Congressional monitoring of the Department of Defense (DOD) is a good example of the problems of congressional oversight. It bogs down in details and special concerns but fails to provide critical scrutiny of the big picture.

Forty years ago, Congress engaged in little oversight of the Pentagon. In fact, the Defense Department witnesses at committee hearings actually submitted to the committee the questions that members should ask them. The practice stopped after 1969, however, when a confused committee member read not only the proposed question, but also the proposed answer to this question!

Now Congress has gone to the other extreme. Dozens of committees and subcommittees oversee the Pentagon. Hundreds of Pentagon witnesses spend hundreds of hours testifying before 84 committees and subcommittees. The Pentagon also annually responds to several hundred thousand congressional requests for information. All four congressional support agencies also monitor the department. In its attempts to make the system more responsible, Congress has bogged it down in red tape.

Congress issues detailed requirements for each weapons system or other equipment it orders. Thus a proposal from a contractor for a new military transport jet weighed three tons (the proposal, not the plane!).

Despite all this, Congress spends little time on the "big picture," the overall organization and strategies of our armed forces. Many critics believe these problems are potentially much more damaging to our national security than waste and corruption in weapons purchasing on which congressional oversight focuses. As one military expert noted, "When admirals, officials, and Congressmen gather to examine the Navy in each year's review of the budget, ten minutes of . . . chitchat disposes of the entire question of naval strategy—i.e., the purpose of the Navy, its major tasks . . . before all concerned settle down to many weeks of scrutiny . . . of every single item of expenditure. . . . Debate on each service's chosen operational concepts of war, which actually determine their equipment needs, is almost unknown."

Sources: David Morrison, "Chaos on Capital Hill," *National Journal,* September 27, 1986, pp. 2302–7; J. Ronald Fox, *Arming America* (Cambridge, Mass.: Harvard University Press, 1974); Edward Luttwak, *The Pentagon and the Art of War* (New York: Simon & Schuster, 1984), pp. 152–53.

levels, they do not actually provide the funding. **Appropriations** are the authority to spend money.

After the president makes budget recommendations reflecting agency requests as filtered through his own priorities, authorization requests are reviewed by the particular standing committee whose subject matter encompasses the activities of a particular agency. In essence, almost all standing committees are authorization committees for those agencies whose work they oversee. The House Interior and Insular Affairs Committee and the Senate Energy and National Resources Committee, for example, review the authorization of the Park Service in the Department of Interior; the agriculture committees are authorization committees for the Department of Agriculture.

In reviewing an agency, the authorizing committee is not bound by the administration's request. It is free to expand, shrink, or eliminate it altogether. However, the authorizing committee and the agency being reviewed will have developed close ties over the years so authorizations are likely to be more generous than appropriations.

Appropriations are reviewed by the Appropriations Committee. There is only one appropriations committee in each house and it makes recommendations on the entire budget. Although appropriations subcommittees develop close ties with the agencies they review, the committee as a whole does not have these ties, and thus its recommendations for funding tend to be lower than authorized. Conflicts occur frequently between authorizing committees and the Appropriations Committee.

Both authorizing and appropriations bills must pass each house, and differences must be resolved in a conference. The separation of the authorization and appropriations process is complex and rather uncoordinated. Authorizing committees often make decisions without considering the total budget picture and so the real power to control spending passes to the Appropriations Committee, thus weakening the authorizing committees.

Congress is aided in its budget setting by the Congressional Budget Office (CBO), which provides expertise to Congress on matters related to the budget and economy. Before the establishment of the CBO, members of Congress felt they were junior partners in budget making because they had to depend on information provided by the president, his budget advisors, and the Office of Management and Budget. Because the CBO is responsible to both parties in Congress, it provides a less politically biased set of forecasts about the budget than does the administration.

Each house of Congress also has a budget committee whose function is to monitor the revenue and spending decisions of House and Senate committees and assess their impact on the federal budget. Recently, these committees have had little influence.

Congress and the president talk a lot about balancing the budget. The 1985 Gramm-Rudman-Hollings Bill was designed to balance the budget but was unsuccessful in doing so. This bill called for the annual budget deficits to be reduced to zero by 1993. Unfortunately, the bill did little to limit the real deficit and a lot to increase the dishonesty of the budget process. To keep the official budget from showing a greater deficit than called for by Gramm-Rudman, Congress and the president do make some real budget cuts, but mostly they have taken programs out of the official budget and put them "off budget," moved expenditures from one fiscal year to the next, and sold national assets to generate one year's income. Trust funds for Social Security, highways (money from gas taxes that is supposed to be used to repair and maintain federal highways), and other purposes are being used to cover current expenses.

In 1995, two years after the budget was to be balanced, the president and Congress again called for a balanced budget in several years. The likelihood of that happening seems to be little greater than it was in 1985, when the Gramm-Rudman-Hollings bill was passed with great fanfare.

The budget process has also become less tied to committees. Recent budgets are produced after months of direct negotiations among congressional leaders, their staffs, administration aides, individual members, and the president. Committee hearings became a sideshow, with the real decisions made in private negotiations. Congress is then presented with a "take it or leave it" budget package.

Conclusion: Is Congress Responsive?

Congress is certainly responsive to many individuals with individual problems. The primacy given to constituency service practically guarantees this kind of responsiveness. But is Congress responsive to the nation's policy demands? The primary policy function of Congress seems to be to serve as a check on the president, reviewing, revising, and perhaps killing his policy proposals. The efficiency of Congress in producing its own legislation varies greatly and may be declining.

The media attention that Congress receives probably is eroding its ability to make public policy. Some media attention is good, because we prize open government in a democracy. But some of it is not so good, because in a heterogeneous society we rely on compromise to achieve our public goals and, under the harsh glare of media, there are fewer opportunities to compromise and deliberate without fear of losing votes back home.

Members often feel they have to be too responsive. Now, as never before, every step—or misstep—that members of Congress take is carried to every part of the nation. Or as the *New York Times* commented, "Modern Washington is wired for quadrophonic sound and wide-screen video, lashed by fax, computer, 800 number, overnight poll, FedEx, grassroots mail, air shuttle and CNN to every citizen in every village on the continent and Hawaii too. Its every twitch is blared to the world, thanks to C-SPAN, open meetings laws, financial-disclosure reports, and campaign spending rules, and its every misstep is logged in a database for the use of some future office seeker."[90] As a response to media scrutiny and partisan deadlock, more legislation is being written in secret negotiations between congressional and executive leaders and staffers. This trend is hailed by some but criticized by others who are shut out of the process.

The pressures of elections and of constituency service also undermine Congress's ability to focus on public policy. Said one long-term member, "We see people coming here who do nothing but public relations . . . and that's not good."[91] Pressure to be in the home district meeting constituents competes with legislators' desires to do a good job at lawmaking and to work more efficiently (such as by expanding the work week from three days to five). Pressure to raise money for reelection campaigns incurs obligations to interest groups that may not be consistent with either the members' or constituents' views.

Indeed, part of the congressional Democratic leadership's problems in articulating a clear vision and supporting Clinton's initiatives is that so many of its members have become dependent on the contributions of PACs for their campaign funding. This puts them in the position of having to support some interests that are not consistent with the Democratic voters' views or interests. The lengthy debate and foot dragging by some congressional Democrats on health-care

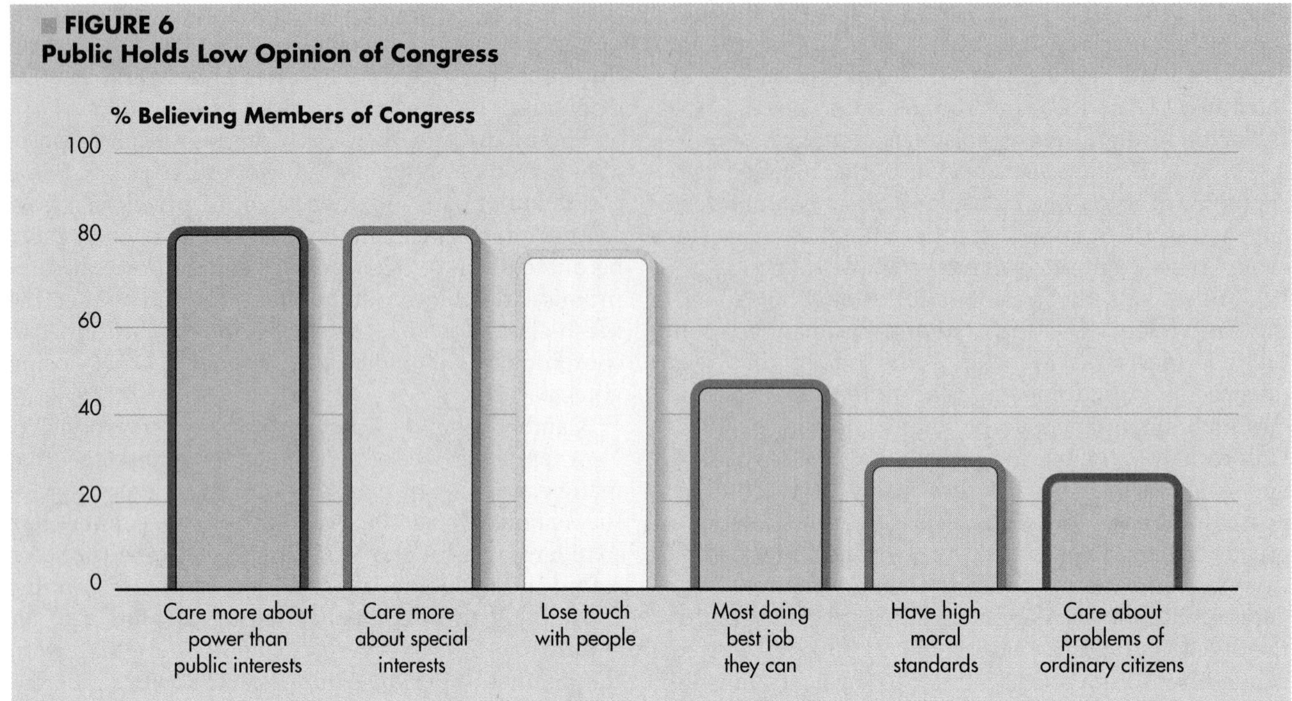

■ **FIGURE 6**
Public Holds Low Opinion of Congress

Source: Washington Post-ABC Polls, reported July 11–17, 1994, p. 7.

reform illustrated this tension, with many major interest groups (insurance companies, hospitals, drug companies, physicians) adamantly opposed to further government involvement in health care, but a huge Democratic constituency desperate for some change that would allow them access to quality health care. For the Republicans, reliance on PACs is not so contradictory, since Republicans have traditionally been the party of the better-off and of business.

The procedures and organization of Congress also give individuals and small groups opportunities to block or redirect action. This is particularly true in the Senate, where procedures allow a minority of senators to engage in unlimited debate, unless an overwhelming majority vote to stop it. The fragmented committee and subcommittee structure in both houses offers many points for action to be killed. Political parties have been strengthened in recent years but are not strong enough to protect against the pressure of lobbyists or outraged constituents. All of these factors mean that Congress continues to be more responsive to individual needs than to more general societal ones.

It is perhaps this nonresponsiveness to overall societal needs that has given rise to the disdain for government expressed so vehemently in the 1994 election. (See Figure 6.) The public wants their Congress to be responsive to their individual needs and those of their group, and then looks down on the institution because this responsiveness leads to inaction and conflict. Moreover, public disdain is fueled by an unrealistic public expectation that there really is one public interest, one majority, and it is only the malfeasance and inefficiencies of Congress that keeps "good" policies from being enacted. The truth is, of course, that there is no set of policies on which everyone agrees. The public does not always agree on the aims of public policy (Are we interested in saving money, or making sure every child has access to health care? Are we interested in making public schools better, or encouraging more education to be taken over by private schools? Are we interested in promoting a woman's right to choose an abortion, or closing off that choice?), let alone how to accomplish those aims.

Moreover, most of the public does not know what Congress has done. They are much more likely to know about bounced checks and sexual improprieties of members of Congress than they are about legislation. For example, in 1994, although two-thirds were aware of new handgun regulations and family leave policy (granting most employees the right to take an unpaid leave for a new baby or family illness), less than one-third of the public knew that Congress had passed a budget bill cutting the deficit by billions, reduced taxes on the working poor and raised them on the very rich, made voting registration nearly automatic when individuals sign up for their driver's licenses, and gave federal workers the right to get involved in politics.[92] Thus, the public evaluation of Congress as having accomplished "not much" or "nothing at all" (from the same poll) was based on the public's lack of awareness of what Congress actually did.

Congress, as confused, inefficient, and conflict-ridden though it may be, is really a reflection of our society. And yet, few would want to replace this crucial democratic institution. The public takes pride, in the abstract, in this feature of constitutional government.

Before 1994, many Republicans felt shut out of the Democrat-dominated Congress, and their anger and institution-bashing stimulated public anger and frustration. It remains to be seen if this new Republican majority, most of whom ran against not only individual members of Congress, but Congress as a whole and indeed government itself, can restore public confidence in this key democratic institution.

EPILOGUE

Margolies-Mezvinsky Supports the President and Loses Her Job

Representative Margolies-Mezvinsky told the president she would vote for the bill only if he was one vote short and hers was the swing vote, and only if he agreed to the entitlement summit. Unfortunately for her, the president needed her vote to pull out a one-vote victory. While many Democrats with safer seats "took a walk" away from supporting Clinton, Margolies-Mezvinsky supported him. As soon as she

Source: Reprinted with special permission King Features Syndicate.

cast her ballot, some Republicans in the House stood up and waved "Goodbye, Marjorie."

Friends, members of the administration, and some media praised her courage for taking a fiscally responsible but politically dangerous position ("Courageous Freshman Saves the President"), but her constituents were infuriated. "Just another run-of-the-mill, cheap, soiled, ward-heeling politician whose word was not worth a spit stain in the street," said one local paper.[93] Phone lines to her offices were tied up for hours with angry constituents. Her proposals to cut entitlements were unpopular and so were tax increases in the bill. Focus groups found most voters thought she had sold her vote for an ambassadorship or some other emolument, when all she received was a promise to hold an economic summit in her district.

Margolies-Mezvinsky was swept out in the Republican landslide of 1994, losing the election by a 45% to 49% margin to Jon Fox, her 1992 opponent. She ran an excellent campaign to pull that close. Most observers attributed her loss to the budget vote.

Did she make the "right" decision? On the one hand, she was not responsive to some demands of her constituents. She promised she would not support Clinton's plan, and she did. But she was responsive in other ways. Her constituents voted for Clinton and she was supporting one of his key programs. Her constituents wanted to reduce the deficit, and the Clinton proposal would. Her constituent focus groups showed none wanted a failed presidency, and a defeat on the budget bill would have contributed to that perception. In other words, her constituents were as torn as she was about what was right. Unfortunately for Margolies-Mezvinsky, nine of ten voters erroneously believed that the deficit could be cut by eliminating waste, thus allowing them to reconcile their contradictory desires for tax cuts, deficit reduction, and maintenance of entitlement programs such as Social Security and Medicare.[94] Mezvinsky knew that belief was an illusion, and cast her vote accordingly.

Clinton's plan did reduce the deficit, and, contrary to Republican warnings, stimulated the economy. But the deficit remains. The new Republican congressional majority wants to go much further than Clinton did in solving the deficit problem. Their proposed spending cuts go much deeper, but they promise tax cuts and not tax increases. Whether voters will find this more palatable remains to be seen.

➤Key Terms

constituencies
reapportionment
redistricting
gerrymander
franking
constituency service
casework
pork barrel
informal norms
institutional loyalty
reciprocity
specialization
going public
Speaker of the House
majority leader
minority leader
whips
standing committees
markup
seniority rule
subcommittee bill of rights
special interest caucuses
Rules Committee
filibuster
cloture
Conference Committee
oversight
legislative veto
authorizations
appropriations

➤Further Reading

Michael Barone et al., *The Almanac of American Politics* (Washington, D.C.: National Journal, since 1980). *A description of each member, his or her district, and voting record. Revised every two years since 1980. A volume similar in format and publication schedule is Alan Ehrenhalt's* Politics in America *(Washington, D.C.: CQ Press).*

Lindy Boggs, *Washington Through a Purple Veil* (New York: Harcourt Brace, 1994). A congressional wife (and mother of NPR reporter Cokie Roberts), then a member of Congress herself for 17 years, Lindy Boggs provides an engrossing narrative of life in the House.

Congressional Quarterly Weekly Report. *Published weekly, provides analyses of the workings of Congress and its members. The Congressional Quarterly also publishes a yearly summary of congressional action called the* Congressional Quarterly Almanac.

Timothy Cook, *Making Laws and Making News* (Washington, D.C.: Brookings, 1989). *A revealing account of how media coverage has affected the legislative process in the United States House.*

Elizabeth Drew, *Senator* (New York: Simon and Schuster, 1979). *Describes the day-to-day life of a former United States senator, John Culver, working in his state and Washington.*

Richard Fenno, *Home Style* (Boston: Little, Brown, 1978). *A readable book based on Fenno's travels with House members to their home districts. Fenno offers interesting and valuable insights into how members present themselves to the home folks. In* The United States Senate: A Bicameral Perspective *(Washington, D.C.: The American Enterprise Institute, 1982), Fenno gives the same attention to senators.*

Linda Fowler, *Candidates, Congress, and the American Democracy* (Ann Arbor: University of Michigan Press, 1993). How the political system affects the recruitment of congressional candidates, and how the candidates affect the system.

Morris Fiorina, *Congress: Keystone of the Washington Establishment,* 2nd ed. (New Haven: Yale University Press, 1989). *A small and significant book that argues that Congress loves the big bureaucracy because it helps their constituents and thereby helps them win reelection.*

Marjorie Margolies-Mezvinsky, *A Woman's Place: The Freshmen Women Who Changed the Face of Congress* (New York: Crown, 1994). *Representative Margolies-Mezvinsky reflects on the changes brought about in Congress by the largest group of women representatives ever.*

Timothy Phelps and Helen Winternitz, *Capitol Games: Clarence Thomas, Anita Hill and the Story of a Supreme Court Nomination* (New York: Hyperion, 1992). *A close look at the Senate hearings on Clarence Thomas's nomination to the Supreme Court.*

Steven Waldman, *The Bill: How the Adventures of Clinton's National Service Bill Reveal What Is Corrupt, Comic, Cynical—and Noble—About Washington* (New York: Viking, 1995). *How a bill becomes a law in the 1990s, with a focus on Clinton's national service and student loan proposals.*

➤NOTES

1. These quotes, and much of this background information, are from Michael Barone and Grant Ujifusa, *The Almanac of American Politics* (Washington: National Journal, 1994), pp. 1108–9; other sources include "Special Report," *Congressional Quarterly Weekly Report* (October 22, 1994), p. 3048; "The Last Stretch," *Congressional Quarterly Weekly Report,* August 7, 1993, pp. 2125, 2129. See also Marjorie Margolies-Mezvinsky, *A Woman's Place: The Freshmen Women Who Changed the Face of Congress* (New York: Crown, 1994).

2. John Hibbing and Elizabeth Theiss-Morse, *Congress as Public Enemy* (Cambridge, Mass.: Cambridge University Press, 1995). The next three paragraphs draw from this source.

3. Ibid.

4. Richard Fenno, "U.S. House Members and Their Constituencies: An Exploration," *American Political Science Review* 71 (September 1977), pp. 883–917. The data in this paragraph are from the Washington Post/ABC Polls, reported in *Washington Post National Weekly Edition,* July 11–17, 1994, p. 7.

5. Hibbing and Theiss-Morse, *Congress as Public Enemy.*

6. Fenno, "U.S. House Members and Their Constituencies."

7. Richard Fenno, "If, as Ralph Nader Says, Congress Is 'The Broken Branch,' How Come We Love Our Congressmen So Much?" in Norman Ornstein, ed., *Congress and Change* (New York: Praeger, 1974), pp. 277–87.

8. Michael Berkman, "State Legislators in Congress," *American Journal of Political Science* 38 (November 1994), pp. 1025–1055.

9. Robert Erikson and Gerald Wright, Jr., "Policy Representation of Constituency Interests," *Political Behavior* 2 (1980), pp. 91–106; Erikson and Wright, "Voters, Candidates, and Issues in Congressional Elections," in Lawrence Dodd and Bruce Oppenheimer, eds., *Congress Reconsidered,* 3rd ed. (Washington, D.C.: CQ Press; Wright, "Policy Voting in the U.S. Senate: Who Is Represented?" *Legislative Studies Quarterly* 14 (November 1989), pp. 465–86. See also Robert Erikson and Norman Luttbeg, *American Public Opinion* (New York: John Wiley & Sons, 1973), p. 257; William Shaffer, "The Ideological and Partisan Linkages between U.S. Senators and Their Constituents," paper prepared at the Annual Meeting of the Midwest Political Science Association, Chicago, 1987; Warren Miller and Donald Stokes, "Constituency Influence in Congress," *American Political Science Review* 56 (March 1963), pp. 45–56.

10. Wright, "Policy Voting in the U.S. Senate."

11. Barbara Vobejda, "Losing the Numbers Game," *Washington Post National Weekly Edition,* September 24–30, 1990, p. 13.

12. 369 U.S. 186 (1962).

13. *Wesberry v. Sanders,* 376 U.S. 1 (1964).

14. Bruce Cain and Janet Campagna, "Predicting Partisan Redistricting Disputes," *Legislative Studies Quarterly* 12 (1987), pp. 265–74.

15. See report in *New York Times,* July 2, 1995, of the *Miller v. Johnson* (94–631) decisions, pp. E1, E4.

16. Steven A. Holmes, "Did Racial Redistricting Undermine Democrats?" *New York Times* (November 13, 1994), p. 32.

17. Kevin A. Hill, "Does the Creation of Majority Black Districts Aid Republicans? An Analysis of the 1992 Congressional Elections in Eight States," *Journal of Politics* 57 (May, 1995), pp. 384–401; Holmes, "Did Racial Redistricting Undermine Democrats?" November 13, 1994; Juan Williams, "How Black Liberal Strategy Failed Its Followers," *Washington Post National Weekly Edition,* November 28–December 3, 1994, p. 25.

18. See Thomas E. Mann, "Elections and Change in Congress," in Thomas Mann and Norman Ornstein, eds., *The New Congress* (Washington, D.C.: American Enterprise Institute, 1981), pp. 32–54; David Mayhew, *The Electoral Connection* (New Haven: Yale University Press, 1974); Glenn Parker and Roger Davidson, "Why Do Americans Love Their Congressmen So Much?" *Legislative Studies Quarterly* (February 1979), pp. 53–62.

19. Thomas Mann and Raymond Wolfinger, "Candidates and Parties in Congressional Elections," *American Political Science Review* 74 (September 1980), pp. 617–32; Patricia Hurley and Kim Q. Hill, "The Prospects for Issue Voting in Contemporary Congressional Elections," *American Politics Quarterly* 8 (October 1980), p. 446.

20. John Alford and John Hibbing, "The Disparate Electoral Security of House and Senate Incumbents," paper presented at the American Political Science meetings, Atlanta, Georgia, September 1989.

21. Richard Fenno, *Home Style* (Boston: Little, Brown, 1978).

22. Susan Trausch, *It Came from the Swamp: Your Federal Government at Work* (New York: Houghton Mifflin, 1986).

23. Tim Miller, "Frankly Free Mail Seems to Help Incumbents," *Washington Post National Weekly Edition,* August 8, 1985, pp. 13–14. For an investigation of the impact of franked mail, see Albert Cover, "The Electoral Impact of Franked Congressional Mail," *Polity* 17 (Summer 1985), pp. 649–63.

24. Miller, "Frankly Free Mail Seems to Help Incumbents."

25. See Glenn Parker, "Sources of Change in Congressional District Attentiveness," *American Journal of Political Science* (February 1980), pp. 115–24.

26. Carol Matlack, "Live from Capitol Hill," *National Journal,* February 18, 1989, p. 390.

27. *Setting Course: A Congressional Management Guide* (Washington, D.C.: American University Congressional Management Program, 1984); *Vital Statistics on Congress*, 1992, p. 161.

28. Norman Ornstein, Thomas E. Mann, and Michael Malbin, *Vital Statistics on Congress*, 1991–1992 (Washington, D.C.: American Enterprise Institute, 1992), tables 5-3, 5-4.

29. Morris Fiorina, "Congressional Control of the Bureaucracy: A Mismatch of Incentives and Capabilities," in Lawrence C. Dodd and Bruce I. Oppenheimer, eds., *Congress Reconsidered*, 2nd ed. (Washington, D.C.: CQ Press, 1981), p. 341.

30. Morris Fiorina, *Congress: Keystone of the Washington Establishment* (New Haven: Yale University Press, 1977), especially pp. 48–49.

31. Robert Sherill, "Squealing on Porcine Politics," *Washington Post National Weekly Edition*, September 7–12, 1992, p. 35; the quote is by Alan Schick from Brian Kelly, "Pigging Out at the White House," *Washington Post National Weekly Edition*, September 14–20, 1992, p. 23.

32. Cass Peterson "Despite Gramm-Rudman Diet, The House Still Likes Its Pork," *Washington Post National Weekly Edition*, November 25, 1985, p. 13.

33. Michael Wines, "Watch out with That Budget Ax. My District NEEDS That Dam," *New York Times*, July 30, 1995, p. E7. "Hypocrites of Pork," *Newsweek*, April 12, 1993, p. 26.

34. Quoted in Kenneth Shepsle, "The Failures of Congressional Budgeting," *Social Science and Modern Society* 20 (1983), pp. 4–10. See also Howard Kurtz, "Pork Barrel Politics," *Washington Post*, January 25, 1982, reported in Randall Ripley, *Congress*, 3rd ed. (New York: W. W. Norton, 1983).

35. See Paul Feldman and James Jondrow, "Congressional Elections and Local Federal Spending," *American Journal of Political Science* 28 (1984), p. 152; Glenn R. Parker and Suzanne Parker, "The Correlates and Effects of Attention to District by U.S. House Members," *Legislative Studies Quarterly* 10 (1985), p. 239.

36. Christopher Buckley, "Hangin' with the Houseboyz," *Washington Monthly*, June 1992, p. 44.

37. Linda L. Fowler, *Who Decides to Run for Congress?* (New Haven: Yale University Press, 1989); Linda L. Fowler, *Candidates, Congress and the American Democracy* (Ann Arbor, University of Michigan Press, 1993).

38. Thomas Mann, *Unsafe at Any Margin: Interpreting Congressional Elections* (Washington, D.C.: American Enterprise Institute, 1978).

39. "Women, Minorities Join Senate," *CQ Almanac*, 1992, pp. 8A–14A; "Wave of Diversity Spared Many Incumbents," *CQ Almanac*, 1992, pp. 15A–21A, 24A; "The Elections" *CQ*, November 12, 1994, p. 3237.

40. Gary Jacobson, *The Politics of Congressional Elections*, 2nd ed. (Boston: Little, Brown, 1987), p. 51.

41. Ibid.

42. Barbara Hinckley, "The American Voter in Congressional Elections," *American Political Science Review* 74 (September 1980), pp. 641–50; Hinckley, "House Reelections and Senate Defeats: The Role of the Challenger," *British Journal of Political Science* 10 (October 1980), pp. 441–60; Mann and Wolfinger, "Candidates and Parties"; Alan I. Abramowitz, "A Comparison of Voting of U.S. Senators and Representatives in 1978," *American Political Science Review* 74 (September 1980), pp. 633–40.

43. Alford and Hibbing, "The Disparate Electoral Security of House and Senate Incumbents."

44. A good review of these arguments is found in John R. Hibbing and Sara L. Brandes, "State Population and the Electoral Success of U.S. Senators," *American Journal of Political Science* 27 (November 1983), pp. 808–19. See also Eric Uslaner, "The Case of the Vanishing Liberal Senators: The House Did It," *British Journal of Political Science* 11 (January 1981), pp. 105–13; Abramowitz, "A Comparison . . . ."

45. Hibbing and Brandes, "State Population . . . ." See also Glenn Parker, "Stylistic Change in the U.S. Senate," *Journal of Politics* 47 (November 1985), pp. 1190–1202.

46. Edie Goldenberg and Michael Traugott, *Campaigning for Congress* (Washington, D.C.: CQ Press, 1984); Gary Jacobson and Samuel Kernell, *Strategy and Choice in Congressional Elections*, 2nd ed. (New Haven: Yale University Press, 1983).

47. Edward Walsh, "Wanted: Candidates for Congress," *Washington Post National Weekly Edition*, November 25, 1985, p. 9.

48. Paul Herrnson, "Do Parties Make a Difference? The Role of Parties in Congressional Elections," *Journal of Politics* 48 (August 1986), pp. 589–615.

49. Alan Ehrenhalt, "Technology, Strategy Bring New Campaign Era," *Congressional Quarterly Weekly Report*, December 7, 1985, p. 2561; Mann, "Elections and Change in Congress"; Jacobson, *The Politics of Congressional Elections.*

50. Paul Hernson, *Party Campaigning in the 1980s* (Cambridge, Mass.: Harvard University Press, 1988).

51. See Gerald Wright, Jr. and Michael Berkman, "Candidates and Policy in United States Senate Elections," *American Political Science Review* 80 (June 1986), pp. 567–88; Erikson and Wright, "Voters, Candidates, and Issues in Congressional Elections."

52. See James Campbell, "Explaining Presidential Losses in Midterm Elections," *Journal of Politics* 47 (November 1985), pp. 1140–57. See also Barbara Hinckley, "Interpreting House Midterm Elections," *American Political Science Review* 61 (1967), pp. 694–700; Samuel Kernell, "Presidential Popularity and Negative Voting," *American Political Science Review* 71 (1977), pp. 44–66; Edward Tufte, "Determinants of the Outcomes of Midterm Congressional Elections," *American Political Science Review* 69 (1975), pp. 812–26; Alan Abramowitz, "Economic Conditions, Presidential Popularity and Voting Behavior in Midterm Elections," *Journal of Politics* 47 (February 1985), pp. 31–43.

53. Herbert Asher, "Learning of Legislative Norms," *American Political Science Review* 67 (June 1973); pp. 499–513. Michael Berkman points out that those freshmen who have had state legislative experience—now more than half of all House members—adapt to the job faster than other members. See "Former State Legislators in the U.S. House of Representatives: Institutional and Policy Mastery," *Legislative Studies Quarterly* 18 (February 1993), pp. 77–104.

54. Minot (North Dakota) *Daily News*, June 17, 1976, quoted in Ripley, *Congress.*

55. Samuel Kernell, *Going Public* (Washington, D.C.: CQ Press, 1986).

56. Quoted in W. Mark Crain and Brian Goff, *Televised Legislatures: Political Information Technology and Public Choice* (Boston: Kluwer, 1988), p. 19. See also R. E. Cohen, "The Congress Watchers," *National Journal*, January 26, 1985, p. 215. For an examination of the Senate debate, see Richard Fenno, "The Senate Thru the Looking Glass: The Debate over Television," *Legislative Studies Quarterly* 14 (August, 1989), pp. 313–48.

57. Cohen, "The Congress Watchers."

58. Ronald Garay, *Congressional Television: A Legislative History* (Westport, Conn.: Grenwood Press, 1984), p. 143; Michael Robinson, "Three Faces of Congressional Media," in Thomas Mann and

Norman Ornstein, eds., *The New Congress* (Washington, D.C.: American Enterprise Institute, 1981), p. 68.

59. Katharine Q. Seelye, "Gingrich Used TV Skills to Be King of the Hill," *New York Times*, December 14, 1994, p. A14.

60. Ibid.

61. Diane Duston, "They're Angry, Conservative, and They're Dialing Right Now," *Centre Daily Times* (AP Release), July 16, 1993, p. 1. The study was done by the Times-Mirror Center for the People and the Press.

62. Richard Fenno, "U.S. House Members in Their Constituencies: An Exploration," *American Political Science Review* 71 (1977), pp. 883–917; and Fenno, *Home Style*.

63. Benjamin Page et al., "Constituency, Party and Representation in Congress," *Public Opinion Quarterly* 48 (Winter 1984), pp. 741–56; Jerrold E. Schneider, *Ideological Coalitions in Congress* (Westport, Conn.: Greenwood Press, 1979).

64. John Kingdon, *Congressmen's Voting Decisions* (New York: Harper & Row, 1973).

65. Congressional Quarterly, *The Origins and Development of Congress* (Washington, D.C.: CQ Press, 1976).

66. Neil McNeil, *Forge of Democracy* (New York: McKay, 1963), pp. 306–309.

67. Susan Welch and John G. Peters, "Private Interests in the U.S. Congress," *Legislative Studies Quarterly* 7 (November 1982), pp. 547–55.

68. See Roger Davidson, "Subcommittee Government," in Mann and Ornstein, *The New Congress*, pp. 110–11. Some of this occurs because members of Congress tend to be wealthy, and the wealthy make investments in corporations. It also occurs because members' financial interests are often similar to the interests in their districts (e.g., representatives of farm districts are likely to be involved in farming or agribusiness).

69. Ehrenhalt, "Media, Power Shifts to Dominate O'Neill's House"; Stephen Hess, "Live from Capitol Hill, It's . . .," *Washington Monthly* (June 1986), pp. 41–43. The Biden quotation is from this article. See also Steven Smith and Christopher Deering, *Committees in Congress* (Washington, D.C.: CQ Press, 1984), p. 67.

70. Eric Planin, "David Obey Appropriates a New Fiefdom," *Washington Post National Weekly Edition*, May 9–15, 1994, p. 11.

71. John Hibbing and Sara Brandes-Crook, "Congressional Reform and Party Discipline: The Effects of Changes in the Seniority System on Party Loyalty in the U.S. House of Representatives," *British Journal of Political Science* 15 (April 1985).

72. Eleanor Clift, "The Prince of Pork," *Newsweek* (April 15, 1991), p. 35.

73. John Fairhall, quoting Thomas Downey (D-N.Y.), "Bureaucratic Bloat Crippling Congress," *Lincoln Journal-Star*, June 7, 1992, p. 7B.

74. Michael J. Malbin, "Delegation, Deliberation, and the New Role of Congressional Staff," in Mann and Ornstein, *The New Congress*, p. 135.

75. Ibid. pp. 170–77.

76. Alan Ehrenhalt, "In the Senate of the '80s, Team Spirit Has Given Way to the Rule of Individuals," *Congressional Quarterly Weekly Report*, September 4, 1982, p. 2175.

77. Ronald Moe and Steven Teel, "Congress as a Policy-Maker: A Necessary Reappraisal," *Political Science Quarterly* 85 (September 1970), pp. 443–70.

78. Bruce Oppenheimer, "The Rules Committee," in Lawrence Dodd and Bruce Oppenheimer, eds., *Congress Reconsidered* (New York: Praeger, 1977), p. 96–116.

79. Stanley Cloud, "Return of the Lions," *Time*, May 31, 1993, p. 28. The quote is by John Dingell (D-Mich.).

80. Thomas Geoghegan, "Bust the Filibuster," *Washington Post National Weekly Edition*, July 12–18, 1994, p. 25.

81. Michael Malbin, "Leading a Filibustered Senate," in *Extensions* (Norman, Okla.: University of Oklahoma, Carl A. Albert Center, Spring 1985), p. 3.

82. Louis Fisher, "A Washington Guidebook," *Public Administration Review* (January/February 1989), p. 86.

83. Morris Ogul, "Congressional Oversight: Structures and Incentives," in Dodd and Oppenheimer, *Congress Reconsidered*. See also Loch Johnson, "The U.S. Congress and the CIA: Monitoring the Dark Side of Government," *Legislative Studies Quarterly* 5 (November 1980), pp. 477–501.

84. Joseph Califano, "Imperial Congress," *New York Times Magazine*, January 23, 1994, p. 41.

85. Morris Fiorina, "Congressional Control of the Bureaucracy: A Mismatch of Incentives and Capabilities," in Dodd and Oppenheimer, *Congress Reconsidered*, pp. 332–48.

86. Aaron Wildavsky, *The Politics of the Budgetary Process* (Boston: Little, Brown, 1964).

87. D. Roderick Kiewiet and Matthew McCubbins, "Congressional Appropriations and the Electoral Connection," *Journal of Politics* 47 (February 1985), pp. 59–82.

88. John Hibbing, "The Liberal Hour: Electoral Pressures and Transfer Payment Voting in the United States Congress," *Journal of Politics* 46 (August 1984), pp. 846–65.

89. Allen Schick, *Congress and Money* (Washington, D.C.: Urban Institute, 1980).

90. Michael Wines, "Washington Really Is in Touch. We're the Problem," *New York Times* (October 16, 1994), section 4, p. 2.

91. Broder, "Who Took the Fun? . . ."

92. Richard Morin and Thomas Edsall, "Bumping Up Against the Public Perception," *Washington Post National Weekly Edition*, April 17–23, 1995, p. 14. See also John Hibbing and Elizabeth Theiss-Morse," Civics Is Not Enough," forthcoming, *PS*.

93. Bill Turque, "Housebroken," *Newsweek*, November 29, 1993, pp. 32ff.

94. Ibid. See also Margolies-Mezvinsky's story in "Freshman Rush—First You Run to Get Elected, Then You Just Keep Running," *Washingtonian Magazine* (April, 1993), pp. 76–80.

11 The Presidency

You Are There

Retreat Again?

It is February 1995, and you are Bill Clinton. Beginning the third year of your presidential term, you are confronted with a tough decision. Should you stick by your nominee for surgeon general, Henry W. Foster, Jr., or should you withdraw the nomination in the face of growing opposition?

This nomination, like many other high-level positions, must be confirmed by a vote of the Senate before the person can take office. Before the Senate votes on the nomination, the candidate must undergo a public hearing before the Senate Labor and Human Resources Committee and win a positive vote from the committee. Because the Republicans are a majority in the Senate, they have a majority on this committee.

You have had trouble with several nominations already. Your first nominee for surgeon general, Joycelyn Elders, was confirmed and served almost two years. But she was controversial throughout her service, speaking out in favor of choice in abortion and about the school's role in sex education to prevent teen-age pregnancy and disease. You finally asked for her resignation when she was quoted as saying that children should be taught about masturbation. Your first nominee for attorney general, Lani Guinier, also proved to be controversial, and you withdrew her nomination before she even was able to appear before a Senate committee hearing. She had been an advocate of consideration of different forms of voting (such as multimember districts and proportional representation) in order to promote the electoral strength of minorities. Opponents of affirmative action led the attack on her. Both Elders and Guinier were black women.

You also withdrew other nominees, including a woman attorney general candidate who had hired an illegal alien to do household work. Overall, you and your staff have been highly criticized for slowness in making nominations and lacking adequate background information on the nominees; having to withdraw nominees gives the impression you are weak and vacillating.

Now the nightmare continues. You are faced with a seemingly no-win situation because of both your political allies and your enemies. Your allies, in particular your own staff, helped cause your problems because of sloppy background work. You choose Dr. Foster because he was a well-known doctor and educator. You believed he could lead a national campaign to reduce teen pregnancy.[1] He had led such a campaign in his hometown of Nashville, Tennessee, through his "I have a future" program. In fact, George Bush awarded him his "thousand points of light" award only four years ago for the success of this campaign. Foster, like you born in Arkansas, was the only black in his medical school class at the University of Arkansas. He had been chair of the Department of Obstetrics and Gynecology at Meharry Medical College in Nashville and later president of the college.

But only a day after you announced his nomination, he became embroiled in the abortion controversy. As an obstetrician, he had delivered over 10,000 babies. But he also performed some abortions. When the question of just how many

CONTINUED 

OUTLINE

Presidential Job Description
- Qualifications
- Tenure
- Succession
- Rewards

Growth of the Modern Presidency
- The Presidency Before the New Deal
- Development of the Personal Presidency

Presidential Power
- Persuading the Washingtonians
- Persuading the Public
- Presidential Popularity
- Limits of Presidential Power

Roles of the President
- Growth of Presidential Staff
- Administrative Leadership
- Domestic Policy Leadership
- Foreign Policy Leadership
- Military Leadership
- Symbolic Leadership
- Party Leadership

Conclusion: Is the Presidency Responsive?

abortions was first raised, White House officials told Nancy Kassebaum, the chair of the Senate Labor and Human Resources Committee, that Dr. Foster had performed only one abortion. Then Foster said he had performed less than a dozen abortions, mostly to save women's lives or because of rape or incest. A few days later, after he did a more thorough check of his records, he said he had done 39 abortions.

These different stories drew fire not only from abortion opponents, but from others who charge that Dr. Foster was not being honest. One opponent called for withdrawal of the nomination, claiming that "The litmus test is truthtelling, and on this point, the president's and Dr. Foster's versions of the truth differ from day to day."[2] But Dr. Foster claimed that it is not a common practice for doctors to keep track in their heads of how many procedures of any kind they have done, and that it was not his intent to deceive. Rather, he said, he was trying to provide a quick answer to a question. But others claim that he and the White House staff should have done better homework on this issue.

Even some Democrats are angry with you and your staff. Joseph Biden (D.-Del.) announced he would vote against Foster, though he later said he would withhold judgment. Paul Simon (D.-Ill.) noted that the nomination was in trouble.

Your enemies seem jubilant; you seem to have botched another key appointment. Many people urged that you withdraw this nomination. Anti-abortion groups quickly lined up against Dr. Foster. A number of prominent Republicans also attacked him for doing abortions. Senator Kassebaum, a moderate Republican and a moderate on the abortion issue, attacked you and your aides for the poor handling of this sensitive issue, and even senators from your own party were critical. Your staff forgot to think about the fact that obstetricians do abortions, and once the question was raised were not able to provide specific answers to the seemingly simple question of how often Dr. Foster did them.

What do you do? On the one hand, you can withdraw the nomination, bowing to the same conservative forces that were vocal in opposing Joycelyn Elders. If you do this, you are sure to lose the battle and your image as a weak and vacillating leader will be confirmed. However, this would be the quickest way to cut your losses and not drag Dr. Foster through what could possibly be a very stressful and embarrassing process. Even if you stick with the nomination, the chances of his winning are slim given Republican opposition.

On the other hand, there are several reasons why you could continue to back Dr. Foster. Withdrawing his nomination could be seen as a slap at African-Americans. As the secretary of the Nashville branch of the NAACP (a civil rights group) said: "The African American community is once again reminded how the Clinton administration has succumbed to pressure by removing support for dedicated African American public servants. We have not forgotten the mistreatment of Lani Guinier, Mike Espy, and Dr. Joycelyn Elders."[3]

Moreover, in his recent comments, Dr. Foster seemed to have recovered his poise and began to spread his message about decreasing teen-age pregnancy. He defended his abortion record, claiming "It's the law of the land," and noting that he, like the president, believed that "abortions should be safe, legal, and rare."[4] And it is not clear that those who were initially upset with you will vote against Foster. For example, though Nancy Kassebaum has expressed her displeasure with White House handling of the abortion issue, she is considered a fair-minded, independent person. With her as chair of the committee that will conduct the hearings on Dr. Foster, perhaps the nomination will squeak through. Sticking by Dr. Foster, if he won, would certainly help improve your image as a strong leader. Even if he loses, you may gain from being steadfast.

What do you do?

The president of the United States is one of the most powerful people in the world. His likes and dislikes, prejudices and preoccupations affect almost everyone. The scope of his power has led some observers to write about an "imperial" presidency.[5] His physical health, activities, ideas, and stamina generate intense media coverage.

Yet all recent presidents have suffered reelection defeats or left office under a cloud. They have seemed powerless to shape events affecting the national interest and their own reputations. A conservative Congress frustrated John Kennedy's policy initiatives before his assassination. Lyndon Johnson's candidacy for reelection was killed by a war that took Richard Nixon six years to end. And Nixon had to resign from office because of his Watergate coverup. Ronald Reagan, one of our most popular presidents, was so frustrated by terrorism and Nicaragua that he condoned illegal activities, producing the Iran-contra scandal and a tarnished personal reputation. Gerald Ford, Jimmy Carter, and George Bush failed to get reelected, the latter hurt by economic problems and doubts about his leadership on domestic issues. And now Bill Clinton is finding out that instead of an imperial presidency, we may have an "impossible" or "imperiled" presidency.[6] Little wonder that a recent survey found that 52% of Americans would rather spend one week in jail than serve one term as president and that many Americans, instead of believing the president is too powerful, believe he is too weak to battle Congress and interest groups.[7]

We will consider the paradox of presidential power and presidential weakness. After describing the requirements for being president, we will examine the office's growth and see why modern incumbents are both powerful and vulnerable. We then will discuss the president's various responsibilities.

➤Presidential Job Description

Pharaohs, consuls, kings, queens, emperors, czars, prime ministers, and councils of various sizes served as executives in other governments before 1787. But no national government had a president, an elected executive with authority equal to and independent of a national legislature, until we did.

Qualifications

There are formal, constitutional qualifications to be president: One must be a "natural born citizen," at least 35 years old, and a resident of the United States for at least 14 years before taking office.

Informally, it also helps to be a white male with roots in small-town America, a Protestant of English, German, or Scandinavian background, from a state with a large population, and a good family man. In recent years, however, this profile has broadened considerably as society has become more tolerant of diversity, though gender and racial barriers still remain.

Tenure

Presidents have four-years terms. The Twenty-second Amendment limits them to serving two terms, or ten years if they complete the term of an incumbent who dies or resigns. Eight presidents have died in office from illness or violence. The first was William Harrison, who caught a fatal cold at his inaugural parade in 1841, and the last was Kennedy, who was assassinated in 1963. In 1974, Nixon was the first to resign.

Congress may remove presidents and other civil officers in a two-step process. The House decides questions of impeachment, or whether to bring charges of "high crimes and misdemeanors" (this phrase includes serious crimes and, depending on the mood of congressional majorities, political abuses). If a House majority favors impeachment, it notifies the Senate, which must mobilize a two-thirds majority to remove an accused president from office.

Two presidents have faced impeachment and removal. One vote in the Senate saved Andrew Johnson from removal after the Civil War. Nixon's role in Watergate crimes led the House Judiciary Committee to recommend his impeachment. He avoided it by resigning.

The Founders meant Congress's impeachment and removal power to be one of the checks and balances, a final weapon against executive unresponsiveness. However, the procedures involved are cumbersome. Presidents usually have enough clout to avoid them, so Congress has rarely used these powers.

Succession

The Constitution says only that presidential powers and duties "shall devolve on the Vice President" if a president dies, resigns, or cannot execute them. It directs Congress to choose a successor if there is no vice president. Congress passed the Presidential Succession Act of 1947 two years after Franklin Roosevelt's death in office. It lists the officers who become president, starting with the Speaker of the House of Representatives and the president pro tempore of the Senate and ending with the head of the most recently created cabinet department.

The Succession Act has never been used because we have always had a vice president when something happened to the president. The Twenty-fifth Amendment was ratified in 1967 to ensure, as much as possible, that this will always be the case. It directs that, if the office falls vacant, the president must name a new vice president acceptable to majorities in the House and Senate. The amendment has been used twice. Nixon chose Gerald Ford to replace Spiro Agnew, who resigned after pleading no contest to charges of taking bribes when he was a public official in Maryland. Ford then named Nelson Rockefeller his vice president after Nixon resigned.

Whether a president is well enough to do his job is not always clear. James Garfield was shot in July 1881 and did not die until mid-September. In 1919, Woodrow Wilson had a nervous collapse in the summer and a stroke in the fall and was incapacitated for many months. No one was sure about his condition, however, because his wife restricted access to him. In both cases, the issue of who was or should have been acting as president was unclear.

Another section of the Twenty-fifty Amendment charges the vice president and a majority of the cabinet (or some other body named by Congress) to determine if a president is able to do his job. The vice president becomes "acting president" if they find the president incapacitated. The president resumes his functions after notifying Congress of his recovery. Reagan followed the spirit of this section in 1985. Before undergoing cancer surgery, he sent his vice president, George Bush, a letter authorizing him to act as president while Reagan was unconscious.

Rewards

The president's salary of $200,000 a year is large by most standards but seems almost small compared to the job's other benefits. These benefits include living in one of the world's most famous mansions, a rural retreat (Camp David), fleets of aircraft and cars, and a generous pension as well as money for an office and staff after leaving office.

Many people believed that Edith Galt Wilson, the president's wife, was making the decisions during President Wilson's illness.

No one argues that the president's material rewards should be slight. However, perhaps daily life on Pennsylvania Avenue is too isolated from the daily realities of most citizens. Shortly after his inauguration, Bill Clinton described the White House as "the crown jewel in the American prison system" when he found he could not do many everyday things (like jogging on public streets and making unplanned trips to fast-food restaurants). Given daily life in the White House, might a president come to think he is more special than we want him to be, that his views are better than others?

Growth of the Modern Presidency

The Presidency Before the New Deal

Most presidents during the 1800s and early 1900s were "ordinary people with very ordinary reputations."[8] James Monroe, who served from 1817 to 1825, wore outdated knee breeches, silk stockings, ink-spotted clothing, and worn-down shoes. He looked, according to a European diplomat, like an unkempt clerk.[9] The nineteenth century was an age of legislative power. Indeed, Woodrow Wilson wrote a book calling national government in the 1880s "congressional government."

The Founders largely viewed the president as a presiding office. Before 1932, most people saw Congress as the representative and policymaking part of government. They saw presidential leadership as a threat to responsive government. As a result, the office tended to attract individuals of average ability who did not try to be leaders and who regarded administering the law as their primary job.

The powerful presidents before the New Deal—Washington, Jackson, Lincoln, Teddy Roosevelt, and Wilson—were the exceptions and not the rule. Washington set many important precedents. For example, he initiated meetings of department heads, or cabinet meetings. Jackson was the first to act assertively to fulfill the popular mandate he saw in his election—the first to veto a bill because *he* did not like it. Lincoln

Vice Presidency

Job

Vice presidents of private corporations work on matters of importance to their firms. This has only recently been true of United States vice presidents. Historically, the only jobs vice presidents have had were to preside over the Senate and cast tie-breaking votes. Presidents have traditionally given vice presidents little information and few opportunities for involvement. Harry Truman did not know about the atom bomb when he became president after Franklin Roosevelt's (FDR's) death, but within months he had to decide about using it on Japan.

Gerald Ford's vice president, Nelson Rockefeller, called the job "standby equipment." Others have been less charitable. Woodrow Wilson's vice president, Thomas R. Marshall, said holding the job is like being "a man in a cataleptic fit: He cannot speak, he cannot move. He suffers no pain. He is perfectly conscious of all that goes on. But he has no part in it." FDR's first vice president, John Nance Garner, was less elegant in observing that his job was not worth a "pitcher of warm spit."

FDR had told Garner, "You tend to your office and I'll tend to mine." The problem was that there was little to tend. Historically, presidents have had difficulty delegating important jobs to their vice presidents because they themselves have wanted to wield all the power.

Until Jimmy Carter, presidents asked their vice presidents to deal mainly with partisan or ceremonial matters. Vice presidents helped mend party fences and criticized the opposition in harsher terms than the president could use without damaging his image as president of all the people. Spiro Agnew gained considerable attention for calling Nixon's opponents "effete intellectuals," among other things.

Carter was the first president to use his vice president, Walter Mondale, for important work. Carter had no national experience before his election and considered Mondale, a former United States senator, a major asset. Carter gave Mondale a White House office (as opposed to one in the Old Executive Office Building next door), scheduled weekly lunches with him, put him on all White House advisory groups, and had him attend all important meetings, lobby Congress, and read the paperwork that crossed Carter's desk. Ronald Reagan and George Bush did much the same with their vice presidents, and Bill Clinton has added to this new tradition. He has let his vice president, Al Gore, influence his political appointments, review and offer suggestions for many of his speeches, and influence issues related to the environment, advanced technology, and bureaucratic reform.

Although tensions sometimes exist between the vice president's staff and the president's, as a reflection of their separate political careers, there is incentive for cooperation. Given the great public exposure of the White House, it is not to either official's interest to appear on bad terms with the other.

Springboard to the White House?

George Bush was the first incumbent vice president to win a presidential election since Martin Van Buren in 1836. That 34 men after Van Buren failed to win the presidency while serving as vice president led to talk of a "Van Buren Jinx." According to it, a vice president cannot win the White House because he is saddled with the negatives of his president's record without being able to take credit for his successes. Evidence for this are the failed presidential bids of Richard Nixon, Hubert Humphrey, and Walter Mondale. In 1960, Nixon received little help from the popular Dwight Eisenhower, who preferred to avoid partisan battles and did not like Nixon personally. Opposition to the Vietnam War and Lyndon Johnson hurt Humphrey in 1968. And Reagan would not let Mondale escape Carter's shadow in 1984.

However, the "jinx" may be a fiction.[1] Only 7 of the 34 vice presidents from Van Buren to Bush actually ran for president while they were vice president. When Nixon lost in 1960 and Humphrey in 1968 (to former vice president Nixon!), they lost by very little. In fact, recent history shows that vice presidents do become presidential frontrunners. Six of the last nine vice presidents were nominated to be president.

The caliber of recent vice presidents indicates that the office may have become more important. Most have been seasoned public servants with considerable experience and personal records of achievement. That they were willing to take the job suggests it has become more than "standby equipment." Perhaps the furor over the qualifications (or lack of them) of Dan Quayle, Bush's vice president, reflects the fact that the public thinks the vice presidency is worth a highly qualified candidate.

---

[1] Michael Nelson, *A Heartbeat Away* (New York: Priority Press, 1988). For more on the vice-presidency, see Paul C. Light, *Vice-Presidential Power: Advice and Influence in the White House* (Baltimore: Johns Hopkins University Press, 1984), and George Sirgiovanni, "The 'Van Buren Jinx': Vice Presidents Need Not Beware," *Presidential Studies Quarterly* 18 (Winter 1988), pp. 61–76.

Although political scientists rank Jefferson as a great president, he did not consider the office, or his performance in it, very important. His instructions for an epitaph listed what he thought were his three main accomplishments in life: authoring the Declaration of Independence and a Virginia law guaranteeing religious freedom and founding the University of Virginia. He did not include his presidential office.

boldly and creatively interpreted the Constitution to say individual states could not legally leave the Union. Teddy Roosevelt understood our growing national power and sent a fleet halfway around the world to show off American strength, although he had only enough money to send it that far and Congress had to pay for bringing it home. Wilson was the first twentieth-century president to lead us into a major foreign involvement, World War I.

Someone once said Americans were lucky because we always got presidential leadership when we needed it: during the birth of the nation, the Civil War, and foreign crises. This implies that our needs change, that we need more government and executive leadership during crises and less at other times. Presidential power was traditionally supposed to return to its "normal" low profile after we resolved special problems.

Development of the Personal Presidency

The presidency has grown considerably since the nineteenth century because people want more services from government and because they look to the president for leadership. Theodore Lowi believes that we have had a **personal presidency** since the New Deal.[10] He argues that, consciously or unconsciously, the American people have had a "new social contract" with the president since the 1930s. In return for getting more power and support from us than we give to other parts of government, the president is supposed to make sure we get what we want from government.

Through the media, presidents amass tremendous personal power directly from the people. Presidents tell us what they think our needs are and give us an opportunity to accept or reject their views. Lowi argues that in the polling booth and in opinion polls we "vote" on each president and his policies. Our views shape presidential policy, power, and the workings of government.

Why did the personal presidency develop? We have already seen in Chapter 3 that the New Deal brought about a large expansion in the role of government, especially the national government. In addition, it brought about a tremendous growth in presidential power. Franklin Roosevelt was elected president in 1932 because people thought he would help them. His policies, which he called the New Deal, put the national government and the presidency in direct contact with many citizens for the first time. People saw presidential leadership as a way to deal with national needs.

Other factors contributed to presidential power too. For example, political parties did not assume a more national character in response to the growth of the national government. As a result, they rarely provide national leadership, and few people look to them for answers to national problems.

Furthermore, Congress has been unable to provide national leadership. Made up of 535 individuals divided into two houses and hundreds of committees and subcommittees, it cannot develop, articulate, or keep its members faithful to national policy goals. Thus, even though the Republican-led House had some early success in "keeping" what its leaders called their "Contract with America" in 1995, the Republican-led Senate often went its own and different way. Congress is also influenced by interest groups that have built effective national organizations. And, of course, it has strong representation from both political parties, another source of divisiveness.

In addition, enacting a flood of New Deal policies to combat Depression-era problems led to the expan-

When President Franklin D. Roosevelt died, most Americans felt a personal loss, as these people showed watching his body being loaded on the train.

sion of the executive branch. New agencies were created and new civil servants hired. This increased the president's power by making him more important as a manager and policymaker.

Finally, radio and television contributed to the expansion of presidential power. As an integral part of national life by the 1930s, broadcasting made the news seem more immediate and compelling. Along with the wire services, it gave people a way to follow presidents and a way for presidents to "sell" their policies and provide leadership. Because it is easier to follow one person than many (as in Congress), the media helped make the presidency the focal point of national politics.

Roosevelt's fireside chats were the first presidential effort to use the media to speak directly and regularly to the nation. They helped make him, and his office, the most important link between people and government. In a personalized style he began, "My friends. . . ." People felt Roosevelt was talking to each of them in their own homes, and they gathered around their radios whenever he was on. Whereas President Herbert Hoover had received an average of 40 letters a day, Roosevelt received 4,000 letters a day after beginning his chats.[11] He even received some addressed not to "The President" but simply to "My Friend, Washington, D.C." More recently, Bush received 2.3 million pieces of mail during his last year in office and Clinton got over 8 million in his first year as well as over 4,000 e-mail messages.

The personal presidency ties government directly to the people and can produce substantial benefits. For example, it gives us something to rally around during times of crisis. The public expressed loyalty to our system after Kennedy's assassination by supporting his successor, Johnson. The personal presidency also contributes to our ability to achieve national goals. Roosevelt was able to build support for New Deal programs because he articulated a persuasive view of what people expected the national government to do. He was the first president to use survey data to identify public needs and to use the media to tell people that he would give them what they wanted. Making himself the major link between public opinion and government often let him overcome the inertia and divisions associated with a system of fragmented powers.

However, Roosevelt's actions also revealed a cost of the personal presidency: Presidents with great power often seek more. Roosevelt won reelection in 1936 by a landslide, confirming popular support for his New Deal. This led him to seek more power by trying to expand the size of an unfriendly Supreme

BERRY'S WORLD. Reprinted by permission of NEA, Inc.

Court so he could appoint judges who supported him. He also tried to get local and state parties to nominate certain congressional candidates by using federal funds as a carrot. The defeat of pro-Roosevelt congressional candidates in 1938 ruined both his plans. People did not want to politicize the Court, and state and local parties wanted to pick their own nominees. Nixon and Reagan also tried to override constitutional limitations on their power after their landslide reelections in 1972 and 1984. The Watergate and Iran-contra scandals were the results.

Incumbents of the personal presidency seek more power because they typically promise more than they can deliver. Their power is based on public support for their programs. The president can increase that support by promising to give people more. Presidents are tempted to do this because they need more power to compete successfully with other parts of government and maintain their public support. Thus, they are caught on a treadmill of making great promises, seeking more power to honor them, and making even greater promises to get more power. Inevitably, they promise more than they can deliver. Bush promised to send astronauts to Mars, protect the environment, be the "education president," and do many other things while cutting the budget deficit without raising taxes. Clinton has also made many promises and said he wants "to do it all as quick as we can."[12]

Given this, Lowi may be right in calling the personal presidency the "victim" of democracy. After Roosevelt's death in 1946, only three of eight presidents left office without experiencing permanently lowered public opinion rations: Eisenhower, Kennedy (who was assassinated in mid-term), and Reagan.[13]

If the personal presidency victimizes presidents, it also victimizes many others. Johnson's promise that he would not be the first president to lose a war not only caused his downfall but also had devastating consequences for many Americans and people in Southeast Asia.

Presidential Power

The presidency has formal powers deriving from the Constitution, acts of Congress, and judicial opinions interpreting them. Thus the Constitution charges presidents with nominating federal judges and members of their administrations, an act of Congress directs them to submit annual budget requests, and judicial decisions have directed presidents to spend money appropriated by Congress.

Although all modern presidents have had the same formal powers, each has used them more or less effectively depending on his native skills and the quality of the people serving him. Circumstances beyond White House control also contribute to the potential for presidential power. The Depression, World War II, and the Cold War contributed to the growth of presidential power because they led Americans to look to the president for leadership against a common threat. Now that these crises are past, Americans are more inclined to criticize presidential initiatives.

Persuading the Washingtonians

To achieve their goals, presidents need more than their formal powers. They need the **power to persuade** people, whom Richard Neustadt called the **Washingtonians,** to support them.[14]

The Washingtonians are members of Congress who vote on a president's proposals, interest group leaders who can mobilize congressional and bureaucratic support, judges who consider challenges to presidential policies, and media leaders who influence public opinion. In short, they are the people the president needs on his side in order to govern. Significantly, these are people over whom the president has no formal authority—he cannot give them orders. Because the Washingtonians also need him to get what they want, a president can bargain and persuade.

The effective president is "one who seizes the center of the Washington bazaar and actively barters . . . to build winning coalitions."[15] Johnson told one member of Congress whose vote he was seeking, "You may need me some time, and I'll remember this if you'll do it." Presidents "remember" their friends by putting their pet projects in the budget, by campaigning for them, and by naming the people they want to public office.

A president's powers give him more favors and penalties to dispense than anyone else. As the chief foreign policymaker, he can seek support from Irish and Jewish Americans by promoting peace in Northern Ireland and the Middle East. As commander-in-chief, he can help local economies by maintaining military bases in some places but not in others. And as chief budget maker, he has many favors to give and withhold. Bush supported new pork barrel projects to get Louisiana Senator J. Bennett Johnson's vote for the multibillion-dollar superconductor project. Clinton penalized Alabama Senator Richard Shelby for criticizing his budget cut proposals (which still left a $31 billion space-station project in Alabama!) by moving a $380 million program to Texas where a Clinton favorite was running for election to the Senate.

Presidential persuasion does not always involve bargaining, however. Presidents also remind fellow Republicans or Democrats of the need to stick together to promote their party platform and achieve party goals. Bush used this tactic in 1990 when he asked former presidents and fellow Republicans Reagan, Ford, and Nixon to call House Republicans to urge them to vote for a budget plan supported by the White House. Bipartisan appeals can be effective too, especially in foreign affairs. In addition, presidents try to convince others of the merits of their positions. For example, having served many years in Congress, Johnson knew how to approach members and was a masterful lobbyist. In working for a foreign aid bill, he invited key members to the White House for one-on-one talks described by an aide as "endless talking, ceaseless importuning, torrential laying on of the facts . . . for several days."[16]

Sometimes presidents are more heavy-handed in seeking support. A Reagan aide described how the White House changed one senator's vote: "We just beat his brains out. We stood him in front of an open grave and told him he could jump in if he wanted to [oppose Reagan]."[17] Such tactics can succeed but make a president look bad. In 1990, Bush was criticized for the way White House staff lobbied Congress for a budget plan. His chief of staff, John Sununu, called Senator Trent Lott (R-Miss.) "insignificant" on television after Lott refused to support the plan, and Sununu alienated others with petty reprisals.

Presidents use the prestige of their office to get support too. In 1975, Ford persuaded 18 House members to change their votes to support one of his vetoes. He took them on his jet, *Air Force One,* and "lectured" them.[18] Because many members rarely, if ever, talk to a president, most consider these conversations memorable events and listen.

Presidents cannot always get the support of those they need, however. Members of Congress have their own constituencies and careers. Interest group leaders have to consider the views of their rank-and-file members. And other Washingtonians have interests that diverge from the president's.

Every president develops a track record of his effectiveness as a leader. Neustadt calls it the president's **professional reputation.**[19] A president with an effective reputation has a record of getting what he wants, helping his allies, and penalizing the opposition.

This reputation contributes to his continuing ability to persuade. Franklin Roosevelt earned his professional reputation because he got Congress to enact much of his legislative program in the first 100 days of his administration. Since Roosevelt, the Washingtonians have expected presidents to make their marks early.

Part of a president's professional reputation is based on how successful he is in getting congressional support. Reagan's effectiveness with Congress and his professional reputation were greatest in his first year in office when he got Congress to make a major tax cut and increase military spending. Economic problems produced in part by these changes and a growing public awareness that he was uninformed about, and uninvolved in, White House routine led to a drop in his effectiveness with Congress and in his professional reputation during the remainder of his administration. As Figure 1 shows, Reagan's congressional support fell after 1981 and was low compared to other presidents.

Compared to other recent presidents, Bush's professional reputation as measured by congressional support was weak throughout his term. Figure 1 shows that his first-year success with Congress was the lowest of any elected president since 1953, when scores were first computed. He also has the lowest two-year record. In part, these scores are products of partisanship. Bush had fewer congressional Republicans to work with than any GOP president in this century. However, low support for Bush among congressional Republicans may have resulted from the absence of a well-articulated White House legislative program.[20] He also failed to capture the public's attention with clear themes, what he once called the "vision thing." One observer wrote, "Nobody ever says 'Let Bush be Bush,' because nobody can be sure what that would be."[21] This prevented Bush from securing more congressional support, even after the Persian Gulf War when his popularity was very high.

Clinton had some early setbacks in dealing with Congress (over two nominees to be attorney general, lifting the ban on gays in the military, and parts of his

FIGURE 1
Presidential Success on Congressional Votes Often Declines Over Time

Presidents usually have the most success with Congress early in their first terms. This figure presents the percentage that presidents won, of the votes on which they took a position. Clinton's 86.4% score in 1993 ranks the highest of any president in his first year since Johnson's 88% in 1964 and Eisenhower's 89% in 1953. President Bush had the smallest first-year success of any of these presidents. In 1995, however, Clinton's score was the lowest since these scores have been kept.

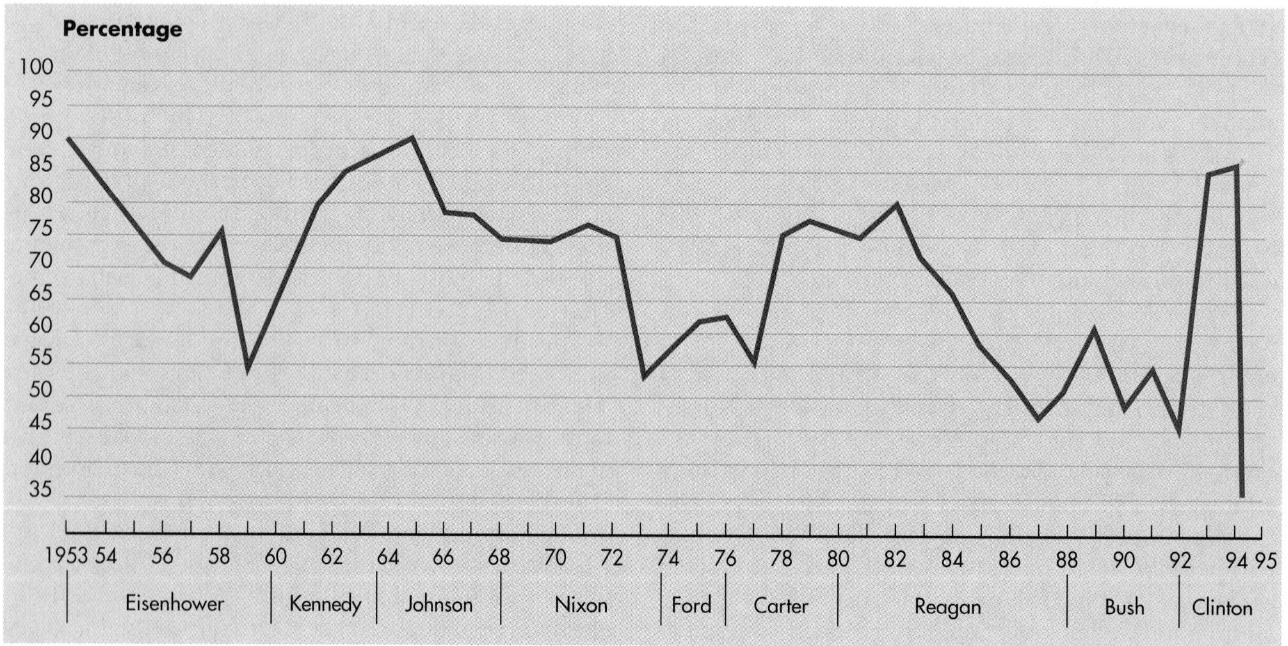

Sources: *Congressional Quarterly Weekly Report,* October 17, 1992, p. 3249; *Congressional Quarterly Weekly Report,* December 18, 1993, pp. 3427–3431; *Congressional Quarterly Weekly Report,* January 27, 1996, p. 239.

economic stimulus package), which raised doubts about his likely effectiveness. He tried, with mixed success, to emulate Reagan's successful first year strategy of asking Congress to vote on a few high-priority bills. This strategy lets presidents define their positions in relatively simple terms and seek congressional support when they are in their postelection honeymoon periods and before other influences on Congress have time to make mobilizing majorities more difficult. Enjoying early successes with Congress can help presidents build their professional reputations.

In dealing with Congress in the first half of his term, Clinton had an advantage neither Reagan nor Bush enjoyed, a partisan majority in each house. Despite substantial disagreements among congressional Democrats, Clinton succeeded in getting most of his early economic proposals passed. In fact, Clinton had the highest first-year success score with Congress (86.4%) since Eisenhower's 89% in 1953 and Johnson's 88% in 1964. And he got more out of Congress in his first two years than Kennedy, Ford, Carter, and Bush combined. Clinton's two-year record of congressional success exceeded that of every president since Johnson, a record that no doubt surprises many people.

Clinton's legislative record was impressive but it did not give him an effective professional reputation. His success was overshadowed by a problem he did not overcome: a failure to articulate larger goals so the American people knew where he wanted to lead them. The congressional defeat of his health care bill in 1994, shortly before the mid-term elections and after he made it his top priority, convinced many Americans that he was an inept leader who could not take advantage of Democratic majorities in Congress when he had them.

Clinton did not have Democratic majorities in the second half of his term. Congress was dominated by Republicans who had their own legislative agenda, their "Contract with America," and Clinton was unable to generate much support for bills he favored. His congressional support score dropped to 36.2% in 1995, the lowest in the forty years these statistics have been kept. Helping Clinton with his professional reputation, however, is the fact that his popularity has actually been rising, while most presidents experience lower popularity toward the end of their terms, as Figure 2 shows.

Persuading the Public

Our earliest presidents typically communicated with Congress in writing and made very few speeches. Abraham Lincoln thought it prudent to avoid giving speeches. He told people gathered at Gettysburg the night before his famous address, "I have no speech to make. In my position it is somewhat important that I should not say foolish things. It very often happens that the only way to help it is to say nothing at all."[22] The development of new transportation and communication technologies gave presidents more opportunities to utilize the presidency as, in Teddy Roosevelt's words, a "bully pulpit." Woodrow Wilson rode a train around the country trying, and failing, to persuade people to support our entry into the League of Nations. Until air travel became commonplace, however, most presidents were tied to Washington. Until radio and television, they had to speak to the nation indirectly through newspapers.

By the 1960s, television and jet travel were no longer novelties. Johnson and his successors used both to put themselves at the center of even routine events. Believing it important "to spread the White House around," Nixon traveled often and used many prime-time television addresses to defend his Vietnam policies. Carter and Reagan matched Nixon's use of television. Of the three, Carter was the least and Reagan the most effective in generating public support with it.

Samuel Kernell calls direct presidential appeals to the people **going public.**[23] It is a strategy whereby presidents try to use their public support to gain cooperation from the Washingtonians. The strategy includes giving prime-time television and radio addresses, holding press conferences, making speeches at events around the country, and using satellite technology to give interviews to local television stations, conventions, and other audiences.

Going public is a way to activate high levels of public support to persuade the Washingtonians to back a presidential policy. Thus, in a 1981 television address to stimulate support for major tax cuts, Reagan asked viewers "to put aside any feelings of frustration . . . about our political institutions . . . [and] contact your senators and congressmen."[24] The public's reaction was swift and overwhelming. Many Democrats decided to support the president and the cuts passed.

Why have some presidents found "going public" attractive? One reason is that the weakness of national political parties forces presidential candidates to appeal as widely as they can for support. They continue doing so after taking office because they have seen its value. In addition, weak national parties have been unable to represent the larger number of interests produced by government's larger role in society. This has helped to disperse power among leaders on congressional committees and subcommittees, in executive agencies, and interest groups. It is difficult for presidents to know, bargain with, and persuade all these Washingtonians. It is often easier to go public.

Finally, Carter, Reagan, and now Clinton, as **outsiders,** or presidential candidates without national political experience, saw the value of going public because they lacked ties with the Washingtonians they needed to govern.[25]

Going public has a number of important effects. It makes the workings of the presidency resemble an election campaign because presidents fly around the country to get their views in the media. Seeking coverage and support, they use the same simple, dramatic style to oversell their positions that they used as candidates. To identify public reactions, presidential staff regularly gather data just as they did on the campaign trail. A White House aide described the Reagan administration as "a P.R. outfit that became President and took over the country."[26] In Reagan's last term, each of his televised speeches and news conferences was monitored by a specially chosen group of people somewhere in the country (called a focus group) using "people meters," little dials they turned to record their positive and negative reactions. The next day, Reagan aides would get an electrocardiogram-like chart indicating exactly which phrases, words, and gestures had evoked positive reactions. In writing future speeches, Reagan's people dropped those elements that did not work and repeated those that did.[27] Despite this, however, after 1982 the public no longer responded to Reagan's policy proposals and hence Congress did not either.

In addition, going public leads presidents to use "sound bites" to simplify their positions to build public support while working behind the scenes to build congressional and interest group support. This worked for Reagan, who publicly described his 1982 budget package as "a line drawn in the dirt" to stress his resolve. He traveled around the country to generate public support and his staff used focus groups to identify popular reactions to his proposals. These analyses told his advisers where he could hold firm and where he should compromise. And he made the necessary changes in his package to build congressional support for it.

Clinton used Reagan's sound-bite and compromise strategy to gain congressional passage of the North American Free Trade Agreement and a ban on assault weapons. However, an observer likened Clinton to "a home-run hitter with a .200 batting average"[28] when he tried to sell health care reform to the nation and to Congress. In his 1994 State of the Union address, Clinton threatened to veto any reform that did not offer universal coverage. However, his proposal was complex and difficult to understand. This made it an

Rating the Presidents

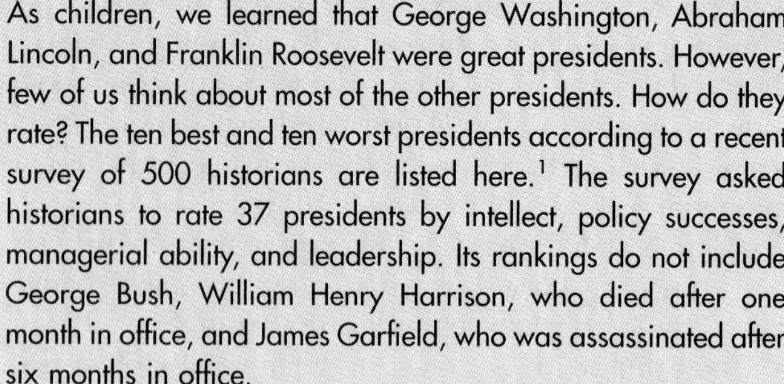

As children, we learned that George Washington, Abraham Lincoln, and Franklin Roosevelt were great presidents. However, few of us think about most of the other presidents. How do they rate? The ten best and ten worst presidents according to a recent survey of 500 historians are listed here.[1] The survey asked historians to rate 37 presidents by intellect, policy successes, managerial ability, and leadership. Its rankings do not include George Bush, William Henry Harrison, who died after one month in office, and James Garfield, who was assassinated after six months in office.

The historians ranked Ronald Reagan 28th, or tenth from the bottom, among former presidents. While they graded him highly for leadership, they gave him low marks for intellectual ability, executive branch corruption, and budget deficits. The only recent president they graded lower was Nixon.

These results differ little from public assessments of our last 10 presidents, including Bush.[2] The biggest differences are that public opinion rates Lyndon Johnson as the second worst recent president after Nixon and Reagan third worst (only two points separate him from Carter) and it ranks Kennedy ahead of Franklin Roosevelt and Eisenhower.

What do you think? Did Reagan do a better or worse job than Johnson or Carter? Was Kennedy the best of our last 10 presidents? Will future historians put Clinton in the top ten? Or bottom ten?

Ten Best Presidents	Ten Worst Presidents
1. Lincoln	1. Harding
2. F. Roosevelt	2. Grant
3. Washington	3. Nixon
4. Jefferson	4. Buchanan
5. T. Roosevelt	5. A. Johnson
6. Wilson	6. Pierce
7. Jackson	7. Coolidge
8. Truman	8. Fillmore
9. J. Adams	9. Tyler
10. Eisenhower (tenth best)	10. Reagan (tenth worst)

1. Information was obtained directly from Professor Tim Blessing, who administered the survey, and from Hugh Sidey, "The Presidency: What Links These Six?" *Time,* April 15, 1991, p. 35.
2. Adam Clymer, "Presidents Ask a Place in Posterity; Posterity Keeps Rearranging Them," *The New York Times,* January 24, 1993, p. 3E.

FIGURE 2
Presidential Popularity Usually Declines Over Time

Eisenhower and, to some extent, Reagan are exceptions to the post–World War II tendency for presidential popularity to fall over time. Although Reagan's popularity plunged 20 points at the end of 1986 because of the Iran-contra scandal, it partly rebounded by the end of his term. Most commentators thought this reflected popular fondness for Reagan as a person and Reagan's early successes rather than policy achievements late in his term. Bush began his term with high ratings typical of new presidents; after falling in 1990, his ratings rebounded to record heights during the Persian Gulf War. Bush's popularity began falling dramatically in 1991. Clinton's comparatively low first year popularity reflects the minority share (43%) of the popular vote he received in 1992 and public reactions to his positions on many controversial issues. The increase in his popularity in 1995 was chiefly the result of Clinton winning the public opinion battle with the Republicans in Congress.

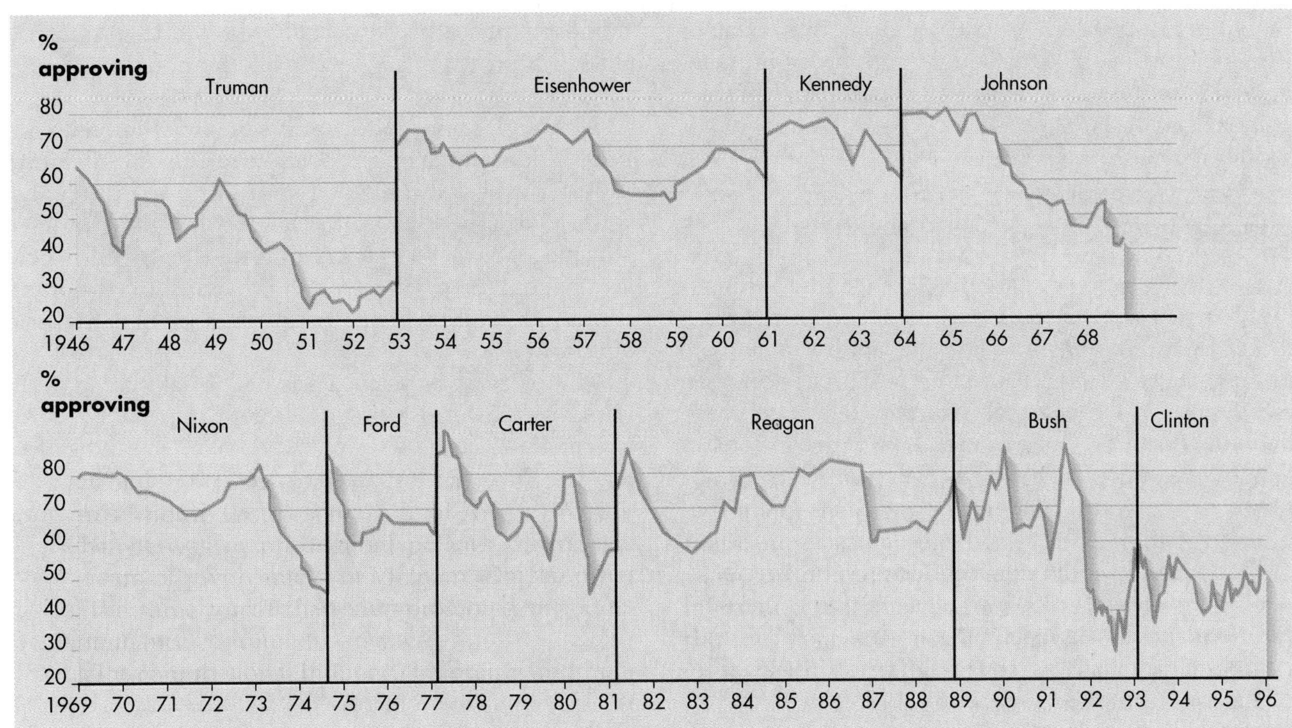

Sources: Caption: William Schneider, "Reagan Now Viewed as an Irrelevant President," *National Journal*, November 28, 1987, p. 3051. See also George Gallup, Jr. and Alec Gallup, "The Former President," *The Polling Report*, January 30, 1989, pp. 1 and 5. Figure data: Gallup Polls, reported in *Public Opinion*, January/February 1989, and updated. The question asked is: "Do you approve or disapprove of the way [name of president] is handling his job as president?" Also: *Gallup Poll Monthly*, December 1995, p. 28.

easy target for interest groups to oppose by playing on fears of an unknown plan. His effort to build support for his position could not overcome the problem, despite focus groups, and Congress defeated his bill.

Going public may sometimes lead presidents to emphasize public relations over results and to blame the media rather than themselves for low poll scores. For example, Nixon and his supporters claimed the media had hounded him from office, Reagan blamed the media for exaggerating the importance of the Iran-contra scandal, and Clinton blamed the media for not getting credit for his first-year accomplishments. He complained that "I have fought more damn battles than any president has in 20 years with the possible exception of Reagan's first budget and not gotten one damn bit of credit from the knee-jerk liberal press. I am sick and tired of it, and you can put that in the damn article."[29]

Bush used going public as a strategy in his handling of events leading up to the Persian Gulf War. He decided to use military force soon after Iraq invaded Kuwait in August 1990. Until January, when Congress approved this option, Bush made many speeches comparing Iraq's Suddam Hussein to Hitler, condemning Hussein's use of chemical and biological weapons on his own people, and warning that Hussein would soon have nuclear weapons. Bush's efforts won more public support for using force and made congressional support more likely.

While Bush went public to build support for the Persian Gulf War, he did not rely on this strategy to get congressional support on other, and especially domestic, matters. As a former member of the House, Republican National Committee chair, ambassador to China, CIA director, and vice president, Bush was the ultimate insider. As such and lacking ex-actor Reagan's media skills, he sought support from members of Congress and other Washingtonians through personal contacts, especially phone calls and handwritten notes.

Presidential Popularity

A president's professional reputation is now based on his ability to work directly with members of Congress to get their support as well as his ability to activate popular support, as measured by public opinion polls (see Figure 2).[30] Some polls ask people to rate presidential efforts on specific issues. Others ask more general questions such as: Do you approve or disapprove of the way President ________ has been handling his job?

Many people are predisposed to support the president. People tend to look at a president's efforts and positions more than his short-run success or how his policies affect them.[31] Failure on specific issues does not always produce low scores on general performance. For example, majorities of respondents simultaneously disapproved of Reagan's handling of environmental and foreign policy issues, which the public thinks are important, *and* registered approval of his overall performance.

Crises called "rally events" affect presidential popularity.[32] President Clinton's approval ratings increased after the bombing of the federal building in Oklahoma City. Public support rises significantly at such times because people do not want to hurt the president, the symbol of national unity. However, the higher levels of support produced by rally events are rarely sustained.[33] Greater support among those who were critical of a president before the event tends to be brief; critics usually return to their earlier negative views shortly after it.

Increasing support for Bush's policies toward Iraq after its invasion of Kuwait also demonstrates public readiness to rally around the president. In November 1990, the public was divided over Bush's decision to send more troops to the Persian Gulf, with 47% approving and 46% disapproving. By January 1991, after fighting began, almost 90% approved of the way he was handling the situation. As Figure 2 shows, this increasing support helped raise Bush's general approval ratings from 54% in October to 89% in February. The unexpectedly swift defeat of Iraq with surprisingly few American casualties kept Bush's poll scores high for some time.[34] However, the effect of the Gulf War faded as Americans began focusing on domestic concerns, especially economic problems. Bush's approval rating fell to 33% by mid-1992, leading to his defeat by Clinton in November.[35]

Although many factors affect public opinion about presidential leadership, a positive image of leadership may be especially good at protecting a president's ratings from serious policy failure. Reagan's ratings survived policy failures because he already had such an image. However, they were lowered by the Iran-contra scandal, which cast serious doubts on his ability to lead.

Clinton's rating at midterm (47%) compared well with the midterm ratings of recent presidents (Ford was at 45%, Carter 43%, and Reagan 37%). But he also had the lowest ratings of any president in his first two years.[36] In 1995, polls reported that 56% of Americans described Clinton as a weak president and 80% expected the Republican Congress to have more influence than Clinton on the nation's direction in the last two years of his term.[37] Although his popularity increased in 1995, it was still lower than that of most presidents in the third year of their terms.

Winning consistently good ratings when public anger and frustration with government are widespread is difficult. Although short-term crises or rally events can help a president's ratings, long-term conditions will continue to influence them. In a time of peace and relative prosperity, the public is less tolerant of perceived personal failings than they are when the nation is facing a crisis. Thus, from the time Clinton began to compete for his party's nomination, he has faced an almost steady stream of accusations of sexual impropriety, financial misdealings, and cover-ups. Regardless of his policy success, his ratings may never be consistently high because of them.

Limits of Presidential Power

Even persuasive presidents do not get everything they want. There is evidence that the public feels presidents have too little power. When asked whether each institution has too much power, not enough, or about the right amount, 43% of the public declare that Congress has too much power, and very few, 9%, say it does not have enough. But when asked about the presidency, 25% of the public says it does not have enough power while only 19% say it has too much.[38] This perception is not a result of the Republican resurgence in the 1994 election and the aggressive "Contract with America" offered by the Republican majority; the survey was done before 1994. It is likely that the perception of a presidency without enough power has grown since the 1994 election.

Some presidents have become very frustrated by limitations on their power, sometimes to the point that they may try to overcome their limitations with aggressive action, either overt or covert. An example of overt action is Carter's failed attempt to free American hostages in Iran by force in 1980 after months of frustration.

The most famous examples of covert presidential action in the face of perceived frustrations are Nixon's secret attempts to know what his "enemies" were doing: invading individual privacy with phone taps, break-ins, and unauthorized reviews of income tax returns. Reagan, frustrated trying to free American hostages in Lebanon, authorized covert arms sales to Iran and supported covert and illegal aid to the Nicaraguan contras.

full-scale bureaucracy around the president, the Executive Office of the President (EOP), whose employees work directly for the president.

Franklin Roosevelt created the EOP by executive order in 1939 because New Deal programs had increased the number of federal agencies and workers and he needed help running a larger and more complex executive branch. The EOP grew rapidly beginning in the Nixon administration. Bush's EOP employed more than 1,700 people, over 400 times as many as Lincoln had. Clinton cut this number by 25% in his first year in office to show his commitment to deficit reduction. The White House staff, a part of the EOP, has also grown. To put staff growth in perspective, Nancy Reagan's staff was larger than Roosevelt's at the height of the New Deal.[41]

Presidents have used different styles in running the EOP. Roosevelt and Kennedy cared little for rigid lines of responsibility. They gave staffers different jobs over time and fostered a competitive spirit: Who could serve the president best?

Eisenhower and Nixon valued formal lines of authority. Eisenhower's military experience led him to rely on a chief of staff, Sherman Adams. Adams so dominated White House routine that one newspaper story was headlined, "Adams Insists Ike Is Really President."[42] Nixon's chief of staff, H. R. Haldeman,

➤Roles of the President

We have seen that the president's role in government has grown with government's role in society. Here we examine the many roles of the president, sometimes called the president's many hats. Clinton Rossiter identified the president's roles in administrative, domestic and foreign policy leadership, military matters, promoting national unity, and party leadership.[39] Before discussing them, however, we will describe how the president's own office has grown to handle the larger workload.

Growth of Presidential Staff

George Washington paid a nephew out of his own pocket to be his only full-time aide. Congress did not appropriate funds for a presidential clerk until 1857. Lincoln's staff "exploded" to four people, but he often opened and answered the daily mail himself. Cleveland answered the White House telephone, and Wilson typed many of his own speeches.[40] Today, demand for presidential leadership has produced a

Source: Feiffer © 1968, Jules Feiffer. Reprinted with permission of Universal Press Syndicate. All rights reserved.

ran the White House for his president and took much of the heat when people did not get what they wanted. He saw his job this way: "Every president needs a son of a bitch, and I'm Nixon's. I'm his buffer and his bastard. I get done what he wants done and I take the heat instead of him."[43]

The Watergate scandal led presidents Ford and Carter to avoid the appearance of strong staff chiefs, although both eventually saw a need for a chief of staff to manage their schedules and the huge flow of paper that passes through the White House. Reagan prided himself on delegating authority to the best people and letting them do their work without interfering.[44] Serious problems developed, however, because no one had enough authority to make final decisions on more important matters and Reagan was too removed from daily affairs to do so. This detached management style had its costs, most noticeably the Iran-contra scandal.[45] Problems produced by his detached management style led Reagan to appoint a series of strong staff chiefs.

Unlike Reagan, Bush was involved in White House operations. However, he spent more time on foreign policy matters and less time on domestic issues, which he largely left to his staff. This produced problems for Bush by the 1992 election when most voters were more interested in domestic problems.

Clinton's White House organization puts him in the center of decision making. He directed his first staff chief, businessman and friend Thomas McLarty, to channel all paperwork to him so his appointees would not repeat the frustration of a Bush cabinet member who had to mail his views to Bush because Bush's first staff chief, John Sununu, sat on them. This

Decisions ultimately rest on the president. Here President Kennedy is alone with his thoughts in the Oval Office.

decision, coupled with his choice of many staffers with little Washington experience and diverse views, and his selection of his wife, Hillary Rodham Clinton, to develop and help sell his health reform proposal, shows his determination to be in command and to immerse himself in policy details.

However, Clinton knows that running the White House this way makes it difficult to keep his and the nation's focus on important issues. Four months into his term, he directed that low-priority issues be kept off his desk. In 1994, he told his second staff chief, former congressman Leon Panetta, to tighten lines of authority and communication and to manage the flow of paper to him more closely than was done earlier. But Clinton's White House operation still reflects his love of policy details and inability to stick to a few clear policy themes in communicating with the public and the media. A pundit wrote, "Each White House reflects the personality of its leader, and [Clinton], immune to punctuality and discipline, will always have a Pigpen cloud of chaos around him."[46]

Presidents seek advice from different people. Although their advisers differ from issue to issue, they consult some more than others. Thus, Reagan went to close friends from California when he was in particular need of good advice. Andrew Jackson was the first to call such groups of advisers "kitchen cabinets."

Members of the White House staff also have great influence on presidents because the president appoints them, works daily with them, and tends to trust them more than others. They are often people who helped him get elected or worked for him when he held other offices.

Other EOP members can also have influence on the president. For example, Reagan's and Bush's directors of the Office of Management and Budget had tremendous influence on budget policy. Career civil servants have less influence because presidents tend to rely on their own staffs.

Today's EOP mirrors America's diversity of needs and interests. Its offices deal with national security, energy, economics, consumers, and drug abuse, for example. It employs special assistants with responsibilities for foreign trade, civil rights, the elderly, physical fitness, labor relations, women, Wall Street, and the District of Columbia, among others.

The growth of the EOP reflects the growth of government generally. Because departments and agencies often have policy interests independent of the president's, a president wants his "own" people around him, staffers he can trust. Many EOP jobs boil down to a ceaseless effort to monitor and control agency operations.

Administrative Leadership

Administrative powers were very important to the Founders. They expected a representative Congress to make policy and a representative president to administer it. Although they gave the president other tasks as well, they gave executive tasks the highest priority in creating the presidency.

The Constitution has very few provisions that describe the president's administrative duties. It does not call for the creation of bureaucratic departments and agencies directly, but it does invest the president with executive power and authorizes him to demand written reports from his "principal officers." The Constitution also directs the president to nominate the most important officers of the executive branch.

Presidential control of the executive branch is difficult, however, because of Congress's legislative and budgetary powers, the huge number and diversity of executive jobs, and interest group influence. This difficulty and the pressures associated with the need to attract popular support have led recent presidents to spend less time on the administrative side of their job.[47] Nevertheless, presidents have a number of ways to try to control executive agencies. They can appoint and remove key administrators, formulate budget recommendations, and reorganize agencies.

Appointing Officials

The president nominates about 1,300 people to policy-making jobs in executive agencies and to positions as United States attorneys and marshals, ambassadors, and members of part-time boards and commissions. The Senate must confirm all of them, and, with a few exceptions, does. Another 1,140 presidential appointments to senior civil service jobs do not need Senate approval.

Presidents have little freedom in naming people to many positions. The custom of **senatorial courtesy** gives senators of the president's party a virtual veto over appointments to jobs, including judicial appointments, in their states. Senatorial courtesy limits a president's ability to promote his policy preferences through his appointments because it gives senators opportunities to push their own policy preferences, which might not be in tune with the president's.

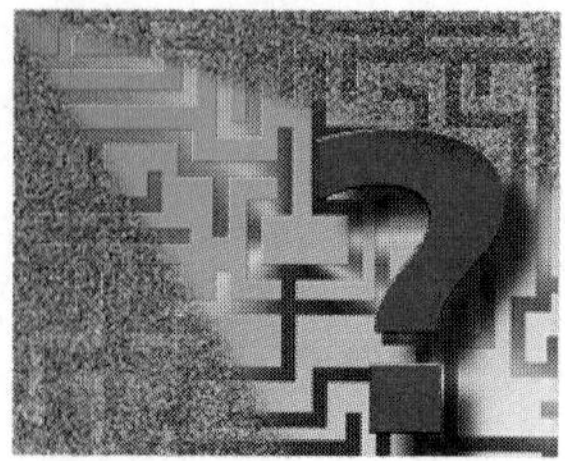

Symbolic Solutions for Complex Problems?

The Line-Item Veto

Levels of trust that Americans have in their government have fallen dramatically, as we have seen. Among other reasons, many Americans think government is too big, taxes too much, spends too much, and is not accountable to the average citizen. They see "special interest groups" imposing their will on Congress, partly because of their campaign contributions. They see Congress spend money on pork barrel projects and boondoggles, while budget deficits remain high. Congress is a special focus of distrust because of its visible role in government. The messy workings of the democratic process are laid bare for all to see on CNN, C-SPAN, and the nightly news. In our constitutional system of checks and balances, the president can sometimes serve as a check by vetoing legislation Congress passes, but this does not seem to be enough.

The Constitution allows presidents to veto entire bills passed by Congress. They have not had the same power most governors have with their state legislatures, to strike down specific provisions or parts of appropriations bills they dislike. A **line-item veto** would allow presidents to veto one or more provisions of individual spending bills without preventing the remaining provisions from becoming law. Congress could still override a line-item veto if two-thirds of both houses disapprove of a president's action. But, as we note elsewhere in this chapter, overriding a veto is difficult. As a result, supporters of the line-item veto argue, presidents would be able to impose a fiscal discipline on Congress that Congress has been unable to impose on itself.

In the 1980s, Republicans were the strongest advocates for the line-item veto as a way to curb federal spending. Now, many Democrats, including President Clinton, support it, too.

Can the line-item veto do what its supporters say it can? Or is it a symbolic solution, something that cannot work but some elected officials look good?

Supporters of the line-item veto say it would reduce pork barrel spending. Congress would know that the president has more power to kill legislation that primarily benefits special interests. Consequently, members of Congress might be less likely to pass such proposals. The president could resist the tactic sometimes used by opponents in Congress to add spending items that the president does not like to bills that he does support (in these cases the president often swallows hard and signs the bill).

Opponents of the line-item veto counter that Congress would be even less inclined to act "responsibly" because presidents would be the real bosses of the budget process. Congress could vote to fund many pork barrel projects, believing that the president would veto them. This in turn would put all the pressure on the president to make the tough decisions denying benefits to organized constituencies. Few presidents want this pressure.

Presidents have considerable discretion in filling jobs with national jurisdictions, such as cabinet jobs and seats on regulatory commissions. Several traditions govern certain jobs (a westerner to be secretary of the interior and someone with union ties to be secretary of labor), but they are not confining. As a result, presidents can shape the direction and image of their administrations with their appointments. The reputations of Grant, Harding, and Nixon suffered because of the low quality of some of their appointees. Likewise, some of Reagan's and Clinton's appointees hurt their reputations. For example, a Justice Department report found that former Attorney General Edwin Meese had engaged in "conduct which should not be tolerated of any government employee."[48] Reagan aides, including Michael Deaver, John Poindexter, and Oliver North, admitted lying to Congress. And more than 100 high-ranking Reagan appointees resigned under suspicion of unethical behavior.[49] By the middle of his term, Clinton's White House counsel and two Treasury Department appointees had resigned because of alleged illegal contributions to his gubernatorial campaigns from a failed Arkansas savings and loan. Agriculture Secretary Mike Espy resigned after accepting gifts from companies he regulated. Criminal investigations were also pending against Housing Secretary Henry Cisneros and against Commerce Secretary Ron Brown when he died in an airplane crash in Bosnia.

In addition, opponents say that effective presidents have gotten most, though not all, of what they wanted without the line-item veto. In 1983, the appropriations process worked well enough for Reagan that he did not veto a single appropriations bill while getting Congress to cut taxes and domestic spending and increase defense spending. Clinton did not veto a single piece of legislation until he was in his third year of office. In his first two years, he got Congress to pass important debt reduction legislation and other bills related to taxes and spending.

Thus, opponents argue that the line-item veto is an unneeded or symbolic solution when we have effective presidents. And it would not be more realistic solution when we have weak presidents who, by definition, would avoid making tough decisions that might anger organized constituencies.

Opponents add that the line-item veto could be a symbolic solution that produces unexpected and real dangers. They warn us that the veto could give too much power to already effective presidents and produce executive excesses. "It doesn't take much imagination to consider how much more persuasive [the president] would be if his words were buttressed with a veto stamp over individual projects and activities within our districts," Senator Mark Hatfield (R-Ore.) noted.[1] Opponents remind us of the Iran-contra crisis and of Congress's inability to carry out a useful investigation when confronted with a strong president.

Whether supporters or opponents are right, whether the line-item veto is a symbolic solution or a real solution to the budget deficit, remains to be seen. We may see quite soon. A version of the line-item veto, adopted by Congress and signed by the president in 1996, takes effect in 1997 for an eight-year trial. The president may reject any specific appropriation or any tax break that affects fewer than 100 people or 10 businesses. Social Security, Medicare, and other existing entitlement programs are exempt, as is interest on the national debt. If the president uses the line-item veto, Congress can pass a "disapproval bill" to restore the money, but that bill is itself subject to presidential veto (and congressional override of a veto if it comes).

Noting that it took Republicans in Congress a long time to pass a line-item veto and that the law delays its implementation until after the end of Clinton's first term, some conjectured that Clinton's opponents did not want to give him another tool to influence Congress. But congressional Republicans began promoting the veto in the 1980s when they were in the minority and Reagan and Bush were president. That suggests that the line-item veto may be an effective tool for members of a congressional minority with its own president in the White House to, in effect, veto the majority's action.

But because the president may be as much subject to pressures to use pork barrel spending and special tax breaks to put together a majority coalition for his programs as is Congress, a line-term veto may be no more than a symbolic solution. It will still be necessary "to buy votes with money for parochial projects," but the coalitions "will simply be packaged in the White House instead of in Capitol Hill committee rooms."[2] If so, members will still be able to claim credit with their constituents for bringing the pork home but will be able to pin the blame on the president for the budget deficit.

1. Quoted in Roger H. Davidson and Walter J. Oleszek, *Congress and Its Members*, 5th ed. (Washington, D.C.: CQ Press, 1996), p. 302.
2. Marshall Ingwerson, "GOP Irony: Delivering Power Back to President," *Christian Science Monitor*, February 10, 1995, p. 5, quoted in Davidson and Oleszek, *Congress and Its Members*, p. 302.

Removing Officials

Although the power to remove political appointees is not in the Constitution, presidents have it. Their power to name people they trust implies a power to remove those they find wanting. In 1935 the Supreme Court tried to define this power by saying that presidents can remove appointees from purely administrative jobs but not from those with quasi-legislative and judicial responsibilities. Although this ruling protects many appointees, identifying quasi-legislative and judicial jobs can be subjective.[50]

Making the Budget

The Founders gave Congress, and particularly the House of Representatives, the power of the purse. However, the growth of the presidency has increased presidential power in this area.

Although the president is chief administrator, for many years he had a negligible role in managing executive branch funds. Agency budget requests went to the House unreviewed and unchanged by the White House. Until the turn of the century, Congress thought it could handle the budget, but by the end of World War I, a general awareness had developed that a larger government required better management. The Budget and Accounting Act of 1921 gave presidents important priority-setting and managerial responsibilities that contributed to the president's dominance in budgetary politics.

The 1921 act requires the president to give Congress annual estimates of how much money it will take to run the government during the next fiscal year. The president's budget message contains his recommendations for how much money Congress should appropriate for every program of the national government. Formulating the message requires the White House to examine all agency budget requests and to decide which to support or reject. This exercise gives the president a chance to activate public support by recommending budget policies consistent with public expectations. It also allows the president and his staff to initiate the annual budget debate on their own terms.

In addition, the act created the Bureau of the Budget, or BOB. Originally a part of the Treasury Department, BOB was meant to be the president's primary tool in developing budget policy. It was

Presidents and Prime Ministers

Most democratic nations have **parliamentary governments,** that is, systems in which the executive is chosen by the legislature. Americans have long admired Britain's parliamentary system. Woodrow Wilson once proposed that members of the president's cabinet sit in Congress and be able to introduce bills like their British counterparts. Many Americans are frustrated by our system's fragmentation and by a lack of accountability among elected officials, as evidenced by the Watergate and Iran-contra scandals. They have looked enviously across the Atlantic where British heads of government, called prime ministers, seem to be better leaders *and* more accountable to the public.

In recent years, we have heard about "gridlock," the inability of our elected officials to agree about how to solve our nation's problems. These differences are exacerbated when different parties control the White House and Congress. Divided control, which has been the case most years since World War II, makes it more likely that the president and congressional leaders will advocate different policies and priorities. It also makes it easier for elected officials to play the "blame game" and avoid taking responsibility for failed policies and inaction. We even have problems when the White House and Congress are controlled by the same party. The president and members of Congress often have different interests because they are elected by different constituencies at different times. And they can use our system's checks and balances to thwart each other's efforts.

In contrast, the British government is marked by a unity of authority. The prime minister, or PM, is an elected member of the House of Commons, the lower house of Britain's national legislature called the Parliament. (Parliament's other house, the House of Lords, is unelected and has very little power.) The PM is elected like other members of the Commons—by the voters of a constituency—and then is chosen by his or her party as its leader. The PM is always the leader of the majority (or largest) party in the Commons and usually decides when elections to the Commons will occur. However, elections must take place within five years of the last election. As members of the Commons, the PM and the cabinet ministers appointed by the PM must argue for their policies and respond to criticism from minority party members in debate.

Rank-and-file members of the Commons have very little independent power and often do not live in the constituencies that elect them. National party organizations have a great deal of influence over who is selected to run for election to the Commons. Members who do not vote the party line sometimes lose their party's support for reelection. This helps explain why 97% of the bills sponsored by the PM and cabinet from 1945 to 1987 were enacted.[1]

Although this is an attractive picture in some respects, the Founders designed our system to represent the diverse interests of a large, heterogeneous population. While more effective leadership in government is appealing, greater centralization can mean less opportunity to accommodate diverse local interests. Many Americans would not like a party organization to have the major influence on nominations for congressional office. Some would also be angry if representatives advocated positions contrary to local majority opinion on an important issue. America is a much more diverse society than Britain, perhaps making centralization less workable.

Diversity in America is also represented by powerful interest groups. Their close ties to congressional committees and subcommittees and executive branch officials give these interest groups considerable power to obstruct government. While these groups might be weakened by parliamentary-style arrangements, the interests they represent would still exist.

Considering whether parliamentary forms would improve the workings of our government requires us to weigh some difficult trade-offs. Do we want to pay the costs of frequent gridlock and inefficiency to keep a system that is accessible to diverse local and other interests? Or do we want to sacrifice accessibility to government in order to have the efficiency of a stronger, more centralized system?

1. Richard Rose, *Politics in England: Change and Persistence*, 5th ed. (London: Macmillan Press, 1989), p. 113.

made a part of the newly created EOP in 1939. Nixon changed BOB's name to the Office of Management and Budget (OMB) to stress its function of helping the president manage the executive branch.

Employing hundreds of budget and policy experts, OMB works only for the president and is a powerful presidential resource. It begins evaluating agency budget requests more than a year before the start of each fiscal year and helps defend the president's budget message. OMB also regulates when agencies spend their money, what they do with it, what policy ideas they develop, and how they operate. The budget is a huge document allocating billions of dollars to thousands of programs. It is hard—if not impossible—to read and understand it systematically. Using OMB often gives the president an edge in dealing with Congress on budget issues.

In 1995, Congress voted to give the president another edge in budget matters. It passed a bill creating a line-item veto to allow the president to kill individual budget recommendations passed by Congress. This veto was also part of Clinton's set of election promises. For example, the president would be able to kill spending for a weapons system without having to veto spending for an entire package of defense-related spending measures. Advocates of the line-item veto used a "good government" argument for it: that it is needed to bring a discipline to budget policy that a fragmented Congress cannot impose on itself. However, the law included a provision that kept it from going into effect until January, 1997, after the next presidential inauguration. Some observers suspected that the Republican congressional leadership wanted to keep Clinton from having the line-item veto while they were dueling with him over budget issues.

Reorganizing Executive Agencies

Since the 1930s, presidents have had the authority to submit plans to Congress to reorganize parts of the executive branch. Reorganization means redrawing agency boundaries to promote coordination when their actions overlap or duplicate each other. This may involve merging or abolishing offices or creating new ones.

Presidents have also created councils or offices in the White House to oversee departments with overlapping responsibilities. For example, Nixon merged a number of offices to create the Domestic Council to improve White House coordination of domestic programs. Clinton created the National Economic Council to coordinate departments and agencies that shape economic policy and to show that economic issues are a high priority for him.

Domestic Policy Leadership

Polls have consistently shown that Americans consider "leadership" very important in evaluating presidents.[51] Somewhat paradoxically in light of their fear of "big government," most people want a president who can get government to "do" things. Presidents have a difficult position of trying to satisfy popular expectations of executive leadership when popular distrust of government is high.

The Founders, who understood the need for national leadership, required the president to inform Congress and the country of the "State of the Union" and to recommend policies to better it. In the president's State of the Union address at the start of each congressional session, he lists past achievements as well as remaining and new problems.

The Founders' desire to have the president act for the entire nation is also evidenced in his constitutional authority to kill, or veto, bills passed by Congress. Once the president receives a bill from Congress, he can sign it into law, veto it and send his objections to Congress, or not do anything, in which case the bill becomes a law after 10 congressional working days. Congress can enact a vetoed bill if a two-thirds majority in each house votes to override the president's veto. Presidents can avoid override attempts at certain times, however. A bill reaching the president dies if he does not sign it and Congress adjourns within 10 working days. This way of killing a bill is called a pocket veto.

Given expectations of presidential leadership and the presence of White House supporters in Congress, mobilizing two-thirds majorities to override a veto is usually very hard. As a result, presidents can influence Congress to write bills in certain ways by threatening to veto them if they do not conform to presidential wishes.

Only eight presidents never vetoed a bill. Franklin Roosevelt, a very assertive president, holds the record with 635 vetoes in his 14 years in office. That Congress overrode only 9 of his vetoes shows the effectiveness of his leadership. Among more recent presidents, Eisenhower vetoed 181 bills in 8 years. Congress overrode only 2 of them even though his party was in the minority for 6 of those years. Reagan vetoed 78 bills with 9 overridden and Bush vetoed 46 bills with 1 overridden.

Presidents must be careful about using the veto too often to avoid appearing isolated or uncooperative. Vetoes indicate that presidents have failed to win initial support for their positions. Clinton did not use the veto in the first half of his term and still had a number of congressional successes. He used it for the first time in 1995. That presidents are rarely overridden reminds us of their power when they decide they really want something.

Executive orders are another vehicle of presidential leadership. Based on constitutional provisions and congressional acts, they are issued by the president and executive agencies and contain binding policy. Their rationale is that Congress often lacks the expertise and ability to act quickly when technological or other developments require fast action and flexibility. However, recent presidents have used executive orders to make policies opposed by congressional majorities. Thus, Reagan and Bush issued executive orders to ban abortion counseling in federally financed clinics and financial aid to United Nations-sponsored family planning programs. Clinton canceled these orders in his first week in office.

Presidential leadership also includes creating and promoting policy packages such as Teddy Roosevelt's Square Deal, Wilson's New Freedom, Franklin Roosevelt's New Deal, and Johnson's Great Society. In 1981, Reagan had a huge impact on policy although he did not use a catchy label. People often evaluate presidential leadership in terms of the content and impact of these programs.

Reagan's leadership style in dealing with Congress involved going public to pressure it for support. In contrast, Bush used White House staff to negotiate policy matters directly with congressional leaders. Bush lacked Reagan's media skills and, as an insider, already had working relationships with many Washingtonians. This style, as well as a heavy use of the veto to kill bills he opposed, freed him to devote more time to foreign policy.

Clinton tries to generate congressional support by lobbying members himself and by trying to influence opinion in their districts. His aides describe this as combining policy-making and politics. After setting his goals, Clinton tries to influence opinion in those parts of the country and in interest groups most affected by them. One way he and his aides do this is to give interviews to journalists whose work reaches those he wants to influence. Clinton then tries to use popular support to build congressional support by lobbying members of Congress directly and indirectly through intermediaries such as business and union leaders.

Foreign Policy Leadership

Although presidential leadership in domestic policy is important, presidents are even more dominant in foreign policy. Article II of the Constitution gives the president a number of foreign policy powers: to make treaties with other countries, with Senate approval; to appoint ambassadors and consuls to represent us abroad; and to receive ambassadors from other countries. This last power lets presidents recognize or not recognize other governments, an important decision. Recognition may show our approval of a government or a belief that it contributes to our national interest. Recognition is not, therefore, automatic. We did not recognize the Soviet government until 16 years after the Bolshevik Revolution of 1917 or that of the communist government of mainland China until almost 25 years after it took power.

The Constitution also contains implied powers, which were acknowledged by the Supreme Court in a 1936 decision.[52] Congress had authorized Franklin Roosevelt to ban arms sales to warring Bolivia and Paraguay, but a military aircraft manufacturer

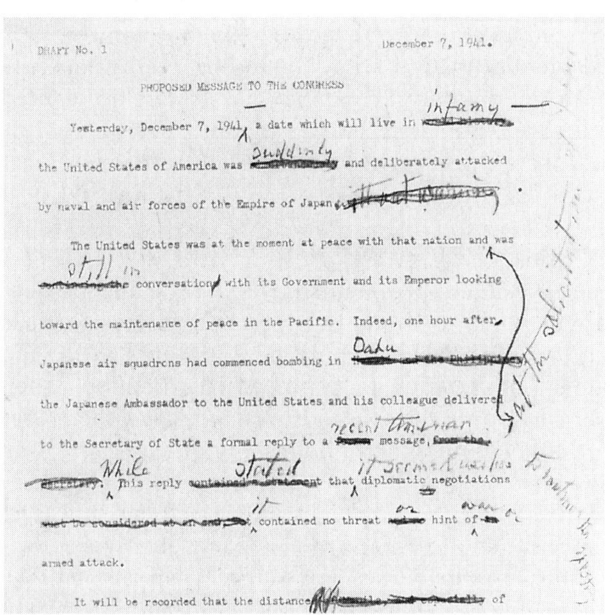

DRAFT No. 1 December 7, 1941.

PROPOSED MESSAGE TO THE CONGRESS

Yesterday, December 7, 1941, a date which will live in infamy the United States of America was suddenly and deliberately attacked by naval and air forces of the Empire of Japan.

The United States was at the moment at peace with that nation and was still in conversation with its Government and its Emperor looking toward the maintenance of peace in the Pacific. Indeed, one hour after Japanese air squadrons had commenced bombing in Oahu the Japanese Ambassador to the United States and his colleague delivered to the Secretary of State a formal reply to a recent American message. While this reply stated that diplomatic negotiations it contained no threat or hint of armed attack.

It will be recorded that the distance of

As the nation's foreign policy leader, President Franklin Roosevelt edited his own speech to Congress about the Japanese attack on Pearl Harbor. He added the word that made memorable his phrase, "a date which will live in infamy."

claimed that Congress lacked the constitutional authority to delegate such power. The Court ruled against the corporation, saying that every nation has implied powers to promote its interests in the world. The Court said there is a logic behind presidential power in foreign policy. A nation's government must be able to speak with one voice; having more than one voice can produce confusion about our ends and actions.

Presidents have their own styles in making foreign policy.[53] Eisenhower preferred using the formal procedures of the National Security Council, Kennedy and Johnson liked face-to-face discussions with many different people, and Nixon isolated himself with staff reports. Bush relied on four or five advisers who had worked together before and knew each other well.

Clinton gave world problems a low priority when he entered office and lacked experience with them. His early attempts at foreign policy leadership produced more criticism than praise, as when he seemed unable to choose between a forceful or hands-off response to bloody "ethnic cleansing" campaigns in Bosnia. By midterm, Clinton found that foreign policy issues can free presidents from the often messy partisan wrangles of domestic politics. He enjoyed higher ratings for a time after a showdown with Iraq and sending troops to Haiti to replace its military leaders with elected civilian leaders in 1994. These and later actions to work for peace in Bosnia and in the Middle East suggest that foreign policy is now a higher priority for him. Success with it can benefit both the nation and his professional reputation.

Over the years, the president has become more powerful than Congress in foreign policy-making, assuming powers that were not explicitly given to either the legislative or the executive branch. As one observer commented:

> The President's normal problem with domestic policy is to get congressional support for the programs he prefers. In foreign affairs, in contrast, he can almost always get support for policies that he believes will protect the nation—but his problem is to find a viable policy.[54]

Sometimes Congress will not support the president. For example, over President Reagan's veto, Congress passed a law detailing policy toward South Africa; it sometimes opposed Reagan's proposed aid to guerrillas fighting the Nicaraguan government; and it overrode President Wilson's desire for the United States to enter the League of Nations and ratify the Treaty of Versailles ending World War I. Usually, however, even ill-conceived presidential foreign policies win congressional support.

Since World War II, one of the president's most important foreign policy tasks has been to develop policy toward the former Soviet Union. Early in his term, President Reagan took a hard line against the Soviet Union. But as pressure in the United States grew for more amicable relations between the superpowers, and as the Soviet Union moved toward a more open political system, Reagan began to negotiate seriously with Soviet leader Mikhail Gorbachev. Here, Gorbachev and Reagan are shown during Reagan's 1988 visit to Moscow.

Vietnam is a good example of presidential dominance in foreign policy. Kennedy started sending troops there in the early 1960s. By 1968, public opinion polls reported considerable opposition to the war. Nevertheless, American involvement continued until the North Vietnamese victory in 1975. Presidential policy dominated despite demonstrations, mass arrests, opposing editorials, negative opinion polls, and congressional criticism.

President Bush's control of events leading up to the Persian Gulf War is another example of the effectiveness of determined presidential foreign policy leadership. He sent 250,000 troops to the Gulf between August and November 1990 on his own authority. He also delayed announcing his decision to double this number until after the November elections, although he had made the decision in October. This kept the decision that changed our mission from defense (Operation Desert Shield) to offense (Operation Desert Storm) from becoming a campaign issue. And he mobilized United States and world opinion and gained United Nations support. By the time Congress authorized using force in January 1991, the question of whether to do so was, practically speaking, already decided.

One reason for this dominance is that in foreign policy, more than in domestic, the president has more information than others do. He can often stifle debate by saying, "If you knew what I knew, you would agree with me," because of classified or secret information from the CIA, Defense Department, State Department, and other agencies. The president can also share certain information with Congress (and the public) and try to withhold other information. Members of Congress who must often rely on the media are then at a distinct disadvantage in dealing with the president. In 1984, the Reagan administration mined harbors in Nicaragua after telling the Senate Intelligence Committee it was not doing so. When the facts became known, the chair of that committee, Barry Goldwater (R-Ariz.), wrote a blistering public letter to the head of the CIA saying, not so formally, "I am

Presidential Abuse of Power: The Iran-Contra Affair

During the mid-1980s, eight Americans were kidnapped and held hostage in Lebanon by Moslem extremist groups, some of whom were supported by Iran and its leader, the Ayatollah Khomeini. One hostage, a Central Intelligence Agency (CIA) operative assigned to our Beirut embassy, was killed.

This situation was an embarrassment to President Reagan who, in the 1980 election, belittled his predecessor Jimmy Carter for not being able to free hostages who had been kidnapped from the American embassy in Iran. In 1984, Reagan campaigned for reelection using slogans such as "America is back, and standing tall," and our continuing inability to secure the release of the hostages appeared inconsistent with that message.

In an attempt to free the hostages, President Reagan decided to let the CIA secretly sell weapons to Iran for use in its war against Iraq. He hoped this would convince the Iranians to release the hostages. The sale was opposed by Reagan's secretary of state, George Schultz, and his secretary of defense, Caspar Weinberger, but national security advisor John Poindexter and his subordinate, Lieutenant Colonel Oliver North argued for it.

According to federal law, Reagan was required to notify Congress of the secret arms sale. At the urging of North, and perhaps others, he did not do so.[1]

As a result of Reagan's decision, 2,008 antitank missiles were sent to Iran along with parts for antiaircraft missiles.[2] Everything was kept secret until a pro-Syrian Lebanese publication broke the news in November. This led to more revelations. News surfaced that we had also shipped arms to Iran earlier, in September 1985. Robert McFarlane, then national security adviser, told a congressional committee the president had approved these sales orally. Reagan said he did not remember. And Attorney General Edwin Meese revealed that profits from the sales were used to aid the Nicaraguan contras, again in violation of the law.

Reactions were overwhelmingly negative. Reagan's popularity plummeted.[3] Most did not believe him when he said he did not know what was going on. Media analyses appeared comparing what was being called Irangate to Watergate. The public and Congress asked what the president knew and when he knew it. Comedians asked what he forgot and when he forgot it. At first the president called North a "national hero." Then he fired him.

For the next several years, various investigations tried to find out if the president had authorized breaking the law (and hence violated his constitutional oath) and if Vice President George Bush knew about it. A presidential fact-finding commission reported that Reagan was removed from day-to-day business and that his management of foreign policy was lax and ineffective. Reagan reported to the commission that he could not remember when he authorized arms sales to Iran and that he knew nothing about diversion of funds to the contras. But in 1987, Reagan contradicted his earlier claim by declaring, "I was very definitely involved in the decisions about support to the freedom fighters [i.e., contras]—my idea to begin with."

The congressional hearings investigating the matter suggested that Reagan did know what was going on, and opinion surveys continued to report that most people thought Reagan was lying when he said he didn't remember.[4]

pissed off."[55] Later the Iran-contra hearings and the report of the special prosecutor revealed that Reagan administration officials, including Vice President George Bush, deliberately lied to Congress and the press about a whole series of actions taken with respect to Iran and Nicaragua.[56]

The administration also has a large role in shaping the agenda of debate. Alternatives acceptable to the administration are advanced through public statements, background briefings of the press and Congress, and "national" newspapers such as the *New York Times* or *Washington Post.* Many reasonable alternatives may never be suggested or receive support. Thus, media outlets did little to initiate discussions of our goals in the Persian Gulf when they covered troop commitments largely as a logistical challenge and human interest story. Media acceptance of Pentagon restrictions on news gathering also helped Bush generate support for his policies by producing news of successful, not unsuccessful, attacks and by concealing information describing casualties on both sides.

Although different presidential advisers sometimes advocate conflicting views publicly, it is much easier for a president to have a coherent policy than for Congress to do so. Thus, another advantage the president has over Congress is that he can act decisively, whereas Congress must talk in order to act and this takes time. President Bush sent American troops to Somalia in December 1992. The House Foreign Affairs Committee met in May 1993 to authorize this

In well-publicized criminal trials, North and Poindexter claimed they had followed the orders of their superiors, including Reagan. North also said that Bush knew about illegal contra supply efforts and had helped get other countries to assist the contras in return for U.S. aid. Thus, the North and Poindexter trials also became Reagan's and Bush's. Evidence showed that Bush had not been "out of the loop," as he had claimed earlier. Bush regularly attended meetings from 1984 to 1986 dealing with the arms sales, hostages, and contra aid.[5]

Fearing what some of his aides described as a "political witch hunt" after Clinton's victory,[6] Bush pardoned six Reagan-era officials, each of whom had been charged with or convicted of crimes related to the Iran-contra scandal. Bush decried what he saw as the "criminalization of policy differences" and argued that "the common denominator of their motivation—whether their actions were right or wrong—was patriotism. . . . [and] they did not profit or seek to profit from their conduct."[7]

Reactions to the pardons were quick and critical. The special prosecutor declared, "The Iran-contra coverup has now been completed."[8] Some critics charged that Bush had misused his pardon power. Others rebuked him for arguing that the prosecutor had criminalized policy differences when those who were pardoned had been accused or convicted of lawbreaking and lying to congressional and other investigators. A poll found that only 15% of those surveyed thought Bush's main reason for issuing the pardons was "to protect people he felt acted honorably and patriotically from unfair prosecution."[9]

The Irangate incident reveals the temptations offered to presidents to use illegal means to increase their own power. Although presidents have an inherent advantage over Congress in making foreign policy, they cannot legally operate in defiance of Congress.

The Iran-contra affair, like Watergate, raises serious questions about the accountability of the personal presidency. In some ways "Irangate" is more serious than Watergate in that while President Nixon resigned in disgrace rather than face impeachment, the public seemed willing to allow Reagan to serve his full term and then elected Bush to replace him.

1. Much of the information in this section comes from James M. McCormick and Steven S. Smith, "The Iran Arms Sale and the Intelligence Oversight Act of 1980," *PS* 20 (Winter 1987), pp. 29–37.
2. Robert Pear, "The Story Thus Far: Assembling Some of the Pieces of the Puzzle," *New York Times,* December 14, 1986, Section 4, p. 1. "Reagan's Crusade," *Newsweek,* December 15, 1986, pp. 26–28.
3. Elizabeth Drew, "Letter from Washington," *The New Yorker,* August 31, 1987, p. 72.
4. For a critique of the congressional hearings, see Seymour M. Hersh, "The Iran-Contra Committees: Did They Protect Reagan?" *New York Times Magazine,* April 29, 1990, pp. 46–78; Louis Harris, "Iran-Contra Hearings Erode Faith in Reagan," *Lincoln Star,* May 25, 1987.
5. See Tom Blanton, "Iran-Contradictions: It's Time to Ask Where George Was," *Washington Post National Weekly Edition,* June 18–24, 1990, pp. 24–25; Richard Cohen, "What Did Bush Know?"; and Walter Pincus, "Has Bush Come Clean About Iran-Contra?" *The Washington Post National Weekly Edition,* September 28–October 4, 1992, pp. 29 and 31–32.
6. "Pardon Me," *Newsweek,* January 4, 1993, p. 15.
7. Leslie H. Gelb, "Bush's Ethical Manure," *The New York Times,* December 27, 1992, p. E11.
8. Ibid.
9. "Pardon Me." See also George Lardner, Jr., and Walter Pincus, "Dear Diary: Now, About Iran-Contra . . . ," *The Washington Post National Weekly Edition,* January 25–31, 1993, p. 31; and George Lardner Jr.and Walter Pincus, "The Source of the Iran-Contra Mess Is Tracked to Reagan," *Washington Post National Weekly Edition,* January 24–30, 1994, p. 13.

action, on the day after the United Nations had assumed responsibility in Somalia and most of our troops had come home.

Because the president is one and Congress is many, the president is usually more effective in appealing for public support. There is almost always a "rally 'round the flag" effect on both Congress and the public when the president takes a strong stance in foreign policy, especially if troops are involved. Our 1989 invasion of Panama is a good example of this. There was very little negative media coverage of the invasion, and public opinion was strongly supportive.

A final advantage for the president is that members of Congress hesitate to oppose major presidential foreign or military policies because they fear doing so may be seen by other nations as a sign of United States weakness.

Military Leadership

Using the military to achieve national goals is one way presidents conduct foreign policy. The Founders made the president "commander-in-chief." By this they meant that the president would be the "first general" and "first admiral," as Alexander Hamilton wrote in *Federalist #69.*

But the Founders did not want to give the president the sole power to make war. In the words of Connecticut's Roger Sherman, they believed "the Executive should be able to repel and not to commence war." The founders feared that presidents, like the English kings from whom they had recently freed themselves, would be too eager to go to war.[57] So they gave Congress the power to declare war. James Madison expressed the view of several of the Founders when he argued that "the executive is the branch of power most interested in war and most prone to it. [The Constitution] has, accordingly, with studied care, vested the question of war in the legislature."[58] Thus, the Founders created a system of checks and balances in military affairs; the president commands the troops, but Congress has the power to declare war and, of course, decides whether to authorize funds to pay for it. Thomas Jefferson thought this arrangement would be an "effectual check to the dog of war, by transferring the power of letting him loose from the executive to the legislative body, from those who are to spend to those who are to pay."[59]

Although every president is commander-in-chief, no president has ever led troops into battle. However, modern weapons have led to more presidential involvement. The decision to use certain weapons has become important politically as well as militarily. The

President Lincoln, as commander-in-chief, consults his generals at the Antietam battlefield during the Civil War. Lincoln wanted a more active role in Civil War battles, but his generals worried about his safety and made sure he was gone when there was fighting. Limited by an inability to maintain close communications with field commanders, he could not direct ongoing battles as recent presidents have been able to do.

FIGURE 3
Presidential Support Rises with Military Action

Americans normally rally around the president when he uses military action, sometimes even when the action fails. (Vietnam was an exception because the war dragged on for so long.) Yet the increased support for the president does not last long because of other problems back home.

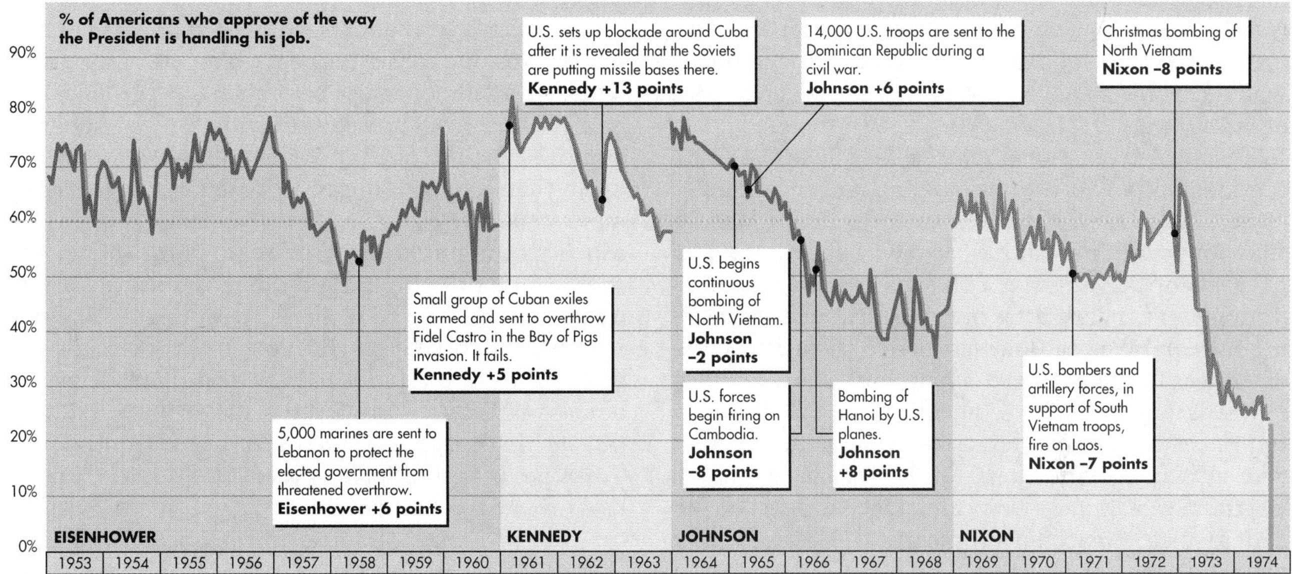

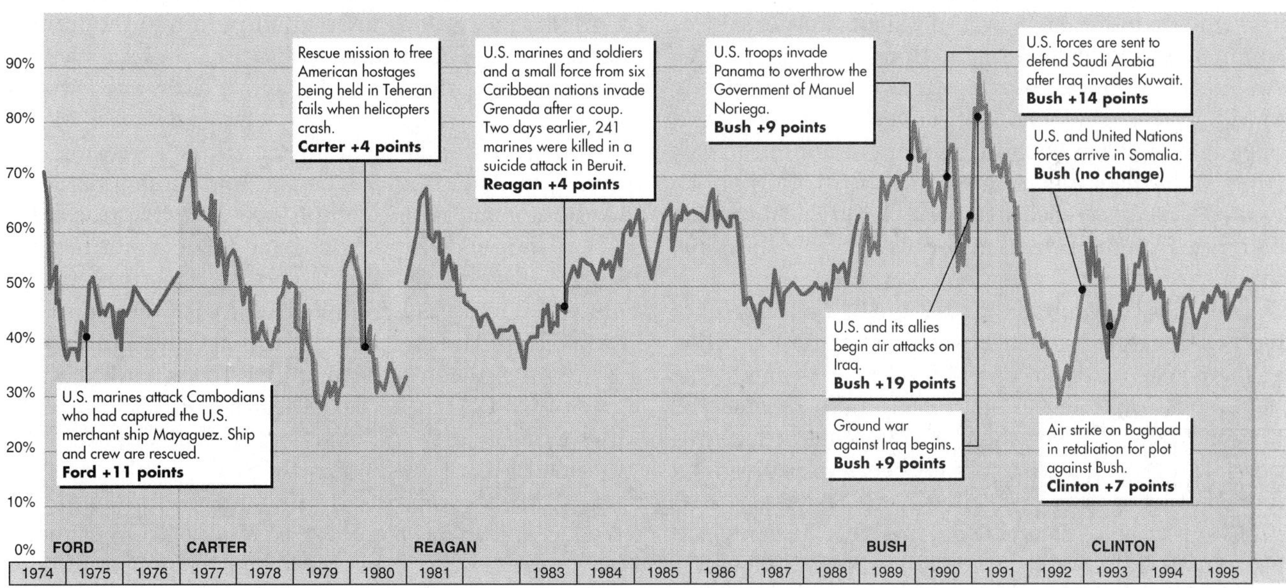

Source: Based on Gallup Polls. *The New York Times,* Sunday, September 18, 1994, pp. E. 4–5.

decision to wage a "limited" war in Vietnam, that is, not to use nuclear weapons, was political and based on presidential beliefs that Vietnam was not worth a nuclear holocaust.

Other technological developments also have given presidents more military leadership opportunities. Johnson and Nixon used sophisticated communications equipment to select targets in Vietnam. In the

Persian Gulf War, Bush used modern transportation facilities to send large numbers of troops to the Gulf quickly with the latest "smart" weapons. His White House sent so many orders to General Norman Schwarzkopf in the Gulf (from how to stop a blockade-running Iraqi tanker to ending the ground war before Iraq's army was destroyed) that the general complained of "a total vacuum of guidance" when disagreements in Washington stopped the flow of instructions.[60]

Despite congressional power in military affairs, presidential power is wide ranging and increasingly controversial as we more frequently use troops in situations when no war has been declared. Presidents have historically assumed the most military power during wars endangering our national survival. During the Civil War, Lincoln suspended the use of writs of habeas corpus, seized control of some eastern railroads, and blockaded southern ports. He did these things on his own authority as commander-in-chief and without congressional authorization. The war jeopardized national unity, and Lincoln believed he had to take extraordinary measures. Because most people in the North agreed with him, he was able to do what he thought necessary.

Acting under his self-defined authority as commander-in-chief, Franklin Roosevelt put 100,000 Americans of Japanese descent into camps during World War II. He had the government seize and operate more than 60 industries important to the war effort and vulnerable to union strikes. In addition, he created special agencies to control the consumption and price of important materials such as gasoline, meat, and shoes.

Wars not threatening our national survival do not tend to generate high levels of support for executive actions. When Truman had his secretary of commerce seize most of the nation's steel mills during the Korean conflict to keep them operating in the face of a possible labor strike, one of the steel companies took him to court to stop him. In 1952, the Supreme Court sided with the company by ruling that Truman had not exhausted other, legal remedies to the problem.[61]

The Vietnam War raised major questions about presidential authority in foreign and military policy. Although Congress never declared war in Vietnam, it routinely appropriated money for it. Nonetheless, many members of Congress believed the president exceeded his authority in pursuing the war. This painful experience led Congress to assert itself by trying to supervise presidential foreign and military policy more closely.

In 1973, Congress passed the **War Powers Act** to limit the president's ability to commit troops to combat. It says the president can use troops abroad under three conditions: when Congress has declared war, when Congress has given him specific authority to do so, or when an attack on the United States or its military creates a national crisis. If a president commits troops under the third condition, he is supposed to consult with Congress beforehand, if possible, and notify it within 48 hours afterwards. Unless Congress approves the use of troops, the president must withdraw them within 60 days, or 90 days if he needs more time to protect them. Congress can pass a concurrent resolution (not subject to presidential veto) at any time ordering the president to end the use of military force.

Congress passed the War Powers Act over Nixon's veto. He believed it violated the president's constitutional authority to protect the nation from military threats. Although presidents have not questioned Congress's constitutional authority to declare war, all have fought congressional influence in the use of troops. As a result, enforcement of the act has been controversial. For example, President Carter did not inform, let alone consult, Congress before using United States troops in an attempt to free the Iranian hostages in 1980. Congress did not protest. Neither did it protest after Bush sent troops to invade Panama in 1989. Bush did not even refer to the act in the two-page letter he sent to Congress justifying the invasion 60 hours after it began. And no congressional leader demanded his compliance with its provisions.

On the whole, then, the War Powers Act has not stopped presidents from sending American troops abroad. This was certainly true in the Persian Gulf crisis. Bush did not refer to the act and ignored its procedures when he sent troops there. Few in Congress pressed him to do otherwise. It was not until five months after the crisis began that Congress authorized Bush to use force. By then, Bush's efforts to build public support for military action had succeeded and many members went along. Other members were ready to let Bush take responsibility for what they expected to be a long and unpopular war. Such an attitude among members is unlikely to produce more congressional influence.

In addition to passing the War Powers Act, Congress has sought to increase its power by trying to control CIA covert operations, by limiting the president's ability to make agreements with other nations without congressional approval, and by requiring congressional approval of major arms sales.

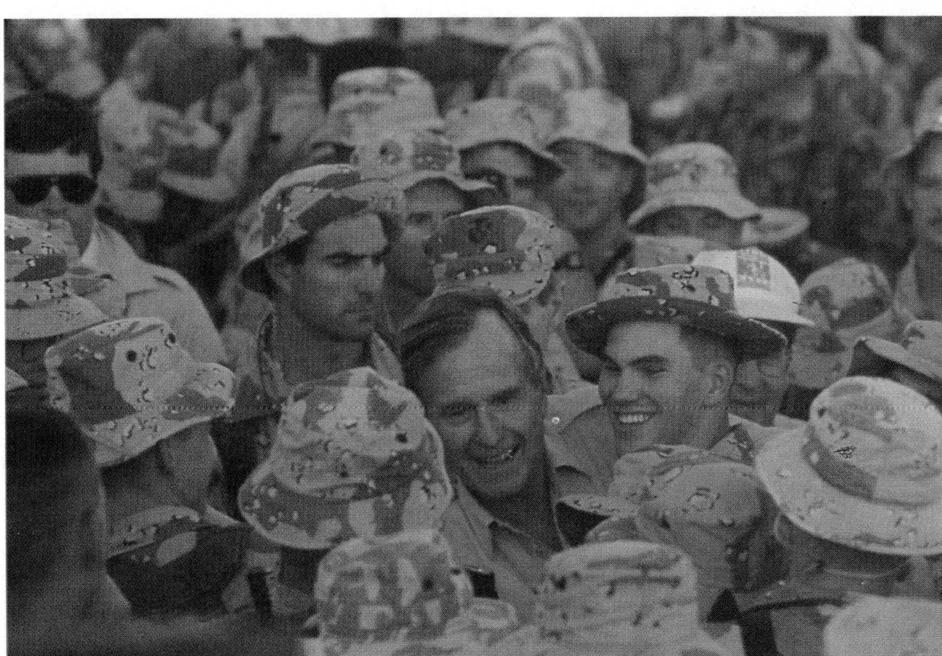

President Bush, as commander-in-chief, greets the troops in the Persian Gulf.

These efforts have had mixed success. On the one hand, Congress was more interested and involved in Reagan's Middle Eastern and Central American policies than it was in presidential policies during the early years of involvement in Vietnam. On the other hand, the same forces that have promoted presidential dominance continue to exist.

Finally, congressional influence in foreign and military policy may be limited by presidents concerned about their popularity. Low presidential public opinion scores, especially before national elections, are related to the president's use of military force abroad.[62] Presidents may be tempted to use rally events to increase their popularity and congressional support for their policies (see Figure 3). A White House aide, acknowledging low presidential popularity in October 1983, said Reagan needed "a major victory somewhere to show that we can manage foreign policy." Another added, "We need a win . . . whether it's in Central America, the Middle East or with the Russians."[63] The United States invaded Grenada that month. When Bush's scores were falling in 1990, his staff chief told associates that a short successful war against Iraq would guarantee Bush's reelection (he was wrong!).[64]

Historically, a president's use of military force tends to raise his congressional support for about a month.[65] This led one observer to note that, based on U.S. experiences in Vietnam and Grenada, presidents who start military actions abroad must win them in a hurry if they want to stay popular.[66] Presidents worried about their popularity must target weak nations that can be beaten quickly.

We want a president able to act decisively in international affairs. But we also want to make sure the president does not act against our wishes. Congress has historically served as the most important check on the president, but its clout in foreign and military policy is, as we have seen, limited. This uneasy balance between presidential powers adequate to do the job and controls necessary to maintain democracy will continue to concern us.

Symbolic Leadership

The president serves as a national symbol of collective unity and pride. Political scientists call this symbolic role **chief of state.**

In this role the president must say and do things on behalf of all Americans. Reagan opened the 1984 Olympic Games and welcomed athletes and spectators from abroad. Every president also attends the funerals of foreign leaders or sends a representative such as the vice president. Bush's first trip abroad was to attend the funeral of Japanese Emperor Hirohito. Whether it involves phoning the winners of the Super Bowl or lighting the White House Christmas tree, all presidents perform symbolic tasks.

As symbolic leaders, presidents often congratulate national sports heroes. President Calvin Coolidge (a Republican, who served from 1924 to 1928, and was aptly known as "Silent Cal") presents a trophy to a Marine team after its victory over Army.

Knowing that symbolic responsibilities are very important, the Founders gave the president power to grant reprieves and pardons for crimes under national law. During the Civil War, Lincoln pardoned soldiers who were sentenced to die for sleeping on guard duty. Such humane acts allow presidents to express the sympathetic spirit of the nation. Ford used his authority to pardon Nixon for his part in the Watergate scandal. His justification was that trying Nixon would have served no useful purpose and divided the nation. He thought the pardon expressed a national feeling. However, opinion polls showed that most people disagreed, and the pardon hurt Ford in the 1976 election.

The more a president can link his personal reputation with popular feelings of patriotism and national unity, the more persuasive he might be in getting support for his policies.The job of chief of state does not involve presidents in policy matters directly, but it can give successful practitioners more leverage in achieving their policy goals.

Party Leadership

In addition to roles representing the entire nation, the presidency includes a more partisan set of tasks. Presidents are elected only after being nominated by a political party. As "party leader," a president leads his party, confronts the opposition, and represents his party's interests when they are his own. For example, traditional Republican support for the Equal Rights Amendment changed when Reagan came out against it. In addition, a president seeking reelection typically has tremendous influence in writing his party's platform. In an extreme example of this, the 1972 Republican platform was mostly written in Nixon's White House and not at the party's convention.

To improve the electoral chances of their party, presidents help recruit good candidates for House and Senate races. In addition, presidents help raise money by being the guest star at fund-raising events, by staying on good terms with major contributors, and by looking like a winner generally. Thus, Bush raised $80 million at fund-raising events for Republican candidates in 1990. They also send their aides around the country to help fellow Democrats or Republicans with their campaigns and sometimes even go themselves. Seeing a president in person—seeing a little history in the making—is exciting and almost always draws a crowd and good media coverage. Candidates for any office are usually eager for a presidential visit, although in 1992 some Republican candidates avoided being photographed with Bush when he visited their districts, and in 1994 some Democratic candidates preferred to campaign without Clinton's support.

Presidential partisanship has a purpose: The more members of a president's party who sit in Congress, the more support he gets for his policies. However, a president's support, when he chooses to give it, is no guarantee of electoral success for congressional candidates, especially in off-year elections (see Table 1). Since 1932, the president's party has lost an average of 29 House and 4 Senate seats in off-year elections; in presidential election years, the average gains for the winning presidential candidate's party in Congress are almost a mirror image, 21 in the House and 3 in the Senate. The 1994 election followed the historical pattern, except that the loss of Democratic seats was substantially greater than normal, but recent presidential elections did not. When Bush was elected in 1988, Republicans lost three House seats and one Senate seat, and Democrats lost ten House seats and stayed even in the Senate in 1992. When Clinton was reelected, Democrats gained back over ten seats, but they lost two in the Senate.

TABLE 1 Congressional Candidates Fall Off the President's Coattails in Off-Year Elections

		SEATS GAINED OR LOST BY PRESIDENT'S PARTY IN	
Year	President	House	Senate
1934	Roosevelt (D)	+ 9	+ 10
1938	Roosevelt (D)	− 71	− 6
1942	Roosevelt (D)	− 45	− 9
1946	Truman (D)	− 55	− 12
1950	Truman (D)	− 29	− 6
1954	Eisenhower (R)	− 18	− 1
1958	Eisenhower (R)	− 47	− 13
1962	Kennedy (D)	− 4	+ 4
1966	Johnson (D)	− 47	− 3
1970	Nixon (R)	− 12	+ 2
1974	Ford (R)	− 48	− 3
1978	Carter (D)	− 11	− 3
1982	Reagan (R)	− 26	0
1986	Reagan (R)	− 6	− 8
1990	Bush (R)	− 8	− 1
1994	Clinton (D)	− 52	− 9
Average, all off-year elections		− 29	− 4
Average, all presidential election years		+ 21	+ 3

D = Democrat; R = Republican.

Sources: *Congressional Quarterly Guide to U.S. Elections, 1985,* p. 1116; Harold W. Stanley and Richard G. Niemi, *Vital Statistics on American Politics,* 3d ed. (Washington, D.C.: CQ Press, 1992), table 7-4; *Congressional Quarterly Guide to Current American Government Spring 1991* (Washington, D.C.: CQ Press, 1991), p. 1; and *Lincoln Star,* November 10, 1994, p. 1.

The president usually tries to camouflage his actions as party leader when trying to persuade people to support him or to vote for his party's candidates. People are more likely to listen to him when they see the president in terms of his other jobs, such as chief of state.

Few presidents were as good as Reagan at hiding their partisan performances. When he tilted his head, winked, and smilingly advised his audiences to ignore attacks on his policies, he implied that the attacks were clearly partisan and should be ignored. Moreover, he implied that he was above party differences, that his only concern was the national interest.

➤Conclusion: Is the Presidency Responsive?

The presidency has become the most consistently powerful part of government. Americans expect leadership from it because of societal changes resulting in more government and because of our larger interests abroad.

Neustadt called twentieth-century public opinion about the presidency "monarchical." Johnson's and Nixon's "imperial" styles certainly were consistent with it. After a ceremony for Marines going to Vietnam, Johnson was directed to a helicopter by an airman who said, "That's your helicopter over there, sir." Johnson responded, "Son, they are all my helicopters." He once called the State of the Union speech the "State of My Union address."

The public does not believe the president has such power. They see him limited by a Congress heavily influenced by "special interests." More people think the president has too little power (25%) than too much (19%).[67] Most recent presidents eventually learned hard lessons about the limits of presidential power. Indeed, the moral of the personal presidency suggests we have an "impossible" or "imperiled" presidency. Presidents who become popular by making exaggerated promises have trouble keeping them and their popularity in a system of fragmented power.

We have all become Washingtonians. We pay more attention to the president than to anyone else, and we typically link government's success to the effectiveness of his leadership. America was critical of the presidency in the 1970s. Vietnam and Watergate showed the dangers of placing too much faith in one part of government. By 1980, Americans were demanding presidential leadership again. They are still demanding it now.

Is our personal presidency responsive? It is in that the president has an almost direct relationship with the public. Using the media, the president can tell us what he wants and attempt to shape our opinion. Through public opinion polls and the ballot box, we tell the president what we think. There are limits and dangers in this relationship, however. To remain popular, a president may seek short-term solutions to the nation's problems and neglect long-term interests. Short-term responsiveness catering to public opinion may not always represent responsiveness to the real needs of the nation.

EPILOGUE

The President Stands Firm

President Clinton did not withdraw the Foster nomination, continuing to support him enthusiastically. Dr. Foster's impressive performance at the hearings, and his strong support from many doctors, public health workers, and social services advocates pulled him through with a narrow majority vote in the committee. Though Nancy Kassebaum voted against Foster, two other Republicans on the committee voted in his favor, yielding a 9–7 favorable vote.[68]

But the nomination soon became entangled not just in partisan rivalries between Democrats and Republicans and not just in the national debate over abortion rights, but in intra-Republican presidential politics. Trying to convince the religious right of the party that he was safe on the abortion issue, Bob Dole (R-Kan.), majority leader of the Senate and presidential candidate, declared he would not let the nomination come to a floor vote. Phil Gramm (R-Tex.), another Repub-

Dr. Foster and President Clinton heading back to the White House after the press conference acknowledging the nomination was dead.

lican candidate for the 1996 nomination, also vying for support of the conservative anti-abortion wing of the party, declared that he would lead a filibuster to see that the Senate would not have a chance to vote.

And, nearly five months after the initial nomination, these threats became true. Although the nomination needed only a simple majority vote to be confirmed, stopping a filibuster requires 60 votes. The president could only muster 57 votes, including all 46 Democrats and 11 of 54 Republicans. Though it was clear that Dr. Foster would be confirmed if a vote were held, the filibuster prevented that.

The president attacked the anti-abortion lobbyists for the defeat, while opponents of Dr. Foster cited both his role in abortions and his waffling admissions about them. Bob Dole attacked the president while Phil Gramm attacked Bob Dole.

Political observers declared Clinton both a winner and a loser. He "won" by sticking by his nominee and not waffling as he had with some earlier nominations. In the process of fighting for the nomination, Clinton, and Dr. Foster himself, turned the battle into a near win from a lopsided loss. The president also solidified his support among pro-choice advocates and blacks, and led the Democrats in a united front. On the other hand, the president lost because the nominee lost. The defeat brought back into the public eye his record of controversial choices and poor staff work that had plagued him earlier. On the whole, however, sticking with his choice did work to undermine his image as a vacillator who tried to please everyone and gave members of his party a rallying point.

Key Terms

personal presidency
power to persuade
Washingtonians
professional reputation
going public
outsiders
line-item veto
senatorial courtesy
parliamentary government
executive orders
War Powers Act
chief of state

Further Reading

Colin Campbell and Margaret Jane Wyszomirski, eds., *Executive Leadership in Anglo-American Systems* (Pittsburgh: University of Pittsburgh Press, 1991). *Comparisons of presidential government in the United States and British and Canadian cabinet government with respect to domestic and foreign policy-making, the roles of political appointees and civil servants, and media relations.*

Theodore Draper, *A Very Thin Line: The Iran-Contra Affairs* (New York: Hill & Wang, 1991). *A detailed account of the Iran-contra scandal, how it was investigated, and what it tells us about presidential and congressional roles in foreign policy matters.*

Doris Kearns Goodwin, *No Ordinary Time* (New York: Simon & Schuster, 1994). *An engaging study of life in the White House and the leadership of Franklin Roosevelt during World War II.*

Charles O. Jones, *The Presidency in a Separated System* (Washington, D.C.: Brookings Institution, 1994). *A book for post-Cold War times, it argues that constitutional limits make popular expectations of presidential leadership unrealistic and that responsibility for public policy must be shared by all branches of government.*

Richard E. Neustadt, *Presidential Power and the Modern Presidents* (New York: The Free Press, 1990). *The most cited book on the presidency, it argues that presidential power is based on the ability to persuade.*

Peggy Noonan, *What I Saw at the Revolution: A Political Life in the Reagan Era* (New York: Random House, 1990). *A lively description by a Reagan speechwriter of White House life and an analysis of why Reagan could not turn his election victories into a major party realignment.*

Bradley H. Patterson, Jr., *The Ring of Power: The White House Staff and Its Expanding Role in Government* (New York: Basic Books, 1988). *This book sees White House operations as so complex and involving so many officials that "the only decision a president carries out himself is to go to the bathroom."*

Bob Woodward, *The Commanders* (New York: Simon & Schuster, 1991). *An account of how Bush's White House brought the nation to war in the Persian Gulf that reveals divisions of high-level opinions that did not surface in the months before the war.*

Notes

1. Much of the material for this You Are There was drawn from the following stories in the *Congressional Quarterly Weekly Report:* Colette Fraley, "Foster's Fate May Rest in the Hands of Three GOP Senators," April 29, 1995, p. 1182; and "Foster's Answers Keep His Bid for Surgeon General Alive," May 6, 1995, p. 1244; "Pending Vote on Foster Places Sen. Frist in Quandary," May 13, 1995, p. 1332; Robert Marshall Wells with Peter MacPherson,

"Foster's Problems Illustrate Anti-Abortion Strength," February 11, 1995, p. 460.

2. Fraley, "Foster's Fate May Rest in Hands of Three GOP Senators," p. 1182.

3. "Excerpts from Testimony," compiled by Jeanne Ponessa, *Congressional Quarterly Weekly Report,* May 6, 1995, p. 1246.

4. Wells with MacPherson, "Foster's Problems Illustrate Anti-Abortion Strength," p. 460.

5. Arthur M. Schlesinger, Jr., *The Imperial Presidency* (Boston: Houghton Mifflin, 1973).

6. Harold M. Barger, *The Impossible Presidency* (Glenview, Ill.: Scott-Foresman, 1984).

7. Richard Morin, "A Pollster's Worst Nightmare: Declining Response Rates," *The Washington Post National Weekly Edition,* July 5–11, 1993, p. 37; John Hibbing and Elizabeth Theiss-Morse, *Congress as Public Enemy* (Cambridge: Cambridge University Press, 1995).

8. Theodore J. Lowi, *The Personal President* (Ithaca, N.Y.: Cornell University Press, 1985).

9. Paul F. Boller, Jr., *Presidential Anecdotes* (New York: Oxford University Press, 1981), p. 50.

10. Lowi, *The Personal President.*

11. David Halberstam, *The Powers That Be* (New York: Dell, 1980), p. 30.

12. "A Talk with Clinton," *Newsweek,* January 25, 1993, p. 37.

13. Bush's ratings fluctuated considerably. They achieved record highs during the Persian Gulf War after being fairly low in mid-1990.

14. Richard E. Neustadt, *Presidential Power: The Politics of Leadership from FDR to Carter* (New York: John Wiley & Sons, 1980).

15. Samuel Kernell, *Going Public: New Strategies of Presidential Leadership* (Washington, D.C.: CQ Press, 1986), p. 15.

16. Reported in George C. Edwards III, *Presidential Influence in Congress* (San Francisco: W. H. Freeman, 1980), p. 125.

17. Quoted in Dick Kirschten, "Reagan Warms Up for Political Hardball," *National Journal,* February 9, 1985, p. 328.

18. Edwards, *Presidential Influence,* p. 127.

19. Neustadt, *Presidential Power,* p. 130.

20. "Presidential Support: Bush's Success Rate Sinks to Near-Record Low," *Congressional Quarterly,* December 22, 1990, pp. 4183–87.

21. William Safire, "Bush's Gamble," *New York Times Magazine,* October 18, 1992, p. 41.

22. Garry Wills, *Lincoln at Gettysburg* (New York: Simon & Schuster, 1992), p. 31, quoting from Roy P. Basler, ed., *The Collected Works of Abraham Lincoln,* Vol 7 (n.p.: Rutgers, 1955), pp. 16–17.

23. Kernell, *Going Public.*

24. Ibid., p. 120.

25. Ibid., pp. 38–42.

26. "Notes and Comments," *The New Yorker,* November 7, 1988, p. 29.

27. Paul Taylor, "Pigsty Politics," *Washington Post National Weekly Edition,* February 13–19, 1989, p. 7.

28. From presidential scholar Fred I. Greenstein, quoted in "White House Notebook: When Clinton Speaks . . . Does Anyone Listen?"*National Journal,* February 11, 1995, p. 378.

29. "The Presidency," *Newsweek,* December 20, 1993, p. 46.

30. Dennis M. Simon and Charles W. Ostrom, Jr., "The Politics of Prestige: Popular Support and the Modern Presidency," *Presidential Studies Quarterly* 18 (Fall 1988), pp. 741–59.

31. George C. Edwards III, *The Public Presidency* (New York: St. Martin's Press, 1983), p. 253.

32. John Mueller, *War, Presidents and Public Opinion* (New York: John Wiley & Sons, 1970).

33. For example, see Edwards, *The Public Presidency,* pp. 239–47.

34. Poll scores reported here are from the following *National Journal* issues: December 8, 1990, p. 2993; January 19, 1991, p. 185; and February 16, 1991, p. 412.

35. For more on the Gulf War's impact on Bush's ratings, see John A. Krosnick and Laura A. Brannon, "The Impact of the Gulf War on the Ingredients of Presidential Evaluations: Multidimensional Effects of Political Involvement," *American Political Science Review* 87 (December, 1993), pp. 963–975.

36. Richard Morin, "A-Not-So-Bad Midterm Grade," *The Washington Post National Weekly Edition,* February 20–26, 1995, p. 37.

37. These survey results are from "Opinion Outlook," *National Journal,* February 18, 1995, p. 452.

38. Hibbing and Theiss-Morse, ibid.; Bruce Buchanan, *The Presidential Experience: What the Office Does to the Man* (Englewood Cliffs, N.J.: Prentice-Hall, 1978).

39. Clinton Rossiter, *The American Presidency* (New York: Harcourt Brace, 1956).

40. Thomas F. Cronin, *The State of the Presidency* (Boston: Little, Brown, 1975), p. 118.

41. James Reston, "Cut the Public Relations Budget," *Lincoln Star,* February 7, 1989, p. 6.

42. Fred I. Greenstein, *The Hidden-Hand Presidency* (New York: Basic Books, 1982), p. 139.

43. Quoted in Richard Pious, *The American Presidency* (New York: Basic Books, 1979), p. 244.

44. Ann Reilly Dowd, "What Managers Can Learn from Manager Reagan," *Fortune,* September 15, 1986, pp. 32–41.

45. See John H. Kessel, "The Structures of the Reagan White House," *American Journal of Political Science 28* (May 1984), pp. 231–58.

46. Maureen Dowd, "On Washington: Beached," *The New York Times Magazine,* June 19, 1994, p. 18.

47. See Ronald Moe, "Traditional Organizational Principles and the Managerial Presidency: From Phoenix to Ashes," *Public Administration Review,* March/April, 1990, pp. 129–40.

48. "Justice Says Meese's Conduct Intolerable," *Lincoln Journal,* January 17, 1989, p. 1.

49. "Beyond Sound Bites," *Newsweek,* October 17, 1988, pp. 27–28.

50. For discussion of the president's removal powers in light of a 1988 Supreme Court decision regarding independent counsels, see John A. Rohr, "Public Administration, Executive Power, and Constitutional Confusion" and Rosemary O'Leary, "Response to John Rohr," *Public Administration Review 49* (March/April 1989), pp. 108–15.

51. Associated Press, "Poll Shows Americans Want a Strong Leader," *Lincoln Journal,* June 16, 1992, p. 5.

52. *United States v. Curtiss-Wright Export Corporation,* 299 U.S. 304 (1936).

53. For a discussion of these styles, see John P. Burke and Fred I. Greenstein, *How Presidents Test Reality: Decisions on Vietnam, 1954 and 1965* (New York: Russell Sage Foundation, 1989), and Burt Solomon, "Making Foreign Policy in Secret May Be Easy, But It Carries Risks," *National Journal,* January 12, 1991, pp. 90–91.

54. Aaron Wildavsky, "The Two Presidencies," *Transaction* 4 (December 1966), pp. 6–7.

55. "A Furor over the Secret War," *Newsweek,* April 23, 1984, p. 22.

56. Shanto Iyengar, *Is Anyone Responsible? How Television Frames Political Issues* (Chicago: University of Chicago, 1991), pp. 107–13;

George Lardner Jr. and Walter Pincus, "The Source of the Iran-Contra Mess Is Tracked to Reagan," *Washington Post National Weekly Edition,* January 24–30, 1994, p. 13.

57. See the discussion in the *Federalist Paper #69,* written by Alexander Hamilton.

58. Quoted in "Notes and Comment," *New Yorker,* June 1, 1987, p. 23.

59. Ibid.

60. John Barry, "What Schwarzkopf's Book Leaves Out," *Newsweek,* September 28, 1992, p. 68.

61. *Youngstown Sheet and Tube Co. v. Sawyer,* 343 U.S. 579 (1952).

62. Charles W. Ostrom, Jr., and Brian I. Job, "The President and the Political Use of Force," *American Political Science Review* 80 (June 1986), pp. 541–66.

63. Quoted in Lowi, *The Personal President,* p. 133.

64. Elizabeth Drew, "Letter from Washington," *The New Yorker,* February 4, 1991, p. 83.

65. Richard J. Stoll, "The Sound of the Guns," *American Politics Quarterly* 15 (April 1987), pp. 223–37.

66. Richard J. Barnet, *The Rockets' Red Glare: When America Goes to War—The Presidents and the People* (New York: Simon and Schuster, 1990).

67. Hibbing and Theiss-Morse, *Congress as Public Enemy.*

68. Colette Fraley, "Foster Clears One Hurdle, Hopes for Floor Vote," *Congressional Quarterly Weekly Report,* May 27, 1995, p. 1508.

12 The Bureaucracy

You Are There

Attacking AIDS

You are the surgeon general of the United States, C. Everett Koop. It is 1986 and President Reagan has asked you, the government's top medical officer, to report to him on what has become a major problem: AIDS, or acquired immune deficiency syndrome. AIDS involves a virus that weakens the body's immunity, making it vulnerable to deadly infections.

There have been more than 35,000 cases of AIDS so far in the United States, 493 of them children. Those who contract AIDS inevitably die, as 20,000 Americans have so far. You estimate that 1.5 million people have been exposed to the virus and that 270,000 will develop AIDS by 1991.[1] In the United States, people with the most risk of getting it are intravenous drug users and homosexual men.[2] However, AIDS has begun to appear among heterosexual men and women through contact with intravenous drug users, prostitutes, bisexuals, and those who had multiple blood transfusions before the spring of 1985, when blood banks began testing for AIDS.

As long as the first two groups provided almost all the victims, most people did not worry about AIDS. As it began to spread, however, it became a major issue arousing considerable public anxiety. For example, real estate agents trying to sell Rock Hudson's house found that clients would not enter it because they knew he had died of AIDS. And some parents have tried to bar child victims of AIDS from the schools their children attend.

Now the president has asked for a report advising him what to do. You do not expect an effective vaccine to be available until the mid-1990s at the earliest. A major issue that your report must deal with is whether we should require mandatory testing for AIDS. A blood test can reveal exposure to the AIDS virus, but it cannot predict who will get the disease because some who carry the virus will not contract the disease. Still, finding out who has been exposed to the virus can help limit the exposure of others to it.

Already, military recruits and Foreign Service officers must take a blood test to determine if they have been exposed to AIDS. Proposals have been made to test many others, such as convicted prostitutes and intravenous drug users, hospital patients from 15 to 49 years of age, venereal disease patients, and couples seeking marriage licenses. Secretary of Education William Bennett, whose views often echo the president's, also wants to include prison inmates and people planning to immigrate here. He says the government should notify spouses and past sexual partners if test results are positive—that is, if evidence of exposure to AIDS is found.

Many conservatives view AIDS as a moral issue. They think AIDS is a punishment for homosexuality and drug use. Some charge that public health officials are "intimidated by the homosexual lobby." One called AIDS the "first politically protected disease in the history of mankind."[3] They want you to recommend mandatory testing to identify who is infected so government can quarantine those who will not change their sexual or drug habits to protect society.

Most public health experts reject mandatory testing as unworkable. They argue that many people will go underground to avoid being tested. They also say mandatory testing of huge

CONTINUED 

Bureau of Engraving and Printing employees check the quality of $20 bills. The woman at the right is holding $8,000 worth of mistakes.

OUTLINE

Bureaucracy
- Nature of Bureaucracy
- Public and Private Bureaucracies

Federal Bureaucracy
- Growth of the Bureaucracy
- Why the Bureaucracy Has Grown
- Types of Bureaucracy

Bureaucratic Functions
- Making Policy
- Administering Policy
- Other Functions

Expectations About the Federal Bureaucracy
- Responsiveness
- Neutral Competence

Controlling the Bureaucracy
- President
- Congress
- Courts
- Interest Groups and Individuals

Conclusion: Is the Bureaucracy Responsive?

Former Surgeon General Koop visits an AIDS patient.

numbers of people will produce mistakes in test results. Further, most experts oppose mandatory testing as a violation of doctor/patient confidentiality and doubt that most people will identify their sexual partners. They add that mandatory testing will only increase discrimination against homosexuals and others who have been exposed to AIDS and who may or may not contract it.

Few experts agree with Secretary Bennett, who argues that the key to stopping AIDS is to teach sexual abstinence to our children. Most experts recommend educating young people about "safe sex" and contraception. They say abstinence as a policy is unrealistic given the emphasis on sex in our society, as illustrated by studies showing that television programming refers to sexual intercourse at least once an hour. Their views reflect Senator Paul Simon's (D-Ill.) remark that, "It's been too long since [Bennett] was a teenager."

Many conservatives object strongly to sex education in schools. Referring to "safe sodomy" instead of "safe sex," they say "condomania" means we have given up trying to raise our children properly.

The president is comfortable with conservative views on AIDS. When he appointed you, you were a surgeon in Philadelphia, known for having pioneered techniques to separate Siamese twins and for being a born-again Christian with conservative views on abortion and birth control. You know your views were more important to the president than your surgical innovations. You agree with him on many issues and want to write a report he will like. Your political instincts push you this way.

On the other side of the coin, and in government there is always another side to the coin, you are a doctor who respects the views of health-care professionals. You want to write a report that will help fight AIDS, without political interference. What should you do?

Americans expect their government to deliver billions of dollars worth of services to them, from highways for fast-moving cars to Social Security payments on time, from clean running water to safe neighborhoods, from protection from foreign enemies to cures for cancer. At the same time, most Americans denigrate their government and its bureaucracy, and some even express hatred toward it. In 1995, in Oklahoma City, scores of people were murdered because they were federal bureaucrats (or happened to be in the same building with bureaucrats).

Despite the strong emotions sometimes directed toward them, federal bureaucrats are ordinary people. But the jobs they are asked to do and the number of different groups to which they are responsible makes them a target for public distress with society's problems.

The federal bureaucracy employs over three million civilians, who work in more than 800 different occupations in 100 agencies, and over two million uniformed military personnel. The bureaucracy executes or enforces policies made by Congress and the president. Because policymakers have given government many different goals, the bureaucracy has many different jobs. It analyzes the soil, runs hospitals and utilities, fights drug abuse, checks manufacturers' claims about their products, and does many other things.

To some, the bureaucracy is the fourth branch of government—powerful, uncontrollable, and often seeming to have a life of its own. As the part of government that carries out the law, the bureaucracy is also political. People disagree about whether it does its job well, largely because they disagree about the goals policymakers set for it. One person's lazy, red tape-ridden, uncaring bureaucracy is another's responsive agency.

➤BUREAUCRACY

Around the turn of the century, the German social scientist Max Weber predicted that bureaucracy would someday dominate society. That future is now. Bureaucracy affects almost everything we do.

Nature of Bureaucracy

Although individual bureaucracies differ in many ways, all share some common features.[4] For example, all have hierarchies of authority; that is, everyone in a bureaucracy has a place in a pyramidal network of jobs with fewer near the top and more near the bottom. Almost everyone in a bureaucracy has a boss and, unless one is at the bottom of a hierarchy, some subordinates.

Individuals with more expertise and experience tend to have more authority. As a result, bureaucracy is not always consistent with democratic principles, which hold that everyone should have the same opportunity to influence events. Indeed, bureaucracy can endanger individual opportunities to express opinions, raise doubts about the value of individual opinions, and jeopardize the availability of information to individuals. In effect, bureaucratic tendencies, if unrestrained, can transform "citizens" into "subordinates."

Public and Private Bureaucracies

Many people associate public bureaucracies with monotony and inefficiency. A Virginia company sold a "Bureaucrat" doll, calling it "a product of no redeeming social value. Place the Bureaucrat on a stack of papers on your desk, and he will just sit on them."[5]

Although stereotyping the public service can produce some laughs, it misses the similarities shared by public and private bureaucracies. For example, both involve a good deal of routine. Auditing expense vouchers is as routine in a business firm as in a public

"I'm sorry, dear, but you knew I was a bureaucrat when you married me."

agency. Both also have workers who are productive and efficient and others who are not. Executives in the Defense Department bought $600 toilet seats and $650 ashtrays. Their private counterparts at Chrysler, Lockheed, Penn Central, and hundreds of banks and savings and loans ran their businesses into the ground.

To some extent, the distinction between private and public bureaucracies has become blurred.[6] However, Americans typically distinguish public from private bureaucracies by looking at goals and openness.

Goals

Businesses are supposed to make a profit while public agencies are supposed to promote the "public interest." Although people disagree over what the "public interest" is, they know public agencies do not exist to make a profit.

Public and private bureaucratic goals differ in another way too. It is usually easier to measure and put a value on efforts to achieve private goals than public ones. We can identify the value of a chair or a house by computing the cost of building them. Placing a value on such public goals as consumer safety or education is much harder. How many children must die from eating the contents of medicine bottles before government should require pharmaceutical manufacturers to use childproof caps on bottles? How many lives saved make it worthwhile for government to require auto manufacturers to install mandatory seat belts, thereby raising auto prices?

Difficulties in measuring what government agencies do and disagreements over defining the public interest often produce charges that public bureaucracy is wasteful. Indeed, over two-thirds of the American public believes government programs are usually inefficient and wasteful.[7] Of course, private corporations may waste far more than government.[8] But government spending is so great that even if it wastes only proportionally as much money as a typical citizen does, the sums are vast.

Discussions of government "waste" are confusing because they refer to two quite different things. One involves inefficient or corrupt government agencies, those that, for example, do not get competitive bids and therefore pay more than they need to for supplies. Waste also occurs when more employees are hired than are necessary to do a job, when consultants are paid to do little, or when errors are made in making welfare or farm subsidy payments so that recipients are overpaid.

A second kind of government "waste" is a program that some people find objectionable, no matter how well run it is. This meaning of waste has little to do with mismanagement or fraud. Waste in this sense may mean that a particular program serves relatively few people at a large cost. For example, a government commission labeled the operation of hundreds of very small post offices "wasteful." The commission did not allege fraud or mismanagement but said the post offices cost a lot for the small number of people served. However, residents of small communities argued that their post offices were not a waste but an important source of community pride.

The average citizen probably does not think much about waste, particularly this second kind, in private bureaucracies. If a business or industry makes a profit, we assume it is not being wasteful. We may not like chocolate-covered raisins, but we do not consider their manufacturer wasteful for making them as long as the product is profitable.

Openness

The openness of public bureaucracy is a second way of distinguishing it from private bureaucracy. Both

---

The Under Secretary of Energy
Washington, DC 20585

December 3, 1992

MEMORANDUM FOR SECRETARIAL OFFICERS

SUBJECT: NE/NE-60 Concurrence

Recently, memoranda have been prepared for my signature or directed to departmental offices from other departmental offices which contain statements regarding whether the direction contained in the memorandum is applicable to Naval Reactors (NE-60). Several memoranda have been incorrect in their assumption regarding the effects on NE-60, resulting in unnecessary further correspondence to correct the misunderstanding.

Applicability to NE-60 of a contemplated action is not always obvious. In many cases, the impact is either indirect or the direct impact is not appreciated due to lack of understanding of the scope of NE-60 responsibility. To avoid misunderstandings in the future, you are requested to consult NE regarding applicability statements before they are made and before memoranda are presented to me, the Secretary, or Deputy Secretary for signature.

I appreciate your attention to this matter.

Hugo Pomrehn
Hugo Pomrehn

Sometimes real examples of bureaucratic thinking are stranger than ones we might imagine. Every issue, *Washington Monthly* reprints a memo that parodies bureaucratic language. Is it any wonder ordinary people do not trust—or understand—the bureaucracy?

Some local post offices are economically inefficient, but residents of small towns lobby Congress to keep them open.

often have internal disagreements about their goals, but differences about public agency goals are usually more visible. This visibility, or openness, is important in making public agencies responsive.

The question, of course, is openness to whom? Because the bureaucracy is doing the public's business, one answer is being open to the public. But being open to the public also means being open to the media who want to report significant conflicts and decisions made in the executive branch and open to interest groups who want to influence agencies' decisions.

In the Sunshine Act of 1977 and the Freedom of Information Act of 1966, as amended in 1974, Congress recognized the importance of keeping public bureaucracies open. The Sunshine Act requires regularity agencies, such as the Interstate Commerce Commission, to give advance notice of the date, time, place, and agenda of their meetings and to follow certain rules to prevent unwarranted secrecy. The Freedom of Information Act lets people obtain information from agencies if it is not classified or concerned with sensitive matters.

The Freedom of Information Act was intended to make agencies more open to the public, but most requests for information come from businesses, interest groups, lawyers, and the media. Very few members of the general public take advantage of it. But groups that are directly affected by an agency's decisions have a strong incentive to use the act. Thus, in 1985, 85% of the requests for information submitted to the Food and Drug Administration came form companies that it regulates. That information enables those companies to evaluate their strategies for influencing the agency's decisions that affect them. And media want to uncover disagreements and conflicts in the agency's internal decision-making process, something no agency would welcome.

Efforts to make government agencies more open often run up against a desire to limit the distribution of critical or embarrassing information. It is the rare public or private bureaucracy that wants to reveal its failures. Thus, an evaluation of the Freedom of Information Act in 1972 found that agencies used many tactics to discourage people from seeking information, such as delaying responses to requests, charging high fees for copies of records (the State Department once charged $10 a page for copying records), and requiring detailed descriptions of material in requests for information.[9] In 1993, the Federal Bureau of Investigation (FBI) refused to expedite the release of information to a prisoner on death row who was afraid he would be executed before the information was available. (The FBI's judgment that his situation did not show "exceptional need or urgency" was overruled by a federal court.)[10]

As the chief executive, a president's views of how open agencies should be have also been important. Recent presidents have had different views. Under Reagan and Bush, federal agencies adopted a narrow reading of the act, making it more difficult to get information.[11] Carter and Clinton attempted, somewhat unsuccessfully, to open the bureaucracy more and to classify fewer pieces of information. President Carter banned the classification of files lacking a clear relation to national security. In 1995, President Clinton issued an executive order that directs the declassification of most documents 25 years old or older and puts a 10-year limit on how long documents can remain classified unless a review determines that they should remain so.[12]

Finally, problems with the Freedom of Information Act have surfaced because it was written with the expectation that all information would be on paper. But the federal government, like private businesses, stores an increasing amount of information on computer tapes and disks. The federal bureaucracy now has over 1.25 million microcomputers, compared to only 17,500 in 1985. Retrieving the growing mass of information stored on computer can be easier than

Symbolic Solutions for Complex Problems?

Slashing the Bureaucracy

Government bureaucrats have a long history of getting under Americans' skins (recall that opposition to the king's tax collectors helped to fuel the American Revolution). Despite this perennial irritation, government continues to grow. Most Americans think government is too big, and there are many proposals to cut it. The Clinton administration plans to cut nearly 300,000 federal government positions by 1999. Republicans have proposed the end of the Departments of Education, Commerce, Housing and Urban Development, and Labor, as well as scores of government programs located in other agencies. But is cutting the size of the bureaucracy a real solution to our country's problems? Or is it a symbolic solution?

Cutting the size of the bureaucracy is a real solution if it would make government more efficient, save money, and allow us to direct more resources to attack the nation's problems or to reduce the deficit. For example, Clinton's proposed "reinvention of government," led by Vice President Gore, would cut 2,400 jobs from Health and Human Services by eliminating a layer of management, consolidating dozens of programs, turning some work over to private business, and giving states a bigger role in these programs. The vice president argues that this would create a more "customer friendly" agency.[1]

Some of those who wish to cut some of the federal agencies mentioned above believe that services can be improved by merging programs that duplicate each other, cutting some programs that no longer serve an urgent need, and increasing resources for other, more pressing needs, including deficit reduction.

Other institutions, particularly some large corporations, have found that they can operate more efficiently and serve their customers better by consolidations, cutting, and reducing the layers of management. If government achieves these successes, cutting government could be a real solution.

On the other hand, cries to cut government may be mostly a symbolic solution that does not really help us solve our nation's problems more effectively. Cutting government might not save money. For example, if private firms take over the provision of services, costs could fall, but they could also increase. Those who can pay will get the services, though not necessarily for a lower cost.[2]

Some advocates of cutting the size of government think local government can handle problems more efficiently. This is likely true in some instances but not in others. After all, the federal government got into the programs it did because some constitu-

finding information on paper. However, the act neither defines when computerized information is in the public domain nor requires agencies to save and release it. Thus the act does not say whether electronic messages used by officials to schedule meetings or exchange opinions are their private property or public records. Reagan, Bush, and Clinton aides used e-mail extensively. Bush took his aides' e-mail tapes with him when he left office and argued that the tapes were not public property. A federal appeals court ruled that these tapes are public records and must be preserved. The Clinton administration sided with Bush and argued that White House officials have a right to erase the e-mail messages they send to each other.[13] Defining such messages as public helps hold officials accountable. The act also fails to address problems created by the use of incompatible hardware and software and to protect against the loss of data over time because tapes and disks deteriorate. Congress has been trying to remedy computer-related problems for several years without success.

Some agencies are more open than others. Agencies that depend on public support and agreement with their goals are more likely to respond to media requests for information and news. The Food and Drug Administration, for instance, is much more accessible than the State Department.[14] Other agencies prefer less coverage. For them, no news is good news. The balance between openness and responsiveness to the public, and undue access for interest groups and the media has been difficult to strike.

encies were not satisfied with local or state handling of programs.

And, though we can all point to some agencies that seem ineffective, many agencies do their jobs well, and eliminating them would increase, not decrease, problems—for example, the Social Security Administration, the Securities and Exchange Commission, the air traffic control system, the Secret Service, among others. In fact, there is little evidence that, on the whole, public bureaucracies are less effective than private ones.[3]

Moreover, if we eliminated those agencies the Republicans have targeted, would our nation's problems be closer to solution? Would crime be reduced, more families be intact, our country's defense strengthened, teen-aged pregnancies decreased, or racism ameliorated? Probably not. This is not to suggest that eliminating some federal agencies might not be a bad idea, but only that doing so in and of itself is not a solution to the country's most pressing problems.[4]

Despite years of vociferous debate about whether government is too big, too intrusive, and too expensive, it is difficult to reach a conclusion about what the "right" size of government is. Government has grown considerably over the past 60 years, but so has the size and wealth of the nation. The federal government employs about 2% of all employees in the U.S.; excluding the Department of Defense, it employs 1%. Whether this is too big probably depends on your view of what government should be doing rather than of the size of government itself. That being the case, slashing the bureaucracy is likely to be predominantly a symbolic solution.

After all, if we agree that government is an appropriate agency to solve an important problem, but does it poorly, we should think about fixing the bureaucracy, not eradicating it. For example, if the military slips up (consider Pearl Harbor, the Bay of Pigs, or the bombing of the Marine barracks in Beirut), we do not argue that we should do away with it. We look for ways to make it work better.[5]

This sounds like a sensible approach. But it is easier to agree with than to implement. For example, most Americans criticize the bureaucracy in the abstract but say they are satisfied with the services they receive from particular agencies (e.g., the Postal Service and Social Security Administration).[6] But agreeing to fix the bureaucracy will not work if we do not agree on what government should do and we do not admit that some agencies work well—that government can work—and that our attention must be on agencies that work poorly.

1. For more about "reinventing" government, see: Al Gore, Jr., "The New Job of the Federal Executive," *Public Administration Review* (July/August, 1994), pp. 317–321; Ronald C. Moe, "The 'Reinventing Government' Exercise: Misinterpreting the Problem, Misjudging the Consequences," *Public Administration Review* (March/April, 1994), pp. 111–122; James Q. Wilson, "Reinventing Public Administration," *PS: Political Science & Politics* (December, 1994), pp. 667–673; and "Clinton Team Plans to Redesign HHS," *Omaha World-Herald*, May 12, 1995, p. 5.
2. Rob Gurwit, "Social Services and Reality," *Governing* (May, 1995), p. 13.
3. Nicolas Lemann, "Government *Can* Work," *The Washington Monthly* (January/February, 1994), p. 37; see also Charles Goodsell, *The Case for Bureaucracy*, 3rd ed. (Chatham, N.J.: Chatham House, 1994).
4. This point is drawn from Herbert Stein, "Shrinking Government May Not Be the Answer," *Washington Post National Weekly Edition*, March 6–12, 1995, p. 28.
5. Lemann, "Government *Can* Work," p. 36.
6. Goodsell, *The Case for Bureaucracy*, Chapter 2.

Federal Bureaucracy

Growth of the Bureaucracy

The Founders did not discuss the federal "bureaucracy," but they did recognize the need for an administration to carry out laws and programs. They envisioned administrators with only a little power, charged with "executive details" and "mere execution" of the law. But the growing size and complexity of modern society and increasing demands that government do more have dramatically changed the nature of the federal bureaucracy.

George Washington's first cabinet included only three departments and the offices of attorney general and postmaster general, employing a few hundred people. More people worked at Mount Vernon, his plantation, than in the executive branch in the 1790s.[15] The Department of State had just nine employees. By 1800, the bureaucracy was still small, with only 3,000 civil servants. Since then, the bureaucracy has grown continuously, though not always at the same rate. Three eras of especially large growth have occurred.

The first period of rapid growth followed the Civil War. This era of industrialization, westward expansion, and population growth saw increasing demands for government to provide benefits to business, labor, and farmers. So Congress established the Departments of Commerce, Labor, and Agriculture. Worries about abuses by big business also led to the creation of new bureaucracies, such as the Interstate Commerce Commission, and expanded powers for others, such as antitrust law enforcement in the Justice Department.

A second surge of bureaucratic growth took place during the Great Depression. With New Deal programs, such as Social Security and bank deposit insurance, came an expansion of bureaucracy to administer them.

A third era of bureaucratic growth came during the 1960s and 1970s as a response to public demands that government do more to fight poverty, protect the environment, promote civil rights, and ensure consumer and worker safety. During this time Congress created several new cabinet departments (Housing and Urban Development, Transportation, Energy, and Education) and agencies (Environmental Protection Agency [EPA], Occupational Safety and Health Administration [OSHA], and the Equal Employment Opportunity Commission [EEOC]).

Why the Bureaucracy Has Grown

President Reagan once expressed the popular dissatisfaction with big government by noting that he liked flying over Washington because being in the air made government look smaller. Despite Reagan's pronounced feelings about the bureaucracy, it grew by over 200,000 employees during his administration. Although many agencies lost personnel (the biggest loser was the Department of Housing and Urban Development), others such as the Defense, Justice, and Treasury Departments gained. The continued growth of the bureaucracy suggests that powerful forces in society view it as a source of benefits.

One scholar explained the bureaucracy's growth by pointing to Americans' discovery that "government can protect and assist as well as punish and repress."[16] Thus, at the same time we criticize government's growth, we demand educational services, irrigation projects, roads, airports, job training, consumer protection, and many other benefits. Each of us might be willing to cut benefits for someone else, but most of us want government benefits for ourselves.

Sometimes bureaucracies grow in response to external threats. Though World War II was won 50 years ago, our Department of Defense has never returned to its prewar size or scope. The Cold War gave us a new reason to support a massive military establishment. And of course, from the war as well as later ones came demands for services for veterans, another area of government growth.

Because the bureaucracy has grown in response to demands for public services, its growth has not been uncontrolled as some have charged. Every agency needs congressional and presidential approval of its programs, appropriations, staffing, and procedures. In fact, government also grows, ironically, because the president and Congress want it to be more accountable. The number of managerial layers in it has almost doubled in the last 30 to 40 years because of presidential and congressional efforts to control agency rule making and enforcement. This has produced waste, inefficiency, and, ironically, more difficulty in holding agencies accountable.[17] Bureaucrats cannot produce growth on their own. Every agency exists because it is valuable to enough people with enough influence to sustain it.

The growth of the bureaucracy should be seen in the perspective of the overall growth of our economy and population. For example, the number of federal bureaucrats for every 1,000 people in the United States decreased from 16 in 1953 to 11.2 in 1994.[18] This trend will continue. A 1994 law requires cuts of almost 273,000 bureaucratic jobs by 1999. By 1995, 78,000 people had left the bureaucracy as a result of hiring freezes, buyouts, and layoffs. Another 60,000 will follow in 1996. Total personnel costs were only 15% of total federal spending in 1994. If the government fired all its employees and used only volunteers, it would still run a deficit.

The major growth in public employment has been at the state and local levels. Over 37% of all government workers were federal employees in 1953; in 1994 only 14% were. Only 12% of these federal civil servants work in the Washington, D.C. metropolitan area.

Some of these trends are illustrated in Figure 1, showing the growth in the size, cost, and regulatory activities of the executive branch. Although the size of the bureaucracy has been relatively stable, its production of regulations has grown more, especially from about 1968 to 1980, and its expenditure of funds has doubled since 1961.

Types of Bureaucracy

Although the Constitution says little about the organization of the executive branch, the Founders probably expected all bureaucratic jobs to be included in only a few departments, each headed by one person. Yet the bureaucracy has become much more complex than this. There are several major types of federal bureaucracy.[19]

Departments

Fourteen departments are directly responsible to the president and headed by his appointees (see Figure 2).

FIGURE 1
Federal Government Growth: Money, Rules, and People

The numbers listed vertically on the left are percentages, comparing each year with 1961. They indicate the growth of federal regulatory activity, federal spending, and the size of the civil service, each on a per person basis.

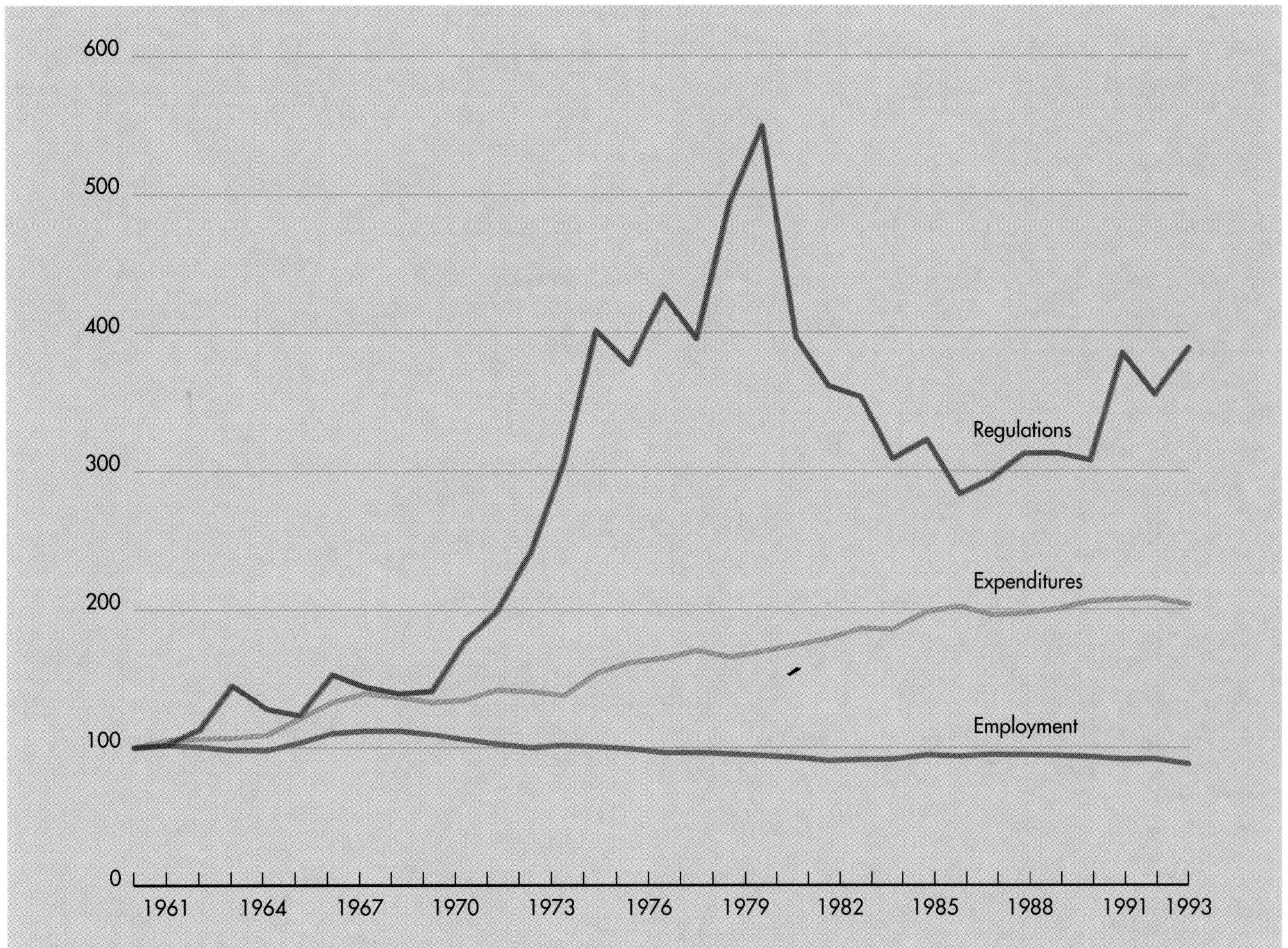

Sources: Idea for chart from Hugh Heclo, "Issue Networks and the Executive Establishment," in Anthony King, ed., *The New American Political System* (Washington, D.C.: American Enterprise Institute, 1978), p. 90. Federal employment statistics from *Budget of the United States Government: Fiscal Year 1994*, p. 42. Data on expenditures are from the Bureau of Economic Analysis, Department of Commerce, *Budget of the United States: Fiscal Year 1994* (Washington, D.C.: U.S. Government Printing Office, 1993), p. 101 and *Budget of the United States: Fiscal Year 1995*, p. 251. Federal regulations information is based on the number of pages in *The Federal Register for each year.*

Thirteen of these appointees, called secretaries, comprise the president's cabinet, along with the attorney general who runs the Justice Department. Departments constitute the lion's share of the executive branch, with over 60% of all civilian workers. The largest employer is the Defense Department. The Department of Veterans Affairs is the newest department, created in 1989 from an independent agency.

Independent Agencies

Independent agencies are independent only in that they are not parts of departments. Their heads are appointed by and responsible to the president. In this, independent agencies resemble departments. They differ from departments, however, in that they are often smaller and their heads do not sit in the cabinet. The largest of these agencies are the National Aero-

FIGURE 2
The Development and Size of Cabinet Departments

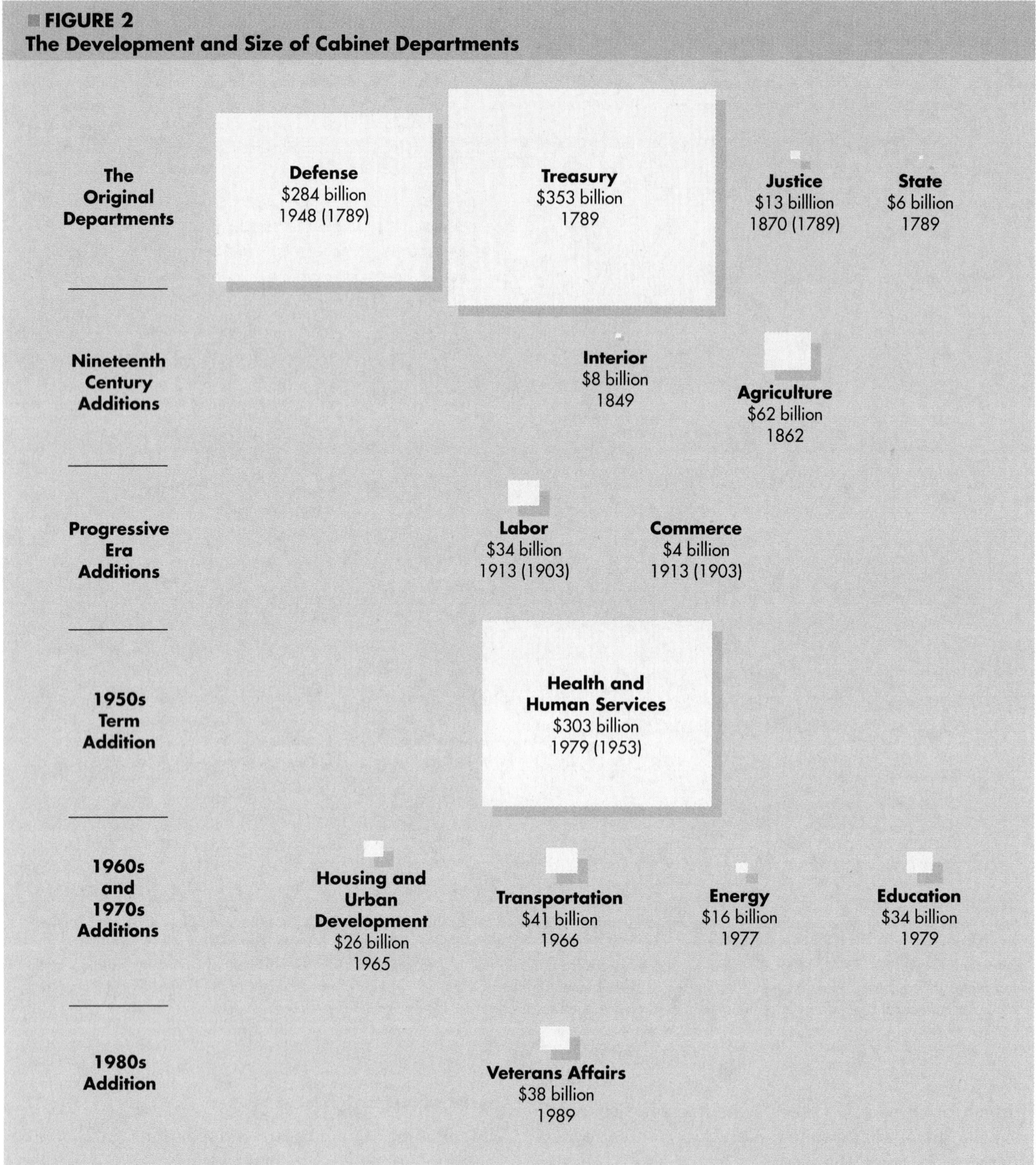

Note: The figures in each box include 1994 budget estimates and year of founding. Some departments have undergone a name change or major reorganization. The date of their initial founding is in parentheses. The modern Defense Department replaced the Departments of War (1789) and Navy (1798); the Justice Department replaced the Attorney General (1789); the Commerce and Labor Departments were first established in 1903 as a joint enterprise; and the Health and Human Services Department and the Education Department replaced the Department of Health, Education, and Welfare (1953).

Source: *Budget of the United States Government: Fiscal Year 1996* (Washington, D.C.: U.S. Government Printing Office, 1995), p. 215.

New Populism

Are Bureaucrats the Enemy?

When George Wallace ran as a third-party candidate for president in 1968, he campaigned against "pointy-headed bureaucrats" in Washington making decisions that regulated good people's lives. Bureaucrats, according to Wallace, were out of touch with everyday citizens and their concerns. A historian describes how populists see government workers: "The federal bureaucrat, overeducated and amoral, scoffs at the God-fearing nuclear family in its modest home, a crucifix on the wall and a flagpole in the yard."[1] The conflict between presumed governmental goals and citizens' true values cannot be made clearer. Bureaucrats became symbols of big government and everything populists dislike about big government.

Similar charges and criticisms abound today. Patrick Buchanan and Ross Perot are only the latest in a long line of politicians who run for office by criticizing government and the people who work for it. When they refer to "Washington," we all understand the reference: Big government using too much money to do things that are not needed. Why does big government do so many unneeded things? Populists would answer, "Because bureaucrats do not understand how people live. They are not like you and me." Instead, they are busybodies committed to expanding government's size, spending taxpayers' money, and designing regulations to make life more difficult for individuals and business.

Are government bureaucrats really like this? Are they different from other citizens? A comparison using a large national sample found that public employees are like everyone else in most ways. They are no more likely to favor raising taxes or government spending; they have about the same confidence in government and other institutions—such as organized religion, business, labor, and the press—as other citizens; and they are about as likely to favor busing and gun control.

When civil servants do differ from other citizens, they seem more open to diversity. For example, they are more likely to say they would vote for a black or woman as president and less likely to accept traditional gender roles. And they are somewhat *less* likely than other Americans to approve government intrusions into people's private lives. They are less likely to approve censoring people with unpopular views or laws banning pornography or interracial marriage. On only one issue are they more liable to favor "big government." They are somewhat more likely to favor wiretapping.

Not only do federal bureaucrats resemble us, they live around us, too. A small number—fewer than 10%—work in Washington, D.C.,[2] but the rest work in branch offices scattered throughout the nation. Check the U.S. Government listing in your telephone book and see how many offices are located in or near your home town. All the people who work there are bureaucrats in one sense or another. But they are your neighbors, pretty ordinary people you meet on the street every day.

Populist appeals affect us more deeply, however, when bureaucrats are depicted as colorless drudges, small cogs in vast impersonal machines, interested only in their paperwork. When we distrust big government, we easily assume that people who work for it must be different from the rest of us and do not care about us. That irritates us, making populist rhetoric that much more attractive. It is easier to criticize big government and the faceless bureaucrats who run it than to acknowledge that bureaucrats are no different than the rest of us.

1. Michael Kazin, *The Populist Persuasion: An American History* (New York: Basic Books, 1995), p. 1.
2. U.S. Department of Commerce, Bureau of the Census, *Statistical Abstract of the United States, 1995*, 115th ed. (Washington, D.C.: U.S. Government Printing Office, 1995), p. 352, table 544.

Source: Gregory B. Lewis, "In Search of the Machiavellian Milquetoasts: Comparing Attitudes of Bureaucrats and Ordinary People," *Public Administration Review* (May/June, 1990): 220–27.

nautics and Space Administration and the General Services Administration.

Independent Regulatory Boards and Commissions

These boards and commissions regulate some aspect of the economy. Five to 10 presidential appointees head every independent regulatory board and commission. By law, each board and commission must be balanced with members of both major political parties. Appointees serve staggered terms and cannot be removed by presidents who dislike their decisions. Examples of such boards include the Federal Communications Commission, which regulates the electronic media and interstate telephone and telegraph rates. The Securities and Exchange Commission makes and enforces rules regarding stocks, bonds, and securities.

In its early years Washington was described as "a miserable little swamp." When this photo was taken in 1882, the government was still comparatively small.

And the National Labor Relations Board regulates labor-management relations.

These and other regulatory agencies are "independent" because they are supposed to work free of partisan influences and presidential control. Many people believe regulatory problems are technical, not political, and should be removed from politics insofar as possible. Others point out that technical decisions may also be political. Just how strict or lax the regulations for nuclear power plants should be is a political as well as a technical question because it involves value judgments, weighing costs, health, and safety. Because the voice of the public is heard through elected officials, the immunity of regulators from "politics" means immunity from public, as well as presidential or congressional, control.

As a result, in recent years Congress has tended to place regulatory functions in the hands of agencies within the executive branch, which are more responsive to the president through his power of removal.

Government Corporations

Although government corporations charge for their services or products like private firms, their charges are not meant to make a profit. Historically, these corporations were created when government decided a service was important to the public interest but no private company could profit from providing it. The first government corporation, the Tennessee Valley Authority, supplies electricity to its part of the country. COMSAT markets satellite communications capabilities to businesses and other governments. The Postal Service and AMTRAK (passenger railroad service) are other examples.

The operating costs and incomes of government corporations are not counted as expenditures and revenues in the annual budget. Thus they have become an attractive device for elected officials who want to spend without enlarging the deficit. Real spending and deficits are put "off budget" to make the deficit look smaller. For example, when the Post Office showed a projected $2 billion deficit in 1990, it was taken out of the official budget.[20] Moving spending off the budget can be done with any government program, but officials find it easier to do with government corporations.

➤Bureaucratic Functions

After elected officials make a law, someone must carry it out. That is the job of the bureaucracy. Bureaucrats convert laws passed by Congress and signed by the president into rules and activities that have an actual impact on people and things. We call this process **policy implementation.**

For example, the Americans with Disabilities Act directs employers to make a "reasonable accommodation" for a competent worker with a disability that "substantially limits" a major life activity such as seeing or walking, except when this causes "undue hardship."[21] Although the act went into effect in 1992 and a bureaucracy, the Equal Employment Opportunity Commission (EEOC), is still trying to determine what the act means, much is unclear. What is the difference between a "reasonable accommodation" and an "undue hardship"? When voters want local governments to spend less, is the $2 million Des Plaines, Illinois, spent for sidewalks and curb cuts an "undue hardship" or not?[22] Will the EEOC let colleges and universities make only some classrooms accessible to students and staff in wheelchairs or must every classroom be accessible to people with disabilities, by elevators, for example, at a cost of millions of dollars on older campuses?

Exercising its rule-making function, the U.S. Customs Service classified G. I. Joe as a doll rather than a toy soldier. Consequently, G. I. Joe imports are subject to a 12% import tax (toy soldiers are not taxed).

After the answers to such questions are developed and formulated into rules, implementation involves carrying out the rules and negotiations over interpretations of the rules. State and local counterparts of the EEOC and their clients must be informed of the rules, assisted in their attempts to use the rules, and monitored in their progress. Bills must be paid, disputes resolved, and information collected as to how successful the program is.

As this example illustrates, the general process of policy implementation has two major components: making policies and administering them.

Making Policy

Over time, the policymaking functions of public bureaucracies have grown. Industrialization, population growth, urbanization, and profound changes in science, transportation, and communications have put problems of a more complex nature on government's agenda. The large number and technical nature of these problems, as well as policy differences among its members, have often limited Congress's ability to draft specific policy responses.

Congress often responds to this situation by enacting a general statement of goals and identifying actions that would help achieve them. Congress then has an agency with the relevant expertise draft specific rules that will achieve these goals. Thus, Congress gives agencies **delegated legislative authority,** the authority to draft, as well as execute, specific policies. The Tax Reform Act of 1986, for example, required thousands of rules to be written by the Internal Revenue Service (IRS) and the Treasury Department.

Agency-made policy is just as binding as acts of Congress because agencies make it on Congress's behalf. In strictly numerical terms, agencies make much more policy than Congress. On average, for example, executive agencies issue about 7,000 new rules and regulations a year compared to Congress's annual production of about 300 new laws.

Many political scientists believe Congress abdicates its authority and acts in an irresponsible manner by refusing, because of political pressures and its heavy work load, to develop specific guidelines for agencies.[23] This congressional inaction has contributed to partisan conflicts. From 1980 to 1993, intense policy differences divided Democratic congressional majorities

American Diversity

Women and Minorities in the Civil Service

Americans expect their public bureaucracies to be open and responsive. Andrew Jackson recognized this when he opened the civil service to frontiersmen of "common" origins. He hoped to make the bureaucracy more responsive by putting his frontier supporters in office. In the twentieth century, the expectation that public agencies should be open to all qualified applicants has given some groups, such as the Irish, Jews, and blacks, more job opportunities than in the more restricted private corporate world.

Although progress has been made, the federal bureaucracy does not yet fully reflect the diversity of the American people. There seems to be a "glass ceiling" in the bureaucracy that keeps women and minority men out of top management positions.[1] In 1992, most women worked in lower civil service grades doing mostly clerical and service jobs; women held only 13% of the top-level jobs. Women tend to earn several thousand dollars less and to be in jobs one to three grades lower than men with the same levels of education and federal job experience. Women are also less likely to be promoted in their first five years of federal employment than men with the same qualifications and background. And fewer women than men get to Grade 13, the gateway to supervisory jobs. Thus, women are less likely than men to be in grades from which they can be promoted to top-level jobs. Similarly, blacks comprised 28% of the lowest four grades and only 5% of the executive level. Seven percent of the lowest 4 grades were Hispanics compared to 2% at the top level. Regarding minorities, a government report found that minority workers are almost three times as likely to be fired as white workers.[2]

In the 1970s, both women and minorities made progress in filling high-level civil service jobs. In the 1980s, women made more progress than minorities, though in proportion to their population percent, minorities are better represented than women. Major discrepancies remain, in part, because those who enforced equal opportunity and nondiscrimination regulations were white men

Percentage of Women in White-Collar Full-Time Jobs in the Federal Civil Service by Job Grade[3]

GENERAL SCHEDULE Grades:	1970	1980	1990	1992
1–6 (clerical and service jobs)	72	74	75	74
Grades 7–10	33	46	55	57
Grades 11–12	10	19	35	35
Grades 13–15	3	8	19	21
Grades 16–18 (top-level jobs)	1	4	11	13

Sources: U.S. Department of Commerce, Bureau of the Census, *Statistical Abstract of the United States: 1987,* 107th ed. (Washington, D.C.: U.S. Government Printing Office, 1986), pp. 311–12; U.S. Office of Personnel Management, Federal Civilian Workforce Statistics, *Employment and Trends as of January 1989;* and U.S. Office of Personnel Management, *Central Personnel Data File,* September 30, 1990. The Office of Personnel Management provided figures for 1992.

and Republican executive branch officials. Committed to cutting domestic spending, the latter ignored or only partially implemented legislative directives they disliked. The administration justified this by arguing that Congress's directions were unclear. This was sometimes true. For example, a section of a bill prohibiting discrimination against people with disabilities in federally subsidized programs had no congressional hearings, no mention in committee reports and floor debates, and no explanation elsewhere.[24]

However, sometimes these complaints about Congress were just an excuse not to implement disliked policies. In response, Congress began to adopt more detailed directives to agencies. Although this resulted in less agency-made policy (see Figure 1), executive officials still argued that congressional directives they disliked were too complex and unrealistic to follow.

In effect, the competitions associated with legislative policymaking continued when Congress delegated legislative authority to agencies. This compe-

opposed to affirmative action policies. Indeed, the Justice Department backed white males who sued the government for reverse discrimination.

Problems also remain because performance evaluations in the bureaucracy favor employees who work overtime and who have worked in different offices as a result of transfers. These criteria limit the careers of many women. For example, the government's poor record of providing job-site child care means that many women cannot work overtime because they, more than men, must juggle work and family commitments. Moreover, for many women the work environment is still hostile. They believe they are not as respected as men and have to meet higher standards to be promoted and rewarded.

Some factors limit the ability of policymakers to diversify public service employment. For example, offices in parts of the country with small minority populations may have problems hiring minorities. However, other factors suggest that the diversification of the public service is inevitable. By the year 2000, 2 out of 3 new entrants into the labor force will be women, including many Hispanic and black women. What is not inevitable is that more women and minorities will hold top-level jobs. For this to happen, policymakers must set clear goals, adopt effective recruitment and training programs, and treat complaints of discrimination sympathetically.

Eleanor Roosevelt, in her role as wife and adviser to her husband Franklin Delano Roosevelt, prodded him to appoint women to high levels of the federal government. Roosevelt, here with John Kennedy and Lyndon Johnson at the 1960 Democratic National Convention, was also a Democratic leader and activist in her own right.

1. For summaries of the studies see Joanne Desky, "Women Bump Into Glass Ceiling in Government," *PA Times*, December 1, 1992, pp. 1 & 16; Pan Suk Kim and Gregory B. Lewis, "Asian Americans in the Public Service: Success, Diversity, and Discrimination," *Public Administration Review* (May/June, 1994), pp. 285–290; Gregory B. Lewis, "Is It Time to Drop the Glass Ceiling Metaphor?," and Katherine C. Naff, "A Questionof Equity in the Federal Government," both in *PA Times*, November 1, 1992, p. 8; Bill McAllister, "Female Bureaucrats, Up Against It,"*The Washington Post National Weekly Edition*, November 9–15, 1992, p. 34; and Mary E. Guy, "Three Steps Forward, Two Steps Backward: The Status of Women's Integration into Public Management," *Public Administration Review* (July/August, 1993) pp. 285–92.

2. Stephen Barr, "In the Line of Firings," *The Washington Post National Weekly Edition*, February 21–27, 1994, p. 34; and Craig Zwerling and Hilary Silver, "Race and Job Dismissals in a Federal Bureaucracy," *American Sociological Review* (October, 1992), pp. 651–660.

tition subsided when the Democrats won the White House in 1992 and reemerged after the Republicans won congressional majorities in 1994. The competition will likely continue regardless of who controls the White House and Congress because officials in both branches often have different priorities and policy positions. This puts agencies in the difficult position of having to satisfy diverse interests. To figure out what Congress, the president, and others want, agency officials read congressional debates and testimony and talk to members of Congress, committee staffers, White House aides, lobbyists, and others. While agencies also try to determine what the public wants, they are more likely to respond to well-organized and well-funded interests that closely monitor their actions. As a result, agency-made policy is often less responsive to the general public than to particular interests.

Regulation

A special kind of policymaking is called **regulation.** Though regulation is hard to define, in general, it is an action of a regulatory agency. Regulatory agencies have authority to establish standards or guidelines conferring benefits and imposing restrictions on business conduct, have heads or members appointed by the president, and have legal procedures generally governed by the Administrative Procedure Act (discussed later). Regulatory agencies include not only independent regulatory boards and commissions but also some independent agencies, such as the Environmental Protection Agency, and some agencies within cabinet departments, such as the Food and Drug Administration in Health and Human Services and OSHA within the Labor Department.

Some regulatory policies require businesses to meet standards, such as for clean air, safe disposal of toxic wastes, or safe workplaces. Failure to do so results in legal penalties. Other regulations control who can own certain goods. For example, the Federal Communications Commission licenses people to own and operate radio and television stations. Regulations may require businesses to provide information, such as the cancer warnings on cigarette packages and the labels noting sugar, salt, and vitamin content on canned food.

At J.F.K. International Airport in New York, a Department of Agriculture inspector searches for illegal aliens—insects—in fruits and vegetables that travelers bring into the United States.

Regulatory actions include two steps: making rules and adjudicating their enforcement. Rulemaking is the establishment of standards that apply to a class of individuals or businesses. For example, the Interstate Commerce Commission sets standards that apply to interstate carriers such as railroads, trucking firms, and bus lines. Adjudication occurs when agencies try individuals or firms charged with violating standards. To do this, they use procedures that are very similar to those of courts.

Because of the dangers inherent in having one agency be the lawmaker, judge, and jury, in 1946 Congress passed the Administrative Procedure Act (APA) to establish fair and open procedures. For example, agencies must publish a description of their rulemaking procedures in the *Federal Register* and hold open hearings on proposed rules or provide for another means of public input. Those who believe they have been treated unfairly by an agency have the right to take their case to court.

Antiregulation feeling helps to fuel public distrust of government. Surveys report that the number of people who think government controls too much of our daily lives has risen from 57% to 69% since 1987.[25] As Figure 1 shows, regulation has increased since then. This is largely because of the passage of the Clean Air Act, the Civil Rights Act, and the Americans with Disabilities Act during the Bush years and a reversal by Bush and Clinton appointees of the antiregulatory fervor of the Reagan years. Most Americans support the goals of these laws (e.g., 78% of the public says government should do "whatever it takes to protect the environment"[26]). But many also think the regulations produced to implement these and other laws produce wasteful paperwork and more costs than benefits. For example, officials in Madison, Wisconsin report they spend 14% of their transit budget obeying regulations to ensure bus service to the disabled, who make up 1.5% of their users.[27]

Most regulations are based on laws that direct agencies to take certain actions to accomplish certain ends. Thus, Congress gave the Environmental Protection Agency (EPA) authority to tell business to use or not use certain processes to reduce pollution. This "command and control" strategy is expensive because agencies have to employ many experts to design rules to achieve the desired ends and then have to get those they regulate to obey the rules. The strategy also allows little flexibility for the agencies and the people they regulate.

Many people believe there may be better ways to achieve the goals of clean air, fairness to the disabled,

Your Hamburger: 41,000 Regulations

Protesting "overregulation" is a popular pastime of Americans. The 41,000 regulations that accompany a hamburger may seem an obvious example of the absurdity of too much regulation. But the issue is more complicated than it seems at first glance. If government does not regulate pesticide use on crops, there is a significant risk of serious illness to consumers who eat the crops. If the government does not inspect to make sure livestock are free of tuberculosis, the incidence of TB bacteria in meat will be higher.

When examined closely, most of the regulations have a plausible rationale. But regulation is not free. The cost of regulating hamburger is about 8¢ to 11¢ per pound. Is this a high cost? It depends on the probability of contracting a serious disease and the value you as a consumer place on having some confidence in the quality of products you buy.

And then, of course, there are some regulations that are mystifying even to those not especially opposed to government regulation. What is the danger in eating a pickle sliced too thin? Only Uncle Sam knows!

Source: *U.S. News & World Report,* February 11, 1980, p. 64. Copyright 1980, U.S. News & World Report, Inc.

The hamburger, staple of the quick, inexpensive meal, is the subject of 41,000 federal and state regulations, many of those stemming from 200 laws and 111,000 precedent-setting court cases.

These rules, cited in a three-volume study by Colorado State University, touch on everything involved in meat production–grazing practices of cattle, conditions in slaughterhouses and methods used to process meat for sale to supermarkets, restaurants and fast-food outlets. Here is just a sampling of the rules and regulations governing the burger.

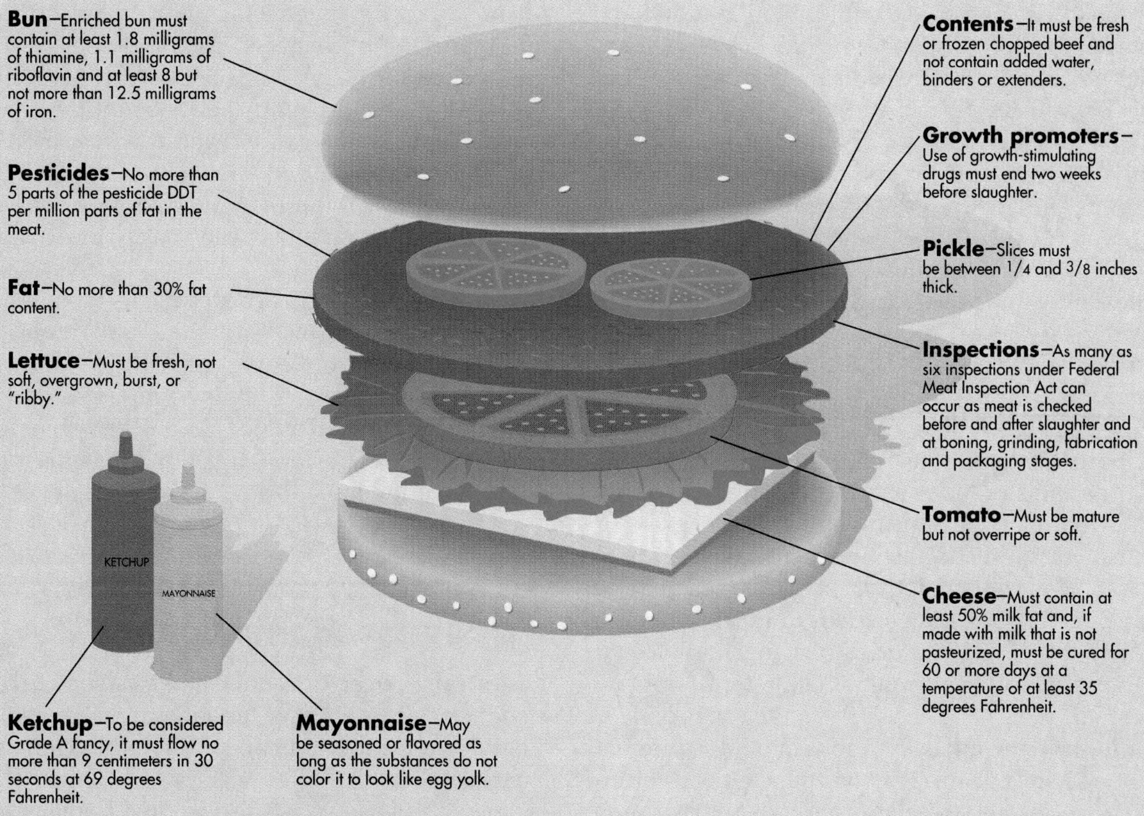

Bun—Enriched bun must contain at least 1.8 milligrams of thiamine, 1.1 milligrams of riboflavin and at least 8 but not more than 12.5 milligrams of iron.

Pesticides—No more than 5 parts of the pesticide DDT per million parts of fat in the meat.

Fat—No more than 30% fat content.

Lettuce—Must be fresh, not soft, overgrown, burst, or "ribby."

KETCHUP

MAYONNAISE

Ketchup—To be considered Grade A fancy, it must flow no more than 9 centimeters in 30 seconds at 69 degrees Fahrenheit.

Mayonnaise—May be seasoned or flavored as long as the substances do not color it to look like egg yolk.

Contents—It must be fresh or frozen chopped beef and not contain added water, binders or extenders.

Growth promoters—Use of growth-stimulating drugs must end two weeks before slaughter.

Pickle—Slices must be between 1/4 and 3/8 inches thick.

Inspections—As many as six inspections under Federal Meat Inspection Act can occur as meat is checked before and after slaughter and at boning, grinding, fabrication and packaging stages.

Tomato—Must be mature but not overripe or soft.

Cheese—Must contain at least 50% milk fat and, if made with milk that is not pasteurized, must be cured for 60 or more days at a temperature of at least 35 degrees Fahrenheit.

and other desirable objectives.[28] Some argue that we should eliminate agency regulations and rely on lawsuits by private citizens to protect public health and safety by proving in court that they have been harmed by something, like pollution. A problem with this idea is that it could pit individuals with limited means against industries with vast resources. It also moves problems to the courts more quickly. Other critics say we should entrust regulation to the states, who would finance their own efforts. Still others call for Washington to give block grants to states to set their own priorities and devise solutions consistent with broad goals set at the federal level. And others argue we should make business and industry comply with goals and standards (for example, in environmental cleanups) but leave them more discretion on how to do it.

Since the 1994 elections, some change, perhaps significant, in the regulatory process seems certain. Congress signalled its opposition to command-and-control regulation by threatening to pass bills to stop the making of new regulations for one year and to force agencies to give greater weight to the costs of new regulations (to kill those based on "minute or exaggerated risks"[29]). And Clinton issued an executive order to cut paperwork, void many regulations, and create a pilot program to give business more flexibility to comply with clean air and water requirements. These actions indicate that less regulatory activity is likely now given the influence of policymakers' preferences. However, titanic political battles lie ahead because advocates of a cleaner environment, more rights for the disabled and other interests protected by regulations point out that giving businesses more flexibility and weakening regulations is likely to erode progress toward goals they desire.

Administering Policy

Public bureaucracy's oldest job is to administer the law. To "administer" is to execute, enforce, and apply the rules that have been made either by Congress or the bureaucracy itself. Thus if policymakers decide to go to war, they must empower an agency to acquire weapons, recruit and train soldiers, and lead them in battle with a winning strategy. Policymaking without administration is usually tantamount to having no policy at all.

Administration involves thousands of different kinds of activities. It involves writing checks to farmers who receive payments for growing—or not growing—crops, providing direct services to the public, evaluating how well programs are working, prosecuting those who try to defraud the government, and maintaining buildings and offices. For forest rangers, administration involves helping backpackers in the Grand Canyon or putting out a forest fire in northern Minnesota. For postal employees, it includes delivering the mail or repairing an automatic sorting machine.

Other Functions

In the course of policymaking and administration, the bureaucracy performs other functions. It collects data, such as in the census, and makes information available to us. Much of what we know about ourselves comes from the government's collection of data on births and deaths, occupations and income, housing and health, crime, and many other things.

The bureaucracy does research too. A prime example is the Department of Agriculture, which for over 100 years has conducted research on how to grow bigger and better crops, raise healthier animals, and transport and market products more effectively.

In addition, providing continuity is an important offshoot of the bureaucracy's activities. Presidents and members of Congress come and go, and political appointees in the bureaucracy stay an average of two years. Many barely learn their jobs by the time they leave. Career civil servants tend to know more about government's past and current efforts, which can make government more productive. At the same time, the presence of careerists can make the bureaucracy less responsive.

Bureaucracy also teaches citizens about government. First, it informs us about public policies and programs. For example, we contact the National Park Service if we want to know the rules governing camping in national parks. Second, the bureaucracy performs a socialization function. It helps us learn about government and our role as citizens.

Expectations About the Federal Bureaucracy

Historically, Americans have had two sometimes contradictory expectations about public bureaucracy. They have wanted bureaucracies to be responsive to their needs, which often means responsive to majority views. But they have also wanted bureaucracies to be competent enough to do an effective job. They want fair, apolitical competence applied so that, for example, Social Security recipients who are Democrats do not receive favors when Democrats are in office and Republican recipients do not receive favors when Republicans are in office. For the bureaucracy to have both political responsiveness and neutral competence is often difficult.

Responsiveness

Responsiveness refers to a democratic desire that public agencies do what we want. We have shown how highly we value bureaucratic responsiveness in three major ways.

First, Americans elect more bureaucrats than citizens of other nations do. By the mid-1800s voters were electing numerous state and local executive officers from ballots (called long ballots) having hundreds of names. Many states and localities still have long ballots electing not only chief executives, such as governors and mayors, but also treasurers, clerks, sheriffs, surveyors, auditors, engineers, and other administrative officers. Electing rather than appointing these officials is supposed to make them responsive, though in reality it may have the opposite effect by making it unclear who is really in charge.

The second way Americans have encouraged bureaucratic responsiveness is through **patronage.** Under the patronage system elected officials appoint their supporters to administrative jobs in order to build their own political strength. Newly elected presidents and other executives replace everyone appointed by their predecessors with their own supporters: "To the victor belong the spoils." Andrew Jackson's presidential election in 1828 was a watershed in using the patronage system. Jackson and others believed any white male citizen of average intelligence and goodwill could do a government job well. He reversed the existing practice of naming mostly well-off people from the East Coast by appointing less well-off supporters from frontier areas.

Andrew Jackson opened the doors to the White House as well as to the government bureaucracy. The guests at a White House party open to the public consumed or carried away much of a 1400-pound cheese.

A major problem with patronage is that it can lead to corruption, in particular to deal making between candidates and voters or, more unfortunately, individuals who control blocks of voters. Voters may support candidates who promise them jobs or other favors. Such corruption increasingly sullied city councils, state legislatures, and Congress during the 1800s.

Another problem with patronage is incompetence. People got bureaucratic jobs because they supported winning candidates, not because they knew how to do the jobs. This became a major problem as government jobs became more technical.

The third way Americans have sought bureaucratic responsiveness is by giving legislatures great authority over the bureaucracy. Before the Revolution and for a long time after, the bureaucracy performed a few relatively simple jobs and was relatively easy to control. Now the job of controlling the bureaucracy is much more difficult as government has become larger and more complex.

Neutral Competence

Neutral competence can be a contradictory objective to responsiveness. It holds that bureaucrats should be uninvolved or neutral in policymaking and chosen only for their expertise in executing policy. It assumes there is no Republican or Democratic way to build a sewer, collect customs, or fight a war. In effect, it says politics has no place in bureaucracy. It also implies that bureaucrats should not profit personally from the decisions they make.

Woodrow Wilson, who was a major advocate of neutral competence, wrote that we can learn to execute policy both expertly and responsively.[30] He believed government jobs are either political or administrative in nature, and that if we know which are which, we can create a bureaucracy that policymakers can control. Most current observers believe it is impossible to separate the political from the administrative completely, however.[31]

The first impact of the desire for neutral competence was the creation of the **Civil Service Commission** by the Pendleton Act in 1883. Patronage was a serious problem by the 1880s. Given the strength of political machines that had grown powerful through its use, it took the assassination of President James Garfield in 1881 by an unsuccessful job seeker to get Congress to do something.

The commission's job was to fill certain bureaucratic jobs with people who had proven their competence in competitive examinations. It was also supposed to protect these people from having to support or oppose particular candidates. The jobs under the commission's jurisdiction were part of the **merit system.**

The act authorized the president to extend merit system coverage to additional federal jobs by executive order. The merit system covered about 10% of the jobs in the federal bureaucracy in 1884. That figure is over 90% today; most of the remainder are covered by some other merit system such as that in the State Department's Foreign Service.

A merit system protects individuals from dismissal for partisan reasons. However, the system does not give "merit" a monopoly. The system favors veterans by adding a 5-point bonus to their test scores (disabled veterans get 10 points). People already in the system are also favored because they know about job openings first. Sometimes, job descriptions are written to fit particular individuals.

The creation of independent regulatory boards and commissions was also a result of the push for neutral competence. In 1887, Congress created the Interstate Commerce Commission to decide, on the basis of expert, not partisan, factors, such things as interstate freight rates, railroad ticket prices, conditions of service, and which companies could operate between different places. Some partisan influences remain: The president names and the Senate confirms board and commission members, and Congress and the presi-

The Politics of Breast Implants

Bureaucracies affect most things in life, including sometimes the shape of one's body. The debate over how government should regulate silicone-gel breast implants illustrates the pervasiveness, slowness, and political responsiveness of the regulatory process.

Breast surgery is a $300 million industry and accounts for more than 130,000 surgical operations annually. It is one of the most frequently used forms of plastic surgery in the United States. Some plastic surgeons obtain more than 50% of their income from this operation.[1] Fifteen to 20% of these operations involve replacing breast tissue lost to cancer surgery. The rest are elective surgeries to augment the size and change the shape of the breasts of women who are not pleased with their natural shape.[2]

When silicone-gel implants were introduced in the 1960s, the Food and Drug Administration (FDA), which has the regulatory responsibility for food and drugs, did not have specific legislative authority to regulate medical devices such as implants. Thus manufacturers did not have to obtain FDA approval before marketing implants. In 1976, Congress gave the FDA responsibility for regulating the safety of medical devices but exempted more than 100,000 existing medical devices. The FDA could, however, ask manufacturers to submit safety data on existing devices for the purpose of deciding if regulation was needed.[3]

In 1987, the FDA asked silicone-gel implant manufacturers to provide evidence of their safety by 1991. If the devices were found safe, the FDA would allow them to be sold and used as in the past.[4] If not, the FDA could impose restrictions on their use or even ban them altogether. The FDA requested this safety information after the medical literature began to report that the implants did not always perform as advertised (they sometimes leaked or became lumpy or hard). Even more seriously, silicone from leaky or ruptured implants appeared to be causing arthritic conditions and autoimmune diseases.

In 1991, three of the four manufacturers of the implants submitted millions of pages of documentation on implant safety

Karen Berger holds a silicone-gel breast implant. Berger, an author of a book on implants, testified at an FDA hearing on the safety of implants.

dent determine their funding. But partisanship is supposed to end there.

Limits on the partisan political activities of federal workers are another result of attempts to achieve neutral competence. The **Hatch Act** of 1939 says federal employees can do very little in partisan campaigns, even in state and local ones. They can vote, attend rallies, and talk privately to others. But they cannot participate in party-sponsored voter registration drives, endorse party candidates, or work for or against them in any way. These prohibitions also apply to state and local government workers supported by federal funds.

The Hatch Act has been the subject of considerable controversy. Supporters argue that it protects the neutral competence of civil servants from partisan influences. Critics of the act say it makes civil servants second-class citizens by denying them the First Amendment guarantees of freedom of speech and association. In 1993 Congress changed the law to allow most federal employees to run for office within political parties, to participate in political campaigns, and to raise funds for political action committees when they are off-duty. However, all employees of law enforcement and national security agencies remain under the earlier, more stringent prohibitions.[32]

The 1980s were troubled years for the entire civil service. Reagan's belief that "government isn't the solution, it's the problem" endorsed negative views of the public service and indicated a commitment to cut government activity. This and publicity glorifying private business made hiring and keeping good people in government difficult; the work of many agencies suffered. For example, the Food and Drug Administration (FDA) tests products that represent about a quarter of consumer spending. Yet in a decade that saw the onset of AIDS and the development of many new products, FDA staffing dropped 9% and

(the fourth manufacturer discontinued the product). They argued that these studies of patients' medical records and their other research found silicone-gel implants harmless. The American Society of Plastic and Reconstructive Surgeons reported that over 90% of breast implant patients were happy with the results.[5]

Critics presented a different picture. They pointed out that despite the documentation presented, manufacturers had not studied many patients. Dow Chemicals, one of the largest manufacturers, had studied only about 1,000 women. More important, the patients had not been studied over a long time period. Most were followed only a year or two after the operation, a time that would not begin to reveal long-term effects. Only one-third of the subjects in the biggest test had been studied more than 2 years, and only 46 women were checked after 7 years. Even without long-term studies, the companies' data showed problems with one-third of the implants.[6] And there were many personal accounts from women who told stories of pain and serious disease after implant surgery.[7]

When it was apparent that serious regulation was contemplated, the American Society of Plastic and Reconstructive Surgeons launched a multimillion-dollar lobbying initiative to fight proposed regulations. Each member was assessed $1,050 to pay for the campaign, which included recruiting 400 women to travel to Washington to state how important the breast implants were to their health and well-being.[8] On the other side, a network of women whose implants were unsuccessful formed a group called Command Trust Network to continue to publicize the negative aspects of implants.

After committee hearings highlighting these disagreements and in the context of a larger discussion over whether government agencies were giving women's health concerns equal weight to those of men, the FDA commissioner decided that silicone-gel breast implants would be restricted while additional safety data were collected. Implants will be limited to women who are part of FDA-approved safety studies. The studies will be open to all women seeking implants following breast cancer surgery, but the number of implants for cosmetic purposes will be drastically reduced until safety questions are answered.[9]

1. Jean Seligmann, Mary Hager, and Karen Springen, "Another Tempest in a C Cup," *Newsweek*, March 23, 1992, p. 67.
2. Diana McLellan, "Rethinking Big," *The Washingtonian* (June 1991), pp. 57–59; Laura Shapiro, Karen Springen, and Jeanne Gordon, "What Is It with Women and Large Breasts?" *Newsweek*, January 20, 1992, p. 57.
3. Malcolm Gladwell, "FDA Set to Begin Hearings on Silicone Breast Implants," *Washington Post*, February 17, 1992, p. A1.
4. Malcolm Gladwell, "Silicone Breast Implants," *Washington Post* (Health Supplement), March 3, 1992, p. 10.
5. McLellan, "Rethinking Big," p. 57.
6. Philip Hilts, "Under Pressure, US Weighs Ban on Use of Breast Implants," *New York Times*, October 21, 1991, p. 1.
7. "Reprieve for Breast Implants," *Time*, November 25, 1991, p. 81.
8. Hilts, "Under Pressure . . ."
9. Malcolm Gladwell, "FDA Will Allow Limited Use of Silicone-Gel Breast Implants," *Washington Post*, April 17, 1992, p. A2.

A disappointed office seeker assassinates President Garfield.

food and drug inspections fell 40%. In 1990, the FDA took 31 months, not the 6 months required by law, to review new drug applications.[33]

Although Bush noted his "very high regard for the overall competence of career civil servants and for [their] vital role,"[34] he did little to overcome the trends of the 1980s. Clinton sent mixed signals to the bureaucracy. He described government, and by implication the bureaucracy, as a valuable tool for social change, but recommended freezing civil service salaries and vowed to cut 100,000 federal jobs. The number of new workers is declining in the 1990s as the "baby bust" generation enters the job market and as one-quarter of the federal work force reaches retirement age. Government will have trouble competing with the private sector for workers because federal salaries lag behind comparable nongovernment jobs and this gap widens at higher levels.

Neutral competence also includes the idea that bureaucrats should not profit personally from their decisions. Civil servants should be experts in what they do but should not have a personal stake in it. For example, bureaucrats who are stockholders in chemical companies should not make policy about chemical waste. Even if policymakers could completely divorce themselves from their financial interests, their ties with a regulated firm would still produce an appearance of conflict of interest. Critics of policy could point to it, lowering public confidence in government.

Responding to concerns about conflicts of interest, Congress passed the Ethics in Government Act in 1978. The act sought to prevent ex-public officials with inside information about specific issues from using it and their contacts to give their private employers an unfair competitive advantage. The act barred ex-public servants from lobbying their former agencies for one year and, on matters in which they "personally and substantially" participated as public officials, for life. In 1989, news that ex-Reagan officials had used their government service for substantial financial gain led to the passage of a law designed to strengthen the 1978 act. It will have little impact if it is enforced as weakly as its predecessor.

To address these concerns, President Clinton signed an executive order requiring many of his political appointees to sign a pledge that they will not lobby the agencies in which they worked for five years and will never lobby for foreign political parties

American Diversity

Presidential Administrative Appointments

Bill Clinton, as a candidate for the presidency, promised that his administration would reflect American diversity. After one year, with more than two-thirds of his appointments filled, Clinton's choices almost exactly represented gender and minority groups, with small exceptions for women and Hispanics.

Perhaps even more importantly for the representation of these groups, many were also included among top-level appointees. These are the officials who participate in the shaping of policy, rather than serving in low-level service positions. If we examine the proportion of top-level appointees in each group and compare it with that group's population of college educated, 30–64-year-olds, we find both women and minorities to be reasonably well represented among the higher echelons of the Clinton administration when compared with the overall population and very well represented when compared with the highly educated population.

Source: Martha Farnsworth Riche, "An Administration That Mirrors America," *Washington Post National Weekly Edition*, January 31–February 6, 1994, p. 25.

Clinton Administration Appointments of Minorities and Women

	% of Total Appointments	**% of Total Population**
Women	46	50
African Americans	14	12
Hispanics	6	10
Asian Americans	3	3
Native Americans	1	1
	% of Total Top-Level Appointments	**% of Total College-Educated Population, Ages 30-64**
Women	30	35
African Americans	14	6
Hispanics	5	3
Asian Americans	3	5
Native Americans	3	.3

and governments. Analysts noted that the rules apply to only one-third of his appointees, that lobbying for foreign corporations is unaffected, and that Clinton said nothing about how he will enforce the rules. These points suggest that the new rules may have little more impact than the old ones.[35]

Although responsiveness and neutral competence contribute to an effective bureaucracy, each has problems and ultimately works against the other. The most neutrally competent bureaucracy is not always the most responsive one and vice versa.

➤Controlling the Bureaucracy

To whom is the bureaucracy responsible? Although many bureaucratic decisions significantly affect our lives, most are not made in the public eye, and most citizens know little about them. No "ADM-SPAN" channel televises agency activities as C-SPAN covers Congress.[36] Nevertheless, many compete to influence public agencies: the president, parts of Congress, interest groups, and individual citizens. Whether they succeed depends on their resources, agency reactions, and agency ability to resist unwanted outside influence.[37]

■ President

The development of the bureaucracy led to demands for **executive leadership.** The president, constitutionally the "chief executive," has several tools to control the bureaucracy. One is budgeting. Presidents can try to limit agency appropriations to keep agencies from doing certain things, or they can tie conditions to appropriations to make them do things. Using these strategies effectively can be difficult, although President Reagan was able to weaken some regulatory agencies by significantly cutting their budgets.[38]

President Bush's 1991 budget for the Internal Revenue Service proposed that the IRS target middle- and lower-income taxpayers for audits (to check the honesty of their tax returns) rather than wealthy individuals and companies. He cut the IRS's budget request to target rich tax cheats by over 90%.[39]

Second, presidents can try to control agencies by appointing people to them with views like their own. This is obvious in the case of cabinet departments. Reagan and Bush filled health care-related positions in the Department of Health and Human Services with people who were pro-life.[40] Clinton filled these jobs with people who are pro-choice. In appointments to regulatory agencies, Republican presidents tend to appoint pro-business people and Democratic presidents pro-consumer and pro-labor individuals.[41] Reagan's appointees to regulatory agencies such as OSHA, the Consumer Products Safety Commission, and the EPA agreed with his goal of reducing government regulation. Clinton's appointees to these agencies believe, with him, that government can be a valuable agent of social change.

Often, however, presidential appointees end up representing agency interests rather than presidential ones. This can happen because most appointees have less expertise and experience in agency operations than career civil servants and often come to rely on career officials for information about agency history, procedures, and policy questions.

Administrative reform is a third presidential opportunity to control the bureaucracy. Generally, the more sweeping a president's recommendation for change, the more he must anticipate congressional and interest group resistance. For example, Reagan wanted to abolish the Departments of Education and Energy and merge the Commerce and Labor Departments, but Congress would not support him.

Fourth, the White House can try to influence agencies not under presidential control by lobbying and mobilizing public opinion. For example, presidents try to influence Federal Reserve Board decisions on interest rates.

Despite these powers, there are many limits on the president's ability to control the bureaucracy. Given its size and complexity, the president cannot possibly control every important decision. Moreover, presidents have found it increasingly difficult to lead an executive branch containing large numbers of merit system employees deliberately insulated from presidential control.

Presidential control problems became much more serious in the 1930s with the establishment of many new programs and agencies. In 1935, Franklin Roosevelt appointed the Brownlow Committee, named after its chair and composed of public administration specialists, which wrote an excellent statement of the principles of executive leadership in its 1937 report.

The report was very influential. At its suggestion, the Bureau of the Budget, created in 1921, was put into the new Executive Office of the President to help the president cope with the bureaucracy. Congress also passed legislation in 1939 permitting the president to create, merge, or dissolve agencies subject to Congress's disapproval.

In 1978, the Civil Service Reform Act replaced the Civil Service Commission with two agencies. One promotes executive leadership by working with the president in writing and administering civil service regulations. The other is supposed to protect civil servants from violations of these regulations. In addition, the act gave managers more opportunity to fire incompetent subordinates, authorized bonuses and a new pay scale for managers to encourage better performance, and created the Senior Executive Service (SES).

Despite this legislation, executive leadership is still thwarted by the difficulty of removing incompetents from the civil service. Although job security is not meant to shield public servants who do poor work, it does make firing incompetent workers difficult and time-consuming. The organization of public employees into unions contributes to this. The government's rate of discharging people for inefficiency is .01% a year. The 1978 reform has made little difference. As one public employee said, "We're all like headless nails down here—once you get us in you can't get us out."[42]

Another limit to presidential leadership are agencies' own connections. Presidents have more success trying to control agencies that lack strong congressional allies and domestic clientele groups, such as the Treasury and State departments, than agencies *with* such allies, such as the Agriculture and Health and Human Services departments.

Congress

Creating and reorganizing agencies and enacting laws gives Congress opportunities to tell agencies what to do and how to do it. In recent years, Congress took away some of the powers of the Federal Trade Commission to regulate used-car sales, practices of the insurance industry, and children's television advertising. In doing so, Congress was responding to complaints (and campaign donations) from used-car dealers, the insurance industry, and other businesses who found their actions being circumscribed by the commission's new or proposed regulations. In 1995, congressional interest in cutting the bureaucracy and regulatory activity led Clinton to propose the elimination of the Interstate Commerce Commission, the original independent regulatory commission. Despite these examples, however, the existence of complex, technical issues and generally stated congressional goals often gives agencies considerable leeway in doing their jobs.

Legislative oversight is another congressional tool of control, but it too has problems. Just as an agency's connections can work to thwart presidential control, they can also limit congressional oversight. Agencies frequently work closely with certain congressional committees and interest groups for mutual support; agencies adjust their actions to the preferences of the congressional committees that authorize their programs and appropriate their funds. For example, decisions by members of independent regulatory commissions are sensitive to the views of members of their congressional oversight committees. When the membership of the committees becomes more liberal, so too do the decisions regulators make.[43]

Constituent service is also a congressional tool for controlling the bureaucracy. Members of Congress often try to influence agencies on behalf of constituents. This becomes a problem when it leads to inefficiencies such as keeping unneeded military bases open to boost the economy of a member's district or when it impedes necessary government regulation, as it did when several prominent senators delayed investigation of corrupt and careless savings and loan operations.

Courts

The courts also influence the bureaucracy. Judicial decisions shape agency actions by directing agencies to follow legally correct procedures. Of course, the courts cannot intercede in an agency's decision making unless some aggrieved person or corporation files a suit against the agency. Nevertheless, in almost any controversial agency action, there will be aggrieved parties, and possibly some with sufficient resources to bring a court action.

The courts interpret lawmakers' intentions by deciding what congressional majorities and the president had in mind when they made a law. This can be difficult. Sometimes, in their haste, lawmakers may have left out parts of a law or, as a Supreme Court justice put it, "agreed to disagree."[44] Lawmakers may have also written a law so agencies can adapt it to unknown future conditions. How the courts read a law may add to or reduce the relative power of Congress and the president or expand the courts' own powers. We discuss these issues in Chapter 13.

Regulators as well as other agency policymakers appear to be quite sensitive to court decisions. For example, when the courts begin overturning the National Labor Relations Board's decisions in a pro-labor direction, NLRB decisions soon become more pro-labor. Similarly, decisions drift the other way when courts begin to overturn decisions in a pro-business direction.[45]

Interest Groups and Individuals

Interest groups want to make sure bureaucracies adopt rules and enforcement practices they favor. A law establishing new safeguards in toxic waste disposal may be applauded by environmental and citizen groups, but the job of these groups is not over until they make sure the Environmental Protection Agency writes strict rules to carry out the law and then enforces them. Thus it is not enough to get a law passed that responds to your interests; the law must be implemented in a responsive way too.

How do groups seek to make sure this happens? One way is through relationships with Congress. If an agency seems to be sabotaging the intent of Congress, interest groups can work with friendly congressional committees to put pressure on the agency to mend its ways. Interest groups can also try to rally public opinion to their side and pressure Congress or the president to do something about the agency.

Interest groups try to influence agencies directly, too. For example, the broadcasting industry tries to shape Federal Communications Commission decisions to enable the industry to compete more effectively with cable television companies. Sometimes interest groups are so effective at pressuring agencies that the agency is said to be "captured."[46] This term is used most frequently in regard to regulatory agencies said to be controlled by the groups they are supposed to be regulating. Thus the Nuclear Regulatory Commission looks out for the interests of the nuclear industry, which it is supposed to be regulating.

Studies of voting by regulatory commissioners also show the indirect influence of industry. Some commissioners come to their regulatory agencies from the

The FBI Runs Amok

J. Edgar Hoover helped the Federal Bureau of Investigation (FBI) develop a reputation for being *the* leading crime fighter in America. Hollywood made movies about the FBI and television carried a popular weekly series describing its exploits. What became known only later is that under Hoover's leadership the FBI consistently did things that were illegal and violated citizens' rights.

- It conducted over 500,000 investigations of "subversive" activity between 1960 and 1974, none of which resulted in a prosecution. Those investigated included Washington, D.C., high school students who had complained about the quality of school food, the women's liberation movement, all black student groups, and antiwar activists.
- It played "dirty tricks" on what it thought were subversive people. For example, it harassed Martin Luther King, Jr., by discouraging colleges from giving him honorary degrees; putting wiretaps and bugs in his hotel rooms, home, and offices; circulating information obtained with these devices to the media and executive branch officials; and mailing King a tape suggesting he kill himself or face public exposure of material on his extracurricular sex life the agency had collected about him. (After King's assassination, the FBI worked against congressional proposals to commemorate him with a national holiday.)
- Hoover "blackmailed" President Kennedy into signing an order permitting wiretapping of King by threatening to expose Kennedy's extracurricular sex life to the public. Hoover had gotten this evidence by tapping White House telephone conversations between Kennedy and a woman with Mafia ties.
- It conducted burglaries, forged letters, disrupted marriages, got people fired from jobs and ousted from apartments, and supplied violent groups like the Ku Klux Klan with arms and explosives.

The FBI's usual justification for doing these things was that they were necessary to fight those wanting to overthrow the government. But, in fact, the agency aimed its effort at anyone Hoover disliked—people such as Albert Einstein, Ernest Hemingway, and John Lennon. Hoover had the FBI keep files on leading political figures to protect himself and the agency from criticism.

Hoover led the FBI for 48 years, until 1972. "Hoover used his confidential files to hang on to power long past retirement age. Once when an aide suggested Johnson get rid of Hoover, the President replied, 'Son, when you have a skunk it is better to have him inside the tent pissing out than outside pissing in.' "[1]

Although his successors have acknowledged the need to prevent abuses, progress is slow. For example, from 1981 to 1985, the FBI harassed labor unions, churches, and individuals (including nuns and students) opposed to White House Central American policies. It infiltrated their meetings and took and circulated photographs of them without finding any criminal activity. In 1988, criticism that the FBI was violating privacy rights forced it to retreat from looking for Soviet spies by asking librarians to finger library users with foreign-sounding names or accents and those who acted in "suspicious" ways.[2] And, during the Persian Gulf crisis, FBI investigations into the political beliefs of Arab Americans frightened many into recalling the internment of Japanese Americans during World War II.

Hoover was a master organizer who created a paranoid agency environment that stifled those who disagreed with him or did not conform to his idea of what an FBI agent should do or look like. He hired agents who would adapt to this environment and, as an opponent of the civil rights movement, hired mostly whites. His preferences still dominate the agency. Even today, the FBI has few black (4.7%) and Hispanic (5.3%) agents and even fewer Asian and Native American agents. Black agents resign at twice the rate of white agents. Only 10% of its agents are women.

Before we can control an agency, we need to know what it is doing. Most Americans had little idea these activities were taking place. This indicates that controlling the bureaucracy is a never-ending job.

---

1. Hugh Sidey, "Reach Out and Twist an Arm," *Time*, December 13, 1993, p. 43.
2. Herbert N. Foerstel, *Surveillance in the Stacks* (Westport, Conn.: Greenwood Press, 1991).

Source: Robert Justin Goldstein, "The FBI and American Politics Textbooks," *PS* 18 (Spring 1985), pp. 237–46. For more on Hoover and the FBI, see Taylor Branch, *Parting the Waters: America in the King Years, 1954–1963* (New York: Simon and Schuster, 1988), which examines the FBI and the civil rights movement; Herbert Mitgang, *Dangerous Dossiers* (New York: Donald I. Fine, 1988); and Kenneth O'Reilly, *"Racial Matters": The FBI's Secret File on Black America, 1960–1972* (New York: Free Press, 1989).

industry they are regulating. These commissioners are more likely than others to take a pro-industry position in cases before the agency. Furthermore, commissioners leaving a regulatory agency to take jobs in a regulated industry become more pro-industry in their last year as regulators than others who are not leaving for such jobs.[47] They apparently anticipate a move to industry and, in a sacrifice of their neutral competence, try to make their decisions more acceptable to possible employers.

Can individual citizens influence the bureaucracy too? It is difficult for citizens acting as individuals to influence public agencies. Not surprisingly, as we have seen, few individuals take advantage of their right to get information from the bureaucracy.

However, individual bureaucrats, called **whistle-blowers,** can sometimes open their agencies to public view. Their purpose is usually to expose mismanagement and abuse of discretion to make their agencies more responsive and productive. The most famous whistleblower is Ernest Fitzgerald. In 1968, as an Air Force cost accountant, he exposed bad management by revealing problems with the Lockheed C-5A transport plane. The plane vibrated so much in flight that its wings actually fell off if they were not replaced after only 200 hours of flying time. Saying it wanted "to save expenses"—his $32,000 salary—the Air Force reacted by firing Fitzgerald. He sued to get his job back and won, but all he got was his title, office, and pay. The Air Force gave him nothing to do, and he had to wait for a court order in 1982 before the Air Force gave him responsibilities equal to his qualifications. The wings were repaired, and the C-5A operated succesfully for many years.[48] In 1987, the Air Force was still trying to neutralize what one Pentagon veteran called "the most hated man in the Air Force" by juggling staff assignments.[49]

The 1978 Civil Service Reform Act created an agency to protect whistleblowers. During its first decade, the agency was ineffective because the act defined whistleblowers' rights narrowly and because of budget cuts and morale problems in the 1980s. In 1988, Reagan vetoed a bill designed to strengthen it. Congress passed the bill again in 1989 and Bush signed it into law. It gives whistleblowers more protection from agencies they accuse of mismanagement and harassment. A law passed in 1986 allows private citizens to be whistleblowers too by suing companies with government contracts that defraud the government.[50]

Relying on brave people like Fitzgerald to get agencies to operate properly is a mistake. A study reported in 1993 that over one-third of federal whistleblowers alleged they suffered some form of reprisal or threat of reprisal.[51] It is the rare person who will lay aside an ambition for promotion and relations with colleagues to challenge the status quo. Most people, whether in the private or the public sector, find it difficult to expose the dirty laundry of the bureaucracy employing them.

➤Conclusion: Is the Bureaucracy Responsive?

Is the federal bureaucracy the uncontrollable fourth branch of government, as some portray it? Our fragmented political system has created an environment of uncertainty and competition for public agencies. They have many bosses: a president, his appointees, Congress, and its many committees and subcommittees. In addition, numerous interest groups try to influence them. The often contradictory expectations of responsiveness and neutral competence contribute to the uncertainty of the bureaucracy's environment too.

As a result, agencies try to protect themselves by cultivating the support of congressional committees and interest groups. Even presidents have trouble influencing agencies because of these alliances. Although some presidents, such as Franklin Roosevelt and Lyndon

"It's not mailmen per se. I'm just very anti-government these days."

Source: Richter, *The New Yorker Magazine*, September 18, 1995, p. 50.

Johnson, have occasionally rearranged the status quo, their successes in representing a vision of national priorities are more the exception than the rule.

Well-organized interest groups and Congress can also influence agencies, often through the iron triangles that help stabilize agency environments. But interest groups do not represent everyone. Likewise, not everyone feels represented by members of Congress or can take advantage of the Sunshine and Freedom of Information Acts. As a result, agencies may not represent those who fall through the "safety net" of interest group and congressional representation.

Thus diverse expectations of what government should do make the federal bureaucracy seem unresponsive. Even well-run agencies represent waste, and therefore a lack of responsiveness and executive leadership, to people unaware of, lacking need of, or opposed to their services.

Despite people's negative feelings about the bureaucracy, the mail is delivered, bridges get inspected, and passports are issued. As Charles Goodsell points out, "Unmistakably, . . . bureaucracy works most of the time."[52] It usually does what it is supposed to do. But when what the bureaucracy is supposed to do is unclear, it is harder for the bureaucracy to respond to our wishes.

EPILOGUE

The Surgeon General Chooses Neutral Competence

In 1986 Surgeon General Koop issued a report proposing expanded sex education and better education on the dangers of AIDS for schoolchildren. The 36-page report ignored conservative views. It concluded that a lack of sex education impedes the effort to stop AIDS in the absence of a vaccine or cure. The report noted that testing all hospital patients is unnecessary because many of the 37 million people hospitalized each year are children or the elderly, who face low risks of infection.

Later, in a radio broadcast, Koop called on the nation's networks to lift their self-imposed ban on condom advertising. He argued that "anyone who is sexually active should use a condom from start to finish. AIDS kills and sexually active people have to be told this." The networks indicated they would leave policy changes to their local affiliates.

The government's most visible response to AIDS was a brochure mailed to 107 million households in 1988 describing how AIDS is contracted and how to avoid it. That same year, a presidential commission and a National Academy of Sciences panel made recommendations about dealing with AIDS that echoed Koop's. Both criticized the government, and especially Reagan's White House, for a lack of leadership. At the same time, many conservatives were disappointed and angry, accusing Koop of not promoting chastity.

By 1995, AIDS had killed more than 204,000 people. And the demographics of the disease were changing. A majority of victims were still gay men, but there were signs that the spread of AIDS among gays had peaked. Increasingly, the new high-risk populations were intravenous drug users and poor inner city blacks and Hispanics. In 1993, over 40% of all Americans with the disease were minorities. It is now the second leading cause of death of men and the fourth leading killer of women aged 25 to 44. It is also the seventh leading cause of death of young children. Koop acknowledged that health workers have been "singularly unsuccessful in penetrating the drug-addicted culture" with educational messages.[53] An observer noted that heterosexual AIDS is becoming a "poor people's disease."[54]

Civil servants are supposed to be responsive to public opinion and their superiors, in Koop's case the president. At the same time, they are supposed to do their jobs in a neutrally competent way. As surgeon general, Koop said, "I'm not afforded the luxury of bringing ideology or morals into my job, especially with the sort of threat we have with AIDS."[55] He could not satisfy presidential expectations because his professional expertise led him to different conclusions.

➤Key Terms

independent agencies
policy implementation
delegated legislative authority
regulation
patronage
neutral competence
Civil Service Commission
merit system
Hatch Act
executive leadership
whistleblowers

➤Further Reading

David Burnham, *A Law Unto Itself: Power, Politics and the IRS* (New York: Random House, 1990). *An analysis of the enforcement of the federal tax code, a code so complex it seems to invite bureaucratic inefficiency and abuses.*

Hugh Heclo, *A Government of Strangers* (Washington, D.C.: The Brookings Institution, 1977). *A thorough study of the small number of political appointees in the federal bureaucracy and of the challenges they face trying to control it.*

Irving L. Janis, *Victims of Groupthink* (Boston: Houghton Mifflin, 1972). *Explaining why people often prefer getting along to making hard decisions, he helps us see why whistleblowers are rare souls.*

James H. Jones, *Bad Blood* (New York: Free Press, 1981). *Award-winning account of the Public Health Service's experiment in which black men with syphilis were left untreated so doctors could see the effects of the disease. The book is revealing about the nature of both bureaucratic behavior and racial discrimination.*

Steven Kelman, *Making Public Policy: A Helpful View of American Government* (New York: Basic Books, 1987). *A defense of government and bureaucracy as imperfect forces for good in a complex and imperfect world.*

Robert N. Kharasch, *The Institutional Imperative: How to Understand the United States Government and Other Bulky Objects* (New York: Charterhouse Books, 1973). *A witty and insightful study of such topics as the "irrelevance" of bureaucratic morality and purpose, Pentagon "busyness," and the "Sweet Uses of Stupidity."*

Jonathan Kwitny, *Acceptable Risks* (New York: Poseidon Books, 1992). *A fast-paced and well-written story of two men who prodded and fought the Food and Drug Administration to make potentially helpful medicines available to AIDS patients. A good illustration both of agency rigidity and, ultimately, responsiveness.*

➤Notes

1. "AIDS: Who Should Be Tested?" *Newsweek,* May 11, 1987, pp. 64–65.
2. Stephen Jay Gould, "The Exponential Spread of AIDS Underscores the Tragedy of Our Delay in Fighting One of Nature's Plagues," *New York Times Magazine,* April 19, 1987, p. 33.
3. "AIDS Becomes a Political Issue," *Time,* March 23, 1987, p. 24.
4. For a description of Weber's view of bureaucracy, see H. H. Gerth and C. Wright Mills, trans., *From Max Weber: Essays on Sociology* (New York: Oxford University Press, 1946), pp. 196–239.
5. Taken from Bruce Adams, "The Frustrations of Government Service," *Public Administration Review* 44 (January/February 1984), p. 5. For more discussion of public attitudes about the civil service, see Herbert Kaufman, "Fear of Bureaucracy: A Raging Pandemic," *Public Administration Review* 41 (January/February 1981), p. 1.
6. Barry Bozeman, *All Organizations Are Public: Bridging Public and Private Organizational Theories* (San Francisco: Jossey-Bass, 1987).
7. Donald S. Kellermann, Andrew Kohut, and Carol Bowman, *The People, The Press & Politics on the Eve of '92: Fault Lines in the Electorate* (Washington, D.C.: Times Mirror Center for The People & The Press, December 4, 1991), p. 39.
8. Mark Green and John Berry, *The Challenge of Hidden Profits: Reducing Corporate Bureaucracy and Waste* (New York: Wm. Morrow, 1985).
9. Reported in Sam Archibald, "The Early Years of the Freedom of Information Act—1955–1974," *PS: Political Science & Politics* (December 1993), p. 730.
10. Debra Gersh Hernandez, "Many Promises, Little Action," *Editor & Publisher* (March 26, 1994), p. 15.

11. General Accounting Office, *Freedom of Information Act: State Department Request Processing* (Washington, D.C.: U.S. Government Printing Office, January 23, 1989).

12. "President Declassifies Old Papers," *Omaha World-Herald,* April 18, 1995, p. 1.

13. Hernandez, "Many Promises, Little Action," p. 12; and George Lardner Jr., "Hit That 'Save' Button," *The Washington Post National Weekly Edition,* August 23–29, 1993, p. 32.

14. Stephen Hess, *The Government/Press Connection: Press Officers and Their Offices* (Washington, D.C.: The Brookings Institution, 1984), p. 101.

15. Joyce Appleby, "That's General Washington to You," *The New York Times Book Review,* February 14, 1993, p. 11. This is a review of Richard Norton Smith, *Patriarch* (Boston: Houghton Mifflin, 1993).

16. Leonard D. White, *Introduction to the Study of Public Administration,* 4th ed. (New York: Macmillan, 1955), p. 4.

17. Paul C. Light, *Thickening Government: Federal Hierarchy and the Diffusion of Accountability* (Washington, D.C.: Brookings Institution, 1995).

18. Office of Management and Budget, *Special Analyses: Budget of the United States: Fiscal Year 1990* (Washington, D.C.: U.S. Government Printing Office, 1989), pp. 1–13; and *Historical Tables: Budget of the United States: Fiscal Year 1996* (Washington, D.C.: U.S. Government Printing Office, 1995), p. 245.

19. Harold Seidman and Robert Gilmour, *Politics, Position and Power: The Dynamics of Federal Organization,* 4th ed. (New York: Oxford University Press, 1986), pp. 249–92. See also Herbert Kaufman, "Emerging Conflicts in the Doctrines of Public Administration," *American Political Science Review* 50 (December 1956), pp. 1057–73, for a study of the growth of American public bureaucracy focusing on the conflicting expectations people have of it.

20. See Lawrence J. Haas, "Dodging the Budget Bullet," *National Journal,* October 1, 1988, pp. 2465–69; Donald F. Kettl, "Expansion and Protection in the Budgetary Process," *Public Administration Review* 49 (May/June 1989), pp. 231–39; and Harold Seidman and Robert Gilmour, *Politics, Position, and Power,* 4th ed. (New York: Oxford University Press, 1986), pp. 281–92.

21. For a discussion of these issues see Peter T. Kilborn, "Big Change Likely As Law Bans Bias Toward Disabled," *The New York Times,* July 19, 1992, pp. 1 & 16.

22. Jill Smolows, "Noble Aims, Mixed Results," *Time,* July 31, 1995, p. 54.

23. Theodore Lowi, *The End of Liberalism* (New York: W. W. Norton, 1969).

24. Thomas J. Anton, *American Federalism and Public Policy* (Philadelphia, Pa.: Temple University Press, 1989).

25. Virginia I. Postrel, "Red (Tape) Alert," *The Washington Post National Weekly Edition,* February 20–26, 1995, p. 23.

26. Ibid.

27. John M. Goshko, "The Big-Ticket Costs of the Disabilities Act," *The Washington Post National Weekly Edition,* March 20–26, 1995, p. 31.

28. For more, see Margaret Kriz, "A New Shade of Green," *National Journal,* March 18, 1995, pp. 661–665.

29. Gary Lee, "Deregulating Regulations," *The Washington Post National Weekly Edition,* February 20–26, 1995, pp. 6–7.

30. Woodrow Wilson, "The Study of Administration," *Political Science Quarterly* 56 (December 1941), pp. 481–506. This was reprinted from the article's original publication in *The Academy of Political Science* in 1887.

31. See David H. Rosenbloom, "Editorial: Have an Administrative Rx? Don't Forget the Politics!" *Public Administration Review* (November/December, 1993), pp. 503–507.

32. "Hatch Act Revamped," *PA Times,* November 1, 1993, p. 3; "Hatch Act Political Curbs Retained for Some Workers," *Lincoln Star,* July 16, 1993, p. 3.

33. Walter Williams, "So, You Like Government on Cheap?" *Lincoln Sunday Journal-Star,* October 21, 1990, p. 6B. See also E. J. Dionne, Jr., "Are We Getting the Kind of Public Servants We Deserve?" *Washington Post National Weekly Edition,* August 13–19, 1990, p. 31; and Gregory B. Lewis, "Turnover and the Quiet Crisis in the Federal Civil Service," *Public Administration Review* (March/April 1991), pp. 145–55.

34. Reported in "Bush Commits to Support the Public Service," *PA Times,* November 25, 1988, p. 1. See also Judith Havemann, "Panel Seeks Raises for Civil Service," *Washington Post,* March 30, 1989, p. A20.

35. Information about conflict-of-interest matters is in Ronald Brownstein, "Agency Ethics Officers Fear Meese Ruling Could Weaken Conflict Laws," *National Journal,* March 23, 1985, pp. 639–42; and W. John Moore, "Ethics Plan: Too Stingy or Humbug?" *National Journal,* December 19, 1992, p. 2898.

36. Steven Maynard-Moody, "Beyond Implementation: Developing an Institutional Theory of Administrative Policy Making," *Public Administration Review* 49 (March/April 1989), p. 139.

37. B. Dan Wood, "Principals, Bureaucrats, and Responsiveness in Clean Air Enforcements," *American Political Science Review* 82 (March 1988), pp. 213–34.

38. George C. Eads and Michael Fix, *Relief or Reform?* (Washington, D.C.: Urban Institute Press, 1984), chapter 7.

39. David Ellis, "White House to IRS: Hands Off the Rich," *Time,* April 1, 1991, p. 15.

40. Richard Lacayo, "Pro-Choice? Get Lost," *Time,* December 4, 1989, pp. 43–44.

41. Jeffrey Cohen, "The Dynamics of the Revolving Door," *American Journal of Political Science* 30 (November 1986), pp. 689–708.

42. Charles Peters, *How Washington Really Works* (Reading, Mass.: Addison-Wesley, 1980), p. 46–47.

43. Terry Moe, "Regulators' Performance and Presidential Administrations," *American Journal of Political Science* 26 (May 1982), pp. 197–224; Terry Moe, "Control and Feedback in Economic Regulation," *American Political Science Review* 79 (December 1985), pp. 1094–1116.

44. Joan Biskupic, "Asking the Court to Read Between the Lines," *The Washington Post National Weekly Edition,* May 9–15, 1994, p. 32.

45. Moe, "Control and Feedback."

46. The term "capture" is widely used but its use by political scientists studying regulation seems to have originated with Samuel Huntington, "The Marasmus of the ICC," *Yale Law Journal* 61 (April 1952), pp. 467–509; it was later popularized by Marver Bernstein, *Regulating Business by Independent Commission* (Princeton, N.J.: Princeton University Press, 1955).

47. Bernstein, *Regulating Business;* William Gormley, "A Test of the Revolving Door Hypothesis in the FCC," *American Journal of Political Science* 23 (November 1979), pp. 665–83; Jeffrey Cohen, "The Dynamics of the Revolving Door," *American Journal of Political Science* 30 (November 1986), pp. 689–708.

48. See "C-5As with Wing Modifications Planned for September Delivery," *Aviation Week & Space Technology,* December 22, 1969, p. 13; and "Whatever Happened to the C-5A 'White Elephant'?" *U.S. News and World Report,* June 19, 1972, p. 63.

49. David C. Morrison, "Extracting a Thorn, Air Force-Style," *National Journal,* March 7, 1987, p. 567. For more on Fitzgerald's experiences, see A. Ernest Fitzgerald, *The Pentagonists: An Insider's View of Waste, Mismanagement, and Fraud in Defense Spending* (Boston: Houghton Mifflin, 1989).

50. W. John Moore, "Citizen Prosecutors," *National Journal,* August 18, 1990, pp. 2006–10.

51. "Whistleblowing in the Federal Government: An Update," Merit Systems Protection Board, Office of Policy and Evaluation (Washington, D.C., 1993).

52. Charles T. Goodsell, *The Case for Bureaucracy: A Public Administration Polemic,* 2d ed. (Chatham, NJ: Chatham House, 1985), p. 140.

53. Lawrence K. Altman, "Who's Stricken and How: AIDS Pattern Is Shifting," *New York Times,* February 5, 1989, pp. 1 and 16. See also Sandra Panem, *The AIDS Bureaucracy* (Cambridge, Mass.: Harvard University Press, 1988).

54. Ibid.

55. Koop's 1987 remark is quoted in Julie Kosterlitz, "Health Focus," *National Journal,* January 28, 1989, p. 259.

13 The Judiciary

You Are There

Friend or Foe?

You are Justice William Douglas of the Supreme Court facing a decision in the case of ***Korematsu v. United States.*** Fred Korematsu, a Japanese American, was born and raised in California. He was working as a welder when Japan bombed Pearl Harbor and forced the United States into World War II. As an American citizen, he tried to enlist in the army but was rejected because of ulcers. A few months later President Franklin Roosevelt issued an executive order, which Congress ratified, that allowed the secretary of war to exclude persons of Japanese ancestry from the three West Coast states and part of Arizona to prevent espionage and sabotage. Under the order, these persons were required to report to assembly centers—often fairgrounds, racetracks, or stockyards, from which the animals had been removed days before.[1] Allowed to take only what possessions they could carry, 120,000 persons were then relocated to camps in deserts and swamps further inland for, presumably, the duration of the war. Enclosed by barbed wire and patrolled by armed guards, these camps resembled prisoner-of-war camps.

Korematsu did not leave with the others. He had fallen in love with an Italian American woman, and they planned to marry. He had had plastic surgery to look Spanish Hawaiian instead of Japanese. But the surgery was not successful, and while walking down the street in his hometown, he was identified and arrested for violating the order. At trial he was convicted, and on appeal his conviction was upheld. On further appeal his case has reached the Supreme Court.

On one hand, the government claims the order is justified. Although officials do not expect an invasion of the West Coast, they do fear espionage and sabotage. Before the war some Japanese Americans supported Japan's efforts to expand its territory in Asia. Some contributed money, tinfoil, and scrap metal, while a few formed an espionage ring. Intelligence officials crushed the ring but now fear renewed attempts. Already Japanese submarines have attacked American merchant ships off our coast, sinking two and damaging another. Officials speculate that Japanese Americans were signaling Japanese ships (The *Los Angeles Times* even reported that local Japanese farmers were guiding Japanese airplanes to their targets: "Caps on Japanese Tomato Plants Point to Air Base."[2])

Officials question Japanese Americans' loyalty. Most, born here, are U.S. citizens, but they have been granted citizenship by Japan as well because of their ancestry. And they have formed semiclosed communities and adhered to Old World cultural patterns. The army general in charge of evacuation expressed the prevalent attitude toward them: "There isn't such a thing as a loyal Japanese."[3]

Many groups characterized the Japanese as rats. West Coast restaurants placed signs in their windows: "This Restaurant Poisons Both Rats and Japs." Groups distributed pamphlets—"Slap the Jap Rat"—and put stickers with pictures of a rat with a Japanese face on their cars. A patriotic parade in New York City included a float the crowd reportedly "loved"—an eagle leading a squadron of American bombers toward a herd of yellow rats trying to escape.[4]

On the other hand, Korematsu claims the order discriminates against him on the basis of his race and thereby violates his Fifth Amendment right to due process of law. As evidence, Korematsu

CONTINUED 

OUTLINE

Development of the Courts' Role in Government
- Founding to the Civil War
- Civil War to the Depression
- Depression to the Present

Courts
- Structure of the Courts
- Jurisdiction of the Courts

Judges
- Selection of Judges
- Tenure of Judges
- Qualifications of Judges
- Independence of Judges

Access to the Courts
- Wealth Discrimination in Access
- Interest Group Help in Access
- Restrictions on Access
- Proceeding Through the Courts

Deciding Cases
- Interpreting Statutes
- Interpreting the Constitution
- Restraint and Activism
- Following Precedents
- Making Law

The Power of the Courts
- Use of Judicial Review
- Use of Political Checks Against the Courts

Conclusion: Are the Courts Responsive?

notes that the order does not apply to persons of German or Italian ancestry. (Although the order was general, the military commander was told not to remove the many persons of Italian descent on the West Coast. The mayor of San Francisco was Italian, and baseball star Joe DiMaggio, whose parents were aliens, was a national idol. Anyway, President Roosevelt said he was not worried about the Italians. "They are a lot of opera singers. . . ."[5])

Korematsu also notes that there has been widespread discrimination against Asians on the West Coast. For decades there has been talk of the "yellow peril." In 1913 Congress refused to allow more Japanese to become citizens and in 1924 refused to allow more to immigrate. The discrimination has resulted in segregated neighborhoods and schools and, in at least one city—Bakersfield—even the omission of their names from the telephone directory. The hostility has fueled efforts to drive Japanese Americans off their productive farmland. Many Japanese, brought over as cheap laborers, worked hard enough to become successful owners. At the outbreak of the war, according to some estimates, they grew about half the fruits and vegetables in California, and an acre of their land was worth more than seven times the average value of farmland on the Coast. Competitors covet their land.

You are torn. You were appointed by President Roosevelt, yet you are strongly committed to individual rights. What do you decide?

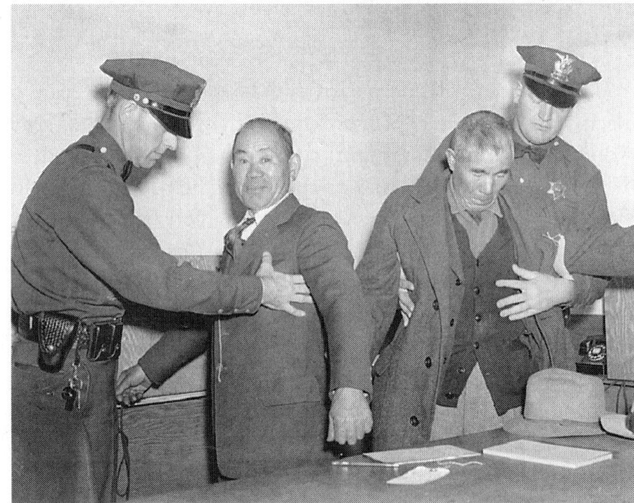

Los Angeles police frisk Japanese Americans who did not report for relocation.

Most people assume that courts are nonpolitical and that judges are objective. People say we have "a government of laws, not of men." This is a myth. At any time in our history, "It is individuals who make, enforce, and interpret the law."[6] When judges interpret the law, they are political actors and courts are political institutions.

As political institutions, courts make policy, although not all make policy to the same degree. Among the federal courts, the Supreme Court makes national policy in most of its cases. As the highest court, it decides difficult legal questions and resolves important national controversies that the lower courts could not settle to the litigants' satisfaction. The lower courts make regional and local policy in some of their cases, although most of their cases are routine because the law is clear and the decisions are of little consequence except to the litigants.

That the judiciary is part of the political process can be seen in the history, structure, jurisdiction, composition, operation, and impact of the courts.

➤Development of the Courts' Role in Government

The Founders expected the judiciary to be the weakest branch of government. In the *Federalist Papers,* Alexander Hamilton wrote that Congress would have power to make the laws and appropriate the money; the president would have power to execute the laws; but the courts would have "merely judgment," that is, only authority to resolve disputes in cases brought to them. In doing so, they would exercise "neither force nor will." They would not have any means to enforce decisions, and they would not use their own values to decide cases. Rather, they would simply apply the Constitution and laws as written. Consequently, the judiciary would be the "least dangerous" branch.[7]

This prediction was accurate for the early years of the Republic. The Supreme Court was held in such low esteem that some distinguished men refused to accept appointment, or they accepted appointment but refused to attend sessions. The first chief justice thought the Court was "inauspicious,"[8] without enough "weight and dignity" to play an important role.[9] So he resigned to be governor of New York. The second chief justice resigned to be envoy to France. To add insult, when the capital was moved to Washington in 1801, the planners overlooked the Court and forgot to provide a place for it to hold sessions. The justices had to meet in the office of the clerk of the Senate for some years.

However, the status of the Court changed after the appointment of the third chief justice—John Marshall. Under the leadership of Marshall and later chief justices, the Court gradually developed "weight and dignity" and came to play an important role in government. The lower courts eventually did as well.

The development of the courts' role in government can be shown by dividing the courts' history into three eras—from the Founding to the Civil War, from the Civil War to the Depression, and from the Depression to the present.

Chief Justice John Marshall.

Founding to the Civil War

The primary issue for the courts in the era from this country's founding to the Civil War was the relationship between nation and state. In addressing this issue, the Supreme Court established judicial review and national dominance.

Judicial Review

Judicial review is the authority to declare laws or actions of government officials unconstitutional. The Constitution does not mention judicial review, but the Founders apparently expected the courts to exercise it. In the *Federalist Papers,* Hamilton said the courts would have authority to void laws contrary to the Constitution,[10] and at the time some state courts had such authority. Yet the Founders did not expect the courts to exercise it vigorously.

The Supreme Court asserted itself to exercise judicial review in the case of ***Marbury v. Madison*** in 1803.[11] The case had its origins in 1800, when President John Adams was defeated in his bid for reelection by Thomas Jefferson, and Federalist members of Congress were defeated by Jeffersonians. With both the presidency and Congress lost, the Federalists tried to ensure continued control of the judiciary. The lame duck president and Congress added more judgeships to which they appointed Federalists, working feverishly to install these "midnight judges" before the new president and Congress took over. Adams named his secretary of state, John Marshall, to be chief justice. Although Marshall, still secretary of state, was responsible for delivering the commissions to the new judicial appointees, he failed to deliver 17 of the 42 commissions for District of Columbia justices of the peace. He assumed that his successor would deliver the rest. But Jefferson, angry at the Federalists' efforts to pack the judiciary, told his secretary of state, James Madison, not to deliver the commissions. Without the signed commissions, the appointees could not prove that they had in fact been appointed.

William Marbury and three other intended appointees petitioned the Supreme Court for a writ of mandamus, a writ that orders government officials to do something they have a duty to do. In this case it would order Madison to deliver the commissions.

This portrait of William Marbury reflects the importance of *Marbury v. Madison*. It is the only portrait of a litigant owned by the Supreme Court Historical Society.

As chief justice, Marshall was in a position to rule on his own negligence. Today this would be considered a conflict of interest and he would be expected to disqualify himself. But at the time people were not as troubled by such conflicts.

Marshall could issue the writ, but surely Jefferson would tell Madison to disobey it and the Court would be powerless to enforce it. Or he could not issue the writ, and the Court would appear to cave in to Jefferson. Either way the Court would demonstrate weakness rather than strength. But Marshall, in his genius, found a way out of the dilemma.

Marbury had petitioned the Court for a writ of mandamus under the authority of a provision of the Judiciary Act of 1789 that permitted the Court to issue this type of writ. But Marshall maintained that the Court could issue the writ only in cases that came to it on appeal from a lower court rather than in ones, like Marbury's, that started at the High Court. The Constitution gives the Court original jurisdiction over cases involving a state or foreign ambassador, which Marbury's case did not. By expanding the Court's original jurisdiction, Marshall argued, the Judiciary Act contradicted the Constitution. This interpretation was questionable because the Constitution does not say that the Court shall have original jurisdiction *only* over cases involving a state or foreign ambassador. Many of those who had drafted and voted for the Judiciary Act had been delegates to the Constitutional Convention, and it is unlikely they would have initiated a law that contradicted the Constitution. But this interpretation allowed Marshall a way out of the dilemma.

Speaking for a unanimous Court, Marshall insisted that Marbury had a right to the commission. But Marshall concluded that the Court could not order the administration to give the commission because the provision of the act was unconstitutional. Thus, Marshall exercised judicial review. He wrote, in a statement that would be repeated by courts for years to come, "It is emphatically the province and duty of the judicial department to say what the law is."

Marshall justified judicial review this way: The Constitution is the supreme law of the land. If other laws contradict it, they are unconstitutional. So far, few of his contemporaries would quarrel with his reasoning. Marshall continued: Judges decide cases, and to decide cases they have to apply the Constitution. To apply it they have to say what it means. They can be trusted to say what it means because they take an oath to uphold it. Here many would quarrel with his reasoning. Other officials who have to follow the Constitution and who take an oath to uphold it could interpret it as appropriately as judges could.

But Marshall was persuasive enough to convince many people. A sly fox, he sacrificed the commissions—he could not have gotten them anyway—and established the power of judicial review instead. In doing so, with one hand he gave the Jeffersonians what they wanted, while with the other he gave the Federalists something much greater. And all along he claimed he did what the Constitution required him to do.

Jefferson saw through this. He said the Constitution, in Marshall's hands, was "a thing of putty."[12] But the decision did not require Jefferson to do anything, so he could not do anything but protest. Most of Jefferson's followers were satisfied with the result. They were not upset that the Court invalidated a Federalist law or concerned with the means used to do so.

Of course, they were shortsighted because this decision laid the cornerstone for a strong judiciary. Thus, the case that began as a "trivial squabble over a few petty political plums" became perhaps the most important case the Court ever decided.[13]

However, the case was not treated as a landmark until late in the century. (It was not even cited by the Court for its use of judicial review until 1887.) Apparently the opinion reflected a common view, except among the most ardent Jeffersonians, that the Court would exercise judicial review. Thus, the opinion became more important for articulating and justifying judicial review than for creating it.[14]

National Dominance

After *Marbury* the Court did not declare any other congressional laws unconstitutional during Marshall's tenure, although it did declare numerous state laws unconstitutional.[15]

The Court also furthered national dominance by broadly construing Congress's power. In *McCulloch v. Maryland* (see Chapter 3), the Court interpreted the "necessary and proper clause" to allow Congress to legislate in many matters not mentioned in the Constitution. The Court also furthered national dominance by narrowly construing states' power to regulate commerce.[16]

When President Andrew Jackson named Roger Taney to replace Marshall, proponents of a strong national government worried that Taney would undo what Marshall had done. But, although Taney did not further expand national power, he upheld national supremacy and thus solidified most of Marshall's doctrine.

Even so, in one case Taney severely undermined the Court's reputation and effectiveness. In the Dred Scott case,[17] the Court jumped into the thick of the slavery conflict and declared the Missouri Compromise of 1820, which controlled slavery in the territories, unconstitutional.

This was only the second time the Court had declared a congressional law unconstitutional, and it could not have come in a more controversial area or at a less opportune time. The slavery issue had polarized the nation, and the ruling polarized it further. Southerners were disenchanted with the Court because of its emphasis on a strong national government. Now northerners became disenchanted too. The Court's prestige dropped so precipitously that it could play only a weak role for two decades. President Abraham Lincoln refused to enforce one of its rulings,[18] and Congress withdrew part of its jurisdiction.[19] As a result, the Court avoided important issues.

The Taney Court naively thought it could resolve the clash over slavery and thereby resolve the conflict between nation and state. But no court could achieve this. It took the Civil War to do so.

Civil War to the Depression

With the controversy between nation and state dampened after the war, the next primary issue for the courts was the relationship between government and business in cases involving regulation of business.

After the war, industrialization proceeded at a breakneck pace, bringing not only benefits but many problems. Some corporations abused their power over their employees, their competitors, and their customers. Some legislatures passed laws to regulate these abuses, but the corporations challenged the laws in court. The Supreme Court, dominated by

Although many children worked long days in unhealthy conditions, the Supreme Court declared initial laws prohibiting child labor unconstitutional. This boy worked in coal mines at the turn of the century.

justices who had been lawyers for corporations, reflected the views of corporations and struck down laws regulating them.

Beginning in the 1870s, intensifying in the 1890s, and continuing in the 1900s, the Court invalidated laws that regulated child labor,[20] maximum hours of work,[21] and minimum wages for work.[22] It also discouraged employees from joining unions and striking,[23] and it limited antitrust laws.[24] In just one decade, the Court invalidated 41 state laws that regulated railroads.[25]

In 1935 and 1936, the Court struck down 12 congressional laws,[26] nearly nullifying President Franklin Roosevelt's New Deal program to help the country recover from the Depression.

The Court's action precipitated another major crisis. Roosevelt was reelected resoundingly in 1936. Heady from his victory and frustrated by the Court's decisions and his lack of opportunities to appoint new justices in his first term, he retaliated against the Court by proposing what was soon labeled a **court-packing plan.** The plan would have authorized the president to nominate and the Senate to confirm a new justice for every justice over 70 who did not retire, up to a total of 15. At the time, there were 6 justices over 70, so Roosevelt could have appointed 6 new justices and assured himself a friendly Court. Roosevelt claimed the plan was to help the Court cope with its increasing caseload, but virtually everyone could see through this. Even many of his supporters criticized him for tampering with the Court.

Before Congress could vote on the plan, two justices who often sided with four conservative justices against New Deal legislation switched positions to side with three liberal justices for the legislation. Chief Justice Charles Evans Hughes and Justice Owen Roberts apparently thought the Court would suffer if it continued to oppose the popular president and his popular programs. Their "conversion" tipped the scales from votes of 6 to 3 against New Deal legislation to 5 to 4 for similar legislation. As a result, Roosevelt's plan became unnecessary, and Congress scuttled it. Hughes's and Roberts's switch was dubbed "the switch in time that saved nine."

Thus the Court resolved this issue in favor of government over business. Since then it has permitted most efforts to regulate business.

Depression to the Present

With the controversy between government and business subdued, the next primary issue for the courts has been the relationship between government and the individual in cases involving civil liberties and rights.

Especially since the 1950s, individuals have demanded an expansion of the rights in the Bill of Rights and the guarantees of due process and equal protection in the Fourteenth Amendment.

Traditionally the Supreme Court had not supported civil liberties and rights very much. But in 1953 President Dwight Eisenhower appointed Earl Warren to be chief justice. For the rest of the 1950s and 1960s, Warren led the Court more effectively than any chief justice since Marshall. The **Warren Court** completely overhauled doctrine in three areas—racial segregation, criminal defendants' rights, and reapportionment. It also significantly altered doctrine in other areas—libel, obscenity, and religion. In the process it held many laws unconstitutional. It was more activist in these areas than the Court had ever been (see Figure 1).

Because its decisions generally favored a minority or unpopular individual, such as an alleged subversive or a criminal defendant, over government, the

Chief Justice Earl Warren, flanked by Justices Hugo Black (*left*) and William Douglas.

FIGURE 1
Number of Laws Regulating Economic Activity and Restricting Civil Liberties and Rights Declared Unconstitutional by the Supreme Court Since 1900

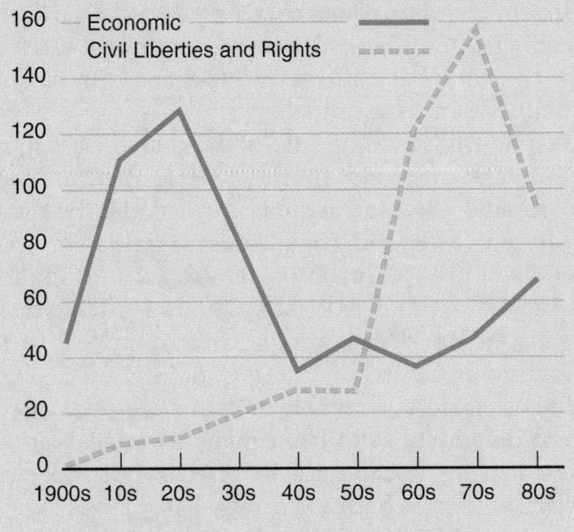

The Supreme Court was nearly as activist in striking down laws in the 1910s, 1920s, and 1930s as it was in the 1950s, 1960s, and 1970s. But in the former years it was activist in economic cases, while in the latter years it was activist in civil liberties and rights cases.

Sources: Congressional Research Service, *The Constitution of the United States: Analysis and Interpretation* (Washington, D.C.: U.S. Government Printing Office, 1973 and 1982); Lawrence Baum, *The Supreme Court,* 3rd ed. (Washington, D.C.: CQ Press, 1989), p. 188.

Court brought about a backlash by the majority that peaked in the late 1960s. President Richard Nixon vowed to change the direction of the Court, and in 1969 he appointed Warren Burger to be chief justice. Then Nixon and the next Republican president appointed four more justices. They wanted to slow, halt, or even reverse the Warren Court's actions. They expected the **Burger Court** to make a "constitutional counter-revolution."

But the Court did not. Although it eroded some of the Warren Court's doctrine, particularly in the area of criminal defendants' rights, it left most of the doctrine intact. Further, it overhauled doctrine in two areas where the Warren Court was silent—sexual discrimination and abortion. In these and other areas, the Burger Court held numerous laws unconstitutional. Although not as committed to civil liberties and rights as the Warren Court, the Burger Court was more committed to them than any earlier Court.

President Reagan sought to erode the Warren Court's doctrine further by appointing three more conservatives to fill vacancies and in 1986, when Burger retired, by naming William Rehnquist, the most conservative associate justice, to be chief justice. President Bush also had an opportunity to erode the Warren Court's doctrine by appointing two more conservatives when the only two consistent liberals retired. By the end of his administration, Republican presidents had named 10 straight justices and the **Rehnquist Court** had seven conservatives. Yet conflicts among the conservatives—some are willing to uphold precedents they would not have agreed to set in the first place, while others vote to sweep them away—have splintered the bloc. In some terms, the former group dominates, but in other terms the latter group dominates. Overall, the Rehnquist Court, though markedly more conservative than the Burger Court, has not overturned most of the Warren Court's doctrine.[27]

The election of President Clinton, a Democrat, in 1992 probably will keep the Court from tilting any more to the right as long as he is in office.

In sum, throughout its history the Court's role in government has been that of a policymaker—in relationships between nation and state, government and business, and government and the individual. In the first and second eras, the Court was a solidly conservative policymaker, protecting private property rights and limiting government regulation of business; in the third era the Court has been a generally liberal policymaker, permitting government regulation of business and supporting civil liberties and rights for individuals. The third era, however, might be coming to a close.

➤Courts

Most countries with a federal system have one national court over a system of regional courts. In contrast, the United States has a complete system of national courts side by side with complete systems of state courts, for a total of 51 separate systems. This makes litigation far more complicated than in other countries.

Structure of the Courts

The Constitution mentions only one court—a supreme court—although it allows Congress to set up additional, lower courts, which it did in the Judiciary Act of 1789. The act was a compromise between Federalists, who wanted a full system of lower courts with extensive jurisdiction—authority to hear and decide cases—in order to strengthen the national government, and Jeffersonians, who wanted only a partial system of lower courts with limited jurisdiction in order to avoid strengthening the national government. The compromise established a full system of lower courts with limited jurisdiction. These courts were authorized to hear disputes involving citizens of more than one state but not disputes relating to the U.S. Constitution and laws. The state courts were permitted to hear all these.

In 1875, Congress granted the federal courts extensive jurisdiction. Sixteen years later Congress created another level of courts, between the Supreme Court and the original lower courts, to complete the basic structure of the federal judiciary.

The **district courts** are trial courts. There are 94, based on population but with at least 1 in each state. They have a number of judges, although a single judge or jury decides each case.

The **courts of appeals** are intermediate appellate courts. There are 12, based on regions—"circuits"—of the country. A group of three judges decides their cases.

The Supreme Court is the ultimate appellate court. Although it can hear some cases (those involving a state or diplomat) that have not proceeded through the lower courts first, in practice it hears nearly all of its cases on appeal. A group of nine justices decides its cases.

The district courts conduct trials. The courts of appeals and Supreme Court do not; they do not have juries or witnesses to testify and present evidence—just lawyers for the opposing litigants. Rather than determine guilt or innocence, these courts evaluate arguments about legal questions arising in the cases.

The state judiciaries have a structure similar to the federal judiciary. In most states, though, there are two tiers of trial courts. The lower tier is usually for criminal cases involving minor crimes, and the upper tier is for criminal cases involving major crimes and for civil cases. In about three-fourths of the states, there are intermediate appellate courts, and in all of the states there is a supreme court (although in a few it is called another name).

Jurisdiction of the Courts

Jurisdiction is the authority to hear and decide cases. According to the Constitution, the federal courts exercise jurisdiction over cases in which the subject involves either the U.S. Constitution, statutes, or treaties; maritime law; or cases in which the litigants include either the U.S. government, more than one state government, one state government and a citizen of another state, citizens of more than one state, or a foreign government or citizen. The state courts exercise jurisdiction over the remaining cases. These include most criminal cases because the states have authority over most criminal matters and pass most criminal laws.

Despite this dividing line, some cases begin in the state courts and end in the federal courts. These involve state law and federal law, frequently a state statute and a federal constitutional right. For these cases there are two major paths from the state judiciary to the federal judiciary. One is for the litigant who lost at the state supreme court to appeal to the U.S. Supreme Court.

The other path, available only in a criminal case, is for the defendant who has exhausted appeals in the state courts to appeal to the local federal district court through a writ of **habeas corpus.** Latin for "Have ye the body!" this writ demands that the state figuratively produce the defendant and justify his or her incarceration. If the district court decides that the state courts did not grant the defendant's federal constitutional rights, it will reverse the conviction. From the district court's decision, the losing side can try to appeal to the courts of appeals and Supreme Court. Jurisdiction in these cases is complicated, and appeals may be numerous (see Figure 2).

Judges

Selection of Judges

Benjamin Franklin proposed that judges be selected by lawyers because lawyers would pick "the ablest of the profession in order to get rid of him, and share his practice among themselves."[28] The Founders rejected this unique idea in favor of a plan whereby the president nominates judges and the Senate confirms them. There are no other requirements in the Constitution, although there is an unwritten requirement that judges be lawyers and an expectation that they be members of the president's political party. Most have been active party members who have served in office or contributed to candidates. In this century presidents nominated members of their party from 82% of the time (Gerald Ford) to 99% of the time (Woodrow Wilson). Thus the process of selecting federal judges is highly political.

FIGURE 2
Federal and State Court Systems

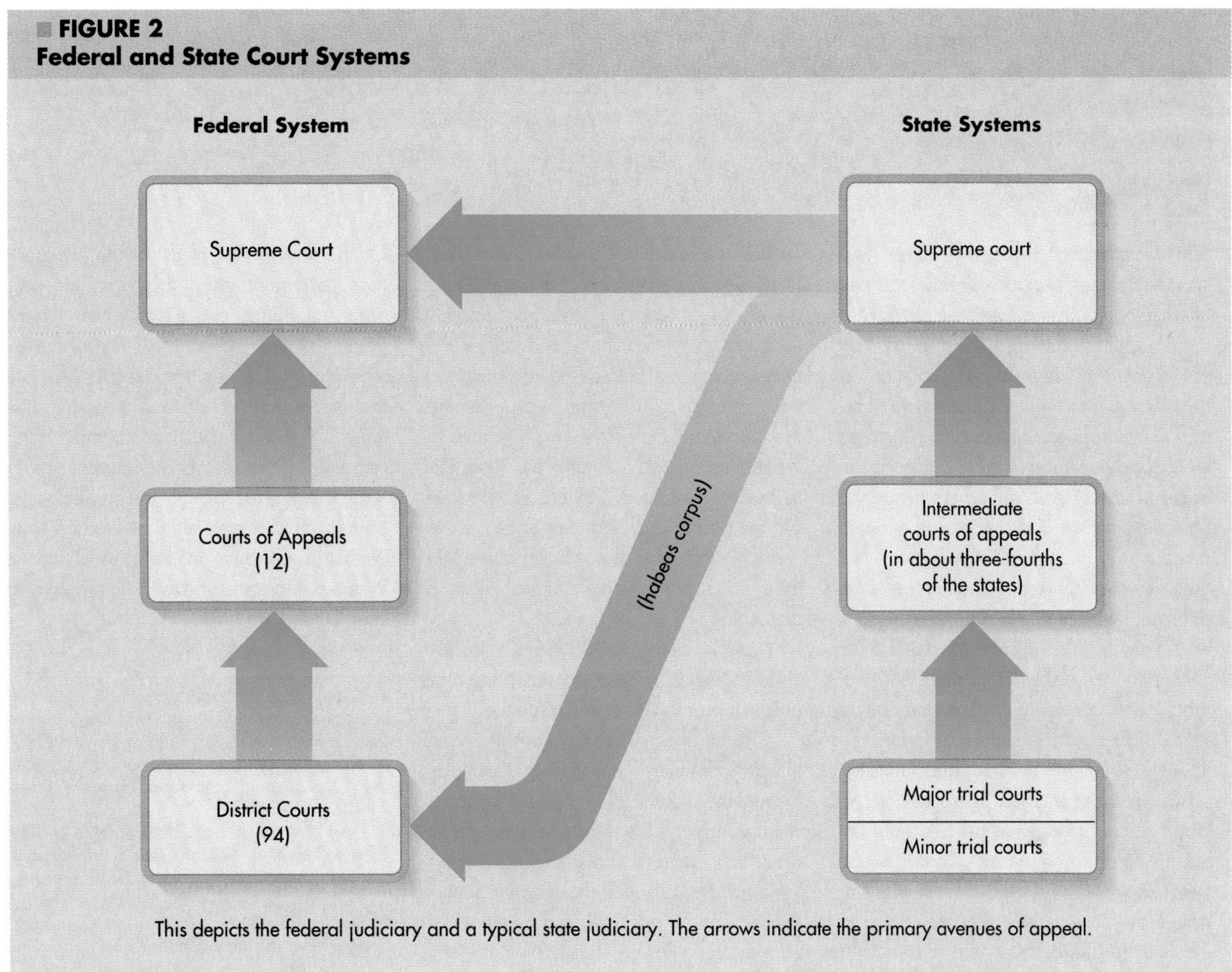

This depicts the federal judiciary and a typical state judiciary. The arrows indicate the primary avenues of appeal.

Mechanics of Selection

For lower court vacancies, administration officials recommend candidates, but senators also play a key role through the practice of senatorial courtesy. This tradition allows senators of the president's party to veto candidates for positions in their state and to recommend other candidates instead.

Senatorial courtesy can tie the president's hands. In deference to southern senators, President John Kennedy, who advocated civil rights, appointed southern judges who advocated segregation. One characterized the Supreme Court's desegregation ruling as "one of the truly regrettable decisions of all time," and another called blacks "niggers" and "chimpanzees" in court.[29]

Senatorial courtesy applies not only to district courts, which lie within individual states, but also to courts of appeals, which span several states. For these courts, senators informally divide the seats among the states in the circuit. The practice does not apply to the Supreme Court, however, because this court is a national court and there are too few seats to divide among the states.

For Supreme Court vacancies, administration officials conduct a search for acceptable candidates. Prominent politicians and lawyers recommend persons, and interest groups lobby for their preferences.

Once the president has settled upon a candidate, he submits the nomination to the Senate, where it goes to the Judiciary Committee for hearings. Senators question the nominee about his or her judicial philosophy, and interest groups voice their concerns. If a majority of the committee consents, the nomination goes to the whole Senate. If a majority of the Senate consents, the nomination is confirmed.

American Diversity

Do Women Judges Make a Difference?

Some argue that there should be more women judges because women are entitled to their "fair share" of all governmental offices, including judgeships. Others argue that there should be more so that women as well as men would feel that courts represent them and, therefore, would believe that courts' decisions are fair and legitimate. Still others argue that there should be more because women, compared to men, have somewhat different views and would make somewhat different decisions.

A study of Justice Sandra Day O'Connnor's behavior shows that although she generally votes on the conservative side of issues, she usually votes in a liberal direction in sex discrimination cases. Moreover, her presence on the Court apparently sensitizes her male colleagues to gender issues. All but two of them began to vote against sex discrimination more frequently after she joined the Court (and one of these two already had voted against sex discrimination regularly).[1]

Some studies reflect similar results for women justices on state supreme courts. These justices tend to support a broad array of women's rights in cases ranging from sex discrimination to child support and property settlement. On these issues even women justices from opposing political parties tend to agree.[2]

But studies that compare voting patterns on issues less obviously related to gender have less clear findings. Women judges appear more liberal than men in cases involving employment discrimination and racial discrimination. Perhaps the treatment they have experienced as women has made them more sympathetic to the discrimination others have faced. On the other hand, women judges do not appear more liberal or conservative than men in cases involving criminal rights or obscenity.[3]

A study of the sentences of state trial court judges found that compared to male judges, women judges sentenced men defendants the same way, but they sentenced women defendants to prison more frequently. That is, in borderline cases, women judges ordered women defendants to prison, while men judges gave them probation. Where women judges treated men and women defendants equally, men judges treated women defendants more leniently and more paternalistically, permitting them to avoid prison.[4]

In addition, women judges seem to make a difference in a less direct way. They help protect the credibility of women lawyers and witnesses. In court some men judges and lawyers refer to women lawyers and witnesses by their first names or by such terms as "young lady," "little girl," "sweetie," or "honey." Or the men, in the midst of the proceedings, comment upon the women's perfume, clothing, or appearance. "How does an attorney establish her authority when the judge has just described her to the entire courtroom as 'a pretty little thing'?"[5] Even if the men consider their remarks harmless compliments rather than intentional tactics, their effect is to undermine the credibility of women lawyers and witnesses in the eyes of jurors. Women judges have attempted to squelch such remarks.[6]

1. Karen O'Connor and Jeffrey A. Segal, "Justice Sandra Day O'Connor and the Supreme Court's Reaction to Its First Female Member," in Naomi B. Lynn, ed., *Women, Politics and the Constitution* (New York: Haworth Press, 1990), pp. 95–104.
2. David W. Allen and Diane E. Wall, "Role Orientations and Women State Supreme Court Justices," *Judicature* 77 (November/December, 1993), pp. 156–65.
3. Sue Davis, Susan Haire, and Donald R. Songer, "Voting Behavior and Gender on the U.S. Courts of Appeals," *Judicature* 77 (November/December, 1993), pp. 129–33; Thomas G. Walker and Deborah J. Barrow, "The Diversification of the Federal Bench," *Journal of Politics* 47 (1985), pp. 596–617.
4. John Gruhl, Cassia Spohn, and Susan Welch, "Women as Policymakers: The Case of Trial Judges," *American Journal of Political Science* 25 (May 1981), pp. 308–22.
5. William Eich, "Gender Bias in the Courtroom: Some Participants Are More Equal Than Others," *Judicature* 69 (April–May 1986), pp. 339–43.
6. Georgia Dullea, "Women on the Bench Increase," *New York Times*, April 26, 1984.

Criteria Used in Selection

The Founders expected judges to be selected by merit; they did not foresee the policymaking role of the courts or the development of political parties and senatorial courtesy, which have thrust political criteria into the process of selection.

CRITERIA USED BY PRESIDENTS Although presidents prefer judges with merit, usually they select them on the basis of other factors—friendship, favors, political experience, or ideological views. President Reagan emphasized ideology in an effort to mold the bench more than any president since Franklin

Roosevelt. His administration screened candidates for conservative views on controversial issues. For example, the administration looked for those who, in the language of the Republican party platform, "respect the sanctity of innocent human life"—code words for opposition to Supreme Court decisions allowing abortion. President Bush also sought candidates with conservative views, although he tried to avoid those who would be controversial.

Presidents also select justices to balance representation on the Supreme Court. They choose persons from groups who do not have a member on the Court already. As the country expanded, presidents were urged to nominate persons from the West. Eventually, they were pressured to nominate Catholics, Jews, blacks, and women. Presidents bowed to these pressures because they sought support from diverse groups of people and feared that ignoring them would make confirmation of their nominees difficult.

When Thurgood Marshall, the first black to sit on the Supreme Court, retired in 1991, President Bush felt obligated to nominate another black for this seat. He chose Clarence Thomas, a conservative Republican court of appeals judge. But where Marshall was an ardent champion of civil rights, Thomas, as head of the Equal Employment Opportunity Commission in the Reagan administration, criticized affirmative action and drew the ire of most black leaders.

Indeed, individual justices do not always reflect their group's views. In abortion cases Justice Sandra Day O'Connor has voted against the feminist groups' position in some cases, and former Justice William Brennan, a Catholic, voted against the Catholic Church's policy consistently. Sometimes groups have to satisfy themselves with the symbolic benefits of having a "member" on the Court.

CRITERIA USED BY SENATORS Although senators normally confirm presidential nominations to the lower courts, occasionally they refuse to confirm Supreme Court nominations. Because the high Court is more important and appointments to it are more visible, these nominations are more likely to become embroiled in politics. Since the late 1960s senators have rejected six nominations to the Court—two of President Lyndon Johnson, two of President Nixon, and two of President Reagan.

Senators decide whether to confirm a nomination primarily on the basis of the qualifications and ideology of the nominee. If a nominee is highly qualified and ideologically moderate, he or she sails through. If a nominee is less well qualified or ideologically extreme, he or she faces more problems.[30] (Even then, however, senators are reluctant to admit they consider ideological views because most of the public thinks politics is not or at least should not be involved.)

When Nixon chose Court of Appeals Judge G. Harold Carswell, law scholars familiar with his record were dismayed. At Senate hearings they testified that he was undistinguished, as well as opposed to civil rights. Nixon's floor manager for the nomination, Senator Roman Hruska (R-Neb.), blurted out in exasperation, "Even if he is mediocre there are a lot of mediocre judges and people and lawyers. They are entitled to a little representation, aren't they and a little chance? We can't have all Brandeises, Cardozos, and Frankfurters, and stuff like that there."[31] This was the kiss of death. Once Carswell's supporters admitted his mediocrity, senators who objected to his views on civil rights could vote against him more freely, and his nomination was doomed.

Yet when Nixon and Reagan nominated conservatives with unquestioned qualifications, they rarely faced a problem. One exception was Reagan's nomination of Robert Bork in 1987. Bork had criticized Court doctrine in his writings and speeches, and the debate focused on his ideology. In addition to rejecting a right to privacy, which is the basis of Court decisions allowing birth control and abortion, he had criticized Court decisions and congressional laws advancing racial equality. Bork's positions struck many Americans as extreme, and his nomination was voted down.

This battle prompted some observers to ask whether anyone with a record could be nominated again. Indeed, when Bush had his first vacancy, he chose a man who had left no trail of controversial writings and speeches. David Souter, though a former New Hampshire attorney general and then state supreme court justice, was called the "Stealth candidate" (after the bomber designed to elude radar).[32] Souter was a private person, living alone in a house at the end of a dirt road and not answering his neighbors' phone calls some nights. He had expressed few positions and made few decisions reflecting his views on federal constitutional doctrine. Even in his confirmation hearings he refused to reveal his views. It was assumed that he was another conservative, because of his lifestyle and because of his support from conservative aides to the president, yet he offered a small target and won confirmation easily.

When Bush had his second vacancy and chose Thomas, he realized that the nomination could be controversial (even before the charges of sexual harassment surfaced) but saw that it would split the Democratic coalition: Some Democrats would be sympathetic because of his race, while others would be critical because of his views. For insurance the administration instructed Thomas to soft-pedal his views. Thomas told senators he made his previous statements as a representative of the administration but would be impartial as a justice. On abortion he insisted, incredibly, that he had no position and, in fact, had never discussed the issue with anyone.

Both Souter and Thomas said they could not reveal their views because they would have to decide these issues and so would need to preserve their impartiality. Yet both stated their support for capital punishment, although they would also have to decide these cases. The difference is that their view on capital punishment coincided with that of three-fourths of the public, whereas their views on other issues probably did not.

When Clinton had his first vacancy, he was wary because the Senate had forced him to withdraw several nominations to other positions and because Republicans had vowed to avenge Bork's defeat. The president chose Ruth Bader Ginsburg, a court of appeals judge for 13 years. The nomination satisfied Republicans because Ginsburg had often voted with Republicans on the bench, yet it also pleased some Democratic constituencies. Women's groups, of course, expected more seats, and Jews, who had not had a representative on the Court since 1969, also wanted a seat.

Racial and Sexual Stereotypes in Thomas versus Hill

With a combustible mixture of politics, race, and sex, the battle over the nomination of Clarence Thomas to the Supreme Court was enticing theater; it was bound to play on television. In this medium, which oversimplifies complex issues, dividing competitors into two camps—pro and con—and then encouraging them to attack and counterattack, perhaps it was inevitable that the key participants would be assigned roles that were not nearly as subtle and complex as the real people were. But these roles, actually stereotypes, would determine the outcome of the battle.[1]

Bush administration officials began with a nonracial stereotype—the heroes of nineteenth-century writer Horatio Alger, the boys who overcame insurmountable odds (for example, *From Canal Boy to President*). In interviews with reporters, officials emphasized, and Thomas stressed, how he began life in Pin Point, Georgia, and overcame poverty and injustice along the way. Thomas, in fact, had far more to say about prejudice against him when young than about any prejudice against blacks today. But officials did not stop with Horatio Alger. They also invoked Booker T. Washington, the late-nineteenth-century black educator who urged blacks to become self-reliant rather than dependent on the government for help. Like Washington, officials said, Thomas had pulled himself up by his own bootstraps. Although he had benefited from affirmative action to gain admission to Yale Law School, Thomas later had rejected affirmative action and other vigorous government initiatives and instead had called for more self-reliance. Thomas had even used the stereotype of the "welfare queen" to deride his sister, who for a time received welfare, and to distance himself from many blacks and their leaders.

Blacks critical of the nomination thought the stereotypes did not stop with Horatio Alger and Booker T. Washington. Some believed that the whites were looking for an "Uncle Tom" (without, of course, using the phrase), a loyal and trustworthy, even compliant, black man who was willing to cater to white prejudices.

During the first round of confirmation hearings, blacks critical of the nomination saw another stereotype—"Sambo," a grinning, mindless minstrel who could remember nothing without his master's help.[2] Thomas did come across as affable and, under the coaching of his handlers, refused to divulge his views on judicial doctrine.

After Anita Hill's charges of sexual harassment, and all their sordid details, became public, blacks cringed as another stereotype surfaced—"Buck," an oversexed black male who has casual sex with black women but who lusts after white women.[3] According to Hill, Thomas talked about the size of his penis and scenes in pornographic movies, and he pressured her to go out with him before he eventually married a white woman.

During the second round of confirmation hearings, after the charges of harassment, Thomas himself invoked the stereotype of the "uppity black." Characterizing himself as rebellious, because he disagreed with black leaders and liberal activists about the role of government in civil rights, he angrily proclaimed that the country was witnessing a "high-tech legal lynching" of an "uppity black man." The image of lynching an

Ginsburg refused to discuss doctrine at her hearings, but her record showed a commitment to abortion rights and sexual equality. Although she had tied for first in her graduating class from Columbia Law School in 1959, she was turned down for a clerkship by Justice Felix Frankfurter and for a job by New York City law firms. The firms, just beginning to hire Jews, were not ready to hire mothers with young children. She taught law and then served as an attorney for the American Civil Liberties Union (ACLU). In the 1970s she argued six sex discrimination cases before the Supreme Court and, with an innovative approach, won five.

When Clinton had his second vacancy, he was still wary of a confirmation fight. Instead of the people he most desired, he chose Stephen Breyer, a court of appeals judge with a reputation as a moderate.

Nominations to the Court, which were contentious during the nineteenth century but not during the first half of the twentieth century, have become contentious again partly because of the Court's activism—both liberals and conservatives saw what the Court can do—and partly because of the struggle for control of the divided government since the late 1960s. In most years Republicans have dominated the presidency while Democrats have dominated Congress, so both have fought over the judiciary to tip the balance. Republicans, especially, have been frustrated by their inability to push their civil liberties and rights policies through Congress, so they have hoped that their appointees to the Court would do what their members in Congress have not been able to do.

uppity black man, seared into the black consciousness for generations, was calculated to arouse the sympathy of African Americans. Indeed, this particular stereotype was decisive in persuading most of the black public to support Thomas and, in turn, persuading the undecided senators to vote for confirmation. Senators, especially those with large black constituencies, did not want to be accused of racism.

Hill was also the beneficiary and victim of stereotypes. Feminist critics of the nomination rallied around Hill, with some calling her the "Rosa Parks of sexual harassment," after the woman whose refusal to accept segregation on the bus sparked the Montgomery boycott. Yet Hill waited many years to air her charges and even then did so reluctantly. And, like Thomas, she had worked in the Reagan administration and supported the Bork nomination that so many of her new champions had assailed.

Although white professional women were impressed with Hill, many black workers were not. Some lower-class black women distrusted her because of her Yale education and her standard English diction. Neither the "nurturing mammy" nor the "surly black wife with the frying pan in her hand," according to one black writer, she was not recognizable as a black woman to some of them.[4] Others criticized her for airing the dirty laundry of the African American community in front of the larger white society.

Hill was also the target of sexual stereotypes promoted by Republicans on the Senate Judiciary Committee. Worried that her charges would cause senators to abandon Thomas, they characterized her as a "scorned and vengeful woman" who was attracted to Thomas and who sought revenge when he did not return her feelings. They also characterized her as a "whiny and weak woman" who wanted to do traditional male jobs but who could not put up with common problems in the workplace; a woman who complained about minor things but was not strong enough to voice her objections at the time.

Most of these stereotypes were promoted, not by Thomas and Hill, but by the warring forces—Republicans and Democrats, conservatives and liberals—who were using them as the weapons of their opposing agendas. And all of these stereotypes were effective because they played off sharp divisions in society—between blacks and whites, women and men, feminist women and traditional women, the professional classes and the working classes.

1. See, generally, Robert Chrisman and Robert L. Allen, eds., *Court of Appeal: The Black Community Speaks Out on the Racial and Sexual Politics of Thomas vs. Hill* (New York: Ballentine, 1992), an extensive collection of essays by black writers reflecting on the confirmation battle.
2. Llenda Jackson-Leslie, "Tom, Buck, and Sambo or How Clarence Thomas Got to the Supreme Court," in Chrisman and Allen, *Court of Appeal*, p. 106.
3. Jackson-Leslie, "Tom, Buck, and Sambo," in Chrisman and Allen, *Court of Appeal*, p. 108; Henry Vance Davis, "The High-Tech Lynching and the High-Tech Overseer," in Chrisman and Allen, *Court of Appeal*, pp. 59–62.
4. Rosemary L. Bray, "Taking Sides Against Ourselves," in Chrisman and Allen, *Court of Appeal*, p. 53. See also Melba Joyce Boyd, "Collard Greens, Clarence Thomas, and the High-Tech Rape of Anita Hill," in Chrisman and Allen, *Court of Appeal*, pp. 43–46.

Results of Selection

Judges are drawn primarily from the lower federal and state courts, the federal government, or large law firms. These established legal circles are dominated by white men so, not surprisingly, most judges have been white men. Before President Jimmy Carter took office, only eight women had ever served on the federal bench.[33] Carter, however, made a concerted effort to appoint more women and racial minorities. Sixteen percent of his appointees were women, and 21% were racial minorities. President Reagan, despite the impression he created by naming a woman to the Supreme Court, named mostly white men to the lower courts. Eight percent of his appointees were women, and 6% were racial minorities. Seventeen percent of President Bush's appointees were women, and 11% were racial minorities.[34]

President Clinton, in his first three years, nominated 30% women and 30% racial minorities among 165 vacancies.[35]

Most judges have been wealthy. Most of Bush's appointees were worth more than a half million dollars; a fourth of Reagan's and a third of Bush's appointees were millionaires.

Despite some efforts to balance representation on the Supreme Court, presidents have not sought actual representatives of all socioeconomic groups. Throughout history, justices have come from a narrow, elite slice of society. Most have been born into families of Western European stock (especially English, Welsh, Scotch, and Irish), profess the Protestant religion (especially Episcopalian, Presbyterian, Congregational, and Unitarian), and are upper middle or upper class. Moreover, they have been born into families with traditions of political or even judicial service, families with prestige and connections as well as expectations for achievement.[36]

With the power to nominate judges, presidents have a tremendous opportunity to shape the courts and their decisions. By the time Carter finished his term, he had appointed about 40% of the lower court judges, although he had no opportunity to appoint Supreme Court justices. By the time Bush finished his term, he and Reagan had appointed about 65% of the lower court judges and five Supreme Court justices (in addition to elevating Rehnquist from associate to chief justice). Most of Carter's appointees were moderates or liberals, whereas most of Bush's and Reagan's were conservatives (see Tables 1 and 2).

In addition to ideological differences in broad categories of cases, appointees of recent presidents also reflect differences in the narrower categories of abortion and the environment. Carter's appointees to the

TABLE 1 Appointees of Democrats and Republicans Think Differently

	PERCENT WHO AGREE		
	Democratic Appointees	Republican Appointees	Difference
Big corporations should be taken out of private ownership.	10%	2%	8%
U.S. institutions need complete restructuring.	24	13	11
The more able should earn more.	86	98	12
America would be better off if it moved toward socialism.	19	4	15
Private enterprise is fair to workers.	70	87	17
The poor are such due to circumstances beyond their control.	50	33	17
America offers an opportunity for financial security to all who work hard.	59	85	26
Government should ensure a good standard of living.	57	27	30
Less regulation of business is good for the country.	54	85	31
Government should not guarantee jobs.	36	70	34
Government should reduce the income gap between rich and poor.	78	44	34

A survey of the economic attitudes of federal lower court judges shows that most hold opinions accepting the economic status quo. Even so, there are significant differences according to the political party of the appointing president. Judges appointed by Republican presidents tend to think individuals are largely responsible for their financial success or failure and that government should do less to equalize conditions.

Source: Althea K. Nagai, Stanley Rothman, and S. Robert Lichter, "The Verdict on Federal Judges," *Public Opinion* (November/December 1987), p. 54.

district courts voted against abortion rights in just 13% of their cases, whereas Reagan's appointees voted against abortion rights in 77% of their cases.[37] Carter's appointees to the appellate courts sided more often with environmental groups, whereas Reagan's and Bush's appointees sided more often with businesses.[38] Reagan's appointees to the appellate courts voted to narrow existing air and water pollution laws and to resist recognizing new environmental obligations.[39]

Tenure of Judges

Once appointed, judges can serve for "good behavior." This means for life, unless they commit "high crimes and misdemeanors." These are not defined in the Constitution but are considered serious crimes or, possibly, political abuses. Congress can impeach and remove judges as it can presidents, but it has impeached only 13 and removed only 6.[40] The standard of guilt—"high crimes and misdemeanors"—is vague, the punishment drastic, and the process time consuming, so Congress has been reluctant to impeach judges.

As an alternative, Congress established other procedures to discipline lower federal court judges in 1980. Councils made up of district and appellate court judges can ask judges to resign or can prevent them from hearing cases, but they cannot actually remove them. The procedures have been used infrequently, although their existence has prompted some judges to resign before being disciplined.

Qualifications of Judges

Given the use of political criteria in selecting judges, are judges well qualified?

Political scientists who study the judiciary consider federal judges generally well qualified. This is especially true of Supreme Court justices, apparently because presidents think they will be held responsible for the justices they nominate and do not want to be embarrassed by them. Also, because presidents have so few vacancies to fill, they can confine themselves to persons of their party and political views, and even to persons of a particular region, religion, race, and sex, and still locate good candidates. This is less true of lower court judges. Presidents and senators jointly appoint them, so both can avoid full responsibility for them. These judges are also less visible, so a lack of merit is not as noticeable.

Presidents do appoint some losers. President Truman put a longtime supporter on a court of appeals who was "drunk half the time" and "no damn good." When asked why he appointed the man, Truman candidly replied, "I . . . felt I owed him a favor; that's why, and I thought as a judge he couldn't do too much harm, and he didn't . . . he wasn't the worst court appointment I ever made. By no means the worst."[41]

Sometimes presidents appoint qualified persons who later become incompetent. After serving for many years they incur the illnesses and infirmities of old age, and perhaps one-tenth become unable to perform their job well.[42] Yet they hang on because

TABLE 2 Appointees of Democrats and Republicans Vote Differently

	PERCENT LIBERAL* VOTES BY APPOINTEES OF				
Issue	**Nixon (R)**	**Ford (R)**	**Carter (D)**	**Reagan (R)**	**Bush (R)**
Criminal justice	27%	37%	39%	28%	26%
Civil rights and civil liberties	40	40	53	31	23
Labor and economic regulation	49	52	61	47	48

A study of the votes of federal district court judges appointed by President Nixon through President Bush shows marked differences according to the political party of the president. The study also shows some differences, especially in civil rights and liberties cases, among appointees of Republicans. Compare the appointees of Bush and Reagan with those of earlier Republicans. These results reflect the effort that the Bush and Reagan administrations made to nominate candidates who held conservative views on these issues.

*Liberal votes were defined as ones in favor of criminal defendants' or prisoners' rights in criminal justice cases; individuals' rights, involving freedom of expression or religion and equality between the races or sexes, in civil rights and liberties cases; and workers' or economic underdogs' interests, rather than businesses' or economic upper-dogs' interests, in labor and economic regulation cases. Cases through 1991 are included.

Source: Robert A. Carp, Donald Songer, C. K. Rowland, Ronald Stidham, and Lisa Richey-Tracy, "The Voting Behavior of Judges Appointed by President Bush," *Judicature* 76 (April–May, 1993), pp. 298–302.

they are allowed to serve for "good behavior." The situation has prompted proposals for a constitutional amendment setting a mandatory retirement age of 70. This would have a substantial impact because fully one-third of all Supreme Court justices, for example, have served past 75. But constitutional amendments are difficult to pass, and mandatory retirement ages are out of favor now. Further, some of the best judges have done some of their finest work after 70.

Independence of Judges

Given the use of political criteria in selecting judges, can judges be independent on the bench? Can they decide cases as they think the law requires? Or do they feel pressure to decide cases as presidents or senators want them to?

Because judges are not dependent upon presidents for renomination or senators for reconfirmation, they can be independent to a great extent. In the Watergate tapes case, Chief Justice Burger wrote the majority opinion and three other Nixon appointees joined the decision against President Nixon. In a case involving a law authorizing a special prosecutor to investigate and prosecute misconduct by governmental officials, Chief Justice Rehnquist wrote the majority opinion and another Reagan appointee joined the decision upholding the law against a challenge by President Reagan (whose aides had been prosecuted under the law).[43]

After surveying Warren and Burger Court decisions involving desegregation, obscenity, abortion, and criminal defendants' rights, one scholar observed, "Few American politicians even today would care to run on a platform of desegregation, pornography, abortion, and the 'coddling' of criminals."[44]

Presidents have scoffed at the notion that their appointees become their pawns. A study concluded that one-fourth of the justices deviated from their president's expectations.[45] Theodore Roosevelt placed Oliver Wendell Holmes on the Court because he thought Holmes shared his views on trusts. But in an early antitrust case, Holmes voted against Roosevelt's position, which prompted Roosevelt to declare, "I could carve out of a banana a judge with more backbone than that!"[46] Holmes had plenty of backbone; he just did not agree with Roosevelt's position in this case. Likewise, President Eisenhower placed Earl Warren on the Court, in part because he thought Warren was a moderate. But Warren turned out to be a liberal. Later Eisenhower said his appointment of Warren was "the biggest damn fool thing I ever did."[47] President Truman concluded that "packing the Supreme Court simply can't be done. . . . I've tried it and it won't work. . . . Whenever you put a man on the Supreme Court he ceases to be your friend."[48]

Truman exaggerated, although some presidents have had trouble "packing" the courts. They have not been able to foresee the issues their appointees would have to rule on or predict the ways their appointees would change on the bench. Nevertheless, presidents who have made a serious effort to find candidates with similar views usually have not been disappointed.

Access to the Courts

In this litigation-prone society, many individuals and groups want courts to resolve their disputes. Whether these individuals and groups get their "day in court" depends on their type of case, their wealth, and the level of court involved.

Courts hear two kinds of cases. **Criminal cases** are those in which governments prosecute persons for violating laws. **Civil cases** are those in which persons sue others for denying their rights and causing them harm. Criminal defendants, of course, must appear in court. Potential civil litigants, however, often cannot get to court.

Wealth Discrimination in Access

Although the courts are supposed to be open to all, most individuals do not have enough money to hire an attorney and pay the related costs necessary to pursue a case. Only corporations, wealthy individuals, or seriously injured victims suing corporations or wealthy individuals do. (Seriously injured victims with a strong case can obtain an attorney by agreeing to pay him or her a sizable portion of what they win in their suit.) In addition, a small number of poor individuals supported by legal aid programs can pursue a case.

The primary expense is paying an attorney. In most places attorneys charge over $100 per hour for their services. Other expenses include various fees for filing the case, summoning jurors, paying witnesses—doctors might demand $500 or $1,000 to testify in a simple case and more in a complex one, and also lost income from the individual's job due to numerous meetings with the attorney and hearings in court.

Even if individuals have enough money to initiate a suit, the disparity continues. Corporations or wealthy individuals sued by middle class or lower class individuals often use tactics to prolong the suit and delay a trial as a way to pressure the plaintiffs to settle for less money than they likely would have recieved from a judge or jury at a trial several years later. Many individuals, especially if injured, need some money sooner.

Even if individuals have enough persisitence to continue the suit, the disparity continues in court. Those with more money can develop a full case, whereas others must proceed with a skeletal case that is far less likely to persuade judges or jurors. This is true not only for civil litigants but also for criminal defendants. Our legal system, according to one judge, "is divided into two separate and unequal systems of justice: one for the rich, in which the courts take limitless time to examine, ponder, consider, and deliberate over hundreds of thousands of bits of evidence and days of testimony, and hear elaborate, endless appeals and write countless learned opinions" and one for the nonrich, in which the courts provide "turnstile justice."[49] (During the week that a judge spent conducting the preliminary hearing to determine if there was sufficient evidence to require O. J. Simpson to stand trial for murdering his ex-wife and her friend, other judges in Los Angeles disposed of 474 preliminary hearings for less wealthy defendants.) Consequently many individuals are discouraged from pursuing a case in the first place.

Interest Group Help in Access

Because of the expense of litigation interest groups, with greater resources than most individuals, have come to play a crucial role in helping individuals gain access. The groups sponsor and finance cases that relate to their goals. Some groups, especially civil liberties organizations such as the American Civil Liberties Union (ACLU), civil rights organizations such as the National Association for the Advancement of Colored People (NAACP), environmental groups such as the Sierra Club, and consumer and safety groups such as Ralph Nader's organizations, use litigation as a primary tactic to advance their goals. Interest groups have become so ubiquitous in the judicial process that most major court decisions involve an interest group. About 50% of all Supreme Court cases from 1969 to 1980 involved a liberal or conservative interest group.[50] Many lower court cases do as well.

Despite their activity and successes, interest groups can help only a small portion of individuals without the resources to finance their own suits.

Restrictions on Access

Even if litigants have enough wealth or interest group help, they must overcome various restrictions on access imposed by the courts. According to the Constitution, litigants can get access only for a "case" or "controversy." Courts interpret this to mean a real dispute—one in which the litigants themselves have lost rights and suffered harm. This major restriction is called **standing to sue.**

This principle is illustrated by a series of cases challenging Connecticut's birth control law. Passed in 1879, the law prohibited giving advice about, or using, birth control devices. Actually the law was not enforced much; women with a private doctor could get advice and a prescription. But the law effectively prevented opening birth control clinics that would help poor women without a private doctor or young women who did not want to go to their family doctor.

In the 1940s a doctor challenged the law, arguing that it prevented him from advising patients whose health might be endangered by childbearing. The courts said he did not have standing because he could not point to any injury he had suffered.[51] In the 1960s a doctor and two patients, who had had dangerous pregnancies in the past, challenged the law, claiming that it forced them to choose between stopping sexual activity or risking more dangerous pregnancies. Again the courts said they did not have standing because they could not point to any injury they had suffered, or would suffer, because the law was rarely enforced.[52] Finally, the head of Connecticut's Planned Parenthood League and the head of Yale's obstetrics and gynecology department opened a birth control clinic. Within days they were arrested. Although they could not get access in a civil suit, they could in the criminal case. In the process of defending themselves, they claimed the law was unconstitutional, and the Supreme Court agreed.[53]

Although this doctrine is technical, its implications are highly political. Without access, of course, individuals and groups have no chance to get courts to rule in their favor. And whether they get access depends, to a considerable extent, on the ideology of the judge presiding. According to one study, Reagan's appointees to the district courts denied access to underdogs (individuals, groups representing individuals, or unions) in 78% of the cases in which they sued but denied access to upper-dogs (governments or corporations) in only 41% of the cases in which they sued. These rulings contrast with those of

Law and Politics in a Coffee Cup

When Stella Liebeck and her grandson pulled into a McDonald's drive-through in Albuquerque for breakfast, she was about to have an accident that would lead to a lawsuit that would generate headlines across the country. The 79-year-old woman ordered a McBreakfast. She had trouble pulling the lid off the cup of coffee, so she put the cup between her knees and tugged, spilling scalding coffee all over her lap. By the time she reached the emergency room, the 170-degree coffee had caused second- and third-degree burns across her thighs, labia, and buttocks.

After seven days in the hospital and three weeks at home, she returned to the hospital for skin grafts that were almost as painful as the burn.

She wrote to McDonald's, asking the company to reduce the temperature of the coffee and to pay her out-of-pocket expenses (about $2000) and her daughter's lost wages from staying home and helping her. Liebeck did not want to sue—until McDonald's offered only $800. Then she hired a lawyer to sue, claiming McDonald's was negligent by serving such hot coffee.

The lawyer asked the jury to award her $100,000 in compensatory damages (to compensate her for her expenses and her pain and suffering) and triple this amount in punitive damages (to punish McDonald's and deter other restaurants).

The jury heard a McDonald's lawyer say the restaurants served coffee hot because most customers wanted it that way. Further, the cups caution, "CONTENTS HOT!" (though in small print). The jury also heard a doctor testify that 170-degree coffee would cause second-degree burns in 3.5 seconds, and a McDonald's official admit that the restaurants had received 700 complaints from people burned by the coffee in the past 10 years. (However, these complaints represented just one injury for every 24 million cups.)

The jurors, although initially annoyed for having to spend time on such a "ridiculous" case, found McDonald's negligent, awarding Liebeck $200,000 in compensatory damages and $2.7 million in punitive damages—about two days' coffee sales.

The judge reduced to $640,000 the punitive damages, and McDonald's settled with Liebeck for some other amount (the exact amount was kept secret) rather than appeal. Still, the headlines and the stories about the case focused on the $2.9 million figure, and tongues across the country clucked about the "outrageous verdict."

Although Liebeck's decision to sue and the jury's decision to award her so much money were atypical, this case was touted as a representative example of our legal system's problems. For years business groups and medical associations had been pushing for tort reform. A tort is a personal injury, usually caused by negligence. These interests wanted to reduce the number of lawsuits and the size of awards levied against corporations for harmful products and doctors for malpractice. The reform would, among other things, limit the amount of punitive damages that juries could grant. (Consumer groups and trial lawyers' associations, demanding that corporations and doctors be held accountable for injuries they cause, were fighting against such limits.) This case became the prime exhibit in the effort to enact reform in Congress. Business lobbyists talked about greedy lawyers and stupid jurors, and their marchers waved a banner: "SHE SPILLED IT ON HERSELF." Republicans, who tend to be sympathetic to corporations and doctors, included tort reform in their "Contract with America."

Stella Liebeck.

Yet both Liebeck and the judge, who had reduced the damages but still insisted that McDonald's be punished and other restaurants be deterred, described themselves as conservative Republicans. More ironically, if tort reform had been in effect, the final damages would have been within the limits specified in the proposed bill. Thus, the case would not have turned out differently. However, the bill was complicated and its provisions were difficult to evaluate, so the case was used as a symbol to sway public opinion.[1]

Source: Aric Press, "Are Lawyers Burning America?" *Newsweek,* March 20, 1995, pp. 32–35.

---

1. In 1996, in a case involving a defective paint job on a new car, the Supreme Court declared punitive damages of $2 million "grossly excessive." It is not clear whether this ruling will affect punitive damages in more typical cases. (BMW v. Gore, 134 L.Ed.2d 809)

Carter's and Nixon's appointees, who were both less strict in denying access and more evenhanded in treating underdogs (46% and 51%) and upper-dogs (46% and 65%).[54]

Proceeding Through the Courts

Individuals with a case normally start in the district courts. Those who lose have a right to have their case decided by one higher court to determine if there was a miscarriage of justicc. They normally appeal to the courts of appeals.

Those who lose at this level can appeal to the Supreme Court, but they have no *right* to have their case decided by it. No matter how important or urgent an issue seems, the Court does not have to hear it. It can exercise almost unlimited discretion in accepting cases to review.

Litigants who want the Court to hear their case file petitions for review. Most petitions are for a **writ of certiorari** (Latin for "made more certain"). The writ is granted—that is, the Court agrees to hear the case—if four of the nine justices vote to do so. The rationale for this "rule of four" is that a substantial number, but not necessarily a majority, of the justices should think the case important enough to review. Generally the Court agrees to review a case when the justices think an issue has not been resolved consistently or satisfactorily by the lower courts.

From about 8,000 petitions each year, the Court selects less than 100 to hear, thus exercising considerable discretion.[55] The oft-spoken threat, "We're going to appeal all the way to the Supreme Court," is usually just bluster. Likewise, the notion that the Court is "the court of last resort" is misleading. The vast majority of cases never get beyond a district court or court of appeals.

That the Supreme Court grants so few writs means the Court has tremendous power to control its docket and therefore to determine which policies to review. It also means the lower courts have considerable power because they serve as the court of last resort for most cases.

Deciding Cases

In deciding cases judges need to interpret statutes and the Constitution and determine whether to follow precedents. In the process they make law.

Interpreting Statutes

In deciding cases judges start with statutes—laws passed by legislatures. If the statutes are ambiguous, judges need to interpret them in order to apply them to their cases.

Sometimes statutes are ambiguous because of their nature. To be broad enough to cover many situations, their words and phrases must be so general that they might not be clear. Other times statutes are ambiguous because of the nature of the legislative process. To satisfy public demand for action on problems, legislators are urged to move quickly, even if they are not prepared. They are encouraged to act symbolically, even if they cannot alleviate the problems this way. They are pressed to compromise, even if they must include fuzzy provisions in statutes to avoid upsetting fragile agreements negotiated among themselves. These pressures tend to result in ill-conceived legislation.

When statutes are ambiguous, judges try to ascertain the legislators' intent in passing them. They scrutinize the legislators' remarks and debates. But they often find that different members said different things, even contradictory things, and most members said nothing about the provisions in question. This gives judges considerable leeway in construing statutes. A member of Congress admitted to one justice that they purposely use "unintelligible language" in statutes so the courts will "tell us what we mean."[56]

Interpreting the Constitution

After interpreting statutes, judges determine whether they are constitutional. Or, if the cases involve actions of government officials rather than statutes, judges determine whether the actions are constitutional. To do this they need to interpret the Constitution.

Compared to constitutions of other countries, our Constitution is short and therefore necessarily ambiguous. It speaks in broad principles rather than in narrow details. The Fifth Amendment states that persons shall not be "deprived of life, liberty, or property without due process of law." The Fourteenth Amendment states that persons shall not be denied "the equal protection of the laws." What is "due process of law"? "Equal protection of the laws"? Generally the former means that people should be treated fairly and the latter means that they should be treated equally. But what is fairly? Equally? These are broad principles that need to be interpreted in specific cases.

Chief Justice William Rehnquist dons his robe in the Supreme Court's robing room.

Sometimes the Constitution uses relative terms. The Fourth Amendment provides that persons shall be "secure . . . against unreasonable searches and seizures." What are "unreasonable searches and seizures"? Other times the Constitution uses absolute terms. These appear more clear-cut but are deceptive. The First Amendment provides that there shall be "no law . . . abridging the freedom of speech." Does "no law" mean literally no law? Then what about the proverbial example of the person who falsely shouts "Fire!" in a crowded theater? Whether relative or absolute, the language needs to be interpreted in specific cases.

Occasionally politicians assert that judges ought to be "strict constructionists"; that is, they ought to interpret the Constitution "strictly." This is nonsense. Judges cannot possibly interpret ambiguous language strictly.

When the language does not give sufficient guidance, some judges believe they should follow the intentions of the Framers.[57] Yet these intentions are difficult to ascertain. James Madison's notes of the Constitutional Convention or the *Federalist Papers* are considered the most authoritative sources, but relying upon them is fraught with problems. Because Madison edited his notes many years after the convention, his experiences in government or lapses of memory in the intervening years might have colored his version of the intentions of the delegates. Because Madison, Hamilton, and Jay published the *Federalist Papers* to persuade New York to ratify the Constitution, their motive might have affected their account of the intentions of the delegates. Further, there were 55 delegates to the Constitutional Convention and many more to the state ratifying conventions, and the sources do not indicate what most thought about any of the provisions. Undoubtedly, all did not think the same.[58]

Indeed, we know that even some framers disagreed among themselves. James Madison, who would be called the "Father of the Constitution," and George Washington, who presided at the Constitutional Convention and would be called the "Father of the Country," disagreed over the scope of presidential authority in foreign affairs.[59]

Other judges believe they need not follow the intentions of the framers. They maintain the Constitution was designed to be flexible and adaptable to changes in society.[60] These judges try to distill the general meaning of the provisions of the Constitution and apply this meaning to the contemporary situations facing them. The Fourteenth Amendment's equal protection clause does not refer to schools, and its framers did not intend it to relate to schools. However, they did intend it to grant blacks greater equality than before, and therefore the Court applied this meaning to segregated schools. Then the Court applied it to other segregated facilities, then to other racial minorities, and then to women. In short, the Court extracted the general meaning of equality and extended it to prohibit discrimination in many situations. In this way the Court put into practice Chief Justice John Marshall's statement that the Constitution is "intended to endure for ages to come."[61]

When judges interpret the Constitution, they exercise discretion. As former Chief Justice Hughes candidly acknowledged, "We are under a constitution, but the Constitution is what the Supreme Court says it is."[62]

Restraint and Activism

All judges exercise discretion, but not all engage in policymaking to the same extent. Some, classified as restrained, are less willing to declare statutes or actions of government officials unconstitutional, whereas others, classified as activist, are more willing to do so.

Restrained judges argue that the judiciary is the least democratic branch because judges are appointed for life rather than elected and reelected. Consequently, they should be reluctant to overrule the other branches. "Courts are not the only agency of government that must be presumed to have the capacity to govern," Justice Harlan Stone said. "For the removal of unwise laws from the statute books appeal lies not to the courts, but to the ballot and the processes of democratic government."[63] Restrained judges also contend that the judiciary is the branch least capable of making policy because judges are generalists. They lack the expertise and resources that many bureaucrats and legislators use to help make policy. Restrained judges further maintain that the power to declare laws unconstitutional is more effective if it is used sparingly. Justice Louis Brandeis concluded that "the most important thing we do is not doing."[64] That is, the most important thing judges do is declare laws constitutional and thereby build up political capital for the occasional times that they declare laws unconstitutional.

Activist judges do not share these qualms. Instead, they seem more outraged at injustice. Court of appeals judge David Bazelon, of the District of Columbia, said the test should be "Does it make you sick?" If so, the law or action should be struck down.[65] Activist judges also seem more concerned about obtaining results than following technical procedures. Chief Justice Warren asked lawyers who emphasized technical procedures during oral arguments, "Yes, yes, yes, but is it right? Is it good?"[66] In addition, activist judges seem more pragmatic. District court judge Frank Johnson, who issued sweeping orders for Alabama's prisons and mental hospitals, replied to critics, "I didn't ask for any of these cases. In an ideal society, all of these . . . decisions should be made by those to whom we have entrusted these responsibilities. But when governmental institutions fail to make these . . . decisions in a manner which comports with the Constitution, the federal courts have a duty to remedy the violation."[67]

The distinction between restrained and activist judges does not necessarily parallel that between conservative and liberal judges. In the 1950s and 1960s, it did; the Supreme Court was both activist and liberal. But in the early 1930s, the Court was activist and conservative; it struck down regulations on business. In the late 1930s, it was restrained and liberal; it upheld similar regulations on business.

But we should not make too much of the distinction between restraint and activism. It is probably

FIGURE 3
Ideological Blocs on the Rehnquist Court

Now the Court has a very conservative bloc of Chief Justice Rehnquist and Justices Thomas and Scalia; a moderately conservative bloc of Justices O'Connor and Kennedy; a moderately liberal bloc of Justices Breyer, Souter, and Ginsberg; and the liberal Justice Stevens. (There are no very liberal justices since the retirements of Justices Brennan and Marshall.) As a result of these blocs, the conservative side usually wins. However, Justice O'Connor or Kennedy occasionally switches, providing the margin of victory for the liberal side.

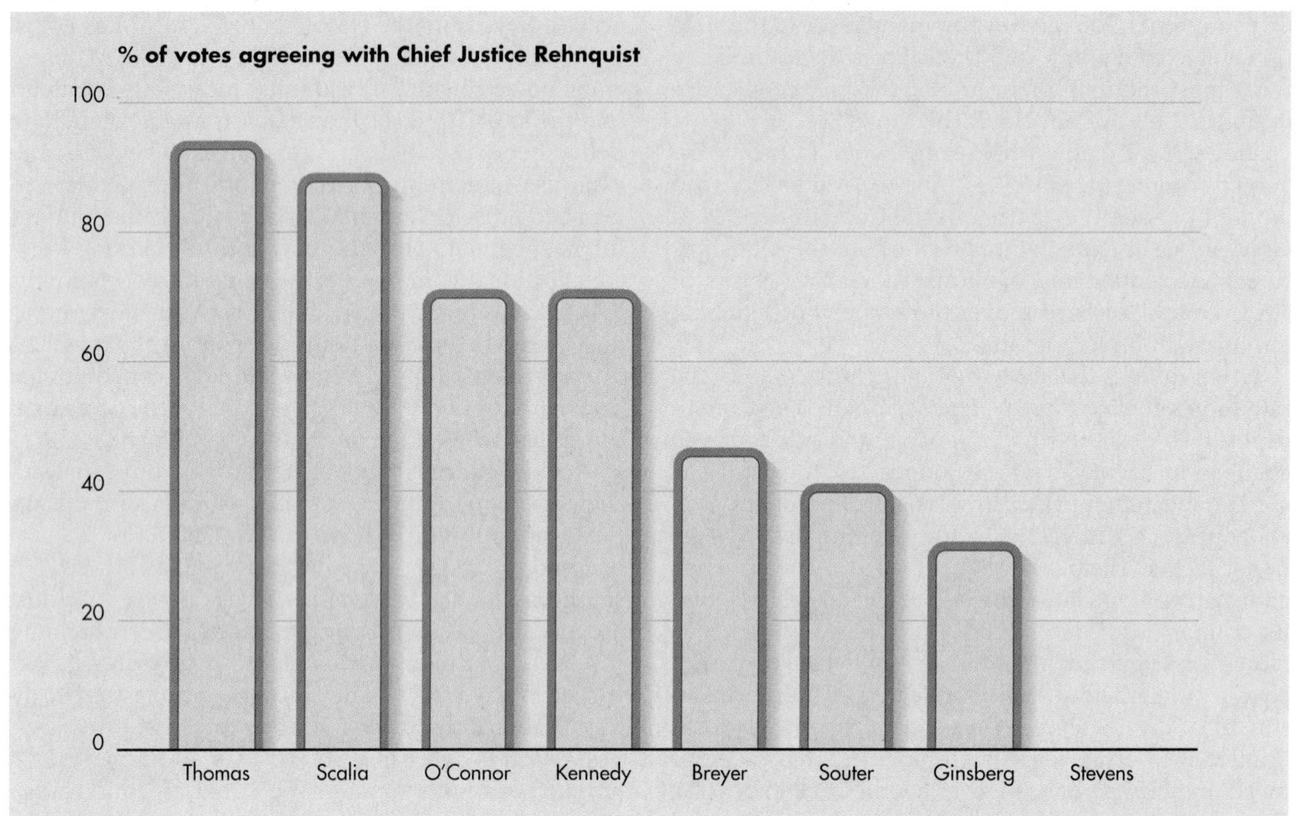

Source: *New York Times,* July 3, 1995, Section 3, p. 1ff. Based on 35 votes on which Justices Rehnquist and Stevens disagreed in 1995.

more important to know whether a judge is conservative or liberal. Sometimes a restrained conservative might vote differently than an activist conservative, but the two conservatives are likely to vote the same in most cases. A study of the justices appointed to the Supreme Court from 1953 through 1987 found that their conservative or liberal attitudes accounted for most of their individual votes, regardless of their restraint or activism (and regardless of the existence of relevant precedent or unique facts in the cases).[68] Some researchers conclude that "judicial restraint" is little more than "a cloak for the justices' policy preferences."[69] That is, justices justify their decisions on the basis of "judicial restraint" because that is considered appropriate by many people who do not think ideology or politics should play a role.

Following Precedents

In interpreting statutes and the Constitution, judges are expected to follow precedents established by their court or higher courts in previous cases. This is the rule of **stare decisis** (Latin for "stand by what has been decided").

The primary advantage of stare decisis is that it provides stability in the law. If different judges were to decide similar cases in different ways, the law would be unpredictable, even chaotic. "Stare decisis,"

Justice Brandeis said, "is usually the wise policy; because in most matters it is more important that the applicable rule of law be settled than that it be settled right."[70] Another advantage of this practice is that it promotes equality in the law, ensuring that judges treat comparable cases similarly. Otherwise, judges might appear to be arbitrary and discriminatory.

The primary disadvantage of stare decisis is that it produces excessive stability—inflexibility—in the law when it is adhered to strictly. Times change and demand new law, but precedents of past generations bind present and future generations. Justice Holmes declared, "It is revolting to have no better reason for a rule of law than that it was laid down in the time of Henry IV. It is still more revolting if the grounds upon which it was laid down have vanished long since, and the rule simply persists from blind imitation of the past."[71]

Judges need to decide not only whether to follow precedents but also which ones to follow. There might not be any that are controlling but several that are relevant, and these might point in contrary directions. For some cases there are "plenty of precedents to go around," Justice Douglas remarked, and judges can use the ones they want to reach the results they want.[72]

Making Law

Many judges deny that they make law. They say that it is already there, that they merely "find it or, occasionally, "interpret" it with their education and experience. They imply that they use a mechanical process. Justice Roberts wrote for the majority that struck down a New Deal act in 1936.

> It is sometimes said that the Court assumes a power to overrule . . . the people's representatives. This is a misconception. The Constitution is the supreme law of the land. . . . All legislation must conform to the principles it lays down. When an act of Congress is appropriately challenged in the courts as not conforming to the constitutional mandate, the judicial branch of government has only one duty—to lay . . . the Constitution . . . beside the statute . . . and to decide whether the latter squares with the former.[73]

In other words, the Constitution itself dictates the decision.

However, by now it should be apparent that judges do not use a mechanical process, and that they do exercise discretion. They *do* make law—when they interpret statutes, when they interpret the Constitution, and when they determine which precedents to follow or disregard.

In doing so, they reflect their own political preferences. As Justice Benjamin Cardozo said, "We may try to see things as objectively as we please. Nonetheless, we can never see them with any eyes except our own."[74] That is, judges too are human beings with their own perceptions and attitudes and even prejudices. They do not, and cannot, shed these the moment they put on their robes.

To say that judges make law is not to say that they make law as legislators do. Judges make law less directly. They make it in the process of resolving disputes brought to them. They usually make it by telling governments what they cannot do, rather than what they must do and how they must do it. More significantly, judges make law less freely. They start not with clean slates but with established principles embodied in statutes, the Constitution, and precedents. They have to address these, and if they do not accept them, they have to state their reasons. If their reasons are not persuasive, they open themselves to criticism or political checks against their authority.

The Power of the Courts

Alexis de Tocqueville observed that unlike in other countries, "Scarcely any political question arises in the United States that is not resolved, sooner or later, into a judicial question."[75] Because Americans are more inclined than other people to bring suits, courts have many opportunities to try to wield power.

This does not in itself guarantee that the courts can wield power, but they have been able to because the public venerates the Constitution and the courts interpret it, and because the courts enjoy relative, though not absolute, independence from the political pressures on the other branches.

The use of judicial review and the use of political checks against the courts reveal the extent of the power of the courts.

Use of Judicial Review

Judicial review—the authority to declare laws or actions of government officials unconstitutional—is the tool that courts use to wield power. When courts declare a law or action unconstitutional, they not only void that particular law or action, but they also might put the issue on the public agenda, and they might speed up or slow down the pace of change in government policies.

The Supreme Court Decides a Case

When the Supreme Court agrees to hear a case, it asks the litigants to submit written arguments. These "briefs" identify the issues and marshall the evidence—statutes, the Constitution, precedents—for their side. After the Court receives the briefs, it sets a date for oral arguments.

On that date the justices gather in the robing room behind the courtroom. They put on their black robes and, as the curtains part, file into the courtroom and take their places at the raised half-hexagon bench. The chief justice sits in the center, and the associate justices extend out in order of seniority. The crier gavels the courtroom to attention and announces:

> The Honorable, the Chief Justice and Associate Justices of the Supreme Court of the United States! Oyez, oyez, oyez! [Give ear, give ear, give ear!] All persons having business before the Honorable, the Supreme Court of the United States are admonished to draw near and give attention, for the Court is now sitting. God save the United States and this Honorable Court.

The chief justice calls the case. The lawyers present their arguments. Those who read from a prepared text find the justices bored or even hostile; those who speak extemporaneously find them willing to engage in a lively dialogue. They interrupt with questions whenever they want. When Thurgood Marshall, as counsel for the NAACP, argued one school desegregation case, he was interrupted 127 times. Some lawyers are so unnerved by this practice that occasionally one faints on the spot.

The chief justice usually allots half an hour per side. When time expires, a red light flashes on the lectern, and the chief justice halts any lawyer who continues. Chief Justice Hughes was so strict he reportedly cut off one lawyer in the middle of the word "it."

The Court holds Friday conferences to make a tentative decision and assign the opinion. The decision affirms or reverses the lower court decision; it indicates who wins and who loses. The opinion explains why. It expresses principles of law and thereby establishes precedents for other cases, so it is very important.

A portrait of Chief Justice Marshall presides over the conference. To ensure secrecy, no one is present but the justices. They begin with handshakes. (During his tenure Chief Justice Marshall suggested that they begin with a drink anytime it was raining anywhere in the Court's jurisdiction. Perhaps this accounts for his extraordinary success in persuading his colleagues to adopt his views.) Then the justices battle. The chief justice initiates the discussion of the case. He asserts what he thinks the issues are and how they ought to be decided, and he casts a vote. The associate justices follow in order of seniority. The discussion might become heated. When the justices reach a tentative decision, if the chief justice is in the majority, he assigns a justice to write the opinion of the Court. If not, the most senior associate justice in the majority assigns one to write it.

These procedures reveal the chief justice's power. Although his vote counts the same as each associate justice's vote, his

Law clerks of the Supreme Court, recent law school grads who ranked high in their classes, are chosen by the justices each year to help read petitions for review, research statutes and precedents, and draft opinions. Here two clerks meet with Justice John Paul Stevens.

authority to initiate the discussion and assign the opinion is significant. The former can influence what the other justices think about the case; the latter can determine what the opinion expresses.

Before Marshall became chief justice, each justice wrote his own opinion. But Marshall realized that one majority opinion would have more clout. He often convinced the other justices to forsake their own opinions and subscribe to his; he authored almost half of the Court's approximately 1,100 opinions during his years. Chief Justices Warren and Burger assigned more than 80% of the Court's opinions during their years, though they wrote only some of them.[1] Burger reportedly used his authority to punish several colleagues who voted opposite him in other cases. Justice Powell told another justice, "I'm resigned to writing nothing but Indian affairs cases for the rest of my life."[2] Chief Justice Rehnquist is so conservative that he has dissented more than most chief justices and consequently has left the most senior associate to assign numerous opinions.[3]

After the conference the Court produces the opinion. This is the most time-consuming stage in the process. Because the justices are free to change their vote anytime until the decision is announced, there is much maneuvering and politicking. The justice assigned the opinion tries to write it to command support of the justices in the original majority and possibly even some in the original minority. The writer circulates the draft among the others, who suggest revisions. The writer circulates more drafts. These go back and forth, as the justices attempt to persuade or cajole, nudge or push their colleagues toward their position. Justice Brennan was especially adept at this and is considered by some scholars "the best coalition builder ever to sit on the Supreme Court."[4]

If the opinion does not command the support of some of the justices in the original majority, they write a concurring opinion. This indicates that they agree with the decision but not the reasons for it. Meanwhile, the justices in the minority write a dissenting opinion. This indicates that they do not agree even with the decision. Both concurring and dissenting opinions weaken the force of the majority opinion. They question the validity of it, and they suggest that at a different time with different justices there might be a different ruling.

The Court's own print shop in the basement prints the opinions. Then the Court announces the decision and opinions in the hushed courtroom.

This process shows the individual responsibility expected of Supreme Court justices. They not only vote for one decision rather than another, but they state their reasons among the many that could justify their decision. If they disagree with other

"My dissenting opinion will be brief: "You're all full of crap."

justices, even on minor points, they say so and explain why. (In one case Justice O'Connor joined a justice's opinion except for one sentence, while in another case Justice Thomas joined a majority opinion except for one footnote.[5]) Thus, each justice's behavior can be assessed by the legal community and the general public. Contrast this with how Congress passes a law. It is much harder to determine responsibility, and pin accountability, on members of Congress. No doubt it is easier for the justices to accept personal responsibility because they have judicial independence. They do not need to be as responsive to the public as members of Congress do.

1. David W. Rhode and Harold J. Spaeth, *Supreme Court Decision Making* (San Francisco, W. H. Freeman, 1976), p. 177; Harold J. Spaeth, "Distributive Justice: Majority Opinion Assignments in the Burger Court," *Judicature* 67 (December/January 1984), pp. 299–304.
2. Nina Totenberg and Fred Barbash, "Burger's Colleagues Won't Be Sorry to See Him Go," *Washington Post National Weekly Edition*, July 7, 1986, p. 8.
3. Al Kamen, "The Scalia Surprise," *Washington Post National Weekly Edition*, March 23,1987, p. 6.
4. Michael S. Serrill, "The Power of William Brennan," *Time*, July 22, 1985, p. 62.
5. Ronald Suresh Roberts, *Clarence Thomas and the Tough Love Crowd* (New York: New York University Press, 1995), p. 84.

When the Supreme Court declared a Texas abortion law unconstitutional in *Roe v. Wade* in 1973, the Court put abortion on the public agenda.[76] The issue had not been a national controversy before the decision.

The Court used judicial review as a catalyst to speed up change in the desegregation cases in the 1950s. At the time President Eisenhower was not inclined to act, and while many members of Congress were, they were unable to act because the houses were dominated by southerners who, as committee chairs, blocked civil rights legislation. The Court broke the logjam.

The Court used judicial review as a brake to slow down change in the business regulation cases in the first third of the twentieth century. The Court delayed some policies for several decades.

When courts exercise judicial review, they help shape the country's vision of itself. They might push the country forward to a better future, or they might pull it backward to an idealized past.[77]

Judicial review, an American contribution to government, was for years unique to this country. It is now used in numerous other countries but not as extensively or as effectively as in the United States.

The Supreme Court alone has struck down more than 100 provisions of federal laws and more than 1,000 provisions of state and local laws. The Court has struck down more of the latter for several reasons: State and local legislatures enact more laws; these legislatures reflect parochial, rather than national, interests, so they enact more laws that the national Court considers in conflict with the national Constitution; and these legislatures are less risky to confront than Congress.

The number of laws struck down, however, is not the true measure of the importance of judicial review. Instead, the ever-present threat of review has undoubtedly prevented legislatures from enacting many laws they feared would be struck down.

By using judicial review to play a strong role in government, the Court has contradicted the Founders' expectation that the judiciary would be the weakest branch. Although it has been the weakest at times, it has been the strongest at other times. Arguably, these include some years during the early nineteenth century, when the Court established national dominance; the late nineteenth century and early twentieth century, when the Court thwarted efforts to regulate business; and the 1950s and early 1960s, when the Court extended civil liberties and rights.

Nevertheless, the extent to which the Court has played a strong role in government should not be exaggerated. The Court has not exercised judicial review over a wide range of issues; in each of the three eras of its history, it has exercised review over one dominant issue and paid relatively little attention to other issues. Moreover, the one dominant issue always has involved domestic policy. Traditionally the Court has been reluctant to intervene in foreign policy.[78] For example, although the war in Vietnam was the hottest issue in the country for years and its constitutionality was challenged repeatedly, the Court never reviewed the issue.

Even when the Court has tackled an issue, it has been cautious. Of the provisions of congressional laws held unconstitutional, more than half were voided more than 4 years after they had been passed, and more than one-fourth were voided more than 12 years after they had been passed.[79] These laws were voided years after many of the members of Congress responsible for them had left Congress; the Court confronted Congress when it was safer to do so.

Use of Political Checks Against the Courts

Although the courts enjoy relative independence from the political pressures brought to bear on the other branches, they by no means enjoy absolute independence. Because they are part of the political process, they are subject to political checks, which limit the extent to which they can wield judicial review.

Checks by the Executive

Presidents can impose the most effective check. If they dislike judges' rulings, they can appoint new judges when vacancies occur. And a sizable proportion of these appointees remain on the bench even two decades after presidents leave the White House.[80] Even so, it can be difficult to get judges to reverse precedents or to make decisions beyond the existing political consensus, as Presidents Reagan and Bush discovered.

Presidents and state and local executives, such as governors and mayors and even school officials and police officers, can refuse to enforce courts' rulings. School officials have disobeyed decisions requiring desegregation and invalidating class prayers. Police officers have ignored decisions invalidating some kinds of searches and interrogations.

Yet executives who refuse to enforce courts' rulings risk losing public support, unless the public also opposes the rulings. Even President Nixon complied when the Court ordered him to turn over the incriminating Watergate tapes.

Checks by the Legislature

Congress and the state legislatures can overturn courts' rulings by adopting constitutional amendments or, sometimes, new statutes. (When courts base decisions on particular interpretations of statutes, or when they make decisions in the absence of statutes, legislatures can pass new statutes to negate the decisions. In 1986 the Supreme Court ruled that the air force did not have to allow an ordained rabbi to wear his yarmulke with his uniform.[81] The next year Congress passed a statute permitting military personnel to wear some religious apparel while in uniform.) From 1967 through 1990, Congress passed statutes to negate 121 Supreme Court rulings.[82] Legislatures can refuse to implement courts' rulings, especially when money is needed to implement them. The legislators might simply fail to appropriate the money.

Although these checks are the most common, Congress has invoked others, although only rarely: It can alter the structure of the lower federal courts; it can limit the appellate jurisdiction of the Supreme Court; and it can impeach and remove judges.

Checks by the Public

Judges come from the public, so it is not surprising that their decisions tend to reflect the views of the public. A study that compared 110 Supreme Court rulings from 1936 through 1986 with public opinion polls on the same issues found that the rulings mirrored the polls in 62% of the cases.[83]

But when court rulings do not reflect the views of the public, opinion toward the courts can turn negative. Although research shows that citizens know little about the cases, they do remember especially controversial decisions, and they do recognize broad trends in decisions. A study of opinion toward the Supreme Court from 1966 to 1984 found that opinion became more negative when the Court struck down more congressional laws and when it upheld more criminal rights. (On the other hand, opinion grew more positive immediately after Watergate; people saw the Court as the bastion of law in the face of the Nixon administration's efforts to circumvent the law.)[84]

Yet opinion toward the courts retains a reservoir of support. In recent years, for example, attitudes about the Supreme Court have been more positive than attitudes about the presidency or Congress.[85] Because the public believes in the myth that courts are nonpolitical or because the public does not see the ways in which the courts are political—the inner workings of the courts, and the politicking among the judges, are not as visible as such processes are in the other branches—the public has not gotten as disgusted with the justices as it has with presidents and members of Congress.

However, when opinion toward the courts turns negative, the president or Congress is more likely to impose checks on the courts. This possibility has made the courts wary. As one political scientist concluded, the Supreme Court has "learned to be a political institution and to behave accordingly." It has "seldom lagged far behind or forged far ahead" of public opinion.[86] When it has, notably in the Dred Scott case and in the business regulation cases in the 1930s, it has lost some of its support and consequently some of its power.

In response to the occasional checks threatened or imposed on them, the courts have developed a strong sense of self-restraint to ensure self-preservation. This, more than the checks themselves, limits their use of judicial review.

➤Conclusion: Are the Courts Responsive?

The judiciary, appellate court judge Learned Hand said, stands as a bulwark against "the pressure of public panic." It provides a "sober second thought."[87] The Founders did not intend the judiciary to be responsive. They gave judges life tenure so courts would be independent to a large extent.

Indeed, the judiciary is more independent of pressures from the rest of the political process than the other branches are. Consequently, courts sometimes act on behalf of the relatively powerless individuals and small groups that lack clout with the executive and legislative branches. Courts have extended important civil liberties and rights to these individuals and groups.

Although relatively independent, the judiciary is part of the political process and is sensitive to others in the process. It is responsive to the president and Congress—or at least to one of these. Ultimately, it is responsive to the majority of the public. Even when courts act on behalf of nonelites, they rarely challenge the fundamental principles of society. They ordinarily uphold "the system." They simply give nonelites a place in it. Thus, in most cases, decisions by the courts reflect the attitudes of society.

EPILOGUE

Exclusion of Japanese Is Upheld

In *Korematsu v. United States,* the Supreme Court, by a six-to-three vote, upheld the order excluding Japanese Americans from the West Coast.[88] Justice Douglas voted against the order in conference but switched to the majority just before the Court announced its decision.[89] The Court noted that the president and Congress agreed that the order was necessary, and it emphasized that the government could take precautions to prevent espionage and sabotage during wartime.

Thus the majority was restrained, deferring to the combined force of the other two branches. These justices did not question the validity of officials' fear of espionage or sabotage or the scanty evidence of such acts by Japanese Americans. Nor did they question the discrimination against these persons. In contrast, the minority was activist, challenging the other two branches. These justices disputed the charges of disloyalty and suspected that discrimination against these persons led to the order.

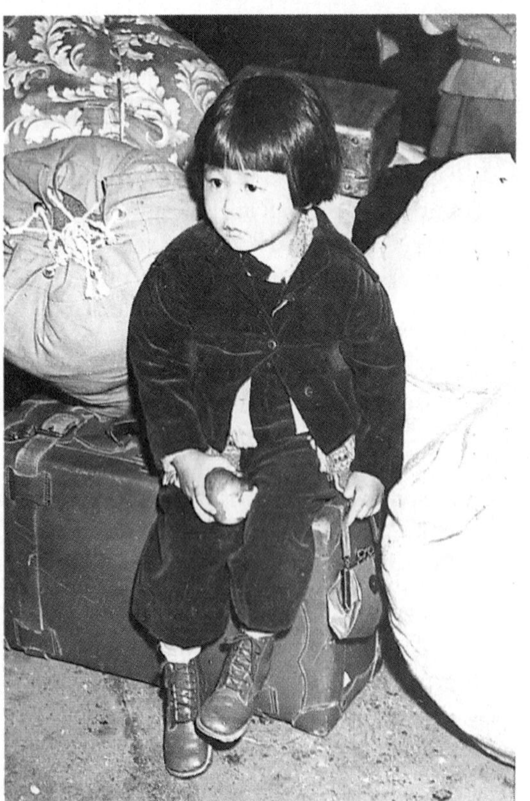

This three-year old awaits relocation to a detention camp in northern California. Yukiko Llewellyn is now an assistant dean of students at the University of Illinois.

The minority raised the specter that the Court's ruling would set a dangerous precedent. "A military order, however unconstitutional, is not apt to last longer than the military emergency," Justice Robert Jackson wrote. "But once a judicial opinion rationalizes such an order . . . the Court for all time has validated the principle of racial discrimination . . . and of transplanting American citizens. The principle then lies about like a loaded weapon ready for the hand of any authority that can bring forward a plausible claim of an urgent need."

In December 1944—two-and-a-half years after it began the evacuation and one day before it heard the Court's decision—the military ordered release of all "loyal" Japanese Americans.

Upon release they discovered that the government had failed to keep its promise to protect their property. Many of their possessions stored in warehouses had been vandalized or stolen. Some of their homes had been taken over by strangers, and some of their land had been seized for unpaid taxes.

"They did me a great wrong," Korematsu said. But he returned to live in the same town where he was arrested. "I love this country and I belong here."[90]

Near the end of his career, Justice Douglas expressed regret that he and others in the majority went along with the government. The case "was ever on my conscience."[91] Douglas did not live long enough to learn about research that revealed that the War Department had presented false information to the Court. The department had altered some reports and destroyed others demonstrating the loyalty of the Japanese Americans.[92] From Pearl Harbor until the end of the war, the government had no record of a single incident of sabotage by a Japanese American citizen or alien in this country.

With help from the lawyer who discovered the false information, Korematsu reopened his case through a rarely used procedure available only when the original trial was tainted with prosecutorial misconduct and fraud. In 1983 a federal judge reversed his conviction.[93]

In 1988 Congress passed a law offering a public apology for the internment and $20,000 compensation to each surviving internee.[94]

➤Key Terms

Korematsu v. United States	jurisdiction
judicial review	habeas corpus
Marbury v. Madison	criminal cases
court-packing plan	civil cases
Warren Court	standing to sue
Burger Court	writ of certiorari
Rehnquist Court	restrained judges
district courts	activist judges
courts of appeals	stare decisis

➤Further Reading

Peter Irons, *Justice at War* (New York: Oxford University Press, 1983). *The story of Korematsu and other cases involving the Japanese American relocation by the attorney who uncovered the government's false information.*

Lauren Kessler, *Stubborn Twig: Three Generations in the Life of a Japanese American Family* (New York: Random House, 1993). *A chronicle of a family, beginning with a 16-year-old boy who arrived in the U.S. to work on the building of the railroad and who established a business, only to see it collapse and himself arrested in the wake of Pearl Harbor.*

David M. O'Brien, *Storm Center,* 3rd ed. (New York: W. W. Norton, 1993). *A lively account of the Supreme Court and its very human justices.*

Bob Woodward and Scott Armstrong, *The Brethren* (New York: Simon & Schuster, 1979). *Behind-the-scenes look at the politicking among Supreme Court justices for major cases during the 1970s.*

➤Notes

1. John W. Dower, *War Without Mercy* (New York: Pantheon, 1986), p. 82.
2. Ibid., p. 112.
3. Peter Irons, *Justice at War* (New York: Oxford University Press, 1983), p. 269.
4. Dower, *War Without Mercy,* p. 92.
5. John Hersey, "Behind Barbed Wire," *New York Times Magazine,* September 11, 1988, p. 120.
6. John R. Schmidhauser, *Justices and Judges* (Boston: Little, Brown, 1979), p. 11.
7. *Federalist Paper # 78.*
8. Henry J. Abraham, *Justices and Presidents* (New York: Oxford University Press, 1974), p. 74.
9. Henry J. Abraham, *The Judicial Process,* 3rd ed. (New York: Oxford University Press, 1975), p. 309.
10. *Federalist Paper #78.*
11. 1 Cranch 137 (1803). *Marbury* was not the first use of judicial review by the Court, but it was the first use that was fully articulated and widely reported.
12. Walter F. Murphy and C. Herman Pritchett, *Courts, Judges, and Politics,* 3rd ed. (New York: Random House, 1979), p. 4.
13. John A. Garraty, "The Case of the Missing Commissions," in John A. Garraty, ed., *Quarrels That Have Shaped the Constitution* (New York: Harper & Row, 1962), p. 13.
14. Wallace Mendelson, "The Judiciary Act of 1789: The Formal Origin of Judicial Review," *Judicature* 76 (October–November, 1992), pp. 133–36.
15. *Fletcher v. Peck,* 6 Cranch 87 (1810); *Martin v. Hunter's Lessee,* 1 Wheaton 304 (1816); *Cohens v. Virginia,* 6 Wheaton 264 (1821).
16. *Gibbons v. Ogden,* 9 Wheaton 1 (1824).
17. *Scott v. Sandford,* 19 Howard 393 (1857).
18. *Ex parte Merryman,* 17 Federal Cases 9487 (1861).
19. *Ex parte McCardle,* 7 Wallace 506 (1869).
20. *Hammer v. Dagenhart,* 247 U.S. 251 (1918).
21. *Lochner v. New York,* 198 U.S. 45 (1905).
22. *Adkins v. Children's Hospital,* 261 U.S. 525 (1923).
23. *Adair v. United States,* 208 U.S. 161 (1908). *In re Delis,* 158 U.S. 564 (1895).
24. *United States v. E. C. Knight Co.,* 156 U.S. 1 (1895).
25. Lawrence Baum, *The Supreme Court,* 2nd ed. (Washington, D.C.: CQ Press, 1985), p. 177.
26. C. Herman Pritchett, *The American Constitution,* 2nd ed. (New York: McGraw-Hill, 1968), p. 166.
27. For elaboration of this point and analysis of Rehnquist Court decisions, see James F. Simon, *The Center Holds* (New York: Simon & Schuster, 1995).
28. Henry Abraham, "A Bench Happily Filled," *Judicature* 66 (February 1983), p. 284.
29. Victor Navasky, *Kennedy Justice* (New York: Atheneum, 1971), pp. 245–46.
30. Charles M. Cameron, Albert D. Cover, and Jeffrey A. Segal, "Senate Voting on Supreme Court Nominees: A Neoinstitutional Model," *American Political Science Review* 84 (June 1990), pp. 525–34.
31. Abraham, *Justices and Presidents,* pp. 6–7.
32. Ruth Marcus and Joe Pichirallo, "The Noncontemporary Judge," *Washington Post National Weekly Edition,* September 17–23, 1990, p. 6; Margaret Carlson, "An 18th Century Man," *Time,* August 6, 1990, p. 19; Richard Lacayo, "A Blank Slate," *Time,* August 6, 1990, p. 16.
33. M. Nejelski, *Women in the Judiciary: A Status Report* (Washington, D.C.: National Women's Political Caucus, June 1984).
34. Sheldon Goldman, "Reagan's Second Term Judicial Appointments," *Judicature* 70 (April/May 1987), pp. 324–39. Al Kamen and Ruth Marcus, "The Next Species for the Endangered List: Liberal Judges," *Washington Post National Weekly Edition,* February 6–12, 1989, p. 31; "Clinton Begins Undoing the Reagan-Bush Judiciary," *Time,* January 10, 1994, p. 10.
35. Joan Biskupic, "No Tilting at Windmills Here," *Washington Post National Weekly Edition,* November 6–12, 1995, pp. 14–15.
36. Schmidhauser, *Justice and Judges,* pp. 55–57.
37. Steve Alumbaugh and C. K. Rowland, "The Links Between Platform-Based Appointment Criteria and Trial Judges' Abortion Judgments," *Judicature* 74 (October/November 1990), pp. 153–62.
38. Lettie M. Wenner and Cynthias Ostberg, "Restraint in Environmental Cases by Reagan-Bush Judicial Appointees," *Judicature* 77 (January/February 1994), pp. 217–20.
39. William E. Kovacic, "The Reagan Judiciary and Environmental Policy," *Environmental Affairs* 18 (1991), pp. 669–713.
40. These numbers include a recent impeachment that was overturned by a district court because the Senate, to streamline procedures, had just the Judiciary Committee hear the charges and then allowed all senators to vote. The removal was reinstated by a court of appeals.

41. Merle Miller, *Plain Speaking* (New York: Berkeley Publishing/ G. P. Putnam's Sons, 1974), p. 121.

42. Harold W. Chase, *Federal Judges* (Minneapolis: University of Minnesota Press, 1972), pp. 189.

43. *Morrison v. Olson,* 487 U.S. 654 (1988).

44. Martin Shapiro, "The Supreme Court: From Warren to Burger," in Anthony King, ed., *The New American Political System* (Washington, D.C.: American Enterprise Institute, 1978), pp. 180–81.

45. Robert Seigliano, *The Supreme Court and the Presidency* (New York: Free Press, 1971), pp. 147–48.

46. Abraham, *Justices and Presidents,* p. 62.

47. Earl Warren, *The Memoirs of Earl Warren* (Garden City, N.Y.: Doubleday, 1977), p. 5.

48. Abraham, *Justices and Presidents,* p. 63.

49. Lois G. Forer, *Money and Justice* (New York: W. W. Norton, 1984), pp. 9, 15, 102.

50. Karen O'Connor and Lee Epstein, "The Rise of Conservative Interest Group Litigation," *Journal of Politics* 45 (May 1983), p. 481. See also Richard C. Cortner, *The Supreme Court and the Second Bill of Rights* (Madison, Wis.: University of Wisconsin Press, 1981), p. 282.

51. *Tileston v. Ullman,* 318 U.S. 44 (1943).

52. *Poe v. Ullman,* 367 U.S. 497 (1961).

53. *Griswold v. Connecticut,* 381 U.S. 479 (1965).

54. C. K. Rowland and Bridget Jeffery Todd, "Where You Stand Depends on Who Sits," *Journal of Politics* 53 (February 1991), pp. 175–85.

55. Although the Court accepted about 150 cases for oral argument and written opinions (and about an equal number to decide summarily—without oral arguments and written opinions) each term during the mid-1980s, the Rehnquist Court has shrunk the docket. It heard only 75 cases in the 1995 term.

56. Fred Barbash and Al Kamen, "Supreme Court, 'A Rotten Way to Earn a Living,'" *Washington Post National Weekly Edition,* October 1, 1984, p. 33.

57. Robert Bork, *The Tempting of America* (Touchstone/Simon & Schuster, 1990).

58. For an extended examination of the difficulties of ascertaining the intentions of the Founders, see Leonard W. Levy, *Original Intent and the Framers' Constitution* (New York: Macmillan, 1988).

59. Jeffrey M. Shaman, "Interpreting the Constitution," *Judicature* 71 (August–September, 1987), p. 86.

60. Lawrence Tribe, *On Reading the Constitution* (Harvard University Press, 1992).

61. *Osborn v. U.S. Bank,* 9 Wheaton 738 (1824), at 866.

62. Abraham, *Judicial Process,* p. 324.

63. *U.S. v. Butler,* 297 U.S. 1, at 94.

64. Murphy and Pritchett, *Courts, Judges, and Politics,* p. 586.

65. "Judicial Authority Moves Growing Issue," *Lincoln Journal,* April 24, 1977.

66. Alexander Bickel, *The Morality of Consent* (New Haven, Conn.: Yale University Press, 1975), p. 120.

67. "Judicial Authority Moves Growing Issue."

68. Jeffrey A. Segal and Albert D. Cover, "Ideological Values and the Votes of U.S. Supreme Court Justices," *American Political Science Review* 83 (June 1989), pp. 557–64. For different findings for state supreme court justices, see John M. Scheb II, Terry Bowen, and Gary Anderson, "Ideology, Role Orientations, and Behavior in the State Courts of Last Resort," *American Politics Quarterly* 19 (July, 1991), pp. 324–35.

69 Harold Spaeth and Stuart Teger, "Activism and Restraint: A Cloak for the Justices' Policy Preferences," in Stephen P. Halpern and Clark M. Lamb, eds., *Supreme Court Activism and Restraint* (Lexington, Mass.: Lexington, 1982), p. 277.

70. *Burnet v. Coronado Oil and Gas,* 285 U.S. 293 (1932), at 406.

71. Abraham, *Judicial Process,* p. 13.

72. William O. Douglas, "Stare Decisis," *Columbia Law Review* 32 (1949), pp. 735–55.

73. *U.S. v. Butler,* 297 U.S. 1 (1936), at 79.

74 Murphy and Pritchett, *Courts, Judges and Politics,* p. 25.

75. Baum, *The Supreme Court,* p. 4.

76. 410 U.S. 113.

77. Ronald Suresh Roberts, *Clarence Thomas and the Tough Love Crowd* (New York: New York University Press, 1995), p. 78.

78. Craig R. Ducat and Robert L. Dudley, "Federal Appellate Judges and Presidential Power," paper presented at the Midwest Political Science Association Meeting, April, 1987.

79. Baum, *The Supreme Court,* p. 158.

80. Sheldon Goldman, "How Long the Legacy?" *Judicature* 76 (April/May 1993), p. 295.

81. *Goldman v. Weinberger,* 475 U.S. 503 (1986).

82. William N. Eskridge, Jr., "Overriding Supreme Court Statutory Interpretation Decisions," *Yale Law Journal* 101 (1991), p. 338.

83. Thomas R. Marshall, "Public Opinion, Representation, and the Modern Supreme Court," *American Politics Quarterly* 16 (July 1988), pp. 296–316.

84. Gregory A. Caldeira, "Neither the Purse nor the Sword," paper presented at the American Political Science Association Meeting, August, 1987.

85. John Hibbing and Elizabeth Theiss-Morse, *Congress as Public Enemy: Public Attitudes Toward American Political Institutions* (Cambridge University Press, 1995), chs. 2 and 3.

86. Robert G. McCloskey, *The American Supreme Court* (Chicago: University of Chicago Press, 1960), p. 225.

87. Abraham, *Justices and Presidents,* pp. 342–43.

88. 323 U.S. 214 (1944).

89. Peter Irons, "Race and the Constitution: The Case of the Japanese American Internment," *This Constitution* (Winter 1986), p. 23.

90. William O. Douglas, *The Court Years* (New York: Random House, 1980), p. 279.

91. Irons, *Justice at War,* pp. vii–ix, 186–218.

92. Ibid., pp. vii, 367; Hersey, "Behind Barbed Wire," p. 73.

93. *Korematsu v. United States,* 584 F.Supp. 1406 (1983).

94. In 1948 Congress passed a law providing $37 million to settle damage claims by internees, but this was less than one-tenth of the amount that the government estimates internees had lost.

PART FOUR

Civil Liberties and Rights

14 Civil Liberties

You Are There

Does Religious Liberty Include Animal Sacrifice?

You are Justice Anthony Kennedy of the U.S. Supreme Court facing an unusual case from Hialeah, Florida. The Church of the Lukumi Babalu Aye has brought suit against the city because of ordinances that restrict the church's practices.

The church follows the Santeria religion, which originated in Nigeria 4000 years ago. The religion spread to Cuba when Nigerians were brought as slaves and eventually to Florida when Cubans fled their communist government. Santeria now blends ancient African rites and Roman Catholic rituals, but its distinguishing and most provocative practice is animal sacrifice. Adherents believe animal sacrifice is necessary to win the favor of the gods, and they practice it at births, marriages, and deaths, and at initiations of new members and priests. Chickens, ducks, doves, pigeons, sheep, goats, and turtles are killed by knife, their blood is drained into pots, and their meat is prepared for eating.

Santeria long existed underground, but the church decided to bring it into the open in 1987, leasing a used-car lot and announcing plans for a church building, cultural center, museum, and school in the Miami suburb. Then "the neighborhood went ape," according to one resident.[1] The city council held an emergency session, at which one council member stated that devotees "are in violation of everything this country stands for," while another quoted the Bible in opposition. The council president asked, "What can we do to prevent the church from opening?"

The city attorney's office drafted a series of ordinances, which the city council passed, that essentially deny adherents the opportunity to practice their religion. Although the ordinances do not explicitly refer to Santeria, they prohibit ritualistic animal sacrifice. They make exception for kosher slaughter for persons who follow Jewish dietary laws.

The church filed suit, claiming that the ordinances impinge on members' free exercise of their religion guaranteed by the First Amendment of the Constitution. The free exercise clause allows individuals to practice their religion as they see fit. Governments cannot restrict a particular religion or practice, unless there is a compelling reason to do so. The city countered that there were compelling reasons: First, animal sacrifice presents a health risk to the adherents, because the animals are uninspected and might be unsanitary, and to the public, because the carcasses sometimes are found rotting in the streets and floating in the canals. (The church responded that it properly disposes of the remains but adherents of Santeria who are not members of the church might not.) Second, animal sacrifice entails cruelty to animals. (The church responded that it humanely kills the animals by slicing their carotid artery, as kosher slaughter does.) Third, animal sacrifice results in emotional injury to children who witness it.

The church's priest, Ernesto Pichardo, suggested that town officials were hypocrites. "You can kill a turkey in your backyard, put it on the table, say a prayer, and serve it for Thanksgiving. But if we pray over the turkey, kill it, then eat it, we violated the law."[2]

CONTINUED 

Ernesto Pichardo, priest of the Santeria church.

OUTLINE

The Constitution and the Bill of Rights
- Individual Rights in the Constitution
- The Bill of Rights

Freedom of Expression
- Freedom of Speech
- Freedom of the Press
- Libel and Obscenity
- Freedom of Religion

Rights of Criminal Defendants
- Search and Seizure
- Self-Incrimination
- Counsel
- Jury Trial
- Cruel and Unusual Punishment
- Rights in Theory and in Practice

Right to Privacy
- Birth Control
- Abortion
- Homosexuality
- Right to Die

Conclusion: Are the Courts Responsive in Interpreting Civil Liberties?

But the federal district court ruled for the city, and the federal court of appeals affirmed. Now it is 1993, and the Supreme Court is deciding the case.

You were appointed by President Reagan because of your conservatism. Actually, you were not Reagan's first choice for this seat. Robert Bork was, but he was denied confirmation because of his more extreme conservatism. Eventually you were nominated because you were less flamboyant and less likely to antagonize the groups and senators who opposed Bork. But in most cases you have voted the way observers predicted Bork would have voted—generally against individual rights and for government authority. (Even now you are relatively unknown. A group of tourists at the Court, thinking you were also sightseeing, asked you to take their picture.)

You are a Roman Catholic—you even served as an altar boy—and you seem inclined to accommodate people's religious desires or demands, yet your views appear uncertain. A year ago, for instance, you wrote the majority opinion that invalidated prayers at graduation ceremonies for public elementary, middle, and high schools.[3] In cases involving minority religious practices, you voted to allow Hare Krishnas the right to distribute literature at public airports, yet you voted to deny members of the Native American church the right to use peyote, a hallucinogen, in worship ceremonies.[4] In this case you joined an opinion that could make it difficult for members of minority religions to adhere to their practices.

So how do you decide this case?

Americans value their "rights." Eighteenth-century Americans believed that people had "natural rights" by virtue of being human. Given by God, not by government, the rights could not be taken away by government. Contemporary Americans do not use this term, but they do think about rights much as their forebears did.

Yet Americans have a split personality about their rights. As Chapter 4 described, most people tell pollsters they believe in various constitutional rights in the abstract, but many do not accept these rights when applied to concrete situations. For example, most people say they believe in free speech, but many would not allow Communists, socialists, or atheists to speak in public or teach in schools.

Surveys in the 1990s show that Americans remain divided over their support for civil liberties. Thirty-one percent say freedom of expression should not apply to network television; 28% say it should not apply to newspapers; and 26% say it should not apply to art, film, or music. Fifty-five percent think songs with sexually explicit lyrics should be barred from radio and television, and 50% think books with "dangerous ideas" should be banned from school libraries.[5] Forty percent believe police should be able to search homes of suspected drug dealers without search warrants.[6]

Conflicts over civil liberties and rights have dominated the courts since the Depression. This chapter, covering civil liberties, and the next, covering civil rights, describe how the courts have interpreted these rights and tried to resolve these conflicts. We will explain the most important rights and recount the struggles by individuals and groups to achieve them. We will see how judges act as referees between litigants, brokers among competing groups, and policymakers in the process of deciding these cases.

The Constitution and the Bill of Rights

Individual Rights in the Constitution

Although the term *civil liberties* usually refers to the rights in the Bill of Rights, a few rights are granted in the body of the Constitution. The Constitution bans religious qualifications for federal office and guarantees jury trials in federal criminal cases. It bans **bills of attainder,** which are legislative acts rather than judicial trials pronouncing specific persons guilty of crimes, and **ex post facto laws,** which are legislative acts making some behavior illegal that was not illegal when it was done. The Constitution also prohibits suspension of the writ of habeas corpus, except during rebellion or invasion of the country. These rights are significant, but they by no means exhaust the rights people believed they had at the time the Constitution was written.

The Bill of Rights

Origin and Meaning

The Constitution originally did not include a bill of rights; the Founders did not think traditional liberties needed specific protections because federalism, separation of powers, and checks and balances would prevent the national government from becoming too powerful. But to win support for ratification, the Founders promised to adopt amendments to provide such rights. James Madison proposed 12, Congress passed them, and in 1791 the states ratified 10, which came to be known as the Bill of Rights.[7] Of these, the first 8 grant specific rights. (The Ninth says the listing of these rights does not mean they are the only ones the people have; and the Tenth clarifies the relationship between the federal and state governments.)

The Bill of Rights provides rights against the government. According to Justice Hugo Black, it is "a collection of Thou shalt nots" directed at the government.[8] Essentially, the Bill of Rights provides rights for minorities against the majority, because government policies affecting civil liberties tend to reflect the views of the majority.

As Chapter 2 explained, the Founders set up a government to protect property rights for the well-to-do minority against the presumably jealous majority. Separation of powers, checks and balances, and various specific provisions of the Constitution were intended to limit the ability of the masses to curtail the rights of the elites. However, as Americans became more egalitarian and attained more opportunity to participate in politics, the importance of property rights has declined while the importance of other rights has increased. At the same time, the role of the Bill of Rights has increased to protect the "have-nots" of society—the unpopular, powerless minorities in conflict with the majority.

Responsibility for interpreting the Bill of Rights generally falls on the federal courts. Because their judges are appointed for life, they are more independent from majority pressure than elected officials are. The greatest responsibility rests on the Supreme Court, as the highest of the federal courts.

Application

For many years the Supreme Court applied the Bill of Rights only to the federal government—not to state governments (or local governments, which are under the authority of state governments). The Court ruled that the Bill of Rights restricted only what the federal government could do.[9]

The Founders thought that states, being closer to the people, would be less likely to violate their liberties. Also, they knew that many states had their own bills of rights, and they expected the rest to follow.

The Founders did not realize that states would come to violate people's liberties more frequently than the federal government. State governments, representing smaller, more homogeneous populations,

Civil Liberties in the Bill of Rights

- First Amendment
  freedom of religion
  freedom of speech, assembly, and association
  freedom of the press
- Second Amendment
  right to keep and bear arms (for individuals in a militia at a time when there was no standing army to protect the country)
- Third Amendment
  forbids quartering soldiers in houses during peacetime
- Fourth Amendment
  forbids unreasonable searches and seizures
- Fifth Amendment
  right to grand jury hearing in criminal cases
  forbids double jeopardy (more than one trial for the same offense)
  forbids compulsory self-incrimination
  right to due process
  forbids taking private property without just compensation
- Sixth Amendment
  right to speedy trial
  right to public trial
  right to jury trial in criminal cases
  right to cross-examine adverse witnesses
  right to present favorable witnesses
  right to counsel
- Seventh Amendment
  right to jury trial in civil cases
- Eighth Amendment
  forbids excessive bail and fines
  forbids cruel and unusual punishment

tended to reflect majority sentiment more closely than the federal government, and they often rode roughshod over criminal defendants or racial, religious, or political minorities. When disputes arose, state courts tended to interpret their bills of rights narrowly.

However, starting in 1925[10] and continuing through 1972,[11] the Supreme Court gradually applied most provisions of the Bill of Rights to the states, using the Fourteenth Amendment's due process clause as justification. This clause, adopted after the Civil War to protect blacks from southern governments, reads, "Nor shall any state deprive any person of life, liberty, or property, without due process of law." The clause refers to states and "liberty." It is ambiguous, but the Court interpreted it to mean that states also have to provide the liberties in the Bill of Rights.

The Court has applied all but two provisions of the First and the Fourth through the Eighth Amendments to the states: guarantee of a grand jury in criminal cases and guarantee of a jury trial in civil cases. In addition, the Court has established some rights not in the Bill of Rights, and it has applied these to the states too: presumption of innocence in criminal cases, right to travel within the country, and right to privacy. Thus, most provisions in the Bill of Rights, and even some not in it, now restrict what both the federal and state governments can do.

To see how the Court has interpreted these provisions, we will look at three major areas—freedom of expression, rights of criminal defendants, and right to privacy.

"Let me give you a lesson in American history: James Madison never intended the Bill of Rights to protect riffraff like you."

Source: Drawing by Handelsman, © 1990 the New Yorker Magazine, Inc.

➤Freedom of Expression

The First Amendment provides freedom of expression, which includes freedom of speech, assembly, and association;[12] freedom of the press; and freedom of religion.

The amendment states that "Congress shall make no law" abridging these liberties. The language is absolute, but few justices interpret it literally. They cite the example of the person who falsely shouts "Fire!" in a crowded theater and causes a stampede that injures someone, and they say the amendment does not protect this expression. So the Court needs to draw a line between expression the amendment protects and that which it does not.

Freedom of Speech

Freedom of speech, Justice Black asserted, "is the heart of our government."[13] First, by allowing an open atmosphere, it maximizes the opportunities for every individual to develop his or her personality and potential to the fullest. Second, by encouraging a variety of opinions, it furthers the advancement of knowledge and discovery of truth. Unpopular opinions could be true or partially true. Even if completely false, they could prompt a reevaluation of accepted opinions. Third, by permitting citizens to form opinions and express them to others, it helps them participate in government. It especially helps them check inefficient or corrupt government. Fourth, by channeling conflict toward persuasion, it promotes a stable society. Governments that deny freedom of speech become inflexible; they force conflict toward violence.[14]

Seditious Speech

The first controversies to test the scope of freedom of speech involved **seditious speech,** speech that encourages rebellion against the government. The government historically prosecuted individuals for seditious speech during or shortly after war, when society was most sensitive about loyalty.

Numerous prosecutions came with World War I and the Russian Revolution, which brought the Communists to power in the Soviet Union in 1917. The Russian Revolution prompted a "Red Scare," in which people feared conspiracies to overthrow the U.S. government. Congress passed the Espionage Act of 1917, which prohibited interfering with military recruitment, inciting insubordination in military forces, and mailing material advocating rebellion; and the Sedition Act of 1918, which prohibited "disloyal, profane, scurrilous, or abusive language about the form of government, Constitution, soldiers and sailors, flag or uniform of the armed forces." Many states passed similar laws. In short, government prohibited a wide range of speech.

During the war the federal government prosecuted almost 2,000 and convicted almost 900 persons under these acts, and the states prosecuted and convicted many others. They prosecuted individuals for saying that war is contrary to the teachings of Jesus, that World War I should not have been declared until after a referendum was held, and that the draft was unconstitutional. Officials even prosecuted an individual for remarking to women knitting clothes for the troops, "No soldier ever sees those socks."[15]

These cases gave the Supreme Court numerous opportunities to rule on seditious speech. In six major cases, the Court upheld the federal and state laws and affirmed the convictions of all the defendants.[16] The defendants advocated socialism or communism, and some advocated the overthrow of the government to achieve it. Except for one—Eugene Debs, the Socialist party's candidate for president—the defendants did not command a large audience. Even so, the Court concluded that these defendants' speech constituted a "clear and present danger" to the government. Justice Edward Sanford wrote, "A single revolutionary spark may kindle a fire that, smouldering for a time, may burst into a sweeping and destructive conflagration."[17] In reality, there was nothing clear or present about the danger; the defendants' speech had little effect.

More prosecutions came after World War II. Congress passed the Smith Act in 1940, which was not as broad as the World War I acts because it did not forbid criticizing the government. But it did forbid advocating overthrow of the government by force and organizing or joining individuals who advocated overthrow.

The act was used against members of the American Communist party after the war. The uneasy alliance between the United States and the Soviet Union had given way to the Cold War between the countries. Politicians, especially Senator Joseph McCarthy (R-Wis.), exploited the tensions. McCarthy charged various government officials with being Communists. He had little evidence, and his tactics were called "witch-hunts" and, eventually, **McCarthyism.** Other Republicans too accused the Democratic administration of covering up Communists. They goaded it into prosecuting members of the Communist party so it would not appear "soft on communism."

In 1951 the Court upheld the Smith Act and affirmed the convictions of 11 top-echelon leaders of the Communist party.[18] These leaders organized the party and the party advocated overthrowing the government by force, but the leaders had not attempted overthrowing it. (If they had, they clearly would have been guilty of crimes.) Even so, the Court majority concluded that they constituted a clear and present danger, and Chief Justice Fred Vinson wrote that the government does not have to "wait until the putsch is about to be executed, the plans have been laid and the signal is awaited" before it can act against the party. The minority argued that the Communist party was not a danger. Justice William Douglas said that the party was "of little consequence. . . . Communism has been so thoroughly exposed in this country that it has been crippled as a political force. Free speech has destroyed it as an effective political party."

Eugene Debs, the Socialist party's candidate for president, criticized American involvement in World War I and the draft. He was convicted for violating the Espionage Act and sentenced to 10 years in prison. When President Harding pardoned him early, Debs commented, "It is the government that should ask *me* for a pardon."

At congressional hearings Senator Joseph McCarthy identified locations of alleged Communists and "fellow travelers."

Following the Court's decision, the government prosecuted and convicted almost 100 other Communists.

But the Cold War thawed slightly, the Senate voted to condemn McCarthy, and two new members, including Chief Justice Earl Warren, joined the Court. In a series of cases in the 1950s, the Court made it more difficult to convict Communists,[19] thereby incurring the wrath of the public, Congress, and President Eisenhower. In a private conversation, Warren asked Eisenhower what he thought the Court should do with the Communists. Eisenhower replied, "I would kill the S.O.B.s."[20]

The government took other action against Communists. The federal government ordered Communists to register, and then some state governments banned them from public jobs such as teaching, or private jobs such as practicing law or serving as union officers. Legislative committees held hearings to expose and humiliate them. The Court heard numerous cases involving these actions and usually ruled against the government.

The Vietnam War did not prompt the same fears that World Wars I and II did. Congress did not pass comparable laws, perhaps because many "respectable" people opposed this war and also because the Court in the 1950s and 1960s increasingly allowed seditious speech.

The Court developed new doctrine for seditious speech in 1969. A Ku Klux Klan leader said at a rally in Ohio that the Klan might take "revengeance" on the president, Congress, and Supreme Court if they continued "to suppress the white, Caucasian race." The leader was convicted under a statute similar to those upheld after World War I, but this time the statute was unanimously struck down by the Court.[21] The justices said people can advocate—enthusiastically, even heatedly—as long as they do not incite illegal action. This broad protection for seditious speech remains in effect today.

Thus, after many years and many cases, the Court concluded that the First Amendment protects seditious speech as much as other speech. Justice Douglas noted that "the threats were often loud but always puny."[22] Even the attorney general who prosecuted the major Communist cases later admitted that the cases were "squeezed oranges. I didn't think there was much to them."[23] Nevertheless, the Court had permitted a climate of fear to overwhelm the First Amendment for many years.

Public Forum

People usually communicate with each other in private. But sometimes speakers want more listeners and they use public places where people congregate. This means speakers will be heard by some listeners who do not like their message or their use of public places to disseminate it, and it also means speakers might disrupt the normal purposes of these places.

The Court holds that individuals have a right to use public places, such as streets, sidewalks, and parks, to express their views on public issues. These places constitute the **public forum** and serve as "the poor person's printing press."

When speakers seek to use other public facilities, the Court has to determine which ones are also part of the public forum. It decided that federal and state capitol grounds,[24] Supreme Court grounds,[25] and public school grounds[26] are part of the forum. It decided that blacks could protest library segregation at a public library[27] and promoters could show the rock musical *Hair* at a public theater[28] because these too are part of the forum.

On the other hand, the Court decided that civil rights activists could not demonstrate against jail segregation outside a jail because of the need for security,[29] and Dr. Benjamin Spock—the baby doctor—and other antiwar activists could not encourage opposition to the Vietnam War at an army base because of the need for discipline in the army.[30]

Normally only publicly owned facilities are considered part of the public forum, but the proliferation of shopping centers and malls prompted speakers to use these privately owned facilities to reach crowds of shoppers. The Warren Court permitted them to do so, saying that shopping centers and malls are similar to downtown shopping districts where streets and sidewalks are part of the public forum.[31] But the Burger Court overruled the Warren Court, emphasizing property rights rather than First Amendment rights in this situation.[32]

Even in public forums people cannot speak whenever and however they want. The Court has divided speech into three kinds—pure speech, speech plus conduct, and symbolic speech—and established doctrine for each.

Pure Speech

Pure speech is speech without any conduct (besides the speech itself). Individuals can say what they want as long as they do not cause a breach of the peace or a riot, or hurl "fighting words" at specific persons, except at police officers, who are supposed to be trained and disciplined to take abuse.[33]

Before the Court's ruling in 1972, arrests for swearing were common. In the District of Columbia, for example, more than half of the 15,000 to 20,000 arrests for "disorderly conduct" each year involved swearing, usually at police.[34]

Individuals can use offensive language in many situations.[35] During the Vietnam War, a man walked through the corridors of the Los Angeles County courthouse wearing a jacket with the words "Fuck the Draft" emblazoned on the back. Police arrested him. The Court reversed his conviction, and 72-year-old Justice John Harlan remarked that "one man's vulgarity is another's lyric."[36]

The media, however, cannot broadcast some offensive language. A California radio station broadcast a monologue by comedian George Carlin. Titled "Filthy Words," it lampooned society's sensitivity to seven words that "you couldn't say on the public airwaves . . . the ones you definitely wouldn't say, ever." The seven words, according to the Federal Communications Commission report, included "a four-letter word for excrement" repeated 70 times in 12 minutes. In a close vote, the Court ruled that although the monologue was part of a serious program on contemporary attitudes toward language, it was not protected under the First Amendment because people, including children, tuning the radio could be subjected to the language in their home.[37]

Yet the Court struck down a Utah law restricting "indecent material" on cable television. The difference apparently is that people choose to subscribe and pay for cable television.[38]

Speech Plus Conduct

Speech plus conduct is speech combined with conduct that is intended to convey ideas—for example, a demonstration in which protesters chant slogans or carry signs with slogans (the speech) and march, picket, or sit-in (the conduct).

Individuals can demonstrate, but they are subject to some restrictions. Places in the public forum are used for other purposes besides demonstrating, and individuals cannot disrupt these activities. They cannot, Justice Arthur Goldberg remarked, hold "a street meeting in the middle of Times Square at the rush hour."[39] To avoid this, governments can require them to obtain a permit, which can specify the place, time, and manner of the demonstration. However, officials cannot allow one group to demonstrate but forbid another, no matter how much they dislike the group or its message. They cannot forbid the group even if they say they fear violence, unless the group actually threatens violence. In short, officials may establish restrictions to avoid disruption, but they may not use these restrictions to censor speech.

Accordingly, lower federal courts required the Chicago suburb of Skokie to permit the American Nazi party to demonstrate in front of the town hall in 1978.[40] About 40,000 of Skokie's population of 70,000 were Jews. Of these, hundreds had survived the German Nazi concentration camps during World War II, and thousands had lost relatives who died in the camps. The city, edgy about the announced demonstration, passed ordinances that prohibited wearing "military-style" uniforms and distributing material that "promotes and incites hatred against persons by reason of their race, national origin, or religion." These ordinances were thinly disguised attempts to bar the demonstration, and the courts threw them out. One quoted Justice Oliver Wendell Holmes's statement that "if there is any principle of the Constitution that more imperatively calls for attachment than any other it is the principle of free thought—not free thought for those who agree with us but freedom for the thought we hate."[41]

The Rehnquist Court, however, did uphold a Milwaukee suburb's ordinance that prohibited picketing at a residence.[42] The city passed the ordinance after antiabortionists had picketed, six times in one month, the home of a doctor who performed abortions. Although protesters can march through residential neighborhoods, the Court said, a city can prohibit them from focusing on a particular home. Thus the Court emphasized the right to privacy at home over the right to demonstrate in this situation.

The Rehnquist Court addressed another potential restriction on demonstrations when homosexual groups demanded to be included in the St. Patrick's Day parade in Boston. The parade, though not as political as most demonstrations, was a form of expression, and the Court unanimously concluded that the private sponsors cannot be forced to include an unwanted message—recognition or acceptance of gay groups.[43] These groups could hold their own parade.

Symbolic Speech

Symbolic speech is the use of symbols, rather than words, to convey ideas.

During the Vietnam War, men burned their draft cards to protest the draft and the war. This was powerful expression, and Congress tried to stifle it by passing a law prohibiting destruction of draft cards. The Supreme Court was uncomfortable with symbolic speech and reluctant to protect it. Even Chief Justice Warren worried that this would mean that "an apparently limitless variety of conduct can be labeled 'speech.'" The court upheld the law.[44]

One year later, however, the Court was willing to protect symbolic speech. A junior high and two senior high school students in Des Moines, Iowa, including Mary Beth Tinker, wore black armbands to protest the war. They were suspended, and they sued school officials. Public schools, Justice Abe Fortas said, "may not be enclaves of totalitarianism." They must allow students freedom of speech, providing students do not disrupt the schools.[45]

In the 1960s and 1970s, many students wore long hair or beards in violation of school policy. Some claimed they did so to protest "establishment culture." Blacks and Indians claimed they wore Afros and braids to show racial pride. Federal courts of appeals split evenly as to whether this was symbolic speech. The Supreme Court refused to hear any of these cases, so there was no uniform law across the country.

Some individuals treated the American flag disrespectfully to protest the Vietnam War. A Massachusetts man wore a flag patch on the seat of his pants and was sentenced to six months in jail. A Washington student taped a peace symbol on a flag and then hung the flag, upside down, outside his apartment. The Court reversed both convictions.[46]

When a member of the Revolutionary Communist Youth Brigade burned an American flag outside the Republican Convention in Dallas in 1984, the justices

Mary Beth Tinker, here with her mother and brother, wore a black armband at school to protest the Vietnam War.

faced the issue of actual desecration of the flag. The Rehnquist Court surprisingly permitted this symbolic speech.[47] Two Reagan-appointed conservatives, Justices Anthony Kennedy and Antonin Scalia, joined the three most liberal members of the Court to forge a bare majority. The foremost free speech advocate on the bench, Justice William Brennan, wrote that the First Amendment cannot be limited just because this form of expression offends some people. "We do not consecrate the flag by punishing its desecration, for in doing so we dilute the freedom that this cherished emblem represents." The ruling invalidated laws of 48 states (not Alaska or Wyoming) and the federal government.

Chief Justice Rehnquist emotionally criticized the decision. He said the First Amendment should not apply because the flag is a unique national symbol. He recounted the history of the "Star-Spangled Banner" and the music of John Philip Sousa's "Stars and Stripes Forever"; he quoted poems by Ralph Waldo Emerson and John Greenleaf Whittier that refer to the flag; and he discussed the role of the "Pledge of Allegiance."

Civil liberties advocates praised the decision. One lawyer for the defendant said, "If free expression is to exist in this country, people must be as free to burn the flag as they are to wave it." Another said veterans should cheer the decision because it shows that the values in the Bill of Rights that they fought for are intact. Yet veterans groups were outraged.

After administration officials assessed public opinion by monitoring talk shows, President Bush stood in front of the Iwo Jima Memorial and proposed a constitutional amendment to override the decision.[48] Members of Congress, always anxious to appear patriotic, lined up in support. But some, especially Democrats, later came out in opposition. They criticized the proposal for creating an unprecedented exception to the First Amendment. Instead of the proposed amendment, Congress passed a statute prohibiting flag desecration. Apparently a majority felt that this less permanent substitute would be an adequate shield against the public's wrath. Yet in 1990, the justices, dividing the same way, declared the statute unconstitutional for the same reasons they reversed the Dallas conviction.[49] President Bush, this time waving a model of the Iwo Jima Memorial, proposed another constitutional amendment, and Senate Republican leader Robert Dole (Kan.) warned Democrats that their opposition to the amendment "would make a good 30-second spot" for the upcoming elections, but Congress rejected the amendment. Members sensed less pressure from the public. By this second year of debate on this issue, the initial emotional reaction of the public had ebbed. More voices had spoken out against dilution of the First Amendment. In 1995 Republican majorities in Congress renewed effeorts to adopt a constitutional amendment but fell three votes short in one house.

Protesters torch flags in Chicago.

Freedom of the Press

Unlike most civil liberties cases, which pit a relatively powerless individual or group against the government, freedom of the press cases usually feature a more powerful publisher or broadcaster against the government. Even so, these cases still involve rights against the government.

Prior Restraint

The core of freedom of the press is freedom from **prior restraint**—censorship. If the press violates laws prohibiting, for example, libelous or obscene material, it can be punished after publishing such materials. But freedom from prior restraint means the press at least has the opportunity to publish what it thinks is appropriate.

Freedom from prior restraint is not absolute. At the height of the Vietnam War, the secretary of defense in the Johnson administration, Robert McNamara, became disenchanted with the war and ordered a thorough study of our involvement. The study, called "The Pentagon Papers," laid bare the reasons the country was embroiled—reasons not as honorable as the ones officials had been giving the public—and it questioned the effectiveness of military policy. The study was so revealing that McNamara remarked to a friend, "They could hang people for what's in there."[50] He printed only 15 copies and classified them "Top Secret" so few persons could see them. One of the 36 authors, Daniel Ellsberg, originally supported the war but later turned against it. In 1971 he photocopied the papers and gave them to the *New York Times* and *Washington Post*, which published excerpts.

The Nixon administration sought injunctions to restrain the newspapers from publishing more excerpts, but the Supreme Court refused to grant them.[51] Most justices said they would grant injunctions if publishing the papers clearly jeopardized national security. But information in the papers was historical; it did not directly hinder the war effort. Thus, the rule remained—no prior restraint—but exceptions were possible.

The chief of the presses of the *Washington Post* hails the Supreme Court's decision allowing publication of the Pentagon Papers.

The Rehnquist Court did approve prior restraint in a situation far removed from national security. When journalism students at a St. Louis high school wrote articles for their newspaper about the impact of pregnancy and of parents' divorce on teenagers, the principal deleted the articles and three of the students sued. The Court, noting that students below the college level have fewer rights than adults, decided that officials can censor school publications.[52]

Principals have exercised their authority typically over articles covering school policies or social issues. A Colorado principal blocked an editorial criticizing his study hall policy while allowing another editorial praising it. A Texas principal banned an article about the class valedictorian who succeeded despite the death of her mother, the desertion of her father, and her own pregnancy. An editorial urging students to be more responsible about sex was censored by a Kentucky principal, who feared it could be interpreted as condoning sex, while a survey on AIDS was censored by a Maryland principal, who prohibited students from defining the term "safe sex." A North Carolina high school newspaper was shut down and its advisor was fired because of three articles, including a satirical story about the "death" of the writer after eating a cheeseburger from the school cafeteria.

High school newspaper advisers, according to a 1994 survey, said principals have tightened their control in recent years. Over a third of the advisers reported that principals have rejected articles or required changes in articles for their paper.[53]

Despite these exceptions to freedom from prior restraint, the press in the United States is freer than that in Great Britain, where freedom from prior restraint began. Britain has no First Amendment and tolerates more secrecy. In 1987 the government barred publication of controversial and embarrassing memoirs by a former security service agent, even though they were being published in the United States at the time. A year later the government banned radio and television interviews with all members of the outlawed Irish Republican Army (IRA) and its political party, including its one representative in Parliament.[54] The government even banned broadcast of a song by a popular folk group because the lyrics supported people convicted of IRA bombings. During the Persian Gulf War, the French government banned sale of a song—"Go For It Saddam"—that criticized the West. After neo-Nazi violence in 1992, the German government banned the sale of music by skinhead groups.

Leanne Tippell and Leslie Smart, two of the St. Louis high school students who sued their school for suppressing their student newspaper story, meet with their attorney, Leslie Edwards (left).

Restrictions on Gathering News

Although prior restraint is an obvious limitation on freedom of the press, restrictions on gathering news in the first place are less obvious but no less serious. They also keep news from the public.

The Burger Court was not vigilant in guarding the press from these restrictions. Most important, it denied reporters a right to keep the names of their sources confidential. In investigative reporting, reporters frequently rely on sources who demand anonymity in exchange for information. The sources might have sensitive positions in government or relations with criminals that would be jeopardized if their names were publicized. A Louisville reporter was allowed to watch persons make hashish from marijuana if he kept their names confidential. But after publication of the story, a grand jury demanded their names. When the reporter refused to reveal them, he was cited for contempt of court, and his conviction was upheld by the Supreme Court.[55] The majority said reporters' need for confidentiality is not as great as the judicial system's need for information about crimes. So either reporters cannot guarantee potential sources anonymity, or reporters might have to choose between breaking their promise or being cited for contempt and jailed for an indefinite period of time.

Invasion of Privacy

The right to a free press can conflict with an individual's right to privacy when the press publishes personal information. The Supreme Court has permitted the press to publish factual information. For example, although a Georgia law prohibited the press from releasing names of crime victims to spare them embarrassment, an Atlanta television station announced the name of a high school girl who was raped by six classmates and left unconscious on a neighbor's lawn to die. The girl's father sued the station, but the Court said the press needs freedom to publish information that is a matter of public record so citizens can scrutinize the workings of the judicial system.[56]

In 1975 a man in a crowd of people watching President Gerald Ford noticed a woman pull out a gun. He grabbed the gun and prevented the assassination. Reporters wrote stories about this hero, including the fact that he was a homosexual. This caused the man embarrassment and some practical problems and he sued. The courts sided with the press again. The man's good deed made him newsworthy, whether he wanted to be or not.[57] Persons who become newsworthy are permitted little privacy. Justice Brennan said this is a necessary evil "in a society which places a primary value on freedom of speech and of press."[58]

Libel and Obscenity

Despite broad protection for the press overall, courts grant much less protection for libelous and obscene material. Traditionally, they considered such material irrelevant to the exposition of ideas and search for truth envisioned by the framers of the First Amendment. Whatever benefit such material might have was outweighed by the need to protect persons' reputations and morals. Courts thus allowed states to adopt and implement libel and obscenity laws as they saw fit.

Libel

Libel consists of printed or broadcast statements that are false and that tarnish someone's reputation. Victims are entitled to sue for money to compensate them for the damage.

The Warren Court decided that traditional state libel laws infringed on freedom of the press too much and forced radical changes in these laws. Its landmark decision came in *New York Times v. Sullivan* in 1964.[59]

The *Times* ran an ad by black clergymen who criticized Montgomery, Alabama, officials for their handling of racial protests. The ad contained some trivial inaccuracies. It did not mention any officials by name, but the commissioner of police claimed it referred to him implicitly, and he sued. The local jury ordered the *Times* to pay him a half million dollars! The Court could see that the law was used to punish a detested northern newspaper for an ad that criticized the handling of controversial civil rights protests. And the Court could not ignore the size of the award or the fact that another jury had ordered the *Times* to pay another commissioner a half million dollars for the same ad. It was apparent that libel laws could be used to wreak vengeance on a critical press.

The Court ruled against the police commissioner and made it harder for public officials to win libel suits. It said officials must show not only that the statements about them were false but also that the statements were made with "reckless disregard for the truth." This provides the press some leeway to make mistakes and print false statements, as long as the press is not careless to the point of recklessness.

This protection for the press is necessary, according to Justice Brennan, because "the central meaning of the First Amendment" is that individuals should have the right to criticize officials' conduct. This statement prompted one legal scholar to herald the decision "an occasion for dancing in the streets."[60]

In later cases the Court extended this ruling to public figures—persons other than public officials who have public prominence or who thrust themselves into public controversies. The court held several persons to be public figures: candidates for public

Hate Speech on Campus and the First Amendment

A student puts a sign on her dorm room door that announces, "People who will be shot on sight—preppies, bimbos, men without chest hair, and homos."

A fraternity holds a "slave auction" as a fund-raiser. White pledges in blackface and Afro wigs perform skits. Afterward, audience members bid on the performers.

Two black students find the letters "KKK" carved into their dorm room door and a note saying, "African monkeys, why don't you go back to the jungle."

After a class discussion of media treatment of African Americans, a black woman receives a card asking her to have "a very bad Christmas" and calling her a "nigger."

Such incidents have forced members of college and university communities—students, faculty, and administrators—to consider in a real and personal way the meaning of the First Amendment. Many conclude that hate speech should be prohibited and that students who engage in it should be punished. They argue that students who hurl epithets or slurs at others, especially anonymously, are more interested in intimidating than in initiating a dialogue about issues. They also argue that civility and tolerance must be maintained. Otherwise, victims of such speech are made to feel unwelcome on campus and in some cases are kept from concentrating on their studies. A student who was jeered nightly by students taunting "Faggot!" said, "When you are told you are not worth anything, it is difficult to function."[1]

Some legal scholars believe hate speech could be a violation of the Fourteenth Amendment's equal protection clause—which guarantees "equal protection of the laws" and restricts discrimination in society—if it creates a hostile and intimidating environment for minority students.[2]

However, other scholars believe such speech is protected by the First Amendment. Precedents described in this chapter emphasize that even repulsive speech is allowed. Indeed, the First Amendment would be meaningless if only speech acceptable to everybody were protected.

Critics of speech codes point to history: The First Amendment has helped minorities make their case against discrimination. By thwarting southern law enforcement officials' efforts to censor and intimidate the media, the amendment helped the civil rights movement gain national support. On the other hand, censorship has been used against minorities. It is shortsighted to expect new censorship to be used primarily for minorities against majorities. New censorship could be directed at students and speakers who say the sorts of things Malcolm X once said. During the year and a half that the University of Michigan's speech code was in effect, more than 20 black students were charged with violations by white students, and no white students were charged with violations.[3]

Critics also say the codes could be directed at students who make relatively innocuous comments. A Brown University student was the first casualty. He was expelled for shouting "nigger" and "faggot" to no one in particular while drunk. A University of Pennsylvania student faced disciplinary action for yelling, "Shut up, you water buffalo. If you're looking for a party, there's a zoo a mile from here," to a dozen sorority sisters singing loudly outside his dorm window while he was writing a paper one night. It turns out that the women were black and the remark was considered a racial slur.[4] (The women who filed the grievance later dropped it.)

office,[61] a retired general who spoke for right-wing causes,[62] a real estate developer,[63] and a university athletic director.[64] The Court justified making it harder for public figures to win libel suits by saying that they sometimes influence public policy as much as public officials do. They also are newsworthy enough to get coverage to rebut any false charges against them.

The Burger Court was less inclined to consider various persons public figures,[65] but it maintained the core of the Warren Court's doctrine, which shifted the emphasis from protection of personal reputation to protection of press freedom.

This shift in emphasis has aided the press tremendously at a time when its coverage of controversial events has angered much of the public. Increasingly since the 1960s, individuals and groups have sued the press not primarily to win compensation for damage to personal reputations but to punish it. A lawyer for a conservative organization admitted that the organization sought "the dismantling" of CBS by suing the network for its depiction of the army general commanding the U.S. military in Vietnam.[66]

Although the press has an advantage in the law when public officials or figures bring suits, lawsuits are expensive to defend against. A recent case cost the *Washington Post* more than a million dollars in defense expenses at the trial court level alone.[67] The expense puts pressure on the press to refrain from publishing controversial material. Large news organizations

Critics observe that more than any other institutions, colleges and universities traditionally have fostered free inquiry and free expression. They have allowed, even encouraged, a variety of views so the views could be debated.

The answer to the problem, these critics contend, is more, not less, speech. According to the theory of free expression, the remedy for bad ideas is more speech to demonstrate why the ideas are wrong. Four black women at Arizona State University passed a dorm room door with a "job application form" for minority applicants. The form asked for:

- Sources of income: (1) theft, (2) welfare, (3) unemployment;
- Marital status: (1) common law, (2) shacked up, (3) other;
- Number of legitimate children (if any).

Although ASU had a speech code, the women did not try to invoke it or even approach the administration. First they knocked on the door and told one of the occupants what they thought of the form. Then they organized an open meeting in the dorm. Eventually there was a news conference, a rally, and a program on African American history in the dorm. All along there was a lively exchange in the campus newspaper. The women accomplished more, and in the process kept the focus on racism rather than on a speech code.[5]

Many schools enacted speech codes, but federal district courts struck down codes at the universities of Michigan and Wisconsin on grounds that they were overly broad and inherently vague.[6] The Supreme Court has not ruled on the constitutionality of these codes, but it struck down a St. Paul, Minnesota, ordinance that prohibited people from writing graffiti and displaying objects such as a Nazi swastika or a burning cross on public or private property.[7] This ruling probably means that the Court would invalidate campus speech codes as well.

However, the Court did say that illegal *conduct* associated with the speech can be punished. A person who erects a burning cross on private property can be prosecuted for trespassing, starting an open fire, and littering, or for such major crimes as arson and making terroristic threats. Similarly, students who engage in hate speech in some situations might be punished for defacing public property or making terroristic threats.

---

1. Mary Jordan, "Free Speech Starts to Have Its Say," *Washington Post National Weekly Edition*, September 21–27, 1992, p. 31.
2. Mary Ellen Gale, "On Curbing Racial Speech," *The Responsive Community* (Winter 1990–91), pp. 53, 57.
3. Nadine Strossen, *Defending Pornography: Free Speech, Sex, and the Fight For Women's Rights* (New York: Scribners, 1995).
4. Mike Littwin, "Penn's Water Buffalo Debate," *Lincoln Journal* (Baltimore Sun), May 13, 1993.
5. Nat Hentoff, "The Right Thing at ASU," *Washington Post National Weekly Edition*, July 1–7, 1991, p. 28.
6. *Doe v. University of Michigan,* 721 F.Supp. 852 (E.D. Mich., 1989); Jordan, "Free Speech Starts To Have Its Say." A California court also struck down Stanford University's antiharassment code, which was similar to a speech code.
7. *R.A.V. v. St. Paul,* 120 L.Ed.2d 305 (1992). Yet the Court has upheld state laws that provide longer sentences for violent crimes motivated by bias than for the same crimes without evidence of bias. *Wisconsin v. Mitchell,* 124 L.Ed.2d 436 (1993).

can withstand most of this pressure, but many small ones cannot. After 12 libel suits in as many years, the publisher of 6 weekly newspapers in suburban Philadelphia halted his papers' investigative reporting. "I found myself vigorously defending the First Amendment and watching my business go to hell," he said. "Now the communities our papers serve no longer learn about the misconduct of their officials."[68]

Obscenity

Obscenity also pits conservative groups against the media, albeit a small and specialized part of the media. Yet there are important differences. Whereas it is relatively clear what libel is and who the victim is, it is not at all clear what obscenity is and who, if anyone, the victim is. It is not even clear why the law needs to deal with it. Some say it is necessary because obscenity is immoral; others say it is necessary because obscenity leads to improper behavior (although this link is uncertain). The justices themselves have disagreed, perhaps more than in any other area, and their decisions reflect this. They have been neither clear nor consistent.

The Warren Court decided that state obscenity laws restricted publication of sexual material that should be allowed. While maintaining that the First Amendment does not protect obscenity, the Court narrowed the definition of obscenity in a series of cases in the 1950s and 1960s.[69]

The Burger Court, however, thought the Warren Court went too far. When a man and his mother received an ad for a book entitled *Orgies Illustrated*, their suit gave the justices an opportunity to broaden the definition of obscenity somewhat.[70] Now the Court defines obscenity as sexual material that is patently offensive to the average person in the community and that lacks any serious literary, artistic, or scientific value. The Court generally permits state legislatures and local juries, in passing statutes and deciding cases, to determine if this definition applies to certain types of material.

But some local officials got carried away. A prosecutor in Charlottesville, Virginia, announced that he would prosecute persons who sold *Playboy* magazine. Jurors in Albany, Georgia, convicted a theater manager who showed the movie *Carnal Knowledge*. The movie, which featured explicit language and occasional nudity, was nominated for an Academy Award as the best film of the year. The Burger Court reversed the conviction and announced that local communities have discretion but not "unbridled discretion."[71]

In 1990 a prosecutor in Cincinnati put the director of an art gallery on trial for an exhibit of photographs by Robert Mapplethorpe. The homoerotic pictures, which the director called "tough, brutal, sometimes disgusting," included three showing penetration of a man's anus with various objects. Yet the prosecutor could not prove that they lacked serious artistic value, because the photographer has received praise from art critics and the pictures, of course, were displayed in an art gallery, so the jury acquitted the director.

The Burger Court did not succeed in its efforts to reduce the availability of sexual material. A survey asking prosecutors across the country to compare the years immediately before the Burger Court redefined obscenity with those immediately after found, surprisingly, that they prosecuted fewer cases. Prosecutors said the public is less concerned about obscenity, so jurors are less likely to convict.[72]

The continuing flow and increasing violence of pornography prompted some radical feminists, in alliance with religious fundamentalists, to advocate new antipornography statutes. They maintain that pornography discriminates against women by degrading them and portraying them as willing targets for violent sex. In response, Indianapolis passed a statute that defined pornography as "the sexually explicit subordination of women"—material in which women were "sexual objects for domination . . . or use" or depicted in "positions of servility or submission or display." The statute allowed women who believed themselves victims of pornography to sue for a court order banning such material and, possibly, for monetary damages. The proponents' aim was to encourage enough women to sue to drive the purveyors out of business.

A coalition of book and magazine publishers, distributors, and sellers challenged the law. They said it was so broad and vague it could apply to many nonpornographic books and magazines. The American Civil Liberties Union (ACLU) maintained that it could apply to books such as Ian Fleming's James Bond stories and movies like *Last Tango in Paris*. Some feminist writers said it could apply to feminist literature.

The federal district court judge, a woman, ruled the statute unconstitutional. She said its breadth and vagueness would prohibit much sexual material now permitted by the Supreme Court and would severely

American Diversity

Can They Be "As Nasty as They Wanna Be"?

When the rap group 2 Live Crew released its album "As Nasty As They Wanna Be," a Florida lawyer who is a born-again Christian and a crusader against pornography sent copies of the lyrics to the governor and every sheriff in the state. The lawyer likens himself to Batman—he wears a Batman watch and distributes copies of his driver's license with Batman's photograph pasted over his own—and says he needs to help law enforcement officials. The Cuban-born Broward County sheriff, who as a public official has a history of flamboyant actions that attract publicity, mobilized his deputies to protect citizens against the album. They arrested a record store owner for selling the album and then arrested members of the group for singing lyrics from the album in an adult nightclub in Fort Lauderdale.[1]

Is the album obscene? According to current doctrine, it is obscene if it is patently offensive to the average person in the community and if it lacks serious artistic value. This doctrine from the Burger Court differs from that of the Warren Court primarily in its emphasis on the local community. Where the Warren Court based the definition on the views of the average person in the country, the Burger Court spoke of the average person in the community. The Warren Court reasoned, "It is, after all, a national Constitution we are expounding."[2] But the Burger Court countered that the Constitution should not require "the people of Maine or Mississippi [to] accept public depiction of conduct found tolerable in Las Vegas or New York."[3] So the decision in these cases would be made according to the views of the average person in Broward County.

Is the album patently offensive? The songs are about sex, and they feature explicit lyrics, including descriptions of oral sex, group sex, and masturbation, moans at appropriate moments, and a beat that mimics sexual passion. According to an evangelical group, the 79-minute album refers to genitalia 117 times (1.4 times per minute).[4] In addition, the songs are mean-spirited and sometimes violent; they exhibit, in the words of one critic, "a knuckle sandwich approach to women."[5] The rappers, who use the word "bitch" 163 times, speak of rape and ripping open women's vaginas.

Does the album lack serious artistic value? According to some students of African American culture, the album reflects the vernacular tradition of this culture.[6] In particular, it reflects the oral tradition of inner-city speech, with its profanity, satire, and exaggeration. This tradition includes pretense—acting out the folklore of the streets. Other African Americans, however, are offended by the lyrics and the depiction of women in them.

The residents of the county were called upon to decide. In a civil suit preceding the criminal cases, a Hispanic male judge found the album obscene, making it the first musical recording ever banned by a court in this country. Then a jury of six whites, mostly women, convicted the record store owner. Just two weeks later a jury of five whites and one black, also mostly women, acquitted the members of the group for their live performance. These jurors said they thought the album had artistic value.

These decisions have implications for the Court's obscenity doctrine. Is it possible to define a single "community standard" anywhere, let alone in cities or counties with ethnically and religiously diverse populations? Who or what determines the community standard? Men or women? Whites or blacks or Hispanics? Middle-class norms or those of the ghetto? When the jury convicted the record store owner, he yelled, "They don't know nothing about the . . . ghetto! . . . The verdict does not reflect my community standards as a black man in Broward County."[7] Even assuming it is possible to define a single "community standard," is it reasonable to expect laypersons to assess the artistic value of material they find offensive? Is it reasonable to ask a Hispanic judge and white jurors to gauge the artistic merit of black rap music?

Meanwhile, the controversy propelled the album toward the two-million sales mark.

1. Laura Parker, "How Things Got Nasty in Broward County," *Washington Post National Weekly Edition,* June 25–July 1, 1990, p. 10.
2. *Jacobellis v. Ohio,* 378 U.S. 184 (1964).
3. *Miller v. California,* 413 U.S. 15 (1973).
4. Paul Gray, "Grapevine," *Time,* July 2, 1990, p. 13.
5. Richard Lacayo, "The Rap Against a Rap Group," *Time,* June 25, 1990, p. 18.
6. For a good discussion, see David Mills, "The Judge vs. 2 Live Crew," *Washington Post National Weekly Edition,* June 25–July 1, 1990, pp. 9–10.
7. "Which Community's Standards?" *Lincoln Journal,* October 10, 1990.

restrict the First Amendment. The Supreme Court affirmed the decision.[73]

Despite the Court's refusal to broaden its definition of obscenity further, it does allow cities, through zoning ordinances, to scatter "adult" theaters and bookstores to avoid seedy districts that might attract criminals, or to concentrate them to avoid location in neighborhoods where they might offend residents or passersby.[74] The Court acknowledged that such ordinances help preserve the quality of urban life.

Overall the court seems close to saying, in the words of one scholar, "If people want it, they can have it. But they shouldn't subject everyone else to it."[75]

Freedom of Religion

Some people came to America for religious liberty, but once they got here many did not want to allow others this liberty. Some communities here were as intolerant as the ones in the Old World from which people had fled. But people came with so many different religious views that the diversity gradually led to tolerance, and by the time the Bill of Rights was adopted there was widespread support for religious liberty. The First Amendment states, "Congress shall make no law respecting an establishment of religion, or prohibiting the free exercise thereof." The two clauses concerning religion—the establishment clause and the free exercise clause—were intended to work in tandem to provide freedom of religion and, by implication, freedom from others' religions.

The Founders' recoiled from the Europeans' experience of continuous conflict and long wars fought over religious differences. Thus, Thomas Jefferson said, the clauses were designed to build "a wall of separation between church and state." Each would stay on its own side of the wall and not interfere or even interact with the other.

However, as society became more complex and government became more pervasive, church and state came to interact, sometimes interfere, with each other. Inevitably, the high wall began to crumble, and courts had to devise new doctrine to accommodate both church and state.

Free Exercise of Religion

The **free exercise clause** allows individuals to practice their religion without government coercion. Government occasionally has restricted free exercise of religion directly. Early in the country's history, some states prohibited Catholics or Jews from voting or holding office, and as late as 1961 Maryland prohibited nonbelievers from holding office.[76] In the 1920s Oregon prohibited students from attending parochial schools.[77] More recently prisons in Illinois and Texas prohibited black Muslims and Buddhists from receiving religious publications and using the prison chapel.[78] The Supreme Court invalidated each of these restrictions.

Government also has restricted free exercise of religion indirectly. As society has become more complex, some laws inevitably have interfered with religion, even when not designed to. The laws usually have interfered with minority religions, which do not have many members in legislatures looking out for their interests.

At first the Court distinguished between belief and action: Individuals could believe what they wanted, but they could not act accordingly if such action was against the law. In 1878 male Mormons who believed their religion required polygamy could not marry more than one woman.[79] The Court rhetorically asked, "Suppose one believed that human sacrifices were a necessary part of religious worship?" Of course, belief without action gave little protection and scant satisfaction to the individuals involved.

In the 1960s the Warren Court realized this and began to broaden protection by granting exemptions to laws. A Seventh-Day Adventist who worked in a textile mill in South Carolina quit when the mill shifted from a five- to six-day workweek that included Saturday—her Sabbath. Unable to find another job, she applied for unemployment benefits, but the state refused to provide them. To receive them she had to be "available" for work, and the state said she was not available because she would not accept jobs that required Saturday work. The Court ordered the state to grant an exemption to its law.[80] Yet the Burger Court ruled that employers need make only a minimal effort to accommodate employees' request to fit work schedules around their Sabbath.[81]

Amish in Wisconsin withheld their children from high school, although the law required attendance until age 16. The parents sent their children to elementary and junior high school to learn basic reading, writing, and arithmetic, but they complained that high school would subject their children to worldly influences that would interfere with their semi-isolated agricultural life. The Warren Court ruled that the Amish could be exempt from the additional one to two years the law required beyond junior high school.[82]

The country's religious diversity has led to demands for some exotic exemptions. Inspired by the Bible's statement that Jesus' followers "shall take up serpents" and "if they drink any deadly thing, it shall not hurt them," members of the Holiness Church of God in Jesus' Name handle snakes and drink strychnine. Some become enraptured and entranced to the point of hysteria, and occasionally some die. In 1975 the Tennessee Supreme Court forbade such practices, saying that the state has "the right to guard against the unnecessary creation of widows and orphans." However, the practices continue in some places.

Congress too has granted some exemptions. It excused the Amish from participating in the Social Security program, because the Amish support their own elderly. And in every draft law it excused conscientious objectors from participating in war.

The Court has been most reluctant to exempt individuals from paying taxes. It did not excuse either the Amish[83] or Quakers, who as pacifists tried to withhold the portion of their income taxes that would go to the military.[84] The Court worried that many other persons would try to avoid paying taxes, too.

The Rehnquist Court has been especially reluctant to grant exemptions.[85] The Native American church uses peyote, a hallucinogen from a cactus, in worship ceremonies. Members believe the plant embodies their deity and eating it is an act of communion. Although peyote is a controlled substance, Congress has authorized its use on Indian reservations and almost half the states have authorized its use off reservations by members of the church. But when two members in Oregon, a state that did not allow its use, were fired from their jobs and denied unemployment for using the substance, the Court refused to grant them an exemption.[86] In an opinion with broad implications, a five-justice majority explicitly rejected the doctrine and precedents of the Warren and Burger courts. Justice Scalia, a Catholic, admitted that denying exemptions will put minority religions at a disadvantage but said that this is an "unavoidable consequence of democratic government." That is, denying minority rights is acceptable because of majority rule. This rationale, of course, could be used to emasculate not only the free exercise clause but other provisions of the Bill of Rights as well.

Adherents of minority religions felt the effects of the ruling in various ways. Some families of deceased Jews and Laotian immigrants who reject autopsies on religious grounds were overruled. Muslim prisoners whose religion forbids them from eating pork were refused other meat instead. Members of the Sikh religion, who wear turbans, had been exempted from the federal law requiring construction workers to wear hard hats, but the Occupational Safety and Health Administration (OSHA) rescinded the exemption in the wake of the ruling.[87]

Even mainstream churches worried about the implications of the ruling, and a coalition of religious groups lobbied Congress to overturn it. In 1993 Congress passed and President Clinton signed the Religious Freedom Restoration Act, which reversed the ruling and substituted the previous doctrine. Now when a law impinges on an individual's free exercise of religion, the law must reflect a compelling government interest and it must use the least restrictive means to reach this interest.

Amish children head for the cornfields to avoid school officials in Iowa.

Establishment of Religion

Two competing traditions regarding the role of government have led to conflict over the **establishment clause.** Many early settlers in America wanted government to reinforce their religion, yet the framers of the Constitution were products of the Enlightenment, which deemphasized the role of religion. The two individuals most responsible for the religious guarantees in the First Amendment, Jefferson and Madison, wanted strict separation of church and state, advocating not only freedom *of* religion for believers but freedom *from* religion for others.[88]

Early decisions by the Supreme Court usually reflected the first of these traditions. In 1892 Justice David Brewer smugly declared that "this is a Christian nation."[89] But as the country became more pluralistic, the Court moved toward the second of these traditions. Since the early 1960s, the Court generally has interpreted the establishment clause not only to forbid government from designating an official church, like the Church of England in England, but also to forbid government from aiding one religion over another or even from aiding religion over nonreligion.

Courts have used the clause to resolve disputes about prayer in public schools. In 1962 and 1963, the Supreme Court issued its famous, or infamous, prayer rulings. New York had students recite a nondenominational prayer at the start of every day, and Pennsylvania and Baltimore had students recite the "Lord's Prayer" or Bible verses. The Court, with only one justice dissenting, ruled that these practices violated the establishment clause.[90] The prayers technically were voluntary; students could leave the room. But the Court doubted that the prayers really were voluntary. It noted that nonconforming students would face tremendous pressure from teachers and peers, and that leaving the room usually connotes being bad and being punished. Thus, the Court said the prayers fostered religion. According to Justice Black, "Government in this country should stay out of the business of writing and sanctioning official prayers and leave that purely religious function to the people themselves and to those the people choose to look to for religious guidance." Schools could teach about religion, but they cannot promote it.

Many people sharply criticized the rulings. A representative from Alabama lamented, "They put the Negroes in the schools, and now they've driven God out."[91] Actually, the justices had not driven God out because students could pray on their own anytime they felt the need.

Alfred Smith, fired for using peyote in religious ceremonies, challenged Oregon's law.

A survey of teachers two years after the rulings found that prayers and Bible readings had decreased but by no means disappeared. Schools in the West, East, and, to a lesser extent, the Midwest generally complied with the rulings, but schools in the South overwhelmingly refused to.[92] For example, just 1 of 121 districts in Tennessee fully complied. A local official said, "I saw no reason to create controversy," and another asserted, "I am of the opinion that 99% of the people in the United States feel as I do about the Supreme Court's decision—that it was an outrage. . . . The remaining 1% do not belong in this free world."[93]

Despite the passage of time, periodic news reports indicate that many schools, especially in the rural South, still use prayers or Bible readings in violation of the Court's rulings.

Congress considered a constitutional amendment to overturn the rulings but did not pass one for several reasons. Some people support the rulings. Others support the Court and do not want to challenge its authority and thereby set a precedent for other groups on other matters. Some religious leaders doubt that groups would ever agree about specific prayers. America's religious diversity means that the prayers would offend some students or parents. Prayers that suit Christians might not suit Jews; those that suit Jews might not suit persons of other faiths. Recent immigrants from Asia and the Middle East, practicing Buddhism, Shintoism, Taoism, and Islam, have made the country even more pluralistic. Now, according to one researcher, America's religious diversity is greater than that of any country in recorded history.[94] Thus, asking students in this country to say a prayer would be like "asking the members of the United Nations to stand and sing the national anthem of one country."[95] Other religious leaders expect that officials anxious to avoid controversy would adopt the religious equivalent of canned peas—bland and watered-down prayers. And they expect that prayers would become rote exercises while students were daydreaming or checking out their classmates. In either event, the prayers would trivialize religious faith.

In lieu of an amendment, about half the states have passed laws providing for a "moment of silence" to begin each school day. Although the laws ostensibly are for meditation, some legislators admit they really are for prayer. In 1985 the Supreme Court invalidated Alabama's law that authorized a moment of silence "for meditation or voluntary prayer" because the wording of the law endorsed and promoted prayer.[96] Yet a majority of justices indicated that they would approve a moment of silence if students were not encouraged to pray.

Although the Rehnquist Court's support for the prayer rulings was uncertain, the Court did reaffirm them and even extend them in 1992. It held that clergy cannot offer prayers at graduation ceremonies for public elementary, middle, and high schools.[97] The prayers in question were brief and nonsectarian, but the majority reasoned, "What to most believers may seem nothing more than a reasonable request that the nonbeliever respect their religious practices, in a school context may appear to the nonbeliever or dissenter to be an attempt to employ the machinery of the state to enforce a religious orthodoxy." Although attendance at the ceremony was voluntary, like participation in school prayers, the majority did not consider it truly voluntary. Justice Kennedy

Source: Don Wright, *The Miami News*.

wrote, "Everyone knows that in our society and in our culture high school graduation is one of life's most significant occasions. . . . Graduation is a time for family and those closest to the student to celebrate success and express mutual wishes of gratitude and respect. . . ." The Court decided this case by a bare majority, but its wording was very emphatic.

Yet later that year the Court refused to review a federal court of appeals ruling that allowed student-led prayers at graduation ceremonies.[98] When a Texas school board faced a lawsuit for planning to include an invocation and benediction during graduation ceremonies, it modified its policy to permit the senior class to decide whether to have a prayer and, if so, which student to give it. The appellate court held that this policy was not precluded by the Supreme Court's ruling, because the decision was not made by officials and the prayer was not given by a clergy member, so there would not be any official coercion. Of course, there would be a great deal of peer pressure. Yet the court said a majority of students could do what the state could not. But graduation would still be an official event sponsored by the state, and the opportunity to include a prayer would be offered by the state. Thus, the legality of this policy is in doubt.

Such doubt, however, did not prevent the American Center for Law and Justice, a conservative religious organization funded by televangelist Pat Robertson, from sending bulletins to 15,000 administrators and 500,000 parents and students advising them that graduation prayers, if led by students, were lawful after all. This mailing prompted the American Civil Liberties Union to notify administrators that the issue was not really resolved after all.[99] Meanwhile, confused school boards reached contradictory conclusions and made varying decisions.

The appellate court's holding encouraged opponents of the Supreme Court's school prayer rulings to use the same approach to circumvent these rulings as well. A high school principal in Jackson, Mississippi, let students vote whether to have a daily prayer and then he let them give it over the intercom. After ignoring a warning from the school board, he was suspended, prompting thousands of students in 15 counties to walk out of their schools in protest. Then the legislature passed a law allowing students to initiate and give prayers. Several other southern states followed Mississippi. The legality of these laws is in doubt.

The public demand is fueled by the symbolism of school prayer and a nostalgia for the less troubling times before the 1960s. As one writer perceived, the demand "doesn't have much to do with prayer anyway, but with a time, a place, an ethos that praying and pledging allegiance at the beginning of school each day represent."[100] Many people echo the feelings of a Pennsylvania school board member who said, "The country has certainly gone downhill since they took it out."[101] For these people, reinstitutionalization of school prayer would be a symbol that our society stands for appropriate values. For some religious leaders, however, calls for school prayer are "a cynical exploitation" of the public by politicians who imply that "two-minute pieties" will make up for the decline of values in society.[102]

In a related matter, the Court said that the University of Missouri at Kansas City had to make its meeting rooms available to students' religious organizations on an equal basis with other organizations, even if the religious organizations used the rooms for prayer or worship.[103] Otherwise, the university would be discriminating against religion. After this decision, Congress passed a law that requires public high schools as well to allow meetings of students' religious, philosophical, or political groups outside class hours. The Court accepted this law in 1990.[104] Justice O'Connor said high school students "are likely to understand that a school does not endorse or support student speech that it merely permits on a nondiscriminatory basis." Students have established 12,000 Bible clubs in public schools, according to an estimate in 1994.[105]

The Rehnquist Court also said that the University of Virginia had to provide financial aid, from students' fees, to students' religious organizations on an equal basis with other campus organizations, even if a religious organization sought the money to print a religious newspaper.[106]

Despite its prayer rulings, the Court has been reluctant to invalidate traditional religious symbols. It has not questioned the motto "In God We Trust," on our money since 1865, or the phrase "One nation under God," in the Pledge of Allegiance since 1954.

The Rehnquist Court upheld the display of a nativity scene on government property, at least if it is part of a broader display for the holiday season.[107] Pawtucket, Rhode Island, had a creche, Santa Claus, sleigh with reindeer, Christmas tree, and talking wishing well. Although the nativity scene was an obvious symbol of Christianity, the Court said it was a traditional symbol of a holiday that has become secular as well as religious. Moreover, the presence of the secular decorations diluted any religious impact the nativity scene would have. A creche by itself, however, would be impermissible.[108]

Courts also have used the establishment clause to resolve disputes about teaching evolution in schools. In 1968 the Supreme Court invalidated Arkansas' 40-year-old law forbidding schools from teaching evolution.[109] Arkansas and Louisiana then passed laws requiring schools that teach evolution to also teach "creationism"—the biblical version of creation. In 1987 the Court invalidated these laws, because their purpose was to promote the fundamentalist Christian view.[110]

Courts also have used the establishment clause to resolve disputes about aid to parochial schools, most of which are Catholic. Millions of students attend, and their parents pay tuition and other expenses. In recent decades, costs have risen and enrollments have dropped. Schools have asked legislatures to provide money to defray part of the costs of their nonreligious activities. Courts have had to decide whether providing the money helps religion or whether denying it hinders religion. In addition, courts have had to determine if providing the money leads to excessive entanglement of church and state because of the monitoring required to ensure that the money is not spent for religious purposes.

In its first modern case, in 1947, the Court upheld New Jersey's program to reimburse both public and parochial students for bus fares to school.[111] Then the Court upheld New York's and Pennsylvania's

A Buddhist priest in California lowers the American flag at the end of the day.

programs to provide both public and parochial students with textbooks.[112] Because the government already provided public schools with textbooks, the programs aided parochial schools, allowing them to use more of their scarce resources for religious purposes. But the Court said providing transportation and textbooks for all students is little different than providing police and fire protection for all schools.

The Court has struck down most other forms of aid, however.[113] Because these kinds of assistance have entailed sizable sums of money, the Court has said they could help Catholicism significantly and entangle church and state excessively. Yet the Court, reflecting shifting coalitions of justices, has not been consistent. The Burger Court, for example, struck down tax credits but upheld tax deductions to reduce tuition costs for parents.[114]

At the same time the Court struck down most forms of aid to parochial schools, it permitted aid to church-related colleges.[115] The Court noted that colleges are less likely to be under direct control of church officials and are less likely to try to indoctrinate their students, who are less impressionable than younger students.

Rights of Criminal Defendants

The Fourth, Fifth, Sixth, and Eighth Amendments provide numerous **due process** rights for criminal defendants. When the government prosecutes defendants, it must give them the process—that is, the procedures—they are due; it must be fair and "respect certain decencies of civilized conduct,"[116] even toward uncivilized people.

One defense attorney said many of his clients "had been monsters—nothing less—who had done monstrous things. Although occasionally not guilty of the crime charged, nearly all my clients have been guilty of something."[117] Then why do we give them rights? Partly we do so to avoid convicting innocent defendants. But mostly we do so because defendants are citizens, and we give all citizens rights. As Justice Douglas observed, "respecting the dignity even of the least worthy citizen . . . raises the stature of all of us."[118]

Search and Seizure

England fostered the notion that a family's home is its castle, but Parliament made exceptions for the American colonies. It authorized writs of assistance, which allowed customs officials to conduct general searches for goods colonists had imported without paying taxes to the crown. The English tradition combined with the colonists' resentment of the writs of assistance led to adoption of the Fourth Amendment, which forbids **unreasonable searches and seizures.**

One type of seizure is the arrest of a person. Police must have evidence to believe that a person committed a crime. Another type of seizure is the confiscation of illegal contraband. The general requirement is that police should get a search warrant from a judge by showing evidence that a particular thing is in a particular place.

However, the Court has made exceptions to this requirement that complicate the law. These exceptions account for the vast majority of searches. If persons consent to a search, police can conduct one without a warrant. If police see contraband in plain view, they can seize it; they do not need to close their eyes to it. If police have suspicion that persons are committing a crime but lack evidence to arrest them, they can "stop and frisk" them—give them a pat-down search. If police have evidence to arrest them, they can search them and the area within their immediate control. If police face an emergency situation, they can search for weapons. And if police want to search motor vehicles in some situations, they can do so because vehicles are mobile and could be gone by the time police get a warrant.

Customs and border patrol officials can search persons and things coming into the country to enforce customs and immigration laws. Airport guards can search passengers and luggage to prevent hijackings. And prison guards can search prisoners to ensure security.

In defining reasonable and unreasonable searches and seizures, the Court has tried to walk a fine line between acknowledging officials' need for evidence and persons' need for privacy.

Exclusionary Rule

To enforce search and seizure law, the Court has established the **exclusionary rule,** which bars from court any evidence obtained in violation of the Fourth Amendment. The rule's goal is to deter police from illegal conduct.

Although the Court issued the rule for federal courts in 1914,[119] it did not impose the rule on state courts until 1961. Even so, the Warren Court's decision, in the case of *Mapp v. Ohio*,[120] was one of its most controversial. Until this time, police in many states had ignored search and seizure law.

The decision still has not been widely accepted. The Burger Court in 1984 created an exception to it. In a pair of cases, the justices allowed evidence obtained illegally to be used in court because the police had acted in "good faith."[121] The Rehnquist Court probably will define the scope of this exception more fully.

Electronic Surveillance

The Fourth Amendment traditionally applied to searches involving a physical trespass and seizures producing a tangible object. Electronic surveillance, however, does not require a physical trespass or result in a tangible object.

This posed a problem for the Supreme Court when it heard its first wiretapping case in 1928. Federal prohibition agents tapped the telephone of bootleggers by installing equipment on wires in the basement of the bootleggers' apartment building. The majority of the Court rigidly adhered to its traditional doctrine, saying this was not a search and seizure so the agents did not need a warrant.[122]

In a classic example of keeping the Constitution up to date, the Warren Court overruled this precedent in 1967.[123] Because electronic eavesdropping might threaten privacy as much as traditional searching, officials must get judicial authorization, similar to a warrant, to engage in such eavesdropping.

Self-Incrimination

The Fifth Amendment provides that persons shall not be compelled to be witnesses against themselves, that is, to incriminate themselves. Because defendants are presumed innocent, the government must prove their guilt.

This right means that defendants on trial do not have to take the witness stand and answer questions, and neither prosecutor nor judge can call attention to their failure to do so. Neither can suggest that defendants must have something to hide and thereby imply that they must be guilty. (But if defendants do take the stand and testify, this constitutes a waiver of their right, so the prosecutor can cross-examine them and they must answer.)

This right also means that prosecutors cannot introduce into evidence any statements or confessions from defendants that were not voluntary. However, the meaning of "voluntary" has changed over time.

For years law enforcement officials used physical brutality—"the third degree"—to get confessions. After 1936, when the Supreme Court ruled that confessions obtained this way were invalid,[124] officials resorted to more subtle techniques. They held suspects incommunicado, so the suspects could not notify anyone about their arrest, and delayed bringing them to court, so the judge could not inform them of their rights.[125] They interrogated suspects for long periods of time without food or rest, in one case with alternating teams of interrogators for 36 hours.[126] They tricked suspects. In one case, they told a man they would jail his wife if he did not talk, although they knew she was not involved, and in another they told a woman they would take away her welfare benefits and even her children if she did not talk, although they did not have authority to do either.[127] The Court ruled that these techniques, designed to break the suspects' will, were psychological coercion, so the confessions were invalid.

The Warren Court still worried that many confessions were not truly voluntary, so it issued a landmark decision in 1966. Arizona police arrested a poor, mentally disturbed man, Ernesto Miranda, for kidnapping and raping a woman. After the woman identified him in a lineup, police interrogated him for two hours, prompting him to confess. He had not been told that he could remain silent or be represented by an attorney. In *Miranda v. Arizona*, the Court decided that his confession was not truly voluntary.[128] Chief Justice Warren, himself a former district attorney, noted the tremendous advantage police have in interrogation and said suspects needed more

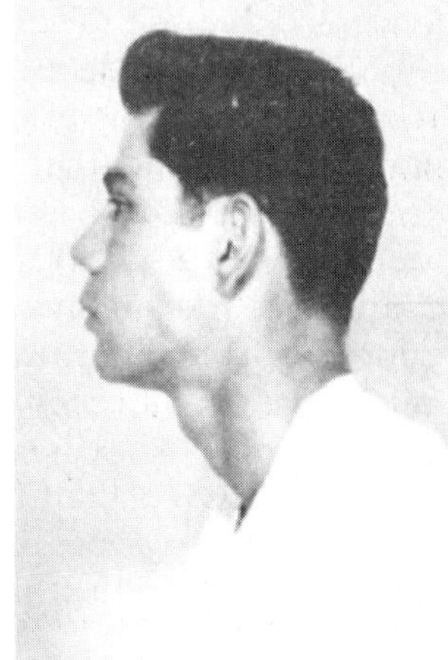

Ernesto Miranda.

protection. The Court ruled that officials must advise suspects of their rights before interrogation. These came to be known as the **Miranda rights:**

- You have the right to remain silent.
- If you talk, anything you say can be used against you.
- You have the right to be represented by an attorney.
- If you cannot afford an attorney, one will be appointed for you.

The Burger and Rehnquist courts have not required police and prosecutors to follow *Miranda* as strictly as the Warren Court did but, contrary to expectations, have not abandoned *Miranda*.

When a Court Reverses a Conviction . . .

. . . the defendant does not necessarily go free. An appellate court normally only evaluates the legality of the procedures used by officials; it does not determine guilt or innocence. Therefore, when it reverses a conviction, it only indicates that officials used some illegal procedure in convicting the defendant—for example, they may have used evidence from an improper search and seizure. Then the prosecutor can retry the defendant, without this evidence, if the prosecutor thinks there is enough other evidence. Often prosecutors do retry the defendants, and in about half the cases judges or juries reconvict them.[1]

1. Robert T. Roper and Albert P. Malone, "Does Procedural Due Process Make a Difference? A Study of Second Trials," *Judicature* 65 (1981), pp. 136–41.

Counsel

The Sixth Amendment provides the **right to counsel** in criminal cases. Historically, it permitted defendants to hire an attorney to represent them in court, but it was no help to most defendants because they were too poor to hire one.

Consequently, the Supreme Court required federal courts to furnish an attorney to all indigent defendants as long ago as 1938.[129] But most criminal cases are state cases, and although the Court required state courts to furnish an attorney in some cases, it was reluctant to impose a broad requirement on these courts.[130]

In 1963 the Warren Court accepted the appeal of Clarence Earl Gideon. Charged with breaking into a pool hall and stealing beer, wine, and change from a vending machine, Gideon asked the judge for a lawyer. The judge refused to appoint one, leaving Gideon to defend himself. The prosecutor did not have a strong case, but Gideon was not able to point out its weaknesses. He was convicted and sentenced to five years. On appeal, the Warren Court unanimously declared that Gideon was entitled to be represented by counsel.[131] Justice Black explained that "lawyers in criminal courts are necessities, not luxuries." The Court finally established a broad rule: State courts must give an attorney to indigent defendants in felony cases.

Gideon proved the Court's point. Given a lawyer and retried, he was not convicted. The lawyer did the effective job defending him that he had not been able to do himself.

In 1972 the Burger Court expanded the rule: State courts must give an attorney to indigent defendants in misdemeanor cases too, except those that result in no incarceration at all,[132] because even misdemeanor cases are too complex for defendants to defend themselves. In addition, the Court decided that courts must provide an attorney for one appeal.[133]

Receiving counsel does not necessarily mean receiving effective counsel, however. Some assigned attorneys are inexperienced, some are incompetent, and most are overworked and have little time to prepare the best possible defense.

Jury Trial

The Sixth Amendment also provides the **right to a jury trial** in "serious" criminal cases. The Supreme Court has defined "serious" cases as those that could result in more than six months' incarceration.[134]

The right was adopted to prevent oppression by a "corrupt or overzealous prosecutor" or a "biased . . . or eccentric judge."[135] It also has served to limit governmental use of unpopular laws or enforcement procedures. Regardless of the extent of evidence against a defendant, a jury can refuse to convict if it feels the government has overstepped its bounds.

The jury is to be "impartial," so persons who have made up their minds before trial should be dismissed. It also is to be "a fair cross section" of the community, so no group should be systematically excluded.[136] But the jury need not be a perfect cross section and, in fact, need not have a single member of a particular group.[137] Most courts use voter registration lists to obtain names of potential jurors. These lists are not

Clarence Earl Gideon, convinced he was denied a fair trial because he was not given an attorney, read law books in prison so he could petition the Supreme Court for a writ of certiorari. Although he had spent much of his life in prison, he was optimistic. "I believe that each era finds an improvement in law each year brings something new for the benefit of mankind [*sic*]. Maybe this will be one of those small steps forward."

No. 990 Misc.
OCT. TERM 1961
U. S. Supreme Court

DIVISION OF CORRECTIONS

CORRESPONDENCE REGULATIONS

MAIL WILL NOT BE DELIVERED WHICH DOES NOT CONFORM WITH THESE RULES

No. 1 -- Only 2 letters each week, not to exceed 2 sheets letter-size 8 1/2 x 11" and written *on one side only*, and if ruled paper, do not write between lines. *Your complete name* must be signed at the close of your letter. *Clippings, stamps, letters* from other people, *stationery* or *cash must not be enclosed* in your letters.

No. 2 -- All *letters* must be addressed in the *complete prison name* of the inmate. *Cell number*, where applicable, and *prison number* must be placed in lower left corner of envelope, with your complete name and address in the upper left corner.

No. 3 -- *Do not send any packages without a Package Permit.* Unauthorized *packages* will be destroyed.

No. 4 -- *Letters* must be written in English only.

No. 5 -- *Books, magazines, pamphlets*, and *newspapers* of reputable character will be delivered *only if* mailed direct from the publisher.

No. 6 -- *Money* must be sent in the form of *Postal Money Orders* only, in the inmate's complete prison name and prison number.

INSTITUTION ______ CELL NUMBER ______

NAME ______ NUMBER ______

RECEIVED JAN 8 1962 OFFICE OF THE CLERK SUPREME COURT U.S.

In the Supreme Court of The United States
Washington D.C.
Motion for leave to proceed in Forma Pauperis
Clarence Earl Gideon, Petitioner
VS.
H. G. Cochran Jr, Director, Divisions of corrections State of Florida Respondent

Petitioner, Clarence Earl Gideon, who is now held in the Florida state penitentiary, asks leave to file the attached petition for a Writ of Certiorari to the United States Supreme Court, directed to the Supreme Court of The State of Florida, without prepayment of costs and to proceed in Forma Pauperis. The petitioner's affidavit in support is attached hereto.

Clarence Earl Gideon
counsel for Petitioner

Affidavit in support of petition for leave to proceed in Forma Pauperis
Clarence Earl Gideon, petitioner
VS.
H. G. Cochran Jr, Director, Divisions of corrections State of Florida, Respondent

I, Clarence Earl Gideon, being duly sworn according to law, depose and say that I am

truly representative because poor people do not register at the same rate as others, but courts have decided that the lists are sufficiently representative. And Congress passed and President Clinton signed the "motor voter bill," which requires drivers' license and welfare offices to offer voter registration forms. Presumably more poor people will register and be eligible for serving on juries.

Cruel and Unusual Punishment

The Eighth Amendment forbids **cruel and unusual punishment** but does not define it. The Supreme Court had defined it as torture or any punishment grossly disproportionate to the offense, but the Court had seldom used the provision until applying it to capital punishment in the 1970s.

Because the death penalty was used at the time the amendment was adopted and had been used ever since, it was assumed to be constitutional. In fact, in the nineteenth century the Court ruled that two methods of execution—the firing squad and the electric chair—were not so inhumane as to be torture.[138]

But in 1972 the Burger Court, albeit with Chief Justice Burger and the other three Nixon appointees in dissent, held that capital punishment as it was then being administered was cruel and unusual.[139] The Court said the laws and procedures allowed too much discretion for those who administered the punishment and too much arbitrariness and discrimination for those who received it. It was imposed so seldom, according to Justice Potter Stewart, that it was "cruel and unusual in the same way that being struck by

Symbolic Solutions for Complex Problems?

Capital Punishment

Public opinion, which opposed capital punishment in the 1960s and early 1970s, flip-flopped as the crime rate soared. Since the early 1970s, 70–80% of the people have supported this punishment. Many people see it as one solution to the crime problem, especially to the homicide rate. That is, they consider the death penalty a deterrent.[1] Others believe the death penalty is only a symbolic solution.

The theory of deterrence rests on the assumption that people are rational actors who weigh the costs and benefits of their actions. They try to avoid unpleasant or painful consequences. If society does not want them to do something, society imposes such consequences. If these do not work, society increases the consequences. Thus, because almost no one wants to die, capital punishment in theory ensures that almost no one will take a life. But does capital punishment actually deter murder?

The death penalty, of course, does deter the killer who receives it from killing again. This penalty, however, is not necessary to deter most killers. Studies of killers who were not executed and who were eventually paroled show that they rarely kill again. And those released in states without capital punishment are no more likely to kill again than those released in states with it.[2]

But does the death penalty deter potential killers from killing in the first place? This is extremely difficult to measure. Many factors contribute to the homicide rate—poverty, unemployment, brutality at home, brutality in the community, availability of guns, number of males in their teens or early 20s (the most criminal- and violent-prone people in society), and so forth. It is difficult to identify, let alone take into account, all of the relevant factors.

Social science studies do not prove that capital punishment is a deterrent.[3] (Nor do they conclusively prove that it is not.) Comparisons of neighboring states with and without the death penalty found that the murder rates are similar and increase or decrease at about the same time, suggesting that the rates reflect broad social trends rather than official executions.[4] Examinations of states that abolished or reinstated the death penalty and comparisons with neighboring states that did not change their punishment found that the murder rates seem unaffected by the changes.[5]

Numerous studies looked at the possibility of deterrence in the murder of police officers. These murderers have a high rate of apprehension, and because their victims are officers, they have a good chance of facing the death penalty. And these crimes and their punishment receive much publicity. Thus, if capital punishment is a deterrent, it should be seen here. Yet the studies found no higher murder rates of police officers in states that have abandoned capital punishment.[6]

Some proponents of capital punishment have hypothesized that it would also deter crimes beside murder by educating people in general to obey the law or face the consequences. Yet a study found no such impact on other serious crimes.[7]

Some proponents acknowledge that capital punishment is not a deterrent now because it is not used soon enough after arrest or conviction. There are, on average, delays of 8 years between a murder and the execution. These are due to additional appeals afforded defendants who face this ultimate and irrevocable punishment. Although most convicted criminals do not take advantage of their appeals, those facing the death penalty have the most incentive to do so. Because the punishment is irrevocable—and reports of new evidence exonerating inmates on death row periodically surface—it is unlikely that society would tolerate much reduction in these safeguards.

There are good reasons why we should not expect capital punishment to be a deterrent. Before defendants can be given this sentence, they must be arrested and convicted. Otherwise, the sentence on the books is irrelevant.

Further, the alternative sentence—life in prison, with or without the possibility of parole—already is steep. Perhaps it already provides as much deterrence as possible. Capital punishment presumably would be a deterrent only to the extent that a potential killer thought life in prison was acceptable but execution was not.

Moreover, consider the typical killers. "Professional" killers are rare and are rarely caught. When caught, they are usually offered leniency in exchange for information about those who employ them.[8] Unlike professionals, most killers do not plan their crimes. Murders frequently occur in a fit of rage, as an outgrowth of an argument with an acquaintance, often a partner or ex-partner in a sour domestic relationship. The killers normally do not calculate their eventual punishment; they do not even think of getting caught and being convicted. Often they are high on alcohol or drugs so they are even less rational. Murders also frequently occur in the drug trade. Drug dealers realize that rivals, wannabes, or others might kill them for drugs, money, territory, or "respect" any day, yet the the dealers continue to traffic in drugs and sometimes commit violent acts. If their immediate fears do not prompt them to quit, the remote possibility of capital punishment is not likely to, either. If capital punishment is not a deterrent, then it is a symbolic rather than a real solution to crime.

There is actually some evidence that official executions slightly increase the homicide rate in the month or two afterward.[9] Perhaps executions convey the message that violence is an acceptable solution to problems—just enough to push people already on the brink. Or perhaps executions show potential killers that they, too, can get public attention by committing such acts.

Many people also consider the death penalty just retribution. The theory of retribution is the secular equivalent of the biblical phrase, "an eye for an eye." It is a payment to society, to satisfy the moral indignation of society, for the act the defendant committed. If the act was taking a life, the payment should be forfeiting one's life. (Taken literally, the execution should be performed in the same manner as the murder was committed.)

Opponents of retribution say society, rather than being more moral for using the death penalty, is less moral. Society is supposed to reflect appropriate standards of behavior, not imitate the lowest standards of its worst members. They also maintain that society is less moral because the death penalty, unlike the typical murder, is undertaken in a rational and cold-blooded way. Essentially, in response to "an eye for an eye," opponents say that "two wrongs don't make a right."

As a moral, rather than a pragmatic argument, the theory of retribution cannot be refuted by studies the way the theory of deterrence can be.

If the death penalty is accepted as retribution, it is a symbolic reflection of society's morality and as such is also a symbolic solution to crime. This might be a sufficient basis to persuade many people to support capital punishment. Indeed, polls find that many people who support capital punishment do not want it used much. Apparently they want it on the books as a symbol. But these people should not expect it to reduce the homicide rate, let alone the overall crime rate.

Regardless of one's own preference for or opposition to capital punishment, this issue reflects the inherent problems of symbolic solutions in our politics. Some sponsors of such solutions are merely trying to score political points, pointing out their stand in favor, or their opponent's stand against, the penalty. Other sponsors are sincerely hoping to do some good. Either way, the debate about symbolic measures usually takes precedence over and interferes with efforts to adopt more substantive solutions. Mario Cuomo, who as governor of New York vetoed capital punishment and lost reelection in part as a result, called it "the ultimate political cop-out." It lets legislators convince constituents that they are doing something about the crime problem. When Congress adopted the death penalty for federal courts in 1994, sponsors claimed that they made the country safer by allowing the penalty for 50 different crimes. But one crime was murder of egg inspectors, another was murder of poultry inspectors, and so on. Many members privately conceded that they voted for the penalty only to avoid appearing "soft on crime."[10] Yet many legislators who claim to be so worried about the crime problem refrain from proposing substantive solutions. Such programs would cost more money, require more taxes, and take years to reap the benefits. Instead, Cuomo said, "It is easier to hold out a quick fix, the idea that all will be well if we just burn people."[11] But the crime problem did not develop quickly, and it will not be resolved quickly.

---

1. K. M. Jamieson and T. J. Flanagan, *Sourcebook of Criminal Justice Statistics, 1988* (Albany, NY: Hindelang Criminal Justice Research Center, 1989), p. 229.
2. Hugo Adam Bedau, ed., *The Death Penalty in America,* 3rd ed. (New York: Oxford University Press, 1982), p. 180.
3. Victor E. Kappeler, Mark Blumberg, and Gary W. Potter, *The Mythology of Crime and Criminal Justice* (Prospect Heights, IL: Waveland, 1993), pp. 213–22; Samuel Walker, *Sense and Nonsense about Crime and Drugs,* 3rd ed. (Belmont, CA: Wadsworth, 1994), pp. 103–108.
4. Thorsten Sellin, *The Penalty of Death* (Beverly Hills, CA: Sage, 1980).
5. Hans Zeisel, "The Deterrent Effect of the Death Penalty: Facts v. Faith," in Philip B. Kurland, ed., *The Supreme Court Review, 1976* (Chicago: University of Chicago Press, 1977).
6. See numerous sources cited in Kappeler, et. al., *Mythology of Crime and Criminal Justice,* p. 218. Isaac Ehrlich claimed that every execution from 1930 to 1969 deterred 7 or 8 murders. Although he took into account some variables that could affect the homicide rate, such as the probabilities of apprehension, conviction, and execution, there were flaws in the study that led later researchers to dismiss his conclusions. See Ehrlich, "The Deterrent Effect of Capital Punishment," *American Economic Review* 65 (1975): 397–417; and numerous sources cited in Kappeler, et al., *Mythology of Crime and Criminal Justice,* pp. 220–21.
7. William C. Bailey, "The General Prevention Effect of Capital Punishment for Non-Capital Felonies," in R. M. Bohm, ed., *The Death Penalty in America: Current Research* (Cincinnati: Anderson Publishing and Academy of Criminal Justice Sciences, 1991).
8. John Kaplan, "The Problem of Capital Punishment," *University of Illinois Law Review* 31 (1963): p. 565–70.
9. W. J. Bowers, G. L. Pierce, and J. F. McDevitt, *Legal Homicide: Death as Punishment in America, 1864–1982* (Boston: Northeastern University Press, 1984), p. 284.
10. Helen Dewar, "It's Better to Look Good Than to Do Good," *Washington Post National Weekly Edition,* December 2–8, 1991, p. 12.
11. Michael Kramer, "Cuomo, the Last Holdout," *Time,* April 2, 1990, p. 20.

lightning is cruel and unusual." Yet when imposed, it was given to blacks disproportionately to their convictions for murder.

The decision invalidated the laws of 40 states and commuted the death sentences of 629 inmates. But because the Court did not hold capital punishment cruel and unusual in principle, about three-fourths of the states adopted new laws that permitted less discretion in an effort to be less arbitrary and discriminatory.

These changes satisfied a majority of the court. In 1976 and 1977, the Court said capital punishment is not cruel and unusual for murder if the punishment is administered fairly.[140] But the punishment cannot be imposed automatically for everyone convicted of murder, for the judge or jury must consider any mitigating factors that would call for a lesser punishment.[141] Also, the punishment cannot be imposed for rape, because it is disproportionate to that offense.[142]

The new laws apparently have reduced but not eliminated discrimination. Although past studies showed discrimination against black defendants, recent studies show discrimination against black or white defendants who murder whites. People who affect the decision to impose capital punishment—prosecutors, defense attorneys, judges, and jurors—appear to value white lives more. Despite evidence that in Georgia those who kill whites are more than four times as likely to be given the death penalty as those who kill blacks, the Rehnquist Court, by a five to four vote, upheld capital punishment in the state in 1987.[143] The majority, in part reflecting the views of lawyers untrained in and uncomfortable with social science, expressed reluctance to use such evidence in reaching decisions. They acknowledged that the study showed discrimination but said it did not show that this particular defendant, a black man who killed a white cop, was a victim of the discrimination.

Rights in Theory and in Practice

Although the Supreme Court has interpreted the Bill of Rights to provide an impressive list of rights for criminal defendants, not all rights are available for all defendants in all places. Some trial court judges, prosecutors, and police do not comply with Supreme Court rulings. If defendants appeal to a high enough court, they probably will get their rights, but most defendants do not have the knowledge, the resources, or the perseverance to do this.

When rights are available, most defendants do not take advantage of them. About 90% of all criminal defendants plead guilty, and many of them do so as part of a **plea bargain.** This is an agreement between the prosecutor, the defense attorney, and the defendant, with the explicit or implicit approval of the judge, to reduce the charge or the sentence in exchange for a plea of guilty. A plea bargain is a compromise. For officials it saves the time, trouble, and uncertainty of a trial. For defendants it eliminates the fear of a harsher sentence. However, it also reduces due process rights. A plea of guilty waives defendants' rights to a trial by a jury of their peers, in which defendants can present their own witnesses and cross-examine the government's witnesses, and in which they cannot be forced to incriminate themselves. A plea of guilty also waives the right to counsel to some extent because most attorneys appointed to represent defendants are overworked and inclined to pressure defendants to plead guilty so they do not have to prepare a defense. Despite these disadvantages for due process rights, the Court allows plea bargaining because of its practical advantages.[144]

Right to Privacy

Neither the Constitution nor the Bill of Rights mentions "privacy." Nevertheless, the **right to privacy,** Justice Douglas noted, is "older than the Bill of Rights,"[145] and the framers undoubtedly assumed that people would have it. The framers did include amendments that reflect a concern for privacy: The First Amendment protects privacy of association, the Third privacy of homes from quartering soldiers, the Fourth privacy of persons and places where they live from searches and seizures, and the Fifth privacy of knowledge or thoughts from compulsory self-incrimination.

So far the Court's right-to-privacy doctrine reflects a right to autonomy—what Justice Louis Brandeis called "the right to be left alone"—more than a right to keep things confidential. As noted earlier in the chapter, the Court has been reluctant to punish the press for invasion of privacy.[146]

Birth Control

The Warren Court established the right to privacy in 1965 when it struck down a Connecticut law that

Norma McCorvey, alias "Jane Roe," whose suit prompted the landmark abortion ruling.

prohibited distributing or using contraceptives.[147] To enforce the law the state would have had to police people's bedrooms, and the Court said the very idea of policing married couples' bedrooms was absurd. Then the Court struck down Massachusetts and New York laws that prohibited distributing contraceptives to unmarried persons.[148] "If the right of privacy means anything," Justice Brennan said, "it is the right of the individual, married or single, to be free from unwarranted governmental intrusion into matters so fundamentally affecting a person as the decision whether to bear or beget a child."[149]

Abortion

When 21-year-old Norma McCorvey became pregnant in 1969, she was divorced and already had a 5-year-old daughter, and she sought an abortion. But Texas, where she lived, prohibited abortions unless the mother's life was in danger. She discovered, "No legitimate doctor in Dallas would touch me.... I found one doctor who offered to abort me for $500. Only he didn't have a license, and I was scared to turn my body over to him. So there I was—pregnant, unmarried, unemployed, alone, and stuck."[150]

Too poor to go to a state that permitted abortions, McCorvey decided to put her baby up for adoption. But the state law still rankled her. With the help of two women attorneys recently out of law school, she used her case to challenge Texas's law. She adopted the name Jane Roe to conceal her identity.

In *Roe v. Wade* in 1973, the Burger Court extended the right to privacy from birth control to abortion. The majority concluded that because doctors, theologians, and philosophers cannot agree when life begins, judges should not assert that life begins at conception, thus deeming a fetus a person and abortion murder. Amidst such uncertainty, the majority decided that a woman's right to privacy of her body is paramount.

The Court ruled that women can have an abortion during the first three months of pregnancy and, subject to reasonable regulations for health, during the middle three months. States can prohibit an abortion during the last three months. Thus the right is broad though not absolute.

The justices, as revealed in memos discovered years later, acknowledged that their division of pregnancy into trimesters was "legislative," but they saw this as a way to balance the rights of the mother in the early stages of pregnancy with the rights of the fetus in the later stage.[151]

The Court's ruling invalidated the abortion laws of 45 states (see Figure 1). Far from settling the issue, however, it stimulated more controversy. The right-to-life movement, spearheaded initially by Catholics and later by fundamentalist Protestants, organized to protest the ruling. The movement also pressured legislators to overturn or circumvent the ruling. Although Congress failed to pass a constitutional amendment banning abortions or allowing states to regulate them, many state legislatures did pass statutes restricting abortions in various ways.

The Burger Court invalidated most of these laws.[152] It held that states cannot require abortions to be performed in hospitals rather than clinics, where they are cheaper.[153] They cannot require consent by either the parents of unmarried minors[154] or the husband of married women (Table 1).[155]

The Burger Court, however, upheld a major restriction on the right to abortion. It allowed laws that bar the use of government funds to pay for abortions for poor women. The Medicaid program, financed jointly by the federal and state governments, had paid for abortions for poor women. Before these laws, the program had paid for about one-third of the abortions in the country each year.[156] These laws put a safe abortion, by a doctor in a clinic or hospital, beyond the financial reach of some women. Regardless, a majority of the Burger Court ruled that governments

FIGURE 1
The Number of Abortions Has Leveled Off

The number of abortions in the United States was already increasing before the Supreme Court's *Roe* decision because some states had liberalized their laws. After the *Roe* decision, the number increased sharply but leveled off in the 1980s. The rate of abortions is about 29% of all pregnancies (excluding miscarriages and stillbirths). This compares with 13% for West Germany, 14% for Canada, 27% for Japan, and 68% for the former Soviet Union.

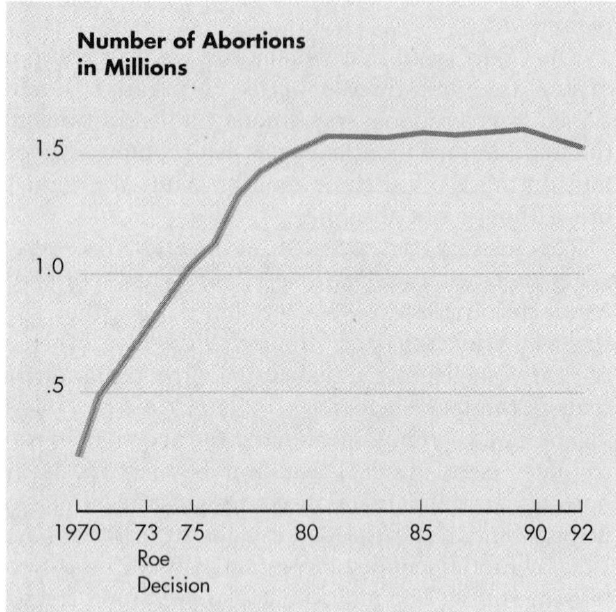

Sources: 1970–1972: Susan Hansen, "State Implementation of Supreme Court Decisions: Abortion Rates since *Roe v. Wade*," *Journal of Politics* 42 (May 1980), pp. 372–95; 1973–1981: Stanley K. Henshaw and Ellen Blaine, *Abortion Services in the United States, Each State, and Metropolitan Area, 1981–1982* (New York: Alan Guttmacher Institute, 1985), p. 64; 1982–1983: Stanley K. Henshaw, "Characteristics of U.S. Women Having Abortions, 1982–1983," *Family Planning Perspectives* 19 (1987), pp. 6–7; 1984–1985: Stanley K. Henshaw, Jacqueline Darroch Forrest, and Jennifer Van Vort, "Abortion Services in the United States, 1984 and 1985," *Family Planning Perspectives* 19 (1987), p. 64; 1986–1988: *Abortion Fact Book* (New York: Alan Guttmacher Institute, 1992); "Number of Abortions at Lowest Level Since '79," *Lincoln Journal* (AP), June 16, 1994.

have no obligation to finance abortions, even if this means that some women cannot take advantage of their right to have them.[157]

Congress and over half the states now prohibit use of their funds to pay for abortions for poor women, except for those whose pregnancy threatens their life or whose pregnancy is the result of rape or incest. However, about a fifth of the states do provide funds for all poor women who want abortions.[158]

One effect of the laws barring use of government funds is to delay abortions, making them more risky and expensive, while the women search for the money.[159] Another effect is to deny abortions to an estimated 20% of the women who cannot obtain the money. The women, then, bear their unwanted children. As a result, state medical and welfare expenditures for the additional children increase. According to one analysis of states that do provide funds for poor women, the states incur the cost of the abortions initially but save money in the long run. For every $1 spent for the abortions, $4 is saved in medical and welfare expenses in what would have been just the first two years of the child's life.[160]

Presidents Reagan and Bush sought justices who opposed *Roe* and, after they filled their fifth vacancy on the Court, pro-life advocates expected the Court to overturn it. Yet the Rehnquist Court, while narrowing *Roe*, has not overturned it.[161] In *Planned Parenthood of Southeastern Pennsylvania v. Casey* in 1992, a bare majority of five justices reaffirmed the right to abortion.[162] At the same time, the majority signaled a willingness to allow more restrictions on the right—as long they do not place an "undue burden" on women seeking abortions.

The majority upheld Pennsylvania's 24-hour waiting period between the time a woman indicates her desire to have an abortion and the time a doctor can perform one. Although a 24-hour waiting period will not be much burden for many women, it will for some. Poor women who live in rural areas and must travel to cities to obtain abortions will have to make one trip, turn around and go home, then turn around and come back the next day. Or they will have to spend the night and pay for food and lodging. One woman in Mississippi hitch-hiked and planned to sleep on outdoor furniture in the K Mart parking lot across the street (until the clinic offered to pay for her motel room).[163]

Teenagers will also be affected. Pro-life groups often note the license numbers of cars driven to clinics by teenagers. They look up the name and address of the family and then inform the parents in hope the parents will pressure the daughter to change her mind during the waiting period.

The majority struck down Pennsylvania's requirement that married women notify their husband before having an abortion. This was an undue burden because women who fear physical abuse from their

TABLE 1 Why Women Have Abortions

Reason	Percent
Child would change life (job, school)	76%
Cannot afford child	68
Problems with husband or partner, or do not want to be single parent	51
Do not want people to know I had sex or am pregnant	31
Too young, or cannot handle the responsibility	30
Husband or partner wants me to	23
Concerned for fetus's health	13
Concerned for own health	7
Pregnancy was due to rape or incest	1

Women gave these reasons for having abortions. Because many gave more than one, the percents total more than 100.

Source: 1985 data from Alan Guttmacher Institute, published in *Lincoln Sunday Journal-Star*, April 30, 1989.

husband would be deterred from seeking an abortion. Justice O'Connor said a state "may not give to a man the kind of dominion over his wife that parents exercise over their children."

The Rehnquist Court upheld various states' requirement that unmarried minors notify their parents before having an abortion.[164] If a daughter does not want to tell her parents, she can try to get permission from a judge. She must convince the judge that an abortion would be in her best interest or that she is mature enough to make the decision herself. If she is not mature enough, she must become a mother. These laws, Justice Marshall wrote in dissent, force "a young woman in an already dire situation to choose between two fundamentally unacceptable alternatives: notifying a possibly dictatorial or even abusive parent or justifying her profoundly personal decision in an intimidating judicial proceeding to a black-robed stranger."

Pro-life groups advocated these laws with the expectation that they would result in fewer abortions. They believed many teenagers would go to their parents rather than face the forbidding atmosphere of a court hearing and their parents would persuade or pressure them not to have the abortion. Some evidence indicates that the laws have had this effect.[165] When teenagers do go to court, they routinely get waivers in some states, such as Pennsylvania, but do not in others, such as Indiana. There they are advised to go out of state.[166]

Despite the dissatisfaction of some people, it is worth noting that the unelected, nonmajoritarian Supreme Court has come closer to forging a policy reflective of public opinion than have most politicians. Polls show the majority of the people want to keep the right to abortion but would like to discourage it somewhat.[167] The Court's doctrine now essentially articulates this view.

The pro-life movement, growing increasingly frustrated in recent years, has adopted more militant tactics. Organizations such as Operation Rescue engage in civil disobedience, blockading clinics and harassing workers and patients as they come and go. Some organizations spray chemicals inside clinics, ruining carpets and fabrics and leaving a stench that makes the clinics unusable. Such incidents occurred 50 times in one recent year alone.[168]

Protestors in Charleston, South Carolina, distributed fliers in the city's poorest neighborhood encouraging residents to rob an abortion clinic: "The killers accept only cash! They kill about 60 babies each week. That is $16,500 of CASH taken to the bank each week. That means that an average of $5,500 is waiting there each day of business in cash before closing hours."[169]

Organizations also target doctors, nurses, and other workers of the clinics. Operation Rescue runs a training camp in Florida that instructs members how to use public records to locate personal information about employees, how to tail them to their homes, and how to organize demonstrations at their homes. Organizations put up "Wanted" posters, with a doctor's picture, name, address, and phone number. They encourage others to harass the doctor, his or her spouse, and even their children. (One 13-year-old was confronted in a restaurant and was told that he was going to burn in hell.)[170] Some activists have come out in favor of killing abortion doctors. One organization released a "deadly dozen" list of abortion doctors—a quasi-hit list. One minister wrote a book—*A Time to Kill*—and markets a bumper sticker—"EXECUTE ABORTIONISTS-MURDERERS."[171]

In this climate, two doctors, two clinic receptionists, and one clinic volunteer have been killed, and seven other doctors, employees, and volunteers have been wounded.[172] Numerous clinics have been firebombed. The tactics have had their intended effect on doctors. Although surveys show that most gynecologists and obstetricians are pro-choice, fewer do abortions now than a decade ago.[173] While many doctors consider abortions routine work that pays little, others worry about the consequences.

Abortions remain available in most metropolitan centers but not in most rural areas. Eighty-three

Which Women Have Abortions

More than half of all pregnancies in the U.S. are unintended, and half of these are terminated by abortions.

Twenty-six percent of the abortions are for females in their teens and 55% for those in their twenties. The highest rate is for 18–19 year-olds—64 abortions per 1,000 women.

About a fourth of the teens under 18 who get abortions have never used birth control. Almost half of the teens under 18 who get abortions have not told their parents before doing so.

The majority of women who get abortions are not married. The majority are white, but the rate is twice as high for nonwhites. (This is not a contradiction. The majority are white because there are more whites, but a smaller percentage of them have abortions.)

Catholics, perhaps surprisingly, have a higher rate than Protestants or Jews. Born-again or evangelical Christians do not have a higher rate; even so, one of six abortion patients in recent years has described herself as a born-again or evangelical Christian.

Almost all women have their abortion during the first trimester of pregnancy, when it is safest and easiest to obtain. Fifty percent have it within the first two months, and 39% within the third month.

Source: "Facts in Brief: Abortion in the United States" (New York: Alan Guttmacher Institute, 1992).

percent of U.S. counties have no doctor who performs abortions. Some states have only one or two places where women can obtain abortions.[174]

The leaders of pro-life groups have admitted their strategy. One proclaimed, "We've found the weak link is the doctor." Another acknowledged that they have not succeeded in the Supreme Court or Congress, but, "When you get doctors out, you can have all the laws on the books you want and it doesn't mean a thing."[175]

Still, a million and a half women have abortions each year. Almost 1 in 10 women in college has had an abortion, and 1 in 4 women between 20 and 24 has had one. Many more women see the right as a symbol of the struggle for equality.

Although in the day after the ruling, *Roe* was not even the lead story in the news it has had an enormous impact on politics. It put abortion on the public agenda, and it galvanized conservative groups, who saw it as a symbol of "a whole range of societal restraints being removed."[176] Disparate groups, such as evangelical Protestants and Roman Catholics (and even some Orthodox Jews), rural residents and urban ethnics, who normally did not see eye to eye, coalesced around this issue and exercised leverage within the Republican party.

Meanwhile, Norma McCorvey lived in relative anonymity for some years. However, feeling proud of her involvement in the landmark case, she decided to go public. As a result, she received hate mail, found baby clothes scattered across her lawn, and was shot at through the window of her home.[177]

Pro-choice groups considered McCorvey a useful symbol and gave her a job at an abortion clinic. But Operation Rescue also considered her a useful symbol and wooed her away. It gave her a job at its headquarters. In 1995 she declared that she was "pro-life" (but at the same time said she favored the right to abortion for the first three months of pregnancy). So the woman whose case was used to further the pro-choice cause now is being used to advance the pro-life cause. She says she wants to be a "regular person," but the two sides are fighting as though she were "a flag to be captured or lost."[178]

Homosexuality

The Court has not extended the right to privacy to protect homosexual acts. Almost half the states have laws prohibiting sodomy—oral and anal sex. Although applicable to heterosexuals as well, these laws are seen as restrictions on homosexuals. Although they are primarily symbolic and rarely enforced, they can be applied at any time. For example, a case arose in Georgia in 1986 when police, delivering a summons to residents of a house, discovered two men violating the law. Police arrested them, but prosecutors declined to press charges. Nevertheless, one of the men sued to have the law declared unconstitutional. In a five-to-four decision, the Court refused to go this far.[179]

Justice Powell reportedly agreed during the Court's conference that the law was unconstitutional, but he changed his mind before the decision was announced because the man had not been prosecuted. Powell was leery of the Court issuing a highly controversial decision involving a law that might never be enforced. After retiring, however, he admitted making a mistake in the case.[180]

Despite the efforts of gay groups to have the laws repealed or declared unconstitutional, the appointment of conservatives to the bench and the spread of AIDS make extension of the right to privacy to homosexual acts unlikely anytime soon. However, some

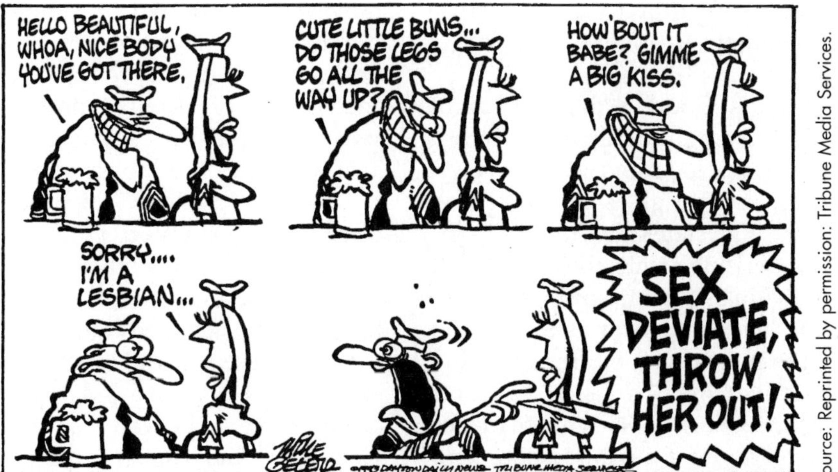

Source: Reprinted by permission: Tribune Media Services.

states and localities have passed laws barring discrimination against homosexuals in employment, housing, credit, insurance, and public accommodations.

Colorado voters adopted a constitutional amendment *prohibiting* laws that bar discrimination against homosexuals, but the Supreme Court in 1996 invalidated this amendment.[181] The six-justice majority said it denied homosexuals a right enjoyed by everyone else—the opportunity to seek protection from discrimination. The ruling, however, did not establish this protection or address the legality of homosexual conduct.

President Clinton, trying to keep a campaign pledge, announced that he would issue an executive order barring discrimination against homosexuals in the military.[182] Since World War II, the U.S. military has rejected recruits who admit to being homosexual and discharged troops who are found to be homosexual. (During the Korean and Vietnam wars, when it needed more troops, the military relaxed its policy.) Officials insist that the presence of homosexuals would disrupt the discipline and morale essential for combat.[183] The president had to back down in the face of strong opposition from military officials, congressional members, and the public.

Instead, the two sides compromised. Now the military (including the Reserves and National Guard) is not allowed to ask questions about sexual orientation on enlistment or security questionnaires but is allowed to discharge members for statements admitting homosexuality or conduct reflecting homosexuality (or bisexuality). Such conduct is defined broadly to encompass not only sexual actions, but also holding hands, dancing, or trying to marry someone of the same sex. The restrictions apply off-base as well as on. They do not encompass reading gay publications, associating with gay people, frequenting gay bars or churches, or marching in gay rights parades.

The new policy of "don't ask—don't tell" does not resolve the issue and does not satisfy either side. For example, homosexuals who receive death threats cannot report these to their commanding officers without risking violation of the policy.[184] And the new policy has not reduced the number of homosexuals discharged.[185]

Most other democracies allow homosexuals in their military. These include Canada, most Western European countries, Japan, and Israel, which, of course, has a battle-tested military.[186]

Right to Die

The Court has broadened the right to privacy to provide a limited right to die. When Nancy Cruzan's car skidded off an icy road and flipped into a ditch in 1983, doctors were able to save her life but not her brain. She never regained consciousness. She lived in a vegetative state, similar to a coma, and was fed through a tube. Twenty-five at the time of the accident, she was expected to live another 30 years. When her parents asked doctors to remove the tube, the hospital objected and the state of Missouri, despite paying $130,000 a year to support her, also objected. This issue, complicated enough in itself, became entangled in other controversial issues. Pro-life groups said denying life support was analogous to abortion; disability groups said her condition was merely a disability, and withholding food and water from her would lead to withholding treatment from other people with disabilities.[187]

In this case the Rehnquist Court established a right to die.[188] The justices ruled that individuals can refuse medical treatment, including food and water, even if this means they will die. But the right is limited. It does not encompass suicide, and states can require individuals to make their decision while competent and alert. (Presumably individuals can also prepare a "living will" or designate another person as a proxy to make the decision in the event that they are unable to.)

Several months after the Court's decision, Cruzan's parents returned to a Missouri court with evidence that their daughter would prefer death to being kept alive by medical machines. Three of Cruzan's former co-workers testified that they recalled conversations in which she said she never would want to live "like a vegetable." Her parents asked for permission to remove her feeding tube and the court agreed. She died 12 days later.[189]

The Supreme Court ruling, however, does not affect most of the approximately 10,000 Americans in irreversible comas who did not indicate their decision beforehand.[190]

But lower courts are moving faster than the Supreme Court. In 1996 two federal courts of appeals struck down laws in New York and Washington, similar to ones in a majority of states, prohibiting physician-assisted suicide. Now, in these two circuits, terminally ill but mentally competent adults can receive doctors' help in committing suicide.

➤Conclusion: Are the Courts Responsive in Interpreting Civil Liberties?

The Supreme Court has interpreted the Constitution to provide many important civil liberties. The Warren Court in the 1950s and 1960s expanded civil liberties more than any other Court in history. It applied many provisions of the Bill of Rights to the states. It substantially broadened rights in the areas of speech, libel, obscenity, and religion. It enormously broadened rights of criminal defendants in the areas of search and seizure, self-incrimination, counsel, and jury trial. And it established a right to privacy.

Observers predicted the Burger Court would lead a constitutional counterrevolution. However, it did not. The Burger Court in the 1970s and 1980s narrowed rights in the areas of freedom of the press, libel, and obscenity. It narrowed rights of criminal defendants in the areas of search and seizure, self-incrimination, and jury trial. And it narrowed opportunities for convicted defendants to appeal on the basis that their rights were violated.[191] But the Court accepted the core of the Warren Court's doctrine and, in fact, even extended it in two areas—right to counsel and right to privacy.

Then observers predicted the Rehnquist Court would produce a constitutional counterrevolution. So far it has not. It has narrowed rights further in some areas, but it too has accepted most of the Warren Court's doctrine.

The decisions of these Courts show the extent to which the Supreme Court is responsive to the people in civil liberties cases. The majority of the people support civil liberties in general but not necessarily in specific situations. The elites support civil liberties more than the masses. As the Court has expanded civil liberties, it has not been very responsive to the majority. But it has been more responsive to the elites, and it has been very responsive to minorities.

The Court, given relative independence from the rest of the political process, was not intended to be responsive to the majority. Therefore, it does not have to mirror public opinion, although it cannot ignore this opinion either. It must stay within the broad limits of this opinion, or it will be pulled back. Thus, the Warren Court, which was not very responsive to majority opinion, went too far too fast for too many people. It produced a backlash that led to the Burger and Rehnquist courts, which have been more responsive to majority opinion.

EPILOGUE

The First Amendment Protects Animal Sacrifice

Although the case of *Church of the Lukumi Babalu Aye v. Hialeah* was bizarre, it did not prove difficult for the justices to decide. The justices unanimously struck down the ordinances.[192] Justice Kennedy wrote the opinion, concluding that the ordinances restricted the Santeria religion without compelling reasons.

Although the ordinances did not mention the Santeria religion, they were written in such a way that they restricted this religion and its practices but virtually no others. The ordinances exempted Jewish kosher slaughter and also a variety of other animal killings—slaughter primarily for food (not primarily for religious purposes), hunting, fishing, euthanasia, and eradication of insects. State law even allowed the use of live rabbits to train greyhound dogs for racing. Thus, the argument that restriction of animal sacrifice was necessary to prevent cruelty to animals rang hollow.

The ordinances also made no effort to regulate the disposal of carcasses from hunting and fishing or the disposal of garbage from restaurants, which would be more voluminous than the carcasses from Santeria ceremonies. Thus, the argument that restriction of animal sacrifice was necessary to prevent a public health risk also rang hollow.

In short, the Court concluded that Hialeah had targeted the Santeria religion because officials and citizens disapproved of it. "Although the practice of animal sacrifice may seem abhorrent to some," Kennedy wrote, "religious beliefs need not be acceptable, logical, consistent, or comprehensible to others in order to merit First Amendment protection." And, he reminded, "it was historical instances of religious persecution and intolerance that gave concern to those who drafted the free exercise clause."

Key Terms

bills of attainder
ex post facto laws
freedom of speech
seditious speech
McCarthyism
public forum
pure speech
speech plus conduct
symbolic speech
prior restraint
libel
obscenity
free exercise clause
establishment clause
due process
unreasonable searches and seizures
exclusionary rule
Miranda rights
right to counsel
right to a jury trial
cruel and unusual punishment
plea bargain
right to privacy

Further Reading

Dan T. Carter, *Scottsboro: A Tragedy of the American South* (Baton Rouge: Louisiana State University Press, 1979). *An examination of the infamous Scottsboro, Alabama, rape case that prompted the Supreme Court to begin to provide counsel to poor defendants.*

Fred W. Friendly, *Minnesota Rag* (New York: Random House, 1981). *A lively chronicle of the Court's first important freedom of the press case—*Near v. Minnesota *in 1927.*

David J. Garrow, *Liberty and Sexuality: The Right to Privacy and the Making of* Roe v. Wade (New York: Macmillan, 1994). *An exhaustive account of the hard road to* Roe.

Franz Kafka, *The Trial* (numerous editions, 1937). *One of the great novels of the twentieth century, which shows, perhaps more dramatically than anything else written, what life without due process rights would be like.*

James Kirby, *Fumble: Bear Bryant, Wally Butts, and the Great College Football Scandal* (New York: Dell, 1986). *Law for football fans—the story of the libel suit against a national magazine for writing that the coach of Alabama and athletic director of Georgia fixed a football game between the two schools. The author, a lawyer, was hired by the Southeastern Conference to determine what really happened in the dispute.*

Anthony Lewis, *Gideon's Trumpet* (New York: Vintage, 1964). *A wonderful account of Clarence Earl Gideon's suit and the Court's landmark decision.*

Patricia G. Miller, *The Worst of Times* (New York: HarperCollins, 1992). *Recollections of women who had abortions before* Roe *made them legal—and interviews with abortionists, doctors, and police who witnessed the effects.*

Notes

1. Bob Cohn and David A. Kaplan, "A Chicken on Every Altar?" *Newsweek*, November 9, 1992, p. 79. Previously Santeria had been praticed semi-openly in parts of New York City and Puerto Rico.
2. Ibid.
3. *Lee v. Weisman*, 112 S.Ct. 2649 (1992).
4. *International Society for Krishna Consciousness v. Lee*, 120 L.Ed2d 541 (1992); *Employment Division v. Smith*, 494 U.S. 872 (1990).
5. Richard Morin, "Is There a Constitutional Right to Rap Rambunctiously?" *Washington Post National Weekly Edition*, September 24–30, 1990, p. 37.
6. "Poll: 33% of Americans Can Identify Bill of Rights," *Lincoln Journal-Star* (AP), December 15, 1991.
7. The states did not ratify a proposed amendment that would have required at least one representative in Congress for every 50,000 people. That amendment would have put about 5,000 members in today's Congress. The states did not ratify, until 1992, another proposed amendment that would have prohibited a salary raise for members of Congress from taking effect until after the next election to Congress.
8. *Reid v. Covert*, 354 U.S. 1 (1957).
9. *Barron v. Baltimore*, 32 U.S. 243 (1833).
10. *Gitlow v. New York*, 268 U.S. 652 (1925).

11. *Argersinger v. Hamlin,* 407 U.S. 25 (1972).

12. Freedom of association is not listed in the First Amendment, but the Court has interpreted freedom of speech and assembly to imply such a right.

13. *Milk Wagon Drivers Union v. Meadowmoor Dairies,* 312 U.S. 287 (1941).

14. Thomas I. Emerson, *The System of Freedom of Expression* (New York: Random House/Vintage, 1971), pp. 6–8.

15. Zechariah Chafee, Jr., *Free Speech in the United States* (Cambridge, Mass.: Harvard University Press, 1941), pp. 51–52.

16. *Schenk v. United States,* 249 U.S. 47 (1919); *Frohwerk v. United States,* 249 U.S. 204 (1919); *Debs v. United States,* 249 U.S. 211 (1919); *Abrams v. United States,* 250 U.S. 616 (1919); *Gitlow v. New York,* 268 U.S. 652 (1925); *Whitney v. California,* 274 U.S. 357 (1927).

17. *Gitlow v. New York.*

18. *Dennis v. United States,* 341 U.S. 494 (1951).

19. *Yates v. United States,* 354 U.S. 298 (1957); *Scales v. United States,* 367 U.S. 203 (1961).

20. Earl Warren, *The Memoirs of Earl Warren* (Garden City, N.Y.: Doubleday, 1977), p. 6.

21. *Brandenburg v. Ohio,* 395 U.S. 444 (1969).

22. *Brandenburg v. Ohio.*

23. *Esquire* (November 1974).

24. *Jeannette Rankin Brigade v. Chief of Capital Police,* 409 U.S. 972 (1972); *Edwards v. South Carolina,* 372 U.S. 229 (1963).

25. *United States v. Grace,* 75 L.Ed.2d 736 (1983).

26. *Grayned v. Rockford,* 408 U.S. 104 (1972); *Tinker v. Des Moines School District,* 393 U.S. 503 (1969).

27. *Brown v. Louisiana,* 383 U.S. 131 (1966).

28. *Southeastern Promotions v. Conrad,* 420 U.S. 546 (1975).

29. *Adderley v. Florida,* 385 U.S. 39 (1966).

30. *Greer v. Spock,* 424 U.S. 828 (1976).

31. *Amalgamated Food Employees v. Logan Valley Plaza,* 391 U.S. 308 (1968).

32. *Lloyd v. Tanner,* 407 U.S. 551 (1972); *Hudgens v. NLRB,* 424 U.S. 507 (1976).

33. *Gooding v. Wilson,* 405 U.S. 518 (1972); *Lewis v. New Orleans,* 408 U.S. 913 (1972).

34. C. Herman Pritchett, *The American Constitution,* 2nd ed. (New York: McGraw-Hill, 1968), p. 476, n. 2.

35. *Rosenfeld v. New Jersey,* 408 U.S. 901 (1972); *Brown v. Oklahoma,* 408 U.S. 914 (1972).

36. *Cohen v. California,* 403 U.S. 15 (1971).

37. *FCC v. Pacifica Foundation,* 438 U.S. 726 (1968). In response, Congress and the FCC have considered several proposals to ban offensive speech except for hours when children are not likely to be listening. In 1993 a federal court of appeals ruled that a ban except from midnight until 6 A.M. was too broad. The court said it infringed on the rights of adults.

38. *Wilkinson v. Jones,* No. 86–1125, 1987.

39. *Cox v. Louisiana,* 379 U.S. 536 (1965).

40. *Collin v. Smith,* 447 F.Supp. 676 (N.D. Ill., 1978); *Collin v. Smith,* 578 F.2d 1197 (7th Cir., 1978).

41. *U.S. v. Schwimmer,* 279 U.S. 644 (1929).

42. *Frisby v. Schultz,* 101 L.Ed.2d 420 (1988).

43. *Hurley v. Irish-American Gay, Lesbian and Bisexual Group of Boston,* 132 L.Ed.2d 487 (1995).

44. *United States v. O'Brien,* 391 U.S. 367 (1968).

45. *Tinker v. Des Moines School District.*

46. *Smith v. Goguen,* 415 U.S. 566 (1974); *Spence v. Washington,* 418 U.S. 405 (1974).

47. *Texas v. Johnson,* 105 L.Ed.2d 342 (1989).

48. Walter Isaacson, "O'er the Land of the Free," *Time,* July 3, 1989, p. 15; "What Price Old Glory?" *Time,* July 10, 1989, p. 23.

49. *U.S. v. Eichman,* 110 L.Ed.2d 287 (1990).

50. David Halbertstam, *The Best and the Brightest* (Greenwich, Conn.: Fawcett, 1969), p. 769.

51. *New York Times v. United States,* 403 U.S. 713 (1971).

52. *Hazelwood School District v. Kuhlmeier,* 98 L.Ed.2d 592 (1988).

53. William Glaberson, "Censors and Finances Curb Student Press, Report Says," *New York Times,* May 1, 1994, p. 19. However, a bigger problem for city schools has been a lack of money to publish a paper at all.

54. Then radio and television stations used actors with Irish accents to dub the comments made by IRA members. In 1994 the government lifted the ban.

55. *Branzburg v. Hayes,* 408 U.S. 665 (1972).

56. *Cox Broadcasting v. Cohn,* 420 U.S. 469 (1975).

57. This was not a Supreme Court case.

58. *Time v. Hill,* 385 U.S. 374 (1967).

59. 376 U.S. 254.

60. Harry Kalven, "The *New York Times* Case: A Note on 'the Central Meaning of the First Amendment,' " *Supreme Court Review* 1964, p. 221.

61. *Monitor Patriot v. Roy,* 401 U.S. 265 (1971).

62. *Associated Press v. Walker,* 388 U.S. 130 (1967).

63. *Greenbelt Cooperative Publishing v. Bresler,* 398 U.S. 6 (1970).

64. *Curtis Publishing v. Butts,* 388 U.S. 130 (1967).

65. *Gertz v. Robert Welch,* 418 U.S. 323 (1974), and *Time v. Firestone,* 424 U.S. 448 (1976).

66. Eric Press, "Westmoreland Takes on CBS," *Newsweek,* October 22, 1984, p. 62.

67. William A. Henry III, "Libel Law: Good Intentions Gone Awry," *Time,* March 4, 1985, p. 94.

68. Ibid., p. 71.

69. *Roth v. United States,* 354 U.S. 476 (1957); *Manual Enterprises v. Day,* 370 U.S. 478 (1962); *Jacobellis v. Ohio,* 378 U.S. 184 (1964); *A Book Named "John Cleland's Memoirs of a Woman of Pleasure" v. Attorney General of Massachusetts,* 383 U.S. 413 (1966).

70. *Miller v. California,* 413 U.S. 15 (1973).

71. *Jenkins v. Georgia,* 418 U.S. 153 (1974).

72. "Project—An Empirical Inquiry into the Effects of *Miller v. California* on the Control of Obscenity," *New York University Law Review* 52 (October 1977), pp. 810–939.

73. *Hudnut v. American Booksellers Association,* 89 L.Ed.2d 291 (1986).

74. *Young v. American Mini Theaters,* 427 U.S. 50 (1976); *Renton v. Playtime Theaters,* 89 L.Ed.2d 29 (1986).

75. Richard Lacayo, "Give and Take on Pornography," *Time,* March 10, 1986, p. 67.

76. *Torcaso v. Watkins,* 367 U.S. 488 (1961).

77. *Pierce v. Society of Sisters,* 268 U.S. 510 (1925).

78. *Cooper v. Pate,* 378 U.S. 546 (1963); *Cruz v. Beto,* 405 U.S. 319 (1972).

79. *Reynolds v. United States,* 98 U.S. 145 (1879).

80. *Sherbert v. Verner,* 374 U.S. 398 (1963).

81. Although a congressional statute mandates "reasonable accommodation," the Court interpreted it so narrowly that it essentially requires only minimal accommodation. *T.W.A. v. Hardison,* 432 U.S. 63 (1977). For analysis see Gloria T. Beckley and Paul Burstein, "Religious Pluralism, Equal Opportunity, and the State," *Western Political Quarterly* 44 (March 1991), pp. 185–208. For a related case see *Thornton v. Caldor,* 86 L.Ed.2d. 557 (1985).

82. *Wisconsin v. Yoder,* 406 U.S. 205 (1972).

83. *United States v. Lee*, 455 U.S. 252 (1982).

84. *United States v. American Friends Service Committee*, 419 U.S. 7 (1974).

85. *Goldman v. Weinberger*, 475 U.S. 503 (1986); and *O'Lone v. Shabazz*, 482 U.S. 342 (1986).

86. *Employment Division v. Smith*, 108 L.Ed.2d 876 (1990).

87. Ruth Marcus, "One Nation, Under Court Rulings," *Washington Post National Weekly Edition*, March 18–24, 1991, p. 33.

88. William Lee Miller, "The Ghost of Freedoms Past," *Washington Post National Weekly Edition*, October 13, 1986, pp. 23–24.

89. *Church of Holy Trinity v. United States*, 143 U.S. 457 (1892).

90. *Engel v. Vitale*, 370 U.S. 421 (1962); *Abington School District v. Schempp*, 374 U.S. 203 (1963).

91. C. Herman Pritchett, *The American Constitution*, 3rd ed. (New York: McGraw-Hill, 1977), p. 406.

92. Kenneth M. Dolbeare and Phillip E. Hammond, *The School Prayer Decisions* (Chicago: University of Chicago Press, 1971).

93. Robert H. Birkby, "The Supreme Court and the Bible Belt," *Midwest Journal of Political Science* 10 (1966), pp. 304–15.

94. J. Gordon Melton, quoted in Jon D. Hull, "The State of the Union," *Time*, January 30, 1995, p. 55.

95. Peter Cushnie, "Letters," *Time*, October 15, 1984, p. 21.

96. *Wallace v. Jaffree*, 86 L.Ed.2d 29 (1985).

97. *Lee v. Weisman*, 120 L.Ed.2d 467 (1992).

98. *Jones v. Clear Creek*, 977 F.2d 965 (5th Cir., 1992).

99. Nancy E. Roman, "War over Graduation Prayers Waged by Mail," *Washington Times*, July 18, 1993, p. A6.

100. Anna Quindlen, "School Prayer: Substitutes for Substance, *Lincoln Journal* (New York Times), December 8, 1994.

101. Ibid.

102. James M. Wall, "Keep Faith Voluntarily," *Lincoln Journal-Star (Newsday)*, January 29, 1995.

103. *Widmar v. Vincent*, 454 U.S. 263 (1981). The law requires high schools that receive federal funds to allow meetings of students' religious, philosophical, or political groups if the schools permit meetings of any "noncurriculum" groups. Schools could prohibit meetings of all noncurriculum groups. Thus, a Salt Lake City high school banned all non-academic clubs rather than let students form a homosexual organization in 1996.

104. *Board of Education v. Mergens*, 110 S. Ct. 2356 (1990).

105. William Booth, "Bowing to the Desire for School Prayer," *Washington Post National Weekly Edition*, April 11–17, 1994, p. 32.

106. *Rosenberger v. University of Virginia*, 132 L.Ed.2d 700 (1995).

107. *Lynch v. Donnelly*, 79 L.Ed.2d 604 (1984).

108. *Allegheny County v. ACLU*, 106 L.Ed.2d 472 (1989).

109. *Epperson v. Arkansas*, 393 U.S. 97 (1968).

110. *Edwards v. Aguillard*, 482 U.S. 578 (1987).

111. *Everson v. Board of Education of Ewing Township*, 330 U.S. 1 (1947).

112. *Board of Education v. Allen*, 392 U.S. 236 (1968); *Meek v. Pittinger*, 421 U.S. 349 (1975).

113. *Lemon v. Kurtzman*, 403 U.S. 602 (1971); *Committee for Public Education and Religious Liberty v. Nyquist*, 413 U.S. 756 (1973).

114. Ibid; *Mueller v. Allen*, 463 U.S. 388 (1983).

115. *Tilton v. Richardson*, 403 U.S. 672 (1971); *Hunt v. McNair*, 413 U.S. 734 (1973); *Roemer v. Maryland Public Works Board*, 426 U.S. 736 (1976).

116. *Rochin v. California*, 342 U.S. 165 (1952).

117. Seymour Wishman, *Confessions of a Criminal Lawyer* (New York: Penguin Books, 1981), p. 16.

118. *Stein v. New York*, 346 U.S. 156 (1953).

119. *Weeks v. United States*, 232 U.S. 383 (1914).

120. 367 U.S. 643 (1961).

121. *United States v. Leon*, 82 L.Ed.2d 677 (1984); *Massachusetts v. Sheppard*, 82 L.Ed.2d 737 (1984).

122. *Olmstead v. United States*, 277 U.S. 438 (1928).

123. *Katz v. United States*, 389 U.S. 347 (1967).

124. *Brown v. Mississippi*, 297 U.S. 278 (1936).

125. *McNabb v. United States*, 318 U.S. 332 (1943); *Mallory v. United States*, 354 U.S. 449 (1957); *Spano v. New York*, 360 U.S. 315 (1959).

126. *Ashcraft v. Tennessee*, 322 U.S. 143 (1944).

127. *Rogers v. Richmond*, 365 U.S. 534 (1961); *Lynumn v. Illinois*, 372 U.S. 528 (1963).

128. 384 U.S. 436 (1966).

129. *Johnson v. Zerbst*, 304 U.S. 458 (1938).

130. *Powell v. Alabama*, 287 U.S. 45 (1932).

131. *Gideon v. Wainwright*, 372 U.S. 335 (1963).

132. *Argersinger v. Hamlin*, 407 U.S. 25 (1972); *Scott v. Illinois*, 440 U.S. 367 (1974).

133. *Douglas v. California*, 372 U.S. 353 (1953).

134. *Baldwin v. New York*, 339 U.S. 66 (1970); *Blanton v. North Las Vegas*, 489 U.S. 538 (1989).

135. *Duncan v. Louisiana*, 391 U.S. 145 (1968).

136. *Taylor v. Louisiana*, 419 U.S. 522 (1975).

137. *Swain v. Alabama*, 380 U.S. 202 (1965).

138. *Wilkerson v. Utah*, 99 U.S. 130 (1878); *In re Kemmler*, 136 U.S. 436 (1890).

139. *Furman v. Georgia*, 408 U.S. 238 (1972).

140. *Gregg v. Georgia*, 428 U.S. 153 (1976).

141. *Woodson v. North Carolina*, 428 U.S. 289 (1976).

142. *Coker v. Georgia*, 433 U.S. 584 (1977).

143. *McCleskey v. Kemp*, 95 L.Ed.2d 262 (1987).

144. *Brady v. United States*, 397 U.S. 742 (1970).

145. *Griswold v. Connecticut*, 38 U.S. 479 (1965).

146. For a rare exception, see *Time v. Hill*, 385 U.S. 374 (1967).

147. *Griswold v. Connecticut*.

148. *Eisenstadt v. Baird*, 405 U.S. 438 (1972); *Carey v. Population Services International*, 431 U.S. 678 (1977).

149. *Eisenstadt v. Baird*.

150. Lloyd Shearer, "This Woman and This Man Made History," *Parade* (1983).

151. Bob Woodward, "The Abortion Papers," *Washington Post National Weekly Edition*, January 30–February 5, 1989, pp. 24–25.

152. *Akron v. Akron Center for Reproductive Health*, 76 L.Ed.2d 687 (1983).

153. *Akron v. Akron Center for Reproductive Health; Sendak v. Arnold*, 50 L.Ed.2d, p. N (1976).

154. *Akron v. Akron Center for Reproductive Health*.

155. *Planned Parenthood of Missouri v. Danforth*, 428 U.S. 52 (1976).

156. "The Supreme Court Ignites a Fiery Abortion Debate," *Time*, July 4, 1977, pp. 6–8.

157. *Beal v. Doe*, 432 U.S. 438 (1977); *Maher v. Roe*, 432 U.S. 464 (1977); *Poelker v. Doe*, 432 U.S. 519 (1977); *Harris v. McRae* 448 U.S. 297 (1980).

158. Carlson, "Abortion's Hardest Cases," p. 25.

159. Benjamin Weiser, "The Abortion Dilemma Come to Life," *Washington Post National Weekly Edition*, December 25–31, 1989, pp. 10–11.

160. "Facts in Brief: Abortion in the United States," (New York. Alan Guttmacher Institute, 1992); Stephanie Meneimer, "Ending Illegitimacy as We Know It," *Washington Post National Weekly Edition*, January 17–23, 1994, p. 24.

161. *Webster v. Reproductive Health Services,* 106 L.Ed.2d 410 (1989).

162. 120 L.Ed.2d 674 (1992).

163. William Booth, "The Difference a Day Makes," *Washington Post National Weekly Edition,* November 23–29, 1992, p. 31.

164. *Hodgson v. Minnesota,* 111 L.Ed.2d 344 (1990); *Ohio v. Akron Center for Reproductive Health,* 111 L.Ed.2d 405 (1990).

165. Margaret Carlson, "Abortion's Hardest Cases," *Time,* July 2, 1990, p. 24.

166. "All Things Considered," National Public Radio, June 29, 1992.

167. Susan Estrich, "If Bork Were on the Court . . . Confirmation Battles Do Matter," *Lincoln Journal-Star* (Los Angeles Times), July 5, 1992.

168. Alissa Rubin, "The Abortion Wars are Far From Over," *Washington Post National Weekly Edition,* December 21–27, 1992, p. 25.

169. Sandra G. Boodman, "Bringing Abortion Home," *Washington Post National Weekly Edition,* April 19–25, 1993, p. 7.

170. Richard Lacayo, "One Doctor Down, How Many More?" *Time,* March 22, 1993, p. 47.

171. Douglas Frantz, "The Rhetoric of Terror," *Time,* March 27, 1995, pp. 48–51.

172. Dan Sewell, "Abortion War Requires Guns, Bulletproof Vests," *Lincoln Journal-Star* (AP), January 8, 1995.

173. Richard Lacayo, "Abortion: The Future is Already Here," *Time,* May 4, 1992, p. 29.

174. Cynthia Gorney, "Getting an Abortion in the Heartland," *Washington Post National Weekly Edition,* October 15–21, 1990, pp. 10–11.

175. Randall Terry, quoted in Anthony Lewis, "Pro-Life Zealots 'Outside the Bargain,'" *Lincoln Journal-Star (New York Times),* March 14, 1993; Joseph Scheidler, quoted in Boodman, "Bringing Abortion Home," p. 6.

176. David Von Drehle, "The Opinion that Ignited the Great Abortion War," *Washington Post National Weekly Edition,* April 11–17, 1994, p. 7.

177. Steven Waldman, "Attacking the Real 'Jane Roe,'" *Newsweek,* April 17, 1989, p. 22.

178. Ellen Goodman, "Poster Child for Ambivalence," *Lincoln Journal-Star,* August 17, 1995.

179. *Bowers v. Hardwick,* 92 L.Ed.2d 140 (1986); see also *Doe v. Commonwealth's Attorney,* 425 U.S. 901 (1976).

180. "Ex-Justice's Second Thoughts to Make Heated Debate Hotter," *Lincoln Sunday Journal-Star,* October 28, 1990.

181. *Romer v. Evans,* 134 L.Ed.2d 855 (1996).

182. President Clinton also ordered the FBI to end its policy that made it difficult for homosexuals to be hired.

183. The policy originally was based on psychoanalytic theory, which considered homosexuality a mental illness. This conclusion was rejected by the American Psychiatric Association some years later.

184. "Critics Cite Delay as Illustrating Problem in Gay Policy," *Lincoln Journal* (AP), March 22, 1995.

185. "Group Says Gays Worse Off in Military since New Policy," *Lincoln Journal-Star* (AP), February 28, 1996.

186. Israel drafts every 18-year-old man and woman. It does consider homosexuality in the assignment of jobs. Gays who admit their orientation to their superiors confidentially are restricted from security-sensitive jobs for fear they are susceptible to blackmail. But gays who acknowledge their orientation openly could not be blackmailed, so they are treated the same as straights. Randy Shilts, "What's Fair in Love and War," *Newsweek,* February 1, 1993, pp. 58–59; Eric Konigsberg, "Gays in Arms," *Washington Monthly,* November 1992, pp. 10–13; "Canada Had No Problems Lifting its Military Gay Ban," *Lincoln Journal-Star* (AP), January 31, 1993. See also: Randy Shilts, *Conduct Unbecoming: Gays and Lesbians in the U.S. Military* (New York: St. Martin's, 1993).

187. Al Kamen, "When Exactly Does Life End?" *Washington Post National Weekly Edition,* September 18–24, 1989, p. 31; Alain L. Sanders, "Whose Right to Die?" *Time,* December 11, 1989, p. 80.

188. *Cruzan v. Missouri Health Department,* 111 L.Ed.2d 224 (1990).

189. Malcolm Gladwell, "Women in Right-To-Die Case Succumbs," *Washington Post,* December 27, 1990, p. A3.

190. Otto Friedrich, "A Limited Right to Die," *Time,* July 9, 1990, p. 59.

191. *Stone v. Powell,* 428 U.S. 465 (1976).

192. 124 L.Ed. 2d 472 (1993).

15 Civil Rights

You Are There

Compromise or Continue to Fight?

You are Fannie Lou Hamer, a leader of the Mississippi Freedom Democratic Party (MFDP), a group of mostly African Americans challenging the seating of the regular state Democratic Party delegates at the national Democratic Party Convention in 1964. You have to decide whether to accept a compromise offered by national party officials.

You have come a long way.[1] You were born the youngest in a family of 20 children in the small town of Ruleville, located in the heart of the Mississippi Delta. Like many other African Americans, your parents were sharecroppers, picking cotton on a white family's plantation in exchange for housing and a little money for food.[2] At the age of 6, after the owner enticed you with treats from the plantation store, you began picking cotton too.

You were resigned to your life but never satisfied with it because you had little control. For instance, the owner of the house you lived in refused to fix the indoor toilet, saying you did not need it. When you cleaned his house, you discovered that his family had a separate bathroom for their dog. And when you entered the hospital to have a small tumor removed, you were sterilized without your knowledge or permission.

So when the civil rights movement reached Ruleville in 1962, you were ready. You were 44 years old, yet you could not vote. At a meeting at church, a leader of the Student Non-Violent Coordinating Committee (SNCC) and a minister with Martin Luther King's Southern Christian Leadership Conference (SCLC) spoke. When they asked who would try to register to vote, you raised your hand. Two weeks later you and 17 others were driven to the county seat. You were confronted by many people, you recalled, "and some of them looked like the Beverly Hillbillies . . . but they wasn't kidding down there; they had on, you know, cowboy hats and they had guns; they had dogs."[3] The registrar pulled out a copy of the state constitution and asked you to explain one section. You could not, so he would not register you.

On the way back to Ruleville, the civil rights workers' bus was stopped and the driver was arrested. The charge? The bus was too yellow. (Police said it looked like a school bus.) Once home, the owner of the plantation where you had toiled for 18 years told you to go back and take your name off the registration forms or leave the plantation. You told him, "I didn't go down there to register for you. I went down to register for myself."[4] You left your house on the plantation and moved in with friends in town (and after the cotton season, your husband also was evicted from the plantation).

It was clear that getting your rights would not be easy. But you are deeply religious, and you told people, "Whether I want to do it or not, I got to. This is my calling. This is my mission."[5]

With help from the SNCC workers, you studied the state constitution and several months later returned to register again. This time you passed the "test." At the next election, however, you were not allowed to vote because you had not paid poll taxes in the previous years when you were not allowed to register or vote.

CONTINUED

Many Americans have given up their hopes and efforts to desegregate the schools.

OUTLINE

Race Discrimination

Discrimination Against African Americans

Overcoming Discrimination Against African Americans

Continuing Discrimination Against African Americans

Discrimination Against Hispanics

Discrimination Against Native Americans

Sex Discrimination

Discrimination Against Women

Discrimination Against Men

Affirmative Action

Are Civil Rights Enough?

Conclusion: Is Government Responsive in Granting Civil Rights?

Fannie Lou Hamer leads marchers in song.

You were determined to get your right to vote and to help others get theirs. You attended an SCLC training course. While returning on the bus, you and others in the group sat at a whites-only lunch counter in the station and then complained when a white girl was moved ahead of you in the line. The driver explained that "niggers are not to be in front of the line."[6] When the bus reached the next town, the members of your group were arrested and severely beaten. For the rest of your life, you would be plagued by ailments from this beating.[7]

Yet you continued. You organized throughout the Delta, inspiring your neighbors to be strong and mocking those, such as the "chicken-eating preachers," who were less courageous. You traveled throughout the country to help raise funds for civil rights organizations. Although you are short and overweight and you have little education, you are a charismatic figure in the movement—a rousing speaker, perhaps more than anyone except King, and you are a beautiful singer. After your speeches, you lead the audience in religious hymns and movement songs, breaking down the barriers between strangers.

"We're tired of all this beatin', we're tired of takin' this," you say to anyone who will listen. "All my life I've been sick and tired. Now I'm sick and tired of being sick and tired."[8]

Now, in 1964, you were permitted to vote for the first time, but most blacks still are prevented from voting, and all are prevented from participating in the regular Democratic Party in Mississippi. The state party, whose platform endorses segregation, controls the state legislature, whose laws make voting by blacks nearly impossible. So you and a few others decided to organize your own party.[9]

The Freedom Democrats' immediate goal is to challenge the regular Democrats chosen as delegates to the national convention this year. The Freedom Democrats' claim is that the delegates are unlawful representatives of the state because they were chosen by unlawful means.

The MFDP held its own precinct, county, and state conventions, and allowed whites as well as blacks to participate. You were elected as one of the delegates.

In August your upstart delegation loaded onto buses for the long trip to Atlantic City, New Jersey. Yet when you arrived you learned that national party officials, though sympathetic to your cause, did not want you to challenge the regular delegation.

President Johnson, who took office after President Kennedy was assassinated, is running for his own term. Although a southerner—a Texan—he favors civil rights. He plans to tap Minnesota Senator Hubert Humphrey as his running mate. At the 1948 convention Humphrey gained attention by calling for government to open the door to people of all races. His speech caused many white southerners to walk out in protest.

Johnson will face the Republican, Arizona Senator Barry Goldwater, whose positions are much closer to most white southerners' views. The Democrats are worried, with the civil rights movement and the combination of Humphrey's liberalism and Goldwater's conservatism, that southerners will not vote solidly Democratic this year as they have historically. Now Johnson and other officials are vexed that a challenge by the MFDP, even if unsuccessful, would attract publicity that would upset southerners still more.

So Johnson sent word that he might not pick Humphrey if the Freedom Democrats persisted. Clearly, you would prefer Humphrey to anyone else mentioned as a possible vice presidential candidate, and you would prefer Johnson to Goldwater.

If you gave up your challenge, officials said you could sit as honored guests in the balcony. You rejected this offer; it was too much like the segregated seating in the movie theaters back home. Then officials made their final proposal: You could have two seats as at-large delegates. The regular delegates could keep their seats but would have to pledge loyalty to the national ticket. (It was likely that many would refuse and would leave.) Further, officials promised that in the future delegates would not be seated if their state party did not allow full participation by blacks.

Do you accept this compromise? Some national civil rights leaders urge you to. They have stressed that you are now involved in politics, not protest, and that politics is the art of compromise.[10]

Civil rights refers to equality of rights for persons regardless of their race, sex, or ethnic background. The Declaration of Independence proclaimed that "all men are created equal." The author, Thomas Jefferson, knew all men were not created equal in many respects, but he sought to emphasize that they should be considered equal in rights and equal before the law. This represented a break with England where rigid classes with unequal rights existed; nobles had more rights than commoners. The Declaration's promise did not include nonwhites or women, however. Thus, although colonial Americans advocated equality, they envisioned it only for white men. Others gradually gained more equality, but the Declaration's promise remains unfulfilled for some.

Virtually all minority groups in this country have suffered discrimination. Some religious groups, such as Catholics and Jews, and many ethnic groups, such as the Irish, Italians, and Poles, have made enormous progress against discrimination, but other groups have not. This chapter focuses on the struggle by racial minorities and women to overcome discrimination.

➤Race Discrimination

African Americans, Hispanics, and Native Americans all have endured and continue to face much discrimination.

Discrimination Against African Americans

Slavery

The first blacks came to America in 1619, just 12 years after the first whites. The blacks, like many whites, initially came as indentured servants. In exchange for passage across the ocean, they were bound to an employer, usually for 4 to 7 years, and then freed. But later in the seventeenth century, the colonies passed laws requiring blacks and their children to be slaves for life. Once slavery was established, the slave trade flourished, especially in the South.

As a result of compromises between northern and southern states, the Constitution accepted slavery. It allowed the importation of slaves until 1808, when Congress could bar further importation, and it required the return of escaped slaves to their owners.

Shortly after ratification of the Constitution, northern states abolished slavery. In 1808 Congress barred the importation of slaves but did not halt the practice of slavery in the South. Slavery became increasingly controversial, and abolitionists called for its end.

The Supreme Court tried to quell the antislavery sentiment in the **Dred Scott case** in 1857.[11] Dred Scott, a slave who lived in Missouri, was taken by his owner to the free state of Illinois and the free territory of Wisconsin and, after five years, was returned to Missouri. The owner died and passed title to his wife, who moved but left Scott in the care of people in Missouri. They opposed slavery and arranged to have Scott sue his owner for his freedom. They argued that Scott's time in a free state and a free territory made him a free man even though he was brought back to a slave state. The owner, also opposed to slavery, had the authority to free Scott, so the purpose of the suit was not to win his freedom. Rather, she and others sought a major court decision to keep slavery out of the territories.

In this infamous case, Chief Justice Roger Taney stated that no blacks, whether slave or free, were citizens, and that they were "so far inferior that they had no rights which the white man was bound to

Dred Scott.

respect." Taney could have stopped here—if Scott was not a citizen, he could not sue in federal court— but Taney continued. He declared that Congress had no power to control slavery in the territories. This meant that slavery could extend into the territories Congress already had declared free. It also raised the possibility that states could not control slavery within their borders.[12]

By this time, slavery had become the hottest controversy in American politics, and this decision fanned the flames. It provoked vehement opposition in the North and prompted further polarization, which eventually led to the Civil War. Meanwhile, Scott got his freedom from his owner.

The North's victory in the Civil War gave force to President Lincoln's Emancipation Proclamation ending slavery. But blacks would find short-lived solace.

Civil War Amendments and Reconstruction

After the war, Congress passed and the states ratified three constitutional amendments. The Thirteenth prohibited slavery. (Mississippi became the last state to ratify the amendment—in 1995.) The Fourteenth granted citizenship to blacks, thus overruling the Dred Scott decision, and also granted "equal protection of the laws" and "due process of law." The Fifteenth provided the right to vote for black men. The **equal protection clause** eventually would become the primary guarantee that government would treat people equally.

Congress also passed a series of civil rights acts to reverse the "Black Codes" that southern states had enacted to deny the newly freed slaves legal rights. These civil rights acts allowed blacks to buy, own, and sell property; to make contracts; to sue; and to be witnesses and jurors in court. They also allowed blacks to use public transportation, such as railroads and steamboats, and to patronize hotels and theaters.[13]

Even so, most freed blacks faced bleak conditions. Congress rejected proposals to break up plantations and give former slaves "40 acres and a mule" or to provide aid to establish schools. Without land or education, they had to work for their former masters as hired hands or sharecroppers. Their status was not much better than it had been. Landowners designed a system to keep them dependent. They allowed sharecroppers to sell half their crop and keep the proceeds, but they paid so little, regardless of how hard the farmers worked, that the families had to borrow to tide them over the winter. The next year they had to work for the landowner to pay off their debt. The following year the cycle continued. And, lacking education, most sharecroppers did not keep records of how much they owed and how much the landowner owed them, and many were cheated.

During the period of Reconstruction, the Union army enforced the new amendments and acts. While the army occupied the South, military commanders established procedures to register voters, including the newly freed slaves; hold elections; and ratify the Fourteenth Amendment. The commanders also started schools for children of the newly freed slaves. But in state after state, the South resisted and eventually the North capitulated. After a decade, the two regions struck a deal to end what was left of Reconstruction. The 1876 presidential election between Republican Rutherford Hayes and Democrat Samuel Tilden was disputed in some states. To resolve the dispute, Republicans, most of whom were northerners, and Democrats, many of whom were southerners, agreed to a compromise: Hayes would be named president, and the remaining Union troops would be removed from the South.

Segregation

In both the South and North, blacks came to be segregated from whites.

SEGREGATION IN THE SOUTH The reconciliation between Republicans and Democrats—northerners and southerners—was effected at the expense of blacks. Removing the troops enabled the South to govern itself again, and this enabled the South to reduce blacks to near-slave status.

Slavery itself kept blacks down, and segregation would have been inconvenient when blacks and whites needed to live and work near each other. There was no residential segregation—not in rural areas, where former slaves' shacks were intermixed with plantation houses, and not in urban areas, where few blocks were solidly black. But after slavery, southerners established segregation as another way to keep blacks down. Initially, they did so haphazardly—one law here, another there. By the early 1900s, however, there was a pervasive pattern of **Jim Crow laws.**

Jim Crow laws segregated just about everything. Some segregated blocks within neighborhoods, others neighborhoods within cities. Laws in some small

American Diversity

Black Masters

Although most slaveowners were white, some were black. William Ellison of South Carolina was one. Born a slave, he bought his freedom and then his family's by building and repairing cotton gins. Over time he earned enough to buy slaves and operate a plantation. With 60 slaves, Ellison ranked in the top 1% of all slaveholders, black or white.

Ellison was unusual, but he was not unique. In Charleston, South Carolina, alone, more than 100 African Americans owned slaves in 1860. Most, however, owned fewer than 4.

Although part of the slave-owning class, black slaveholders were not much more acceptable to whites. Ellison's family was granted a pew on the main floor of the local Episcopal church, but they had to be on guard at all times. Failure to maintain the norms of black-white relations—acting deferentially—could mean instant punishment. And as the Civil War approached, free blacks, even slaveholders, were seen as a growing threat by whites trying to preserve the established order. Harsher legislation regulated their lives. For example, they had to have a white "guardian" to vouch for their character, and they had to carry special papers to show their free status. Without these papers, they could be sold back into slavery.

Some black slaveowners showed little sign of shared concerns with black slaves. Indeed, Ellison freed none of his slaves.

Source: Michael P. Johnson and James L. Roark, *Black Masters* (New York: W. W. Norton, 1984).

towns excluded blacks altogether. Some did so explicitly; others by setting curfews that required blacks to be off the streets by 10 P.M. Laws also segregated schools, which blacks had been allowed to attend during Reconstruction, and even textbooks (black schools' texts had to be stored separately from white schools' books). Many laws segregated public accommodations, such as hotels, restaurants, bars, and transportation. At first they required the races to sit in separate sections of streetcars; eventually they required them to sit in separate cars; finally they also forced them to sit in separate sections of waiting rooms. They segregated parks, sporting events, and circuses. Laws segregated black and white checkers players in Birmingham and established districts for black and white prostitutes in New Orleans. They segregated drinking fountains, restrooms, ticket windows, entrances, and exits. They segregated the races in prisons and in hospitals and in homes for the blind. They even segregated the races in death—in morgues, funeral homes, and cemeteries.

Blacks were forced to defer to whites in all informal settings as well, and failure to do so could mean punishment or even death. They were "humiliated by a thousand daily reminders of their subordination."[14]

Meanwhile, northern leaders, who had championed the cause of the slaves before and during the Civil War, abandoned blacks a decade after the war; Congress did not pass new laws, presidents did not enforce existing laws, and the Supreme Court gutted the constitutional amendments and civil rights acts. All acquiesced in "the southern way."

The Supreme Court struck down the civil rights act allowing blacks to use public accommodations, including transportation, hotels, and theaters.[15] Where the Fourteenth Amendment said that "no state" shall deny equal protection, the Court interpreted this to mean that "no government" shall, but private individuals—owners of transportation, hotels, and theaters—could. The Court's interpretation might seem plausible, but it was clearly contrary to Congress's intent.[16]

Then the Court upheld segregation. Louisiana passed "an Act to promote the comfort of passengers," which mandated separate accommodations in trains. New Orleans black leaders sponsored a case to test the act's constitutionality. Homer Adolph Plessy bought a ticket and sat in the white car. When the conductor ordered him to move to the black car, Plessy refused. He maintained that the act was unconstitutional under the Fourteenth Amendment. In ***Plessy v. Ferguson*** in 1896, the court disagreed, claiming that the act was not a denial of equal protection because it provided equal accommodations.[17] Thus the Court established the **separate-but-equal doctrine,** which allowed separate facilities if they were equal. Of course, government required separate facilities only because it thought the races were not equal, but the Court brazenly commented that the act did not stamp "the colored race with a badge of inferiority" unless "the colored race chooses to put that construction on it." Only Justice John Harlan, a former Kentucky slaveholder, dissented: "Our Constitution is color-blind, and neither knows nor tolerates classes among citizens."

Three years later the Court accepted segregation in schools.[18] A Georgia school board turned a black high school into a black elementary school. Although the board did not establish a new high school for blacks or allow them to attend the ones for whites, the Court did not object. This set a pattern in which separate but equal meant separation but not equality.

SEGREGATION IN THE NORTH Although Jim Crow laws were not as pervasive in the North as in the South, northerners imitated southerners to the point where one writer proclaimed, "The North has surrendered!"[19]

Job opportunities were better in the North. Southern blacks were sharecropping—by 1930 80% of those who farmed were still working somebody else's land[20]—and northern factories were offering jobs. Between 1915 and 1940 more than a million southern blacks headed north in the "Great Migration." But they were forced to live in black ghettos because they could not afford better housing and because they could not escape discrimination in the North, either.

Denial of the Right to Vote

With the adoption of the Fifteenth Amendment, many blacks voted and even elected fellow blacks to office during Reconstruction, but southern states began to disfranchise them in the 1890s (as explained in Chapter 7). Thus, they were unable to elect black representatives or even pressure white officials to oppose segregation.

Violence

To solidify their control, whites engaged in sporadic violence against African Americans. In the 1880s and 1890s, whites lynched about 100 blacks a year. In the 1900s vigilante "justice" continued (Table 1). For example, a mob in Livermore, Kentucky, dragged a black man accused of murdering a white man into a

Lynching occurred not only in the South but also in northern cities such as Marion, Indiana, in 1930.

TABLE 1 Why Whites Lynched Blacks in 1907

Whites gave the following reasons for lynching blacks, who may or may not have committed these acts.	Number
Murder	5
Attempted murder	5
Manslaughter	10
Rape	9
Attempted rape	11
Burglary	3
Harboring a fugitive	1
Theft of 75¢	1
Having debt of $3	2
Being victor over white man in fight	1
Insulting white man	1
Talking to white girls on telephone	1
Being wife or son of rapist	2
Being father of boy who "jostled" white women	1
Expressing sympathy for victim of mob	3
	56

Source: Adapted from Ray Stannard Baker, *Following the Color Line* (New York: Harper & Row, 1964), pp. 176-77.

theater. The ringleaders charged admission and hanged the man. Then they permitted the audience to shoot at the swinging body—those in the balcony could fire once; those in the better seats could empty their revolvers.[21] In 1919 there were 25 race riots in six months. White mobs took over cities in the North and South, burning black neighborhoods and terrorizing black residents for days on end.[22]

The Ku Klux Klan, which began during Reconstruction and started up again in 1915, played a major role in inflaming prejudice and terrorizing blacks. It was strong enough to dominate many southern towns and even the state governments of Oklahoma and Texas. It also made inroads into some northern states.

Federal officials said such violence was a state problem—presidents refused to speak out and Congress refused to pass legislation making lynching a federal offense—yet state officials did nothing.

For at least the first third of the twentieth century, white supremacy reigned—in the southern states, the border states, and many of the northern states. It also pervaded the nation's capital, where President Woodrow Wilson instituted segregation in the federal government.[23]

Overcoming Discrimination Against African Americans

African Americans fought white supremacy primarily in three arenas—the courts, the streets, and Congress. In general, they fought in the courts first and Congress last, although as they gained momentum they increasingly fought in all three arenas at once.

The Movement in the Courts

The first strategy was to convince the Supreme Court to overturn the separate-but-equal doctrine of *Plessy v. Ferguson*.

THE NAACP In response to white violence, a group of blacks and whites founded the **NAACP,** the National Association for the Advancement of Colored People, in 1909. In its first two decades, it was led by W. E. B. DuBois, a black sociologist. In time it became the major organization fighting for blacks' civil rights.

Frustrated by presidential and congressional inaction and its own lack of power to force action, the NAACP devised a winning strategy—to converge on the federal courts, which were less subject to pressures from the majority. The association assembled a cadre of lawyers, mainly from Howard University Law School, a black university in Washington, D.C., to bring lawsuits attacking segregation and the denial of the right to vote. In 1915 they persuaded the Supreme Court to strike down the grandfather clause (which exempted persons whose ancestors could vote from the literacy test),[24] and two years later they convinced the court to invalidate laws prescribing residential segregation.[25] But the Court continued to allow most devices to disfranchise blacks and most efforts to segregate.

In 1938 the NAACP chose a 30 year-old attorney, Thurgood Marshall, to head its litigation arm.[26] In the next two decades, presidents appointed more liberals to the Supreme Court. These two developments led to the NAACP's success in the courts.

DESEGREGATION OF SCHOOLS Seventeen states and the District of Columbia segregated their schools (and four other states allowed it by local option). The states gave white students better facilities and paid white teachers more. Overall, they spent from 2 to 10 times more on white schools than on black ones.[27] Few of these states had graduate schools for blacks: As late as 1950 they had 15 engineering schools, 14 medical schools, and 5 dental schools for whites, and none for blacks; they had 16 law schools for whites and 5 for blacks.

The NAACP's tactics were first to show that "separate but equal" really resulted in unequal schools and then to attack "separate but equal" head on, arguing that it led to unequal status.

The NAACP began by challenging segregation in graduate schools. Missouri provided no black law school but offered to reimburse blacks who went to out-of-state law schools. In 1938 the Supreme Court said the state had to provide a black law school.[28] Texas established a black law school clearly inferior to the white law school at the University of Texas in size of faculty, student body, library, and opportunities for students to specialize. In 1950 the Court said the black school had to be substantially equal to the white school.[29] Oklahoma allowed a black student to attend the white graduate school at the University of Oklahoma but designated a separate section of the classroom, library, and cafeteria for the student. The court said this too was inadequate, because it deprived the student of the exchange of views with fellow students necessary for education.[30] The Court did not invalidate the separate-but-equal doctrine in these decisions, but it made segregation almost impossible to implement in graduate schools.

The NAACP continued by challenging segregation in grade schools and high schools. Marshall filed suits in two southern states, one border state, one northern state, and the District of Columbia. The suit in the northern state was brought against Topeka, Kansas, where Linda Brown could not attend the school just 4 blocks from her home because it was a white school. Instead, she had to go to a school 21 blocks away.

When the cases reached the Supreme Court, President Eisenhower pressured his appointee, Chief Justice Earl Warren, to rule in favor of segregation. Eisenhower invited Warren and the attorney for the states to the White House for dinner. When the conversation turned to the segregationists, Eisenhower said, "These are not bad people. All they are concerned about is to see that their sweet little girls are not required to sit in schools alongside some big overgrown Negroes."[31]

However, Warren not only voted against segregation but persuaded other justices, some of whom had supported segregation, to vote against it too.

In the landmark case of ***Brown v. Board of Education*** in 1954, the Court ruled unanimously that school segregation violated the Fourteenth Amendment's equal protection clause.[32] In the opinion, Warren asserted that separate but equal not only resulted in unequal schools but was inherently unequal because it made black children feel inferior. In overruling the *Plessy* doctrine, the Court showed how revolutionary the equal protection clause was—or could be interpreted to be. The Court required the segregated states to change their way of life to a degree unprecedented in American history.

After overturning laws requiring segregation in schools, the court overruled laws mandating segrega-

Linda Brown's kindergarten class. Brown is in the back row, fourth from right.

Outside the Supreme Court, NAACP attorneys George E. C. Hayes, Thurgood Marshall, and James M. Nabrit celebrate the *Brown v. Board of Education* decision.

tion in such places as public parks, golf courses, swimming pools, auditoriums, courtrooms, and jails.[33]

In *Brown* the Court ordered schools to desegregate "with all deliberate speed."[34] This was a compromise between those who wanted schools to do so immediately and those who wanted schools to do so gradually.[35] The ambiguity of the phrase, however, allowed them to take years to desegregate. The ruling prompted much deliberation but little speed.

The South engaged in massive resistance. The Court needed help from the other branches of government to implement its ruling but failed to get any cooperation for some time. President Eisenhower, who had desegregated the military and also public schools and public facilities in Washington, D.C., was reluctant to tell the states to change. In fact, he joined their representatives in Congress in criticizing the decision. With his position and popularity, the president could have speeded implementation by speaking out in support of the decision, yet he did not do so for more than three years. When nine black students tried to attend a white high school under a desegregation plan in Little Rock, Arkansas, the governor's and state legislature's inflammatory rhetoric against desegregation had encouraged local citizens to take the law into their own hands. Finally President Eisenhower acted; he sent federal troops and federalized the state's national guard to quell the riot.

A few years later President Kennedy used federal marshals and paratroopers to quell violence after the governor of Mississippi blocked the door to keep James Meredith from registering at the University of Mississippi. Kennedy again used force when the governor of Alabama, George Wallace, proclaiming "segregation now, segregation tomorrow, segregation forever," blocked the door to keep blacks from enrolling at the University of Alabama.

After outright defiance, some states attempted to circumvent the ruling by shutting down their public schools and providing tuition grants for students to use at private schools, which at the time could segregate. They also provided other forms of aid, such as textbooks and public recreation facilities, for private schools. These efforts hindered desegregation and hurt black education because the black communities seldom had the resources to establish their own schools.

The states also tried less blatant schemes, such as "freedom of choice" plans that allowed students to choose the school they wanted to attend. Of course, virtually no whites chose a black school, and, due to strong pressure, few blacks chose a white school. The idea was to achieve desegregation on paper, or token desegregation in practice, in order to avoid real desegregation. But the Court rebuffed these schemes and even forbade discrimination by private schools.[36]

The Court's firm support gave blacks hope. Thurgood Marshall said, "Chief Justice Warren became the image [of the Court] that allowed the poor Negro sharecropper to say, 'Kick me around Mr. Sheriff, kick me around Mr. County Judge, kick me around Supreme Court of my state, but there's one person I can rely on.' "[37]

Nevertheless, progress was excruciatingly slow. If a school district was segregated, a group like the NAACP had to run the risks and spend the time and money to bring a suit in a federal district court. Judges in these courts reflected the views of the state or local political establishment they came from, so the suit might not be successful. If it was, the school board had to prepare a desegregation plan. Members of the school board reflected the views of the community and the pressures from the segregationists, so the plan might not be adequate. If it was, segregationists would challenge it in a federal district court. If the court upheld the plan, segregationists would appeal to a federal court of appeals. Judges in these courts came from the South, and they sat in Richmond and New Orleans. However, they were not as tied to the state or local political establishment, and they usually decided against the segregationists. But then segregationists could appeal to the Supreme Court. Segregationists knew they would lose sooner or later. But the process took several years, so they were able to delay the inevitable.

Thus, segregationists tried to resist, then to evade, and finally to delay. In this they succeeded. By 1964, a decade after *Brown,* 98% of all black children in the South still attended all-black schools.[38]

By this time, the mood in Congress had changed. Congress passed the Civil Rights Act of 1964, which, among other things, cut off federal aid to school districts that continued to segregate. The following year it passed the first major program providing federal aid to education. This was the carrot at the end of the stick: School districts began to comply to get the federal money.

Finally, by 1970 only 14% of all black children in the South still attended all-black schools. Of course, some went to mostly black schools. Even so, the change was dramatic. Since then, though, many white students have left the public schools for private schools, causing creeping resegregation of the public schools.

BUSING *Brown* and related rulings addressed **de jure segregation**—segregation enforced by law. This segregation can be attacked by striking down the law. *Brown* did not address **de facto segregation**—segregation based on residential patterns—typical of northern cities and large southern cities, where most blacks live in black neighborhoods and most whites live in white neighborhoods. Students attend neighborhood schools, which are mostly black or mostly white. This segregation is much more intractable because it does not stem primarily from a law, so it cannot be eliminated by striking down a law.

Civil rights groups proposed busing some black children to schools in white neighborhoods and some white children to schools in black neighborhoods. They hoped to improve black children's education, their self-confidence and aspirations, and, eventually, their college and career opportunities. They also hoped to improve black and white children's ability to get along together.

Although Chief Justice Warren retired and President Nixon, who opposed busing, appointed Warren Burger to be chief justice, the Supreme Court unanimously upheld busing in Charlotte, North Carolina, in 1971.[39] The Court ruled that busing is appropriate within school districts—ordinarily cities—where there is a history of intentional segregation. The Court brushed off complaints that busing would be too burdensome for students. It noted that 39% of the public school students in the country were already bused for reasons other than desegregation.

Following this decision, the Court upheld busing in northern cities—Columbus, Dayton, and Denver.[40] Although these cities had mostly de facto segregation, school officials had located schools and assigned students in ways that perpetuated this segregation.

But no matter how extensive busing is within a city, it still cannot desegregate most large cities, where blacks and other minorities now are in the majority. There are not enough whites to desegregate the schools, largely because of "white flight" from the city and its public schools. After World War II, affluent whites began to leave central cities for suburbs, and after the courts upheld busing, even more did so. In addition, others transferred their children out of public and into private schools.

Consequently, civil rights groups proposed busing some black children from the city to the suburbs and some white children from the suburbs to the city. This would provide enough of both races to achieve balance in both places.

The Burger Court rejected this proposal by a five to four vote in 1974.[41] It said busing between Detroit and its suburbs was not necessary, although Detroit schools were 70% black and suburban schools were 80% white. The Court said busing is not appropriate between school districts unless there is evidence of intentional segregation in both the city and its suburbs. Otherwise, such extensive busing would require too long rides for students and too much coordination by administrators. Although there has been intentional segregtion by many cities and their suburbs,[42] the evidence is not as clear as that of the de jure segregation by southern states at the time of *Brown,* so it is difficult to demonstrate a pattern by the cities and their multiple suburbs to the extent expected by the judges. Consequently, the Court's ruling makes busing between cities and suburbs much less likely than within the cities alone.

Thurgood Marshall, now on the Court, dissented and predicted that the ruling would allow "our great metropolitan areas to be divided up each into two cities—one white, the other black." Indeed, the ruling did contribute to this result. Only atypical metropolitan areas, such as Louisville, Kentucky, where the city and its suburbs formed a single school district, achieved significant desegregation.

During these years relatively few students were bused for desegregation—4% in one typical year. These students were far fewer than those bused, at public expense, to segregated public and private schools.[43]

Nevertheless, busing ran up against a wall of public opinion. White parents criticized the courts sharply. Their reaction stemmed from prejudice against blacks; bias against poor persons; fear of the crime in inner city schools; worry about the quality of inner city schools; and desire for the convenience of neighborhood schools. Their reaction also arose from resentment against courts for telling local governments what to do. In addition, some black parents opposed busing because of the disruption in their children's lives and the hostility of the white students in their children's new schools. Black parents also resented the implication that their children could learn only if sitting next to white children. But other black parents favored busing because of the opportunity for their children to go to better schools.

Opponents, especially white parents, were so strident that many people assumed busing could not work. In Charlotte, where the Supreme Court first upheld busing, it suffered a rocky start; each of the 10 high schools closed because of racial fighting. But after a period of adjustment, busing won the support of most students and parents.[44] Studies of some other cities, particularly small- and medium-size cities, show similar results.[45]

Busing had less success in big cities. It apparently prompted an increase in white flight, with the result that there are fewer white students to balance enrollments and fewer middle class students to provide stability in the cities' schools. It also contributed to the deterioration of minority communities, because it diminished the neighborhood schools that had helped define and hold together these communities.[46]

Busing, only one part of the education equation, could not accomplish all that civil rights groups and federal judges expected—or at least hoped—it could. Busing could not compensate for massive residential segregation. It could not overcome students' poverty or their parents' lack of involvement in their education. Thus, studies of the performance of minority children bused to white schools show disappointing, mixed results.

Busing led to rioting in some cities, such as Boston. Here protesters assault a black man in 1976.

In 1991 the Rehnquist Court reduced judicial pressure for even the limited busing that was occurring.[47] The majority said busing was "intended as a temporary measure" and districts could stop when "the vestiges of past discrimination had been eliminated to the extent practicable."

As an alternative to busing, some districts established magnet schools, which receive extra resources and offer special programs, often in sciences, languages, or performing arts. These schools are located in the inner city but are designed to attract whites from throughout the city as well as blacks from the neighborhood. Magnet plans can produce some integrated schools, but they can enroll only a fraction of a city's students. These schools are expensive, and they cannot offset the imbalance in the number of whites and blacks in the city's system. Thus, most students continue to attend segregated schools.

A federal district court in Kansas City, Missouri, tried to address this problem by ordering officials to draw up a magnet plan that would lure whites from the suburbs as well as blacks in the city. The plan was ambitious and, of course, expensive—it required funding from the state in addition to the district—and it was challenged in court. In 1995 the Rehnquist Court invalidated it. The majority said federal judges could not order state or local officials to pay for school improvements to attract suburban students.[48]

The Rehnquist Court's rulings came at a time when more minoities began to question the goal of integration. Their communities have deteriorated so much that many minorities voice greater concern about improving the quality and safety of their schools than about sending their children to other schools or bringing white children to their schools.[49]

Martin Luther King, under arrest in 1958.

The Movement in the Streets

After the NAACP's early successes in the courts, other blacks, and some whites, took the fight to the streets. Their bold efforts gave birth to the modern civil rights movement.

The movement began in Montgomery, Alabama, in 1955, when Rosa Parks refused to move to the back of the bus. Her refusal and arrest prompted blacks to boycott city buses. For their leader they chose a young Baptist minister, Dr. Martin Luther King, Jr. The boycott catapulted the movement and King to national attention (as explained in Chapter 5).

King was the first charismatic leader of the movement. He formed the Southern Christian Leadership Conference (SCLC) of black clergy and adopted the tactics of Mahatma Gandhi, who had led the movement to free India from the British. The tactics included direct action, such as demonstrations and marches, and civil disobedience—intentional and public disobedience of laws considered unjust. The tactics were based on nonviolence, even when confronted with violence. The strategy was designed to draw support from whites by contrasting the morality of the movement's position with the immorality of the discrimination and violence against blacks.

For a long time some whites, focusing on civil rights leaders such as King and even fearing foreign "communists," deluded themselves into thinking that "outside agitators" were responsible for the turmoil in their communities. But the movement grew from the grass roots, and it eventually shattered this delusion.

The movement spread, especially among black students. In 1960 four black students of North Carolina A&T College sat at the lunch counter in Woolworth's and asked for a cup of coffee. The waitress refused to serve them, but they stayed and were arrested. On following days, as whites waved the Confederate flag and jeered, more students sat at the lunch counter. Within a year such sit-ins occurred in more than 100 cities.

When blacks asserted their rights, whites often reacted with violence. In 1963 King led demonstrators in Birmingham, Alabama, for desegregation of public facilities. Public Safety Commissioner Eugene "Bull" Connor had police unleash their dogs to attack the marchers. In 1964 King led demonstrators in Selma, Alabama, for voting rights. State troopers clubbed many marchers, and vigilantes beat and shot others.

In the summer of 1964, black and white college students mounted a voter registration drive in Mississippi. By the end of the summer, 1,000 had been arrested, 80 beaten, 35 shot, and 6 killed.[50] These included 1 southern black and 2 northern whites who were murdered by Klansmen, allegedly with aid from a sheriff and deputy sheriff, in Neshoba County. (This incident was fictionalized in the movie *Mississippi Burning*.)

Perpetrators of the violence usually were not caught. When they were, they usually were not punished. Law enforcement was frequently in the hands of bigots, and juries generally were all white. The Supreme Court had struck down discrimination in choosing juries,[51] but discrimination continued through informal means.

Through the 1960s, most whites told pollsters they disliked the civil rights movement's speed and tactics: "They're pushing too fast and too hard." At the same time, most said they favored integration more than ever. And they seemed repelled by the violence. The brutality against blacks generated more support for them.

Although the movement's tactics worked well against southern de jure segregation, they did not work as well against northern de facto segregation or against both regions' job discrimination. By the mid-1960s, a decade after the *Brown* decision, blacks became increasingly impatient. In place of King's advocacy of integration, some leaders called for "black power." This phrase meant different things to different people—black pride to some, violence to others. In general it implied more black self-reliance. And in place of King's advocacy of nonviolence, some leaders called for violence in retaliation for that by whites. The movement splintered further.

When three civil rights workers were murdered in Neshoba County, Mississippi, no one was ever indicted by the state. After an investigation, 18 persons, including the sheriff (*right*) and deputy sheriff (*left*), here in court, were indicted by the federal government for the lesser charge of conspiracy. (There was no applicable federal law for murder.) Ultimately, 7 persons, including the deputy, were convicted by the federal court.

The Movement in Congress

As the civil rights movement expanded, it pressured presidents and members of Congress to act. Presidents Kennedy and Johnson supported civil rights but felt hamstrung by southerners in Congress who through the seniority system had risen to chair key committees and dominate both houses. As a result, the presidents considered civil rights leaders unreasonable and the movement a nuisance that alienated the southerners upon whom the presidents had to rely. But once the movement demonstrated its strength, it was able to prod officials to act. After 200,000 blacks and whites marched in Washington in 1963, President Kennedy introduced civil rights legislation, and President Johnson, with his consummate legislative skills, forged a coalition of northern Democrats and northern Republicans to overcome southern Democrats and pass the Civil Rights Act of 1964. After 1,000 blacks and whites had been arrested and many had been attacked in Selma, the public outcry led Johnson to introduce and Congress to pass the Voting Rights Act of 1965.

Within a span of four years, Congress passed legislation prohibiting discrimination in public accommodations, employment, housing, and voting.

DESEGREGATION OF PUBLIC ACCOMMODATIONS The **Civil Rights Act of 1964** prohibits discrimination on the basis of race, color, religion, or national origin in public accommodations. This time, unlike after the Civil War, the Court unanimously upheld the act.[52]

The act does not cover private clubs, such as country clubs, social clubs, or fraternities and sororities, on the principle that the government should not tell people with whom they must associate in private. (The Court has made private schools an exception to this principle to help enforce *Brown*.)

DESEGREGATION OF EMPLOYMENT The Civil Rights Act of 1964 also prohibits employment discrimination on the basis of race, color, religion, national origin, or sex and (as amended) physical handicap, age, or Vietnam-era veteran status. The act covers employers with 15 or more employees and unions.[53]

In addition to practicing blatant discrimination, some employers practiced more subtle discrimination. They required applicants to meet standards unnecessary for their jobs, a practice that hindered blacks more than whites. A high school degree for a manual job was a common example. The court held that standards must relate to the jobs.[54] However, standards that hinder blacks more than whites are not necessarily unlawful. Washington, D.C., required applicants for police officer to pass an exam. Although a higher percentage of blacks failed to pass, the Court said the exam related to the job.[55]

When the Burger Court held that standards must relate to the job, it placed the burden of proof on employers. (They had to show that their requirements were necessary.) The Rehnquist Court shifted the burden of proof to workers.[56] This technical change had a substantial impact; it made it hard for victims to win in court. In 1991 Congress passed new legislation to override the ruling and clarify its intent that employers should bear the burden of proof.

The Court has allowed employers to reduce their workforce by laying off workers with less seniority, even though these workers often are disproportionately black due to past discrimination.[57] The principle of "last hired, first fired" means that, in hard times, blacks face even harder times.

DESEGREGATION OF HOUSING Although the Supreme Court had struck down laws that prescribed segregation in residential areas, whites maintained segregation by making **restrictive covenants**—agreements among neighbors not to sell to blacks if they sell their house. In 1948 the Court ruled that courts could not enforce these covenants because doing so would involve the government in discrimination.[58]

Realtors also played a role in segregation by practicing **steering**—showing blacks houses in black neighborhoods and whites houses in white neighborhoods. Unscrupulous realtors practiced **blockbusting.** After a black family bought a house in a white neighborhood, realtors would warn white families that more blacks would move in. Because of prejudice and fear that their houses' values would decline, whites would panic and sell to realtors at low prices. Then realtors would resell to blacks at higher prices. In this way neighborhoods that might have been desegregated were instead resegregated—from all white to all black.

Banks and savings and loans also played a role. They were reluctant to lend money to blacks who wanted to buy a house in a white neighborhood. Some engaged in **redlining**—refusing to lend money to those who wanted to buy a house in a racially changing neighborhood. The lenders worried that if buyers could not keep up with their payments, the lenders would be left with a house whose value had declined.

The government also played an important role. The Veterans Administration and the Federal Housing Authority, which guaranteed loans to some buyers, were reluctant to authorize loans to blacks who sought to buy a house in a white neighborhood. And the federal government, which funded low-income housing, allowed local governments to locate such housing in ghettos. In these ways the governments helped perpetuate segregation.

But the **Civil Rights Act of 1968** bans discrimination in the sale or rental of housing on the basis of race, color, religion, national origin, and (as amended) on the basis of sex, having children, or being disabled. The act covers about 80% of the available housing and prohibits steering, blockbusting, and redlining.

RESTORATION OF THE RIGHT TO VOTE After years of skirmishing with the states, the Supreme Court and Congress barred measures designed to keep blacks from voting. The Voting Rights Act of 1965 permitted large numbers of blacks to vote for the first time (as explained in Chapter 7).

Continuing Discrimination Against African Americans

African Americans have overcome much discrimination but still face continuing discrimination. Most overt laws and practices have been struck down, but more subtle manifestations of old attitudes and habits persist—and in ways far more numerous and with effects far more serious than this one chapter can convey.[59] Further, of course, blacks must cope with the legacy of generations of slavery, segregation, and discrimination, and for many of them the effects of generations of poverty.

Discrimination in Education

For Blacks who can afford it, there has been a great deal of desegregation in education. Affluent parents who can pay for private schools or live in expensive neighborhoods with good public schools can send their children to integrated schools. However, for most blacks in big cities, medium cities, or areas where private schools predominate, there has been much less desegregation.

Although de jure segregation of schools has been eliminated, de facto segregation remains. In fact, this segregation is getting worse. After progress in the mid-1960s and 1970s, the trend toward desegregation slowed and then reversed itself in the 1980s. "For the first time since the *Brown v. Board* decision," according to one study, "we are going backwards."[60] (See Table 2.)

The reversal is caused by massive residential segregation that is exacerbated by the flight of whites to the suburbs and the movement of whites to private schools. In our 47 largest cities, only 1 of 4 students in public schools is white. In Detroit, for example, the number of whites in public schools fell from 98,000 in 1970 to 14,000 today; in Atlanta, from 50,000 in the

How Much Is White Skin Worth?

"You will be visited tonight by an official you have never met. He begins by telling you he is extremely embarrassed. The organization he represents has made a mistake, something that hardly ever happens.

"According to their records, he goes on, you were to have been born black—to another set of parents, far from where you were raised.

"However, the rules being what they are, this error must be rectified, and as soon as possible. So at midnight tonight, you will become black. And this will mean not simply a darker skin, but the bodily and facial features associated with African ancestry. However, inside, you will be the person you always were. Your knowledge and ideas will remain intact. But outwardly you will not be recognizable to anyone you now know.

"Your visitor emphasizes that being born to the wrong parents was in no way your fault. Consequently, his organization is prepared to offer you some reasonable recompense. Would you, he asks, care to name a sum of money you might consider appropriate? He adds that his group is by no means poor. It can be quite generous when the circumstances warrant, as they seem to in your case. He finishes by saying that their records show you are scheduled to live another 50 years—as a black man or woman in America.

"How much financial recompense would you request?"

A professor who puts this parable to white college students finds that most feel $1 million per year—$50 million total—would be appropriate. This much would protect them from, and reimburse them for, the danger and discrimination they would face if they were perceived as black. In acknowledging that white skin is worth this much, the students also are admitting that treatment of the races, even today, is not nearly equal.

Source: Andrew Hacker, *Two Nations: Black and White, Separate, Hostile, Unequal* (New York: Charles Scribner's Sons, 1992), pp. 31–32.

TABLE 2 School Segregation of Blacks Is Greatest in the North

States with the largest percentages of black students attending schools with 50% or more minority enrollment.	
Illinois	89%
New York	86
Michigan	85
New Jersey	80
California	79
Maryland	76
Wisconsin	75
Texas	68
Pennsylvania	68
Connecticut	66

Source: Gary Orfield and Franklin Montfort, "Status of School Desegregation: The Next Generation," a report to the National School Boards Association, reprinted in Karen De Witt, "The Nation's Schools Learn a 4th R: Resegregation," *New York Times*, January 19, 1992, p. E5.

1960s to 4,000 today.[61] To a lesser extent, the reversal is due to the Burger and Rehnquist Courts' decisions to restrict busing and financing for desegregation efforts and to the Reagan and Bush administrations' policies not to enforce desegregation orders. School districts got the message that school desegregation was no longer an important national goal.[62]

As a result, in much of the South, where segregation was de jure, desegregation has been substantial. But in the big cities of the South and in most of the North, where segregation now is de facto, desegregation has been minimal. In fact, blacks in the Northeast and Midwest are more likely to attend predominantly minority schools than blacks in the South are.[63]

The persistence of de facto segregation and the waning of commitment to integration have led national, state, and local officials to adopt the attitude, "We still agree with the goal of school desegregation, but it's too hard, and we're tired of it, and we give up."[64]

When reforms are proposed for urban schools, they rarely include desegregation. Officials speak of a ghetto school that is more "efficient" or one that gets more "input" from ghetto parents or offers more "choices" for ghetto children. But the existence of ghetto education as "a permanent American reality" appears to be accepted.[65]

A writer who visited many ghetto classrooms and talked with students, teachers, and administrators observed that Martin Luther King was treated as "an icon, but his vision of a nation in which black and white kids went to school together seemed to be effaced almost entirely. Dutiful references to 'The Dream' were often seen in school brochures and on wall posters in February, when 'Black History' was celebrated in the public schools, but the content of the dream was treated as a closed box that could not be opened without ruining the celebration."[66]

Indeed, many cities have a school named after King—a segregated school in a segregated neighborhood—"like a terrible joke on history," a 14-year-old, wise beyond her years, noted.[67]

UNEQUAL FUNDING In areas where schools are segregated, the quality varies enormously—from "the golden to the godawful," in the words of a Missouri judge.[68] And, of course, minorities are more likely to be in the "godawful."

Schools are financed largely by property taxes paid by homeowners and businesses. Wealthy cities get more in property taxes than poor ones. In modern America, this means suburban school districts get more to spend per pupil than central city school districts. (And although many suburbs tax their residents at a lower rate than cities do, suburbs still bring in more revenue because their property is valued at a higher level. Thus, these suburbs ask their residents to sacrifice less but they still provide their children with an education that costs more.)[69]

Thus, it is common for a city such as Detroit to spend $3,600 per pupil while a suburb spends $6,400 per pupil per year. Camden, New Jersey, with a population over 400,000 but with an entire property value less than that of one casino in Atlantic City, spent $3,500 per pupil while Princeton spent $7,700 per pupil in 1989. In Illinois the range stretched from $2,100 per pupil to more than $10,000 per pupil in 1990.[70]

And spending per pupil figures do not take into account the fact that the needs of poor children, after years of neglect and with scores of problems at home and in the neighborhood, are greater than the needs of other children. Schools for poor children would require *more* funding to provide their students an equal education.

So, many inner city schools are bleak institutions, reflecting disrepair and filth. A Camden school has a fire alarm system that has not worked in 20 years. An East St. Louis, Illinois, school has, a visitor discovered, a boys' bathroom in which "[f]our of the six toilets do not work. The toilet stalls, which are eaten away by red and brown corrosion, have no doors. The toilets have no seats. One has a rotted wooden stump. There are no paper towels and no soap. Near the door is a loop of wire with an empty toilet-paper roll." Yet the visitor was told, "This is the best school we have in East St. Louis." At another school in the city, sewage repeatedly backed up into the bathrooms and kitchen and flooded the gym and parking lot.[71]

Many inner city schools are overcrowded. Classes routinely are held in former coatrooms and closets. At one school two classes are held in converted coal bins while another is held in the current bathroom. Some cities in New Jersey literally ran out of classrooms and tried to rent space in vacant schools in the suburbs. But the cities were turned down because the suburbs did not want the mostly nonwhite children using the empty buildings.[72]

Many inner city schools do not have texts for all their students, texts that are at the appropriate grade levels, or texts that are up to date. A Chicago school has not had a library for 21 years. Some schools cannot afford to hire science, art, music, or physical education teachers. Almost all cannot afford to offer competitive salaries to hire good teachers in the subjects the schools do offer. A New York City principal says he is forced to take the "tenth-best" teachers. "I thank God they're still breathing."[73]

To save money, the Chicago school system relies on substitutes for a fourth of its teaching force. It cannot attract and hold enough substitutes, so on an average morning 5,700 students in 190 classrooms show up to find they have no teacher.[74]

A Chicago alderman, reflecting the prevailing middle class view about local education, said, "Nobody in his right mind would send [his] kids to public school."[75]

Despite the pervasive pattern of unequal funding, cash alone would not solve all the problems. Cultural and economic factors in inner cities also restrict the quality of education available. But cash would help. According to one calculation, if New York City schools had been funded at the same level as the highest spending suburban schools on Long Island, a typical fourth grade class of 36 children would have had $200,000 more invested in their education in 1987. The difference would have been enough to divide the class in half, hire two excellent teachers, and provide the classrooms with computers, new texts, reference books, learning games, carpets, air conditioning, and new counselors to help the children cope with problems in their environment outside school.[76]

Yet moves to redistribute funds are fought fiercely. After the New Jersey Supreme Court in 1990 ordered the state to reduce disparities between districts, the Democratic governor and legislature increased some taxes and cut some spending in other areas. The governor also redirected a portion of state aid from suburban schools to inner city schools to comply with the order. Suburbanites were furious; the next year they elected veto-proof majorities of Republicans to both houses of the state legislature in an attempt to block the program, and in the next election they ousted the governor.

SECOND-GENERATION DISCRIMINATION Even where desegregation of schools has been achieved, segregation within schools exists. This "second-generation discrimination" isolates many minority students by placing them in separate programs or classes from white students. Black children are more likely to be put in "special education" classes for slow learners and less likely to be put in programs for gifted students. They are more likely to be put in classes for the educable mentally retarded (EMR).[77]

These facts by themselves are not necessarily evidence of second-generation discrimination, because the long legacy of discrimination and the dismal living conditions of many blacks make it harder for them to succeed in school. However, in school districts where more minorities are school board members or are administrators or teachers, less disparate treatment occurs.[78] The presence of minorities in authoritative positions apparently discourages white administrators or teachers from discriminating. It prompts them to think twice about relegating black students to "special education" or EMR classes.

Discrimination in Public Accommodations

Most businesses comply with the Civil Rights Act of 1964 prohibiting discrimination in public accommodations. Suits claiming discrimination fell 51% from 1975 to 1984, reflecting increasing compliance with the act.[79]

However, Jim Crow still lives in some places. For example, numerous blue-collar bars and lounges in New Orleans operate as though the act is not on the books. One serves blacks through a side window while it allows whites to drink inside. Others keep separate rooms for blacks and whites. Others use separate entrances—blacks through a back or side door, whites through the front door. "I can go to the front door, now," a black patron says. "But no one is going to let me in. All I'll do is get my feelings hurt. If you want service, you go around to the back room—that's for blacks."[80] Although illegal, these practices persist if no one files a complaint or brings a lawsuit.

In recent years a Denny's restaurant in Maryland refused to serve a group of blacks—unbeknownst to the restaurant, Secret Service agents—but at the same time did serve a group of whites—also Secret Service agents. The Denny's chain in California faced a lawsuit for discriminating against blacks. The plaintiffs said Denny's refused to honor offers for free birthday meals, assessed them a $2 cover on top of the cost of their meals, and asked them to pay in advance for their meals.[81]

Some businesses try to circumvent the act. For instance, restaurants give blacks poor service so they will not return. A suburban mall refused to allow city buses from Buffalo in its parking lot, although it allowed Canadian buses to bring their shoppers from across the border. Mall executives assured shopkeepers that "you'll never see an inner-city bus on the mall premises."[82]

For businesses that try to comply with the act, some employees treat blacks differently and embarrassingly. As one writer notes, "You stroll into a shop to look at the merchandise, and it soon becomes clear that the clerks are keeping a watchful eye on you. Too quickly, one of them comes over to inquire what it is you might want, and then remains conspicuously close as you continue your search. It also seems that they take an unusually long time verifying your credit card. And then you and a black friend enter a restaurant, and find yourselves greeted warily, with what is obviously a more anxious reception than that given to white guests. Yes, you will be served, and your table will not necessarily be next to the kitchen. Still, you sense that they would rather you had chosen some other eating place."[83]

Because the Civil Rights Act does not apply to private clubs, many country clubs and golf clubs discriminate against blacks. One estimate is that three-fourths of these clubs have no black members, and many of the remainder have only one or a few token members.[84] Thus, the business, professional, and political elites who form the membership perpetuate inequality in their circles and also send a message that discrimination is acceptable for others in society.

Discrimination in Employment

Although the Civil Rights Act of 1964 and affirmative action (discussed later in the chapter) have prompted more employers to hire and promote African Americans, discrimination remains.

More than a decade after the Civil Rights Act, one rural county in Georgia with 50% black population had never had a black mayor, sheriff, judge, county commissioner, city council member, or grand jury member. The county had never had a black librarian, firefighter,

A Chicago artist put up this billboard to prompt white motorists to think about how they would feel if discrimination were directed at them instead. By the next day the word NIGER [*sic*] had been scrawled on the billboard, and the mayor had gotten so many complaints that the artist had to take the billboard down.

mail carrier, or state park employee. There were no black employees in the Social Security office, welfare office, courthouse, power company, phone company, or in a convenience store. The county had never had a black salesperson or clerk, bank teller or cashier or bookkeeper. In fact, no employer apparently had ever hired a black for a position above unskilled laborer, maid, or cook.[85] This county might be an extreme example, but no doubt there are others not much different.

Discrimination continues in urban areas as well. A 1991 study of Chicago and Washington, D.C., used pairs of white and black male college students who were matched in education, experience, age, speech, demeanor, and physical build. The men applied for nearly 500 advertised jobs involving retail, service, clerical, or physical labor. The whites advanced farther in the hiring process 20% of the time, while the blacks did 7% of the time. (Neither advanced farther in the remainder.) The blacks found discrimination most in white collar jobs—one who had applied for a job as a hotel desk clerk was offered a job as a bellboy—and those requiring contact with customers.[86] These results not only reflect discrimination against blacks, but they also contradict the perception that there is widespread reverse discrimination against whites.

A 1992 investigation by the Equal Employment Opportunity Commission (EEOC) uncovered discriminatory practices by employment agencies who hire workers for many companies. The agencies devised code phrases the companies could use to screen out applicants of a particular race or sex or age as a way to violate the law without being caught. If, for example, a business did not want any blacks, it was instructed to specify, "No Z." If it simply preferred whites, it was instructed to say, "Talk to Mary." Through these phrases, one Los Angeles agency alone discriminated against 3,900 applicants.[87]

Blacks who are hired sometimes face harassment on the job. For instance, black supervisors and executives at the Miller brewery in Fulton, New York, have endured repeated verbal abuse—racial slurs over the plant's paging and beeper systems; symbolic gestures—a noose and chicken bones left at their desks; and vandalism to their cars. While some white laborers have had trouble accepting black bosses, lax enforcement of employment law by the Reagan and Bush administrations apparently aggravated the problem.[88]

Discrimination in Housing

The Civil Rights Act of 1968 prohibiting discrimination in housing has fostered some desegregation of housing, especially big apartment complexes, which are more visible and therefore more susceptible to pressure from civil rights groups and the government. And the act has resulted in large penalties on individuals found guilty of violations. Lawyers for fair-housing organizations say white jurors think discrimination has been eliminated—until they hear the testimony, which jars them into granting large awards. These awards prompt more lawyers to file more suits.[89]

But the act is working only at a snail's pace to change housing patterns. One reason is economic. Most blacks do not have enough money to buy homes in white neighborhoods. This problem is aggravated by local zoning laws designed to establish a certain type of community. Often these laws require large lots and large houses, which command high prices.

Another reason is continuing discrimination. Occasional violence and considerable social pressure discourage blacks who try to move into white neighborhoods. Actual discrimination by homeowners, realtors, lenders, and insurers also stymies them. A study of 40 metropolitan areas found that blacks who try to buy a house face discrimination 75% of the time, and those who try to rent do so 62% of the time.[90]

Some realtors still practice steering. Many lenders apparently require extra proof that blacks will repay their home loans. A study by the Federal Reserve Board examined 5.3 million mortgage applications to 9,300 financial institutions in 19 major cities in 1990. It found that applications from blacks were denied more than twice as often as those from whites with comparable income. As a result, applications from high-income blacks were rejected about as often as those from low-income whites.[91] Some insurers evidently practice a version of redlining. A 1993 study of five large midwestern cities concluded that insurance companies charged blacks in inner cities twice the rate for homeowners' insurance as they charged whites with similar income.[92] Because lenders normally require borrowers to get homeowners' insurance to qualify for a home loan, higher priced insurance makes it harder to buy the home.

For all of these reasons, residential segregation remains pervasive in metropolitan areas (see Table 3). However, for the first time segregation declined in the 1980s. The percentage of blacks living in nonblack neighborhoods, defined as areas with less than 10% blacks, inched from about 10% to 12%.[93] Still, Asians and Hispanics with third-grade educations are more likely to live in integrated neighborhoods than blacks with Ph.D.s.[94]

TABLE 3 Residential Segregation of Blacks Is Pervasive

Major cities with the largest percentages of black residents who would have to change neighborhoods for the cities to have a desegregated residential pattern.	
Gary	89%
Detroit	88
Chicago	86
Cleveland	85
New York	82
Philadelphia	77
Los Angeles	73
Birmingham	72
Miami	71
Boston	68
San Francisco	66
Washington	66
New Orleans	64
Dallas	63

Source: Douglas Massey and Nancy Denton, *American Apartheid: Segregation and the Making of the Underclass* (Cambridge, Massachusetts: Harvard University Press, 1993), p. 222. Data from 1990 Census reported by Rodrick Harrison and Daniel Weinberg.

Segregation does not continue because blacks "want to live by their own kind," as some whites insist. Surveys show that only about 15% want to live in segregated neighborhoods, while 85% would prefer mixed neighborhoods. (Many say the optimal level would be about half blacks and half whites.) Yet whites tend to move out, and new ones do not move in, when blacks reach 8–10%.[95] These very different views make integration an elusive goal, particularly because blacks make up 12–13% of the American population and a much larger percentage of some cities.

These patterns and attitudes are all the more troublesome because residential segregation, of course, leads to further school segregation.

To add potential injury to the insult for blacks, a study of the Environmental Protection Agency's enforcement of air, water, and hazardous-waste pollution laws from 1985 to 1991 concluded that the government took longer to act in minority communities, imposed smaller fines against polluters in those communities, and required less stringent solutions in those communities.[96]

Discrimination in Other Ways

Discrimination occurs in many other ways. Some police officers stop black drivers without any evidence. Officers claim that drivers of expensive cars might be stealing them while drivers of other cars might be hauling drugs. (African Americans speak of the moving violation "D.W.B."—Driving While Black.)[97] Some police officers arrest or beat black citizens without legal cause. Numerous examples—not just the Rodney King incident—attest to the use of excessive force.[98] Some police officers lie while testifying against black suspects in court. As a result, even prominent African Americans say their "worst fear is to have to go before the criminal justice system."[99] It is little wonder, then, that black jurors hearing the O.J. Simpson trial and black citizens following it put less faith in the police testimony than white observers did.

Most blacks, even those in the upper and middle classes and those in professional occupations, face insults because of their race. Black women tell of being mistaken for hotel chambermaids. One family therapist, invited to speak at a conference, was stopped in the hallway by a white attendee who asked where the restrooms were. When the therapist appeared taken aback, the attendee said she thought the woman worked at the hotel. Although the therapist was wearing her official name tag and presenter's ribbon, the attendee did not look past her black face.[100] Black women also tell of waiting for friends in hotel lobbies and being mistaken for prostitutes by white men and police officers. A distinguished black political scientist tells of being considered a butler, in his own home. Black doctors tell of dressing up when they go shopping to avoid being seen as shoplifters. But even dressing up is no guarantee. A black lawyer, a senior partner in a large law firm, arrived at work early one morning, before the doors were unlocked. As he reached for his key, a young white lawyer, a junior associate in the firm, arrived at work, blocked his entrance and asked, repeatedly and demandingly, "May I help you?" The white associate had taken the black partner for an intruder.[101] Although in these encounters the insults were unintentional, the stings hurt just the same.

Overall, discrimination against African Americans continues. Whites speak of "past discrimination"—sometimes referring to slavery, sometimes to official segregation—but this phrase is misleading. True, there was more discrimination in earlier decades and

Employees of an Orange County, California, shopping mall hear the verdict in the O.J. Simpson trial. The opposite reactions among blacks and whites reveal the gulf between the races in this country.

there is a lot less discrimination now due to the civil rights movement and Supreme Court decisions and congressional acts. However, there is nothing "past" about much "past discrimination."[102] The effects linger and, indeed, the discrimination itself persists.

As African Americans have become frustrated with the slow pace of progress in the 1980s and 1990s, some have been attracted to the black separatist movement. These blacks, seeing themselves as realistic, consider integration a naive ideal from the 1950s and 1960s—an impossibility even in the future. These neoseparatists want to direct their energy toward building up the black community.[103] (Supreme Court Justice Clarence Thomas seems to hold this view.) But most blacks, remaining hopeful, consider separatism premature and risky, playing into the hands of the most prejudiced whites trying to perpetuate discrimination.

Discrimination Against Hispanics

Hispanics, also called Latinos, are people with Spanish-speaking backgrounds. The first Hispanics came to America from Spain in the 1500s. They settled in the Southwest, and when the United States took this landfrom Mexico in 1848, they became U.S. citizens. Other Hispanics came to America more recently.

Hispanics comprise groups with different cultural traditions. About 61% trace their ancestry to Mexico and live mainly in the Southwest, though some live in large cities in the Midwest. About 15% are from Puerto Rico, which is a commonwealth—a self-governing territory—of the United States. As members of the commonwealth, they are U.S. citizens. Most live in New York, Boston, Chicago, and other cities in the North. Another 6% are from Cuba. Following the establishment of a Communist government in Cuba in 1959, many fled to the United States and settled in south Florida. In recent years, Hispanics from other Caribbean or Central American countries have immigrated to the United States to escape turmoil and oppression.

Despite the diversity of their origins, Latinos are heavily concentrated. More than half live in California and Texas.

Hispanics represent about 9% of the U.S. population. Already the United States has the seventh largest Hispanic population in the world, and within the United States this group is the second fastest growing minority (after Asians). Due to a high birthrate, Hispanics are predicted to equal blacks in 2020 even without the increased immigration that is likely.[104]

Hispanics never endured slavery, but they have suffered discrimination. Many Hispanics are Caucasian. However, many Puerto Ricans and Cubans have

African ancestry, and many Mexicans have some Indian ancestry, so they have darker skin than non-Hispanic whites. Like blacks, Hispanics have faced discrimination in education, employment, housing, and voting.[105]

Hispanics also encounter discrimination due to continuing immigration. The illegal immigrants pouring in from Mexico exacerbate hostility and discrimination against Hispanics, especially in the Southwest. U.S. Border Patrol and local law enforcement officials, who cannot tell the difference between Hispanics who are citizens or legal residents and those who are not, often stop Hispanics for questioning not only at the border but inland as well. (Agents stopped the mayor of Pomona, California, more than a hundred miles from the border, and ordered him to produce papers to prove that he is a legal resident.) Even when officials are well intentioned, their conduct is considered harassment by law-abiding legal residents.

Moreover, the 1986 immigration law, which penalizes employers of illegal aliens, has increased discrimination against Hispanics who are legal residents. Some employers, leery of hiring illegal aliens, are reluctant to hire Hispanics.[106]

Discrimination in Education

For years Hispanic children in some areas were not allowed to attend schools at all. In other areas they were segregated into "Mexican" schools whose quality was not comparable with Anglo schools.[107]

In the 1940s, Mexican American organizations asked the courts to find that Mexican Americans were "white" so they could not be segregated. The federal courts agreed. This, however, backfired after the Supreme Court declared segregation by race illegal. Many school districts accomplished "integration" by combining blacks with Hispanics, leaving non-Hispanic whites in separate schools.[108]

Even when admitted to schools, Hispanics faced discrimination due to their language. Traditionally, teachers and administrators forbade students from speaking their native Spanish to each other in school. They reprimanded, spanked, or expelled those who did. Some even anglicized students' names in class and in school records, so "Jesus" became "Jesse" and "Miguel" became "Michael."[109]

Although de jure segregation has been struck down, de facto segregation exists in northern and southwestern cities where Hispanics are concentrated, due to residential segregation and white flight to the suburbs (see Table 4). Many Hispanics attend schools with more than 90% minorities, and most attend schools with more than half minorities.[110] As a result, Latinos in Los Angeles, for example, are more likely to attend segregated schools than blacks in Alabama or Georgia.[111]

Predominantly Hispanic schools, like predominantly black schools, are not as well funded as other schools. Because minority schools are frequently in poor communities, they do not receive as much revenue from property taxes. In San Antonio, Hispanic families were concentrated in the poorest districts, while wealthy families were concentrated in a section that was incorporated as a separate district, though it was in the city and surrounded on four sides by the rest of the city. Its property taxes financed its schools only. When Hispanic parents sued, the Burger Court ruled that the Fourteenth Amendment's equal protection clause does not require states to equalize funding between school districts.[112]

One generation later, per-pupil spending in Texas ranged from about $2,000 in the poorest districts to $19,000 in the wealthiest ones. Yet the 100 poorest districts had a property tax rate more than 50% higher than the 100 wealthiest ones.[113] Faced with these figures, the Texas Supreme Court held in 1989 that state law requires the state to equalize funding.[114] Some other states also have decided to reform financing of schools.

Even where Hispanics attend desegregated schools, often they are segregated within the schools. They face "second-generation discrimination," though not as much as blacks. Hispanics are more likely than Anglos to be put in EMR classes and less likely to be placed in gifted classes.[115] Some Hispanics also face a language barrier because of their inability to speak English. These children are often grouped in bilingual education classes.

Bilingual education gives instruction in substantive subjects such as math, in students' native language for those who do not speak English. (It also provides instruction in English itself.) In 1968 Congress encouraged bilingual education by providing funding, and in 1974 the Supreme Court, in a case brought by Chinese parents, held that schools must teach students in a language they can understand.[116] This can be their native language, or it can be English if they have been taught English. These federal actions prompted many states to establish bilingual education programs.

TABLE 4 School Segregation of Hispanics Is Greatest in North and Southwest

States with the largest percentages of Hispanic students attending schools with 50% or more minority enrollment.	
New York	86%
Illinois	85
Texas	84
New Jersey	84
California	79
Rhode Island	78
New Mexico	74
Connecticut	72
Pennsylvania	67
Arizona	57

Source: Gary Orfield and Franklin Montfort, "Status of School Desegregation: The Next Generation," a report to the National School Boards Association, reprinted in Karen De Witt, "The Nation's Schools Learn a 4th R: Resegregation," *New York Times*, January 19, 1992, p. E5.

Now more than 150 languages, from Chinese to Yapese, are offered nationwide. With almost three-fourths of the students who do not speak English being Hispanic, Spanish is the most common.[117]

These programs are controversial, and the debate revolves around politics as much as education. Some proponents of bilingual education, especially Hispanic groups, see it as a way to preserve their native language and culture. They consider bilingual education to be a component of multiculturalism. So they want it not as a temporary bridge until students learn English but as a permanent fixture through high school. Some proponents also see it as a way to enhance the self-esteem of students with a native language other than English. These students tend to fail in school and drop out of school at higher rates than other students.[118] Hispanic leaders argue that they do so not because they cannot speak English but because they are not part of the dominant group in society.[119] These leaders maintain that students are more likely to succeed in school if bilingual education is integrated throughout the curriculum.

Many opponents of bilingual education, especially Anglos who fear the influx of immigrants, also see it as a way to preserve foreign languages and cultures. They discount the need for multiculturalism. Instead, they want students to be exposed only to English in school as a guarantee that they will assimilate into society.

For both sides, then, bilingual education has become a symbolic issue. It prompts concerns, even fears, about the relative dominance of Anglo culture and Hispanic culture, and about the extent to which Anglo Americans will make room for Hispanic Americans in society.

Meanwhile, Hispanic parents want their children to learn English, and to learn it well, as Chapter 2 explains. Recent research indicates that bilingual education serves this goal.[120] Apparently children learn English faster and other subjects better if they receive instruction in their native language until they are fluent in English. Otherwise, they miss too much of what is said in class.

But bilingual education is expensive, because it requires extra teachers and small classes. And it is impractical for some languages in some places. "It's hard to find someone who can teach math in Korean," an educator in Virginia explained.[121]

In contrast to the difficulty Hispanics historically had getting into public schools, in 1982 the Supreme Court ruled, by a close vote, that children of illegal aliens have the right to attend public schools.[122] The majority assumed that most of these children, although subject to deportation, would remain in the United States, given the large number of illegal aliens who do remain here. Denying them an education would deprive them of the opportunity to fulfill their potential and would deprive society of the benefit of their contribution.

Combating Discrimination Against Hispanics

Hispanics have had some political success at the local level in places where they are heavily concentrated, but they have had less success at the national level. Except for Cesar Chavez, who led a coalition of labor, civil rights, and religious groups to bring better working conditions for migrant farm workers in California in the 1960s, Hispanics have not had highly visible national leaders or organizations.

Hispanics are more diverse and less cohesive than blacks. Most do not even consider themselves part of a large group of Hispanics.[123] They profess strong loyalty to people of their national origin and have little contact with Hispanics with other ancestry. Thus, most do not call themselves "Hispanics" or "Latinos," but "Mexican Americans," "Puerto Ricans," or "Cuban Americans."[124] Also, they have different legal statuses. Puerto Ricans have American

Hispanics are gradually improving their status. This woman toils as a migrant farm worker, but her son graduated from college and now runs personnel management programs for farmers.

citizenship by birth, but many Hispanics do not have it at all. And they lack a common defining experience in their background, such as slavery for blacks, to unite them.

Discrimination Against Native Americans

About one and a half million Native Americans live in the United States. Although some are Eskimos and Aleuts from Alaska, most are Indians, representing more than 300 tribes with different histories, customs, and languages. More than half live off reservations, mostly in urban areas.

Although Native Americans have faced some discrimination similar to that against blacks and Hispanics, they have endured much discrimination of a different nature.

Government Policy Toward Native Americans

The government's policy toward Native Americans has varied over the years, ranging from forced separation at one extreme to forced assimilation at the other.

SEPARATION Initially the policy was separation. For many years people believed the continent was so vast that most of its interior would remain wilderness, populated by Indians who would have ample room to live and hunt. The Constitution reflects this belief. It grants Congress authority to "regulate commerce with foreign nations, and among the several states, and with the Indian tribes." In early cases Chief Justice John Marshall described the tribes as "dependent domestic nations."[125] They were within U.S. borders but outside its political process.

Early treaties reinforced separation by establishing boundaries between Indians and non-Indians. These boundaries were ones the government thought necessary for its growth, the Indians for their survival; they were intended to minimize conflict. White hunters or settlers who ventured across the boundaries could be punished as the Indians saw fit.

But as the country grew, it became increasingly difficult to contain settlers within the boundaries. Mounting pressure to push Native Americans further west led to the Indian Removal Act of 1830, which authorized removal of tribes east of the Mississippi River and relocation on reservations west of the river. At the time people considered the Great Plains to be the great American desert, unfit for habitation by whites but suitable for Indians. At first, removal was voluntary, but eventually it became mandatory for most and was supervised by the U.S. cavalry.

ASSIMILATION As more settlers moved west, the vision of separate Indian country far enough beyond white civilization to prevent conflict faded. In the 1880s the government switched its policy to assimilation. Prompted by Christian churches, officials sought to "civilize" the Indians, that is, to incorporate them into the larger society, whether they wanted to be incorporated or not. In place of their traditional means of subsistence, rendered useless once the tribes were removed from their homeland, the government subdivided reservation land into small tracts and allotted these tracts to tribe members in hopes that they would turn to farming as white and black settlers had. (In the process, the government reclaimed "surplus" land and sold it to white settlers. Ultimately, the Indians lost about two-thirds of their reservation land.)[126] Bureau of Indian Affairs agents, who supervised the reservations, tried to root out Native American ways and replace them with white dress and hairstyles, the English language, and the Christian religion. Government boarding schools separated Native American children from their families to instill these new practices.

CITIZENSHIP Native Americans were not considered citizens but members of separate nations early in the history of the United States. Treaties made exceptions for those who married whites and for those who left their tribes and abandoned their tribal customs. But in 1890, after government policy switched to assimilation, Congress permitted some who remained with their tribes on reservations to become citizens by applying to the U.S. government. Citizenship was sometimes marked by a formal ceremony. In one the Indian shot his last arrow and then took hold of the handles of a plow to demonstrate his assimilation.[127] After World War I, Congress granted citizenship to those who served in the military during the war, and finally in 1924, Congress extended it to all those born in the United States.

Citizenship enabled Indians to vote and hold office, though some states effectively barred them from the polls for decades. Arizona denied them the right to vote until 1948, Utah until 1956.[128]

TRIBAL RESTORATION By the 1930s, the government recognized the negative consequences of coerced assimilation. Most Indians could speak English, but they were poorly educated in other respects. And with their traditional means of earning a living gone, most were poverty stricken. The policy led to destruction of Native American ways without much assimilation in white society. Consequently, Congress implemented a new policy of tribal restoration in 1934 that recognized Indians as distinct persons and tribes as autonomous entities encouraged to govern themselves once again. Traditional cultural and religious practices were accepted, and children, no longer forced to attend boarding schools, were taught some Indian languages.

Reflecting the new policy as well as the efforts by other minorities, Indian interest groups became active in the 1960s and 1970s. Some tried to take over Alcatraz Island, the former federal prison in San Francisco Bay, which they claimed was their land. Others marched to Washington on the "Trail of Broken Treaties" and occupied the Bureau of Indian Affairs (BIA) building. The BIA, controlled by whites, implemented federal policy for Indians. In 1973 members of the American Indian Movement (AIM) seized the village of Wounded Knee, South Dakota—site of the last massacre of Indians by the U.S. cavalry—and demanded review of treaties between native Americans and the government.

Indian law firms pursued varied interests in court, seeking to protect not only tribal independence and traditional practices but also land, mineral, and water resources. Some filed claims for restoration of tribal territory.

In 1975 the Indian Self-Determination Act gave tribes more authority to administer their own educational and social programs. Now they control about 40% of the BIA's budget.[129]

In recent years Indians have fought for an end to digging up old gravesites and for a return of bones

Tom Torlino, before and after his transformation at a boarding school in Carlisle, Pennsylvania. Native Americans were shorn of their hair and clothes and trained to adopt white ways.

and artifacts unearthed from them. With little regard for Native American culture, "pothunters" have searched for artifacts to sell to collectors. Such looting raises the ire of archaeologists who say, "We'll never know what's been taken or how it relates to what remains in the ground. Everything has been scrambled." But digging for scientific purposes itself enrages some Indians, who say that archaeologists are "hardly any better than grave robbers themselves; only difference is they've got a state permit." Until recent years, in fact, many laws about exhumation of bones applied only to those of whites.[130]

Overall, Native Americans enjoy renewed pride. From 1970 to 1990, according to birth and death records, the Indian population increased by 760,000. Yet, according to people's self-identification for the census, this population rose by 1.4 million.[131] Evidently, many people, including those with only distant Indian ancestry, who did not wish to identify themselves as Indians in 1970, did by 1990.

The tribes also enjoy renewed vitality. Some even have become wealthy from revenue from gambling casinos and mineral rights. Although the diversity of tribes—divided by geography and culture and located in many of the remotest and poorest parts of the country—makes it difficult to present a united front, they have been able to wrest some autonomy from the government. They have become a more integral part of American federalism. As one activist sees the situation, "You have a federal government, state governments, and tribal governments—three sovereigns in one country. This is . . . the civil rights movement of Native Americans."[132]

Collectors of ancient Native American artifacts prompt "pothunters" to dig up gravesites.

Sex Discrimination

Discrimination Against Women

Unlike blacks, Hispanics, and Native Americans, women are not a minority—in fact, they are a slight majority—but, like minorities, they were not considered equal. Thomas Jefferson, the most egalitarian of the Founders, insisted, "Were our state a pure democracy there would still be excluded from our deliberations women, who, to prevent deprivation of morals and ambiguity of issues, should not mix promiscuously in gatherings of men."[133] That is, women are too moral—they would be corrupted by politics—and too muddleheaded—they would confuse the issues.

Indeed, women were not considered equal. In 1824 the Mississippi Supreme Court acknowledged a husband's right to beat his wife, and some other state courts followed.[134] According to the "rule of thumb," a husband could not beat his wife with a weapon thicker than his thumb.

Before the Civil War, women were not admitted to public high schools. Because they were being prepared for motherhood, education was considered unnecessary, even dangerous. According to the *Encyclopaedia Britannica* in 1800, women had smaller brains than men.[135] Education would fatigue them and possibly ruin their reproductive organs. Similarly, women were not encouraged to hold jobs. Women who did seek employment were shunted into menial and industrial jobs, mostly in sewing shops and textile mills, where they worked long hours for low wages.

"Kemo sabe, I want you to be official greeter at my new casino."

Source: Drawing by Mankoff © 1994 The New Yorker Magazine, Inc.

(Apparently people were not concerned that such jobs would ruin these women's reproductive organs.)

Women were denied the right to vote in most places, and married women were denied other legal rights. They did not have the right to manage property they owned before marriage, to manage wages they received from jobs, to enter into contracts, or to sue. Beginning in 1839, some states legislated these rights, but when disputes arose, male judges hesitated to tell other men how to treat their wives. Often, then, the rights did not exist in practice. Other states did not even adopt such rights until well into the twentieth century.

The Women's Movement

Early feminists were determined to remedy these inequities. Many had gained political and organizational experience in the abolitionist movement. It was not considered "unladylike" for women to campaign for the end of slavery, because the movement was associated with religious groups. Yet women were barely tolerated by the male leaders of the movement and not allowed to participate fully in the major antislavery society. They formed their own antislavery society, but when they attended a convention of antislavery societies, they were not allowed to sit with the male delegates.

Angry at such treatment, the women held a meeting to discuss the "social, civil and religious rights of women." This first Women's Rights Convention in 1848 adopted a declaration of rights based on the Declaration of Independence. It said, "We hold these truths to be self-evident: that all men and women are created equal." The convention also passed a resolution in favor of women's suffrage.

Following the Civil War, women who had worked in the abolitionist movement expected that women, as well as blacks, would get legal rights and voting rights. When the Fourteenth and Fifteenth Amendments did not include women, they felt betrayed and they disassociated themselves from the black movement. They formed their own organizations to campaign for women's suffrage. This movement, led by Susan B. Anthony and Elizabeth Cady Stanton, succeeded in 1920, when the Nineteenth Amendment gave women the right to vote.

Then dissension developed within the women's movement. Many groups felt the passage of the Nineteenth Amendment was but a first step in the struggle for equal rights. They proposed the Equal Rights Amendment to remedy remaining inequities. Other groups felt the battle had been won. They opposed the Equal Rights Amendment, arguing it would overturn labor laws recently enacted to protect women. Because of this dissension and the conservatism in the country, the movement became relatively dormant.[136]

The movement reemerged in the 1960s. As a result of the civil rights movement, many women recognized their own inferior status. Numerous writers sensitized more women to this. A group of middle-class, professional women formed the National Organization for Women (NOW) in 1966 and installed Betty Friedan as its first president. They resolved "to bring women into full participation in the mainstream of American society now."

Other women, also middle class but veterans of the civil rights and antiwar movements, had developed a taste for political action and gained political experience. They formed other organizations. Where NOW fought primarily for women's political and economic rights, the other organizations fought more broadly for women's liberation in all spheres of life. Together these organizations pushed the issue of discrimination against women back onto the public agenda.

The Movement in Congress

Under pressure from the women's movement, Congress adopted legislation to prohibit discrimination against women in employment, education, and credit. Congress also passed the Equal Rights Amendment, though the states failed to ratify it.

EMPLOYMENT The Civil Rights Act of 1964 forbids discrimination on the basis of sex as well as race in hiring, promoting, and firing. The original bill did not cover sex discrimination, and its inclusion was the result of a joke. Eighty-one-year-old Representative Howard Smith (D-Va.) proposed an amendment to add sex discrimination to the bill. A foe of equal rights for blacks, Smith thought his proposal so ludicrous

During World War II, women were urged into the labor force to replace men called into the military services. "Rosie the Riveter" became a symbol of women working in the war effort. Following the war, they were told that it was patriotic to go home and give up their jobs to returning veterans. This 1955 magazine cover depicts the stereotypical women's role in the postwar era before the beginning of the modern women's movement.

and radical that it would help defeat the entire bill. Indeed, during debate on the amendment, members of Congress laughed so hard that they could barely hear each other speak.[137] But the joke was on them, because the amendment, and then the entire bill, passed. Unlike other legislation prohibiting discrimination against women, Congress adopted this provision without pressure from women.

The act prohibits discrimination on the basis of sex, except where sex is a "bona fide occupational qualification" for the job. The Equal Employment Opportunity Commission (EEOC), which enforces the act, interprets it broadly and accepts sex as a legitimate qualification for very few jobs. For example, employers can seek a man or woman to be a restroom attendant, lingerie salesclerk, model, actor, or performer in the entertainment business where sex appeal is considered necessary. On the other hand, employers cannot seek a male for jobs men traditionally held, such as those that entail heavy physical labor, unpleasant working conditions, late-night hours, overtime, or travel.

Some employers are reluctant to comply. For matched pairs of men and women, resumes were sent to 65 Philadelphia restaurants in 1995. The men were more than twice as likely to get an interview and more than five times as likely to get the job at the higher-priced restaurants than the equally qualified women.[138]

An executive of a Fortune 500 company, in a conversation with business professors at a southwestern university in a recent year, admitted that his company prefers to hire men married to traditional housewives.[139] The men are dependent upon their own job for all their family's income, and they are relieved of most household chores. It is not coincidental that executives who reach the higher rungs of management, according to one research organization, are "almost always men from what used to be the traditional family—men with wives who don't work outside the home."[140]

The **Equal Pay Act** of 1963 requires that women and men receive equal pay for equal work. The act makes exceptions for merit, productivity, and seniority. Yet more than a quarter century after passage of the act, working women earn only 75¢ for every $1.00 working men earn (although young women, from 16 through 24, earn more than 90¢ for every $1.00 young men earn).

Women make less partly because they have less education and experience than men in the same jobs; many stopped their schooling or working to marry and have children (see Table 5). But they make less primarily because they have different jobs than men, and these jobs pay much less.

Traditionally, women have been shunted into a small number of jobs; currently 80% are squeezed into 20 of the 427 jobs identified by the Department of Labor.[141] These "pink-collar" jobs include secretaries (99% are women), household workers (98%), child care workers (97%), nurses (96%), waiters (88%, although waiters in fancy restaurants, who get larger tips, are mostly men), librarians (87%), health technicians (84%), elementary school teachers (83%), and bank tellers (81%).[142] In contrast, few women are plumbers (less than 1%), truck drivers (2%), butchers (7%), or mail carriers (12%).[143]

Although the Equal Pay Act mandates equal pay for equal work, it does not require equal pay for comparable work—usually called **comparable worth.** According to a personnel study in Washington State, maintenance carpenters and secretaries performed comparable jobs, but the carpenters, mostly men, made about $600 a month more than the secretaries, mostly women. Overall, the study found that "men's jobs" paid about 20% more than comparable "women's jobs." These findings prompted unions representing government employees in the state to file a suit and demand an increase in pay for jobs held mostly by women. The federal court of appeals, in an opinion by Judge Anthony Kennedy, now on the Supreme Court, rejected comparable worth. Nevertheless, some state and city governments have begun to implement comparable worth plans for their employees after prodding by unions and women's groups. Most private companies, however, have not adopted comparable worth because it would require them to pay most of their women employees more.

TABLE 5 Women with Children Earn Less

FEMALE-TO-MALE EARNINGS PERCENT	
With Children	Without Children
72%	91%

These figures are for whites, ages 20-44, in 1987. The figures control for age, education, skill level, labor force turnover, and region.

Source: Current Population Survey, 1988. Reprinted in June O'Neill, "Women & Wages," *The American Enterprise*, November-December, 1990, p. 32.

EDUCATION The Education Amendments of 1972 (to the Civil Rights Act of 1964) forbid discrimination on the basis of sex in schools and colleges that receive federal aid. The amendments were prompted by discrimination against women by undergraduate and graduate colleges, especially in admissions and financial aid.

The language of the amendments, often referred to as "Title IX," is so broad that the Department of Education, which administers them, has established rules that cover more aspects of education than their congressional supporters expected.[144] The department has used the amendments to prod institutions into employing and promoting more female teachers and administrators, opening vocational training classes to women and home economics classes to men, and offering equal athletic programs to women. If institutions do not comply, the government can cut off their federal aid.

The amendments have had a substantial impact on athletic programs in particular. Before the amendments, schools and colleges provided fewer sports for women than for men, and they spent far fewer dollars—for scholarships, equipment, and facilities—on those they did provide. Now institutions offer more sports for women and allocate more money for them, although institutions do not provide equal resources, primarily because of the size and cost of men's football programs and the lack of a women's counterpart. To offset this disparity somewhat, more schools are establishing women's teams in sports where they do not have a men's team. The number of schools that offer women's soccer, for example, increased from 133 to 445 during the 1980s and 1990s.[145]

An unintended consequence of the amendments, however, has been a reduction in the number of female athletic administrators and coaches in colleges and universities. In 1972 over 90% of women's athletic programs were headed by a female administrator; by 1988 only 16% were. In 1972 over 90% of women's team coaches were female; by 1988 just 48% were. In response to the amendments, many schools merged their men's and women's athletic programs to cut costs and promote equity. But the head of the men's program became the athletic director, while the head of the women's program became his assistant. Before the amendments, most schools used poorly paid part-time coaches for women's teams. After the amendments, the schools boosted salaries, so more men were attracted to the positions and hired by the male athletic director.[146]

CREDIT The Equal Credit Opportunity Act of 1974 forbids discrimination on the basis of sex or marital status in credit transactions. Historically banks, savings and loans, credit card companies, and retail stores discriminated against women. Typically these businesses determine how much money people can borrow according to how much they earn. Yet the lenders refused loans to single women, regardless of income, because they assumed that the women would work only until they got married and became pregnant. Likewise, the lenders did not count wives' income as part of couples' total income, again because they assumed the wives would work temporarily. Only if women were professionals or in their forties would lenders count their income the same as men's. And when businesses lent money to married couples, they put the transactions just in the husband's name. Upon divorce or widowhood, women had no credit record and little chance to obtain credit.

The Equal Credit Opportunity Act requires lenders to lend to single women and to count wives' income as part of couples' total income. It restricts lenders from asking women if they intend to bear children. And the act requires lenders to put accounts in the names of both spouses if they request.

EQUAL RIGHTS AMENDMENT The **Equal Rights Amendment (ERA)** simply declared, "Equality of rights under the law shall not be denied or abridged by the United States or by any state on account of sex." Introduced in 1923 and every year thereafter, the amendment was passed by Congress in 1972.

Men resisted the expansion of women's athletics. The Boston Marathon traditionally was for men only, and when the first woman tried to participate in 1967, a marathon official assaulted her.

It appeared the amendment would zip through the states. Both parties endorsed it, and the majority of the public supported it. But after about half the states ratified it, the amendment bogged down. Observers noted that it would make women subject to the draft and, possibly, combat duty. Opponents charged that it would result in unisex restrooms and homosexual rights. Legal scholars denied that it would lead to these latter consequences, but after the judicial activism of the 1950s, 1960s, and 1970s, some people distrusted the courts to interpret the amendment.

The main problem, however, proved to be the symbolism of the amendment. For many women the ERA represented an attack on the traditional values of motherhood, the family, and the home. To underscore this, women in conservative groups baked bread for state legislators about to vote on ratification. Because of the symbolism, even some women who favored equality opposed the amendment itself. Although many young women supported it, fewer of their mothers and grandmothers did; and although many working women supported it, fewer housewives did. Women's organizations had not created an effective grass-roots campaign to sway traditional women. Ultimately, the disaffection of many women allowed male legislators to vote according to their traditional attitudes. They did not need to worry that a strong majority of their female constituents would object.[147]

In 1980 the Republican party became the first party not to endorse the ERA since 1940, and President Reagan became the first president not to support the amendment since Truman.

When the deadline set by Congress expired in 1982, the ERA fell three states short of ratification by the necessary three-fourths—38—of the states. Like the Nineteenth Amendment, it was not ratified primarily by southern states.

Despite the defeat, a state equal rights amendment has been adopted by numerous states, and the ERA continues to be favored by a majority of the public.

The Movement in the Courts

Meanwhile, women sought action from the courts as well as the legislatures. Initially they found little success in the courts. In 1873, when Illinois denied a woman a license to practice law solely because she was a woman, the Supreme Court upheld the state's policy.[148] The Court set the tone for almost a century. Justice Joseph Bradley declared,

> Man is, or should be, woman's protector and defender. The natural and proper timidity and delicacy which belongs to the female sex evidently unfits it for many of the occupations of civil life. . . . The harmony . . . of interests and views which belong, or should belong, to the family institution is repugnant to the idea of a woman adopting a distinct and independent career from that of her husband. [The] paramount destiny and mission of woman are to fulfill the noble and benign offices of wife and mother. This is the law of the Creator.

So the Court upheld laws that discriminated against women, and it also upheld some laws that protected women, especially from arduous working conditions.[149] The same attitude underlay both sets of decisions: Women are inferior and weaker, so they can be discriminated against yet also should be protected.

As late as 1970, the Ohio Supreme Court held that a wife is a husband's servant with "no legally recognized feelings or rights."[150]

The Burger Court finally reversed this pattern of decisions. In 1971, for the first time, the Court struck down a law that discriminated against women,[151] heralding a long series of rulings that invalidated a variety of such laws. In these rulings the Court used the congressional statutes and also broadened the Fourteenth Amendment's equal protection clause to apply to women as well as to racial minorities.

The change was especially apparent in a pair of cases involving the selection of jurors. For the pool of potential jurors, some states drew the names of men, but not women, from voter registration or other lists. The states allowed women to serve only if they voluntarily signed up at the courthouse. Consequently, few women served. In 1961 the Court let Florida use these procedures because the "woman is still regarded as the center of home and family life."[152] In 1975, however, the Court forbade Louisiana from using similar procedures,[153] thus overturning a precedent only 14 years old.

The Court's rulings rejected the traditional stereotypes that men are the breadwinners and women the childrearers in society. The Court invalidated Utah's law that required divorced fathers to support their daughters until age 18 but their sons until 21.[154] The state assumed that the daughters would get married and be supported by their husbands, whereas the sons would need to get educated for their careers. But the Court noted, "No longer is the female destined solely for the home."

The Court ruled that the government can forbid newspapers from designating help-wanted ads as "male" or "female."[155] Employers cannot set arbitrary height and weight requirements that screen out women.[156] Industries cannot bar fertile women from jobs that would entail risk to their fetus if they became pregnant.[157] A manufacturer of automobile batteries barred women who could not prove that they were sterile from jobs that would expose them to lead. These high-risk jobs paid more than others in the plant. The company worried about potential lawsuits, yet the Court concluded that the company would not be liable as long as it explained the hazards to employees. The justices said the company must allow employees to make the decisions about their future children.

Employers cannot refuse to hire mothers of preschool children because they fear that these women might miss too much work while caring for their children.[158] Employers cannot force women to take maternity leave,[159] and, if women do take maternity leave, employers cannot cancel the seniority they have accumulated.[160]

Employers cannot require women employees to pay more money per month into pension plans, and they cannot give women retirees less money per month from pension plans.[161] Overall, women tend to live longer than men, so they could collect more money from pension plans, but these policies discriminated against individual women who would not live longer. The Court required companies to base their plans on individual equality rather than group life expectancy.

The Court also upheld state laws that prohibit private organizations such as the Jaycees and Rotary Club from excluding women. These organizations

Sexual Harassment at Work

Although the Supreme Court had ruled that sexual harassment was a form of job discrimination prohibited by the Civil Rights Act of 1964,[1] and Congress had passed a law allowing victims to collect monetary damages from employers for distress, illness, or loss of their job due to harassment, there was little public awareness of the law until Clarence Thomas' confirmation hearings for appointment to the Supreme Court in 1991.

The hearings propelled sexual harassment to the forefront of societal debate. For seven days the public was riveted to the televised hearings. Anita Hill's charges—that Thomas, as her supervisor at the Equal Employment Opportunity Commission, made lewd comments about her, about sex, about finding pubic hairs on Coke cans and watching animals have sex in films—led to many discussions around workplace water coolers.

The hearings illustrated that sexual harassment includes more than just physical acts, such as unwanted touching, or propositions in which sex is demanded in exchange for a job or promotion. It also encompasses other conduct and comments that create a "hostile working environment."

Although some men fear that innocent comments will be construed as harassment by women, other men who do not want women as co-workers intend their behavior to upset women. Sometimes they turn the workplace into a locker room and then say, "What's the matter, you can't handle it? You wanted equality—you got it." For example, the first female skilled crafts worker for Santa Clara County, California, found that in the yard the men kept the women's restroom locked and on the road they refused to stop to let her use a restroom. "You wanted a man's job," a superior told her, "you learn to pee like a man."[2]

The dynamics of sexual harassment do not revolve around sex as much they reflect abuse of power. A supervisor, or a co-worker in a position to cause problems, makes a woman feel vulnerable. Thus, the supervisor or co-worker demonstrates psychological dominance or economic dominance ("You need this job? Then keep quiet.").

Surveys show that a third of female workers say they have been sexually harassed on the job.[3] After 23 women acknowledged in 1992 and 1993 that they had to fend off sexual advances by Senator Bob Packwood (R.-Ore.), the *Washington Post* conducted a survey of women who worked as aides to

Do You Think It Is Sexual Harassment If a Man Who is a Woman's Supervisor . . .

	YES
Insists on discussing pornographic acts with her	91%
Makes remarks to her that contain sexual references or double meanings	80
Pressures her to go out to dinner with him	77
Insists on telling sexual jokes to her	74
Frequently puts his arm around her shoulders or back	64
Flirts with the woman	41

Source: A nationwide survey of men and women by Yankelovich Clancy Shulman for *Time* and CNN. *Time*, October 21, 1991, p. 64.

provide important business contacts and, the Court noted, are not as private as traditional men's clubs, which still may discriminate against women.[162]

In 1996 the Court ordered the Virginia Military Institute to admit women, which it had not done in its 157-year history, or to give up state funding. The Court said there has to be an "exceedingly persuasive justification" for any government policy based on gender. (The ruling apparently applies to The Citadel in South Carolina as well.)

Only occasionally did the Court go in the opposite direction. Most important, the Court ruled that government may give military veterans a preference over nonveterans in obtaining civil service jobs.[163] Because most veterans are men, this benefits many men who seek government jobs at the expense of almost all women who seek them. Nevertheless, the Court said government may adopt this policy to thank veterans for their service.

Although formal restrictions against women have been struck down, informal discrimination continues. Women get hired, but some find it more difficult to get promoted than comparable men. They hit a "glass ceiling."

Many women in masculine workplaces feel pressure to submerge feminist beliefs. "You're not a feminist, are you?" is a familiar query. Women who seek career advancement say they would commit "professional suicide" if they spoke up for their rights or beliefs as women.[164]

Some women also face sexual harassment. "In college, they lied to us twice," one disillusioned young woman said. "They said it would be equal. And they said it would be safe."[165]

members of Congress or staffers for congressional committees. It found the same results: A third of them had been sexually harassed in the hallowed halls of Congress, and a third of these had been harassed by a member of Congress. (The others had been harassed by supervisors, coworkers, or lobbyists.)[4]

Yet few victims file formal complaints, let alone bring lawsuits, because they need their jobs. According to several studies, only 3% of women who have been harassed have filed formal complaints.[5] On Capitol Hill, 80% of the women surveyed said they would lose their job if they did; 80% said they would never find another job there if they did; and 70% said nothing would be done to the harasser anyway.[6]

Sexual harassment can be directed toward men as well. About 15% of male workers say they have been sexually harassed by men or women on the job.[7]

While the public expressed disgust with the Thomas hearings—because of the way they were conducted and the charges they revealed—people were sensitized to sexual harassment. After the hearings, more women recognized that behavior they had dismissed as merely annoying was actually harassment. More workers filed complaints with the EEOC—nearly twice as many annually.[8] And more employers adopted written policies and held training sessions to educate their employees.

The new awareness of sexual harassment apparently affected attitudes toward Thomas and Hill as well. After the hearings, the public thought Thomas had told the truth (40% to 24% for Hill), but a year later the public thought Hill had told the truth after all (44% to 34% for Thomas).[9]

In 1993 the Supreme Court sent a signal to lower courts and employers to take harassment seriously. It ruled unanimously, just 27 days after oral arguments, that victims do not have to prove a severe psychological injury to collect damages.[10] Teresa Harris, the rental manager of an equipment company, had endured repeated comments by her boss—"You're a woman; what do you know?"—and suggestions to accompany him to the Holiday Inn to negotiate her raise. Harris and other female workers also had been asked to retrieve coins from his pants pockets. Although Harris did not suffer any concrete psychological injury, she did feel compelled to quit the job. Justice O'Connor wrote that the law applies if a reasonable person would consider the workplace a hostile environment. (On the other hand, the law does not apply to "merely offensive" conduct short of creating an abusive environment.)

---

1. *Meritor Savings Bank v. Vinson,* 91 L.Ed.2d 49 (1986).
2. Nancy Gibbs, "Office Crimes," *Time,* October 21, 1991, p. 53.
3. Richard Morin, "Think Twice Before You Say Another Word," *Washington Post National Weekly Edition,* December 28, 1992–January 3, 1993, p. 37.
4. Richard Morin, "Jack and Jill Went Up the Hill," *Washington Post National Weekly Edition,* March 1–7, 1993, p. 37.
5. Daniel Goleman, "Sexual Harassment: About Power, Not Sex." *New York Times,* October 22, 1991, p. B8.
6. Morin, "Jack and Jill Went Up the Hill."
7. Janice Castro, "Sexual Harassment: A Guide," *Time,* January 20, 1992, p. 37.
8. Kara Swisher, "Corporations Are Seeing the Light on Harassment," *Washington Post National Weekly Edition,* February 14-20, 1994, p. 21.
9. Jill Smolowe, "Anita Hill's Legacy," *Time,* October 19, 1992, p. 56.
10. *Harris v. Forklift Systems,* 126 L.Ed.2d 295 (1993).

Mothers with young children confront more obstacles. Their male employers and co-workers think women should be responsible for child rearing, but these men do little to accommodate the demands of child rearing. Most companies do not provide paid maternity leaves, flexible schedules, or on-site day care. The United States lags far behind many other countries, 98 of which grant partly paid maternity leaves for at least three months.[166]

When Congress passed a bill requiring employers to grant unpaid maternity leaves, President Bush vetoed it, but then President Clinton signed a similar bill. Companies must allow leaves for up to three months for workers with newborn or recently adopted children or with seriously ill family members. The act applies to companies that have 50 employees and to workers who work 25 hours a week for a year. This covers about 40% of American workers.

So far, however, few workers have taken advantage of maternity leaves or flexible schedules where they are available. Researchers have concluded that managers often do not support such measures, so employees are reluctant to take advantage of them. At a time when many companies have laid off workers to cut costs, "If you look like you are not career-oriented, you can lose your job."[167]

Discrimination Against Men

Although nearly all sex discrimination has been against women, some has been against men. However, laws discriminating against men often have reinforced negative stereotypes about women and in this sense have perpetuated discrimination against them as well.

The Burger Court struck down Oklahoma's law that allowed women to drink beer at 18 but required men to wait until 21.[168] Prior to the law, men 18 through 20 were arrested for drunk driving 10 times more than women in this age group, but the Court said the law penalized all young men for the behavior of a few. The Court also struck down Alabama's law that permitted only women to seek alimony upon divorce and Mississippi's law that barred men from one of the state's three university nursing schools.[169] Thus the Court rejected stereotypes that only women are dependent on their spouses and only women are nurses.

On the other hand, the Burger Court upheld some laws motivated by a desire to protect women. In 1980 President Carter asked Congress to reinstate registration for the draft, though not the draft itself, to show our "toughness" to the Soviet Union and other Communist countries. Carter urged Congress to include women in the program. Although Congress had admitted women to the military academies in 1975, it was not ready to include them here. When young men subject to registration brought suit, the Court was not ready either.[170] It rationalized that registration eventually could lead to the draft and the draft eventually to combat. And it insisted that most women are not capable of combat. Likewise, many states have laws that prohibit statutory rape—intercourse with a minor with consent—by men but not by women. When a young man convicted of statutory rape appealed, the Court affirmed these laws and his conviction.[171] Thus the Court accepted stereotypes that only men are capable of combat and only men initiate intercourse.

In the absence of war, the most significant discrimination against men may occur in divorce cases, where the norm is to grant custody of children to mothers and require payment of support by fathers. Although courts give fathers visitation rights, they permit mothers to move miles away, making visitation difficult and sporadic. And although in the past decade governments have taken steps to enforce support payments, they have done little to enforce visitation rights. This practice reflects the stereotype that fathers are capable of financing their children's upbringing but not of bringing them up themselves. The Court has ignored this problem.

Overall, however, the Court has moved steadily toward legal equality for the sexes. Women, and occasionally men, have accomplished through the Court much of what they would have accomplished with the ERA, although the Court's rulings are not a complete substitute for the ERA. Court decisions make law case by case, slowly and haphazardly, whereas a constitutional amendment would make law across the board, more quickly and thoroughly. Also, Court decisions by justices sympathetic to women's rights can be overruled by later justices not sympathetic, whereas a constitutional amendment could not be repealed without widespread agreement in society. Finally, Court decisions do not give women the same symbolic satisfaction that a constitutional amendment would.

Affirmative Action

Assume there is a track meet. A black runner and a white runner start together. But the officials force the black runner to carry heavy weights, and he falls behind. Eventually, the officials realize this is unfair, and they take the weights off. Of course the black runner is still behind. Would this be fair? Assume, instead, the officials not only take the weights off but allow him to catch up. Would this be more fair? Or would it be unfair to the white runner who was not responsible for the weights and who might have run faster than the black even without the weights?[172]

This scenario captures the dilemma of civil rights policy today. Although most race and sex discrimination has been repudiated by the courts and legislatures, the effects of past discrimination survive. Now the question is whether civil rights policy should ignore race and sex or take race and sex into account to compensate for the effects of past discrimination. That is, should the policy require nondiscrimination only or **affirmative action** as well?

Affirmative action applies to employers in hiring and promoting minorities and women, governments in reserving a portion of their contracts for businesses owned by minorities and women, and colleges and universities in admitting minorities and women.

The Civil Rights Act of 1964, which bars discrimination in employment, does not mention affirmative action, but it does authorize the bureaucracy to make rules to help end discrimination. In 1969 the Department of Labor called for affirmative action by companies doing business with the federal government. Later the Equal Employment Opportunities Commission called for affirmative action by governments and the Office of Education by colleges as well. Despite public hostility to affirmative action, presidents from Nixon through Carter supported it with executive orders, and the Supreme Court sanctioned it in a series of cases.[173] Many state and local governments also adopted it.

Affirmative action applies most extensively to employment. It requires positive steps to ensure that qualified minorities and women receive a fair share of jobs at all levels. Just what the positive steps and the fair share should be are the subject of much controversy.

To meet affirmative action requirements, a job must be advertised publicly in places minorities and women are likely to hear about it, and the qualifications must be related to the job. For instance, a requirement that police officers be a certain height may discriminate against Hispanics and women and is not necessary for the job. On the other hand, a requirement that firefighters be able to drag a heavy hose a certain distance may discriminate against women but is necessary for the job. In hiring, more than one candidate should be interviewed, and, ideally, the interviews should be evaluated as objectively as possible by using preestablished criteria and more than one interviewer.

In addition, if the number of minorities and women in a company or government agency, at any level, is less than the number in the local labor force, the company or agency must agree to recruit more or, in serious cases, draw up an affirmative action plan. The plan must include goals to hire or promote more minorities or women and a timetable to reach these goals. If the company or agency does not reach them, it must explain why. Failure to satisfy the government can result in the loss of future contracts or aid.

Although the requirements for affirmative action plans speak of "goals," some people say they really mean quotas. Critics charge that quotas would result in both lower standards and reverse discrimination. But affirmative action usually does not require actual quotas. Admittedly, the terms blur; if employers are pressured to meet "goals," they might interpret them to be quotas. But only occasionally, and only after a finding of deliberate and systematic discrimination, does affirmative action entail actual quotas.

The Supreme Court has issued mixed rulings on the legality of quotas. In *University of California Regents v. Bakke* in 1978, the Court upheld the policy of the medical school at the University of California at Davis to consider race as a factor in admissions, but it struck down the policy to establish a quota of 16 spaces for minorities out of 100 spaces in the class. On the other hand, the Court upheld the plan of Kaiser Aluminum and Chemical Company and the United Steelworkers union to establish a quota of 50% of the openings in Kaiser's training program for blacks until the percentage of blacks in skilled positions in the company matches the percentage in the local labor force.[174] The Court also upheld quotas for New York City sheet metal workers, Cleveland firefighters, and Alabama state police.[175]

The primary factor in determining the legality of quotas is whether the employer or union discriminated in the past. The University of California at Davis had no history of discrimination, but the other employers did.

In reviewing affirmative action plans, the Court also looks at two crucial elements: They must not prevent all white men from being hired and promoted, and the plans must be temporary. Many are to end when the number of black employees approaches the percentage of black residents in the community.

Because of concern that affirmative action not pose too great a burden on innocent individuals, the Court has struck down affirmative action in laying off workers—that is, struck down protection for minorities and women when employers pare their work force for economic reasons. Instead, the Court has accepted the traditional practice, based on seniority, that the last hired is the first fired.[176]

The Rehnquist Court, however, has signaled a change of direction in affirmative action doctrine. Although the Court has not barred affirmative action programs, a slim majority has made it more difficult for governments to adopt some programs.[177] Governments must demonstrate a "compelling" reason, which apparently means they must have clear evidence of specific discrimination, rather than cite the general pattern of historical discrimination, and they must show how particular programs would ameliorate the problems.

Affirmative action requirements are not very stringent and are not strictly enforced. Employers who are required to file an affirmative action plan but fail to reach their goals ordinarily need to show only that they made a genuine effort to reach them. Employers rarely are penalized. Federal officials are swamped with discrimination complaints and rarely have enough staff to investigate compliance with affirmative action policies. Thus, compliance depends on the good faith of some employers plus the strategic use of a few investigations and penalties to serve as a threat to others.

Some government pressure evidently is necessary. A study of Philadelphia companies found that over half were run by executives whose views on affirmative action ranged from "neutral" to "extremely resistant." They practiced affirmative action because they felt they had to.[178]

Affirmative action programs have helped minorities and women. Companies that do business with the federal government, and therefore are subject to affirmative action, have shown more improvement in hiring minorities and women than other companies. And state and local governments, also subject to affirmative action, have shown more improvement in

Affirmative Action for . . . Alums' Children?

Critics of affirmative action by colleges and universities charge that preferential treatment for racial minorities means that many better-qualified whites are denied admission. Critics then claim that this lowers academic standards at the schools.[1]

But at most elite schools the number of students admitted through affirmative action does not come close to the number admitted because their parents are alums.[2] For more than 40 years, a fifth of Harvard's students have had preferential treatment in admission because their parents attended the school. In the 1980s Harvard's "legacies" were more than two times as likely to be admitted as blacks or Hispanics. A similar advantage exists at other Ivy League schools.[3] Yale's legacies were more than two-and-a-half times as likely to be admitted as nonlegacies. A former dean of admissions at Princeton asserts that having one or both parents as alums "doubles, even trebles the chances of admission."

This advantage exists at other selective schools. Notre Dame reportedly reserves 25% of its openings for legacies. The Universities of Virginia and California-Berkeley treat out-of-state legacies as in-state students, which gives them a competitive edge because most state universities favor state residents.

Schools say legacies have such a high rate of admission because their parents provide the upbringing that makes their children more qualified than other students. Yet the U.S. Department of Education's Office of Civil Rights, investigating Harvard for possible discrimination in admission, found that the average admitted legacy was significantly less qualified than the average admitted nonlegacy. In fact, the number of marginally qualified legacies was greater than the number of black, Mexican American, Puerto Rican, and Native American students combined.

Schools also justify their policies by saying they fear that alums will stop giving money if their children are denied admission. This probably is the main concern.

Regardless of the wisdom of the policies, hypocrisy toward affirmative action is widespread. Opponents ignore the many factors in addition to merit that have always gone into college admissions decisions. Some who have called for the end of affirmative action for minorities, such as a group of Dartmouth alumni, have at the same time demanded that it continue for their children.

1. Thomas Sowell, *Preferential Policies: An International Perspective* (New York: Morrow, 1990); Dinesh D'Souza, *Illiberal Education* (New York: Free Press, 1991).
2. The remaining text is drawn from John Larew, "Why Are Droves of Unqualified, Unprepared Kids Getting into Our Top Colleges?" *Washington Monthly*, June 1991, pp 10–14.
3. Theodore Cross, "Suppose There Was No Affirmative Action at the Most Prestigious Colleges and Graduate Schools," *Journal of Blacks in Higher Education*, Spring 1994, pp. 47, 50.

New Populism

Opposition to Affirmative Action

Trailing his black opponent in his reelection bid in 1990, Senator Jesse Helms (R.-N.C.) ran a simple but devastating television commercial: A white man, rejected for a job, crumpled up his application form while a voice-over said, "You really wanted that job, you really needed that job, but you didn't get it because you're not a minority. Vote for Jesse Helms." After this commercial began, the polls switched, and North Carolina reelected the senator.

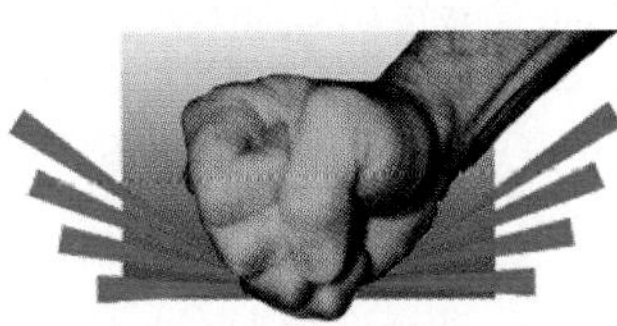

Helms's commercial reopened—actually, reignited—public debate on affirmative action. Politicians in both parties saw how volatile the issue could be. Critics of the programs stepped up their attacks, while white lower-middle class males worried about losing a job or a promotion to blacks and white male executives worried about losing a job or a promotion to women.

According to public opinion polls, a majority of whites agrees with the statement, "We have gone too far in pushing equal rights in this country."[1] More specifically, 75% of Americans oppose giving a "preference" for blacks and other minorities in hiring, promoting, and admitting to college "to make up for past discrimination." And 73% oppose "preference" for women. Although large majorities of whites and males think affirmative action programs have increased opportunities for minorities and women, only 34% of whites and 37% of males think this is "a price worth paying" if these programs result in less opportunity for white men. As a result, about half of Americans want to "change them," while another quarter want to "do away with them entirely." (The remaining quarter want to "leave them as they are.")[2]

Like other racial issues, opinion about affirmative action divides along racial lines. Although 63% of white males thought affirmative action had hurt white men, just 19% of blacks thought so. And although 81% of whites oppose affirmative action for minorities, 46% of blacks do.[3]

Public opposition has been festering for years. There has been little change in responses to questions about affirmative action since they were first asked in the early 1980s.[4] But public debate had been relatively muted, because government policy had been largely initiated by executive orders, implemented by bureaucratic agencies, and sanctioned by court rulings. The legislative branch, controlled by Democrats sympathetic to civil rights, had acquiesced, so Congress had not staged the same debate as it does for many issues. In short, the government had neither tried to persuade those who were uncertain before adopting the policy nor tried to persuade those who were opposed while continuing the policy.

When Republicans wrested control of Congress from the Democrats in 1994, affirmative action was no longer protected. Congressional Republicans called for a review of all affirmative action programs, with an eye toward shrinking or dismantling them. Most Republicans running for president, recognizing the political value of this volatile issue, echoed these views. President Clinton and some Democrats, seeking the return of the white males who left the party in the 1994 elections, proposed reforming the programs.

Rollbacks were also underway in some states. Two California professors, prompted by a legislative proposal (which failed to pass) to establish quotas for admission to and graduation from state universities, launched a petition drive for a public vote on an initiative prohibiting the use of race, sex, or national origin as "a criterion for either discriminating against, or granting preferential treatment to, an individual or group" in state education, employment, or contracting. In 1995 the University of California Board of Regents, over the opposition of many administrators and faculty members, voted to eliminate the use of race and sex as factors for admission to the university. (A majority of the regents were appointed by Governor Pete Wilson (R.), who was running for nomination for president in part on a platform opposed to affirmative action.) Yet several of the regents who voted to stop affirmative action had acted behind the scenes to get relatives, friends, and children of business partners enrolled at the UC schools. One had made 32 requests to UCLA alone.[5]

To evaluate the policies of the government and the arguments in the debate, consider the following questions:

Is Affirmative Action Pervasive?

Public employers and private employers who have government contracts (and who have 50 or more employees and do $50,000 or more of business with the government in a year) are subject to affirmative action. This encompasses thousands of employers responsible for hiring and promoting millions of employees. In addition, public colleges that receive federal aid are subject to affirmative action in hiring and promoting employees and also in admitting students.

However, as the chapter explains, affirmative action requirements are not very stringent and are not strictly enforced. Although affirmative action programs have led to some gains for blacks, they have not displaced many whites. For instance, the number of black employees in 40 cities between 1973 and 1980, the peak years for affirmative action, increased from 28% to 33% of the total employees. The number of black administrators increased from 9% to 16%, which was about half the proportion of black residents in these cities.[6]

In 1995 about 13% of white males told pollsters they think they lost a job or promotion at some time because of their race, while about 10% think they did because of their sex.[7] Many others claim they "heard about" someone else who was a victim of affirmative action. Yet often persons do not know the worker hired or promoted instead of them or do not know the qualifications of this worker (which may have been better than those of the white male).

One analyst concluded that white males' beliefs that they are at a disadvantage come from a concern that "the category I belong to, the group I'm in, doesn't have the same access we used to."[8] This perception is correct though exaggerated, given the limited scope of affirmative action.

Does Affirmative Action Result in Less Merit?

It is difficult to assess merit. The concept means different things to different people, and its characteristics cannot be measured precisely. For example, assume one applicant for a social work position has more years of experience, another has the highest score on the exam, while another seems better able to understand and communicate with the people who are the agency's clients. Which applicant is more qualified? Some people would emphasize the first applicant's experience, others would focus on the second applicant's score—these can be measured—while still others would emphasize the third applicant's ability to understand and communicate—these cannot be measured easily.

The Supreme Court's decision approving affirmative action for women reflects the problems in assessing merit. A woman who applied to be a dispatcher for the transportation agency of Santa Clara County, California, was one of nine considered qualified for the job. She scored 73, and a white man scored 75, on a subjective oral exam administered by a panel of men who had never hired a woman for a skilled position. The county decided that the two-point differential was inconsequential and hired the woman for affirmative action. The man sued for reverse discrimination, but the Court upheld the hiring.[9]

In addition, opponents of affirmative action tend to compare it with an idealized picture of traditional employment practices. Opponents assume these practices were based squarely on merit. In reality, these practices were based only partly on merit.

For government employment, many jobs were open only to those who already worked for that government. Other jobs were open to those who took exams and performed well, but the jobs did not necessarily go to the person who scored highest. Typically they went to the person among the three or five who scored highest and who had the desired political connections, personal connections, personality, or area of residence, or to the person who was a military veteran.

For faculty positions in colleges and universities, the "old boy network" of fellow faculty at other schools was the primary means of hiring. Departments seldom advertised their positions widely.

For private employment, vacancies were advertised by word of mouth to relatives or friends. Union membership was necessary for many skilled blue-collar jobs, and places were reserved for sons and brothers—rarely daughters and sisters—of members. Even when jobs were advertised, usually no effort was made to canvass the locality or region for the most meritorious candidate.

For both public and private employment, jobs often went to persons of particular ethnic groups when members of these groups reached positions of power. Italians and Irish in New York and Boston, for example, hired other Italians and Irish.

Source: Clay Bennett, North America Syndicate.

Nevertheless, there is a legitimate concern that affirmative action might result in lower standards and lower quality employees or students. Affirmative action probably pressures some employers and schools into choosing some minorities or women who lack adequate education, training, or experience because of past discrimination. At the same time, affirmative action provides a larger pool of talent to choose from. According to one executive, before affirmative action, "We were not using all the talent available." With affirmative action, the company found a "goldmine" of untapped talent.[10]

Does Affirmative Action Result in Reverse Discrimination?

By compensating for past discrimination against some, does affirmative action constitute new discrimination against others? If the number of jobs or places in schools are limited and if more are offered to minorities or women, fewer are available for white men. To determine if this is reverse discrimination, consider four possible outcomes of affirmative action: (1) Choosing a minority or woman who is more qualified than a white man. Although the principle of nondiscrimination, rather than affirmative action, should have led to this outcome, often it did not. In fact, the greatest accomplishment of affirmative action may have been to prod employers to hire or promote minorities and women who should have been hired or promoted all along. (2) Choosing a minority or woman who is as qualified as a white man. This occurs frequently in less specialized jobs, where candidates do not differ clearly in qualifications, but rarely in more specialized jobs, where candidates do differ significantly. (3) Choosing a minority or woman who, though qualified, is less qualified than a white man. Here affirmative action is similar to past practices in that both select persons from among qualified candidates but according to some factor other than merit. (4) Choosing a minority or woman who is unqualified. Employers or schools are not required to choose unqualified persons, but undoubtedly they do occasionally.

Of these four outcomes, only the last two result in reverse discrimination. When they occur white men pay for the sins of their fathers and grandfathers. Yet the first two probably occur more often. White men dominate public and private institutions and, as the personnel director of a Fortune 500 company observed, "People tend to hire people like themselves."[11] If reverse discrimination were widespread, minorities and women would hold more jobs, at higher levels, than they do now.

Does Affirmative Action Result in Less Fairness?

When affirmation action prods employers to hire or promote minorities or women who are more qualified than white men (see outcome 1 above), it results in more fairness. When affirmative action prompts employers to hire or promote minorities or women who are as qualified or less qualified than white men (outcomes 2 and 3 above), it appears to result in less fairness. A Chicago police officer complained, "I didn't own slaves, and I shouldn't be penalized for what happened hundreds of years ago."[12]

But, of course, whites benefited from hundreds of years of slavery, segregation, and discrimination. Whites increased their wealth and improved their position in society and then passed these gains on to their descendants. (Sometimes whites gained at the direct expense of blacks. Other times they gained because of the lack of competition from blacks—from a sizable portion of the population.) For instance, after World War II, Levittowns in New York and Pennsylvania developed suburban tract housing and made it available to white GIs—for just $100 down—but not to black GIs. In the 1990s, these houses are worth about $180,000. This wealth will continue to accrue to these white families but never to any black families.[13]

Although many individual whites today are not responsible for the status of blacks today, they continue to benefit from the discrepancy. Without affirmative action or some comparable policy to redress past discrimination, they will continue to benefit from it. The advantages will be locked in. (Even with affirmative action, which is only a modest effort to compensate, most advantages will remain.)

This problem is compounded by society's view that slavery was not just bad luck—one of life's misfortunes that seem to befall people randomly—or even a shortsighted or inefficient policy, but that it was morally wrong behavior. As a black Birmingham, Alabama, firefighter observed: "Say your father robs a bank, takes the money and buys his daughter a Mercedes, and then buys his son a Porsche and his wife a home in the high-rent district. Then they discover [his crime]. He has to give the cars and house back. And the family starts to cry: 'We didn't do anything.' [But] sometimes you have to pay up. If a wrong has been committed, you have to right that wrong."[14] Seen in this light, it is not clear that affirmative action results in less fairness.[15]

Still, the analogy becomes less valid in an increasingly diverse society, with many newcomers whose ancestors were not here during the era of slavery or even Jim Crow, and who may not be white. The recent discussions of affirmative action in the California university system, for example, reveal that the biggest beneficiaries of removal of affirmative action admittances would be Asians, not whites.

Why Are So Many Opposed to Affirmative Action?

If affirmative action has made only modest differences, why is it so opposed by so many people? Affirmative action highlights a conflict between two fundamental American values—egalitarianism and individualism. It emphasizes the former at the expense of the latter. It offers equality of opportunity by opening doors for people who found them closed before. And it offers equality of results by providing jobs for people who were denied them before. In a way, it furthers individuality by helping minorities and women develop their full potential. But, for the most part, it undermines individuality by treating people as members of groups rather than as individuals. Essentially, affirmative action helps group A (minorities or women today) by punishing group B (white men today) for what group C (white men yesterday) did to group D (minorities or women yesterday). Employment practices still consider the abilities and efforts of individuals but do not emphasize them to the extent they would in the absence of affirmative action policies. Perhaps a group remedy, such as affirmative action, is appropriate for the group problem of discrimination, but such a remedy concerns people who value individuality, especially those who value individuality more than equality.

But opposition does not stem from people's abstract values alone. It comes from more concrete factors also. Many people are limited in their historical knowledge. They assume the Civil War not only abolished slavery but also leveled the playing field for blacks and whites. Many people are affected by the pervasive racism in society. Although such feelings are considered socially unacceptable now, at least in some circles, the feelings exist still.[16] In focus groups (which, as Chapter 6 explained, are designed to make participants feel comfortable and free to express their opinions), the racism comes out. Researchers who tried to discover why middle-class whites in a Michigan county were leaving the Democratic Party found that the main reason was the racial policies of the Democratic Party juxtaposed with the racial feelings of the whites. The participants considered affirmative action a threat to their livelihood and the city of Detroit, with its black majority, a sinkhole for their tax dollars. These concerns, by themselves, would not necessarily be evidence of racism, but prejudicial attitudes emerged. When researchers had participants listen to a quotation from Robert Kennedy challenging whites to honor their "special obligation" to blacks, almost all participants reacted angrily. One even remarked, "No wonder they killed him."[17]

These feelings are exacerbated by the economic problems that have prevailed since the 1970s. During the 1960s and 1970s, the economy was robust and affirmative action was not so threatening. But during the 1980s and 1990s, the economy has been sluggish, with more competition for good jobs and decent paychecks. The real earnings (adjusted for inflation) of white men have declined, and the economic status of white men without a college degree

hiring than private companies. Organizations subject to affirmative action have shown even more progress in promoting minorities and women previously kept in low-level positions.[179]

The state of Alabama, for example, made dramatic gains. After a finding that the state troopers had never employed any blacks, the Department of Public Safety was socked with a court order to hire one new black for every new white until the force reached 25% black. The force reached 20% black within 12 years and became the most integrated force in the country. Faced with the threat of a similar order, other departments of the state government quickly hired more blacks at all levels.

Affirmative action has helped middle class and some lower class blacks get jobs in government and business.[180] It has been most successful in increasing the number of blacks in government agencies, police departments, fire departments, and various construction trades. It has been least successful in pulling blacks out of the "underclass." Many, from families with long-term poverty, experience long-term unemployment because they lack the education and skills necessary to compete for the available jobs.[181] Affirmative action also has helped many women get jobs in government and business that traditionally went only to men.

Of course, affirmative action cannot create new jobs or better jobs. Thus, it is not as helpful, either to minorities or women, as a general improvement in the economy would be.

Contrary to the view that affirmative action has helped some blacks, a minority claims that it actually has hindered them by encouraging them to rely on government programs, rather than on their own efforts, and by stigmatizing them. They say affirmative action casts doubt on minorities' credentials—in whites' minds and in minorities' minds as well. One black student complained, "I feel like I have AFFIRMATIVE ACTION stamped on my forehead."

➤Are Civil Rights Enough?

Although minorities and women have advanced toward legal equality, judicial decisions and legislative acts have not produced economic equality. The push for civil rights has opened doors for minorities and has dropped the most. As a result, affirmative action has become very threatening.

Politicians could explain that major economic trends, not affirmative action, account for the precarious position of many workers: corporations have computerized and automated many functions, downsized their workforce, hired part-time employees to whom they do not have to pay benefits, and moved their factories to Third World countries to minimize their payroll. It is easier, however, to blame affirmative action. Some Republicans see affirmative action as a "wedge issue"—an issue that enables them to drive a wedge between the constituencies of their opponents. By focusing on affirmative action, they hope to drive white men, especially laborers, from the Democratic Party, and by emphasizing minorities (rather than women) as the beneficiaries of affirmative action, they hope to drive some white women from the Democratic Party as well.[18]

The debate over affirmative action shows how the parties are trying to be responsive to the voters and to their members. When Republicans discovered that opposition to the policy was intense, they tried to capitalize on it. When Democrats saw that the issue could splinter their party, some called for reform of the policy to retain white men, while others called for continuation of the policy to satisfy minorities and women who constitute key groups in the party. Yet the parties have framed the issue for their own short-term gains rather than as a real examination where the rights and wrongs of both sides could be considered and the polarization of the races could be minimized. Thus, the debate also has reflected the downside of being responsive to the people.

1. Richard Lacayo, "A New Push for Blind Justice," *Time*, February 20, 1995, p. 39.
2. Richard Morin and Sharon Warden, "Poll Says Americans Angry about Affirmative Action," *Washington Post*, March 24, 1995, p. A4. There appears to be majority support for the vague concept of "affirmative action," undefined, but the support evaporates when the questions use language indicating or implying any preference for minorities or women. Richard Morin, "No Place for Calm and Quiet Opinions," *Washington Post National Weekly Edition*, April 24–30, 1995, p. 34.
3. Morin and Warden, "Poll Says Americans Angry about Affirmative Action."
4. Louis Jacobson, "A Speak-No-Evil Veil Lifted," *National Journal*, April 1, 1995, p. 836.
5. "UC Regents Aided Own, Paper Says," *San Diego Tribune*, March 17, 1996, p. A-3.
6. Peter Eisinger, *Black Employment in City Government* (Washington, D.C.: Joint Center for Political Studies, 1983).
7. Donald Kaul, "Privilege in Workplace Invisible to White Men Who Enjoy It," *Lincoln Journal-Star*, April 9, 1995.
8. Richard Morin and Lynne Duke, "A Look at the Bigger Picture," *Washington Post National Weekly Edition*, March 16–22, 1992, p. 9.
9. *Johnson v. Transportation Agency*, 94 L.Ed.2d 615 (1987).
10. Douglas B. Huron, "It's Fashionable to Denigrate Hiring Quotas—But It's Wrong," *Washington Post National Weekly Edition*, Aug. 27, 1984, p. 23.
11. Robert J. Samuelson, "End Affirmative Action," *Washington Post National Weekly Edition*, March 6–12, 1995, p. 5.
12. Thomas B. Edsall, "A Political Powder Keg," *Washington Post National Weekly Edition*, January 14–20, 1991, p. 6.
13. Juan Williams, "White Man's Burden," *Washington Post National Weekly Edition*, April 10–16, 1995, p. 24.
14. Edsall, "A Political Powder Keg."
15. For an extended analysis, see Ronald J. Fiscus (ed. Stephen L. Wasby), *The Constitutional Logic of Affirmative Action* (Durham, NC: Duke University Press, 1992).
16. Jacobson, "A Speak-No-Evil Veil Lifted."
17. Elizabeth Kolbert, "Test-Marketing a President," *New York Times Magazine*, August 30, 1992, p. 18.
18. Rochelle L. Stanfield, "The Wedge Issue," *National Journal*, April 1, 1995, pp. 790–93.

women, but those in the middle class were in a better position to pass through the doors than those in the lower class.

The black middle class has grown dramatically. The percentage of black professionals has nearly tripled, from 1.7% of all professionals in 1966 to about 5% in 1993.[182] The number of black families able to leave the inner cities for the suburbs has sharply increased. One-third of all blacks live in the suburbs now.[183]

But the black lower class could not take advantage of the expansion of civil rights. Economic stagnation and economic changes, beginning in the mid-1970s, hit the poor the hardest. Good-paying manufacturing jobs in the cities—the traditional path out of poverty for immigrant groups—decreased. Chicago lost over 300,000, New York over 500,000.[184] Many jobs were eliminated by automation, while many others were moved to foreign countries or to the suburbs. Although service jobs increased, most were outside the cities also. And most either required more education or paid less wages than the manufacturing jobs had. Thus, for the lower class in the inner cities, the decline of manufacturing jobs was not offset by the growth of service jobs.

As a result, black men, especially, lost their jobs and lost their ability to support a family. This led not only to pressure on intact families but to a decrease in the number of "marriageable" black men and an increase in the number of households headed by black women. These households are among the poorest in the country.[185]

Meanwhile, the black middle class fled the inner cities to the suburbs. Their migration left the ghettoes with fewer healthy businesses, strong schools, or other institutions to provide stability and fewer role models to portray mainstream behavior.[186] By 1996 one Chicago ghetto with 66,000 people had just one supermarket and one bank but 48 state-licensed lottery agents and 99 state-licensed liquor stores and bars.[187] The combination of chronic unemployment in the inner cities and middle class migration from the inner cities created an environment that offers ample opportunity and some incentive to use drugs, commit crimes, and engage in other types of antisocial behavior.

The development of crack, a cheap form of cocaine, in the mid-1980s aggravated these conditions. It led to more drug use and drug trafficking that overwhelmed whole neighborhoods. Crack ravaged the lives of users in ways that other drugs did not, and by producing steady demand by users and huge profits for dealers, it stimulated more violence. As drug gangs multiplied and tangled with each other for control of turf, drug executions and drive-by shootings became commonplace.[188]

The spread of AIDS, rampant among intravenous drug users, further aggravated these conditions.

The plight of young black men is worse than that of any other group in society. In 1990 almost one of every four black men between 20 and 29 was serving a criminal sentence in prison or on probation or parole; by 1995 almost one of every three was.[189] And a black man in Harlem has less chance of living past 40 than a man in Bangladesh.[190]

About a third of the black population lives in poverty—three times the rate among the white population—and about a tenth, the poorest of the poor, exists in a stage of economic and social "disintegration."[191] This "underclass" is trapped in a cycle of self-perpetuating problems from which it is extremely difficult to escape. These people are isolated from the rest of society and demoralized about their prospects for improvement.

After the riots in the 1960s, the Kerner Commission, appointed by President Johnson to examine the cause of the riots, concluded, "What white Americans have never fully understood—but what the Negro can never forget—is that white society is deeply implicated in the ghetto. White institutions created it, white institutions maintain it, and white society condones it." After the riots, however, governments did little to improve the conditions that precipitated the riots. Now, over a quarter of a century later, the conditions are worse.

After the riots that followed the first trial of the Los Angeles police officers who beat Rodney King, there was more talk about improving the conditions in the ghetto. But a columnist who had heard such talk before commented, "My guess is that when all is said and done, a great deal more will be said than done. The truth is we don't know any quick fixes for our urban ills and we lack the patience and resources for slow fixes."[192]

To make these problems more difficult to resolve, the cities have lost political power as they have lost population, because of white flight and black migration. In 1992, for the first time, more voters lived in the suburbs than in the cities. These voters do not urge action on urban problems. Sometimes, in fact, they resist action if it means an increase in their taxes or decrease in their services.

A woman in Simi Valley, the suburb where the first trial of the Los Angeles police officers who beat Rodney King was held, unintentionally revealed a common attitude when she shouted at inner city blacks who came to picket the courthouse, "Why do you bother us? Let us go on with our lives, like you are down there."[193]

Although whites tell pollsters they think conditions for blacks have improved and are continuing to improve, a majority of blacks tell pollsters they think conditions are worsening.[194] Consequently, whites say governments have done enough for blacks, while blacks say governments should do much more.

Hispanics, too, remain disadvantaged. They earn considerably less than Anglos, though more than blacks.[195] But they are moving up the ladder. More attend college and become managers and professionals. At least those who speak educated English appear to be following the pattern of Southern and Eastern European immigrants—arriving poor, facing discrimination, but eventually working their way up.

Native Americans, with a legacy of discrimination and coerced assimilation, continue to suffer extreme poverty and unemployment, which are exacerbated by high rates of alcoholism.

Women in the middle class, like minorities in the middle class, benefited a great deal from the expansion of civil rights. But women are more likely to be poor than men, and almost 40% of all female-headed families are below the poverty line.

Despite the value of civil rights, it should be apparent from the current status of minorities and women that civil rights alone are not enough. As one black leader said, "What good is a seat in the front of the bus if you don't have the money for the fare?"[196]

➤Conclusion: Is Government Responsive in Granting Civil Rights?

Blacks and women have made tremendous progress in obtaining civil rights since the time when a federal official who fired competent blacks could insist, "A Negro's place is in the cornfield,"[197] or employers who refused to hire women could insist, "A woman's place is in the home." The black movement and the women's movement initiated the changes. They protested legal inequality and put the issue on the public agenda. As they grew and garnered support, they pressured the government. Finally, approximately one century after the first significant agitations for change, the government responded.

Within the government, the Supreme Court exercised decisive leadership. Historically, the Court was both activist and restrained toward blacks—whichever was necessary to deny their rights—while it was restrained toward women. Then in the 1950s and 1960s, the Warren Court was activist in striking down segregation. In the 1970s and 1980s, the Burger Court was somewhat less activist in upholding limited busing and affirmative action. At the same time, it was activist in striking down sex discrimination. As with the Warren Court's decisions against race discrimination, the Burger Court's decisions against sex discrimination may go down in history as its major achievement.

But the Court's rulings themselves did not guarantee the rights. Because the Court lacks the means to enforce its decisions, the president and Congress had to help overcome the resistance. The history of the government's efforts to grant civil rights, especially to blacks, shows the limits of the Supreme Court.

The changes in policy illustrate the responsiveness of government. In its subjugation of minorities until the 1950s and treatment of women until the 1970s, government was responding to the majority view. When minorities and women organized to protest their status, government began responding to them and to shifts in the majority view that their protest prompted.

In pressuring government to respond, blacks have benefited from being numerous, visible, and, with their common legacy of slavery, segregation, and discrimination, relatively cohesive. Their concentration in large northern cities and some southern states has helped them exercise political power. Their long legacy, though, has fostered debilitating ghetto conditions and denied them resources to make quicker and greater progress.

Hispanics are less numerous but rapidly growing in number. Their concentration in some western and southwestern states has enabled them to influence state and local governments. Their diversity and lack of cohesiveness, however, has hindered their ability to influence the national government.

Native Americans are the smallest, most isolated, and least organized minority, so they have had the poorest success in pressuring government to respond.

As minority groups grow in size, they will be able to pressure governments more effectively. In the 1980s, blacks increased their population 13%, native Americans 39%, Hispanics 53%, and Asians 108%, while whites increased their population just 6%.[198]

But as minority groups expand, they will increasingly come into conflict with each other, especially if economic conditions remain stagnant. Competition for scarce resources will widen the cracks in the coalition. Already there are tensions. Some blacks resent the faster progress of Hispanics and Asians. Blacks say they were here before most Hispanics and Asians, they suffered more and struggled more, and so they should reap the rewards sooner. On the other hand, some Hispanic leaders resent the reluctance of black groups to help them with their civil rights problems.[199] Occasionally there are conflicts over issues. When Hispanic leaders sought to repeal the sanctions on employers who hire illegal aliens, because of concern that these penalties discourage employers from hiring Hispanic legal residents, some blacks worried that employers once again would hire legal aliens who would take jobs from them. Occasionally, there have been riots. Blacks have rioted in Miami from frustration with the Cuban-dominated leadership. Hispanics have rioted in Washington, D.C., out of anger with their lack of city services and jobs and with gerrymandering by the black power structure.

Nonminority women were never subjugated as much as minority men and women, so they have had less to overcome. Moreover, women are a majority, they vote as frequently as men, and they have well-organized and well-funded interest groups. Consequently, since the 1970s they have made the greatest gains toward equality.

EPILOGUE

Hamer Continues to Fight

Fannie Lou Hamer was not one to back down from a challenge, especially since the first time she tried to register to vote. Indeed, a frequent criticism levied against her, by supporters as well as opponents, was that she was unwilling to compromise. At the Democratic convention in 1964, she and two other women leaders of the Mississippi Freedom Democratic Party urged the delegation to reject the compromise offered by the national Democratic Party. "We didn't come all this way for no two seats," she declared.[200] She also criticized the proposal that the seats be given to two middle-class representatives of the delegation—a professor and a druggist—rather than to any of the poor sharecroppers who formed the bulk of the delegation.

The delegation voted to press its case before the credentials committee of the convention. But the FBI had infiltrated the MFDP and had wiretapped its phones to determine the delegation's plans, and then had forwarded this information to President Johnson. When the credentials committee began its hearing, the president called a press conference to preempt the hearing from television. Without the presence of cameras, the committee voted to seat the regular Democrats.

Furious, the Freedom Democrats entered the convention hall, using their tickets as "guests," and stood silently in a circle to call attention to their issue. The sergeants-at-arms tried to remove them but gave up when officials realized that the effort would cast the wrong image on television. Nevertheless, the protest attracted the press coverage that had been denied at the hearing.

Meanwhile, most of the regular Democrats left for Mississippi. They apparently went to the convention just to keep the Freedom Democrats from getting the seats.

When Johnson wrote his memoirs after retiring, he omitted any mention of the Freedom Democrats' challenge. "Atlantic City in August 1964," he wrote, "was a place of happy surging crowds and thundering cheers. To a man as troubled as I was by party and national divisions, this display of unity was welcome indeed."[201]

Hamer continued to fight. Following the election she and two other Freedom Democrats challenged the seating of all five white men elected to the House of Representatives from Mississippi. Hamer claimed they were elected illegally because the Freedom Democrats' candidates were denied places on the ballot. The House sent 150 lawyers to the state to collect information about violations of election laws. The findings of widespread discrimination prompted enough support to force a roll call vote, but the challenge was defeated.

Change did come, however. In 1965 President Johnson pushed the Voting Rights Act through Congress, and in 1968 the Democratic Party propounded rules against seating delegations that denied full participation to blacks.

Yet Mississippi's regular Democrats refused to change. In 1968 a coalition including Hamer, other Freedom Democrats, and moderate whites challenged the seating of the regular Democrats at the national convention. This time Vice President Humphrey, running for president after Johnson retired, backed the challenge. Finally, an integrated delegation represented Mississippi.

Fannie Lou Hamer, with her boundless energy, still had battles to fight. She brought lawsuits to broaden interpretation of the Voting Rights Act, reconfigure electoral districts in the state, and desegregate schools in her town.

As African Americans began to overcome discrimination, she believed the next step was for the poor, blacks and whites alike, to overcome poverty. She arranged financing for 70 new homes in town, and she helped organize a farm co-op and a "pig bank." (She bought 40 pigs and loaned them to families who would care for them and keep the new piglets—the "dividends"—and then return the pigs—the "principal"—to the bank for other families the next year.)

In her declining years, she felt frustrated because she had not accomplished more and forgotten because people had not come to see her as often when she no longer had the energy for their cause. In 1977 she died.

Yet Fannie Lou Hamer had achieved much. With the increased participation of black voters in Mississippi, black candidates ran for office, and many won; and white candidates began to court black voters as well. In 1986 the first black member of the U.S. House of Representatives was elected from Mississippi since Reconstruction.

Fannie Lou Hamer would not be forgotten. She showed people that although she had much to fear, her oppressors were the ones who came to fear her because she would not be silenced and could not be controlled. "She owed them nothing, and she gave them hell. . . ."[202]

Key Terms

Dred Scott case
equal protection clause
Jim Crow laws
Plessy v. Ferguson
separate-but-equal doctrine
NAACP
Brown v. Board of Education
de jure segregation
de facto segregation
Civil Rights Act of 1964
restrictive covenants
steering
blockbusting
redlining
Civil Rights Act of 1968
bilingual education
Equal Pay Act
comparable worth
Equal Rights Amendment (ERA)
affirmative action

Further Reading

Paul Berman, ed., *Blacks and Jews: Alliance and Arguments* (Delacorte Press, 1992). *Essays about the "love-hate" relationship between these two peoples who have suffered prejudice and who embraced in the civil rights era but tangled in recent decades.*

Taylor Branch, *Parting the Waters: America in the King Years, 1954–63* (New York: Simon & Schuster, 1988). *Extremely readable account of Martin Luther King, Jr., and the first decade of the civil rights movement.*

Seth Cagin and Philip Dray, *We Are Not Afraid: The Story of Goodman, Schwerner, and Chaney and the Civil Rights Campaign for Mississippi* (New York: Macmillan, 1988). *An American crime in the steamy summer of 1964.*

Audrey K. Edwards and Craig K. Polite, *Children of the Dream: The Psychology of Black Success* (New York: Doubleday, 1992). *Interviews with 41 successful professionals who came of age between the Supreme Court's* Brown *decision and Martin Luther King's assassination.*

Melissa Fay Greene, *Praying for Sheetrock* (Reading, Mass. Addison-Wesley, 1991). *A nonfiction story about the clash between "good old boy politics" and black power in a Georgia county in the 1970s.*

Andrew Hacker, *Two Nations: Black and White, Separate, Hostile, Unequal* (New York: Charles Scribner's Sons, 1992). *Perceptive insights about contemporary race relations.*

Jonathan Kozol, *Savage Inequalities: Children in America's Schools* (New York: Crown, 1991). *The impact of unequal school financing upon real students, real teachers, and (unfortunately) real schools.*

Jane Kramer, "Whose Art Is It?" *New Yorker,* December 21, 1992, pp. 80–109. *A fascinating article about the interactions between a white artist, the poor black neighbors he uses as models for his lifelike sculptures, and the middle class black officials in New York City who determine whether, and where, the controversial sculptures can be erected.*

Susan Ware, *Still Missing: Amelia Earhart and the Search for Modern Feminism* (Norton, 1994). *The life of the famous pilot, who disappeared over the Pacific ocean in 1937, as a reflection of American feminism between the two world wars.*

Notes

1. The information for this section is from Kay Mills, *This Little Light of Mine: The Life of Fannie Lou Hamer* (New York: Plume, 1994).
2. In the Delta, as in much of Mississippi, most blacks picked cotton or cleaned or cooked for white people. Black teachers had some status, but they were hired and usually controlled by the white officials of the segregated school systems. Only black preachers and funeral directors had any independence.
3. Mills, p. 36.
4. Ibid., p. 38.
5. Ibid., p. 18.
6. Ibid., p. 57.
7. This incident received little media coverage because no reporters were present. And this result prompted civil rights leaders to seek help from white college students, assuming, correctly, that if any of them were harmed there would be more coverage of the repression blacks encountered. Thus began the recruitment of northern college students for voter registration drives during the summer.
8. Mills, p. 93.
9. The Republican Party was not a viable party in the state at the time. There was a black wing of the party, called the "Black and Tans," but its only role was to help dispense patronage when there was a Republican president. In fact, the head of the Mississippi Black and Tans was an attorney who lived in Washington, D.C. Mills, p. 109.
10. Ibid., p. 128.
11. *Scott v. Sandford,* 19 How. 393 (1857).
12. Despite the ruling, Taney considered slavery "a blot on our national character," and three decades before the case he freed his own slaves, whom he had inherited from his parents. When the South seceded, Taney remained with the Union. Richard Shenkman, *"I Love Paul Revere, Whether He Rode or Not"* (New York: HarperCollins, 1991), p. 168.
13. Civil Rights Act of 1866; Civil Rights Act of 1871; Civil Rights Act of 1875.
14. C. Vann Woodward, *The Strange Career of Jim Crow,* 2nd ed. (London: Oxford University Press, 1966), p. 44.
15. *Civil Rights Cases,* 109 U.S. 3 (1883).
16. C. Herman Pritchett, *The American Constitution,* 3rd ed. (New York: McGraw-Hill, 1977), p. 486.

17. *Plessy v. Ferguson,* 163 U.S. 537 (1896). The Court's ruling prompted states to expand their Jim Crow laws. Before *Plessy* states segregated just trains and schools.

18. *Cumming v. Richmond County Board of Education,* 175 U.S. 528 (1899). Then the Court enforced segregation in colleges. It upheld a criminal conviction against a private college for teaching blacks together with whites. *Berea College v. Kentucky,* 211 U.S. 45 (1908).

19. Woodward, *Strange Career of Jim Crow,* p. 113.

20. Jacqueline Jones, *The Dispossessed: America's Underclasses from the Civil War to the Present* (Basic Books, 1992), p. 83. And they were still being cheated. One sharecropper went to the landowner at the end of the season to settle up but was told he would not receive any money that year because the landowner needed it to send his son to college. The sharecropper moved North. Interview with sharecropper's son, "The Best of Discovery," Discovery Television Channel, June 11, 1995.

21. Richard Kluger, *Simple Justice* (New York: Alfred A. Knopf, 1976), pp. 89–90.

22. Woodward, *Strange Career of Jim Crow,* p. 114.

23. Wilson apparently opposed segregation in government but still allowed it to appease southerners who were a major portion of his Democratic Party and whose support was essential for his economic reforms.

24. *Guinn v. United States,* 238 U.S. 347 (1915).

25. *Buchanan v. Warley,* 245 U.S. 60 (1917).

26. In 1939 the NAACP established the NAACP Legal Defense and Educational Fund as its litigation arm. In 1957 the IRS, pressured by southern members of Congress, ordered the two branches of the NAACP to break their connection or lose their tax-exempt status. Since then they have been separate organizations, and chapter references to the "NAACP" are to the NAACP Legal Defense and Educational Fund.

27. Kluger, *Simple Justice,* p. 134.

28. *Missouri ex rel. Gaines v. Canada,* 305 U.S. 337 (1938).

29. *Sweatt v. Painter,* 339 U.S. 629 (1950).

30. *McLaurin v. Oklahoma State Regents,* 339 U.S. 637 (1950).

31. Earl Warren, *The Memoirs of Earl Warren* (Garden City, N.Y.: Doubleday, 1977), p. 291.

32. 347 U.S. 483 (1954).

33. *Holmes v. Atlanta,* 350 U.S. 879 (1955); *Baltimore v. Dawson,* 350 U.S. 877 (1955); *Schiro v. Bynum,* 375 U.S. 395 (1964); *Johnson v. Virginia,* 373 U.S. 61 (1963); *Lee v. Washington,* 390 U.S. 333 (1968).

34. *Brown v. Board of Education II,* 349 U.S. 294 (1955).

35. Justice Tom Clark later told a political science conference that one justice had proposed desegregating one grade a year, beginning with kindergarten or first grade, but this concrete standard was rejected because the other justices felt it would take too long. In retrospect, it might have been quicker, and easier, than the vague standard used.

36. *Griffin v. Prince Edward County School Board,* 377 U.S. 218 (1964); *Norwood v. Harrison,* 413 U.S. 455 (1973); *Gilmore v. Montgomery,* 417 U.S. 556 (1974); *Green v. New Kent County School Board,* 391 U.S. 430 (1968).

37. James F. Simon, *In His Own Image* (New York: David McKay, 1974), p. 70.

38. William Cohen and John Kaplan, *Bill of Rights* (Mineola, N.Y.: Foundation Press, 1976), p. 622.

39. *Swann v. Charlotte-Mecklenburg Board of Education,* 402 U.S. 1 (1971).

40. *Columbus Board of Education v. Penick,* 443 U.S. 449 (1979); *Dayton Board of Education v. Brinkman,* 443 U.S. 526 (1979); *Keyes v. School District 1, Denver,* 413 U.S. 921 (1973).

41. *Milliken v. Bradley,* 418 U.S. 717 (1974).

42. For example, some suburbs of Kansas City, Missouri, did not allow black students to attend high schools. Some black families, then, moved back to the city, aggravating both school segregation and residential segregation. James S. Kunen, "The End of Integration," *Time,* April 29, 1996, p. 41.

43. Lee A. Daniels, "In Defense of Busing," *New York Times Magazine,* April 17, 1983, pp. 36–37.

44. Daniels, "In Defense of Busing," p. 34.

45. Ibid., p. 97; Susan Chira, "Housing and Fear Upend Integration," *New York Times,* February 14, 1993, p. E3.

46. Rob Gurwitt, "Getting Off the Bus," *Governing* (May 1992), pp. 30–36.

47. *Board of Education of Oklahoma City v. Dowell,* 112 L.Ed.2d 715 (1991).

48. *Missouri v. Jenkins,* 132 L.Ed.2d 63 (1995).

49. Gurwitt, "Getting Off the Bus"; Jervis Anderson, "Black and Blue," *New Yorker,* April 29 and May 6, 1996, p. 64.

50. Woodward, *Strange Career of Jim Crow,* p. 186.

51. *Norris v. Alabama,* 294 U.S. 587 (1935); *Smith v. Texas,* 311 U.S. 128 (1940); *Avery v. Georgia,* 345 U.S. 559 (1952).

52. *Heart of Atlanta Motel v. United States,* 379 U.S. 421 (1964).

53. For discussion of organized labor's ambivalence toward enactment and enforcement of the employment provisions of the act, see Herbert Hill, "Black Workers, Organized Labor, and Title VII of the 1964 Civil Rights Act: Legislative History and Litigation Record," in Herbert Hill and James E. Jones, *Race in America* (Madison: University of Wisconsin Press, 1993), pp. 263–341.

54. *Griggs v. Duke Power,* 401 U.S. 424 (1971).

55. *Washington v. Davis,* 426 U.S. 229 (1976).

56. *Wards Cove Packing v. Atonio,* 490 U.S. 642 (1989).

57. *Firefighters Local Union v. Stotts,* 81 L.Ed.2d 483 (1984).

58. *Shelley v. Kraemer,* 334 U.S. 1 (1948).

59. For more extensive examination, see Andrew Hacker, *Two Nations: Black and White, Separate, Hostile, Unequal* (New York: Charles Scribner's Sons, 1992).

60. Gary Orfield, quoted in Mary Jordan, "Separating the Country from the *Brown* Decision," *Washington Post National Weekly Edition,* December 20–26, 1993, p. 33.

61. Mary Jordan, "On Track Toward Two-Tier Schools," *Washington Post National Weekly Edition,* May 31–June 6, 1993, p. 31.

62. Jordan, "Separating the Country from the *Brown* Decision."

63. J. Harvie Wilkinson, *From Brown to Bakke* (New York: Oxford University Press, 1979), pp. 118–25; "School Segregation Worsens, Study Says," *Lincoln Journal (Los Angeles Times),* December 14, 1993; William Celis 3d, "Forty Years after *Brown,* Segregation Persists," *New York Times,* May 18, 1994, p. A1.

64. Kunen, "The End of Integration," p. 39.

65. Jonathan Kozol, *Savage Inequalities: Children in America's Schools* (New York: HarperPerennial, 1992), p. 4.

66. Kozol, *Savage Inequalities,* p. 3.

67. Ibid., p. 35.

68. "That's Quite a Range," *Lincoln Journal,* January 21, 1993.

69. In addition, cities have numerous nonprofit institutions—colleges, museums, hospitals—that benefit the entire urban area but do not pay property taxes. According to one estimate, 30% of the cities' potential tax base is tax exempt, compared with 3% of the suburbs'. Kozol, *Savage Inequalities,* p. 55.

70. Ibid., pp. 198, 137, 236, 57. (There are a few exceptions, such as Newark, New Jersey, which spent more than $9,000 per pupil in recent years. Jordan, "On Track Toward Two-Tier Schools," p. 31.)

71. Ibid., pp. 140, 36, 23–24.
72. Ibid., pp. 155–56.
73. Ibid., pp. 53, 84.
74. Ibid., p. 52.
75. Ibid., p. 53.
76. Ibid., pp. 123–24.
77. Robert England and Kenneth Meier, "From Desegregation to Integration: Second Generation School Discrimination as an Institutional Impediment," *American Politics Quarterly* 13 (April 1985), pp. 227–47; Charles Bullock and Joseph Stewart, "Incidence and Correlates of Second-Generation Discrimination," in Marian Palley and Michael Preston, eds., *Race, Sex, and Policy Problems* (Lexington, Mass: Lexington Books, 1979); Stephen Wainscott and J. David Woodard, "Second Thoughts on Second Generation Discrimination," *American Politics Quarterly* 16 (April 1988), pp. 171–92.
78. Kenneth Meier and Robert England, "Black Representation and Educational Policy," *American Political Science Review* 78 (June 1984), pp. 392–403; Kenneth Meier, Joseph Stewart, and Robert England, *Race, Class, and Education: The Politics of Second-Generation Discrimination* (Madison: University of Wisconsin Press, 1989.)
79. Marc Galanter, "Beyond the Litigation Panic," in *New Directions in Liability Law, Proceedings of the Academy of Political Science* 37 (New York: Academy of Political Science, 1988), pp. 21, 23.
80. Gary Boulard, "Jim Crow Said Alive in the South," *Lincoln Journal (Los Angeles Times)*, October 3, 1991.
81. Colleen Barry, "Denny's Accused of Discrimination," *San Diego Union-Tribune*, March 25, 1993, p. A–3.
82. Edward Barnes, "Can't Get There from Here," *Time*, February 19, 1996, p. 33.
83. Hacker, *Two Nations*, pp. 48–49.
84. William A. Henry III, "The Last Bastions of Bigotry," *Time*, July 22, 1991, pp. 66–67.
85. Melissa Fay Greene, *Praying for Sheetrock* (Reading, Mass.: Addison-Wesley, 1991), pp. 8, 145.
86. "Study Demonstrates Hiring Discrimination against Blacks," *Lincoln Star (Washington Post)*, May 15, 1991.
87. "Deciphering a Racist Business Code," *Time*, October 19, 1992, pp. 21–22.
88. Michael Janofsky, "Race and the American Workplace," *New York Times*, June 20, 1993, pp. F1, 6.
89. Jerry DeMuth, "Fair-Housing Suits: Color Them Gold," *Washington Post National Weekly Edition*, August 11, 1986, p. 34.
90. Jonathan Kaufman, "In Big-City Ghettos, Life Is Often Worse Than in '60s Tumult," *Wall Street Journal*, May 23, 1980.
91. Jerry Knight, "Coloring the Chances of Getting a Mortgage," *Washington Post National Weekly Edition*, October 28-November 3, 1991, p. 26; "Racial Disparities Seen in Home Lending," *Lincoln Journal* (AP), October 22, 1991.
92. "Possible Redlining Investigated," *Urbana News-Gazette* (AP), February 15, 1993.
93. Barbara Vobejda, "Neighborhood Integration, Inch by Inch," *Washington Post National Weekly Edition*, March 23–29, 1992, p. 37.
94. Nancy Denton and Douglas Massey, "Residential Segregation of Blacks, Hispanics, and Asians by Socioeconomic Status and Generation," *Social Science Quarterly* 69 (December 1988), p. 259.
95. Hacker, *Two Nations*, pp. 35–38.
96. "Study Says EPA Penalties Smaller in Minority Areas," *Lincoln Journal* (Newsday), September 14, 1992.
97. Henry Louis Gates, Jr., "Thirteen Ways of Looking at a Black Man," *New Yorker*, October 23, 1995, p. 59.
98. Pierre Thomas, "Bias and the Badge," *Washington Post National Weekly Edition*, December 18–24, 1995, pp. 6–9.
99. Gates, "Thirteen Ways of Looking at a Black Man," p. 59; Anderson, "Black and Blue," p. 64.
100. Laura M. Markowitz, "Walking the Walk," *Networker* (July/August, 1993), p. 22.
101. William Raspberry, "The Little Things That Hurt," *Washington Post National Weekly Edition*, April 18–24, 1994, p. 29. And see Ellis Cose, *The Rage of a Privileged Class* (New York: HarperCollins, 1993).
102. Kozol, *Savage Inequalities*, pp. 179–80.
103. Juan Williams, "Why Segregation Seems So Seductive," *Washington Post National Weekly Edition*, January 24–30, 1994, p. 24. For an extended examination, see Derrick Bell, *Faces at the Bottom of the Well: The Permanence of Racism* (Basic Books, 1992).
104. C. Davis, C. Haub, and J. Willette, "U.S. Hispanics: Changing the Face of America," *Population Bulletin* 38 (1983), pp. 1–44.
105. Although Hispanics commonly are spoken of as though they are a separate race, they really are not. Most are an amalgam of European, African, and/or Indian ancestry that makes it impossible to identify a race. On the 1990 census forms, where individuals indicate their own race, half of the Hispanics left this line blank. Hacker, *Two Nations*, p. 6.
106. Eloise Salholz, "The Push for Power," *Newsweek*, April 9, 1990, p. 18.
107. Guadaloupe San Miguel, "Mexican American Organizations and the Changing Politics of School Desegregation in Texas, 1945–1980," *Social Science Quarterly* 63 (1982), pp. 701–15. See also Luis R. Fraga, Kenneth J. Meier, and Robert E. England, "Hispanic Americans and Educational Policy: Structural Limits to Equal Access and Opportunities for Upward Mobility," unpublished paper, University of Oklahoma, 1985.
108. San Miguel, "Mexican American Organizations," p. 710.
109. Leo Grebler, Joan W. Moore, and Ralph C. Guzman, *The Mexican-American People* (New York: Free Press, 1970), p. 157.
110. Fraga, Meier, and England, "Hispanic Americans," p. 6.
111. Karen De Witt, "The Nation's Schools Learn a 4th R: Resegregation," *New York Times*, January 19, 1992, p. E5.
112. *San Antonio Independent School District v. Rodriguez*, 411 U.S. 1 (1973).
113. Kozol, *Savage Inequalities*, pp. 223–25.
114. Ibid., p. 229.
115. Luis Ricardo Fraga, Kenneth Meier, and Robert England, "Hispanic Americans and Educational Policy: Limits to Equal Access," *Journal of Politics* 48 (November 1986), pp. 850–73.
116. *Lau v. Nichols*, 414 U.S. 563 (1974).
117. "Many-Tongued Classes," *Newsweek*, February 11, 1991, p. 57.
118. Hispanics have a higher dropout rate than blacks; over a quarter leave high school. "High Hispanic Dropout Rate Language-Related," *Lincoln Journal*, September 14, 1994.
119. Richard Bernstein, "In U.S. Schools a War of Words," *New York Times Magazine*, October 14, 1990, p. 34; Paul Taylor, "Is Bilingual Better?" *Washington Post National Weekly Edition*, April 30, 1984.
120. Margot Hornblower, "Putting Tongues in Check," *Time*, October 9, 1995, pp. 40–50.
121. Paul Gray, "Teach Your Children Well," *Time*, Fall, 1993, p. 70.
122. *Plyler v. Doe*, 457 U.S. 202 (1982).
123. "Survey: Hispanics Reject Cohesive Group Identity," *Lincoln Journal* (AP), December 15, 1992.
124. Lynne Duke, "English Spoken Here," *Washington Post National Weekly Edition* (December 21–27, 1992) p. 37.

125. *Cherokee Nation v. Georgia,* 5 Peters 1 (1831); *Worcester v. Georgia,* 6 Peters 515 (1832).

126. Alfonso Ortiz, *The Pueblo* (New York: Chelsea House, 1994), p. 10.

127. Vine Deloria, Jr. and Clifford M. Lytle, *American Indians, American Justice* (Austin: University of Texas Press, 1983), p. 221.

128. Ibid., pp. 222–25.

129. Michael S. Serrill, "Struggling to Be Themselves," *Time,* November 9, 1992, p. 54.

130. Harvey Arden, "Who Owns Our Past?" *National Geographic,* March 1989, pp. 383, 388, 393.

131. Felicity Barringer, "Ethnic Pride Confounds the Census," *New York Times,* May 9, 1993, p. E3.

132. W. John Moore, "Tribal Imperatives," *National Journal,* June 9, 1990, p. 1396.

133. Ruth B. Ginsburg, *Constitutional Aspects of Sex-Based Discrimination* (St. Paul, Minn.: West Publishing Co. 1974), p. 2.

134. Donna M. Moore, "Editor's Introduction" in Moore, *Battered Women* (Beverly Hills: Sage, 1979), p. 8.

135. Karen DeCrow, *Sexist Justice* (New York: Vintage, 1975), p. 72.

136. Barbara Sinclair Deckard, *The Women's Movement,* 2nd ed. (New York: Harper & Row, 1979), p. 303.

137. DeCrow, *Sexist Justice,* p. 119.

138. "White Men Still First," *Lincoln Journal-Star,* April 1, 1995.

139. From a personal conversation with a business professor in attendance.

140. *Time,* June 28, 1993, p. 55–56.

141. "A New Push to Raise Women's Pay," *New York Times,* January 1, 1984, p. F15.

142. "Battle of the Sexes Over 'Comparable Worth'," *U.S. News & World Report,* February 20, 1984, p. 74.

143. Bureau of Labor Statistics, March 1982.

144. Joyce Gelb and Marian Lief Palley, *Women and Public Policies* (Princeton, N.J.: Princeton University Press, 1982), p. 102.

145. Jeremy L. Milk, "Women's Soccer on a Roll," *Chronicle of Higher Education* (November 3, 1993), p. A39.

146. Matthew Goodman, "Where the Boys Are," *Washington Monthly,* April 1989, pp. 18–20.

147. For a discussion of these points, see Jane Mansbridge, *Why We Lost the ERA* (Chicago: University of Chicago Press, 1986); Mary Frances Berry, *Why ERA Failed* (Bloomington, Ind.: Indiana University Press, 1986); Janet Boles, "Building Support for the ERA: A Case of 'Too Much, Too Late,'" *PS* 15 (Fall 1982): pp. 575–92.

148. *Bradwell v. Illinois,* 16 Wall. 130 (1873).

149. *Muller v. Oregon,* 208 U.S. 412 (1908).

150. Shenkman, "I Love Paul Revere," pp. 136–37.

151. *Reed v. Reed,* 404 U.S. 71 (1971).

152. *Hoyt v. Florida,* 368 U.S. 57 (1961).

153. *Taylor v. Louisiana,* 419 U.S. 522 (1975).

154. *Stanton v. Stanton,* 421 U.S. 7 (1975).

155. *Pittsburgh Press v. Pittsburgh Commission on Human Relations,* 413 U.S. 376 (1973).

156. *Dothard v. Rawlinson,* 97 S.Ct. 2720 (1977).

157. *Automobile Workers v. Johnson Controls,* 113 L.Ed.2d 158 (1991).

158. *Phillips v. Martin-Marietta,* 400 US. 542 (1971).

159. *Cleveland Board of Education v. LaFleur,* 413 U.S. 632 (1974).

160. *Nashville Gas v. Satty,* 434 U.S. 136 (1977).

161. *Los Angeles Department of Water and Power v. Manhart,* 435 U.S. 702 (1978); *Arizona Governing Committee v. Norris,* 82 L.Ed.2d 462 (1983).

162. *Roberts v. United States Jaycees,* 82 L.Ed.2d 462 (1984); *Board of Directors of Rotary International v. Rotary Club,* 95 L.Ed.2d 474 (1987).

163. *Massachusetts v. Feeney,* 442 U.S. 256 (1979).

164. Naomi Wolf, "Stirring the Women's Movement from Its Dormant Decade," *Washington Post National Weekly Edition,* October 21–27, 1991, p. 23.

165. Ibid.

166. Susan Benesch, "The Birth of a Nation," *Washington Post National Weekly Edition,* August 4, 1986, p. 12.

167. Lisa Genasci, "Many Workers Resist Family Benefit Offers," *Lincoln Journal* (A.P.), June 28, 1995.

168. *Craig v. Boren,* 429 U.S. 190 (1976).

169. *Orr v. Orr,* 440 U.S. 268 (1979); *Mississippi University for Women v. Hogan,* 458 U.S. 718 (1982).

170. *Rostker v. Goldberg,* 453 U.S. 57 (1981).

171. *Michael M. v. Sonoma County,* 450 U.S. 464 (1981).

172. A simplified version of this scenario was used by President Johnson in support of affirmative action.

173. Early decisions include *University of California Regents v. Bakke,* 438 U.S. 265 (1978); *United Steelworkers v. Weber,* 443 U.S. 193 (1979); *Fullilove v. Klutznick,* 448 U.S. 448 (1980).

174. *United Steelworkers v. Weber.*

175. *Sheet Metal Workers v. EEOC,* 92 L.Ed.2d 344 (1986); *Firefighters v. Cleveland,* 92 L.Ed.2d 405 (1986); *United States v. Paradise Local Union,* 94 L.Ed.2d 203 (1987).

176. *Firefighters v. Stotts* 467 U.S. 561 (1985); *Wygant v. Jackson Board of Education,* 90 L.Ed.2d 260 (1986).

177. *Richmond v. Croson,* 102 L.Ed.2d 854 (1989); *Adarand Constructors v. Pena,* 132 L.Ed.2d 158 (1995). The perception that minorities are taking over is also reflected in a peculiar poll finding: The average American estimates that 32% of the U.S. population is black and 21% is Hispanic (rather than just 12% and 9%). Richard Nadeau, Richard G. Niemi, and Jeffrey Levine, "Innumeracy about Minority Populations," *Public Opinion Quarterly* 57 (1993) pp. 332–47.

178. Alison M. Konrad and Frank Linnehan, "Formalized HRM Structures: Coordinating Equal Employment Opportunity or Concealing Organizational Practices?" *Academy of Management Journal* 38 (June, 1995), p. 787.

179. James E. Jones, "The Genesis and Present Status of Affirmative Action in Employment," paper presented at the American Political Science Association Annual Meeting, 1984: Robert Pear, *New York Times,* June 19, 1983; Nelson C. Dometrius and Lee Sigelman, "Assessing Progress Toward Affirmative Action Goals in State and Local Government," *Public Administration Review* 44 (May/June 1984) pp. 241–47; Peter Eisinger, *Black Employment in City Government* (Washington, D.C.: Joint Center for Political Studies, 1983); Milton Coleman, "Uncle Sam Has Stopped Running Interference for Blacks," *Washington Post National Weekly Edition,* December 19, 1983.

180. Gertrude Ezorsky, *Racism and Justice: The Case for Affirmative Action* (Ithaca, NY: Cornell University Press, 1991), pp. 48–49, 63–65.

181. William Julius Wilson, *The Truly Disadvantaged* (Chicago: University of Chicago Press, 1987).

182. Andrew Tobias, "Now, the Good News About Your Money," *Parade,* April 4, 1993, p. 5.

183. Joel Garreau, "Candidates Take Note: It's a Mall World After All," *Washington Post National Weekly Edition,* August 10–16, 1992, p. 25.

184. From 1967 to 1987, according to calculations by William Julius Wilson. David Remnick, "Dr. Wilson's Neighborhood," *New Yorker*, April 29 and May 6, 1996, p. 98.

185. Sociologist William Julius Wilson develops this idea extensively in *The Truly Disadvantaged* (1987).

186. Ibid.

187. Remnick, "Dr. Wilson's Neighborhood," p. 98.

188. Samuel Walker, *Sense and Nonsense about Crime and Drugs,* 3rd ed. (Belmont, CA: Wadsworth, 1994), pp. xviii, 3.

189. Connie Cass, "More Young Black Men in Trouble with Law," *Lincoln Journal-Star* (AP), October 5, 1995.

190. "Doctor: Harlem's Death Rate Worse Than Bangladesh's," *Lincoln Journal* (A.P.), January 18, 1990.

191. Orlando Patterson, quoted in Anderson, "Black and Blue," p. 62.

192. Donald Kaul, "Only Surprise Is That Riots Didn't Happen Sooner," *Lincoln Journal* (Tribune Media Services), May 19, 1992.

193. Richard Lacayo, "This Land Is Your Land . . . This Land Is My Land," *Time,* May 18, 1992, p. 29.

194. Anderson, "Black and Blue," p. 64.

195. *U.S. Census* (Washington, D.C.: U.S. Government Printing Office, 1989), *Statistical Abstract of the United States 1989,* Table 713; Naomi Verdugo and Richard Verdugo, "Earnings Differentials among Mexican American, Black, and White Male Workers," *Social Science Quarterly* 65 (June 1984), pp. 417–25; Allen Williams, Peter Beeson, and David Johnson, "Some Factors Associated with Income among Mexican Americans," *Social Science Quarterly* 53 (March 1973), pp. 710–15.

196. *New York Times,* April 2, 1978.

197. Kluger, *Simple Justice,* p. 90.

198. Neal R. Peirce, "It's Later in the Day for a Nation Fashioned by European Immigrants," *Lincoln Sunday Journal-Star,* May 19, 1991.

199. Dick Kirschten, "Not Black-and-White," *National Journal,* March 2, 1991, pp. 496–500.

200. Mills, *This Little Light of Mine,* p. 132.

201. Ibid., p. 114, citing Lyndon Johnson, *The Vantage Point* (New York: Holt, Rinehart and Winston, 1971), p. 101.

202. Mills, *This Little Light of Mine,* p. xiii.

PART FIVE

Public Policies

A federal inspector checks poultry in 1910, and a federal hazardous waste worker trains in his new uniform.

16 The Budget

You Are There

Support the Budget Compromise?

It is April 1996, and you are Representative John Kasich, an Ohio Republican serving as chair of the House Budget Committee. You have been a leader in the battle with President Clinton over the budget for the fiscal year ending September 30, 1996. No budget has yet been adopted, even though the year is more than half over, and now, finally, an agreement between congressional leaders and the president seems imminent. But you are not satisfied with the compromise and not sure you should support it.

The contest between Congress and the president over the budget has been marked by both partisan wrangling and basic disagreements over spending, deficits, and taxes. As chair of the Budget Committee, you have been in the front lines of the battle, arguing both publicly and privately for a seven-year plan that will cut spending and balance the budget by 2002.

You have tackled spending issues before. While you were still in the Ohio state legislature, you opposed a $400 million tax increase. Instead, you proposed $400 million in spending cuts. In 1993, when President Clinton's deficit reduction package included significant tax increases, you and sixteen of your Republican colleagues devised a plan that would have cut the deficit more than Clinton's proposal without raising taxes. That plan generated considerable interest and made you a leading player in the House. Speaker Newt Gingrich became a close ally and used his influence to help you vault over several more senior Republicans on the House Budget Committee. When the GOP took control in 1995, you became the chair of the committee, at 42 the youngest chair in the House.

You are typical of the new generation of Republican members of the House. *Time* said you "embod[y] both the brashness and the energy of the new generation of conservatives."[1] You get excited in your talks to groups of people about the budget, coming across as "part policy wonk, part Dale Carnegie disciple, part stand-up comic."[2] You are also a Deadhead (a devotee of the classic rock group, the Grateful Dead), frequently wearing psychedelic ties and trendy socks. You are ready to make your mark in the House and in the nation.

President Clinton's first proposed budget for 1996 would not have resulted in a balanced budget in seven years, so you and other Republican leaders in Congress prepared your own budget. Despite the president's threats that he would veto appropriations bills he disagreed with, you and the rest of the congressional budget team pressed ahead, secure in the knowledge that Clinton's popularity was low and that you had wide public support for your deficit-cutting efforts. Hopes were high, and you shared the feeling that this time the process would succeed.

But slowly the tide turned. President Clinton took the initiative, arguing that the Republican budget slashed too deeply into important programs, and that he would protect Medicare, the target of the deepest cuts. (The "cuts" in Medicare were actually reductions in the rate of increases for the program, but they

CONTINUED 

John Kasich, chair of the House Budget Committee, tears up the Clinton administration's budget.
Source: Karen Keuhn, Time, *May 22, 1995, pp. 30–31.*

OUTLINE

Fundamentals of Budgeting
- Evolution of Budgeting Processes
- Purposes of Budgeting
- Limits on Budgeting
- Operation of the Current Budgeting Process

Issues in Budgeting
- Where Does the Money Go?
- The Deficit and Its Causes
- Dealing with the Deficit

Budgeting as Politics

Conclusion: Is Government Responsive in Its Budgeting?

were considered cuts because, given the expanding costs of medical care, reductions in the rate of increases would eventually result in reductions in the level of services provided to people.) Public opinion began to flow in the president's direction, with more people voicing displeasure at deep cuts, even while supporting an eventually balanced budget.

The shift in public opinion worried Republicans on Capitol Hill. The effort to cut many programs led one Republican to criticize you personally: "He wants to be secretary of everything."[3] And in the Senate, Republicans did not share the enthusiasm for the deep cuts the House budget plan proposed. There, Republicans wanted to move more slowly, and it took a long time for the Senate and the House to agree on a budget blueprint for fiscal 1996.

By October 1995, when the new budget was supposed to take effect, only one of the thirteen appropriations bills that enable government to spend money had passed. A continuing resolution was needed so that government could operate, even if a budget was not yet in place. Over the course of the next seven months, thirteen different continuing resolutions were passed.

But you and your fellow Republicans in the House pared down the money agencies could spend under these continuing resolutions, and riders—extraneous legislative requirements—were added that limited the purposes for which the money could be spent. President Clinton disagreed vehemently with both the spending limitations and the riders on these continuing resolutions, and he vetoed several of them. Each time he did, government no longer had the funds to operate and had to shut down. On one occasion, the federal government was effectively out of operation for 27 days in a row. Essential operations continued, but national parks were closed, immigration and passport offices did not operate, and other agencies could not conduct their business; and government workers were sent home.

Congress got the blame for these government shutdowns. Although the idea behind the continuing resolutions was to put pressure on President Clinton and force him to accept Republican priorities, he did not blink. The president successfully used his access to the media to place responsibility for the shutdown on congressional shoulders. Public opinion sided with him. People could not understand why politicians in Washington could not simply agree to fund government at a reasonable level so that citizens could get the services they counted on. When it became clear that government workers would later get paid for the days they did not work—as victims of the wrangling, it was not their fault that they did not work—there seemed to be no defensible rationale for refusing to compromise.

By April 1996, the situation was complicated by the presidential bid of Senate majority leader Robert Dole (R-Kan.). Having the 1996 budget still unresolved while work had begun on the 1997 budget put Dole in a bad spot. He could hardly claim to be able to get things done, when the budget was not done. And because the public blamed Congress and the Republicans for the impasse, Dole needed to get the issue behind him. When Clinton said he was willing to negotiate with the Republican leadership, Dole responded almost casually, "You mean more people bargaining? We need fewer. How about the two candidates?"[4] White House chief of staff Leon Panetta quickly answered, "The President accepts."[5] Two days later a compromise was struck.

In the final package, it seemed President Clinton won the big battles. Although he agreed to a seven-year budget balancing target, he got continued funding for some pet projects, including Goals 2000 for education, Americorps for volunteer service, and putting more police on the streets. On the other hand, Republicans got $23 billion in cuts from discretionary spending and the elimination of 200 federal programs, many of which Clinton also had marked for potential elimination.

You are disappointed with the compromise. You thought you could reduce spending more now. Although Republicans got a pledge to balance the budget in seven years, some of the hardest decisions were put off. When the time comes, Republicans might have less leverage. Yet you did get some programs reduced and others eliminated. So do you conclude that this budget is a good first step?

Some congressional Republicans oppose the compromise. The new freshmen came in with a budget balancing fervor unmatched in recent times. They also came with a real disdain for political compromise and "business as usual" in Washington. You want to keep their respect as well as the more experienced members' respect.

You also want to maintain your working relationship with the Democratic members. You have cultivated a reputation as a conservative Republican who is willing and able to work with the Democrats.[6] When the Democrats had controlled Congress, you worked with them to oppose wasteful defense spending (and you proudly called yourself a "cheap hawk").[7]

So how do you balance these competing pressures?

Over the last two decades, Americans have worried about the federal government's budget deficit. Most people cannot imagine how government can spend $150 billion more in one year than it takes in. During one year of the Bush administration, the budget deficit reached almost $300 billion. Citizens struggling to make ends meet have a hard time accepting such deficits.

They are not alone. Many candidates for office, from Ronald Reagan and H. Ross Perot to congressional hopefuls, have made the federal deficit a campaign issue. In his speech accepting the 1980 Republican nomination for president, for example, Ronald Reagan criticized a "government which has utterly refused to live within its means" and promised to "apply to government the common sense that we all use in our daily lives."[8] Some office-holders have used the deficit issue as an excuse to oppose funding projects they did not support. The media have picked up on the controversy. Stories about the deficit frequently appear in the headlines.

For many, the deficit has become the symbol of "big government." If the deficit is too big, the feeling goes, it must be because government is trying to do too much and is spending needlessly and wastefully. One way to cure the deficit problem, the conclusion would be, is to reduce the size of government. Dissatisfaction with government, then, is expressed in concern over the deficit.

Others point out that the deficit results not from big government so much as from the fact that governing a complex society takes a big government, and we have not been willing to pay the price. But because we still want government to provide programs such as Social Security, student loans, new fighter planes, and interstate highways, government borrows to pay for them. The result is a deficit. To cure the deficit problem, these people would say, we need to increase the government's income—in other words, to raise taxes.

The debate over the deficit is thus not really a debate about money. It is a debate over what kind of government citizens want. As Anthony Lewis put it, "It is not . . . about a balanced budget. It is about what the budget will fund: what the government should do."[9] Do we want an active federal government providing many services and administering many programs? Or do we want a smaller national government that taxes less, spends less, and does less? Indeed, when Republicans won control of Congress as a result of the 1994 congressional elections, one Republican leader made it clear: "We're going to fund those agencies that we want to fund. We're not going to fund those we don't want to fund."[10]

In this chapter we will put the deficit problem in the context of government's spending and taxing decisions. These decisions are partially aimed at keeping the economy healthy—or restoring its health, if necessary. They are also intended to fund the programs that we expect government to run. We will explore the budget and the decisions that go into making it. We will then see why the deficit is so difficult to reduce.

➤Fundamentals of Budgeting

Evolution of Budgeting Processes

We have become so used to hearing about the federal budget and about federal budget deficits that we naturally assume the federal government has always had a budget. That is not true. Although Congress always had to approve spending by federal agencies by appropriating money for them, as the Constitution requires, for most of the nation's history there was no overall budget for the federal government. The president did not submit spending requests for the agencies in the executive branch to Congress. Instead, the agencies themselves asked Congress for the money they needed to operate. And because sales of federal lands and high import tariffs brought in a great deal of revenue in the nineteenth century, it did not seem important to worry about budgetary balances. In fact, what to do with the federal government's surplus was a much bigger concern than the government's overall spending. How times have changed!

Actually, by the turn of the century, federal debt began to rise and concerns over spending increased. But because the national government was so much smaller then—its big expansion during the New Deal was still decades away—spending never became a major issue.

But the way spending decisions were made seemed inconsistent with the concept of separation of powers. Because agencies' requests for funds were made directly to Congress, it made the spending decisions, not the president. In that way the legislative branch exercised a great deal of authority over the agencies in the executive branch. With Congress holding the purse strings, agencies were as likely, if

Federal Government Revenues and Spending a Century Ago

The federal government regularly took in more money than it spent between the Civil War and the economically turbulent years of the 1890s. In fact, the surpluses were politically embarrassing. The first table here shows just how large those surpluses were, in proportion to the revenues government was taking in, for some typical years. For example, in 1881, the national government spent only 72.2% of its revenues. By comparison, if government were to spend only 72.2% of what it takes in today, over $400 billion dollars would be left over.

For much of this period, the fastest growing expenditure the national government made was not for defense, for internal improvements such as roads, canals, and railroads, or for interest on the national debt. Instead, it went to pay for pensions for the nation's veterans, most of whom had fought in the Civil War. The second table demonstrates how that sum increased over time. The growth occurred partially because veterans of the wars against Native American nations began to draw compensation, but more because the national government found that paying veterans was a politically acceptable use for the large amounts of money it had available. Funds left over were used to repay the national debt.

During this period that seems so different from today, the same concern was voiced: What is the proper role of the national government? Spending money on veterans' pensions could be defended, because it did not imply an increase in the size and authority of the national government. Spending money to regulate railroads and large business monopolies, however, presented different considerations. Many people were philosophically opposed to the national government regulating the economy in that way. Just because the national government had the funds available did not mean that the public wanted the national government to act. Then, as now, spending decisions reflected people's thinking about the size, purpose, and role of the national government.

Table A
National Government Finances in the Late Nineteenth Century
(in thousands of dollars)

Year	Receipts	Expenditures	Surplus	Total National Debt
1866	558,033	520,809	37,223	2,755,764
1871	383,324	292,177	91,147	2,322,052
1876	294,096	265,101	28,995	2,130,846
1881	360,782	260,713	100,069	2,019,286
1886	336,440	242,483	93,957	1,555,660
1891	392,612	365,774	26,839	1,005,807

Source: U.S. Department of Commerce, *Historical Statistics of the U.S., Colonial Times to 1970,* Part 2 (U.S. Department of Commerce, Bureau of the Census), 1975, Series Y 335-338, p. 1104.

Table B
Federal Government Spending in the late Nineteenth Century (in thousands of dollars)

Year	Total Spending	Military Spending	Interest Payments	Veterans' Benefits	Other
1866	520,809	327,774	133,068	15,605	44,363
1871	292,177	55,231	125,577	34,444	76,926
1876	265,101	57,034	100,243	28,257	79,567
1881	260,713	56,153	82,509	50,059	71,992
1886	242,483	48,232	50,580	63,405	80,266
1891	365,774	74,834	37,547	124,416	128,977

Source: U.S. Department of Commerce, *Historical Statistics of the U.S., Colonial Times to 1970,* Part 2 (U.S. Department of Commerce, Bureau of the Census), 1975, Series Y, 457-465, p. 1114.

not more so, to respond to congressional than to presidential priorities. That put presidents in an awkward position. They were charged with overseeing the bureaucracy, but one of the most useful means of influencing its activity—distributing its money—belonged to Congress.

Change was bound to come, and come it did. President Woodrow Wilson, a political scientist by training, proposed that budgeting should become an executive branch function, where he thought spending decisions could be made rationally, instead of on the basis of political criteria. He argued that politics and administration could and should be kept separate and that the president was in a better position to consider overall revenues and expenditures, in short, to prepare a budget. The distribution of authority between Congress and the president would then make more sense. Wilson's proposal reflected prevailing attitudes of the Progressive Era that political institutions made the wrong decisions because of

In the 1870s, Congress appropriated money to survey, map, and photograph the previously uncharted West, with shots like this 1871 photo of Mammoth Hot Springs in Yellowstone a result. Because the national government funded few programs during the nineteenth century, and because tariffs and sales of western lands to homesteaders and others brought in a lot of revenue, Congress easily found the money to fund the exploration of the West.

political pressures. Reformers thought politics could be removed from many government decisions, including budgeting.

Congress agreed. It passed the Budget and Accounting Act of 1921. Among other things, the act strengthened the appropriations committees in each house of Congress, committees whose authority over spending had gradually been whittled away over the years. It moved the comptroller, who audits governmental expenditures, from the executive branch to the legislative branch. But, most importantly, it established the Bureau of the Budget in the executive branch through which the president would be able to oversee the budgeting process in the bureaucracy. Agencies would have to send requests for appropriations to the bureau rather than directly to Congress. The president could now submit a yearly budget for the federal government as a whole. Congress could still make whatever changes it saw fit, but for the first time the president had a clearly defined role in the process.

The Bureau of the Budget became an important tool for presidents in their efforts to enforce their priorities on government agencies and to develop congressional support for their funding recommendations. Over time, presidents began to give the bureau additional responsibilities in overseeing agencies in the executive branch, and by 1970 Richard Nixon renamed the agency the Office of Management and Budget (OMB) to recognize its greater role. Presidents nowadays channel their budgetary efforts through the OMB. It has become the chief liaison with Congress and with individual agencies on budgeting matters.

Presidential influence over budgeting reached a high point in the late 1960s. Sometimes funds budgeted by Congress for some purposes were "impounded," that is, not spent, because the president disagreed with the projects. Other funds were shifted to unauthorized uses, including the bombing of the Cambodian strongholds of North Vietnamese troops during the Vietnam War.

Members of Congress thought it was time to reassert more congressional control over the federal government's purse strings. The result was the Congressional Budget and Impoundment Control Act of 1974. This act established the Congressional Budget Office with a director appointed by the Speaker of the House and the president pro tempore of the Senate, more or less as a counterweight to the president's OMB. The CBO was to provide Congress with its own analysis of spending and taxing requests, so members would not be dependent on the president for information on the impact of the president's budgetary proposals.

The act also called on Congress to set overall spending limits before it begins to consider actual spending requests for governmental programs. In setting those limits, Congress has to consider available revenues and to reach an agreement on spending priorities for the next year's budget. To stay under the projected budget ceiling, for instance, Congress may have to decide whether to decrease defense spending more than welfare spending. And, importantly, the House and the Senate must negotiate these matters with each other, because these limits and spending priorities have to be adopted in a concurrent resolution by both houses in identical form. For the first time, the two houses have to consider how much money they proposed to spend in the appropriations bills before these bills become law.

As a result, the budget resolutions limit congressional decisions in the appropriations process, but not always successfully. There are always requests for more money than the budget resolutions call for spending. So Congress has to fit its appropriations under the budget ceiling, which turns out to be politically difficult. Members want to provide their constituents with the government services and programs they benefit from. Under this process, it was frequently easier to raise the budget ceiling than to cut funding from politically popular programs. That kept the deficit high.

To control spending, particularly deficit spending, Congress passed the Gramm-Rudman-Hollings bill in 1985 and revised it in 1987. This bill provided for automatic sequestration (withdrawal of authority to spend) of funds if deficit reduction targets were not reached. However, accounting gimmicks enabled the deficit to rise while still technically meeting Gramm-Rudman-Hollings goals. In 1990 Congress passed the Budget Enforcement Act, which substituted more flexible deficit reduction targets and capped discretionary spending (spending not required by law) at predetermined levels. Whereas Gramm-Rudman-Hollings pretended to take deficit-cutting out of politics, the Budget Enforcement Act forces Congress to face up to the hard political choices involved in budgeting.

No one thinks the present process is without difficulties. One is that budgeting is now extremely time-consuming for Congress. Aaron Wildavsky has estimated that Congress spent more time on budgeting in the middle '80s than it did on everything else combined,[11] and the time has not shrunk since then. Legislators have less time, energy, and other resources to deal with other problems facing the nation.

Another is that budgeting is now extremely "Congress-centered" and that presidential influence is again at a relatively low ebb. Once the president has submitted his budget and tried to influence the two houses while they negotiate the budget resolutions, he becomes a frustrated outside observer. But for the foreseeable future, this is the system we have. And how well it works may depend on the ability and motivation of the people representing us in Congress.

Purposes of Budgeting

Is budgeting worth all the time and effort? Not only does it take up most of the time of the staff of the Office of Management and Budget (about 500–600 employees[12]) and the Congressional Budget Office (226 employees in 1991[13]), every agency in the federal government must devote significant resources to provide information relevant to budgeting for upcoming fiscal years. In addition, both the president and Congress are embroiled in negotiations and controversies about budgetary totals as well as appropriations for specific programs.

In theory, budgeting could be simple: Take the expected revenues and distribute the money among the programs government operates. Keep the allocations low enough that total spending is no greater than the money coming in.

That approach may work for our personal budgets. For most of us, budgeting is simply a matter of allocating our income to meet our needs and, if there is any money left, our desires. Although we borrow for expenses we cannot or will not forego, such as a college education or a house, which we cannot easily pay for otherwise, our borrowing capacity is severely constrained. Lenders can be picky about making loans. So for most of us budgeting is a simple matter.

Unfortunately, even in our personal lives, decisions about spending are often a major source of conflict in many families. Do we spend too much on clothes and not enough on entertainment? Should the family eat out more often or give each other less extravagant birthday gifts? When we get down to brass tacks, our personal budgeting does not resemble our image of how we ought to make money decisions. Is it any wonder that governmental budgeting, which reflects the needs and desires of over 250 million Americans, looks a lot different from our simplistic ideal?

The federal government budgets for a variety of reasons. Nevertheless, we may recognize similar motivations in our own budgeting, whether or not we hold ourselves to strict budgets and keep meticulous track of our expenditures. One is that budgeting allows the president and Congress to exert control over the activities of the federal bureaucracy. Another is that budgeting forces the federal government to plan, something governments rarely tend to do. In fact, most private citizens do not plan much better; few people, for instance, set enough money aside for their retirement or for emergencies. Finally, budgeting allows the president and Congress to set priorities among the various programs government administers. If you think about your family's budget, you may recognize similar purposes.

Budgeting gives both the president and Congress a regular, systematic opportunity to influence bureaucratic decision making and to cut funding when an agency's priorities conflict with those of the president or Congress. Presidents have traditionally groused over the difficulty they encounter getting federal agencies to respond to their preferences and priorities. Members of Congress are no more successful. But when agencies must ask for funds to administer their programs and justify their expenditures in the process, presidents and Congress have an opportunity to intervene. Presidents can and do reduce agencies' requests to make their work correspond more closely to the presidents' programs. Members of Congress ask agency heads hard questions about their operations during the hearings on appropriations bills. One political scientist found that budget decisions "carry powerful political signals from elected authorities to the agencies," signals the bureaucracy responds to.[14]

Budgeting also forces the federal government to plan. Many democratically elected governments concern themselves more with the short term—the period until the next election—than the long term. So quick fixes and predictable payoffs have a political advantage among politicians concerned with retaining office. Budgeting shares these characteristics; needed program cuts are deferred and tax cuts hastened, especially in an election year. When gasoline prices rose in the spring of 1996—an election year—politicians of both parties suggested rolling back a federal excise tax on gasoline imposed as a deficit cutting measure in 1993. (A drop in gas prices quieted the calls for rolling back the tax.)

Moreover, many budgetary expenditures form part of a long-term project. In these instances, budgeting requires government to determine how a program will be implemented over time, which steps should follow which others, and how rapidly the program should grow. An agency may, for instance, justify its request for money for an expansion of a pilot child immunization program by developing a plan for the program over the next five years. The current request is but a step in an ongoing process. And budget makers must then consider not only the wisdom of the current funding but the likelihood that the program is going in the right direction. Although agencies plan as a matter of course, Congress would rarely have an occasion to review their plans outside the budgetary process.

Finally, and perhaps most importantly, during consideration of the budget, government must weigh the relative importance of various programs. When a governmental program is first adopted through the policy-making process, it is considered in isolation. The questions are whether the program is worthwhile and whether it is properly structured. But only during the budgeting process does government consider whether it is better to conduct more heart research or build more roads, or whether it is preferable to decrease food stamp allotments or aid to local school districts. Because money spent in one area cannot be spent elsewhere, the president and Congress must set priorities. The budgeting process forces those judgments about priorities each year.

These decisions are political in every sense of the word, despite Wilson's belief that politics and administration could be separated, and despite the implementation of his proposal. Some programs win and others lose. As a result, some groups and individuals come out ahead and others lag behind. In Chapter 1 we defined politics as "the competition to shape government's impact on society's problems and goals." These decisions about planning and priorities certainly fall under that heading, and the attempts to control the bureaucracy's efforts in administering the federal government's policies certainly do, too. People will disagree about what government's impact on society should be, about how government ought to approach a problem, and how rapidly government should attempt to act, if at all. People, parties, and interest groups work out those disagreements every year through the budgetary process. Budgeting seems esoteric and technical, but a more political process would be hard to envision.

Limits on Budgeting

Decisions about spending are constrained by some budgetary facts of life. The first, simply, is that funds are limited. Although the federal government expects to raise almost $1.5 trillion in revenue, it will spend over $1.6 trillion in 1997. It could easily spend more. More defense weapons systems could be developed. More highways could be built. More money could be devoted to cancer research. Many worthwhile programs are not funded because the money is not there. More specifically, some projects have a lower priority and are therefore less likely to be funded than others.

Another budgetary fact of life is that a lot of spending is required by law. We tend to think of all federal spending as optional. If Congress thinks the program is worth funding, it will fund it; otherwise it will not appropriate any money. But that is not correct. Many statutes require Congress to provide money if certain conditions, specified in the law, are met. So people who retire at age 65 can expect a Social Security check, and Congress has no choice but to make the money available.

Recent legislation designed to bring the budget deficit under control divides federal spending into two categories: discretionary, and direct or mandatory. **Direct or mandatory spending** is spending required by law. Even though some of these outlays are provided for by annual appropriation bills, Congress *must* appropriate the money because there are laws that order it to do so. Examples of mandatory spending are payments made for Medicare and Medicaid, various government subsidies such as farm price supports, unemployment insurance, and interest on the national debt.

Entitlements comprise much of mandatory spending. An entitlement is a payment from government to people that they qualify for under the guidelines set by law. Thus, existing law makes aid available to full-time college students coming from families with income under a certain level. Students who meet the requirements are *entitled* to that aid.

Although government can pretty well predict how much money to appropriate for entitlement programs, it cannot determine the exact amount. If, for instance, the economy performs worse than expected, more people will qualify for unemployment compensation, and more money will have to be appropriated for that purpose. And if fewer people retire than expected, Social Security outlays will be lower than expected.

The amount needed to cover entitlements has been growing rapidly over the years. In 1963, entitlements comprised 22.7% of the federal budget. By 1993 they reached 47.3% of the budget, and a federal commission to study entitlements projected that entitlements would consume 58.2% of the budget by 2003.[15] An aging population with a longer life expectancy is one major cause. More people will be benefiting from Social Security and Medicare and for a longer time.

Mandatory spending is not uncontrollable in every instance. In considering the president's budget, Congress cannot simply refuse to fund Medicaid, for example, nor can it decide to drastically lower its funding level. But it can amend the law to change eligibility, or it can repeal the law and remove any need for appropriations. This type of spending, therefore, while not controllable through the budgetary process alone, can be altered through legislation. An expenditure such as interest on the national debt, however, is truly mandatory and can be reduced only by paying down the debt.

Making those changes is politically very difficult, as the new Republican majority in Congress discovered in 1995. When they assumed leadership, they immediately introduced legislation to alter the permanent laws that created, and which order spending for, welfare, farm subsidies, and other programs. People who benefit from these programs, however, mobilized their resources to fight the proposed changes. Entitlement programs, while not untouchable, have strong support that make them difficult to cut.

Quite a few people, however, think that changes are needed—and are inevitable. Take Social Security and Medicare, for example, entitlement programs that just about everybody over the age of 65 benefits from. Contrary to public opinion, these programs are not funded by people's past contributions to the fund; instead, the payments current retirees receive come from payroll taxes on workers. In 1990 there were almost five workers per retiree; in 2030 there will be only about three for each retiree.[16] Your generation will be taxed to provide retirement income for the generations that preceded you.

Discretionary spending, on the other hand, is set by annual appropriations bills passed by Congress, and as the label suggests, amounts are established at the discretion of members of Congress in any given year. Discretionary spending does not mean extra spending on frivolous, unnecessary items. It simply means spending not required by existing law. But much of it is necessary from most perspectives. Discretionary spending, for instance, provides the money for the operation of the Federal Bureau of Investigation, the State Department, the Environmental Protection Agency, and the other programs the national government operates. Spending is limited by the dollar ceilings, or caps, that Congress authorizes for the year (recall the discussion in Chapter 10).

Because mandatory spending makes up so much of each year's budget, pressures for cutting the deficit fall most frequently on discretionary spending. The hard truth is that there is not enough room in discretionary funding for cuts to make a meaningful dent in the deficit.

Operation of the Current Budgeting Process

Decisions about allocating funds to various governmental programs are made in a complex, time-consuming process that involves the bureaucracy, the president, and Congress. Besides these official participants, interest groups pay close attention to budgeting choices that may affect their concerns. State and local government officials also worry about these decisions, because their own budgets and programs are affected. The media, too, follow the process closely, and their reports have political effects, as we found out in Chapter 8. The result is the federal budget, the plan for carrying out the government's purposes for the following twelve months.

The federal budget applies to its fiscal year, which runs from October 1 through September 30 of the following year. It may surprise you to know that the budget process begins about eighteen months before the start of a new fiscal year. The process for fiscal year 1998 (abbreviated FY 1998 to distinguish it from calendar year 1998), which ends September 30, 1998, began in the spring of FY 1996, long before Congress had finished considering the budget for FY 1997. The process is so time-consuming that one year's budget has to be planned before the previous one has been adopted. In fact, in the spring of 1996, President Clinton submitted his FY 1997 budget request to Congress before agreement had been reached on FY 1996 spending.

The first step involves the president and the Office of Management and Budget. They set the basic budgetary parameters: How large should the total be? How large (or small) should the deficit be? What should be the general balance between spending on defense and spending on social programs? These decisions are based both on presidential priorities and on their predictions about probable levels of revenue, inflation, economic growth, and interest rates.

These decisions are not technical decisions on which experts would all agree. They are political and reflect different preferences and political goals. President Reagan, for instance, placed a higher priority on defense than did President Carter. And all presidents have been tempted to adjust economic predictions to match their budgeting goals. Does the budget President Clinton presented to Congress in 1996 lead to a balanced budget by 2002? That depends to a great degree on the economic projections on which it is based, projections that may or may not turn out to be accurate, projections that may or may not be wishful thinking.

The OMB then translates this outline budget into more specific guidelines for the agencies in the executive branch to follow in preparing their requests for funds. These requests are due back to the OMB by the end of the summer. Not surprisingly, the grand total of all these requests usually surpasses the president's goal for total spending, and a number of agencies may have requested significantly more money than the president will support. During the fall, then, agencies may be asked to cut back their requests or to change some priorities. They may comply readily, or they may appeal to the president. Final decisions on agency requests are made by the end of the calendar year. When all requests are in and conform to presidential wishes, the president prepares his formal budget request and submits it to Congress no later than the first Monday in February.

When Congress receives the president's budget, the battle arena shifts to the legislative branch. Democrats in the House in the 1980s were fond of saying that President Reagan's budget was "Dead on Arrival," meaning that they were ready to prepare a budget of their own, despite the president's preferences. When Republicans became the majority in 1995, President Clinton's budgets were also "DOA," with congressional preferences and priorities more important. Although the president tries to influence congressional action on the budget, his success in doing so depends on the resources he can bring to bear on Congress, including "going public."

Congress's first step involves adopting a budget resolution. This resolution, required to be adopted by April 15, sets congressional priorities for thirteen large categories of spending, such as defense, transportation, agriculture, and various social welfare programs (including Social Security and Medicare). Congress also estimates available revenues, overall spending levels, and the size of the deficit. The process forces Congress to examine the budget as a whole. Both the House and the Senate have budget committees in which the budget resolution is considered and then forwarded to the floor for action. The House and the Senate have to agree on the budget resolution, although it does not have to be submitted to the president. Therefore, the president cannot veto Congress's budget resolution.

When changes in existing law have to be made in order to keep spending under the limits set in the resolution, the budget committees require committees in each chamber that have legislative jurisdiction over various areas to submit bills changing the law. That is essentially the only way that Congress can appropriate less money for entitlements and other mandatory spending. In 1995, for instance, when Republicans wanted to spend less on student loans, the Committee on Economic and Educational Opportunities needed to propose changes in the law so that the spending target could be reached. Usually, these changes call for alterations in the criteria by which people qualify for federal funds. If these changes are made, less money need be appropriated.

These kinds of changes are called "reconciliation bills," and from time to time a number of them must be considered. When congressional budgetary goals can be met without changes in authorization, the reconciliation process is not needed. In the last several years, reconciliation has become a major tool of deficit reduction. It has also centralized budgeting authority in Congress, placing more power in the hands of the budget committees and congressional leadership, just as the development of the Office of Management and Budget has centralized budgetary authority in the executive branch. Essentially, reconciliation allows these leaders to negotiate budgetary provisions, leaving the authorizing committees and the Appropriations Committee with much less leeway and room to maneuver.

Reconciliation also shows the vitality of the budget resolutions. Not only do they limit congressional spending, they can force congressional committees to change previously adopted legislation to stay within budget parameters.

Each of the thirteen categories of spending winds up in its own appropriations bill. These thirteen bills comprise the actual budget, even though they are technically separate pieces of legislation. Various subcommittees of the Appropriations Committee in the House will usually hold hearings, often inviting agency personnel to testify about the proposed appropriations, before they mark up the bill and report it to the whole committee. These occasions are the last time agencies can try to influence their budgetary allocations, but the subcommittees are much more constrained by instructions from the Budget Committee than they were in the past.

When members consider these bills, they may make final adjustments to avoid presidential vetoes or to keep the grand total under the budget resolution ceilings. In fact, increases in mandatory spending, such as entitlements, must be balanced by corresponding cuts elsewhere, called "PAYGO" for "pay as you go." Usually appropriations bills cannot be amended on the House floor, although the senators are not so limited. Differences between the two chambers must be reconciled in a conference committee before bills are sent to the president.

If the bills have all been passed by October 1, the new fiscal year can start under a new budget. But the bills are frequently delayed by attempts to work out an agreement on reconciliation bills, by differences in opinion between the Senate and the House, and by a presidential veto. If these appropriations bills have not been adopted by October 1, Congress usually passes "continuing resolutions," signed by the president, that allow the federal government to continue spending as if the previous year's budget were still in effect.

Much of the federal government operated under continuing resolutions for seven months of FY 1996, before the last five appropriations bills were enacted in April 1996. But many continuing resolutions forced agencies to spend at a reduced level—70% or lower than the previous year. Others had attached provisions, called riders, that President Clinton found objectionable. He vetoed several, leading to lengthy government shutdowns because offices could spend no money.

➤Issues in Budgeting

Let's face it: money matters. Everything costs money, and everything government does costs money, too. From telephone lines into government offices to paint for battleships, from paper clips to interstate highway bridges, from printing presidential proclamations to providing emergency assistance for hurricane victims, government programs all entail costs of some sort. We are easily distracted by horror stories about $200 hammers and $500 toilet seats, but even reasonable costs add up. As long as we want government to act, we must expect government to need money.

Although state and local government programs cost money, too, national (or federal) government spending receives the most attention. Indeed, if you ask anyone on the street for an opinion on government spending, you are most likely to hear about the federal budget, not the state or city budget. Pay attention to media coverage of spending issues, and you'll hear about proposals and criticisms of the federal budget. And why not? Federal government spending dwarfs state and local spending. The national budget in 1993 totaled about $1.4 trillion, while that of the largest state, California, was only $104 billion.[17] Even in outlays per person, the federal government's spending was higher than for any one state. The budget totals for all state and local governments combined fall short of the expenditures of the federal government alone, with state and local governments spending $1.2 trillion in 1993.[18] It is not surprising, then, that national government spending gets most of our attention.

Where Does the Money Go?

The overall size of the federal budget may catch our eye first: $1.6 trillion is a lot of money, a sum difficult to imagine. Figure 1 tells us, in broad categories, where that money comes from and where it goes.

FIGURE 1
Estimated Federal Income and Expenditures by Category, 1997

*Does not include interest paid on government securities held by the Social Security Trust Fund. Direct payments to individuals include primarily Medicare and Social Security, but also AFDC and other support for the poor.

Source: Budget of the U.S. Government, 1997, supplement, p. 2.

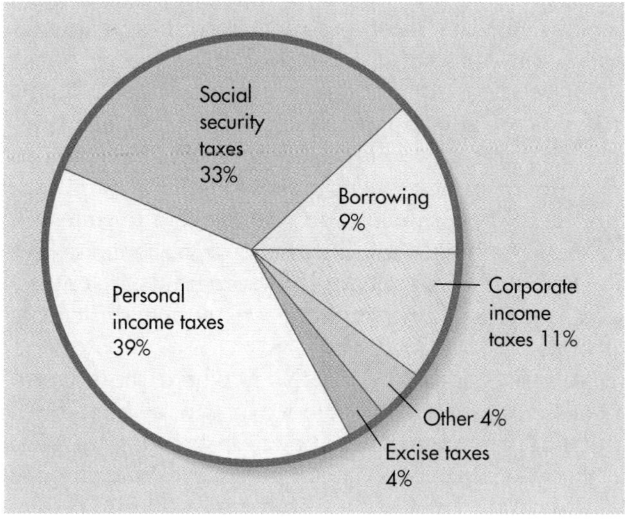

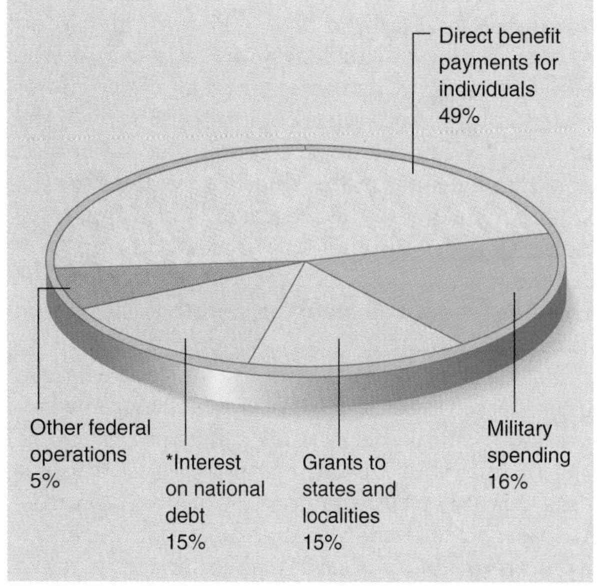

Although the total is important, we must also understand how the money is used. After all, if we have no idea why it is spent, we cannot come to a realistic, balanced position on current budget controversies. Although the federal government, just like individuals, does not always "get what it paid for," we should keep in mind what it hopes to get. So let us take a quick tour of some of the federal government's spending programs to see where the money goes.

It may come as a surprise to you that the federal government funds a lot of programs we take for granted. And it may come as a bigger surprise that many of these programs comprise only a minute proportion of total federal spending.

Some of the spending goes for continuing government operations. The United States, for example, maintains embassies in virtually every nation with which it has diplomatic relations. That's more than 150 embassies, each with a building, clerical staff, a U.S. Marine Corps detachment, and foreign service personnel. For fiscal 1997 President Clinton requested an appropriation of $338 million for the State Department to conduct diplomatic relations, chiefly operating the nation's embassies.[19] Utility bills for government offices across the nation—and most federal employees work outside of Washington, D.C.—must also be paid. Every office needs water service, electrical power, trash collection, and telephone lines. Check your local telephone book to see how many federal agencies operate in your locality. These offices are scattered across the nation because we want government close to the people and because that is where the services are needed. Agricultural Stabilization and Conservation offices should be near farms, and Forest Service offices need to be located near public forests. With any imagination, you can think of further examples.

Other money is spent on maintaining our infrastructure, which includes the basic facilities and installations needed for a society to function. Highway construction is an example—you may have seen "Your Tax Dollars at Work" signs at a road construction site, signs that frequently indicate how much of the cost is being met by the federal government. Many bridge inspections are also federally financed. Maintenance of barge traffic on the Mississippi, dredging the channels and operating the locks, is a federal responsibility. And let's not forget regulating radio and television communication; imagine the chaos that would result if several stations attempted to broadcast on the same frequency. Recent airplane crashes bring to mind the importance of the Federal Aviation Administration in maintaining safety in air transportation.

Still more is spent on defense. Of course, the big costs are weapons systems (a typical bomber costs up to $200 million), salaries, and maintenance of military installations. But think of how the little things add up. Consider the cost of sheets and blankets for the men and women in the barracks. Think of the motor oil, spark plugs, and radiator antifreeze for all the military vehicles. And don't forget the scrambled eggs, the lima beans, and the mashed potatoes for the mess halls. The day-to-day expenses of housing, feeding, and clothing our military forces adds up to a considerable sum.

Then there are the many programs that the federal government administers. It provides assistance to small businesses to help them find markets and grow. It funds heart research, nuclear research, and sociological and political science studies. It helps control the spread of infectious disease through the Centers for Disease Control and Prevention. It warns of blizzards, tornadoes, and hurricanes. It measures earthquake severity and responds to earthquake damage. It fights forest fires, drug trafficking, and smuggling. It inspects working conditions and meat and poultry. It regulates the stock market and the banking system. It funds Head Start and helps school districts pay for new school buildings. It sends shuttles into space and maps the nation by satellite.

Finally, the federal government provides funds. Social Security payments to retirees and disabled persons are the most prominent of these expenditures. But they also include compensating banks when students default on their guaranteed loans, making crop subsidy payments to farmers when commodity prices are too low, and providing food stamps to the poor to help them make ends meet. Similarly, the federal government also provides aid to state and local governments for a variety of reasons. As we have pointed out, many of these programs are entitlements, and spending on them is extremely difficult to control.

Now let's look specifically at where the government's money goes. In Table 1, you can see how much the national government spends in broad categories, from national defense to Social Security and interest on the national debt. These categories refer to sets of programs, not specific government agencies. "Income security," for instance, includes federally financed welfare programs, unemployment compensation, and

TABLE 1 Federal Expenditures in Basic Categories, 1995 (estimate), in Billions of Dollars

NATIONAL DEFENSE			**$271.8**
HUMAN RESOURCES	Social Security	$336.1	
	Income security	223.0	
	Medicare	157.3	
	Health	115.1	
	Education	56.1	
	Veterans' benefits	38.4	
TOTAL HUMAN RESOURCES			**$926.0**
PHYSICAL RESOURCES	Transportation	$39.1	
	Commerce and housing	−12.0[a]	
	Other	39.2	
TOTAL PHYSICAL RESOURCES			**$66.3**
NET INTEREST:			**234.0**
OTHER:			**40.8**
TOTAL:			**$1,538.9**

[a]A negative amount refers to an "offset," which occurs when government takes in money from nongovernment activities, such as rent from public housing.

Source: *Statistical Abstract of the United States: 1994* (Washington D.C.: U.S. Government Printing Office, 1994), p. 335, table 520.

pensions for federal workers. "Physical resources" refers to spending on natural resources such as national forests and clean water, energy, and disaster relief and insurance. Agriculture and support for scientific research fall into the "Other" category at the bottom of the table. Clearly, spending on human resources far exceeds spending on defense or on physical resources, and the largest single category is Social Security. You may be surprised to notice that the nation spends as much on veterans' benefits as it does on transportation, and that Medicare and education expenses combined add up to less money than the interest on the national debt.

More specific breakdowns of federal spending in 1995 for some typical government operations appear in Table 2. Of course, the table does not include all government spending; if it did, it would be too complicated to read. Instead, it reports some instructive totals. For instance, the much-criticized National Aeronautics and Space Administration (NASA) spent just over \$14 billion in 1995, about 1% of total spending. Even less money went to health research: just over \$11 billion. Energy conservation got just under \$700 million, while federal law enforcement received over \$7 billion. Foreign aid was allocated \$7.3 billion, half of the money used for agricultural programs.

TABLE 2 Federal Government Expenditures for Selected Purposes, 1995 (estimated), in Millions of Dollars

PROGRAM	AMOUNT	PERCENT OF FEDERAL BUDGET
Agricultural programs	\$14,401	0.9%
Air transportation programs	10,132	0.7%
Disaster relief	4,845	0.3%
Energy conservation	681	0.04%
Federal law enforcement	7,060	0.5%
Foreign aid	7,311	0.5%
General science and basic research	4,173	0.3%
Health research	11,660	0.8%
Higher education	14,029	0.9%
Legislative branch	2,793	0.2%
Military construction	5,621	0.4%
National Aeronautics and Space Administration	14,241	0.9%
Pollution control and abatement	6,438	0.4%
Unemployment compensation	23,839	2.0%
Veterans' hospital and medical care	16,527	1.1%

Source: *Statistical Abstract of the United States: 1995* (Washington, D.C.: U.S. Government Printing Office, 1995), pp. 337–8, Table 522.

When we examine these allocations, we cannot help but see that most of the federal government's programs contribute relatively little to the overall level of spending. Even if there were tremendous "waste, fraud, and abuse" in NASA, for instance, so much so that perhaps 10% of its funds were mismanaged, eliminating it would reduce overall spending very little. Only a very few categories of government spending contribute significantly to overall budget outlays.

The Deficit and Its Causes

The federal government spends more than it takes in. Figure 2 charts federal spending, revenues, and the size of the deficit for the last twenty years. Although federal revenues have grown consistently, they have not grown enough to close the gap between income and outlays. The result has been a series of budget deficits, an unbroken string since 1969.

Since the mid-1980s, the size of the gap has been so large that many politicians and economists have urged Congress and the president to take action. During this period, the deficit has averaged more than \$200 billion a year—about \$800 annually for every man, woman, and child in the nation. Deficits that size do not lend themselves to a quick fix.

Why is the deficit so large? Three factors are most prominent. One is spending by the government, including for entitlements and for interest on the national debt, and another is revenues received by the government. A related factor is demographics, in particular the aging of the population, which affects both spending and revenues.

Spending

The national government now spends about twice as much as it did in the early 1980s. Where has the increase in spending come from? Traditionally, analysts break spending down into two major categories—national defense and human resources, which includes Social Security, Medicare, health programs, veterans' benefits, and education programs. Defense spending has been virtually constant for the last decade,[20] but social spending has increased. Whereas defense spending overwhelmed social spending in the 1960s and early 1970s, now social spending triples defense spending.

FIGURE 2
Federal Spending, Revenues, and Deficit, in Billions of Dollars

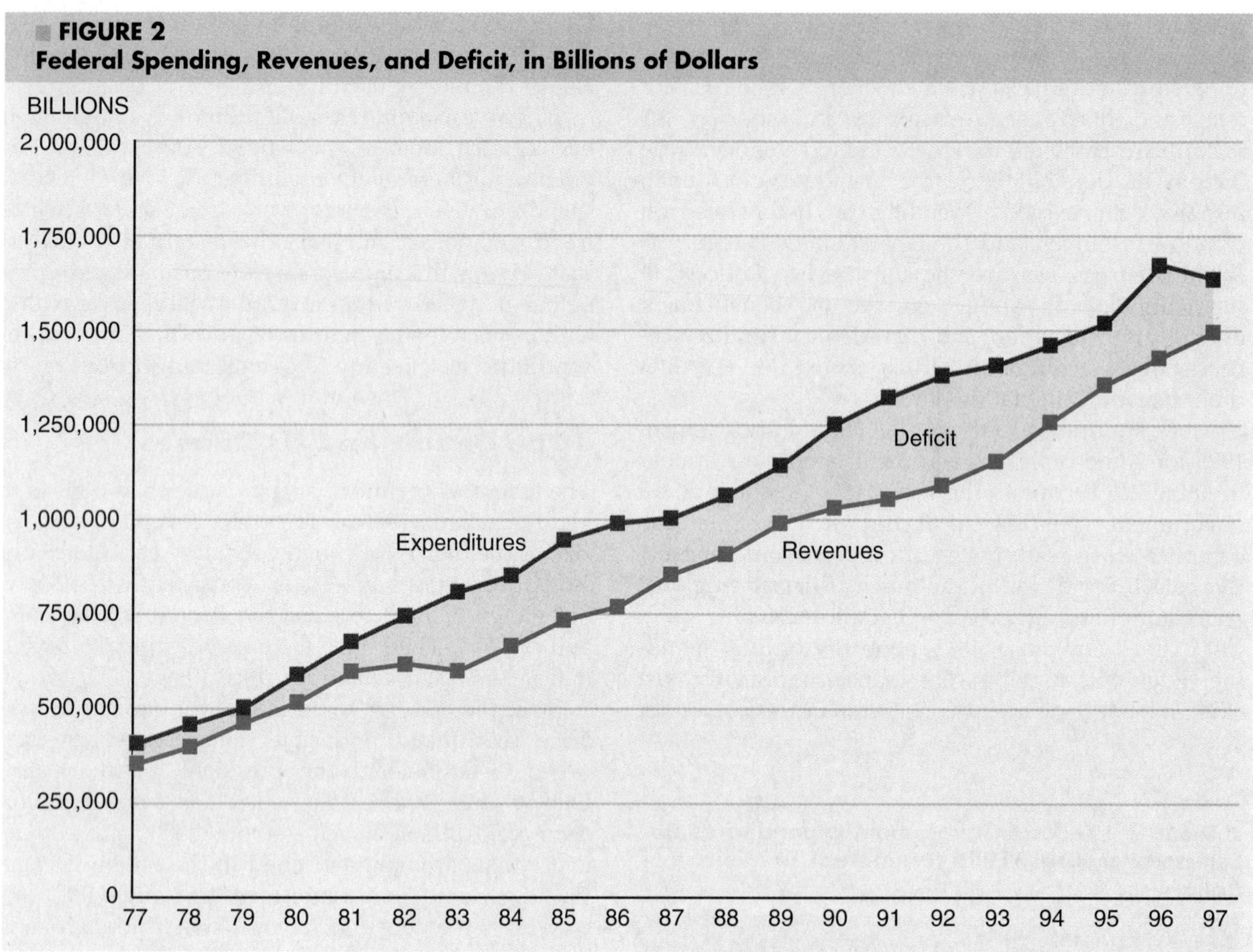

ENTITLEMENTS Many human resources programs are entitlements, in which the government provides the money to everyone who qualifies. As the number of people eligible for these programs increases, so does the amount of money needed to fund these programs. Thus, expenditures for these programs are difficult to limit.

People usually think of entitlements as assistance for poor people, but more than one-third of American families earning more than $40,000 a year receive benefits, and as income goes up, the average benefit also increases. Families with incomes over $100,000 a year receiving entitlement benefits get almost twice as much as families with incomes under $10,000 a year.

Medicare, the program that provides health care for elderly Americans who are eligible for Social Security (not just those who are poor), has especially worried officials. Currently, about 37 million people are covered by the program at a cost of $178 billion.[21] The program is financed in part by payroll taxes and in part by fees paid by participants in the program. But because the cost of medical care has risen dramatically over the last decade and because the number of people eligible for Medicare is increasing rapidly, the cost of the program to the federal government is expected to skyrocket. President Clinton's health care proposals, rejected by Congress in 1994, were intended in part to rein in future Medicare costs. Without health care reforms, Medicare spending will make budget balancing difficult.

We can predict quite accurately how much Social Security and Medicare are going to cost in the future. As the baby boom generation ages, a larger proportion of our population will draw Social Security and benefit from Medicare than ever before. And because people live longer today than they did in the past, these retirees will be "entitled" to payments from government longer than anyone anticipated when the programs were established. Because recipients use their substantial political resources to defend any changes in these programs that would reduce their benefits in the future, spending on entitlements will be hard to reduce.

INTEREST ON THE NATIONAL DEBT The deficits themselves ultimately cost money. The accumulation of money owed by the government from all budget deficits is the **national debt.** Because the government has run continuous and sizable deficits, the national debt has increased rapidly. As a result, interest payments on the national debt have also soared. For instance, in 1977 the federal government paid less than $30 billion in interest on the national debt, but in 1997 these payments are projected to be $239 billion.

As interest payments increase, balancing the budget becomes more and more difficult. In 1980, the federal government devoted about 9% of the budget to interest payments on the national debt. By 1989 the proportion increased to about 15%, and in 1996 it will be about 16%.

These interest payments have had quite an impact on the budget over time. As Figure 3 shows, the budget would be balanced now if no interest were due on the national debt. The massive deficits incurred in the 1980s keep the budget in deficit even today.

FIGURE 3

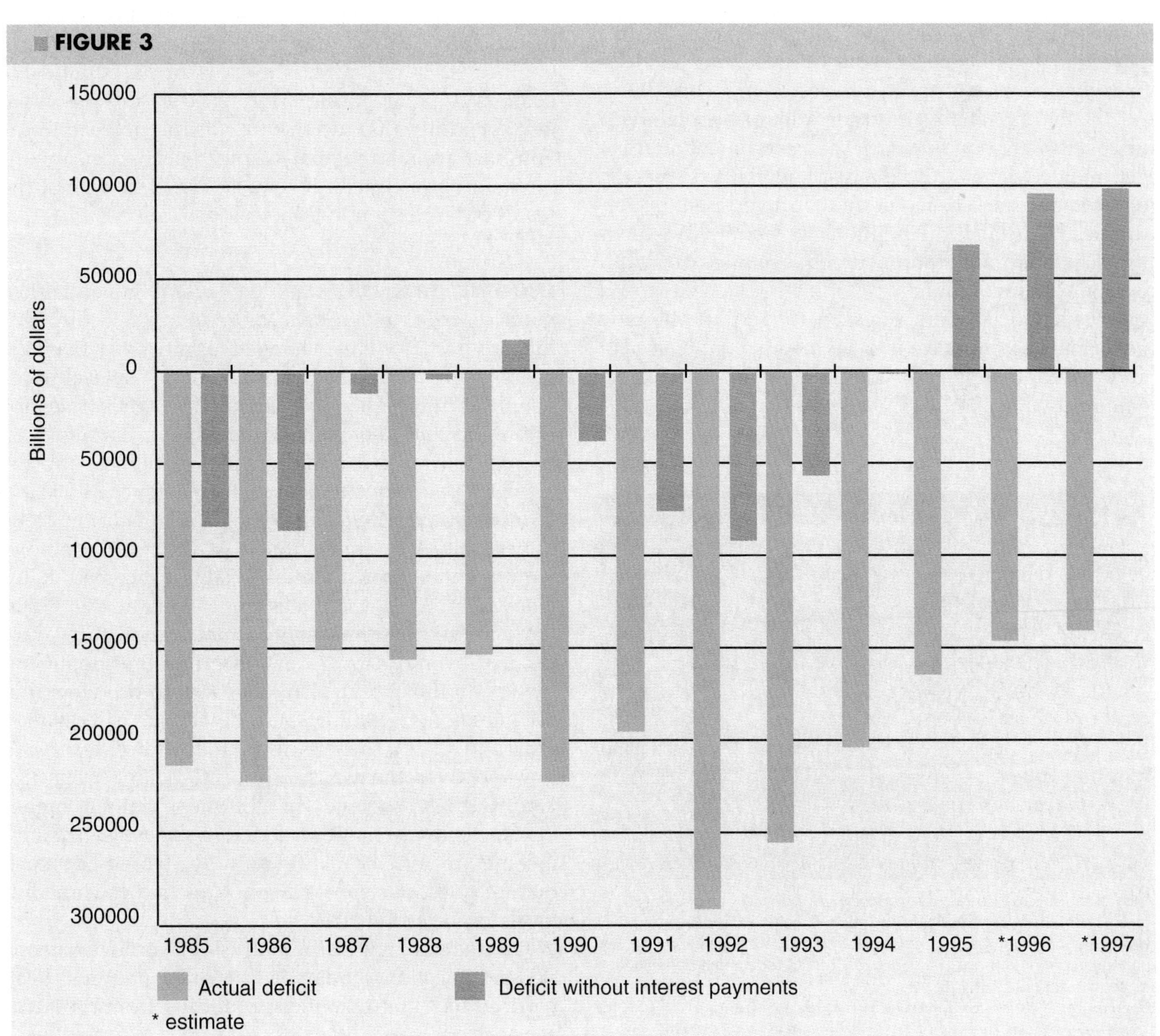

The amount of interest due varies with the rates at which the federal government has to borrow money. Luckily, in recent years, interest rates have been moderating, so the national government has had to pay less in interest than it would have otherwise. Nevertheless, every year the federal government runs a deficit, it has to borrow more money—and pay more interest on the additional borrowing. And, as is the case with entitlement programs, Congress cannot refuse to provide the money to pay this interest.

Balancing the budget will not reduce these interest payments; it would just prevent their increase. Only if the national government were to run a surplus, taking in more in revenues than it spends, would the national debt be reduced and interest payments go down. That is not likely to happen. People dislike paying taxes but expect to continue receiving services. Sharply increasing taxes or decreasing services is politically unpalatable. Further, a lot of people invest in government bonds, which the government offers to get money to make the interest payments, so paying off the national debt would reduce investment opportunities. (Alexander Hamilton, in George Washington's first administration, urged Congress to stand behind the Revolutionary War debt, because it would give economic leaders a reason to support the new government.) Thus, we will have both a national debt and annual payments on the interest for the foreseeable future.

One of the success stories of American public policy, Social Security gives most elderly the freedom to swim in society's mainstream. However, some changes are needed to maintain its benefits for the next generation. Perhaps a "means test" could reduce the benefits to those who do not really need it.
Source: Red Morgan for *Time*, December 19, 1994, p. 36.

Revenues

Federal revenues, the money the national government collects in taxes and fees each year, have increased slowly but steadily over the last several decades. Much of that increase has come from the growth of the economy and from the effect of inflation. As the economy improves, people earn more taxable income and require less assistance; as inflation drives wages and salaries up, federal revenues also go up. The ratio of revenues collected by the government to the total value of the products and services produced by the economy (called the Gross Domestic Product) has stayed pretty constant in the last twenty years, hovering around 19%.

Over the last twenty years, federal revenues have actually risen a little faster than expenditures, except in the early 1980s, when the Reagan Administration engineered large tax cuts as part of its supply-side economics policy. Congress refused to make equivalent spending cuts, and the tax cuts did not lead to the administration's anticipated spurt in economic investment and government revenues. The deficit is not the result of large spending increases.

INCOME TAX RATES The federal government's main source of revenue is the individual income tax. Income tax rates have changed significantly over the years. The rates have come down, especially for people in the higher brackets. In the 1950s, rates for the higher brackets were, in retrospect, astronomical. A family with two children in the highest income category paid up to 85% of its income over $1,000,000 in income tax. (However, these people had numerous opportunities to shield much of their income so it would not be considered "taxable" income.) Rates were reduced in the 1960s and again in the 1970s. Early in President Reagan's administration, rates were reduced even further. After concern in President Clinton's administration that the well-to-do were not paying enough, the highest rate was increased somewhat, to 39.6%, where it is today. Besides being lowered over the years, the tax brackets were also "indexed," so people do not move into a higher bracket because inflation led to an increase in their income. Imagine how differently we would approach budget questions today if tax rates had remained at levels used in the 1950s!

Or imagine how differently we would approach budget questions today if tax rates had not been reduced by Congress, under prodding from President

Reagan, in 1982. The revenues dropped from 1982 to 1983, and the deficit skyrocketed to over $200 billion. Although revenues resumed their gradual growth in subsequent years, expenditures continued to grow, too (though at a lower rate, as noted). Since then, the deficit has remained consistently high. If the Reagan tax cuts had not occurred, the deficit picture would appear substantially different. Reagan's economic policies led to markedly higher budget deficits.

We still think our tax rates are high, yet our tax burden is the smallest in the industrial world (Figure 4). Moreover, we tax our wealthiest citizens at a much lower rate than do other nations. Our tax policies, based on comparatively low income taxes for the well-to-do and increasingly high Social Security taxes for workers, allow the average worker to keep a smaller part of his or her paycheck than counterparts in Europe or Japan.

FIGURE 4
U.S. Has Smallest Tax Burden in Industrial World

The United States government's total tax revenues as a percentage of gross domestic product were less than those of other wealthy nations in 1990, the latest year for which figures are available.

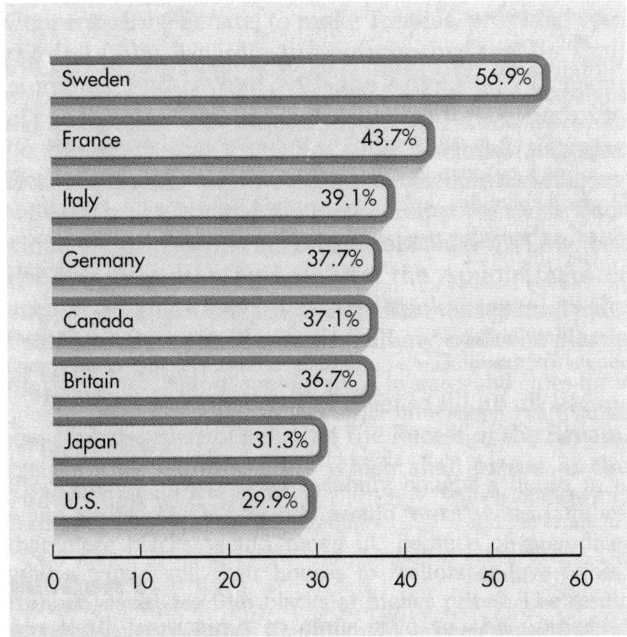

Source: Organization for Economic Cooperation and Development.

TAX EXPENDITURES Although many people assume that the federal government's chronic deficits reflect runaway spending, others think that they are due to incomplete taxing. These people point out that the federal government exempts some income from taxes. Collectively, these exemptions are called **tax expenditures,** and they add up to big sums. Just three tax expenditures add up to almost $180 billion for fiscal 1996, more than the projected deficit. Not taxing interest on the loans people take out to buy their houses, not taxing the health benefits that many employers provide their employees, and not taxing contributions to qualified pension plans reduce federal revenues about $60 billion each. These exemptions are very popular, however, especially with their predominantly middle and upper class recipients, so proposals to eliminate them attract significant political opposition. But the effect on the budget is exactly the same as if government taxed these items fully and then sent recipients a check instead. Few politicians, however, want to risk the political heat that would come if these exemptions were challenged.

No one reason, then, explains the chronic budget deficits of the federal government. The deficits are the result of both spending and taxing decisions that citizens, through pressure on their elected representatives, have made (compounded by demographic trends that have occurred). Over the years citizens have made clear that they want many government services but they do not want high taxes. The upshot is continuing deficits. As the comic strip character Pogo told his compatriots, "We have met the enemy—and he is us."

Contemporary budget battles will center as much on these political choices and these trends as on the actual dollars in the budget. Of course, Congress and the president will fight with each other over allocations for various programs, but changing the allocations and cutting here and there will not end budget deficits. Hard political choices need to be made. The debate is not just about the budget—it is about the nature and direction of government in the future.

Dealing with the Deficit

Pressures on government to deal with the deficit have increased in recent years. Some are self-imposed; when candidates for Congress criticize incumbents for deficit spending and when presidents promise to submit a balanced budget by the end of their first

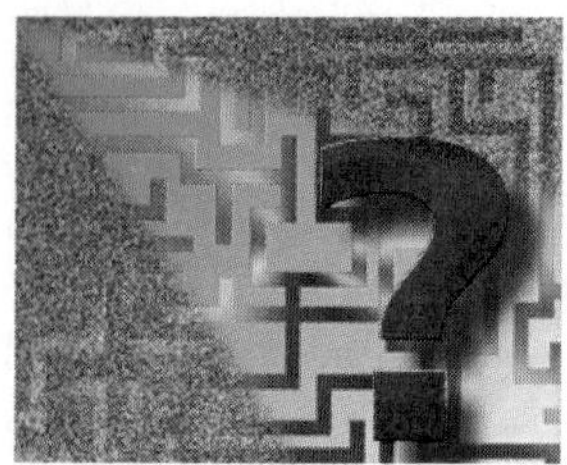

Symbolic Solutions for Complex Problems?

Balancing the Budget by Constitutional Amendment

President Reagan once said, "Balancing the budget is like protecting your virtue: you have to learn to say no."[1] If this is the case, America has been suffering from persistent promiscuity: Balancing the budget has been easy to talk about but nearly impossible to do. Despite his admonition, President Reagan ran up the largest deficits in our country's history. Neither Congress nor the president has yet put together enough spending cuts or tax increases to bring the budget into balance.

One solution that has been offered periodically since the early nineteenth century, and persistently during the past twenty years, is a constitutional amendment to require a balanced budget. Republicans, acting on their "Contract with America," have pushed hard to pass the amendment, thus far without success.

The public strongly appears to favor such an amendment, with 80% typically saying they support it. However, when faced with the possibility of higher taxes or cuts in social insurance programs as conditions for erasing the deficit, the support falls to far less than a majority.[2] Therefore, opponents of the amendment argue that what is needed more than a constitutional mandate is that legislators have the political will and the backbone to face the anger of groups whose favorite programs or tax deductions are cut. Reducing the deficit requires unpopular choices: higher taxes, spending cuts, or both.

Backers of the proposed amendment argue that only a constitutional requirement will give big spenders in Congress and the White House the courage they need to enact big spending cuts. In support of this claim, Senator Nancy Kassebaum (R.-Kan.) pointed out that when an earlier version of the amendment had been introduced in the Senate in 1982, it received 69 votes. Yet two years later only 33 senators had supported her bill to freeze all federal spending for one year.[3] Amendment supporters argue that unless members of Congress can say, "The Constitution made me do it," most will not take the political risk of voting for cuts in popular programs.

By itself the amendment offers no solution to the problems that have contributed to the deficit, such as spiraling health care costs, waste and fraud, and Cold War military spending. However, supporters argue that an amendment would provide an imperative for finding solutions.

Opponents of an amendment argue that it would remove the fiscal flexibility Congress needs to respond to emergencies. What would happen if huge unforeseen expenditures were needed for a war or natural disaster or an economic downturn, for example? The Gulf War, sending troops to Somalia and Haiti, the flooding of the Mississippi River, and the Northridge (California) earthquake all required special budget authorizations. By some estimates, government insistence on a balanced budget during the recession of the early 1990s would have led to an unemployment rate of 9% instead of 7.7%, and $5,000 less per year in unemployment benefits for a laid-off worker.[4] Would Congress refuse to buffer the effects of a recession if the amendment passes? Or, if government-insured pension funds or savings accounts were to fail, would Congress refuse to cover these losses as it is required to do by law? The 1995 amendment bill responded to this concern by including a provision that in the event of war, or if three-fifths of Congress agreed there was a need for spending beyond revenues, the balanced budget requirement could be waived.

Both opponents and supporters of the amendment have also expressed concern over a possible loss of budgetary powers to the federal courts. Even with an amendment in place, Congress still may not be able to agree on a combination of taxes and outlays that balances the budget. In this case, who but the federal courts would be in a position to review the budget and resolve the imbalance? To prevent an unwanted strengthening of the judiciary, the Senate version of the bill denied budgetary review powers to the federal courts.

If the amendment forbids the courts to step in and includes a waiver option allowing an unbalanced budget in emergency situations, and if interest groups continue to demand support for their favorite programs, then will an amendment prevent Congress from engaging in the same kind of budgetary gimmickry used to meet the requirements of the Gramm-Rudman-Hollings Act?

---

terms, everybody expects action. Other pressures come from outside. Investors have recently greeted each substantial move toward a balanced budget with increased enthusiasm for stocks and bonds. Some economists, by no means all, have begun to warn Washington that the economy cannot continue to absorb massive deficits indefinitely. Public opinion has strongly supported a balanced budget in recent

"A billion is a thousand million? Why wasn't I informed of this?"

The real fear is that budgetary gimmicks would reduce the amendment's effect. One political scientist reports that states have used all sorts of tactics, including changing accounting systems, to stay within the law, even though they were actually running deficits.[5] Alice Rivlin, an economist who has served both in the Congressional Budget Office and in the Office of Management and Budget, called a balanced budget amendment "the mother of all budget gimmicks."[6]

Moreover, requiring a balanced budget will not make budget forecasting any more of a science than it is. It will be just as difficult with an amendment as without to discourage wishful thinking by politicians and to prevent budgetmakers from making errors in estimating economic growth and revenues. For example, most of President Reagan's early budgets predicted surpluses. The magnitude of error was huge as year after year rosy estimates of revenue were not realized. A constitutional amendment could encourage such optimistic forecasting in order to make estimated federal revenues match outlays.

The CBO has estimated that, without additional taxes, it would take $1.2 trillion in spending cuts to eliminate the deficit by 2002. This is a huge sum, but for the first time there appears to be a commitment—if not agreement on how to do it—in both Congress and the White House to cut spending and reduce the size of government. In addition in 1995 Congress passed legislation requiring that tax cuts had to be matched dollar for dollar by spending cuts.

The 1995 balanced budget amendment bill was narrowly defeated in the Senate. The following year, the measure was brought up again, in large part because Majority Leader and Republican presidential nominee Robert Dole wanted to force Democratic Senators to vote against it before the fall campaign. Dole did not expect the bill to pass, and it again lost by two votes. Although not adopted, the proposal is likely to come up again in succeeding sessions of Congress.

In the absence of a constitutional amendment, budget plans for fiscal years 1996 and 1997 were submitted containing a combination of spending cuts and changes in entitlement programs. Together, these plans met or surpassed CBO requirements for balancing the budget by 2002, the year Congress and President Clinton agreed on as the target date for ending deficits. These changes are politically difficult, and Congress and President Clinton disagree about specific cuts and changes, but they represent the kinds of changes, not counting new or higher taxes, that would be necessary if a balanced budget amendment were added to the Constitution.

Once the budget is balanced, there will still be the matter of paying off close to $5 trillion of accrued debt. The figure sounds staggering but the picture is not all gloom and doom. By 1790 the fledgling U.S. government had run up a national debt of $75.4 million, mainly from the costs of the Revolutionary War. This figure was fifteen times greater than the new government's annual revenues, whereas in 1995 our national debt was "only" four times larger than the $1.4 trillion in revenues. It took almost 50 years to pay off that first debt, but by 1835 the U.S. was virtually debt free.[7] And during that period of steady debt reduction the country continued to grow and prosper.

1. Quoted in "The Deficit: Out of Control?" *Newsweek,* December 12, 1983, p. 36.
2. David E. Rosenbaum, "In Loss, Republicans Find Seeds of Victory," *New York Times,* March; 5, 1995, p. E16; George J. Church, "Hard Going for the Easy Part," *Time,* January 23, 1995, p. 34.
3. Senator Nancy Kassebaum, quoted by William Rasberry, "Mandating a Destination Without a Hint of How to Get There," *Lincoln Star-Journal,* December 19, 1994.
4. Louis Uchitelle, "The Pitfalls of a Balanced Budget," *New York Times,* February 21, 1995, p. C1.
5. Irene S. Rubin, *The Politics of Public Budgeting: Getting and Spending, Borrowing and Balancing,* 2nd ed. (Chatham, N.J.: Chatham House, 1993), pp. 190–198.
6. Quoted in Jeffrey B. Tramwell and Gary P. Osifchin, *The Clinton 500: The New Team Running America* (Washington, D.C.: Advance Publishing, 1994), p. 54.
7. Thomas K. McCraw, "Deficit Lessons: Hamilton the Hero," *New York Times,* May 2, 1993, p. F13.

Sources: Paul Krugman, *Age of Diminished Expectations* (Cambridge, Ma: MIT Press, 1992), pp. 35–78; *U.S. Budget for Fiscal Year 1996.*

years, although the public is more ambiguous than it seems, as we will soon discover.

In response, our representatives have taken a number of steps. They fall, broadly, into four categories—making structural changes in the process; reducing spending, increasing revenues, and shifting responsibilities to the states.

Structural Changes

Although the budgetary process has undergone some major changes in this century, the changes were not motivated by the need to handle a budget deficit. Today, however, two changes have been put forward for this purpose. One is a balanced budget amendment to the Constitution, and the other is a line-item veto for the president.

The rationale behind the balanced budget amendment is to require the president to propose and Congress to adopt a balanced budget, so that deficit spending is no longer an option. Many states have such a provision in their constitutions. The box in this chapter considers whether this option represents a real change or whether it is merely a symbolic solution. Because in 1995 the Senate rejected the balanced budget amendment by two votes, although the House passed it, we may not know whether it would have worked.

A line-item veto, which allows the president to reject a specific appropriation while still signing the rest of the bill into law, is now being tried. (The box in Chapter 11 presents the details on its operation.) The rationale is that the president will be able to reduce pork barrel and special interest spending that legislators find themselves pressured to include in an appropriations bill. But because the present version exempts entitlement spending from the line-item veto, it is unlikely that this change will dramatically affect the size of future deficits. Even if all pork barrel spending were eliminated—a highly unlikely scenario—deficits would still be high enough to be worrisome.

Even if these two responses are only symbolic and not real solutions to the deficit problem, that symbolism is still important. Adoption of these reforms signals legislators' recognition of the seriousness of the problem and their willingness to take drastic steps to deal with it. How drastic? A line-item veto threatens to change the balance of power between the president and Congress. A balanced budget amendment to the Constitution would alter the basic makeup of our system, something we have usually done only for significant reasons. The symbolism of these proposed reforms, therefore, should not be lightly dismissed.

Spending Cuts

If a family falls deeper and deeper into debt, the first advice financial consultants would give is to cut spending. And so when people consider the federal government's chronic deficits, reducing spending leads the list of solutions.

Republicans who found themselves in the majority after the 1994 congressional elections, buoyed by a large and enthusiastic freshman class, urged deep cuts in spending, especially in such programs as Aid

Source: [first name unknown] Trever, *Albuquerque Journal*, reprinted in *Washington Post National Weekly Edition*, May 6–12, 1996, p. 31.

to Families with Dependent Children (AFDC), the federal government's main welfare program. They also urged cutbacks in the Department of Education and elimination of the Department of Commerce. Even though cutting spending seemed logical enough on the surface, it soon became clear that spending cuts would not come easily.

President Clinton and congressional Democrats resisted large cuts in spending, partly because the proposed cuts ran counter to their views on the proper role of government and partly because the proposed cuts would affect their constituents more than the Republicans' constituents.

U.S. public opinion is remarkably ambiguous on federal spending. As a whole, public opinion is strongly in favor of a balanced budget without an increase in taxes. But the only way to balance the budget without raising more revenues is to reduce spending. Specific proposals for cutting spending, however, hurt programs people want. One group who came to see a senator from Maine gave him a list of nine requests. "The first item was 'Balance the budget' and items 2 through 9 were proposals that would increase the budget," the senator reported.[22]

President Clinton and the Republican-led Congress clashed over many cuts proposed in congressional appropriations bills in 1995 and 1996. It was easier for the president to defend programs such as Medicare from Republicans' attempts to reduce them than it was for Republicans to defend the overall goal of balancing the budget. The agreement for the 1996 budget Congress and the president finally reached included $20 billion cuts in domestic spending, substantial but quite a bit less than Republicans had first proposed. Most politicians conclude that future benefits from balancing the budget rarely outweigh present costs from reduced spending on popular programs.

Another difficulty is that meaningful spending cuts can be made only if entitlements are tackled. Senator Bob Kerrey (D.-Neb.), co-chair of a bipartisan commission to consider entitlements, had argued that Clinton's deficit cutting proposals did not go far enough because they left entitlements untouched. But when the commission issued its final report to the president in 1995, it was unable to agree on specific recommendations. Although the members agreed that projected growth in entitlement spending, chiefly Medicare and Social Security, meant "higher taxes for Americans" or "benefit reductions for retirees," they could not arrive at a consensus about action to take now.[23] This choice entails a generational conflict: Do we tax younger people to pay for benefits for older people? Do we reduce older people's benefits to avoid raising younger people's taxes? The commission found neither choice palatable.

"By the way, Sam, as someday you'll be paying for my entitlements, I'd like to thank you in advance."

Source: [first name unknown] Handelsman, *The New Yorker*, April 1, 1996, p. 67.

A prominent alternative being considered to rein in entitlement spending is to use "means tests" for Social Security and Medicare payments. Essentially, means-testing reduces Social Security and Medicare benefits to those with higher incomes. Because 30% of families earning over $100,000 a year receive such benefits, averaging about $15,000 a year, means tests have the potential of reducing entitlement spending significantly.[24] Opponents argue, however, that a means test would make it more obvious that Social Security and Medicare are welfare programs and, as a result, they would lose their popularity. Opponents also argue that recipients deserve the benefits because they have contributed to the programs through payroll taxes during their working years. However, the average recipient gets far more from these programs than he or she ever paid into them.

Although some steps were taken in 1995 and 1996 to reform Medicare so that future revenues would meet future expected outlays, the steps were small and the rise in health care costs continues.

Raising Revenues

No politician likes to talk about raising taxes. Walter Mondale, the 1984 Democratic candidate for president, did so right after the Reagan tax cuts had led to a massive increase in the yearly deficit, and he was soundly defeated. President Clinton virtually apologized for the tax increases in his 1993 economic package. Politicians are more likely to promise tax cuts, even when the deficit remains high.

Nevertheless, hints at revenue increases come up regularly. Most of them are disguised by referring to "closing loopholes" or eliminating unjustified exemptions in the tax codes. Some businesses have obtained loopholes that most people, if aware of them, would want to close. But many people, including the broad middle class, also benefit from exemptions. One of the largest is the mortgage interest deduction, which makes buying a home easier. (People can deduct the mortgage interest from their taxes.) Similarly, the tax code provides an investment tax credit to encourage businesses to invest more. We could close this "loophole," but then we would lose the gains in productivity that come with increases in investment.

Others argue that we could increase revenues without increasing tax rates if government would spend enough money for the right purposes. Investing in infrastructure, some argue, could raise productivity in the economy enough to increase tax revenues because people would be earning more and spending more. One economist has argued that if productivity over the last two decades had averaged 2% per year, as it has historically, instead of the actual 1%, "higher tax revenues . . . would have erased the deficit and left us with a budget surplus."[25]

Finally, ever since the Reagan tax cuts in the early 1980s, politicians have been calling for an increase in income taxes on the rich. Although President Clinton and the Democratic majorities in Congress in 1993 slightly raised tax rates for the wealthy, the rates remain lower than before the Reagan tax cuts. So there still are calls to make the rich pay more. Politically, the appeal makes sense: There are fewer rich people than poor people. In terms of fairness, the appeal makes sense: The rich benefited disproportionately from the tax cuts in the 1980s. Because of the growing incomes of the very rich, an increase in their taxes would even bring in substantial revenue, something that was not true twenty years ago. However, wealthier people are in a better position to fight an increase in their taxes.

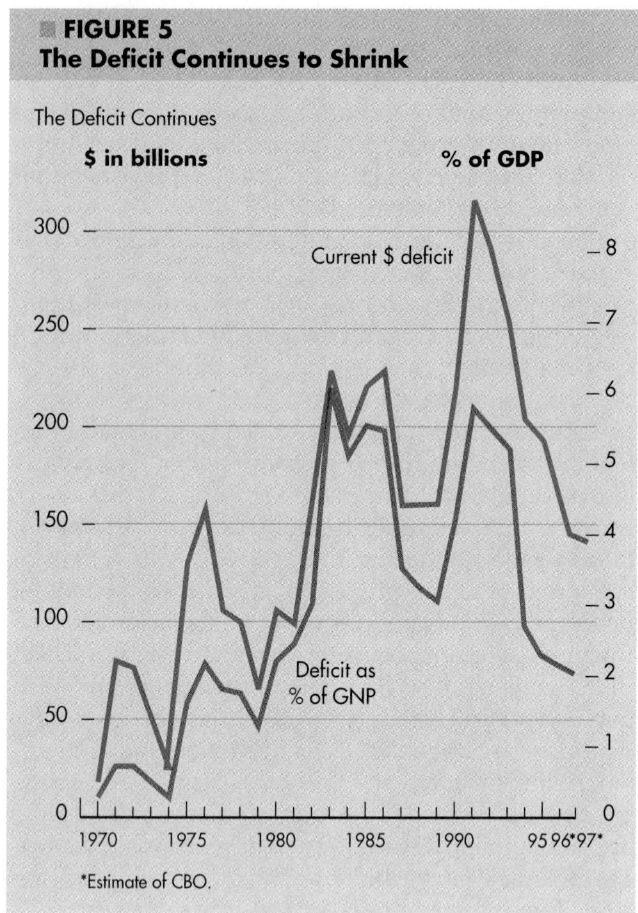

Shifting Costs

Because welfare programs such as AFDC and Medicaid have increased in cost over the years, Republicans in Congress have proposed shifting these programs to the states and providing fixed, limited sums of money for the states to pay for them. Thus, the burden would fall on the states to keep the costs from rising or to pay the additional costs themselves.

A philosophical rationale, as well as a fiscal one, is behind this proposal. If the federal government is too big, it is because it handles matters more appropriately left to the states, so the argument goes. Taking care of the needs of the poor was not a federal responsibility before the Great Depression, and states have greater flexibility to respond to their own unique needs and circumstances.

But states, beset with their own budget problems, are not eager to take on additional burdens. They worry that an economic slump will cause their revenues to decline just as the need for welfare assistance increases. And they generally have fewer resources to cope with a downturn than the national government. If the welfare programs are transferred to the states, the federal deficit would be lower, but state taxes might have to be higher. There might be no net benefit for citizens.

One more factor comes into play when policymakers consider measures to reduce the deficit: Is the battle worth fighting? The president and Congress must decide, each year, whether the costs associated with the deficit outweigh the need, or at least desire for particular programs. A balanced budget is a goal that needs to be weighed against other goals. For many people and politicians, it is not the goal with the highest priority.

In any event, no quick solution is in sight, but the picture is improving. President Clinton's deficit reduction package, which included politically-dangerous tax increases (see You Are There in Chapter 10), has made a real difference. One economist called it a gamble that "turned out far better than anybody had any reason to expect."[25a]

As the budget moves closer to balance—deficits now are lower in percentage of GNP than they have been for years (See Figure 5)—the political pressures to adopt one or more of the approaches we have just discussed diminish considerably and the incentives to fund popular programs with borrowed money increase accordingly.

➤Budgeting as Politics

Just how political is the budgeting process? Earlier, we noted that a more political process than budgeting would be hard to imagine. Are all the disagreements about taxing and spending and all the talk about deficits just political grandstanding? Are the participants concerned at all with societal needs or just with their own interests, like reelection?

To be sure, some of the crass elements of politics are involved in budgeting. Participants are quick to criticize one another's motives, to exaggerate the negative consequences of opponents' proposals, and, generally, to make the other side look bad. It makes for great drama, and it generates a lot of news coverage. It does not help resolve budget conflicts.

Participants are not just motivated by self-interest, however. Rational people of good will can and do disagree about the direction government should take. Democrats sincerely believe that the nation as a whole would be better off if the poor received government help to deal with their poverty. Republicans sincerely believe that the nation as a whole would be better off if government removed the constraints that keep business from expanding and providing jobs for all who want to work. Typically, then, Democrats want government to do more and Republicans want government to do less.

For government to do more, agencies need larger appropriations; for government to do less, agencies do not need as much money. Each year, the budgetary process presents the opportunity to fight over the role government should play in society. Government responds to the winner of the yearly struggle with either greater or lesser activity.

After Republicans won control of Congress in 1994, they quickly proposed remedies for the deficit, counting on painting President Clinton into a corner so that he would have no choice but to agree to their proposals. It did not work. One Republican leader admitted the mistake: "We tried to run the government from Congress. That has only been done once in American history, during Reconstruction when the Republicans had a two-thirds majority in both houses. Political Science 101—you fail if you try to run the government from Congress when you don't have two-thirds and the president is from the other party. But that's what we did last year."[26] Politics calls for compromise.

Compromise represents one of the most common ways political differences can be overcome. However, some think of a balanced budget not simply in economic terms, representing fiscal sanity and clear thinking, but as an end in itself, a sign that all is well in the political world. The quest for a balanced budget becomes "a moral mission."[27] And if one side believes it is moral, it sees compromising with the opposition as close to accepting immorality.

When ideology is involved, compromise is also difficult. Clearly, liberals and conservatives look upon budget deficits differently. Whereas liberals are willing to accept continued budget deficits in order to achieve other political goals, conservatives are not. With Democrats in control, welfare is unlikely to be cut significantly, but wealthy Americans are more likely to have their taxes raised. For conservatives, support for a balanced budget has become a defining characteristic. With Republicans in power, welfare is threatened, but the rich are more likely to benefit. Depending on ideology, a legislator would be more likely to see one rather than another set of proposals as fair and equitable.

Unavoidably, budget decisions are caught up in electoral politics. Right after the 1994 congressional elections, Republicans in Congress wanted to take advantage of their momentum and push their priorities onto the budget. Democrats, however, were not convinced that the GOP won control of Congress because of campaign promises to balance the budget. The next year the presidential contest was in full swing, and Democrats were looking to retain the White House and cut into the Republican advantage in Congress. The Republicans saw an uphill fight to win the presidency and had reason to worry about maintaining control of the House. In 1996 Republicans in Congress decided to back away from the deep spending cuts in domestic programs they aimed for the previous year. One reporter called it a "sort of bending to political reality" in an election year.[28]

While participants in the budget struggle keep one eye on the substantive details of government finance, they keep the other on their electoral chances. To keep their seats, legislators must ultimately satisfy their constituents that they are doing a good job. The more visible the budget battles are, the more likely legislators will want to respond to the views of the people back home. Legislators will have to decide whether sticking to their positions without accommodation is more likely to bring them electoral support in their districts, or whether coming home with a compromise budget is more likely to be seen favorably.

Interest groups attempt to exert their influence, too. They often come to the defense of a program subject to a funding cut. Their pressure reduces policymakers' flexibility. Except for some large business organizations, few groups are active in the efforts to cut the deficit. Overall, then, interest groups exert pressure toward increased spending.

In the background of budget dealings among the major participants lies public opinion. No participant can afford to present and defend a position that cannot be explained and justified to the nation. The president and members of Congress, especially the Speaker of the House, will "go public" to build a case for their positions in the court of public opinion and to try to deflate the case the others make.

For example, in 1995, Republicans and Democrats disagreed about the Republican plan to control Medicare spending. Democrats warned that Republicans were cutting Medicare drastically. Republicans pointed out that they were recommending increased funding for the program for the foreseeable future. Both took their case to the American people. Who was right? They both were. Medicare would not be cut; it would, in fact, receive higher appropriations each year. However, individual recipients would not receive the benefits they would be entitled to under current law. The program would grow, but the benefits individuals receive would be cut.

As you might expect, it is harder to make a case for an abstract concept such as "reducing the rate of growth" in Medicare than it is for a concrete example of Aunt Polly and Uncle Gus getting fewer benefits than before. Public opinion swung around to the Democratic position, and the question of Medicare cuts was postponed.

It is easy to criticize the budgetary process as being too political. On the other hand, its political nature is one of its strong points. The decisions being made concern the direction the nation should go. There is no way to make those choices nonpolitical. Moreover, because the process is so political, it is subject to influences from all those who may be affected. Because it is so political, you and I as citizens are drawn into the discussion. We all form opinions. Our representatives ultimately respond to those opinions. Politics makes the process work.

➤Conclusion: Is Government Responsive in Its Budgeting?

Budget makers attempt to satisfy incompatible demands from the American public. One is to reduce the federal deficit. Another is to maintain or increase government services. Both must be done without raising taxes.

The federal government has been only partially responsive to the demand to reduce or eliminate the federal deficit. The deficit is now markedly lower than in the 1980s. The 1996 budget agreement put the president and Congress on record with a spending plan over the next six years that would lead to a balanced budget. But many hurdles remain. Government will run a deficit for the coming years, and elimination of the deficit by 2002 depends on whether the economy stays healthy and whether sharper cuts in entitlement programs, such as Medicare, projected for the future will stay in place.

But the federal government has also responded to demands that it pay for the many programs citizens benefit from. College students want the Pell Grant program fully funded. Truckers want the interstate highway system kept in good repair. Farmers want crop subsidies. Environmentalists want wildlife protected. Government has found it difficult to reduce spending for these and other programs. The arguments that convinced Congress to establish the program in the first place remain convincing when funding decisions need to be made.

Some argue that government is *too* responsive to outside pressures, including public opinion. Senator Richard Lugar (R.-Ind.) describes Congress as a "hyper weather vane" that changes its direction every time a new poll is released.[29] Rep. David Nagle (D.-Iowa) sees a danger: "Because we are too close, we simply reflect the passing moment rather than the longer interest."[30] Representatives with their ear close to the ground often avoid making the hard choices because they sense that the public wants contradictory goals.

Simultaneous pressures to spend and to cut spending put the federal government in a dilemma. The Gramm-Rudman-Hollings Act was an attempt to force Congress to abide by deficit reduction targets. It did not work. The deficit was artificially reduced by selling off public land and public enterprises, a one-shot infusion of money that does nothing to solve any long-range spending problems (it is like selling your house to pay for a vacation) and by gimmicks like delaying military pay raises for a day. Senator Rudman, a co-sponsor of the bill, got so sick of these games that he decided not to run for reelection.

These games and gimmicks tempt legislators and presidents. These ruses provide a way for government to give the people both a budget that seems on its way to being balanced and the expenditures for the programs they want. It is easy to project a slightly stronger economy than anticipated. After all, economic forecasting is not an exact science. Budgeters can predict greater revenues coming in because people earn more and lower expenditures because fewer people need help. They hold out the hope that a budget more in balance would in fact lead to a stronger economy than predicted, and the rosy outlook becomes, in their minds, a self-fulfilling prophecy.

But a real balanced budget requires more consensus among all of us as to the kind of government we want. If we want an active national government, we should be willing to pay the necessary taxes. If we want a more passive national government, we should be willing to forego some of the programs and services it now funds. Until we decide, government will have a hard time being responsive to the people's wishes.

EPILOGUE

Kasich Goes Along

Kasich supported the compromise for the 1996 budget. With the 1997 budget already under consideration, and with presidential and congressional elections coming up in the fall, he decided that it was better to put the 1996 budget behind him. Further shutdowns of government while fellow Republican Dole was trying to mount a challenge to President Clinton would virtually assure Clinton's reelection. A strong Clinton showing in November would probably benefit Democratic candidates for the House. If that happened, Republicans would have a smaller majority—if they retained control of the House—than they did now.

Kasich knew the choice between fiscal responsibility and party loyalty was a difficult one. But he believed that this budget agreement was about as good as he was going to get. He knew that he had to work with others to succeed, and that frequently means accepting compromises along the way. Here party loyalty works side by side with fiscal responsibility, because the battle lines for future budget struggles have been defined. It is no longer whether a balanced budget is a desirable short- or long-term goal, but rather how soon the budget will be balanced.

And so he made the best of the situation. He portrayed the outcome as a victory—these budget negotiations with the White House were one time where "the President was forced to sit down and achieve a result."[31] That result was one Kasich helped craft: a blueprint for progress toward a balanced budget by 2002. "We are right on schedule with our budget goals," Kasich pointed out, "and we're going to keep right on going."[32]

➤Key Terms

direct or mandatory spending
entitlements
discretionary spending
national debt
tax expenditures

➤Further Reading

Budget of the United States, 1997 (Washington, D.C.: U.S. Government Printing Office, 1996). *A surprisingly readable discussion of presidential budgetary priorities and plans for the federal government over the next fiscal year. A supplement and an appendix contain much technical data.*

Benjamin Friedman, *Day of Reckoning* (New York: Random House, 1988); and Murray Weidenbaum, *Rendezvous with Reality* (New York: Basic Books, 1988). *Two economists, a liberal (Friedman) and a conservative, critique Reagan's economic policy. Both believe something must be done about the biggest Reagan legacy—the deficit—but they disagree about what that something should be.*

William Grieder, *Secrets of the Temple* (New York: Simon & Schuster, 1988). *It is hard to imagine a book about the Federal Reserve Board being interesting, but this one is. Reveals the human face behind this most technical institution.*

Katherine S. Newman, *Decline Fortunes: The Withering of the American Dream* (New York: Basic Books, 1994). *An anthropologist describes the economic fortunes of the baby boom generation.*

Irene S. Rubin, *The Politics of Public Budgeting,* 2nd ed. (Chatham, N.J.: Chatham House Publishing, 1993). *A good, although somewhat jargon-filled discussion of differences and similarities among federal, state, and local budgeting.*

Alan Schick, *The Federal Budget: Politics, Policy, Process* (Washington, D.C.: The Brookings Institution, 1995). *A good, clear overview of the entire budgetary process as it now operates. Schick slights the politics, but he presents the process clearly. A good source for definitions and examples of technical budgeting concepts.*

Edward Tufte, *Political Control of the Economy* (Princeton, N.J.: Princeton University Press, 1978). *An interesting, sophisticated, but readable account of the relationship between trying to win elections and economic policy making.*

Aaron Wildavsky, *The New Politics of the Budgetary Process* (Glenview, Ill.: Scott, Foresman, 1988). *Wildavsky was the first to study budgeting as a political process. An insightful primer into the way participants deal with the complexities of budgeting.*

➤Notes

1. Karen Tumulty, "Budget, Meet Thy Maker," *Time,* February 27, 1995, p. 20.
2. Rich Henderson, "The Energizer," *Reason,* August/September 1993, p. 28.
3. Tumulty, "Budget, Meet Thy Maker," p. 19.
4. Quoted in Jerry Gray, "Dole and Clinton in Budget Face-Off," *New York Times,* April 24, 1996, p. A9.
5. Gray, "Dole and Clinton in Budget Face-Off," p. A1.
6. Weston Kosova, "Hard Kasich," *New Republic,* December 12, 1994, p. 11.
7. Tumulty, "Budget, Meet Thy Maker," pp. 20–21.
8. Ronald Reagan, "Presidential Nomination Acceptance Address," *Vital Speeches,* August 15, 1980, pp. 643, 644.
9. Anthony Lewis, "Chilling Candor in the House," *Lincoln Journal Star,* January 9, 1996, p. 4B.
10. Quoted in Lewis, "Chilling Candor in the House." p. 4B.
11. Aaron Wildavsky, *The New Politics of the Budgetary Process* (Glenview, Ill.: Scott, Foresman, 1988), p. vii.
12. Hugh Heclo, "Office of Management and Budget," *Encyclopedia of the American Presidency* (New York: Simon & Schuster, 1994), p. 1111.
13. *Congressional Quarterly's Guide to Congress,* 4th ed. (Washington, D.C.: CQ Press, 1991), p. 628.
14. Daniel P. Carpenter, "Adaptive Signal Processing, Hierarchy, and Budgetary Control in Federal Regulation," *American Political Science Review* 90 (June 1966), p. 298.
15. Bipartisan Commission on Entitlement and Tax Reform, *Final Report to the President* (Washington, D.C.: U.S. Government Printing Office, 1995), p. 10.
16. Bipartisan Commission, p. 16.
17. *Statistical Abstract of the United States: 1995* (Washington, D.C.: U.S. Government Printing Office, 1995), p. 309, table 489.
18. *Statistical Abstract of the U.S., 1995,* p. 309, table 489; p. 315, table 498.
19. *Budget of the United States Government: Fiscal Year 1997, Appendix* (Washington, D.C.: U.S. Government Printing Office, 1996), p. 695.
20. Defense spending increased substantially under President Reagan, from $135 billion in the last year of the Carter administration to $290 billion in Reagan's last full year in office.
21. Robert Pear, "Democrats Act to Counter G.O.P.'s Medicare Plans," *New York Times,* October 3, 1995, p. A11.
22. Quoted in Helen Dewar, "The Trees Get in the Way of the Forest," *Washington Post National Weekly Edition,* June 15–21, 1992, p. 13.
23. Bipartisan Commission, p. 1.
24. David Hage, David Fischer, and Robert F. Black, "America's Other Welfare State," *U.S. News & World Report,* April 10, 1995, p. 34.
25. Jeffrey Madrick, "It's Productivity, Stupid," *Washington Post National Weekly Edition,* April 8–14, 1996, p. 22.

25a. Alan Blinder, quoted in John Cassidy, "Ace in the Hole," *The New Yorker,* June 10, 1996, p. 37.

26. Donald Devine, quoted in Jerry Gray, "In Congress, GOP Tries New Tactics to Regain Its Edge," *Lincoln Journal Star* (New York Times), February 25, 1996, p. 3A.
27. Madrick, "It's Productivity, Stupid."
28. George Hager, "GOP Adds Billions to Budget after Easing Up on Cuts," *Congressional Quarterly Weekly Report,* May 25, 1996, p. 1446.
29. Quoted in Dewar, "The Trees Get in the Way of the Forest," p. 13.
30. Quoted in Dewar, "The Trees Get in the Way of the Forest," p. 13.
31. Quoted in Michael Wines, "House and Senate Vote to Approve '96 Spending Bill," *New York Times,* April 26, 1996, p. A1.
32. Quoted in George Hager, "Congress, Clinton Yield Enough to Close the Book on Fiscal '96," *Congressional Quarterly Weekly Report,* April 27, 1996, p. 1156.

APPENDIX A

The Declaration of Independence*

In Congress, July 4, 1776.

A Declaration by the Representatives of the United States of America, in General Congress assembled.

When in the Course of human Events, it becomes necessary for one People to dissolve the Political Bonds which have connected them with another, and to assume among the Powers of the Earth, the separate and equal Station to which the Laws of Nature and of Nature's God entitle them, a decent Respect to the Opinions of Mankind requires that they should declare the causes which impel them to the Separation.

We hold these Truths to be self-evident, that all Men are created equal, that they are endowed by their Creator with certain unalienable Rights, that among these are Life, Liberty, and the Pursuit of Happiness—That to secure these Rights, Governments are instituted among Men, deriving their just Powers from the Consent of the Governed, that whenever any Form of Government becomes destructive of these Ends, it is the Right of the People to alter or to abolish it, and to institute new Government, laying its Foundation on such Principles, and organizing its Powers in such Forms, as to them shall seem most likely to effect their Safety and Happiness. Prudence, indeed, will dictate that Governments long established should not be changed for light and transient Causes; and accordingly all Experience hath shewn, that Mankind are more disposed to suffer, while Evils are sufferable, than to right themselves by abolishing the Forms to which they are accustomed. But when a long Train of Abuses and Usurpations, pursuing invariably the same Object, evinces a Design to reduce them under absolute Despotism, it is their Right, it is their Duty, to throw off such Government, and to provide new Guards for their future Security. Such has been the patient Sufferance of these Colonies; and such is now the Necessity which constrains them to alter their former Systems of Government. The History of the present King of Great Britain is a History of repeated Injuries and Usurpations, all having in direct Object the Establishment of an absolute Tyranny over these States. To prove this, let facts be submitted to a candid World.

He has refused his Assent to Laws, the most wholesome and necessary for the public Good.

He has forbidden his Governors to pass Laws of immediate and pressing Importance, unless suspended in their Operation till his Assent should be obtained; and when so suspended, he has utterly neglected to attend to them.

He has refused to pass other Laws for the Accommodation of large Districts of People, unless those People would relinquish the Right of Representation in the Legislature, a Right inestimable to them, and formidable to Tyrants only.

He has called together Legislative Bodies at Places unusual, uncomfortable, and distant from the Depository of their Public Records, for the sole Purpose of fatiguing them into Compliance with his Measures.

He has dissolved Representative Houses repeatedly, for opposing with manly Firmness his Invasions on the Rights of the People.

He has refused for a long Time, after such Dissolutions, to cause others to be elected; whereby the Legislative Powers, incapable of Annihilation, have returned to the People at large for their exercise; the State remaining in the mean time exposed to all the Dangers of Invasion from without, and Convulsions within.

He has endeavoured to prevent the Population of these States; for that Purpose obstructing the Laws for Naturalization of Foreigners; refusing to pass others to encourage their Migration hither, and raising the Conditions of new Appropriations of Lands.

He has obstructed the Administration of Justice, by refusing his Assent to Laws for establishing Judiciary Powers.

He has made Judges dependent on his Will alone, for the Tenure of their offices, and the Amount and payments of their Salaries.

He has erected a Multitude of new Offices, and sent hither Swarms of Officers to harass our People, and eat out their Substance.

*The spelling, capitalization, and punctuation of the original have been retained here.

He has kept among us, in times of Peace, Standing Armies, without the consent of our Legislatures.

He has affected to render the Military independent of, and superior to the Civil Power.

He has combined with others to subject us to a Jurisdiction foreign to our Constitution, and unacknowledged by our Laws; giving his Assent to their Acts of pretended Legislation:

For quartering large Bodies of Armed Troops among us:

For protecting them, by a mock Trial, from Punishment for any Murders which they should commit on the Inhabitants of these States:

For cutting off our Trade with all Parts of the World:

For imposing Taxes on us without our Consent:

For depriving us, in many cases, of the Benefits of Trial by Jury:

For transporting us beyond Seas to be tried for pretended Offences:

For abolishing the free System of English Laws in a neighbouring Province, establishing therein an arbitrary Government, and enlarging its Boundaries, so as to render it at once an Example and fit Instrument for introducing the same absolute Rule into these Colonies:

For taking away our Charters, abolishing our most valuable Laws, and altering fundamentally the Forms of our Governments:

For suspending our own Legislatures, and declaring themselves invested with Power to legislate for us in all Cases whatsoever.

He has abdicated Government here, by declaring us out of his Protection and waging War against us.

He has plundered our Seas, ravaged our Coasts, burnt our towns, and destroyed the Lives of our People.

He is, at this Time, transporting large Armies of foreign Mercenaries to compleat the works of Death, Desolation, and Tyranny, already begun with circumstances of Cruelty and Perfidy, scarcely paralleled in the most barbarous Ages, and totally unworthy the Head of a civilized Nation.

He has constrained our fellow Citizens taken Captive on the high Seas to bear Arms against their Country, to become the Executioners of their Friends and Brethren, or to fall themselves by their Hands.

He has excited domestic Insurrections amongst us, and has endeavoured to bring on the Inhabitants of our Frontiers, the merciless Indian Savages, whose known Rule of Warfare, is an undistinguished Destruction, of all Ages, Sexes and Conditions.

In every state of these Oppressions we have Petitioned for Redress in the most humble Terms: Our repeated Petitions have been answered only by repeated Injury. A Prince, whose Character is thus marked by every act which may define a Tyrant, is unfit to be the Ruler of a free People.

Nor have we been wanting in Attentions to our British Brethren. We have warned them from Time to Time of Attempts by their Legislature to extend an unwarrantable Jurisdiction over us. We have reminded them of the Circumstances of our Emigration and Settlement here. We have appealed to their native Justice and Magnanimity, and we have conjured them by the Ties of our common Kindred to disavow these Usurpations, which, would inevitably interrupt our Connections and Correspondence. They too have been deaf to the Voice of Justice and of Consanguinity. We must, therefore, acquiesce in the Necessity, which denounces our Separation, and hold them, as we hold the rest of Mankind, Enemies in War, in Peace, Friends.

We, therefore, the Representatives of the UNITED STATES OF AMERICA, in General Congress Assembled, appealing to the Supreme Judge of the World for the Rectitude of our Intentions, do, in the Name, and by Authority of the good People of these Colonies, solemnly Publish and Declare, That these United Colonies are, and of Right ought to be, Free and Independent States; that they are absolved from all Allegiance to the British Crown, and that all political Connection between them and the State of Great Britain, is and ought to be totally dissolved; and that as Free and Independent States, they have full Power to levy War, conclude Peace, contract Alliances, establish Commerce, and to do all other Acts and Things which Independent States may of right do. And for the support of this declaration, with a firm Reliance on the Protection of divine Providence, we mutually pledge to each other our Lives, our Fortunes, and our sacred Honor.

APPENDIX B

Constitution of the United States of America*

We the people of the United States, in Order to form a more perfect Union, establish Justice, insure domestic Tranquility, provide for the common defence, promote the general Welfare, and secure the Blessings of Liberty to ourselves and our posterity, do ordain and establish this Constitution for the United States of America.

Article I.

Section 1.

All legislative Powers herein granted shall be vested in a Congress of the United States, which shall consist of a Senate and House of Representatives.

Section 2.

The House of Representatives shall be composed of Members chosen every second Year by the People of the several States, and the Electors in each State shall have the Qualifications requisite for Electors of the most numerous Branch of the State Legislature.

No person shall be a Representative who shall not have attained to the Age of twenty-five Years, and been seven Years a Citizen of the United States, and who shall not, when elected, be an Inhabitant of that State in which he shall be chosen.

Representatives and direct [Taxes][1] shall be apportioned among the several States which may be included within this Union, according to their respective Numbers [which shall be determined by adding to the whole Number of free Persons, including those bound to Service for a Term of Years, and excluding Indians not taxed, three fifths of all other Persons].[2] The actual Enumeration shall be made within three Years after the first Meeting of the Congress of the United States, and within every subsequent Term of ten Years, in such Manner as they shall by Law direct. The Number of Representatives shall not exceed one for every thirty Thousand, but each State shall have at Least one Representative; and until such enumeration shall be made, the State of New Hampshire shall be entitled to chuse three, Massachusetts eight, Rhode Island and Providence Plantations one, Connecticut five, New-York six, New Jersy four, Pennsylvania eight, Delaware one, Maryland six, Virginia ten, North Carolina five, South Carolina five, and Georgia three.

When vacancies happen in the Representation from any State, the Executive Authority thereof shall issue Writs of Election to fill such Vacancies.

The House of Representatives shall chuse their Speaker and other Officers; and shall have the sole Power of Impeachment.

Section 3.

The Senate of the United States shall be composed of two Senators from each State [chosen by the Legislature thereof],[3] for six Years; and each Senator shall have one Vote.

Immediately after they shall be assembled in Consequence of the first Election, they shall be divided as equally as may be into three Classes. The Seats of the Senators of the first Class shall be vacated at the Expiration of the second year, of the second Class at the Expiration of the fourth Year, and of the third Class at the Expiration of the sixth Year, so that one third may be chosen every second Year [and if Vacancies happen by Resignation, or otherwise, during the Recess of the Legislature of any State, the Executive thereof may make temporary Appointments until the next Meeting of the Legislature, which shall then fill such Vacancies.][4]

No Person shall be a Senator who shall not have attained to the Age of thirty Years, and been nine Years a Citizen of the United States, and who shall not, when elected, be an Inhabitant of that State for which he shall be chosen.

The Vice President of the United States shall be President of the Senate, but shall have no Vote, unless they be equally divided.

*The spelling, capitalization, and punctuation of the original have been retained here. Brackets indicate passages that have been altered by amendments to the Constitution.

1. Modified by the Sixteenth Amendment.
2. Modified by the Fourteenth Amendment.
3. Repealed by the Seventeenth Amendment.
4. Modified by the Seventeenth Amendment.

The Senate shall chuse their other Officers, and also a President pro tempore, in the Absence of the Vice President, or when he shall exercise the Office of President of the United States.

The Senate shall have the sole Power to try all Impeachments. When sitting for that Purpose, they shall be on Oath or Affirmation. When the President of the United States is tried, the Chief Justice shall preside: And no Person shall be convicted without the Concurrence of two thirds of the Members present.

Judgment in Cases of Impeachment shall not extend further than to removal from Office, and disqualification to hold and enjoy any Office of honor, Trust or Profit under the United States; but the Party convicted shall nevertheless be liable and subject to Indictment, Trial, Judgment and Punishment, according to Law.

Section 4.

The Times, Places and Manner of holding Elections for Senators and Representatives, shall be prescribed in each State by the Legislature thereof; but the Congress may at any time by Law make or alter such Regulations, except as to the Places of chusing Senators.

[The Congress shall assemble at least once in every Year, and such Meeting shall be on the first Monday in December, unless they shall by Law appoint a different Day.][5]

Section 5.

Each House shall be the Judge of the Elections, Returns and Qualifications of its own Members, and a Majority of each shall constitute a Quorum to do Business; but a smaller Number may adjourn from day to day, and may be authorized to compel the Attendance of absent Members, in such Manner, and under such Penalties as each House may provide.

Each House may determine the Rules of its Proceedings, punish its Members for disorderly Behaviour, and, with the Concurrence of two thirds, expel a Member.

Each House shall keep a Journal of its Proceedings, and from time to time publish the same, excepting such Parts as may in their Judgment require Secrecy; and the Yeas and Nays of the Members of either House on any question shall, at the Desire of one fifth of those present, be entered on the Journal.

Neither House, during the Session of Congress, shall, without the Consent of the other, adjourn for more than three days, nor to any other Place than that in which the two Houses shall be sitting.

Section 6.

The Senators and Representatives shall receive a Compensation for their Services, to be ascertained by Law, and paid out of the Treasury of the United States. They shall in all Cases, except Treason, Felony and Breach of the Peace, be privileged from Arrest during their Attendance at the Session of their respective Houses, and in going to and returning from the same; and for any Speech or Debate in either House, they shall not be questioned in any other Place.

No Senator or Representative shall, during the Time for which he was elected, be appointed to any civil Office under the Authority of the United States, which shall have been created, or the Emoluments whereof shall have been encreased during such time; and no Person holding any Office under the United States, shall be a Member of either House during his Continuance in Office.

Section 7.

All Bills for raising Revenue shall originate in the House of Representatives; but the Senate may propose or concur with Amendments as on other Bills.

Every Bill which shall have passed the House of Representatives and the Senate, shall, before it become a Law, be presented to the President of the United States; If he approves he shall sign it, but if not he shall return it, with his objections to that House in which it shall have originated, who shall enter the Objections at large on their Journal, and proceed to reconsider it. If after such Reconsideration two thirds of that House shall agree to pass the Bill, it shall be sent, together with the Objections, to the other House, by which it shall likewise be reconsidered, and if approved by two thirds of that House, it shall become a Law. But in all such Cases the Votes of both Houses shall be determined by Yeas and Nays, and the Names of the Persons voting for and against the Bill shall be entered on the Journal of each House respectively. If any Bill shall not be returned by the President within ten Days (Sundays excepted) after it shall have been presented to him, the Same shall be a

5. Changed by the Twentieth Amendment.

Law, in like Manner as if he had signed it, unless the Congress by their Adjournment prevent its Return, in which Case it shall not be a Law.

Every Order, Resolution, or Vote to which the Concurrence of the Senate and House of Representatives may be necessary (except on a question of Adjournment) shall be presented to the President of the United States; and before the Same shall take Effect, shall be approved by him, or being disapproved by him, shall be repassed by two thirds of the Senate and House of Representatives, according to the Rules and Limitations prescribed in the Case of a Bill.

Section 8.

The Congress shall have Power To lay and collect Taxes, Duties, Imposts and Excises, to pay the Debts and provide for the common Defence and general Welfare of the United States; but all Duties, Imposts and Excises shall be uniform throughout the United States;

To borrow Money on the credit of the United States;

To regulate Commerce with foreign Nations, and among the several States, and with the Indian Tribes;

To establish a uniform Rule of Naturalization, and uniform Laws on the subject of Bankruptcies throughout the United States;

To coin Money, regulate the Value thereof, and of foreign Coin, and fix the Standard of Weights and Measures;

To provide for the Punishment of counterfeiting the Securities and current Coin of the United States.

To establish Post Offices and post Roads;

To promote the Progress of Science and useful Arts, by securing for limited Times to Authors and Inventors the exclusive Right to their respective Writings and Discoveries;

To constitute Tribunals inferior to the supreme Court;

To define and punish Piracies and Felonies committed on the high Seas, and Offences against the Law of Nations;

To declare War, grant Letters of Marque and Reprisal, and make Rules concerning Captures on Land and Water;

To raise and support Armies, but no Appropriation of Money to that Use shall be for a longer Term than two Years;

To provide and maintain a Navy;

To make Rules for the Government and Regulation of the land and naval Forces;

To provide for calling forth the Militia to execute the Laws of the Union, suppress Insurrections and repel Invasions;

To provide for organizing, arming, and disciplining the Militia, and for governing such Part of them as may be employed in the Service of the United States, reserving to the States respectively, the Appointment of the Officers, and the Authority of training the Militia according to the discipline prescribed by Congress;

To exercise exclusive Legislation in all Cases whatsoever, over such District (not exceeding ten Miles square) as may, by Cession of particular States, and the Acceptance of Congress, become the Seat of the Government of the United States, and to exercise like Authority over all Places purchased by the Consent of the Legislature of the State in which the Same shall be, for the Erection of forts, Magazines, Arsenals, dockYards, and other needful Buildings;—And

To make all Laws which shall be necessary and proper for carrying into Execution the foregoing Powers, and all other Powers vested by this Constitution in the Government of the United States, or in any Department or Officer thereof.

Section 9.

The Migration or Importation of such Persons as any of the States now existing shall think proper to admit, shall not be prohibited by the Congress prior to the Year one thousand eight hundred and eight, but a Tax or duty may be imposed on such Importation, not exceeding ten dollars for each Person.

The Privilege of the Writ of Habeas Corpus shall not be suspended, unless when in Cases of Rebellion or Invasion the public Safety may require it.

No Bill of Attainder or ex post facto Law shall be passed.

[No Capitation, or other direct, Tax shall be laid, unless in Proportion to the Census or Enumeration herein before directed to be taken.][6]

No Tax or Duty shall be laid on Articles exported from any State.

No Preference shall be given by any Regulation of Commerce or Revenue to the Ports of one State over those of another; nor shall Vessels bound to, or from, one State, be obliged to enter, clear, or pay Duties in another.

6. Modified by the Sixteenth Amendment.

No Money shall be drawn from the Treasury, but in Consequence of Appropriations made by Law; and a regular Statement and Account of the Receipts and Expenditures of all public Money shall be published from time to time.

No Title of Nobility shall be granted by the United States; and no Person holding any Office or Profit or Trust under them, shall, without the Consent of the Congress, accept of any present, Emolument, Office, or Title, of any kind whatever, from any King, Prince, or foreign State.

Section 10.

No state shall enter into any Treaty, Alliance, or Confederation; grant Letters of Marque and Reprisal; coin Money; emit Bills of Credit; make any Thing but gold and silver Coin a Tender in Payment of Debts; pass any Bill of Attainder, ex post facto Law, or Law impairing the Obligation of Contracts, or grant any Title of Nobility.

No State shall, without the Consent of the Congress, lay any Imposts or Duties on Imports or Exports, except what may be absolutely necessary for executing its inspection Laws; and the net Produce of all Duties and Imposts, laid by any State on Imports or Exports, shall be for the Use of the Treasury of the United States; and all such Laws shall be subject to the Revision and Controul of the Congress.

No State shall, without the Consent of Congress, lay any duty of Tonnage, keep Troops, or Ships of War in time of Peace, enter into any Agreement or Compact with another State, or with a foreign Power or engage in War, unless actually invaded, or in such imminent Danger as will not admit of delay.

Article II.

Section 1.

The executive Power shall be vested in a President of the United States of America. He shall hold his Office during the Term of four Years, and, together with the Vice President, chosen for the Same Term, be elected, as follows.

Each State shall appoint, in such Manner as the Legislature thereof may direct, a Number of Electors, equal to the whole Number of Senators and Representatives to which the State may be entitled in the Congress; but no Senator or Representative, or Person holding an Office of Trust or Profit under the United States, shall be appointed an Elector.

[The Electors shall meet in their respective States, and vote by Ballot for two Persons of whom one at least shall not be an Inhabitant of the same State with themselves. And they shall make a List of all the Persons voted for, and of the Number of Votes for each; which List they shall sign and certify, and transmit sealed to the Seat of the Government of the United States, directed to the President of the Senate. The President of the Senate shall, in the Presence of the Senate and House of Representatives, open all the Certificates, and the Votes shall then be counted. The Person having the greatest Number of Votes shall be the President, if such Number be a Majority of the whole Number of Electors appointed; and if there be more than one who have such Majority, and have an equal Number of Votes, then the House of Representatives shall immediately chuse by Ballot one of them for President; and if no Person have a Majority, then from the five highest on the List the said House shall in like Manner chuse the President. But in chusing the President, the Votes shall be taken by States, the Representation from each State having one Vote; A quorum for this Purpose shall consist of a Member or Members from two thirds of the States, and a Majority of all the states shall be necessary to a Choice. In every Case, after the Choice of the President, the Person having the greatest Number of Votes of the Electors shall be the Vice President. But if there should remain two or more who have equal Votes, the Senate shall chuse from them by Ballot the Vice President.][7]

The Congress may determine the Time of chusing the Electors, and the Day on which they shall give their Votes; which Day shall be the same throughout the United States.

No person except a natural born Citizen, or a Citizen of the United States, at the time of the Adoption of this Constitution, shall be eligible to the Office of President; neither shall any Person be eligible to that Office who shall not have attained to the Age of thirty five Years, and been fourteen Years a Resident within the United States.

[In Case of the Removal of the President from Office, or of his Death, Resignation, or Inability to discharge the Powers and Duties of the said Office, the same shall devolve on the Vice President, and the Congress may by Law provide for the Case of Re-

7. Changed by the Twelfth Amendment.

moval, Death, Resignation or Inability, both of the President and Vice President, declaring what Officer shall then act as President, and such Officer shall act accordingly, until the Disability be removed, or a President shall be elected.][8]

The President shall, at stated Times, receive for his Services, a Compensation, which shall neither be encreased nor diminished during the Period for which he shall have been elected, and he shall not receive within that Period any other Emolument from the United States, or any of them.

Before he enter on the Execution of his Office, he shall take the following Oath or Affirmation:—"I do solemnly swear (or affirm) that I will faithfully execute the Office of President of the United States, and will to the best of my Ability, preserve, protect and defend the constitution of the United States."

Section 2.

The President shall be Commander in Chief of the Army and Navy of the United States, and of the Militia of the several States, when called into the actual Service of the United States; he may require the Opinion, in writing, of the principal Officer in each of the executive Departments, upon any Subject relating to the Duties of their respective Offices, and he shall have Power to grant Reprieves and Pardons for Offences against the United States, except in Cases of Impeachment.

He shall have Power, by and with the Advice and Consent of the Senate, to make Treaties, provided two thirds of the Senators present concur; and he shall nominate, and by and with the Advice and Consent of the Senate, shall appoint Ambassadors, other public Ministers and Consuls, Judges of the supreme Court, and all other Officers of the United States, whose Appointments are not herein otherwise provided for, and which shall be established by Law; but the Congress may by Law vest the Appointment of such inferior Officers, as they think proper, in the President alone, in the Courts of Law, or in the Heads of Departments.

The President shall have Power to fill up all Vacancies that may happen during the Recess of the Senate, by granting Commissions which shall expire at the end of their next Session.

Section 3.

He shall from time to time give to the Congress Information of the State of the Union, and recommend to their Consideration such Measures as he shall judge necessary and expedient; he may, on extraordinary Occasions, convene both Houses, or either of them, and in Case of Disagreement between them, with Respect to the Time of Adjournment, he may adjourn them to such Time as he shall think proper; he shall receive Ambassadors and other public Ministers; he shall take Care that the Laws be faithfully executed, and shall Commission all the Officers of the United States.

Section 4.

The President, Vice President and all civil Officers of the United States, shall be removed from Office on Impeachment for, and Conviction of, Treason, Bribery, or other high Crimes and Misdemeanors.

Article III.

Section 1.

The judicial Power of the United States, shall be vested in one supreme Court, and in such inferior Courts as the Congress may from time to time ordain and establish. The Judges, both of the supreme and inferior Courts, shall hold their Offices during good Behaviour, and shall, at stated Times, receive for their Services, a Compensation, which shall not be diminished during their Continuance in Office.

Section 2.

The judicial Power shall extend to all Cases, in Law and Equity, arising under this Constitution, the Laws of the United States, and Treaties made, or which shall be made, under their Authority;—to all Cases affecting Ambassadors, other public Ministers and Consuls;—to all Cases of admiralty and maritime Jurisdiction;—to Controversies to which the United States shall be a Party;—to Controversies between two or more States;[—between a State and Citizens of another State;][9]—between Citizens of different States,—between Citizens of the same State claiming Lands under Grants of different States, [and between

8. Modified by the Twenty-fifth Amendment.
9. Modified by the Eleventh Amendment.

a state, or the Citizens thereof, and foreign States, Citizens or Subjects.][10]

In all cases affecting Ambassadors, other public Ministers and Consuls, and those in which a State shall be Party, the supreme Court shall have original Jurisdiction. In all the other Cases before mentioned, the supreme Court shall have appellate Jurisdiction, both as to Law and Fact, with such Exceptions, and under such Regulations as the Congress shall make.

The Trial of all Crimes, except in Cases of Impeachment, shall be by Jury; and such Trial shall be held in the State where the said Crimes shall have been committed; but when not committed within any State, the Trial shall be at such Place or Places as the Congress may by Law have directed.

Section 3.

Treason against the United States, shall consist only in levying War against them, or in adhering to their Enemies, giving them Aid and Comfort. No Person shall be convicted of Treason unless on the Testimony of two Witnesses to the same overt Act, or on Confession in open Court.

The Congress shall have Power to declare the Punishment of Treason, but no Attainder of Treason shall work Corruption of Blood, or Forfeiture except during the Life of the Person attainted.

Article IV.

Section 1.

Full Faith and Credit shall be given in each State to the public Acts, Records, and judicial Proceedings of every other State. And the Congress may by general Laws prescribe the Manner in which such Acts, Records and Proceedings shall be proved, and the Effect thereof.

Section 2.

The Citizens of each State shall be entitled to all Privileges and Immunities of Citizens in the several States.

A Person charged in any State with Treason, Felony, or other Crime, who shall flee from Justice, and be found in another State, shall on Demand of the executive Authority of the State from which he fled, be delivered up, to be removed to the State having Jurisdiction of the Crime.

[No Person held to Service or Labour in one State under the Laws thereof, escaping into another, shall, in Consequence of any Law or Regulation therein, be discharged from such Service or Labour, but shall be delivered up on Claim of the Party to whom such Service or Labour may be due.][11]

Section 3.

New States may be admitted by the Congress into this Union; but no new State shall be formed or erected within the Jurisdiction of any other State; nor any State be formed by the Junction of two or more States, or Parts of States, without the Consent of the Legislatures of the States concerned as well as of the Congress.

The Congress shall have Power to dispose of and make all needful Rules and Regulations respecting the Territory or other Property belonging to the United States; and nothing in this Constitution shall be so construed as to Prejudice any Claimes of the United States, or of any particular State.

Section 4.

The United States shall guarantee to every State in this Union a Republican Form of Government, and shall protect each of them against Invasion, and on Application of the Legislature, or of the Executive (when the Legislature cannot be convened) against domestic Violence.

Article V.

The Congress, whenever two thirds of both Houses shall deem it necessary, shall propose Amendments to this Constitution, or on the Application of the Legislatures of two thirds of the several States, shall call a Convention for proposing Amendments, which, in either Case, shall be valid to all Intents and Purposes, as Part of this Constitution, when ratified by the Legislatures of three fourths of the several States, or by Conventions in three fourths thereof, as the one or the other Mode of Ratification may be proposed by the Congress; Provided that no Amendment which may be made prior to the Year One thousand eight hundred and eight shall in any Manner affect the first and fourth Clauses in the Ninth Section of the first Article; and that no State, without its Consent, shall be deprived of its equal Suffrage in the Senate.

10. Modified by the Eleventh Amendment.
11. Repealed by the Thirteenth Amendment.

Article VI.

All Debts contracted and Engagements entered into, before the Adoption of this Constitution, shall be as valid against the United States under this Constitution, as under the Confederation.

This Constitution, and the laws of the United States which shall be made in Pursuance thereof; and all Treaties made, or which shall be made, under the Authority of the United States, shall be the supreme Law of the Land; and the Judges in every State shall be bound thereby, any Thing in the Constitution or Laws of any State to the Contrary notwithstanding.

The Senators and Representatives before mentioned, and the Members of the several State Legislatures, and all executive and judicial Officers, both of the United States and of the several States, shall be bound by Oath or Affirmation, to support this Constitution; but no religious Text shall ever be required as a Qualification to any Office or public Trust under the United States.

Article VII.

The Ratification of the Conventions of nine States, shall be sufficient for the Establishment of this constitution between the States so ratifying the Same.

Done in Convention by the Unanimous Consent of the States present the Seventeenth Day of September in the Year of our Lord one thousand seven hundred and Eighty seven and of the Independence of the United States of America the Twelfth. In Witness whereof we have hereunto subscribed our Names.

Go. WASHINGTON
Presid't. and deputy from Virginia

Attest
William Jackson
Secretary

Delaware
Geo. Read
Gunning Bedford jun
John Dickinson
Richard Basset
Jaco. Broon

Massachusetts
Nathaniel Gorham
Rufus King

Connecticut
Wm. Saml. Johnson
Roger Sherman

New York
Alexander Hamilton

New Jersey
Wh. Livingston
David Brearley.
Wm. Paterson.
Jona. Dayton

Pennsylvania
B. Franklin
Thomas Mifflin
Robt. Morris
Geo. Clymer
Thos. FitzSimons
Jared Ingersoll
James Wilson
Gouv. Morris

Viriginia
John Blair
James Madison Jr.

North Carolina
Wm. Blount
Richd. Dobbs Spaight.
Hu. Williamson

South Carolina
J. Rutledge
Charles Cotesworth Pinckney
Charles Pinckney
Pierce Butler.

Georgia
William Few
Abr. Baldwin

New Hampshire
John Langdon
Nicholas Gilman

Maryland
James McHenry
Dan of St. Thos. Jenifer
Danl. Carroll.

Amendment I[12]

Congress shall make no law respecting an establishment of religion, or prohibiting the free exercise thereof; or abridging the freedom of speech, or of the press; or the right of the people peaceably to assemble, and to petition the Government for a redress of grievances.

Amendment II

A well regulated militia, being necessary to the security of a free State, the right of the people to keep and bear arms, shall not be infringed.

Amendment III

No Soldier shall, in time of peace be quartered in any house, without the consent of the owner, nor in time of war, but in a manner to be prescribed by law.

Amendment IV

The right of the people to be secure in their persons, houses, papers, and effects, against unreasonable searches and seizures, shall not be violated, and no warrants shall issue, but upon probable cause, supported by oath or affirmation, and particularly describing the place to be searched, and the persons or things to be seized.

12. The first ten amendments were passed by Congress on September 25, 1789, and were ratified on December 15, 1791.

Amendment V

No person shall be held to answer for a capital, or otherwise infamous crime, unless on a presentment or indictment of a Grand Jury, except in cases arising in the land or naval forces, or in the militia, when in actual service in time of war or public danger; nor shall any person be subject for the same offence to be twice put in jeopardy of life or limb; nor shall be compelled in any criminal case to be a witness against himself, nor be deprived of life, liberty, or property, without due process of law; nor shall private property be taken for public use, without just compensation.

Amendment VI

In all criminal prosecutions, the accused shall enjoy the right to a speedy and public trial, by an impartial jury of the State and district wherein the crime shall have been committed, which district shall have been previously ascertained by law, and to be informed of the nature and cause of the accusation; to be confronted with the witnesses against him; to have compulsory process for obtaining witnesses in his favor, and to have the assistance of counsel for his defence.

Amendment VII

In Suits at common law, where the value in controversy shall exceed twenty dollars, the right of trial by jury shall be preserved, and no fact tried by a jury, shall be otherwise reexamined in any Court of the United States, than according to the rules of the common law.

Amendment VIII

Excessive bail shall not be required, nor excessive fines imposed, nor cruel and unusual punishments inflicted.

Amendment IX

The enumeration in the Constitution, of certain rights, shall not be construed to deny or disparage others retained by the people.

Amendment X

The powers not delegated to the United States by the Constitution, nor prohibited by it to the States, are reserved to the States respectively, or to the people.

Amendment XI (Ratified February 7, 1795)

The Judicial power of the United States shall not be construed to extend to any suit in law or equity, commenced or prosecuted against one of the United States by Citizens of another State, or by Citizens or Subjects of any Foreign State.

Amendment XII (Ratified June 15, 1804)

The Electors shall meet in their respective states, and vote by ballot for President and Vice-President, one of whom, at least, shall not be an inhabitant of the same state with themselves; they shall name in their ballots the person voted for as President, and in distinct ballots the person voted for as Vice President, and they shall make distinct lists of all persons voted for as President, and of all persons voted for as Vice-President, and of the number of votes for each, which lists they shall sign and certify, and transmit sealed to the seat of the government of the United States, directed to the President of the Senate;—The President of the Senate shall, in the presence of the Senate and House of Representatives, open all the certificates and the votes shall then be counted;—The person having the greatest number of votes for President, shall be the President, if such number be a majority of the whole number of Electors appointed; and if no person have such majority, then from the persons having the highest numbers not exceeding three on the list of those voted for as President, the House of Representatives shall choose immediately, by ballot, the President. But in choosing the President, the votes shall be taken by states, the representation from each state having one vote; a quorum for this purpose shall consist of a member or members from two-thirds of the states, and a majority of all the states shall be necessary to a choice. [And if the House of Representatives shall not choose a President whenever the right of choice shall devolve upon them, before the fourth day of March next following, then the Vice-President shall act as President, as in the case of the death or other constitutional disability of the President.][13]—The person having the greatest number of votes as Vice-President, shall be the Vice-President, if such number be a majority of the whole number of Electors appointed, and if no person have a majority, then from the two highest numbers on

13. Changed by the Twentieth Amendment.

the list, the Senate shall choose the Vice-President; a quorum for the purpose shall consist of two-thirds of the whole number of Senators, and a majority of the whole number shall be necessary to a choice. But no person constitutionally ineligible to the office of President shall be eligible to that of Vice-President of the United States.

Amendment XIII (Ratified on December 6, 1865)

Section 1.

Neither slavery nor involuntary servitude, except as a punishment for crime whereof the party shall have been duly convicted, shall exist within the United States, or any place subject to their jurisdiction.

Section 2.

Congress shall have power to enforce this article by appropriate legislation.

Amendment XIV (Ratified on July 9, 1868)

Section 1.

All persons born or naturalized in the United States, and subject to the jurisdiction thereof, are citizens of the United States and of the State wherein they reside. No State shall make or enforce any law which shall abridge the privileges or immunities of citizens of the United States; nor shall any State deprive any person of life, liberty, or property, without due process of law; nor deny to any person within its jurisdiction the equal protection of the laws.

Section 2.

Representatives shall be apportioned among the several States according to their respective numbers, counting the whole number of persons in each State, excluding Indians not taxed. But when the right to vote at any election for the choice of electors for President and Vice President of the United States, Representatives in Congress, the Executive and Judicial officers of a State, or the members of the Legislature thereof, is denied to any of the male inhabitants of such State, being [twenty-one][14] years of age, and citizens of the United States, or in any way abridged, except for participation in rebellion, or other crime, the basis of representation therein shall be reduced in the proportion which the number of such male citizens shall bear to the whole number of male citizens twenty-one years of age in such State.

Section 3.

No person shall be a Senator or Representative in Congress, or elector of President and Vice President, or hold any office, civil or military, under the United States, or under any State, who having previously taken an oath, as a member of Congress, or as an officer of the United States, or as a member of any State legislature, or as an executive or judicial officer of any State, to support the Constitution of the United States, shall have engaged in insurrection or rebellion against the same, or given aid or comfort to the enemies thereof. But Congress may by a vote of two-thirds of each House, remove such disability.

Section 4.

The validity of the public debt of the United States, authorized by law, including debts incurred for payment of pensions and bounties for services in suppressing insurrection or rebellion, shall not be questioned. But neither the United States nor any State shall assume or pay any debt or obligation incurred in aid of insurrection or rebellion against the United States, or any claim for the loss or emancipation of any slave, but all such debts, obligations and claims shall be held illegal and void.

Section 5.

The Congress shall have power to enforce, by appropriate legislation, the provisions of this article.

Amendment XV (Ratified on February 3, 1870)

Section 1.

The right of citizens of the United States to vote shall not be denied or abridged by the United States or by any State on account of race, color, or previous condition of servitude.

14. Changed by the Twenty-sixth Amendment.

Section 2.

The Congress shall have power to enforce this article by appropriate legislation.

Amendment XVI (Ratified on February 3, 1913)

The Congress shall have power to lay and collect taxes on incomes, from whatever source derived, without apportionment among the several States, and without regard to any census or enumeration.

Amendment XVII (Ratified on April 8, 1913)

The Senate of the United States shall be composed of two Senators from each State, elected by the people thereof, for six years; and each Senator shall have one vote. The electors in each State shall have the qualifications requisite for electors of the most numerous branch of the State legislatures.

When vacancies happen in the representation of any State in the Senate, the executive authority of such State shall issue writs of election to fill such vacancies: *Provided,* That the legislature of any State may empower the executive thereof to make temporary appointments until the people fill the vacancies by election as the legislature may direct.

This amendment shall not be so construed as to affect the election or term of any Senator chosen before it becomes valid as part of the Constitution.

Amendment XVIII (Ratified on January 16, 1919)

Section 1.

After one year from the ratification of this article the manufacture, sale, or transportation of intoxicating liquors within, the importation thereof into, or the exportation thereof from the United States and all territory subject to the jurisdiction thereof for beverage purposes is hereby prohibited.

Section 2.

The Congress and the several States shall have concurrent power to enforce this article by appropriate legislation.

Section 3.

This article shall be inoperative unless it shall have been ratified as an amendment to the Constitution by the legislatures of the several States, as provided in the Constitution, within seven years from the date of the submission hereof to the States by the Congress.[15]

Amendment XIX (Ratified on August 18, 1920)

The right of citizens of the United States to vote shall not be denied or abridged by the United States or by any State on account of sex.

Congress shall have power to enforce this article by appropriate legislation.

Amendment XX (Ratified on January 23, 1933)

Section 1.

The terms of the President and Vice President shall end at noon on the 20th day of January, and the terms of Senators and Representatives at noon on the 3rd day of January, of the years in which such terms would have ended if this article had not been ratified, and the terms of their successors shall then begin.

Section 2.

The Congress shall assemble at least once in every year, and such meeting shall begin at noon on the 3rd day of January, unless they shall by law appoint a different day.

Section 3.

If, at the time fixed for the beginning of the term of the President, the President elect shall have died, the Vice President elect shall become President. If a President shall not have been chosen before the time fixed for the beginning of his term, or if the President elect shall have failed to qualify, then the Vice President elect shall act as President until a President shall have qualified; and the Congress may by law provide for the case wherein neither a President elect nor a Vice

15. The Eighteenth Amendment was repealed by the Twenty-first Amendment.

President elect shall have qualified, declaring who shall then act as President, or the manner in which one who is to act shall be selected, and such person shall act accordingly until a President or Vice President shall have qualified.

Section 4.

The Congress may by law provide for the case of the death of any of the persons from whom the House of Representatives may choose a President whenever the rights of choice shall have devolved upon them, and for the case of the death of any of the persons from whom the Senate may choose a Vice President whenever the right of choice shall have devolved upon them.

Section 5.

Sections 1 and 2 shall take effect on the 15th day of October following the ratification of this article.

Section 6.

This article shall be inoperative unless it shall have been ratified as an amendment to the Constitution by the legislatures of three-fourths of the several States within seven years from the date of its submission.

Amendment XXI (Ratified on December 5, 1933)

Section 1.

The eighteenth article of amendment to the Constitution of the United States is hereby repealed.

Section 2.

The transportation or importation into any State, Territory, or possession of the United States for delivery or use therein of intoxicating liquors, in violation of the laws thereof, is hereby prohibited.

Section 3.

This article shall be inoperative unless it shall have been ratified as an amendment to the Constitution by conventions in the several States, as provided in the Constitution, within seven years from the date of the submission hereof to the States by the Congress.

Amendment XXII (Ratified on February 27, 1951)

No person shall be elected to the office of the President more than twice, and no person who has held the office of President, or acted as President, for more than two years of a term to which some other person was elected President shall be elected to the office of the President more than once. But this Article shall not apply to any person holding the office of President when this Article was proposed by the Congress, and shall not prevent any person who may be holding the office of President, or acting as President, during the term within which this Article becomes operative from holding the office of President or acting as President during the remainder of such term.

Amendment XXIII (Ratified on March 29, 1961)

Section 1.

The District constituting the seat of Government of the United States shall appoint in such manner as the Congress may direct:

A number of electors of President and Vice President equal to the whole number of Senators and Representatives in Congress to which the District would be entitled if it were a State, but in no event more than the least populous State; they shall be in addition to those appointed by the States, but they shall be considered, for the purposes of the election of President and Vice President, to be electors appointed by a State; and they shall meet in the District and perform such duties as provided by the twelfth article of amendment.

Section 2.

The Congress shall have power to enforce this article by appropriate legislation.

Amendment XXIV (Ratified on January 23, 1964)

Section 1.

The right of citizens of the United States to vote in any primary or other election for President or Vice President, for electors for President or Vice President, or for Senator or Representative in Congress, shall not be denied or abridged by the United States or any State by reason of failure to pay any poll tax or other tax.

Section 2.

The Congress shall have power to enforce this article by appropriate legislation.

Amendment XXV (Ratified on February 10, 1967)

Section 1.

In case of the removal of the President from office or of his death or resignation, the Vice President shall become President.

Section 2.

Whenever there is a vacancy in the office of the Vice President, the President shall nominate a Vice President who shall take office upon confirmation by a majority vote of both Houses of Congress.

Section 3.

Whenever the President transmits to the President pro tempore of the Senate and the Speaker of the House of Representatives his written declaration that he is unable to discharge the powers and duties of his office, and until he transmits to them a written declaration to the contrary, such powers and duties shall be discharged by the Vice President as Acting President.

Section 4.

Whenever the Vice President and a majority of either the principal officers of the executive departments or of such other body as Congress may by law provide, transmit to the President pro tempore of the Senate and the Speaker of the House of Representatives their written declaration that the President is unable to discharge the powers and duties of his office, the Vice President shall immediately assume the powers and duties of the offices as Acting President.

Thereafter, when the President transmits to the President pro tempore of the Senate and the Speaker of the House of Representatives his written declaration that no inability exists, he shall resume the powers and duties of his office unless the Vice President and a majority of either the principal officers of the executive department or of such other body as Congress may by law provide, transmit within four days to the President pro tempore of the Senate and the Speaker of the House of Representatives their written declaration that the President is unable to discharge the powers and duties of his office. Thereupon Congress shall decide the issue, assembling within forty-eight hours for that purpose if not in session. If the Congress, within twenty-one days after receipt of the latter written declaration, or, if Congress is not in session, within twenty-one days after Congress is required to assemble, determines by two-thirds vote of both Houses that the President is unable to discharge the powers and duties of his office, the Vice President shall continue to discharge the same as Acting President; otherwise; the President shall resume the powers and duties of his office.

Amendment XXVI (Ratified on July 1, 1971)

Section 1.

The right of citizens of the United States, who are eighteen years of age or older, to vote shall not be denied or abridged by the United States or by any State on account of age.

Section 2.

The Congress shall have the power to enforce this article by appropriate legislation.

Amendment XXVII (Ratified on May 7, 1992)

No law, varying the compensation for the services of the Senators and Representatives, shall take effect, until an election of Representatives shall have intervened.

APPENDIX C

Federalist Paper #10

Among the numerous advantages promised by a well-constructed Union, none deserves to be more accurately developed than its tendency to break and control the violence of faction. The friend of popular governments never finds himself so much alarmed for their character and fate as when he contemplates their propensity to this dangerous vice. He will not fail, therefore, to set a due value on any plan which, without violating the principles to which he is attached, provides a proper cure for it. The instability, injustice, and confusion introduced into the public councils have, in truth, been the mortal diseases under which popular governments have everywhere perished, as they continue to be the favorite and fruitful topics from which the adversaries to liberty derive their most specious declamations. The valuable improvements made by the American constitutions on the popular models, both ancient and modern, cannot certainly be too much admired; but it would be an unwarrantable partiality to contend that they have as effectually obviated the danger on this side, as was wished and expected. Complaints are everywhere heard from our most considerate and virtuous citizens, equally the friends of public and private faith and of public and personal liberty, that our governments are too unstable, that the public good is disregarded in the conflicts of rival parties, and that measures are too often decided, not according to the rules of justice and the rights of the minor party, but by the superior force of an interested and overbearing majority. However anxiously we may wish that these complaints had no foundation, the evidence of known facts will not permit us to deny that they are in some degree true. It will be found, indeed, on a candid review of our situation, that some of the distresses under which we labor have been erroneously charged on the operation of our governments; but it will be found, at the same time, that other causes will not alone account for many of our heaviest misfortunes; and, particularly, for that prevailing and increasing distrust of public engagements and alarm for private rights which are echoed from one end of the continent to the other. These must be chiefly, if not wholly, effects of the unsteadiness and injustice with which a factious spirit has tainted our public administration.

By a faction I understand a number of citizens, whether amounting to a majority or minority of the whole, who are united and actuated by some common impulse of passion, or of interest, adverse to the rights of other citizens, or the permanent and aggregate interests of the community.

There are two methods of curing the mischiefs of faction: the one, by removing its causes; the other, by controlling its effects.

There are again two methods of removing the causes of faction: the one, by destroying the liberty which is essential to its existence; the other, by giving to every citizen the same opinions, the same passions, and the same interests.

It could never be more truly said than of the first remedy that it was worse than the disease. Liberty is to faction what air is to fire, an aliment without which it instantly expires. But it could not be a less folly to abolish liberty, which is essential to political life, because it nourishes faction than it would be to wish the annihilation of air, which is essential to animal life, because it imparts to fire its destructive agency.

The second expedient is as impracticable as the first would be unwise. As long as the reason of man continues fallible, and his is at liberty to exercise it, different opinions will be formed. As long as the connection subsists between his reason and his self-love, his opinions and his passions will have a reciprocal influence on each other; and the former will be objects to which the latter will attach themselves. The diversity in the faculties of men, from which the rights of property originate, is not less an insuperable obstacle to a uniformity of interests. The protection of these faculties is the first object of government. From the protection of different and unequal faculties of acquiring property, the possession of different degrees and kinds of property immediately results; and from the influence of these on the sentiments and views of the respective proprietors ensues a division of the society into different interests and parties.

The latent causes of faction are thus sown in the nature of man; and we see them everywhere brought into different degrees of activity, according to the different circumstances of civil society. A zeal for different opinions concerning religion, concerning government, and many other points, as well of speculation as of practice; an attachment to different leaders ambitiously contending for pre-eminence and power; or to persons of other descriptions whose fortunes have been interesting to the human passions, have, in turn, divided mankind into parties, inflamed them with mutual animosity, and rendered them much more disposed to vex and oppress each other than to cooperate for their common good. So strong is this propensity of mankind to fall into mutual animosities that where no substantial occasion presents itself the most frivolous and fanciful distinctions have been sufficient to kindle their unfriendly passions and excite their most violent conflicts. But the most common and durable source of factions has been the verious and unequal distribution of property. Those who hold and those who are without property have ever formed distinct interests in society. Those who are creditors, and those who are debtors, fall under a like discrimination. A landed interest, a manufacturing interest, a mercantile interest, a moneyed interest, with many lesser interests, grow up of necessity in civilized nations, and divide them into different classes, actuated by different sentiments and views. The regulation of these various and interfering interests forms the principal task of modern legislation and involves the spirit of party and faction in the necessary and ordinary operations of government.

No man is allowed to be a judge in his own cause, because his interest would certainly bias his judgment, and, not improbably, corrupt his integrity. With equal, nay with greater reason, a body of men are unfit to be both judges and parties at the same time; yet what are many of the most important acts of legislation but so many judicial determinations, not indeed concerning the rights of single persons, but concerning the rights of large bodies of citizens? And what are the different classes of legislators but advocates and parties to the causes which they determine? Is a law proposed concerning private debts? It is a question to which the creditors are parties on one side and the debtors on the other. Justice ought to hold the balance between them. Yet the parties are, and must be, themselves the judges; and the most numerous party, or in other words, the most powerful faction must be expected to prevail. Shall domestic manufacturers be encouraged, and in what degree, by restrictions on foreign manufacturers? Are questions which would be differently decided by the landed and the manufacturing classes, and probably by neither with a sole regard to justice and the public good. The apportionment of taxes on the various descriptions of property is an act which seems to require the most exact impartiality; yet there is, perhaps, no legislative act in which greater opportunity and temptation are given to a predominant party to trample on the rules of justice. Every shilling with which they overburden the inferior number is a shilling saved to their own pockets.

It is in vain to say that enlightened statesmen will be able to adjust these clashing interests and render them all subservient to the public good. Enlightened statesmen will not always be at the helm. Nor, in many cases, can such an adjustment be made at all without taking into view indirect and remote considerations, which will rarely prevail over the immediate interest which one party may find in disregarding the rights of another or the good of the whole.

The inference to which we are brought is that the *causes* of faction cannot be removed and that relief is only to be sought in the means of controlling its *effects*.

If a faction consists of less than a majority, relief is supplied by the republican principle, which enables the majority to defeat its sinister views by regular vote. It may clog the administration, it may convulse the society; but it will be unable to execute and mask its violence under the forms of the Constitution. When a majority is included in a faction, the form of popular government, on the other hand, enables it to sacrifice to its ruling passion or interest both the public good and the rights of other citizens. To secure the public good and private rights against the danger of such a faction, and at the same time to preserve the spirit and the form of popular government, is then the great object to which our inquiries are directed. Let me add that it is the great desideratum by which alone this form of government can be rescued from the opprobrium under which it has so long labored and be recommended to the esteem and adoption of mankind.

By what means is this object attainable? Evidently by one of two only. Either the existence of the same passion or interest in a majority at the same time must be prevented, or the majority, having such coexistent passion or interest, must be rendered, by their number and local situation, unable to concert and carry into effect schemes of oppression. If the impulse and the opportunity be suffered to coincide, we well know that neither moral nor religious motives can be relied on as an adequate control. They are not found to be such on the injustice and violence of individuals, and lose their efficacy in proportion to the number combined together, that is, in proportion as their efficacy becomes needful.

From this view of the subject it may be concluded that a pure democracy, by which I mean a society consisting of a small number of citizens, who assemble and administer the government in person, can admit of no cure for the mischiefs of faction. A common passion or interest will, in almost every case, be felt by a majority of the whole; a communication and concert results from the form of government itself; and there is nothing to check the inducements to sacrifice the weaker party or an obnoxious individual. Hence it is that such democracies have ever been spectacles of turbulence and contention; have ever been found incompatible with personal security or the rights of property; and have in general been as short in their lives as they have been violent in their deaths. Theoretic politicians, who have patronized this species of government, have erroneously supposed that by reducing mankind to a perfect equality in their political rights, they would at the same time be perfectly equalized and assimilated in their possessions, their opinions, and their passions.

A republic, by which I mean a government in which the scheme of representation takes place, opens a different prospect and promises the cure for which we are seeking. Let us examine the points in which it varies from pure democracy, and we shall comprehend both the nature of the cure and the efficacy which it must derive from the Union.

The two great points of difference between a democracy and a republic are: first, the delegation of the government, in the latter, to a small number of citizens elected by the rest; secondly, the greater number of citizens and greater sphere of country over which the latter may be extended.

The effect of the first difference is, on the one hand, to refine and enlarge the public views by passing them through the medium of a chosen body of citizens, whose wisdom may best discern the true interest of their country and whose patriotism and love of justice will be least likely to sacrifice it to temporary or partial considerations. Under such a regulation it may well happen that the public voice, pronounced by the representatives of the people, will be more consonant to the public good than if pronounced by the people themselves, convened for the purpose. On the other hand, the effect may be inverted. Men of factious tempers, of local prejudices, or of sinister designs, may, by intrigue, by corruption, or by other means, first obtain the suffrages, and then betray the interests of the people. The question resulting is, whether small or extensive republics are most favorable to the election of proper guardians of the public weal; and it is clearly decided in favor of the latter by two obvious considerations.

In the first place it is to be remarked that however small the republic may be the representatives must be raised to a certain number in order to guard against the cabals of a few; and that however large it may be they must be limited to a certain number in order to guard against the confusion of a multitude. Hence, the number of representatives in the two cases not being in proportion to that of the constituents, and being proportionally greatest in the small republic, it follows that if the proportion of fit characters be not less in the large than in the small republic, the former will present a greater option, and consequently a greater probability of a fit choice.

In the next place, as each representative will be chosen by a greater number of citizens in the large than in the small republic, it will be more difficult for unworthy candidates to practice with success the vicious arts by which elections are too often carried; and the suffrages of the people being more free, will be more likely to center on men who possess the most attractive merit and the most diffusive and established characters.

It must be confessed that in this, as in most other cases, there is a mean, on both sides of which inconveniencies will be found to lie. By enlarging too much the number of electors, you render the representative too little acquainted with all their local circumstances and lesser interests; as by reducing it too much, you render him unduly attached to these, and too little fit to comprehend and pursue great and national objects. The federal Constitution forms a happy combination in this respect; the great and aggregate interests being referred to the national, the local and particular to the State legislatures.

The other point of difference is the greater number of citizens and extent of territory which may be brought within the compass of republican than of democratic government; and it is this circumstance principally which renders factious combinations less to be dreaded in the former than in the latter. The smaller the society, the fewer probably will be the distinct parties and interests composing it; the fewer the distinct parties and interests, the more frequently will a majority be found of the same party; and the smaller the number of individuals composing a majority, and the smaller the compass within which they are placed, the more easily will they concert and execute their plans of oppression. Extend the sphere and you take in a greater variety of parties and interests; you make it less probable that a majority of the whole will have a common motive to invade the rights of other citizens; or if such a common motive exists, it will be more difficult for all who feel it to discover their own strength and to act in unison with each other. Besides other impediments, it may be remarked that, where there is a consciousness of unjust or dishonorable purposes, communication is always checked by distrust in proportion to the number whose concurrence is necessary.

Hence, it clearly appears that the same advantage which a republic has over a democracy in controlling the effects of faction is enjoyed by a large over a small republic—is enjoyed by the Union over the States composing it. Does this advantage consist in the substitution of representatives whose enlightened views and virtuous sentiments render them superior to local prejudices and to schemes of injustice? It will not be denied that the representation of the Union will be most likely to possess these requisite endowments. Does it consist in the greater security afforded by a greater variety of parties, against the event of any one party being able to outnumber and oppress the rest? In an equal degree does the increased variety of parties comprised within the Union increase this security. Does it, in fine, consist in the greater obstacles opposed to the concert and accomplishment of the secret wishes of an unjust and interested majority? Here again the extent of the Union gives it the most palpable advantage.

The influence of factious leaders may kindle a flame within their particular States but will be unable to spread a general conflagration through the other States. A religious sect may degenerate into a political faction in a part of the Confederacy; but the variety of sects dispersed over the entire face of it must secure the national councils against any danger from that source. A rage for paper money, for an abolition of debts, for an equal division of property, or for any other improper or wicked project, will be less apt to pervade the whole body of the Union than a particular member of it, in the same proportion as such a malady is more likely to taint a particular county or district than an entire State.

In the extent and proper structure of the Union, therefore, we behold a republican remedy for the diseases most incident to republican government. And according to the degree of pleasure and pride we feel in being republicans ought to be our zeal in cherishing the spirit and supporting the character of federalists.

APPENDIX D

Federalist Paper #51

To what expedient, then, shall we finally resort, for maintaining in practice the necessary partition of power among the several departments as laid down in the Constitution? The only answer that can be given is that as all these exterior provisions are found to be inadequate the defect must be supplied, by so contriving the interior structure of the government as that its several constituent parts may, by their mutual relations, be the means of keeping each other in their proper places. Without presuming to undertake a full development of this important idea I will hazard a few general observations which may perhaps place it in a clearer light, and enable us to form a more correct judgment of the principles and structure of the government planned by the convention.

In order to lay a due foundation for that separate and distinct exercise of the different powers of government, which to a certain extent is admitted on all hands to be essential to the preservation of liberty, it is evident that each department should have a will of its own; and consequently should be so constituted that the members of each should have as little agency as possible in the appointment of the members of the others. Were this principle rigorously adhered to, it would require that all the appointments for the supreme executive, legislative, and judiciary magistracies should be drawn from the same fountain of authority, the people, through channels having no communication whatever with one another. Perhaps such a plan of constructing the several departments would be less difficult in practice than it may in contemplation appear. Some difficulties, however, and some additional expense would attend the execution of it. Some deviations, therefore, from the principle must be admitted. In the constitution of the judiciary department in particular, it might be inexpedient to insist rigorously on the principle: first, because peculiar qualifications being essential in the members, the primary consideration ought to be to select that mode of choice which best secures these qualifications; second, because the permanent tenure by which the appointments are held in that department must soon destroy all sense of dependence on the authority conferring them.

It is equally evident that the members of each department should be as little dependent as possible on those of the others for the emoluments annexed to their offices. Were the executive magistrate, or the judges, not independent of the legislature in this particular, their independence in every other would be merely nominal.

But the great security against a gradual concentration of the several powers in the same department consists in giving to those who administer each department the necessary constitutional means and personal motives to resist encroachments of the others. The provision for defense must in this, as in all other cases, be made commensurate to the danger of attack. Ambition must be made to counteract ambition. The interest of the man must be connected with the constitutional rights of the place. It may be a reflection on human nature that such devices should be necessary to control the abuses of government. But what is government itself but the greatest of all reflections on human nature? If men were angels, no government would be necessary. If angels were to govern men, neither external nor internal controls on government would be necessary. In framing a government which is to be administered by men over men, the great difficulty lies in this: you must first enable the government to control the governed; and in the next place oblige it to control itself. A dependence on the people is, no doubt, the primary control on the government; but experience has taught mankind the necessity of auxiliary precautions.

This policy of supplying, by opposite and rival interests, the defect of better motives, might be traced through the whole system of human affairs, private as well as public. We see it particularly displayed in all the subordinate distributions of power, where the constant aim is to divide and arrange the several offices in such a manner as that each may be a check on the other—that the private interest of every individual may be a sentinel over the public rights. These inventions of prudence cannot be less requisite in the distribution of the supreme powers of the State.

But it is not possible to give to each department an equal power of self-defense. In republican government, the legislative authority necessarily predominates. The remedy for this inconveniency is to divide the legislature into different branches; and to render them, by different modes of election and different principles of action, as little connected with each other as the nature of their common functions and their common dependence on the society will admit. It may even be necessary to guard against dangerous encroachments by still further precautions. As the weight of the legislative authority requires that it should be thus divided, the weakness of the executive may require, on the other hand, that it should be fortified. An absolute negative on the legislature appears, at first view, to be the natural defense with which the executive magistrate should be armed. But perhaps it would be neither altogether safe nor alone sufficient. On ordinary occasions it might not be exerted with the requisite firmness, and on extraordinary occasions it might be perfidiously abused. May not this defect of an absolute negative be supplied by some qualified connection between this weaker department and the weaker branch of the stronger department, by which the latter may be led to support the constitutional rights of the former, without being too much detached from the rights of its own department?

If the principles on which these observations are found be just, as I persuade myself they are, and they be applied as a criterion to the several State constitutions, and the federal Constitution, it will be found that if the latter does not perfectly correspond with them, the former are infinitely less able to bear such a test.

There are, moreover, two considerations particularly applicable to the federal system of America, which place that system in a very interesting point of view.

First. In a single republic, all the power surrendered by the people is submitted to the administration of a single government; and the usurpations are guarded against by a division of the government into distinct and separate departments. In the compound republic of America, the power surrendered by the people is first divided between two distinct governments, and then the portion allotted to each subdivided among distinct and separate departments. Hence a double security arises to the rights of the people. The different governments will control each other, at the same time that each will be controlled by itself.

Second. It is of great importance in a republic not only to guard the society against the oppression of its rulers, but to guard one part of the society against the injustice of the other part. Different interests necessarily exist in different classes of citizens. If a majority be united by a common interest, the rights of the minority will be insecure. There are but two methods of providing against this evil: the one by creating a will in the community independent of the majority—that is, of the society itself; the other, by comprehending in the society so many separate descriptions of citizens as will render an unjust combination of a majority of the whole very improbable, if not impracticable. The first method prevails in all governments possessing an hereditary or self-appointed authority. This, at best, is but a precarious security; because a power independent of the society may as well espouse the unjust views of the major as the rightful interests of the minor party, and may possibly be turned against both parties. The second method will be exemplified in the federal republic of the United States. Whilst all authority in it will be derived from and dependent on the society, the society itself will be broken into so many parts, interests and classes of citizens, that the rights of individuals, or of the minority, will be in little danger from interested combinations of the majority. In a free government the security for civil rights must be the same as that for religious rights. It consists in the one case in the multiplicity of interests, and in the other in the multiplicity of sects. The degree of security in both cases will depend on the number of interests and sects; and this may be presumed to depend on the extent of country and number of people comprehended under the same government. This view of the subject must particularly recommend a proper federal system to all the sincere and considerate friends of republican government, since it shows that in exact proportion as the territory of the Union may be formed into more circumscribed Confederacies, or States, oppressive combinations of a majority will be facilitated; the best security, under the republican forms, for the rights of every class of citizen, will be diminished; and consequently the stability and independence of some member of the government, the only other security, must be proportionally increased. Justice is the end of government. It is the end of civil society. It ever has been and ever will be pursued until it be obtained, or until liberty be lost in the pursuit. In a society under the forms of which the stronger faction can readily unite and oppress the weaker, anarchy may as truly be said to reign as in a state of nature, where the weaker individual is not secured against the violence of the stronger; and as, in the latter state, even the stronger individuals are prompted, by the uncertainty of their condition, to submit to a government which may protect the weak as well as themselves; so, in the former state, will the more powerful factions or parties be gradually induced, by a like motive, to wish for a government which will protect all parties, the weaker as well as the more powerful. It can be little doubted that if the State of Rhode Island was separated from the Confederacy and left to itself, the insecurity of rights under the popular form of government within such narrow limits would be displayed by such reiterate oppressions of factious majorities that some power altogether independent of the people would soon be called for by the voice of the very factions whose misrule had proved the necessity of it. In the extended republic of the United States, and among the great variety of interests, parties, and sects which it embraces, a coalition of a majority of the whole society could seldom take place on any other principles than those of justice and the general good; whilst there being thus less danger to a minor from the will of a major party, there must be less pretext, also, to provide for the security of the former, by introducing into the government a will not dependent on the latter, or, in other words, a will independent of the society itself. It is no less certain than it is important, notwithstanding the contrary opinions which have been entertained, that the larger the society, provided it lie within a practicable sphere, the more duly capable it will be of self-government. And happily for the *republican cause*, the practicable sphere may be carried to a very great extent by a judicious modification and mixture of the *federal principle.*

GLOSSARY

Activist judges Those who are more willing to declare statutes or actions of government officials unconstitutional.

Adversarial relationship A close relationship between, for example, the media and politicians, in which they fight each other.

Affirmative action Hiring policies that take race and sex into account to compensate for past discrimination.

Agents of political socialization See **political socialization.**

Antifederalists Those who opposed ratification of the Constitution because they feared it would provide for an overly powerful national government.

Appropriations The authority to spend money.

Articles of Confederation Ratified in 1781 to form a "league of friendship" among the states. Each state retained its "sovereignty" and "independence."

Authorizations Provide agencies and departments with the legal authority to operate.

Beats Organizations or departments that reporters are assigned to cover, such as the White House, Supreme Court, or State Department.

Bilingual education Giving instruction, in substantive subjects such as math, in students' native language for those who do not speak English; also providing instruction in English itself.

Bill of Rights The first 10 amendments to the Constitution, ratified in 1791. They include freedom of expression, rights for those accused of crime, the right to bear arms for a militia, and the right not to have soldiers quartered in homes during peacetime. They state that those rights are not the only ones people have and that the powers not given to the national government are reserved to the states.

Bills of attainder Legislative acts rather than judicial trials that pronounce specific persons guilty of crimes.

Block grants Federal money given to states and cities for a specific purpose, but with less strict limitations than those on grants-in-aid.

Blockbusting After a black family bought a house in a white neighborhood, realtors would warn white families that more blacks would move in. Because of prejudice, whites would sell their houses to realtors at low prices; realtors would resell to blacks at higher prices. The result was that neighborhoods that might have been desegregated were resegregated from all white to all black.

Brown v. Board of Education In 1954, the Supreme Court ruled that school segregation violated the Fourteenth Amendment's equal protection clause.

Burger Court The Supreme Court during the tenure of Chief Justice Warren Burger, from 1969-1986.

Casework See **constituency service.**

Caucus A meeting.

Checks and balances Each branch of government is given some authority over the others. If one branch abuses its powers, the others can check it.

Chief of state The president as a national symbol of collective unity and pride.

Civil cases Those in which persons sue others for denying their rights and causing them harm.

Civil Rights Act of 1964 Prohibits discrimination in public accommodations and employment on the basis of race, color, sex, religion, or national origin.

Civil Rights Act of 1968 Bans discrimination in the sale or rental of housing on the basis of race, color, religion, national origin, and (as amended) on the basis of sex, having children, or being disabled. Prohibits steering, blockbusting, and redlining.

Civil Service Commission Created by the Pendleton Act in 1883 to achieve neutral competence in the bureaucracy by filling certain jobs with people who had proven their competence in competitive examinations and would not have to support or oppose particular political candidates.

Classical democracy A form of government in which citizens participate through debating, voting, and holding office.

Closed primary Limits participation in an election to those who are registered with a party or declare a preference for a party.

Cloture A vote of three-fifths of the Senate to limit debate on a bill to only 20 more hours.

Coalitions Networks of interest groups with similar concerns.

Commercial bias The need to attract an audience and to print or broadcast what advertisers want.

Comparable worth Equal pay for women and men for comparable work.

Confederal system A system in which the central government has only those powers given to it by the subnational governments; it cannot act directly on citizens.

Conference Committee A committee of members of both houses that meets to resolve differences in a bill.

Conflict of interest When an official makes decisions that directly affect his or her own personal livelihood or interests.

Conservative One who believes that the domestic role of government should be minimized and that individuals are responsible for their own well-being.

Constituencies The districts and the people in them that members of Congress represent.

Constituency service Members of Congress answer questions and do personal favors for constituents who write or call for help.

Constitutional Convention Held in Philadelphia in 1787, at first to revise the Articles of Confederation and then to write a new constitution.

Cooperative federalism The continuing cooperation among federal, state, and local officials in carrying out the business of government.

Court-packing plan A plan proposed by President Franklin Roosevelt that would have authorized the president to nominate and the Senate to confirm a new justice for every justice over 70 who did not retire, up to a total of 15.

Courts of appeal Federal intermediate appellate courts. There are 12, based on regions of the country.

Criminal cases Those in which governments prosecute persons for violating laws.

Cruel and unusual punishment Defined as torture or any punishment grossly disproportionate to the offense; also applied to certain provisions of capital punishment laws.

Cumulative voting Members of Congress would not be elected from single-member districts, but from at-large districts in which several members of Congress would be elected at the same time.

De facto segregation Segregation not enforced by law. Normally refers to residential segregation.

De jure segregation Segregation enforced by law.

Dealignment Voters feel that parties are becoming irrelevant and voters feel indifferent toward them.

Delegated legislative authority When Congress gives agencies the authority to draft and execute specific policies.

Democracy In a "direct democracy," the will of the people becomes law. See **republic** and **indirect democracy.**

Direct democracy A form of government that permits citizens to vote on most issues.

Direct or mandatory spending Government spending that is required by law, such as Medicare payments, unemployment insurance, farm price supports, and interest on the national debt.

Direct primary Allows the voters to choose the party's candidates.

Discretionary spending Government spending that is not required by existing law, but is set by annual appropriations bills passed by Congress; for example, to operate departments, agencies, and programs.

District courts Federal trial courts. There are 94, based on population but with at least one in each state.

Divided government When one party controls the White House and the other party controls Congress.

Dred Scott case In 1857, the Supreme Court ruled that no blacks, whether slave or free, were citizens, and that they had no rights.

Dual federalism The idea that the Constitution created a system in which nation and state each have separate grants of power, with each supreme in its own sphere.

Due process When the government prosecutes defendants, it must give them the procedures they are due.

Electoral College Composed of electors, party notables who gather in each state capitol in December after the presidential election to cast their votes for president and vice president. Each state has as many electors as its total representation in Congress (House plus Senate).

Elitism A theory that the holders of a few top jobs in key parts of society rule.

Entitlements Payments from government to people that they qualify for under the guidelines set by law, for example, aid to full-time college students coming from families with income under a certain level.

Equal Pay Act In 1963; requires that women and men receive equal pay for equal work.

Equal protection clause Phrase in the Fourteenth Amendment guaranteeing that government must treat people equally.

Equal Rights Amendment (ERA) Equality of rights under the law shall not be denied or abridged by the United States or by any state on account of sex.

Establishment clause The clause in the First Amendment that forbids government from designating an official church, from aiding one religion over another, or from aiding religion over nonreligion.

Ex post facto laws Legislative acts making a behavior illegal that was legal when it was done.

Exclusionary rule Any evidence obtained in violation of the Fourth Amendment is barred from court.

Executive leadership The president's ability to control the bureaucracy by budgeting, appointing people who share his views, recommending administrative reform, and lobbying public opinion.

Executive orders Issued by the president and executive agencies and containing binding policy.

Executive privilege The president's authority to withhold information from the courts and Congress.

Faithless elector An elector in the Electoral College who decides to cast a ballot for a personal choice, not the choice of his or her state's voters.

Federal Election Campaign Act An attempt by Congress in 1974 to regulate campaign financing. Its major provisions establish public financing of presidential campaigns and limit the amount of political contributions candidates may accept.

Federalism A system in which power is constitutionally divided between a central government and subnational or local governments.

Federalism The division of power between the national and the state governments.

Federalist Papers Essays written by Alexander Hamilton, James Madison, and John Jay to convince delegates to the Constitutional Convention to vote for ratification of the Constitution.

Federalists Those who supported ratification of the Constitution.

Filibuster A continuous speech in the Senate made by one or more members to prevent the Senate from taking action.

Fireside chats A series of radio talks by President Franklin Roosevelt to advocate his policies and reassure his listeners during the Depression.

Franking The free mail privileges of House members.

Free exercise clause The clause in the First Amendment that allows individuals to practice their religion without government coercion.

Freedom of speech The First Amendment guarantee that individuals will be free from governmental prosecution for almost everything they say

Full faith and credit clause A provision of the Constitution establishing rules to govern states' relationships with each other, such as requiring states to recognize contracts.

Game orientation The assumption that politics is a game and politicians are self-interested players who are not concerned about the consequences of their proposals or the government's policies.

General revenue sharing Federal money given to states and cities to spend as they see fit, subject to only a few conditions.

Gerrymander The process of drawing a Congressional district to maximize the political advantage of a party or racial group.

Going public A strategy whereby presidents try to use their public support to gain cooperation from the Washingtonians, by giving prime-time TV and radio addresses, holding press conferences, making speeches, and using satellite technology to give interviews to local TV stations, conventions, and other audiences.

Going public Carrying an issue debate to the public through the media.

Grandfather clause Exempting illiterate people whose grandfathers had the right to vote before 1867 from having to take literacy tests.

Grants-in-aid Federal money given to states (and occasionally to local governments) to set up programs to help people, for example, the aged poor or the unemployed.

Great Compromise The proposal that Congress should have two houses, one in which representation was based on population and members were elected by voters, and the other in which representation was by states and members were selected by state legislatures.

Habeas corpus Latin for "Have ye the body!" A writ demanding that the state figuratively produce the defendant and justify his or her incarceration.

Hatch Act Passed in 1939, it prohibits federal employees (and state and local government workers supported by federal funds) from participating in party-sponsored voter registration drives, endorsing party candidates, or working for or against candidates in any way.

Home rule Charters in some states that give local governments considerable autonomy in such matters as setting tax rates, regulating land use, and choosing their form of local government.

Hyperpluralism A theory that government responds to many but not all groups.

Ideology A highly organized and coherent set of opinions.

Implied powers clause A provision of the Constitution that gives Congress the power to make all laws it considers "necessary and proper" to attain legitimate national objectives; it enables Congress to legislate in areas where it has not been granted explicit authority to act.

Independent agencies Government agencies. Like departments, their heads are appointed by and responsible to the president. Unlike departments, their heads do not sit in the cabinet.

Independent spending Spending by groups not under the control of candidates.

Indirect democracy A form of government in which citizens have an indirect impact because they select policymakers to make decisions for them. See **republic.**

Influence peddling Using one's access to powerful people to make money.

Informal norms The unstated rules for running Congress smoothly by attempting to diminish friction and competition among members.

Institutional loyalty The expectation that members of Congress will respect their fellow members and Congress itself, especially their own house.

Interest groups Organizations that try to achieve at least some of their goals with government assistance.

Jim Crow laws Local segregation laws.

Judicial review The authority of the courts to declare laws or actions of government officials unconstitutional.

Jurisdiction The authority to hear and decide cases.

Korematsu v. United States Supreme Court case stemming from the exclusion of Japanese Americans from the West Coast after the bombing of Pearl Harbor. A majority of justices upheld the exclusion because it occurred during wartime.

Leaks Disclosures of information some officials want to keep secret.

Legislative veto Allows one or both houses of Congress or a committee to block legislative action; declared unconstitutional by the Supreme Court in 1983 but still in use.

Libel Printed or broadcast statements that are false and that tarnish someone's reputation.

Liberal One who believes in a national government active in domestic policies, providing health, education, and welfare help to individuals and communities, and promoting civil rights.

Limited government A government that is strong enough to protect people's rights but not too strong to threaten those rights.

Line-item veto Allows the president to veto one or more provisions of individual spending bills without preventing the remaining provisions from becoming law.

Literacy tests Tests to make sure voters could read and write and thus evaluate political information.

Lobbying The efforts of interest groups to influence government.

Majority leader Second in command to the Speaker in the House.

Mandate A clear direction by the voters for the winning candidate to take a particular course of action.

Marbury v. Madison Supreme Court case in 1803 in which Chief Justice Marshall articulated and justified judicial review.

Market share The number of members in a group compared to its potential membership.

Markup A session during which a congressional subcommittee can rewrite a bill before sending it back to the full committee.

McCarthyism With little evidence, charging various government officials with being Communists.

McCulloch v. Maryland A Supreme Court case about a Maryland state tax on the Bank of the United States in which the Court interpreted the "necessary and proper" clause of Article I, Section 8, of the Constitution broadly, thereby increasing national authority.

Media events Events staged for television, usually pairing a photo opportunity and a speech, to convey a particular impression of a politician's position on an issue.

Media malaise A feeling of cynicism and distrust, perhaps even despair, toward government and officials.

Merit system A system of filling government jobs with people who have passed competitive examinations and who are protected from dismissal for partisan reasons.

Minority leader Leader of the minority party in the House.

Miranda rights The requirement that officials must advise suspects of their rights before interrogation. Suspects have the right to remain silent; if they speak, anything they say can be used against them; they have the right to be represented by an attorney; if they can't afford an attorney, one will be appointed for them.

"Mischiefs of faction" James Madison's idea that it is inevitable that groups of citizens seeking some goal contrary to the rights of other citizens or to the well-being of the whole country will threaten the stability of the nation.

Motor voter law Makes voter registration easier by allowing people to register at public offices and drivers' license bureaus.

Muckrakers Progressive Era reformers and journalists who attacked political corruption and tried to break the financial link between business and politicians.

Multiparty systems There are more than two and sometimes many parties that compete for power.

NAACP National Association for the Advancement of Colored People, founded in 1909 to fight for blacks' civil rights.

National committee Members are selected by state party committees or conventions, usually on the basis of service to the party. The national committee chooses the site of the party's national convention and the formula for determining the number of delegates each state sends to it.

National debt The accumulation of money owed by the government from all budget deficits.

Natural rights Inherent, inalienable rights.

"Necessary and proper" See **implied powers clause.**

Neutral competence The assumption that bureaucrats should be uninvolved or neutral in policymaking and chosen only for their expertise in executing policy, and that they should not profit personally from the decisions they make.

New Deal A program to stimulate economic recovery and aid the victims of the Great Depression by regulating many activities of business and labor, setting up a welfare system, and funding and administering programs through federal **grants-in-aid.**

New Deal coalition Composed of city dwellers, blue-collar workers, Catholic and Jewish immigrants, blacks, and southerners, who elected Franklin Roosevelt to an unprecedented four terms as president.

New federalism A term used to describe various proposals to revitalize federalism in the United States, most frequently through strengthening states' ability to act independently of the national government. Both Richard Nixon and Ronald Reagan made such proposals.

Obscenity As defined by the Supreme Court, sexual material that is patently offensive to the average person in the community and that lacks any serious literary, artistic, or scientific value.

Open primary Regardless of party registration, one may vote in either party's primary.

Outsiders Presidential candidates without national political experience.

Oversight Congress's responsibility to make sure the bureaucracy is carrying out the intent of Congress in administering federal programs.

Parliamentary governments Systems in which the executive is chosen by the legislature.

Party identification A psychological link between individuals and a party.

Party in government Those who are appointed or elected to office as members of a political party.

Party in the electorate Those who identify with the party.

Party organization The party "professionals" who run the party at the national, state, and local levels.

Patronage A system under which elected officials appoint their supporters to administrative jobs in order to build their own political strength.

Patronage Giving jobs to party loyalists when the party controls local government.

Personal presidency In return for getting more power and support from us than we give to other parts of government, the president is supposed to make sure we get what we want from government.

Plea bargain An agreement between the prosecutor, the defense attorney, and the defendant, with the explicit or implicit approval of the judge, to reduce the charge or the sentence in exchange for a plea of guilty.

Plessy v. Ferguson In 1896, the Supreme Court allowed separate but equal facilities.

Pluralism A theory that government is responsive to groups of citizens working together to promote their common interests.

Policy implementation The process of bureaucrats converting laws passed by Congress and signed by the president into rules and activities that have an actual impact on people and things.

Political action committee (PAC) A committee that raises money to support a candidate, a political party, or an interest group.

Political action committees (PACs) Organizations that raise money through direct mail and channel it to political candidates.

Political bias More favorable coverage of one politician or one side of an issue than of others.

Political culture A distinctive way of looking at, and participating in, politics.

Political machine A strong party organization that flourished in some large cities in the late nineteenth and early twentieth centuries; it controlled city politics and provided services to party members.

Political socialization The process of learning about politics by being exposed to new information from parents, peers, schools, the media, political leaders, and the community, which are referred to as **agents of political socialization.**

Political tolerance The willingness of individuals to extend procedural rights and liberties to people with whom they disagree.

Politics The competition to shape government's impact on society's problems and goals.

Poll tax A tax required of prospective voters.

Popular sovereignty Rule by the people.

Populism A movement that celebrates "the people" in contrast with the greed and immorality of the powerful.

Pork barrel Special projects, new programs, buildings, or other public works that members of Congress obtain for their districts.

Power to persuade The president's power to gain support for what he wants to do.

Presidential preference primaries Direct primaries. Voters indicate a preference for a presidential candidate, delegates committed to a candidate, or both.

Presidential press conference When the president meets formally with reporters to make a statement or answer questions.

Prior restraint Censorship.

Private interest groups Groups that pursue mostly economic interests that benefit their members.

Professional reputation The president's track record of his effectiveness as a leader.

Progressive reforms Primary elections, voter registration laws, secret ballots, nonpartisan ballots, denial of voting rights for aliens, and the merit system for public employment.

Proportional representation Seats in the national legislature go to political parties roughly according to the proportion of the popular vote the parties' candidates receive.

Public forum Public places, such as streets, sidewalks, and parks, where individuals may express their views on public issues.

Public interest groups Groups that lobby for benefits that cannot be limited or restricted to their members.

Public opinion The collection of individual opinions toward issues or objects of general interest.

Pure speech Speech without any conduct.

Realignment The transition from one stable party system to another.

Reapportionment The process of distributing the 435 seats in Congress among the states based on population changes.

Reciprocity

Reconstruction Between 1865 and 1870, the northern military presence in the South and the close monitoring of southern politics by the national government.

Redistricting The process of redrawing Congressional district boundaries within states as a result of population shifts.

Redlining Lenders refusing to lend money to those who wanted to buy a house in a racially changing neighborhood.

Regulation In general, an action of a regulatory agency, including making rules and adjudicating their enforcement.

Rehnquist Court The Supreme Court during the tenure of Chief Justice William Rehnquist, from 1986 to the present.

Republic A form of government in which people vote for representatives who make decisions for them.

Responsible party government The idea that parties should take clear and contrasting positions on issues and enforce them on their members.

Restrained judges Those who feel the judiciary should be reluctant to overrule the other branches of government.

Restrictive covenants Agreements among whites not to sell their houses to blacks.

Retrospective voting Voting on the basis of a candidate's or party's past performance.

Right to a jury trial Individuals charged with crimes that could result in incarceration of more than six months can choose to be tried by a jury rather than a judge.

Right to counsel Indigent defendants must be given attorneys to represent them.

Right to privacy Reflected in the First, Third, Fourth, and Fifth amendments and in Supreme Court rulings involving birth control, abortion, and the "right to die."

Rules Committee In the House, this committee sets the terms of the debate on a bill by issuing a rule.

Scoop When a reporter gets information before other reporters.

Seditious speech Speech that encourages rebellion against the government.

Selective perception A tendency for people to screen out information that contradicts their beliefs.

Senatorial courtesy The custom of giving senators of the president's party a virtual veto over appointments to jobs, including judicial appointments, in their states.

Seniority rule The basis for selecting chairs in Congress.

Separate-but-equal doctrine Permitted segregated public facilities if they were "equal." in theory, although they did not have to be equal in actuality.

Separation of powers The national government is split into three branches: legislative, executive, and judicial. In the legislative branch, power is split further into two houses.

Setting the agenda How the media influence the process by which problems are considered important and alternative policies are proposed and debated.

Shays's Rebellion In western Massachusetts in 1786–87, a protest by farmers against high state taxes, and foreclosure and jail for those who could not pay.

Single-issue groups Groups that pursue public interest goals but that focus on a single issue and are usually reluctant to compromise.

Single-member districts Only one individual is elected from a district or state, the one who receives the most votes.

Social contract An implied agreement between the people and their government. The people give up part of their liberty to the government; in exchange, the government protects the remainder of their liberty.

Soft money Donors who want to give more than their legal federal maximum can give to national party committees, which channel money to state parties, which spend under less stringent state regulations.

Sound bite An extremely short time in which a politician can emphasize a few key phrases or sentences on television news.

Speaker of the House The presiding officer of the House of Representatives.

Special interest caucuses Groups of members united by some personal interest or characteristic.

Specialization

Speech plus conduct Speech combined with conduct that is intended to convey ideas.

Standing committees Permanent committees in the House and Senate.

Standing to sue When a litigant has lost rights and suffered harm, and thus is allowed access to court to sue.

Stare decisis Latin for "stand by what has been decided"; the idea that judges should follow precedents established by their court or by higher courts in previous cases.

Steering When realtors show black customers only houses in black neighborhoods and show white customers only houses in white neighborhoods.

Straw polls Unscientific polls developed by newspapers in the nineteenth century; the first attempts to measure popular sentiments on a large scale.

Subcommittee bill of rights In Congress, rules changes that reduced the control of the whole committee, especially its chair, over a subcommittee.

Suffrage The right to vote.

Super Tuesday A day when most southern states held primaries simultaneously.

Supremacy clause A provision of the Constitution that says that treaties, the Constitution, and federal laws are to be supreme whenever they conflict with state laws or state actions.

Symbiotic relationship A close relationship between, for example, the media and politicians, in which they use each other for their mutual advantage.

Symbolic speech The use of symbols, rather than words, to convey ideas.

Tax expenditures Income that is exempted from federal taxation.

Teapot Dome scandal In 1921, President Harding's secretary of the interior accepted $400,000 from two corporations that were then allowed to lease oil reserves in California and Wyoming.

Three-fifths Compromise The proposal to count three-fifths of the slaves when counting population to apportion seats in Congress.

Ticket splitting Voting for a member of one party for one office but a member of another party for a different office.

Two-party system Only two major parties control American local, state, and national governments.

Unfunded mandates Federal laws requiring states to do something, usually to regulate something, but without accompanying federal funds.

Unitary system A system in which the national government creates subnational governments and gives them what power it wishes.

Unreasonable searches and seizures Searches by law enforcement officials who do not have a valid search warrant and in circumstances that do not allow an exception to the need for a warrant.

Voting Rights Act Of 1965. The act made it illegal to interfere with anyone's right to vote and suspended the use of literacy tests. It also sent federal registrars into many southern counties to increase black registration.

War Powers Act Passed by Congress in 1973 to limit the president's ability to commit troops to combat.

Warren Court The Supreme Court during the tenure of Chief Justice Earl Warren, from 1953-1969. The Warren Court issued liberal activist rulings in many civil liberties and rights cases.

Washingtonians Members of Congress who vote on a president's proposals, interest group leaders who can mobilize congressional and bureaucratic support, judges who consider challenges to presidential policies, and media leaders who influence public opinion.

Watergate scandal A variety of illegal actions by Nixon administration officials, and a coverup of these actions by

President Nixon himself, stemming from the 1972 presidential campaign. The public reaction led to prosecution of the officials and resignation of the president.

Whips In the House, those who maintain contact with party members, see which way they are leaning on votes, and attempt to gain their support.

Whistleblowers Individual bureaucrats who try to expose mismanagement and abuse of discretion in their agencies.

White primary Blacks in southern states were barred from voting in primary elections.

Winner-take-all See **single-member districts.**

Writ of certiorari Latin for "made more certain"; a petition to the Supreme Court to hear a case.

INDEX

A

ABC, 217
Abolitionist movement, 491
Abortion, 453–456
  controversy over, 121–122
  public opinion on, 79
Abortion Rights Action League, 122
Abscam, 271–272
Accommodations, discrimination in public, 481–482
Acquired immune deficiency syndrome (AIDS), 361–362, 388–389
Activist judges, 413–414
ACT UP (AIDS Coalition to Unleash Power) or Queer Nation, 120, 213
Adams, Abigail, 27
Adams, Brock (D-Wash.), 263
Adams, Charles Francis, 27
Adams, John, 27
  on democracy, 32
  in election of 1796, 144
  in election of 1800, 395
  and the media, 224
  rating of, as president, 336
  view of, on political parties, 143
Adams, John Quincy
  on Andrew Jackson, 144
  in election of 1824, 80
Adams, Sherman, 339
Administrative Procedure Act (APA), 376
Adult socialization as agent of political socialization, 80
Adversarial relationship with media, 221, 224–225
Affirmative action, 498–500, 504. *See also* Civil rights
  opposition to, 501–504
African Americans. *See* Black Americans
Agnew, Spiro, as vice president, 225, 234, 327, 329
Agnostics, 96, 97
Agriculture, private interest groups in, 112–113
Agriculture, U. S. Department of, 378
Aid to Families with Dependent Children (AFDC), 59, 66, 68, 534–535
Alger, Horatio, 404
Amendments, 38, 40. *See also specific number*
American Agriculture Movement (AAM), 113
American Airlines, 128
American Association of Retired Persons (AARP), 108, 109, 115
American Bar Association (ABA), 114
American Civil Liberties Union (ACLU), 120, 125, 405, 409, 438, 444
American College of Physicians, 128
American Conservative Union, 128
American Council of Education, 108
American democracy, contemporary theories of, 15–17
American diversity, 5–10
American Farm Bureau Federation, 107, 113
  private interest groups in, 112–113
American Federation of Labor-Congress of Industrial Organizations (AFL-CIO), 109, 112, 128
American Independent Party, 151
American Indian Movement (AIM), 489
American Know-Nothing party, 151
American Medical Association (AMA), 107, 114
  lobbying by, 269
American Political Science Association, 114–115
American Soybean Growers, 114
Americans with Disabilities Act (ADA), 376
American system, 154
Americorps, 516
Amish and freedom of religion, 440–441
Amnesty International, 116
AMTRAK, 372
Anderson, John, 151
Animal sacrifice and religious liberty, 425–426, 458–459
Anthony, Susan B., 491
Antifederalists, 37–38
Antiwar protest, 128
AP, 217
Appointees, presidential, 341–342
Appropriations, 316
Aristocracies, 14
Aristotle, 10, 14
Armey, Richard, 139
"Arsenio Hall Show," 219
Articles of Confederation, 53
  national government problems, 25–26
  state government problems, 26
Asian-Americans, immigration of, 7
Assimilation of Native Americans, 488
Authorizations, 315

B

Back pocket PACs, 259
Baird, Zoe, 218, 244
Baker, James, 221–222
Baker v. *Carr,* 285
Ballots, long, 379
Barbour, Haley, 258
Baum, Frank, 8
Bazelon, David, 413
Beard, Charles, 36
Beer Drinkers of America, 127
Beer lobby, 127
Bennett, William, 361–362
Bernstein, Carl, 23, 222
Bias of media, 230–239
Biden, Joseph (D-Del.), 326
Bilingual education, 486–487
Bilirakis, Michael, 265
Bill of Rights, 38, 40. *See also amendments in*
  application, 427–428
  origin and meaning, 427
Bills, congressional handling of, 311–314
Bills of attainder, 426
Birth control and privacy rights, 452–453
Black, Hugo, 427, 428, 442
Black Americans
  assimilation of, 7
  political participation by, 15
  racial discrimination against, 467–485
Black Caucus, 310
Black Codes, 468
Black power, 477
Black Power in Congress, 310
Black slaveowners, 469
Blockbusting, 478
Block grants, 61–63
Blow, 126
Boggs, Thomas H., 126
Bork, Robert, 23, 403, 426
Boschwitz, Rudy, 241
Boucher, Frederick, 265
Bradley, Bill, 241
Bradley, Joseph, 495
Branch Dividians, 111
Brandeis, Louis, 413
Breast implants, politics of, 380–381
Brennan, William, 403, 433, 435, 436, 453
Brewer, David, 442
Breyer, Stephen, 405
Brinkley, David, 234
Brokaw, Tom, 238
Brown, Ron, 342
Brownlow Committee, 384
Brown v. *Board of Education,* 472–473, 474, 479
Bryan, William Jennings, 8, 145
Buchanan, James, rating of, as president, 336
Buchanan, Patrick, 11, 371
  in 1996 elections, 161

Budget. *See* Federal budget
Budget and Accounting Act (1921), 343–345, 519
Budget Enforcement Act (1990), 520
Bunning, Jim, 241
Bureaucracy
computers in, 365–366
controlling, 383
Congress, 384–385
courts, 385
interest groups and individuals, 385, 387
president, 383–384
as enemy, 371
expectations about, 378–379
neutral competence, 379–383
responsiveness, 379
goals of, 364
growth of, 17, 367–368
lobbying, 124–125
making policy functions, 373–375
administering, 378
other functions, 378
regulation, 375–376, 378
nature of, 363
openness of, 364–367
public and private, 363–364
reasons for growth of, 368
responsiveness of, 387–388
size of federal, 362
slashing, 366–367
types of
departments, 368–369
government corporations, 372–373
independent agencies, 369, 371
independent regulatory boards and commissions, 371
Bureau of Land Management (BLM), 60
Bureau of the Budget (BOB), 384, 519
creation of, 344–345
Burger, Warren, Supreme Court under, 24, 44, 399, 408, 435, 438, 439, 447, 449, 453, 474, 478, 480, 507
Bush, George, 336
administration of, 50
budget deficit under, 517
bureaucracy under, 382
and child care legislation, 69
and civil rights, 498
court appointments of, 403, 404–405, 407
in election of 1988, 233
in election of 1992, 3–4, 8, 82, 139–140, 219–220, 233, 234
in election of 1994, 74
foreign policy leadership of, 347, 349–350
and Freedom of Information Act, 365
and going public, 337–338
and handgun control, 121
mail received by, 331
and the media, 221, 223, 227–228
military leadership of, 352, 353
party leadership of, 354
persuasive tactics of, 333
and political gridlock, 160
popularity rating of, 338
presidential staff of, 340
professional reputation of, 334, 335
public perception of, 84, 327
response to King case, 85
and symbolic speech, 433
and "thousand points of light" awards, 325
veto use by, 345
and vice presidency, 328, 329
Business, private interest groups in, 109–110, 112
Business Roundtable, 110
Busing, 474–476
Byrd, Robert (D-W. Va.), 308

C

Cable television, expansion of, 217
Calhoun, John, 57
and *McCulloch* v. *Maryland*, 56
Calhoun, John C., 302
California
English as official national language in, 41
Proposition 187 in, 12
Campaign America, 261
Campaign finance laws, 257–258
loopholes in reforms, 258–259
Campaign money system, reforming, 268–271
Candidates
political bias against all, 234
political bias for particular, 232–234
Cannon, Joseph (Il.), 303, 304, 307
Capital punishment, 450–451
Caraway, Hattie (D-Ark.), 289
Cardozo, Benjamin, 415
Career politician, 3
Cargill, 113
Carlin, George, 431
Carswell, Harold, 403
Carter, Billy, 235
Carter, Jimmy, 4
and budget process, 523
and civil rights, 498
court appointments of, 406, 407
in election of 1976, 146, 147, 233, 236–237, 241
in election of 1980, 84, 233
and Freedom of Information Act, 365
and going public, 336
and Iranian hostages, 352
and the media, 240, 241, 242
persuasive ability of, 335
popularity rating of, 338
presidential staff of, 340
professional reputation of, 335
public perception of, 327
reform efforts of, 17
and size of government, 63
and vice presidency, 329
Casework, 291
Catholic groups, 118
Caucuses, 158
CBS, 217
Centers for Disease Control and Prevention, 526
Chamber of Commerce, 110, 130
Checks and balances, 33–34, 43
Cheney, Richard, and campaign finance, 263
Child-care legislation, 69
Children's Defense Fund, 115, 120
Chinese, immigration of, 7
Christian Coalition, 118–119
Chrysler Corp, 128
Cisneros, Henry, 342
Citizens Against Health Rationing, 128
Citizenship for Native Americans, 489
Civil cases, 408
Civil disobedience, 128–129
Civil liberties
in Bill of Rights, 427
public support for, 426
responsiveness of courts in interpreting, 458
Civil rights. *See also* Affirmative action; Race discrimination
definition of, 467
evaluation of efforts in, 504–506
responsiveness of government in granting, 507
Civil Rights Act (1964), 314, 474, 478, 482, 492, 494, 499
Civil Rights Act (1968), 479, 483
Civil Rights Act, 376
Civil rights movement in courts, 471
Civil service, women and minorities in, 374–375
Civil Service Commission, 379–380, 384
Civil Service Reform Act (1978), 384, 387
Civil War, 57–58
Amendments and Reconstruction, 468
Classical democracy, 14–15
Clay, Henry (Ky.), 302
Clean Air Act, 376
Cleveland, Grover, presidential staff of, 339
Clinton, Bill, 148, 150
and budget process, 515–516, 523, 524, 525, 530, 535, 536, 539
bureaucracy under, 382–383
and campaign finance, 258
and civil rights, 498
court appointments of, 404–405, 406
and deficit reduction package, 537
economic policies of, 281–282, 319–320

in election of 1992, 3–4, 8, 18–19, 82, 147, 219–220, 233, 234
in election of 1994, 74
foreign policy leadership of, 347
and Freedom of Information Act, 365
and going public, 336–337
impact of Whitewater, 273
isolation of, 328
leadership style of, 346
mail received by, 331
and the media, 217, 218, 219, 221, 223, 228–229
and nation's concern over crime, 73–74, 99
nomination for Surgeon General by, 325–326, 356–357
party influence over, 155
and political gridlock, 160
poll use by, 82
popularity rating of, 338
populism of, 9
presidential staff of, 340–341
professional reputation of, 334–335
public perception of, 327
reform efforts of, 17
reputation of, 342
Clinton, Hillary Rodham, 124, 148, 218, 341
and Whitewater, 273
Closed primary, 158–159
CNN Microsoft, 217
Coalition building, 127–128
Commercial bias, 234–239
Committee on Economic and Educational Opportunities, 523
Committee on Political Education (COPE), 112
Committee to Reelect the President (CREEP), 23
Common Cause, 108, 120, 125
Communist parties, 107
Comparable worth, 493
Competition, interstate, 65
COMSAT, 372
Confederal systems, 52
Confederate States of America, 57
Conference Committee, 314
Conflicts of interest, 271–272
Congress, U.S. *See also* House of Representatives, U.S.; Senate, U.S.
Black Power in, 310
budget making in, 315–317
bureaucracy under, 384–385
checks of, against courts, 419
committees
chairs, 306
conference, 314
evaluating government, 308–309
membership, 305–306
other, 308
rules, 311–312
standing, 304–305
subcommittees, 306–308
constituencies of, 285, 287–288
C-SPAN coverage of, 217, 229, 282, 299, 317, 383
leaders in, 304
media in, 299–300
members of, 284
opinions and party identification of, 285, 287–288
organization of, 302
evolution of, 302–304
in overseeing Federal bureaucracy, 314–315
in overseeing Pentagon, 316
party influence in voting, 155
public funding for, 270
public position on, 282–284
relationship between media and, 229–230
responsiveness of, 317–319
social characteristics in, 284–285
staff, 309
impact of, 309, 311
types of, 309
and term limits debate, 286–287
voting by members, 300
voting for, 298
women in, 289–290
working privately and "going public," 299
Congressional Budget Office (CBO), 316–317, 519, 520
Congressional Caucus for Women, 289
Congressional election(s), 259–262
advantages of incumbency, 288, 290–292
campaigns, 295
media, 295
money, 295, 298
challengers in, 294–295
in 1994, 8, 74, 139–140, 161, 296–297
Congressional oversight, 314
Connor, Eugene "Bull," 477
Conservative activists, 95, 96
Conservative Christians, 125
Conservatives, 88–89, 95–97
position of, on social issues, 90–91
Constituencies, 285, 287–288
Constituent service, 291–292, 385
Constitution, United States. *See also specific amendments*
bases of federalism in, 53–55
brevity of, 42–43
changing
by constitutional amendment, 38, 40
by judicial interpretation, 40
by political practice, 40
features of, 31–34
full faith and credit clause, 65
implied powers clause, 54, 57
individual rights in, 426
motives of founders in, 34–36
popularity of, 42
ratification of, 36–38
responsiveness of, 40, 42–44
role of Supreme Court in interpreting, 411–413
supremacy clause, 54
Constitutional Amendment, balancing budget by, 532–533
Constitutional Convention
conflict at, 29–31
consensus at, 29
predicament, 28–29
setting for, 26, 28
Consumer groups, 116–117
Consumer Products Safety Commission, 315, 384
Continental Congress, 25
"Contract with America," 65, 66, 84, 121, 139–140, 161, 286, 330, 335, 339, 410
Conventions, 158
Conviction, court reversal of, 448
Coolidge, Calvin
rating of, as president, 336
as symbolic leader, 354
Cooperation, voluntary, 65
Cooperative federalism, 55
Corporate lobbies, 114
Corruption and scandal
Iran-contra, 222–223, 315, 348–349
Teapot Dome, 256
Watergate, 23–24, 44–45, 76, 146, 340
Whitewater, 273
Costs, shifting, 536–537
Coughlin, Charles, 11
Counsel, right to, 448
Court-packing plan of Franklin Delano Roosevelt, 397–398
Courts. *See also* Judges
and bureaucracy, 385
deciding, 411–415
development of role in government, 394–399
in interpreting civil liberties, 458
jurisdiction of, 400
lobbying, 125
political checks against, 418–419
power of, 415, 418–419
responsiveness of, 419, 458
structure of, 399–400
Courts of appeals, 400
Coverdell, Paul, 120
Cox, Archibald, 23
Crack, 506
Craig, Larry (R-Idaho), 290–291
Cranston, Alan (D-Cal.), and savings and loan crisis, 274
Crawford, William H., in election of 1824, 80
Creationism, 445
Crime, public concerns over, 73–74, 99

Criminal cases, 408
Criminal defendants, rights of, 446–449, 451–452
Cronkite, Walter, 230
  and the media, 240
Crow, Jim, laws, 468–469, 481
Cruel and unusual punishment, 449, 451–452
Cruzan, Nancy, 457–458
C-SPAN, 217, 229, 282, 299, 317, 383
"Current Affair, A," 219

D

Dale, Robert (R-Kan.), 261
Daley, Richard, 158
D'Amato, Alfonse (R-N.Y.), 290, 292
"Daughters of liberty," 27
Daylight Saving Time Coalition, 127
Dealignment, 148
Deaver, Michael, 226, 238, 272, 342
Debates, media commentary about, 242–243
Debs, Eugene, 429
Declaration of Independence, 13, 25, 467
DeConcini, Dennis (D-Ariz), 266
  moral dilemma of, over savings and loan crisis, 253–254, 274–276
De facto segregation, 474, 479, 486
Defense, U.S. Department of, 369
  spending by, 527
Deficit
  causes of, 527
  dealing with, 531–533
De jure segregation, 479, 486
DeLay, Tom, 139
Delegated legislative authority, 373
Democracy, 10
  characteristics of, 12–14
  classical, 14–15
  contemporary theories of Americans, 15–17
  defined, 12
  direct, 14
  distinguishing between republic and, 32
  indirect, 14
  problems with, 4–5
Democratic party, 141
  characteristics of, 153
  dominance of, 145–146
  in 1990s, 148, 149
  rise of, 144
Denial of the right to vote, 470
Desegregation
  of employment, 478
  of housing, 478–479
  of public accommodations, 478
  of schools, 471–474
De Tocqueville, Alexis, 13, 284
Die, right to, 457–458
Direct democracy, 14
Direct lobbying techniques, 123–125
Direct primary, 158
Direct spending, 521–522
Discretionary spending, 522
Discrimination. *See* Race discrimination
District courts, 400
Diversity and public interest, 9–10
Divided government, 160
Dole, Robert (R-Kans), 356, 516
  and campaign finance, 270
  in election of 1996, 83, 161
  as majority leader, 356, 516
  and pork barrel politics, 291
  and symbolic speech, 433
Domestic Council, 345
Donaldson, Sam, 220, 225
Douglas, William, 393, 415, 420, 429, 430, 452
Dowagers, 95, 96
Dred Scott case, 467–468
Dual federalism, 55, 57
DuBois, W. E. B., 471
Dukakis, Michael, 236

E

Early Money Is Like Yeast (EMILY), 118, 260
Earmarking, 291
Earth First, 120
Economic Interpretation of Constitution, An (Beard), 36
Economy
  diversity of, 8–10
  security and party realignment, 147
Education
  bilingual, 486–487
  desegregation of schools, 471–474
  discrimination in, 479–480
    against Hispanics, 486–487
  schools as agents of political socialization, 77–78
  unequal funding of, 480–481
Education, U.S. Department of, 367
Education Amendments (1972), 494
Eighth Amendment, 40, 428, 449, 451–452
  civil liberties in, 427
Einstein, Albert, 386
Eisenhower, Dwight D., 146, 398
  and abortion, 418
  administration of, 24
  and civil rights, 43, 472, 473
  court appointments of, 408
  foreign policy leadership of, 347
  professional reputation of, 335
  rating of, as president, 336
  and size of government, 59
  and Supreme Court, 429
  veto use by, 345
Elderly, private interest groups of, 115
Elders, Joycelyn, 325, 326
Election(s). *See also* Congressional election(s)
  of 1796, 44
  of 1800, 395
  of 1824, 80
  of 1876, 468
  of 1896, 256
  of 1912, 18
  of 1928, 8
  of 1936, 81
  of 1964, 234, 466
  of 1968, 263
  of 1972, 23–24
  of 1976, 146, 147, 233, 236–237, 241
  of 1980, 84, 233
  of 1984, 84
  of 1988, 221–222, 233, 236
  of 1992, 3–4, 8, 18–19, 43–44, 82, 139–140, 218, 219–220, 233, 234, 237
  of 1996, 19, 44, 83, 161
  media impact on, 240–243
  presidential, 259
  role of money in campaigns, 256–262
Electoral College, 33, 40
Electorate of 1990s, 148
Electronic surveillance, 447
Elitism, 16
Ellison, William, 469
Ellsberg, Daniel, 434
Emerson, Ralph Waldo, 433
Employment
  desegregation of, 478
  discrimination in, 482–483
Energy, U.S. Department of, 367
English, making official national language, 41–42
English First, 41
Entitlements, 522, 528–529
Environmental Defense Fund, 267
Environmental groups, 120
Environmental Protection Agency (EPA), 315, 367, 376, 384, 522
Equal Credit Opportunity Act (1974), 494
Equal Employment Opportunity Commission (EEOC), 367, 373
Equal Pay Act (1963), 493
Equal protection clause, 468
Equal Rights Amendment, 491–492
Ervin, Sam, 298
Espionage Act (1917), 429
ESPN, 220
Espy, Mike, 326, 342
Establishment clause, 442
  and teaching of evolution, 445
Ethics in Government Act (1978), 272, 382–383
Ethnic conservatives, 95, 96
Ethnic diversity, 5–8
Evolution, teaching of, 445
Exclusionary rule, 446–447
Executive leadership, 383–384

Executive Office of the President (EOP), 384
growth of, 341
Executive orders, 346
Executive privilege, 24, 44–45
Expertise, providing, 123
Ex post facto laws, 426

■ F

Fair Government Foundation, 120
Fairness & Accuracy in Reporting (FAIR), 232
Falwell, Jerry, 125, 148
Family as agent of political socialization, 76–77
Farmers, conflict with federal government, 60
Farrakhan, Louis, 148
Faster, Vincent, alleged suicide of, 273
Federal budget. *See also* Spending
balancing, by Constitutional Amendment, 532–533
compromise on, 515–516, 539
Congressional role in making, 315–317
evolution of, 517–520
issues in, 524–537
limits on, 521–522
operation of current, 522–524
as politics, 537–538
presidential role in making, 343–345
purposes of, 520–521
responsiveness of government in, 538–539
size of, 524–527
structural changes in, 534
Federal Bureau of Investigation (FBI), 522
and Freedom of Information Act, 365
under J. Edgar Hoover, 386
Federal Communications Commission (FCC), 371, 376, 385
Federal Corrupt Practices Act (1925), 256
Federal Election Campaign Act (1974), 257
as unconstitutional, 258
Federal government, conflict with Western farmers, 60
Federal grants to states, 64
Federal Housing Authority (FHA), 479
Federalism, 32, 43, 51
constitutional bases of, 53–55
contemporary, 63–65, 67–68
cooperative, 55
dual, 55, 57
and growth of government, 55–63
nation-centered, 54
new, 60–63
political bases of, 52–53
responsiveness of, 68–69
state-centered, 54–55
Federalist Papers, 39, 350, 394, 412–413
Federalists, 37, 38
Federal Register, 376
Federal Reserve Board, 384
Federal-state relations, 63–64
Federal systems, 51
Federal Trade Commission (FTC), 384–385
Fifteenth Amendment, 40, 468, 491
Fifth Amendment, 40, 411, 447
civil liberties in, 427
Filibuster, 313–314
Fillmore, Millard, rating of, as president, 336
Fireside chats, 226
First Amendment, 38, 412
civil liberties in, 427
press freedom in, 433–435
religious freedom in, 440–446
speech freedoms in, 381, 428–433, 438–440
and libel, 435–438
and obscenity, 438–440
Fitzgerald, Ernest, 387
Flag as symbolic speech, 432–433
Flowers, Gennifer, 217, 219
Focus groups, 86
Foley, Thomas (D-Wash.), 297
Food and Drug Administration (FDA), 365, 366, 376, 381–382
Forbes, Steve, 19, 82
in 1996 elections, 83, 161
Ford, Gerald, 435
assumption of presidency, 45
in election of 1976, 233
and the media, 435
pardoning of Nixon by, 45
persuasive tactics of, 333
presidential staff of, 340
professional reputation of, 335
public perception of, 327
and selection of judges, 400
as symbolic leader, 354
and vice presidency, 327, 329
Foreign governments, private interest groups for, 115–116
Fortas, Abe, 432
Foster, Henry W., Jr., 325–326, 356–357
Foster, Vince, apparent suicide of, 220
Fourteenth Amendment, 40, 411, 413, 468, 469, 491
equal protection clause of, 495
Fourth Amendment, 40, 412, 447
civil liberties in, 427
Fragmentation, 150
Franking, 290
Franklin, Benjamin, 32
as delegate to Continental Congress, 28, 29, 30–31
and selection of judges, 400
Freedom of Information Act (1966), 365
Free exercise clause, 440
Freemen, 111
Friedan, Betty, 492
Fringe media, rise of, 225
Fulbright, J. William, 93
Full faith and credit clause, 65
Fund-raising, 292

■ G

Gallup, George, 82
Game orientation, 236
Gandhi, Mahatma, 476
Gardner, John, 120
Garfield, James, assassination of, 328
Garn, Jake (R-Utah), moral dilemmas of, over savings and loan crisis, 254
Garner, John Nance, and vice presidency, 329
Gay Men's Health Crisis, 120
Gay rights organizations, 119–120
General revenue sharing, 61
General Services Administration, 369, 371
Gephardt, Richard (D-Mo.), 261
Gerry, Elbridge, on Constitution, 36
Gerrymander, 285
Gideon, Earl, 448
Gingrich, Newt (R-Ga.)
media coverage of, 229–230
and PACS, 259, 261
as populist, 9
and Republican contract, 139–140, 161
as speaker, 268, 296, 299, 304, 306, 307, 515
and teledomocracy, 85
Ginsburg, Ruth Bader, 404–405
Gladstone, William, 31
Glenn, John (D-Ohio), 241, 259, 263
and savings and loan crisis, 274
Going public, 299, 335–338
Goldberg, Arthur, 431
Goldwater, Barry, 147, 348–349
in election of 1964, 234, 466
Goodsell, Charles, 388
GOPAC, 261, 307
Gore, Al
and campaign finance, 258
as Vice President, 304, 329, 366
Government
proper role of, 89–90
responsiveness of, 17–18
in budgeting, 538–539
in civil rights, 507
and interest groups, 132–133
on money, 272–274
and political parties, 160–161
to public opinion, 98–99
spending, 527–530
Government corporations, 372–373
Gramm, Phil (R-Tex.), 261, 356
Gramm-Rudman-Hollings Act, 317, 520, 539
Grandy, Fred, 241

Grant, Ulysses S.
  rating of, as president, 336
  reputation of, 255, 342
Grants-in-aid, 58
Grassley, Charles (R-Iowa), 290
Grassroots lobbying, 125–127
Gray, Edward, 274
Gray lobby, 115
Great Compromise, 29
Great Depression, 58
Great Migration, 470
Great Society, 59
Greenpeace, 120, 128
Greenspan, Alan, and Keating's trial, 276
Greider, William, 221
Gridlock, 17, 18, 43, 160
Gross Domestic Product, 530
Group organizers, role in group formation, 107–108
Guinier, Lani, 325, 326

■ H

Habeas corpus, 400
Haldeman, H. R., 339–340
Hamer, Fannie Lou, 465–466, 508
Hamilton, Alexander, 144, 350, 394, 530
  as author of *Federalist Papers*, 39, 350, 394, 395
  on Constitution, 36
  as delegate to Continental Congress, 28, 29
  as secretary of treasury, 144, 530
Handgun control, 120
Hanna, Mark, 256
Harding, Warren
  rating of, as president, 336
  reputation of, 342
  and Teapot Dome scandal, 256
Harkin, Tom (D-Iowa), 295
Harlan, John, 431, 470
Harris, Teresa, 497
Harrison, William Henry, 336
  death of, in office, 327
Hatch Act (1939), 381
Hate speech, 436–437
Hatfield, Mark (R-Ore.), 343
Hayes, Rutherford, in election of 1876, 468
Health and Human Services, U.S. Department of, 376, 384
Hearings, testifying at, 123–124
Helms, Jesse, 241, 501
Hemingway, Ernest, 386
Henry, Patrick, as delegate to Continental Congress, 28
Henry, Prince (Prussia), 26
Hill, Anita, sexual harassment charges of, 222, 281, 404–405, 496, 497
Hirohito, 353
Hispanic Americans
  discrimination against, 485–486, 506, 507
    combating, 487–488
    in education, 486–487
  immigration of, 7
  political participation by, 15
Holmes, Oliver Wendell, 408, 415, 432
Homosexuality
  media recognition of, for public officials, 213–214, 245–246
  and right to privacy, 456–457
Hoover, Herbert, mail received by, 331
Hoover, J. Edgar, 386
House Judiciary Committee, 327
House of Representatives, U.S. *See also* Congress, U.S.; Senate, U.S.
  debate in, 313
  informal norms in, 298–299
  and separation of power, 33
Housing
  desegregation of, 478–479
  discrimination in, 483–484
Housing, U.S. Department of, 367
Hruska, Roman (R-Neb.), 403
Hudson, Rock, 361
Huffington, Michael (R-Cal.), 264
Hughes, Charles Evans, as Chief Justice, 398, 416
Humphrey, Hubert, 466
  in election of 1968, 263
Hyperpluralism, 17

■ I

Ideology, 88–89
  influence of, on congressional voting, 301
Immigration
  of Africans, 5, 7
  beliefs on, 11
  controlling, 11–12
  and English as official national language, 41–42
  major waves of, 5–6
  numbers in, 6, 11
  problem of illegal, 6
Impeachment, 327
  charges against Nixon, 24
Implied powers clause, 54
Income tax rates, 530–531
Incumbency, advantages of, 288, 290–292
Incumbents, media attention for, 290–291
Independence Hall, 28
Independent Action PAC (IAPAC), 267
Independent agencies, 369, 371
Independent regulatory boards and commission, 371–372
Independent spending, 257
Independent spending loophole, 258–259
Indian Affairs, Bureau of (BIA), 489
Indian Removal Act (1830), 488
Indian Self-Determination Act (1975), 489
Indirect democracy, 14
Indirect lobbying techniques, 125–128
Individual, value of, in democracy, 12–13
Influence peddling, 272
Informal norms, 298–299
Institutional loyalty, 298
Institutions, political bias for established, 231–232
Interest, on national debt, 529
Interest groups, 106, 302. *See also* Lobbying; Political action committees (PAC)
  and budget process, 538
  and court cases, 409
  formation of, 106–107, 106–108
    decline of members in, 109
    identifying members, 108–109
  and individuals and bureaucracy, 385, 387
  reasons for joining, 108
  and responsiveness of government, 132–133
  success of, 129–132
  tactics of, 123–129
  types of
    private, 109–110, 112–116
    public, 116–123
Interfaith Alliance, 119
Internal Revenue Service (IRS), 373, 384
Interstate Commerce Commission (ICC), 376, 380–381, 385
Interstate competition, 65
Interstate relations, 65, 67
Iran-contra affair, 315, 348–349
  media coverage of, 222–223

■ J

Jackson, Andrew
  appointment of Taney by, 397
  in election of 1824, 80
  in election of 1828, 8
  kitchen cabinet of, 341
  and the media, 224, 241
  patronage under, 379
  power of, as president, 328
  rating of, as president, 336
Jackson, Jesse, 49, 310
  populism of, 9
Jacksonian Democrats, 142, 144
Japanese Americans, treatment of, in World War II, 393–394, 420
Jaworski, Leon, 24
Jay, John, as author of *Federalist Papers*, 39
Jefferson, Thomas, 27, 33, 330
  as author of Declaration of Independence, 467
  and discrimination against women, 490
  in election of 1796, 144
  in election of 1800, 395
  and freedom of religion, 440
  and judicial review, 395, 396
  and the media, 241
  military leadership of, 350
  rating of, as president, 330, 336
  and separation of church and state, 442

Jeffersonian Republicans, 144
Jewish groups, 118
Johnson, Andrew
impeachment proceedings against, 327
rating of, as president, 336
Johnson, Frank, 413
Johnson, J. Bennett, 333
Johnson, Lyndon B.
bureaucracy under, 387–388
and civil rights, 478
court appointments of, 403
effectivenss of, 333
in election of 1964, 466
foreign policy leadership of, 347
and Great Society, 59
leadership style of, 346, 355
and the media, 220–221, 243
military leadership of, 351–352
persuasive ability of, 335
professional reputation of, 335
public perception of, 326
Johnson, Nancy (R-Conn.), 289
Jordan, Hamilton, 4
Judges. *See also* Courts
activist, 413–414
criteria used in selection, 402–405
independence of, 408
mechanics of selection, 401
qualifications of, 407–408
restrained, 413–414
selection of, 400, 406–407
tenure of, 407
women as, 402
Judicial interpretation in changing Constitution, 40
Judicial review, 395, 415, 418
Judiciary Act (1789), 396, 400
Judiciary Committee, 401
Jury trial, right to, 448–449
Justice, U.S. Department of, 369

K

Kasich, John, 515–516, 539
Kassebaum, Nancy, 326, 356
Keating, Charles, 238–239, 253–254, 266
Kemp, Jack, 241
and campaign finance, 263
Kennedy, Anthony, 425, 433, 493
Kennedy, John F., 148
assassination of, 327, 331
and civil rights, 473, 478
foreign policy leadership of, 347
and the media, 223, 225, 242
presidential staff of, 339
professional reputation of, 335
public perception of, 326
and senatorial courtesy, 401
use of polls by, 82
Kennedy, Justice, 443–444
Kerner Commission, 506
Kerrey, Bob (D.-Neb.), 236, 535
King, Martin Luther, Jr., 105, 130, 131, 386, 476, 477, 480
King, Rodney, 85, 506
Know-Nothings, 6
Kohl, Herbert, 150
Koop, C. Everett, 361, 388
Korematsu v. *United States*, 393–394, 420
Ku Klux Klan, 430, 471

L

Labor, private interest groups in, 112
Labor, U.S. Department of, 376
Landon, Alfred, in election of 1936, 81
"Larry King Live," 3, 219
Laws
development of, to regulate money and politics, 255–256
role of Supreme Court in making, 415
Leadership Conference on Civil Rights, 128
League of Women Voters, 120, 128
Leaks to media, 221–222
Legislative oversight, 385
Legislative veto, 314–315
Legislature. *See* Congress, U.S.
Lennon, John, 386
Lewis, Anthony, 517
Libel, 435–438
Liberal activists, 96
Liberals, 88–89, 95–97
on social issues, 90–91
Liebeck, Stella, 410
Limbaugh, Rush, 148, 218, 220
Limited government, 35
Lincoln, Abraham, 14, 144
and the media, 241
military leadership of, 350, 352
persuasive ability of, 335
power of, as president, 328, 330
presidential staff of, 339
rating of, as president, 336
as symbolic leader, 354
Line-item veto, 342–343, 534
Lippman, Walter, 271
Literary Digest, 81, 82
Little Rock, Arkansas, desegregation of schools in, 473
Lobbying, 106. *See also* Political action committees (PACs)
states and localities in, 64–65
ten commandments of, 124
Localities as lobbyists, 64–65
Locke, John, 35
Logrolling, 298
Long ballots, 379
Los Angeles Times, 216
Lott, Trent (R-Miss.), 333
Lowi, Theodore, 330, 332
Lugar, Richard, 539
Lynching, 470–471

M

Machine politician, 157
Madison, James, 133, 271
as author of *Federalist Papers*, 39, 255, 742–413
on Constitution, 13, 36, 427
as delegate to Continental Congress, 28–29
on interest groups, 106
on political parties, 143, 144
and separation of church and state, 442
on separation of power, 32–33
Majority leader, 304
Majority rule in democracy, 14
Mandates, unfunded, 65
Mandatory spending, 521–522
Mapplethorpe, Robert, 438
Mapp v. *Ohio*, 446–447
Marbury, William, 395–396
Marbury v. *Madison*, 395
Margolies-Mezvinsky, Marjorie (D-Pa.), 281–282, 319–320
Market share, 130
Markup sessions, 305
Marshall, John, as Chief Justice, 56–57, 395–397, 413
Marshall, Thomas R., and vice presidency, 329
Marshall, Thurgood, 403, 416, 471, 473, 474
Mass media as agent of political socialization, 80
Mathematical principles of probability, application of, in development of scientific polling, 81–82
Mayflower Compact, 24, 31
McCain, John (R-Ariz.), 254
and savings and loan crisis, 274
McCarthy, Joseph, 213–214, 429
McCarthyism, 429
McCorvey, Norma, 453, 456
McCulloch v. *Maryland*, 56–57, 397
McDougal, James, 273
McFarlane, Robert, 348
McLarty, Thomas, 340
McMillen, Tom, 241
McNamara, Robert, 434
Media. *See also* Press
atomization of, 217, 219–220
attention for incumbents, 290–291
and bias of, 230–239
concentration of, 216–217
in congressional campaigns, 295
coverage of homosexuality by, 213–214, 245–246
events, 223–224
impact of, on politics, 239–243
public exposure to, 215
relations between House of Representatives and, 299–300
and relationship
with Abraham Lincoln, 241
with Andrew Jackson, 224, 241

with Bill Clinton, 217, 219, 221, 223, 228–229
with Congress, 229–230
with Franklin Roosevelt, 223, 225–226, 242
with George Bush, 221, 223, 227–228
with George Washington, 224, 241
with Harry Truman, 242
with Jimmy Carter, 240, 241, 242
with John Adams, 224
with John F. Kennedy, 223, 225, 242
with Lyndon Johnson, 220–221, 243
with Richard Nixon, 221, 225
with Ronald Reagan, 224, 225, 226–227, 242
with Thomas Jefferson, 241
with Walter Cronkite, 240
relationship between politicians and, 220–230
responsiveness of, 243–245
roles of, 215–216
and talk radio, 218–219
Media malaise, 240
Medicare, 528, 535
and federal budget, 515–516
Meese, Edwin, 342, 348
Melting pot, efficiency of, 7
Membership committee, 305–306
Men, sexual discrimination against, 498
Meredith, James, 473
Merit system, 380
Mfume, Kweisi, 105–106, 133
Military, president's role as leader of, 350–353
Minorities
in civil service, 374–375
rights in democracy, 14
Minority leader, 304
Minority whips, 304
Miranda rights, 448
Miranda v. *Arizona*, 447
Mississippi Freedom Democratic Party (MFDP), 465–466, 508
Moderation, 150–151
Monarchies, 14
Mondale, Walter
in election of 1984, 84
media coverage of, 242–243
and vice presidency, 329
Money
as corrupting influence on politics, 254–255
development of laws to regulate, 255–256
in creating conflict of interest, 271–272
in election campaigns, 256–266, 268, 295, 298
giving, 124
in Nineteenth-Century American politics, 255–256
and responsiveness of government, 272–274
soft, 258
Monroe, James, 328
Montesquieu, Charles de, 35
Montgomery bus boycott, 130–131
Mormons and freedom of religion, 440
Morris, Gouverneur, as delegate to Continental Congress, 30
MTV, 217
Muckrakers, 256
Mudd, Roger, 235
Multiparty systems, 150
Multiple-issue groups, 116–120
"Murphy Brown," 237
Mutual Network, 217

N

Nader, Ralph, 116, 409
"Nader's Raiders," 117
Nagle, David, 539
Nashville Network, 220
National Aeronautics and Space Administration (NASA), 369, 371, 527
National Association for the Advancement of Colored People (NAACP), 107, 125, 130, 409, 416, 471
Kweisi Mfume as leader of, 105–106, 133
National Association of Evangelicals, 118
National Association of Manufacturers, 110
National Audubon Society, 120
National committee, 156
National Council of Churches, 118
National Council of Senior Citizens, 108
National Council to Control Handguns, 131
National debt, interest on, 529
National Disease Control Center, 64
National dominance, 397
National Economic Council, 345
National Education Association, 114
National Farmers' Union, 113
National Federation of Independent Business, 110, 125
National Funeral Directors and Morticians Association, 128
National Governors Association, 108
National Highway Traffic Safety Administration, 124
Nationalist period, 56–57
National Labor Relations Board (NLRB), 112, 372, 385
National Organization for Women (NOW), 109, 117–118, 492
National Rifle Association (NRA), 108, 120, 125
National Right to Life Committee, 121
National Small Business Association, 112
National Taxpayers Union, 116
National Women's Political Caucus, 118
Nation-centered federalism, 54
Native Americans, 5, 6
discrimination against, 488, 506, 507
assimilation, 488
citizenship, 489
government policy toward, 488–490
separation, 488
tribal restoration, 489–490
and freedom of religion, 441
Naturalist Society, 108
Natural Resources Defense Council, 120
Natural rights, 35
NBC, 217
Necessary and proper clause, 54
Neustadt, Richard, 333
Neutral competence, 379–383, 388–389
New Deal, 58–59
legislation in, 61
New Deal coalition, 146
New Jersey Plan, 29
New Populism, 8–9, 111, 296–297
and controlling immigration, 11–12
Newsmagazine shows, 217
Newspapers, 215
trends in, 216
Newsweek, 217
Newsweeklies, 215
Newton, Isaac, 35
New York Times, 215, 216, 230
political bias of, 232, 233
New York Times v. *Sullivan*, 435–436
Nicaraguan contras, 315
"Nightline," 232
Nineteenth Amendment, 40, 491
Ninth Amendment, 40, 427
Nixon, Richard, 234
and civil rights, 474
court appointments of, 403
in election of 1968, 263
in election of 1972, 23–24
and executive privilege, 44–45
and going public, 337
impeachment proceedings against, 327
leadership style of, 355
and the media, 221, 225
military leadership of, 351–352
new federation under, 61–62
and Office of Management and Budget, 519
party leadership of, 354
persuasive tactics of, 333, 335
poll use by, 82
presidential power of, 332
presidential staff of, 339
public perception of, 326
rating of, as president, 336
reputation of, 342

resignation of, 45
as symbolic leader, 354
Nominating process
caucuses, 158
conventions, 158
primaries, 158–160
Noriega, Manuel, 227
Norris, Frank, 8
North, Oliver (R-Va.), 148, 222, 264, 315, 342, 348–349
North, segregation in, 470
North American Free Trade Agreement (NAFTA), 112, 115–116, 150, 336
Nuclear Regulatory Commission, 385
Nudists, 108

■ O

Obscenity, 438–440
Occupational Safety and Health Administration (OSHA), 367, 376, 384, 441
O'Connor, Sandra Day, 402, 403, 445, 455, 497
Octopus, The (Norris), 8
Offensive language, Supreme Court on, 431
Office of Management and Budget (OMB), 341, 345, 519, 520, 523
O'Neill, Tip, 254, 299
Open primary, 159
Operation Desert Shield, 348
Operation Desert Storm, 348
Operation Rescue, 121
Outsiders, 336
Oversight, congressional, 314

■ P

Packwood, Bob, 496
Panama, media coverage of invasion of, 227
Panetta, Leon, 123, 341, 516
Parks, Rosa, 130, 131, 405, 476
Parliamentary governments, 344
Party identification, 153
Party in electorate, 153
Party in government, 141, 153–155
Party in the electorate, 141
Party organization, 141
Paterson, William, as delegate to Continental Congress, 29
Patronage, 158, 379
Patton, 126
Paxon, Bill, 139
Peers as agent of political socialization, 78–79
Pendleton Act, 380
Pentagon, overseeing, 316
Pentagon Papers, 434
Perception, selective, 242
Perot, H. Ross, 259, 371
in election of 1992, 3–4, 18–19, 82, 151, 152, 153, 219–220, 233
in election of 1994, 84
in election of 1996, 19
and federal deficit, 517
populism of, 9
Persian-Gulf War, media coverage of, 216, 227, 232
Personal contacts, making, 123
Personal presidency, 330–332
Pharmaceutical Manufacturers Association, 125
"Phil Donahue Show," 219
Phillips Petroleum, 132
Pichardo, Ernesto, 425
Pierce, Franklin, rating of, as president, 336
Planned Parenthood League, 122, 409
Planned Parenthood of Southeastern Pennsylvania v. *Casey*, 454
Plea bargain, 452
Plessy v. *Ferguson*, 469–470
Plunkitt, George Washington, 257
Pluralism, 15–16
Pocket veto, 345
Poindexter, John, 342, 348–349
Policy implementation, 373
Political action committees (PACs). *See also* Interest groups; Lobbying
back pocket, 259
for business, 258
and campaign contributions, 124, 128, 149
and congressional elections, 259–260
for labor groups, 256, 258
for trade, 258
Political bias, 231
Political campaigns
media concerns on candidates, 241–242
media coverage of, 242–243
Political cultures
individualistic, 52
moralistic, 52
traditionalistic, 52
Political equality in democracy, 13–14
Political machine, 158
Political magazines, 215
Political participation, reasons for lack of, 15
Political parties. *See also specific*
characteristics of, 149–153
definition of, 141–142
development and changes in, 142–149
and government responsiveness, 160–161
identification of, in Congress, 285
media impact on, 240–243
nominating process, 158–160
organization of, 155–158
president as leader of, 354–355
today, 149
and voting by members, 301
Political practice in changing Constitution, 40
Political socialization
agents of, 75
adult, 80
family, 76–77
mass media, 80
peers, 78–79
school, 77–78
impact of, 80
Political tolerance in public tolerance, 93–94
Politicians, relationship between media and, 220–230
Politics
budgeting as, 537–538
defined, 9
impact of media on, 239–243
money as corrupting influence on, 254–255
development of laws to regulate, 255–256
and polls, 82–85, 87
role of money in creating conflict of interest, 271–272
Popular sovereignty, 14
Populist movement of late 1800s, 8–9
Populist party, 151
Populist traditionalists, 95, 96
Pork barrel politics, 291, 292, 343
Powell, Colin, 124, 148
Powell, Lewis F.
as Justice, 456
Prayer in public schools, 442–443
Precedents, role of Supreme Court in following, 414–415
Pre-Civil War period, 57
Presidency. *See also presidents by name*
growth of modern
development of personal, 330–332
before New Deal, 328, 330
responsiveness of, 355–356
Presidential abuse of power, 348–349
Presidential action and congressional response, 314
Presidential administrative appointments, 383
Presidential elections, 259
Presidential job description
qualifications, 327
rewards, 328
succession, 327–328
tenure, 327
Presidential power, 332–333
limits of, 338–339
persuading public, 335

persuading Washingtonians, 333–335
popularity, 338
Presidential press conference, 223
Presidential staff, growth of, 339–341
Presidential Succession Act (1947), 327
Presidents. *See also presidents by name*
in administrative leadership, 341
in appointing officials, 341–342
budget making role of, 343–345
bureaucracy under, 383–384
checks of against courts, 418–419
in domestic policy leadership, 345–346
in foreign policy leadership, 346–350
influence of, on congressional voting, 301–302
in military leadership, 350–353
in party leadership, 354–355
rating of, 336
in removing officials, 343
in reorganizing executive agencies, 345
responsiveness of, 355–356
in symbolic leadership, 353–354
Press. *See also* Media
freedom of, 433–435
Press conference, presidential, 223
Primaries, 158–160
Prime ministers, 344
Prior restraint, 433–434
Privacy
invasion of, 435
right to, 452–458
Private bureaucracies, 363–364
Private interest groups, 109–110, 112–116
Pro-choice groups, 456
Professionals
private interest groups of, 114–115
reputation of, 333–334
Progressives, 145
Pro-life groups, 455
Proportional representation, 150
Protest, 128–129
PTA, 109
Public accommodations, discrimination in, 478, 481–482
Public Affairs Act (1975), 87
Public agenda,
media impact on, 239
Public bureaucracies, 363–364
Public Citizen, 117
Public forum, 430–431
Public interest
and diversity, 9–10
groups, 116–123
Public opinion
on abortion, 79
definition of, 74
formation of, 75–80
ideology in, 88–89
information in, 87–88
measuring, 80–85, 87
media impact on, 240
molding, 127
nature of, 74
race, 91–93
responsiveness of government to, 98–99
social issues in, 90–91
social welfare and proper role of government in, 89–90
trust in government in, 94, 97–98
Public opinion polls
and politics, 82–85, 87
problems in designing questions for, 81
Public tolerance, political tolerance in, 93–94
Pure speech, 431
Push poll, 83

■ Q

Quayle, Dan, 237
and campaign finance, 263

■ R

Race
and party realignment, 147
in public opinion, 91–93
Race discrimination. *See also* Civil rights
and Civil War amendments and reconstruction, 468
in Congress
desegregation of employment, 478
desegregation of housing, 478–479
desegregation of public accommodations, 478
restoration of right to vote, 479
continuing, 479
denial of right to vote, 470
in education, 479–480
in employment, 482–483
against Hispanics, 485–486
combating, 487–488
in education, 486–487
in housing, 483–484
against Native Americans, 488
assimilation, 488
citizenship, 489
government policy toward, 488–490
separation, 488
tribal restoration, 489–490
in other ways, 484–485
overcoming, 471–479
busing, 474–476
desegregation of schools, 471–474
NAACP, 471
in public accommodations, 481–482
second-generation, 481
segregation, 468
in the North, 470
in the South, 468–470
and slavery, 467–468
in the streets, 476–477
violence, 470–471
Racial riots, Kerner Commission on, 506
Radio, 215
contribution to spread presidential power, 331
talk, 218–219
Radio stations, trends in, 216
Randolph, Edmund, 25
as delegate to Continental Congress, 29
Rankin, Jeannette, 289
Reagan, Ronald, 4, 148
administration of, 49
and balancing budget, 532
budget of, 523
and budget process, 530–531
bureaucracy under, 368
court appointments of, 402–403, 406, 407
and Freedom of Information Act, 365
and going public, 336, 337
and Iran-contra affair, 348–349
leadership style of, 346
and the media, 221, 224, 225, 226–227, 242, 299
military leadership of, 353
new federation under, 61–62
party leadership of, 354
persuasive tactics of, 333, 335
popularity rating of, 338
presidential power of, 332
presidential staff of, 340
public perception of, 326–327
rating of, as president, 336
reform efforts of, 17
reputation of, 334, 342
and size of government, 63
as symbolic leader, 353
and trust in government, 97
veto use by, 345
Realignment, 142, 146–149
Reapportionment, 285
Reciprocity, 298, 299
Reconciliation bills, 523–524
Reconstruction, 147, 468, 469
Redistricting, 285, 287–288
Redlining, 478
Reed, Ralph, 118
Reed, Thomas (Me.), 302, 303
Regulation, bureaucratic, 375–376, 378
Rehnquist, William, Supreme Court under, 399, 408, 432, 434, 441, 443, 445, 452, 455, 458, 476, 478, 480, 500
Religion
establishment of, 442–446
freedom of, 440–446
free exercise of, 440–441
Religious Freedom Restoration Act (1993), 441
Religious groups, 118–119
Religious liberty and animal sacrifice, 425–426, 458–459

Religious right, 149
Representation, conflict over, at Constitutional Convention, 29
Republic, 14
distinguishing between democracy and, 32
Republican party, 141, 149
characteristics of, 153
"Contract with America," 65, 66, 84, 121, 139–140, 161, 286, 330, 335, 339, 410,
dominance of, 145
in 1990s, 148
rise of, 144–145
takeover of Congress in 1994, 8
Responsible party government, 154
Responsiveness
of bureaucracy, 379, 387–388
in civil rights, 507
of Congress, 317–319
of Constitution, 40, 42–44
of courts, 419, 458
of Federalism, 68–69
of government, 17–18
in budgeting, 538–539
and interest groups, 132–133
on money, 272–274
and political parties, 160–161
to public opinion, 98–99
of media, 243–245
of presidency, 355–356
Restrained judges, 413–414
Restrictive covenants, 478
Revenues, 530–531
raising, 536
Reverse discrimination, 503
Riegle, Donald (D-Mich.), and savings and loan crisis, 274
Robber barons, 255–256
Roberts, 415
Roberts, Owen, 398
Robertson, Pat, 118, 444
populism of, 9
Robinson, Jo Ann, 130
Rockefeller, Nelson, and vice presidency, 327, 329
Roe v. *Wade*, 418, 453
Rollins, Ed, 4
Roosevelt, Franklin Delano
appointment of Brownlow Committee by, 384
bureaucracy under, 387–388
death of, 327, 331
in election of 1932, 145–146, 330
in election of 1936, 81, 331
fireside chats of, 331
foreign policy leadership of, 346–347
leadership style of, 346
mail received by, 331
and the media, 223, 225–226, 242, 331
military leadership of, 352
and New Deal, 58–59, 61
persuasiveness of, 334
presidential staff of, 339
rating of, as president, 336
and Supreme Court, 331–332
veto use by, 345
and vice presidency, 329
Roosevelt, Theodore
in election of 1912, 18–19
leadership style of, 346
persuasive ability of, 335
power of, as president, 328, 330
and public funding, 270
rating of, as president, 336
Ros-Lehtinen, Ileana, 49, 69
Rossiter, Clinton, 339
Rules committee, 311–312

■ S

Sanford, Edward, 429
"Saturday Night Massacre," 23–24
Saving and loan crisis, 253–254, 274–276
Scalia, Antonin, 433
Scandal. *See* Corruption and scandal
Schattschneider, E. E., 141
Schmitt, Harrison, 241
Schools. *See* Education
Schwarzkopf, Norman, 352
Scientific polling, emergence of, 81–82
Scott, Dred, 467–468
Search and seizure, 446–447
Sea Shepherds, 120
Second Amendment, 40
civil liberties in, 427
Second-generation discrimination, 481
Securities and Exchange Commission (SEC), 371
Sedition Act (1798), 224
Sedition Act (1918), 429
Seditious speech, 428–430
Segregation
in the North, 470
in the South, 468–470
Selective perception, 242
Self-incrimination, 447–448
Senate, United States, 313–314
and separation of power, 33
Senate, U.S. *See also* Congress, U.S.; House of Representatives, U.S.
Senatorial courtesy, 341, 401
Senior Executive Service (SES), 384
Seniority chairs, 306
Separate-but-equal doctrine, 470, 472
Separation and Native Americans, 488
Separation of powers, 32–33, 43
Seventeenth Amendment, 33, 40
Seventh Amendment, 40
civil liberties in, 427
Seventh-Day Adventist and freedom of religion, 440
Sex discrimination, against women, 490–491
Sexual harassment, 496–497
Sharecropping, 468
Shays, Daniel, 26
Shays's Rebellion, 26
Shelby, Richard, 333
Sherman, Roger, 350
Sierra Club, 120, 125, 409
Simon, Paul (D-Ill.), 326, 362
Simpson, O. J., 409
Single-issue groups, 120–123
Single-member districts, 150
Sirica, John, 23, 24
Sit ins, 476–477
Sixth Amendment, 448–449
civil liberties in, 427
"60 Minutes," 217
Slaveowners, black, 469
Slavery, 467–468
conflict over, at Constitutional Convention, 29–30
and party realignment, 147
SLOP surveys, 83
Smith, Howard, 492–493
Smith, Margaret Chase, 289
Smith Act (1940), 429
Social contract, 31–32
Social issues in public opinion, 90–91
Socialist parties, 107
Social Security, 535
Social spending, 527
Social welfare and proper role of government, 89–90
Soft money loophole, 258
Somalia, media coverage of, 223–224
Sound bite, 224
Sousa, John Philip, 433
Souter, David, 403
South, segregation in, 468–470
Southern Christian Leadership Conference (SCLC), 465, 476
Speaker of the House, 302, 304
Specialization, 298–299
Speech, freedom of, 428–433
Speech plus conduct, 431–432
Spending, 524–527. *See also* Federal budget
cuts in, 534–536
defense, 527
direct, 521–522
discretionary, 522
government, 527–530
mandatory, 521–522
social, 527
Split-ticket voting, 161
Spock, Benjamin, 430
Standing committees, 304–305
Standing to sue, 409
Stanton, Elizabeth Cady, 491
Stare decisis, 414–415
State, U.S. Department of, 522
State-centered federalism, 54–55
State-local relations, 67–68

States
  as lobbyists, 64–65
  prohibition of certain powers to, 54
Statute of Liberty, 6
Statutes, role of Supreme Court in interpreting, 411
Steering, 478
Stewards, 95, 96
Stewart, Potter, 449, 451
Stockman, David, 221, 292
Stone, Harlan, 413
Straw polls, 80–81
Student Non-Violent Coordinating Committee (SNCC), 465
Subcommittee bill of rights, 306
Sunkist Growers, Inc., 114
Sunshine Act (1977), 365
Sununu, John, 333, 340
Supremacy clause, 54
Supreme Court, U.S., 400
  under Burger, 24, 44, 399, 408, 431, 435, 437, 438, 439, 447, 448, 449, 453, 474, 478, 480, 507
  deciding of cases by, 416–417
  filling vacancies in, 401
  and Franklin Roosevelt, 331–332
  under Hughes, 398, 416
  under Marshall, 56–57, 395–397, 413
  under Rehnquist, 399, 408, 432, 434, 441, 443, 445, 452, 455, 458, 476, 480, 500
  under Taney, 397
  Thomas nomination to, 222
  under Warren, 398, 408, 429, 431, 432, 435, 438, 439, 440, 447, 448, 452–453, 472, 507
Supreme Court cases
  Brown v. *Board of Education*, 472–473, 474, 479
  Dred Scott, 467–468
  Korematsu v. *United States*, 393–394, 420
  Mapp v. *Ohio*, 446–447
  Marbury v. *Madison*, 395
  McCulloch v. *Maryland*, 56–57, 397
  Miranda v. *Arizona*, 447
  Planned Parenthood of Southeastern Pennsylvania v. *Casey*, 454
  Plessy v. *Ferguson*, 469–470
  Roe v. *Wade*, 418, 453
  United States v. *Nixon*, 24, 44
  University of California Regents v. *Bakke*, 499
Symbiotic relations with media, 221–224
Symbolic speech, 432–433

■ T

Talk radio, 218–219
Talk shows, popularity of radio and television, 217
Tammany Hall, 257
Taney, Roger, 397
  as Chief Justice, 467–468
Taxation, conflict over, at Constitutional Convention, 30–31
Tax expenditures, 531
Tax Reform Act (1986), 373
Teapot Dome scandal, 256
Teledemocracy, 84–85
Television, 215
  contribution to spread presidential power, 331
  trends in, 216
Tennessee Valley Authority (TVA), 372
Tenth Amendment, 40, 54
Term limits, 286–287
Third Amendment, 40
  civil liberties in, 427
Third parties, 151–153
Thirteenth Amendment, 40, 468
Thomas, Clarence, 281, 403, 404–405, 496, 497
  nomination of, to Supreme Court, 222
  nomination of, to Supreme Courts, 404–405
Thompson, Fred (Tenn.), 259
Three-fifths Compromise, 30
Ticket splitting, 146
Tilden, Samuel, in election of 1876, 468
Time, 217
Time Warner, 217
Tinker, Mary Beth, 432
Tort reform, 410
Town meeting, 84
Trade, conflict over, at Constitutional Convention, 30–31
Treasury, U.S. Department of, 373
Tribal restoration for Native Americans, 489–490
Truman, Harry
  court appointments of, 407, 408
  and the media, 242
  military leadership of, 352
  rating of, as president, 336
Trusts, 303
  in government in public opinion, 94, 97–98
Turner Broadcasting, 217
Twenty-fifth Amendment, 327, 328
Twenty-fourth Amendment, 40
Twenty-sixth Amendment, 40
Twenty-third Amendment, 40
2 Live Crew, 439
Two-party system, 149–150
Tyler, rating of, as president, 336

■ U

Unfunded mandates, 65
Unitary systems, 51–52
United Seniors Union, 128
United States Chamber of Commerce, 107
U.S. English, 41
United States v. *Nixon*, 24, 44
United We Stand America, 19
University of California Regents v. *Bakke*, 499
Urban Development, U.S. Department of, 367
U.S. News and World Report, 217

■ V

Values, political bias for established, 231–232
Vanderbilt, Cornelius, 256
Veterans Administration, 479
Veterans Affairs, U.S. Department of, 369
Veto
  legislative, 314–315
  line-item, 342–343, 534
  pocket, 345
Vice presidency
  job of, 329
  as springboard to White House, 329
Vietnam War, 43, 352, 519
Vinson, Fred, 429
Violence, 470–471
  in race relations, 470–471
  racial, 477
Virginia Plan, 29
Voluntary cooperation, 65
Voting members, 300
Voting rights
  denial of, to African Americans, 470
  restoration of, 479
Voting Rights Act (1965), 478, 508

■ W

Wallace, Chris, 222
Wallace, George, 11, 151, 152, 371
Wall Street Journal, The, 216
War Powers Act (1973), 352
Warren, Earl, Supreme Court under, 398, 408, 429, 432, 435, 438, 439, 440, 447, 448, 452–453, 472, 474
Warren, Mercy Otis, 27
Washington, Booker T., 404
Washington, George, 33
  administration of, 57
  in campaign for Virginia House of Burgesses, 255
  as delegate to Continental Congress, 28, 29
  in election of 1788, 144
  first cabinet of, 367
  as first president, 38
  and the media, 224, 241
  on political parties, 141
  power of, as president, 328
  presidential staff of, 339
  rating of, as president, 336
Washingtonians, 333–335

Washington Post, 215, 216
political bias of, 232
Watergate, 23–24, 44–45, 146
impact of, 76, 340
media coverage of, 222
Weber, Max, 363
Webster, Daniel (Mass.), 276, 302
Weinberger, Caspar, 348
Welch, Ted, 252
Welfare reform, debate over, 66–67
Whistle-blowers, 387
White fight, 474
Whitman, Walt, 5
Whittier, John Greenleaf, 433
Wilson, Edith Galt, 328
Wilson, Pete (R.), 501
Wilson, Woodrow
as author, 328
and civil rights, 471
incapacitation of, 328
leadership style of, 346
and neutral competence, 379
persuasive ability of, 335
as political scientist, 518–519
power of, as president, 328, 330
presidential staff of, 339
rating of, as president, 336
and selection of judges, 400
on Supreme Court, 40
Winner-take-all arrangement, 150
Wizard of Oz, The (Baum), 8
Women
in civil service, 374–375
in Congress, 289–290
as judges, 402
sex discrimination against, 490–498
Women's groups, 117–118
Women's movement, 491–492
in Congress
credit, 494
education, 494
employment, 492–493
Equal Rights Amendment, 494–495
in Courts, 495–498
against men, 498
Wood, Kimba, 244
Woodward, Bob, 23, 222
Working privately and "going public," 299
Wounded Knee, South Dakota, 489
Wright, Jim (D-Tex.), 261
Writ of certiorari, 411

X

Xenophobia, 42

Y

Young, Milt, 298

Photo Credits—*Continued*

the New York Historical Society; **157** Newsweek—Wally McNamee; **166** Newsweek—Wally McNamee; **169** The Granger Collection; **171** UPI/Bettmann Newsphotos; **174** Brown Brothers; **175** AP/Wide World Photos; **176** Courtesy of Smithsonian Institute; **177** Courtesy of Smithsonian Institute; **180** Courtesy of Smithsonian Institute; **181** Tracey Litt/Impact Visuals; **184** AP/Wide World Photos; **185** Courtesy of Smithsonian Institute; **188** Bettmann; **189** Courtesy of Smithsonian Institute; **193** Steve Leonard/Black Star; **194** © 1995 Tim Dillon—USA Today; **197** Ira Wyman/Sygma; **200** UPI/Bettmann; **212** Alex Webb/Magnum Photos, Inc.; **214** Jodi Buren/Time Magazine; **216** Dane Penland; **220** Phil Huber/Black Star; **222** (top) Dan Adams/George Eastman House; **222** (bottom) Cynthia Johnson/Liaison International; **224** JB Pictures LTD/Stephen Terry; **226** Bettmann; **230** Time Magazine; **231** Time Magazine; **252** Alex Webb/Magnum Photos, Inc.; **255** The Granger Collection; **256** The Byron Collection, Museum of the City of New York; **272** UPI/Bettmann Newsphotos; **271** The Granger Collection; **275** AP/Wide World Photos; **279** (top) Reuters/Bettmann; **279** (bottom left) Laura Pedrick; **279** (bottom right) Reuters/Bettmann; **280** Terry Ashe/Time Magazine; **282** John Ficara; **298** Courtesy of Ailes Communications; **300** Mark Hess Illustration; **303** Engraving by Whitechurch, copyright 1855; courtesy of Library of Congress; **305** George Tames, New York Times Pictures; **324** Associated Press; **328** Historical Pictures Chicago/Stock Montage; **330** The Granger Collection; **331** Edward Clark; **340** George Tames, New York Times Pictures; **346** FDR Library; **347** AP/Wide World Photos; **350** National Archives; **353** © 1990 Wally McNamee, Woodfin Camp & Associates; **354** New York Times; **356** AP/Wide World Photos; **360** Ted Thai/Time Magazine; **362** © Rick Browne/Photoreporters; **365** Ted Thai/Time Magazine; **372** National Archives; **373** AP/Wide World Photos; **375** UPI Photo; **376** Charles Krebs; **380** Reuters/Bettmann; **379** The Granger Collection; **382** The Granger Collection; **386** Fred Ward Prod, Inc./Black Star; **388** Courtesy of New York City Department of Health; **392** Lynn Johnson; **394** UPI/Bettmann; **395** Bettmann; **396** Supreme Court Historical Society; **397** Courtesy of the Utah State Historical Society; **398** Dennis Brack, Black Star; **410** Photoreporters; **412** Ken Regan/Regan Pictures, Inc.; **416** © 1986 Ken Heinen; **420** Courtesy of National Archives; **423** (top) Photo by Harris & Ewing, Courtesy of Library of Congress; **423** (bottom) © 1993 David Burnett/Contact Press; **424** Tom Salyer; **429** UPI/Bettmann; **430** UPI/Bettmann; **432** UPI/Bettmann; **433** Bob Kusel; **434** AP/Wide World Photos; **435** © 1994 Bob Sacha; **442** Tom Defeo © 1965, The Des Moines Register and Tribune Co.; **441** Courtesy of National Archives; **443** © Phil Schofield; **445** Gamma Liaison; **447** Mark Solomon/Time Magazine; **449** (left) National Archives; **449** (right) National Archives; **453** Bill Janscha; **464** Michael Eastman; **466** © Charmian Reading 1966; **467** The Granger Collection; **470** AP/Wide World Photos; **472** AP/Wide World Photos; **473** AP/Wide World Photos; **475** Stanley R. Forman Pulitzer Prize, 1977; **476** Charles Moore/Black Star; **477** AP/Wide World Photos; **482** © Mark Heckman; **485** Cindy Yamanaka, Orange County Register/SABA for Time; **488** © Mario Pignata-Monti; **489** (left) Courtesy of Smithsonian Institute; **489** (right) Courtesy of Smithsonian Institute; **490** © 1989 Steve Wall; **492** (left) Printed by the permission of The Estate of Norman Rockwell; **492** (right) © The Curtis Publishing Company; **494** UPI/Bettmann; **521** American Heritage Center, University of Wyoming; **532** Mary Ellen Mark/Library.

Presidents, Elections, and Congresses, 1789–1993

Year	President	Vice President	Party of President	Election Year	Election Opponent with Most Votes*
1789–1797	George Washington	John Adams	None	(1789)	None
				(1793)	None
1797–1801	John Adams	Thomas Jefferson	Fed	(1797)	Thomas Jefferson
1801–1809	Thomas Jefferson	Aaron Burr (to 1805)	Dem-R	(1801)	John Adams
		George Clinton (to 1809)		(1805)	Charles C. Pinckney
1809–1817	James Madison	George Clinton (to 1813)	Dem-R	(1809)	Charles C. Pinckney
		Elbridge Gerry (to 1817)		(1813)	DeWitt Clinton
1817–1825	James Monroe	Daniel D. Tompkins	Dem-R	(1817)	Rufus King
				(1821)	John Q. Adams
1825–1829	John Quincy Adams	John C. Calhoun	Nat-R	(1824)	Andrew Jackson
1829–1837	Andrew Jackson	John C. Calhoun (to 1833)	Dem	(1828)	John Q. Adams
		Martin Van Buren (to 1837)		(1832)	Henry Clay
1837–1841	Martin Van Buren	Richard M. Johnson	Dem	(1836)	William H. Harrison
1841	William H. Harrison	John Tyler	Whig	(1840)	Martin Van Buren
1841–1845	John Tyler	(No VP)	Whig	(1840)	Took office upon death of Harrison
(1845–1849)	James K. Polk	George M. Dallas	Dem	(1844)	Henry Clay
1849–1850	Zachary Taylor	Millard Fillmore	Whig	(1848)	Lewis Cass
1850–1853	Millard Fillmore	(No VP)	Whig		Took office upon death of Taylor
1853–1857	Franklin Pierce	William R. King	Dem	(1852)	Winfield Scott
1857–1861	James Buchanan	John C. Breckinridge	Dem	(1856)	John C. Fremont
1861–1865	Abraham Lincoln	Hannibal Hamlin (to 1865)	Rep	(1860)	Stephen Douglas
		Andrew Johnson (1865)		(1864)	George B. McClellan
1865–1869	Andrew Johnson	(No VP)	Rep		Took office upon death of Lincoln
1869–1877	Ulysses S. Grant	Schuyler Colfax (to 1873)	Rep	(1868)	Horatio Seymour
		Henry Wilson (to 1877)		(1872)	Horace Greeley
1877–1881	Rutherford B. Hayes	William A. Wheeler	Rep	(1876)	Samuel Tilden
1881	James A. Garfield	Chester A. Arthur	Rep	(1880)	Winfield S. Hancock
1881–1885	Chester A. Arthur	(No VP)	Rep		Took office upon death of Garfield
1885–1889	Grover Cleveland	Thomas A. Hendricks	Dem	(1884)	James G. Blaine

(Table continued inside back cover.)

* In some cases more than one opponent received Electoral College votes. In these cases only the opponent with the most votes is listed.
** Electoral College system before the 12th Amendment (1804). The original Constitutional provisions called for the person with the second highest total Electoral College vote to be the Vice President.

† During the administration of George Washington, Congress was not organized by formal parties; the figures are of supporters and opponents of the administration.
†† Party balance as of beginning of Congress. Only members of the two major parties in Congress are shown.
††† Received fewer popular votes than an opponent.
HR Election decided in House of Representatives.

Winner's Electoral College Vote %	Winner's Popular Vote %	Congress	*House* Majority Party	*House* Minority Party	*Senate* Majority Party	*Senate* Minority Party
**	No popular vote	1st	38 Admin †	26 Opp	17 Admin	9 Opp
		2nd	37 Fed ††	33 Dem-R	16 Fed	13 Dem-R
**	No popular vote	3rd	57 Dem-R	48 Fed	17 Fed	13 Dem-R
		4th	54 Fed	52 Dem-R	19 Fed	13 Dem-R
**	No popular vote	5th	58 Fed	48 Dem-R	20 Fed	12 Dem-R
		6th	64 Fed	42 Dem-R	19 Fed	13 Dem-R
HR**	No popular vote	7th	69 Dem-R	36 Fed	18 Dem-R	13 Fed
		8th	402 Dem-R	39 Fed	25 Dem-R	9 Fed
92.0	No popular vote	9th	116 Dem-R	25 Fed	27 Dem-R	7 Fed
		10th	118 Dem-R	24 Fed	28 Dem-R	6 Fed
69.7	No popular vote	11th	94 Dem-R	48 Fed	28 Dem-R	6 Fed
		12th	108 Dem-R	36 Fed	30 Dem-R	6 Fed
59.0	No popular vote	13th	112 Dem-R	68 Fed	27 Dem-R	9 Fed
		14th	117 Dem-R	65 Fed	25 Dem-R	11 Fed
84.3	No popular vote	15th	141 Dem-R	42 Fed	34 Dem-R	10 Fed
		16th	156 Dem-R	27 Fed	35 Dem-R	7 Fed
99.5	No popular vote	17th	158 Dem-R	25 Fed	44 Dem-R	4 Fed
		18th	187 Dem-R	26 Fed	44 Dem-R	4 Fed
HR	39.1 †††	19th	105 Admin	97 Dem-J	26 Admin	20 Dem-J
		20th	119 Dem-J	94 Admin	28 Dem-J	20 Admin
68.2	56.0	21st	139 Dem	74 Nat R	26 Dem	22 Nat R
		22nd	141 Dem	58 Nat R	25 Dem	21 Nat R
76.6	54.5	23rd	147 Dem	53 AntiMas	20 Dem	20 Nat R
		24th	145 Dem	98 Whig	27 Dem	25 Whig
57.8	50.9	25th	108 Dem	107 Whig	30 Dem	18 Whig
		26th	124 Dem	118 Whig	28 Dem	22 Whig
79.6	52.9					
–	52.9	27th	133 Whig	102 Dem	28 Whig	22 Dem
		28th	142 Dem	79 Whig	28 Whig	25 Dem
61.8	49.6	29th	143 Dem	77 Whig	31 Dem	25 Whig
		30th	115 Whig	108 Dem	36 Dem	21 Whig
56.2	47.3	31st	112 Dem	109 Whig	35 Dem	25 Whig
–	–	32nd	140 Dem	88 Whig	35 Dem	24 Whig
85.8	50.9	33rd	159 Dem	71 Whig	38 Dem	22 Whig
		34th	108 Rep	83 Dem	40 Dem	15 Rep
58.8	45.6	35th	118 Dem	92 Rep	36 Dem	20 Rep
		36th	114 Rep	92 Dem	36 Dem	26 Rep
59.4	39.8	37th	105 Rep	43 Dem	31 Rep	10 Dem
		38th	102 Rep	75 Dem	36 Rep	9 Dem
91.0	55.2					
–	–	39th	149 Union	42 Dem	42 Union	10 Dem
		40th	143 Rep	49 Dem	42 Rep	11 Dem
72.8	52.7	41st	149 Rep	63 Dem	56 Rep	11 Dem
		42nd	134 Rep	104 Dem	52 Rep	17 Dem
81.9	55.6	43rd	194 Rep	92 Dem	49 Rep	19 Dem
		44th	169 Rep	109 Dem	45 Rep	29 Dem
50.1	47.9 †††	45th	153 Dem	140 Rep	39 Rep	36 Dem
		46th	149 Dem	130 Rep	42 Dem	33 Rep
58.0	48.3	47th	147 Rep	135 Dem	37 Rep	37 Dem
–	–	48th	197 Dem	118 Rep	38 Rep	36 Dem
54.6	48.5	49th	183 Dem	140 Rep	43 Rep	34 Dem
		50th	169 Dem	152 Rep	39 Rep	37 Dem

Source for election data: Svend Peterson, *A Statistical History of American Presidential Elections*. New York: Frederick Ungar Publishing, 1963. Updates: Richard Scammon, *America Votes* 19. Washington D.C.: Congressional Quarterly, 1991; *Congressional Quarterly Weekly Report*, Nov. 7, 1992, p. 3552.

Abbreviations:

Admin = Administration supporters
AntiMas = Anti-Masonic
Dem = Democratic
Dem-R = Democratic-Republican
Fed = Federalist
Dem-J = Jacksonian Democrats
Nat R = National Republican
Opp = Opponents of administration
Rep = Republican
Union = Unionist

Presidents, Elections, and Congresses, 1789–1993 (cont.)

Year	President	Vice President	Party of President	Election Year	Election Opponent with Most Votes*
1889–1893	Benjamin Harrison	Levi P. Morton	Rep	(1888)	Grover Cleveland
1893–1897	Grover Cleveland	Adlai E. Stevenson	Dem	(1892)	Benjamin Harrison
1897–1901	William McKinley	Garret A. Hobart (to 1901)	Rep	(1896)	William Jennings Bryan
		Theodore Roosevelt (1901)		(1900)	William Jennings Bryan
1901–1909	Theodore Roosevelt	(No VP, 1901–1905)	Rep		Took office upon death of McKinley
		Charles W. Fairbanks (1905–1909)		(1904)	Alton B. Parker
1909–1913	William Howard Taft	James S. Sherman	Rep	(1908)	William Jennings Bryan
1913–1921	Woodrow Wilson	Thomas R. Marshall	Dem	(1912)	Theodore Roosevelt
				(1916)	Charles Evans Hughes
1921–1923	Warren G. Harding	Calvin Coolidge	Rep	(1920)	James Cox
1923–1929	Calvin Coolidge	(No VP, 1923–1925) Charles G. Dawes (1925–1929)	Rep	 (1924)	Took office upon death of Harding John Davis
1929–1933	Herbert Hoover	Charles Curtis	Rep	(1928)	Alfred E. Smith
1933–1945	Franklin D. Roosevelt	John N. Garner (1933–1941)	Dem	(1932)	Herbert Hoover
		Henry A. Wallace (1941–1945)		(1936)	Alfred Landon
		Harry S. Truman (1945)		(1940)	Wendell Willkie
				(1944)	Thomas Dewey
1945–1953	Harry S. Truman	(No VP, 1945–1949) Alban W. Barkley	Dem		Took office upon death of Roosevelt
				(1948)	Thomas Dewey
1953–1961	Dwight D. Eisenhower	Richard M. Nixon	Rep	(1952)	Adlai Stevenson
				(1956)	Adlai Stevenson
1961–1963	John F. Kennedy	Lyndon B. Johnson	Dem	(1960)	Richard M. Nixon
1963–1969	Lyndon B. Johnson	(No VP, 1963–1965) Hubert H. Humphrey (1965–1969)	Dem	 (1964)	Took office upon death of Kennedy Barry Goldwater
1969–1974	Richard M. Nixon	Spiro T. Agnew	Rep	(1968)	Hubert H. Humphrey
		Gerald R. Ford (appointed)		(1972)	George McGovern
1974–1977	Gerald R. Ford	Nelson A. Rockefeller	Rep		Took office upon Nixon's resignation
1977–1981	Jimmy Carter	Walter Mondale	Dem	(1976)	Gerald R. Ford
1981–1989	Ronald Reagan	George Bush	Rep	(1980)	Jimmy Carter
				(1984)	Walter F. Mondale
1989–1993	George Bush	J. Danforth Quayle	Rep	(1988)	Michael Dukakis
1993–	Willam J. Clinton	Albert Gore	Dem	(1992)	George Bush

* In some cases more than one opponent received Electoral College votes. In these cases only the opponent with the most votes is listed.

** Electoral College system before the 12th Amendment (1804). The original Constitutional provisions called for the person with the second highest total Electoral College vote to be the Vice President.

† During the administration of George Washington, Congress was not organized by formal parties; the figures are of supporters and opponents of the administration.

†† Party balance as of beginning of Congress. Only members of the two major parties in Congress are shown.

††† Received fewer popular votes than an opponent.

HR Election decided in House of Representatives.

Winner's Electoral College Vote %	Winner's Popular Vote %	Congress	House Majority Party	House Minority Party	Senate Majority Party	Senate Minority Party
58.1	47.8 †††	51st	166 Rep	159 Dem	39 Rep	37 Dem
		52nd	235 Dem	88 Rep	47 Rep	39 Dem
62.3	46.0	53rd	218 Dem	127 Rep	44 Dem	38 Rep
		54th	244 Rep	105 Dem	43 Rep	39 Dem
60.6	51.0	55th	204 Rep	113 Dem	47 Rep	34 Dem
		56th	185 Rep	163 Dem	53 Rep	26 Dem
64.7	51.7					
–	–	57th	197 Rep	151 Dem	55 Rep	31 Dem
		58th	208 Rep	178 Dem	57 Rep	33 Dem
70.6	56.4	59th	250 Rep	136 Dem	57 Rep	33 Dem
		60th	222 Rep	164 Dem	61 Rep	31 Dem
66.4	51.6	61st	219 Rep	172 Dem	61 Rep	32 Dem
		62nd	228 Dem	161 Rep	51 Rep	41 Dem
81.9	41.9	63rd	291 Dem	127 Rep	51 Dem	44 Rep
		64th	230 Dem	196 Rep	56 Dem	40 Rep
52.2	49.3	65th	216 Dem	210 Rep	53 Dem	42 Rep
		66th	240 Rep	190 Dem	49 Rep	47 Dem
76.1	60.3	67th	301 Rep	131 Dem	59 Rep	37 Dem
–	–	68th	225 Rep	205 Dem	51 Rep	43 Dem
71.9	54.0	69th	247 Rep	183 Dem	56 Rep	39 Dem
		70th	237 Rep	195 Dem	49 Rep	46 Dem
83.6	58.2	71st	267 Rep	167 Dem	56 Rep	39 Dem
		72nd	220 Dem	214 Rep	48 Rep	47 Dem
88.9	57.4	73rd	310 Dem	117 Rep	60 Dem	35 Rep
		74th	319 Dem	103 Rep	69 Dem	25 Rep
98.5	60.8	75th	331 Dem	89 Rep	76 Dem	16 Rep
		76th	261 Dem	164 Rep	69 Dem	23 Rep
84.6	54.7	77th	268 Dem	162 Rep	66 Dem	28 Rep
		78th	218 Dem	208 Rep	58 Dem	37 Rep
81.4	53.4					
–	–	79th	242 Dem	190 Rep	56 Dem	38 Rep
		80th	245 Rep	188 Dem	51 Rep	45 Dem
57.1	49.5	81st	263 Dem	171 Rep	54 Dem	42 Rep
		82nd	234 Dem	199 Rep	49 Dem	47 Rep
83.2	55.1	83rd	221 Rep	211 Dem	48 Rep	47 Dem
		84th	232 Dem	203 Rep	48 Dem	47 Rep
86.1	57.4	85th	233 Dem	200 Rep	49 Dem	47 Rep
		86th	283 Dem	153 Rep	64 Dem	34 Rep
58.0	49.7	87th	263 Dem	174 Rep	65 Dem	35 Rep
–	–	88th	258 Dem	177 Rep	67 Dem	33 Rep
90.3	61.6	89th	295 Dem	140 Rep	68 Dem	32 Rep
		90th	247 Dem	187 Rep	64 Dem	36 Rep
55.9	43.4	91st	243 Dem	192 Rep	57 Dem	43 Rep
		92nd	254 Dem	180 Rep	54 Dem	44 Rep
96.7	60.7					
–	–	93rd	239 Dem	192 Rep	56 Dem	42 Rep
		94th	291 Dem	144 Rep	60 Dem	37 Rep
55.2	50.1	95th	292 Dem	143 Rep	61 Dem	38 Rep
		96th	280 Dem	155 Rep	58 Dem	41 Rep
90.9	50.7	97th	243 Dem	192 Rep	53 Rep	47 Dem
		98th	269 Dem	166 Rep	54 Rep	46 Dem
97.4	59.8	99th	253 Dem	182 Rep	53 Rep	47 Dem
		100th	258 Dem	177 Rep	55 Dem	45 Rep
79.0	53.4	101st	260 Dem	175 Rep	55 Dem	45 Rep
		102nd	267 Dem	167 Rep	56 Dem	44 Rep
68.8	43.2	103rd	259 Dem	175 Rep	57 Dem	43 Rep

Source for election data: Svend Peterson, *A Statistical History of American Presidential Elections.* New York: Frederick Ungar Publishing, 1963. Updates: Richard Scammon, *America Votes* 19. Washington D.C.: Congressional Quarterly, 1991; *Congressional Quarterly Weekly Report*, Nov. 7, 1992, p. 3552.

Abbreviations:

Admin = Administration supporters
AntiMas = Anti-Masonic
Dem = Democratic
Dem-R = Democratic-Republican
Fed = Federalist
Dem-J = Jacksonian Democrats
Nat R = National Republican
Opp = Opponents of administration
Rep = Republican
Union = Unionist